D1709182

Contemporary Authors®

NEW REVISION SERIES

ISSN 0275-7176

Contemporary Authors®

A Bio-Bibliographical Guide to
Current Writers in Fiction, General Nonfiction,
Poetry, Journalism, Drama, Motion Pictures,
Television, and Other Fields

DANIEL JONES
JOHN D. JORGENSON
Editors

NEW REVISION SERIES
volume 72

DETROIT • LONDON

STAFF

Daniel Jones and John D. Jorgenson, *Editors, New Revision Series*

Thomas Wiloch, *Sketchwriting Coordinator and Online Research Specialist*

Tim Akers, Catherine V. Donaldson, Jeff Hunter, Jerry Moore, Polly A. Vedder, Tim White, and Kathy Wilson, *Contributing Editors*

Bruce Boston, Mary Gillis, Lane A. Glenn, Joan Goldsworthy, Anne Janette Johnson, Judson Knight, David Kroeger, Cindy Nurak, Jani Prescott, Trudy Ring, Bryan Ryan, Susan Salter, Pamela L. Shelton, Arlene True, Shanna Weagle, and Christina Werth, *Sketchwriters*

Tracy Arnold-Chapman, Patricia Onorato, Pamela L. Shelton, and Kenneth R. Shepherd, *Copyeditors*

James P. Draper, *Managing Editor*

Victoria B. Cariappa, *Research Manager*

Jeffrey D. Daniels, Tamara C. Nott, Tracie A. Richardson, Cheryl L. Warnock, and Robert Whaley, *Research Associates*

27500 Drake Rd.
Farmington Hills, MI 48331-3535

Library of Congress Catalog Card Number 81-640179
ISBN 0-7876-2009-2
ISSN 0275-7176

Printed in the United States of America

10 9 8 7 6 5 4 3 2 1

Contents

Indexing note: All *Contemporary Authors New Revision Series* entries are indexed in the *Contemporary Authors* cumulative index, which is published separately and distributed twice a year.

As always, the most recent *Contemporary Authors* cumulative index continues to be the user's guide to the location of an individual author's listing.

Preface

The *Contemporary Authors New Revision Series* (*CANR*) provides updated information on authors listed in earlier volumes of *Contemporary Authors* (*CA*). Although entries for individual authors from any volume of *CA* may be included in a volume of the *New Revision Series, CANR* updates only those sketches requiring significant change. However, in response to requests from librarians and library patrons for the most current information possible on high-profile writers of greater public and critical interest, *CANR* revises entries for these authors whenever new and noteworthy information becomes available.

Authors are included on the basis of specific criteria that indicate the need for a revision. These criteria include a combination of bibliographical additions, changes in addresses or career, major awards, and personal information such as name changes or death dates. All listings in this volume have been revised or augmented in various ways and contain up-to-the-minute publication information in the Writings section, most often verified by the author and/or by consulting a variety of online resources. Many sketches have been extensively rewritten, often including informative new Sidelights. As always, a *CANR* listing entails no charge or obligation.

The key to locating an author's most recent entry is the *CA* cumulative index, which is published separately and distributed twice a year. It provides access to all entries in *CA* and *CANR*. Always consult the latest index to find an author's most recent entry.

For the convenience of users, the *CA* cumulative index also includes references to all entries in these Gale literary series: *Authors and Artists for Young Adults, Authors in the News, Bestsellers, Black Literature Criticism, Black Writers, Children's Literature Review, Concise Dictionary of American Literary Biography, Concise Dictionary of British Literary Biography, Contemporary Authors Autobiography Series, Contemporary Authors Bibliographical Series, Contemporary Literary Criticism, Dictionary of Literary Biography, Dictionary of Literary Biography Documentary Series, Dictionary of Literary Biography Yearbook, DISCovering Authors, DISCovering Authors: British, DISCovering Authors: Canadian, DISCovering Authors: Modules* (including modules for Dramatists, Most-Studied Authors, Multicultural Authors, Novelists, Poets, and Popular/Genre Authors), *Drama Criticism, Hispanic Literature Criticism, Hispanic Writers, Junior DISCovering Authors, Major Authors and Illustrators for Children and Young Adults, Major 20th-Century Writers, Native North American Literature, Poetry Criticism, Short Story Criticism, Something about the Author, Something about the Author Autobiography Series, Twentieth-Century Literary Criticism, World Literature Criticism, World Literature Criticism Supplement,* and *Yesterday's Authors of Books for Children.*

A Sample Index Entry:

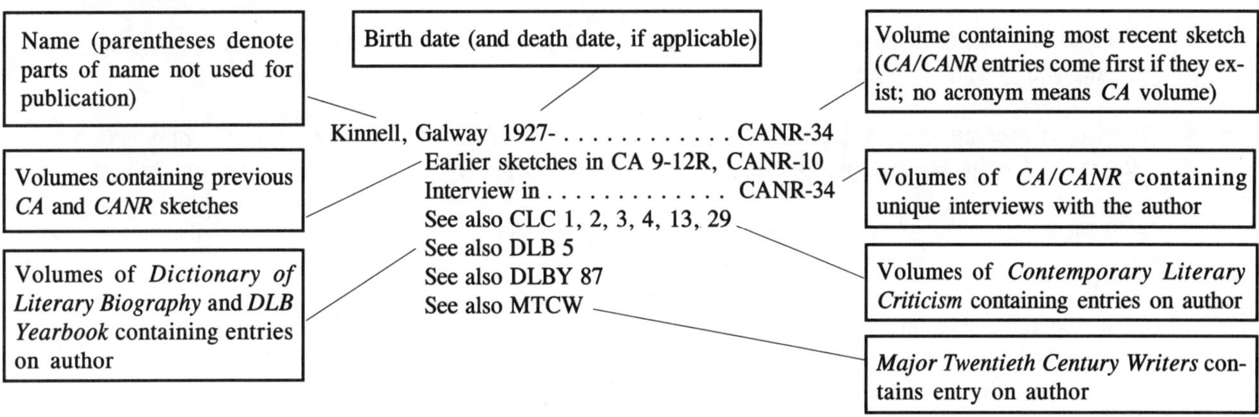

For the most recent *CA* information on Kinnell, users should refer to Volume 34 of the *New Revision Series,* as designated by "CANR-34"; if that volume is unavailable, refer to CANR-10. If CANR-10 is also unavailable, refer to CA 9-12R, published in 1974, for Kinnell's first revision entry.

How Are Entries Compiled?

The editors make every effort to secure new information directly from the authors. Copies of all sketches in selected *CA* and *CANR* volumes previously published are routinely sent to listees at their last-known addresses, and returns from these authors are then assessed. For deceased writers, or those who fail to reply to requests for data, we consult other reliable biographical sources, such as those indexed in The Gale Group's *Biography and Genealogy Master Index,* and biobliographical sources, such as *Magazine Index, Newspaper Abstracts, LC MARC,* and a variety of online databases. Further details come from published interviews, feature stories, book reviews, online literary magazines and journals, author web sites, and often the authors' publishers supply material.

* *Indicates that a listing has been compiled from secondary sources but has not been personally verified for this edition by the author under review.*

What Kinds of Information Does an Entry Provide?

Sketches in *CANR* contain the following biographical and bibliographical information:

- **Entry heading:** the most complete form of author's name, plus any pseudonyms or name variations used for writing
- **Personal information:** author's date and place of birth, family data, ethnicity, educational background, political and religious affiliations, and hobbies and leisure interests
- **Addresses:** author's home, office, or agent's addresses, plus e-mail and fax numbers, as available
- **Career summary:** name of employer, position, and dates held for each career post; resume of other vocational achievements; military service
- **Membership information:** professional, civic, and other association memberships and any official posts held
- **Awards and honors:** military and civic citations, major prizes and nominations, fellowships, grants, and honorary degrees
- **Writings:** a comprehensive, chronological list of titles, publishers, dates of original publication and revised editions, and production information for plays, television scripts, and screenplays
- **Adaptations:** a list of films, plays, and other media which have been adapted from the author's work
- **Work in progress:** current or planned projects, with dates of completion and/or publication, and expected publisher, when known
- **Sidelights:** a biographical portrait of the author's development; information about the critical reception of the author's works; revealing comments, often by the author, on personal interests, aspirations, motivations, and thoughts on writing
- **Biographical and critical sources:** a list of books and periodicals in which additional information on an author's life and/or writings appears

Related Titles in the *CA* Series

Contemporary Authors Autobiography Series complements *CA* original and revised volumes with specially commissioned autobiographical essays by important current authors, illustrated with personal photographs they provide. Common topics include their motivations for writing, the people and experiences that shaped their careers, the rewards they derive from their work, and their impressions of the current literary scene.

Contemporary Authors Bibliographical Series surveys writings by and about important American authors since World War II. Each volume concentrates on a specific genre and features approximately ten writers; entries list works written by and about the author and contain a bibliographical essay discussing the merits and deficiencies of major critical and scholarly studies in detail.

Available in Electronic Formats

CD-ROM. Full-text bio-bibliographic entries from the entire *CA* series, covering approximately 101,000 writers, are available on CD-ROM through lease and purchase plans. The disc combines entries from the *CA, CANR,* and *Contemporary Authors Permanent Series* (*CAP*) print series to provide the most recent author listing. It can be searched by name, title, subject/genre, nationality/ethnicity, personal data, and as well as advanced searching using boolean logic. The disc is updated every six months. For more information, call 1-800-877-GALE. *CA* is also available on CD-ROM from SilverPlatter Information, Inc.

Online. The *Contemporary Authors* database is made available online to libraries and their patrons through online public access catalog (OPAC) vendors. Currently, *CA* is offered through Ameritech Library Services' Vista Online (formerly Dynix).

GaleNet. *CA* is available on a subscription basis through GaleNet, a new online information resource that features an easy-to-use end-user interface, the powerful search capabilities of the BRS/Search retrieval software, and ease of access through the World Wide Web. For more information, call 1-800-877-GALE.

Magnetic Tape. *CA* is available for licensing on magnetic tape in a fielded format. The database is available for internal data processing and nonpublishing purposes only. For more information, call 1-800-877-GALE.

Suggestions Are Welcome

The editors welcome comments and suggestions from users on any aspects of the *CA* series. If readers would like to recommend authors for inclusion in future volumes of the series, they are cordially invited to write the editors; call toll-free at 1-800-347-GALE; fax at 1-248-699-8054; or email at john.jorgenson@gale.com.

CA Numbering System and Volume Update Chart

Occasionally questions arise about the *CA* numbering system and which volumes, if any, can be discarded. Despite numbers like "29-32R," "97-100" and "157," the entire *CA* print series consists of only 167 physical volumes with the publication of *CA* Volume 168. The following charts note changes in the numbering system and cover design, and indicate which volumes are essential for the most complete, up-to-date coverage.

***CA* First Revision**

- 1-4R through 41-44R (11 books)
  Cover: Brown with black and gold trim.
  There will be no further First Revision volumes because revised entries are now being handled exclusively through the more efficient *New Revision Series* mentioned below.

***CA* Original Volumes**

- 45-48 through 97-100 (14 books)
  Cover: Brown with black and gold trim.
- 101 through 168 (68 books)
  Cover: Blue and black with orange bands.
  The same as previous *CA* original volumes but with a new, simplified numbering system and new cover design.

***CA* Permanent Series**

- *CAP*-1 and *CAP*-2 (2 books)
  Cover: Brown with red and gold trim.
  There will be no further *Permanent Series* volumes because revised entries are now being handled exclusively through the more efficient *New Revision Series* mentioned below.

***CA* New Revision Series**

- *CANR*-1 through *CANR*-72 (72 books)
  Cover: Blue and black with green bands.
  Includes only sketches requiring significant changes; **sketches are taken from any previously published *CA, CAP,* or *CANR* volume.**

If You Have:	You May Discard:
CA First Revision Volumes 1-4R through 41-44R **and** *CA Permanent Series* Volumes 1 and 2	*CA* Original Volumes 1, 2, 3, 4 Volumes 5-6 through 41-44
CA Original Volumes 45-48 through 97-100 **and** 101 through 168	**NONE:** These volumes will not be superseded by corresponding revised volumes. Individual entries from these and all other volumes appearing in the left column of this chart may be revised and included in the various volumes of the *New Revision Series.*
CA New Revision Series Volumes *CANR*-1 through *CANR*-72	**NONE:** The *New Revision Series* does not replace any single volume of *CA*. Instead, volumes of *CANR* include entries from many previous *CA* series volumes. All *New Revision Series* volumes must be retained for full coverage.

A Sampling of Authors and Media People Featured in This Volume

Steven Berkoff

An accomplished writer-actor-director who challenges audience expectations and actors' limitations, Berkoff has overseen production of a number of well-received adaptations and original plays. Perhaps better known in America as a character actor in such potboilers as *Beverly Hills Cop* and *Rambo: First Blood, Part II,* Berkoff is the founding director of the London Theatre Group, with which many of his plays have made their debut. His titles include *East, Greek, West,* and *I Am Hamlet.*

Tom Bower

Bower is the author of nonfiction works that focus on Nazi crimes and criminals during and after World War II. Bower claims that many Germans in powerful positions during the War escaped official retribution through a combination of disagreements between military and civilian personnel about how best to handle the situation, a lack of planning by the Allies, and a lack of cooperation by the German people. His titles include *The Pledge Betrayed: America and Britain and the Denazification of Postwar Germany* and *The Paperclip Conspiracy: The Hunt for the Nazi Scientists.*

Dennis Cooper

Poet, playwright, novelist, and author of short fiction, Cooper has earned the reputation of a creative stylist because of his unique prose that incorporates elements of poetry. Some critics have categorized his works as disturbing glimpses of a male homosexual subculture filled with despair, while others have championed his work as "a bold, dystopian vision of sexual desire and moral laxity in contemporary life." His titles include *He Cried, Frisk,* and *Guide.*

Charles Ludlam

Educator, actor, producer, director, and playwright Ludlam, co-founder of New York's Ridiculous Theatrical Company, was known as the author of innovative and sometimes outrageous stage productions characterized by his own blend of satire, camp, and parody. Praised by many critics for bringing new life to the theater, Ludlam's works include *When Queens Collide, Bluebeard: A Melodrama in Three Acts,* and *Love's Tangled Web.*

David Mamet

Mamet has acquired a great deal of critical recognition for his plays, each a microcosmic view of the American experience. Since 1976, his plays have been widely produced in regional theaters and in New York City. During his career, Mamet has received much critical acclaim, including two New York Drama Critics' Circle Awards, a Pulitzer Prize, and two Academy Award nominations. Called "a pure writer" by one critic and "that rare bird, an American playwright who's a language playwright" by another, his plays include *Sexual Perversity in Chicago, American Buffalo, Glengarry Glen Ross,* and *Oleanna.*

Camille Paglia

Paglia's unorthodox feminist views on the role of sexuality in the development of art and culture in Western civilization became the subject of heated debate with the publication of her first book, *Sexual Personae: Art and Decadence from Nefertiti to Emily Dickinson.* Known for accusing the contemporary feminist establishment of suppressing the aesthetics of art and beauty and the dangers of sexuality, her other works include *Sex, Art, and American Culture: Essays.*

Kevin Starr

The author of the highly-regarded "Americans and the California Dream" historical series, Starr examines how myth and reality combined to shape the development of the Golden State. In the series, he interprets the history and lore of the region through the writings of such early Californians as novelists Jack London and Mary Austin and philosopher Josiah Royce. His titles include *Inventing the Dream: California through the Progressive Era* and *The Dream Endures: California Enters the 1940s.*

Helen Vendler

Vendler is regarded by many as one of America's foremost critics of poetry. Since the mid-1960s she has contributed numerous reviews and articles on poetry to prominent literary publications, in particular the *New York Times Book Review,* and since 1978 has served as poetry critic for the *New Yorker.* Her works include *Yeats's Vision and the Later Plays, The Poetry of George Herbert,* and *Seamus Heaney.*

A

**** Indicates that a listing has been compiled from secondary sources believed to be reliable but has not been personally verified for this edition by the author sketched.***

ABBOTT, George (Francis) 1887-1995

PERSONAL: Born June 25, 1887, in Forestville, NY; died January 31, 1995, in Miami Beach, FL; son of George Burwell (in business) and Mary (McLaury) Abbott; married Ednah Levis, 1914 (died, 1930); married Mary Sinclair, 1946 (divorced, 1951); married Joy Moana Valderrama, 1983; children: (first marriage) Judith Ann. *Education:* University of Rochester, B.A., 1911; graduate study at Harvard University, 1911-12.

CAREER: Actor, playwright, director, and producer. Actor in plays, including *The Misleading Lady,* 1913, *Daddies,* 1918, and *Hellbent for Heaven,* 1924, and in television productions, including *The Skin of Our Teeth,* 1955; director of plays, including *Chicago,* 1926, *Twentieth Century,* 1932, *Brown Sugar,* 1937, *Pal Joey,* 1940, *Sweet Charity,* 1942, *On the Town,* 1944, *Call Me Madam,* 1950, *A Funny Thing Happened on the Way to the Forum,* 1962, and *The Education of H*Y*M*A*N K*A*P*L*A*N,* 1968. Director of films, including *All Quiet on the Western Front,* 1930. Founder, with Philip Dunning, of Abbott-Dunning, Inc., 1931-34.

AWARDS, HONORS: Boston Globe award, 1912, for *Man in the Manhole;* Donaldson Awards for direction, 1946, for *Billion Dollar Baby,* and 1948, for *High Button Shoes;* New York Drama Critics Circle award for best musical, Antoinette Perry (Tony) Award, and Donaldson Award, all 1953, all for *Wonderful Town;* Antoinette Perry Award and Donaldson Award, both 1955, both for *The Pajama Game;* Antoinette Perry Award, 1956, for *Damn Yankees;* Pulitzer Prize in drama, and Antoinette Perry Award, both 1960, and New York Drama Critics Circle award, 1961, all for *Fiorello!;* honorary doctorate, University of Rochester, 1961; Outer Circle award for "most effective individual contribution," 1962, and Antoinette Perry Award for best director, 1963, both for *A Funny Thing Happened on the Way to the Forum;* Society of Stage Directors award of merit, 1968; elected to Theater Hall of Fame and Museum, New York City, 1972; "Distinguished Career Achievement" Antoinette Perry Award, 1976; Kennedy Center Award, 1982.

WRITINGS:

PLAYS

Head of the Family (one-act), produced in Cambridge, MA, 1912.

Man in the Manhole (one-act), produced in Boston at Bijou Art Theatre, 1912.

(With James Gleason) *The Fall Guy* (three-act; produced in New York City at Eltinge Theatre, 1925), Samuel French (New York City), 1928.

(With Winchell Smith) *A Holy Terror: A None-Too-Serious Drama* (produced in New York City at George M. Cohan Theatre, 1925), Samuel French, 1926.

(With John V. A. Weaver, and director) *Love 'Em and Leave 'Em* (three-act; produced in New York City at Harris Theatre, 1926), Samuel French, 1926.

(With Pearl Franklin) *Cowboy Crazy,* produced in New York City, 1926.

PLAYS; AND DIRECTOR

(With Philip Dunning) *Broadway* (produced on Broadway, 1926), Doran (New York City), 1927.

(With Dana Burnett) *Four Walls* (produced on Broadway, 1927), Samuel French, 1928.
(With Ann Preston Bridgers) *Coquette* (three-act; produced in New York City at Maxine Elliott's Theatre, 1927), Longmans, Green, 1928.
(With Edward A. Paramore Jr. and Hyatt Daab) *Ringside,* produced on Broadway, 1928.
(With S. K. Lauren) *Those We Love,* produced on Broadway, 1930.
(With Dunning) *Lilly Turner,* produced on Broadway, 1932.
(With Leon Abrams) *Heat Lightning,* produced on Broadway, 1933.
Ladies' Money, produced on Broadway, 1934.
Page Miss Glory, produced in New York City, 1934.
(With John Cecil Holm) *Three Men on a Horse* (produced on Broadway, 1935), Samuel French, 1935.
On Your Toes, produced on Broadway, 1936.
Sweet River (adapted from the novel *Uncle Tom's Cabin,* by Harriet Beecher Stowe), produced in New York City, 1936.
The Boys from Syracuse (adapted from *A Comedy of Errors* by William Shakespeare; produced on Broadway, 1938), Chappell, 1965.
(With Holm) *Best Foot Forward,* produced on Broadway, 1941.
(With George Marion Jr.) *Beat the Band,* produced on Broadway, 1942.
Where's Charley? (adapted from the play *Charley's Aunt,* by Brandon Thomas; produced on Broadway, 1948), Samuel French, 1965.
(With Betty Smith) *A Tree Grows in Brooklyn* (adapted from the novel by Betty Smith), produced on Broadway, 1951.
(With Richard Bissell) *The Pajama Game* (adapted from the novel *7 1/2 Cents,* by Bissell; produced on Broadway, 1954), Random House (New York City), 1954.
(With Douglass Wallop) *Damn Yankees* (adapted from the novel *The Year the Yankees Lost the Pennant,* by Wallop; produced on Broadway, 1955), Random House, 1956.
New Girl in Town (adapted from the play *Anna Christie,* by Eugene O'Neill; produced on Broadway, 1957), Random House, 1958.
(With Jerome Weidman) *Fiorello*! (produced on Broadway, 1959), Random House, 1960.
(With Weidman) *Tenderloin* (adapted from the work of Samuel Hopkins Adams; produced on Broadway, 1960), Random House, 1961.
(With Robert Russell) *Flora, the Red Menace,* produced on Broadway, 1965.
(With Guy Bolton) *Anya* (adapted from the play *Anastasia,* by Marcelle Maurette and Bolton), produced on Broadway, 1965.
Music Is (adapted from *Twelfth Night,* by Shakespeare), produced in Seattle, WA, 1976.

OTHER

Mister Abbott (autobiography), Random House, 1963.
Tryout (novel), Playboy Press, 1979.
(With Richard Rodgers and Lorenz Hart) *Rodgers and Hart's "On Your Toes,"* Rodgers & Hammerstein Theatre Library (New York City), 1985.

SCREENPLAYS; AND DIRECTOR

The Pajama Game, Warner Bros., 1957.
Damn Yankees, Warner Bros., 1958.

SIDELIGHTS: George Abbott's theatrical career ran through nearly every decade of the twentieth century and over 125 professional productions, earning him countless accolades, the respect of legions of actors, directors, producers and critics, and the applause of generations of audience members.

"Mister Abbott," as Abbott was universally known in his profession, got his start as a Broadway actor in a 1913 production of *The Misleading Lady,* and spent the next several years on stage, becoming a very popular leading man. He was named one of the top ten performers of 1923 for his portrayal of Tex, a cowboy, in *Zander the Great.*

Abbott's greatest talent, however, lay behind the scenes, writing, directing, and producing hit after hit after hit. As a playwright, he arrived on the Great White Way in 1925 with *The Fall Guy,* co-authored with James Gleason. The following year, 1926, he debuted as a writer/director with the smash *Broadway,* a melodrama combining backstage life with prohibition and gang warfare of the roaring twenties. Then, after a string of similarly styled comedies and melodramas, songwriters Richard Rodgers and Lorenz Hart lured the prolific Abbott to his theatrical destiny: the Broadway musical.

Originally asked to write the book for Rodgers and Hart's *On Your Toes,* Abbott ended up assuming the helm as director and rescuing the floundering production during rehearsals, turning a near flop into a giant hit. As a result, he became one of the most sought-after talents in U.S. theater and dominated

Broadway for the next thirty years. From 1935 to 1963 he always had at least one play running, either as director or writer. In one amazing season, 1962, Abbott directed three Broadway shows at the same time: *A Funny Thing Happened on the Way to the Forum, Take Her, She's Mine,* and *Never Too Late.*

Among Abbott's successes in those halcyon years of New York theater were *The Boys from Syracuse* (1938), an adaptation of Shakespeare's *Comedy of Errors; The Pajama Game* (1954), which earned him one of an amazing six career Antoinette Perry Awards; and *Damn Yankees* (1955), about a man who sells his soul to the devil for a season of fame as a baseball dynamo.

First and foremost, Abbott was an entertainer. He felt it was his task not to challenge audiences with symbolism and complicated inner meaning, but to excite them with action and tickle them with wit. Though high-minded critics occasionally groaned at his low-comedy approach to theatre, none could dispute his popular appeal. Writing for *Contemporary Dramatists,* Foster Hirsch grudgingly noted, "Abbott is a professional showman whose canon is undisturbed by the least suggestion of intellect. The Abbott production is a good show, a farce, a melodrama, a musical comedy; briskly paced, it is geared for the big laugh, the big climax, and its light-fingered, high-stepping rhythm naturally does not translate well to the library."

Abbott was so successful as a Broadway producer and director that he was often described as "the sole possessor of a superhuman faculty called 'the Abbott Touch.'" In a 1970 interview for *Cue* magazine, however, he denied such miraculous theatrical power. "I never knew what they were talking about when people wrote about the Abbott Touch," he insisted. "I direct for economy. I strip a show to its essentials and then do it, that's all." Then he added, "I have not been infallible, you know."

In his autobiography, *Mister Abbott,* Abbott discussed not only his triumphs but his failures, professional as well as personal. The book, which many critics described as "candid," is a detailed account of the author's childhood, his education in a Nebraskan military school and at the University of Rochester, and his participation in Professor Baker's famous theater workshop at Harvard University. Some critics objected to the frankness with which he portrayed his adult personal life. Lenore Philbin, for example, accused him of "shocking his reader by revealing too much and reporting in detail the unfortunate results of his personal promiscuity."

Still, critics generally agreed on the merit of Abbott's account of the theatrical world. In her contribution to *America,* Claire McGlinchee wrote that "the worthwhile parts of the book—and they are excellent—are those that define for present-day aspirants to theater fame, or the sidelines devotees of this art, such things as the nature of stage-fright or the types of directors who may be met at auditions." Calling Abbott the personification of the term "man of the theater," George Oppenheimer concluded in *Saturday Review* that in his autobiography the author added to his "prodigious record with an extremely well-written, honest, and absorbing book."

The venerable man of the theater once took a turn at fiction with *Tryout,* which began as a play but evolved into a novel. In an article in *Library Journal,* Abbott discussed his first and only novel: "My novel has no message, nor do I have any message. *Tryout* is about people and situations. It is, I think what is called a well-made story, with a beginning, a middle and an end. It attempts to deal truthfully with situations in the theater and in Palm Beach."

Never one to rest on his laurels, Abbott was still collaborating on new projects well past his hundredth birthday. Just a year before his death, the 106-year-old playwright/director supervised the New York revival of *Damn Yankees.* When the show opened in spring, 1994, Abbott's third wife, Joy, accompanied him down the aisle of the Marriott Marquis Theatre to receive a thunderous standing ovation. Gwen Verdon, who Abbott cast as the lead in the original *Yankees* production, told *People Weekly,* without exaggeration, "Everybody on Broadway today has been influenced by George Abbott."

BIOGRAPHICAL/CRITICAL SOURCES:

BOOKS

Contemporary Dramatists, fifth edition, St. James Press (Detroit), 1993.
Newsmakers, Gale (Detroit), 1995.

PERIODICALS

America, January 11, 1964.
American Theatre, April, 1995.
Best Sellers, December 15, 1963.
Cue, January 10, 1970.

Dance, February, 1994.
Fortune, February, 1938.
Library Journal, June 15, 1979.
Life, January 18, 1960; December 13, 1963.
Literary Digest, August 15, 1936.
Newsweek, November 1, 1937.
New Yorker, October 30, 1978.
New York Herald Tribune, July 1, 1962, July 5, 1964.
New York Post Magazine, May 20, 1962.
New York Times, June 25, 1962.
New York Times Book Review, November 24, 1963.
Saturday Review, November 23, 1963.
Theatre Arts, February, 1936.
Time, November 1, 1937; September 26, 1938; March 14, 1994.

OBITUARIES:

PERIODICALS

Los Angeles Times, February 1, 1995, p. A13.
Newsweek, February 13, 1995.
New York Times, February 2, 1995.
People Weekly, February 13, 1995.
Time, February 13, 1995.
Times (London), February 2, 1995.*

Sketch by Lane A. Glenn

* * *

ACUNA, Rodolfo
See ACUNA, Rodolfo F(rancis)

* * *

ACUNA, Rodolfo F(rancis) 1932-
(Rodolfo Acuna, Rudy Acuna)

PERSONAL: Born May 18, 1932, in Los Angeles, CA; son of Francisco and Alicia (Elias) Acuna; married Guadalupe Compean, 1984; children: (former marriage) Frank, Walter; Angela. *Education:* California State University, Los Angeles, B.A. (social science), 1957, B.A. (general), 1958, M.A., 1962; University of Southern California, Ph.D., 1968. *Politics:* "Radical." *Religion:* Catholic.

ADDRESSES: Office—Department of Chicano Studies, California State University, Northridge, 18111 Nordhoff St., Northridge, CA 91324.

CAREER: Worked as columnist for the *Los Angeles Herald-Examiner;* California State University, Northridge, professor of Chicano Studies, 1969—. Member of board of Labor/Community Strategy Center; member of Committee in Solidarity with the People of El Salvador.

AWARDS, HONORS: Community service award from Liberty Hill Foundation; Rockefeller Humanities fellowship; Ford grant; outstanding scholar awards from American Council of Learned Societies and National Association of Chicano Studies; award from University of Guadalajara/state of Jalisco (Mexico) for contributions to border research.

WRITINGS:

(Under name Rudy Acuna) *The Story of the Mexican Americans: The Men and the Land,* American Book Co. (New York City), 1969.
(With Peggy Shackelton, under name Rudy Acuna) *Cultures in Conflict: Problems of the Mexican Americans* (children's textbook), Charter School Books, 1970.
(Under name Rudy Acuna) *A Mexican-American Chronicle,* American Book Co., 1971.
(Under name Rodolfo Acuna) *Occupied America: The Chicano's Struggle Toward Liberation,* Canfield Press, 1972, third edition, Harper (New York City), 1987.
Sonoran Strongman: Ignacio Pesqueira and His Times, University of Arizona Press (Tucson), 1974.
A Community Under Seige: A Chronicle of Chicanos East of the Los Angeles River, 1945-1975, University of California, Los Angeles, Chicano Studies Research Center, 1984.

Contributor to periodicals, including *Arizona and the West, Los Angeles Times,* and *Texas Observer,* and to the Pacific News Service.

WORK IN PROGRESS: A collection of previously published newspaper essays on Los Angeles in the 1980s; *When the Moment Comes: The Revolt of the Mexican Cotton Pickers, 1933; Anything but Mexican,* a study of Los Angeles politics.

SIDELIGHTS: Professor of Chicano studies at the University of California, Northridge, Rodolfo F. Acuna is the author of several books and textbooks on Chicano and Mexican history. Acuna founded the

Chicano Studies program at Northridge and has played a part in making it one of the largest departments of its kind in the United States. His own writings reveal the plight of Hispanic Americans in a racist environment, and as a person who grew up speaking Spanish as a first language, he has been a proponent of bilingual education. To quote James McCarthy in the *Dictionary of Hispanic Biography,* Acuna "has remained a controversial figure throughout his academic career, and continues to challenge American society for what he calls its 'endemic racism.'"

Born in Los Angeles in 1932, Acuna grew up with a strong sense of the unjust aspects of American life. In a *Nation* piece on bilingual education he recalled "having to sit through English-only sessions and being pinched by teachers for speaking Spanish" as a schoolboy. His firsthand experience of racism continued after he volunteered for military service during the Korean War and suffered hostile treatment by white soldiers. He has spent the rest of his career as a teacher and writer trying to draw attention to "inequity and systematic unfairness directed at racial minorities," to quote McCarthy.

Acuna earned his Ph.D. from the University of Southern California in 1968. The following year he joined the faculty of California State University at Northridge, where he created the Chicano Studies program and developed much of the curriculum for it. After being denied tenure by the institution in 1991, Acuna sued his university, claiming that he was the victim of the same sort of racism that he had been writing about. The lawsuit garnered quite a bit of media attention in California, and Acuna told the *Dictionary of Hispanic Biography* that his case "will make it easier for others to sue on the basis of discrimination."

As an author Acuna is perhaps best known for *Occupied America: The Chicano's Struggle Toward Liberation,* a historical study in which he argues that the United States's acquisition of the Southwest from Mexico was an act of imperialism. Referring to the Chicano population in the United States as an "internal colony," Acuna contends that Mexican Americans continue to suffer the effects of economic exploitation and racism perpetrated upon them by an Anglo majority. "My purpose is to bring about an awareness . . . of the forces that control and manipulate seven million people in this country," he notes in the book. "If Chicanos can become aware of *why* they are oppressed and *how* the exploitation is perpetuated, they can work more effectively toward ending their colonization." Acuna told *CA* that in later editions of *Occupied America* he "broke with the internal colonial model, giving a more materialist interpretation."

Occupied America elicited contrasting responses from reviewers. Some critics found the book lacking in objectivity, while others appreciated the study's challenge to traditional historical interpretations of the Chicano experience. Writing in the *Western Historical Quarterly,* Victor C. Dahl, for example, called the work "an angry polemic," and charged that it "abounds with generalizations defying either substantiation or refutation." On the other hand, Robert W. Blew's *Southern California Quarterly* review of *Occupied America* praised the study's scholarly content and found it to contain "an intimacy and vigor that is frequently lacking in secondary studies." Blew declared that Acuna "has presented a provocative, stimulating, and challenging interpretation and view of the history of the southwestern portion of the United States." Similarly impressed were Carrol Hernandez and Nathaniel N. Wagner, who concluded in the *International Migration Review* that while Acuna's perspective may be unpopular, he "is trying to rectify myths and distortions that came about as a result of the 'objective academic' writing of past American historians."

BIOGRAPHICAL/CRITICAL SOURCES:

BOOKS

Acuna, Rodolfo, *Occupied America: The Chicano's Struggle Toward Liberation,* Canfield Press, 1982.

Contemporary Literary Criticism, Volume 2, Gale (Detroit, MI), 1974.

Dictionary of Hispanic Biography, Gale, 1996, pp. 3-5.

PERIODICALS

Black Issues in Higher Education, July 27, 1995, pp. 27-30.

International Migration Review, Volume 7, number 4, 1973.

Los Angeles Times Book Review, January 20, 1985.

Nation, June 29, 1998, pp. 2-3.

Southern California Quarterly, fall, 1973.

Western Historical Quarterly, July, 1973.

ACUNA, Rudy
See ACUNA, Rodolfo F(rancis)

* * *

AICKMAN, Robert (Fordyce) 1914-1981

PERSONAL: Born June 27, 1914, in London, England; died February 27, 1981; son of William Arthur (an architect) and Mabel Violet (Marsh) Aickman. *Education:* Attended Highgate School, London, England. *Politics:* Social Credit and Independent. *Avocational interests:* Drama, literature, music, and travel.

CAREER: Writer. Director and chair, London Opera Society Ltd., 1954-69; chair of Balmin Productions Ltd. (which administers traveling Ballets Minerva), 1963-68. General director of Market Harborough Festival 1950 of Boats and Arts; director of Thames Tour 1961 of American Wind Symphony Orchestra; director of City of London Festival waterborne concert, 1962.

MEMBER: National Council on Inland Transport, World Wildlife Fund (member of advisory panel), Inland Waterway Association (founder; past chair; vice-president), Railway Development Association (vice-president), Lower Avon Navigation Trust (member of council), Upper Avon Navigation Trust (chair, 1969-75), Stratford-upon-Avon Canal Society (vice-president), Kehnet and Avon Canal Trust (vice-president), Residential Boat Owners Association (president), River Stour Trust (vice-president), Northampton Drama Club (vice-president), Great Ouse Restoration Society (vice-president), Leeds University Waterways Society (vice-president).

AWARDS, HONORS: World Fantasy Award for best short story, 1973-74, for "Pages from a Young Girl's Diary."

WRITINGS:

NOVELS

The Late Breakfasters, Gollancz (London), 1964.
The Model, Arbor House (New York City), 1987.

STORY COLLECTIONS

(With Elizabeth Jane Howard) *We Are for the Dark,* J. Cape (London), 1951.
Dark Entries, Collins (London), 1964.
Powers of Darkness, Collins, 1966.
Sub Rosa: Strange Tales, Gollancz, 1968.
Cold Hand in Mine, Gollancz, 1976, Scribner (New York City), 1978.
Tales of Love and Death, Gollancz, 1977.
Painted Devils: Strange Stories, Scribner, 1979.
Intrusions: Strange Tales, Gollancz, 1980.
Night Voices, Gollancz, 1985.
The Wine-Dark Sea, Arbor House, 1988, abridged edition, Mandarin (London), 1990.
The Unsettled Dust, Mandarin, 1990.

EDITOR

The Fontana Book of Great Ghost Stories, eight books, Collins, 1964-72.

OTHER

Know Your Waterways, Temprint, 1954.
The Story of Our Inland Waterways, Pitman, 1955.
The Attempted Rescue, Gollancz, 1966.
The River Runs Uphill: A Story of Success and Failure, Pearson (Burton-on-Trent, Staffordshire), 1986.

Former drama critic, *Nineteenth Century and After;* former film critic, *Jewish Monthly.* Contributor to *The Third Ghost Book, The Fourth Ghost Book,* and of an essay on the Avon to *Portraits of Rivers;* frequent contributor of articles and fiction to newspapers and magazines.

SIDELIGHTS: Robert Aickman wrote a total of forty-eight stories, most of them ghost stories. "This is a relatively small body of work," admitted S. T. Joshi in the *St. James Guide to Horror, Ghost and Gothic Writers,* "but it is not Aickman's quantity of output but his exceptional gifts as a writer—a prose style of impeccable fluidity, urbanity and elegance; a high sensitivity to those nuances and details productive of a weird scenario; a keen insight into all aspects of human psychology, not merely those touching upon the strange; and some very powerful weird conceptions that do not require copious, or any, bloodletting for their effectiveness—that distinguish him. The chief quality of Aickman's tales is, however, simply their indefinableness: some are ghost stories, although hardly conventional ones; in others it is difficult even to specify what makes them horrific in the utter absence of supernatural manifestations. Perhaps the subtitle Aickman himself used for most of his collections—'strange stories'—is as precise a definition as one can have."

BIOGRAPHICAL/CRITICAL SOURCES:

BOOKS

St. James Guide to Horror, Ghost and Gothic Writers, St. James Press (Detroit), 1998.*

* * *

AINSWORTH, Harriet
See CADELL, (Violet) Elizabeth

* * *

ALEGRIA, Ciro 1909-1967

PERSONAL: Born November 4, 1909, in Trujillo, Peru; died of a heart attack, February 17, 1967, in Lima, Peru; son of Jose Alegria Lynch and Herminia Bazan Lynch; married Rosalia Amezquita (marriage dissolved); married Ligia Marchand (marriage dissolved); married Dora Varona (a poet). *Education:* Attended Colegio Nacional de San Juan, Trujillo, and University of Trujillo.

CAREER: Writer. *El Norte,* Trujillo, Peru, newspaper reporter, 1926-27 and 1930-31; construction worker, 1928-30; joined Aprista Party and participated in 1931 revolt; imprisoned, 1931-33; exiled to Chile, 1934; lived in the United States, 1941-48; teacher at University of Puerto Rico, 1949-53; returned to Peru, 1957, and joined Accion Popular Party, 1960, serving in Chamber of Deputies, beginning 1963. *Wartime service:* Worked for Office of War Information and Coordinator of Inter-American Affairs, World War II.

AWARDS, HONORS: First prize, Nascimento (publishers) Contest, 1935, for *La serpiente de oro;* first prize, Latin-American Novel Contest, Pan-American Union/Farrar & Rinehart/*Redbook* Magazine, 1941, for *El mundo es ancho y ajeno.*

WRITINGS:

La serpiente de oro (novel), Nascimento (Santiago, Chile), 1935, translation by Harriet de Onis published as *The Golden Serpent,* Farrar & Rinehart (New York City), 1943.

Los perros hambrientos (novel), Zig-Zag (Santiago, Chile), 1939, revised edition, 1942.

La leyende del nopal (for children), Zig-Zag, 1940.

El mundo es ancho y ajeno (novel), Ercilla (Santiago, Chile), 1941, translation by Onis published as *Broad and Alien Is the World,* Farrar & Rinehart, 1941.

Novelas completas (collected novels), Aguilar (Madrid), 1959.

Duelo de caballeros; cuentos y relatos (short stories), Populibros Peruanos (Lima, Peru), 1963.

Panki y el guerrero (for children), Coleccion Infantil (Lima, Peru), 1968.

Gabriela Mistral intima, compiled by Dora Varona, Universo (Lima, Peru), 1968.

La ofrenda de piedra, compiled by Varona, Universo, 1968.

Sueno y verdad de America, compiled by Varona, Universo, 1969.

Lazaro (novel), Losada (Buenos Aires, Argentina), 1973.

La revolucion cubana: Un testimonio personal, Peisa (Lima, Peru), 1973.

Mucha suerte con harto palo: Memorias, edited by Varona, Losada, 1976.

Siete cuentos quiromanticos (stories), Varona (Lima, Peru), 1978.

El dilema de Krause: Penitenciaria de Lima (novel), Varona, 1979.

El sol de los jagurares, Varona, 1979.

Fabulas y leyendas americanas, Espasa-Calpe (Madrid), 1982.

Relatos (stories), Alianza (Madrid), 1983.

Contributor of poems and stories to various periodicals in Peru.

SIDELIGHTS: Peruvian Ciro Alegria expressed a concern for the Indians of his native country through his writing and political activity. While in exile from Peru in the 1930s, Alegria wrote three well-received novels, all of which deal with the plight of native peoples in the harsh environment of the Andes Mountains. Although a member of the ruling class himself, Alegria clearly sympathized with the exploited workers on his country's haciendas and in its overcrowded cities. According to Antonio Cornejo-Polar in the *Dictionary of Literary Biography,* Alegria's work "is a painful eulogy that bids a nostalgic farewell to a humane way of life, at the same time angrily recognizing that personal interests and the interests of those in power have taken over

Peru." The critic continued: "Ciro Alegria produced literary transformations of considerable significance. As do all great authors, he took on a tradition that suited him and then changed and superseded it within the limits of the awareness possible in his time."

The son of Spanish-Irish parents, Alegria grew up alongside the Indians of the Maranon River. His father owned several haciendas, but unlike other landowners, he treated his Indian and mestizo workers with respect. Along with his formal education, Alegria learned to farm amongst the peasants, and he absorbed their culture and folklore with great interest. "Alegria . . . was more than a mere witness of this world," wrote Cornejo-Polar. "Alegria remembered the limitless admiration with which he listened to the stories and happenings told to him by the Indian and mestizo farmers who worked on his father's haciendas. It is from them he claims that he learned the art of narration."

Alegria's sympathy for the working class grew into indignation. As a young man he became involved in the *Aprista* party, which advocated social and economic reforms, particularly with regard to the country's poorer classes. Arrested for organizing revolutionary movements in several Peruvian provinces, he was imprisoned and tortured, and in 1934 he was deported to Chile. There he began to write of his boyhood home, composing his three best-known works, *La serpiente de oro, Los perros hambrientos,* and *El mundo es ancho y ajeno,* between 1934 and 1941.

In *La serpiente de oro* (translated as *The Golden Serpent*), Alegria related the trials of a tribe of Indians as they "adapt their skills and philosophies to the rough demands of their life," Mildred Adams summarized in the *New York Times*. Episodic in nature, *La serpiente de oro* reveals the life of the *cholos* (or "civilized" natives) along the banks of the Maranon River. Carleton Beals, who called *The Golden Serpent* "a strong and beautiful book," noted in his *Book Week* review that Alegria's tale "has the firm texture of things and people loved and understood, and at the same time is epic in its setting and scope."

Cornejo-Polar wrote of *La serpiente de oro:* "Alegria's first novel represents a transformation of the bases of regionalist literature. . . . Faced with [a] unique world, Alegria does not hide his admiration. In this place distanced from civilization he finds values and forms of social relationships more honorable than those of modern society. One might say that, while distressed in his exile, by attempting to forge an image of a lost nation, Alegria regained his faith and was able to question the unjust and powerful social order that had expelled him."

The author continued his indictment of Peruvian social forces in *Los perros hambrientos,* a novel set in the remote Andean high plateau. Faced with prolonged drought and deteriorating relationships with the wealthy landowners, the Indians endure numerous crises but cling to life through their solidarity. According to Cornejo-Polar, in this novel Alegria "observes how collective misfortune destroys customs and institutions that are in one way or another superficial and unjust. . . . As an antithesis to this process of deterioration, the novel affirms the preservation of the most elemental social values: love, pity, and solidarity among sufferers."

Alegria was best known, however, for *El mundo es ancho y ajeno,* a book that brought him fame in the United States when it won the Pan American Union's Latin-American Novel Contest. Translated as *Broad and Alien Is the World,* the novel concerns a group of North Andean Indians whose way of life is destroyed when powerful landowners move into the area and exploit the land and local work force. The book was compared to John Steinbeck's *The Grapes of Wrath,* and while *New Yorker* reviewer Clifton Fadiman noted that the book could be termed "a class-warfare novel," he stated that "it is very different from the mechanical mintings of our own early nineteen-thirties. There is more poetry than dogma in it." Milton Rugoff similarly observed the theme of class conflict in *Broad and Alien Is the World,* but noted in *Books* that "what makes it so satisfying . . . is not symbolism, but fullness, authenticity, compassion. . . . Rich and strange, the material almost always justifies itself."

Other reviewers, including Fadiman and *Nation* contributor M. J. Benardete, found *Broad and Alien Is the World* somewhat congested with detail. As Benardete commented, "Story and thesis do not get in each other's way, but the overwhelming regional knowledge of the author considerably retards the flow." Nevertheless, the critic admitted that "the abundance of songs, fables, fairy tales, and legends in the novel gives it a folksy tang which sustains it and makes it a memorable introduction to Peru and the Indians." "The narrative is both easy and intricate," P. M. Jack claimed in his *New York Times* review. "The dozen stories of various village characters are sharply focused in themselves, yet they melt into the total life of the community, which is everything." Jack went on to remark that "it is not enough to say that this is the novel through which every reader will understand something fundamental in South America, though that is true and important; it is a fine work of the imagination." As critic John Dos Passos, one of the Latin-American Novel Contest judges, stated in the committee's citation: "I can say without any hesitation that *El mundo es ancho y ajeno* is one of the most impressive novels I've ever read in Spanish."

To quote Cornejo-Polar, *El mundo es ancho y ajeno* "not only reveals and denounces a real situation but also postulates something of an exercise in social consciousness for a nation. The eulogy for a disappearing social order is transformed into a violent opposition of the dominant social system and an appeal for the old values. Within this context Alegria is the first Indianist novelist to defend consistently the indigenous community, not only with regard to political, social, and economic factors but also, in an often more intense way, with his attention to ethnic and cultural viewpoints."

In the wake of *El mundo es ancho y ajeno,* Alegria continued to publish short stories and essays, but none of his subsequent works drew the critical response attendant upon his first three novels. During World War II, he lived in the United States, and from 1949 until 1953 he taught literature at the national university in Puerto Rico. Through the rest of the 1950s he lived in Havana, Cuba, where he wrote and lectured. There he married poet Dora Varona, who would ultimately oversee the posthumous publication of much of his later work.

Twenty-three years after he was exiled from Peru, Alegria returned as a respected man of letters. He and his wife lived in Peru until his death in 1967. Biographer Eileen Early eulogized Alegria as a principled man whose fiction "is of a piece with his nonfiction and, indeed, with his life as journalist, novelist, politician, and professor of literature."

BIOGRAPHICAL/CRITICAL SOURCES:

BOOKS

Alegria, Ciro, *Mucha suerte con alto palo: Memorias,* edited by Dora Varona, Losada (Buenos Aires, Argentina), 1976.

Bunte, Hans, *Ciro Alegria y su obra,* Mejia Baca (Lima, Peru), 1961.

Cornejo-Polar, Jorge, editor, *La obra de Ciro Alegria,* Universidad de San Agustin (Arequipa, Peru), 1976.

Dictionary of Hispanic Biography, Gale (Detroit, MI), 1996, pp. 9-10.

Dictionary of Literary Biography, Volume 113: *Modern Latin-American Fiction Writers, First Series,* Gale, 1992, pp. 3-8.

Early, Eileen, *Joy in Exile,* University Press of America (Washington, DC), 1980.

Escajadillo, Tomas G., *Ciro Alegria y "El mundo es ancho y ajeno,"* Universidad de San Marcos (Lima, Peru), 1983.

Hispanic Writers, Gale, 1991.

Latin American Writers, Scribner's (New York City), 1989.

Onis, Harriet de, editor, *The Golden Land,* Knopf (New York City), 1948.

Tocilovac, Goran, *La communidad indigena y Ciro Alegria,* Biblioteca Universitaria (Lima, Peru), 1972.

Varona, Dora, *La sombra del condor,* Diselpsea, 1993.

PERIODICALS

Americas, February, 1963.

Books, November 9, 1941.

Book Week, October 31, 1943.

Nation, November 29, 1941.

New Yorker, November 15, 1941.

New York Times, November 16, 1941; October 3, 1943.

New York Times Book Review, March 30, 1941; June 22, 1941.

Saturday Review of Literature, March 29, 1941.*

* * *

ALEGRIA, Fernando 1918-

PERSONAL: Born September 26, 1918, in Santiago, Chile; son of Santiago Alegria Toro (in business) and Julia Alfaro; married Carmen Letona Melendez, January 29, 1943; children: Carmen, Daniel, Andres, Isabel. *Education:* Bowling Green State University, M.A., 1941; University of California, Berkeley, Ph.D., 1947.

ADDRESSES: Home—55 Arlmonte Dr., Berkeley, CA 94707. *Office*—Department of Spanish and Portuguese, Stanford University, Stanford, CA 94305.

CAREER: University of Chile, Santiago, Chile, professor of Spanish, 1939; Bowling Green State University, Bowling Green, OH, Extension Division, instructor in Spanish, 1940-41; University of California, Berkeley, instructor, 1947-49, assistant professor, 1949-55, associate professor, 1955-63, professor of Spanish and Portuguese, 1964-67; Stanford University, Stanford, CA, professor of Spanish, 1967-87, professor of Portuguese, 1976-87, professor emeritus, 1987—. Consultant in Spanish American literature, UNESCO, 1968. Cultural attache in Chilean Embassy, Washington, DC, 1970-73.

MEMBER: Instituto Internacional de Literatura Iberoamericana, American Association of Teachers of Spanish, Sociedad de Escritores (Chile).

AWARDS, HONORS: Latin American Prize of Literature, 1943, for *Lautaro: Joven libertador de Arauco;* Guggenheim fellow, 1947-48; Premio Atenea and Premio Municipal (both Chile), for *Caballo de copas.*

WRITINGS:

Recabarren, Antares, 1938.

Ideas esteticas de la poesia moderna, Multitud, 1939.

Leyenda de la ciudad perdida, Zig-Zag (Santiago, Chile), 1942.

Lautaro: Joven libertador de Arauco (juvenile fiction), Zig-Zag, 1943, 5th edition, 1965.

Ensayo sobre cinco temas de Tomas Mann, Funes, 1949.

Camaleon, Ediapsa, 1951.

La poesia chilena: Origenes y desarollo del siglo XVI al XIX, University of California Press (Berkeley), 1954.

Walt Whitman en hispanoamerica, Studium, 1954.

El poeta que se volvio gusano, Cuadernos Americanos, 1956.

Caballo de copas, Zig-Zag, 1957, 2nd edition, 1961, reprinted, Casa de las Americas, 1981, translation by Carlos Lozano published as *My Horse Gonzales,* Casa de las Americas, 1964.

Breve historia de la novela hispanoamericana, Studium, 1959, 2nd edition published as *Historia de la novela hispanoamericana,* De Andrea, 1965, published as *Nueva historia de la novela hispanoamericana,* Ediciones del Norte (Hanover, NH), 1985.

El cataclismo (short stories), Nascimento, 1960.

Las noches del cazador, Zig-Zag, 1961.

Las fronteras del realismo: Literatura chilena del siglo XX, Zig-Zag, 1962, 2nd edition published as *La literatura chilena del siglo XX,* 1967.

(Editor) *Novelistas contemporaneos hispanoamericanos,* Heath (New York City), 1964.

Manana los guerreros (novel), Zig-Zag, 1964.

Viva chile M!, Editorial Universitaria (Santiago), 1965.

(Editor and translator) Rene Marill, *Historia de la novela moderna,* Union Tipografica Editorial Hispano Americana, 1966.

Genio y figura de Gabriela Mistral, Editorial Universitaria de Buenos Aires (Buenos Aires, Argentina), 1966.

La novela hispanoamericana, siglo XX, Centro Editor de America Latina, 1967.

(Translator with others) Nicanor Parra, *Poems and Antipoems,* edited by Miller Williams, New Directions (New York City), 1967.

Los dias contados (novel), Siglo XXI, 1968.

Ten Pastoral Psalms (poetry; bilingual edition; English versions by Bernardo Garcia and Matthew Zion), Kayak (Santa Cruz, CA), 1968.

Como un arbol rojo, Editora Santiago, 1968.

La maraton del palomo (short stories), Centro Editor de America Latina, 1968.

Los mejores cuentos de Fernando Alegria, edited with prologue by Alfonso Calderon, Zig-Zag, 1968.

La literatura chilena contemporanea, Centro Editor de America Latina, 1969.

Instructions for Undressing the Human Race/Instrucciones para desnudar a la raza humana (poem; bilingual edition; English version by Matthew Zion and Lennart Bruce; also see below), Kayak, 1969.

Amerika (manifiestos de Vietnam), Editorial Universitaria, 1970.

(With others) *Literatura y praxis en America Latina,* Monte Avila Editores, 1974.

Retratos contemporaneos, Harcourt (New York City), 1979.

Coral de guerra, Nueva Imagen, 1979.

El paso de los gansos, Laia, 1980.

The Chilean Spring, translated by Stephen Fredman, Latin American Literary Review Press (Pittsburgh, PA), 1980.

(Contributor of poetry) Moraima de Semprun Donahue, *Figuras y contrafiguras en la poesia de Fernando Alegria,* Latin American Literary Review Press, 1981.

(Author of prologue) Pablo Neruda, *Canto general,* 2nd edition, Biblioteca Ayacucho, 1981.

(Editor and contributor) *Chilean Writers in Exile: Eight Short Novels,* Crossing Press (Trumansburg, NY), 1982.

Una especie de memoria, Editorial Nueva Imagen, 1983.

Changing Centuries: Selected Poems of Fernando Alegria (includes selections from *Instrucciones para desnudar a la raza humana*), translated by Stephen Kessler, Latin American Literary Review Press, 1984, 2nd edition, 1988.

Los trapecios, Ediciones Agua Pesada, 1985.

The Funhouse, translated by Kessler, Arte Publico (Houston, TX), 1986.

(Editor with Jorge Ruffinelli) *Paradise Lost or Gained? The Literature of Hispanic Exile,* Arte Publico, 1992.

Allende: A Novel (English translation of *Allende: Mi vecino, el presidente),* Stanford University Press (Stanford, CA), 1994.

Also author of *La venganza del general, La prensa, Literatura y revolucion,* 1970.

SIDELIGHTS: "The most distinguished Chilean writer living in the United States," reports Victor Perera in the *Nation,* "is the critic and novelist Fernando Alegria, who was [former Chilean President Salvador] Allende's cultural attache in Washington." Noted for his important critical works on Latin American literature, his poetry, and his novels, Alegria has been living in exile since a military junta overthrew Allende's government on September 11, 1973. His own experience as an expatriate—as well as his deeply felt opinions on the course of Chilean politics—have informed his writings throughout the years, particularly in the most recent decades.

A native of Santiago, Chile, Alegria was an avid reader as a child and was encouraged in his writing by his mother and grandmother. While still in high school he began to publish pieces in *La Nacion,* Santiago's daily newspaper, and by the time he was twenty he had completed his first full-length book, the biography of a Chilean labor movement leader entitled *Recabarren.* Alegria continued his studies at Bowling Green State University, majoring in literature. He put himself through graduate school by teaching Spanish and Portuguese, and after earning his Ph.D. he served as a professor at the University of California, Berkeley and at Stanford.

Alegria made a name for himself in Chile after publishing *Caballo de copas,* an extended essay on the similarities between life among the Chilean working class and Hispanic laborers in California. The work was a bestseller in Chile, enabling Alegria to return to his homeland with a ready audience for his books. Once there, the author became actively involved in the Popular Unity Movement, led by his old friend Salvador Allende. When Allende was elected president of Chile in 1970, Alegria became the nation's cultural attache in Washington, DC.

The high expectations attending Allende's election were dashed just three years later when a military junta overthrew the government and assassinated Allende. Alegria was in Chile at the time of the coup but managed to escape and return to the United States. He has lived in California ever since.

The Chilean Spring, Alegria's fictionalized account of a young photographer's ordeal and death at the hands of the junta, is a "tribute to a modestly heroic photographer [that] becomes a poignant elegy to a nation whose future has been taken from it," declared *New York Times Book Review* contributor Jeffrey Burke. "That Mr. Alegria accomplishes so much so effectively in so few pages," Burke continued, "is a remarkable achievement." Alegria also addressed the Allende overthrow in his book *Allende: A Novel,* a part-fictional, part-factual biography of the socialist hero. "Alegria manages to provide interesting glimpses into Allende's complex personality," observed Jorge Heine in the *Journal of Latin American Studies.* "We are enriched by a book that makes one of Latin America's most significant leaders come alive in a way that only somebody who knew him so well as Alegria could have done."

His own experience as an exile led Alegria to seek out the writings of other Latin American expatriates, and the result was *Paradise Lost or Gained? The Literature of Hispanic Exile,* which he edited with Jorge Ruffinelli. "The stories, poems and essays in this collection—some in English, some in Spanish—focus on different phases of [the exile] process," wrote Barbara Mujica in *Americas.* "Surprisingly, few of these pieces are nostalgic or angry. The best treats the dilemma of the exile with warmth and humor." Mujica concluded that Alegria and Ruffinelli "have done an excellent job of compiling material that increases our understanding of the trauma of exile. Through the intimate testimonies in *Paradise Lost or Gained?,* millions of exiles who have been uprooted from their native soil cease to be faceless statistics and become flesh and blood men and women whose stories move and enlighten us."

BIOGRAPHICAL/CRITICAL SOURCES:

BOOKS

Dictionary of Hispanic Biography, Gale (Detroit, MI), 1996, pp. 10-12.

Epple, Juan Armando, *Nos reconoce el tiempo y silba su tonada* (interview), Ediciones LAR, 1987.

PERIODICALS

Americas, November/December, 1992, pp. 30-38, 39; May/June, 1993, pp. 60-61.

Books Abroad, winter, 1970.

Carleton Miscellany, Number 3, 1969.

Chicago Review, Number 1, 1968; January/February, 1971.

Journal of Latin American Studies, October, 1995, pp. 748-49.

Nation, February 11, 1978.

New York Times Book Review, May 11, 1980.

Poetry, March, 1970.

Publishers Weekly, April 5, 1993, pp. 66-67.*

* * *

ALEGRIA, Ricardo E(nrique) 1921-

PERSONAL: Born April 14, 1921, in San Juan, Puerto Rico; son of Jose S. and Celeste (Gallardo) Alegria; married Mela Pons (an artist), December 7, 1947; children: Ricardo, Jose Francisco. *Education:* University of Puerto Rico, B.A., 1943; University of Chicago, M.A., 1947; Harvard University, Ph.D., 1955. *Religion:* Roman Catholic.

ADDRESSES: Home—San Jose 101, San Juan, PR 00901. *Office*—Department of History, University of Puerto Rico, Rio Piedras, PR 00901.

CAREER: University of Puerto Rico, Rio Piedras, associate professor of history, 1947-55, director of archaeological museum and research center, 1947-55; Instituto de Cultura Puertorriquena (Institute of Puerto Rican Culture), San Juan, director, 1955-73; University of Puerto Rico, professor of anthropology and history, 1955—. Director, Office of Cultural Affairs, San Juan, 1973-76.

MEMBER: American Anthropological Association (fellow), Society for American Archaeology.

AWARDS, HONORS: Guggenheim Foundation fellow, 1953-55; Doctorate Honoris Causae, humanities, Catholic University (Puerto Rico), 1971; Doctorate Honoris Causae, law, New York University, 1971; National Trust for Historic Preservation award, 1973; Ph.D., University of Puerto Rico, 1974.

WRITINGS:

Historia de nuestros indios, illustrated by wife, Mela Pons de Alegria, Seccion de Publicaciones e Impresos, Departamento de Instruccion (San Juan, PR), 1950, 8th edition, Coleccion de Estudios Puertorriquenos (San Juan), 1972, translation by C. Virginia Matters published as *History of the Indians of Puerto Rico,* Coleccion de Estudios Puertorriquenos, 1970, 3rd edition, 1974.

La fiesta de Santiago Apostol en Loiza Aldea, prologue by Fernando Ortiz, Artes Graficas (Madrid), 1954.

El Instituto de Cultura Puertorriquena: Los primeros cinco anos, 1955-1960, Instituto de Cultura Puertorriquena, 1960.

El tema del cafe en la literature puertorriquena, Instituto de Cultura Puertorriquena, 1965.

(With others) *Cafe,* Instituto de Cultura Puertorriquena, 1967.

(Collector and editor) *Cuentos folkloricos de Puerto Rico,* Editorial El Ateneo (Buenos Aires, Argentina), 1967.

(Selector and adaptor) *The Three Wishes: A Collection of Puerto Rican Folktales,* translated by Elizabeth Culbert, illustrated by Lorenzo Homar, Harcourt (New York City), 1968.

Descubrimiento, conquista y colonizacion de Puerto Rico, 1493-1599, Coleccion de Estudios Puertorriquenos, 1969, translation published as *Discovery, Conquest and Colonization of Puerto Rico, 1493-1599,* 1971.

El fuerte de San Jeronimo del Boqueron, Instituto de Cultura Puertorriquena, 1969.

A History of Our Indians, Urban Media Materials, 1970.

Apuntes en torno a la mitologia de los indios tainos de las Antillas Mayores y sus origenes suramericanos, Centro de Estudios Avanzados de Puerto Rico y el Caribe, Museo del Hombre Dominicano (Santo Domingo, Dominican Republic), 1978.

Las primeras representaciones graficas del indio americano, 1493-1523, Centro de Estudios Avanzados de Puerto Rico y el Caribe, Instituto de Cultura Puertorriquena, 1978.

El Instituto de Cultural Puertorriquena, 1955-1973: 18 anos contribuyendo a fortalecer neustra conciencia nacional, Instituto de Cultura Puertorriquena, 1978.

Fort of San Jeronimo Del Boqueron, Gordon Press (New York City), 1979.

Institute of Puerto Rican Culture, Gordon Press, 1979.

Utuado Ceremonial Park, Gordon Press, 1979.

Cristobal Colon el tesoro de los indios tainos de La Espanola, Fundacion Garcia-Arevalo (Santo Domingo), 1980.

El uso de la incrustacion en la escultura de los indios antillanos, Centro de Estudios Avanzados de Puerto Rico y el Caribe con la colaboracion de la Fundacion Garcia Arevalo, 1981.

Las primeras noticias sobre los indios Caribes, Editorial Universidad de Puerto Rico, en colaboracion con el Centro de Estudios Avanzados de Puerto Rico y el Caribe, 1981.

Ball Courts and Ceremonial Plazas in the West Indies, Yale University Publications in Anthropology (New Haven, CT), 1983.

(With Lucas Moran Arce and others) *Historia de Puerto Rico,* Librotex (San Juan), 1985, 2nd edition, 1986.

(With Irving Rouse) *Excavations at Maria de la Cruz Cave and Hacienda Grande Village Site, Loiza, Puerto Rico,* Yale University Publications in Anthropology, 1993.

(Contributor) *Taino: Pre-Columbian Art and Culture from the Caribbean,* Monacelli Press, 1998.

Also author of *Cacicazgo among the Aborigines of the West Indies,* 1947, and *La poblacion aborigen antillana y su relacion con otras areas de America,* 1948. Contributor of articles on archaeology and folklore to journals in Puerto Rico, the United States, and Mexico, including *Revista del Instituto de Lutural Puertorriquena, American Antiquity,* and *Revista Mexicana de Estudios Antropologicos.*

WORK IN PROGRESS: Writing on the folklore and history of Puerto Rico and on archaeology of the West Indies.

SIDELIGHTS: Ricardo E. Alegria is a noted Puerto Rican historian and anthropologist who, from 1955 through 1973, served as director of the prominent Instituto de Cultura Puertorriquena (Institute of Puerto Rican Culture). Alegria has also directed archaeological excavations at one of Puerto Rico's most important sites, comprising the Maria de la Cruz Cave and Hacienda Grande. At that site Alegria and his colleagues have found Archaic-age and very early Ceramic-age deposits that have broadened understanding of ancient Puerto Rican history. "Hacienda [Grande] is one of the earliest Ceramic-age sites in Puerto Rico, and is therefore of enormous importance," wrote William F. Keegan in *American Antiquity.* Keegan found Alegria's monograph *Excavations at Maria de la Cruz Cave and Hacienda Grande Village Site, Loiza, Puerto Rico* "a cogent expression of . . . senior scholars' interpretations of the earliest periods of Puerto Rican prehistory. It is essential reading for students of Caribbean archaeology."

In addition to his archaeological work, Alegria has compiled books of Puerto Rican folklore and has written histories of the European discovery era. He is an authority on the Indians of Puerto Rico and has written a comprehensive summary of his native country's legacy in *Historia de Puerto Rico.*

BIOGRAPHICAL/CRITICAL SOURCES:

BOOKS

Dictionary of Hispanic Biography, Gale (Detroit, MI), 1996, pp. 13-14.

PERIODICALS

American Antiquity, October, 1993, p. 777.
Book World, August 17, 1969.
Horn Book, August, 1969.
New York Times Book Review, May 4, 1969.*

* * *

ALLBEURY, Ted
See ALLBEURY, Theodore Edward le Bouthillier

* * *

ALLBEURY, Theodore Edward le Bouthillier 1917- (Ted Allbeury; pseudonyms: Richard Butler, Patrick Kelly)

PERSONAL: Born October 24, 1917, in Stockport, England; son of Theo and Florence (Bailey) Allbeury; married third wife, Grazyna Felinska, May 13, 1971; children: David, Kerry, Lisa, Sally. *Education:* Attended schools in Birmingham, England.

Avocational interests: Travel (has visited Europe, the Middle East, Africa, and the United States).

ADDRESSES: Home—Cheriton House, Furnace Lane, Lamberhurst, Kent, England. *Agent*—Blake Friedmann Literary Agency, 37-41 Gower St., London WC1E 6HH, England.

CAREER: E. Walter George Ltd. (advertising agency), London, England, creative director, 1950-57; W. J. Southcombe Ltd. (advertising agency), London, managing director, 1957-62; Allbeury, Coombs & Partners (public relations and marketing consultants), Tunbridge Wells, Kent, England, co-founder and senior partner, 1964—. Radio 390 ("pirate" radio station), managing director, 1964-67; broadcaster for British Broadcasting Corp. (BBC) Network 4 and BBC Radio Medway. *Military service:* British Intelligence Corps, 1939-47; became lieutenant colonel.

MEMBER: Society of Authors, Crime Writers Association, Special Forces Club, TVS Supervisory Board.

WRITINGS:

NOVELS UNDER NAME TED ALLBEURY

A Choice of Enemies, St. Martin's (New York City), 1972.
Snowball, Lippincott (Philadelphia, PA), 1974.
The Special Collection, Mayflower (New York City), 1975.
Omega Minus, Viking (New York City), 1975 (published in England as *Palomino Blonde,* P. Davies (London), 1975), published as *Palomino Blonde,* Harper (New York City), 1983.
The Only Good German, P. Davies, 1976, published as *Mission Berlin,* Walker & Co. (New York City), 1986.
Moscow Quadrille, P. Davies, 1976.
The Lantern Network, P. Davies, 1977, Mysterious Press (New York City), 1987.
The Man with the President's Mind, P. Davies, 1977, Simon & Schuster (New York City), 1978.
The Alpha List, Methuen (New York City), 1979.
Consequence of Fear, Hart Davis, MacGibbon (London), 1979, published as *Smokescreen,* Medallion (New York City), 1986.
The Reaper, Mayflower, 1980, published as *The Stalking Angel,* Mysterious Press, 1988.
The Twentieth Day of January, Granada Publishing (London), 1980.
The Other Side of Silence, Scribner (New York City), 1981.
Shadow of Shadows, Scribner, 1982.
All Our Tomorrows, Granada Publishing, 1982, Mysterious Press, 1989.
Pay Any Price, Granada Publishing, 1983.
The Judas Factor, New English Library, 1984, Mysterious Press, 1987.
The Girl from Addis, Granada Publishing, 1984.
No Place to Hide, New English Library (London), 1984.
Children of Tender Years, Beaufort Books (New York City), 1985.
The Seeds of Treason, Mysterious Press, 1986.
The Choice, New English Library, 1986.
The Crossing, New English Library, 1987.
A Wilderness of Mirrors, New English Library, 1988.
Deep Purple, New English Library, 1989, Mysterious Press, 1990.
A Time without Shadows, New English Library, 1990.
Dangerous Edge, New English Library, 1991.
Show Me a Hero, New English Library, 1992.
The Line Crosser, New English Library, 1993.
As Time Goes By, Hodder & Stoughton (London), 1994.
Beyond the Silence, Hodder & Stoughton, 1995.

SHORT STORIES UNDER NAME TED ALLBEURY

Other Kinds of Treason, Hodder & Stoughton, 1990.

NOVELS UNDER PSEUDONYM RICHARD BUTLER

Where All the Girls Are Sweeter, P. Davies, 1975.
Italian Assets, P. Davies, 1976.

NOVELS UNDER PSEUDONYM PATRICK KELLY

Codeword Cromwell, Granada Publishing, 1980.
The Lonely Margins, Granada Publishing, 1981.
The Secret Whispers, Granada Publishing, 1981, Medallion, 1987.

OTHER

Contributor to *Murder Ink: The Mystery Reader's Companion,* edited by Dilys Winn, Workman, 1977. Contributor to anthologies, including *The Mystery Guild Anthology,* edited by John Waite, Book Club Associates, 1980; *Winter's Crimes 12,* edited by Hilary Watson, Macmillan, 1980. Contributor to periodicals, including *New Statesman,* and to newspapers.

ADAPTATIONS: No Place to Hide, 1984, adapted as the film *Hostage,* 1992.

SIDELIGHTS: British thriller novelist Ted Allbeury is a highly regarded writer whose realistic espionage books have often been praised by critics. Allbeury has had first-hand experience in the world of espionage as a member of the British Intelligence Corps from 1939 to 1947, but his personal knowledge of government intelligence operations is not what first inspired him to write. Rather, as he once told *CA,* he began writing novels in 1970 after the kidnapping of his four-year-old daughter. With his first book, *A Choice of Enemies,* the author said, "I wanted my daughter to know that I cared and tried to find her." This sad chapter in the author's life, along with his belief that all wars inevitably result in disaster for everyone concerned, has strongly influenced his stories, many of which end in tragedy.

Dictionary of Literary Biography contributor Michael J. Tolley observed that Allbeury's stories feature "not the world of le Carre's Smiley, a top professional 'control' who makes the large decisions, but that of the subordinate agent, operating in the no-man's-land between the superpowers, as much exposed to betrayal by his masters as by his colleagues or the ever-deceitful enemy." The essayist declared that Allbeury "has produced some of the chilliest, most depressing endings since the Berlin Wall claimed its archetypal victim." The author himself had this to say about his works: "I have tried in my novels to show that people employed in espionage or in intelligence work have private lives, and that their work affects their lives," he said in the *St. James Guide to Crime and Mystery Writers.* "The man who is tough in his intelligence work may compensate by always picking lame ducks so far as his ladies are concerned. Although so far I have had the nicest of reviews in all countries, there is sometimes a comment that my books have sad endings. This, of course, is deliberate. I believe that all wars have sad endings for both losers and winners, and that those who are concerned with espionage and counterespionage tend to have sad endings even in peacetime."

A Choice of Enemies, Allbeury's first book, is about a British spy named Ted Bailey who defects to Poland after learning that his missing daughter is there under the control of a Belgian double-agent named Berger. Reasoning during his defection that personal loyalties are more important than national interests, he nonetheless makes one last attempt to thwart Berger's plans. In the novel's conclusion, Bailey is forced to leave his daughter in Poland under the protection of an American agent. Praised by Newgate Calendar in the *New York Times Book Review* as a first novel "handled with the skill of a veteran," *A Choice of Enemies* is similar to later Allbeury thrillers in several ways. Beginning with Ted Bailey, the author has used autobiographical elements to create the background for a number of his main characters. Bailey's "background in working-class Birmingham, used here to set him against the typical 'Oxbridge' breed of spy, derives from Allbeury's own," Tolley reported.

Another feature of *A Choice of Enemies* and other thriller and suspense books by the author is the ruthless abilities of agents on both sides to torture or kill their enemies. There is also the common motif of the intelligence superior who puts national interests ahead of personal ones, usually to the detriment of the protagonist. In *A Choice of Enemies,* Tolley observed, "The master spies are the experts in cruel manipulation of the weaknesses of agents, whatever side they are on, though authorial bitterness about this does not obtrude as in some later Allbeury novels."

Cynical endings are the rule in Allbeury's *The Only Good German, The Alpha List, The Lonely Margins, The Secret Whispers, Pay Any Price,* and other works in which errors in judgment, betrayal, and the inhumanity of master spies (the novelist especially portrays the British Special Intelligence Service disparagingly), lead to torture, suicide, and murder. Books such as *Palomino Blonde, The Special Collection,* and *The Girl from Addis* also share the kidnapping motif first addressed in *A Choice of Enemies.*

Grimly realistic as they are, Allbeury's novels have drawn praise from critics for their uncompromising look at the emotional and physical dangers of espionage. To quote Greg Goode in the *St. James Guide to Crime and Mystery Writers,* Allbeury "has become known as the spy writer's spy writer. . . . In humanity of tone, depth of character, and variety of plot, he is unmatched by any spy writer. . . . [His work] depicts the perils of the espionage professon for those who love."

Allbeury has also written a mainstream novel, *The Choice,* that reviewers considered more optimistic than his earlier work. As with many of his spy thrillers, this book concerns a World War II veteran; but instead of becoming involved in espionage, the story simply involves the protagonist's difficult private life. The title refers to the choice the main character, David, must make between his wife and another woman. Eventually, he ends up with neither, marrying instead a young journalist and living happily in his hometown. "With *The Choice,*" Tolley remarked, "Allbeury may have effectively worked out of his system the characteristic life pattern which has informed so many of his novels. This pattern, reiterated so often, enabled him to express his anguish about the constrictions of modern life."

After *The Choice,* the author's *The Seeds of Treason* and *The Crossing* "convey a more affirmative mood," according to Tolley. However, the dark realism that has become an Allbeury trademark has not entirely disappeared. In his 1990 book, *A Time without Shadows,* as London *Times* critic Michael Hartland pointed out, a "wartime atmosphere of bitterness and mistrust pervades everything."

In a 1975 *New York Times Book Review* article, Callendar called Allbeury "a skilled practitioner of espionage and suspense novels," and *Times* reviewer John Nicholson contended that the novelist may be "one of our most convincing writers in this field," yet he is not widely known outside of his native England. In a *Washington Post Book World* review of *The Judas Factor,* Robin W. Winks hypothesized that Allbeury has not become as popular as Ian Fleming, John le Carre, and other luminaries in the genre because he "tells it as it is." Allbeury does not see the world in black and white, good versus evil; his stories are often sad, and "he does not rely on repetitive car chases, torture scenes, kinky sex, descriptions of mechanical wonders, cataclysmic countdowns, or excessive tradecraft to keep his story moving." Perhaps, Winks later added, the novelist merely lacks "that distinctive mark" that has brought other writers fame. But Callendar concluded in a 1983 *New York Times Book Review* article that Allbeury "deserves more attention than he has been getting."

Greg Goode seemed to take exception to the notion that Allbeury remains relatively obscure as a writer. Goode noted that while Allbeury's books are cited for their realism, "they do not sag with overwritten secrets about tradecraft. Instead, they penetrate the shadowy themes of espionage in a clean, lucid prose style reminiscent of Ross MacDonald. The earlier novels bristle with plot and high-tech background and the later ones focus on character and history, but with fluent writing and fascinating themes throughout." The critic concluded that, in the span of some two decades and more than thirty novels, "Allbeury has become one of the finest, most consistent, and most inventive modern espionage craftsmen in the English language."

BIOGRAPHICAL/CRITICAL SOURCES:

BOOKS

Dictionary of Literary Biography, Volume 87: *British Mystery and Thriller Writers since 1940,* Gale (Detroit, MI), 1989.

St. James Guide to Crime and Mystery Writers, fourth edition, St. James (Detroit, MI), 1996.

PERIODICALS

Globe and Mail (Toronto), July 21, 1984; February 23, 1985.

Los Angeles Times Book Review, January 17, 1988.

New Republic, November 25, 1981.

New York Times Book Review, June 2, 1974, p. 20; June 15, 1975; April 16, 1978; November 9, 1980; January 24, 1982; January 2, 1983; October 5, 1986; April 10, 1988; September 25, 1988; May 7, 1989; April 15, 1990.

Times (London), July 28, 1983; March 15, 1984; January 22, 1987; February 3, 1990.

Times Literary Supplement, September 6, 1974; February 21, 1975; December 26, 1975; May 28, 1976; August 26, 1977; April 17, 1981; April 16, 1982; December 10, 1982.

Tribune Books (Chicago), June 25, 1989.

Washington Post Book World, September 13, 1987; February 21, 1988.

* * *

ALLPORT, Susan 1950-

PERSONAL: Born July 5, 1950, in New Haven, CT; daughter of Alexander Wise (an administrator) and Jane (Raible) Allport; married David C. Howell (an artist and product designer), September 10, 1978; children: Liberty, Cecil. *Education:* Pitzer College, B.A., 1972; Tulane University of Louisiana, M.S., 1977. *Politics:* Independent. *Religion:* None.

ADDRESSES: Home—Upstate New York. *Agent*—Virginia Barber, 101 Fifth Ave., New York, NY 10003.

CAREER: Writer.

MEMBER: American Medical Writers Association, National Association of Science Writers.

WRITINGS:

Explorers of the Black Box: The Search for the Cellular Basis of Memory, Norton (New York City), 1986.

Sermons in Stone: The Stone Walls of New England and New York, illustrated by David Howell, Norton, 1990.

A Natural History of Parenting: From Emperor Penguins to Reluctant Ewes: A Naturalist Looks at Parenting in the Animal World and Ours, Harmony (New York City), 1997, reprinted as *A Natural History of Parenting: A Naturalist Looks at Parenting in the Animal World and Ours,* Three Rivers (New York City), 1998.

Also contributor to the *New York Times.*

SIDELIGHTS: Susan Allport lives in upstate New York with her husband, two daughters, and a handful of sheep. She is interested in the history of the things that surround her, especially scientifically, and uses this interest in her writing. Besides writing for the *New York Times,* Allport is the author of *Explorers of the Black Box: The Search for the Cellular Basis of Memory, Sermons in Stone: The Stone Walls of New England and New York,* and *A Natural History of Parenting: From Emperor Penguins to Reluctant Ewes: A Naturalist Looks at Parenting in the Animal World and Ours.*

Allport published *Explorers of the Black Box: The Search for the Cellular Basis of Memory* in 1986, and *Sermons in Stone: The Stone Walls of New England and New York* in 1990. In the latter, Allport reports on the origins and reasons for the more than 250,000 miles of stone walls that existed in New England and New York following the Civil War. In *Sermons in Stone,* described Rolland Foster Miller in the *New York Times,* Allport "tells many stories. She traces a history of the eons, of the great glaciations that threw these stones in our path in the first place. She outlines the early need for walls, the laws that grew up around them and the dramatic shifts in agriculture that signaled the end of their early usefulness." Some of the old stone walls still exist throughout New England and New York, 1000 yards of which remain on Allport's land, noted Miller "with some walls serving an old purpose—fencing the family's . . . sheep."

Allport's third publication, *A Natural History of Parenting: From Emperor Penguins to Reluctant Ewes: A Naturalist Looks at Parenting in the Animal World and Ours,* addresses the child-rearing practices of a wide variety of species. Inspired by her observations of ewes raised on her upstate New York property, Allport gives both personal perspectives and scientific information about a variety of parenting activities, from birthing the young to abandonment. Intermingling information about human behavior with that of other animals, such as bats, wasps, dolphins, and baboons, *A Natural History of Parenting* looks at both the why's and how's associated with parents' care of their off-spring.

"Readers are taken on a journey of discovery," declared Gloria Maxwell in *Library Journal,* "learning that . . . [for example,] flamingos form daycare centers." Allport's "writing is clear and often lovely. . . . in this erudite [book]," proclaimed a *Publishers Weekly* reviewer who warned that the work is "occasionally too technical for the average reader." However, other reviewers, such as Maxwell and *Booklist* contributor Nancy Bent, judged the book very readable. And although Bent noted "minor mistakes in detail" and wished for more direct citation for particular facts, the critic concluded that in *A Natural History of Parenting* "Allport shows how well popular writing can explain science."

BIOGRAPHICAL/CRITICAL SOURCES:

PERIODICALS

Atlantic Monthly, March, 1991.
Booklist, February 1, 1997.
Boston Magazine, November 30, 1990.
Library Journal, February 1, 1997.
Los Angeles Times, October 28, 1986.
Nature, January, 1987.
New Yorker, January 28, 1991.
New York Times, March 10, 1991.
Publishers Weekly, January 13, 1997.
Washington Post Book World, February 22, 1987.*

ALMODOVAR, Pedro 1949(?)-
(Pati Difusa, Patty Diphusa)

PERSONAL: Born September 25, 1949 (one source says 1951), in Calzada de Calatrava, Spain; son of Francisca Caballero. *Education:* Educated in Caceres, Spain.

CAREER: Screenwriter and director. Telephone company worker; singer in rock band, Almodovar and McNamara; actor with independent theater troupe, Los Goliardos; writer of comic strips and columns for underground newspaper, all in Madrid, Spain, all in the 1970s.

AWARDS, HONORS: Best screenplay award from Venice International Film Festival and best foreign film awards from National Board of Review of Motion Pictures and New York Film Critics Circle, all 1988, all for *Women on the Verge of a Nervous Breakdown;* special citation for originality from National Society of Film Critics, 1988; named Man of the Year by Spanish magazine *Cambio 16,* 1989; Academy Award nomination for best foreign film from the Academy of Motion Picture Arts and Sciences, 1989, for *Women on the Verge of a Nervous Breakdown.*

WRITINGS:

SCREENPLAYS; AND DIRECTOR

Pepi, Lucy, Bom y otros chicas del monton, Figaro, 1980.

Laberinto de pasiones, Musidora S.A., 1982, released in the United States as *Labyrinth of Passion,* 1990.

Entre tinieblas, Tesauro P.C., 1983, released in the United States as *Dark Habits* (also titled *Dark Hideout* and *Sisters of Darkness*), Cinevista, 1988.

Que he hecho yo para merecer esto?, Tesauro S.A./ Kaktus P.C., 1984, released in the United States as *What Have I Done to Deserve This?,* Cinevista, 1985.

Matador, Iberoamericana, 1986, released in the United States under same title, Cinevista/Promovision International, 1988.

La ley del deseo, El Deseo/Laurenfilms, 1986, released in the United States as *Law of Desire,* Cinevista, 1987.

Mujeres al borde de un ataque de nervios, El Deseo/ Laurenfilm, 1988, released in the United States as *Women on the Verge of a Nervous Breakdown,* Orion Classics, 1988.

Atame!, El Deseo/Laurenfilm, 1990, released in the United States as *Tie Me Up! Tie Me Down!,* Miramax, 1990.

Tacones lejanos, El Deseo, 1991, released in the United States as *High Heels,* Warner Bros., 1991.

Kika, El Deseo, 1993.

La Flor de mi secreto, El Deseo, 1995, released in the United States as *The Flower of My Secret,* Sony Pictures Classics, 1996.

Carne tremula, El Deseo, 1997, released in the United States as *Live Flesh,* MGM, 1998.

OTHER

Pati Difusa y otros textos, Editorial Anagrama (Barcelona), 1991, translation by Kirk Anderson published as *Patty Diphusa and Other Writings,* Faber (Boston, MA), 1991.

Also author of photonovella *Todo Toya.* Contributor of articles to Spanish periodicals.

WORK IN PROGRESS: More feature films.

SIDELIGHTS: A provocative figure in European cinema, Spanish screenwriter and director Pedro Almodovar rose from underground filmmaker to internationally renowned auteur during the course of the 1980s. With a distinctive blend of raw emotion and camp humor, his unconventional motion pictures defy classification and frequently incite controversy among moviegoers and critics. In an interview with Marsha Kinder for *Film Quarterly,* Almodovar explained: "My films are about pleasure, sensuality, and living—about the celebration of living," and added, "I prefer just to inspire, to suggest, not to explain." Indeed, *Film Criticism* contributor Patricia Hart observed that in his films, Almodovar "plays with a series of impossible (and for some, unspeakable) fantasies, constructing tenuous implausibilities where for a few moments on screen, if not in life, complimentary 'perversions' can be aligned, shortcomings matched with corresponding excesses, and one desiring domination can be lined up with a benevolent sexpot despot."

Frequent entries at various European and American film festivals, Almodovar's movies routinely topple traditional theories of culture and morality and consequently attract extensive criticism and analysis. The filmmaker's works embody a bold and satiric vision that allows for the satisfaction of even the most bizarre human desires and fetishes. Known for his use of stunning and intense imagery, Almodovar frequently juxtaposes fantasy and reality, creating a world on film in which the outrageous seems ordinary and individual freedom is exalted. His movies reflect the influence of diverse masters of the medium, including Alfred Hitchcock, Billy Wilder, surrealist Luis Bunuel, and several neorealist filmmakers of Italy and Spain.

Several critics have suggested that Almodovar's avant-garde motion pictures border on the grotesque and are designed primarily to jolt and disturb his viewers. But he insists that his works are merely exaggerated depictions of universal themes. In an interview with Vito Russo for *Film Comment,* Almodovar capsulized his filmmaking philosophy: "I make movies for my needs. My goal has never, never, never, been to make shocking movies."

With the end of the oppressive, authoritative rule of Spanish dictator Francisco Franco in 1975, a new wave of creativity infused the Spanish arts. Almodovar exploits this post-Franco mentality—popularly known as "la movida"—in his films, emphasizing tolerance and acceptance of individuality over the repression and divisiveness inherent in a totalitarian state. When asked by *Interview* writer David Lida for his reaction to the end of the Franco era, Almodovar recalled that he—and many other Spanish citizens "waiting for that moment to celebrate"—had been "chilling [champagne] in the Frigidaire for a week while Franco lay in agony." In the *Film Comment* interview with Russo, Almodovar asserted that while his films are not overtly political in content, they "are political in the sense that [they] always defend the autonomy and absolute freedom of the individual—which is very dangerous to some people."

Almodovar's motion pictures generally focus on the lives, loves, and desires of women. While the filmmaker, a candid homosexual, suggests that his sexuality has heightened his sensitivity, he rejects the notion that his fascination with women is rooted in his being gay. "Women are more spontaneous and more surprising as dramatic subjects," he told Marcia Pally in *Film Comment,* "and my spontaneity is easier to conduct through them."

Inspired by classic Hollywood stars, including Bette Davis and Katharine Hepburn, and films of the 1950s such as *Cat on a Hot Tin Roof,* Almodovar was attracted to the cinematic scene as a youth. Following a parochial education in a western province of Spain, he moved at age seventeen to Madrid and worked for the next decade as a typist for the telephone company. Simultaneously, he dabbled in the arts by acting with an independent theater troupe, singing in a rock band, writing articles and x-rated comics for an avant-garde newspaper, and composing the memoirs of fictitious porn queen Pati Difusa (*patidifusa* means "flabbergasted" in Spanish). By the mid-1970s, without having attended film school, he was already shooting experimental short films, which he showed at bars, parties, and small film festivals.

Almodovar completed his first full-length feature, the raunchy *Pepi, Lucy, Bom y otros chicas del monton,* in 1980. Eighteen months in the making, the film was shot only on weekends, because Almodovar worked at the national telephone company during the week. A movie "devoted almost exclusively to topics banned from cinema screens only a few years earlier, . . . [seeking] shamelessly to offend the sensibility of the average viewer," to quote Hart, *Pepi* was an underground hit. Its success enabled Almodovar to find funding for his next project, the equally perverse *Labyrinth of Passion,* a work that attained cult status in Spain.

The 1984 film *What Have I Done to Deserve This?*—Almodovar's fourth feature, but his first to be distributed in the United States—effectively explodes the Mediterranean myth of machismo. The story of an overworked woman's attempts to support her family, *What Have I Done to Deserve This?* offers sharp commentary on life in the crowded housing projects of Madrid. The film's heroine, Gloria, subsists mainly on amphetamines, juggling her responsibilities as a housewife with an outside job as a cleaning woman. Her unsupportive family consists of a crude and boorish taxi driver husband, two sons—the elder a drug dealer, the younger a homosexual—and a daffy mother-in-law. Sexually and emotionally unsatisfied and desperate for a change in her life, Gloria takes sudden action, killing her husband with a frozen ham and selling her younger son to a homosexual dentist. In a *New York* review, David Denby surmised, "*What Have I Done to Deserve This?* is bitterly funny, but it never feels nihilistic or merely cruel. . . . Every frame of it breathes freedom and pleasure in freedom." *Variety* correspondent Jonathan Holland called *What Have I Done to Deserve This?* "one of the most hilarious and despairing of Spanish films, establishing a delightful yet dangerous blend that would become a later [Almodovar] hallmark."

Almodovar's 1986 film *Law of Desire* became another cult classic in Madrid. Released the following year in the United States, the film concerns homosexual film director Pablo and his transsexual sibling Tina (who had undergone a sex change to more conventionally facilitate incestuous relations with her father). Tina becomes a lesbian after her father abandons her. Pablo falls in love with Juan, a bisexual, but also finds himself drawn to the obsessive Antonio. In a jealous rage, Antonio tracks and murders Juan, then holds Tina hostage in exchange for a single hour with Pablo. Moved by Antonio's uncompromising passion, Pablo consents. Remarking in *Film Comment* on the seemingly disastrous implications of the story, Almodovar reasoned, "It would have been a tragedy if [Antonio] couldn't have had that one hour."

Dark Habits, Almodovar's third film, and his first to be marketed outside Spain, was not released in the United States until 1988. *Dark Habits* begins with a nightclub singer-stripper fleeing to the safety of a convent following the drug-overdose death of her lover. The film, which takes its title from the unusual activities the nuns engage in during their spare time, then focuses on the irregularities of life inside the convent walls. Oddly named nuns—Sister Damned, Sister Sin, Sister Rat, to list a few—indulge in everything from drugs to exotic pets and thrive on saving the souls of the downtrodden. Several critics have contended that *Dark Habits* lacks the polish and bravura of Almodovar's later works, but most concede that the film served as an important step in his growth as a filmmaker.

Matador, one of the top grossing Spanish films of 1986, also received its first American showing in 1988. A controversial story of indulgence and obsession, *Matador* was both censured as a twisted and offensive study in psychosexual brutality and celebrated as an exaggerated and outrageously lavish comedy of passion. The film centers on the warped alliance between a former matador and a murderous female lawyer, both of whom can only experience sexual fulfillment in conjunction with killing. The pair's own relationship culminates in ecstasy and death. A *Newsweek* reviewer judged *Matador* "a twisted, oddly invigorating comedy." And Pauline Kael, writing in the *New Yorker,* deemed the film "all lush, clownish excess," adding, "Everything is eroticized—the colors, the violence. It's all too much—it's sumptuously sick and funny."

In *The Advocate,* Jan Stuart wrote: "The Almodovar signature invariably signals an elaborate network of the desired and the desirous, a maze of ardor that coils back on itself in unexpected ways. His resourceful lovers seem prepared for anything, as if betrayal, revenge, and unlikely sexual encounters were their daily bread. Handguns are always within easy reach—in the drawer next to the condoms and the diaphragms, we figure—and they tend to go off in homicidal orgasms."

In his conversation with Kinder, Almodovar justified his use of violence in his oeuvre: "The moral of all my films is to get to a stage of greater freedom. . . . I have my own morality. And so do my films. If you see *Matador* through the perspective of traditional morality, it's a dangerous film because it's just a celebration of killing. *Matador* is like a legend. I don't try to be realistic; it's very abstract, so you don't feel identification with the things that are happening, but with the sensibility of this kind of romanticism."

Almodovar earned international acclaim with his next film, *Women on the Verge of a Nervous Breakdown,* which was the second largest box office draw in Spain in 1988. Winner of numerous international film awards, the fast-paced comedy-melodrama chronicles Spanish television and radio actress Pepa's attempts to contact her suave and evasive ex-lover Ivan, also an actor. Ivan leaves a message on Pepa's answering machine informing her of his decision to end their relationship. Upon discovering the farewell message, the vulnerable Pepa heaves her telephone and answering machine out her window and proceeds to contemplate her options: reconciliation, murder, or suicide (with barbiturate-laced gazpacho, which she never gets a chance to drink). *Women on the Verge* features a myriad of supporting characters, including Pepa's friend Candela, who fears arrest because of her involvement with a Shiite terrorist; Ivan's demure son, Carlos, who falls for Candela; and Carlos's overbearing fiancee, Marisa, who experiences her first orgasm in a gazpacho-induced sleep. The film culminates in Pepa and Ivan's final confrontation, following a hectic chase and gunplay.

Women on the Verge scored a resounding critical and popular success. Denby credited Almodovar with creating in Pepa "perhaps the most lovable movie heroine in years." In a *Newsweek* review, David Ansen suggested that *Women on the Verge,* probably the most mainstream of Almodovar's films, exemplifies the refinement of the filmmaker's cinematic skills: "With each film Almodovar's technical assurance grows: he makes stylized high comedy look easy, unforced. . . . Some aficionados may miss the more outrageous edges of [the filmmaker's] earlier works, but the *enfant terrible* has not gone soft; he's just in a holiday mood, and his new comic optimism is infectious." Reviewing the film for *Interview,* Luc Sante pointed to an underlying compassion in Almodovar's treatment of his characters' trials: "*Women on the Verge of a Nervous Breakdown* may be camp, but it is camp of the highest order, *haut* camp, in fact. It exaggerates, but it does not mock; its humor is a weapon used on behalf of the protagonists, not turned against them."

Almodovar followed *Women on the Verge* with *Tie Me Up! Tie Me Down!,* which *New Republic* critic Stanley Kauffmann pronounced "his pinnacle so far." Released without a rating because of allegedly objectionable sex scenes, *Tie Me Up! Tie Me Down!* turns on the abduction of a former porno film star who eventually falls in love with her kidnapper, a recently released mental patient. Though faulted by some critics for its predictability and lack of originality, *Tie Me Up! Tie Me Down!* clearly impressed several other reviewers, including *Rolling Stone* contributor Peter Travers, who called the film "disturbing and invigorating . . . , another masterwork from Spain's most explosive talent." Addressing the supposedly objectionable theme of the movie, Hart concluded: "Viewers may share in the fantasy or not, but only the tacky would condemn a director for sharing with us in witty fashion what turns him on."

Subsequent Almodovar features have revealed a maturation and a world view that is "hopeful without being rosy-tinted," to quote Joseph Cunneen in *National Catholic Reporter.* In *The Flower of My Secret,* for instance, a disenchanted romance writer finds a degree of peace and self-respect even as her marriage disintegrates and her career unravels. In *The Flower of My Secret,* declared Stuart Klawans in *Nation,* Almodovar "has made a thoroughly heartfelt melodrama, one that revels in color and hyperbole not only for their own sake but also because they're garments that shield a human need so abashed that it dares show itself only in the gaudiest disguise." The critic concluded: "How strange that the bad boy should have turned into a benevolent god who respects his creature even though she disagrees with him. How surprising; how just."

With his 1998 comedy *Live Flesh,* Almodovar has established himself as "spiritual padre to a whole new wave of Spanish filmmakers," in Holland's view. Another study of violence, passion, and obsession, *Live Flesh*—an adaptation of a Ruth Rendell crime novel—weaves a web of intrigue and interrelationship between a hapless petty criminal named Victor, two police officers, and two women variously involved with the officers and with Victor. "Almodovar normally focuses on women on the verge, but *Live Flesh* is more about men and their mess," maintained James Greenberg in *Los Angeles Magazine.* "These guys are literally crawling at the feet of their women, struggling to find a way out of the skin they were born into." Declared Lisa Schwarzbaum in *Entertainment Weekly:* "In *Live Flesh* Almodovar is positively mature, adapting a novel by Ruth Rendell so deftly that the plot now also describes the invigorating and sometimes disorienting effects of democracy after long years of repression under the Franco regime." *Time* film critic Richard Corliss described *Live Flesh* as "sensuous [and] delirious," adding: "Obsession has seldom looked as gaudy or thrilling as here. . . . Few films these days are about sex, let alone love. Almodovar is that rare moviemaker who still thinks they are as important as a space invasion or a sinking ship."

Though generally regarded as the exemplar of modern Spanish cinema, Almodovar takes a modest view of his international renown. Reflecting on his career in the *Film Comment* interview with Russo, the filmmaker revealed: "What's wonderful is to notice that people want to see my movies. And that by the miracle of communication I am able to put my obsessions, my problems, my life on the screen and have them reach my audience. That impresses me tremendously. But curiously, it doesn't make me feel more sure of myself as an artist. Each time I start a new movie I know that I want to make that movie, but I don't know if I will know *how* to do it."

BIOGRAPHICAL/CRITICAL SOURCES:

BOOKS

Besas, Peter, *Behind the Spanish Lens: Spanish Cinema under Fascism and Democracy,* Arden Press (Denver, CO), 1985.

Cowie, Peter, editor, *International Film Guide,* Tantivy Press, *1982,* 1981, *1983,* 1982, *1984,* 1983, *1986,* 1985, *1987,* 1986, *1988,* 1987.

Dictionary of Hispanic Biography, Gale (Detroit, MI), 1996, pp. 22-24.

Hopewell, John, *Out of the Past: Spanish Cinema after Franco,* British Film Institute (London), 1986.

Smith, Paul Julian, *Desire Unlimited: The Cinema of Pedro Almodovar,* Verso (New York City), 1994.

PERIODICALS

Advocate, February 3, 1998, pp. 47, 49.
America, January 21, 1989.
American Film, March, 1988.
Entertainment Weekly, December 6, 1996, pp. 76-77; January 23, 1998, p. 41; January 30, 1998, p. 47.
Film Comment, November/December, 1988.
Film Criticism, winter, 1997, pp. 71-74.
Film Quarterly, fall, 1987.
Guardian, May 8, 1998, p. T10.
Interview, July, 1988; November, 1988.
Los Angeles Magazine, February, 1998, p. 100.
Nation, April 1, 1996, pp. 35-36.
National Catholic Reporter, April 26, 1996, p. 10.
New Republic, May 20, 1985; June 6, 1988; December 12, 1988; May 14, 1990.
Newsweek, July 18, 1988; December 5, 1988.
New York, April 29, 1985; November 21, 1988.
New Yorker, June 3, 1985; April 20, 1987; May 16, 1988.
New York Times, April 22, 1990; May 4, 1990.
People Weekly, January 26, 1998, p. 22.
Playboy, January, 1998, p. 19.
Rolling Stone, May 8, 1986; May 17, 1990.
Time, January 30, 1989; February 23, 1998, p. 90.
Variety, April 20, 1998, pp. 39-40.*

* * *

ALONSO, Damaso 1898-1990

PERSONAL: Born October 22, 1898, in Madrid, Spain; died of a respiratory ailment, January 24, 1990, in Madrid, Spain; married Eulalia Galvarriato (a writer), 1929. *Education:* Received LL.L, M.A., Ph.D. (1928), University of Madrid.

ADDRESSES: *Home*—Ave. Alberto Alcocer 23, Madrid 16, Spain.

CAREER: Centro de Estudios Historicos, Madrid, Spain, professor, 1923-36; University of Valencia, Valencia, Spain, professor of Spanish language and literature, 1933-39; University of Madrid, Madrid, professor of Romance philology, 1939-68; writer. Lecturer and visiting professor at universities throughout the world, including Berlin, Cambridge, Columbia, Harvard, Johns Hopkins, London, Stanford, and Yale Universities.

MEMBER: International Association of Hispanists (president), Royal Academy of the Spanish Language (president, 1968-82; director emeritus), Royal Academy of History, Higher Council for Scientific Research, American Association of Teachers of Spanish and Portuguese, Hispanic Society of America, American Philosophical Society, Modern Language Association, Modern Humanities Research Association (president).

AWARDS, HONORS: Premio Nacional de Literatura, c. 1935, for *La lengua poetica de Gongora;* award from the Royal Spanish Academy of the Language, c. 1942, for *La poesia de San Juan de la Cruz;* Premio Miguel de Cervantes from Spain's Ministerio de Cultura, 1978; numerous honorary degrees from universities, including Oxford University and the universities of Madrid, San Marcos, Bordeaux, Hamburg, Freiburg, Rome, Massachusetts, and Leeds.

WRITINGS:

NONFICTION

(Editor and author of text and notes) Luis de Gongora y Argote, *Soledads,* Revista de Occidente (Madrid), 1927, reprinted, Alianza (Madrid), 1982.

(Editor) Desiderius Erasmus, *El Enquiridion; o, Manual del caballero cristiano,* Consejo Superior de Investigaciones Cientificas, Instituto Miguel de Cervantes (Madrid), 1932, reprinted, 1971.

La lengua poetica de Gongora, S. Aguirre (Madrid), 1935, 3rd edition, Consejo Superior de Investigaciones Cientificas, Instituto Miguel de Cervantes, 1961.

(Editor and author of prologue, notes, and vocabulary) *Poesia espanola, antologia,* [Madrid], 1935 (also see below).

(Editor) Luis Carrillo de Sotomayor, *Poesias completas,* Signo (Madrid), 1936.

(Editor) *Poesia de la edad media y poesia de tipo tradicional* (originally published as first volume of *Poesia espanola, antologia*), Losada (Buenos Aires), 1942.

La poesia de San Juan de la Cruz (desde esta ladera), Consejo Superior de Investigaciones Cientificas, Instituto Antonio de Nebrija (Madrid), 1942.

(Editor) Gil Vicente, *Tragicomedia de Don Duardos,* Consejo Superior de Investigaciones Cientificas, 1942.

Ensayos sobre poesia espanola, Revista de Occidente (Madrid), 1944.

Vida y obra de Medrano (about Francisco de Medrano), Volume 1: *Estudio,* Volume 2 (editor, with Stephen Reckert): *Edicion critica,* Consejo Superior de Investigaciones Cientificas, Instituto Miguel de Cervantes, 1948-58.

Poesia y novela de Espana: Conferencias, Departamento de Extension Cultural, Universidad Nacional Mayor de San Marcos (Lima), 1949.

Poesia espanola, ensayo de metodos y limites estilisticos: Garcilaso, fray Luis de Leon, San Juan de la Cruz, Gongora, Lope de Vega, Quevedo, Gredos, 1950.

(With Carlos Bousono) *Seis calas en la expresion literaria espanola (prosa, poesia, teatro),* Gredos, 1951, 2nd edition, 1956, 3rd edition, 1963.

Poetas espanoles contemporaneos, Gredos, 1952, 3rd edition, 1965.

La primitiva epica francesca a la luz de una Nota Emilianense, Consejo Superior de Investigaciones Cientificas, Instituto Miguel de Cervantes, 1954.

Estudios y ensayos gongorinos, Gredos, 1955, reprinted, 1982.

Menendez Pelayo, critico literario, Gredos (Madrid), 1956.

Antologia: Creacion, edited by Vicente Gaos, Escelicer (Madrid), 1956.

Antologia: Critica, edited by Gaos, Escelicer, 1956.

(Editor, with Jose M. Blecua) *Antologia de la poesia espanola: Poesia de tipo tradicional,* Gredos, 1956, 2nd edition, 1964.

En la Andalucia de la e: Dialectologia pintoresca, [Madrid], 1956.

De los siglos oscuros al de Oro: Notas y articulos a traves de 700 anos de letras espanolas, Gredos, 1958, reprinted, 1982.

Dos espanoles de Siglo de Oro: Un poeta madrilensta, latinista, y francesista en la mitad del siglo XVI. El Fabio de la "Epistola moral": Su cara y cruz en Mejico y en Espana, Real Academia de la Historia, 1959 (also see below).

Dos espanoles del Siglo de Oro (includes *El Fabio de la "Epistola moral"*), Gredos, 1960.

Gongora y el "Polifemo," Gredos, 1960, 4th edition published in two volumes, 1961, 5th edition published in three volumes, 1967, 6th edition, 1974, 7th edition, 1985.

Primavera temprana de la literatura europea: Lirica, epica, novela, Guadarrama (Madrid), 1961.

Cuatro poetas espanoles: Garcilaso, Gongora, Maragall, Antonio Machado, Gredos, 1962.

(Editor, with wife, Eulalia Galvarriato de Alonso) *Para la biografia de Gongora: Documentos desconocidos,* Gredos, 1962.

(Editor and author of prose version) Luis de Gongora y Argote, *Romance de Angelica y Medoro,* Ediciones Acies (Madrid), 1962.

Del siglo de Oro a este siglo de siglas: Notas y articulos a traves de 350 anos de letras espanolas, Gredos, 1962.

(Author of introduction) *Antologia de poetas ingleses modernos,* Gredos, 1963.

(With others) *Homenaje a don Ramon Carande,* Sociedad de Estudios y Publicaciones, 1963.

(With Galvarriato) *Poesias completas y comentarios en prosa a los poemas mayores* (poetry of San Juan de la Cruz), Aguilar (Madrid), 1963.

(With Luis Rosales) *Pasion y muerte del Conde de Villamediana* (debate), Real Academia Espanola (Madrid), 1964.

(With Pedro Lain Entralgo) *La amistad entre el medico y el enfermo en la Edad Media* (debate), Real Academia de la Historia (Madrid), 1964.

(With Martin de Riquer) *Vida caballeresca en la Espana del siglo XV* (debate), Real Academia Espanola, 1965.

(With Galvarriato and Luis Rosales) *Primavera y flor de la literatura hispanica,* 4 volumes, Selecciones de Reader's Digest, 1966.

Cancionero y romancero espanol, Salvat (Madrid), 1969, reprinted, 1985.

La novela cervantina, Universidad Internacional Menendez Pelayo (Santander), 1969.

(With others) *Homenaje a Menendez Pidal,* Prensa de la Universidad de Madrid (Madrid), 1969.

Libro de indices, Gredos, 1969.

En torno a Lope: Marino, Cervantes, Benavente, Gongora, los Cardenios, Gredos, 1972.

Obras completas, Gredos, ten volumes, 1972-93.

(Editor) *Antologia de Gongora,* Gredos, 1974.

La Epistola moral a Fabio, de Andres Fernandez de Andrada: Edicion y estudio, Gredos, 1978.

(Author of essay) Vicente Gaos, *Obra poetica completa,* Institucion Alfonso el Magnanimo, Diputacion Provincial de Valencia (Valencia), 1982.

(With others) Federico Garcia Lorca, *Llanto por Ignacio Sanchez Mejias* (critical study of the work by Lorca), Casona de Tudanca (Santander), 1982.

(With Gerardo Diego and Luis Rosales) *Antonio Machado: Conferencias pronunciadas en la Fundacion Universitaria Espanola,* Fundacion Universitaria Espanola, 1983.

Reflexiones sobre mi poesia, Universidad Autonoma de Madrid (Madrid), 1984.

Antologia de nuestro monstruoso mundo: Duda y amor sobre el Ser Supremo, edited by Margarita Smerdou Altolaguirre, Catedra (Madrid), 1985.

Also author of *El viento y el verso,* 1925, *La tragicomedia de Don Duardos* (critical study of the work by Gil Vicente), 1942, and *Un poeta madrilenista, latinista y francesista en la mitad del siglo XVI,* c. 1957; author of *La poesia del Petrarca e il petrarchismo,* Italian edition published by L. S. Olschki, 1959.

POETRY

Poemas puros, poemillas de la ciudad, Galatea (Madrid), 1921.

Oscura noticia (also see below), Hispanica (Madrid), 1944.

Hijos de la ira: Diario intimo (originally published c. 1944), Espasa-Calpe (Buenos Aires), 1946, reprinted, Castalia (Madrid), 1986, translation by Elias L. Rivers published in a bilingual edition as *Hijos de la ira/Children of Wrath,* Johns Hopkins University Press (Baltimore, MD), 1970.

Hombre y dios (also see below), Arroyo de los Angeles (Malaga), 1955.

Oscura noticia [and] *Hombre y dios* (first title originally published in 1944), Espasa-Calpe (Madrid), 1959.

Poemas escogidos, Gredos, 1969.

Antologia poetica, edited by Jose Luis Cano, Plaza y Janes (Espluguas de Llobregat), 1973.

Antologia poetica, edited by Philip W. Silver, Alianza, 1979.

Gozos de la vista, Espasa-Calpe (Madrid), 1981.

Vida y obra (contains *Poemas puros: Poemillas de la ciudad* and *Hombre y dios*), Caballo Griego para la Poesia (Madrid), 1984.

OTHER

Translator of works from English into Spanish, including *A Portrait of the Artist as a Young Man* and poems by James Joyce, *Marie Antoinette,* by Hilaire Belloc, and the poetry of Gerard Manley Hopkins.

SIDELIGHTS: "Damaso Alonso was one of the strongest forces in the intellectual and cultural history of twentieth-century Spain," wrote Jerry Phillips Winfield in the *Dictionary of Literary Biography.* "His contributions to literary and stylistic analysis inspired a new approach to literary criticism, particularly in poetry." Alonso was widely hailed in his native Spain for both his works of literary criticism and his poetry. As a critic, he was considered without equal in twentieth-century Spain, and as a poet he "restored the human condition as a vital theme in Spanish poetry and offered a new freedom of technique and style," to quote Winfield. In a career spanning six decades, Alonso wrote, lectured, and befriended many of the important literary voices in Spain. He was by any measure a distinguished intellectual, respected all over the world for his scholarship and verse.

Alonso was perhaps best known for his studies on the poetry of Spain's Golden Age—the sixteenth and seventeenth centuries. Alonso's edition of Luis de Gongora's poem, "Soledades," which included a prose version that explained the meaning of a poem long considered incomprehensible, rescued both Gongora and his poem from oblivion. Among the other poets that Alonso examined are Saint John of the Cross, Garcilaso, and Fray Luis de Leon. Eventually, Alonso's criticism encompassed the entire range of Spanish literature—early and modern, poetry and prose. Winfield declared the author to be "the dominant figure in literary scholarship in postwar Spain, initiating entirely new schools of criticism. He was one of the greatest intellectual influences on Spanish culture in [the twentieth] century."

As a poet, Alonso was an instrumental part of the renaissance of Spanish verse that occurred in the decades after the civil war of 1936 to 1939. Alonso first began to publish his poetry during the 1920s, when he was a member of the group of poets known as the "Generation of 1927," a group that included Federico Garcia Lorca and Rafael Alberti. It wasn't until the 1940s, however, that Alonso began to attract attention as a major poet. In his two most important collections of poetry, *Hijos de la ira* and *Oscura noticia*—both published in the mid-1940s—the author examines humanity's "search for religious and personal transcendence on the one hand, and [its] temptation to egotism, pettiness and destruction on the other," according to Andrew P. Debicki in his biography, *Damaso Alonso.*

Winfield saw several constant themes in Alonso's poetry, most notably anxiety over death, love, loneliness, and—as the poet matured—humankind's existential struggle. Particularly after the horrors of the Spanish civil war and World War II, Alonso mounted "an anguished, bitter outcry against the particular circumstances of his life and a universal protest against the injustice inherent in life," to quote Winfield. Alonso's poetry also addressed the relationship between man and God, revealing the artist to be deeply religious but still perplexed by the concept of deity. In *Duda y amor sobre el Ser Supremo,* for instance, Alonso finds "meaning in the incessant desire to know and love," in Winfield's words. The critic continued: "In the tension of the constant struggle among doubt, love, and desire, Alonso elicits the participation of the reader in order to solve a mystery of intuition, not logic. . . . The book is a tribute to human nobility in the desperate attempt to endure."

Beginning with *Hijos de la ira,* Alonso challenged the stylistic direction and aesthetics of Spanish poetry, some of which he himself had embraced in his earlier work. Winfield observed that Alonso "was influential in motivating a new and authentic voice in postwar Spain. He stretched the limits of theme and technique, [rebelling] . . . against the existing apathetic schools of surrealism and 'pure' poetry." Through free verse, multiple layers of imagery, and courageous exploration of reality, the author removed traditional boundaries and led Spanish poetry in novel directions." Winfield concluded: "The profound themes of his poetry—existence, God, and humankind's role in the universe—achieved an intensity, precision, and emotive force that was equaled by few Spanish poets of his time. His poems reflect the natural languages of the people in a desolate atmosphere of loneliness and chaos. Yet, amid guilt and injustice, and facing a silent God, Alonso found humans to be wondrous creations who were fragile yet strong in their courage to survive."

As a testament to his importance as a poet, Alonso was awarded the 1978 Miguel de Cervantes prize, Spain's highest literary honor. He was elected to the Royal Academy of the Spanish Language in 1945 and served four terms as its director. In addition to his works of poetry and criticism, he was a respected translator. His own writings have been translated into several languages, including English, German, Portuguese, and Italian. Alonso died early in 1990 after a long battle with respiratory disease.

BIOGRAPHICAL/CRITICAL SOURCES:

BOOKS

Alvarado de Ricord, Elsie, *La obra de Damaso Alonso,* Gredos (Madrid), 1968.

Contemporary Literary Criticism, Volume 14, Gale (Detroit, MI), 1980, pp. 18-20.

Debicki, Andrew P., *Damaso Alonso,* Twayne (Boston, MA), 1970.

Dictionary of Hispanic Biography, Gale, 1996, pp. 27-29.

Dictionary of Literary Biography, Volume 108: *Twentieth-Century Spanish Poets, First Series,* Gale, 1991, pp. 30-41.

Flys, Miguel Jaroslaw, *La poesia existencial de Damaso Alonso,* Gredos, 1969.

Homenaje a Damaso Alonso, El Club (Madrid), 1978.

Manach, Jorge, *Visitas espanolas,* Revista de Occidente (Madrid), 1960.

Modern Spanish and Portuguese Literatures, Continuum (New York City), 1988.

Vivanco, Luis Felipe, *Introduccion a la poesia espanola contemporanea,* Guadarrama (Madrid), 1957.

PERIODICALS

Arbor, Volume 45, number 172, 1960, pp. 38-50.

Cuadernos Hispanoamericanos, November-December, 1951, pp. 113-26.

Papeles de Son Armadans, November-December, 1958, pp. 256-300; Volume 36, 1965, pp. 167-96.

Times Literary Supplement, May 31, 1974.

OBITUARIES:

New York Times, January 27, 1990.

Times (London), January 27, 1990.

Washington Post, January 27, 1990.*

* * *

ALTMAN, Thomas
See BLACK, Campbell

* * *

ARD, William (Thomas) 1922-1960
(Ben Kerr, Mike Moran, Jonas Ward, Thomas Wills)

PERSONAL: Born July 7, 1922, in Brooklyn, NY; died of cancer, March 12, 1960; son of Robert E.

and Rose F. (Doran) Ard; married Eileen A. Kovara, 1945; children: Eileen, William T, Jr. *Education:* Attended Admiral Farragut Naval Academy, 1936-38; Dartmouth College, B.A., 1944. *Avocational interests:* Golf, bowling, croquet.

CAREER: Buchanan Advertising Agency, New York City, copywriter, 1944-46; Warner Brothers, New York City, copywriter, 1946-50; writer, 1950-60.

MEMBER: Sigma Chi; Carlouel Yacht Club, Pelican Golf Club (both Clearwater, FL)

WRITINGS:

CRIME NOVELS; "TIMOTHY DANE" SERIES

The Perfect Frame, Mill and Morrow (New York City), 1951.

.38, Rinehart (New York City), 1952, published as *This Is Murder,* Hammond (London), 1954.

The Diary, Rinehart, 1952, Hammond, 1954.

A Private Party, Rinehart, 1953, published as *Rogue's Murder,* Hammond, 1955.

Don't Come Crying to Me, Rinehart, 1954.

Mr. Trouble, Rinehart, 1954.

Hell Is a City, Rinehart, 1955.

Cry Scandal, Rinehart, 1956, Digit (London), 1960.

The Root of His Evil, Rinehart, 1957, published as *Deadly Beloved,* Dell (New York City), 1958.

CRIME NOVELS

(Under pseudonym Ben Kerr) *Shakedown,* Holt (New York City), 1952.

(Under pseudonym Thomas Wills) *You'll Get Yours,* Lion (New York City), 1952.

(Under pseudonym Mike Moran) *Double Cross,* Popular Library (New York City), 1953.

A Girl for Danny, Popular Library, 1953.

No Angels for Me, Popular Library, 1954.

(Under pseudonym Ben Kerr) *Down I Go,* Popular Library, 1955.

(Under pseudonym Thomas Wills) *Mine to Avenge,* Fawcett (New York City), 1955.

(Under pseudonym Jonas Ward) *The Name's Buchanan,* Fawcett, 1956.

(Under pseudonym Ben Kerr) *Damned If He Does,* Popular Library, 1956.

(Under pseudonym Ben Kerr) *I Fear You Not,* Popular Library, 1956.

(Under pseudonym Ben Kerr) *Club 17,* Popular Library, 1957.

(Under pseudonym Jonas Ward) *Buchanan Says No,* Fawcett, 1957.

(Under pseudonym Ben Kerr) *The Blonde and Johnny Malloy,* Popular Library, 1958.

(Under pseudonym Jonas Ward) *One-Man Massacre,* Fawcett, 1958.

(Under pseudonym Jonas Ward) *Buchanan Gets Mad,* Fawcett, 1958.

All I Can Get ("Lou Largo" series), Monarch (Derby, CT), 1959.

As Bad as I Am ("Danny Fontaine" series), Rinehart, 1959, published as *Wanted: Danny Fontaine,* Dell, 1960.

(Under pseudonym Jonas Ward) *Buchanan's Revenge,* Fawcett, 1960.

Like Ice She Was ("Lou Largo" series), Monarch, 1960.

When She Was Bad ("Danny Fontaine" series), Dell, 1960.

(Under pseudonym Jonas Ward; novel completed by Robert Silverberg) *Buchanan on the Prod,* Fawcett, 1960.

The Sins of Billy Serene, Monarch, 1960.

Babe in the Woods, Compact, 1960.

The Naked and the Innocent, Digit, 1960.

Make Mine Mavis, Compact, 1961.

And So to Bed, Compact, 1962.

Give Me This Woman, Compact, 1962.

SIDELIGHTS: William Ard published more than thirty crime and mystery novels in the course of his very brief career, which was cut short by his death from cancer at the age of thirty-seven. Ard is remembered not so much because of the literary excellence of his work—his novels are largely considered uneven—but because his writing is infused with a romantic sensibility not usually found in crime fiction of the 1950s. In an era when most popular mystery writers were imitating the formula of rough-and-tumble trigger-happy machismo perfected by Mickey Spillane (in his Mike Hammer novels), Ard was writing in the tradition of Dashiell Hammett and Raymond Chandler, creating fictional detectives who, although "hard-boiled," stood out as beacons of honesty and decency in a corrupt world. He was also deeply influenced by the novelist and short story writer John O'Hara, whose straight-forward yet colorful prose style Ard emulated, and from whom Ard borrowed the technique of using flashbacks to explore his characters' socio-economic backgrounds.

Ard created several different series detectives, and published under four pseudonyms (in addition to his real name). Timothy Dane, his principal series detective, embodies all the elements of romanticism that distinguish Ard's work from that of the "Mickey Spillane school." Loath to resort to violence, Dane is young and somewhat callow, tender toward women, and generally incapable of superhuman feats of derring-do. All in all, he is very unlike Spillane's Mike Hammer. In a *New York Herald Tribune Book Review* notice of *The Diary,* Ard's third Dane novel, James Sandoe pinpointed the difference between Ard and most of his contemporaries: "This one involves itself in sex and sadism, but it has two advantages over the current seedy crop of hardboiled novels. Mr. Ard has something like a sense of style and he gives his angry private investigator a sense of recognizable righteousness." Reviewing *Don't Come Crying to Me,* a later Dane novel, *New York Times* critic Anthony Boucher noted, "William Ard continues to display an economy and originality rare (and vastly welcome)in the hard-boiled field." *Hell Is a City,* which Francis Nevins, writing in *The St. James Guide to Crime and Mystery Writers,* called "[t]he most powerful and exciting Dane novel," unfolds in corruption-drenched New York City where the mayor, the police commissioner, and various other city officials are allied with powerful mobsters in an attempt to influence municipal elections. Dane is called upon to investigate the circumstances surrounding the shooting of a Brooklyn vice cop. The dead cop is elevated to the status of a martyr by the corrupt police department, but Dane discovers the awful truth: the shooter was the brother of a girl the cop was about to rape. Dane has to go up against an array of crooked politicians and gun-toting mobsters, all of whom are determined to use any means necessary to keep this truth covered up.

Francis Nevins argued in *The St. James Guide to Crime and Mystery Writers,* that Ard was "far from a model of all the literary virtues," and that even *Hell Is a City,* which "could easily have been a masterpiece" was marred by a "grotesquely bad denouement." According to Nevins, however, "even his worst efforts are enjoyable, and his best are miracles of storytelling economy, blending tough-guy elements with a singular warmth and tenderness."

BIOGRAPHICAL/CRITICAL SOURCES:

BOOKS

St. James Guide to Crime and Mystery Writers, fourth edition, St. James Press (Detroit), 1996.

PERIODICALS

Armchair Detective, Volume 15, number 2, 1982.
Booklist, March 1, 1955.
Canadian Forum, August, 1952.
Chicago Sunday Tribune, June 17, 1951, p. 6; October 12, 1952, p. 6; August 9, 1953, p. 10; February 20, 1955, p. 7.
Kirkus Reviews, April 1, 1951; January 1, 1952; July 1, 1952; May 1, 1953; April 15, 1954; November 15, 1954; April 15, 1955; June 15, 1956; May 15, 1957; December 15, 1958.
New York Herald Tribune Book Review, July 29, 1951, p. 9; March 9, 1952, p. 23; September 28, 1952, p. 20; August 30, 1953, p. 12; July 4, 1954, p. 11; February 6, 1955, p. 12; August 26, 1956, p. 9; August 4, 1957, 9; March 22, 1959, p.11.
New York Times, March 9, 1952, p. 24; September 21, 1952, p. 26; January 23, 1953, p. 26; July 26, 1953, p. 17; July 4, 1954, p. 11; June 26, 1955, p. 21; September 2, 1956, p. 15; August 4, 1957, p. 19; March 8, 1959, p. 22.
Saturday Review, March 22, 1952; October 11, 1952; July 24, 1954; July 23, 1955; September 22, 1956; April 18, 1959.
San Francisco Chronicle, June 10, 1951, p. 22; March 23, 1952, p. 24; October 12, 1952, p. 22; July 26, 1953, p. 13; August 8, 1954, p. 20; February 27, 1955, p. 13; July 3, 1955, p. 16; September 16, 1956, p. 29; August 11, 1957, p. 23; March 29, 1959, p. 13.
Springfield Republican, July 21, 1951, p. 5D; August 23, 1953, p. 6D; October 28, 1956, p. 8C.
Time, August 1, 1955.*

* * *

ARMSTRONG, Campbell
See BLACK, Campbell

* * *

AULETTA, Ken 1942-

PERSONAL: Born April 23, 1942, in New York, NY; son of Pat Auletta and Nettie Tenenbaum (ran sporting goods store); married Amanda "Binky" Urban (literary agent), around 1977, children: Kate. *Education:* State University of New York College at Oswego, B.S., 1963; Syracuse University, M.A., 1965. *Politics:* "Registered Independent."

ADDRESSES: Home—544 East 86th St., New York, NY 10028. *Office—New York Daily News,* 220 East 42nd St., New York, NY 10017; and *New Yorker,* 43 West 43rd St., New York, NY 10017.

CAREER: Worked as bag-carrier, speech writer, and campaign strategist for Robert F. Kennedy and Howard Samuels (New York Democrat), early 1970s; Off-Track Betting Corporation, New York City, executive directorship, early 1970s; *New York Post,* political columnist, two weeks in 1970; *New York* magazine, New York City, contributing editor, 1975-76; *Village Voice,* New York City, staff writer and weekly columnist, 1975-76; *New Yorker,* New York City, writer, 1977—; *New York Daily News,* New York City, political columnist, 1977—. Co-host of a weekly WNET-TV interview program, 1976—.

AWARDS, HONORS: American Bar Association media award, 1976; Public Relations Society of America media award, 1976, for an article on New York's fiscal crisis, and 1977, for an article outlining an agenda to save the city; Amos Tuck Award for national economic reporting, Dartmouth College; finalist in the National Magazine Awards, Columbia University School of Journalism.

WRITINGS:

The Streets Were Paved with Gold, Random House (New York City), 1979.

Hard Feelings: Reporting on the Pols, the Press, the People and the City (collection of essays), Random House 1980.

The Underclass, Random House 1982.

The Art of Corporate Success: The Story of Schlumberger, Putnam (New York City), 1984.

Greed and Glory on Wall Street: The Fall of the House of Lehman, Random House, 1986.

Three Blind Mice: How the TV Networks Lost There Way, Random House, 1991, Vintage Books (New York City), 1992.

(Contributor) *1-800-PRESIDENT: The Report of the Twentieth Century Fund Task Force on Television and the Campaign of 1992,* Twentieth Century Fund Press (New York City), 1993.

The Highwaymen: Tycoons, Technology, and the Coming World of Electronic Communications, Random House, 1997.

Correspondent for *Frontline*'s November 7, 1995 PBS television program "Who's Afraid of Rupert Murdoch?," directed by Jim Gilmore and produced by William Cran and Gilmore, copyright held by WGBH Educational Foundation. Contributor of articles to *New York Times, New York Review of Books, More,* and *Esquire.*

SIDELIGHTS: Ken Auletta has made his career as a reporter, columnist, and author. Auletta once told *CA:* "Most of my work is concerned with political and economic and governmental matters, though I do stray off and write of the media frequently and, more recently, of multinational corporations. I very much enjoy having a regular magazine and newspaper outlet." Before resigning, that was the case at *New York* magazine and the *Voice;* it is again the case at the *New Yorker* and the *Daily News.* The longtime writer and columnist for the *New Yorker* and the *New York Daily News* quit the *Village Voice* and *New York* magazine after both periodicals were purchased by Rupert Murdoch, "rather than work for a man he believes turns publications into political weapons," reported James S. Kunen in *People Weekly.*

Auletta's *The Streets Were Paved with Gold* is an analysis of the financial turmoil that plagued New York City during the 1970s. Bob Kuttner wrote in the *New York Times Book Review:* "For too many of our best political writers, politics itself becomes the central fascination. . . . But the point of politics, after all, is government. And unlike many of his colleagues who stay hooked on the easy adrenaline of day-to-day politics, Ken Auletta has gone on to explore government." Kuttner feels that *The Streets Were Paved with Gold* has "established Mr. Auletta as an astute critic of New York City government, with the patience and intellectual curiosity to plumb the fiscal muck and pull out an instructive, entertaining story." Unlike many observers that blame the near-bankruptcy on a variety of factors outside of the control of the city, Kuttner explained that "rejecting all of the devil theories of New York's fiscal collapse, Mr. Auletta ascribed New York's woes to both the city's corrupt permanent government *and* the municipal unions; to New York's own overly generous version of the New Deal *and* to Washington's raw deal."

Julia Vitullo-Martin, in a *New York Review of Books* article, maintained that much of Auletta's 1979 publication, *The Streets Were Paved with Gold,* is a condemnation of the affluent lifestyle enjoyed by some highly visible New Yorkers rather than an analysis of the city's financial situation and that the author ignores New York's partially successful attempts to correct its own fiscal ills. She wrote: "On the west side of Manhattan, once called Hell's Kitchen, a storefront church's neon sign flashes the message 'Sin will find you out.' *That* should have been the title of Ken Auletta's new book . . . because that is his theme. . . . He is distressed by what he sees as the city's blind revelry in the face of financial doom in 1975, a revelry that has started up once again with the influx of enormous private wealth to the city. He writes with the pain and the passion of one offended by sin." The free-spending attitude of affluent citizens, Auletta feels, helped to influence the city government toward fiscal irresponsibility. Furthermore, stated Vitullo-Martin, "Auletta goes on at length about the fall of New York but gives short shrift to its salvation, temporary as that may be. The city *was* on the verge of catastrophe in June 1975. . . . Today the city has paid off all but a tiny amount of notes. . . . Default is remote. What happened? In 1975, the Municipal Assistance Corporation (MAC) was created by the state to save the city by forcing or cajoling—whichever worked—investors to trade in their short-term debt for long. They did. MAC solved the city's financing." And she feels that Auletta short-changes the effectiveness of this organization: "Anyone unfamiliar with MAC will not understand how it works from Auletta's description."

But many other observers agree with Auletta's assessment in *The Streets Were Paved with Gold* that the city was largely to blame for its financial difficulty. Alan K. Campbell (former dean of the Maxwell School of Citizenship and Public Affairs at Syracuse University), reviewing the book for the *New York Times Book Review,* stated: "New York City used every financial and debt gimmick known to man and even invented some new ones to fill the budget gap, to the point that borrowing came to be considered a normal way to finance current services—in ordinary language, the city was living beyond its means." In addition to out-of-control borrowing, wrote Friedman in the *Chicago Tribune Book World,* "Outrageous municipal union demands and settlements gave a new and disastrous meaning to collective bargaining in a governmental setting. How could political leaders bargain with unions who offered financial backing to those same politicians?"

Friedman called *The Streets Were Paved with Gold* "an informed, impressive, multi-faceted examination of the people and events that led to the city's fiscal decline [and] near demise. . . . It is a classic study of opportunities lost, municipal profligacy, wasted labors, and technically balanced budgets, of well-meaning social goals and not-so-honest political realities." Campbell believes that the book is "a unique analysis of the causes of the New York City fiscal crisis" and stated that "it substantially advances our understanding of the problem of New York City and clarifies the relevance of that problem to the rest of the nation." Concluded Friedman: "Auletta's book is a masterpiece—a shocking look backward and an equally frightening look ahead for this nation's ever-growing-older urban centers."

In another book dealing with problems facing big cities, Auletta looks at a group of people who exemplify hard-core poverty in the United States. As Charles Peters explained in the *New York Times Book Review,* Auletta's *The Underclass* "is not about poor people in general. It's about the underclass, those at the bottom—the long-term welfare recipients, street criminals, addicts and drifters who live outside the world of work and whose problems are not likely to be solved simply by the offer of a job." In researching the book, Auletta studied a number of job training programs, particularly those operated by the Manpower Demonstration Research Corporation (the M.D.R.C.), an institution funded by the federal government among other sources. According to Peters, the author "spent seven months with one group of 26 trainees in New York City attending classes designed, in his words, 'to instill the habit of work and to expunge bad habits.' He also visited M.D.R.C. programs in Mississippi and West Virginia and has read widely in the literature of poverty." The result, wrote Max Benavidez in the *Los Angeles Times Book Review,* is "a responsible, in-depth study of people who have 'disappeared from the system.' The author has amassed and absorbed an extraordinary range of literature on the topic. He has talked with experts and has chronicled daily, direct experiences with the underclass. To his credit, he paints an unromanticized picture of the destitution that America so neatly ignores. . . . Auletta has written a first-rate sourcebook."

Juan Williams, in the *Washington Post Book World,* is bothered by the fact that "there is some inconclusive end to the people Auletta observes. They graduate, don't graduate. They find jobs, lose jobs, can't get a job. Overall, the program that sponsored Auletta's sample finds that it has some success with long-term welfare recipients and former drug addicts but fails with former convicts and school dropouts." And Christopher Lehmann-Haupt of the *New York*

Times maintained that this conclusion, stated by Auletta, is hardly surprising, considering that the M.D.R.C. program "puts welfare mothers in the same class as 'street criminals and hustlers' and 'traumatized ex-mental patients and alcoholics.'. . . Mothers on welfare are about the most direct and uncomplicated victims of poverty-through-unemployment that are possible to imagine." Still, *The Underclass* has been widely praised for its thoroughness, for the seriousness of its subject matter, and for its author's dedication to his task. "It offers a prodigious quantity of facts, statistics and argument, all of urgent concern to us all," wrote Peter S. Prescott of *Newsweek.* In the *New York Times Book Review,* Peters credited Auletta for his fair-minded approach, noting that the author "is equally open to Oscar Lewis, a liberal anthropologist, and to Edward Banfield, a conservative political scientist." And even though he wished Auletta's study had proven more conclusive, Williams stated that the author "brings a reporter's touch and an unbiased mind [to] *The Underclass.* That combination alone would be enough to set his book apart from the ones that preceded it, but Auletta goes a step further by bringing into the argument the people being argued about. By talking to poor people, by watching them—without voyeurism—push to the limits, he insists on testing the human ability to leave a bad way of life behind. . . . As an introduction and overview to the contemporary debate over American poverty—its roots and proposed solutions—Auletta's book is invaluable."

Auletta's 1986 *Greed and Glory on Wall Street: The Fall of the House of Lehman* grew out of a two-part article he wrote for the *New York Times Magazine* the previous year. Lawrence Minard described the book in *The New York Times Book Review* as "a riveting chronicle of the lust for money, power and reputation that drove a handful of Lehman Brothers' partners to liquidate at a bargain price Wall Street's oldest continuing partnership." "But Ken Auletta has managed to transform the recent acquisition of an investment bank by a financial conglomerate into a compelling melodrama. What's more, he doesn't rely on colorful New Journalism techniques such as imagined conversations and interior monologues. Instead, he bases his reconstructions on transcripts of interviews he conducted with members of the Lehman Bothers board, corporate financiers and traders, all notorious tight-lipped folks. Auletta is so scrupulous that he's reported (in footnotes) conflicting assertions made to him," wrote Marc Granetz in *The New Republic.*

In addition to talking to over forty Lehman partners, Auletta conducted about fifty hours of interview with Pete Peterson and thirty-five with Lewis Glucksman. Key figures of Lehman Brothers in 1983, Glucksman, president of Lehman, forced out then-chairperson Pete Peterson. Kunen reported that neither Peterson nor Glucksman are "enthusiastic about the book" and quoted each man, writing: "'There's a great deal of accuracy in it,' admits Glucksman, 'and a certain amount of inaccuracy.' Peterson is less circumspect: 'Mr. Auletta reduced a complicated business story to a simplistic morality play.'" Comments made by critics seem to support Peterson's remark. Granetz, who called the book a "compelling melodrama, also noted that the book "tend[s] to rely on the obvious human vices to explain what motivates the characters." Granetz, along with other critics, also faulted the book for, what Minard stated as "fail[ing] to grapple seriously with the larger forces reshaping Wall Street." Granetz specified: "To understand the forces at work on Wall Street one would have to know something about what Auletta tries to explain in two pages: why investment banks need more capital." Nevertheless, Granetz described the book as "entertaining" and "revealing" calling the book "a well-researched contribution." *Time* contributor William A. Henry II indicated: "the [book's] narrative is slow in starting, repetitive, dotted with clichs and awkward syntax. It lacks detailed explanations of Lehman's management structure, and is overburdened with irrelevant details. . . . Still, the book's eventual energy is propulsive, and even at its weakest, Auletta's tale is buoyed by the sheer venom of its gossip."

More recent books by Auletta, *The Highway Men: Warriors of the Information Superhighway* and *Three Blind Mice: How the Networks Lost Their Way* focus on the communications industry. A *Publishers Weekly* review of *The Highway Men* recognized Auletta as a proficient journalist and concluded the book was "an ideal way to catch up" on the events in the "communication world." *The Highway Men* is a collection of 16 pieces by Auletta published in the *New Yorker* between February 1993 and May 1996. The book "roams all over the communications landscape in these pieces" with "too many [pieces] to cohere," although Auletta attempts "to pull everything together in his Introduction by proclaiming a series of overarching maxims," according to Christopher Lehmann-Haupt in the *New York Times Book Review. Booklist*'s Jennifer Henderson noted "the dated nature of the articles" as a "major drawback." Similarly, Lehmann-Haupt said that " postscripts following each piece occasionally "contain more pertinent news than the pieces themselves." However, added Lehmann-Haupt, "large benefits stem from both the datedness and the variety of Mr. Auletta's material. The chief one is that he clarifies all the confusion surrounding his subject, which is to say, he makes clear why the communications revolution is so terribly confusing."

Three Blind Mice is "an exhaustive behind-the-scenes look at the three broadcast networks" with "serviceable, and usually quite lucid" writing, according to Richard Zoglin in a review for *Time.* Auletta was critically recognized for his unprecedented "fly-on-the-wall" access to all happenings in the mid- to late-1980s at NBC, ABC, and CBS during his six year research of the major networks which furnished him with incredible details. Although the book received positive reviews from critics, almost unanimously, critics faulted the book's length and excessive use of unnecessary details. Todd Gitlin colorfully noted this common complaint in the *New York Times Book Review:* "Over all, *Three Blind Mice* lacks a sense of proportion, For scores of pages, the fly buzzes around the trivia of office politics. Like a sports announcer frightened of dead air, Mr. Auletta clogs his story with stray statistics. Details, pungent the first time, get repeated like twitches of the dying dinosaur's fail. We are flooded with ineffectual and inept atmospherics."

"Still," concluded Zoglin, "if he is occasionally too fascinated by the tree, Auletta never loses sight of the forest. . . . his is the network book to beat." A review for *The Economist* praised Auletta for "see[ing] things [players in the networks] do not. . . . [Auletta] lucidly lays out the structural forces that are working against the networks." This reviewer remarked that the book's "tediousness" is counteracted by the "compelling and important" nature of the "big story that arches over all the corporate hubbub." In contrast, *Commentary* contributor George Russel and *Newsweek* critic Joshua Hammer believed the book lacked focus. "Auletta's analysis gets lost amid all the anecdotes," remarked Hammer. Russel, disappointed with Auletta's performance in this book, wrote: Auletta's method—the numbing, *New Yorker*-style compilation of facts, irrespective of their larger significance—robs the narrative of any compelling focus." Looking outside of *Three Blind Mice,* Russel repeatedly commended Auletta's journalistic skills and acknowledged: "Auletta is one of our most energetic and resourceful business journalists, with a cool eye for the technical complexities that underlie business reality and economic policy-making."

BIOGRAPHICAL/CRITICAL SOURCES:

PERIODICALS

Booklist, April 1, 1997, p. 1362.
Chicago Tribune Book World, April 8, 1979.
Commentary, January, 1992, pp. 63-64.
Economist, October 19, 1991, p. 103.
Library Journal, September 15, 1991, p. 90.
Los Angeles Times Book Review, June 13, 1982, p. 150.
Maclean's, March 31, 1986.
New Republic, April 28, 1986, pp. 36-38.
Newsweek, June 7, 1982; February 10, 1986, pp. 73A-73C; September 9, 1991, p. 66.
New York Review of Books, May 17, 1979, p. 6.
New York Times, May 11, 1982, p. 25.
New York Times Book Review, March 25, 1979, p. 12; August 10, 1980, p. 11; June 27, 1982, p. 11; January 19, 1986, p. 6; August 25, 1991, p. 3; May 19, 1997, p. C16.
People Weekly, March 24, 1986, p. 12; April 14, 1986, p. 87.
Publishers Weekly, April 14, 1997, p. 67.
Time, January 13, 1986; August 12, 1991, p. 60.
Washington Post Book World, July 11, 1982.*

* * *

AUTH, Tony
See AUTH, William Anthony, Jr.

* * *

AUTH, William Anthony, Jr. 1942-
(Tony Auth)

PERSONAL: Born May 7, 1942, in Akron, OH; son of William Anthony and Julia Kathleen (Donnally) Auth; married Eliza Drake (an artist), August 28, 1982. *Education:* University of California, Los Angeles, B.A., 1965. *Avocational interests:* Reading fiction (especially childrens' books, science fiction, and fantasy), swimming, travelling, watching movies, and spending time with friends.

ADDRESSES: Home—1137 Rodman St., Philadelphia, PA 19147. *Office*—400 North Broad St., Philadelphia, PA 19101.

CAREER: Rancho Los Amigos Hospital, Downey, CA, chief medical illustrator, 1964-70; *Philadelphia Inquirer,* Philadelphia, PA, editorial cartoonist, 1971—.

AWARDS, HONORS: Overseas Press Club Award, 1975 and 1976; Pulitzer Prize, Society of Professional Journalists Award, Sigma Delta Chi Award, and Columbia University Trustees Award, all 1976, all for editorial cartooning.

WRITINGS:

UNDER NAME TONY AUTH

Behind the Lines: Cartoons, Houghton (Boston), 1977.
The Gang of Eight, Faber & Faber (Boston), 1985.
Lost in Space: The Reagan Years, Andrews & McMeel (Kansas City, MO), 1988.
Sleeping Babies, Golden Book (New York City), 1989.

ILLUSTRATOR

Stephen Manes, *That Game from Outer Space: The First Strange Thing That Happened to Oscar Noodleman,* Dutton (New York City), 1983.
Nathan Zimelman, *Mean Murgatroyd and the Ten Cats,* Dutton, 1984.
Linda K. Harris, *Kids' Talk,* Andrews & McMeel, 1993.
Chaim Potok, *The Tree of Here,* Knopf (New York City), 1993.
Chaim Potok, *The Sky of Now,* Knopf, 1995.

SIDELIGHTS: Tony Auth's editorial cartoons earned him a Pulitzer Prize, and the talented artist has also illustrated numerous children's books. According to Laurence J. Peter in the *Washington Post Book World,* "Whatever Auth touches is put into a new context, seen in a fresh perspective, simultaneously funny and dead-serious." A *New York Times Book Review* critic found Auth's work to be "acridly witty graphic commentary" and deemed Auth "a bright . . . star in the world of editorial cartooning."

Auth began drawing at the age of five, and went on to study biological illustration in college. He worked as a medical illustrator for some time and enjoyed the work, but the Vietnam War eventually convinced him to become a political cartoonist. "I had always in my youth thought that I would probably be a cartoonist, but I was totally apolitical, so that throughout high school and college the cartoons I was drawing were not political in nature at all, but social commentary," he remarked in a *Contemporary Authors* interview. "It was really very rewarding suddenly to find that the same talents I was using in medical illustration, where I was in fact doing a lot of cartooning, could be turned toward politics."

Auth mused: "Cartooning is an excellent medium for making one point at a time, and the point may be one that I anticipate will provoke a reaction of sadness or joy or laughter or nostalgia or any number of things. As far as changing people's minds, I tend to think of what we call information as being really a torrent of particles: some of them are public relations material; some of them are half-truths; many are honest. Everybody's putting out information, and people get subjected to a torrent of it and then form an opinion of what's going on. I contribute one particle a day to the torrent."

Auth's illustrations for children's books have also won praise from reviewers. He worked with novelist Chaim Potok on two books, *The Sky of Now* and *The Tree of Here.* Reviewing the former, which is a story about a boy's fear of heights, Julie Corsaro noted in *Booklist* that Auth's pastel wash-and-line pictures "are spare yet evocative." In Nathan Zimelman's *Mean Murgatroyd and the Ten Cats,* Auth brought to life the tale of a cat-hating dog and the little girl who foils him. Olga Richard and Donnarae MacCann, reviewers for *Wilson Library Bulletin,* cited his pictures in that book as "an example of how humor and stylistic originality can blend. Auth's art is spontaneous, fresh, bold. He combines color and line in a unique manner, using line to contour some objects, but a combination of line and color in other images. . . . This technique—a studied incompleteness—brings tremendous action and energy to the illustration."

BIOGRAPHICAL/CRITICAL SOURCES:

PERIODICALS

Booklist, January 1, 1996, p. 848.
Newsweek, October 13, 1980.
New York Times Book Review, October 9, 1977.
Publishers Weekly, August 30, 1993, p. 96; November 27, 1995, p. 69.

School Library Journal, October, 1993, p. 108; January, 1996, p. 93.
Washington Post Book World, October 16, 1977.
Wilson Library Bulletin, May, 1985, p. 609.

* * *

AYRES, E. C. 1946-
(Gene Ayres)

PERSONAL: Born May 8, 1946, in Summit, NJ; son of John Underwood (a statistical supervisor) and Alice (a painter; maiden name, Hutchinson) Ayres; married Joyce Newkirk, April, 1984 (divorced April, 1988); children: Jonathan Michael. *Education:* Attended Cornell College, Mount Vernon, IA; Syracuse University, B.A., 1968. *Politics:* "Liberal on most issues." *Religion:* Society of Friends (Quakers). *Avocational interests:* Sailing, tennis, films, books, computers, art, travel.

ADDRESSES: *Agent*—Donald Maas, Donald Maas Literary Agency, 157 West 57th St., New York, NY 10019. *E-mail*—lowellpi@aol.com.

CAREER: Producer, writer, and director of educational films, 1969-72; Children's Television Workshop, New York City, producer, writer, and director for episodes of *Sesame Street* and *Feelin' Good,* 1973-74; producer, writer, and director for television network documentaries and public television programs, 1975-80; Jack Arnold Productions, Universal City, CA, writer and associate producer, 1980-82; Roll Over Beethoven Productions, Los Angeles, CA, feature film development writer, 1983-89; WTSP-TV, St. Petersburg, FL, television film critic, 1990-91; 2020 Productions, Santa Fe, NM, writer and creative producer, 1992-94; freelance novelist, 1994—. International Digital Books, Inc., creative director; Future Wave, Inc., writer and creative producer, 1992-94. Eckerd College, guest lecturer for Elderhostel Program of Continuing Education. Supporter of environmental causes. *Military service:* Performed alternative service as a conscientious objector to military duty, 1968-71.

MEMBER: Writers Guild of America West, Mystery Writers of America, Private Eye Writers of America.

AWARDS, HONORS: Ford Foundation junior fellowship, 1969-72; grant from Carnegie Corp., 1970-72; Silver Medals in the documentary film category, from Atlanta International Film Festival, 1972, for writing, producing, and directing *Reading Is Pride* and *3, 4, Open the Door;* winner of Best First Private Eye Novel Contest, from Private Eye Writers of America, 1992, for *Hour of the Manatee.*

WRITINGS:

MYSTERY NOVELS

Hour of the Manatee, St. Martin's (New York City), 1994.
Eye of the Gator, St. Martin's, 1995.
Night of the Panther, St. Martin's, 1997.
Lair of the Lizard, St. Martin's, 1998.

OTHER

Author of the feature film *Hunter* (also co-producer), 1994, the unreleased film *Andy Warhol's "Tacky Women,"* and several documentary films. Author of television episodes for series such as *Smurfs, Scooby Doo, Benji,* and *Dennis the Menace.* Author of a film and video column, *Berkshire Record,* 1991, and a humor column on single parenting, *Berkshire Eagle,* 1991-92. Contributor to periodicals, including *Harper's* and *Sesame Street.*

WORK IN PROGRESS: *Red Tide,* a novel.

SIDELIGHTS: E. C. Ayres worked for two decades as a writer for television and newspapers before publishing his first novel, a mystery thriller entitled *Hour of the Manatee.* It introduced the character of Tony Lowell, a photographer who also works as a private investigator. Lowell's friend and foil is Lena Bedrosian, a detective on the Manatee City police force. Lowell is a survivor of the 1960s, "a wacky but likable guy who is sort of Travis McGee, Don Quixote, and Willie Nelson rolled into one," writes Emily Melton in *Booklist.* Long-haired Lowell is a divorced Vietnam veteran who loves boats and hates guns. Once a photographer for the UPI news service, Lowell took an early retirement and, in his forties, spends most of his time taking it easy in the Florida Gulf Coast country he calls home.

In *Hour of the Manatee,* Lowell gets a phone call from an old friend who claims to have the real story on the death, years before, of a rich playboy. Before the two can meet and discuss the matter further, Lowell's friend is murdered. He sets out to avenge her. "Ayres writes entertainingly about the idle rich and the sleazy methods they use in the race for power, money, and fame," affirms Melton, adding that "Lowell is an appealing renegade who enjoys bucking the system."

In Ayres's next book, *Night of the Panther,* Lowell is enlisted by Bedrosian to help solve the murder of her cousin, Marge Pappas—a dedicated game warden who might have been killed for her dedication in protecting a mother panther in a nature preserve. Poachers, militia members, corrupt deputies, businessmen, and politicians are all part of the tangled web that surround's Pappas's death. In another *Booklist* review, Melton notes that the characters "are almost too perfectly stereotypical," but admits that "Ayres knows how to make them leap off the page. There's also no denying that his style and tone are as close to that of the beloved John D. MacDonald as anyone writing today. A fine mystery."

Ayres once told *CA:* "Like many authors, I began my writing career with something akin to a sense of purpose, which was considerably different from the purveyor of fictional entertainment that I would become. I had all the fiery idealism spawned of the sixties, tempered with time, and disappointment, and experience, mellowed with realism. I still wanted to change the world, and writing detective fiction is not necessarily the best way to attempt such a goal. Yet, it was what I ended up doing, after years of languishing, often foundering, in television.

"It came about by accident. I had left television in disgust, particularly over the issue of violence. Ironically, my new medium was also steeped in a violent tradition, but I saw in this an interesting challenge. Unlike the television experience, I had total control over the outcome.

"I do not try to pretend that violence is not a part of our lives, our world. After all, crime detection invariably plunges the reader into the realm of violence. I make full use of the tools of my trade: suspense, terror, and the chase, as well as investigative procedure. What I choose to do, however, is to limit violent behavior to the perpetrators, not the heroes.

"My principal character is a private eye who does not carry a weapon. Interestingly, in a survey of Miami-area real-life private investigators, not one actually carried a gun in the line of work. I made this deliberate choice, not so much in an effort to redefine my newly adopted genre but, for my own part, to take away the prurient voyeurism inherent in the vivid depiction of violent conflict and its results that, in my opinion, has pervaded our culture.

"We have come to assume that heroes are, by definition, violent men (or, now, women), whose success is based on being a better shot, a harder hitter, or simply a more ruthless person than their adversaries. What I would far prefer, especially since our heroes have become role models to so many, is that they triumph with wits, with courage, yes, and endurance, and ultimately, simply because they are better human beings than their foes."

BIOGRAPHICAL/CRITICAL SOURCES:

PERIODICALS

Booklist, January 10, 1994, p. 48; February 15, 1994, p. 1062; June 1, 1994, p. 1778; October 15, 1995, p. 387; May 1, 1997, p. 1481.

Library Journal, May 1, 1997, p. 144.

Publishers Weekly, October 2, 1995, p. 59; May 12, 1997, p. 62.

* * *

AYRES, Gene

See AYRES, E. C.

B

BAILEY, Fred Arthur 1947-

PERSONAL: Born March 28, 1947, in Dumas, AR; son of Fred L. (in sales) and Dorothy M. (in sales; maiden name, Austin) Bailey; married Bonnie M. Pitt (a university academic affairs administrator), August 22, 1968; children: Amber, Alex, Stan. *Ethnicity:* "White." *Education:* Harding College (now University), B.A., 1970; University of Tennessee, Knoxville, M.A., 1972, Ph.D., 1979. *Politics:* "High Federalist." *Religion:* Church of Christ.

ADDRESSES: *Home*—1400 Compere Blvd., Abilene, TX 79601. *Office*—Department of History, Box 28130, Abilene Christian University, Abilene, TX 79699; fax: 915-674-2369. *E-mail*—baileyf@nicanor.acu.edu.

CAREER: Freed-Hardeman College, Henderson, TN, associate professor of history, 1983-84; Abilene Christian University, Abilene, TX, associate professor, 1984-87, professor of history, 1988—, chair, 1996.

MEMBER: Organization of American Historians, Southern Historical Association.

AWARDS, HONORS: Marshall Wingfield Award, West Tennessee Historical Society, 1983, for article in the *West Tennessee Historical Society Papers,* "The Poor, Plain Folk, and Planters: A Social Analysis of Middle Tennessee Respondents to the Civil War Veterans Questionnaires"; John Trotwood Moore Award, Tennessee Historical Society, 1987, for article in the *Tennessee Historical Quarterly,* "Class Contrasts in Old South Tennessee"; Tennessee History Book Award, Tennessee Library Association and Tennessee Historical Commission, 1988, for *Class and Tennessee's Confederate Generation;* E. Merton Coulter Award, 1991, for article in the *Georgia Historical Quarterly,* "Textbooks of the Lost Cause: Censorship and the Creation of Southern State Histories"; H. Bailey Carroll Award, 1994, for article in the *Southwestern Historical Quarterly*, "Free Speech and the 'Lost Case' in Texas: A Study of Censorship and Social Control in the New South"; A. Elizabeth Taylor Award, Southern Association of Women's Historians, 1994, for article in the *Georgia Historical Quarterly,* "Mildred Lewis Rutherford and the Patrician Cult of the Old South."

WRITINGS:

Class and Tennessee's Confederate Generation, University of North Carolina Press, 1987.

William Edward Dodd: The South's Yeoman Scholar, University Press of Virginia, 1997.

Contributor of approximately eighty articles, encyclopedia entries, and reviews to various history journals, including *Georgia Historical Quarterly, Southwestern Historical Quarterly, Tennessee Quarterly,* and *West Tennessee Historical Society Papers.*

WORK IN PROGRESS: The Southern Quest for a Suitable Past: Historiography and Social Control in the Modern South.

SIDELIGHTS: Fred Arthur Bailey once told *CA:* "To a great extent my own interest in Southern class studies derives from my youth in southeastern Arkansas, where I witnessed the dynamics of the country store in which both blacks and impoverished whites were bonded to the credit system. My grandparents' store encompassed Southern class values. An unpainted structure split in half lengthwise by a single aisle, it had three main divisions. The first third of the structure stretched from the porch to the produce scales with a post office on one side and a counter on the others. Black sharecroppers never went beyond this section. There they were waited on by my grandmother, but when a white landowner entered they either stepped outdoors, or in inclement weather crossed to the other side of the aisle, remaining without voiced complaint until the local planter completed his business. The store's middle third was an open visiting area built around an old kerosene stove. Whites—farmers, fishermen, and hunters—played dominoes or checkers (with overturned soda bottle caps) and swapped stories mixing truth and lies about farming, fishing, and fox hunting. A larger screen partitioned the last third off from the visiting area. This was the kitchen and dining room where only family members and invited guests entered.

"My boyhood memories are filled with thoughts of enormous pecan trees, fresh fish from the Arkansas River, and cotton plants taller than myself. It also brings to mind a land of family, class, and race that seemed at odds with the themes of respect and freedom taught in my schools. Later at college and graduate school my professors were almost all consensus historians whose pronouncements of American unity and democratic felicity ran counter to my own personal experience. My search into the South's past suggests that it was more a land of social seams than a region of social seamlessness."

BIOGRAPHICAL/CRITICAL SOURCES:

PERIODICALS

Anderson Independent-Mail, June 26, 1987.
Richmond News Leader, April 8, 1987.

* * *

BAITZ, Jon Robin 1961-

PERSONAL: Born in 1961, in Los Angeles, CA; son of a businessman. *Education:* Attended schools in the United States, Brazil, and South Africa.

ADDRESSES: *Agent*—William Morris Agency, Inc., 1350 Avenue of the Americas, New York, NY 10019.

CAREER: Playwright, 1986—. New York Stage and Film Company, New York City, playwright-in-residence, 1989; co-artistic director, Naked Angels, New York City. Worked variously as a short-order cook, tractor driver, painter, and assistant to film producers.

AWARDS, HONORS: Playwrights Horizon Revson fellow; Playwrights USA Award, Theatre Communications Group, 1987; runner-up for outstanding regional play in the United States, American Theater Critics Association, 1987; Rockefeller fellowship; New York *Newsday* Oppenheimer Award, 1987; Humanitas award, 1990.

WRITINGS:

Mizlansky/Zilinsky, produced in Los Angeles, 1985.
The Film Society (two-act play; produced in Los Angeles, 1987, produced in London, 1988, produced off-Broadway, 1988), Theatre Communications Group, 1987.
Dutch Landscape, produced in Los Angeles, 1989.
Substance of Fire, produced in New York, 1992, adapted for film, 1996.
The End of the Day (produced in Seattle, 1990; produced in New York and London, 1992) Samuel French (New York City), 1993.
Three Hotels (produced in New York, 1993) Samuel French (New York City), 1993.
The Substance of Fire and Other Plays, Theatre Communications Group (New York City), 1993.
A Fair Country (produced in Chicago, 1997) Theatre Communications Group, 1996.

Work represented in *The Best Plays of 1986-1987,* edited by Otis L. Guernsey Jr. and Jeffrey Sweet, Dodd, 1988, and *New Plays USA Four,* edited by James Leverett, Theatre Communications Group, 1988.

SIDELIGHTS: For six years of his youth, Jon Robin Baitz lived in South Africa, a republic filled with mounting racial tensions due to its white-dominated government's continued practice of apartheid among a predominantly black population. Baitz used his observations, which included a glimpse of the racially motivated riots in Soweto, near Johannesburg, in 1976, as the foundation for his 1987 play, *The Film Society.* Set in the conservative Blenheim School for Boys in Durban, South Africa, in 1970, the work presents a look at apartheid through the eyes of white, middle-class adults. Students, blacks, and other minorities are not featured. Delving into the passive attitudes of some middle-class whites toward segregation policies, the play also charts the quest of these people to remain isolated from such controversial politics.

The young playwright described the experiences that helped shape *The Film Society* to Mervyn Rothstein of the *New York Times:* "Like many children of Americans abroad, I was quite sheltered. . . . On a certain level, I understood what South Africa was about, but it was sort of abstract. The presence of apartheid was always real, but I never felt it as keenly as people back home might imagine. But awareness does grow. What happens is you try and fight a process of assimilation." That process faces the play's protagonist, Jonathon Balton. Head of the school's film society, Balton uses the extracurricular group as an escape from the realities of apartheid, school politics, and his ambivalence toward such matters.

Balton's apathy, however, is tested when fellow teacher and close friend Terry Sinclair is fired after arranging to have a black priest speak at the centenary celebration of Blenheim—a prep school that has remained a distant outpost from the nation's racial strife, much to the pleasure of its financial supporters. When some patrons perceive Sinclair's gesture as a radical departure and threaten to withdraw their children and monetary backing, Balton's mother offers to aid the school's headmaster, Neville Sutter, provided her son's career is advanced. The film teacher must then decide whether to accept the promotion to headmaster and the school's political stance or assert his objections.

Produced in cities including London and New York City, *The Film Society* was applauded by many critics and frequently compared to the works of notable twentieth-century playwrights Simon Gray and Athol Fugard. "What distinguishes Mr. Baitz's writing, aside from its wit and its manifest, if sometimes showy, literacy, is its ability to embrace the ambiguities of political and moral dilemmas," noted Frank Rich in the *New York Times.* The critic deemed Baitz "a new talent to watch." John Simon, writing in *New York,* praised the play for its "love of language," adding, "It is not always as poetic or muscular as it wants to be, but it is real language, fitted to each character. . . . Though it's riskier to gamble on writers' futures than on pork bellies, I would invest in Jon Robin Baitz."

Although Baitz's next play, an autobiographical family portrait titled *Dutch Landscape* that premiered in Los Angeles in 1989, was deemed a failure, the twenty-eight-year-old writer bounced back with the resiliency of his youth. He returned to New York and his next production, *The Substance of Fire,* opened off-Broadway in March of 1991 to rave reviews. The play, which examines the decay of a publishing empire run by a once-influential family, found critics comparing the cosmopolitan author to Shakespeare, Chekhov, and Edward Albee. This time around, Baitz was able to parlay his success into a new medium: he was invited to write and direct several movies, including the film version of *Substance of Fire,* which made it to the screen in 1996.

Baitz's next widely acclaimed work was all about the revelation of terrible, dangerous secrets. *Three Hotels,* which premiered in New York in 1993, is a play in the form of three confessional monologues, each set in a different hotel room in exotic corners of the world. The first act/monologue belongs to Kenneth Hoyle, an executive for a U.S. company that markets a powdered-milk formula baby supplement to third world countries (or, in corporate lingo "developing nations.") Hoyle has been sent to Tangier, Morocco on a mission that has become his specialty: the mass layoff of white collar "dead wood" in the name of lean-and-mean, '90s-style corporate competition. Hoyle is cold, matter-of-fact, and seemingly impervious to the emotions he stirs. He boasts, "They go quietly when I do it." Although Hoyle is being groomed for the company presidency, his job, his travels, and his family life seem to be wearing him down. He drinks his way continuously through his first speech, getting steadily more vulgar and brave.

A beachfront cabana in St. Thomas, Virgin Islands is the setting for the second act/monologue, which belongs to Hoyle's fragile and frazzled wife, Barbara. Her high-powered husband's high-pressure company has met on the island paradise for a conference ("a sort of baby formula summit," Barbara wryly calls it), and she has just delivered a speech to the "Wives of Executives Stationed in the Third World" or, more simply, "the 3-W club." Her speech marks the beginning of the end of her husband's career. In it, she reveals all the frustration, terror, and anguish that have been building inside her for years as she has dutifully followed her husband from one port of call to the next. She warns the new wives not to become attached to foreign luxuries like maids and lavish homes, to preserve some semblance of their own careers and, more importantly she tells them: Be careful. Barbara's son, we learn, was stabbed to death on a Copacabana beach in broad daylight, for the price of a watch he received as a birthday present and her husband, it seems, has been lost to her ever since.

After her presentation, Barbara is lost to Kenneth. The third act/monologue finds Hoyle in the Hotel Principal in Oaxaca, Mexico, licking his wounds and searching desperately for his vanished wife. The tables were turned and he was summarily fired, as coldly and ruthlessly as he himself might have done, by the presidents of his firm. He relates the tale of his dismissal into a tape recorder for his senile mother, confined to the Jewish Home for the Aged in Baltimore, and hopes Barbara will find him, or he will find her, on the Day of the Dead in Mexico, at the hotel where they spent their honeymoon.

Reviewing *Three Hotels* for *Time,* William A. Henry III declared, "With these speeches Jon Robin Baitz, 31, vaults into the top rank of U.S. dramatists." What makes the play so memorable, Henry wrote, "is Baitz's ability to render people specific and real." Lawrence Bommer noted in the *Windy City Times,* "As a gadfly playwright, Baitz chronicles the small sellouts that amount to a lost life. The unwitting exposures of his complex characters typify a divided-and-conquered culture that feels increasingly more corporate than individualistic."

Although Baitz has begun doing more work among the Hollywood set (he took his first turn in front of the camera in the role of a charming gay playwright in the 1995 film *Last Summer in the Hamptons*), the lure of filmmaking will not likely draw him away from his true passion: the theatre. In the theatre, Baitz told the *Windy City Times,* "You see these subversive secrets playing themselves out as truth, revelations that on the deepest level work on us communally and sink us into new depths. You get to share terrible secrets together, wonderfully and dangerously in a way that doesn't happen at the movies."

In some way, and to different degrees, all of Baitz' plays have emerged from his own experiences which, like the playwright himself, are constantly changing. "I think that people discover that they are alive very gradually," Baitz told *American Theatre,* "Part of the process of discovering that one is actually living is the discovery of one's politics. That frequently means that you're being surprised by yourself, that your politics are not the politics or the notions or the ideals that you thought you had, but rather something altogether strange." Describing his personal politics, Baitz predicted, "I see myself becoming increasingly reclusive, heard from less frequently . . . less public, more internal. And getting older."

BIOGRAPHICAL/CRITICAL SOURCES:

BOOKS

Contemporary Dramatists, fifth edition, St. James Press (Detroit), 1993.

Guernsey, Otis L., Jr., and Jeffrey Sweet, editors, *The Best Plays of 1986-1987,* Dodd, 1988.

Leverett, James, editor, *New Plays USA Four,* Theatre Communications Group, 1988.

PERIODICALS

American Theatre, March, 1993, p. 66.

Los Angeles Magazine, March, 1993, p. 96.

New Leader, September 6, 1993, p. 22.

New York, August 1, 1988.

New Yorker, August 8, 1988.

New York Times, July 22, 1988; August 2, 1988.

Time, April 19, 1993, p. 66; December 30, 1996, p. 160.

Times (London), February 6, 1988; April 19, 1993.

Wall Street Journal, October 4, 1995, p. A12.

Windy City Times, July 17, 1997.

* * *

BAKER, Denys Val 1917-1984
(David Eames)

PERSONAL: Born October 24, 1917, in Poppleton, Yorkshire, England; died June 6, 1984; son of Valentine Henry and Dilys (Eames) Baker; married Jess Margaret Bryan (a self-employed potter), January 28, 1948; children: Martin, Gillian, Jane, Stephen, Demelza, Genevieve. *Politics:* Pacifist. *Avocational interests:* Surfing and boating.

CAREER: Writer on British daily and trade newspapers, 1935-41; freelance writer, 1941-84.

WRITINGS:

STORY COLLECTIONS

Worlds without End, Sylvan Press, 1945.

The Return of Uncle Walter, and Other Stories, Low, 1948.

The Flame Swallower and Other Tales from Cornwall, Lake (London), 1963.
The Strange and the Damned (short stories), Pyramid, 1964.
Bizarre Loves, Brown Watson (London), 1966.
Strange Journeys, Pyramid, 1969.
The Face in the Mirror, Arkham House (Sauk City, WI), 1971.
The Woman and the Engine Driver, United Writers (Zennor, Cornwall), 1972.
A Summer to Remember: Cornish Stories, Kimber (London), 1975.
Echoes from the Cornish Cliffs, Kimber, 1976.
The Secret Place and Other Cornish Stories, Kimber, 1977.
Passenger to Penance and Other Stories from Cornwall, Kimber, 1978.
At the Sea's Edge and Other Stories, Kimber, 1979.
Thomasina's Island: A Novella of Cornwall and Other Short Stories, Kimber, 1981.
The House on the Creek and Other Stories of Cornwall, Kimber, 1981.
The Girl in the Photograph and Other Stories, Kimber, 1983.
Martin's Cottage: A Novella of Cornwall and Other Stories, Kimber, 1983.
A Work of Art and Other Stories, Kimber, 1984.
The Tenant and Other Stories, Kimber, 1985.

NOVELS

The White Rock, Sylvan Press, 1945, Appleton, 1947.
The More We Are Together, Low, 1947.
The Widening Mirror, Low, 1949.
(Under pseudonym David Eames) *The Title's My Own,* Bles (London), 1955.
As the River Flows, Milton House (Aylesbury), 1974.
A Company of Three, Milton House, 1974.
Don't Lose Your Cool, Dad, Milton House, 1975.
Barbican's End: A Novel of Cornwall, Kimber, 1979.
Rose: A Novel of Cornwall, Kimber, 1980.
Karenza: A Novel of Cornwall, Kimber, 1980.
One Summer at St. Merry's, Kimber, 1984.

NONFICTION

Paintings from Cornwall, Cornish Library, 1950.
Britain Discovers Herself, Christopher Johnson, 1950.
How to Be an Author, Harvill Press, 1952.
(With wife, Jess Baker) *The Pottery Book: An Introduction to an Individual Art and Craft,* Cassell, 1959.
Britain's Art Colony by Sea, George Ronald, 1959.
The Minack Theatre, George Ronald, 1960.
How to Be a Parent, Boardman & Co., 1960.
Pottery Today, Oxford University Press, 1961.
The Sea's in the Kitchen, Phoenix House, 1962.
The Door Is Always Open, Phoenix House, 1963.
The Young Potter: A How-It-Is-Done Book of Pottery, Warne, 1963, published as *Fun with Pottery,* 1975.
(Under pseudonym David Eames) *Pottery for Profit and Pleasure,* Museum Press, 1963.
We'll Go 'Round the World Tomorrow, John Baker, 1965.
To Sea with Sanu, John Baker, 1967.
Adventures before Fifty, John Baker, 1969.
Lift Up the Creek, John Baker, 1971.
The Petrified Mariner, Kimber, 1972.
Timeless Land: Creative Spirit in Cornwall, Adams, 1973.
An Old Mill by the Stream, Kimber, 1973.
Spring at Land's End, Kimber, 1974.
Sunset over the Scillies, Kimber, 1975.
A View from the Valley, Kimber, 1976.
It's a Long Way to Land's End, Kimber, 1977.
The Wind Blows from the West, Kimber, 1977.
All This and Cornwall Too, Kimber, 1978.
A Family for All Seasons, Kimber, 1979.
As the Stream Flows By, Kimber, 1980.
The Spirit of Cornwall, W. H. Allen, 1980.
A Family at Sea, Kimber, 1981.
Let's Make Pottery, Warne, 1981.
Upstream at the Mill, Kimber, 1981.
The Waterwheel Turns: A Retrospect, Kimber, 1982.
Summer at the Mill, Kimber, 1982.
Family Circles, Kimber, 1983.
Down a Cornish Lane, Kimber, 1983.
A Mill in the Valley, Kimber, 1984.
When Cornish Eyes Are Smiling, Kimber, 1984.
My Cornish World, Kimber, 1985.
Cornish Prelude, Kimber, 1985.

EDITOR

Little Reviews, 1914-1943, Allen & Unwin, 1943.
Little Reviews Anthology, Volume I, Allen & Unwin, 1943, Volume II-IV, Eyre & Spottiswoode, 1945, 1946, 1948, Volume V, Methuen, 1949.
Writing Today, Staples, Volume I (with Peter Ratazzi), 1943, Volumes II-IV, 1944-46.
International Short Stories, two volumes, W. H. Allen, 1944-45.
Modern Short Stories, Staples, 1944.
Voyage: An Anthology of Selected Stories, Sylvan Press, 1945.

Writers of Today, two volumes, Sidgwick & Jackson, 1946-48.
Modern British Writing, Vanguard, 1947.
One and All: A Selection of Stories from Cornwall, Museum Press, 1951.
The Ways of Love, New English Library, 1969.
The Dreams of Love, New English Library, 1969.
Haunted Cornwall: A Book of Supernatural Stories, Kimber, 1973.
Cornish Harvest: An Anthology, Kimber, 1974.
Stories of the Sea, Kimber, 1974.
Stories of Country Life, Kimber, 1975.
Cornish Short Stories, Penguin, 1976.
Stories of the Macabre, Kimber, 1976.
Personal Choices: An Anthology, Kimber, 1977.
Twelve Stories by Famous Women Writers, W. H. Allen, 1977.
Stories of Horror and Suspense: An Anthology, Kimber, 1977.
Stories of the Occult and Other Tales of Mystery, Kimber, 1978.
Stories of the Supernatural, Kimber, 1979.
The Sea Survivors, W. H. Allen, 1979.
Women Writing: An Anthology, W. H. Allen, 1979.
Stories of Fear, Kimber, 1980.
Cornish Ghost Stories, Kimber, 1981.
Ghosts in Country Houses, Kimber, 1981.
A View from Land's End: Writers against a Cornish Background, Kimber, 1982.
When Churchyards Yawn, Kimber, 1982.
Ghosts in Country Villages, Kimber, 1983.
Stories of Haunted Inns, Kimber, 1983.
Phantom Lovers, Kimber, 1984.
Haunted Travellers, Kimber, 1985.
Something Special, Crescent, 1986.

OTHER

Contributor of short stories to *Argosy, Pick of Today's Stories, Esquire, Town and Country, Chicago Review, Western Review, Good Housekeeping, Home, Evening News, Evening Standard, Punch,* and other publications; author of nearly one hundred stories broadcast on British Broadcasting Corp. programs.

SIDELIGHTS: A prolific writer of regional and supernatural fiction, and the editor of many anthologies, Denys Val Baker is probably best remembered for his stories of ghostly hauntings. Chris Morgan, writing in the *St. James Guide to Horror, Ghost and Gothic Writers,* acknowledged that "quite a few of Val Baker's stories feature ghosts." Baker's subtle writing often confuses whether his characters have encountered the supernatural or whether they are suffering from their own psychological delusions. In a number of stories, Morgan noted, a character's "obsession is so extreme that the explanation must be either a mental imbalance or a manifestation of the supernatural. The novelette "The Girl in the Photograph" shows how a middle-aged man . . . finds a photo of people who lived in [his] house, an old mill, over 60 years before and falls in love with one of them, a young woman. Clearly he is haunted by her face, though not in the supernatural sense. As he has a portion of the photograph secretly enlarged and tries to discover more about her, his behaviour becomes more extreme and irrational. He tries to strangle his wife, and he comes to believe that the young woman is still out there and returns his love."

Another such story, Morgan noted, is "The Face in the Mirror," the title story of a collection Baker published with the horror press Arkham House. In this story, Morgan explained, a man finds himself being followed by a disturbingly fearsome man. No matter where he goes, the man is there, following him. Finally he confronts the pursuer and attempts to strangle the man. He wakes in a hospital room with neck injuries; he has attempted to kill himself, and finds that he himself is the stranger who has been pursuing him relentlessly. "The sense of blind panic," Morgan noted, "is well conveyed; the narrator is so gripped by his need to escape that he never considers why the other man is pursuing him, nor does he think to call on the assistance of a policeman. . . . Baker's intention is not to suggest some implausible fantasy scenario of exchanged personalities, but to demonstrate mental imbalance, the hysterical effects of paranoia."

BIOGRAPHICAL/CRITICAL SOURCES:

BOOKS

St. James Guide to Horror, Ghost and Gothic Writers, St. James Press (Detroit), 1998.

PERIODICALS

Book and Magazine Collector, number 78, September, 1990.
Times Literary Supplement, March 28, 1980; January 2, 1981.

OBITUARIES:

PERIODICALS

Times (London), July 10, 1984.*

BAKER, Scott (MacMartin) 1947-

PERSONAL: Born September 29, 1947, in Oak Park, IL; son of Robert MacMartin (a lawyer) and Sally (an antique clothing collector; maiden name, Underwood) Baker; married. *Education:* New College, Sarasota, FL, B.A., 1969; attended University of California, Irvine, 1969-70; Goddard College, M.A., 1978; attended Sorbonne, University of Paris, 1978-81.

ADDRESSES: Home—4 rue St. Sulpice, Paris 75006, France.

CAREER: Writer, 1972—; Editions Jean-Claude Lattes, Paris, France, currently a reader.

MEMBER: Science Fiction Writers of America, World SF.

AWARDS, HONORS: World Fantasy Award, 1985, for short story "Still Life with Scorpion."

WRITINGS:

NOVELS

Symbiote's Crown, Berkley Publishing (New York City), 1978.
Nightchild, Berkley Publishing, 1979, revised edition, Pocket Books (New York City), 1983.
Dhampire, Pocket Books, 1982, revised edition published as *Ancestral Hungers,* Tor Books (New York City), 1995.
Firedance, Tor Books, 1986.
Drink the Fire from the Flames, Tor Books, 1987.
Webs, Tor Books, 1989.

OTHER

(Editor) Robert Silverberg, *La Fete de St. Dionysos* (short stories), Editions Jean-Claude Lattes, 1980.

Contributor of short stories to *New Infinity Review, Interzone, Omni,* and *Isaac Asimov's Science Fiction Magazine.*

SIDELIGHTS: Scott Baker, according to Chris Morgan in the *St. James Guide to Horror, Ghost and Gothic Writers,* "tends to allow each of his novels or stories to include elements of horror, fantasy and science fiction. . . . Baker has not always chosen the most propitious subject matter for his horror novels; nor has he always tackled his plots and characters in a way that would make them easy for the reader to follow or enjoy. Obviously he expects rather too much of his readers; or, to put it another way, he can be too oblique for his own good."

In *Dhampire,* revised as *Ancestral Hungers,* Baker tells the story of a strange family related distantly to Vlad the Impaler and the complex machinations they employ in a battle for family power. David Bathory, a cocaine addict and snake breeder, sets the tale in motion when, following the death of his wife, he seeks to reacquaint himself with his estranged family. While the critic for *Publishers Weekly* believes that Baker "introduces too much arcane material throughout the narrative, and his convoluted story line . . . proves difficult to follow," Michelle Guthrie in *Booklist* concludes" Baker spins a gothic tale that blends the influences of Bram Stoker's Dracula and the general lore of vampires with sensual imagery and occult themes to create a unique novel well worthy of horror fans' attention."

Baker writes: "I am far more interested in writing about things I haven't done, won't do, or wouldn't do, than about things that have any sort of real-life connection with my personal experience. I have little interest in simplistically realistic or naturalistic fiction, or in fiction whose relationship with the 'world of consensus reality' can be taken for granted. I write out of a need to do so, and for my own personal satisfaction."

BIOGRAPHICAL/CRITICAL SOURCES:

BOOKS

St. James Guide to Horror, Ghost and Gothic Writers, St. James Press (Detroit), 1998.

PERIODICALS

Booklist, March 15, 1995, p. 1306.
Publishers Weekly, March 13, 1995, p. 64.

* * *

BALSEIRO, Jose Agustin 1900-

PERSONAL: Born August 23, 1900, in Barceloneta, Puerto Rico; son of Rafael and Dolores (Romos-Casellas) Balseiro; married Mercedes Pedreira, March 3, 1924; children: Yolanda Buchanon, Liliana

Mees. *Education:* University of Puerto Rico, LL.B., 1921.

ADDRESSES: *Home*—408 Valencia 4, Coral Gables, FL 33134.

CAREER: University of Illinois, Urbana, professor of romance languages, 1930-33 and 1936-38; University of Puerto Rico, Rio Piedras, visiting professor of Spanish literature, 1933-36; U.S. delegate to First International Congress on Teaching Ibero-American Literature, 1938; U.S. representative to First International American Conference on Libraries and Publications, 1939; senator-at-large to Puerto Rican Senate, 1942-44; University of Miami, Coral Gables, FL, professor of Hispanic literature, 1946-67; University of Arizona, Tucson, visiting professor of Spanish literature, 1967-72. Consultant on Hispanic literature at University of Miami. Summer lecturer, Northwestern University, 1937, Duke University, 1947, 1949, and 1950, Inter-American University, Puerto Rico, 1957-63, University of Mexico, 1959, University of North Carolina at Chapel Hill, 1973, Bryn Mawr College, 1973, Yale University, 1973, and Emory University, 1975. U.S. State Department, International Educational Exchange Program, lecturer in South America, 1954, in Spain and England, 1955-56, and in Puerto Rico, 1956; member of U.S. consultative committee of UNESCO, 1957; vice-president of Fourth Congress of the Academies of the Spanish Language, 1964.

MEMBER: International Institute of Ibero-American Literature (president, 1955-57), North American Academy of Spanish Languages, Modern Language Association of America (president of contemporary Spanish literature section, 1938), National Association of Authors and Journalists (honorary member), Spanish Royal Academy of Language (corresponding member), Spanish-American Academy of Sciences and Arts, Colombian Academy of Letters (corresponding member), Instituto Sarmiento of Argentina, Puerto Rican Academy.

AWARDS, HONORS: Spanish Royal Academy prize for best collection of essays of the year, 1925, for *El vigia,* Volume 1; Litt.D., Inter-American University, 1950; Sc.D., Catholic University, Chile, 1954; L.H.D., Belmont Abbey, 1962; Litt.D., Catholic University, Puerto Rico, 1972; diploma of honor, Mexican Academy of Letters; D.H.L., Polytechnic Institute of Puerto Rico; decorated commander of the Order of Queen Isabel La Catolica, Spain; member of the Order of Vasco Nunez of Balboa, Panama.

WRITINGS:

IN ENGLISH

Eugenio Maria de Hostos: Hispanic America's Public Servant, [Coral Gables, FL], 1949.

The Americas Look at Each Other, translated by Muna Munoz Lee, University of Miami Press (Miami, FL), 1969.

(Editor) *The Hispanic Presence in Florida,* E. A. Seeman (Miami, FL), 1976.

POETRY

Flores de primavera (title means "Flowers of Spring"), [San Juan], 1919.

Las palomas de Eros (title means "The Doves of Eros"), [Madrid], 1921.

Al rumor de la fuente (title means "To the Murmur of the Fountain"), [San Juan], 1922.

La copa de Anacreonte (title means "The Crown of Anacreon"), Editorial Mundo Latino (Madrid), 1924.

Musica cordial (title means "Friendly Music"), Editorial Lex (Havana), 1926.

Sonetos (title means "Sonnets"), [San Juan], 1933.

La pureza cautiva (title means "Captive Purity"), Editorial Lex, 1946.

Saudades de Puerto Rico (title means "Homesickness for Puerto Rico"), Aguilar, 1957.

Visperas de sombras y otros poemas (title means "Eves of Shadow and Other Poems"), Ediciones de Andre (Mexico), 1959.

NOVELS

La maldecida (title means "The Cursed Woman"), [Madrid], 1922.

La ruta eterna (title means "The Eternal Way"), [Madrid], 1926.

En vela mientras el mundo duerme (title means "Vigil While the World Sleeps"), Mnemosyne Publishing, 1969.

La gratitud humana Mnemosyne Publishing, 1969.

Also author of *El sveno de Manon,* 1922.

EDITOR

Novelistas espanoles modernos (title means "Modern Spanish Novelists"), Macmillan (New York

City), 1933, 8th revised and enlarged edition, University of Puerto Rico Press, 1977.

(With J. Riis Owre and others) Alejandro Casona, *La barca sin pescador* (title means "The Boat without a Fisherman"), Oxford University Press (New York City), 1955.

(With Owre) Casona, *Corona de amor y muerte* (title means "Crown of Love and Death"), Oxford University Press, 1960.

(With Eliana Suarez-Rivero) Casona, *El Cabellero de las espuelas de oro* (title means "The Cowboy of the Golden Spurs"), Oxford University Press, 1968.

OTHER

El vigia (title means "The Watchman"), Volume 1, Editorial Mundo Latino, 1925, Volume 2, [Madrid], 1926, reprinted, Biblioteca de autores Puertorriquenas, 1956, Volume 3, [San Juan], 1942.

El Quijote de la Espana contemporanea: Miguel de Unamuno (title means "The Quixote of Contemporary Spain"), E. Gimenez, 1935.

Blasco Ibanez, Unamuno, Valle Inclan y Baroja, cuatro individualistas de Espana (title means "Four Spanish Individualists"), University of North Carolina Press (Chapel Hill, NC), 1949.

Mediciones fisicas: calculo de errores, approximaciones, metodos graficos (title means "Physical Measurements: Calculation of Errors, Approximations, Graphic Methods"), Lebreria Machette (Buenos Aires), 1956.

Expresio de Hispanoamerica (title means "Expression of Spanish America"), Instituto de Cultura Puertorriquena, Volume 1, 1960, Volume 2, 1963, 2nd edition, 1970.

Seis estudios sobre Ruben Dario (title means "Six Studies about Ruben Dario"), Editorial Gredos (Madrid), 1967.

Contributor to periodicals, including *Cuadernos Americanos, Nosotros, Hispanic Review,* and *La Torre.* Editor of numerous Spanish periodicals.

SIDELIGHTS: Jose Agustin Balseiro has brought a multitude of talents to his work. He is internationally known as a writer and critic, a musician whose compositions have been performed at Carnegie Hall, and a respected lecturer on Hispanic cultures in North America. Balseiro has published poetry and novels while teaching language and literature at colleges in America and abroad. As Jane Stewart Cook noted in the *Dictionary of Hispanic Biography,* Balseiro "became a kind of cultural ambassador to the world. His lectures on the arts and the role of the artist as a conduit between the Hispanic and American cultures earned him praise throughout the world, especially within the Spanish-speaking countries."

Although once invited to play professional baseball, Balseiro set out at a young age to become a writer. He was born in Puerto Rico in 1900 and educated there, gaining his bachelor's degree from the University of Puerto Rico in 1921. Balseiro studied law but also loved literature, especially poetry. Even before earning his bachelor's degree he published his first work of poetry, *Flores de primavera* ("Flowers of Spring"). After living for some time in Spain, he accepted a job at the University of Illinois, Urbana, and taught there for five years during the 1930s, spending the rest of the decade at home in Puerto Rico. His most notable career milestone was passed when he accepted a teaching position at the University of Miami in Coral Gables, Florida. He taught there from 1946 until 1967.

Balseiro was always more than a college professor. He authored novels, criticism, and more poetry. He traveled extensively, giving lectures on the connections between Hispanic and American cultures, "and set himself the goal of interpreting the spirit of each of those cultures to the other," to quote Cook. Eventually, he came to be regarded world-wide as a kind of cultural ambassador whose topics have included the philosophies and biographies of poets, public leaders, artists, and musicians.

Critics have acknowledged Balseiro's importance to people both within and without the Spanish-speaking world. One such reviewer from the *South Atlantic Bulletin,* as quoted in the *Dictionary of Hispanic Biography,* called the author "an international scholar who knows no boundaries, and whose criterion is world literature."

During a lecture at the University of Miami in the 1950s, Balseiro explained the reason for his emphasis on internationalism. *Miami Herald* staff writer Sandy Flickner quotes the author's speech: "The nearer we approach our neighbors by the disinterested paths of art, literature, scholarship, and open-hearted friendship, the sooner will we demolish the prejudices that hamper the constructive development of human nature." In his honor, the University of Miami established the Jose A. Balseiro Award, an essay contest, in 1967.

BIOGRAPHICAL/CRITICAL SOURCES:

BOOKS

Dictionary of Hispanic Biography, Gale (Detroit, MI), 1996, pp. 94-96.
Hill, Marnesba D., and Harold B. Schleifer, *Puerto Rican Authors,* Scarecrow (Metuchen, NJ), 1974.

PERIODICALS

Miami Herald, April 29, 1974.*

* * *

BARBER, Richard (William) 1941-

PERSONAL: Born October 30, 1941, in Dunmow, Essex, England; married Helen Tolson, 1970; children: Humphrey, Elaine. *Education:* Corpus Christi College, Cambridge, M.A., 1967, Ph.D., 1982.

ADDRESSES: Home—Stangrove Hall, Alderton, Woodbridge, England.

CAREER: Writer and publisher. Founder, Boydell Press, 1969.

MEMBER: Royal Society of Literature (fellow), Royal Historical Society (fellow), Society of Antiquaries (fellow).

AWARDS, HONORS: Somerset Maugham Award, Society of Authors, 1971, for *The Knight and Chivalry*; *Times Educational Supplement* Junior Information Book Award, 1979, for *Tournaments.*

WRITINGS:

Arthur of Albion: An Introduction to the Arthurian Literature and Legends of England, Barrie & Rockliff, 1961, second revised and extended edition published as *King Arthur in Legend and History,* Cardinal Publications (Davis, CA), 1973, third revised and extended edition published as *King Arthur: Hero and Legend,* St. Martin's (New York City), 1986.
Henry Plantagenet: A Biography, Barrie & Rockliff, 1964.
(With Francis E. Camps) *The Investigation of Murder,* M. Joseph (London), 1966.
Knighthood and Chivalry, Scribner (New York City), 1970, revised edition, Cardinal Publications, 1974 (published in England as *The Knight and Chivalry,* Longmans, Green [London], 1970, revised edition, Boydell Press, 1974).
Samuel Pepys Esq., University of California Press (Berkeley), 1970, second revised edition, Boydell Press, 1996.
(Translator with E. C. Elstob) *Russian Folktales,* Bell, 1971.
(With Anne Riches) *A Dictionary of Fabulous Beasts,* Macmillan (New York City), 1971.
The Figure of Arthur, Longmans, Green, 1972, Rowman & Littlefield (Totowa, NJ), 1973.
Cooking and Recipes from Rome to the Renaissance, Lane, 1974.
(Editor) John Aubrey, *Brief Lives,* Folio (London), 1975, revised and enlarged edition, Boydell Press, 1982.
A Strong Land and a Sturdy: England in the Middle Ages (juvenile), Seabury (New York City), 1976.
Edward, Prince of Wales and Aquitaine: A Biography of the Black Prince, Scribner, 1976.
The Companion Guide to South West France: Bordeaux and the Dordogne, Collins (London), 1977.
Tournaments (juvenile), Kestrel (London), 1978.
(Editor) *The Life and Campaigns of the Black Prince,* Folio, 1978.
The Devil's Crown: Henry II, Richard I, John, BBC Publications (London), 1978, Combined Books, 1997.
A Companion to World Mythology, Kestrel, 1979, Delacorte (New York City), 1980.
(Editor) *The Arthurian Legends: An Illustrated History,* Boydell, 1979, Rowman and Littlefield, 1979.
Living Legends, BBC Publications, 1980.
The Reign of Chivalry, St. Martin's, 1980.
(Editor) *The Pastons: A Family in the Wars of the Roses,* Folio, 1981, Boydell, 1993.
(Editor) *The Penguin Guide to Medieval Europe,* Penguin (New York City), 1984.
The Worlds of John Aubrey, Folio, 1986.
(With Juliet Barker) *Tournaments,* Weidenfeld & Nicolson (London), 1989.
Pilgrimages, Boydell, 1991.
British Myths and Legends, Folio, 1998.

Editor, *Arthurian Literature* (annual volume on Arthurian studies), 1981—.

WORK IN PROGRESS: The Grail, Penguin, publication expected in 2000.

SIDELIGHTS: In several volumes, scholar Richard Barber has explored the various myths and truths surrounding medieval history, in particular that of the celebrated King Arthur. His *Arthur of Albion,* a review of Arthurian legends, was published by the time he was twenty, and since then the author has undertaken two major revisions of the work. In his *King Arthur: Hero and Legend,* Barber "spices up the usual procession of romances and evidences (of the elusive 'real' Arthur) with generally solid perspective and occasionally pointy opinions," Terry Atkinson summarizes in the *Los Angeles Times Book Review.* As Toronto *Globe and Mail* contributor James P. Carley explains, *King Arthur* is "deceptively straightforward in narrative: Barber so smoothly negotiates his way through the labyrinth of Arthurian theses and countertheses that many of the controversies seem never to have existed." The critic adds that "nobody will be shocked by what Barber says, but all his readers will be charmed and stimulated by how he says it. It is only after finishing the book that one realizes what a fine and learned synthesis the urbane prose and elegant illustrations provide." Barber performs a similar uncovering in *The Knight and Chivalry,* showing "how, century by century, Christianity and heresy and technology transformed a barbarian war party into a social elite whose military skills became less important than its genealogy and elegance," as a *New Yorker* critic describes. The result, states Vincent Cronin in *Book World,* is "a useful, well-documented book about what knights actually did and what writers liked to think they did."

BIOGRAPHICAL/CRITICAL SOURCES:

PERIODICALS

Book World, December 27, 1970.
Globe and Mail (Toronto), February 21, 1987.
Los Angeles Times Book Review, March 8, 1987.
New Yorker, December 26, 1970.
Times Literary Supplement, April 16, 1971.

* * *

BARNOUW, Erik 1908-

PERSONAL: Born June 23, 1908, in The Hague, Netherlands; moved to U. S. in 1919, naturalized citizen, 1928; son of Adrian Jacob (a teacher) and Ann Eliza (Midgley) Barnouw; married Dorothy Maybelle Beach, June 3, 1939; children: Jeffrey, Susanna, Karen. *Education:* Princeton University, A.B., 1929; University of Vienna, studied at Reinhardt Seminar, 1930.

ADDRESSES: Home—6 West Park Place, Fair Haven, VT 05743. *Office*—Columbia University, New York, NY 10027. *Agent*—Harold Ober Associates, 40 East 49th St., New York, NY 10017.

CAREER: During early career, worked as broadcasting program director and writer for advertising agencies, including Erwin Wasey and Company; Columbia Broadcasting System, New York City, writer and editor, 1939-40; National Broadcasting Company, New York City, editor of Script Division, 1942-44; commentator overseas br. OWI, 1943-44; U.S. War Department, Washington, DC, supervisor of education unit, Armed Forces Radio Service, 1944-45; Columbia University, New York City, 1946—, member of faculty, began as assistant professor, became professor of dramatic arts in charge of film, radio and television, 1964-69, professor emeritus, 1973—, editor, Center for Mass Communication of Columbia University Press, 1948-72; U.S. Public Health Service, consultant on communication, 1947-50; Theatre Guild, television and radio adapter, 1954-61; National Educational Television, writer and producer for series: *Decision,* 1957-59; International Film Seminars, Inc., president, 1960-67; Library of Congress, Washington, chief of motion picture, broadcasting, and recorded sound division, 1978-81. Also has worked as a song writer and union leader.

MEMBER: Writers Guild of America (national chair, 1957-59), Radio Writers Guild of America (national chair, 1957-59), Authors League of America (secretary, 1949-53), Society of American Historians, Society for Cinema Studies, National Academy of Television Arts and Sciences (member of board of governors, New York, 1958-61, 1966-68), American Civil Liberties Union (member of television-radio panel, 1946-73), Phi Beta Kappa, PEN Club, Public Affairs Committee (member of board, 1961-65).

AWARDS, HONORS: George Foster Peabody Award for achievement in radio or television, 1944, for National Broadcasting Co. radio series, *Words at War;* Ohio State Institute for Education by Radio award, for best single program, 1948, for "The Conspiracy of Silence"; "Freedom to Read" was Edinburgh Film Festival selection, 1954; Gavel Award of American Bar Association and Sylvania

Television Award for best noncommercial television series, 1959, for *Decision: The Constitution in Action;* Fulbright grant, 1961-62, for research in India on use of mass media; Guggenheim fellowship, 1969; Bancroft Prize, 1971, for *The Image Empire;* George Polk Award, 1971, and Frank Luther Mott Award for *A History of Broadcasting in the United States;* Silver Dragon award of Cracow Film Festival, 1972, for *Fable-Safe;* John D. Rockefeller III Fund fellowship, 1972; Woodrow Wilson Centre for Scholars fellowship, 1976; Indo-American fellowship, 1978-79; Eastman Kodak Gold Medal Award, 1982, for significant contributions as an innovative educator.

WRITINGS:

Handbook of Radio Writing, Little, 1939, 2nd edition, 1947.

(Editor) *Radio Drama in Action,* Rinehart, 1945.

Mass Communication: Television, Radio, Film, Press, Rinehart, 1956.

The Television Writer, Hill & Wang (New York City), 1962.

(With S. Krishnaswamy) *Indian Film,* Columbia University Press (New York City), 1963, 2nd edition, Oxford University Press (New York City), 1980.

A History of Broadcasting in the United States, Oxford University Press, Volume I: *A Tower in Babel,* 1966, Volume II: *The Golden Web,* 1968, Volume III: *The Image Empire,* 1970.

Documentary: A History of the Non-Fiction Film, Oxford University Press, 1974, revised editions, 1983, 1993.

Tube of Plenty: The Evolution of American Television, Oxford University Press, 1975, revised edition, 1982, 1990.

The Sponsor: Notes on a Modern Potentate, Oxford University Press, 1978.

The Magician and the Cinema, Oxford University Press, 1981.

(Editor) *International Encyclopedia of Communications,* four volumes, Oxford University Press, 1989.

House with a Past, Vermont Historical Society (Montpelier, VT), 1992.

Documentary: A History of the Non-Fiction Film, Oxford University Press, 1993.

(Author of foreword) Albert Abramson, *Zworykin, Pioneer of Television,* University of Illinois Press (Urbana), 1995.

Media Marathon: A Twentieth-Century Memoir, Duke University Press (Durham), 1996.

FILMS

(Producer) *Freedom to Read,* Columbia University Bicentennial film, 1954.

(And producer, in consultation with Herbert Wechsler) *Decision: The Constitution in Action,* (series of seven films), Center for Mass Communication and National Educational Television, 1957-59.

Memento, Center for Mass Communication, 1968.

(Producer) *Hiroshima-Nagasaki, August 1945,* Center for Mass Communication, 1970.

(And director) *Fable-Safe,* Center for Mass Communication, 1971.

TELEVISION; ADAPTOR; ALL FOR U.S. STEEL HOUR

Patterson Greene, *Papa Is All.*

Roger Eddy, *The Women of Hadley.*

Henrik Ibsen, *Hedda Gabler.*

Also, author of *Open Collars* (3 act play, parody of "Kingston University" life), 1928, and a musical with Joshua Logan, *Zuider Zee,* both produced at Princeton University, 1928; author of radio documentary, *The Conspiracy of Silence,* produced by ABC, 1948; and *Handbook of Radio Production,* 1949.

SIDELIGHTS: In his *New York Review of Books* article about Erik Barnouw's *A History of Broadcasting in the United States,* Leonard Ross recounted an anecdote involving Philo T. Farnsworth, the inventor of television. In 1927, Farnsworth and financial backer George Everson "gathered for a demonstration of Farnsworth's television apparatus. For the first time [the inventor] successfully transmitted several graphic designs, including a dollar sign. As Everson recalled later, "It seemed to jump out at us on the screen.' " The overwhelming influence of money on the American broadcasting industry is an important theme of Barnouw's writings, including *A History of Broadcasting in the United States* and *The Sponsor: Notes on a Modern Potentate.*

A History of Broadcasting in the United States, which *New York Times Book Review* critic John Leonard called the work that "everybody who writes about television steals from," covers, in three chronological categories, the high and low points of American radio and television history. Volume one, *A Tower in Babel,* recalls radio from its infancy until 1933; volume two, *The Golden Web,* examines the years 1933-1953, the peak period of radio programming; volume three, *The Image Empire,* takes up the story from 1953, when television was just beginning to hit its stride as the most formidable communication source in the world. The books illustrate events both dramatic (David Sarnoff's 72-hour marathon at the Wanamaker department store telegraph booth in 1912; as Sarnoff reports the sinking of the S.S. *Titanic,* President William Howard Taft orders all other wave lengths off the air) and whimsical (a profile of National Broadcasting Corp.'s "discovery," chimpanzee J. Fred Muggs, who almost single-handedly rescues the fledgling "Today" show in 1953). Governmental controls of the air, technological achievements, and the study of broadcasting as a purely commercial enterprise are explored at length.

In a *New York Times Book Review* article, Eric F. Goldman described Barnouw's "system" of the broadcasting industry as a "subtle one of men with inevitable instincts for money, status, power and a sense of fulfillment controlling powerful instruments which neither they nor most others have really tried to understand. The exploration of this theme permits the volumes to make their most salient contributions. Mr. Barnouw finds truth less on the flat surfaces than in the interstices; his emphasis is on complexity, conflicting interests, colliding drives, shadings, inherent difficulties. He spells out the full ambivalence of the figure who had so much to do with stating the original pattern of all broadcasting, Secretary of Commerce Herbert Hoover. [Barnouw] describes the rise of the corporate structures in a way which makes clear that men were fighting over a good many things apart from who makes money from the airwaves."

Nevertheless, the practice of making money from the airwaves pervades the entire broadcast industry. Thus it is the sponsor who perhaps exudes the greatest influence on the corporate structure; often the advertisers, as much as the government, control the content of the programs being broadcast. Barnouw's book *The Sponsor,* according to *Nation* critic John S. Rosenberg, is "the most incisive and well-written study to date of the economic structure and ideological impact of modern broadcasting." The author uses examples of advertiser influence throughout the book. One such story is of a 1950s dramatic presentation of the Nuremberg trials; the show's sponsor, a natural gas association, demanded that all references to "gas" (i.e. gas chambers) be deleted from the script.

"Barnouw is particularly effective in explaining what this [kind of] total sponsor control means," stated *Washington Post Book World* reviewer Joel Swerdlow. Even today, "'newsmen' are selected via devices like the 'galvanic skin response tests' to make sure the audience will like them. 'Public service announcements' must be approved by the Advertising Council, the very people they're supposed to counterbalance." Another manifestation of sponsor control, according to Swerdlow's review, "is a revisionism that would make even Stalinist historians blush. The stories are legend. One program portrayed the Civil War and never mentioned blacks or slavery. Lobbying by florists is notorious for keeping bereaved characters everywhere from saying, 'Send a charitable contribution instead of flowers.'"

Rosenberg summed up: "Although most viewers tend to view commercials as necessary interruptions in their favorite programs, Barnouw makes it abundantly clear [in *The Sponsor*] that the very purpose of the programs—a purpose that governs them from inception to airing—is to bring us to the commercials. Others have argued, as Barnouw does, that "a network commercial is likely to promote not only a product but a way of life, a view of the world, a philosophy. . . .' What is unique about *The Sponsor* is the skill, subtlety and wisdom with which [the author's] observations on the structure of the media are woven together in such a slim and immensely readable volume."

Barnouw's wealth of experience in various media and entertainment venues and roles is chronicled in his 1996 publication, *Media Marathon: A Twentieth-Century Memoir.* "Mr. Barnouw's soft-spoke, enjoyable memoir, shaped as a series of character sketches of interesting and distinguished people he has encountered, reveals a 'white-collar vagabond' career that has lurched from theater to radio to teaching to television and film. . . . [it is] the overarching story of the media century," wrote *New York Times Book Review* contributor Nathan Ward. Because he has worked in a variety of functions, remarked Michael Curtin in *The Journal of American History,* "Barnouw's vantage point for assessing the media of this century is unique." Curtin called the book "a captivating read about a fascinating life," although he stated that it needed "a more expansive analysis of [certain] media moments." Curtin summarized: "the critical analysis offered by *Media Marathon* is somewhat sparing by comparison to the rich narrative texture of Barnouw's reminiscences." In *Journalism & Mass Communication Quarterly,* Diane L. Borden positively reviewed this behind-the-scenes look at twentieth century mass media. However, she criticized Barnouw for almost entirely omitting his personal life and discussion of some outside influences on the media. More specifically, Borden faulted *Me-*

dia Marathon for failing to include important "historical events or social and cultural movements of the mid-twentieth century—civil rights, women's liberation, antiwar protests, environmental awareness . . . either in their own right or as they intersected with the burgeoning institution of the mass media." A *Kirkus Reviews* critic noted that *Media Marathon* displays Barnouw's "deep knowledge and intimate, jargon-free style."

BIOGRAPHICAL/CRITICAL SOURCES:

BOOKS

Barnouw, Erik, *The Sponsor: Notes on a Modern Potentate,* Oxford University Press, 1978.

PERIODICALS

Commonweal, December 17, 1971.
Journal of American History, December, 1996, pp. 1082-83.
Journalism & Mass Communication Quarterly, summer, 1996, pp. 493-94.
Kirkus Reviews, December 1, 1995, p. 1676.
Nation, October 21, 1978.
New York Review of Books, April 8, 1971; March 9, 1972; April 6, 1978.
New York Times, June 6, 1981.
New York Times Book Review, November 21, 1971; November 30, 1978; April 28, 1996, p. 35.
Spectator, February 14, 1976.
Washington Post Book World, June 18, 1978.*

* * *

BARRE, Richard 1943-

PERSONAL: Born March 10, 1943, in Los Angeles, CA; son of Ruth (Groves) Barre; married Susan E. Dwan (a word processor and editor), August 19, 1967. *Education:* California State University, Sacramento, B.A., 1966.

ADDRESSES: Home—6156 Coloma Dr., Santa Barbara, CA 93117. *Agent*—Philip Spitzer, 50 Talmage Farm Ln., East Hampton, NY 11937.

CAREER: Barre Advertising, Santa Barbara, CA, owner, 1975-90. *Military service:* U.S. Coast Guard, 1967-70; became lieutenant.

AWARDS, HONORS: Shamus Award, 1995, for *The Innocents.*

WRITINGS:

MYSTERY NOVELS

The Innocents, Walker and Co. (New York City), 1995.
Bearing Secrets, Walker and Co., 1996.
The Ghosts of Morning, Berkley (New York City), 1998.

SIDELIGHTS: Richard Barre's mystery novels feature a hard-drinking, motorcycle-riding, surfer named Wil Hardesty. Angst-ridden from a past that includes the death of his child and a tour of duty in Vietnam, Hardesty has nearly ruined his business and his marriage. The dark tone of the Hardesty books, which are set in California, reminded a *Rapport* reviewer of Raymond Chandler's detective fiction. In his first appearance, the detective investigates the death of several children whose long-dead bodies are unearthed after a flash flood in the desert. "Barre writes with great passion, giving his characters a depth of feeling that draws us in at once," declared the reviewer. "He is also a skilled storyteller." *Los Angeles Times Book Review* critic Charles Champlin criticized the book for "improbabilities" in the plot, but credited the author with generating "a narrative drive that, as sometimes happens, is stronger than the originating premise."

In *Bearing Secrets,* Hardesty is hired to look into the alleged suicide of a 1960s radical. Dick Lochte, a contributor to *Los Angeles Times Book Review,* praised Barre's creation of "a sensitive, introspective private eye" and called the author a man of "obvious skill and sensitivity." *Library Journal*'s reviewer also approved of *Bearing Secrets,* stating: "Good narrative, inventive plot, striking characters, and psychological depth make this a keeper."

In his third novel, *The Ghosts of Morning,* Barre has Hardesty confront more demons from his past when he is hired to search for his childhood friend Danny, who was apparently killed in Vietnam years before. The soldier's dying mother has begun receiving notes offering to tell her where the man is—for a price. The case also summons up an old love affair Hardesty experienced with Danny's younger sister. A *Publishers Weekly* reviewer faulted the story for depending too much on overworked plot elements, but noted that "Barre's language strikes eloquent chords of pain and regret, and he writes as well about surfing as anyone since Kem Nunn. . . . It adds up to a steamy, evocative stew, although many of the items in the pot have seen better days."

BIOGRAPHICAL/CRITICAL SOURCES:

PERIODICALS

Armchair Detective, fall, 1995, p. 413.
Booklist, May 1, 1995, p. 1554; June 1, 1996, p. 1678; April 15, 1998.
Library Journal, May 1, 1995, p. 134; May 1, 1996, p. 137.
Los Angeles Times Book Review, May 14, 1995, p. 11; June 23, 1996, p. 10.
Publishers Weekly, April 3, 1995, p. 49; April 15, 1996, p. 53; March 30, 1998, p. 72.
Rapport, January, 1995, p. 33.
Wilson Library Bulletin, April, 1995, p. 96.

* * *

BARRINGTON, John
See BROWNJOHN, Alan

* * *

BARYSHNIKOV, Mikhail (Nikolayevich) 1948-

PERSONAL: Surname sometimes transliterated as Barishnikov or Barichnikov; born January 27 (some sources say January 28), 1948, in Riga, Latvia, U.S.S.R.; immigrated to Canada, 1974; immigrated to United States, 1974; naturalized U.S. citizen, 1986; son of Nikolai and Alexandra (Kisselov) Baryshnikov; companion of Jessica Lange (an actress), mid-1970s-early 1980s; companion of Lisa Rinehart (a dancer), early 1980s—; children: (with Lange) one daughter; (with Rinehart) three children. *Education:* Trained in ballet at School of Theatre Opera Ballet, Riga, and Agrippina Vaganova Choreographic Institute, graduating in 1967. *Avocational interests:* Fishing.

CAREER: Dancer and choreographer. Kirov Ballet, Leningrad, U.S.S.R., soloist, 1969-74; American Ballet Theatre, New York City, principal dancer, 1974-78; New York City Ballet, principal dancer, 1978-79; American Ballet Theatre, principal dancer, 1979-90, director designee, 1979-80, artistic director, 1980-89; White Oak Dance Project, director and dancer, 1990—. Guest artist with numerous groups, including National Ballet of Canada, Royal Ballet, Hamburg Ballet, Ballet Victoria, Stuttgart Ballet, Vienna Opera Ballet, Alvin Ailey Company, Eliot Feld Ballet, Martha Graham Dance Company, and Mark Morris Dance Company. Performer in numerous television programs or specials, including *The Nutcracker, In Performance at Wolf Trap, Live from Lincoln Center, Baryshnikov at the White House, Baryshnikov on Broadway, Baryshnikov in Hollywood,* and *Baryshnikov by Tharp.* Actor in motion pictures, including *The Turning Point, White Nights,* and *Dancers.* Choreographer of productions of many full-length ballets, including *The Nutcracker,* 1976, *Don Quixote (Kitri's Wedding),* 1978, *Cinderella,* 1984, and *Swan Lake,* 1989. Has self-titled fragrance, *Misha,* and line of dance and exercise clothing. Part owner of Russian Samovar restaurant, New York City.

AWARDS, HONORS: Gold Medal from Varna Dance Competition, 1966; Gold Medal from First International Ballet Competition, 1969, and Nijinsky prize from Paris Academy of Dance, 1969, both for performance in *Vestris;* Academy Award nomination for best supporting actor from Academy of Motion Picture Arts and Sciences, 1977, for *The Turning Point;* award from *Dance Magazine,* 1978; D.F.A. from Yale University, 1979.

WRITINGS:

(With Charles Engell France) *Baryshnikov at Work: Mikhail Baryshnikov Discusses His Roles,* photographs by Martha Swope, Knopf (New York City), 1976.
Baryshnikov in Color, edited by Charles Engell France, photographs by Martha Swope and others, Abrams (New York City), 1980.
(Written by Peter Anastos; based on an idea by Baryshnikov) *The Swan Prince,* photographs by Arthur Elgort, Bantam (New York City), 1987.

SIDELIGHTS: Mikhail Baryshnikov is widely hailed as one of ballet's greatest performers. Born in 1948 in the Soviet Union, he showed both athletic and musical prowess in childhood. But at the encouragement of his mother, an avid ballet fan, he commenced dance studies upon reaching adolescence. After three years at a dance academy in his hometown of Riga, Baryshnikov was selected, along with other promising students, to travel to Leningrad. Once there, he applied to the Agrippina Vaganova Choreographic Institute, the school of the prestigious Kirov Ballet, and he began studying there in 1963.

Baryshnikov's mentor at the school was Alexander Pushkin, a distinguished teacher who had already trained the great dancer Rudolph Nureyev. Baryshnikov studied with Pushkin for three years before making his professional debut with the Kirov Ballet in 1966. Bypassing the usual apprenticeship in the corps, he appeared first as a soloist in *Giselle.* Word soon spread throughout Leningrad of the Kirov's exciting new performer, and only two years later Baryshnikov began dancing leading roles. His first lead was in *Gorianka,* created especially for him by choreographer Oleg Vinograd. An immense triumph, *Gorianka* was followed by Baryshnikov with *Vestris,* which choreographer Leonid Jacobson devised for him. *Vestris* proved an even greater success, earning Baryshnikov both the revered Nijinsky Prize and the First International Ballet Competition's Gold Medal.

By the late 1960s Baryshnikov was dancing principal roles in the great ballet classics, including *Sleeping Beauty, Don Quixote,* and *Giselle.* His success in these ballets established him among the Kirov's most popular, and thus most powerful, dancers. "I had the theatre in my pocket," he recalled in a 1987 *Rolling Stone* interview. "I was one of the few leading dancers, and I was pretty much in command."

With the acclaim and authority came considerable rewards, including relatively spacious living quarters and greater access to goods than that of most Soviet citizens. But despite his seemingly enviable position, Baryshnikov gradually became dissatisfied with what he perceived as the alienating nature of Soviet life. "I didn't like the way people treated each other," he told *Rolling Stone.* "You had to pretend something you didn't feel."

In 1974, while touring Canada with the Kirov, Baryshnikov decided to escape from Soviet authority. After an evening performance, he exited into a mob of adoring fans at the rear of the theatre. Suddenly he broke from the throng and sprinted toward a car waiting two blocks away. The fans, thinking that he merely sought to elude them, gave chase. Baryshnikov evaded them, however, jumped into the car, and sped away to a new life. Soon after his dramatic escape, the Canadian government granted Baryshnikov political immunity and allowed him to work there for one year. Only a few weeks after his defection, he made his first non-Soviet dance appearance by performing in a televised production of *La Sylphide.* Through fellow expatriate and former lover Natalia Makarova, then a leading ballerina with the American Ballet Theatre, Baryshnikov was already engineering a career in the United States. Within one month of his appearance on Canadian television, he was dancing with Makarova in New York City, where his stirring performances during a two-week stint prompted public clamoring for a more extended engagement.

North American critics found in Baryshnikov an unequaled combination of acting and athletic talents. His expressions, unlike those of many great dancers, were hailed as utterly convincing and stirring, while his technical capabilities—including an extraordinary leaping capacity—were acclaimed as unmatched. *New York Post* reviewer Frances Herridge, for instance, called his acting "superb" and his technique "flawless." "His body," Herridge declared, "exudes expression."

Before the summer of 1974 came to its hectic close for Baryshnikov, he returned to Canada and made a particularly memorable appearance in Toronto, where he gave his substantial fee to the Canadian National Ballet School out of gratitude. Another important Canadian engagement came in Winnipeg, where in early autumn Baryshnikov first partnered celebrated ballerina Gelsey Kirkland, who reportedly left the New York City Ballet for the opportunity to work with him. Soon Baryshnikov and Kirkland were romantically, as well as professionally, linked. Together they joined the American Ballet Theatre in late October, and almost immediately they began astonishing audiences with performances in such classics as *Don Quixote* and *Coppelia.* But their best work together, according to some critics, may be in Baryshnikov's interpretation of *The Nutcracker,* which has been televised frequently at Christmastime.

By the late 1970s Baryshnikov had reached another pinnacle in his profession, for he had become the major performer in a company composed exclusively—at its highest level—of internationally renowned dancers. But he proved restless with mere success, and in 1978 he left the company to dance in choreographer George Balanchine's relatively group-oriented New York City Ballet. There Baryshnikov was content to recede somewhat from the limelight and subordinate himself to Balanchine's expertise. "I had a very good time in that company," Baryshnikov later told *Rolling Stone.* "It was a great experience just to be next to Balanchine, just to see the way he ran a company, treated people."

In 1979, despite a satisfactory, if uncharacteristically low-key, role within the New York City Ballet, Baryshnikov returned to the American Ballet Theatre, where he resumed performing in the company's largely classic repertoire. The following year he was offered the company's artistic directorship, which he accepted. During the next ten years Baryshnikov served the dual roles of principal and artistic director, though he accepted no salary in the latter position.

The ten years of Baryshnikov's leadership at the American Ballet Theatre were marked by both great successes and substantial failures. Highlights of the company under Baryshnikov would almost certainly include productions of *Swan Lake,* in which Baryshnikov partnered Cynthia Harvey, and *Giselle,* in which he danced with Alessandra Ferri. In addition, the company distinguished itself by both reviving works of its own choreographer, Antony Tudor, and commissioning new pieces by contemporary masters such as Twyla Tharp. Less successful were revivals—or reinterpretations—of classic works, most notably *Cinderella,* the production of which was criticized as overly expensive and the performance confusing.

Critics are divided on the merits of what was perhaps Baryshnikov's most ambitious enterprise, the diminishing of the company's star system in favor of greater opportunity for the group's younger dancers. Some reviewers hailed this Balanchine-like approach as a necessity to the company's longevity, but others decried the consequent scarcity of performances by the company's biggest box-office draws, including Baryshnikov. To *Rolling Stone* Baryshnikov conceded the difficulties involved in his dual responsibilities, observing that "you have to deal with dignity, human weakness, ugliness, beauty, sincerity, mediocrity, as well as simply extraordinary human beings." He added, "It makes you grow up very fast."

Despite his considerable duties with the American Ballet Theatre in the 1980s, Baryshnikov also worked in many outside projects. He appeared in motion pictures, earning an Academy Award nomination for best supporting actor for his first film, *The Turning Point,* and he appeared in numerous televised dance programs. In addition, he danced as a guest artist with several companies in North America and Europe, and he even toured at various times with his own groups.

In 1990, after leaving the American Ballet Theatre, Baryshnikov co-founded the White Oak Dance Company with choreographer Mark Morris. Named after the home of Howard Gilman, a wealthy arts patron and longtime friend of Baryshnikov, the modern-dance troupe broke many of the dance world's conventions. The company consists of an ever changing caste of dancer, with Baryshnikov as the only constant, and often features older dancers in their 30s or, more commonly, 40s. White Oak lists no artistic directory, is run democratically, and seems to exist as a forum to allow Baryshnikov to work with a variety of choreographers and to tackle new projects. The company does not accept corporate or government grants, as Baryshnikov has contended that doing so would force the group to compromise its artistic integrity. It is supported instead with Baryshnikov's own money—including his earnings from his *Misha* perfume and his line of dancewear—and by ticket sales. "White Oak specializes in two sorts of dances—solos for Baryshnikov and group works—with the odd historical rarity for high-profile seasons," observed Lynn Garafola in *Dance* magazine. The troupe has presented works by such prominent modern-dance choreographers as Tharp, Merce Cunningham, and Martha Graham, but its efforts have met with mixed reviews. Garafola, for instance, critiquing a 1997 performance, denounced White Oak's "haphazardly assembled repertory," finding few of the works good enough for the company's talented dancers. "White Oak remains a vanity enterprise in search of artistic direction."

Baryshnikov continues to perform, eager to attempt new pieces and to continue to develop his talents, most notably by exploring minimalism nd improvisation. Early in 1998, at the age of fifty, he presented his first all-solo dance program in New York City and California. The program consisted of four modern-dance pieces; in one, "HeartBeat: mb," he danced to the sound of his heartbeat, amplified by a device created by sound designer Christopher Janney. *Los Angeles Times* dance critic Lewis Segal praised Baryshnikov's performance and described him as "sustaining at 50 the same miraculous fusion of speed, precision and unearthly lightness that made him the icon of virtuosity in his prime." Writing for *Newsweek,* Laura Shapiro argued that Baryshnikov's current efforts require more depth than his work of twenty years ago. Baryshnikov remarked in Cigar Aficionado that he is in good physical condition but admits that one day he will have to quit dancing. In a 1998 interview with *Los Angeles Times* writer Eleanor Randolph, Baryshnikov summarized his plans for the future: "I'm having a very good time just continuing working with White Oak. . . . I'm thinking about commissioning a few more [pieces] for the spring season. It's always fun to try to work with somebody for the first time."

BIOGRAPHICAL/CRITICAL SOURCES:

BOOKS

Alovert, Nina, *Baryshnikov in Russia,* translated by Irene Huntoon, Holt (New York City), 1984.

Aria, Barbara, *Misha: The Mikhail Baryshnikov Story,* St. Martin's (New York City), 1989.

Baryshnikov, Mikhail, with Charles Engell France, *Baryshnikov at Work: Mikhail Baryshnikov Discusses His Roles,* photographs by Martha Swope, Knopf (New York City), 1976.

Baryshnikov, Mikhail, *Baryshnikov in Color,* edited by France, photographs by Martha swope and others, Abrams (New York City), 1980.

Baryshnikov, Mikhail, with Peter Anastos, *The Swan Prince: A Fairy Tale,* photographs by Arthur Elgort, Bantam (New York City), 1987.

Fraser, John, *Private View: Inside Baryshnikov's American Ballet Theatre,* Bantam (New York City), 1988.

Glassman, Bruce, *Mikhail Baryshnikov,* Silver Burdett (Englewood Cliffs, NJ), 1990.

Goodman, Saul, *Baryshnikov: A Most Spectacular Dancer,* Harvey House (New York City), 1979.

Klein, Norma, *Baryshnikov's Nutcracker,* photographs by Ken Regan, Christopher Little, and Martha Swope, Putnam (New York City), 1983.

LeMond, Alan, *Bravo, Baryshnikov!,* photographs by Lois Greenfield and others, Grosset (New York City), 1978.

Paeres, Louis, *Mikhail Baryshnikov,* photographs with text by Patricia Barnes, Dance Horizons (Brooklyn, NY), 1975.

Pollock, Sean R., ed. *Newsmakers: The People Behind Today's Headlines,* Issue 3, Gale (Detroit), 1997.

Smakov, Gennady, *Baryshnikov: From Russia to the West,* Farrar, Straus (New York City), 1981.

Smakov, *The Great Russian Dancers,* Knopf, 1985.

Swope, Martha, *Baryshnikov on Broadway,* foreword by Walter Terry, Harmony Books (New York City), 1980.

Townsend, Alecia Carol, *Mikhail Baryshnikov,* Rourke (Vero Beach, Fla.), 1993.

Victor, Thomas, *The Making of a Dance: Mikhail Baryshnikov and Carla Fracci in Medea,* introduction by Clive Barnes, Holt, 1976.

PERIODICALS

Chicago Tribune, June 22, 1989.

Cigar Aficionado, November-December, 1997.

Dance, April, 1978; July, 1997, p. 70.

Hudson Review, autumn, 1981.

Los Angeles Times, June 27, 1989; September 29, 1989; February 1, 1998, "Calendar" section, pp. 3, 58-59; February 9, 1998, section F, pp. 1, 8.

Newsweek, January 19, 1998, p. 50.

New Yorker, January 20, 1975.

New York Post, December 26, 1974.

New York Times, June 20, 1976; June 22, 1989; September 29, 1989; September 9, 1990.

New York Times Magazine, April 11, 1982.

People, April 26, 1982.

Rolling Stone, October 8, 1987.

Saturday Review, December, 1980.

Time, August 12, 1974; January 3, 1977; July 8, 1985; January 12, 1998, p. 28.

Vogue, December, 1983.

Washington Post, July 11, 1989; September 29, 1989.*

* * *

BEAN, Gregory (K.) 1952-

PERSONAL: Born April 13, 1952, in Rock Springs, WY; son of Keith and Phyllis (maiden name, Fordyce; present surname, Harris) Bean; married Pamela Sue Bower (divorced, 1974); married second wife, Linda (a reporter), June 18, 1982; children: Coleman, Padraic. *Education:* University of Wyoming, B.A. (with honors), 1975, M.A., 1977. *Politics:* Independent. *Religion:* Christian. *Avocational interests:* Fly fishing, camping, reading.

ADDRESSES: Agent—Helen Rees, 308 Commonwealth Ave., Boston, MA 02115.

CAREER: Wyoming News, Cody, WY, began as reporter, became associate editor, 1978-80; Howard Publications, Casper, WY, began as police reporter for *Casper Star Tribune,* became assistant city editor, 1980- 83, and editor of *Wyoming Horizons,* 1983-85; *Freeport Journal Standard,* Freeport, IL, editor, 1985-86; Community Newspapers Co., Boston, MA, editor of *North Shore Sunday,* Danvers, MA, 1986-91, *Region,* Ipswich, MA, 1990-91, *Merrimack Valley Sunday,* 1991-92, and *Seacoast Sunday,* 1991-92, editor for the parent company, 1992; Greater Media

Newspapers, East Brunswick, NJ, executive editor, 1993—. University of Wyoming, instructor, 1979-85.

MEMBER: New Jersey Press Association (member of board of directors).

AWARDS, HONORS: First place award, Northern Illinois Newspaper Association, 1985, for best local editorial; first place award for column writing, and award for the best newspaper in Illinois, Associated Press, 1986; first place award, Illinois Press Association, 1986, for best editorial; Special Award, Massachusetts Alliance for the Mentally Ill, 1988, and Audubon A Award, 1990, both for *North Shore Sunday;* first place award, New England Press Association, 1991, for column writing.

WRITINGS:

MYSTERY NOVELS

No Comfort in Victory, St. Martin's (New York City), 1995.
Long Shadows in Victory, St. Martin's, 1996.
A Death in Victory, St. Martin's, 1997.
Grave Victory, St. Martin's, 1998.

SIDELIGHTS: Gregory Bean is an award-winning journalist as well as the creator of a series of detective novels featuring Harry Starbranch—a burnt-out homicide detective who takes a job as a small-town police chief in Wyoming. Naturally, Starbranch is unable to escape becoming involved in murders, even when he leaves the big city police force in Denver for what he hopes will be a quiet life in rural town of Victory.

In Bean's first book, *No Comfort in Victory,* a sixteen-year-old girl is raped and murdered, and the man who apparently attacked her is found dead alongside her with his head blown away by a long-distance rifle. Rustlers seem to be involved, giving a traditional western twist to the tale. "This is a mature, polished, and powerful first novel that bodes very well for the future of both Starbranch and his creator," Wes Lukowsky notes in a *Booklist* review.

In the next entry in the series, *Long Shadows in Victory,* Starbranch must cope with the discovery of a long-dead body in a mine-shaft and the subsequent torture and murder of the man who found the corpse. Vandalism against Mexican and Jewish residents, and the arrival of the FBI, lead Starbranch to suspect that a militant, antigovernment, racist group is behind the crime wave in his town. The story is told in the voice of the protagonist, and a *Publishers Weekly* reviewer finds that his "chatty narration sometimes slows the action, but it nicely evokes a close-knit Western town. Bean . . . weaves in history of authentic militant groups, adding timely realism."

The series continues with *A Death in Victory,* in which the town's mayor, Curly Ahern—who is also Starbranch's best friend—is charged with murder, after Liam O'Bannion is found shot to death with the mayor's gun. O'Bannion was the lover of Curly's daughter, and had been beaten and threatened by the mayor after he had abused her; but Starbranch digs deep to uncover the truth, which involves illegal traffic in bear paws and bladders. "The novel offers interesting and sympathetic characters, nail-biting suspense, eloquent outrage about wildlife poaching, and a mystery plot that is unsettling and surprising," applaudes John Rowen in *Booklist.* "Starbranch is a modern knight errant, using wit and strength to cut pompous, bullying, and arrogant people down to size." A *Publishers Weekly* reviewer concurs that Bean has created a "solid series," and adds: "Harry Starbranch rings true as the fiercely independent Westerner who stands by his friends and does the right thing, no matter the cost to himself."

BIOGRAPHICAL/CRITICAL SOURCES:

PERIODICALS

Booklist, August, 1995, p. 1931; May 15, 1997, p. 1566; April 15, 1998, p. 1375.
Publishers Weekly, July 10, 1995, p. 48; July 8, 1996, p. 77; April 28, 1997, p. 53; March 16, 1998, p. 57.

* * *

BEATON, George
See BRENAN, (Edward Fitz)Gerald

* * *

BELL, Arthur 1939-1984

PERSONAL: Born November 14, 1939, in Brooklyn, NY; died of complications from diabetes, June 2, 1984, in New York, NY; son of Samuel (a manufacturer of children's clothing) and Claire (a designer; maiden name, Bodan) Bell. *Education:* Attended commercial high school in Montreal, Ontario, Canada. *Politics:* Democrat. *Religion:* Jewish.

CAREER: Viking Press, Inc., New York City, publicity director for children's books, 1960-68; Random House, Inc., New York City, publicity director for children's books, 1968-70; *Village Voice,* New York City, feature writer and author of column "Bell Tells," 1970-84.

AWARDS, HONORS: Runner-up award in nonfiction from *Playboy* for adaptation of *Kings Don't Mean a Thing* and best nonfiction award from *Where It's At* for *King Don't Mean a Thing,* both 1978.

WRITINGS:

Dancing the Gay Lib Blues: A Year in the Gay Liberation Movement, Simon & Schuster (New York City), 1971.

Kings Don't Mean a Thing: The John Knight Murder Case, Morrow (New York City), 1978.

Contributor to *Gay Source: A Catalog for Men,* Coward (New York City), 1977. Contributor to magazines and newspapers, including *Esquire, Playboy, Cosmopolitan,* and *New York Times.*

SIDELIGHTS: Arthur Bell was one of the twelve founding members of the Gay Activists' Alliance, a homosexual rights group based in New York City. He joined the staff of the *Village Voice* in 1976 and began writing a column, "Bell Tells," about night life in New York City and show business. Bell produced two books, *Dancing the Gay Lib Blues: A Year in the Homosexual Liberation Movement* and *Kings Don't Mean a Thing.*

Dancing the Gay Lib Blues was described by Joseph M. Eagan in *Gay and Lesbian Literature* as "one of the first books about the gay liberation movement published by a mainstream American publisher." Recounting Bell's first year as a gay activist, the book contains valuable insights into the politics of the movement in the early 1970s. Bell was a founder of the Gay Activists' Alliance, a group with "an open membership, a militant agenda, and a confrontational style that differentiated it from many earlier homophile groups," as Eagan noted. Bell's role as the organization's publicity contact made him a prominent media figure. In 1970, a New York television station broadcast a three-part feature on Bell's work as a gay activist. Eagan concluded: "*Dancing the Gay Lib Blues* remains one of the most important documents written by a gay male about the post-Stonewall gay liberation movement in America."

Bell once told *CA:* "I've probably had more articles on the gay lifestyle published in non-gay media than anyone else in America. Additionally, I cover crime stories and write a good deal about the entertainment world. I'm published weekly in the *Weekly Voice,* and the subjects and personalities in my column really run the gamut. When time permits, I write features for other magazines."

BIOGRAPHICAL/CRITICAL SOURCES:

BOOKS

Gay and Lesbian Literature, Volume 2, St. James Press (Detroit), 1998.

Teal, Donn, *The Gay Militants,* Stein & Day (New York City), 1971.

PERIODICALS

America, January 8, 1972.

Christopher Street, February, 1979.

Library Journal, June 1, 1972; September 15, 1978.

New Republic, January 6, 1979.

New York Times Book Review, February 20, 1972; December 17, 1978.

OBITUARIES:

PERIODICALS

New York Times, June 5, 1984.

Village Voice, June 12, 1984; June 26, 1984.*

* * *

BELL, (Arthur) Clive (Howard) 1881-1964

PERSONAL: Born September 16, 1881, in East Shefford, Bedfordshire, England; died September 18, 1964, in London, England; son of William Heyward Bell (a mining engineer); married Vanessa Stephen; children: Julian. *Education:* Attended Trinity College, Cambridge.

CAREER: Writer, poet, and critic of politics, literature, and art.

AWARDS, HONORS: Chevalier of the Legion of Honor, 1936.

WRITINGS:

Art (criticism and history), Stokes (New York City), 1914, reprinted, Oxford University Press, (New York City), 1987.
Peace at Once (history), National Labour Press (Manchester), 1915.
Ad Familiares, Pelican Press (London), 1917.
Pot-Boilers (criticism), Chatto & Windus (London), 1918.
Poems, Hogarth Press (Richmond, Surrey, England), 1921.
Since Cezanne (criticism), Harcourt (New York City), 1922, reprinted, Books for Libraries Press (Freeport, NY), 1969.
The Legend of Monte della Sibilla; or, Le Paradis de la reine Sibille (poem), Hogarth, 1923.
On British Freedom, Harcourt, 1923.
Landmarks in Nineteenth-Century Painting (criticism), Harcourt, 1927, reprinted, Books for Libraries Press, 1967.
Civilization: An Essay (philosophy; also see below), Harcourt, 1928.
Proust (criticism), Hogarth, 1928, Harcourt, 1929, reprinted, Richard West (Philadelphia), 1977.
An Account of French Painting (criticism), Chatto & Windus, 1931, Harcourt, 1932, reprinted, Richard West, 1979.
Enjoying Pictures: Meditations in the National Gallery and Elsewhere (criticism), Harcourt, 1934.
Warmongers, Peace Pledge Union (London), 1938.
Victor Pasmore, Penguin (Harmondsworth, England), 1945.
Modern French Painting: The Cone Collection, Johns Hopkins Press (Baltimore), 1951.
Old Friends: Personal Recollections (autobiographical; also see below), Chatto & Windus, 1956, Harcourt, 1957.
Civilization and Old Friends, University of Chicago Press, 1973.
Aesthetics [and] *Post-Impressionism: A New Theory of Art,* two volumes, Foundation for Classical Reprints (Albuquerque, NM), 1985.

Contributor of articles to *New Statesman and Nation.* Collections of Clive Bell's papers are housed at Trinity College, Cambridge, England, and in the Tate Gallery Archive.

SIDELIGHTS: Clive Bell was a member of the Bloomsbury Group of writers, which included such luminaries as the novelists E. M. Forster, V. Sackville-West, and Virginia Woolf, biographer Lytton Strachey, economist John Maynard Keynes, and art critic Roger Fry. Married to the elder sister of Virginia Woolf, Bell was associated with the informal group of artists by marriage, but also through his literary style. Like many of the group's writers, Bell endeavored to write intellectually and objectively about strong emotions. His treatment of art in this manner established him as a prominent critic and writer. Bell's work was also a major force in obtaining recognition for modern art. He asserted that form and design were the most important aspects of a work of art. Subject was no longer the focus; instead, the feelings and ideas expressed were emphasized. Bell coined "significant form" as a term of value with which to appraise the purely aesthetic quality of a work of art.

In 1914, Bell recorded his theory about art in his first book, appropriately entitled *Art.* As a reviewer for the *Saturday Review* explained it, "The root of Mr. Bell's argument is that a work of art produces in us aesthetic ecstasy and emotion, and by doing so awakens and stimulates the spiritual side of our nature." Such a view generated a bit of controversy at the time it was published. An *Athenaeum* critic foresaw that "several different kinds of people will be violently irritated by this book. It has a malignant ingenuity which will put most painters, art-critics, art-historians, archaeologists, and connoisseurs beside themselves." As a *New York Times* reviewer commented: "It is in this insensitiveness to art of a kind that does not reveal its significance by means of the formulas he has learned that Mr. Bell shows his lack of the deep insight often called tolerance which marks the highest order of mind." For the *Athenaeum* critic, however, Bell's work was worthy of high praise. This critic maintained that *Art* represented "the first book, since [John] Ruskin began to publish [his five-volume] 'Modern Painters' in 1843, that could even conceivably convince a serious-minded person of good judgment that Art is something more than an agreeable ornamentation and seasoning of life."

Since Cezanne, a 1922 volume of art criticism, offered Bell's views on this late nineteenth-century French painter, those who influenced him, and those he influenced. L. Baury, a contributor to *Freeman,* observed that in this book "the field upon which he enters . . . is a wide one." All the more reason, continued the reviewer, that "the deftness and delicacy of perception with which he picks his way across it are matters for constant delight." H. L. Seaver, of

Atlantic's Bookshelf, had a similar reaction. "Mr. Bell's criticism is delightfully agile jumping, and so attains its end," commented this critic. Reviewers for journals such as *Literary Review* and the *Spectator* conceded Bell's deftness but faulted him for "lacking balance and real seriousness" and "crudities and the complacent dealing out of haloes of immortality" respectively. *Dial* contributor Raymond Mortimer recognized that Bell's views would not win over everyone interested in painting. "You may hate it. You are certain to disagree with some of it. But," noted the reviewer, "you can neither neglect it, nor be bored by it." Burton Rascoe, of the *New York Tribune,* concluded, "Mr. Bell is honest, he is sincere, and he is a servitor of beauty, a champion of good taste, a valiant defender of culture, and he would not let vanity stand in the way of the universal good. In this book he lends his fine emotional sensibility, his alert intelligence and his happy prose style in the service of beauty, taste and culture. He provokes ideas and images, he aides sensitivity, and he entertains."

Bell's *Account of French Painting,* published in 1932, traced the development of that French art over a period of almost nine centuries, culminating in analysis of his contemporaries on the continent. A number of reviewers commended Bell for covering so well such a broad span of art history in the space of 220 pages. E. A. Jewell wrote in the *New York Times,* "Clive Bell's book is almost uninterruptedly amusing. And it is remarkable what a deal of worthwhile information he has been able to sandwich into this adroit, appetizing literary snack." *Spectator* reviewer David Fincham called the book "a brilliant, amusing, and devastatingly learned introduction to the painting of France." He went on to compare Bell's *Account of French Painting* to a novel. "It is so good a book about painting that anyone can read it with as much amusement and enjoyment as a good novel." Fellow art critic and Bloomsbury Group member Roger Fry went even farther. He concluded in a *New Statesman and Nation* piece, "Mr. Bell's style is so lively, his movement so rapid and exhilarating, that it would be less than the truth to say that one devours it like a novel, since it is more lucid and more readable than the vast majority of such books."

Bell followed his *Account of French Painting* with *Enjoying Pictures,* a collection of three essays offering Bell's aesthetic of painting through his analysis of paintings in Britain's National Gallery and in the Vatican. This overview of Bell's judgments on painting was faulted by Anthony Blunt of the *Spectator* for "a certain cheapness of style" and by Robert Morse of the *Nation* for insufficient use of illustrations. Yet, a reviewer for the *Times Literary Supplement* commented, "Mr. Bell can be read by any intelligent person with profit to his appreciation of art, of whatever kind it may be." And Roger Fry—writing in the *New Statesman and Nation*—responding especially to Bell's analysis of Raphael's frescoes in the Vatican, maintains that *Enjoying Pictures* "is perhaps the best piece of critical writing which he has ever done and certainly brings us into closer contact with the real quality of the work than ever before."

In addition to his role as an art critic, Clive Bell was also a keen observer of politics, society, and civilization. Critics praised *On British Freedom* as "a brilliant piece of writing" and "the most spirited, swift, admirably written onslaught" since Shaw's prefaces. *Civilization* was applauded by a *New Statesman* reviewer as "a perfectly clear definition of Civilisation which no one can ignore. It is not only the best and most comprehensible. It is a really brilliant piece of authentic analysis." *International Journal of Ethics* contributor C. D. Burns found the book "alive," adding, "It should be read by all lecturers and students of ethics." T. Craven distinguished Bell from his contemporaries. This reviewer commented in *New York Herald Tribune Books,* "Unlike most critics of art, he has wit, scholarship and engaging effrontery." Continued Craven, "He is neither long-winded nor obscure; he has ideas, and he presents them not only with cleverness but with stimulating assurance." Leonard Woolf, husband to Virginia Woolf and himself a member of the Bloomsbury Group, wrote of *Civilization*'s author, "To write such a fresh and readable book on the subject of civilization is a feat of which he may well be proud and for which we may well be grateful."

Bell was not known for his literary criticism, but as a member of the Bloomsbury Group, he was steeped in the literary sensibility. In 1929, he combined his literary sensibility with his deep interest in French culture in *Proust,* a profile of the author of *Remembrance of Things Past.* Bell's analysis drew close scrutiny as the first book-length treatment of Proust in English. Some reviewers, including Edgar Johnson of the *New York Evening Post* were disappointed. He claimed that "as a contribution either to criticism or art, Mr. Bell's 'Proust' is negligible." R. E. Roberts found fault with Bell for "excusing himself for his admiration for Proust." Even so, the *New Statesman* contributor admitted, "His essay, of course, is exceedingly intelligent; in some passages, in which he is stating and agreeing with what he believes to be Proust's philosophy of life, Mr. Bell attains real eloquence and passion." And, in the opinion of a *Times Literary Supplement* critic, "Bell is to be congratulated upon having written . . . the most intelligent commentary upon Proust since the publication of 'Le Temps Retrouve,'" an essay by Edmund Wilson in the *New Republic.*

Bell's only autobiographical work, *Old Friends,* contains letters and reminiscences about his fellow artists of the Bloomsbury Group. Overall, the book drew praise as a readable account of the relationships, both emotional and intellectual, of this group. "Tolerant, affectionate, humorous, and, for the most part, an able story-teller, those same qualities that made him a good friend, make his book excellent reading. *Old Friends* was also a source of insights for scholars into the lives of some of the most influential thinkers of early twentieth-century Britain. David Daiches of the *New York Herald Tribune Book Review* commented that though the book "occasionally irritates by its tone of condescending elegance and its gentlemanly scorn for a younger generation of writers and critics who lack the social advantages possessed by Bloomsbury, it is full of interest for its first-hand account of people, places, and things in a fascinating period of English . . . culture. It will remain an important source in the rapidly growing literature of Bloomsbury."

BIOGRAPHICAL/CRITICAL SOURCES:

BOOKS

Bywater, William G., *Clive Bell's Eye,* Wayne State University Press (Detroit), 1975.

Dictionary of Literary Biography Documentary Series, Volume 10: *The Bloomsbury Group,* Gale (Detroit), 1992.

Laing, Donald A., *Clive Bell: An Annotated Bibliography of the Published Writings,* Garland (New York City), 1983.

PERIODICALS

ARTnews, September, 1989, p. 87.

Athenaeum, February 21, 1914, p. 280.

Atlantic, March, 1957, p. 76.

Atlantic's Bookshelf, November, 1922.

Bookman, September, 1922; October, 1928, p. 226.

Boston Transcript, November 17, 1923; October 20, 1928; March 16, 1929.

Christian Science Monitor, February 14, 1957, p. 5.

Dial, August 19, 1922, p. 215.

Freeman, October 4, 1922, p. 91.

Independent, December 8, 1923.

International Journal of Ethics, October, 1928, p. 118.

Literary Review, August 12, 1922, p. 874.

Nation, February 11, 1915, p. 179; September 6, 1922, p. 234; January 4, 1928; December 12, 1928, p. 662; January 2, 1935, p. 25; March 9, 1957, p. 218.

Nation and Athenaeum, June 9, 1928, p. 331; December 8, 1928, p. 362.

New Republic, August 9, 1922, p. 311; March 21, 1928; September 26, 1928, p. 156; June 1, 1932, p. 80.

New Statesman, June 23, 1923; June 9, 1928, p. 287; November 24, 1928, p. 224.

New Statesman and Nation, November 14, 1931, p. 614; April 21, 1934, p. 606.

New York Evening Post, February 16, 1929.

New York Herald Tribune, September 30, 1928; September 16, 1934.

New York Herald Tribune Book Review, February 10, 1957, p. 3.

New York Times, November 15, 1914, p. 500; October 14, 1923; October 14, 1928, p. 2; March 24, 1929, p. 2; March 20, 1932, p. 10; February 10, 1957, p. 6.

New York Tribune, June 25, 1922, p. 5.

Outlook, October 24, 1928, p. 1034; February 13, 1929, p. 272.

Saturday Review, March 21, 1914, p. 4; February 16, 1957, p. 20.

Saturday Review of Literature, November 24, 1928, p. 397; April 2, 1932, p. 639; September 22, 1934, p. 133.

Spectator, July 18, 1914, p. 97; May 6, 1922, p. 563; August 18, 1923; December 19, 1931, p. 856; March 30, 1934, p. 511.

Times Literary Supplement, March 16, 1922, p. 167; June 21, 1928, p. 465; January 24, 1929, p. 58; December 10, 1931, p. 997; January 7, 1932, p. 1; April 19, 1934; December 7, 1956, p. 721.

World Tomorrow, December, 1928, p. 521.

OBITUARIES:

PERIODICALS

Illustrated London News, September 26, 1964.

New York Times, September 20,1964.

Spectator, September 25, 1964.
Time, October 2, 1964.*

* * *

BENARY, Margot
See BENARY-ISBERT, Margot

* * *

BENARY-ISBERT, Margot 1889-1979
(Margot Benary)

PERSONAL: Born December 2, 1889, in Saarbrucken, Germany; died May 27, 1979, in Santa Barbara, CA; became U.S. citizen in 1957; daughter of Adolf and Toni (maiden name, Ippel) Isbert; married Wilhelm Benary (a psychologist and seed firm executive), 1917 (deceased); children: Eva Toni (Mrs. Peter Hearst). *Education:* Attended College St. Carolus St. Carolus and University of Frankfurt.

CAREER: Museum of Ethnology and Anthropology, Frankfurt, Germany, secretary, 1910-17; bred Great Danes on husband's family estate in Thuringia, Germany; fled to West Germany when Russians took over estate area at the end of World War II; writer in United States, 1952-79.

MEMBER: Schutzverband Deutscher Schriftsteller, International PEN.

AWARDS, HONORS: First prize, *New York Herald Tribune* Spring Book Festival, 1953, for *The Ark;* Jane Addams Children's Book Award of Women's International League for Peace and Freedom, 1957, for *Blue Mystery.*

WRITINGS:

CHILDREN'S NOVELS

Die Arche Noah, F. Ehrenwirth, 1948, translation by Clara Winston and Richard Winston published as *The Ark,* Harcourt (San Diego), 1953.

Die Ebereschenhof (sequel to *Die Arche Noah*), F. Ehrenwirth, 1949, translation by C. Winston and R. Winston published as *Rowan Farm,* Harcourt, 1954.

Heiligenwald, D. Gundert, 1953, translation by Joyce Emerson and Margot Benary-Isbert published as *A Time to Love,* Harcourt, 1962.

Schloss an der Grenze, D. Gundert, 1956, translation by C. Winston and R. Winston published as *Castle on the Border,* Harcourt, 1956.

OTHER

Annegret und Cara, D. Gundert, 1951, translation by C. Winston and R. Winston published as *Blue Mystery,* Harcourt, 1967.

Madchen fuer Alles: Sieben Jahre Sekretarian im Volkerkindemuseum, E. Heimeran, 1953, reprinted, J. Knecht, 1969.

The Shooting Star, translation by C. Winston and R. Winston, Harcourt, 1954.

The Wicked Enchantment, translation by C. Winston and R. Winston, Harcourt, 1955.

Die Grossmutter und ihr erster Enkel, E. Heimeran, 1957.

The Long Way Home, translation by C. Winston and R. Winston, Harcourt, 1959.

Dangerous Spring, translation by James Kirkup, Harcourt, 1961.

Under a Changing Moon, translation by Rosaleen Ockenden and M. Benary-Isbert, Harcourt, 1964.

Das Abenteuer des Alterns, Knecht, 1965, translation by M. Benary-Isbert published as *These Vintage Years,* Abingdon, 1968.

Gefahrlichen Fruhling, D. Gendert, 1966.

Anemone und der bose Kauz, D. Gundert, 1968.

Ein heitrer Abend kront den reichen Tag, J. Knecht, 1968.

Ich reise mit meinen Enkeln, J. Knecht, 1971.

Das ewige Siegel: Eine Legende um den Dichter Li Tai Pe, J. Knecht, 1974.

Also translator of *The Vision of Francois* and *Macaroon,* both by Julia Cunningham.

SIDELIGHTS: Margot Benary-Isbert's fiction often focuses on postwar Germany, depicting the hardships of German refugees. The author is considered to have drawn upon her own war experiences for these works; she and her family fled to West Germany to avoid the Russian occupation troops following World War II. Some of Benary-Isbert's novels for young adults offer a portrait of nineteenth-century Germany, before it became a unified country, and the author has been praised for providing richly detailed, historical narratives of a high quality for discerning young adults. Evan Commager, a reviewer for *Book Week,* wrote that *Under a Changing Moon,* a coming of age novel set in southern Germany in the 1860s, "stands head and shoulders and maybe elbows above most teen-age novels."

Called "a born storyteller" by Anne Carroll Moore of *Horn Book Magazine,* Benary-Isbert's critics particularly admire her for her depictions of humane, realistic characters. A reviewer for the *Times Literary Supplement,* writing of the book *A Time to Love,* notes that "Benary's people are people; they are solid, real characters [and] their lives and their hopes and their sorrows matter to the reader." Moore finds Benary-Isbert's award-winning novel *The Ark* to be "a true picture of life and death among a homeless people, . . . lighted by a courage and a warm human sympathy and understanding that leave a glow in the heart of the reader." In reviewing *Rowan Farm,* the sequel to *The Ark,* the critic for *Horn Book* concluded: "The two books belong together as one of the most satisfying of our family chronicles—warm, lively, full of courage, and a deep understanding that comes from the author's own experiences."

In *Shooting Star,* a novel for a younger audience, Benary-Isbert tells the story of a German girl and her mother recovering from pneumonia in Switzerland. "It is a simple, leisurely, everyday tale, but is touched with bits of gentle wisdom," wrote L.S. Bechtel in the *New York Herald Tribune Book Review.* For the same age group, the author produced *Blue Mystery,* which concerns the theft of a rare plant and earned accolades from critics who considered it of a higher quality than most in the genre. "The book mirrors Mrs. Benary-Isbert's feeling for time and place and her love of people, animals, and the out-of-doors," according to A.O. Murphy in *Saturday Review.* Although some critics have faulted Benary-Isbert for sentimentality and even self-pity in her depiction of the trials and tribulations of German people, others insist that the author succeeds in avoiding such pitfalls. Polly Goodwin remarked in her *Chicago Sunday Tribune* review of *Blue Mystery:* "Mrs. Benary understands children and animals and nature as well as anyone writing for young people today and reading her stories is a delight for any age."

BIOGRAPHICAL/CRITICAL SOURCES:

BOOKS

Children's Literature Review, Volume 12, Gale (Detroit), 1987.

Contemporary Literary Criticism, Volume 12, Gale, 1980.

PERIODICALS

America, November 21, 1964.

Booklist, March 15, 1953; March 15, 1954; September 1, 1954; June 1, 1956; June 15, 1957.

Bookmark, April, 1953; April, 1954.

Book Week, November 15, 1964, p. 27.

Chicago Sunday Tribune, May 17, 1953, p. 14; February 28, 1954, p. 12; October 10, 1954, p. 12; June 24, 1956, p. 5; June 2, 1957, p. 5.

Christian Century, September 2, 1953.

Christian Science Monitor, May 9, 1957, p. 11.

Cleveland Open Shelf, December, 1954, p. 39.

Commonweal, November 20, 1953.

Horn Book Magazine, April, 1953; April, 1954; October, 1954; August, 1956; October, 1964.

Kirkus Reviews, January 15, 1953; February 1, 1954; June 1, 1954; February 15, 1956; March 15, 1957.

Library Journal, May 1, 1953; April 15, 1954; September 15, 1954; September 15, 1957; September 15, 1964.

New Yorker, November 28, 1953; November 27, 1954.

New York Herald Tribune Book Review, March 22, 1953, p. 10; February 28, 1954, p. 12; August 22, 1954, p. 7; October 2, 1955; May 13, 1956, p. 35; June 16, 1957, p. 8; August, 1957; May 14, 1961.

New York Times, March 1, 1953, p. 32; February 28, 1954, p. 24; October 10, 1954, p. 38; May 6, 1956, p. 34.

New York Times Book Review, March 1, 1953; February 28, 1954; October 10, 1954; May 6, 1956; May 10, 1959; November 11, 1962.

Publishers Weekly, June 25, 1979.

Saturday Review, April 4, 1953; April 17, 1954; August 21, 1954; August 18, 1956; May 11, 1957.

Spectator, May, 1972.

Springfield Republican, March 29, 1953, p. 7C; April 25, 1954, p. 6C; September 5, 1954, p. 5C; September 23, 1956, p. 8C; September 29, 1957, p. 8C.

Times Literary Supplement, November 28, 1963; December 9, 1965, p. 1145.

Wilson Library Bulletin, May, 1953; May, 1954; October, 1954; May, 1956; September, 1957.

OBITUARIES:

PERIODICALS

Publishers Weekly, June 25, 1979.*

BENEZRA, Barbara (Beardsley) 1921-

PERSONAL: Born April 2, 1921, in Woodman, CO; daughter of Earl (a dentist) and Alice (a teacher; maiden name, Smith) Beardsley; married Leo L. Benezra (a chemist); children: Heather Lee, Paul Louis, Judith Ann, David Allen. *Religion:* Scientology. *Education:* Attended San Francisco State College (now University), 1939-40; University of California, Berkeley, General Secondary Certificate, 1944; University of the Pacific, A.B., 1943; San Jose State College (now University of California), Librarian Degree, 1960. *Avocational interests:* Singing, painting, traveling, entertaining friends.

ADDRESSES: Home—7170 Hawthorn Dr., Mentor, OH 44060.

CAREER: Elementary school librarian in Sunnyvale, CA, 1960-68; Kennedy Junior High School, East Lake, OH, librarian, 1968; Dianetic auditor, beginning 1975.

MEMBER: American Library Association, National Education Association, Ohio State Library Association.

WRITINGS:

NOVELS

Gold Dust and Petticoats, Bobbs-Merrill (New York City), 1964.
Nuggets in My Pocket, Bobbs-Merrill, 1966.
Fire Dragon, Criterion Books (New York City), 1970.

OTHER

Contributor to library journals.

SIDELIGHTS: Barbara Benezra's books are historical novels set in California. In *Gold Dust and Petticoats,* the author gave young readers a colorful tale of San Francisco in the Gold Rush days. *Nuggets in My Pocket* covers the same period, but focuses on the remote gold fields of the time. In *Fire Dragon,* Benezra explored American-Oriental relations against the backdrop of the great San Francisco earthquake of 1906.

Thirteen-year-old Marcy Miller is the main character in *Gold Dust and Petticoats.* Marcy's father, a doctor, made the long trip to the West Coast hoping to establish a medical practice there. Many exciting adventures befall Marcy, who is described by Olivia R. Way in the *Instructor* as "well-meaning, lovable, and sometimes impulsive." Fires, runaway horses, and kidnapping are only some of the events in the book. "The style and dialogue are invigorating," approved a *Best Sellers* reviewer.

Marcy's brother Jeb was the focal character in *Nuggets in My Pocket.* Some of the same events that occurred in *Gold Dust and Petticoats* are described again, but from the boy's point of view. Eventually, he runs away to the gold fields for new adventures. "There is some moderately interesting detailing of the techniques of gathering gold," allowed a *Kirkus Reviews* contributor, who went on to complain of stereotyped characters and an overused storyline. Emma Kirby in *Library Journal* concurred that *Nuggets in My Pocket* suffered from a "pot-boiler plot," but she felt that "the story has good pace and color."

In *Fire Dragon,* seventeen-year-old Sam Watkins embodies the bigoted attitudes prevalent toward Oriental immigrants during the early years of this century. But when a massive earthquake and the ensuing fire separate him from his family, he forges a bond with a Chinese family as they work together to survive and save others.

Commenting on her own work, Benezra once said: "I have always been fascinated by history, and feel since history is about people, that is how it should be studied. I wanted my readers to realize that people of a hundred years ago had many of the same problems and all of the emotions we experience today.

"In order to write my books, all historical novels, I read many books about the colorful, exciting times of the California gold rush. I haunted museums and even took a trip into the Mother Lode country of the Sierras to try and recapture the flavor of the times of 1853. By the time I sat down to write my books I felt as though I had walked through the mud that paved the streets of San Francisco then, or walked behind a mule into the Sierras, carrying my pick on my back."

She further commented: "When young people ask me how to learn to write, I usually tell them to sharpen their wits, learn their basic skills from school, but above all, *to write.* Although it is a demanding occupation and very few books are published from all of the manuscripts sent in by hopeful authors, there is always room for a good book."

BIOGRAPHICAL/CRITICAL SOURCES:

PERIODICALS

Best Sellers, February 15, 1965, p. 453.

Bulletin of the Center for Children's Books, November, 1965, p. 42.

Instructor, May, 1965, p. 30.

Kirkus Reviews, October 15, 1966.

Library Journal, October 15, 1966, p. 5221.

New York Times Book Review, May 9, 1965, p. 6.

* * *

BERESFORD, Maurice Warwick 1920-

PERSONAL: Born February 6, 1920, in Sutton, Coldfield, Warwickshire, England; son of Harry Bertram (a clerk) and Nora Elizabeth (Jefferies) Beresford. *Education:* Jesus College, Cambridge, B.A., 1941, M.A., 1945. *Politics:* Socialist. *Avocational interests:* The cinema as a serious art, music, walking, travel, theatre, maps.

ADDRESSES: Home—10 Holt Close, Leeds, 16, Yorkshire, England. *Office*—University of Leeds, Leeds, England.

CAREER: University of Leeds, Leeds, England, lecturer in economic history, 1948-55, reader, 1955-59, professor of economic history, 1959—, dean, 1958-60, chair of School of Economic Studies, 1965-68 and 1971-72, chair of faculty board, 1968-70. Adult Education Centre, Rugby, warden, 1943-48; Yorkshire Citizens Advice Bureau Committee, chair, 1962—; Yorkshire Dales National Park Committee, 1964-71; Leeds Probation Committee member, 1972—.

WRITINGS:

The Leeds Chamber of Commerce, E. J. Arnold, 1951.

The Lost Villages of England, Lutterworth, 1956, reprinted, A. Sutton, 1989.

History on the Ground: Six Studies in Maps and Landscapes, Lutterworth, 1957, revised edition, Methuen, 1971.

(With J. K. S. St. Joseph) *Medieval England: An Aerial Survey,* Cambridge University Press, 1958, reprinted, 1979.

Lay Subsidies and Poll Taxes, Phillimores, 1963.

(Editor with G. R. Jones) *Leeds and Its Region,* British Association for the Advancement of Science, 1967.

New Towns of the Middle Ages: Town Plantation in England, Wales, and Gascony, Praeger, 1967, reprinted, A. Sutton, 1988.

(Editor with John G. Hurst) *Deserted Medieval Villages: Studies,* Lutterworth Press, 1971, St. Martin's, 1972, reprinted, A. Sutton, 1989.

(With H. P. R. Finberg) *English Medieval Boroughs: A Hand-List,* Rowman & Littlefield, 1973.

Time and Place: Collected Essays, Hambledon Press, 1984.

East End, West End: The Face of Leeds during Urbanisation, 1684-1842, Thoresby Society, 1988.

(With John Hurst) *English Heritage Book of Wharram Percy,* B.T. Batsford, 1990, published as *Wharram Percy: Deserted Medieval Village,* Yale University Press, 1991.

Contributor to economics and history journals.

SIDELIGHTS: Maurice Warwick Beresford is an historical geographer, one who utilizes the tools of the geographer in order to speculate on questions of historical significance. His first major work, *The Lost Villages of England,* was considered groundbreaking in this regard when it first appeared. N. J. G. Pounds, who reviewed the work for the *Geographical Review,* contended: "To the historical geographer this study is especially welcome because it demonstrates how geographical methods of field work and mapping can help to form conclusions in economic and social history that might not have been reached without them."

Reviewers noted the significance of Beresford's reliance on aerial photographs of sites where it is believed a village once stood, and praised the author for including information on those villages not yet located, along with advice on how to investigate these sites further. For his efforts, the author earned glowing reviews. "Mr. Beresford has produced a pioneer study of such grasp and quality that it will, beyond question, take a deserved place among the historical classics of our countryside," Nigel Harvey predicted in the *New Statesman and Nation.*

Almost twenty years later, Beresford and John G. Hurst edited *Deserted Medieval Villages: Studies,* a collection of essays updating the information contained in *Lost Villages of England.* A reviewer in the *Times Literary Supplement* concluded: "It is an expensive book, handsomely produced, but is well worth every penny, for it is packed with new knowledge and speculations and guidance for future work."

Beresford paired up with John Kenneth Sinclair St. Joseph to produce *Medieval England,* which relies heavily upon photographs of England taken from the air to document the history of the land. This book demonstrated to a reviewer in the *New Statesman* the value of air photography to historical researchers: "To the teacher it is invaluable in saving time and arousing curiosity; to the professional historian it gives a new precision to old truths and raises new questions." As in his earlier efforts, Beresford's prose earned special note for its clarity to general readers as well as specialists in the field. Thus, concluded the reviewer for the *Times Literary Supplement, Medieval England* is "important for the specialist and both instructive and entertaining for the general reader."

New Towns of the Middle Ages, does for Europe what Beresford's earlier books did for England alone, tracing the history of settlements with the help of geographical traces as well as historical documents. "No college library should be without this book," averred I.M. Berger in *Library Journal,* who applauded the author's "exhaustive" investigation into the eleventh-century urban expansion throughout Europe. "Not only is this an excellent history and invaluable for reference, it is beautifully written and copiously illustrated."

Beresford is considered a pioneering geographical historian whose methods, as generously outlined in his first book, *The Lost Villages of England,* have been widely emulated in the field. In particular, he is noted for bringing to the fore the utility of aerial photographs in the search for the buried sites of lost towns and villages of ancient England. In addition, he has garnered praise for his readable prose, which makes his texts accessible to the interested lay reader as well as the specialist.

BIOGRAPHICAL/CRITICAL SOURCES:

PERIODICALS

American Historical Review, October, 1955; July, 1958.
Choice, May, 1968; November, 1972.
Encounter, October, 1971.
Geographical Review, July, 1955.
Library Journal, October 1, 1967.
New Statesman, April 26, 1958.
New Statesman and Nation, September 4, 1954.
Spectator, May 9, 1958, p. 601.
Times Literary Supplement, August 20, 1954, p. 532; April 25, 1958, p. 233; June 6, 1968, p. 573; October 15, 1971, p. 1268.

* * *

BERGREEN, Laurence R. 1950-

PERSONAL: Born February 4, 1950, in New York, NY; son of Morris H. (a lawyer) and Adele (a lawyer; maiden name, Gabel) Bergreen; married Elizabeth Freeman (a musician), June, 1975. *Education:* Harvard University, A.B., 1972.

ADDRESSES: Office—15 East 10th St., New York, NY 10003. *Agent*—Wylie, Aitken and Stone, 250 West 57th St., Suite 2106, New York, NY 10107.

CAREER: Museum of Broadcasting, New York City, assistant to president, 1977-78; New School for Social Research, New York City, faculty member, 1981-82; writer. Consultant on television documentaries, including *Prohibition,* BBC-TV, 1997.

WRITINGS:

Look Now, Pay Later: The Rise of Network Broadcasting, Doubleday (Garden City, NY), 1980.
James Agee: A Life, Dutton (New York City), 1984.
As Thousands Cheer: The Life of Irving Berlin, Viking (New York City), 1990.
Capone: The Man and the Era, Simon & Schuster (New York City), 1994.
Louis Armstrong: An Extravagant Life, Broadway Books (New York City), 1997.

Also contributor to *Academic American Encyclopedia.* Contributor to magazines, including *American Film, Newsweek, Quest, Television Quarterly,* and *TV Guide.*

SIDELIGHTS: When Laurence R. Bergreen turned to writing nonfiction and biography, he discovered a pleasant surprise. He once told *CA:* "When writing my first book [*Look Now, Pay Later: The Rise of Network Broadcasting*], a history of the American broadcasting industry, I found myself becoming more imaginatively engaged in the story of the rise of a business venture than I would have guessed possible at the outset. After a while it struck me that the networks served as a huge metaphor for the craggy face of American enterprise. It was a microcosm of society—at least as it looks to me here in New York—a fascinating, discordant combination of remarkable elements and people." *Look Now, Pay Later* represents a kind of collective biography, containing sketches of major journalists and broadcasting executives, including Edward R. Murrow, Eric Sevareid, Edwin Armstrong, and Fred Silverman. Writing for the *Washington Journalism Review,* E. William Henry praises Bergreen for both his "highly readable, perceptive study of the broadcasting industry" and his "compelling portraits of the broadcast pioneers and their successors." Blaik Kirby of the Toronto *Globe and Mail* recommends *Look Now, Pay Later* for "anyone interested in broadcasting," declaring, "It is often an exciting tale and it is so thorough that I have complete faith in its accuracy and fairness."

Bergreen continued to explore the lives of twentieth-century Americans in *James Agee: A Life*. Here, the biographer chronicles the Pulitzer Prize-winning author's varied career and tumultuous personal life. Melvin Maddocks points out in *Time* that Bergreen "spent three years in research and interviews amassing the minute data of Agee's life," and the reviewer asserts that the book is a "solid, unassuming biography." Jonathan Yardley states in *Washington Post Book World,* "It is a terribly familiar story, and a terribly sad one, and it is told exceptionally well by Laurence Bergreen in what is, rather surprisingly, the first full Agee biography." Yardley also praises Bergreen for not "succumb[ing] to the literary biographer's temptation to overrate his subject's work."

Bergreen's next biography, *As Thousands Cheer: The Life of Irving Berlin,* traces the life of the songwriter known for such classics as "God Bless America," "White Christmas," "There's No Business Like Show Business," and "Puttin' on the Ritz." As Alex Witchel points out in the *New York Times,* the fact that his subject was still alive did not make this biography any easier for Bergreen, for Berlin and his three daughters "refused to cooperate with Mr. Bergreen, who began his research when the songwriter was 97." Witchel adds, however, that Bergreen "did not feel that the family's lack of cooperation hurt his work." Gene Lees stresses in the *New York Times Book Review,* "In view of how hard Berlin tried to keep anyone from writing about him, Mr. Bergreen's vivid portrait is impressive indeed." In a Chicago *Tribune Books* review, Gerald Bordman calls the work "a complete, carefully researched biography" and a "major accomplishment. It will probably stand as the definitive biography of a man whose fathomless well of unforgettable melody and rare gift for simple, homey, touching lyrics made his songs among the best that Tin Pan Alley, Broadway, and Hollywood had to offer." Witchel notes, nonetheless, that Bergreen has revealed "a darker side of Mr. Berlin's character," and Lees finds in *As Thousands Cheer* a Berlin who was "a mystery, and for the last three decades he was a crabby recluse, enveloped in a cocoon of memories, ingratitude, egotism and self-doubt." The *New York Times*'s Michiko Kakutani concludes, "The reader finishes this biography with the feeling that there is often no correlation between genius and sensitivity, talent and temperament. The man who wrote such wonderfully romantic songs as 'Cheek to Cheek,' 'Always,' and 'What'll I Do?' appears to have been an egotist and a boor."

In *Capone: The Man and the Era,* Bergreen turns his attention to a notorious figure whose story has grown to almost mythical proportions as the battle of good and evil between gangsters and G-men moved from the headlines to the silver screen to popular culture. Yet, as Digby Diehl observes in *Playboy,* Bergreen "extracts Al Capone from decades of mythology and misinformation to reveal him in the context of his times." As the biographer notes, Capone was born into a tough neighborhood in Brooklyn, New York, in 1899. He moved to Chicago in 1921. There, he became an entrepreneur and businessman, but one on the wrong side of the law. Within a decade, he had built an empire, selling alcohol in violation of Prohibition and running other very profitable illegal and legal operations. "Capone, as portrayed by Laurence Bergreen," George F. Will observes in *National Review,* "was a cunning creature more or less sincerely convinced that his enterprises, principally bootlegging but also gambling and prostitution, produced jobs for deserving men and women and satisfied appetites that he did not create and which someone else would satisfy if he did not." But, as his biographer shows, the government thought differently of his dealings. Capone was deposed in 1931 when the Feds convicted him for failure to pay taxes on his earnings. He died in 1947 of syphilis in Alcatraz Prison. Stephen Birmingham, in a review in *Insight on the News,* faults Bergreen for speculation on Capone's private thoughts and the gangster's use of cocaine, but a *Publishers Weekly* reviewer recognizes that Bergreen "has done a prodigious amount of research.

Perhaps Bergreen's most pleasant experience as a biographer came in writing *Louis Armstrong: An Extravagant Life.* As he explained in a *Publishers Weekly* interview, "This is the first biography I have written in which my opinion of my subject kept improving as I worked." Armstrong was born in 1901 in New Orleans where he heard all around him the music of the diverse peoples who made their homes in this Mississippi Delta city. In addition to all these other influences, Armstrong was encouraged by a Jewish family named Karnofsky to pursue music himself. He picked up the coronet. He left New Orleans for Chicago in 1922 and joined King Oliver and his band. Over the next thirty years, he travelled the world and became an international star. He died in 1971. David Ostwald, writing in *Commentary,* is impressed with the eloquence of Bergreen's "opening chapter—one of the best six-page summaries of Armstrong ever written." And, as Paul de Barros points out in *Down Beat,* "Based on intimate, previously ignored writings by Armstrong himself, mostly about his four wives and various girlfriends, this new biography boasts as vivid and cinematic a description of early New Orleans as you'll read anywhere."

Bergreen is not credited with the definitive biography of this jazz legend, however. Ostwald faults the biographer for not adequately developing the last twenty-five years of Armstrong's life and argues that the book does contain some factual errors. For *Entertainment Weekly* contributor David Hajdu "it fails to illuminate the peculiarly American miracle of [Armstrong's] genius." Yet, in the opinion of de Barros, "Bergreen is a fluid and engaging writer who gets the often complex and contradictory details right." And, concludes David Yaffe in the *Nation,* "The prose throughout is lucid and stylish, and Bergreen's love for his subject comes through on every page."

BIOGRAPHICAL/CRITICAL SOURCES:

PERIODICALS

Bestsellers, Volume 90, number 4, pp. 13-15.
Chicago Tribune, July 23, 1988; July 8, 1990, section 13, pp. 12-13.
Chicago Tribune Book World, July 29, 1984.
Commentary, November, 1997, p. 68.
Detroit Free Press, July 1, 1990, p. Q7.
Down Beat, December, 1997, p. 96.
Economist, September 6, 1997, p. 18.
Entertainment Weekly, August 8, 1997, p. 74.
Globe and Mail (Toronto), June 28, 1980; October 6, 1984; July 28, 1990.
Insight on the News, August 29, 1994, p. 30.
Los Angeles Times, July 28, 1988.
Los Angeles Times Book Review, July 15, 1984, p. 2; July 1, 1990, pp. 6, 8.
Nation, July 14, 1997, p. 30.
National Review, December 31, 1994, p. 55.
Newsweek, July 7, 1997, p. 66.
New York Times, June 30, 1984; June 19, 1990; August 18, 1990.
New York Times Book Review, July 8, 1984, pp. 1, 31; July 1, 1990, pp. 1, 23.
Playboy, September, 1994, p. 32.
Publishers Weekly, July 4, 1994, p. 48; June 9, 1997, p. 32; July 14, 1997, p. 59.
Time, July 2, 1984, p. 85; July 23, 1990, pp. 74-5.
Times Literary Supplement, August 31, 1990.
Tribune Books (Chicago), July 8, 1990, pp. 1, 5.
Washington Journalism Review, July/August, 1980.
Washington Post Book World, June 10, 1984, pp. 3-4; June 24, 1990, p. 3.*

* * *

BERKOFF, Steven 1937-

PERSONAL: Born August 3, 1937, in London, England; son of Alfred (a tailor) and Pauline (Hyman) Berkoff; married Shelley Lee (a dancer and choreographer), August 21, 1976. *Education:* Studied acting at Webber-Douglas Academy in London, England, 1958-59, and at Ecole Jacques Lecoq in Paris, France, 1965.

ADDRESSES: Agent—Joanna Marston, Rosica Colin Ltd., 1 Clareville Grove Mews, London SW7 5AH, England.

CAREER: Actor, director, writer, and adapter of plays for London Theatre Group, London England, and New York Shakespeare Festival, New York City. Founder of London Theatre Group, 1973. Principal stage appearances include *Hamlet,* 1980; *Metamorphosis,* 1982; and *Salome,* 1988. Actor in motion pictures, including *A Clockwork Orange,* 1971; *Barry Lyndon,* 1975; *McVicar,* 1980; *Outland,* 1981; *Octopussy,* 1983; *Beverly Hills Cop,* 1984; *Rambo: First Blood, Part II,* 1985; *Revolution,* 1985; *Absolute Beginners,* 1986; *Under the Cherry Moon,* 1986; and *The Krays,* 1990. Actor in television films, including

Sins, 1987; *War and Remembrance,* 1990; *Tell-Tale Heart,* 1991; and *Silent Night,* 1991.

AWARDS, HONORS: Los Angeles Drama Critics Circle award for directing, 1983.

WRITINGS:

In the Penal Colony (also see below), based on a story by Franz Kafka, first produced in London, 1968.
Metamorphosis (also see below), based on a story by Kafka, first produced in London, 1968, produced in Los Angeles, CA, 1982, New York, 1989.
The Trial (also see below), based on a story by Kafka, first produced in the Netherlands, 1971, produced in London, 1973.
Agamemnon (also see below), based on a play by Aeschylus, first produced in London, 1971, revised version produced in London, 1976.
Knock at the Manor Gate, based on a story by Kafka, first produced in London, 1972.
Miss Julie Versus Expressionism, based on a play by Strindberg, first produced in London, 1973.
Mr. Prufrock's Songs (also see below), first produced in London, 1974, revised version, as *Lunch,* produced in London, 1981.
The Fall of the House of Usher (also see below), based on a story by Edgar Allan Poe, first produced in Edinburgh, Scotland, 1974, produced in London, 1975.
East (also see below), first produced in London, 1975.
East, Agamemnon, The Fall of the House of Usher, Calder (London), 1977, Riverrun Press (New York City), 1982.
Gross Intrusions and Other Stories, Calder, 1977, Riverrun Press, 1979.
Greek (also see below), first produced in London, 1980, produced in Los Angeles, 1982.
West (also see below), first produced in London, 1980.
Decadence (also see below), first produced in London, 1981.
Decadence [and] *Greek,* Calder, 1982, Riverrun Press, 1983.
Harry's Christmas (also see below), first produced in London, 1985.
The Tell-Tale Heart, based on a story by Poe, first produced in London, 1985.
West, Lunch, Harry's Christmas, Grove Press (New York City), 1985.
Kvetch (also see below), first produced in Los Angeles, 1986.
Sink the Belgrano! (also see below), first produced in London, 1986.
Acapulco (also see below), first produced in Los Angeles, 1986, produced in London, 1992.
Acapulco [and] Kvetch, Faber (London), 1986, Grove Press, 1987.
The Trial, Metamorphosis, In the Penal Colony: Three Theatre Adaptations from Franz Kafka, Amber Lane (Oxford, England), 1988.
Steven Berkoff's America, Hutchinson (London), 1988.
A Prisoner in Rio, Hutchinson, 1989.
Decadence and Other Plays (includes *East, West,* and *Greek),* Faber, 1989.
I Am Hamlet, Faber, 1989, Grove Press, 1990.
Theatre of Steven Berkoff, Methuen (London), 1992.

Also author or adapter of such plays as *Greek, Agamemnon, Decadence,* and *The Fall of the House of Usher.*

SIDELIGHTS: "This is the age of the mundane, and I just stand out in it because I don't like the mundanity," Steven Berkoff once told *Theatre Quarterly*'s Bruce Elder. An accomplished writer-actor-director who challenges audience expectations and actors' limitations, Berkoff has overseen production of a number of well-received adaptations and original plays. Perhaps better known in America as a character actor in such potboilers as *Beverly Hills Cop* and *Rambo: First Blood, Part II,* Berkoff is the founding director of the London Theatre Group, with which many of his plays have made their debut. To quote Jeremy Gerard in the *New York Times,* "Part theatrical triple-threat . . . part unashamed snake-oil salesman, Mr. Berkoff writes plays that compel an audience to face without mercy contemporary stereotypes and prejudices."

Berkoff's plays fly in the face of traditional theatre, even as some of them are adapted from playwrights such as Aeschylus and Shakespeare. According to Ned Chaillet in *Contemporary Dramatists,* Berkoff "established his own dedicated following, an audience primed to admire the violent flow of his language as a dramatist and the physicality of his theatrical style. Where realism struggled to represent the inarticulacy of ordinary life, Berkoff gave his characters pages of poetic diatribe driven by profane imagery and obscene rhyme. He combined the street language of London's East End with Shakespearean grandiloquence. His visual images shared the urgent violence of his language, through the threatening presence of motorcycles and muscular actors in leather and denim."

Berkoff began his career by adapting some of the best known works of Franz Kafka for the stage, including *In the Penal Colony* and *Metamorphosis.* Elder felt that the Berkoff treatment of *Metamorphosis* in particular "breathes life into Kafka's world with terrifying effectiveness. . . . He always seems to relish the psychological parable and *Metamorphosis,* with its resonances of human cruelty, of prejudice, of familial cruelty and insensitivity, stretches his imaginative powers to their limit." Chaillet wrote: "[Berkoff's] adaptation of Kafka's *Metamorphosis,* originally tailored to his own athletic performance as the man who is transformed into a giant insect, has proved exceptionally durable and has been staged by Berkoff in several languages. . . . That adaptation has paved the way for his particular use of the human body and voice as the prime elements in his productions, powerfully demonstrating his concern for the expression of text through physical images which imprint themselves on the audience's memory."

While his adaptations have been lauded for their nightmare vision and strong political viewpoints, Berkoff has also made a mark as an original playwright. His own full-length plays—including *East, West, Kvetch,* and *Decadence,* portray the violence and corruption, writ small or large, that infects Great Britain today. His works make use of graphic imagery, creatively evocative language, and even pantomime as characters satirize the various social classes. In *Plays and Players,* Dave Robins observed: "*East* shows the East End [of London] as it is—a city of violent, comic, deeply frustrated people, a hard place to grow up and develop in. . . . It certainly tears holes in our accepted stage version of the East End." Elder maintained that *East* "is total theatre, gut reaction theatre, call it what you will. . . . [I]t is a great theatrical scream of pain and resentment, a kaleidoscope of images of life in the East End." *Kvetch* also forms itself around family pain, as the characters speak both the formal words with which they frame a polite dinner and the far more anxious and nihilistic thoughts that are churning in their heads. Gerard declared that some audience members watching *Kvetch* "are bound to think they've died and gone to family hell, as Mr. Berkoff's characters dredge up deep-seated feelings about sex, identity and race."

Chaillet concluded of Berkoff's original productions: "Visionary as his adaptations might be . . . it is the original writing which has proved most influential. . . . [His plays have] become a model for younger playwrights seeking to escape the limits of conversational drama." Elder, too, commented that "Berkoff has created a theatrical form that is uniquely his. He is out on a limb, but he enjoys being there."

"Out on a limb" could also describe Berkoff's work as a director. In the 1990s he adapted and directed two Shakespearean dramas, *Coriolanus* and *Richard II,* as well as *Salome,* the Oscar Wilde play about a woman who connives to have John the Baptist killed. All of these productions were staged in America, the first two at the New York Shakespeare Festival and the latter at the Next Wave Festival. In a *Newsday* review of Berkoff's *Coriolanus,* Linda Winer cited the play for its "updated and truncated, impertinent, overboard but overwhelmingly beautiful production," adding that the work "is powered by a sweep and vision that . . . seem truer to the life of Shakespeare than a dozen earnestly faithful readings of the text." *American Theatre* contributor Stephen Haff declared Berkoff's reading of *Richard II* a "satire," noting: "Berkoff's staging unfolds as tense, tableau-punctuated choreography. The production is a single-minded, mocking, mechanized, choral attack on the empty world it portrays, with a smoothly sinister Richard its polished, hollow heart."

Berkoff has committed much of his Hollywood earnings to theatrical productions and continues to be an imposing figure in the British theatre world especially. To quote Chaillet, "his plays are still intended to tap the full potentiality of actors and clear away the trivial routines and reenactments of ordinary activity. With the use of his dialogue and monologues, "acting becomes a compulsive medium because I can touch primeval forces and release them—madness and maybe enlightenment.'"

Berkoff once told *CA* that "getting up in the morning" has been his motivation and that "the bailiffs" were the circumstances surrounding his writing. Writing to be "notorious," Berkoff hopes to achieve "fame, money, and sex" through his books. His writing habits include "avoiding it," and he advises aspiring writers to "get out of my way." The author revealed that he has no views on his contemporaries, although he sees the current literary scene as "pathetic."

He commented: "My main motivation is to write well and to create theatrical works that do not send people to sleep. I write for the sheer pleasure of it and as a hobby. Writing should never be work—the closest thing to writing is loving or day-dreaming or eating a salt-beef sandwich with a pickle."

BIOGRAPHICAL/CRITICAL SOURCES:

BOOKS

Contemporary Dramatists, fifth edition, St. James Press (Detroit), 1993.
Contemporary Literary Criticism, Volume 56, Gale (Detroit), 1989.
International Dictionary of Theatre-2: Playwrights, St. James Press, 1994.

PERIODICALS

American Theatre, September, 1994, pp. 72-75.
Educational Theatre Journal, March, 1977, pp. 110-11; December, 1978, pp. 547-48.
Independent, April 26, 1997, p. S4.
Newsday, February 19, 1987; November 23, 1988.
New Statesman & Society, July 8, 1988, p. 48.
New York Daily News, February 19, 1987.
New Yorker, December 12, 1988, pp. 139-40.
New York Post, February 19, 1987; November 23, 1988.
New York Times, February 15, 1987, p. H3; February 19, 1987, p. C26; November 23, 1988, p. C9.
Plays and Players, September, 1977, pp. 28-29; November, 1986, pp. 32-33.
Spectator, July 9, 1988, pp. 72-73.
Theatre Journal, May, 1983, pp. 241-43.
Theatre Quarterly, autumn, 1978, pp. 37-43.
Time, March 20, 1989, p. 90.
Wall Street Journal, November 29, 1988.

* * *

BERNAYS, Anne
See KAPLAN, Anne Bernays

* * *

BERNE, Stanley 1923-

PERSONAL: Born June 8, 1923, in Staten Island, NY; son of William (a businessman) and Irene (Daniels) Berne; married Arlene Zekowski (a writer and university professor), May 17, 1953. *Education:* Rutgers University, B.S., 1951; New York University, M.A., 1952; Louisiana State University, additional study, 1958-62.

ADDRESSES: Home—P. O. Box 4595, Santa Fe, NM 87502-4595. *Office*—Department of English, Eastern New Mexico University, Portales, NM 88130.

CAREER: Eastern New Mexico University, Portales, assistant professor, 1963-67, associate professor of English, beginning 1968, University Professor of the History of Literature. Guest lecturer at University of the Americas, 1965, University of South Dakota, 1968, and Styrian Hauptschulen Paedagogische Akademie (Graz, Austria), 1969. Producer and host with wife, Arlene Zekowski, of television series, *Future Writing Today,* for Public Broadcasting System. Has participated in lecture tour through Mexico, sponsored by U.S. Department of State and U.S. Embassy, 1965; has appeared on over 150 radio and television interview programs in the United States and Canada, speaking about art and literature, and on television programs including *Avant-Garde Goes West* and *Noonday. Military service:* U.S. Army Air Forces, 1942-45; served in South Pacific theater; received Philippine Liberation Medal.

MEMBER: PEN, Committee of Small Magazine Editors and Publishers, Western Independent Publishers.

WRITINGS:

(With wife, Arlene Zekowski) *A First Book of the Neo-Narrative,* Wittenborn (New York City), 1954.
(With A. Zekowski) *Cardinals and Saints,* Wittenborn, 1958.
The Dialogues, Wittenborn, 1962.
The Multiple Modern Gods and Other Stories, Wittenborn, 1964.
The Unconscious Victorious and Other Stories, Wittenborn, 1968.
The New Rubaiyat of Stanley Berne (poetry), American-Canadian Publishers (Portales, NM), 1973.
Future Language, Horizon Press (New York City), 1977.
The Great American Empire, Horizon Press, 1979.
(With A. Zekowski) *Every Person's Little Book of P-L-U-T-O-N-I-U-M,* Rising Tide Press (Santa Fe, NM), 1992.
To Hell with Optimism!, Rising Tide Press, 1997.

Work represented in anthologies, including *Breakthrough Fictioneers,* edited by Richard Kostelanetz, Something Else Press, 1973, and *First Person Intense* edited by Sasha Newborn, Mudborn Press, 1978.

SIDELIGHTS: Stanley Berne has written a number of books of experimental fiction with his wife, Arlene Zekowski. Writing in *Dictionary of the Avant-Gardes,* Richard Kostelanetz states that the couple "customarily publish their books in tandem and reflect a common esthetic, which holds that the conventional sentence is esthetically outmoded. Usually classified as 'fiction,' their books are typically difficult, in the tradition of Gertrude Stein at her most opaque."

Speaking of Berne's *To Hell with Optimism!,* Constance Dial in *Small Press Review* states that it "is really a fun book to read. It's filled with *real people* Berne knows and has met, like the very richest man on Earth, brothel queens, famous authors like Edward Dahlberg . . . , ruthless media moguls . . . , retired ex-Presidents of the United States, phony Russian ballet dancers, [and] Hollywood 'stars'." Speaking of *Every Person's Little Book of P-L-U-T-O-N-I-U-M,* Ramadev Levine in *Small Press Review* notes that Berne presents his argument that plutonium is "pure evil and his book makes a very strong case for that conclusion."

Berne once told *CA:* "We [Berne and his wife, Alene Zekowski] proposed in our books that grammar be reformed for purposes of artistic communication in prose. We proposed . . . that grammar be made sensibly simpler. Everybody got angry. They thought we were advocating anarchy. Does reducing the 300 rules and elements of grammar to two sound anarchic? Well, that's what we proposed. We simply called attention to the four great writers of the 20th century who, working by artistic instinct, had already indicated the direction of English (and all modern language communication) for the future. They are Virginia Woolf, Gertrude Stein, William Faulkner, and James Joyce. Some think these writers were eccentrics, or merely interesting but impractical dreamers. We discovered, in the course of writing*Future Language* [by Berne] and *Image Breaking Images* [by Zekowski], that they were harbingers of the future.

"It is clear that people will resist change in language as passionately as in religion. But it appeared to us unthinkable, that in the age of space travel, jet aircraft, new electronic storage and retrieval systems, that language would remain frozen in the linear form of the sentence. It cannot be, because of the assault on our sensibilities by electronic communication devices, and the overwhelming flood of information coming at us as we approach the year 2000. Above all, we, as authors, are interested in the beauty of language, in its elasticity as a human organ, and in authors and poets providing solutions to the stunning and compounding loss of interest in reading and in books rather than in linguistitioners and grammarians making rules, from which masses of people are daily fleeing. I believe with Shelley that writers and poets are the true legislators of the spirit. If we are, then we must turn our minds to the problem of the fading away of reading interest (which is nothing more than the failure of language forms to communicate contemporary thought and feeling) and to the solution of providing new and reliable forms for the future of communication."

BIOGRAPHICAL/CRITICAL SOURCES:

BOOKS

Kostelanetz, Richard, *Dictionary of the Avant Gardes,* a cappella books (Chicago), 1993.

PERIODICALS

Denver Quarterly, autumn, 1969.
New World Writing, number 11, 1958.
Saturday Review, September 29, 1979.
Small Press Review, December, 1993, p. 12; April, 1996, pp. 10-11.
Times Literary Supplement, August 6, 1964.
X: A Journal of the Arts, winter, 1979.

* * *

BEYER, Audrey White 1916-1985

PERSONAL: Born November 12, 1916, in Portland, ME; died November, 1985; daughter of William Joseph and Hermon (Brand) White; married Walter Archer Beyer (a teacher of mathematics), July 20, 1940; children: Henry G. II, Edmund Brand. *Education:* Westbrook Junior College (now Westbrook College), diploma, 1937; University of Maine, A.B., 1939, graduate study. *Politics:* Independent (registered Republican). *Religion:* Episcopalian. *Avocational interests:* Reading, walking.

CAREER: Teacher of English at Westbrook Junior College (now Westbrook College), Portland, ME, 1939-43, Milton Academy Girls' School, Milton, MA, 1956, and Waynflete Summer School, 1957-59; Northeastern University, Boston, MA, instructor in English, 1967-72; Milton Academy Boys' School, Milton, MA, teacher of composition, 1973-74; private tutor in English.

MEMBER: Maine Historical Society.

AWARDS, HONORS: *Jack and Jill* Award, 1958; Westbrook College Award for Alumnae Achievement, 1960.

WRITINGS:

JUVENILE

Capture at Sea (serialized in *Jack and Jill* magazine), illustrated by H. Tom Hall, Knopf (New York City), 1959.

The Sapphire Pendant, illustrated by Robin Jacques, Knopf, 1961.

Katharine Leslie, illustrated by Polly Bolian, Knopf, 1963.

Dark Venture, illustrated by Leon and Diane Dillon, Knopf, 1968.

SIDELIGHTS: Audrey White Beyer wrote historical novels for young adults. *Capture At Sea* deals with two Yankee boys, impressed into British naval service during the War of 1812. M. S. Libby, in the *New York Herald Tribune Book Review,* says: "the reader will learn much of conditions in the British Navy of the time." A *Horn Book* reviewer calls the book "an exciting story. . . . [*Capture At Sea* is] a high-interest book for older reluctant readers." And L. E. Cathon in the *Library Journal* labels it a "fast-moving story."

The Sapphire Pendant takes place in 1803. A sixteen-year-old orphan, Elizabeth Montgomery, travels from Portsmouth, England, to France, in disguise as a sailor. The story involves espionage during the Napoleonic Wars and Elizabeth's relationship with her guardian, Paul. "Equal parts of romance, intrigue, and mystery make up this teen-age novel," writes Elizabeth Hodges in the *New York Times Book Review.* Cathon thinks the "characterizations are good and descriptions vivid: action, if a bit contrived moves swiftly."

The novel, *Katharine Leslie* deals with a sixteen-year-old governess falsely incarcerated in Newgate Prison. Through the help of a young doctor, she escapes to America and goes to work as a tutor for a Tory family, only to find herself in the middle of the Revolutionary War. "The good writing, interesting historical background, and complexities of the characters make this romantic story unusually convincing," writes a *Horn Book* contributor. A *Library Journal* reviewer calls *Katharine Leslie* "eye-opening and fascinating reading. . . . [A] good romance and suspense story." C. H. Bishop, in *Commonweal,* mentions the book's "thrilling plot" and "sensitive psychological study."

In *Dark Venture,* Beyer took on slavery in the late eighteenth century. The hero, Demba is a twelve-year-old from West Africa, who wanders away from home. Another tribe captures him, and sells him to a slaver. Beyer "is at her best when she is with Demba, following his nightmarish journey up the Gambia River to the slave stockade," writes Jean Fritz in the *New York Times Book Review.* A *Horn Book* reviewer considers the tale "well written," and feels "the book vividly recreates the horror of slavery, and illustrates the great meaning for one's fellows of individual deeds."

BIOGRAPHICAL/CRITICAL SOURCES:

BOOKS

Something about the Author, Volume 9, Gale (Detroit), 1976.

PERIODICALS

Best Sellers, December 15, 1963, p. 339; June 1, 1968, p. 111.

Booklist, July 15, 1961, p. 701.

Chicago Sunday Tribune, June 18, 1961, p. 6.

Christian Science Monitor, May 11, 1961, p. B4.

Commonweal, November 15, 1963, p. 234; May 24, 1968, p. 306.

Horn Book, August, 1959, p. 286; February, 1964, p. 64; August, 1968, p. 426.

Kirkus, February 1, 1961, p. 109.

Library Journal, May 15, 1959, p. 1692; March 15, 1961, p. 1326; June 15, 1964, p. 2665; September 15, 1968, p. 3311.

New York Herald Tribune Book Review, July 5, 1959, p. 9.

New York Herald Tribune Lively Arts, May 14, 1961, section 12, p. 14.

New York Times Book Review, June 4, 1961, p. 24; May 12, 1968, p. 30.*

* * *

BILLSON, Anne 1954-

PERSONAL: Born November 22, 1954, in Southport, Lancashire, England; daughter of Thomas Billson (a civil servant) and Ruby (Lonsdale) Billson (a civil servant). *Education:* Central School of Art and Design, B.A. (with honors), 1976.

ADDRESSES: Agent—Antony Harwood, Curtis Brown, Ltd., 162-168 Regent St., London W1R 5TB, England.

CAREER: Time Out, London, England, literary editor, 1985-86; *Sunday Correspondent,* London, film critic, 1989-90; *New Statesman & Society,* London, film critic, 1991-92; *Sunday Telegraph,* London, film critic, 1992—. British *GQ,* contributing editor.

AWARDS, HONORS: Received Best Young British Novelists award for *Suckers.*

WRITINGS:

NOVELS

Dream Demon (novelization of screenplay), New English Library (London), 1989.
Suckers, Atheneum (New York City), 1993.
Stiff Lips, Macmillan (London), 1996.

NONFICTION

Screen Lovers, St. Martin's (New York City), 1988.
My Name Is Michael Caine: A Life in Film, Muller, 1991.
The Thing (film criticism), Indiana University Press, 1997.

SIDELIGHTS: "Anne Billson," Chris Morgan maintains in the *St. James Guide to Horror, Ghost and Gothic Writers,* "is a clever and extremely witty writer, perhaps the wittiest currently working in the horror genre."

Billson's novel *Suckers* concerns yuppie vampires in London who are attempting to seize control of Britain's media. "The novel," Morgan writes, "is very sharp and cleverly told." The book is narrated by Dora, an advertising executive who is, Morgan explains, "cynical, vindictive, streetwise to the point of criminality, and almost completely amoral, yet the reader, male or female, cannot help but sympathize with her plight and support her wholeheartedly in her battle against life's problems. Wit and humour in the face of even the worst of horrors . . . make her an original and superior heroine in an outstanding example of the usually cliched vampire sub-genre."

BIOGRAPHICAL/CRITICAL SOURCES:

BOOKS

St. James Guide to Horror, Ghost and Gothic Writers, St. James Press (Detroit), 1998.

PERIODICALS

Film Quarterly, summer, 1998, p. 65.
New Statesman and Society, March 27, 1992, p. 39.
Publishers Weekly, August 16, 1993, p. 87; August 30, 1993, p. 67.
Times Literary Supplement, December 20, 1991, p. 18; January 24, 1993, pp. 8-9; March 5, 1993, p. 22.

* * *

BIRKIN, Charles (Lloyd) 1907-1986
(Charles Lloyd)

PERSONAL: Born September 24, 1907, in Nottinghamshire, England; died November 9, 1986; son of Charles Wilfrid (a colonel) and Claire (Howe) Birkin; married Janet Johnson, June 16, 1940; children: Jennifer Claire de Clermont, Amanda Jane, John Christian. *Education:* Attended private secondary school in England. *Politics:* Conservative. *Religion:* Church of England.

CAREER: Freelance writer, 1934-86. Worked for Philip Allan & Co. (publishers), 1933-35; advertising copywriter for Bernard & Co., 1936-38. *Military service:* British Army, Eighth Sherwood Foresters, 1940-46; became captain.

MEMBER: Carlton Club.

AWARDS, HONORS: Second prize from *Argosy,* 1968, for "Fairy Dust."

WRITINGS:

STORY COLLECTIONS

Devil's Spawn, Philip Allan (London), 1934.
The Kiss of Death (includes stories first published singly under pseudonym Charles Lloyd), Tandem (London), 1964, Award Books (New York City), 1969.

The Smell of Evil, Tandem, 1965, Award Books, 1969.
My Name Is Death and Other New Tales of Horror, Panther (London), 1966, Award Books, 1970.
Where Terror Stalked and Other Horror Stories, Tandem, 1966.
Dark Menace, Tandem, 1968.
So Pale, So Cold, So Fair, Tandem, 1970.
Spawn of Satan, Award Books, 1970.

EDITOR

The Tandem Book of Ghost Stories, Tandem, 1965.
The Tandem Book of Humor Stories, Tandem, 1965.

ANONYMOUS EDITOR

Creeps, W. H. Allan (London), 1932.
Shivers, W. H. Allan, 1932.
Shudders, W. H. Allan, 1932.
Horrors, W. H. Allan, 1933.
Nightmares, W. H. Allan, 1933.
Quakes, W. H. Allan, 1933.
Terrors, W. H. Allan, 1933.
Monsters, W. H. Allan, 1934.
Panics, W. H. Allan, 1934.
Powers of Darkness, W. H. Allan, 1934.
Thrills, W. H. Allan, 1935.
Tales of Fear, W. H. Allan, 1935.
The Creeps Omnibus, W. H. Allan, 1935.
Tales of Dread, W. H. Allan, 1936.
Tales of Death, W. H. Allan, 1936.

OTHER

I'll Have My Gun (animal story), privately printed, 1940.

Also author of radio scripts. Work represented in anthologies, including *Quiver of Horror,* edited by Dennis Wheatley, Arrow, 1964; and *John Creasey's Mystery Bedside Book,* edited by Herbert Harris, Hodder & Stoughton, 1971. Contributor of stories to magazines, including *Tatler, Sketch,* and *Bystander.*

SIDELIGHTS: According to Chris Morgan in the *St. James Guide to Horror, Ghost and Gothic Writers,* Charles Birkin wrote over one hundred short stories in a career lasting from the 1930s until the late 1970s. "Birkin," Morgan explained, "concentrated on non-supernatural horror. His tales feature grotesque means of death, murderous madmen, torture, cannibalism, sex with lepers, embalmed corpses kept by people who love them, and similar accounts of nastiness. It should not be supposed that his stories are mere catalogues of atrocity; in fact they are mostly well-developed accounts of character interaction against a wide variety of atmospheric backgrounds. The *grand guignol* elements are frequently only to be found in the last page or two."

Sir Charles Birkin (5th Baronet Birkin) once told *CA:* "With the post-war closedown of most magazines in England, I specialized in short stories of a *grand guignol* character."

BIOGRAPHICAL/CRITICAL SOURCES:

BOOKS

St. James Guide to Horror, Ghost and Gothic Writers, St. James Press (Detroit), 1998.*

* * *

BLACK, Campbell 1944-
(Thomas Altman, Campbell Armstrong; Jeffrey Campbell, a joint pseudonym)

PERSONAL: Born February, 1944, in Glasgow, Scotland; son of Thomas and Mary (Campbell) Black; married Eileen Altman, December, 1964; children: Iain, Stephen, Keiron. *Education:* University of Sussex, B.A. (with honors), 1967. *Politics:* None. *Religion:* None.

ADDRESSES: Home and office—411 East Cornell, Tempe, AZ 85283. *Agent*—International Creative Management, 40 West 57th St., New York, NY 10019.

CAREER: Granada Publishing, London, England, editor, 1967-71; State University of New York at Oswego, instructor in creative writing, 1971-75; Arizona State University, Tempe, instructor in creative writing, 1975-78; full-time writer, 1978—.

AWARDS, HONORS: Scottish Arts Council Award, 1970, for *The Punctual Rape.*

WRITINGS:

Assassins and Victims, Macmillan (London), 1969, Harper's Magazine Press (New York City), 1970.
The Punctual Rape, Macmillan, 1970, Lippincott (Philadelphia), 1971.

Death's Head, Lippincott, 1972.

And They Used to Star in Movies (one-act play), first produced in London at Soho Poly Theatre, October, 1975.

The Asterisk Destiny, Morrow (New York City), 1978.

Brainfire, Morrow, 1979.

Dressed to Kill (novelization of screenplay), Bantam, 1980.

(With Jeffrey Caine under joint pseudonym Jeffrey Campbell) *The Homing,* Putnam, 1980.

Radiers of the Lost Ark (novelization of screenplay), Ballantine (New York City), 1981.

Mr. Apology, Ballantine, 1984.

Letters from the Dead, Villard (New York City), 1985.

The Wanting, McGraw-Hill (New York City), 1986.

The Piper, Pocket Books (New York City), 1986.

UNDER PSEUDONYM THOMAS ALTMAN

Kiss Daddy Goodbye, Bantam, 1980.

The True Bride, Bantam, 1982.

Black Christmas, Bantam, 1983.

Dark Places, Bantam, 1984.

The Intruder, Bantam, 1985.

UNDER PSEUDONYM CAMPBELL ARMSTRONG

Jig, Hodder & Stoughton (London), 1987.

Mazurka, Hodder & Stoughton, 1988.

Mambo, Hodder & Stoughton, 1990.

Agents of Darkness, Hodder & Stoughton, 1991.

Concert of Ghosts, Hodder & Stoughton, 1992.

Jigsaw, Hodder & Stoughton, 1994.

Heat, Doubleday (London), 1996.

Silencer, Doubleday, 1997.

SIDELIGHTS: Campbell Black, according to Don D'Ammassa in the *St. James Guide to Horror, Ghost and Gothic Writers,* "moved to horror fiction after beginning his career as a writer of spy thrillers, an unusual progression in some ways. It was not as great a leap as it might seem, however, because some of Black's early novels blended international espionage with the fantastic, anticipating to some extent the trend that would later develop in the popular television series *The X-Files.*"

Black's two most successful horror novels, D'Ammassa believes, are *Letters from the Dead* and *The Wanting. Letters from the Dead* concerns two single mothers who take their children to a long-abandoned country house for a quiet vacation. When one woman begins hearing strange voices in the night, and one of the children discovers a ouija board, the group believe that the house is haunted. The story, D'Ammassa explains, is "effective because Black takes the time to flesh in the small plot details that lead inevitably to the climactic scene."

In *The Wanting* a couple's young son is seemingly taken over by elderly neighbors who have a strange power over him. D'Ammassa praises the mother's character in particular: "Louise Untermeyer is an interesting, credible character and her systematic unravelling of the mystery and ultimate reaction to her discovery are convincing enough to hold the reader's interest."

Black once told *CA:* "I write in the hope of entertaining, to tell a story. If there are other merits—literary, stylistic, etc.—they seem like accidental by-products of the entertainment. In a review of my last book, *Brainfire,* the *New York Times* critic mentioned that I had a 'gift for understanding character.' It's good when reviewers or readers notice such stylistic subtleties as might exist, but they do seem to me secondary to the unfolding of the story, which is my main interest. I don't deliberately set out to write stylishly. Like most other writers, I rely heavily on that magic we commonly call intuition; I let that faculty do the writing for me. I don't understand it, and I don't think I even want to, but it does exist. And without it, writing would be impossible."

BIOGRAPHICAL/CRITICAL SOURCES:

BOOKS

St. James Guide to Horror, Ghost and Gothic Writers, St. James Press (Detroit), 1998.

* * *

BLAKENEY, Jay D.
See CHESTER, Deborah

* * *

BLECHMAN, Burt 1927-

PERSONAL: Born March 2, 1927, in Brooklyn, NY. *Education:* University of Vermont, Burlington, B.A. 1949; Columbia University, M.S.

ADDRESSES: Home—200 Waverly Pl., New York, NY 10014.

CAREER: Fulltime professional writer. Former instructor, New York University Medical School, New York City.

MEMBER: Phi Beta Kappa.

AWARDS, HONORS: Merrill Foundation Award, 1965.

WRITINGS:

How Much?, Obolensky (New York City), 1961.
The War of Camp Omongo, Random House (New York City), 1963.
Stations, Random House, 1963.
The Octopus Papers, Horizon (New York City), 1965.
Maybe, Prentice-Hall (Englewood Cliffs, NJ), 1967.

ADAPTATIONS: How Much? was adapted for the stage by Lillian Hellman and renamed *My Mother, My Father and Me,* Random House, 1963.

SIDELIGHTS: Burt Blechman has produced a collection of comic novels that mock the absurdities of everyday life. Whether set in summer camp, the subway system or senior citizen dens, Blechman's books embody many universal themes: search for meaning, coming of age and dealing with life's misery and pain. However heavy—and at times grotesque—the subject matter, Blechman keeps the tone light by using clever word play and sprightly dialog.

The War of Camp Omongo depicts the experiences of young Randy Levine at summer camp. Far from a play house, Camp Omongo proves to be a microcosm of the adult world: "a cesspool of complicated intrigues, teen-age crudities, management hypocrisies, fascistic indoctrination, philistine insensitivities, petty cruelties, and the worst form of snobbery," according to *Commonweal* reviewer W. J. Smith.

Though the book relies on well-worn literary tropes—the angst-ridden teen and the morally decrepit value system, for instance—it nonetheless transcends the restrictions of its genre. Blechman enlivens the story with "little firecrackers of wit and malice and grace notes of appalled social observation," according to Smith, and has "the air of a man who knows what he is doing and his wry jumble of ginger and wormwood has a distinctive tang."

Stations is an apocalyptic novel that parallels the life of a nameless homosexual protagonist—identified simply as 901—with the human condition. As his own life closes in on him, the Bomb is dropped on the world. Blechman draws heavily on Catholic symbols, such as Mother Superior, the Madonna, and of course, the Stations (of the Cross) themselves. He describe the torture-wracked existence of a community of faithful "who make their restless, unsatisfied way from subway station to subway station," according to David Boroff in the *New York Times Book Review.*

Some reviewers have complained that the allegory in *Stations* is overwrought and the plot difficult to follow. Blechman's style, however, offers partial redemption for the book's flaws. Blechman writes "so astonishingly well," said F. C. Crews in the *New York Review of Books,* who considered the book "as powerful as it is grotesque." A reviewer in *Time* echoed this praise: "Every step of the book is dense in meanings and associations, helped on by rhymes, incantatory metrical effects, and puns that ring with a wild echolalia."

The Octopus Papers satirizes the art world through the sorry tale of Sarah Chickel. In her quest to secure funding for her projects, Chickel accumulates various articles, telegrams, and tape transcriptions, which are dutifully recorded in the novel. She also encounters the dubious doorkeepers of fame, including musical maestro Hambone Fireschulz and pornography writer Jack Krack, whom Blechman playfully skewers with his pen. In the *New York Times Book Review,* Arno Karlen called the novel "brilliant, uneven, exasperating in its loss of control."

In *Maybe,* 59-year-old Myra Russell tries desperately to escape boredom by signing up for numerous clubs and activities: chess lessons, museum courses, membership in birth control, antiwar and conservationist klatches, among others. Upon publication, the book met with mixed reviews. G. A. Woolf in *Book Week* called the tone "strained and petulant," while a critic for the *Times Literary Supplement* considered Myra, "rather touching . . . despite her silliness." Martin Levin wrote in the *New York Times Book Review,* "the novel is a well-sustained *tour de force,* whose boldly drawn caricatures and high speed allow for no lulls for the reader."

BIOGRAPHICAL/CRITICAL SOURCES:

BOOKS

Contemporary Novelists, sixth edition, St. James Press (Detroit), 1996, pp. 116-7.

Guttman, Allen, *The Jewish Writer in America,* Oxford University Press (New York City), 1971.

PERIODICALS

Book Week, April 2, 1967, p. 11.
Commonweal, September 20, 1963.
Library Journal, September 1, 1963.
New Leader, July 3, 1967.
New York Review of Books, December 3, 1964.
New York Times Book Review, November 29, 1964; November 7, 1965.
Observer, May 14, 1967.
Time, October 9, 1964.
Times Literary Supplement, May 18, 1967.*

* * *

BLESH, Rudi
See BLESH, Rudolph Pickett

* * *

BLESH, Rudolph Pickett 1899-1985
(Rudi Blesh)

PERSONAL: Born January 21, 1899, in Guthrie, OK; died of a stroke, August 25, 1985, in Gilmanton, NH; son of Abraham Lincoln (a surgeon) and Belle (Pickett) Blesh; married Editha Tuttle, February 22, 1925; married second wife, Barbara Lamont, July, 1938 (divorced); children: (first marriage) Hilary (Mrs. Peter W. Morton). *Education:* Attended Dartmouth College, 1917-20; University of California, Berkeley, A.B. (honors), 1924. *Avocational interests:* American architecture, all periods; collecting Americana, including country antiques; collecting American and other modern art.

CAREER: Industrial, furniture, and architectural designer, 1924-43; abstract artist, with one-man show of paintings, New York City, 1946; lecturer on Afro-American music and jazz at Queens College of the City University of New York, 1956-85, and New York University, New York City, 1957-85; writer on jazz and other subjects.

WRITINGS:

UNDER PSEUDONYM RUDI BLESH

This Is Jazz, San Francisco Museum, 1943.
Shining Trumpets: A History of Jazz, Knopf (New York City), 1946, revised edition, 1958.
(With Harriet Janis) *They All Played Ragtime: The True Story of an American Music,* Knopf, 1950, revised edition, Oak Publications (New York City), 1966, fourth edition, 1971, reprinted the edition published by Chilton (Philadelphia), Da Capo Press (New York City), 1979.
Modern Art, U.S.A.: Men, Rebellion, Conquest, 1900-1956, Knopf, 1956.
O Susanna, Grove (New York City), 1960.
Stuart Davis, Grove, 1960.
(With Janis) *De Kooning,* Grove, 1960.
(With Janis) *Collage: Personalities, Concepts, Techniques,* Chilton, 1962, revised edition, 1967.
Dimensions of Jazz, Queens College Press, 1964.
Keaton, Macmillan (New York City), 1966.
Combo U.S.A.: Eight Lives in Jazz, Chilton, 1971.
(Author of new preface) Sidney Bechet, *Treat it Gentle: An Autobiography,* Da Capo Press, 1978.

Also writer and narrator of radio programs, "This Is Jazz," WOR-Mutual Broadcasting Co., 1947, "Our Singing Land," WYNC, 1949, "Jazz Saga," WFDR, 1950, and "Dimensions of Jazz," WYNC, 1964. A Rudesh interview by Howard Brucker was made into a sound recording for use by the Voice of America.

SIDELIGHTS: Although Rudolph Pickett Blesh worked as an artist, designer, broadcaster, educator, concert promoter, and author, Blesh is perhaps best known for his expertise in jazz and Afro-American music. His work in the field included writing and narrating radio shows such as "This Is Jazz" and "Jazz Saga" and lecturing on the subject at Queens College of the City University of New York and New York University. As Rudi Blesh, he wrote several books on jazz, including *This Is Jazz, Shining Trumpets: A History of Jazz,* and *They All Played Ragtime: The True Story of an American Music,* written with Harriet Janis. He also wrote books on modern art, including *Modern Art, U.S.A.,* and a biography of comedian Buster Keaton.

Shining Trumpets "takes the reader, by means of narrative, well-constructed charts, and pictures, as well as samples of jazz scores, from the early days to modern times," described R. B. Gehmen in the *Saturday Review of Literature.* At the time it was originally published, critics generally agreed it was a valuable contribution to music literature. However, a common complaint with some reviewers was, as stated by Wilder Hobson in the *Nation,* that Blesh "declares, in effect, that anything outside the New Orleans style is not 'real jazz.'" Furthermore, Hobson faulted: "He will not rest with jazz as a musical language which may be used intensely and poetically; he must have it conquer all. And like most critics who are not content to illumine an art, but must also pound the drum for it, his style is sometimes deafening." Although "*Shining Trumpets* does not quite come up to the cosmic enthusiasm and assertions of its author," remarked *New York Times* contributor Frederic Ramsey, "Its organization is essentially sound. . . . [And] the work is fully equipped with scholarly impedimenta." "On the whole, he is accurate," remarked Gehmen, complementing: "[Blesh's] book is one that should stand as a rich source of material for historians for some time to come. There are also a warmth and a quality of admiration about the book which make it a pleasure to read." Similarly, Bucklin Moon lauded in *New Republic*: "*Shining Trumpets* is by far the best critical work on jazz which has thus far appeared, and if it is not the definitive one, it is at least a long step in the right direction. Moreover, it is written with charm, wit and spirit."

Perhaps an even more significant resource in music history is *They All Played Ragtime,* written by both Blesh and Harriet Janis. "This will be an important reference book for the enthusiast for a long time to come," exclaimed *San Francisco Chronicle* reviewer J. H. Jackson at the time of the book's original publication. In fact, the book has been revised and reprinted several times since it first appeared. Despite noting in the *New York Times* that "some passages are dull and others uneven in style," C. E. Smith echoed Jackson's belief and praised the book for it's "thorough exploration of the ragtime field. When commenting on *They All Played Ragtime* in the *Saturday Review of Literature,* Hobson stated the work was"lovingly"told and contains"a great deal of research and plentiful detail."

In addition to *They All Played Ragtime,* Blesh and Janis worked together on other books. One collaboration, *Collage: Personalities, Concepts, Techniques,* is "a highly informative and generally well written work. . . . That stands in many ways as a model of how to write about modern art," according to *New York Herald Tribune Books* critic B. S. Meyer. A *Booklist* review recognized most information in the book was from primary sources; and Meyer reports that the book covers a time period which includes "pre-World War I cubism to post-World War II abstract-expressionism and neo-dada or 'junk art.'" In a review of a revised edition, a *Choice* contributor highly recommended the book: "The definitive work on collage—its history, significance, and particularly it meaning in the corpus of the art of our time. [It has been] extensively expanded and revised. . . . The text is thoughtful, penetrating, informative, and provocative throughout and should proved to be stimulating to artists, teachers and students."

Blesh individually addressed the art world with *Modern Art, U.S.A.: Men, Rebellion, Conquest, 1900-1956.* This book received mixed reviews. The content of it's primary subject, modern art, was generally positively judged, however, the style and secondary statements were criticized by some reviewers. Alfred Frankenstein commented in the *New Republic*: "Its principal weakness is its frequent use of a burbling, archly colloquial style. . . . The book's principle virtue is its strong emphasis on the institutions of modern art in America." "The facts are here (together with some naive remarks on government and art)," stated *Library Journal* reviewer R. L. Enequist, "but the presentation is deplorable: sarcasms are mixed with slang, and serious writing is confused with ostentation and then peppered with flip remarks." J. T. Soby in the *New York Times* recognized that the book's "chief fault" is "its lack of measure," however the critic also stated: "About the art of our own century, his writing is hard hitting and quick."

BIOGRAPHICAL/CRITICAL SOURCES:

PERIODICALS

Chicago Sunday Tribune, October 28, 1956.
Choice, October, 1967.
Christian Science Monitor, July 26, 1962; June 2, 1966.
Library Journal, September 15, 1956.
Nation, December 28, 1946.
New Republic, November 4, 1946; October 22, 1956.
New York Herald Tribune Book Review, October 22, 1950; November 25, 1956.
New York Herald Tribune Books, February 4, 1962.
New York Review of Books, December 15, 1966.
New York Times, December 8, 1946; October 15, 1950; September 23, 1956.
New York Times Book Review, May 15, 1966.
San Francisco Chronicle, December 1, 1946; October 19, 1950;

Saturday Review of Literature, December 7, 1946; November 25, 1950; September 15, 1956.
Weekly Book Review, December 22, 1946.

OBITUARIES:

PERIODICALS

Los Angeles Times, August 31, 1985.
New York Times, August 28, 1985.*

* * *

BLOCK, Eugene B. 1890-1988

PERSONAL: Born June 12, 1890, in Oakland, CA; died February 24, 1988; son of Joseph (a merchant) and Juliette (Haas) Block; married Ruth Weinshenk, March 27, 1915; children: George S., Edwin J., Charles W. *Education:* Attended public schools in San Francisco, CA.

ADDRESSES: Home—2533 Turk St., San Francisco, CA. *Office*— 870 Market St., San Francisco, CA 94102. *Agent*—Bertha Klausner, 71 Park Ave., New York, NY 10016.

CAREER: Writer and editor on San Francisco daily newspapers for thirty-five years; Jewish Community Relations Council, San Francisco, CA, executive director, 1939-65, and editor of *Jewish Community Bulletin.*

MEMBER: Mystery Writers of America, California Writers Club, Public Relations Round Table, Press and Union League Club.

WRITINGS:

The Wizard of Berkeley (crime, nonfiction), Coward, 1958, published in England as *The Chemist of Crime,* Cassell (London), 1958.
Great Train Robberies of the West (crime, nonfiction), Coward, 1959.
Great Stagecoach Robbers of the West, Doubleday (New York City), 1961.
And May God Have Mercy: The Case against Capital Punishment, S. F. Fearson, 1962.
The Vindicators (crime, nonfiction), Doubleday, 1963.
Fifteen Clues: True Stories of Great Crime Detection, Doubleday, 1965.
Above the Civil War, Howell-North Books (Burbank, CA), 1966.
Famous Detectives: True Stories of Great Crime Detection, Doubleday, 1967.
The Fabric of Guilt: True Stories of Criminals Caught in a Net of Circumstantial Evidence, Doubleday, 1968.
Fingerprinting: Magic Weapon against Crime, McKay (New York City), 1969.
The Immortal San Franciscans for Whom the Streets were Named, Chronicle Books (San Francisco), 1971.
Voiceprinting: How the Law Can Read the Voice of Crime, McKay, 1975.
Hypnosis: A New Tool in Crime Detection, McKay, 1976.
Lie Detectors: Their History and Use, McKay, 1977.
Science Versus Crime: The Evolution of the Police Lab, Cragmont (San Francisco), 1979.
When Men Play God: The Fallacy of Capital Punishment, Cragmont, 1983.

SIDELIGHTS: Journalist and author Eugene Block has written numerous books presenting crime, criminal figures, law enforcement professionals, and scientific procedures used in criminal investigations. His first book, *The Wizard of Berkeley,* profiles many of the difficult cases that Edward Oscar Heinrich, a scientist and pioneer of many police laboratory techniques, helped to solve. "These stories are told delicately, with the actual crimes stated in brief, matter-of-fact terms. What emerges is a carefully detailed account of Heinrich's scientific method . . . Mr. Block's account of Oscar Heinrich is done with sympathy and a deep understanding of the interesting figure's contribution to police work," wrote *Christian Science Monitor* contributor J. N. Goodsell. In contrast, Anthony Boucher presented an unfavorable view of the work in the *New York Times*: "Heinrich . . . has been poorly served by his first biographer. . . . Mr. Block writes the sort of journalese even journalists no longer employ . . . and stands in ignorant awe of Science, which he considers a mystery not to be understood by laymen. He has attempted neither a portrait of Heinrich as a man nor an analysis of his place in the history of criminalistics. . . . All Block offers is inadequate, colorless sketches of some fourteen cases in which Heinrich was involved."

Boucher's negative review of Block's debut book did not stop Block from publishing more than fifteen books of similar nature. In fact five books and seven years after Boucher's unfavorable account of *The*

Wizard of Berkeley, Boucher more positively recognized Block's *Fifteen Clues: True Stories of Great Crime Detection*: "These essays, of worldwide range, stress the details of police detection rather than the nature of the crime and criminal; the attitude is one of almost naive wonder and the prose is Early Journalese, but the tellings are lively and there are some good unfamiliar crimes."

Great Train Robberies of the West, Block's second book, profiles some sensational train robberies of the American West, such as those by Jesse James. "Vivid but far from lurid, this book does much to dispel the fictional glamour surrounding this gallery of deperadoes," described a *Kirkus Reviews* critic. Although, as G. M. Gressley pointed out in *Library Journal,* "this volume is largely a rehash" of previous tellings, *San Francisco Chronicle* critic R. H. Dillon commented: "A few of the little known sketches here are most interesting and will be quite new to even the most well-read aficionado. . . . This is fine, new Western Americana, both the stories unearthed by Mr. Block and presented to the public for the first time and the better-known incidents which he treats without great detail but with great interest."

The Fabric of Guilt: True Stories of Criminals Caught in a Net of Circumstantial Evidence is, according to D. W. Harrison in *Library Journal,* "another of Eugene Block's fascinating crime books for the layman. . . . The book will provide suspense for the mystery fan and succinct accounts of the trails flavored with just enough dialogue, will attract the legal buff." Harrison notes that in the book "Block contends that [circumstantial evidence] is often more certain than direct evidence," despite what the public may believe.

BIOGRAPHICAL/CRITICAL SOURCES:

PERIODICALS

Christian Science Monitor, March 3, 1958.
Kirkus Reviews, March 1, 1959.
Library Journal, May 1, 1959; July, 1968.
New York Times, March 23, 1958; May 17, 1959.
New York Times Book Review, November 10, 1963; November 21, 1965; August 6, 1967.
San Francisco Chronicle, March 16, 1958; April 26, 1959.
Saturday Review of Literature, April 5, 1958; June 13, 1959; November 30, 1963; September 30, 1967, September 28, 1968.
Springfield Republican, June 7, 1959.*

BLUM, John Morton 1921-

PERSONAL: Born April 29, 1921, in New York, NY; son of Morton G. (a salesman) and Edna (LeVino) Blum; married Pamela Zink, June 28, 1944; children: Pamela P., Ann S., Thomas Tyler. *Education:* Harvard University, A.B., 1943, M.A., 1947, Ph.D., 1950. *Politics:* Democratic.

ADDRESSES: Home—34 Edgehill Rd., New Haven, CT. *Office*—Department of History, Yale University, New Haven, CT 06520.

CAREER: Massachusetts Institute of Technology, Cambridge, 1948-57, began as assistant professor, became associate professor; Yale University, New Haven, CT, professor of history, 1957—; Cambridge University, Pitt Professor of American History and Institutions, 1963-64; Oxford University, Harmsworth Professor, 1976-77. Member of Alumni council, Phillips Academy, 1957-60, and Harvard Corp., 1970-79. *Military service:* U.S. Naval Reserve, 1943-46; became lieutenant.

MEMBER: American Academy of Arts and Science, American Historical Association, Organization of American Historians, Massachusetts Historical Society, Connecticut Academy of Arts and Science.

AWARDS, HONORS: D.H.L., Trinity College, 1970; L.L.D., Colgate University, 1978, Harvard University, 1980.

WRITINGS:

Joe Tumulty and the Wilson Ear, Houghton (Boston), 1951.
The Republican Roosevelt, Harvard University Press (Cambridge, MA), 1954, second edition, 1962.
(With others) *Trends in Modern American Society,* edited by Clarence Morris, Greenwood (Westport, CT), 1962, reprinted 1986.
Woodrow Wilson and the Politics of Morality, Little, Brown (Boston), 1956.
From the Morgenthau Diaries, Houghton, Volume I: *Years of Crisis,* 1959, Volume II: *Years of Urgency,* 1965, Volume III: *Years of War, 1941-1945,* 1967.
(With others) *The National Experience: A History of the United States,* Harcourt, 1963, reprinted 1981, 1985, 1989, published as *The American Experience,* Hart-Davis, 1963.
The Promise of America (essays), Houghton, 1966.
Roosevelt and Morgenthau, Houghton, 1970.

V Was for Victory: Politics and American Culture during World War II, Harcourt (New York City), 1976.

The Burden of American Equality: An Inaugural Lecture Delivered before the University of Oxford on 26 April, 1977, Clarendon (Oxford, England), 1978.

The Progressive Presidents: Roosevelt, Wilson, Roosevelt, Johnson, Norton (New York City), 1980.

Years of Discord: American Politics and Society, 1961-1974, Norton, 1991.

Liberty, Justice, Order: Essays on Past Politics, Norton, 1993.

EDITOR, EXCEPTED AS NOTED

(Associate editor) *Letters of Theodore Roosevelt,* Harvard University Press, eight volumes, 1951-54.

(And selector) *Yesterday's Children: An Anthology Compiled from Our Young Folks Pages, 1865-1873,* Houghton, 1959.

(Co-editor) *Trends in Modern American Society,* University of Pennsylvania Press (Philadelphia, PA), 1962.

The Price of Vision, Houghton, 1973.

Henry F. Bedford and Trevor Colbourn, *The Americans: A Brief History,* Harcourt, 1980.

Walter Lippmann, *Public Philosopher: Selected Letters of Walter Lippmann,* Ticknor & Fields (New York City), 1985.

SIDELIGHTS: John Morton Blum's debut book, *Joe Tumulty and the Wilson Era,* was published in 1951 and profiles Joe Tumulty, President Woodrow Wilson's political mentor and White House Secretary. "This is both a learned and an interesting book," remarked H. S. Commager in the *New York Times*; which according to W. V. Shannon in the *New Republic,* is "written with grace and spirit and with genuine insight into the workings of practical politics." Described as sympathetically written in many reviews, this "single volume . . . is in fact three books," wrote *New York Herald Tribune Book Review* critic G. W. Johnson: "First, a factual account of a remarkable and attractive personality; second a study in loyalty, and, third a handbook of practical politics." "The tendency to make a hero of his subject works against Professor Blum's otherwise impressive marshaling of evidence in answer to the charges which . . . made Tumulty so controversial a figure," noted E. B. Orr in the *Christian Science Monitor*. However, Orr concluded: "The book is undoubtedly a valuable addition to the literature of American History."

Other books Blum edited and authored focused on different presidents and elements of American history. "Apart from its central emphasis on Roosevelt the conservative, *The Republican Roosevelt* offers a fresh, well-written biographical treatment of one of the most arresting figures of modern American life," lauded E. F. Goldman in the *New York Times.* H. F. Pringle commented in the *New York Herald Tribune Book Review*: "Mr. Blum is in a unique position to know whereof he writes. He was a principal aid to Elting E. Morison in compiling the vast eight-volume correspondence of Theodore Roosevelt. He wrote many of the footnotes and appendices for that excellent series. He has probably read as many T. R. letters as any man alive." In *Saturday Review,* J. D. Hicks commended *The Republican Roosevelt* for not "repeating the facts we already know so well," and explained that "the book is an interpretation, not another biography. And it is convincing. Most readers will agree with the author that when Roosevelt is finally weighed he will not be found wanting."

From the Morgenthau Diaries, published in three separate volumes, looks at the Franklin Delano Roosevelt years from the perspective of then Secretary of the Treasury Henry Morgenthau. Volume I: *Years of Crisis,* was reviewed by *New York Times* critic Frank Freidel, who wrote: "It is written in the third person [and]. . . . It quotes from the diaries lengthily and with scrupulous accuracy. Yet it differs from what Blum might have written entirely independently in that it seems to present Morgenthau's hindsights and conclusions rather than the writer's. . . . If the result is something less than biography it is also more than autobiography, since the detailed quotations create for the reader vivid images of Secretary Morgenthau, his contemporaries and their policies." "Yet," J. M Burns similarly commented in the *New York Herald Tribune Book Review,* "as biography it does not have the critical judgments that a dispassionate outsider would bring to bear on his subject." According to Jonathan Daniels in the *Saturday Review,* "this book's chief weakness was in [presenting] the personal life, personality, and struggles" of Morgenthau. Dexter Perkins criticized in the *Yale Review* that "Professor Blum's literary gifts shine to less advantage here than in some of his earlier works." However, Perkins concluded that "the net result is admirable and there are exciting moments and bits of whimsey in this complicated story." Daniels went even further in his 1959 review when he stated: "John Blum has produced probably the best-documented story of the financial center of the domestic and foreign policies of Roosevelt's New Deal."

BIOGRAPHICAL/CRITICAL SOURCES:

PERIODICALS

American History Review, October, 1954.
American Political Science Review, December 1951.
Chicago Sunday Tribune, May 16, 1954; November 11, 1956; September 20, 1959.
Choice, July, 1966; October, 1970.
Christian Science Monitor, July 31, 1951; June 30, 1954; September 24, 1959; November 19, 1959.
Commonweal, August 17, 1951.
Horn Book, February, 1960.
New Republic, September 3, 1951.
New Yorker, August 4, 1951.
New York Herald Tribune Book Review, July 15, 1951; April 11, 1954; October 18, 1959.
New York Times, August 4, 1951, December 30, 1956; April 11, 1954; September 13, 1959; September 20, 1959.
New York Times Book Review, February 6, 1966; May 31, 1970.
Political Science Quarterly, December, 1951.
San Francisco Chronicle, July 24, 1959.
Saturday Review, May 1, 1954; December 22, 1956; September 19, 1959; January 15, 1966.
Saturday Review of Literature, July 14, 1951.
Springfield Republican, August 12, 1951; December 23, 1956.
Yale Review, summer, 1954; December, 1959; June, 1966.*

* * *

BOARDMAN, Fon Wyman, Jr. 1911-

PERSONAL: Born July 28, 1911, in Bolivar, NY; son of Fon Wyman and Lena (Sternberg) Boardman; married Dorothea Reber, March 11, 1935; children: Constance Mary. *Education:* Columbia University, A.B., 1934.

ADDRESSES: Home—16 West 16th St., New York, NY 10011.

CAREER: Columbia University Press, New York City, copy writer, 1934-42, advertising and publicity manager, 1942-45, sales promotion manager, 1945-51; Oxford University Press, New York City, advertising and publicity manager, 1951-68, secretary, 1960-68, vice-president and marketing director, 1968-72. Lecturer in English, Columbia University, 1954-59. *Military service:* U.S. Army, 1943-46; became master sergeant. U.S. Army Reserve, captain in Military Intelligence.

MEMBER: Publishers' Adclub (secretary, 1952-54; president, 1954-56), Phi Beta Kappa.

WRITINGS:

JUVENILE NONFICTION; PUBLISHED BY WALCK (NEW YORK CITY), EXCEPT AS NOTED

Castles, Oxford University Press (New York City), 1957.
Roads, 1958.
Canals, 1959.
Tunnels, 1960.
History and Historians, 1965.
Economics: Ideas and Men, 1966.
The Thirties: America and the Great Depression, 1967.
America and the Jazz Age: A History of the 1920's, 1968.
America and the Progressive Era: 1900-1917, 1970.
America and the Gilded Age: 1876-1900, 1972.
America and the Virginia Dynasty: 1800-1825, 1974.
America and the Jacksonian Era: 1825-1850, 1975.
Around the World in 1776, 1975.
America and the Civil War Era: 1850-1875, 1976.
Tyrants and Conquerors, 1977.
Against the Iroquois: The Sullivan Campaign of 1779 in New York State, 1978.
America and the Robber Barons: 1865-1913, 1979.

Contributor to *What Happens in Book Publishing,* edited by Chandler Grannis; *Sales on a Shoestring; Encyclopedia of American Facts and Dates,* 1987; *Facts and Dates of American Sports,* 1988; *Encyclopedia of World Facts and Dates,* 1993; *Young Readers Companion,* 1993; and *Volume Library,* 1993. Editor of *Columbia University in Pictures;* general editor of "Careers for Tomorrow," a series of twenty-four guidance books for young people, published by Walck; chair of editorial advisory board, *Columbia University Forum,* 1958-60.

SIDELIGHTS: Fon Wyman Boardman, Jr. is the author of numerous American history books for juveniles. In *History and Historians,* one of his earliest publications, Boardman defines history and explores various approaches historians have taken to document it. *Commonweal* critic E. M. Graves called the book "a unique and absorbing view of history—as seen by the changing vogues in history writing." Following this introduction to the subject of history, Boardman's *Economics: Ideas and Men* was published, educating his juvenile readers about the influential theories and individuals involved with developing the science of economics. "Boardman's account treats explosive controversies, like Keynesianism, with temperance and detachment. Detailed examples help to clarify the differing interpretation," wrote W. J. Jacobs in the *New York Times Book Review.* Madalynne Schoenfeld warned in *Library Journal* that the broad scope of the material is "somewhat bewilder[ing]" as written and the material covered is better presented in a previous adult publication. However, *Best Sellers* contributor W. M. Gallop contended that the book is "an excellent starting point" to learn "the fundamentals of economics," exclaiming: "At last, here is a book about economics that presumes the reader is a complete novice in the field."

Like *Economics: Ideas and Men,* many of Boardman's books present historical accounts of specific subjects. However, in about half of his publications, Boardman features entire historical time periods in America. For example, in *The Thirties: America and the Great Depression,* "[Boardman] takes a large, calm view of the whole decade, complete with movies, song hits, etc.," reported David Cort in the *New York Times Book Review. Library Journal* critic M. S. Bart positively concluded: "[*The Thirties*] is especially noteworthy because of the lucidity of the exposition." However, Cort complained, "[Boardman] is objective and 'fair.' But he has excluded all passion, and so the events are unrecognizable."

In some reviews for *America and the Jazz Age: A History of the 1920's,* Boardman's writing, although recognized as informative, was again faulted for lacking depth. Similar to Cort's remarks about *The Thirities,* critic Robert Cormier stated in the *New York Times Book Review*: "A conscientious craftsman, Boardman . . . fails to evoke the scents and sounds, the frenzies and fantasies, the Prohibition hiccups of that vivacious era. Too often, these pages read like a telephone book. . . . The author fails to dramatize or characterize. When he bends occasionally . . . the book leaps to life. Most of the time, however, he merely summarizes in stuffy, no-nonsense prose." In *America and the Progressive Era: 1900-1917,* "Mr. Boardman offers a wide-angle view of an era. . . . [However,] the sheer quantity of material and the somewhat encyclopedic presentation do not always make for exciting or even meaningful reading," wrote *New York Times Book Review* contributor N. K. Burger. "The book covers not only politics but manifold aspects of personal, community and national life," described Burger, who also remarked on the book's "carefully researched detailed prose arranged in orderly, topical chapters. E. M. Porter recommended the book in *Library Journal,* calling it an "enthusiastic, readable account" of the early-1900s.

Boardman once told *CA:* "I . . . find [American history] a fascinating subject. On the basis of my experience, though, I have a feeling that it is not being taught as much in the schools as it once was. I regret this because I don't see how anyone can understand present-day America and its problems unless he or she knows something about our unique history."

BIOGRAPHICAL/CRITICAL SOURCES:

PERIODICALS

Best Sellers, January 1, 1967.
Christian Century, December 10, 1968.
Commonweal, May 28, 1965.
Horn Book, February, 1967.
Library Journal, June 15, 1965; December 15, 1966; February, 15, 1968; February 15, 1969; September, 1970.
New York Times Book Review, November 20, 1966; March 24, 1968; February 2, 1969, August 9, 1970.
Young Readers Review, February, 1969.*

* * *

BOARDMAN, John 1927-

PERSONAL: Born August 20, 1927, in Ilford, England; son of Frederick Archibald and Clara (Wells) Boardman; married Sheila Joan Lyndon Stanford, October 26, 1952; children: Julia, Mark. *Education:* Magdalene College, Cambridge, B.A., 1948, M.A., 1951.

ADDRESSES: Home—11 Park St., Woodstock, Oxon., England.

CAREER: British School at Athens, Athens, Greece, assistant director, 1952-55; Oxford University, Oxford, England, assistant keeper at Ashmolean Museum, 1955-59, reader in Classical Archaeology, 1959-78, Lincoln Professor of Classical Archaeology and Art, 1978-94; University of Aberdeen, Geddes-Harrower Professor, 1974. Merton College, fellow, 1963-78; British Academy, fellow, 1969—; Lincoln College, fellow, 1978—. Conducted excavations at Chios, 1953-55, and Tocra, Libya, 1964-65. *Military service:* British Army, Intelligence Corps, 1950-52; became second lieutenant.

MEMBER: Society of Antiquaries (fellow), British Academy (fellow), Hellenic Society, Libya Exploration Society.

WRITINGS:

(Translator from Greek) Spyridon N. Marinatos, *Crete and Mycenae,* Thames & Hudson, 1960.

The Cretan Collection in Oxford: The Dictaean Cave and Iron Age Crete, Clarendon Press (Oxford, England), 1961.

Island Gems: A Study of Greek Seals in the Geometric and Early Archaic Periods, Society for the Promotion of Hellenic Studies, 1963.

(With Leonard Robert Palmer) *On the Knossos Tablets,* Clarendon Press, 1963.

Greek Art, Praeger (New York City), 1964, revised edition, 1973, Thames & Hudson (New York City), 1980, fourth revised and expanded edition, 1996.

The Greeks Overseas: The Archaeology of Their Early Colonies and Trade, Penguin (Harmondsworth), 1964, second edition, 1973, new and enlarged edition published as *The Greeks Overseas: Their Early Colonies and Trade,* Thames & Hudson (New York City), 1980, fourth revised and expanded edition, 1999.

(With Jose Doerig, Werner Fuchs, and Max Hirmer) *Die griechische Kunst,* Hirmer Verlag, 1966, translation published as *Greek Art and Architecture,* Abrams (New York City), 1967, published in England as *The Art and Architecture of Ancient Greece,* Thames & Hudson (London), 1967.

(With John Hayes) *Excavations at Tocra, 1963-1965,* Thames & Hudson, Volume I: *The Archaic Deposits,* 1966, Volume II: *Archaic Deposits II and Later Deposits,* 1973.

Excavations in Chios, 1952-1955: Greek Emporio, Thames & Hudson, 1967.

Pre-Classical: From Crete to Archaic Greece, Penguin, 1967.

Archaic Greek Gems: Schools and Artists in the Sixth and Early Fifth Centuries B.C., Northwestern University Press (Evanston, IL), 1968.

Engraved Gems: The Ionides Collection, photographs by Robert L. Wilkins, Northwestern University Press, 1968.

Greek Painted Vases: Catalogue of an Exhibition in the Mappin Art Gallery, Mappin Art Gallery (Sheffield), 1968.

Greek Gems and Finger Rings: Early Bronze Age to Late Classical, photographs by Wilkins, Abrams, 1970.

(With Donna C. Kurtz) *Greek Burial Customs,* Cornell University Press (Ithaca, NY), 1971.

Athenian Black Figure Vases, Oxford University Press (New York City), 1974, published in England as *Athenian Black Figure Vases: A Handbook,* Thames & Hudson (London), 1974, Thames & Hudson (New York City), 1988.

(With Eugenio La Rocca) *Eros in Greece,* photographs by Antonia Mulas, originally published in 1975, Erotic Art Book Society (New York City), 1978, Italian translation published as *Eros in Grecia,* A. Mondadori (Milan), 1975.

Intaglios and Rings: Greek, Etruscan, and Eastern, from a Private Collection, Thames & Hudson (London), 1975.

Oxford, Ashmolean Museum, Oxford University Press, 1975.

Athenian Red Figure Vases: The Archaic Period, a Handbook, Thames & Hudson (London), 1975, Oxford University Press (New York City), 1979.

(With Ashmolean Museum) *Corpus vasorum antiquorum: Great Britain, Oxford—Ashmolean,* Oxford University Press (New York City), 1975.

(With Diana Scarisbrick) *The Ralph Harari Collection of Finger Rings,* Thames & Hudson (London), 1977.

(With Marie-Louise Vollenweider) *Catalogue of the Engraved Gems and Finger Rings: Ashmolean Museum, Oxford,* Volume I: *Greek and Etruscan,* Oxford University Press (New York City), 1978.

Greek Sculpture: The Archaic Period, a Handbook, Oxford University Press (New York City), 1978, revised edition, Thames & Hudson (New York City), 1988.

(With Martin Robertson) *Corpus vasorum antiquorum: Great Britain, Northampton—Castle Ashby,* Oxford University Press (Oxford, England), 1979.

(With Miriam Astruc and Jorge H. Hernandez) *Escarabeos de piedra procedentes de Ibiza,* Ministerio e Cultura (Madrid), 1984.

Greek Sculpture: The Classical Period, a Handbook, Thames & Hudson (New York City), 1985.

The Parthenon and Its Sculptures, photographs by David Finn, University of Texas Press (Austin), 1985.

Athenian Red Figure Vases: The Classic Period, a Handbook (continuation of *Athenian Red Figure Vases: The Archaic Period, a Handbook*), Thames & Hudson, 1989.

The Diffusion of Classical Art in Antiquity, Princeton University Press (Princeton, NJ), 1994.

Greek Sculpture: The Late Classical Period and Sculpture in Colonies and Overseas, Thames & Hudson, 1994.

The Great God Pan: The Survival of an Image: Thames & Hudson, 1998.

Also author of *Excavations in Chios, 1952-1955.* Contributor to scholarly journals and to *Lefkandi I, the Iron Age,* edited by M. R. Popham and L. H. Sackett, Thames & Hudson, 1979. Featured art expert on *Art of the Western World: Program I, The Classical Ideal,* produced and directed by Geoffrey Dunlop and Bayley Silleck for New York City television station WNET, published by Intellimation (Santa Barbara, CA), 1989. Work has been published outside the U.S. and England.

EDITOR

Thomas James Dunbabin, *The Greeks and Their Eastern Neighbours: Studies in the Relations between Greece and the Countries of the Near East in the Eighth and Seventh Centuries B. C.*, Society for the Promotion of Hellenic Studies, 1957, reprinted, Greenwood Press (Westport, CT), 1979.

(With M. A. Brown and T. G. E. Powell) *The European Community in Later Prehistory: Studies in Honour of C. F. C. Hawkes,* Rowman & Littlefield (Totowa, NJ), 1971.

(With I. E. S. Edwards) *The Cambridge Ancient History: Plates to Volume 3: The Middle East, the Greek World, and the Balkans to the Sixth Century B.C.,* Cambridge University Press (New York City), 1977.

(With C. E. Vaphopoulou-Richardson) *Chios: A Conference at the Homereion in Chios, 1984,* Oxford University Press (New York City), 1986.

(With Jasper Griffin and Oswyn Murray) *The Oxford History of the Classical World,* Oxford University Press, 1986, published as two paperback volumes, 1988.

(With Griffin and Murray) *The Oxford History of Greece and the Hellenistic World,* Oxford University Press, 1991.

(Editor with Griffin and Murray) *The Oxford History of the Roman World,* Oxford University Press, 1991.

The Oxford History of Classical Art, Oxford University Press, 1993.

Editor of *Journal of Hellenic Studies,* 1958-65; co-editor of *Oxford Journal of Archaeology,* 1982 ; and co-editor of *Oxford Monographs in Classical Archaeology.*

SIDELIGHTS: John Boardman is the author or editor of numerous works dealing with classical and archaic Greek art. Reviews for Boardman's work have commonly given high praise for the books' illustrations and positively recognized Boardman's succinct, effective prose. A *Times Literary Supplement* offered the following praise for *Greek Art*: "The text is skillfully interwoven with 251 excellent illustrations. . . . The pace is necessarily brisk, but the author has taken great trouble to avoid the hackneyed approach. Even when he is speaking of well-known statues, temples and vases, his commentary is packed with fresh observation." Of the same book, *Library Journal*'s F. D. Lazenby wrote: "Though compact, [it] is replete with information and discriminating comment, and sometimes subtle observations. It is lively, knowledgeable history. . . . The excellent photographs are closely integrated with a text which is never marred by deviations into cloudy abstractions."

The illustrations in *Engraved Gems: The Ionides Collection,* according to and *Economist* critic, are also "ample reason for anyone to be drawn to the book." However, the critic faults Boardman's inability to reach an amateur audience: "This unusual book attempts, presumably, to attract the attention of people who are not collectors. . . . Lovely as it is, and fascinating as are the glimpses it gives of the beauties of this specialist's world the book is not altogether successful as a work of popularization."

Boardman's *Archaic Greek Gems: Schools and Artists in the Sixth and Early Fifth Centuries B.C.*, which Paul von Khrum described in *Library Journal* as a "scholarly work, the result of years of painstaking research," was commended by the *Times Literary Supplement* not only for being "exceptionally well illustrated," but also for "map[ping] out the work of local schools and studios with a sure touch, drawing on a wide range of comparative material (especially coins), and adding several new attributions to the work of the few known and named engravers." The *Times Literary Supplement* contributor wrote: "Far from being designed for the general reader, [*Archaic Greek Gems*] demands the utmost concentration of the professional archaeologist. Much of the material is hitherto unpublished or inaccessible. . . . Many of the ideas and hypotheses are equally new, and will need to be weighed carefully."

Again recognizing Boardman's expertise, another *Times Literary Supplement* review called *Greek Gems and Finger Rings: Early Bronze Age to Late Classical* "magnificent work . . . scholarly, readable, and beautifully produced." And in *Athenian Black Figure Vases,* "Boardman demonstrates a broad and penetrating grasp of Greek art and archaeology," stated a *Times Literary Supplement* review. An *Economist* contributor explained that "Boardman's achievement [in *Athenian Black Figure Vases*] is to bring present knowledge, including his own contributions, into the form of a handbook . . . for connoisseurs and students," further remarking: "It is admirably done . . . for all readers. . . . Naturally it is not easy or fluent reading—no handbook of this kind could be—but all students will find it useful for their work, and all connoisseurs for skimming and reference." The reviewer for the *Times Literary Supplement* recognized the work as "comprehensive and concise yet never offers less than adequate discussion in crisp, lucid prose," and concluded that "the supreme merit of this book lies in the illustrations. . . . Integrated closely with the text, they offer an admirably representative selection illustrative of chronology, style, shapes, scenes, and decorations."

BIOGRAPHICAL/CRITICAL SOURCES:

PERIODICALS

Choice, May, 1972.
Classical World, April, 1965; September, 1979.
Economist, April 27, 1968; July 27, 1974.
Library Journal, February 15, 1965; October 1, 1968; October 15, 1974.
New Statesman, February 19, 1965.
Times Literary Supplement, January 7, 1965; August 22, 1968; March 12, 1971; August 23, 1974.

* * *

BOATRIGHT, Mody Coggin 1896-1970

PERSONAL: Born October 16, 1896, in Colorado City, TX; died August 20, 1970, in Abilene, TX; son of Eldon (a ranchman) and Frances Ann (McAulay) Boatright; married Elizabeth Reck, 1925; married second wife, Elizabeth E. Keefer (an artist), September 12, 1931; children: (first marriage) Frances (Mrs. W. E. Bridges); (second marriage) Mody K. *Education:* West Texas State College (now University), B.A., 1922; University of Texas, M.A., 1923, Ph.D., 1932. *Politics:* Democrat.

CAREER: University of Texas at Austin, began as instructor, 1926, professor of English, 1950-63, chair of department, 1952-61. *Military service:* U.S. Army, 1918-19.

MEMBER: American Folklore Society (fellow; vice-president, 1962), Texas Folklore Society, Texas Institute of Letters, Writers Guild.

WRITINGS:

Tall Tales from Texas, Southwest Press, 1934, published as *Tall Tales from Texas Cow Camps,* Southern Methodist University Press (Dallas), 1982.
(Associated editor, with J. Frank Dobie, editor) *Straight Texas,* Steck, 1937, Folklore Associates (Hatboro, PA), 1966, Southern Methodist University Press, 1977.
Accuracy in Thinking, Farrar & Rinehart, 1938.
(With D. R. Long) *Manual and Workbook in English,* Holt (New York City), 1943.
Gib Morgan, Minstrel of the Oil Fields, illustrated by Betty Boatright, University Press in Dallas, 1945, reprinted, Southern Methodist University Press, 1965.
Folk Laughter on the American Frontier, Macmillan (New York City), 1949.
Folklore of the Oil Industry, Southern Methodist University Press, 1963.
(With William A. Owens) *Tales from the Derrick Floor: A People's History of the Oil Industry,* illustrations by William D. Wittliff, Doubleday (Garden City, NY), 1970, University of Nebraska (Lincoln), 1982.
Mody Boatright, Folklorist: A Collection of Essays, edited by Ernest B. Speck, University of Texas Press (Austin), 1973.

COEDITOR, EXCEPT AS NOTED

Coyote Wisdom, Texas Folklore Society, 1938.
(With Dobie and Harry H. Ransom) *In the Shadow of History,* Texas Folklore Society, 1939, Folklore Associates (Hatboro, PA), 1966, Folklore Associates (Detroit), 1971, Southern Methodist University Press, 1980.
Mustangs and Cow Horses, Texas Folklore Society, 1940.
Freshman Prose Annual, Houghton (Boston), 1940-42.

(With Dobie and Ransom) *Texian Stomping Grounds,* Texas Folklore Society, 1941, Southern Methodist University Press, 1967.

(With Donald Day) *Backwoods to Border,* Texas Folklore Society, 1943, Southern Methodist University Press, 1967.

(With Day) *From Hell to Breakfast,* Texas Folklore Society, 1944, Southern Methodist University Press, 1967.

(Editor) *Mexican Border Ballads, and Other Lore,* Texas Folklore Society, 1946, Southern Methodist University Press, 1967.

(Editor) *The Sky Is My Tipi,* Texas Folklore Society, 1949, Southern Methodist University Press, 1966.

Folk Travelers: Ballads, Tales, and Talk, Southern Methodist University Press, 1953.

Texas Folk and Folklore, drawings by Jose Cisneros, Southern Methodist University Press, 1954.

(With Leo Hughes) *College Prose,* Houghton, 1956.

Mesquite and Willow, Southern Methodist University Press, 1957.

Madstones and Twisters, Southern Methodist University Press, 1958.

Family Saga and Other Phases of American Folklore, University of Illinois Press (Champaigne, IL), 1958.

And Horns on the Toads, Texas Folklore Society, 1959.

(With Wilson M. Hudson and Allen Maxwell) *Singers and Storytellers,* Texas Folklore Society, 1961.

The Golden Log, Texas Folklore Society, 1962.

A Good Tale and a Bonnie Tune, Southern Methodist University Press, 1964.

SIDELIGHTS: Educator and folklorist Mody Coggin Boatright authored and edited numerous books that are primarily focused on Texan folklore. Throughout the majority of his publishing career, he produced titles for the Texas Folklore Society and Southern Methodist University Press. In fact, starting in the mid-1960's many of his earlier works were reprinted by the Southern Methodist University Press, among them: *Tall Tales From Texas, Straight Texas, In the Shadow of History,* and *Texian Stomping Grounds.*

Texas Folk and Folklore, lauded *New York Times* critic B. A. Botkin, is "an excellent introduction to the folklore and the folk-regional spirit of Texas. As such it will please both the folklore audience and the Texas audience." Although strongly connected to Texas folklore, Boatright produced books with broader appeal than to just the Texans or folklore enthusiasts. Of *Folk Travelers: Ballads, Tales, and Talk, Saturday Review* critic Robert Halsband wrote: "Altogether the pieces in the collection should have great appeal beyond the borders of its state and its subject." According to a *Christian Science Monitor* reviewer, "Oil executives on the lookout for a gift item might consider [*Folklore of the Oil Industry*] . . . a natural. It's not calculated to enlighten . . . but it makes entertaining reading."

Boatright also features the oil industry in *Tales from the Derrick Floor: A People's History of the Oil Industry,* a book containing transcriptions of over 100 pioneers in the oil industry. It is recommended by *Library Journal*'s T. M. Bogie as "popular reading and as a supplement to standard histories of the oil industry." However, "the book is less valuable for scholars" because of "the lack of notes to identify the contributors and the persons, places, and events in [the] pieces." However, a *Choice* reviewer ranked the publication as a valuable addition to higher education: "The undergraduate should experience many a thrill when he turns the pages of this fascinating study, and often he will have a much better understanding of, and a clearer insight into, the human fabric of the petroleum industry."

Many critics recognized *Folk Laughter on the American Frontier* as a scholarly work. This "well-documented and highly readable book," described *New York Times* contributor Rex Lardner, was lauded by J. H. Jackson in the *San Francisco Chronicle* as "a wonderful collection of American folk-humor and a scholarly study of how it developed on the frontier. The reader may approach the book either way, or both ways, and enjoy every bit of it." *New York Herald Tribune Book Review* critic Stanley Walker commented: "[*Folk Laughter on the American Frontier* is] a brief, concise, scholarly and workmanlike job, dripping with scholarly footnotes and replete with bibliography, index and so on. It is rich stuff, and by the very nature of the material almost impossible to read at one sitting—too much like trying to listen to the same vaudeville team, no matter how good, for three hours."

BIOGRAPHICAL/CRITICAL SOURCES:

BOOKS

Speck, Ernest B., *Mody C. Boatright,* Steck-Vaughn (Austin, TX), 1971.

PERIODICALS

Chicago Sun, January 1, 1950.

Choice, October, 1971.

Christian Science Monitor, January 5, 1950; November 29, 1963.
Journal of American Folklore, April, 1971.
Library Journal, September 15, 1949; September 1, 1961; February 1, 1964; August, 1970.
New York Herald Tribune Book Review, December 18, 1949; July 30, 1961.
New York Times, December 11, 1949; April 24, 1955.
San Francisco Chronicle, December 20, 1949; February 8, 1954; January 30, 1955
Saturday Review, March 20, 1954; November 26, 1955.

OBITUARIES:

PERIODICALS

AB Bookman's Weekly, September 21, 1970.*

* * *

BOAZ, Noel T(homas) 1952-

PERSONAL: Born February 8, 1952, in Martinsville, VA; son of T. Noel (a businessman) and Elena More (a social worker; maiden name, Taylor; present surname, Robertson) Boaz; married Dorothy Dechant (marriage ended); married Meleisa McDonell (a podiatrist); children: Lydia Elena, Peter Vernon, Alexander McDonell. *Education:* University of Virginia, B.A. (with distinction), 1973; University of California at Berkeley, M.A., 1974, Ph.D., 1977.

ADDRESSES: Home—19470 Dusty Loop, Bend, OR 97701. *Office*—International Institute for Human Evolutionary Research, Central Oregon University Center, 2600 Northwest College Way, Bend, OR 97701.

CAREER: University of California at Los Angeles, lecturer in anthropology, 1977-78; New York University, New York City, assistant professor of anthropology, 1978-83; Virginia Museum of Natural History, Martinsville, director and curator, 1983-90; International Institute for Human Evolutionary Research, Bend, OR, founder, research professor of anthropology and director of the institute, 1990—. Field work includes direction of International Sahabi Research Project in Libya, Senliki Research Expedition in Zaire, and Western Rift Research Expedition in Uganda. Virginia Museum of Natural History Foundation, president, 1984-89; International Foundation for Human Evolutionary Research, president, 1990—.

MEMBER: American Association of Physical Anthropologists, American Anthropological Association, Explorers Club (fellow).

AWARDS, HONORS: Rolex Award honorable mention, 1981.

WRITINGS:

Quarry: Closing in on the Missing Link, Free Press (New York City), 1993.
(With Alan J. Almquist) *Biological Anthropology: A Synthetic Approach to Human Evolution,* Prentice Hall (Upper Saddle River, NJ), 1997.
Eco Homo: How the Human Being Emerged from the Cataclysmic History of the Earth, Basic Books (New York City), 1997.

EDITOR

(With A. E. Arnanti, A. Gaziry, and others) *Neogene Paleontology and the Geology of Sahabi, Libya,* Alan Liss (New York City), 1987.
The Evolution of Environments and Hominidae in the African Western Rift Valley, Virginia Museum of Natural History (Martinsville, VA), 1990.

SIDELIGHTS: Noel T. Boaz once described himself to *CA:* "I am an anthropologist who writes professional papers and monographs on subjects relating to early hominid evolution, paleoecology, and biological anthropology. I have been doing research and publishing the results for about twenty years."

Discussing his book *Quarry: Closing in on the Missing Link,* Boaz once related to *CA:* "In 1993 I published my first book intended for a general audience, *Quarry: Closing in on the Missing Link.* I did this for several reasons. I believe that I have learned something in the last twenty years or so about why we are the way we are and how we got that way. Almost everyone is an anthropologist at some level: people have their own classification of the human species into types and 'races'; they have their own (usually intensely felt) ideas about their own origins, and they feel that they know better than anyone else how their minds and bodies work. So, it is not necessarily an easy task to attempt to tell people about themselves. Many times, however, our closely held folk beliefs about who we are and where we came from are wrong, and these misconceptions can have significant effects on how we deal with the rest of the world. In *Quarry* I attempted to tell something of how biological anthropologists go about their work, using a semi-autobiographical vehicle for this. It was my hope that, by understanding the methods, one might become more convinced of the conclusions.

"I believe that much of what anthropologists do, particularly biological anthropologists, is of clear relevance to a wide range of human concerns and problems. Yet very little of an evolutionary perspective has made it into most discussions of public issues. Part of my mission as a writer is to help correct this situation. There is a widely held misconception that creationism and evolutionism are diametrically opposed polarities when it comes to looking at our origins, and this confusion has clouded the wider acceptance of our biological evolution. But creationism is not science, and evolutionism is not theology, and the twain will never meet. Because they are different, they are both compatible. It is time to move past this phantom barrier to more effective public education in science. A good national public school program in human biology could do wonders for such wide-ranging practical problems as teenage pregnancy, drug and alcohol abuse, and obesity, for example. People do not, in general, change their behavior because they are told to. They must understand their biology and gain a grasp of how their bodies work and have worked over the past millions of years.

In *Eco Homo: How the Human Being Emerged from the Cataclysmic History of the Earth,* "Boaz draws heavily from paleoecology and evolutionary biology, arguing forcefully that responses to global climatic changes provide answers [to many human evolution questions]," described a *Publishers Weekly* critic. Specifically, Boaz maintains that about six or seven million years ago the Mediterranean dried up, causing the forests in northern Africa to change into the Sahara. "The crucible of human evolution . . . may have been provided by fragmenting forests in an increasingly arid north Africa at that time," relayed Mark Ridley in the *New York Times Book Review,* adding that "this is an unorthodox view." "Most anthropologists think humans originated in eastern Africa—in Ethiopia, Kenya, and Tanzania." In *Eco Homo,* Boaz also suggests, as do many other scientists, that the transition to walking on two legs occurred in response to the shift from living in a forest to surviving in a savanna. Ridley reports that Boaz further explains how "climatic fluctuations in ice ages . . . [and] the glacial extremes and minimum temperatures of the ice age" resulted in "the large human brain and the origin of culture."

"The idea that all major changes in hominid anatomy and behavior arose strictly from climate is difficult to prove, since the climate shifted many times within the uncertain dates of evolution events," stated Will St. John in the *Chicago Tribune,* a concern which Ridley also noted. Reviewers of *Eco Homo* commonly recognized, and Boaz openly states in the book, that the book contains just hypotheses. Ridley more extremely warns that "Boaz's hypotheses remain not much more than conjectures. . . . I do suspect he has exaggerated the importance of the weather in the formative events of modern humanity." Nevertheless, Ridley commented that "Boaz has original ideas . . . [which] surely [contain] some truth" and concluded that *Eco Homo* is "stimulating and enjoyable to read" and is written with a "pleasant personal touch." And despite "[occasional] errors of explanation," St. John also believed the book to be "rich in ideas."

The book is "full of entertaining stories about the personalities behind the science. . . . [and] end[s] with nervous glances toward the future," pointed out *Earth* contributor Robert J. Coontz Jr., adding: "Boaz warns us not to take our own survival for granted." Boaz once commented to *CA:* "Most people accept that climate and the environment exert tremendous effects on human life today, but they are unaware of the even greater effects that climate change had on the evolutionary career of our species. With our greatly expanded view of past climates, we can now assess much more fully the correlation of climatic changes and human evolution. With this perspective of immense time depth to our adaptations, we can better understand our modern adaptations."

BIOGRAPHICAL/CRITICAL SOURCES:

PERIODICALS

Booklist, July, 1997, p. 1784.
Chicago Tribune, September 15, 1997, p. 3.
Choice, January, 1996, pp. 831-32.
Earth, February, 1998, p. 62.
New York Times Book Review, August 17, 1997, p. 7.
Publishers Weekly, June 2, 1997, p. 61.*

* * *

BOGART, Stephen Humphrey 1949-

PERSONAL: Born January 6, 1949, in Los Angeles, CA; son of Humphrey Bogart (an actor) and Lauren

Bacall (an actor); married Dale Gemmelli, 1969 (divorced, 1984); married second wife, Barbara Bruchmann (a real-estate agent), 1985; children: (first marriage) Jamie, (second marriage) Richard, Brooke. *Education:* University of Hartford, B.A., 1979. *Politics:* Independent. *Religion:* "None." *Avocational interests:* Golf, working out, skiing, travel.

ADDRESSES: Office—c/o Tor/Forge Books, 175 Fifth Ave., 14th Fl., New York, NY 10010. *Agent*—Crawford Literary Agency.

CAREER: Producer in television, including *Court TV* and of news at the National Broadcasting Company (NBC); author, 1995—.

WRITINGS:

MEMOIR

(With Gary Provost) *Bogart: In Search of My Father* Dutton (New York City), 1995.

"R.J. BROOKS" MYSTERY SERIES

Play It Again, Forge (New York City), 1995.
The Remake: As Time Goes By, Forge, 1997.

SIDELIGHTS: Author and television producer Stephen Humphrey Bogart is the son of two American film icons—Humphrey Bogart and Lauren Bacall. As he recounts in his 1995 book *Bogart: In Search of My Father,* he was only eight years old when his movie-star father died of cancer. "As if that weren't tragic and terrifying enough," observes Caryn James in the *New York Times Book Review,* "when he arrived at church for the funeral, hundreds of people were massed on the sidewalk, gawking and waiting to take his picture."

As the title indicates, *Bogart: In Search of My Father* is the author's attempt to understand the famous father he lost so soon; James went on to praise the book as a "poignant and rawly painful memoir." Some reviewers thought that Bogart's relatively short time with his father made his book less informative on the actor himself than were other Bogart biographies. Other critics, however, found significant value in the author's recollections of childhood as well as his account of coming back as an adult to the home where his father had died. Donna Seaman in *Booklist* labels *Bogart: In Search of My Father* "revealing" and predicts that it "will please movie buffs."

In the same year that *Bogart: In Search of My Father* saw print, Bogart also published his first mystery novel, *Play It Again.* The title comes from a line credited to Humphrey Bogart, who was widely believed to have uttered the words in one of his most well-known roles in the film *Casablanca* (the actor never spoke those exact words onscreen). Bogart's protagonist in *Play It Again,* R. J. Brooks, shares a background similar to the author's and a style similar to many of his father's screen characters, but he makes his living as a private detective specializing in taking evidence pictures of cheating marital partners. When his estranged movie star mother, Belle, is murdered, he tries to solve the case. With the help of a woman who has been putting together a documentary about Belle's career, Brooks picks up the trail of the serial killer for whom his mother was a target. Bogart admits in a *Publishers Weekly* interview that "part of my mother is in Belle . . . but *our* relationship is good. She said, 'You know, Steve, everybody will think you hate me.' I said, 'Mom, they won't. This is fiction.'"

Play It Again received a number of positive reviews. Neal Rubin, writing in the *Detroit Free Press,* hails the novel as "a first-rate first effort." James offers praise as well, and judges Bogart to be "a promising if not yet accomplished mystery writer." Fellow mystery author Kinky Friedman reviews *Play It Again* for the *Washington Post Book World,* and declares: "The characters feel real, the dialogue is killer bee, and, for better or worse, the book smells like New York. Possibly more important, the book satisfies Raymond Chandler's famous criterion for all good fiction: 'it creates the illusion of life.'" Friedman went on to conclude that Bogart's "talent, toughness and charm . . . are uniquely his own."

Bogart brought back R. J. Brooks in a second novel, entitled *The Remake: As Time Goes By.* Once again, the author made full use of his parents' legend. In the story, the Andromeda movie studio plans to remake one of the greatest films ever made, *As Time Goes By*—which starred Brooks's parents. Brooks makes his rage public, saying that he wishes those who plan to make the new movie were dead. Thus, when some of them are killed, he becomes the prime suspect. Brooks's problems are compounded when his girlfriend, Casey, accepts a job working on the movie project and leaves for California. When the real killer begins to threaten everyone involved with the remake, Brooks heads for Hollywood to protect Casey. "Fortunately, as a gumshoe in the grand noir tradition, he is well able to discover the truth," states Dennis

Winters in *Booklist.* "Bogart is equally well able, thanks to both heritage . . . and natural storytelling ability, to delineate the tawdry convergence of show business, greed, and passion in a taut, action-filled thriller full of well-drawn innocents, devils, patsies, and toughs." A *Publishers Weekly* reviewer describes the book as "a tale full of set pieces from the movies" and muses that "Bogart seems to be playing a bit of a con here. As the son of Humphrey Bogart and Lauren Bacall, he's capitalizing on their life . . . as surely as the fictional Andromeda is exploiting R. J.'s parents and their work. Still, readers willing to overlook this harmless hypocrisy will be rewarded with a creditable whodunit."

BIOGRAPHICAL/CRITICAL SOURCES:

BOOKS

Bogart, Stephen Humphrey, and Provost, Gary, *Bogart: In Search of My Father,* Dutton, 1995.

PERIODICALS

Booklist, March 15, 1995, p. 1311; August, 1995, p. 1921; February 1, 1997, p. 927.

Detroit Free Press, April 12, 1995, p. E3.

Entertainment Weekly, September 8, 1995, p. 76.

New York Times, November 9, 1995.

New York Times Book Review, September 10, 1995, p. 14.

People Weekly, September 25, 1995, p. 13.

Publishers Weekly, January 23, 1995, pp. 40-41; March 20, 1995, p. 47; July 3, 1995, p. 40; January 13, 1997, p. 58.

Times (London), October 12, 1995, p. 41.

Washington Post Book World, April 9, 1995, p. 8.

* * *

BOMBAL, Maria Luisa 1910-1980

PERSONAL: Born June 8, 1910, in Vina del Mar, Chile; died May 6, 1980, in Chile; married Count Raphael de Saint-Phalle (a Wall Street financier), c. 1945. *Education:* Attended Ecole Notre Dame de l'Assomption, Lycee La Bruyere, and the Sorbonne, University of Paris.

CAREER: Writer. Worked as a screenwriter for Sonofilm in Argentina, 1937-40. Chilean representative to the International PEN conference held in the United States, 1940.

MEMBER: International PEN.

AWARDS, HONORS: Annual prize from the Chilean Academy of Arts and Letters, 1977, for *La historia de Maria Griselda;* municipal prize from the city of Santiago, Chile, 1942, for the novella *La amortajada.*

WRITINGS:

La ultima niebla (novella; title means "The Final Mist"; originally published alone, 1935; subsequent editions also contain the short stories "El arbol" and "Las islas nuevas"), 2nd edition, Nascimento, 1941, 8th edition, Editorial Orbe, 1975, translation of title story, revised with husband, Raphael de Sainte-Phalle, published separately as *The House of Mist,* Farrar, Straus (New York City), 1947, reprinted, University of Texas Press (Austin, TX), 1996.

La amortajada (novella), Sur, 1938, reprinted, Editorial Universitaria, 1981, translation by Bombal published as *The Shrouded Woman,* Cassell (New York City), 1950, reprinted, University of Texas Press, 1996.

(Translator) Jules Supervielle, *La desconocida del Sena,* Editorial Losada, 1962.

La historia de Maria Griselda, Editorial "El Observador," 1976.

OMNIBUS VOLUMES

La ultima niebla (contains *La ultima niebla,* "El arbol," "Las islas nuevas," and "Lo secreto"), introduction by Amado Alonso, Andina, 1981.

La ultima niebla, El arbol, Las islas nuevas, Lo secreto: Textos completos, Editorial Andres Bello, 1982.

New Islands, and Other Stories (contains "The Final Mist," "The Tree," "Braids," "The Unknown," and "New Islands"), translated by Richard and Lucia Cunningham, preface by Jorge Luis Borges, Farrar, Straus, 1982.

La ultima niebla [and] *La amortajada,* Seix Barral, 1984.

La amortajada; y, El arbol, Zig-Zag, 1984.

Author of screenplay, *La Casa del Recuerdo (The House of Memories),* filmed in Argentina, c. 1938.

SIDELIGHTS: The late Maria Luisa Bombal was one of the most esteemed Latin American writers of the twentieth century. Although she produced only a small body of work during her lifetime and was relatively unknown in English-speaking countries until after her death, Bombal is credited with changing the style, tone, and substance of Hispanic literature. Her avant-garde works—considered early examples of feminist writing—deviated from the exaggeratedly masculine, regionalistic, and realistic trends that dominated South American fiction through the 1930s. According to Barbara Mujica in *Americas,* Bombal's principal works "have long been considered essential components of the Hispanic canon."

Composed in reaction to the confines of her patriarchal society, Bombal's lyrical prose writings center on women who escape their lonely, boring, and unfulfilled existences through fantasy. The works expose the hypocrisies of life in a class-conscious society through interior monologues by female characters. Mujica asserted that Bombal's stories and novels "are revered by both partisans of the canon and feminists, for they are key works in early twentieth-century Latin American literature and, at the same time, represent an important step toward the creation of a feminine literary presence."

A native Chilean of Argentine and German descent, Bombal was born and raised in Vina del Mar, Chile. After spending most of the 1920s in Paris—where she earned a degree from the Sorbonne—she moved to Buenos Aires. There she shared an apartment with poet Pablo Neruda and his wife, composing her first fiction at their kitchen table. The bulk of Bombal's subsequent work was created while the author lived in Chile during the 1930s. Her works, which are characterized by the use of powerful imagery, recurring themes, and fantastic symbolism, illuminate the conflicts of being a woman in a South American society dominated by males.

Bombal's first novella, *La ultima niebla,* was first published in Spanish in 1935; twelve years later, it was revised, enlarged, and published in English as *The House of Mist.* Set in South America, the tale revolves around Helga, a woman who resorts to a dream life for satisfaction after realizing that her new husband, Daniel, remains devoted to his dead wife. The novella is titled for the white mist that rolls up from the lagoon where Daniel's first wife was drowned. Helga finds the fog suffocating, as indicated in a passage from the story excerpted in the *New York Times Book Review:* "[It enshrouds and obscures] the color of the walls, the contours of the furniture, entwining itself in my hair, clinging to my body, smothering everything . . . everything."

American critics found the tale somewhat oversentimentalized but nonetheless intriguing. In a review for the *New York Times* Richard Sullivan noted, "Bombal's heroine dwells far too steadily on her raptures," but conceded that the book's "familiar substance [is] ingeniously twisted"; he judged *The House of Mist* to be "dexterous, amoral, delicate," and suffused with "a kind of engaging breathlessness of manner." Mujica noted of the work: "This psychologically complex novel reveals a repressed, melancholic woman who buries her past in the deepest recesses of her mind in order to survive." The critic described *The House of Mist* as "exquisitely lyrical."

Bombal's 1938 novella *La amortajada* is an unusual story told from the point of view of a dead woman. Ana Maria reflects on her life, her loves, and her feelings of hopelessness as she lies in state at her own funeral. Several critics praised Bombal for her insightful portrait of human conflict and stunning use of lush prose. Marjorie Brace, reviewing the English translation of the work (titled *The Shrouded Woman*) for the *Saturday Review,* commented that the story was at once "amazingly horrid and uncommonly dreadful." She went on to describe Bombal's writing as "a kind . . . seldom produced in [the United States], the ideology of which does not encourage a mysticism of destructiveness." Argentine novelist and art critic Marta Traba, writing in *Americas,* dubbed Bombal's work "the literature of despair." According to Traba, "Death is welcome, not as a romantic figure but as a practical solution" for Ana Maria in *La amortajada,* as "it separates her from those who used, ignored, or humiliated her" during her life.

Mujica concluded: "Both *The House of Mist* and *The Shrouded Woman* are mesmerizing novels that lure the reader into other dimensions, while at the same time exposing disturbing social realities. Even in her second language [English], Bombal is a master craftsman."

In 1941 Bombal shot and seriously wounded Eulogio Sanchez Errazuriz, her anti-communist lover. She was jailed and, upon Errazuriz's recovery, banished from Chile. Bombal then immigrated to the United States. In an article for *Americas* Cuban art critic Jose Gomez-Sicre recalled his affiliation with Bombal, which began in 1944 when they were introduced by a mutual friend. Gomez-Sicre, Bombal, and Cuban painter Mario Carreno—who had an unrequited romantic interest in the author—spent the winter of 1944 together, watching old films shown at New York City's Museum of Modern Art. They passed cold afternoons in neighborhood bars, debating and discussing topics that ranged from the chances for a democratic victory in World War II to the new trends in European cinema. Gomez-Sicre related, "Maria Luisa reasoned that the only way to get warm on those freezing February [days] was to have a properly chilled and decidedly dry martini. . . . She could handle four with no difficulty."

Although a Hollywood studio had purchased the rights to *La ultima niebla* and asked Bombal to compose the script, the film version was never produced. This disappointment, suggested Gomez-Sicre, along with her predisposition to melancholia, may have contributed to Bombal's eventual battle with alcoholism. She remained in the United States until her husband, Raphael de Saint-Phalle, died in 1970. Ten years after returning to Chile, the writer died in her sleep and "like [the corpse in] *La amortajada,*" noted Gomez-Sicre, was cremated.

Bombal's English-speaking audience expanded after her death with the release of *New Islands, and Other Stories* in 1982. Containing the English translation of five stories, including the original, unlengthened version of *La ultima niebla* published as *The Final Mist,* the entire collection is informed by the author's preoccupation with the powers of the imagination. "Of earth and sea and sky," wrote Bombal as quoted by James Polk in *The Nation,* "I know an infinity of small and magic secrets." One enchanting story in the *New Islands* volume, "The Unknown," is about a pirate ship lost in a whirlpool at the bottom of the sea. A frequently anthologized piece titled "The Tree" chronicles a woman's growing alienation from her husband. The man "is emotionally dead, incapable of responding to her need for love," noted Rona Berg in the *Village Voice Literary Supplement.* As excerpted by Ronald De Feo in the *New York Times Book Review,* the closing lines of "The Tree" capture Bombal's basic philosophy: "It may be that true happiness lies in the conviction that one has irremediably lost happiness. It is only then that we can begin to live without hope or fear, able finally to enjoy all the small pleasures, which are the most lasting."

New Islands was well received in the United States. Critics were particularly impressed by Bombal's ability to elicit empathy in her readers. Berg stated, "We drown in silence along with [the author's] characters," and asserted, "Bombal's writing is subtle and beautiful, sensual, yet restrained. . . . It has the rhythm of somnolent breathing. Her tone emulates the murmur of the subconscious."

Bombal's writings changed the face of Hispanic fiction and prefigured magic realism—a South American literary movement whose fiction aims to depict imaginary and fantastic scenes in a realistic way. Having influenced other Spanish writers, including Carlos Fuentes, Gabriel Garcia Marquez, and Jose Donoso, Bombal remains, according to some observers, the most innovative female voice in twentieth-century Latin American literature. Polk, for one, concluded that Bombal's work "takes the daring imaginative flights we have come to expect from a later generation of Latin Americans, for whom she must rank . . . as a Founding Mother."

BIOGRAPHICAL/CRITICAL SOURCES:

BOOKS

Adams, Ian, *Three Authors of Alienation: Bombal, Onetti, and Carpentier,* University of Texas Press (Austin), 1975.

Dictionary of Hispanic Biography, Gale (Detroit, MI), 1996, pp. 128-29.

Kostopulos-Cooperman, Celeste, *The Lyrical Vision of Maria Luisa Bombal,* Tamesis Books (London), 1988.

Reference Guide to Short Fiction, St. James Press (Detroit, MI), 1994.

PERIODICALS

Americas, February, 1981, pp. 49-51; January-February, 1996, pp. 61-62.

Bilingual Review, 1987, p. 33.

Hispanist, Volume 3, number 21, 1977, pp. 5-6.

Nation, December 11, 1982, pp. 634-35.

New York Times Book Review, April 13, 1947; December 19, 1982.

Saturday Review, May 1, 1950.

Sur, August, 1938, p. 80.

Symposium, winter, 1995, pp. 251-56.

Times Literary Supplement, December 9, 1983, p. 1372.

Village Voice Literary Supplement, October, 1982.*

BONNER, Paul Hyde 1893-1968

PERSONAL: Born February 14, 1893, in New York, NY; died December 14, 1968, in Charleston, SC; son of Paul Edward and Theodora (Hall) Bonner; married Lilly Stehli, 1917 (deceased); married Elizabeth McGowan, 1962; children: (first marriage) Paul Hyde, Jr., John T., Henry S., Anthony E. *Education:* Phillips Exeter Academy, graduated, 1911; Harvard University, graduated, 1915. *Avocational interests:* Bird shooting, trout and salmon fishing.

CAREER: Stehli Silks Corp., New York City, 1919-31, rising to vice president; U.S. State Department, posts in Paris, France, and Rome, Italy, 1946-52; writer of fiction. *Military service:* U.S. Army, 1917-19; became second lieutenant; U.S. Army Air Corps, 1941-45; became colonel.

MEMBER: Union Club and Brook Club (both New York City), Travellers Club (Paris), Carolina Yacht Club (Charleston).

WRITINGS:

NOVELS; ALL PUBLISHED BY SCRIBNER (NEW YORK CITY)

S.P.Q.R., 1953.
Hotel Talleyrand, 1954.
Excelsior!, 1955.
The Glorious Mornings, 1956.
With Both Eyes Open, 1957.
Amanda, 1958.
Aged in the Woods, 1959.
The Art of Llewellyn Jones, 1960.
Ambassador Extraordinary, 1962.

OTHER

Stories and essays have appeared in the *Atlantic, Holiday, New Yorker, Sports Illustrated, Esquire,* and *Vogue.*

SIDELIGHTS: Paul Hyde Bonner's novels are exciting tales of international political intrigue and his best-known titles include *Hotel Talleyrand, The Art of Llewellyn Jones,* and *Ambassador Extraordinary.* In *Hotel Talleyrand,* Bonner weaves a complicated web of plotlines involving the lives of American government personnel working in Paris. One of them, Walter Haines, has a tragic affair with a Communist agent. Numerous reviewers approved of the book as light entertainment. *Commonweal* contributor C. H. Weiss called it a "highly palatable concoction," while W. K. Harrison in *Library Journal* described it as "very continental and highly sophisticated." More serious claims for the book came from *San Francisco Chronicle* writer D. A. Pitt, who considered *Hotel Talleyrand* a "fine social observation, forming in its wholeness a tragi-comic picture of modern American innocents abroad," but Virginia Peterson in the *New York Herald Tribune Book Review* found it simply "swift-moving, clever, imbued with a pleasant worldliness," with "implications just serious enough to keep the mind from straying."

In *The Art of Llewellyn Jones,* Bonner created F. Townsend Britton, a wealthy, married ambassador who sheds his wife and his high-class life to take on the identity of Lew Jones. Under this name, he travels to Paris where he ultimately finds romance and success as a painter. A *Booklist* reviewer lauded Bonner's treatment of art in the book, noting that it would appeal "to a sophisticated audience." A *Chicago Sunday Tribune* writer stated that the story, "even when it strains at the seams of credulity, is amusing and exciting." *New York Herald Tribune Book Review* critic Caroline Tunstall rated Bonner a "fluent and entertaining" storyteller, and a *New Yorker* commentator summed up: "In this generally amusing flight of fancy, the detail is sophisticated, the atmosphere is naive, and the tone is boyish."

In *Ambassador Extraordinary,* Bonner creates a fictional Caribbean republic called Antilla, where American ambassador Sherman Biggs becomes entangled with the beautiful wife of a powerful general. The woman, Juanita, is working as a spy not only for the country's dictator, but also for the rebels hiding in the hills, waiting to overthrow the government. *Atlantic* reviewer William Barret mused that Bonner's style is as "sure, adult, and relaxed as ever." The *Chicago Sunday Tribune*'s Fanny Butcher approved of the book, calling it "a good rousing story of diplomatic intrigue and scandal." *Library Journal* contributor Earl Tannenbaum criticized it as "heavy-handed," but John Barkham differed strongly in his *New York Times Book Review* assessment. While allowing that *Ambassador Extraordinary* is improbable, Barkham noted that "the author glides gracefully, performing his verbal arabesques, tending his flowers, choosing his wines, displaying his antiques and gently guiding his characters through their courtly conversations. . . . It is always agreeable."

BIOGRAPHICAL/CRITICAL SOURCES:

PERIODICALS

Atlantic, June, 1956; June, 1962.
Booklist, April 1, 1953; April 15, 1953; March 15, 1956; April 15, 1956; September 15, 1957; November 1, 1958; September 1, 1959; May 1, 1962.
Bookmark, October, 1957; July, 1959; May, 1962.
Catholic World, June, 1953; June, 1956; November, 1957; December, 1959.
Chicago Sunday Tribune, April 12, 1953, p. 5; September 22, 1957, p. 1; July 19, 1959, p. 6; April 22, 1962, p. 3.
Commonweal, May 8, 1953.
Guardian, October 19, 1962, p. 7.
Kirkus Reviews, February 1, 1953; February 15, 1956; July 1, 1957; August 1, 1958; May 1, 1959; February 1, 1962.
Library Journal, April 1, 1953; February 15, 1956; August, 1957; October 1, 1958; August, 1959; March 15, 1962.
Manchester Guardian, November 27, 1953, p. 8.
New Republic, June 29, 1953.
New Yorker, April 11, 1953; August 8, 1959; April 14, 1962.
New York Herald Tribune Book Review, April 12, 1953, p. 8; May 6, 1956, p. 2; December 22, 1957, p. 6; July 19, 1959, p. 10; April 15, 1962.
New York Times, April 12, 1953, p. 5; May 6, 1956, p. 33; September 22, 1957, p. 40; July 19, 1959, p. 4.
New York Times Book Review, April 15, 1962, p. 5.
San Francisco Chronicle, June 7, 1953, p. 17; June 10, 1956, p. 25; November 24, 1957, p. 39; September 6, 1959, p. 21.
Saturday Review, April 11, 1953; May 12, 1956; August 1, 1959.
Time, July 20, 1959.
Times Literary Supplement, December 11, 1953, p. 797; November 23, 1962, p. 925.

OBITUARIES:

PERIODICALS

Detroit Free Press, December 16, 1968.
New York Times, December 15, 1968.
Publishers Weekly, January 13, 1969

BONSALL, Crosby Barbara (Newell) 1921-1995 (Crosby Newell)

PERSONAL: Born January 2, 1921, in Queens, NY; died following a stroke, January 10, 1995, in Boston, MA; married George Bonsall. *Education:* Attended American School of Design and New York University.

CAREER: Author and illustrator of books for children. Also worked for advertising agencies.

AWARDS, HONORS: I'll Show You Cats was named a best illustrated children's book for 1964 by the *New York Times.*

WRITINGS:

SELF-ILLUSTRATED UNDER NAME CROSBY BONSALL; PUBLISHED BY HARPER (NEW YORK CITY), EXCEPT AS INDICATED

Who's a Pest?, 1962.
The Case of the Hungry Stranger, 1963.
What Spot?, 1963.
It's Mine!, 1964.
The Case of the Cat's Meow, 1965.
The Case of the Dumb Bells, 1966.
The Day I Had to Play with My Sister, 1972.
Mine's the Best, 1973.
Piggle, 1973.
And I Mean It, Stanley, 1974.
Twelve Bells for Santa, 1977.
The Case of the Double Cross, 1980.

UNDER NAME CROSBY BONSALL; PUBLISHED BY HARPER (NEW YORK CITY), EXCEPT AS INDICATED

Listen, Listen! (photographs by Ylla), 1961.
Tell Me Some More (illustrated by Fritz Siebel), 1961.
Look Who's Talking (photographs by Ylla), 1962.
Let Papa Sleep (reader; illustrated by Emily Reed), Grosset (New York City), 1963.
I'll Show You Cats (photographs by Ylla), 1964.
Here's Jellybean Reilly (photographs by Ylla), 1966.
Whose Eye Am I? (photographs by Ylla), 1968.
The Case of the Scaredy Cats, 1971.
The Goodbye Summer, Greenwillow (New York City), 1979.
Who's Afraid of the Dark?, 1980.
The Amazing, the Incredible Super Dog, 1986.

UNDER NAME CROSBY NEWELL

(With husband, George Bonsall) *What Are You Looking At?,* Treasure Books (New York City), 1954.

(With G. Bonsall) *The Helpful Friends,* Wonder Books (New York City), 1955.

The Surprise Party (self-illustrated), Wonder Books, 1955.

Captain Kangaroo's Book (illustrated by Evan Jeffrey), Grosset, 1958.

Polar Bear Brothers (illustrated by Ylla), Harper, 1960.

Kippy the Koala (illustrated by George Leavens), Harper, 1960.

Hurry up, Slowpoke (self-illustrated), Grosset, 1961.

ILLUSTRATOR UNDER NAME CROSBY BONSALL

Joan L. Noodset, *Go Away, Dog,* Harper, 1963.

Phil Ressner, *August Explains,* Harper, 1963.

Joan Kahn, *Seesaw,* Harper, 1964.

Ralph Underwood, editor, *Ask Me Another Riddle,* Grosset, 1964.

Oscar Weigle, editor, *Great Big Joke and Riddle Book,* Grosset, 1970.

ILLUSTRATOR UNDER NAME CROSBY NEWELL

George Bonsall, *The Really Truly Treasure Hunt,* Treasure Books, 1954.

G. Bonsall, *The Big Joke,* Wonder Books, 1955.

SIDELIGHTS: During her writing career, Crosby Barbara Bonsall penned more than forty stories for youngsters. She began writing and illustrating for juvenile readers after working for advertising firms, sometimes working under the name Crosby Newell. She had many successful collaborations with photographer Ylla, including *Listen, Listen!, Here's Jellybean Reilly,* and the award-winning *I'll Show You Cats.*

Almost all of Bonsall's work was done in the "I Can Read" and "Early I Can Read" book series. Because of this, she has been unfairly overlooked, according to *Twentieth-Century Children's Writers* essayist John Gough. Gough argued that "many of Bonsall's books are excellent readers and also impressive picture story books. . . . Even her simplest stories transcend the extremely limited and repetitious vocabulary, letting the pictures and the setting carry almost the whole story."

Gough further noted that although many of Bonsall's books were picture oriented, she was also skilled in her use of language. In his opinion, "Bonsall's most significant contribution to children's literature is in the wit and invention of her characters' verbal clashes." The critic pointed to *Who's a Pest?* as an example of the author's best work. It features some elaborate, humorous wordplay, prompting Gough to write, "At this level of readership there is nothing else like it. It is a little like Lewis Carroll for kindergarten!"

In several popular books including *The Case of the Hungry Stranger* and *The Case of the Cat's Meow,* Bonsall presents the adventures of four young detectives: Skinny, Wizard, Tubby, and Snitch. They solve such mysteries as a stolen pie and a missing cat. I. S. Black, a writer for the *New York Times Book Review,* commented on Bonsall's "deceptively simple style" as well as her "wealth of artistry, skillful characterization, suspense and humor." "One scarcely resents the vocabulary limitations, for the author has combined real humor, suspense, and even definite characterization to achieve a result that is . . . irresistible," wrote a *Horn Book* reviewer of *The Case of the Hungry Stranger.*

Of Bonsall's drawing, Gough commented: "Her style is not the zany stereotyped grins and exuberance of Steven Kellogg, or the mannered nostalgia of Mercer Mayer, or the artistic streetwise cartoons of Maurice Sendak. Her characters are simple line drawings of robust little kids, a little like Charles Shultz's Charlie Brown mixed with a kewpie doll. They are immediately identifiable and appealing, and match the stories well."

The Goodbye Summer was one of Bonsall's few departures from her series work. It is a novel for older school-age children, featuring an eccentric heroine with a fantastic imagination. The girl, Allie, lost her father before she was born, and throughout the book, she struggles to learn how to say good-bye and how to treasure her memories of the past. "This is a good lesson, very simply, naturally taught, with no didacticism," approved Gough. "*The Goodbye Summer* stands comparison with Louise Fitzhugh's *Harriet the Spy,* Mary Rodger's *Freaky Friday,* or some of Betsy Byars's novels, but with a lighter touch. It deserves to be much better known."

BIOGRAPHICAL/CRITICAL SOURCES:

BOOKS

Twentieth-Century Children's Writers, St. James Press (Detroit), 1995.

PERIODICALS

Booklist, June 1, 1961; July 1, 1961.
Bookmark, April, 1961.
Book Week, November 10, 1963, p. 43.
Chicago Sunday Tribune, May 14, 1961, section 2, p. 2.
Christian Science Monitor, March 30, 1961, p. 7; May 11, 1961, p. B1; November 14, 1963, p. B2; May 7, 1964, p. 3B.
Commonweal, May 22, 1964.
Horn Book, March 1, 1961; June, 1961; February, 1964; August, 1965.
Kirkus Reviews, February 1, 1961.
Library Journal, April 15, 1961; October 15, 1963; March 15, 1964; May 15, 1965.
New York Herald Tribune Lively Arts, May 21, 1961, p. 31.
New York Times Book Review, November 10, 1963; April 26, 1964; May 9, 1965.
San Francisco Chronicle, May 14, 1961, p. 28.
Saturday Review, April 22, 1961; June 19, 1965.
Wilson Library Bulletin, July, 1961.

OBITUARIES:

PERIODICALS

New York Times, January 20, 1995, p. B8.*

* * *

BOURJAILY, Vance (Nye) 1922-

PERSONAL: Born September 17, 1922, in Cleveland, OH; son of Monte Ferris (a journalist and publisher) and Barbara (a novelist and journalist; maiden name, Webb) Bourjaily; married Bettina Yensen, 1946; children: Anna (deceased), Philip, Robin. *Education:* Bowdoin College, B.A., 1947.

ADDRESSES: Home—New Orleans, LA. *Office*—210H Allen, 525 Ursuline Dr., Louisiana State University, Baton Rouge, LA 70808-4767. *Agent*—William Morris Agency, 1350 Avenue of the Americas, New York, NY 10019.

CAREER: Novelist, playwright, journalist, and lecturer. University of Iowa, Writers Workshop, Iowa City, IA, creative writing instructor, associate professor, and professor, 1957-1980; Distinguished Visiting Professor, Oregon State University, summer, 1968; University of Arizona, creative writing professor, 1980-1985; Louisiana State University, M.F.A. program, professor of creative writing, and Boyd Professor of English, 1985—. Served as American specialist in North American literature on cultural missions of U.S. State Department to South America, 1959, 1972. *Military service:* American Field Service, 1942-44. U.S. Army, 1944-46.

AWARDS, HONORS: National Book Award nomination, 1970, for *Brill among the Ruins;* American Academy of Arts and Letters Award, 1993.

WRITINGS:

NOVELS; EXCEPT AS INDICATED

The End of My Life, Scribner (New York City), 1947.
The Hound of Earth, Scribner, 1955.
(Author of text) *The Girl in the Abstract Bed* (cartoons), Tiber Press (New York City), 1954.
The Violated, Dial Press (New York City), 1958, reprinted, 1978.
Confessions of a Spent Youth, Dial Press, 1960.
The Unnatural Enemy: Essays on Hunting, (essays), Dial Press, 1963, reprinted, University of Arizona Press, 1984.
The Man Who Knew Kennedy, Dial Press, 1967.
Brill among the Ruins, Dial Press, 1970.
Country Matters: Collected Reports from the Fields and Streams of Iowa and Other Places, (essays), Dial Press, 1973.
Now Playing at Canterbury, Dial Press, 1976.
A Game Men Play, Dial Press, 1980.
The Great Fake Book, Weidenfeld & Nicolson (New York City), 1986.
Old Soldier: A Novel, Donald I. Fine (New York City), 1990.
(With son Philip Bourjaily) *Fishing By Mail: The Outdoor Life of a Father and Son,* (nonfiction), Atlantic Monthly Press (New York City), 1993.

Also author of opera libretto for *$4,000,* music by Tom Turner, first produced at the University of Iowa, July 29, 1969; author of plays. Author of the teleplays *A Baby Named X,* NBC-TV, 1956, and *Divorcees Anonymous,* NBC-TV, 1957. Drama critic, *Village Voice.* Contributor of short stories to *New Yorker, Saturday Evening Post, Dial, Transatlantic Review,* and other periodicals. Editor and co-founder, *Discovery,* 1951-53.

A collection of Bourjaily's manuscripts is housed at the library of Bowdoin College in Brunswick, Maine.

WORK IN PROGRESS: Another novel, *The More Fool.*

SIDELIGHTS: Novelist, playwright, essayist, short story writer, and journalist Vance Bourjaily has been a presence on the American literary scene for more than fifty years. Yet, despite his treatment of significant and timely American themes—his work is literary, though hardly abstruse—and numerous favorable reviews, he has achieved neither large-scale popular success nor widespread critical attention. Born in Cleveland, Bourjaily grew up in Connecticut, New York, and Virginia. His parents, who separated when he was eleven, were both writers; his Lebanese-born father a journalist and publisher, and his mother a journalist and author of romance fiction. Expelled from a Pennsylvania prep school for smoking, he graduated from Handley High School in Winchester, Virginia in 1939, after which he enrolled in Bowdoin College. Leaving college in 1942, he spent two years as a volunteer ambulance corpsman in the Middle East and Italy, then served for two years in the U.S. Army. Those four years of wartime service abroad were a crucible of sorts for Bourjaily; World War II and its meaning for Americans of his generation are central themes of his early fiction. His first novel, *The End of My Life,* which traces the wartime experiences of four young friends, appeared in 1947, the same year in which Bourjaily received his degree from Bowdoin.

The End of My Life was, in most respects, an auspicious debut for the twenty-five-year-old author, although most critics were quick to point out his obvious debts to Hemingway. The novel's protagonist, Skinner Galt, is a young man in the throes of a painful transition. Once a carefree and irresponsible youth, Galt has been exposed to the horrors of war; he copes with life, though never very successfully, by adopting a truculent nihilism. In his critical study *After the Lost Generation,* John W. Aldridge called *The End of My Life* "the most neglected but, in many ways, the most promising" of the novels to emerge in the immediate aftermath of World War II. "No book since [Fitzgerald's] *This Side of Paradise* has caught so well the flavor of youth in wartime," Aldridge wrote, "and no book since [Hemingway's] *A Farewell to Arms* has contained so complete a record of the loss of that youth in war."

Bourjaily's second novel, *The Hound of Earth,* is a portrait of America during the Cold War, and focuses on the last days of a seven-year-long flight by Allerd Pennington, an army scientist who goes AWOL after discovering that he had contributed to the development of the atomic bomb that destroyed Hiroshima. Bourjaily's third novel, *The Violated,* more ambitious than either of his previous books, was greeted with considerable critical fanfare. The novel examines the lives of four characters over a period of more than twenty-five years, from the early 1930s to 1957, when the child of one of them is seen leading a performance of *Hamlet.* Watching the play, the four troubled adults are forced to confront the barrenness and isolation of their lives. The characters in this novel are all enmeshed in cycles of violation, all have deep emotional scars, and all suffer physically and psychologically as a result. "With his third novel, . . . Vance Bourjaily joins that select band of writers equipped with antenna-like perception enabling them to project the heart and pulse of their generation," Harding Lemay wrote in a *New York Herald Tribune Book Review* notice of *The Violated.* Although he considered the novel "a failure, but an interesting one," Irving Howe, writing in the *New Republic,* hailed Bourjaily as "one of the few serious young novelists who has tried to go directly toward the center of post-war experience."

In *Confessions of a Spent Youth,* a long, picaresque, and explicitly autobiographical novel, the narrator examines his wartime experiences, particularly his youthful sexual exploits, from the perspective of early middle age. World War II is seen from an even greater distance in Bourjaily's next novel, *The Man Who Knew Kennedy.* Dave Doremus, the protagonist, is a contemporary of John F. Kennedy, with whom he was briefly acquainted when both were recovering in a military hospital during the war. Although he is a quintessential American "golden boy," with looks, money, and a Harvard Law degree, Doremus nevertheless finds his life unraveling in the 1960s, and his decline and eventual demise (by suicide) parallel the increasing turbulence and discontent in America following the Kennedy assassination. The novel received only mixed reviews, but was a solid commercial success.

Brill among the Ruins, nominated for a National Book Award in 1970, is widely regarded as Bourjaily's strongest novel. Set during the late 1960s, when America was being torn asunder over the war in Vietnam, the novel focuses on the inner conflicts of Bob Brill, a hard-drinking, middle-aged lawyer from a small town in Illinois. Appalled by the vulgarity of his country's leaders, and looking on in despair as a variety of commercial interests ravage his beloved rural Midwest, Brill sets out on an archaeological expedition to pre-Columbian Mexico, where his meditations upon the devastation of aboriginal Americans at the hands of Spanish colonialists become intertwined with his thoughts on the decline of his own culture. While reviews of the novel were not uniformly favorable, most critics did acknowledge that *Brill among the Ruins* was a breakthrough book for Bourjaily. Writing in the *New York Times Book Review,* James R. Frakes observed, "Vance Bourjaily belongs to an unfortunate group of American novelists who have been for too many years . . . 'almosting it.'" Calling it Bourjaily's "most finished, most wholly satisfying novel," Frakes concluded, "I wish *Brill among the Ruins* would promote Vance Bourjaily out of the ranks of the also-rans. He has earned much more than a nod in passing. He matters." *New York Times* reviewer John Leonard ended his favorable review on virtually the same note: "Brill matters." *Saturday Review* contributor James Kelly, although he complained of the book's "breezy shorthand style," nonetheless concluded: "Here is a novel for people puzzled by abrasive, contemporary life . . . and for those who would like a fictional look at what it would be like to be a free agent (Brill) on life's highway."

Like Chaucer's *Canterbury Tales,* whose structure it mirrors, *Now Playing at Canterbury,* Bourjaily's seventh novel, brings together a disparate collection of stories and narrators. Instead of pilgrims on their way to Canterbury, however, the characters in Bourjaily's novel are gathering at a newly constructed cultural center at a large midwestern university. The hero of *A Game Men Play,* which is part thriller and part novel of ideas, examines the human condition by reflecting upon his eventful career as an espionage agent, first with the OSS during World War II, and later with the CIA. Reviews of the novel alternated between extremes of praise and derogation. Raymond Carver, writing in the *Chicago Tribune Book World,* hailed it as "far and away Bourjaily's best fictional creation to date," and noted, "The novel is Conradian in its entanglements of motive and its intricacy of plot." But *New York Times* critic Anatole Broyard insisted, "It is difficult to determine what this novel is trying to do. Filled with improbable violence and all-too-probable sentimentality, it vacillates between seriousness and sensationalism."

In his later fiction, Bourjaily has continued to experiment with new styles and new themes. In his epistolary novel *The Great Fake Book,* which *Chicago Tribune Books* critic John Seelye deemed "a tour de force of considerable complexity," Bourjaily draws upon his extensive knowledge of jazz to tell the story of a man's search for his father. The "fake book" of the title refers to a book of chord changes and melodies that professional musicians use to play standard tunes at a glance. The novella *Old Soldier,* whose plot unfolds during a fishing trip in Maine, examines the bond between two brothers, one an ex-soldier and the other a gay musician suffering from AIDS.

Contemporary Novelists contributor David Sanders has noted that despite Bourjaily's "remarkable variety of subject and technique," he has failed to gain "the popularity or the critical recognition that many have thought his due over the past 35 years." According to William A. Francis in the *Dictionary of Literary Biography,* "Bourjaily's reputation rests on his ability to tell wonderful stories with vivid surprising details. . . . [His] novels depict the common man struggling—often heroically, often paradoxically—to live with the contradictions that define society." For his own part, Bourjaily, a reticent man who has rarely sought publicity, has remained philosophical about his own lack of recognition. In a 1977 interview with Matthew Bruccoli, he remarked, "Each time there has been a book I've been, if not optimistic, at least hopeful that I would make some money and get more general recognition. . . . But meanwhile, I suppose, one constructs a life of what satisfactions are available."

BIOGRAPHICAL/CRITICAL SOURCES:

BOOKS

Aldridge, John W., *After the Lost Generation,* McGraw (New York City), 1951.

Contemporary Literary Criticism, Gale (Detroit), Volume 8, 1978, Volume 62, 1991.

Contemporary Novelists, sixth edition, St. James Press (Detroit), 1991.

Conversations with Writers, Gale, 1977.

Dictionary of Literary Biography, Volume 143: *American Novelists since World War II, Third Series* Gale, 1994.

Friedman, Melvin and John B. Vickery, editors, *The Shaken Realist,* Louisiana State University Press, 1970.

Madden, Charles F., editor, *Talks with Authors,* Southern Illinois University Press, 1968.

PERIODICALS

Arizona Quarterly, autumn, 1955, pp. 272-75.

Atlantic Monthly, January, 1971; October, 1976.

Centennial Review, spring, 1984, pp. 100-05.

Chicago Tribune Books, February 15, 1987, pp. 6-7.

Chicago Tribune Book World, January 20,1980.
Commonweal, March 18, 1955, p. 639; August 29, 1958, pp. 550-51; March 17, 1961, pp. 641-43; June 16, 1967, pp. 373-75.
Commentary, April, 1961, pp. 360-63.
Hudson Review, summer, 1967, pp. 325-39.
Lively Arts and Book Review, November 20, 1960, p. 31.
New Leader, January 17, 1977, pp.21-22.
New Republic, February 21, 1955, pp. 18-19; November 10, 1958, pp. 16-18; December 19, 1960, pp. 17-18.
New Statesman, June 16, 1967; June 13, 1971.
Newsweek, January 30, 1967; September 13, 1976.
New York Herald Tribune Book Review. August 24, 1947, p. 3; March 6, 1955, p. 4; August 24, 1958, p. 7.
New York Times, November 10, 1970, p. 45; January 19, 1980, p. 21.
New York Times Book Review, August 31, 1958, p. 12; January 29, 1967, p. 4; November 1, 1970, p.5; September 12, 1976; January 27, 1980, pp. 14-15; January 18, 1987, p. 35; October 28, 1990.
Publishers Weekly, February 6, 1976; September 6, 1993.
Saturday Review, February 4, 1967; December 5, 1970, p. 40; September 18, 1976, pp. 26-28.
Saturday Review of Literature, August 30, 1947, pp. 17-18.
Time, September 13, 1976.
Times Literary Supplement, June 22, 1967.
Washington Post Book World, September 12, 1976, pp. H1-H2; February 4, 1980; January 11, 1987, p. 6.
World Journal Tribune Book Week, February 5, 1967, p. 17.*

* * *

BOWER, Tom 1946-

PERSONAL: Born September 28, 1946, in London, England; son of George and Sylvia Bower; married Veronica Wadley (a newspaper editor) in 1984; children: four. *Education:* London School of Economics, LLB. *Avocational interests:* Skiing, walking, reading.

ADDRESSES: Home—10 Thurrow Rd., London NW3 5PL, England. *Office*—British Broadcasting Company Television Centre, Kensington House, London W14, England. *Agent*—Curtis Brown, 162-168 Regent St., London W1R 5TB, England.

CAREER: British Broadcasting Company (BBC), London, England, correspondent and television documentary producer; writer.

WRITINGS:

Blind Eye to Murder: Britain, America and the Purging of Nazi Germany—A Pledge Betrayed, Andre Deutsch (London), 1981, published as *The Pledge Betrayed: America and Britain and the Denazification of Postwar Germany,* Doubleday (Garden City, NY), 1982.
Klaus Barbie: The "Butcher of Lyons," Pantheon (New York City), 1984.
The Paperclip Conspiracy: The Hunt for the Nazi Scientists, Little, Brown (Boston), 1987, published as *The Paperclip Conspiracy: The Battle for the Spoils and Secrets of Nazi Germany,* M. Joseph (London), 1987.
Maxwell: The Outsider, Aurum (London), 1988, Viking (New York City), 1992.
The Red Web: MI6 and the KGB Mastercop, Aurum, 1990.
Tiny Rowland: A Rebel Tycoon, Heinemann (London), 1993.
Maxwell: The Final Verdict, HarperCollins (London), 1995.
The Perfect English Spy: Sir Dick White and the Secret War, 1935-90, St. Martins (New York City), 1995.
Nazi Gold: The Full Story of the Fifty-Year Swiss-Nazi Conspiracy to Steal Billions from Europe's Jews and Holocaust Survivors, HarperCollins (New York City), 1997.

SIDELIGHTS: Tom Bower is the author of several works of nonfiction that focus on National Socialist (Nazi) crimes and criminals during and after World War II. His first book, *Blind Eye to Murder: Britain, America and the Purging of Nazi Germany—A Pledge Betrayed,* details the attempts to bring the Nazis and their collaborators to justice after World War II. Bower claims that many Germans in powerful positions during the War escaped official retribution through a combination of disagreements between military and civilian personnel about how best to handle the situation, the lack of planning by the Allies, the chaos of the postwar period, and the lack of cooperation of the German people themselves. James Rowe, writing in the *New York Times Book Review,* claimed that "there was in fact no way to accomplish the justice and the reform that almost everyone in England and the United States had wanted." *Listener* contributor Phillip Whitehead called *Blind Eye to Murder* "a massive and scholarly study" and *Los Angeles Times Book Review* critic Allan M. Winkler asserted that "Bower confronts the basic issue of personal responsibility for actions taken in time of war." In *Publishers Weekly,* Genevieve Stuttaford commented that "this forcefully written account is a distressing picture of justice gone astray."

Bower's next book, *Klaus Barbie: The "Butcher of Lyons,"* focuses on the crimes of a man who killed and gave orders to kill for the Nazis during World War II and later had clients ranging from Bolivian cocaine growers to United States counterintelligence forces. "Barbie obsesses us because of the way in which his extraordinary career weaves together so many varieties of evil, cruelty and deceit, and connects up so many apparently separate sources of public paranoia," wrote Neal Ascherson in the *Observer.* Because the book is based in part on transcripts of interviews with the subject, who died in 1991, some reviewers questioned the reliability of some of Bower's conclusions, since Barbie is generally considered a consummate liar. J. E. Talbott also criticized what he calls "Bower's hastily assembled book" for its failure to distinguish the pivotal from the trivial in his account of Barbie's life. "'For the first time the full story . . .' reads the blurb on the cover," wrote Richard Dowden in the *Times Educational Supplement,* "but one feels, having read Bower's excellent story, it is only the beginning of the thread."

Bower continued to expose the fates of Nazis after World War II in his next book, *The Paperclip Conspiracy: The Hunt for Nazi Scientists* (also published as *The Paperclip Conspiracy: The Battle for the Spoils and Secrets of Nazi Germany*). In this work, Bower reveals the Allies' attempts to claim German technological advances by rescuing its scientists—many of whom participated or collaborated in Nazi War atrocities—from attempts to bring them to justice after the War. The U.S. government under President Harry S. Truman devised Operation Paperclip, which allowed Nazi scientists to be brought to the U.S. to work in the military-industrial complex. Of *The Paperclip Conspiracy,* David Wise wrote in the *New York Times Book Review:* "Although his narrative is often obscured by a sea of quoted documents, Mr. Bower reconstructs a significant and disturbing story." *Los Angeles Times* reviewer Jonathan Kirsch concluded that the volume "reads almost like a World War II thriller, but it's also a work of investigative reporting that bristles with righteous indignation."

In his next book, *The Red Web: MI6 and the KGB Mastercop,* Bower relates the early history of the British Secret Intelligence Service's enmity of the former Soviet Union, including an elaborate plan to infiltrate and financially support nationalist and anti-communist movements in the satellite countries of Eastern Europe. David Stafford of the Toronto *Globe and Mail* remarked, "The Cold War added urgency to this historic vision, while freshly minted nostalgia about resistance exploits in Nazi Europe colored hopes about the prospects for similar triumphs behind the Iron Curtain." Unfortunately, the KGB, the intelligence agency of the former Soviet Union, was aware of these efforts, and by 1955 the British undercover agents were all either dead or in prison. While touting the usefulness of Bower's efforts in *The Red Web* to uncover a little-known historical occurrence, Stafford concluded that "Bower's style is pedestrian, and his dense undergrowth of facts and names is rarely relieved by clearings of insight or imagination." On the other hand, Anthony Cavendish wrote in the London *Sunday Times* that *The Red Web* is "a fine, well-researched book which may be the first in a new genre of espionage literature."

Robert Maxwell, who has been described as a charming though unscrupulous businessperson, is the subject of Bower's next expose, *Maxwell: The Outsider.* Maxwell was a victim of the Nazis who became an officer in the British army, a member of its parliament, and eventually a wealthy publishing magnate whose death occurred just as his empire was dissolving. "Maxwell's life was so turbulent, so noisy, so full of storm and strife that it makes the lives of most of the rest of us seem hopelessly pallid," remarked John Taylor in the *New York Times Book Review.* Martin Walker of the *Washington Post Book World* concluded that *Maxwell: The Outsider* "is well-researched, and sometimes almost sympathetic, showing an understanding of the snobbish and anti-semitic obstacles placed in Maxwell's way by a complacent British Establishment." The unauthorized biography, published before its subject's death, greatly angered Maxwell. Bower once explained to *CA:* "*Maxwell: The Outsider* caused an enormous furor in Britain. Maxwell not only started litigation against me but against every bookshop in Britain that attempted to sell the book. It was the first denunciation of him as a crook when he was at the height of his power and wealth and was not widely believed."

"Written in the shadow of threatened writs, about a man who was compulsively secretive about his business affairs, [*Maxwell: The Outsider*] stands as one of the great journalistic achievements of our time," judged Andy McSmith in a *Observer* review of Bower's subsequent book, *Maxwell: The Final Verdict.* McSmith urged people to read *Maxwell: The Final Verdict,* "a 400-page account of the last year of Maxwell's life and its aftermath," in lieu of his Bower's original biography on Maxwell, because "there is a mass of detail which either was not known before or could not be told." *Maxwell: The Final Verdict* is "a story which has everything: greed, intrigue, fraud, sex, spies, famous names and a mysterious and violent death. It is, though, a profoundly serious and unsensational narrative. . . . the known facts are sensational enough: they do not need to be embellished with wild supposition," according to McSmith, who noted: "All it lacks is a fitting ending and a decent title."

Maxwell: The Final Verdict discusses a variety of activities occurring prior to and after Maxwell's death, including Maxwell's hostile reactions to *Maxwell: The Outsider* and the trial of his two sons. Central to Bower's second book on Maxwell is the various and extensive list of people associated with Maxwell's underhanded business activities, specifically his use of pension funds to repay massive business loans. "Bower's initial list of characters is helpful, but it could be enlarged as well as supplemented by brief summaries of the many transactions mentioned," commented John Chown in the *Times Literary Supplement.* Nevertheless, Chown concluded: "[*Maxwell: The Final Verdict*] has a complex story to tell and is not always easy to follow, but it is well worth the effort." Paul Foot asserted in *Spectator* that Bower's "relentless research has produced something much more than an expose of a single rogue." As Chown stated, "Maxwell's frauds would never have succeeded without his supporting cast."

The Perfect English Spy: Sir Dick White and the Secret War, 1935-90 is "an authoritative account of the crises and scandals that plagued Britain's secret service throughout the Cold War," described a *Publishers Weekly* reviewer. Writing more than just a biography of Dick White, a British intelligence agent who "was undoubtedly one of the outstanding civil servants of the postwar period," according to Oleg Gordievsky in *Spectator,* "Bower sets about the worthy task of giving Dick White his due, while along the way creating a sketch of postwar British intelligence and counter-intelligence. . . . His tribute to Dick White is generous. . . . [and his history of British intelligence reports] a series of mistakes, accidents, fiascoes, even catastrophes." Gordievsky believed the book, which is based largely on interviews with White, contains "fascinating . . . accurate. . . . informative" information.

Not as enthusiastic about the work, *Times Literary Supplement* contributor Keith Jeffery faulted Bower's presentation for being "suffused with a persistent ambivalence concerning White's qualities as an intelligence expert." "Bower (who appears to have found White a charming man) seems unable to make up his mind about him. . . . [And] as might be expected, Tom Bower has succumbed to the temptation to gild his narrative by rendering recollected conversations in the present tense," Jeffery wrote, concluding that "*The Perfect English Spy* is not an academic volume, though with a very welcome 'scholarly apparatus' of source notes and bibliography it goes further than most journalistic efforts in this field." More positively, Robin Rasay maintained in *New Statesman & Society:* "Though it is patchy—nothing on nuclear weapons—[*The Perfect English Spy*] is a very interesting and, in places, very important work. It is a significant contribution to our understanding of postwar British foreign policy as well as to the history of our secret services."

A more recent book by Bower returns to his commonly addressed subject—crimes associated with World War II Nazi activities. "Bower's masterly chronicle [*Nazi Gold: The Full Story of the Fifty-Year Swiss-Nazi Conspiracy to Steal Billions from Europe's Jews and Holocaust Survivors*] makes clear [that] the Nazis could never have prevailed as long as they did without the Swiss. Indeed, as Bower makes clear, the war would most likely have ended a full year earlier had it not been for the financial intervention of Swiss bankers," declared Ann Louise Bardach in the *Los Angeles Times Book Review.* Gold, cash, art, and various valuables were looted by Nazis, stated Bardach, explaining: "Billions of dollars of the looted gold and cash and an estimated $2.5 billion in stolen art were sent to Switzerland, where the Reich's Swiss bankers attended to its purchase, care and investment. Nazi Germany was, after all, the most important client in the history of Swiss banking. . . . Thanks to the Third Reich, Switzerland emerged from the war as the second-richest country in the world."

Nazi Gold was characterized by a Booklist contributor as a "fast-paced expose. . . . [a] unique and invaluable volume." Although Randall J. Schroeder declared in a *Library Journal* review that the work was "tedious" at times and was written with unrestrained "contempt for the Swiss," the critic recommended the book and praised the author's ability to "[relate] the victim's story." Donna Seaman suggested in the *New York Times Book Review* that the book, perhaps to a fault, lacked a fair balance of information on "Swiss who opposed the Nazis." Seaman also expressed disappointment that the book "was rushed" and did not include declassified documents released with a report by Clinton's Administration. According to Seaman "Bower is at his best describing the interaction of the American and Swiss negotiators, and the pressures the Swiss banks place on their Government."

BIOGRAPHICAL/CRITICAL SOURCES:

PERIODICALS

Booklist, September 11, 1995; October 1, 1995, p. 235; April 15, 1997.
Globe and Mail (Toronto), September 30, 1989.
Library Journal, October 1, 1995; May 15, 1997, p. 85.
Listener, August 6, 1981, pp. 117-18.
London Review of Books, September 23, 1993, p. 7.
Los Angeles Times, March 15, 1982; December 17, 1987.
Los Angeles Times Book Review, June 3, 1984, p. 16; July 6, 1997, p. 8.
New Statesman & Society, January 10, 1992, p. 36; April 7, 1995, p. 52.
New York Times, February 9, 1988, p. C20.
New York Times Book Review, February 14, 1982, pp. 13, 27; February 14, 1988, p. 13; April 12, 1992, p. 10; June 22, 1997, p. 25.
Observer, January 29, 1984, p. 52; March 27, 1994, p. 22; February 4, 1996, p. 15.
Publishers Weekly, November 13, 1981, p. 82; September 11, 1995, p. 67; November 4, 1996.
Spectator, April 1, 1995, pp. 36-37; February 17, 1996, p. 34.
Sunday Times (London), September 24, 1989.
Times (London), August 20, 1981.
Times Educational Supplement, March 25, 1983, p. 29; July 20, 1984, p. 20.
Times Literary Supplement, May 12, 1995, p. 4; March 22, 1996, p. 31.
Virginia Quarterly Review, spring, 1996.
Washington Post Book World, May 3, 1992, p. 5.*

BOWYER, (Raymond) Chaz 1926-

PERSONAL: Born September 29, 1926, in Weymouth, England; son of Reginald (a builder) and Dorothy (Northam) Bowyer; widowed; children: Katharin, Jeff, Lisa Janine. *Education:* Attended high school in Solihull and Nelson, England.

ADDRESSES: Home and office—77 Southern Reach, Mulbarton, Norwich NR14 8BU, England.

CAREER: Royal Air Force, 1943-69, retired as sergeant; served as armament technician, airman, and instructor in explosives and armaments; stationed in Egypt, Libya, Palestine, Singapore, and Aden; writer, 1958—.

MEMBER: Royal Air Force Association (life member).

WRITINGS:

The Flying Elephants, Macdonald & Co., 1972.
Mosquito at War, Ian Allan, 1973.
(Editor) *Bomber Pilot, 1916-18,* Ian Allan, 1974.
(Editor) *Fighter Pilot on the Western Front,* William Kimber, 1975.
Hurricane at War, Ian Allan, 1975.
Airmen of World War I, Arms & Armour Press, 1975.
Sunderland at War, Ian Allan, 1976.
(Editor) *Wings over the Somme,* William Kimber, 1976.
Beaufighter at War, Ian Allan, 1976.
Hampden Special, Ian Allan, 1977.
Path Finders at War, Ian Allan, 1977.
Albert Ball, V.C., William Kimber, 1977.
History of the R.A.F., Hamlyn, 1977.
Sopwith Camel: King of Combat, Glasney Press, 1978.
For Valour: The Air V.C.s, William Kimber, 1978.
Guns in the Sky: The Air Gunners, Dent, 1979.
Coastal Command at War, Ian Allan, 1979.
Fighter Command, 1936-38, Dent, 1980.
Spitfire: A Tribute, Arms & Armour Press, 1980.
Bomber Group at War, Ian Allan, 1980.
(Editor) *Fall of an Eagle: Ernst Udet,* William Kimber, 1980.
Eugene Esmonde, V.C., D.S.O., William Kimber, 1981.
Desert Air Force at War, Ian Allan, 1981.
Age of the Biplane, Bison Books, 1981.
Air War over Europe, 1939-45, William Kimber, 1981.

Encyclopedia of British Military Aircraft, Arms & Armour, 1982.
Wellington at War, Ian Allan, 1982.
Bomber Barons, William Kimber, 1983.
Images of Air War, 1939-45, Batsford, 1983.
R.A.F. Handbook, 1939-45, Ian Allan, 1984.
Bristol Blenheim, Ian Allan, 1984.
Fighter Pilots of the R.A.F., 1939-45, William Kimber, 1984.
Mosquito Squadrons of the R.A.F., Ian Allan, 1984.
Men of the Desert Air Force, William Kimber, 1984.
Gloster Meteor, Ian Allan, 1985.
Men of Coastal Command, William Kimber, 1985.
Bristol F2B: King of the Two-Seaters, Ian Allan, 1985.
Tales from the Bombers, William Kimber, 1985.
The Wellington Bomber, William Kimber, 1986.
Beaufighter, William Kimber, 1987.
RAF Operations, 1918-38, William Kimber, 1988.
The Short Sunderland, Aston Publications, 1989.
Handley Page Bombers of World War I, Aston Publications, 1990.
(Editor) *Enemy Coast Ahead,* Bridge Books, 1995.
(Editor) *RFC Communiques, 1917-18,* Grub Street, 1998.
RAF Calshot, 1913-61, F. Smith, 1998.

Author of booklets. Former editor, *Journal of the Cross and Cockade Society.*

SIDELIGHTS: Chaz Bowyer once told *CA:* "My motivation? Primarily to place on permanent record *accurate* accounts of men, deeds, and events connected with Royal Air Force history. This is exemplified (perhaps) by *For Valour: The Air V.C.s* which is now accepted as the standard reference work on the subject. I am tired of reading historical drivel as perpetrated by 'well-known' authors, most of whom are simply novelists or journalists with no background knowledge of genuine aviation history. Too many 'military historians' are simply writers jumping on the history bandwagon only for profit."

* * *

BOXER, Charles Ralph 1904-

PERSONAL: Born March 8, 1904; son of Hugh and Jane (Patterson) Boxer; married Emily Hahn, 1945; children: two daughters. *Education:* Attended Wellington College and Royal Military College, Sandhurst, England.

ADDRESSES: Home—Ringshall End, Little Gaddesden, Hertfordshire HP4 1NF, England.

CAREER: University of London, London, England, Camoens Professor of Portuguese, 1947-51, professor of history of the Far East, 1951-53, Camoens Professor of Portuguese, 1953-67, professor emeritus, 1968—, fellow of King's College, 1967, honorary fellow of School of Oriental and African Studies, 1974; Yale University, New Haven, CT, professor of history of expansion of Europe overseas, 1969-72, professor emeritus, 1972—. Indiana University, visiting research professor, 1967-76; lecturer at colleges and universities, including Johns Hopkins University, Bryn Mawr College, University of Virginia, and University of Wisconsin. National Maritime Museum, trustee, 1961-68. *Military service:* Served, 1939-47; Japanese prisoner of war in Hong Kong, 1941-45; became major.

MEMBER: British Academy (fellow), Royal Netherlands Academy of Sciences.

AWARDS, HONORS: Received honorary degrees from universities of Utrecht, 1950, Lisbon, 1952, Bahia, 1959, Liverpool, 1966, and Hong Kong, 1971; Order of Santiago da Espada (Portugal); Grand Cross of the Order of the Infante Dom Henrique (Portugal); Knight of the Order of St. Gregory the Great, 1969.

WRITINGS:

IN ENGLISH

(Editor and translator) Goncalo de Siqueira de Sousa, *A Portuguese Embassy to Japan, 1644-1647,* K. Paul, Trench, Truebner, 1928, published as *The Embassy of Captain Goncalo de Siqueira de Sousa to Japan in 1644-1647,* Oficinas Graficas da Tipografia Mercantil, 1938.
The Affair of the Madre de Deus: A Chapter in the History of the Portuguese in Japan, K. Paul, Trench, Truebner, 1929.
(Editor and author of introduction) Paul Craesbeeck, *Commentaries of Ruy de Andrada,* George Routledge and Sons, 1930.
(Editor and translator) *The Journal of Maerten Hampertszoon Tromp, Anno 1639,* Cambridge University Press, 1930.
(Author of introduction and notes) Frans Caron, *A True Description of the Mighty Kingdoms of Japan and Siam,* Argonaut Press, 1935.
Jan Compagnie in Japan, 1600-1817: An Essay on the Cultural, Artistic, and Scientific Influence Exer-

cised by the Hollanders in Japan from the Seventeenth to the Nineteenth Centuries, M. Nijhoff, 1936, 2nd edition, 1950.

The Topasses of Timor, Indisch Instituut, 1947.

Fidalgos in the Far East, 1550-1770: Fact and Fancy in the History of Macao, M. Nijhoff, 1948, 2nd edition, Oxford University Press, 1968.

The Christian Century in Japan, 1549-1650, University of California Press (Berkeley, CA), 1951.

Salvador de Sa and the Struggle for Brazil and Angola, 1602-1686, Athlone Press, 1952, Greenwood Press (Greenwood, CT), 1975.

(Editor) *South China in the Sixteenth Century: Being the Narratives of Galeote Pereira, Friar Gaspar da Cruz, and Friar Martin de Rada,* Hakluyt Society, 1953.

The Dutch in Brazil, 1624-1654, Clarendon Press, 1957.

The Great Ship from Amacon: Annals of Macao and the Old Japan Trade, 1555-1640, Centro de Estudos Historicos Ultramarinos, 1959.

(Editor and translator) Bernardo Gomes de Brito, editor, *The Tragic History of the Sea, 1589-1622: Narratives of the Shipwrecks of the Portuguese East Indiamen Sao Thome (1589), Santa Alberto (1593), Sao Joao Baptista (1622), and the Journeys of the Survivors in South East Africa,* Cambridge University Press, 1959.

(With Carlos de Azevedo) *Fort Jesus and the Portuguese in Mombasa, 1593-1729,* Hollis & Carter, 1960.

The Golden Age of Brazil, 1695-1750: Growing Pains of a Colonial Society, University of California Press, 1962.

(With J. S. Cummins) *The Dominican Mission in Japan, 1602-1622, and Lope de Vega,* Archivum Fratrum Praedicatorum, 1963.

Race Relations in the Portuguese Colonial Empire, 1415-1825, Clarendon Press, 1963.

Two Pioneers of Tropical Medicine: Garcia d'Orta and Nicolas Monardes, Hispanic and Luso-Brazilian Councils (London), 1963.

The Dutch Seaborne Empire, 1600-1800, Knopf (New York City), 1965.

Portuguese Society in the Tropics: The Municipal Councils of Goa, Macao, Bahia, and Luanda, 1510-1800, University of Wisconsin Press (Madison, WI), 1965.

An African Eldorado: Monomotapa and Mocambique, 1498-1752, Central African Historical Association, 1966.

Francisco Vieira de Figueiredo: A Portuguese Merchant-Adventurer in South East Asia, 1624-1667, M. Nijhoff, 1967.

Some Literary Sources for the History of Brazil in the Eighteenth Century, Clarendon Press, 1967.

(Editor and translator) de Brito, editor, *Further Selections from the Tragic History of the Sea, 1559-1565: Narratives of Shipwrecks of the Portuguese East Indiamen,* Cambridge University Press, 1968.

Four Centuries of Portuguese Expansion, 1415-1825: A Succinct Survey, Witwatersrand University Press, 1961, University of California Press, 1969.

The Portuguese Seaborne Empire, 1415-1825, Knopf, 1969.

The Anglo-Dutch Wars of the Seventeenth Century, 1652-1674, Her Majesty's Stationary Office, 1974.

Women in Iberian Expansion Overseas, 1415-1815: Some Facts, Fancies, and Personalities, Oxford University Press, 1975 (published in England as *Mary and Misogyny: Women in Iberian Expansion Overseas, 1415-1815; Some Facts, Fancies, and Personalities,* Duckworth, 1975).

The Church Militant and Iberian Expansion, 1440-1770, Johns Hopkins University Press (Baltimore, MD), 1978.

OTHER

(Editor) *A aclamacao del Rei D. Joao IV em Goa e um Macau: Relacoes contemporaneas reeditados e anotadas,* [Lisbon, Portugal], 1932.

(Editor) *Embaixada de Macau ao Japao em 1640,* Imprensa de Armada, 1933.

(Editor) Caetano de Sousa Pereira, *O plano da reconquista da provincia do Norte,* Tipografica Rangel, 1936.

O coronel Pedro de Mello e a sublevacao geral de Timor em 1729-1731, Escola Tipografica do Orfanato Salesiano (Macao), 1937.

Sisnando Dias Bayao: Conquistador da "Mae de Ouro," [Lisbon], 1938.

(With J. M. Braga) *Algumas notas sobre a bibliografia de Macau,* Escola Tipografica Salesiana, 1939.

Antonio Coelho Guerreiro, e as relacoes entre Macau e Timor, no comeco do secule XVIII, Tipografica do Orfanato da Imaculada Conceicao de Macau, 1940.

Breve relacao da vida e feitos de Lopo e Inacio Sarmento de Carvalho, Imprensa Nacional (Macao), 1940.

As viagens de Japao e os seus capitaes mores, 1550-1640, Escola Tipografica do Oratorio de S.J. Bosco, 1941.

(Editor) *Macau na epoca da restauracao,* Imprensa Nacional, 1942.

Subsidios para a historia dos capitais gerais e governadores de Macau, 1557-1770, [Macao], 1944.

A proposito dum livrinho xilografico dos Jesuitas de Pequim (secolo XVIII): Ensaio historico, Imprensa Nacional, 1947.

"Adonde hay valor hay honor": Esboco biografico do almirante Luis Velho, 1624-1669, [Lisbon], 1948.

(Editor) Joao Rodrigues Girao, *Antes quebrar que torcer; ou, Pundonor portugues em Nagasaqui, 3-6 de Janeiro de 1610,* Imprensa Nacional, 1950.

(With Frazao de Vasconcelos) *Andre Furtado de Mendonca, 1558-1610,* Diviso de Publicacoes Biblioteca, Angencia Geral do Ultramar, 1955.

Contributor of articles to numerous scholarly journals.

SIDELIGHTS: An authority on European territorial expansion, Charles Ralph Boxer has written numerous books on the Dutch and Portuguese colonization in Brazil, Angola, Japan, and China. *The Dutch in Brazil, 1624-1654,* for example, is an account of Holland's rise to power in the early 1600s. Because the Portuguese closed their ports to Dutch trade, the Dutch were forced to obtain salt, sugar, and other necessities from friendlier ports such as Africa and America. Unintentionally, this act was the catalyst that brought Holland fame and glory as it rose to become the most powerful maritime and colonial faction of the early seventeenth century.

The Dutch continued their expansion into both Brazil, where they commandeered the profitable sugar industry, and Angola, where they obtained slaves to work the mills. Ironically, it was the Portuguese, then under Spanish domination, who were finally able to drive the Dutch out of Brazil. In a review of *The Dutch in Brazil* for the *New Statesman and Nation,* H. R. Trevor-Roper compared it to Boxer's earlier work, *Salvador de Sa and the Struggle for Brazil and Angola, 1602-1686.* Whereas the earlier book presented new information and fresh insights into the Dutch occupation of Brazil, Trevor-Roper maintained that the newer work, "just as scholarly, just as well-written, is more squarely built, and sheds its light directly on the central problem." A writer for the *Times Literary Supplement* concluded: "The merit of Professor Boxer's accomplishment rests on the clear and methodical ordering of the subject-matter, on his proved impartiality and, not least, on the assurance of his historical judgment."

The Golden Age of Brazil, 1695-1750: Growing Pains of a Colonial Society, according to *Library Journal* reviewer F. L. Cinquemani, "is more than a social, political, and economic narrative." It is also "a well-written, thoroughly researched study" that transcends more formal historical accounts by addressing both the strengths and weaknesses of the colony in its heyday. Boxer's research penetrated original sources and included details of the Duguay-Trouin expedition that seized the port of Rio de Janeiro for France. In the *New York Times Book Review,* R. M. Morse reported: "Mr. Boxer concedes neither to romance nor to pedantry. His book abounds in vignettes of the seven deadly sins and, less frequently, their opposite virtues." Morse recommended the work as a "reminder of the complexities, ironies and recalcitrancies of any transition from colony to nation." "It is also," he concluded, "that rare history which rewards [both] general readers and the most specialized scholars."

Another of Boxer's works, *The Dutch Seaborne Empire, 1600-1800,* details the development, prosperity, and subsequent decay of the Dutch empire. Boxer rationalized in this book that wide-spread political squabbling, racism that held back colonization and expansion, and insufficient supplies of coal required to carry Holland into the industrial nineteenth century were all factors that contributed to its decline. Reviewer E. K. Welsch commended the author for "skillfully [introducing] the reader not to kings and battles but to the people who lived [through that time]." A writer for *New Yorker* likewise praised Boxer's presentation as "far more than just theories of history; he offers an astonishing amount of statistical information, and uses it to give us a sense of the quality of life in the Netherlands' golden age."

In addition to the history of Dutch expansion, Boxer wrote of Portugal and her colonial activities from 1415 to 1825. In *The Portuguese Seaborne Empire, 1415-1825* he discusses the motivations behind Portuguese colonization. Portugal, he explains, was not interested in finding a new route to the Far East by sailing west, as her native son Christopher Columbus was, but wished instead to round the Cape of Good Hope in order to open up trade from the Indian Ocean. Spurred on by fantastic tales of an enormously wealthy priest-king residing in splendor somewhere in the vast expanse of Africa, the Portuguese pursued colonization in hopes of obtaining for themselves the riches of that world.

The Portuguese Seaborne Empire was highly praised for its portrayal of four centuries of expansion and motivations that inspired it. A reviewer for the *Times Literary Supplement* commented that "the author's familiarity with the onion-and-garlic side of Portuguese idealism, and perhaps also a temperamental scepticism, makes his tribute to the achievements of Portuguese Christianity all the more impressive." Robert Rea hailed the book as "a magnificent new study." He added that "this volume is a great work of synthesis, an illuminating introduction packed with challenging interpretations and insights."

Consisting of a series of lectures given by Boxer at the University of Wisconsin, *Portuguese Society in the Tropics: The Municipal Councils of Goa, Macao, Bahia, and Luanda, 1510-1800,* is an examination of the character and composition of the municipal councils of Portugal in the period between 1510 and 1800. One of the major points Boxer discusses in the book is the high degree of local autonomy enjoyed by the councils due to the lack of qualified Portuguese statesmen to fill the seats of administration. As with his many other books, Boxer was again commended for presenting keen insights into previously slighted issues. The *Times Literary Supplement,* for instance, declared, "Treading once more on virgin soil, Professor Boxer gives an admiringly succinct and readable account of the functions and importance of these municipal councils."

In *Race Relations in the Portuguese Colonial Empire, 1415-1825* Boxer attacked the popular notion that Portugal refrained from promoting racial superiority during its era of colonization. He argues that this was simply not the case, that the Portuguese were in fact no worse, yet no better, than the other European colonizing powers. According to the author, they engaged in slave trade, mistreatment of black subjects, and other common practices of the time. Although the work was considered controversial in Portugal, it was well received in other European countries and in the United States as well. A writer for the *Virginia Quarterly Review* assessed that "this sincere, scholarly book restores a much needed authenticity to the study of Portuguese global conquest and colonization." The *Times Literary Supplement* concurred: "Professor Boxer writes with refreshing directness. If only all works of learning were as sensible, pungent and sparing of verbiage."

Related to Boxer's studies on Portuguese colonization, *Women in Iberian Expansion Overseas, 1415-1815: Some Facts, Fancies, and Personalities* probes the role of women during that era. The book was praised for revealing a long-ignored portion of the historical record, for as one writer pointed out, "exploration of the role of women has much to say about culture, society, religious and intellectual history, and the economy." Reviewer John Lynch deemed the work "a bibliographical and narrative masterpiece" and added: "Scholarship allied to lucid narrative and a sense of humour—these are the qualities we have come to expect from the prolific pen of Professor Boxer."

Boxer's research also followed the Portuguese into the Far East. *The Christian Century in Japan, 1549-1650,* based partly on research among original, once-confidential Jesuit documents, explored the impact of the Roman Catholic church and its philosophy of mission on medieval Japanese society. It was the Portuguese explorers who bore the missionary priests to Tokugawa Japan and, according to *Christian Science Monitor* reviewer Randall Gould, "played the leading, probably decisive role" in a period of far-reaching historical significance. K. S. Latourette reported in the *Annals of the American Academy of Political and Social Science* that Boxer "writes in thoroughly readable style and with as much objectivity as is given to most of us," calling the book "the best comprehensive account which we have." *Catholic World* reviewer Joseph McSorley praised the author for a style that is "simple, clear, even colloquial at times" and for "his admirable objectivity." A *San Francisco Chronicle* critic described *The Christian Century in Japan* as "a beautiful book. It is a handsome volume in its physical appearance and the author combines superb scholarship with a naturalness and humor in his writing."

Another study of the Far East was *Jan Compagnie in Japan, 1600-1817: An Essay on the Cultural, Artistic, and Scientific Influence Exercised by the Hollanders in Japan from the Seventeenth to the Nineteenth Centuries.* This scholarly review of early Japanese documents on arts and the sciences was first published in the Netherlands in 1936. Critics especially appreciated its illustrations in the form of woodcuts and other materials drawn from Boxer's personal collection of rare books and original art.

BIOGRAPHICAL/CRITICAL SOURCES:

PERIODICALS

American Historical Review, January, 1958; October, 1970.

Annals of the American Academy of Political and Social Science, November, 1951.

Book Week, January 30, 1966, p. 5.
Book World, February 1, 1970, p. 10.
Catholic World, October, 1951.
Choice, December, 1975.
Christian Science Monitor, July 3, 1951, p. 11.
Commonweal, July 6, 1951.
Economist, January 1, 1966; December 13, 1969.
Library Journal, May 15, 1962; October 15, 1965; November 1, 1969; November 1, 1970.
New Statesman and Nation, February 23, 1957.
New Yorker, November 6, 1965; April 11, 1970.
New York Times Book Review, June 17, 1962, p. 7; November 28, 1965, p. 24.
San Francisco Chronicle, September 16, 1951, p. 13.
Spectator, November 8, 1969.
Times Literary Supplement, September 14, 1951, p. 585; April 12, 1957, p. 227; September 21, 1962, p. 722; June 4, 1964; June 2, 1966; September 4, 1969, p. 985; December 18, 1969; October 3, 1975.
Virginia Quarterly Review, summer, 1964.*

* * *

BOYLE, Gerry 1956-

PERSONAL: Born May 20, 1956, in Chicago, IL; son of Emmet J. and Jeanne (McGowan) Boyle; married Mary Victoria Foley (a teacher), June 21, 1980; children: Emily, Carolyn, Charles. *Education:* Colby College, B.A., 1978. *Avocational interests:* Tennis, birding, canoeing.

ADDRESSES: Home—Maine. *Agent*—Helen Brann Agency, 94 Curtis Rd., Bridgewater, CT 06752.

CAREER: Rumford Falls Times, Rumford, ME, reporter and editor, 1979; *Central Maine Morning Sentinel,* Waterville, reporter and editor, 1981-87, columnist, 1987—.

AWARDS, HONORS: Various awards from New England press associations, for newspaper columns.

WRITINGS:

"JACK McMORROW" MYSTERY SERIES

Dead Line, North Country Press (Belfast, ME), 1993.
Bloodline, Putnam (New York City), 1995.
Lifeline, Putnam, 1996.
Potshot, Putnam, 1997.
Borderline, Berkley Books (New York City), 1998.

SIDELIGHTS: Novelist Gerry Boyle has won a considerable reading audience for his fictional detective Jack McMorrow. In books such as *Bloodline, Lifeline,* and *Potshot,* McMorrow is portrayed as an alienated reporter who has left the *New York Times* to live as a freelance writer/bum in the back woods of Maine. Reviewers frequently praise Boyle's gritty, realistic view of life in rural New England.

Deadline, the first book in the McMorrow series, is praised as "a bone-cracking first novel" by Marilyn Stasio of the *New York Times Book Review.* It shows the jaded reporter taking a job as editor of the *Androscoggin Review,* a weekly newspaper in "a gritty mill town where the snow starts falling around Labor Day and the hearts of the citizenry stay frozen all year round," as Stasio puts it. When McMorrow's staff photographer is found dead, the townspeople seem indifferent, but there is strong reaction when he starts to investigate the local paper mill. Stasio finds that the author's guarded writing style perfectly conveyed the "stark terror of isolation," and she adds: "There's a steel backbone in his lean plot, and the clipped prose and flinty characterizations are to this rugged literary landscape what the black woods and craggy cliffs are to the contours of Maine—a daunting kind of beauty."

Bloodline, the sequel to *Deadline,* was a superior effort in which the protagonist became "less a collection of traits and quirks and much more a fully realized character," in the estimation of *Booklist* contributor Wes Lukowsky. In this book, McMorrow is at work on a magazine article about teenaged mothers. One of his interview subjects turns up dead, and the reporter becomes the prime suspect. The critic for *Publishers Weekly* notes: "Boyle deftly establishes mood and setting, clearly defines his characters and offers lots of reflection from Jack, whose subdued first-person narration gives this solid mystery an intimate, small-town air."

In *Potshot* McMorrow accepts a $300 paycheck from some Maine hippies to write a story about their campaign to legalize marijuana. His story leads to an assassination attempt by some vicious urban gangsters. "Boyle provides a big cast of quirky down-easters as he authoritatively guides us through the Maine woods," approves a *Publishers Weekly* reviewer. "The climactic chase is a stunner." In *Borderline,* Boyle interweaves the tale of Benedict

Arnold's doomed 1775 trek to Quebec (the subject of an article being researched by McMorrow) with McMorrow's investigation into the disappearance of a tourist. Rex E. Klett, writing in *Library Journal,* declares *Borderline* an example of more "solid writing" from Boyle, and *Booklist* contributor Thomas Gaughan asserts that Boyle's "best work comes in lovely, evocative passages about rural, remote Maine; the horrific story of Arnold's doomed effort to bring Quebec into the war against the British; and McMorrow's ruminations about mortality."

Boyle once told *CA:* "I began my fiction writing career after several years as a newspaper reporter, covering the events and lives of Maine mill towns. My newspaper writing takes me to courtrooms and police stations and the streets, where life is very different from the Maine that people know from postcards. This immersion in the tougher side of life led me to look for an escape of sorts, which I found in mystery writing.

"My mysteries, featuring big-city newsman Jack McMorrow, are gritty and realistic, and have been described as a stark contrast to the Maine that has been dubbed 'vacationland.' For me, however, they offer a respite from the boundaries of newspaper writing (everything has to be true) and from a world where usually there is no McMorrow to solve the crime or come to the rescue. The novels may be realistic, but they contain a strong element that is missing in real life, and that is justice.

"I have been influenced by Robert Parker and Raymond Chandler, with additional inspiration from the works of John D. McDonald, Tony Hillerman, and Dick Francis, all of whom write beautifully and mysteriously. It is not easy to do both."

BIOGRAPHICAL/CRITICAL SOURCES:

PERIODICALS

Booklist, March 15, 1995, p. 1311; July, 1996, p. 1806; January 1, 1997, p. 780; March 1, 1997, p. 1113.

Library Journal, March 15, 1997, p. 87; January, 1998, p. 147.

New York Times Book Review, November 18, 1993; March 16, 1997.

Publishers Weekly, March 20, 1995, p. 47; June 17, 1996, p. 50; February 3, 1997, p. 98; December 1, 1997, p. 47.

Writer, April, 1994, p. 23.

BRACKEEN, Steve
See FARRIS, John

* * *

BRAND, Garrison
See BRANDNER, Gary

* * *

BRAND, Millen 1906-1980

PERSONAL: Born January 19, 1906, in Jersey City, NJ; died March 19, 1980, in New York, NY; son of Elmer (an electrician, carpenter, and farmer) and Carrie (a nurse; maiden name, Myers) Brand; married Pauline Leader (an author), 1932 (divorced); married Helen Mendelsohn, 1943; children: Elinor (Mrs. Paul Marion), Jonathan, Daniel, Carol. *Education:* Columbia University, B.A., 1929, B.Litt. (journalism), 1929.

CAREER: New York Telephone Co., copywriter, 1929-37; Writing Center, New York University, New York City, instructor, c. 1940-50; Office of Civilian Defense, Washington, DC, copywriter, 1942-43; Magazine Institute, New York City, instructor, c. 1958; Crown Publishers, New York City, editor, 1953-74. Worked for one and one-half years as a psychiatric aide in treatment centers and with private physicians.

MEMBER: Authors League, PEN, Society of American Historians.

AWARDS, HONORS: Co-recipient of Robert Meltzer plaque, Screenwriters Guild award, and an Academy Award for best screenplay, all for *The Snake Pit.*

WRITINGS:

NOVELS

The Outward Room (Book-of-the-Month Club selection), Simon & Schuster (New York City), 1937.

The Heroes, Simon & Schuster, 1939.

Albert Sears, Simon & Schuster, 1947.

Some Love, Some Hunger, Crown (New York City), 1955.

Savage Sleep, Crown, 1968.

OTHER

(With Frank Partos) *The Snake Pit* (screenplay), 20th Century-Fox, 1948.

Dry Summer in Provence (poems), C. N. Potter (New York City), 1966.

This Little Pig Named Curly (juvenile), Crown, 1968.

(Author of text; photographs by George Tice) *Fields of Peace: A Pennsylvania German Album,* Doubleday (New York City), 1970.

Local Lives (poems), C. N. Potter, 1975.

Also contributor to numerous literary magazines and anthologies.

ADAPTATIONS: The Outward Room was adapted as a Broadway play entitled *The World We Make.*

SIDELIGHTS: Millen Brand was best known for his works about mental hospitals, including the novels *The Outward Room* and *Savage Sleep* and the critically-acclaimed screenplay *The Snake Pit.* Brand, who worked for a short time as a psychiatric aide, often explored the fascinating world of mental illness in his works. He also sought to expose the poor conditions and inhumane practices prevalent at many mental hospitals.

The Outward Room was Brand's first novel. Its central character is Harriet Demuth, who entered an insane asylum after the death of her brother, seven years before the story opens. Partially cured, but unwilling to return to normal life, Harriet runs away from the asylum to New York City. Unable to find work, she moves in with a man and eventually falls in love and completes her cure. "I cannot recall a first novel of recent years that shows more original or important potentialities than [*The Outward Room*]," enthused Mary Ross in *Books.* Fanny Butcher, a reviewer for the *Chicago Daily Tribune,* found it to be "terribly tense, and yet strangely and beautifully simple. . . . It is the story of one human being's emergence into life from death." *New York Times* reviewer E. H. Walton declared that *The Outward Room* had "a purity of poetic feeling which moves one consistently and intangibly."

Brand's next book *The Heroes* is set in another kind of institution: a home for disabled soldiers. George Burley, the book's hero, lost an arm in World War I, but was able to find work until the Great Depression, when he was forced to take refuge in the Soldier's Home. He and his fellow veterans eventually begin to doubt that they will ever return to normal lives or happiness, but by the end of the book, George has found a new job and the right woman. Alfred Kazin, writing in *Books,* praised "[*The Heroes*'] tone, a warm and humming prose at once deft and tender, glowing and bitter." He added: "It is not often that one is moved by a novel as a whole, in which one is excited by the very sense of life caught at sudden pitch, so that one knows that what has been said is good, and that what will be said is true."

Brand continued to demonstrate his social conscience in *Some Love, Some Hunger,* which depicted the search for love in New York City's slums. *Library Journal* reviewer H. L. Roth called it "a highly sensitive portrayal of life on the poorer plane of society"; Rose Feld, writing in the *New York Herald Tribune Book Review,* decided that it "holds the warm essence of human experience." Richard Sullivan, contributor to *Chicago Sunday Tribune,* remarked that it was "gratifying to read a quiet novel, carefully and deliberately composed," but he complained that *Some Love, Some Hunger* was so restrained "that the effect one feels ought to be forthcoming simply doesn't come forth."

With *Savage Sleep,* Brand returned to familiar ground—mental illness and its treatment—and again received critical praise. Modeled on the work of the psychotherapist Dr. John N. Rosen, with whom Brand worked in Bucks County, Pennsylvania, "the book reads like an exciting detective thriller," wrote Paul Zimmerman in *Newsweek.* The book's main thrust is to examine the use of shock treatments for catatonic schizophrenia. Haskel Frankel, writing in the *Saturday Review,* described *Savage Sleep* as "an eye-opening picture of life within our mental institutions that Millen Brand creates as he moves Dr. Marks from case to case, cure to cure."

Brand began writing when he was six years old. He once told *CA:* "*Dry Summer in Provence* resulted from a nine-month stay in the South of France. I'm reasonably competent in French, speak it fairly well, read it fluently. I lived in Monaco and Le Rouret. I wrote*Dry Summer* in six weeks, revised it for six years. My main interest is poetry. *Local Lives* is a portrait of a Pennsylvania German community in which I lived for ten years (I'm of Pennsylvania German descent on my mother's side). It took thirty-four years to write along with other work, and records the final flowering of a way of life."

The Outward Room, The Heroes, and *Savage Sleep* have been published in foreign editions.

BIOGRAPHICAL/CRITICAL SOURCES:

PERIODICALS

America, May 3, 1969.
Best Sellers, December 15, 1968.
Booklist, June, 1937; May 1, 1939; May 15, 1955.
Books, May 2, 1937, p. 4; April 16, 1939, p. 2.
Book World, February 23, 1969, p. 10.
Chicago Daily Tribune, May 1, 1937, p. 12.
Chicago Sunday Tribune, March 27, 1955, p. 4.
Choice, October, 1966; November, 1969.
Christian Science Monitor, August 30, 1947, p. 10.
Cleveland Open Shelf, May, 1937, p. 12; June, 1939, p. 12.
Commonweal, May 19, 1939.
Forum, July, 1937; July, 1939.
Kirkus Reviews, July 1, 1946; January 1, 1955.
Library Journal, June 15, 1947; February 1, 1955; June 15, 1966; October 15, 1968; August, 1970.
Manchester Guardian, June 8, 1937, p. 7.
Nation, May 8, 1937.
National Review, February 11, 1969.
New Republic, May 19, 1937; June 7, 1939.
New Statesman & Nation, June 19, 1937.
Newsweek, November 25, 1968.
New Yorker, April 22, 1939; July 5, 1947.
New York Herald Tribune, April 16, 1939.
New York Herald Tribune Book Review, June 29, 1947, p. 2; March 20, 1955, p. 3.
New York Times, May 2, 1937, p. 7; April 16, 1939, p. 7; July 13, 1947, p. 21; March 20, 1955, p. 5; October 31, 1968; November 5, 1968.
New York Times Book Review, April 16, 1939; October 27, 1968, p. 64; June 7, 1970, p. 16; May 18, 1975.
Publishers Weekly, May 12, 1975.
Saturday Review, December 7, 1968.
Saturday Review of Literature, May 1, 1937; April 15, 1939; July 5, 1947.
Spectator, June 4, 1937; May 26, 1939.
Springfield Republican, May 23, 1937, p. 7E; April 23, 1939, p. 7E.
Time, May 10, 1937; April 17, 1939; December 20, 1968.
Times Literary Supplement, June 12, 1937, p. 445; June 10, 1939, p. 339.

OBITUARIES:

PERIODICALS

New York Times, March 22, 1980.
Publishers Weekly, April 4, 1980.*

BRANDNER, Gary (Phil) 1933-
(Garrison Brand, Nick Carter, Phil Garrison, Barnaby Quill; joint pseudonyms: Clayton Moore, Lee Davis Willoughby)

PERSONAL: Born May 31, 1933, in Sault Ste. Marie, MI; son of Henry Phil and Beada (Gehrman) Brandner; married Paula Moon, 1958 (divorced, 1963); married Barbara Grant Nutting, 1979 (divorced, 1983); married Martine Frances Wood, 1988. *Education:* University of Washington, B.A., 1955.

CAREER: Dan B. Miner (advertising agency), Los Angeles, CA, copywriter, 1955-57; Douglas Aircraft, Santa Monica, CA, technical writer, 1957-59; North American Rockwell, Downey, CA, technical writer, 1959-67; freelance writer, 1969—.

MEMBER: Mystery Writers of America, Private Eye Writers of America, Horror Writers of America, Writers Guild of America West.

AWARDS, HONORS: Saturn Award, Academy of Science Fiction, Fantasy and Horror Films, 1981 and 1988.

WRITINGS:

NOVELS

(With Clayton Matthews) *Saturday Night in Milwaukee,* Curtis Books (New York City), 1973.
(With Robert Colby under joint pseudonym Nick Carter) *The Death's Head Conspiracy,* Award Books (New York City), 1973.
(Under pseudonym Clayton Moore) *Wesley Sheridan,* Berkley Publishing (New York City), 1974.
The Aardvark Affair, Zebra Publications (New York City), 1975, published as *The Big Brain,* Severn House (London), 1991.
The Beelzebub Business, Zebra Publications, 1975.
The Players, Pyramid Publications (New York City), 1975.
London, Pocket Books (New York City), 1976.
Billy Lives!, Manor (New York City), 1976.
The Howling, Fawcett (New York City), 1977.
The Howling II, Fawcett, 1978, published as *Return of the Howling,* Hamlyn (London), 1979.
Offshore, Pinnacle Books (New York City), 1978.
Walkers, Fawcett, 1980, published as *Death Walkers,* Hamlyn, 1980.
The Sterling Standard, Popular Library (New York City), 1980.
Hellborn, Fawcett, 1981.

A Rage in Paradise, Playboy Paperbacks (New York City), 1981.
Cat People (novelization of screenplay), Fawcett, 1982.
(Under pseudonym Lee Davis Willoughby) *The Express Riders,* Dell (New York City), 1982.
Quintana Roo, Fawcett, 1984, published as *Tribe of the Dead,* Hamlyn, 1984.
The Brain Eaters, Fawcett, 1985.
The Howling III, Fawcett, 1985, published as *The Howling III: Echoes,* Hamlyn, 1985.
Carrion, Fawcett, 1986.
Cameron's Closet, Fawcett, 1987, published as *Cameron's Terror,* Severn House, 1988.
Floater, Fawcett, 1988.
Doomstalker, Fawcett, 1989.

SCREENPLAYS

(With Robert Sarno) *The Howling II* (based on his novel of the same title), Granite Productions, 1982.
Cameron's Closet (based on his novel of the same title), Smart Egg Productions, 1987.

CHILDREN'S FICTION

(Under pseudonym Phil Garrison) *The Good Luck Smiling Cat,* Pitman (Belmont, CA), 1984.
(Under pseudonym Phil Garrison) *The Disappearing Man,* Pitman, 1984.
Dressed Up for Murder, Pitman, 1986.
The Wet Goodbye, Lake (Belmont, CA), 1986.
The Experiment, Lake, 1987.
Mind Grabber, Lake, 1987.

OTHER

Vitamin E: Key to Sexual Satisfaction, Nash Publishing, 1971, revised edition, Paperback Library, 1972.
Living off the Land, Nash Publishing, 1971.
Off the Beaten Track in London, Nash Publishing, 1972.
(Anonymous editor) *Illusions,* Lake, 1988.
(Anonymous editor) *Claws & Feathers,* Lake, 1989.

Contributor to anthologies, including *Year's Best Horror Stories,* edited by Richard Davis, Sphere Books, 1971. Contributor of over fifty short stories, sometimes under pseudonyms, to periodicals, including *Ellery Queen's Mystery Magazine, Alfred Hitchcock's Mystery Magazine, Mike Shayne Mystery Magazine, Cavalier, Gem, New Blood,* and *Twilight Zone.*

ADAPTATIONS: A movie based on *The Howling* was filmed by Avco Embassy Pictures Corp., 1981; an Australian-made movie based on *The Howling III* was released by Square Pictures, 1987; a movie based on *Cameron's Closet* was filmed and released in 1989; a television mini-series based on *Walkers* was produced by NBC, 1990.

SIDELIGHTS: Writing in the *St. James Guide to Horror, Ghost and Gothic Writers,* Don D'Ammassa explains that Gary Brandner "is best known for his werewolf story, *The Howling,* and the series of at least six cheap films that derived from it. Although the original novel and its two sequels . . . represent some of Brandner's best work, it is unfortunate that he has become so identified with that theme that the best of his other horror fiction is largely ignored."

The Howling, D'Ammassa argues, is one of the best werewolf stories to appear in the recent past. "Even with the flood of horror fiction that has been published in the last two decades," D'Ammassa notes, "there are very few novels of lycanthropy that stand out. *The Howling* is one of these, partly because Brandner constructed a tight, suspenseful plot, partly because he hiy upon a novel idea. There's a colony of werewolves living right with human society, led by a prominent scientist whose influence helps protect their idiosyncratic lifestyles. A tough-minded reporter discovers the truth, but only after her husband has been seduced and infected with lycanthropy."

Brandner once told *CA:* "More than twenty years as a writer has taught me that you had better kiss security goodbye. No more paid vacations, sick leave, health insurance, Christmas bonuses. In return you get to create your own fictional world, reward the good guys, and punish the bad as doesn't always happen in real life.

"My advice to a writer starting out: Get it on paper and get it out to market and start the next one. Don't talk it away. And respect your reader. Without him you do not exist."

BIOGRAPHICAL/CRITICAL SOURCES:

BOOKS

St. James Guide to Horror, Ghost and Gothic Writers, St. James Press (Detroit), 1998.
Wood, Martine, *The Work of Gary Brandner,* Borgo Press (San Bernardino, CA), 1995.

PERIODICALS

Los Angeles Times, May 25, 1989.
New York Times, November 13, 1987.

* * *

BRANFIELD, John (Charles) 1931-

PERSONAL: Born January 19, 1931, in Burrow Bridge, Somerset, England; son of Allan Frederick (a civil servant) and Bessie (Storey) Branfield; married Kathleen Elizabeth Peplow, 1955; children: Susan, Frances, Stephen, Peter. *Education:* Queens' College, Cambridge, M.A., 1957; University of Exeter, M.Ed., 1972. *Avocational interests:* Walking, sailing, art.

ADDRESSES: Home—Mingoose Villa, Mingoose, Mount Hawke, Truro, Cornwall TR4 8BX, England. *Agent*—A. P. Watt & Son, 20 John St., London WC1N 2DR, England.

CAREER: Writer. Camborne Grammar School, Cornwall, England, English teacher and head of department, 1961-76; affiliated with Camborne Comprehensive School, 1976-81.

AWARDS, HONORS: Walter Hines Page Scholar, 1974; Arts Council Writers' Award, 1978; Carnegie Gold Medal commendation, Library Association (Britain), 1980.

WRITINGS:

A Flag in the Map, Eyre & Spottiswoode, 1960.
Look the Other Way, Eyre & Spottiswoode, 1963.
In the Country, Eyre & Spottiswoode, 1966.
The Poison Factory (young adult novel), Harper (New York City), 1972 published in England as *Nancekuke,* Gollancz, 1972.
Why Me? (young adult), Harper, 1973, published in England as *Sugar Mouse,* Gollancz, 1973.
The Scillies Trip, Gollancz, 1975.
The Day I Shot My Dad (teleplay), British Broadcasting Corp. (BBC-TV), 1975 Heinemann, 1991.
Castle Minalto, Gollancz, 1979.
The Fox in Winter (young adult novel), Gollancz, 1980, Atheneum, 1982.
Brown Cow, Gollancz, 1983.
Thin Ice (young adult novel), Gollancz, 1983.
The Falklands Summer (young adult novel), Gollancz, 1987.
The Day I Shot My Dad and Other Stories, Gollancz, 1989.
Lanhydrock Days, Gollancz, 1991.

SIDELIGHTS: British writer John Branfield is noted for his young adult novels, several of which deal with social issues while presenting believable characters. *The Poison Factory,* for example, follows a teenager after her father's suspicious death from cancer inspires her to become an activist against poison gas. A *Times Literary Supplement* critic observes that "what gives [the novel] a special quality is the feeling of other lives going on around Helen and her obsession. The minor characters . . . are all credible and sometimes very funny." Similarly, *The Fox in Winter* portrays "in a mature and sensitive manner, the blooming of an affectionate and respectful friendship" between a teenager and a nonagenarian, as Jennifer Moody summarizes in the *Times Literary Supplement.* Margery Fisher of *Growing Point* calls the novel "honest," praising it for "using humour, domestic verisimilitude and vividly drawn landscape to give credibility to the characters." Branfield "has proved triumphantly that the twentieth century's 'great unmentionable' *can* be spoken of in front of the children, and to their great advantage," Moody concludes. *The Fox in Winter* "is a worthwhile addition to teenage literature."

BIOGRAPHICAL/CRITICAL SOURCES:

PERIODICALS

Growing Point, March, 1981.
Times Literary Supplement, April 28, 1972; December 14, 1979; September 19, 1980; November 25, 1983; March 6, 1987.

* * *

BRECHER, Michael 1925-

PERSONAL: Born March 14, 1925, in Montreal, Quebec, Canada; son of Nathan and Gisella (Hopmeyer) Brecher; married Eva Danon, 1950; children: Leora, Diana, Seegla. *Education:* McGill University, B.A., 1946; Yale University, M.A., 1948, Ph.D., 1953.

ADDRESSES: Office—Department of Political Science, McGill University, Montreal, Quebec, Canada.

CAREER: McGill University, Montreal, Quebec, lecturer, 1952-54, assistant professor, 1954-58, associate professor, 1958-63, professor of political science, 1963—. Visiting professor, University of Chicago, 1963, Hebrew University, Jerusalem, Israel, 1970-75, University of California, Berkeley, 1979-80, and Stanford University, 1980.

MEMBER: Canadian Political Science Association, International Political Science Association, Association for Asian Studies, American Political Science Association, International Studies Association.

AWARDS, HONORS: Watumull Prize of American Historical Association for best work on India, 1960, for *Nehru: A Political Biography;* traveling fellowships from Nuffield Foundation, 1955-56, Rockefeller Foundation, 1964-65, Guggenheim Foundation, 1965-66, and Canada Council; Killam senior research scholarships, 1970-74, 1976-79; Woodrow Wilson Foundation Award for best book on politics, government, or international affairs from American Political Science Association, 1973, for *The Foreign Policy System of Israel.*

WRITINGS:

The Struggle for Kashmir, Oxford University Press (New York City), 1953.

Nehru: A Political Biography, Oxford University Press, 1959.

The New States of Asia, Oxford University Press, 1963.

Nehru's Mantle: The Politics of Succession in India, Praeger (New York City), 1966, Greenwood Press (Westport, CT), 1976.

India and World Politics; Krishna Menon's View of the World, Praeger, 1968.

Political Leadership in India: An Analysis of Elite Attitudes, Praeger, 1969.

The Foreign Policy System of Israel, Yale University Press (New Haven, CT), 1972.

Israel, the Korean War and China: Images, Decisions and Consequences, Jerusalem Academic Press (Jerusalem), 1974.

Decisions in Israel's Foreign Policy, Oxford University Press (London), 1974, Yale University Press, 1975.

(Editor) *Studies in Crisis Behavior,* Transaction Books (New Brunswick, NJ), 1979.

Decisions in Crisis: Israel, 1967 and 1973, University of California Press (Berkeley, CA), 1980.

(With Patrick James) *Crisis and Change in World Politics,* Westview Press (Boulder, CO), 1986.

(With Jonathan Wilkenfeld and Sheila Moser) *Handbook of International Crises,* Pergamon Press (New York City), 1988.

(With Wilkenfeld and Moser) *Crises in the Twentieth Century,* Pergamon Press, 1988.

(With Wilkenfeld and Moser) *Handbook of Foreign Policy Crises,* Pergamon Press, 1988.

(With Wilkenfeld) *Crisis, Conflict and Instability,* with contributions by Patrick James and others, Pergamon Press, 1989.

Crises in World Politics: Theory and Reality, Pergamon Press, 1993.

(With Wilkenfeld) *A Study of Crisis,* University of Michigan Press (Ann Arbor), 1997.

Contributor to *Pacific Affairs, World Politics, International Journal, British Journal of International Studies, Asian Survey,* and other journals.

SIDELIGHTS: Michael Brecher's books on India, often based on firsthand observations and interviews, have won praise for their careful scholarship and for the insights of their political analyses. Reviewing *Nehru: A Political Biography* for *Nation,* T. M. Greene states: "I know of no book on India as illuminating or authoritative for the Western reader. It is excellently written, fully documented and well indexed and illustrated." R. L. Park in *Pacific Affairs* notes Brecher's "devotion . . . to the sifting of mountains of details," and credits the book with being "without doubt, the best biography of Nehru."

In *Nehru's Mantle: The Politics of Succession in India* Brecher examines the post-Nehru era from 1964-66, arguing that the peaceful successions of the period demonstrate India's political maturity. According to George Woodcock in *Canadian Forum,* the book is "a carefully arranged, shrewd and sober reconstruction." *Library Journal* contributor R. S. Dillon finds it "solidly-based" and "highly readable," while Park, writing in the *Annals of the American Academy of Social and Political Science* calls Brecher "a superb journalist" and believes that *Nehru's Mantle* provides "a more detailed and accurate picture of the interrelationships between the upper levels of the Indian political establishment than has ever before appeared in print."

Brecher based *Political Leadership in India* on interviews with 80 members of India's political elite regarding their opinions of the 1967 elections. R. S. Robins points out in *American Political Science Review* that this is the first "serious examination of how the Indian national elite perceives its role and how it interprets the political system in which it operates." Robins also notes that "Brecher has as keen an ear for what is not said as what is." However, a reviewer for *Choice* finds Brecher's analysis too cautious and the scope of the book too narrow, arguing that *Political Leadership in India* could have profited from a "more precise research design, more reliance on other sources, and a general discussion of the 1967 election."

Brecher has also written books on Israel and the emerging states of Asia, and has edited a number of volumes dealing with political crises throughout the world.

BIOGRAPHICAL/CRITICAL SOURCES:

PERIODICALS

American Political Science Review, March, 1970, p. 197.
Annals of the American Academy of Social and Political Science, September, 1964. p. 193; May, 1967, p. 238.
Choice, October, 1967, p. 890; July, 1969, p. 692; November, 1969, p. 1302.
Encounter, November, 1968, p. 79.
Library Journal, October 1, 1966, p. 4672; May 1, 1972, p. 1722.
Nation, June 25, 1960, p. 555.
Pacific Affairs, March, 1960, p. 76.
Times Literary Supplement (London), July 28, 1966, p. 682; August 22, 1968, p. 890; September 1, 1972, p. 1028.
Yale Review, June, 1964, p. 584.

* * *

BRECHT, Arnold 1884-1977

PERSONAL: Born January 26, 1884, in Luebeck, Germany; came to United States, 1933, naturalized citizen; died September 11, 1977, in Eutin, West Germany; married wife, Clara (deceased). *Education:* Educated in Germany.

CAREER: Served as judge and counselor in German ministry of justice before World War I; held posts in ministries of interior and finance during Weimar Republic; representative from Prussia in German Reichsrat until 1933; New School for Social Research, New York, NY, faculty member of University in Exile and professor of political science, international law, and public finance, 1933-54; writer. Visiting professor at Yale University, Harvard University, Princeton University, Barnard College, and Wellesley College. Served with U.S. military government in Germany, 1950. *Military service:* Supervised U.S. Army area-training program for Germany during World War II.

WRITINGS:

Die Geshaeftsordnung der reichsministerien, ihre staatsrechtliche und geschaeftstechnische bedeutung, zugleich ein lehrbuch der bueroreform, Heymann, 1927.
(With Theodor Kutzer) *Neuordnung der dezentralisation im Deutschen Reich,* Deutscher Kommunal-Verlag, 1928.
(With Comstock Glaser) *The Art and Technique of Administration in German Ministries,* Harvard University Press (Cambridge, MA), 1940, reprinted, Greenwood Press (Westport, CT), 1971.
(Principal in charge) *Public Health Administration in Germany, 1919-1945,* prepared by Hedwig Wachenheim, Institute of World Affairs (New York), 1945.
Prelude to Silence: The End of the German Republic, Oxford University Press (New York), 1944, reprinted, H. Fertig (New York), 1968.
Federalism and Regionalism in Germany: The Division of Prussia, Oxford University Press, 1945, reprinted, Russell (New York), 1971.
The Political Philosophy of Arnold Brecht (essays), edited by Morris D. Forkosch, Exposition Press (Smithtown, NY), 1954.
Wiedervereinigung, Nymphenburger Verlagshandlung, 1957.
Political Theory: The Foundations of Twentieth-Century Political Thought, Princeton University Press (Princeton, NJ), 1959.
Lebenserinnerungen, Deutsche Verlagsanstalt, Volume I: *Aus naechster Naehe,* 1966, Volume II: *Mit der Kraft des Geistes,* 1967, abridged translation by the author of both volumes published as *The Political Education of Arnold Brecht: An Autobiography, 1884-1970,* Princeton University Press, 1970.

SIDELIGHTS: It was Arnold Brecht, representative of Prussia in the Reichsrat, who responded to Adolph Hitler's first address as Chancellor to the German parliament in 1933. Brecht's reminder to Hitler of his oath "to abide by the Constitution and the law of the land" provoked Hitler to walk out of the legislative chambers and to dismiss Brecht from his position several days later. Brecht emigrated to the United States shortly thereafter and joined the faculty of the New School for Social Research. In a review of Brecht's autobiography, *The Political Education of Arnold Brecht,* which records his experiences as an "inside" government official during the Weimar Republic and the rise of Hitler, a reviewer for the *Virginia Quarterly Review* notes: "A sensitive writer, Brecht has transferred his political acumen to the printed page, and the result is an important, delightful memoir." According to A. F. Peterson of *Library Journal:* "Any student of modern German history can count himself lucky to have this lucid, intelligent, and balanced account."

Brecht's other works include books on political science and political philosophy, the former dealing with modern German history. In *The Art and Technique of Administration in German Ministries* Brecht, with co-author Comstock Glaser, examines the code of procedures which he helped developed in 1926 for German ministries. Although this code reflected both monarchical and democratic elements, Brecht notes that it survived essentially unchanged under Hitler's totalitarian rule. He concludes that techniques of administration are independent of the form of government under which they function. William Anderson, writing in the *Annals of the American Academy of Social and Political Science,* feels that American administrators could "profit greatly from an intensive study of this little volume."

Brecht explores the legal and constitutional means by which Hitler rose to power in *Prelude to Silence: The End of the German Republic.* W. F. Sollman, writing in *American Political Science Review,* finds it to be a "splendid, scholarly contribution to the understanding of German politics." However, Waldemar Gurain, reviewing the book for *Commonweal,* states that "Brecht makes the mystery of Hitler's success, not only against democrats but also against conservative forces, only more mysterious." *Federalism and Regionalism in Germany: The Division of Prussia,* published at the end of World War II, describes the make-up of pre-Hitler Germany in the late twenties and includes Brecht's suggestions on how Germany should be reconstructed. In his *Library Journal* review, H. H. A. Bernt praises the book as a "[p]enetrating analysis, with rather strong emphasis on legal-administrative aspect, which merits serious consideration in the building of Germany's postwar structure."

In *Political Theory: The Foundations of Twentieth-Century Political Thought,* Brecht draws upon both historical events and the work of other political scientists in an attempt to put forth a comprehensive theory of modern political thought. C. J. Friedrich in *American History Review* finds it to be "a very orderly treatment, well organized and lucid," while William Anderson in *American Political Science Review* describes the book as a "major work . . . significant and impressive." William Ebenstein, reviewing *Political Theory* for the *Annals of the American Academy of Social and Political Science,* predicts that "this book will henceforth be studied by every serious student of political theory, whether or not he agrees with the author's findings and conclusions."

BIOGRAPHICAL/CRITICAL SOURCES:

PERIODICALS

American History Review, January, 1960, p. 340.
American Political Science Review, April, 1941, p. 383; October, 1944, p. 1005; March, 1960, p. 203.
Annals of the American Academy of Social and Political Science, January, 1941, p. 236; November, 1944, p. 187; November, 1959, p. 171.
Bookweek, December 16, 1942, p. 2.
Choice, January, 1971, p. 1562.
Columbia Law Review, September, 1944, p. 800.
Commonweal, July 7, 1944, p. 284.
Library Journal, October 12, 1945, p. 977; October 15, 1970, p. 3464.
New York Times, June 25, 1944, p. 4.
Saturday Review of Literature, July 22, 1944, p. 32; June 20, 1959, p. 14.
Times Literary Supplement (London), February 5, 1971, p. 165.
Virginia Quarterly Review, spring, 1971, p. lxx.

OBITUARIES:

PERIODICALS

AB Bookman's Weekly, January 30, 1978.
New York Times, September 15, 1977.
Time, September 26, 1977.*

* * *

BRELIS, Dean 1924-

PERSONAL: Born April 1, 1924, in Newport, RI; son of Christopher and Mary (Phillips) Brelis; married

Nancy Burns, December 10, 1949; married second wife, Isabel O'Donnell, June 5, 1967; married third wife, Mary Anne Weaver, March 21, 1973; children: (first marriage) Doron, Jane, Tia, Matthew. *Education:* Harvard University, A.B., 1949.

ADDRESSES: Home—27 West 44th St., New York, NY 10036. *Office*—Valaoritou, 9B, Athens, 134, Greece. *Agent*—Harold Ober Associates, Inc, 40 East 49th St., New York, NY 10017.

CAREER: Boston Globe, Boston, MA, reporter 1946-49; Time-Life, Inc., New York, NY, correspondent, 1949-54; Harvard College and Radcliffe College, Cambridge, MA, instructor, 1958-63; National Broadcasting Co., New York, NY, foreign correspondent in Middle East, North Africa, Cyprus, Vietnam, 1963-70; Columbia Broadcasting System, special correspondent to Greece, 1970—. *Military service:* U.S. Army, Office of Strategic Services, 1942-45; received battlefield commission as second lieutenant; awarded Bronze Star, Presidential Unit Citation, and Bronze Arrowhead.

MEMBER: PEN, Authors Guild, Dramatists Guild, Signet Society, Harvard Club (New York).

AWARDS, HONORS: Nieman fellow, 1958-59; Overseas Press Club award, 1964, for best radio reporting from abroad; Emmy award for distinguished television news reporting, "Odyssey House," 1970.

WRITINGS:

The Mission (novel), Random House (New York City), 1958.

Shalom (novel), Little, Brown (Boston, MA), 1959.

Run, Dig or Stay?: A Search for an Answer to the Shelter Question, Beacon Press (Boston, MA), 1962.

My New-Found Land (novel), Houghton (Boston, MA), 1963.

(With William R. Peers) *Behind the Burma Road: The Story of America's Most Successful Guerilla Force,* Little, Brown, 1963.

The Face of South Vietnam, photographs by Jill Krementz, Houghton, 1967.

WORK IN PROGRESS: A novel.

SIDELIGHTS: Dean Brelis's first novel, *The Mission,* while not strictly autobiographical, draws upon his own experience in World War II. The action takes place behind enemy lines in 1943 Burma where a young OSS officer, along with the son of a local leader, organizes resistance to the Japanese occupation. "This is a good, direct, cleanly written, brief novel," according to a reviewer for *Booklist,* while a reviewer for *Kirkus* describes it as "told briefly and with a finesse of style and presentation singular among the war novels of today." However, several reviewers were critical of Brelis's approach as too sketchy. Gene Baro of the *New York Herald Tribune* feels that "[t]oo much is left out . . . too much that we want to know."

Before writing his second novel, *Shalom,* Brelis voluntarily entered a Displaced Persons camp in postwar Europe and subsequently traveled to Israel with Jewish refugees. The book details the experiences and adventures of similar refugees on a freighter bound for Palestine. A reviewer for *Booklist* describes it as a "memorable account of people united in a common purpose." In contrast, R. T. Bresler of *Library Journal* states: "The book, sincere and graphic as it is, lacks any dramatic conflict on the personal level."

For the subject matter of *My New-Found Land,* Brelis harkened back to his own boyhood. The novel is set in Newport, Rhode Island in 1932 on the eve of Franklin Roosevelt's election to the presidency. Its story centers around the young Dimitri, the son of Greek immigrants, and the travails faced by himself and his family. Echoing criticism of *The Mission,* some reviewers find Brelis' text too brief. Others, like K. G. Jackson in *Harper's,* note, "One lives that exciting day in that boy's life in that special town, and in the process learns everything important to him that has come before and much that will come later."

In *The Face of South Vietnam* Brelis provided the text for photographs by Jill Krementz that depict the effect of the Vietnam War on both soldiers and civilians. Collin Clark of *Library Journal* feels the text and photos are a "patched-up job" that fail to complement one another. However, Howard Junker of *Newsweek* praises Brelis' text, and R. H. Fifield of the *Saturday Review* credits the book with providing "a better understanding of Vietnam in terms of human beings and their experiences."

BIOGRAPHICAL/CRITICAL SOURCES:

PERIODICALS

Best Sellers, May 15, 1963, p. 78.

Booklist, September 1, 1958, p. 21; November 15, 1959, p. 183.

Chicago Sunday Times, June 15, 1958, p. 5.
Christian Science Monitor, June 26, 1958, p. 7; May 9, 1963, p. 8B.
Harper's, June, 1963, p. 109.
Kirkus, April 1, 1958, p. 297; September 15, 1959, p. 707.
Library Journal, July, 1958, p. 2049; November 15, 1959, p. 3585; January 15, 1968, p. 194.
Newsweek, February 5, 1968, p. 78.
New Yorker, June 28, 1958, p. 92.
New York Herald Tribune Book Review, June 8, 1958, p. 7; January 10, 1960, p. 8; May 12, 1963, p. 8.
New York Times, July 27, 1958, p. 16.
New York Times Book Review, November 15, 1959, p. 55.
Saturday Review, June 7, 1958, p. 12; October 31, 1959, p. 14; February 17, 1968, p. 34.
Springfield Republican, November 22, 1959, p. 4D.

* * *

BRENAN, (Edward Fitz)Gerald 1894-1987 (George Beaton)

PERSONAL: Born April 7, 1894, on Island of Malta; died of heart failure, January 16 (some sources say January 19), 1987, in Alhaurin el Grande, Malaga, Spain; son of Hugh Gerald and Helen (Graham) Brenan; married Elisabeth Gamel Woolsey, 1931 (died January, 1968); children: Miranda Helen Corre. *Education:* Attended Radley College. *Avocational interests:* Reading, walking.

CAREER: Author. *Military service:* British Army, Infantry, 1914-19; became captain; received Military Cross and Croix de Guerre.

WRITINGS:

The Spanish Labyrinth: An Account of the Social and Political Background of the Civil War, Cambridge University Press (New York City), 1943, reprinted, 1990.
The Face of Spain (travel), Turnstile Press, 1950, reprinted, Octagon Books (New York City), 1976.
The Literature of the Spanish People: From Roman Times to the Present, Cambridge University Press, 1951.
South from Granada: Seven Years in an Andalusian Village (memoir), Hamish Hamilton (London), 1957, reprinted, Cambridge University Press, 1980, Kondansha International (New York City), 1998.
A Holiday by the Sea (novel), Hamish Hamilton, 1961, Farrar, Straus (New York City), 1962.
A Life of One's Own: Childhood and Youth (autobiography), Hamish Hamilton, 1962.
The Lighthouse Always Says Yes, Hamish Hamilton, 1966.
(With poetry translations by Lynda Nicholson) *St. John of the Cross: His Life and Poetry,* Cambridge University Press, 1973.
Personal Record, 1920-1972 (autobiography), J. Cape (London), 1974, Knopf (New York City), 1975.
Thoughts in a Dry Season: A Miscellany, Cambridge University Press, 1978.
The Magnetic Moment: Poems, Warren House Press, 1978.
Best of Friends: The Brenan-Partridge Letters, selected and edited by Xan Fielding, Chatto & Windus (London), 1986.

UNDER PSEUDONYM GEORGE BEATON

Jack Robinson (picaresque novel), Chatto & Windus, 1933.
Doctor Partridge's Almanack, Chatto & Windus, 1934.

SIDELIGHTS: Although of English background and educated in England, Gerald Brenan spent most of his life in Spain. At the age of sixteen Brenan ran away to France and traveled on foot to Eastern Europe. After serving as a captain in the British infantry during World War I, he left Britain for Spain to become a writer. Brenan took up residence in Andulusia where he subsequently owned his own farm and became a widely respected scholar of Spanish culture and history. During the Spanish Civil War he worked as a foreign correspondent for the *Manchester Guardian.* Brenan's many books on Spain include literary and historical studies, travelogues and memoirs, biography and autobiography.

Reviewing Brenan's *The Spanish Labyrinth* for *Book Week* John Cournos states: "This book, ostensibly 'an account of the social and political background of the Spanish Civil War,' . . . is actually a far more profound undertaking. . . . The roots of Spain, the mystery of the Spanish character and Spain's uniqueness on the European scene are admirably delineated and analyzed in a penetrating study which should take its place beside the recognized classics dealing with the people who inhabit the Iberian peninsula." B. D.

Wolfe of *Weekly Book Review* finds *The Spanish Labyrinth* to be "an honest book, rigorously objective despite the frank expression of the author's own views." In contrast, Joseph McSorley of *Catholic World* notes, "Not limiting himself to the presentation of discreditable facts, [Brenan] draws unjustifiable deductions. . . . He reveals himself as prone to intemperate and extreme statements."

In *Literature of the Spanish People* Brenan examines the works of leading prose writers, dramatists, and poets of the area from Roman times to the present. According to Geoffrey Bereton in *New Statesman & Nation,* "Mr. Brenan reduces to manageable proportions that tangle of lyricism, sadism, punctilio and imbroglio, the Spanish drama. . . . Few histories of literature so successfully avoid both dogma and neutralism." Hershel Brickell of *Saturday Review* finds *Literature of the Spanish People* to be "among the most readable and most useful" books on Spanish literature.

In *The Face of Spain* Brenan offers a travelogue/memoir, relating his return to Andulusia after more than a decade's absence and his travels throughout other parts of Spain. Brickell describes the book as "a first-rate piece of work, timely, penetrating, exceptionally well-written, and memorable for the amount of pure truth it contains." A reviewer for *Manchester Guardian* praises Brenan's "[f]ine descriptive passages, of men and women, of landscape and flora, of jewels of art and architecture." In a later travelogue/memoir, *South from Granada,* Brenan tells of his travels on foot through the Spanish countryside. Like *The Face of Spain* the book received uniform praise from reviewers, and prompted J. G. Harrison of the *Christian Science Monitor* to state, "It is not merely possible, it is now probable that Gerald Brenan is the most perceptive writer on Spain in the English language today."

Brenan's venture into fiction with *A Holiday by the Sea* was less well-received by critics. The novel concerns a holiday at an English seaside resort as related by its central character, a middle-aged intellectual and failed novelist. Incest, love affairs, and a death by drowning figure in the plot. Matthew Hodgart of *New Statesman* feels that "the human relationships remain insignificant," and William Barret states in the *Atlantic:* "Its failure is one of human substance rather than of literary skill."

Brenan's two-volume autobiography, *A Life of One's Own* and *Personal Record,* covers his life through World War I in the first volume and his life in Spain in the second. Reviewing *A Life of One's Own* for *Library Journal,* R. R. Rea notes that Brenan's "early life did not possess sufficient objective interest nor is his memory sufficiently objective to make this . . . really outstanding." However, V. S. Prichett of *New Statesman* finds the book compelling and believes that it contains "flashes of the best war writing I have ever read."

BIOGRAPHICAL/CRITICAL SOURCES:

BOOKS

Gathorne-Hardy, Jonathan, *Gerald Brenan: The Interior Castle; A Biography,* Norton (New York City), 1993.

PERIODICALS

Atlantic, February, 1962, p. 118.
Book Week, August 15, 1943, p. 4.
Booklist, November 1, 1951, p. 83; October 15, 1957, p. 101..
Catholic World, October, 1943, p. 103.
Chicago Sunday Tribune, January 14, 1962, p. 5.
Christian Century, December 26, 1951, p. 1513.
Christian Science Monitor, October 10, 1957, p. 11.
Commonweal, December 3, 1943, p. 157.
Kirkus, September 1, 1957, p.664; December 1, 1961, p. 1055.
Library Journal, April 1, 1963, p. 1518; October 15, 1973, p. 3002.
Manchester Guardian, May 5, 1943, p. 3.
New Statesman & Nation, November 10, 1951, p. 536; April 20, 1957, p. 519.
New Yorker, October 13, 1951, p. 150; August 10, 1963, p. 90.
New York Herald Tribune Books, November 3, 1957, p. 6; January 7, 1961, p. 4.
New York Review of Books, November 1, 1971, p. 8.
New York Times, December 9, 1951, p. 36; October 6, 1957, p. 6.
New York Times Book Review, January 7, 1962, p. 36.
Saturday Review of Literature, January 5, 1952, p. 15; October 19, 1957, p. 59; January 20, 1962, p 21.
Spectator, April 26, 1957, p. 552.
Times Literary Supplement (London), May 15, 1943, p. 230; January 19, 1951, p. 31; April 15, 1957, p. 243; August 10, 1962, p. 603; August 24, 1973, p. 977.
Weekly Book Review, August 15, 1943, p. 4.

OBITUARIES:

PERIODICALS

Chicago Tribune, January 22, 1987.
Des Moines Register, January 21, 1987.
Detroit Free Press, January 21, 1987.
Detroit News, January 21, 1987.
New York Times, January 24, 1987.
Sun (Baltimore), January 22, 1987.
Times (London), January 21, 1987.
Washington Post, January 24, 1987.*

* * *

BRENNAN, Joseph Payne 1918-1990

PERSONAL: Born December 20, 1918, in Bridgeport, CT; died in 1990; son of Joseph Payne and Nellie (Holborn) Brennan; married Doris M. Philbrick, October 24, 1970. *Education:* Self-educated.

CAREER: New Haven Journal-Courier, New Haven, CT, staff member in display advertisement department, 1937-39; assistant editor, *Theatre News,* 1940; Yale University Library, New Haven, assistant in reserve book room, 1941-42, senior assistant in acquisitions department, 1946-85. Founder, Macabre House (publisher). *Military service:* U.S. Army, 1943-45; received four battle stars.

MEMBER: Poetry Society of America, New England Poetry Club.

AWARDS, HONORS: Leonora Speyer Memorial Award, Poetry Society of America, 1961, for "New England Vignette"; Clark Ashton Smith Poetry Award, 1978, for life work; World Fantasy Convention award, 1982, for life achievement.

WRITINGS:

POETRY

Hearts of Earth, Decker Press, 1950.
The Humming Stair, Big Mountain Press, 1953.
The Wind of Time, Hawk & Whippoorwill Press, 1962.
Nightmare Need, Arkham House (Sauk City, WI), 1964.
A Sheaf of Snow Poems, Pendulum Press, 1973.
Edges of Night, Pilot Press Books, 1974.
Death Poems, Pilot Press Books, 1974.
Five Connecticut Poets, Fireside Press, 1975.
As Evening Advances, Crystal Visions Press, 1978.
Webs of Time, Macabre House (New Haven, CT), 1978.
Creep to Death, Donald M. Grant (West Kingston, RI), 1981.
Sixty Selected Poems, New Establishment Press (Amherst, NY), 1985.
Look Back on Laurel Hills, Jwindz (Minneapolis), 1989.

STORY COLLECTIONS

Nine Horrors and a Dream, Arkham House, 1958.
The Dark Returners, Macabre House, 1959.
Scream at Midnight, Macabre House, 1963.
The Casebook of Lucius Leffing, Macabre House, 1973.
Stories of Darkness and Dread, Arkham House, 1973.
The Chronicles of Lucius Leffing, Donald M. Grant, 1977.
The Shapes of Midnight, Berkley Publishing (New York City), 1981.
The Borders Just Beyond, Donald M. Grant, 1986.
The Adventures of Lucius Leffing, Donald M. Grant, 1990.

OTHER

H. P. Lovecraft: A Bibliography, Biblio Press, 1952.
H. P. Lovecraft: An Evaluation, Macabre House, 1955.
(With Donald M. Grant) *Act of Providence* (novelette), Donald M. Grant, 1978.
Evil Always Ends (novel), Donald M. Grant, 1982.

Contributor to anthologies, including *Stories Not for the Nervous,* Random House, 1965; *Travellers by Night,* Arkham House, 1967; *Great Occasions,* Beacon Press, 1968; *Every Child's Book of Verse,* F. Watts, 1968; *The Owl Book,* Kaye & Ward, 1970; *Dark Things,* Arkham House, 1971; *Stories to Stay Awake By,* Random House, 1971; *The Seventh Fontana Book of Great Ghost Stories,* Fontana, 1971; *The Freak Show,* Thomas Nelson, 1972; *A Tide of Terror,* Taplinger, 1973; *Nameless Places,* Arkham House, 1975; *Night Chills,* Avon, 1975; *Living in Fear: A History of Horror in the Mass Media,* Scribner, 1975; *Dying of Fright: Masterpieces of the Macabre,* Scribner, 1976; *Alfred Hitchcock's Tales to Keep You Spellbound,* Dial Press, 1976; *The Year's Best Horror Stories,* Series IV, DAW Books, 1976; *The Disciples of Cthulhu,* DAW Books, 1976; *Thirteen Tales of Terror,* Scribner, 1977; *Whispers: An*

Anthology of Fantasy and Horror, Doubleday, 1977; *The Year's Best Horror Stories,* Series V, DAW Books, 1977; *Alfred Hitchcock's Tales to Make Your Blood Run Cold,* Davis Publications, 1978; *Sixty-five Great Tales of Horror,* Octopus, 1981; *The Dodd, Mead Gallery of Horror,* Dodd, 1983; *Shadows 7,* Doubleday, 1984; and *Night Visions 2,* Dark Harvest, 1985. Also contributor to *Stories to Be Read with the Door Locked,* edited by Hitchcock, 1975.

Contributor to numerous journals and magazines, including *Commonweal, Beloit Poetry Journal, New York Times, Esquire, Weird Tales, Twilight Zone,* and *Yale Literary Magazine*. Editor of *Essence,* 1950-77, and *Macabre,* 1957-76.

ADAPTATIONS: Two stories from *The Dark Returners* were adapted for NBC's *Thriller* television series; the short story "Levitation" was adapted for the television series "Tales from the Dark Side." Another short story, "The Calamander Chest," was recorded by Vincent Price for Caedmon Records in 1978.

SIDELIGHTS: Joseph Payne Brennan "is unusual among modern horror writers for having built a distinguished reputation from mostly non-commercial work," as Stefan R. Dziemianowicz stated in the *St. James Guide to Horror, Ghost and Gothic Writers.* Brennan published short stories and poems in genre magazines and his work was gathered into collections by small press publishers.

Many of Brennan's stories "are simple tales of average human beings confronting the supernatural," as Dziemianowicz explained. His story "Slime," for example, tells of a strange ocean slime which "rampages through a seaside town," Dziemianowicz relates. The story shows Brennan at "the top of his form," Dziemianowicz continued, "building a powerful sense of the uncanny through shifts in the viewpoint between the mindless monster and the horrified human beings unfortunate enough to cross its path."

Brennan was also known as a poet of the macabre whose first collections, Dziemianowicz believed, "rank as high watermarks of modern macabre verse. His more atmospheric stories are laced with poetic images and several read like narrative expansions of poetic moments, among them the sublime 'Mr. Octbur,' a prose poem of delicate beauty all the more remarkable for the simplicity of its language."

Brennan once told *CA:* "In a brief introductory note to my book *Sixty Selected Poems,* issued by a small press publisher, I criticized the academic establishment for its insular and sometimes arrogant attitude toward 'outsider' poets such as myself. Although I was assured by a critic friend who read the note before publication that I would be committing 'literary suicide' if I published it, I nevertheless included it in the book. Perhaps my friend's prediction was a trifle melodramatic, but he was not far wrong. While a number of little-magazine editors reviewed the book with enthusiasm and warm praise, the major literary journals received it—and probably trashed it—in stony silence. I was disappointed, but scarcely surprised.

"How does an outsider, lacking university-establishment credentials and connections, achieve anything approaching national recognition in the United States today? I haven't yet found out. An acquaintance facetiously told me that I had made the mistake of not dying young. He said that was a timetested, sure-fire way of drawing attention to one's work. Well, that option is no longer open to me—I'm already sixty-seven.

"How does a sixty-seven year-old poet, ignored by the academic establishment, achieve mainstream recognition? Anyone sending me the correct answer will receive a postpaid autograph. (That's about all I can afford.) In any case, it certainly appears that the kind of times which enabled poets to attain attention and even honors without the blessing of academia are long gone.

"As a footnote, let me say that, yes, I have received some recognition for my 'dark fantasy' stories, detective stories and 'macabre' poetry—but I fear that recognition in these realms serves only to intensify the indifference and/or hostility of those ivy-entrenched individuals who decide whose turn it is next in the jealously-guarded world of mainstream poetry."

BIOGRAPHICAL/CRITICAL SOURCES:

BOOKS

St. James Guide to Horror, Ghost and Gothic Writers, St. James Press (Detroit), 1998.*

* * *

BRENNAN, Maeve 1917-1993

PERSONAL: Born January 6, 1917, in Dublin, Ireland; came to the United States in 1934; died 1993;

daughter of Robert (one source says James) and Anastasia (Bolger) Brennan; married St. Clair McKelway (a writer; divorced). *Education:* Attended a convent school in Ireland.

CAREER: Harpers Bazaar, New York City, copywriter, 1943-49; *New Yorker,* New York City, writer, 1949-93.

WRITINGS:

In and Out of Never-Never Land (short stories; also see below), Scribner (New York City), 1969.
The Long-Winded Lady, Morrow (New York City), 1969.
Christmas Eve (short stories; also see below), Scribner, 1974.
The Springs of Affection: Stories of Dublin (contains stories previously published in *In and Out of Never-Never Land* and *Christmas Eve*), Houghton (Boston), 1997.

Contributor to Philip Larkin, *A Lifted Study-Storehouse: The Brynmor Jones Library, 1929-1979,* Hull University Press (Hull, England), 1987.

SIDELIGHTS: Maeve Brennan's books are collections of short stories or other writings, most of which were published in the *New Yorker* through the years. Critics have generally agreed with Joyce Carol Oates' description of Brennan's writing as "polished, gentle, highly feminine," and that her talent was in transforming the commonplace into something quite meaningful.

In and Out of Never-Never Land is a collection of twenty-two tales, many based on every-day middle-class life in Dublin, Ireland. "They are conventional short stories, expertly realized, expertly controlled and very moving," commented Anne O'Neill-Barna in the *New York Times Book Review.* Oates wrote in *Saturday Review* that, despite the book's merits, "one does expect from fiction something more than the carefully controlled 'cute' dullness" of *In and Out of Never-Never Land.*

Brennan's vignettes are based on "the overheard and the glimpsed and the guessed at," wrote John Updike in a review of *The Long-Winded Lady.* The author "is constantly alert, sharp-eyed as a sparrow for the crumbs of human event." W. G. Rogers observed: "The pieces all together give a clearer understanding of her feminine aptitude for proving that what looks unimportant is often very important. Her speciality is the stuff of New York City itself." Disagreeing, a *New York* reviewer said simply that reading it "is like being trapped with a dread dinner companion on a 21-day cruise."

Christmas Eve contains both stories set in a working-class area of Dublin, Ireland, and in an affluent New York City suburb. In critic Robert Kiely's opinion, expressed in the *New York Times Book Review,* "the Irish stories, though unsensational, have a fine, mature, well-knit quality to them," while the American tales are "shallow, obvious, ill-composed and all but devoid of fresh observation, intellectual subtlety and emotional depth." Helen Rogan wrote in *Time* that Brennan's stories are marked by a "steady accumulation of detail and alternate flashes of passionate statement and raw insight. The accomplishment is formidable—something few writers attempt without sounding precious, dull, or both."

Several years after Brennan's death, a new collection of her work was published. *The Springs of Affection* contained pieces formerly printed in the *New Yorker* and collected in *In and Out of Never-Never Land* and *Christmas Eve.* Jim O'Laughlin noted that *The Springs of Affection* traced Brennan's development as a writer over three decades. Often, several stories work together to form a story cycle, creating fiction of considerable depth. "Against a backdrop of considerable realistic detail in small Irish towns or in suburban Dublin, most of these characters struggle with their past and with the limitations of self-perception or their intimacy with others, limits that these stories draw with considerable subtlety and style," approved O'Laughlin.

Noting that most of the stories in *The Springs of Affection* are set in the Dublin neighborhood of Ranelagh, *New York Times* reviewer Jay Parini commented that "both the strength and weakness of these stories derive from this insularity, this obsessive retracing of familiar boundaries. Like a tongue returning to a broken tooth, Brennan's imagination flicks back compulsively to the same place, reliving the little hurts, the faint joys, the unrealized dreams sealed away in its seemingly identical houses." He called the title story "wide-ranging, savage," and "poignant" and concluded that the book "is full of small miracles presented in elegant but simple prose. *The Springs of Affection* should bring her back to the table of modern fiction, where her place has been empty for too long."

Thomas Flanagan of the *Washington Post Book World* was also hopeful that *The Springs of Affection* would spark a renaissance of appreciation for Brennan's work. "The fiction that emerged at her hands is extraordinarily good, moving and strange. . . . The language in all of the stories is clear, simple as glass, apparently as transparent—and they record disappearance of feeling, losses, life-sustaining illusions. They assume that families come into being, are sustained, by manifold unstated magic thoughts, attitudes toward objects. Small happinesses come without warning, leave quickly. They are stories that quietly, without airs or pretenses, challenge the stability of being itself."

BIOGRAPHICAL/CRITICAL SOURCES:

BOOKS

Contemporary Literary Criticism, Volume 5, Gale (Detroit), 1976.

PERIODICALS

Atlantic, October, 1969.
Best Sellers, November 15, 1969; April 15, 1974.
Booklist, December 1, 1997, p. 608.
Choice, June, 1974.
Kirkus Reviews, September 15, 1997, p. 1403.
Library Journal, October 15, 1997, p. 96.
New Republic, April 27, 1974.
New York, September 15, 1969.
New York Times Book Review, November 6, 1969; August 4, 1974; December 14, 1997, p. 38.
Publishers Weekly, February 4, 1974; September 22, 1997, p. 68; November 3, 1997, p. 20.
Saturday Review, March 22, 1969; March 23, 1974.
Time, July 1, 1974.
Village Voice, May 16, 1974.
Washington Post Book World, January 11, 1998, pp. 1, 14.*

* * *

BRENNERT, Alan (Michael) 1954-
(Michael Bryant)

PERSONAL: Born May 30, 1954, in Englewood, NJ; son of Herbert Edward (an aviation writer and sheet metal operator) and Almyra (an apartment rentals manager; maiden name, Wittmer) Brennert. *Education:* Attended William Paterson State College, 1972-73; California State University, Long Beach, B.A., 1977; graduate study at the University of California, Los Angeles, 1977-78.

ADDRESSES: *Home*—Los Angeles, CA. *Agent*—Howard Morhaim Literary Agency, 501 Fifth Ave., New York, NY 10017.

CAREER: Freelance writer, 1978—.

MEMBER: Writers Guild of America, Authors Guild.

AWARDS, HONORS: Writers Guild of America Award nomination for outstanding teleplay in a dramatic series, 1983, for "Closed Circuit," premier episode of American Broadcasting Company (ABC) television series *Darkroom; Kindred Spirits* was named one of the most outstanding books of the year by the University of Iowa's Books for Young Adults Program, 1985.

WRITINGS:

NOVELS

City of Masques, Playboy Press, 1978.
Kindred Spirits, Tor Books, 1984.
Time and Chance, Tor Books, 1990.
Batman: Holy Terror (graphic novel), Warner Books (New York City), 1991.

STORY COLLECTIONS

Her Pilgrim Soul and Other Stories, Tor Books, 1990.
Ma Qui and Other Phantoms, Pulphouse (Eugene, OR), 1991.

OTHER

(With David Spenser) *Weird Romance: Two One-Act Musicals of Speculative Fiction,* Samuel French (New York City), 1993.

Author of more than thirty television scripts, sometimes under the pseudonym Michael Bryant, for such series as *The Twilight Zone, Darkroom, Outer Limits,* and *Simon and Simon, The New Adventures of Wonder Woman, Buck Rogers in the Twenty-Fifth Century, L.A. Law, China Beach,* and *The Mississippi*. Screenplay writer for producers, including ABC Circle Films and Four D Productions. Author of comic book scripts for *Detective Comics, Brave and the Bold, Daredevil, Christmas with the Super Heroes,* and *Secret Origins*.

SIDELIGHTS: According to Gary Westfahl in the *St. James Guide to Horror, Ghost and Gothic Writers,* Alan Brennert "believes in ghosts. Not literally, perhaps, but he recognizes that most people's lives are perpetually haunted by images of 'phantoms': the people we've lost touch with, the people we've never met, the people we no longer are, the people we may or may not become. And while conveying this philosophy in fiction logically leads Brennert to forms of the ghost story, the results are rarely horrific, for his spirits are usually benign, ready to help characters better understand themselves and possibly gain a second chance in life."

Brennert's most popular novel is probably *Kindred Spirits,* the story of a man and woman who separately attempt suicide at Christmas and who, while lying in the hospital from the attempts, meet on a spiritual place and become friends. Upon reawakening again, the pair forget their otherworldly meeting and go their separate ways. "Though the novel is not without cloying moments," Westfahl admits, "especially in the opening chapters chronicling the characters' cloistered, miserable lives, Michael and Ginny soon transcend self-pity to emerge as concincing characters, and their final happiness seems fully earned."

Brennert once told *CA:* "I try to divide my time between writing books and writing for the screen; each has its own rewards and its own drawbacks. In television, one of my favorite scripts is 'Going Back to Hannibal,' produced on a short-lived and little-seen series called 'The Mississippi.' Donald Moffat appeared as a Mark Twain scholar so traumatized by his wife's death that he retreats behind the persona of a man he knows as well as himself—Twain, or rather Samuel Clemens. The episode was one of those rare instances when a writer's work is respected and left intact, and then vastly improved upon by a skilled set of actors.

"Unfortunately, this particular series had too few episodes produced to warrant syndication and is consigned to video oblivion. It sits recorded on videotape on my shelf at home, and every once in a while a residual check trickles in, hinting that the show is being seen in South Yemen, perhaps, or on a cable channel somewhere in Botswana, but for all intents and purposes the program is in limbo—except for the original broadcast signals which should be reaching the star Proxima Centauri and day now.

"Even so, I would gladly write the same script all over again. I became a writer because I wanted to move people in some way, and even a failed series like 'The Mississippi' reaches perhaps ten million viewers. If just one-tenth of 1 percent of those people were touched by my story, it was well worth it. I'd much rather write a good script for a low-rated show than a script that moves no one and touches no one for a more popular series.

"Currently, I serve as executive story consultant on 'The Twilight Zone'—an unparalleled working experience for me. I've had the pleasure of seeing not one but as many as five or six of my teleplays realized brilliantly by talented actors, directors, and craftspeople. Our ratings have been somewhat shaky, and it's uncertain whether we will last beyond a single season; but even if we don't, I can still point with pride to episodes like 'Her Pilgrim Soul,' 'A Message From Charity,' 'The Star,' 'Shatterday,' and others (some originals by me, some adapted by me from other authors' short stories). As with 'The Mississippi,' one must take satisfaction in the creation and try not to worry about the finished product's life after initial broadcast—that, in any event, is outside my control. No matter what the final fate of 'The Twilight Zone,' I'm proud of my yearlong association with it and would happily repeat the experience.

"Of my books, I take most pride in *Kindred Spirits.* It's the story of two lonely people, strangers to one another, who become so despondent that each attempts suicide on Christmas Eve. Something goes wrong, their astral bodies are yanked from their physical bodies, and it is in this astral state that they meet and forge a sometimes turbulent friendship. (Ultimately, I suppose, everything I write is about friendship, in some way; it seems to be one of the dominant themes of my work.) The novel was born of a certain despair in my own life, many years ago, which I managed somehow to transcend. I guess that is one of the other themes of the book: It is possible, after all, to transcend despair. And if my work is remembered at all after I die, I hope it will be in the context of that novel: 'Brennert? Oh, yeah; he wrote *Kindred Spirits.*'"

BIOGRAPHICAL/CRITICAL SOURCES:

BOOKS

Lofficier, Randy and Jean-Marc, *Into the Twilight Zone: The Rod Serling Programme Guide,* Virgin (London), 1995.

St. James Guide to Horror, Ghost and Gothic Writers, St. James Press (Detroit), 1998.

PERIODICALS

Magazine of Fantasy and Science Fiction, April, 1996, p. 4.

* * *

BRODRIBB, (Arthur) Gerald (Norcott) 1915-

PERSONAL: Born May 21, 1915, in St. Leonards, Sussex, England; son of Arthur Williamson (a doctor) and Violet Brodribb; married Jessica Barr, April 3, 1954; children: Michael Bryan. *Education:* Received Diploma in Education, 1939; Oxford University, M.A., 1950; Institute of Archaeology, London, Ph.D., 1983.

ADDRESSES: Home—Stubbles, Ewhurst Green, Robertsbridge, Sussex, England.

CAREER: Canford Boys' Public School, Wimborne, England, assistant master, 1944-54; Hydneye House, East Sussex, England, headmaster, 1954-72; Beauport Park Roman Excavation, East Sussex, co-director, 1972—. Manager of Ewhurst United Football Club, 1978—.

MEMBER: Society of Antiquaries (fellow), Cricket Writers Club, Marylebone Cricket Club, Sussex County Cricket Club (vice president), Beauport Park Archaelogical Trust.

WRITINGS:

Next Man In: A Study of Cricket Law, Putnam (New York City), 1952, revised editions, Pelham Books, 1985, Souvenir Press, 1995.

The Bay and Other Poems, Mountjoy Press, 1953.

(Editor) *Book of Cricket Verse,* Rupert Hart-Davis, 1954.

(With Henry Sayen) *A Yankee Looks at Cricket,* Putnam, 1956.

Hit for Six, Heinemann, 1960.

The Croucher: A Biography of Gilbert Jessop, London Magazine Editions, 1974.

Maurice Tate: A Biography, London Magazine Editions, 1978, revised edition, Constable & Co., 1985.

Roman Brick and Tile, Alan Sutton Publishing, 1987.

Cricket at Hastings: The Story of a Ground, Spellmount, 1989.

The Lost Art: A History of Underhand Bowling, Boundary Books, 1997.

Felix and the England Eleven, Boundary Books, 1998.

Also author of *Hastings and Men of Letters,* 1954, revised edition, Old Hastings Preservation Society, 1971, *Felix on the Bat,* 1962, *Stamped Tiles of Classic Britannia,* 1969, revised edition, 1978, and *The Art of Nicholas Felix,* 1985. Contributor of more than 200 articles to cricket and archaeology periodicals.

WORK IN PROGRESS: A History of Beauport Park and further work on Gilbert Jessop and Nicholas Felix.

SIDELIGHTS: Gerald Brodribb told *CA:* "I was fortunate enough to have C. S. Lewis as my tutor at Oxford and always remembered his dictum that, without clarity of meaning, any writing is a waste of time. As a historian, I believe it is essential to go back to original sources of information and not just to quote from others. I find research very exciting—the odd letter or news cutting can be like treasure.

"Every piece I write is from the start written in England with plenty of space for amendments. Each draft must be left for days to 'simmer,' and I am sure that all amendments make for a better result. It is essential that someone else—my wife was 'the common reader'—should read the pieces and make suggestions. I find the whole construction a source of delight. If I did not enjoy the business of writing I would not do it—and I have never made use of the services of any agent.

"I enjoyed cricket from a very early age, and at age 7 I used to copy out the county teams in colored inks—my first offering appeared in *The Cricketer* at the age of 14. It's not all cricket—there have been studies of local literary workers and of children's books—verse, history and so on. One thing leads to another—my archaeological interest led to the find of a unique Roman Bathhouse and the first study of Roman brick and till for which I obtained a Doctorate. There are several new books in preparation—I enjoy it."

BIOGRAPHICAL/CRITICAL SOURCES:

PERIODICALS

Times Literary Supplement, November 15, 1985.

BRONER, E(sther) M(asserman) 1930-

PERSONAL: Born in 1930 in Detroit, MI; daughter of Paul (a journalist and historian) and Beatrice (Weckstein) Masserman; married Robert Broner (a painter-printmaker); children: Sari, Adam and Jeremy (twins), Nahama. *Education:* Wayne State University, B.A., 1950, M.A., 1962; Union Graduate School, Ph.D., 1978.

ADDRESSES: *Office*—Department of English, Wayne State University, Detroit, MI 48202; and Sarah Lawrence College, Bronxville, NY 10708.

CAREER: Wayne State University, Detroit, MI, 1962—, began as instructor in creative writing, currently associate professor and writer in residence; Sarah Lawrence College, Bronxville, NY, visiting teacher, 1982—. Visiting professor at Haifa University, 1972 and 1975, Hebrew University, Oberlin College, 1979, and University of California, Los Angeles, 1979. Lecturer at numerous universities throughout the U.S.

AWARDS, HONORS: Two Wayne State University faculty research grants for creative work; Emma Lazarus Shaver Fund grant; O. Henry Awards, second prize, 1968; first prize in bicentennial playwriting contest, 1976, for *Body Parts of Margaret Fuller;* writing fellowships from *Esquire* magazine, National Endowment for the Arts in literature, 1980 and 1987, Michigan Council for the Arts, 1981 and 1987, and Foundation for the Arts, 1982; Wonder Woman Award, 1983.

WRITINGS:

PLAYS

Summer Is a Foreign Land (first produced in Detroit at Studio Theatre, Wayne State University, 1962), Wayne State University Press (Detroit), 1966.

Wait Till I Swallow My Saliva (television play), broadcast on WXYZ-TV, Detroit, 1968.

Body Parts of Margaret Fuller, first produced in Detroit at Hillberry Theatre, Wayne State University, 1976.

Playwrights Horizons, first produced in New York, 1976.

Letters to My Television Past, staged reading in New York at Y on 92nd St., 1985.

Safe Haven, staged reading in New York at Y on 92nd St., 1986.

OTHER

Journal-Nocturnal and Seven Stories, Harcourt (New York City), 1968.

Her Mothers, Holt (New York City), 1975, reprinted, Indiana University Press (Bloomington), 1985.

A Weave of Women (novel), Holt, 1978, reprinted, Indiana University Press, 1985.

(Editor with Cathy N. Davidson) *The Lost Tradition: Mothers and Daughters in Literature* (essays), Ungar (New York City), 1981.

The Telling: The Story of a Group of Jewish Women Who Journey to Spirituality through Community and Ceremony, Harper (San Francisco), 1993.

Mornings and Mourning: A Kaddish Journal, Harper, 1994.

(With Naomi Nimrod) *The Women's Haggadah,* Harper, 1994.

Ghost Stories (short stories), Global City Books (New York City), 1995.

Also author of film script *Dilatory Ship,* and of several one-act plays performed at Raven's Theatre in Birmingham, MI. Contributor of numerous short stories, book reviews, and articles to literary magazines, including *North American Review, Commentary, Story Quarterly, Nimrod, Mother Jones, Ms.,* and *New Letters.*

WORK IN PROGRESS: A novel entitled *The Repair Shop.*

SIDELIGHTS: "In her fiction, Esther Masserman Broner simultaneously experiments with narrative form and emphasizes the continuity of myth, folklore, and tradition," writes Cathy N. Davidson in a *Dictionary of Literary Biography* essay. The new forms that Broner finds for her fiction, says Davidson, "incorporate both dramatic presentation and poetic language and, at the same time, encompass a radical feminist reordering of social and fictional hierarchies." Broner's early short stories were rejected by male editors who, according to *Monthly Detroit*'s Henrietta Epstein, offered "condescending advice about 'masculine experience' or 'male characterization.'" But, says Epstein, once Broner replaced her given name with the initials E. M. she "discovered she could write on virtually any topic she chose and have her stories accepted for publication." This experience led Broner to make a clear distinction between Esther—"a loving wife, a giving mother, a caring teacher"—and E. M.—a disciplined artist who cuts herself off from "all ordinary contacts and connections." In her writing, as in her life, Broner maintains a feminist point of view: "My work is largely about the unchartered course of women: their history, genealogy, pilgrimage, literature, connections, and holidays," she told *CA*.

Each of these subjects is addressed in *A Weave of Women,* which Broner describes in her opening chapter as "the story of sanity and madness in the house of women." A "militant feminist novel," according to *Washington Post*'s Michele Slung, the story concerns the exploits and tribulations of fifteen women who share a communal home in the Old City of Jerusalem. Together the women, who come from all parts of the world, invent new ceremonies, which include ways of exorcising demons, getting married, and burying the dead. In all their actions, the women oppose the state and the rabbinate for what official politics and religion have done to women. "*A Weave of Women* is a technically innovative work, written in prose but also, by turns, poetic, lyrical, and dramatic," explains Davidson. "Each of the characters has a story to tell and only gradually do the fifteen tales interweave into a saga of oppression and joy, revenge and celebration."

New York Times critic John Leonard describes the novel as "an astonishment," in which Broner "seeks nothing less than to achieve, in a kind of epic poem, a recapitulation of the rhythms of female consciousness." Though he notes similarities between her work and that of eminent feminists Marge Piercy, Doris Lessing, and Monique Wittig, he points out one crucial difference: "Miss Broner is interested in health; she proposes a myth of nurture." Praising her ability to create a "geography" as well as an ideology, Leonard continues: "Not the least of her accomplishments is this sense of place, of fact, on which the mysticism drapes itself. . . . When such . . . a way with detail joins with a sneaky sense of humor, we are no longer in the countries of Marge Piercy, Monique Wittig, and Doris Lessing. War and madness yield to healing and music. Humor is subversive, just as beauty is beyond discussion. [The story's] rhythm, its heartbeat, is renewal." The *Nation*'s Sheila Schwartz also offers high praise for the book: "*A Weave of Women* is an extraordinary novel, an original and beautiful work, musical in its conception, dreamlike in form, terrible, wonderful, and haunting." Describing the book as "an extended epic poem," she postulates that it "should become a classic."

Not all the reviewers are so unequivocal in their praise. *New York Times Book Review* writer Jane Larkin Crain admires *A Weave of Women*'s "narrative drive," but ultimately dismisses the work as "an essentially silly book, stuffed with all the cant of contemporary sexual politics." Slung, on the other hand, accepts Broner's treatment of subject but criticizes the way she has structured the story. "The presence of so many equal characters is distracting and the movement is not always smooth," Slung says. Despite these flaws, she commends Broner's efforts, concluding that the book has "enough moments of vulnerability, triumph and epiphany so that a woman reader may find herself, in spite of herself, being won over to the sensibility of its motley sisterhood."

Ghost Stories, Broner's 1995 publication, is a series of stories about Bronya—a Jewish mother whose life begins in Russia, passes through Detroit, and ends in Southern California—and her daughter. The mother haunts her daughter in life, throughout her dying, and even after death. "Because *Ghost Stories* is a series of tales with a commonality of incident and character, the collection reads like a novel. But a novel very different from Broner's *A Weave of Women,*" notes Celia McGee in the *Nation.* In these stories, she adds, "the parent and child go at each other with recriminations, fashion critiques, philosophical differences and disparate versions of the past."

"In the process," Suzanne Berne finds in the *New York Times Book Review,* "Ms. Broner herself delivers a terse, wry and occasionally comic examination of the relationship between mothers and daughters." Like the relationships of other mothers and daughters, this one begins with neither honesty nor understanding. But, as Bronya moves toward death and beyond, these two become brutally honest with each other. "But if the end of life is honesty," observes McGee, "Broner also wants it to be reconciliation, a liberating consciousness that may break the sin chain." McGee continues, "Frankness dispels the misunderstandings and hostility that constitute family relationships; it transforms the universal mismatch of influential parent and impacted child into a dialogue between two separate but equal individuals." According to a reviewer for *Publishers Weekly,* "The lack of invention in their telling, the . . . step-by-step recording of mundane details, render her litany more burdensome than enlightening." McGee arrives at a different evaluation. "Both women reveal secrets," writes the reviewer, "and thereby themselves. Enlightenment follows." She concludes, "Mostly Broner beautifully describes the game of life and death playing tricks on her creations."

In a profile of Broner's writing in *Contemporary Novelists,* fellow writer Marge Piercy comments, "Broner's world-view is thoroughly Judaic and religious, a living and sensuous and intelligent battle fought with her religion through all of her books with the intent of making Judaism extend justice to and become a home for women." The result, concludes Piercy, is that "she is a writer in whom a passionate experimentation comes together with serious political and religious inquiry." For this and other reasons, "Broner's fiction has gained increasing critical attention and is at the forefront of a contemporary burgeoning of fiction by Jewish feminists," states Davidson. "As a reviewer for *Ms.*, a frequent speaker at women's conferences, a playwright, and a novelist, Broner has added an important counterbalance to the prevailing masculine tradition in contemporary American-Jewish writing."

BIOGRAPHICAL/CRITICAL SOURCES:

BOOKS

Contemporary Literary Criticism, Volume 19, Gale (Detroit), 1981.
Contemporary Novelists, 6th edition, St. James Press (Detroit), 1996.
Dictionary of Literary Biography, Volume 28: *Twentieth-Century American-Jewish Fiction Writers,* Gale, 1984.

PERIODICALS

Detroit News, October 23, 1975.
Monthly Detroit, February, 1980.
Ms., July, 1976; July, 1978.
Nation, November 4, 1978; July 3, 1995, p. 22.
New York Times, July 25, 1978.
New York Times Book Review, September 29, 1968; August 13, 1978; July 2, 1995.
Publishers Weekly, March 8, 1993, p. 64; April 3, 1995, p. 56.
Saturday Review, November 23, 1968.
Washington Post, June 3, 1978.*

* * *

BRONNER, Stephen Eric 1949-

PERSONAL: Born August 19, 1949, in New York, NY; son of Harry and Edith (Kirchheimer) Bronner. *Education:* City College of the City University of New York, B.A., 1971; University of California, Berkeley, M.A., 1972, Ph.D., 1975.

ADDRESSES: Home—200 Cabrini Blvd., New York, NY 10033. *Office*—Department of Political Science, Rutgers University, New Brunswick, NJ 08903; fax: 908-932-7170.

CAREER: Rutgers University, New Brunswick, NJ, assistant professor, 1983-89, associate professor, 1983-89, professor of political science, 1990—. Appointment to the Program of Comparative Literature, 1995. New School for Social Research, visiting professor, 1989.

MEMBER: American Political Science Association. On Editorial Boards of *New Politics, New Political Science,* and *Capitalism Nature Socialism.*

AWARDS, HONORS: Fulbright fellowship, 1973, for study in Tuebingen, West Germany; Michael Harrington Book Award of the Caucus for New Political Science.

WRITINGS:

A Beggar's Tales (novel), Pella Publishing (New York City), 1978.
(Editor, translator, and author of introduction) *The Letters of Rosa Luxemburg,* Westview (Boulder, CO), 1978, second revised edition, Humanities Press International (Atlantic Highlands, NJ), 1993.
Rosa Luxemburg: A Revolutionary for Our Times, Pluto (London), 1981, Columbia University Press (New York City), 1987, third edition, Pennsylvania State University Press (University Park), 1997.
(Editor with Douglas Kellner) *Passion and Rebellion: The Expressionist Heritage,* Bergin & Garvey (South Hadley, MA), 1983, second edition, Columbia University Press, 1988.
(Editor and author of introduction) *Socialism in History: The Political Essays of Henry Pachter,* Columbia University Press, 1984.
Leon Blum: A Popular Biography, Chelsea House (New York City), 1987.
(Editor with Kellner) *Critical Theory and Society: A Reader,* Routledge & Kegan Paul (Boston), 1989.
Socialism Unbound, Routledge & Kegan Paul, 1990.
Moments of Decision: Political History and the Crises of Radicalism, Routledge & Kegan Paul, 1992.
Of Critical Theory and Its Theorists, Basil Blackwell (London), 1994.

Albert Camus: The Thinker, The Artist, The Man, F. Watts (New York City), 1996.

Twentieth Century Political Theory: A Reader, Routledge & Kegan Paul, 1996.

(Edited with F. Peter Wagner) *Vienna: The World of Yesterday, 1889-1914,* Humanities Press International, 1997.

A Preface to Political Theory in the Twentieth Century, Routledge & Kegan Paul, 1998.

A Rumor about the Jews: Reflections on Antisemitism and the "Protocols of Zion," Propylaen Verlag (Berlin), in press.

Also contributor of articles to periodicals, including *New Politics, Access, Global Justice, Capitalism, Nature, Socialism, Aesthetik und Kommunikation, New Political Science, Politics and Society, Telos, The Journal of the Hellenic Diaspora, The Boston University Journal, Twentieth-Century Literary Criticism, Minnesota Review, Politics and Society, The Politics and Society Reader, New German Critique, Colloquia Germanica, Review of Politics, Social Research, Salmagundi, Enclitic, Minnesota Review,* and *Political Theory*. Editorial Director of the Social Sciences, Humanities Press; Editor of the Westview Press series, "Interventions: Social Theory and Contemporary Politics."

SIDELIGHTS: "Whatever the personal and philosophical changes that I have undergone," Stephen Eric Bronner once told *CA,* "it is still an aspect of the 1960s which has fundamentally shaped my intellectual and political project. In essence, this involves the recognition that a basic connection between politics and culture exists, and that it must be addressed in a critical fashion.

"It was this insight that influenced my early choice of political aesthetics as the topic of inquiry for my early articles and my first novel. *A Beggar's Tales* has not received a great deal of notice, despite the fact that Charles Webel, writing for *Telos,* pointed out that its 'provocative' prose, its critical ideas, and its 'creativity . . . merit attention.' The novel grew out of the collapse of the old movement as it recognized and sought to discuss the motivations and the need for a new one. In the novel this was done by creating a 'pessimistic superstructure on a utopian base' through a broken-down narrator who cannot act, but rather lives only through the fictional stories that he tells in a shabby cafe. Politically influenced by the works of Sartre, Brecht, Walter Benjamin, and Ernst Bloch, the novel's literary use of the *recit* form derives from Benjamin Constant, Gide, and Camus.

"My concern with Marxian and critical thought must also be seen as a response to the collapse of the student movement. This concern was spurred on by the noted socialist, historian, and essayist, Henry Pachter, whom I met while a student at the City College of New York. My views also reflect the influence of the great maverick, Marxist philosopher Ernst Bloch, with whom I studied at the University of Tuebingen.

"My own political position is in sharp contrast to the reformism of Western social democracy and the orthodoxy of Soviet or Chinese Communism. The great socialist, activist, and theorist Rosa Luxemburg also stands apart from both these camps and, in my opinion, her work constitutes a beginning for any revitalization of *socialist* thought. *A Revolutionary for Our Times* is an attempt to show the relevance of her thought for contemporary socialist politics.

"Thus, reappropriating the socialist tradition for the political demands of the present becomes a dominant theme within my work. This theme is continued in *Socialism Unbound,* which deals with the failures, consequences, and possibilities of traditional socialist thinkers and movements in the light of contemporary events."

* * *

BROWN, Christy 1932-1981

PERSONAL: Born in 1932 in Dublin, Ireland; died of asphyxiation, September 6, 1981, in Parbrook, England; son of a bricklayer and Bridget Brown; married Mary Carr (a dental receptionist), October, 1972.

CAREER: Novelist and poet.

AWARDS, HONORS: Christopher Award from Christopher Society for *My Left Foot.*

WRITINGS:

My Left Foot (autobiography), foreword and epilogue by Robert Collis, Secker & Warburg (London), 1954, Simon & Schuster (New York City), 1955, published as *The Childhood Story of Christy Brown,* Pan Books (London), 1972.

Down All the Days (novel; Book-of-the-Month Club alternate selection), Stein & Day (New York City), 1970.

Come Softly to My Wake: The Poems of Christy Brown, Stein & Day, 1971.
Background Music (poetry), Stein & Day, 1973.
A Shadow on Summer (novel), Stein & Day, 1974.
Wild Grow the Lilies (novel), Stein & Day, 1976.
Of Snails and Skylarks (poetry), Secker & Warburg, 1977, Stein & Day, 1978.
A Promising Career (novel), Secker & Warburg, 1982.
Collected Poems, Secker & Warburg, 1982.

ADAPTATIONS: *My Left Foot* was filmed in 1989 and released in the United States by Miramax Films.

SIDELIGHTS: Born with cerebral palsy, the tenth of twenty-two children, Christy Brown was so disabled that he could not eat, drink, or dress by himself. He did have the use of his left foot, however, and he used it to paint pictures and to type books and poetry on a typewriter. Because Brown was unable to communicate or to move by himself, he was presumed to be totally disabled for his first five years. The first indication of his potential appeared, said *Newsweek's* S. K. Oberbeck, when "at age five, sitting on the floor watching his sister do sums on a chipped slate, Christy Brown's left foot reached out and snatched the chalk from her hand." Although Brown did not master speech until he was eighteen, he soon learned to write—with his left foot—in chalk on the linoleum floor.

"From very early on I had the urge to write," Brown told *New York Times* reporter Desmond Rushe. "As far back as I can remember I was always writing bits and pieces. . . . I had to compensate for being handicapped and the only way I could do it was to put my thoughts down on paper." Brown's urge to write resulted in *My Left Foot,* an autobiography published when the author was twenty-one years old. The book, a chronicle of Brown's struggle to overcome his staggering handicap, begins with the author's birth in an Irish slum. Brown later dismissed the work as "the kind of book they expected a cripple to write, too sentimental and corny," but Oberbeck appraised it as "an engaging, inspiring autobiography."

Brown wrote *My Left Foot* in hopes of earning enough money to buy an electric typewriter. The title succeeded far beyond his wildest dreams and brought him some literary celebrity. "This warm and mature autobiography shows that at age 22 Christy Brown already had more understanding of himself and the world than many of us ever achieve," noted E. J. Taylor in the *New York Times. Library Journal* correspondent E. P. Nichols styled the work "an absorbing, beautifully written story of a boyhood in Dublin, Ireland." Concluded Carol Stewart in *Spectator:* "[*My Left Foot*] is not a book only for those directly concerned with cerebral palsy. We can all learn from the writer's refusal to be shut in by self-pity and bitterness over his limitations."

Brown's next book, *Down All the Days,* took fifteen years to complete. This fictionalized autobiography was, according to Robert Ostermann of *National Observer,* "an astonishing achievement, for it poured out in a verbal flood the coming to physical, imaginative, and intellectual life of a Dublin slum child born into the same crippling prison as its author." Brown once described *Down All the Days* as "just a slice of life, a very raw slice of life," and most critics agreed. A *Times Literary Supplement* reviewer observed that "Christy Brown's Dublin slums are larger than life, dens of roistering blasphemy and fornication." Often focusing on the sexuality of its seedy characters, the book contains "a goodly number of O'Portnoyesque sexual gropings," noted a *Time* reporter, who also pointed out that Brown "too often confuses the artificial throbbing of sex for thematic development."

Eugene A. Dooley of *Best Sellers* praised *Down All the Days* for its "picturesque language and the phrasing of incidents" and commended its literary style. A *Times Literary Supplement* critic thought Brown's style was "too facilely romantic and anecdotal," but admitted that "Brown writes with a breadth of understanding that makes him already one of the most discerning and lively observes of Irish life." Oberbeck concurred, stating that the book is "tender, gritty, immensely warm in its penetration of the hair-trigger tempers and passions that explode, recoil and reverberate in . . . [Brown's] deftly etched episodes." In another *National Observer* review, Robert Osterman declared: "The very fact that it exists at all gives *Down All the Days* an unassailable value; it would be worth attention if it had no literary merit, which is far from the truth." Osterman concluded that the book provides "an unforgettable literary experience."

Down All the Days became a best-seller and was translated into fourteen languages. It was followed by two books of poetry that Ostermann described as "more poetic ore than refined metal." Brown's collection of love lyrics, *Come Softly to My Wake,* fared well. According to Desmond Rushe, the book's "first issue of five thousand copies . . . sold out, which is remarkable for a volume of poetry." While popular with readers, Brown's verse drew some pointed criticism from reviewers. In the *Dictionary of Literary Biography,* Cathleen Donnelly wrote: "Brown's poetry is pleasant, containing many a lilting phrase and reflecting his keen eye and flair for imagery. But, like his novels, his poems are undisciplined and unpolished. The three volumes published before his death are enjoyable rather than brilliant, interesting rather than provocative." *British Book News* contributor Robert Greacen perhaps best summed up Brown's poetry when he stated that, "though not outstanding in a purely literary sense, [it] scores highly for humanity and sincerity."

Brown's second book of poems, *Background Music,* was followed by a novel, *A Shadow on Summer.* While highly anticipated, the novel failed to find favor with the critics, who especially faulted it for its verbosity. The story of a disabled Irish writer who seeks perspective by visiting America—where he becomes infatuated with two American women—*A Shadow on Summer* revisits many of Brown's previous preoccupations, including an absorption in the writing process. To quote Donnelly, "None of the characters is quite fully drawn and much of the novel is taken up with [the protagonist's] excruciating self-consciousness—about his sexual inadequacy, about the literary process, about his own response to the people and environment that surround him."

America's Peter LaSalle maintained that *A Shadow on Summer* "demonstrates again that Brown is a master word-wielder." *New York Times* critic Anatole Broyard, however, criticized Brown's overuse of adjectives and cliches. "The author is not trying to make us feel what he describes," Broyard wrote, "he is trying to impress us with his description of it. His 'eloquence' is not urgent, but complaisant." Conversely, *New Statesman* essayist Valentine Cunningham observed of the novel: "At its best, and worst, Christy Brown's prose is static, given lengthily to pursuing and explicating the sensations of each slow moment: very much the product of living at the edge of immobility. It's a marvelously apt medium for rendering the feelings of a hero who is also marooned on crutches or stuck at a table, familiar most of all with the stench of his own armpits and the race of his own thoughts."

Brown's novel *Wild Grow the Lilies* was also faulted for its excessive verbiage. Again in the *National Observer,* Ostermann pointed out that Brown "has barely stayed the flood of words so fitting for *Down All the Days,* and can't resist muffling every sentence in *Lilies* with five adjectives where one would do." Valentine Cunningham, in another *New Statesman* piece, agreed that the novel is wordy and filled with "blarneyfied eloquence" but still found delight in Brown's "filthy-minded pun-palace."

The success of his writing brought Brown a life of comparative comfort with his wife in a home in the English countryside. He died there of asphyxiation at the age of 49. A manuscript he had just turned over to his publisher was released posthumously as *A Promising Career.* The first of his books to be set outside of Irish concerns, *A Promising Career* follows the efforts of two aspiring singers and their dissolute and venal manager. "There could be no more fitting title for a final manuscript," noted Donnelly. "The words clearly characterize Brown's own career: he had much promise, but he never achieved the greatness of which he seemed capable."

Frank Tuohy expressed a similar sentiment in the *Times Literary Supplement.* "Christy Brown's early writing triumphed over devastating physical disability and an impoverished background," the critic stated. "He was fortunate only in that the moral traditions of Catholic Dublin provided him with twenty-two siblings who helped him to survive. In addition, as a native Irishman, he had the ability to translate into coherent and rhythmic prose some of the untiringly fluent speech—that sense of talking your way into life—which was part of the surrounding scene. His later separation from this source was perhaps inevitable, but the abandonment of whatever experience, even indirect, that it gave him proves in the event to have been disastrously mistaken."

BIOGRAPHICAL/CRITICAL SOURCES:

BOOKS

Brown, Christy, *My Left Foot,* foreword and epilogue by Robert Collis, Secker & Warburg, 1954.

Contemporary Literary Criticism, Volume 63, Gale (Detroit), 1984, pp. 46-57.

Dictionary of Literary Biography, Volume 14: *British Novelists since 1960,* Gale, 1982, pp. 147-50.

Rafroidi, Patrick and Maurice Harmon, editors, *The Irish Novel in Our Time,* Publications de l'Universite de Lille III, 1976, pp. 287-95.

PERIODICALS

America, March 22, 1975, p. 217.

Best Sellers, June 15, 1970; January 15, 1972, p. 459.

Booklist, November 1, 1973; June 15, 1976; October 15, 1978; April 15, 1983, p. 1071.
British Book News, December, 1982, p. 763.
Christian Science Monitor, March 26, 1975.
Critic, January, 1974.
Listener, August 1, 1974, pp. 156-57.
National Observer, June 29, 1970, p. 19; September 25, 1976, p. 21.
New Statesman, August 2, 1974, p. 163; April 16, 1976, p. 514.
Newsweek, June 8, 1970; October 16, 1972.
New York Times, May 30, 1970; October 18, 1971; February 3, 1975, p. 23.
New York Times Book Review, June 14, 1970, pp. 4, 20.
Reader's Digest, June, 1982, pp. 71-77.
Saturday Review, August 20, 1955, pp. 17, 33; August 1, 1970, p. 28.
Spectator, February 18, 1955, p. 201; May 16, 1970, pp. 652-53; April 17, 1976, pp. 20-21.
Time, June 15, 1970; October 16, 1972.
Times Literary Supplement, February 4, 1955, p. 75; May 28, 1970, p. 577; April 16, 1976, p. 455; May 19, 1978, p. 550; August 13, 1982, p. 888.

OBITUARIES:

PERIODICALS

AB Bookman's Weekly, October 19, 1981.
Detroit Free Press, September 8, 1981.
Detroit News, September 8, 1981.
New York Times, September 8, 1981.
Publishers Weekly, September 18, 1981.
Times (London), September 8, 1981.*

* * *

BROWN, Harry (Peter McNab, Jr.) 1917-1986 (Harry Peter M'nab Brown, Artie Greengroin)

PERSONAL: Born April 30, 1917, in Portland, ME; died of emphysema, November 3, 1986, in Los Angeles, CA; son of Harry McNab and Bessie (Hiles) Brown; married June Jollie Clark, 1959 (divorced); children: Jarred. *Education:* Attended Harvard University, 1936-38. *Avocational interests:* Hunting, fishing, guns, "avoiding work, being dull at parties, and not answering letters."

CAREER: Copyboy for *Time* Magazine and sub-editor for *New Yorker* magazine, both before World War II; *Yank* magazine, writer in New York City, 1941-42, in London, England, 1942-44; Office of War Information, London, England, worked in Films Division, 1944-45; poet, novelist, playwright, and screenwriter, 1945-86. *Military service:* U.S. Army, Corps of Engineers, member of Anglo-American Film Unit, 1941-45; served in England.

AWARDS, HONORS: Co-winner of "Oscar" from Motion Picture Academy, 1952, for screenplay of *A Place in the Sun.*

WRITINGS:

FICTION

It's a Cinch, Private Finch (humorous sketches), illustrated by Ralph Stein, McGraw (New York City), 1943.
A Walk in the Sun (novel), Knopf (New York City), Secker & Warburg (London), 1944, reprinted, University of Nebraska Press (New York City), 1998.
Artie Greengroin, P.F.C. (stories originally published in *Yank,* under pseudonym Artie Greengroin), Knopf, 1945, published in England as *Artie Greengroin: Some Episodes in His Life in the Army,* Secker & Warburg, 1945.
The Stars in Their Courses (novel), Knopf, 1960.
A Quiet Place to Work (novel), Knopf, 1968.
The Wild Hunt (novel), Harcourt (New York City), 1973.

POETRY

The End of a Decade, New Directions (Norfolk, CT), 1940.
The Poem of Bunker Hill, Scribner (New York City), 1941.
The Violent: New Poems, New Directions, 1943.
Poems, 1941-44, Secker & Warburg, 1945.
The Beast in His Hunger, Knopf, 1949.

DRAMA

A Sound of Hunting (three-act play; first produced Lyceum Theatre, New York, November 20, 1945), Knopf, 1946.

SCREENPLAYS

The True Glory, Columbia, 1945.
The Other Love, United Artists, 1947.
Arch of Triumph, United Artists, 1948.

(With Kenneth Gamet) *The Wake of the Red Witch,* Republic, 1949.

(With James Edward Grant) *Sands of Iwo Jima,* Republic, 1949.

The Man on the Eiffel Tower, RKO, 1950.

Kiss Tomorrow Goodbye, Warner Bros., 1950.

Only the Valiant, Warner Bros., 1951.

(With Michael Wilson) *A Place in the Sun* (adapted from Theodore Dreiser's novel *An American Tragedy*), Paramount, 1951.

Bugles in the Afternoon, Warner Bros., 1952.

The Sniper, Columbia, 1952.

Eight Iron Men (adapted from Brown's play *A Sound of Hunting*), Columbia, 1952.

All the Brothers Were Valiant, Metro-Goldwyn-Meyer, 1953.

Many Rivers to Cross, Metro-Goldwyn-Meyer, 1955.

The Virgin Queen, Twentieth Century-Fox, 1955.

(With Ivan Moffat) *D-Day, the Sixth of June,* Twentieth Century-Fox, 1956.

Between Heaven and Hell, Twentieth Century-Fox, 1956.

The Deep Six, Warner Bros., 1958.

The Fiend Who Walked the West, Twentieth Century-Fox, 1958.

(With Charles Lederer) *Ocean's Eleven,* Warner Bros., 1960.

OTHER

Contributor to poetry journals and popular magazines, including *New Yorker, Atlantic Monthly, Vogue, Harper's Bazaar, Town and Country,* and *Horizon.*

ADAPTATIONS: A Walk in the Sun was adapted for film by Robert Rossen and released in 1946; *The Stars in Their Courses* was adapted for film by Leigh Brackett as *El Dorado* and released by Paramount, 1967.

SIDELIGHTS: Harry Brown was an eclectic author who penned novels, screenplays, books of poetry, books of humor, and a play. Some of Brown's works met with unqualified critical and commercial success; others failed abysmally on both fronts. Brown attended Harvard University in the late thirties where he won several awards for his poetry. He left Harvard after two years, but his first book of poems, *The End of a Decade,* soon appeared from New Directions.

Brown enlisted in the U. S. Army in 1941. Through most of World War II he was stationed in England, where he wrote for the Army magazine *Yank.* His major contribution to the magazine was a series of humorous sketches about an Army private. These were collected and published in book from in 1945 as *Artie Greengroin, P. F. C.* According to Maurice Baseches writing in *Saturday Review:* "Few things in Army humorous writing can touch the best episodes. . . . A laugh-filled mixture of witty lines and character drawing that have a flavor all their own." However, Herbert Lyons of the *New Republic* stated: "Artie Greengroin may have some value as evidence that men in uniform do not necessarily write freshly or knowingly about the business of soldiering."

A year before the "Greengroin" collection, Brown's first novel, *A Walk in the Sun,* had appeared. Richard Watts of the *New York Times* observed: "Despite the fact that both deal . . . with American soldiers of the second World War, two books could hardly be more different." *A Walk in the Sun* tells the story of an American platoon that meets heavy opposition as it lands on an Italian beach. After the lieutenant and sergeants of the platoon become casualties, a corporal takes charge of the mission. Orville Prescott of *Yale Review* credited Brown with "such superb powers as a writer that he can portray men in battle wonderfully well, better than any other author writing of the Second World War." Henry Reed of *New Statesman & Nation* felt the book provided "the excitement given by the progress and fulfillment of a work of art." Numerous reviewers praised the clarity and effectiveness of Brown's writing style, which Harvey Breit of the *New York Times* characterized as "poetic and realistic." *A Walk in the Sun* became a bestseller and was soon adapted as a motion picture.

The success of the film version of *A Walk in the Sun* had a profound effect upon Brown's career as a writer. He was not to produce another novel for sixteen years; instead, the bulk of his creative energy was devoted to writing screenplays adapted from the work of others. Essayist Joseph R. Millichap in the *Dictionary of Literary Biography* described Brown as "a literary figure captivated by Hollywood." In terms of genre Brown's films ranged the entire gamut, encompassing war stories, westerns, romantic comedies, mysteries and serious dramas. The high point of his stint in Hollywood was the 1951 *A Place in the Sun* for which he received an Academy Award. There were also low points, such as the 1948 *Arch of Triumph,* adapted from an Erich Maria Remarque novel. According to Millichap, this "soap opera" was "an artistic failure and a financial disaster," losing more than two million dollars. Brown stated that his own favorite among his screenplays was "The Enchanted Cup," an updated retelling of the Tristan and Isolde legend. Unfortunately, the script was judged to be too downbeat and was never filmed.

In 1960 Brown returned to the novel with *Stars in Their Courses,* a western that derives its plot from the legends of the Trojan Wars. Reviewers were not impressed. Frank O'Neill of the *Chicago Sunday Times* observed: "there is a flash of promise here . . . [of] a drama of epic scope and stature. But the promise, alas, soon is dissipated in a formula ravaged by age and abuse." The following book, *A Quiet Place to Work,* a story of American ex-patriots in Mexico, fared better with critics. J. M. Carroll of *Library Journal* dubbed it "a well-written novel of suspense. . . . Substantial and of lasting interest." Brown's last novel, the satiric *The Wild Hunt,* tells the story of an Army sergeant caught in an affair with his colonel's wife. The sergeant subsequently embarks upon a wild cross-country flight. Although Phoebe Adam's of the *Atlantic* thought *The Wild Hunt* was "fine disrespectful fun," T. N. Jewell of *Library Journal* described it as "a pointless novel; too forced and mean-spirited to entertain, too shallow and simple-minded to enlighten."

Brown's later novels never received the acclaim or success of *A Walk in the Sun,* and he remains best known for his screenplays. Summing up Brown's Hollywood career, Millichap found him to be "in every sense a professional screenwriter—a literate, intelligent, creative craftsman."

BIOGRAPHICAL/CRITICAL SOURCES:

BOOKS

Dictionary of Literary Biography, Volume 26: *American Screenwriters,* Gale (Detroit), 1984.

PERIODICALS

Atlantic, September, 1944; September, 1945; July, 1960; March, 1973, p. 107.
Best Sellers, May 1, 1968.
Booklist, April 15, 1943; July 1, 1944; July 15, 1945; July 15, 1960.
Book Week, April 4, 1943, p. 4; July 2, 1944, p. 1; July 22, 1945, p. 2.
Book World, May 19, 1968, p. 8; June 16, 1968.
Chicago Sunday Tribune, June 19, 1960, p. 3.
Christian Science Monitor, September 6, 1944, p. 14.
Cleveland Open Shelf, July, 1943, p. 10.
Commonweal, June 17, 1960.
Horn Book, September, 1944.
Hudson Review, autumn, 1968.
Kirkus, May 1, 1944; June 1, 1945.
Library Journal, June 15, 1944; May 1, 1960; March 1, 1968, p. 1017; January 15, 1973, p. 182.
Nation, July 15, 1944.
New Republic, March 15, 1943; January 3, 1944; July 3, 1944; August 13, 1945, p. 198; March 17, 1973.
New Statesman & Nation, December 2, 1944, p. 374.
New Yorker, March 20, 1943; November 20, 1943; July 1, 1944; July 21, 1945.
New York Herald Tribune Book Review, June 12, 1960, p. 3.
New York Times, November 30, 1941; March 28, 1943, p. 5; June 25, 1944, p. 3; July 15, 1945, p. 6.
New York Times Book Review, June 19, 1960, p. 26; April 28, 1968, p. 44.
Poetry, January, 1948.
Publishers Weekly, February 12, 1968.
San Francisco Chronicle, June 21, 1960, p. 25.
Saturday Review, June 11, 1960; April 20, 1968.
Saturday Review of Literature, December 4, 1943; July 1, 1944, p. 11; July 21, 1945, p. 17; December 24, 1949; April 20, 1968.
Spectator, November 24, 1944.
Springfield Republican, March 7, 1943, p. E7; July 2, 1944, p. D4; July 15, 1945; July 24, 1960, p. D5.
Time, July 23, 1945; July 4, 1960.
Times Literary Supplement, January 13, 1945, p. 22.
Virginia Quarterly Review, winter, 1969; summer, 1973.
Weekly Book Review, March 21, 1943, p. 6; June 25, 1944, p. 3; July 15, 1945, p. 2.
Yale Review, autumn, 1944, p. 191.

OBITUARIES:

PERIODICALS

Chicago Tribune, November 6, 1986; November 9, 1986.
Los Angeles Times, November 4, 1986.
New York Times, November 4, 1986.
Washington Post, November 8, 1986.*

* * *

BROWN, Harry Peter M'nab
See BROWN, Harry (Peter McNab, Jr.)

BROWN, Judith M(argaret) 1944-

PERSONAL: Born July 9, 1944, in India; daughter of Wilfred George (a parson) and Joan Margaret (Adams) Brown; married Peter James Diggle, July 21, 1984; children: James Wilfred Lachlan Diggle. *Education:* Girton College, Cambridge, M.A. (with honors), 1965, Ph.D., 1968.

ADDRESSES: Home—Oxford, England. *Office*—Balliol College, Oxford University, Oxford OX1 3BJ, England.

CAREER: Cambridge University, Girton College, Cambridge, England, research fellow, official fellow in history, and director of studies in history, 1968-71; University of Manchester, Manchester, England, lecturer, beginning 1971, senior lecturer in history, 1982-90, advisor in the central academic advisory service, 1978-90; Oxford University, Balliol College, Beit Professor of Commonwealth History, 1990—. Lecturer on Hinduism in Northern Ordination Course, 1982.

MEMBER: Royal Historical Society (fellow).

WRITINGS:

Gandhi's Rise to Power: Indian Politics, 1918-1922, Cambridge University Press, 1972.

Gandhi and Civil Disobedience: The Mahatma in Indian Politics, 1928-1934, Cambridge University Press, 1977.

Men and Gods in a Changing World: Some Themes in the 20th Century Experience of Hindus and Christians, SCM Press (London), 1980.

Modern India: The Origins of an Asian Democracy, Oxford University Press, 1984.

Gandhi: Prisoner of Hope, Yale University Press, 1989.

(Editor with Rosemary Foot) *Migration: The Asian Experience,* Macmillan (New York City), 1994.

(Editor with Martin Prozesky) *Gandhi in South Africa: Principles and Politics,* St. Martin's (New York City), 1996.

(Editor with Foot) *Hong Kong's Transitions, 1842-1997,* Macmillan, 1997.

Contributor to texts, including *The Making of Politicians: Studies from Africa and Asia,* 1976, *Leadership in South Asia,* 1977, and *Congress and Indian Nationalism,* 1988. Member of editorial advisory panel on politics and current affairs, *The Modern Churchman.*

SIDELIGHTS: Focusing on the country of her birth and its most famous modern leader, Judith M. Brown's books "are very useful not only for scholars of India and of [Mohandas] Gandhi, but also for handy references for anyone generally knowledgable in these crucial periods (and apparently inexhaustible subjects) who may want to check out specific details," A. M. Davidon comments in a *New Republic* review of *Gandhi and Civil Disobedience: The Mahatma in Indian Politics, 1928-1934.* Brown deftly manages a great number of sources, as *Times Literary Supplement* contributor Ainslie Embree remarks; the result is "a work that will enhance Brown's reputation as one of the most interesting of the scholars now interpreting recent Indian history." "Seeping through all the tightly-packed data," concludes Davidon, "are delicately tentative, objectively formulated expressions of Brown's sensibility and sympathies which raise the narrative above a dry tedious history to a cautiously positive assessment of this ungainly little man of mammoth spiritual proportions." Because Gandhi's life "was a vast and varicolored mix of service, spirituality, idealism, politics and nonviolent force that puts him well beyond the breadth of ordinary biography," Colman McCarthy asserts in *Washington Post Book World,* in *Gandhi: Prisoner of Hope* Brown "offers what she calls modestly 'a study and interpretation' of Gandhi. The modesty is appreciated but not necessary," the critic continues, for Brown "has written commandingly and refreshingly of a man whom dozens of writers . . . have gone at." Bhikhu Parekh similarly praises the author's "four-dimensional" approach, writing in the *New Statesman and Society* that *Gandhi* "is a fairly comprehensive book that does justice to the complexity of Gandhi's life and thought. . . .[Brown] has an intuitive feel for the man and grasps him as a whole, using his personal and political life to illuminate each other."

In addition, Parekh finds "valuable chapters" born of the new material Brown has brought to her work; *Newsweek* critic Jim Miller likewise states that the author "paints a compelling portrait of an elusive personality" due to her "drawing on a wealth of new sources." Radhakrishnan Nayar, however, faults Brown for not resolving Gandhi's two contrasting roles as political strategist and as proponent of modest economic reform; "yet if Brown's overall assessment of Gandhi's role does not convince, there is no doubt that this a valuable work," the critic admits in the *Times Literary Supplement,* "with thought-provoking descriptions of every phase of Gandhi's career. It is a lucidly written analysis and summary of Gandhi's political and social reform activities," the critic continues, "which takes account of documentary sources and relevant studies published since the last major scholarly biography [in 1958]." Despite the limitations "inevitable in such a wide-ranging book," Parekh concludes, "this is the best biography of Gandhi so far and deserves to be read by everyone interested in him and in modern India."

Brown told *CA*: "I write as an integral part of my research and teaching. I was motivated into the field of Indian history because of my birth in India. I believe historians need to be good communicators, therefore the art and craft of writing is essential to the historian. I find it a satisfying, if demanding process. I believe the best writing happens when one writes for a specific audience (i.e. a person or a particluar group)."

BIOGRAPHICAL/CRITICAL SOURCES:

PERIODICALS

New Republic, July 9-16, 1977.
New Statesman and Society, November 3, 1989.
Newsweek, March 12, 1990.
Times Literary Supplement, August 5, 1977; August 2, 1985; June 8-14, 1990.
Washington Post Book World, January 7, 1990.

* * *

BROWN, Patricia Fortini 1936-

PERSONAL: Born November 16, 1936, in Oakland, CA; daughter of Jack Gino (a chemist) and Mary Lillian (an executive secretary; maiden name, Wells; present surname, Forester) Fortini; married Peter Claus Meyer, May 28, 1957 (divorced August 30, 1978); married Peter Robert Lamont Brown (a historian), August 16, 1980 (divorced July 5, 1989); children: (first marriage) Paul Wells, John Jeffrey. *Education:* Attended Brigham Young University, 1954-57; University of California at Berkeley, A.B., 1959, M.A., 1978, Ph.D., 1983. *Religion:* Episcopalian.

ADDRESSES: Home—54 Humbert St., Princeton, NJ 08542-3319. *Office*—Department of Art and Archaeology, Princeton University, Princeton, NJ 08544-1018.

CAREER: State of California, Department of Employment, employment and claims specialist in San Francisco and San Rafael, 1960-65; painter and graphic designer in San Rafael, 1963-76; Mills College, Oakland, CA, lecturer in Italian Renaissance art, spring, 1983; Princeton University, Princeton, NJ, assistant professor, 1983-89, associate professor of art and archaeology, 1989—; Andrew W. Mellon associate professor in art and archaeology, 1991-95. Fellow at American Academy in Rome, 1989-90; Guggenheim Fellow, 1992-93. Member of San Rafael Cultural Affairs Commission, 1975-77; co-curator of Municipal Art Gallery, Falkirk Community Cultural Center, San Rafael, 1976-77.

MEMBER: College Art Association of America, Renaissance Society of America (member of advisory council; representative of the discipline of the visual arts, 1988-90).

AWARDS, HONORS: Fulbright fellow in Italy, 1980-81; Social Science Research Council fellow, 1980-82; Gladys Krieble Delmas Foundation grant for Venice, 1982; second prize for Premio Salotto Veneto, 1989, for *Venetian Narrative Painting in the Age of Carpaccio;* Rome Prize fellow, 1989-90; Guggenheim fellow, 1989-90.

WRITINGS:

Venetian Narrative Painting in the Age of Carpaccio, Yale University Press (New Haven, CT), 1988.
(Contributor) *Rome: Tradition, Innovation, and Renewal,* edited by Clifford Brown, Chandler Kirwin, and John Osborne, Centro Di (Florence), 1989.
Venice & Antiquity: The Venetian Sense of the Past, Yale University Press, 1996.
Art and Life in Renaissance Venice, Prentice Hall (New York City), 1997, published as *Art and Life in Renaissance Venice: A World Apart,* Weidenfeld & Nicolson (London), 1997.

Also author of *La pittura nell' eta di Carpaccio: I grandi cicli narrativi,* 1992. Contributor to *Macmillan Encyclopedia of Art, Enciclopedia Italiana,* and to various art history journals.

SIDELIGHTS: After reading *Venice & Antiquity: The Venetian Sense of the Past,* one of Patricia Fortini Brown's critically acclaimed art history books, "no one can revisit familiar scenes in Venice . . . without seeing new aspects to the Venetian performance," according to *New York Times Book Review* contributor Gary Wills. Brown analyzes thirteenth through sixteenth century Venetian "arts, crafts, and literature to explore . . . 'a Venetian view of time . . . history and . . . historical change,'" noted Mary Morgan Smith in *Library Journal.* "Of all the major medieval cities in Italy, only Venice lacked a classical past. It had no Roman foundations to unearth, build on or celebrate," explained Wills.

Venice & Antiquity presents "themes [that] may not seem either new or profound. But," the reviewer lauded, "she shows, in sensitive detail, how the perpetual reinvention of Venice made the City reinvent the Rome, Constantinople and Jerusalem over against which it was defining itself. This led to a peculiarly shifting and illusionistic view of the past, undergoing subtle changes like the light of the city's own watery atmosphere." Although John Julius Norwich warned in *Observer* that "This book is not an easy read. There were moments when I felt that the author had got a little carried away by her own scholarship and allowed herself to become slightly ponderous," he overwhelmingly praised the work as a "superbly produced and beautifully produced book" with virtually no inaccuracies. Norwich maintained that Brown is "alarmingly well-informed" and "writes . . . with fluency and style." In his review, Norwich also positively notes Brown's remarkable first book, *Venetian Narrative Painting in the Age of Carpaccio.*"

In her prize-winning debut, "Brown shows how narratives of the lives of saints, miracles, and state processions all yield to the eyewitness style of Gentile Bellini and Vittore Carpaccio," described Thomas D'Evelyn in *Christian Science Monitor.* "Narrative has preoccupied art historians of the Renaissance ever since Vasari recounted his fascination with storytelling pictures in *The Lives of the Artists,* but the very ubiquity of narrative in Renaissance art seems to forestall critical reassessment," wrote a reviewer for *Art Bulletin* who declared *Venetian Narrative Painting in the Age of Carpaccio* to be "a welcome focus on the study of visual narrative in Renaissance art history." Charles Hope praised the book in the *New York Review of Books* for "not just [dealing] very competently with the many specific problems raised by individual works, but also [looking] at more general issues, such as the stylistic origins of the genre." Her work, according to *Times Literary Supplement* contributor David Rosand, "offers a dynamic portrait of a society and its self-imaging." "She has assembled a mass of information, and she has characterized the preoccupations and values of the patrons with skill and sympathy," assessed Hope, qualifying: "But we still need to know much more, not about their piety or their attitudes to Venetian society as a whole, but about their responses to paintings."

Brown once told *CA:* "The central concern of my scholarly work has been the manner in which works of art can materialize and 'sum up' significant aspects of the culture in which they were produced. More specifically, I have sought to understand the formal and iconographical qualities of Renaissance art through a study of the perceptual skills, the ideological assumptions, and the social situation that engendered its production. This approach, exemplified by my book, *Venetian Narrative Painting in the Age of Carpaccio,* has been strongly influenced by the particular background out of which I began my academic career.

"After receiving an bachelor of arts degree in political science in 1959, I seriously pursued a career as a studio artist while raising a family. During this period I also became active in historical preservation activities, and in 1976 I began graduate work in the history of art after an interim of about seventeen years away from the academic world.

"While my late reentry into a graduate program presented a number of difficult hurdles—among them, regaining competency in foreign languages and learning how to think, research, and write as a historian—my studio background proved a positive asset. For during my graduate training I was encouraged to develop an interdisciplinary approach that combined my practical experience as a working artist with my earlier interests in history and political theory. The foundation for this approach had been laid in the studio. There I had been in the habit of confronting the work of art as a 'solution': as the end result of a process of problem solving. Thus, while I was learning in the course of my graduate studies to approach art in a consciously analytical, rather than a purely intuitive, manner, the formal analysis of paintings was already a familiar, embedded skill for me.

"Becoming a historian, however, was another matter. It meant a shift in viewpoint to a position opposite to that of the artist: that is, to the position of the original patrons and viewers of the art. Here my earlier interests in political theory and behavior, kept alive in a practical way by my community service, developed into a concern for the broader dynamics of art: its place in a larger social and cultural context of human experience. Essentially, then, I sought to balance in my work the competing claim of the historian and the artist. It is this combination that has challenged me to deal both with the aesthetic and formal elements of works of art and with the contextual concerns of social, political, religious, and cultural history."

BIOGRAPHICAL/CRITICAL SOURCES:

PERIODICALS

Art Bulletin, March, 1992, pp. 161-62.
Art History, December, 1988.
Choice, November, 1988, p. 474.
Christian Science Monitor, September 2, 1988, p. B2.
Library Journal, October 1, 1988, p. 82; February 15, 1997, p. 145.
New York Review of Books, December 22, 1988, p. 42.
New York Times Book Review, April 20, 1997, p. 34.
Observer, February 23, 1997, p. 16.
Times Educational Supplement, October 26, 1990, p. R2.
Times Literary Supplement, October 21, 1988, p. 1178.*

* * *

BROWNJOHN, Alan 1931-
(John Berrington)

PERSONAL: Born July 28, 1931, in London, England; son of Charles Henry (a managing printer) and Dorothy (Mulligan) Brownjohn; married Shirley Toulson (a poet), February 6, 1960 (divorced, 1969); married Sandra Willingham (a teacher), August 26, 1972; children: (first marriage) Steven. *Education:* Merton College, Oxford, B.A., 1953, M.A., 1961. *Politics:* Member of Labour Party. *Religion:* Atheist.

ADDRESSES: Home—2 Belsize Pk., London NW3, England.

CAREER: Beckenham and Penge Boys' Grammar School, teacher, 1957-65; Wandsworth Borough Councillor, London, 1962-65; Battersea College of Education (now Polytechnic of the South Bank), London, senior lecturer in English, 1965-79; writer, 1979—. Labour Party parliamentary candidate, Richmond, Surrey, 1964; chair of Literature Panel of the Greater London Arts Association, 1973-77, deputy chair, 1979-82, chair, 1982-88, and deputy president, 1988-91.

MEMBER: Poetry Society (London).

AWARDS, HONORS: Cholmondeley award, 1979; Society of Authors travel scholarship, 1985; Authors' Club (London) award for the best first novel of 1990, for *The Way You Tell Them.*

WRITINGS:

POETRY

Travellers Alone, Heron Press (Liverpool, England), 1954.
The Railings, Digby Press (London), 1961.
The Lions' Mouths, Macmillan (London), 1966, Dufour (Chester Springs, PA), 1968.
Woman Reading Aloud, Sycamore Press (Oxford, England), 1969.
Being a Garoon, Sceptre Press (Frensham, Surrey, England), 1969.
Sandgrains on a Tray: Poems, Dufour, 1969.
(With Michael Hamburger and Charles Tomlinson) *Penguin Modern Poets 14,* Penguin (London), 1969.
(Editor) *First I Say This: A Selection of Poems for Reading Aloud,* Hutchinson (London), 1969.
A Day by Indirections, Sceptre Press, 1969.
Brownjohn's Beasts (juvenile), illustrations by Carol Lawson, Scribner (New York City), 1970.
Synopsis, Sceptre Press, 1970.
Frateretto Calling, Sceptre Press, 1970.
An Equivalent, Sceptre Press (Rushden, Northamptonshire), 1971.
(Editor with Seamus Heaney and Jon Stallworthy) *New Poems, 1970-1971,* Hutchinson, 1971.
Warrior's Career, Macmillan (London), 1972.
A Song of Good Life, Secker & Warburg (London), 1975.
A Night in the Gazebo, Secker & Warburg, 1980.
Collected Poems, 1952-1983, Secker & Warburg, 1983.
The Old Flea Pit, Hutchinson (London), 1987.
Collected Poems, 1952-1988, Hutchinson, 1988.
The Observation Car, Hutchinson, 1990.
The Cruel Arcade, Sinclair-Stevenson (London), 1994.

NOVELS

(Under pseudonym John Berrington) *To Clear the River* (juvenile), Heinemann (London), 1964.
The Way You Tell Them: A Yarn of the Nineties, A. Deutsch (London), 1990.

OTHER

Oswin's Word (libretto for children), British Broadcasting Corporation (London), 1967.

The Little Red Bus Book, Inter-Action (London), 1972.
She Made It, Sceptre Press, 1974.
Philip Larkin (criticism), Longmans (London), 1975.
(Editor with Maureen Duffy) *New Poetry 3,* Arts Council (London), 1977.
(Editor) *New Year Poetry Supplement,* Poetry Book Society (London), 1982.
(Editor with wife, Sandy Brownjohn) *Meet and Write,* three volumes, Hodder & Stoughton (London), 1985-87.
(Translator) Goethe, *Torquato Tasso,* Angel (London), 1985.
(Editor with K. W. Gransden) *The Gregory Anthology, 1987-1990,* Hutchinson, 1990.

Poetry critic, *New Statesman* (London), 1968—, and *Times* (London), 1989—.

SIDELIGHTS: In a long career marked by social consciousness and sensitive morality, Alan Brownjohn has emerged as "one of the major talents of contemporary British poetry," to quote John Cotton in *Contemporary Poets*. Brownjohn's verse ranges widely in subject matter, but, as the poet said himself, his work mainly concerns "love, politics, culture, time." He was one of the first British writers to put art to use as a protest against the Cold War and nuclear armament, and, as Roger Garfitt noted in the *Dictionary of Literary Biography,* he has subsequently become "postwar British society's most accurate recorder and its most penetrating satirist." Garfitt added that Brownjohn "brings a similar questioning intelligence to bear on personal relationships, winning an increasing reputation as a subtle and inventive love poet."

During his early years Brownjohn taught school while publishing poetry and children's books. He attended meetings of The Group, a poetry workshop that met weekly under the direction of Philip Hobsbaum and Edward Lucie-Smith. When that workshop was succeeded by the Poetry Society, Brownjohn took a more active role in the proceedings and became chair in 1968. His 1967 volume of poems, *The Lions' Mouths,* enhanced his personal reputation as an artist with a political and moral agenda. As a *Times Literary Supplement* reviewer put it, "Mr. Brownjohn's best work comes from his mature political concerns." Garfitt quoted London *Times* correspondent Christopher Ricks, who found Brownjohn's "hesitant scrupulousness a crisp achievement."

Garfitt cited a recurring theme in Brownjohn's work as "the fantasies with which we sidestep reality or compensate for it." The critic added: "Disappointment is mandatory in Brownjohn's poems as it is in [Philip] Larkin's, but if Larkin's gift is for registering those moments when disillusion takes us by surprise, Brownjohn's is for observing the sleights of mind by which we evade it once again." Cotton observed that Brownjohn takes the stand "that a society is to be judged by the quality of life it engenders. . . . While [his] view is compassionate it is, nevertheless, allied to an uncompromising critical stance."

Several collections of Brownjohn's poems were published in the 1980s, and critics appreciated the opportunity to take a comprehensive view of his work. *Observer* essayist Peter Porter wrote: "The historian of our age's tics and signals will have to read Brownjohn as well as our more sprawling novelists. . . . He catches the tone of the decades we have lived through." In the *Times Literary Supplement,* William Scammell spoke to Brownjohn's growth "over a long period . . . into one of our very best makers."

Brownjohn once told *CA* that he considers himself "a poet of the mainstream, rather than a traditionalist or *avant-gardist.*" He notes that, as yet, he has traveled extensively only in Scandinavia and that he is an admirer of Swedish civilization. He holds strong left-wing Labour opinions in politics but adds that he is "not an active politician any more." He is a "lover of Faure, Debussy and modern jazz," and a "lover of cats."

Brownjohn says that he is "interested in [the] possibility of diversity in form and subject-matter in [his] verse," and that he hopes "to write more novels." Brownjohn enjoys reading poetry aloud and has given many readings in England.

BIOGRAPHICAL/CRITICAL SOURCES:

BOOKS

Contemporary Poets, sixth edition, St. James Press (Detroit), 1996, pp. 125-27.
Dictionary of Literary Biography, Volume 40: *Poets of Great Britain and Ireland since 1960,* Gale (Detroit), 1985, pp. 57-64.
Schmidt, Michael and Grevel Lindop, editors, *British Poetry since 1960,* Carcanet Press (Manchester, England), 1972.

PERIODICALS

Kenyon Review, Volume 30, number 5, 1968.
Literary Review, November, 1983.

London Magazine, March, 1967; October, 1969.
New Statesman, June 27, 1969, p. 914.
Observer (London), March 26, 1967; January 18, 1984.
Poetry, November, 1970, p. 108.
Times Literary Supplement, February 16, 1967, p. 125; October 23, 1969, p. 1231; February 17, 1984, p. 168.*

* * *

BRYANT, Arthur (Wynne Morgan) 1899-1985

PERSONAL: Born February 18, 1899, in Dersingham, Norfolk, England; died January 22, 1985, in Salisbury, England; son of Sir Francis Bryant (a sergeant-at-arms to King George V); married Sylvia Mary Shakerley, 1924 (divorced, 1939); married Anne Elaine Brooke, 1941. *Education:* Received M.A. from Queen's College, Oxford. *Avocational interests:* Collecting old furniture, pictures, and books.

CAREER: Cambridge School of Arts, Crafts, and Technology, England, headmaster, 1923-25; Oxford University, Oxford, England, lecturer in history and English literature, 1925-35; editor of *Ashridge Journal,* 1930-39; London University, London, England, Watson Professor of American History, 1935; *Illustrated London News,* London, writer of column "Our Note Book," beginning 1936. Served as a governor of Ashridge, 1936-49, chair of council, 1946-49. Lecturer in Europe and the United States; lecturer to H.M. forces, 1940-46; editor of speeches for Neville Chamberlain. Producer of pageants. Chair of St. John and Red Cross Hospital Library; trustee of Historic Churches Preservation Council; president of Common Market Safeguards Campaign and Tyneham Action Group. Vice-president of Royal Literary Fund; member of Advisory Talks Council of the British Broadcasting Corp. (BBC); trustee of English Folk Music Fund. *Military service:* Royal Flying Corps and Royal Air Force; served in World War I.

MEMBER: English Association (past president), Royal Historical Society (fellow), Royal Society of Literature (fellow), Society of Authors, Wisbech Society, Friends of the Vale of Aylesbury, Athenaeum Club, Beefsteak Club, Grillion's Club, Pratt's Club, MCC Club.

AWARDS, HONORS: Commander of the Order of the British Empire, 1949; knight of Grace St. John of Jerusalem, 1954; companion of honor, 1967; Chesney Gold Medal from Royal United Service Institute, 1955; gold medal for literature from *London Sunday Times;* gold medal from Royal Institute of Chartered Survivors; honorary member of Southampton Chamber of Commerce; LL.D. from University of Edinburgh, University of St. Andrews, and University of New Brunswick.

WRITINGS:

Rupert Buxton—A Memoir, Cambridge University Press (New York City), 1926.
The Spirit of Conservatism, Methuen (London), 1929.
King Charles II, Longmans, Green (London), 1931, revised edition, Collins (London), 1955.
Macaulay, P. Davies (London), 1932, revised edition, Barnes & Noble (New York City), 1979.
The Man in the Making (part I of "Samuel Pepys" trilogy), Cambridge University Press, 1934, revised edition, Collins, 1947.
The England of Charles II, Longmans, Green, 1934, reprinted, Books for Libraries (Freeport, NY), 1972, published as *Restoration England,* Collins, 1960.
(Editor) *The Man and the Hour: Studies of Six Great Men of Our Times,* P. Allan, 1934, Kennikat Press (Port Washington, NY), 1972.
The National Character, Longmans, Green, 1934.
The Years of Peril (part II of "Samuel Pepys" trilogy), Cambridge University Press, 1935, revised edition, Collins, 1948.
(Editor) King Charles II, *The Letters, Speeches and Declarations of King Charles II,* Cassell (London), 1935, Funk & Wagnalls (New York City), 1968.
The American Ideal, Longmans, Green, 1936, reprinted, Books for Libraries, 1969.
George V, P. Davies, 1936.
(Editor) *Postman's Horn: An Anthology of the Letters of Latter Seventeenth Century England,* Longmans, Green, 1936, revised edition, Home & Von Thal (London), 1946, reprinted, Books for Libraries, 1970.
Humanities in Politics, Hutchinson (London), 1938.
The Saviour of the Navy (part III of "Samuel Pepys" trilogy), Cambridge University Press, 1938, revised edition, Collins, 1967.
(Editor) Arthur Neville Chamberlain, *In Search of Peace,* Hutchinson, 1939, revised and enlarged as *The Struggle for Peace,* 1939.
Britain Awake, Collins, 1940.
English Saga (1840-1940), Collins, 1940, published as *Pageant of England,* Harper (New York),

1941, abridged edition published as *Only Yesterday: Aspects of English History, 1840-1940,* Collins, 1965.

Unfinished Victory, Macmillan (London), 1940.

Years of Endurance, 1793-1802, Harper, 1942.

The Summer of Dunkirk, Kemsley Press (London), 1943.

The Battle of Britain, Kemsley Press, 1944.

Trafalgar and Alamein, Kemsley Press, 1945.

Years of Victory, 1802-1812, Collins, 1944, Harper, 1945, reprinted, Collins, 1975.

The Art of Writing History, Oxford University Press (New York City), 1946.

Historian's Holiday, Dropmore Press (London), 1946, revised edition, Collins, 1951.

A Historian's View of the War, RUSI (London), 1947.

Age of Elegance, 1812-1822, Collins, 1950, Harper, 1951.

The Story of England: Makers of the Realm, Collins, 1953, Houghton (Boston, MA), 1954, published as *Makers of England: The Atlantic Saga,* Doubleday (New York City), 1962 (original volume also published as *Makers of the Realm: The Story of Britain's Beginnings,* Fontana [London], 1972).

The Turn of the Tide: A History of the War Years Based on the Diaries of Field Marshal Lord Alanbrooke, Doubleday, 1957.

Triumph in the West: A History of the War Years Based on the Diaries of Field Marshal Lord Alanbrooke, Doubleday, 1959, reprinted, Greenwood Press, 1974.

Jimmy, the Dog in My Life, Lutterworth (London), 1960.

Liquid History: To Commemorate Fifty Years of the Port of London Authority, [London], 1960.

A Choice for Destiny: Commonwealth and Common Market, Collins, 1962.

(Author of introduction) King James II, *The Memoirs of James II,* Chatto & Windus (London), 1962.

The Age of Chivalry, Collins, 1963, Doubleday, 1964.

Only Yesterday, Collins, 1965.

The Fire and the Rose: Dramatic Moments in British History, Collins, 1965, Doubleday, 1966, revised edition, Fontana, 1972.

The Medieval Foundation, Collins, 1966, published as *The Medieval Foundation of England,* Doubleday, 1967, Collier (New York City), 1968.

Protestant Island, Collins, 1967.

Set in a Silver Sea, Doubleday, 1968, Morrow (New York City), 1984.

The American Ideal, Books for Libraries, 1969.

The Lion and the Unicorn: A Historian's Testament, Collins, 1969, Doubleday, 1970.

Nelson, Collins, 1970.

The Great Duke; or, The Invincible General, Collins, 1971, Morrow, 1972.

Jackets of Green: A Study of the History, Philosophy, and Character of the Rifle Brigade, Collins, 1972.

A Thousand Years of British Monarchy, John Pinches, 1973, Collins, 1975.

Pepys and the Revolution, Collins, 1979.

The Elizabethan Deliverance, Collins, 1980, St. Martin's (New York City), 1982.

Spirit of England, Collins, 1982, Parkwest Publications (New York City), 1985.

A History of Britain and the British People, Morrow, 1984.

Freedom's Own Island, Morrow, 1986.

The Search for Justice, Collins, 1990.

Contributor to periodicals, including *London Sunday Times, Sunday Express,* and *Illustrated London News.*

SIDELIGHTS: Arthur Bryant was a renowned British historian whose ability to make the past come alive for modern readers gained him both critical acclaim and popular success. His great love for his country permeates his work; one writer said that Bryant's patriotism is "a passion that runs in his blood." Although some critics find him overly sentimental, many consider his work accurate, useful, and informative. He was generally recognized for his skill in condensing large amounts of information into what one critic called "eminently readable" works.

Bryant was one of the original officers to serve in the newly formed Royal Air Force during World War I. After the war, he won a scholarship from Cambridge but decided to attend Oxford instead. Upon leaving Oxford, he ran a children's library in a house that had once belonged to Charles Dickens. He was eventually appointed headmaster of the Cambridge School of Arts, Crafts, and Technology, becoming the youngest headmaster in England. It was shortly after he resigned from that post that he began writing.

The 1931 publication of *King Charles II* won him immediate popular success. His reputation as a historian was quickly established, and in a career spanning sixty years he proceeded to publish more than fifty historical and biographical works. *King Charles II* gives "a better understanding of the period in which modern England came into being," wrote Charles Petrie of *Saturday Review. Spectator's* John Buchan called the biography "the best study of the man yet published," but a writer for *Times Literary Supple-*

ment suggested that Bryant portrayed Charles as being more virtuous than he actually was.

Bryant is especially known for his biographical writings. One of his more extensive biographies is his three-volume series on the life of Samuel Pepys, a famous seventeenth-century English diarist. The first volume is taken largely from the diaries; for the later volumes Bryant used official correspondence and naval documents. Graham Greene of *Spectator* felt that Bryant's portrayal of Pepys was "a little too rosy," but he applauded the manner in which Bryant selected and arranged "the vast material of the diary." With W. P. Lipscomb, Bryant later adapted the Pepys story for the stage, and the production ran for one hundred fifty performances.

Bryant's three-volume history of England's wars with Revolutionary and Napoleonic France—*Years of Endurance, Years of Victory,* and *Age of Elegance*—offers a detailed account of the years 1793 to 1822. Critics praised the trilogy for its lively style and its vivid recreation of both battle scenes and the daily life of the period. Reviewing *Years of Endurance* for *New Statesman & Nation,* J. L. Hammond stated: "Mr. Bryant's book serves its immediate purpose well, for it paints a picture of Britain at war with great skill and knowledge, and its vivid touches of the life and mind of the time make it attractive reading." Regarding *Years of Victory,* a reviewer for the *Manchester Guardian* contended: "Mr. Bryant's great story has purified and refined his style and has lifted him above his earlier level. This is undoubtedly his best book, and a very good book too." Geoffrey Bunn, discussing *Age of Elegance* in the *New York Herald Tribune Book Review,* observed: "History presented in this glittering fashion will always have its readers. The rush of images, the flashing style, the epigrams and intrigues, the moments of hot heroic action have the similitude of a living pageant." While disagreeing with Bryant's analysis on several counts, Christopher Sykes concluded his *Spectator* review of *Age of Elegance* by stating: "If these points can be taken against him, as I believe they can, they are trifling blemishes in a magnificent panorama, and I am left finally with a sense of unreserved admiration for the finish, capaciousness, efficiency and the pleasant design of Dr. Bryant's high-powered Time Machine."

Bryant's two-volume *Story of England,* which includes *Makers of England* and *The Age of Chivalry.* is considered by many critics to be one of his greatest accomplishments. *Makers of England* deals with the birth of England as a nation, how it major institutions came into being and how its various peoples were joined together as one. "Endowed with a style beautiful in its simple lucidity," noted S. C. Chew in the *New York Herald Tribune Book Review,* "and with a gift for organizing vast quantities of material, this historian possesses also the faculty of distinguishing the substance from the accidental, the significant from the merely factual." *The Age of Chivalry* covers the high Middle Ages, from the twelfth century reforms of Edward I to the Peasant's Revolt of 1381. C. V. Wedgewood of *Book Week* called Bryant "a Scheherazade among historians" and stated: "There is not a dull moment in this splendid book. . . . The remote century comes vividly alive."

Ambrose Agius of *Best Sellers* called Bryant's *The Medieval Foundation of England* a "work full of intricate historical lore." He recommended the book for anyone planning to visit England, as they will find their "pleasure and profit immeasurably enhanced by a previous reading of this account of the people and events that went into her [England's] making." The *New York Times Book Review's* Charles Ferguson declared *Medieval Foundation* a great book, and he marveled at Bryant's thoroughness in tracing English history through thousands of years. In the book, Bryant tells of the influx and invasions of various peoples, including Romans, Saxons, Vikings, and Normans, and he describes the effect each group had on the growth and development of English agriculture, trade, and law. A writer for the *Economist* suggested that Bryant was guilty of oversimplification, but conceded that this was probably inevitable, given the vast scope of his subject.

In *Set in a Silver Sea,* Bryant takes up the telling of English social history where he left off in *Medieval Foundation.* He traces British life from the Restoration through the reign of Queen Victoria, creating what Agius called a "colorful and engaging . . . portrait" of the English character. Among other things, he describes the sports, food, and farming of the period and discusses both country and city life. Bryant's analysis of the English character caused *Christian Science Monitor's* Eric Forbes-Boyd to praise his "ability to plumb the deeper currents of thought and emotion underlying the scenes he so brilliantly reconstructs."

The Lion and the Unicorn contains selections from Bryant's weekly column "Our Note Book," which was published in the *Illustrated London News* for thirty-three years. The book, "running as it does dead counter to fashions, attitudes and modes of thought current in these late 'sixties, says much that still needs saying, is unaffected, civilised and deeply pondered," wrote David Williams in *Punch.* Williams went on, however, to call Bryant "square," and asked if he is not "sometimes perhaps deliberately blind to the way things are going?" Williams noted that Bryant, accustomed as he is to "scrutinising the once slow process of historical change," is reluctant to realize that people today must adapt to change much more rapidly that their ancestors had to. "We are going down the rapids fast, and what we should concentrate on is navigation, not nostalgia."

With *The Great Duke,* Bryant returned to biography, offering a portrait of the Duke of Wellington during his years as a soldier and commander. Burke Wilson of *Christian Science Monitor* described the book as "military history by a master of the medium." However, a reviewer for the *Times Literary Supplement* noted that much of the material was reproduced verbatim from previous work by Bryant and that the volume as a whole offered "no new interpretation of a perennially fascinating man."

When reviewers find fault with Bryant's work, it is usually to criticize his tendency to be unduly generous when reviewing British history; they suggest that he sometimes allowed his fierce patriotism to color his judgment. Others find his deep love for his mother country admirable, and nearly all agree that he was a distinguished and able historian.

BIOGRAPHICAL/CRITICAL SOURCES:

BOOKS

Dictionary of Literary Biography. Volume 149: *Late Nineteenth- and Early Twentieth-Century British Literary Biographers,* Gale (Detroit), 1995.

Street, Pamela, *Arthur Bryant: Portrait of an Historian,* Collins (London), 1979.

PERIODICALS

Best Sellers, May 15, 1968; July 15, 1976.

Book Week, September 27, 1964, p. 5.

Book World, May 12, 1968.

Christian Science Monitor, November 25, 1933; May 11, 1968; September 20, 1972, p. 11.

Economist, November 12, 1966.

Manchester Guardian, January 17, 1945, p. 3.

Nation, May 25, 1957.

New Statesman, October 20, 1967.

New Statesman & Nation, November 28, 1942.

New York Herald Tribune Book Review, May 27, 1951, p. 3; December 12, 1954, p. 2.

New York Times, February 12, 1939.

New York Times Book Review, September 17, 1967; December 10, 1972.

Punch, December 31, 1969.

Saturday Review, October 24, 1931; May 19, 1962.

Spectator, October 10, 1931; November 24, 1933; November 24, 1950, p. 566.

Times Literary Supplement (London), October 15, 1931; November 2, 1933; December 23, 1944; December 18, 1953; December 3, 1971, p. 1498.

OBITUARIES:

PERIODICALS

Los Angeles Times, January 26, 1985.

New York Times, January 24, 1985.

Time, February 4, 1985.

Washington Post, January 28, 1985.*

* * *

BRYANT, Edward (Winslow, Jr.) 1945-
(Lawrence Talbot)

PERSONAL: Born August 27, 1945, in White Plains, NY; son of Edward Winslow (a postal employee) and Anne (Van Kleeck) Bryant. *Education:* University of Wyoming, B.A., 1967, M.A., 1968. *Politics:* Independent. *Religion:* Protestant.

ADDRESSES: *Agent*—William Morris Agency, 1325 Avenue of the Americas, New York NY 10019.

CAREER: Writer of science fiction and fantasy. Worked as disc jockey for KYCN-Radio, 1961-63, and as broadcaster, disc jockey, and news director for KOWB-Radio, 1965-66; shipping clerk, Blevins Manufacturing Co., 1968-69; taught high school and college courses in science fiction and in writing; lecturer for Science Fiction Writers Speakers Bureau and Western States Art Foundation; attended Clarion Science Fiction and Fantasy Writers Workshop, 1968, 1969.

MEMBER: Science Fiction Writers of America.

AWARDS, HONORS: General Motors scholar; First Place, New American Library Fiction Competition, 1971; Science Fiction Writers of America, nominated for Nebula awards for best novelette and for best short story, both 1978, received Nebula award for best short story, 1979; nominated for Hugo award for best short story, World Science Fiction Convention, 1979; Living Legend Award, International Horror Guild, 1997.

WRITINGS:

Among the Dead: And Other Events Leading up to the Apocalypse, Macmillan (New York City), 1973.
(With Harlan Ellison) *Phoenix without Ashes,* Fawcett (New York City), 1975.
Cinnabar, Macmillan, 1976.
(Editor) *2076: The American Tricentennial,* Pyramid (New York City), 1977.
Wyoming Sun, Jelm Mountain Press (Laramie, WY), 1980.
Particle Theory, Pocket Books (New York City), 1981.
(With Dean R. Koontz and Robert R. McCammon) *Night Visions 4,* Dark Harvest (Arlington Heights, IL), 1987, published as *Night Visions: Hardshell,* Berkley (New York City), 1988.
Trilobyte: An Easter Treasure, Axolotl (Seattle), 1987.
Neon Twilight, Pulphouse (Eugene, OR), 1990.
The Man of the Future, Roadkill Press (Arvada, CO), 1990.
The Cutter, Pulphouse, 1991.
Fetish, Pulphouse, 1991.
Darker Passions, Roadkill Press, 1992.
The Thermals of August, Pulphouse, 1992.

Also author of *The Synar Calculation,* a film script for CVD Studios, 1973. Work represented in many anthologies, including *Universe,* edited by Terry Carr, Random House, 1971, *Prejudice,* edited by Roger Elwood, Prentice-Hall, 1974, *High Terror,* edited by Kirby McCauley, Viking, 1980, *Interfaces,* edited by Ursula K. LeGuin, Ace Books, 1980, *Splatterpunks: Extreme Horror,* edited by Paul M. Sammon, 1990. Author of column, "The Screen Game," *Cthulhu Calls,* 1973-77; author of quarterly column, "Film," *Eternity* Magazine. Contributor of short stories, reviews and articles to science fiction magazines, popular national journals, and literary publications, including *National Lampoon, Rolling Stone, Omni, Locus, Twilight Zone, Mile High Futures, Penthouse,* and *Magazine of Fantasy and Science Fiction.*

SIDELIGHTS: Edward Bryant has earned a reputation for his short stories in the science fiction and horror genres. Gary Westfahl in the *St. James Guide to Horror, Ghost and Gothic Writers* notes: "Bryant specializes almost exclusively in short fiction and has gradually shifted from science fiction to horror. . . . While his stories may offer little in the way of pyrotechnics, they often manifest a quiet, understated strength. What is most striking in Bryant's horror fiction is that his characters rarely seem terrified, or even surprised, by the terrors they confront; instead, they calmly deal with them, then prepare themselves for another day's work."

Bryant has written two novels: *Phoenix without Ashes,* based on a Harlan Ellison television script about a giant starship, and *Cinnabar,* a series of interconnected stories set in a future city which is "the focal point of all time." He has also worked as a film actor, appearing in *Flesh Gordon,* 1974, and *The Laughing Dead,* 1989.

Bryant once told *CA:* "I keep finding myself arguing both with science fiction readers who feel my stories are not science-fictional enough and general readers who shy off because of the science fiction or fantasy label. My contention is that good science fiction possesses the same virtues and acquiesces to the same demands of art and craft as any other sort of fiction. I attempt to adhere to that: I write about people and their problems and relationships. But in addition, I'm intensely curious about what the future's influence through science and technology will be when applied to the basic human relationships of person-to-person and person-to-society. My wish for the moment is that more good writers in all fields would toss aside the knee-jerk anti-technology reaction and exercise a healthy, non-judgmental curiosity about this increasingly complex and fascinating universe."

BIOGRAPHICAL/CRITICAL SOURCES:

BOOKS

Edward Bryant Bibliography, Swigart (Los Angeles), 1980.
St. James Guide to Horror, Ghost and Gothic Writers, St. James Press (Detroit), 1998.

* * *

BRYANT, Michael
See BRENNERT, Alan (Michael)

BRYSON, Bill
See BRYSON, William

* * *

BRYSON, William 1951(?)-
(Bill Bryson)

PERSONAL: Born c. 1951, in Des Moines, IA; son of William Bryson (a sports columnist); married, wife's name Cynthia (a nurse); children: four. *Education:* Attended Drake University.

ADDRESSES: Home—Hanover, NH and North Yorkshire, England.

CAREER: Journalist and author. Worked at a newspaper in Bournemouth, England, beginning in 1977, and for the business sections of London *Times* and London *Independent;* free-lance writer. Guest on television programs, including *Good Morning, America* and *Sunday Morning.*

WRITINGS:

UNDER NAME BILL BRYSON, EXCEPT AS INDICATED

The Facts on File Dictionary of Troublesome Words, Facts on File (New York City), 1984, revised edition, 1987 (published in England as *The Penguin Dictionary of Troublesome Words,* Penguin, 1984).

(Under name William Bryson) *The Palace under the Alps, and Over Two-Hundred Other Unusual, Unspoiled, and Infrequently Visited Spots in Sixteen European Countries,* Congdon & Weed, 1985.

The Lost Continent: Travels in Small-Town America, Harper (New York City), 1989.

The Mother Tongue: English and How It Got That Way, Morrow (New York City), 1990.

Neither Here Nor There: Travels in Europe, Secker & Warburg (London, England), 1991, Morrow, 1992.

The Penguin Dictionary for Writers and Editors, Viking (New York City), 1992.

Made in America: An Informal History of the English Language in the United States, Morrow, 1994.

Notes from a Small Island: An Affectionate Portrait of Britain, Morrow, 1995.

A Walk in the Woods: Rediscovering America on the Appalachian Trail, Broadway Books (New York City), 1998.

Author of "Notes from a Big Country," a weekly column in *Mail on Sunday.* Contributor to periodicals, including *Travel and Leisure, National Geographic,* and *New York Times.*

SIDELIGHTS: William Bryson's works can be divided into two categories, according to some reviewers. "In his adoptive Britain," Norman Oder explained in *Publishers Weekly,* "Bryson reached bestseller status with wiseacre travelogues. . . . In the United States, he's best-known for excursions into the lore of the English language."

For the first of the travelogues, the American-born journalist returned from his home in North Yorkshire, England, to his native Iowa and set out on a journey by car across the North American continent to write *The Lost Continent: Travels in Small-Town America.* The work is an account of a thirty-eight-state tour Bryson began in 1987, having decided to embark on the kind of motor trip his family once took in their blue Rambler station wagon. Bryson's quest was to find the perfect small town in which, as Bryson explains in *The Lost Continent,* "Bing Crosby would be the priest, Jimmy Stewart mayor, Fred MacMurray the high school principal, Henry Fonda a Quaker farmer. Walter Brennan would run the gas station, a boyish Mickey Rooney would deliver groceries, and somewhere, at an open window, Deanna Durbin would sing."

Throughout his travels, however, Bryson offers descriptions of what he finds as "parking lots and tallish buildings surrounded by a sprawl of shopping centers, gas stations and fast-food joints." His observations about small-town America are laced with a sharp-edged humor; at one point he notes that "talking about a scenic route in southeast Iowa is like talking about a good Barry Manilow album," which alienated some reviewers. *Los Angeles Times Book Review* contributor Wanda Urbanska termed *Lost Continent* "merely a forum for the put-down humor so popular these days." A *Newsweek* critic, however, noted that the book "is paradoxically touching—a melancholy memoir in the form of a snide travelogue." *The Lost Continent* proved more popular with readers, becoming a Book-of-the-Month Club alternate selection. "You have to be able to laugh at yourself to understand this book, and I know that is asking a lot of some people," Bryson explained in the *Chicago Tribune.* "It really is a fond portrait."

Bryson again took to the road with his next book, although this time journeying the European continent. *Neither Here Nor There: Travels in Europe* describes his adventures in places such as France, Italy, Norway, and Turkey. As with *The Lost Continent,* some reviewers expressed reservations about *Neither Here Nor There,* complaining that the book's humor sometimes wears thin. A *Los Angeles Times* critic, however, found some of Bryson's descriptions "amusing and accurate" and noted that Bryson occasionally "provides the perfect telling detail." Dervla Murphy in the *Times Literary Supplement* found that "sometimes Bill Bryson's humour recalls [P. G.] Wodehouse, sometimes Flann O'Brien. More often it is distinctive, depending on his cunning use of flamboyant exaggerations, grotesque but always successful metaphors and the deft juxtapositions of incongruous images—the whole presented in a style that boldly veers from laid-back colloquial American to formal clean-cut English."

In the mid-1990s, Bryson moved back to the United States, where he settled with his family in Hanover, New Hampshire. Before leaving England, where he had lived for more than twenty years, the author toured the island one last time, confining himself to public transportation and foot travel. *Notes from a Small Island: An Affectionate Portrait of Britain* represents what some reviewers have likened to a fond farewell. "This affectionate valediction lauds British eccentricity, endurance, and genius for adversity," Oder wrote. British critic Boyd Tonkin reported in *New Statesman & Society* that, beneath the humor of Bryson's "all-smiles, easyreading jaunt," there flows an undercurrent of lament for days gone by. "The Britain he loves is quaint, quiet and deeply welfare-statist," Tonkin wrote, and Bryson's criticisms of "the damage wrought by market-minded dogmas," however witty, left the critic "unpersuaded. . . . He seldom reads our mustn't-grumble tolerance as a sign of surrender, not just of civility." In the United States, on the other hand, some reviewers were delighted with Bryson's "trenchant, witty and detailed observations," as a *Publishers Weekly* critic noted. *Publishers Weekly* recommended *Notes from a Small Island* as an "immensely entertaining" account, and *Booklist* reviewer Alice Joyce hailed Bryson's writing as "delightfully irreverent."

Bryson marked his return to the land of his birth with an exploration of one of America's longest and oldest footpaths—the Appalachian Trail. His goal was to walk the entire trail, more than two-thousand miles long, from Georgia to Maine. He set out optimistically from a Georgia state park with a companion of his boyhood and completed the first hundred miles with relative ease. "Initially, it didn't seem an impossible task," Bryson told Oder in an interview. "But your expectations cannot match reality." Citing difficulties ranging from "drudgery" to the whimsical reliability of maps and map makers to the defection of his partner Stephen Katz, Bryson abridged his plan. According to *New Statesman* critic Albert Scardino, "[h]e decides he doesn't have to walk the whole trail to absorb its spirit." In various segments over a period of time, Bryson eventually completed more than eight-hundred miles of hiking and observation. *A Walk in the Woods: Rediscovering America on the Appalachian Trail* is the memoir of his journey. A *Forbes* reviewer remarked that the author's "humor is winning and succinct" and displays a talent "for boiling down his observations to their absurd essences." *Library Journal* critic Nancy J. Moeckel wrote: "Bryson shares some truly laugh-outloud moments" in his "amiable" account of the journey and the people he met along the way. A British reviewer for the *Economist* compared Bryson's talents to the "droll American mix of folksy intelligence and awshucks wit" of Garrison Kellor, and Roy Antonucci recommended the memoir to *Booklist* readers as "a marvelous description and history of the trail." Oder suggested that *A Walk in the Woods* represents a combination of both sides of Bryson's career: "picaresque traveler and lore-gatherer." The lore-gatherer emerges in several books about words and language, beginning with *The Penguin Dictionary of Troublesome Words.*

The Mother Tongue: English and How It Got That Way is an anecdotal, historical survey of what Bryson calls "the most important and successful language in the world." *The Mother Tongue* was warmly received by critics, who considered the book lively and engaging. *New York Times Book Review* contributor Burt Hochberg found reading Bryson's presentation of such topics as etymology, pronunciation, spelling, dialects, grammar, origins of names, and wordplay "an enthralling excursion." *Los Angeles Times Book Review* contributor Fred S. Holley called the volume "a vastly informative and vastly entertaining consideration, not only of the language's history but also of its position today."

In *Made in America: An Informal History of the English Language in the United States,* Bryson, according to Oder, "uses the evolution of American English to slalom through American history and culture." The *Economist* described Bryson as "an easy, intelligent and good-humoured writer" but warned: "Towards its end the book threatens to become little more than a history of consumption and consumer goods: how the automobile, shopping mall, aeroplane, hamburger, came to America." That reviewer also warned of errors in fact, a caution echoed by other critics as well. A *Publishers Weekly* reviewer called *Made in America* "a treasure trove of trivia about American culture past and present," but in *People Weekly,* Elaine Kahn identified some of the mistakes that could lead an unwary reader astray. Others were less critical. Kim Albert of *Entertainment Weekly* was engaged by Bryson's "unabashed curiosity" about the English language and the "sheer delight" he derives from transmitting the information to his readers. George W. Hunt summarized the work in *America* as, overall, "a leisurely history . . . of a nation's growth as dramatized by its changing vocabulary."

BIOGRAPHICAL/CRITICAL SOURCES:

BOOKS

Bryson, Bill, *The Lost Continent: Travels in Small-Town America,* Harper, 1989.

Bryson, *The Mother Tongue: English and How It Got That Way,* Morrow, 1990.

PERIODICALS

America, November 25, 1995, p. 2.

Booklist, May 1, 1996, p. 1486; April, 1998, pp. 1297-1299.

Chicago Tribune, September 20, 1989, pp. 1, 10; July 11, 1990, section 5, p. 3.

Economist, August 20, 1994, p. 69; November 15, 1997, p S5-S7.

Entertainment Weekly, May 5, 1995, p. 63; June 7, 1996, p. 54.

Forbes, September 26, 1994, p. S32; May 4, 1998, p. S140.

Library Journal, April 1, 1998, pp. 114-116.

Los Angeles Times, August 23, 1990, section E, pp. 1, 13.

Los Angeles Times Book Review, September 3, 1989, pp. 1, 5; September 30, 1990, p. 8; February 16, 1992, p. 6.

New Statesman, December 12, 1997, pp. 43-45.

New Statesman & Society, October 4, 1991, pp. 35-36; September 15, 1995, p. 34.

Newsweek, August 14, 1989, p. 51.

New York, September 18, 1989, p. 26.

New York Times, July 16, 1990.

New York Times Book Review, September 17, 1989, p. 26; August 5, 1990, p. 8.

People Weekly, April 17, 1995, p. 32.

Publishers Weekly, February 13, 1995, p. 71; March 4, 1996, p. 40; February 23, 1998, p. 57; May 4, 1998, pp. 191-193.

Times Literary Supplement, October 18, 1991, p. 28.

Times (London), September 25, 1991, p. 13.

Times Saturday Review (London), October 5, 1991, p. 57.

Washington Post Book World, September 3, 1989, p. 3.*

* * *

BUCHANAN, Marie 1922-
(Clare Curzon, Rhona Petrie)

PERSONAL: Born in Hastings, England, 1922; married Jimmy Duell; children: Karen, Lois, Fergus. *Education:* University of London, B.A. (with honors), 1944, and associateship of King's College, 1944. *Politics:* None. *Religion:* Christian.

ADDRESSES: *Home*—Fairlight, 52 Latenmoor Way, Gerrards Cross, Buckinghamshire SL9 8LT, England. *Agent*—Harvey Klinger, 301 West 53rd St., New York, NY 10019; David Grossman Literary Agency, 110-114 Clerkenwell Rd., London EC1M 5SA, England.

CAREER: Writer. Has worked as interpreter, translator, language teacher, lecturer, and social secretary in various European countries.

MEMBER: Crime Writers Association.

WRITINGS:

NOVELS

Anima, St. Martin's (New York City), 1972 (published in England as *Greenshards,* Gollancz [London], 1972).

An Unofficial Death, St. Martin's, 1973.

The Dark Backward, Coward (New York City), 1975.

Morgana, Doubleday (New York City), 1977.

The Congress of Sedgwick, Collins (London), 1980, Doubleday, 1990.

UNDER PSEUDONYM CLARE CURZON

A Leaven of Malice, Collins, 1980.
Special Occasions, Collins, 1981.
I Give You Five Days, Collins, 1983.
Masks and Faces, Collins, 1984.
The Trojan Hearse, Collins, 1985.
The Quest for K, Collins, 1986.
Trail of Fire, Collins, 1987.
Shot Bolt, Collins, 1988.
Three-Core Lead, Collins, 1988, Doubleday, 1990.
The Face in the Stone, Collins, 1989.
The Blue-Eyed Boy, Collins, 1990.
Cat's Cradle, HarperCollins (London), 1991, St. Martin's, 1992.
First Wife, Twice Removed, Little, Brown (London), 1992, St. Martin's, 1993.
Death Prone, Little, Brown, 1992, St. Martin's, 1994.
Nice People, Little, Brown, 1993.
Past Mischief, Little, Brown, 1994, St. Martin's, 1996.
Close Quarters, St. Martin's, 1997.
All Unwary, St. Martin's, 1998.

UNDER PSEUDONYM RHONA PETRIE

Death in Deakins Wood, Dodd (New York City), 1963.
Murder by Precedent, Gollancz, 1964.
Running Deep, Gollancz, 1965.
Dead Loss, Gollancz, 1966.
Foreign Bodies, Gollancz, 1967.
Maclurg Goes West, Gollancz, 1968.
Despatch of a Dove, Gollancz, 1969.
Come Hell and High Water (story collection), Gollancz, 1970.
Thorne in the Flesh, Gollancz, 1971.

SIDELIGHTS: In her mysteries featuring Superintendent Mike Yeadings and Inspector Angus Mott of the Thames Valley Police, and written under the pseudonym Clare Curzon, Marie Buchanan has created what Judith Rhodes in the *St. James Guide to Crime and Mystery Writers* calls "pleasant, unexceptionable policemen. The reader does not receive any impression of distinctive personalities or of any quirks of character; these men go about their detecting in a fairly unhurried, relaxed fashion, and appear able to concentrate on one case at a time. . . . It is in fact a welcome change in the early novels of this series to meet policemen who are not so harassed that one cares more about what happens to them (or their wives or their cats) than about the eventual solution of the crime."

The Yeadings books fall into the police procedural tradition, in which realistic police officers are shown methodically investigating crime. In *First Wife, Twice Removed,* for example, Yeadings and his men are called in when a divorcee dies after eating a food sample anonymously mailed to her. The death of a young Dutch girl seems at first unrelated, but Yeadings soon finds an unlikely connection between the two crimes. The critic for *Publishers Weekly* notes that the novel is an "intriguing English procedural" and a "grimly realistic drama." In *Past Mischief,* Yeadings investigates a hit-and-run accident in which a young woman is almost killed, then discovers that two of the woman's friends have recently been found dead. Emily Melton in *Booklist* asserts: "Curzon's competent writing and keen understanding of the human psyche—plus an ingenious plot and a cast of fascinating characters—add up to a story that's sure to be a favorite among procedural fans."

Buchanan once told *CA:* "Having started with [writing] crime as Rhona Petrie, and 'gone straight' as Marie Buchanan, [I] have returned to crime as Clare Curzon, [my] interest lying not in the debased professional criminal but in the human creature pushed too far by intolerable pressures."

Buchanan describes herself as an avid reader but one who dislikes category fiction, appreciating form but despairing of formula. She says she particularly admires the work of Carl Jung, Marcel Proust, William Faulkner, Arthur Koestler, Arthur Guirdham, and Jean Rhys. In the literary sense, she hopes never to "arrive, but for long to remain hopefully travelling." Buchanan told *CA* that, as a student, her subjects were European languages and psychology, two aspects of communication that she feels provide the fabric and the theme of her novels. She adds that her present aim is to "write with greater compassion and less cleverness."

BIOGRAPHICAL/CRITICAL SOURCES:

BOOKS

St. James Guide to Crime and Mystery Writers, 4th edition, St. James Press (Detroit), 1996.

PERIODICALS

Booklist, May 15, 1996, p. 1572; February 1, 1997, p. 927.

New York Times Book Review, September 21, 1975; July 2, 1995.
Publishers Weekly, April 26, 1993, p. 59; May 1, 1995, p. 46.
Times Literary Supplement, May 12, 1972.

* * *

BUDD, Lillian (Peterson) 1897-1989

PERSONAL: Born July 21, 1897, in Chicago, IL; died April 6, 1989; daughter of Charles A. and Selma (Nelson) Peterson; married Fred H. Budd (a Navy officer), 1918 (deceased); children: Richard Nelson. *Education:* Attended Chicago public schools. *Avocational interests:* Collecting antiques.

CAREER: Writer and lecturer. Western Electric Company, Hawthorne, IL, secretary, 1915-18; U.S. Government, Selective Service System, Geneva, IL, chief clerk, 1940-47; Campana Sales Company, Batavia, IL, promotion manager, 1947-51. Member of Fredrika Bremer committee, American-Swedish Foundation, Philadelphia, PA. *Military service:* U.S. Navy, 1918-20; became chief yeoman.

MEMBER: Women in Communications, Midland Authors, Friends of Literature, Phi Gamma Nu, Sigma Kappa, Delta Kappa Gamma, Theta Sigma Pi, American Legion, Geneva (IL) Woman's Club (former president).

AWARDS, HONORS: Friends of Literature Fiction award, 1959; Award of Merit from Illinois State Historical Society, 1978, for *Footsteps on the Tall Grass Prairie.*

WRITINGS:

April Snow (also see below), Lippincott (Philadelphia, PA), 1951.
Land of Strangers (also see below), Lippincott, 1953.
April Harvest (also see below), Duell (New York City), 1959.
The Pie Wagon (picture book for children), Lothrop (New York City), 1960.
The Bell of Kamela (historical novel for young people), Rand McNally (Chicago, IL), 1960.
Tekla's Easter (for young people), Rand McNally, 1962.
The People on Long Ago Street (picture book for children), Rand McNally, 1964.
One Heart, One Way (novel for young adults), McKay (New York City), 1964.
Calico Row (juvenile), Whitman, Albert (Niles, IL), 1965.
Larry (juvenile), illustrated by Leonard Vosburgh, McKay, 1966.
Full Moons (adaptation of Indian legends for young people), illustrated by George Armstrong, Rand McNally, 1971.
Footsteps on the Tall Grass Prairie: A History of Lombard, Illinois, introduction by Walter Havighurst, Lombard Historical Society (Lombard, IL), 1978.
April Snow Trilogy (contains *April Snow, Land of Strangers,* and *April Harvest*), Avon (New York City), 1979-80.

Contributor to American, Swedish, and Norwegian magazines.

SIDELIGHTS: Lillian Budd's first three books comprise a novelistic trilogy that portrays life in Sweden in the late-nineteenth century and the Swedish immigrant experience in America in the early-twentieth century. Reviewing the third book in the trilogy for the *New York Herald Tribune Book Review,* David Tilden stated: "One need not doubt that the nobility which animates nearly everyone in *April Harvest* and its several fortunate coincidences had their prototypes in actual persons and incidents in the chronicle of the melting pot."

The first book of the trilogy, *April Snow,* is set entirely in Sweden and tells the story of Sigrid, a peasant woman married to a tyrannical and self-centered husband. Sigrid's life is not an easy one. She bears a child nearly every year, works incessantly, and must confront tragedies involving her children. Yet her courage and her joy in living sustain her throughout. According to Fanny Butcher writing in the *Chicago Sunday Tribune:* "*April Snow,* despite its privations, its bitterness, its cruelties of man and nature, is actually an idyll. It is a reliving of a legendary past." M. L. Mueller of the *San Francisco Chronicle* found "passion in the characters" and "tenderness in the narrative." Reviewing the novel for the *New York Times,* Lily van Amerigen noted that the reader "will certainly come away from this book with a deeper understanding of Sweden and its ways." However, Amerigen believed that Budd "lacks the *sin qua non* of the novelist—an ability to dramatize, to convey the reactions of her characters to the teeming life about them." *Land of Strangers,* the second book of the trilogy, tells of Carl Christianson and his immigration to America. In Chicago, Carl finds and marries Ellen, a woman he had first loved in Sweden. The remainder of the novel deals with their experiences adjusting to and learning to live in a new land. M. B. Snyder of the *Chicago Sunday Tribune* described *Land of Strangers* as "a tender personal story and a universal one of the many who came from the old country to make American strong." A reviewer for *Saturday Review* praised the book's descriptions of both Sweden and "the gaslit atmosphere of . . . nineteenth century New York," but felt that Budd "loses control of her novel in a maze of coincidence, catastrophe, and sheer, unbroken misery."

The trilogy concludes with *April Harvest,* the story of Sigrid Christianson, the daughter of Carl and Ellen. Covering the period up to and including World War I, the novel details Sigrid's passage into adulthood and the influence of immigrants from other backgrounds—Dutch, German, Irish—upon her. The trilogy comes full circle when Sigrid returns to Sweden to visit her grandmother's home. A reviewer for *Bookmark* described *April Harvest* as a "tender, richly detailed portrayal," while a reviewer for *Kirkus* characterized it as a "woman's book written with warmth and emotionalism." However, Tilden found the story "rather too idyllic to be convincing."

Lillian Budd once told *CA:* "I am not one who yearned a lifetime to write a book. It was not until I was fifty years old that, through a set of humorous circumstances, I was precipitated into writing what became my first novel, *April Snow.* My experience—that, without classroom instruction or special education, I could accomplish such a project after reaching middle age, while working at a full-time job, that the manuscript was published by the first publisher to whom I sent it, that my twelfth book was well-received—should certainly offer encouragement to those who 'want to write.'"

BIOGRAPHICAL/CRITICAL SOURCES:

PERIODICALS

Atlantic, December, 1960.
Booklist, May 1, 1951; November 15, 1953; April 15, 1959; June 15, 1962.
Bookmark, June, 1951; December, 1953; March, 1959, p. 149.
Chicago Sunday Tribune, May 20, 1951, p. 3; September 27, 1953, p. 3; March 29, 1959, p. 3; October 30, 1960, p. 12; April 15, 1962, p. 8.
Christian Science Monitor, November 3, 1960, p. B2; May 10, 1962; May 7, 1964, p. B3.
Commonweal, May 25, 1962.
Horn Book, August, 1962.
Kirkus, March 15, 1951; August 1, 1953; January 1, 1959, p. 20; August 1, 1960; March 1, 1962.
Library Journal, March 15, 1959; September 15, 1960; May 15, 1962; March 15, 1964.
New York Herald Tribune Book Review, May 20, 1951, p. 10; September 27, 1953, p. 7; March 22, 1959, p. 8; October 9, 1960, p. 10; April 22, 1962, p. 9.
New York Times, June 24, 1951, p. 16; October 4, 1953, p. 30.
New York Times Book Review, November 13, 1960, p. 58; April 15, 1962, p. 32; May 24, 1964, p. 26.
San Francisco Chronicle, July 1, 1951, p. 24.
Saturday Review, June 23, 1951; November 14, 1953, p. 56; April 28, 1962.*

* * *

BUHLER, Charlotte B(ertha) 1893-1974
(Charlotte Malachowski Buhler)

PERSONAL: Born December 20, 1893, in Berlin, Germany; died, 1974; came to United States in 1940, naturalized citizen, 1945; daughter of Hermann and Rose (Kristeller) Malachowski; married Karl L. Buhler (a psychologist), April 4, 1916; children: Ingeborg (Mrs. Alf-Jorgen Aas), Rolf D. *Education:* Attended Universities of Freiburg, Berlin, and Munich; University of Munich, Ph.D., 1918; postdoctoral study at University of Vienna and Columbia University.

CAREER: University of Vienna, Vienna, Austria, instructor, later associate professor of psychology, 1923-38; University of Oslo, Oslo, Norway, professor of psychology, 1938-40; director of child guidance clinics in Vienna, 1930-38, London, 1930-35, and Oslo, 1938-40; College of St. Catherine, St. Paul, MN, professor of psychology, 1940-42; Minneapolis General Hospital, Minneapolis, MN, chief clinical psychologist, 1942-45; Los Angeles County General Hospital, Los Angeles, CA, chief clinical psychologist, 1945-53; University of Southern California, School of Medicine, Los Angeles, assistant clinical professor of psychiatry, 1953-58, professor emeritus, beginning, 1958. Psychologist in private practice, Los Angeles and Beverly Hills, CA.

MEMBER: International Psychological Association (board member; director), American Association for Humanistic Psychology (director, beginning, 1961; president, 1965-66), American Psychological Association (fellow), American Orthopsychiatric Association (fellow), American Association for Gerontology, Psychologists Interested in the Advancement of Psychotherapy (fellow; member of board of directors), American Group Psychotherapy Association (fellow), Society for Projective Techniques (fellow), California State Psychological Association (fellow), Southern California Group Psychotherapy Association (president, 1958-59), Los Angeles Society of Practicing Psychologists.

AWARDS, HONORS: Rockefeller Foundation fellowships, 1924-25, 1935; medal of honor from the city of Vienna, 1964.

WRITINGS:

Das Maerchen und die Phantasie des Kindes, J. A. Barth (Leipzig), 1918, fourth edition, with J. Bilz and Hildegard Hetzer, 1958.

(As Charlotte Malachowski Buhler) *Das Seelenleben des Jugendlichen: Versuch einer Analyse und Theorie der psychischen Pubertaet,* G. Fischer (Jena, Germany), 1923, sixth edition, 1967, reprinted, Fischer-Taschenbuch (Frankfurt am Main), 1975

(With Hetzer and Beatrix Tudor-Hart) *Soziologische und psychologische Studien ueber das erste Lebensjahr,* G. Fischer, 1927.

(As Charlotte Malachowski Buhler; with Hetzer) *Inventar der Verhaltungsweisen des ersten Lebensjahres,* [Germany], 1927, translation by Pearl Greenberg and Rowena Ripin published as *The First Year of Life,* Day, 1930, Greenwood (Westport, CT), 1974, Arno (New York City), 1975.

Kindheit und Jugend, Hirzel (Leipzig), 1928, fourth edition, Verlag fuer Psychologie Hogrefe, 1967.

Kleinkinder Tests, J. A. Barth, 1932, translation by Henry Beaumont published as *Testing Children's Development from Birth to School Age,* Farrar & Rinehart, 1935.

Der menschliche Lebenslauf als psychologisches Problem, Hirzel, 1933, third edition, Verlag fuer Psychologie Hogrefe, 1960.

Drei Generationen im Jugendtagebuch, G. Fischer, 1934.

From Birth to Maturity: An Outline of the Psychological Development of the Child, translated by Esther Menaker and William Menaker, Paul, Trench, Trubner & Co., 1935, eighth edition, 1950.

(As Charlotte Malachowski Buhler; with Edeltrud Baar and others) *Kind und Familie,* G. Fischer, 1937, translation by Beaumont published as *The Child and His Family,* Harper, 1939, reprinted, Greenwood Press (Westport, CT), 1972.

Praktische Kinderpsychologie, O. Lorenz (Prague and Vienna), 1938.

(With E. Hoehn) *The World Test: Manual and Material,* New York Psychological Corp., 1941.

(With D. Welty Lefever) *A Rorschach Study on the Psychological Characteristics of Alcoholics,* Hillhouse Press for Section of Studies on Alcohol, Yale University, 1948.

(With G. Kelly Lumry and H. Carroll) *World Test Standardization Studies,* Child Care Monograph, 1951.

(As Charlotte Malachowski Buhler; with Faith Smitter, Sybil Richardson, and Franklyn Bradshaw) *Childhood Problems and the Teacher,* Holt (New York City), 1952, Greenwood (New York City), 1969.

(With M. P. Manson) *The Five-Task Test,* Western Psychological Services (Los Angeles), 1955.

(With Manson) *The Picture World Test* (with manual), Western Psychological Services, 1956.

(With others) *Values in Psychotherapy,* Free Press of Glencoe, 1962.

(As Charlotte Malachowski Buhler) *Die Psychologie im Leben unserer Ziet,* Droemer Knar (Munich), 1962, fifth edition, 1964, republished, 1975, translation by Hella Freud Bernays published as *Psychology for Contemporary Living,* Hawthorn (New York City), 1969.

Psychologische Probleme unserer Zeit: Drei Vortraege, G. Fischer (Stuttgart), 1968.

(As Charlotte Malachowski Buhler) *Wenn das Leben gelingen soll: Psychologische Studien ueber Lebens-wartungen und Lebensergebnisse,* Droemer Knaur, 1969, translation by David J. Baker published as *The Way to Fulfillment: Psychological Techniques,* Hawthorn (New York City), 1971.

(As Charlotte Malachowski Buhler; with Melanie Allen) *Introduction to Humanistic Psychology,* Brooks/Cole (Monterey, CA), 1972.

Author of *Die ersten socialen Reaktionen des Kindes,* 1927.

EDITOR

Tagebuch eines jungen Maedchens, G. Fischer, 1922, second edition published as *Jugendtagebuch und Lebenslauf: Zwei Maedchentagebuecher,* 1932.

Zwei Knabentagebuecher, G. Fischer, 1925.

(As Charlotte Malachowski Buhler; with James F. T. Bugental, Fred Massarik, and others) *The Course of Human Life: A Study of Goals in the Humanistic Perspective,* Springer Publishing (New York City), 1968.

Coeditor of *Journal of Humanistic Psychology,* and *The Nervous Child,* both published in America, and the British *Journal of Educational Psychology.*

CONTRIBUTOR

C. A. Murchison, editor, *A Handbook of Child Psychology,* second edition, Clark University Press (Worchester, MA), 1931.

G. Seward, editor, *Clinical Studies in Culture Conflict,* Ronald, 1958.

Handbuch der Neurosenlehre und Psychotherapie, Urban & Schwarzenberg (Munich), 1960.

R. W. Kleemeier, editor, *Aging and Leisure,* Oxford University Press (New York City), 1961.

Lotte Schenk-Danzinger, editor, *Gegenwartsprobleme der Entwicklungspsychologie,* Verlag fuer Psychologie (Goettingen), 1963.

Frank T. Severin, editor, *Humanistic Viewpoints in Psychology,* McGraw (New York City), 1965.

Clark Moustakas, editor, *Existential Moments in Psychotherapy,* Basic Books (New York City), 1966.

Herbert A. Otto, editor, *Explorations in Human Potentialities,* C. C. Thomas (Springfield, IL), 1966.

Contributor to *Encyclopedia for Child Guidance,* and about 150 articles to professional journals in United States and Europe; also writer of popular articles and studies on the psychology of art.

OTHER

(Author of introduction) R. Wisser, editor, *Sinn und Sein,* Niemeyer (Tuebingen), 1960.

SIDELIGHTS: Psychologist Charlotte B. Buhler was a prolific writer whose works addressed both the academic and general audience. She published many books, edited and contributed to professional journals and books, and contributed to popular periodicals. Buhler, a German who came to the United States in 1940, married another psychologist, Karl Buhler, in 1916, and later lost their entire Viennese library to the Nazis. However, Charlotte Buhler's record of almost fifty years of writings in developmental, humanistic, and clinical psychology has survived. There have been more than sixty translations of her works into some fifteen languages, including Hungarian, Icelandic, Russian, Hebrew, and most western European languages.

The First Year of Life, the English translation of Buhler's 1927 German publication *Verhaltungsweisen des ersten Lebensjahres,* is "one of the most fundamental as well as representative works of the distinguished Viennese authority," praised a *Boston Transcript* reviewer, who proclaimed: "Dr. Buhler's book is the result of the most exacting kind of research, carried on at the famous Psychological Institute of Vienna." Buhler's 1935 *Testing Children's Development from Birth to School Age,* the first English translation of her 1932 German publication *Kleinkinder Tests,* is "a detailed series of tests which aim at disclosing the child's personality in all its fundamental dimensions," described a *Nature* contributor, explaining: "The tests are in six categories which include all the fundamental dimensions of human behavior, and cover the essential steps indispensable to the individual's development."

Well over three decades later, Buhler was still publishing her knowledge and perspectives in psychology. *Psychology for Contemporary Living,* an overview of modern psychological theories of human development, addresses "the general reader in practical, nontechnical terms with numerous interesting case histories and illustrations," wrote a *Choice* reviewer. Although *Library Journal*'s C. E. Wadsorth complained that some portions of the book seem "oversimplified or emphasize the obvious," the critic recognized that other parts of the book are "enlightening" and recommended *Psychology for Contemporary Living* as "an introductory psychology book with a different approach [that] will also appeal to the general reader."

BIOGRAPHICAL/CRITICAL SOURCES:

PERIODICALS

Books, September 21, 1930.

Boston Transcript, October 1, 1930.

Choice, October, 1969.

Library Journal, December 1, 1968.

Nature, January 25, 1936.

Times Literary Supplement, April 11, 1936.*

* * *

BUHLER, Charlotte Malachowski

See BUHLER, Charlotte B(ertha)

BULATOVIC, Miodrag 1930-1991

PERSONAL: Born February 20, 1930, in Okladi, Montenegro, Yugoslavia; died after a heart attack, March 14, 1991, in Igalo, Montenegro, Yugoslavia; son of Milorad (a forest ranger) and Milica (Culikovic) Bulatovic; married former wife Vera Milanovic, 1955; married second wife, Kansky Nusa, 1964; children: two sons, one daughter. *Education:* Studied psychology at University of Belgrade. *Avocational interests:* "Travel, contacts with ordinary people, avoidance of fools, scoundrels and careerists of all kinds."

CAREER: Writer. Worked in hospitals and Red Cross centers.

MEMBER: PEN, Yugoslav Association of Writers.

AWARDS, HONORS: Association of Serbian Writers prize, 1958; NIN Prize for best Yugoslavian novel, 1976; Center Library of Servia Prize, 1977.

WRITINGS:

NOVELS

Crveni Petao leti Prema Nebu, Naprijed (Zagreb) for Kalman Vajs, 1959, translation by E. D. Goy published as *The Red Cock Flies to Heaven,* Bernard Geis Associates, 1962, published in England as *The Red Cockrel,* Weidenfeld & Nicolson, 1962.

Heroj na magarcu, translation by Goy published as *Hero on a Donkey,* Secker & Warburg (London), 1966, original version serialized in *Savremenik,* 1967, translation by Goy published as *A Hero on a Donkey,* World Publishing (New York City), 1969.

The War Was Better, translated from the original Serbo-Croatian by B. S. Brusar, McGraw (New York City), 1972.

Ljudi sa cetiri prsta (title means "The Thumbless"), Beogradski Izdavacko-Graficki Zavod (Belgrade), 1975.

Peti prst (title means "The Fifth Finger"), Beogradski Izdavacko-Graficki Zavod, 1977.

Gullo, Gullo, Prosveta (Belgrade), 1983.

OTHER

Djavoli dolaze (short stories; title means "The Devils Are Here"), Nolit (Belgrade), 1956.

Vuk i Zvono (prose poem; title means "The Wolf and the Bell"), Zora (Zagreb), 1958.

Godo je dosao (play; title means "Godot Has Arrived"), first produced in Germany, 1966, first produced in English translation at the Edinburgh Festival, 1970, serialized in *Savremenik,* Volume 11, numbers 10-12, 1965, Volume 12, 1, 1966, DBR International (Belgrade), 1994.

Rat je bio bolji, Prosveta, 1977.

Najveca tajna sveta, Srpska knjizevna zadruga (Belgrade), 1971.

Jahac nad jahacima, Partizanska knjiga (Belgrade), 1980.

Godo je dosao i druge drame, 2 volumes, DBR International, 1994.

Also author of radio plays. English translations of some of Bulatovic's short fiction have appeared in anthologies, including *New Writing from Yugoslavia,* edited by Bernard Johnson, 1970, and in such periodicals as *Atlantic Monthly, Evergreen Review, New Writers, Relations, Slavic and East European Arts,* and *Zavicaj.*

SIDELIGHTS: Yugoslavian writer Miodrag Bulatovic "was a fresh and original genius," according to *Dictionary of Literary Biography* contributor E. D. Goy. "His early works are among the best produced in postwar Yugoslavia." These early works—which include the short stories of *Djavoli dolaze* ("The Devils Are Here"), the novel-like prose poem *Vuk i Zvono* ("The Wolf and the Bell"), and the novel *Crveni Petao leti Prema Nebu* ("The Red Cock Flies to Heaven")—represent, in the words of Joseph Hitrec of *Saturday Review,* a "continuing dialogue with evil, an obsession clearly going back to the trauma of a brutal childhood and the anguished years of genocide in his native Montenegro" during World War II. Goy explained in his *DLB* profile of the author that in addition to Montenegro's ethnic strife, internal political fighting, and occupation by Italians, the young Bulatovic had to cope with the memory of seeing his father murdered by his uncle. All of this experience made its way into the author's writing. Bulatovic himself once told *CA* that in his earliest writing, "I described my life, the tragedy of my family, and the fate that seemed to await me. I wrote and I cried; I cried and I wrote."

Bulatovic's personal experience and the influence of twentieth-century French-language writers such as Jean Genet and Samuel Beckett and the Russians Nikolai Gogol and Fyodor Dostoyevsky created an author who believed "that life was a struggle against a world that was essentially fire, murder, and hatred. There was no room for optimism," observed Goy, "and Bulatovic was fascinated with literature and the need (and delight) of expressing the human predicament in what was a living hell." This living hell manifested itself in Bulatovic's mature work as writing full of profanity and relentless political satire, characteristics which caused the suppression of his books in Yugoslavia. Even so, Bulatovic was well-received throughout Europe and in the United States, with translations of his works appearing in over twenty languages. Among the earliest of his works to be translated into English were "Prica o sreii i nesreii" ("A Tale of Happiness and Unhappiness") and "Ljubavnici" ("The Lovers"), both stories from *Djavoli dolaze.* These stories of the individual struggling against the hell of life "convey a sadomasochism yet also a great tenderness," suggested Goy.

Bulatovic's first widely reviewed novel in the United States was *Crveni Petao leti Prema Nebu,* translated as *The Red Cock Flies to Heaven.* The action of the novel takes place in a poverty-stricken Montenegran village over the course of a couple of hours on a hot summer day. During these two hours, the guests at a peasant wedding, a pair of grave-diggers and the deceased, a woman whose slow-wittedness makes her a victim of rape, two vagabonds, a young Muslim man (Muharem) and his rooster, and the father he has never known come together in a scene that "resembles a naive village painting, or rather, a painting by Marc Chagall or even Pieter Brueghel," commented Goy. A *Times Literary Supplement* writer called the English translation "a very strange book indeed," while *New York Times Book Review* contributor Stoyan Christowe asserted that to call *The Red Cock Flies to Heaven* "a strange book is to put it mildly." Besides being drunk, noted the *Times Literary Supplement* reviewer, "all the characters are degraded, vicious, deformed or mad." Even the central character, the Christ-like Muharem, is on the verge of death from tuberculosis. "The story, if story it may be called, is nothing more than a succession of cruelties, torments, brutalities, horrors, and depravities," according to Christowe's description. At the novel's conclusion, even the bright red rooster—carried tenderly everywhere in the arms of Muharem, and functioning as a symbol for the human heart—is snatched from its keeper and tortured. It breaks free from its tormentors, but its flight to freedom ends with a shotgun blast.

Some critics admitted their confusion over Bulatovic's message, and both the *Times Literary Supplement* reviewer and Christowe found Bulatovic's symbolism somewhat heavy handed. Yet Christowe asserted that *The Red Cock Flies to Heaven* is "the work of a man of talent and of fevered imagination. . . . [He] has sharp eyes for detail and has learned the trick of giving his writing solidity and tangibility through the use of imagery. He can make you touch sleep and hunger and pain." And, although he suggested that the village in the novel is strange, the *Times Literary Supplement* reviewer concluded that Bulatovic "achieves an imaginative *tour de force* in creating from it so compelling a world."

The bleak tone of *The Red Cock Flies to Heaven* also dominated Bulatovic's play *Godo je dosao* ("Godot Has Arrived"). The drama is meant to be a continuation of Samuel Beckett's *Waiting for Godot,* in which characters await the mysterious "Godot"—a symbol often interpreted as hope for mankind's future. In Bulatovic's extension of Beckett's play, Godot arrives, only to be greeted with slander, distrust, and hatred. *Godo je dosao*'s American production was halted by an injunction from Grove Press, Beckett's U.S. publisher, but the play was successfully produced in Germany and later in Scotland. *Books Abroad* contributor Vasa D. Mihailovich noted: "Bulatovic's play is laden, as are all his works, with robust, at times opaque, symbolism, transparent allusions, and striking metaphors." The reviewer concluded that though marred by excessive profanity and a highly pessimistic ending, *Godo je dosao* is "an interesting and gallant first try in a new medium for Bulatovic."

The writer attracted international attention in 1965 when he sued his Yugoslavian publisher, Kultura, for refusing to honor an agreement to publish his novel *Heroj na magarcu.* The work had met with acclaim when serialized in a Yugoslavian periodical. Kultura had already printed two thousand advance copies when a government commission advised the company against its publication. "Its blending of politics and sex, of pacifism and biting satire were the main reason for governmental condemnation," reported a *New York Times Book Review* writer. Downplaying the political aspects of their decision, Kultura informed Bulatovic that the project had been dropped because of forty-two "shocking scenes" in the novel. The author sued, winning 500,000 dinars (about 660 dollars) in damages. The court, however, rejected his claim that Kultura had defaulted on its contract, and *Heroj na magarcu* was never published in Yugoslavia.

Heroj na magarcu was translated and published in the United States as *A Hero on a Donkey.* This satirical saga of saloonkeeper Gruban Malic's doomed efforts to ally himself with resistance forces in Italian-occupied Montenegro is "full of humor, action, surrealistic imagery, and sex," *DLB* contributor Goy explained. These elements come together to convey the theme of the novel, Goy added, "that war and pornography are parallel expressions of the same human aspiration to impose upon others. . . . Sex and power both serve as confirmations of the ego." Joseph Hitrec found the novel "existential at the core but textured with a poet's compassion and sometimes disconcerting imagination."

Although *A Hero on a Donkey* concludes with Gruban Malic's suicide in a chicken coop, the saloonkeeper returns as the main character in Bulatovic's next translated novel, *The War Was Better*. Malic's miraculous resurrection is just one of many bizarre happenings in *The War Was Better*. Elsewhere in the book, the hero single-handedly invades Italy after routing the Italians from his own country and begets a child (identical to Lenin) with Agatha Christie; Italian officers open brothels and fornicate with turtles. Comparing *The War Was Better* to *A Hero on a Donkey*, Joseph Hitrec commented in the *New York Times Book Review:* "Where the earlier novel still observed some amenities of realism, 'War Was Better' moves beyond the opaque surfaces of literalness and zeroes in on the outre, the flagrant and monstrous in contemporary experience, and does it with a will that for sheer invention and energy might leave a Genet or a Burroughs exhausted." Mihailovich also referred to the fantastic quality of the novel, this time in *Saturday Review:* "This wild work demands of the reader a frequent suspension of disbelief in order to experience the novel as a dream, a nightmare, or a drug trip."

"Its sheer zaniness and heady flights of fantasy make [*The War Was Better*] a delight to read," asserted Mihailovich. The reviewer emphasized the serious moral message underlying Bulatovic's farce, however: "*The War Was Better* is a firstclass surrealistic trip backward into the war and postwar days, an emotional circus replete with atrocities, absurdities, and dementia. It is not, however, a war novel in the true sense of the term, nor is it a typical antiwar novel. Rather, Bulatovic uses the war in the Balkans as a pretext to mock war in general and to show what it does to man. . . . It is an eloquent and important protest against the failures of modern civilization."

Bulatovic once told *CA:* "My heart is always as vast as a black mountain. I feel, almost physically, the approach of death—horrible and sickening—but I want to write some sincere and human books. . . . Will I ever finish the novel on my family, the poem on liberty and my people, the novel of sad laughter, which I intend to write? Isn't this perhaps too much, for the brief and painful life of a man?"

BIOGRAPHICAL/CRITICAL SOURCES:

BOOKS

Bulatovic, Miodrag, *Najveca tajna sveta,* Srpska knjizevna zadruga (Belgrade), 1971.

Boskov, Zivojin, editor, *Leksikon pisaca Jugoslavije,* Volume 1, Matica srpska (Novi Sad, Yugoslavia), 1972.

Dictionary of Literary Biography, Volume 181: *South Slavic Writers since World War II,* Gale (Detroit), 1997.

Dzadzic, Petar, *Kritike i ogledi,* Srpska Knjizevna zadruga, 1973.

Jeremic, Dragan, *Prsti nevernog Tome,* Nolit (Belgrade), 1965.

Mihajlovic-Mihiz, Borislav, *Knjizevni razgovori,* Srpska knjizevna zadruga, 1991.

Velmar-Jankovic, Svetlana, *Savremenici,* Prosveta (Belgrade), 1967.

PERIODICALS

Atlantic Monthly, January, 1963, p. 110.

Best Sellers, June 15, 1972, p. 144.

Books Abroad, winter, 1967.

Comparative Drama, Number 4, 1970, p. 3.

Knjizevnost, Volume 15, number 4, 1960, p. 314; number 8, 1968, p. 179.

Letopis Matice srpske, Volume 394, number 5, 1964, p. 432.

L'Express, February 14, 1963.

London Review, number 7, 1968, p. 584.

New Statesman, November 11, 1966.

New York Times, July 17, 1965.

New York Times Book Review, November 4, 1962, p. 55; January 9, 1966; July 16, 1972, p. 34.

Saturday Review, March 14, 1970; May 13, 1972, 84.

Savremenik, June, 1972, p. 554.

Slavic and East European Journal, Volume 12, number 3, 1968, p. 323.

Times Literary Supplement, May 4, 1962, p. 320; December 15, 1966.

World Literature Today, summer, 1978.*

OBITUARIES:

PERIODICALS

New York Times, March 19, 1991.
Washington Post, March 16, 1991.*

* * *

BUNCH, Charlotte (Anne) 1944-
(Charlotte Bunch-Weeks)

PERSONAL: Born October 13, 1944, in West Jefferson, NC; daughter of Charles Pardue (a physician) and Marjorie (a social worker; maiden name, King) Bunch; married James L. Weeks, March 25, 1967 (divorced, 1971). *Education:* Attended University of California, Berkeley, 1965; Duke University, B.A. (magna cum laude), 1966; attended Institute for Policy Studies, 1967-68. *Politics:* "Feminist."

ADDRESSES: Home—392 Third St., No. 6, Brooklyn, NY 11215. *Office*—Center for Women's Global Leadership, Douglass College, Rutgers University, New Brunswick, NJ 08903.

CAREER: University Christian Movement, New York, NY, co-founder and national president, 1966-67, consultant to experimental education groups on fifty college campuses, 1967-68; Case Western Reserve University, Cleveland, Ohio, member of campus ministry staff, 1968-69; Institute for Policy Studies, Washington, DC, visiting fellow, 1969-70, resident fellow, 1971- 75, tenured fellow, 1975-77; Public Resource Center, Washington, DC, founder and director, 1977-81; Interfem Consultants, New York City, founder, director, and consultant to various organizations, 1979-87; Douglass College, Rutgers University, New Brunswick, NJ, Laurie New Jersey chair in women's studies, 1987-89, founder and director of Center for Women's Global Leadership, 1989—. Guest lecturer at universities and colleges, including American University, Bowling Green State University, George Washington University, Graduate Theological Union, and University of Maryland. Organizer of or participant in numerous conferences, workshops, and seminars in several countries, including Australia, Canada, Chile, Denmark, Ethiopia, Finland, India, Japan, Kenya, Mexico, the Netherlands, New Zealand, Peru, the Philippines, Sri Lanka, Switzerland, Tanzania, Thailand, and the United States.

MEMBER: Isis International (associate, 1985—), National Organization for Women (NOW), National Gay and Lesbian Task Force (member of board of directors, 1974-81; member of executive committee, 1976-78), National Women's Studies Association, National Women's Conference Committee, American Friends Service Committee (member of National Women's Program Committee, 1980-83), Women's Liberation Movement (co-founder of Washington, D.C., group, 1968), Women's Institute for Freedom of the Press (associate, 1978- 86), New York Feminist Art Institute (member of advisory board, 1979—), New York City Commission on the Status of Women (chair of United Nations Decade committee, 1982-86).

AWARDS, HONORS: Community service awards from Lambda Legal Defense Fund, 1982, and National Lesbian and Gay Health Foundation, 1986; Wise Woman Award, Center for Women's Policy Studies, 1989; Lesbian Rights Award, Southern California Women for Understanding, 1991; Resourceful Woman Award, 1992; inducted into National Women's Hall of Fame, Seneca Falls, NY, 1996.

WRITINGS:

(Under name Charlotte Bunch-Weeks) *A Broom of One's Own,* Women's Liberation Movement (Washington, DC), 1970.

(With Shirley Castley) *Developing Strategies for the Future: Feminist Perspectives,* International Women's Tribute Centre (New York City), 1980.

Feminism in the '80s (pamphlets), Antelope Publications (Denver), Book 1: *Facing Down the Right,* 1981, Book 2: *Going Public with Our Vision,* 1983, Book 3: *Bringing the Global Home,* 1985.

Passionate Politics: Feminist Theory in Action—Essays, 1968-1986, St. Martin's (New York City), 1987.

(With Roxanna Carrillo) *Gender Violence: A Development and Human Rights Issue,* Center for Women's Global Leadership (New Brunswick, NJ), 1991.

(With Niamh Reilly) *Demanding Accountability: The Global Campaign and Vienna Tribunal for Women's Human Rights,* United Nations Developments Fund for Women (New York City), 1994.

EDITOR

(Under name Charlotte Bunch-Weeks; with Joanne Cooke and Robin Morgan) *The New Women: A Motive Anthology on Women's Liberation,* Bobbs-Merrill (Indianapolis), 1970.

(With Nancy Myron) *Class and Feminism: A Collection of Essays from the Furies,* Diana Press (Baltimore), 1974.

(With Myron) *Women Remembered: A Collection of Biographies from the Furies,* Diana Press, 1974.

(With Myron) *Lesbianism and the Women's Movement,* Diana Press, 1975.

(With J. Flax, A. Freeman, N. Hartsock, and M. Mautner) *Building Feminist Theory: Essays from Quest,* Longman (New York City), 1981.

(With Sandra Pollack) *Learning Our Way: Essays in Feminist Education,* Crossing Press (Trumansburg, NY), 1983.

(With Kathleen Barry and Shirley Castley) *International Feminism: Networking against Female Sexual Slavery,* International Women's Tribune Centre, 1984.

OTHER

Contributor to anthologies, including *Liberation NOW!: Writings From the Women's Liberation Movement,* Dell, 1971; *Our Right to Love,* Prentice-Hall, 1978; *Feminist Frameworks,* McGraw, 1978; *The Women Say, the Men Say,* Delacorte, 1979; *What Women Want: From the Report on International Women's Year in Houston,* Simon & Schuster, 1979; *Lavender Culture,* Jove, 1979; *Issues in Feminism: A First Course in Women's Studies,* Houghton, 1980; *Take Back the Night: Women on Pornography,* Morrow, 1980; *Women in Print II,* Modern Language Association of America, 1982; *Current Issues in Organizational Leadership,* Ginn Press, 1983; *First Harvest: Institute for Policy Studies, 1963-83,* Grove, 1983; *Crimes against Women: Proceedings of the International Tribunal,* Frog in the Well, 1984; and *Studies International Forum,* Pergamon, 1985.

Author or co-author of pamphlets on feminist topics, including "Sweet Sixteen to Soggy Thirty-six: Saga of American Womanhood," "Facing Down the Right," "Going Public with Our Visions," "Bringing the Global Home," and "The Ferraro Factor: Symbolism or Substance?" Contributor to numerous feminist, gay, and Christian periodicals, including *Broadsheet, Nation, Progressive, Christianity and Crisis, Christopher Street, Heresies, IKON, Interact, Isis, Ms., Nouvelles Questions feministes, New Student, Response, Signs, Sinister Wisdom, Sojourner, Student World,* and *Women's World.*

Co-founder and editor of *The Furies,* 1972-73, and *Quest: A Feminist Quarterly,* 1974-81. Member of editorial board of *Motive,* 1967-73. Editor of special editions of *Motive* and *Off Our Backs.* Consultant to Daughters, Inc. (feminist publishing company), 1976-78.

SIDELIGHTS: "Within the Women's Movement, Charlotte Bunch is a touchstone," wrote former *Ms.* editor Gloria Steinem in 1977. "Sooner or later—and especially when any hard question of feminist theory or tactics comes up—one is likely to hear the question, 'But what does Charlotte think?'" Writing in *Gay and Lesbian Literature,* Carolynne Myall calls Bunch "one of the foremost organizers and theorists of the lesbian and global feminist movements."

Bunch became involved in feminism during the late 1960s and eventually devoted herself full-time to the movement. She is especially known for her ability to organize and motivate groups and for the timely insights she conveys in her many speeches. "She is often the first to articulate trends of thought as they percolate unevenly to the surface of various segments of the women's movement," observed interviewer Torie Osborn in *Commonground,* adding that Bunch "is one of the warmest and most accessible feminist leaders in the country, and she is a natural teacher."

Bunch became active in civil rights and student Christian organizations while an undergraduate at Duke University during the early 1960s. "The civil rights movement became my education," she told Osborn, and the campus ministry became her vocation for a time. After earning her bachelor's degree in 1966 Bunch helped found the University Christian Movement and became its national president, and she also joined the campus ministry staff of Case Western Reserve University. If there had been no women's movement, she reflected to Osborn, "I'm convinced I would have become one of those women who work in the Methodist Church bureaucracy for liberal causes. . . . I never was into the religion of Methodism; I was into the social action of it. I was into the notions of love and justice." Bunch, who was raised a Methodist, explained, "When I was a child, the only image I had of my life was that I would be a missionary. It was the only way I knew girls could travel around the world and do exciting things."

Bunch was married in 1967 to a man who had worked with her in civil rights projects, but they divorced in 1971 when Bunch discovered her lesbianism. Bunch "discovered her lesbianism in the context of the feminist movement and, following a very public 'coming out' in 1971, immediately experienced the movement's traumatic 'gay-straight' split," according to Myall. "Believing there was no hospitable space within the existing women's movement to develop a lesbian feminist politics and culture, Charlotte Bunch, Rita Mae Brown, and several others formed a small lesbian separatist community."

Bunch helped found the Furies, a lesbian-feminist collective in Washington, DC, that published a short-lived magazine by the same name. A few years later she helped found another magazine, *Quest: A Feminist Quarterly*. As a fellow of the Washington, DC, Institute for Policy Studies from 1969 to 1977, a consultant to several international women's and human rights organizations through Interfem Consultants beginning in 1979, and a speaker and organizer for numerous conferences and seminars, Bunch gained the opportunity to voice her opinions on feminism, lesbianism, and global concerns.

"Often called into some of the power struggles and debates that sporadically rend communities," observed Karla Dobinski in a 1983 *Feminist Connection* article, "Charlotte consistently emerges as a respected peacemaker and problem-solver, able to foster honest inquiry into the conflicts that arise." During the 1970s, differences between homosexual and heterosexual feminists, or separatist and non-separatist feminism, created a furor within the movement. Explaining the separatist point of view to Steinem in 1977, Bunch said, "Of course, nothing exists outside the system in the pure sense. We pay taxes, and obey certain rules. But the creation of institutions, projects, and movements that are essentially outside the system seems more important than ever now." She acknowledged the need to work occasionally within accepted social, political, and economic institutions to "see just how far we can make the system budge," but added that "we need to keep a base outside. We need a place to create ourselves."

Eventually, however, Bunch decided that feminism must move beyond mere separatism. "We saw separatism as a vehicle to bring attention to important issues being overlooked," Dobinski quoted her as saying. Once the problems were defined, however, "it [was] important to bring the issues into the perspective of a global picture" by applying feminist principles to non- feminist contexts. Bunch was one of the first to question separatism as an effective primary means of social change. "It was practically a national event in the women's liberation circles," declared Osborn, "when, in 1975 at a national conference, Charlotte declared herself no longer a separatist—that speech signaled the end to intense gay/straight and separatist/non-separatist splits which had swept through the movement." At another famous speech in Berkeley, California, in 1979, reported Osborn, Bunch called the lesbian-feminist subculture a "ghetto" and implored the group to "get out of the ghetto and into the mainstream."

"Feminists listened to Charlotte then," observed the interviewer, "and do now, because we *trust* her." Bunch notes that although women are beginning to apply what they've learned to areas outside the feminist movement, they tend to feel disloyal instead of adaptable when they take this approach. "Women are getting regular jobs for the first time in years," she explained to Osborn in their 1983 interview, "[but] they're still viewing it as the job they have INSTEAD of being a feminist. It's not being seen as valid political work." Emphasizing the importance of an inclusive feminist approach as opposed to the former separatist movement, Bunch declared, "We need to . . . let go of our possession of the past—not let go of what we learned from our past, but let go of our dependence on it. We must trust that our past will take us to our future."

As part of her feminist action, Bunch has co-edited a number of anthologies of women's writings, including *International Feminism: Networking Against Female Sexual Slavery, Learning Our Way: Essays in Feminist Education,* and *Lesbianism and the Women's Movement*. "To read *Learning Our Way* in the 1980s," commented Helene V. Wenzel in a *Women's Review of Books* article, "is to understand where feminist learning has come from and what it has been through. The editors [Bunch and Sandra Pollack] have been unusually conscientious in presenting the fullest political panorama of feminist education."

Bunch has also written numerous essays, many of which are included in her 1987 collection *Passionate Politics: Feminist Theory in Action—Essays, 1968-1986.* "My life as an activist and organizer lies at the heart of this book," she writes, as quoted in the Toronto *Globe and Mail.* Naomi Black of the *Globe and Mail* asserted that "[Bunch's] voice, as it has been before, is the voice of the most innovative and important part of American feminism." Blanche Wiesen Cook in *Women's Review of Books* praised the essay collection as "a very personal theoretical odyssey which will serve as an organizing handbook far into the future." Noting Bunch's significant influence on the development of feminist ideology, Cook declared: "*Passionate Politics* is more than a collection of theoretical essays that touch on the most vital issues of our lives; it is a history of those issues as one feminist activist has lived through them, and vigorously helped to inform and to shape them."

"I see my own personal quest or search as very connected to the period of transition I see the women's movement to be in," she told Torie Osborn. Comparing the temporary stagnation of feminism during the late 1970s and early 1980s to her own "movement activist mid-life crisis" at that time, Bunch noted that both she and the movement seemed "discouraged and bored" and "stuck." She asserted: "I strongly believe that the primary way the movement in this country will get 'unstuck' will be by connecting with international feminism." Bunch's own worldwide activities involve consulting with a number of organizations, including the International Women's Tribune Centre, the Asian and Pacific Center for Women and Development, and the National Women's Studies Association; coordinating the "Global Feminist Workshop Against Trafficking in Women," held in the Netherlands in 1983; and organizing and participating in several other international workshops in Denmark, Ethiopia, Japan, Kenya, Mexico, Peru, Thailand, and other countries. "I see feminism as a movement of people working for a change across and despite national boundaries, not of representatives of nation-states or national governments," Dobinski quoted Bunch as saying. "We must be global, recognizing that the oppression of women in one part of the world is often affected by what happens in another, and that no woman is free until the conditions of oppression of women are eliminated everywhere."

BIOGRAPHICAL/CRITICAL SOURCES:

BOOKS

Douglas, Carol Anne, *Love and Politics: Radical Feminist and Lesbian Theories,* Ism Press (San Francisco), 1990.

Gay and Lesbian Literature, Volume 2, St. James Press (Detroit), 1998.

PERIODICALS

Commonground, April, 1983.

Feminist Connection, March, 1983.

Globe and Mail (Toronto), December 19, 1987.

Lesbian Tide, May/June, 1977.

Ms., July, 1977.

New Directions for Women, November/December, 1987.

Off Our Backs, October, 1987.

Signs, winter, 1987; Volume 21, number 4, 1996.

Women's Review of Books, October, 1984; November, 1987.

* * *

BUNCH-WEEKS, Charlotte
See BUNCH, Charlotte (Anne)

* * *

BURCHETT, Wilfred (Graham) 1911-1983

PERSONAL: Born September 16, 1911, in Melbourne, Australia; died of liver disease, September 27, 1983, in Sofia, Bulgaria; son of George Harold (a writer and farmer) and Mary Jane (Davy) Burchett; married Vesselina Ossikovska (a journalist and art historian), December 24, 1949; children: Peter, George, Anna. *Education:* Educated in Australia and England. *Politics:* Independent radical.

CAREER: Daily Express, London, England, war correspondent in China, Burma, India, and Pacific Theater, 1941-45, in Berlin and Central Europe, 1945-49; *Times,* London, foreign correspondent in Budapest, 1949-50; *Ce Soir,* Paris, France, foreign correspondent in China and Korea, 1951-53; freelance correspondent in Hanoi, North Vietnam, 1954-57; *Daily Express,* London, foreign correspondent in Moscow, 1957-61; foreign correspondent in Moscow for *Financial Times,* London, and *National Guardian,* New York, NY, 1961-65; *Guardian,* New York, foreign correspondent in Phnom Penh, Cambodia, 1965-68, and in Paris, 1968-79.

MEMBER: National Union of Journalists.

WRITINGS:

Pacific Treasure Island, F. W. Cheshire, 1941.

Bombs over Burma, F. W. Cheshire, 1943.

Wingate Adventure, F. W. Cheshire, 1944.

Democracy with a Tommygun, F. W. Cheshire, 1946.

Cold War in Germany, World Unity Publications, 1951.

China's Feet Unbound, World Unity Publications, 1952.

This Monstrous War, Jo Waters, 1953.

North of the Seventeenth Parallel, Red River Publishing (Wichita Falls, TX), 1955.
Mekong Upstream, Red River Publishing, 1957.
Gagarin: First Man into Outer Space, Panther Books, 1961.
Titov's Flight into Space, Panther Books, 1962.
The Furtive War, International Pubs. Co. (New York), 1963.
Vietnam: Inside Story of the Guerilla War, International Pubs. Co., 1965.
Vietnam North, International Pubs. Co., 1966, reprinted with an introduction by Bertrand Russel, 1967.
My Visit to the Liberated Zones of South Vietnam, Foreign Language Publishing House (Hanoi, North Vietnam), 1966.
Again Korea?, International Pubs. Co., 1968.
Vietnam Will Win, Guardian Publishing (New York City), 1968.
Passport, Thomas Nelson (Melbourne, Australia), 1969.
Second Indochina War, Lorrimer, 1970.
(With Prince Norodom Sihanouk) *My War with the C.I.A.; The Memoirs of Prince Norodom Sihanouk,* Pantheon (New York City), 1973.
(With Rewi Alley) *China: The Quality of Life,* Penguin (London), 1976.
Grasshoppers and Elephants, Urizen Books (New York City), 1977.
(With Derek Roebuck) *The Whores of War,* Penguin, 1977.
Catapult to Freedom, Quartet (New York City), 1978.
Southern Africa Stands Up, Urizen Books, 1978.
Both Eyes Open (memoirs), Times Books (New York City), 1980.
At the Barricades: Forty Years on the Cutting Edge of History, introduction by Harrison E. Salisbury, Times Books, 1981.
The China-Cambodia-Vietnam Triangle, Vanguard Books (Chicago), 1981.
Shadows of Hiroshima, Verso (London), 1983.
Burchett Reporting on the Other Side of the World, 1939-1983, edited by Ben Kiernan, Quartet, 1986.

Author of about a dozen documentary television films on Indochina and North Korea. Contributor to *Afrique-Asie, Paris, Nation-Review,* and *Le Monde Diplomatique.*

SIDELIGHTS: Australian journalist and author Wilfred Burchett was best known for his interest in national labor movements and independence struggles in Southeast Asia and throughout the rest of the world. In a career spanning forty years his articles and books covered a wide variety of subjects, including World War II, China, Korea, Vietnam, South Africa, and the Russian space program. Many reviewers took strong exception to Burchett's obvious Communist sympathies. Others, while admitting that his perspective was slanted, found much of value in his writings and even contended that Burchett's leftist bias often provided insights that could not be found in more objective accounts.

Writing in the *New York Times Book Review* in 1965, Peter Grose stated: "[Burchett] is able to report a side of the Vietnam war not available through Western newsmen. His present book [*Vietnam: Inside Story of the Guerilla War*] contains vivid and personal impressions gathered during two visits to Vietcong Headquarters and units in South Vietnam." Discussing the same volume, a reviewer for *Choice* noted: "Most Americans are likely to be infuriated by the ridicule directed toward their past leaders and armed forces." He then went on to add: "This book is perhaps most useful to the Vietnam scholar who could cut out the propaganda and the sentimentalism to gain a deeper comprehension of the way of life, the thought processes, and the decision-making processes of the Vietnamese Communists."

In *Vietnam North,* Burchett reported on two trips he took to North Vietnam in 1966 during which he traveled widely throughout the country. According to Hyman Kublin, reviewing the book for *Library Journal:* "[Burchett's] account of conditions north of the 17th Parallel, where he is anything but unwelcome, is zippy and interesting, though markedly slanted. . . . There are nuggets here. But finding them requires a careful search." William Henderson of *Saturday Review* called *Vietnam North* "little more than a Communist Party tract." Nevertheless, he qualified this by saying: "Burchett writes well and easily; his report . . . ought to be interesting and worthwhile, even if . . . basically unreliable. . . . However, the text is so overstated, so laudatory of everything the Communists are doing . . . and so denunciatory of the United States policy and action, as to stretch the credulity of any normally skeptical reader."

During the Korean War Burchett had served as a foreign correspondent for the Paris-based *Ce Soir.* His reports at that time had accused the United Nations of using germ warfare and had praised the humane conditions in North Korean prisoner-of-war camps. After the Korean War, Burchett's passport was temporarily revoked by the Australian Government because he had allegedly helped the Communists interrogate captured U.N. troops. In 1967 Burchett returned to North Korea, and in *Again Korea* he gave his assessment of the state of the country a decade and a half after the war's conclusion. The book also compares the Korean and Vietnam conflicts and puts forth the views of North Korean Communists on the latter. As with Burchett's other works, critics seemed to agree that the reader who could sift through the propaganda aspects of *Again Korea* would find much valuable information on the material being discussed. According to Murray Fromson of *Saturday Review:* "In some ways [this book] sounds like an essay on paradise rather than a report on what may be the poorest, most isolated regime in the Communist world apart from Albania. Nevertheless, it is a useful work."

In 1973 Burchett collaborated with Cambodia's exiled Prince Norodom Sihanouk on *My War with the C.I.A.* Subtitled *The Memoirs of Prince Norodom Sihanouk,* the book covers the period from the 1950s to the early 1970s. Sihanouk contends that the United States was unhappy with his failure to take a stronger stand against Communism and blames the overthrow of his neutralist regime in 1970 on a series of C.I.A. conspiracies. "Whether there was any war against Sihanouk by the American Central Intelligence Agency is not proved by this short, self-justified account of his political life, though the evidence is widely accepted," observed a reviewer for the *Times Literary Supplement.* "These memoirs show Sihanouk to be an astute, dramatic, and opinionated leader," noted D. D. Buck of *Library Journal.*

Burchett is also known for being the first Western journalist to survey the Hiroshima atomic-bomb site and file an account of the holocaust for Western readers.

BIOGRAPHICAL/CRITICAL SOURCES:

BOOKS

Burchett, Wilfred, *Both Eyes Open,* Times Books, 1980.

Maine, Robert, *Agent of Influence: The Life and Times of Wilfred Burchett,* Mackenzie Institute for the Study of Terrorism, Revolution and Propaganda (Toronto, Canada), 1989.

PERIODICALS

Choice, December, 1977; October, 1978.

Library Journal, February 1, 1967, p. 572; June 15, 1968, p. 2509; December 1, 1970, p. 4181; April 15, 1973, p. 1267.

Nation, April 14, 1969, p. 470.

New Statesman, November 25, 1977.

New York Times Book Review, May 2, 1965, p. 30; May 5, 1968, p. 10; July 10, 1977.

Saturday Review, December 17, 1966, p. 32; June 1, 1968, p. 29.

Times Literary Supplement (London), February 23, 1973, p. 198.

OBITUARIES:

PERIODICALS

Chicago Tribune, September 29, 1983.

London Times, September 29, 1983.

Los Angeles Times, September 30, 1983.

New York Times, September 28, 1983.

Time, October 10, 1983.

Washington Post, September 28, 1983.*

* * *

BURLAND, C. A.
See BURLAND, Cottie (Arthur)

* * *

BURLAND, Cottie (Arthur) 1905-
(C. A. Burland)

PERSONAL: Born September 17, 1905, in Kensington, London, England; married Maud March, June 20, 1928; children: Poppy Anne (Mrs. Cyril Martin), Christopher van Tromp, Julian Cornelis. *Education:* Attended schools in London, England. *Religion:* Roman Catholic.

ADDRESSES: Home and office—246 Molesey Ave., West Molesey, Surrey, KT8 OET, England.

CAREER: British Museum, London, ethnographer, 1925-65. Abbey Art Centre Museum, New Barnet, Hertfordshire, England, honorary curator, 1950-55. *Military service:* Royal Air Force, 1940-44.

MEMBER: Royal Anthropological Institute (fellow), British Society of Aesthetics, Societe des Americanistes de Paris, Folk-Lore Society (London).

AWARDS, HONORS: Imago Mundi Award, 1965.

WRITINGS:

Life and Art in Ancient Mexico, Cassirer, 1948.
Magic Books from Mexico, Penguin, 1953.
The Art of Primitive Peoples, Bannisdale Press, 1955.
The Selden Roll, Gebruder Mann, 1955.
The Four Directions of Time, Santa Fe, 1956.
Man and Art, Studio Books, 1959.
(Contributor) *Great Private Collections,* Weidenfeld & Nicolson (London, England), 1964.
Bases of Religion in Aztec Mexico, Guild of Pastoral Psychology, 1964.
(Author of introduction) *Codex Egerton 2895,* Akademische Druck-u. Verlagsanstalt (Graz, Austria), 1965.
North American Indian Mythology, Hamlyn (London), 1966, new edition, 1968.
The Magical Arts: A Short History, Horizon Press (New York City), 1966.
(Contributor) *Arts of the Navigators,* Cassell, 1966.
Codex Mexicanus caractere hieroglyphi, Akademische Druck-u, 1966.
The Gods of Mexico, Putnam (New York City), 1967.
The Arts of the Alchemists, Weidenfeld & Nicolson, 1967, Macmillan (New York City), 1968.
Peru under the Incas, Evans Brothers, 1967, Putnam, 1968.
The Exotic White Man: An Alien in Asian and African Art, with photographs by Werner Forman, McGraw (New York City), 1969.
What Became of the Maori?, illustrated by Denis Wrigley, Wheaton, 1969.
The Travels of Marco Polo, with photographs by Forman, McGraw, 1970.
The People of the Ancient Americas, Hamlyn (Feltham, England), 1970.
Mythology of the Americans, Hamlyn, 1971.
Beyond Science: A Journey into the Supernatural, Grosset (New York City), 1972.
Echoes of Magic: A Study of Seasonal Festivals through the Ages, Rowman & Littlefield (Totowa, NJ), 1972.
Secrets of the Occult, Ebury Press (London), 1972.
Montezuma: Lord of the Aztecs, with photographs by Forman, Putnam, 1973.
Gods and Demons in Primitive Art, with photographs by Forman, Hamlyn (New York City), 1973.
Eskimo Art, Hamlyn, 1973.
Gods and Heroes of War, illustrated by Honi Werner, Putnam, 1974.
Myths of Life and Death, Crown (New York City), 1974.
(With Forman) *Feathered Serpent and Smoking Mirror,* Putnam, 1975.
Peoples of the Sun: The Civilizations of Pre-Columbian America, Weidenfeld & Nicolson, 1976.
The Incas, Silver, 1979.

JUVENILES

Mexico, Rhodesia, and Java, three volumes, Hawthorn Press, 1950-53.
Ancient Egypt, Hulton Educational Publications, 1956.
Ancient Peru, Hulton Educational Publications, 1957.
Ancient Greece, Hulton Educational Publications, 1958.
Ancient Rome, Hulton Educational Publications, 1958.
Ancient China, Hulton Educational Publications, 1959.
The Vikings, illustrated by R. G. Botting, Dufour (Chester Springs, PA), 1960.
Finding Out about the Incas, Lothrop (New York City), 1960.
The Aztecs, Weidenfeld & Nicolson, 1961.
Adventuring with Archaeology, Warne (New York City), 1963.
Time, 1964.
Men before History, 1964.
Men without Machines: The Story of Primitive Peoples, Aldus, 1965, Natural History Press (Garden City, NY), 1969.
The Ancient Maya, illustrated by Elizabeth Hammond, Weidenfeld & Nicolson, 1967.
James Cook R.V., Hulton Educational Publications, 1967.
The First Zulus, Hulton Educational Publications, 1967.
Fun with Archaeology, Kaye & Ward, 1971.
The Way of the Buddha, Hulton Educational Publications, 1972.
See Inside an Aztec Town, illustrated by Charlotte Snook, Warwick Press (New York City), 1980.

Contributor to journals, including *Man, Natural History, Mariners Mirror, Ethnos,* and *Graphis.* Contributor to popular publications, including *Everybody's Weekly* and *Studio.* Critic for *Arts Review* (London). Burland's works have been translated into German, Spanish, and Italian.

SIDELIGHTS: Cottie Burland has written many books about ancient civilizations and primitive peoples, focusing his attention on the peoples of the ancient Americas in particular. The study of these peoples—

the Mayans, the Incas, and the Aztecs—is especially difficult since little information is available about them. The Incas, for example, had no written language, while the Mayan language is as yet undeciphered. Irreplaceable Aztec manuscripts were destroyed by Spanish missionaries. Scientists must rely solely upon the archaeological remains of these civilizations for their information, a situation which severely hinders their work.

Despite these difficulties, Burland's book *The Gods of Mexico* deals with the ancient religions of that area and relates what has been learned of them. I. R. Blacker of the *New York Times Book Review* finds the project "incredible: [Burland] has attempted to organize and to clarify what little is actually known about the several thousand-year-old religions of ancient Mexico." Blacker calls it "astonishing that anyone could tread so carefully through the quicksands of Mexican theology as has C. A. Burland." A reviewer for the *Times Literary Supplement* believes Burland "has succeeded in illuminating not only Mexican religion but also pre-Columbian society as a whole." This reviewer praises Burland for his ability "to lead us within [Mexican religion], and show us not only how it worked but also why it worked as well as it did." Burland's account reflects his own research among the pre-Columbian religious codices, some of which he published in Austria. He also interprets for the general reader some surviving accounts of missionaries who postdated the Columbian conquest. The *Times Literary Supplement* reviewer remarks: "For those of us who have struggled with the symbolism of the pictures in the surviving religious Codices, or vainly tried to grasp the meaning of pre-Columbian artefacts, this book . . . provides the tools for working out the answers."

Burland's studies have often led him beyond the boundaries of formal religious practice. In *The Magical Arts: A Short History,* he discusses a variety of occult and eclectic practices that sometimes resemble religious worship. His wide range of topics includes astrology, animism, telepathy, voodoo, witchcraft, and even herbalism and folklore. His history proceeds from prehistoric times to the present century and ranges around the globe. A *Times Literary Supplement* critic complains that Burland "touches on a great deal that scarcely qualifies as magic in the strict sense at all" but also comments that the work "is fundamentally sane in its approach, and manages to get across a surprising amount of piecemeal information." To A. W. Gardner of the *Library Journal,* this piecemeal approach amounts to "little more than an outline" or "a summary and review for the initiate."

The Arts of the Alchemists focuses on a single arcane practice, which has been variously described as religious heresy, scientific research, and a comprehensive philosophy of life. The conviction that ordinary materials can be transformed into gold has consumed the attention of believers as old as ancient Egyptians and as distinguished and credible as the seventeenth-century British physicist, chemist, and inventor Robert Boyle. Scientists and religious leaders have for centuries denounced alchemists as frauds, but Burland's sympathetic history, writes *Library Journal* reviewer Lee Ash, "make[s] the seriousness of the alchemists' weird approaches seem as logical to us as they did to the practitioners."

The Exotic White Man: An Alien in Asian and African Art is a comparative study of primitive art, in which Burland attempts to view the intruding European colonizers through the eyes of native observers. Some critics suggest that Burland's interpretation falls short of objective honesty, presenting a primitive view that is surprisingly lacking in anger, hate, and fear. An *Economist* reviewer would have preferred "an attempt to interpret the European impact as Asians and Africans may have seen it, rather than as Europeans of this half century may think they ought to have seen it." *The Exotic White Man* includes descriptions of the methods and techniques used by primitive artists and artisans, not only in Africa and Asia, but in Polynesia and the Americas. For this reason, perhaps, *Choice* recommends the book as "indispensable to students of art."

Montezuma: Lord of the Aztecs, Burland's biography of the famous emperor who confronted the Spanish conquerors, has been received with warm praise. The *Economist* critic states: "Burland has produced a beautiful account of the astonishing but little-understood Montezuma. He portrays the poetic and spiritual side of him, and his justness as a judge, as well as the better known pornographic side." Duncan Fallowell of *Books and Bookmen* finds the story of Montezuma "told with clear insight linked to the dramatic pace of an historical novel."

Other books by Burland have also been critically acclaimed. Alan Hull Walton of *Books and Bookmen,* speaking of *Myths of Life and Death,* writes: "Those who are interested in folklore, in the history of religions, and the multifarious nature of human personality in various races and civilizations, will find the well-written and informative text of lasting value." Burland has also written several books for young people. These include *The Ancient Maya,* which M. B. Stephenson of *Library Journal,* for example, calls "the best extant brief introduction to the Maya."

BIOGRAPHICAL/CRITICAL SOURCES:

PERIODICALS

Atlantic, March, 1976.
Books and Bookmen, January, 1974; December, 1975; March, 1976.
Choice, April, 1970.
Economist, January 3, 1970; November 10, 1973; September 4, 1976.
Georgia Review, winter, 1977.
Library Journal, January 15, 1962; February 1, 1967; October 15, 1967; June 15, 1967; April 1, 1968; February 1, 1970; February 15, 1970.
Manchester Guardian, July 24, 1959.
Natural History, November, 1964.
New York Herald Tribune Books, August 26, 1962, p. 10.
New York Times, September 12, 1968.
New York Times Book Review, July 15, 1962, p. 22; April 30, 1967, p. 18; January 11, 1970, p. 35.
Observer, December 14, 1969.
Spectator, December 13, 1969.
Times Literary Supplement, April 27, 1967, p. 363; July 6, 1967, p. 602; November 30, 1967, p. 1162; December 28, 1967, p. 1266; May 9, 1968; October 16, 1969; April 30, 1970, p. 472; November 24, 1972; August 6, 1976.
Washington Post Book World, December 14, 1969.*

* * *

BURLINGAME, (William) Roger 1889-1967

PERSONAL: Born May 7, 1889, in New York, NY; died March 19, 1967; son of Edward Livermore and Ella Frances (Badger) Burlingame; married Angeline Whiton, 1933. *Education:* Harvard University, A.B., 1913; studied at Sorbonne, University of Paris, 1919. *Politics:* Independent.

CAREER: Independent, New York City, member of editorial staff, 1913-14; Charles Scribner's Sons, New York City, publicity manager, 1914-17, book editor, 1919-26; freelance writer, 1926-67. Barnard College, instructor, 1948-49; Massachusetts Institute of Technology, visiting lecturer, 1954-55. Served with Office of War Information, 1942-43; U.S. Army Air Forces, correspondent from European and Mediterranean theaters, 1945. *Military service:* National Guard, Mexican Border Patrol, 1916. U.S. Army, Infantry, served overseas with American Expeditionary Forces in a machine gun battalion, 1918-19; became lieutenant.

AWARDS, HONORS: Poor Richard's Almanack Award, 1956, for *Benjamin Franklin, The First Mr. American.*

WRITINGS:

You Too (novel), Scribner (New York City), 1924.
Susan Shane (novel), Scribner, 1926.
(Compiler) *From Gallegher to The Deserter: The Best Stories of Richard Harding Davis,* Scribner, 1927.
High Thursday (novel), Scribner, 1928.
The Heir (novel), Scribner, 1930.
Peace Veterans, Minton, Balch, 1932.
Cartwheels (novel), Doubleday (New York City), 1935.
Three Bags Full (novel), Harcourt (New York City), 1936.
March of the Iron Men: A Social History of Union through Invention, Scribner, 1938, reprinted, Grosset (New York City), 1960.
Engines of Democracy: Inventions and Society in Mature America, Scribner, 1940.
Whittling Boy: The Story of Eli Whitney, Harcourt, 1941.
(With Alden Stevens) *Victory without Peace,* Harcourt, 1944.
Of Making Many Books (centennial history of Scribner's Sons), Scribner, 1946, reprinted as *Of Making Many Books: A Hundred Years of Reading, Writing, and Publishing,* Pennsylvania State University Press (University Park, PA), 1997.
Inventors behind the Inventor, Harcourt, 1947.
Backgrounds of Power: The Human Story of Mass Production, Scribner, 1949.
Mosquitoes in the Big Ditch (juvenile), Winston, 1952.
General Billy Mitchell, Champion of Air Defense, McGraw (New York City), 1952.
Machines That Built America, Harcourt, 1953.
Henry Ford, a Great Life in Brief, Knopf (New York City), 1954.
Benjamin Franklin, The First Mr. American, New American Library (New York City), 1955.
The American Conscience, Knopf, 1957.

Beyond the Call of Duty: The Story of a Company's Ninety Years of Service, Metropolitan Life Insurance Co., 1958.

I Have Known Many Worlds (autobiography), Doubleday, 1959.

Endless Frontiers: The Story of McGraw-Hill, McGraw, 1959.

Scientists behind the Inventors, Harcourt, 1960.

Don't Let Them Scare You: The Life and Times of Elmer Davis, Lippincott (Philadelphia, PA), 1961.

The Sixth Column, Lippincott, 1962.

Out of Silence into Sound: The Life of Alexander Graham Bell (juvenile), Macmillan, 1964.

Dictator Clock: Five Thousand Years of Telling Time (juvenile), Macmillan, 1966.

Benjamin Franklin, Envoy Extraordinary, Coward (New York City), 1967.

Other books include *Heredity and Social Problems,* 1940, and *Victory without Peace,* 1941. Contributor of short stories, articles, and light verse to magazines, including *Harper's, Atlantic, Harper's Bazaar, Collier's, Ladies' Home Journal, Esquire, Woman's Home Companion, McCall's,* and *American Mercury.*

SIDELIGHTS: Roger Burlingame is "best known for his American social histories, in which invention and technology play the leading role," wrote J. W. Krutch in the *New York Times Book Review.* In a review of the autobiography *I Have Known Many Worlds,* Krutch reported: "The history of our times . . . is never far from the author's thoughts."

In *Inventors behind the Inventor,* Burlingame defends his thesis, according to *New York New Technical Books,* that "inventing is a social process rather than the act of especially gifted individuals." In a chapter titled "Behind Henry Ford," for example, he discusses the events and discoveries that led eventually to the development of the mass-produced automobile. In other chapters devoted to major inventions like the telegraph and the steam engine, Burlingame revives the names of contributors long forgotten or rarely acknowledged, and he discusses the failed attempts that served as stepping stones to success. The *Saturday Review of Literature* called *Inventors behind the Inventor* a "continuously interesting record."

In *Machines That Built America,* the author focuses on United States machine production and the individuals who made it possible. Critics commented on Burlingame's ability to explain complex technology to the general reader in a meaningful way. E. B. Garside reported in the *New York Times:* "Mr. Burlingame has handled a tricky subject with ease and dispatch." Another similar study is *Scientists behind the Inventors,* which not only covers two hundred years of scientific research and discovery, but also, according to *Booklist,* identifies "America's changing attitude" to science, particularly "after World War I."

Often Burlingame turned his attention to individuals who, he believed, had made a significant contribution to social history. One of these is the subject of *General Billy Mitchell, Champion of Air Defense. Library Journal* reviewer M. K. Walraven found the work valuable on two counts: as the life story "of a controversial, contradictory, prophetic figure" and also as a perceptive description of the historical and social events that preceded World War II and America's belated effort to dominate the skies in defense of peace. Eddie Rickenbacker, the World War I flying ace, wrote in the *Chicago Sunday Tribune:* "'General Billy Mitchell' could be read with profit by every American to supply a check against complacency and unthinking acceptance of the 'inevitable' too often presented as political fact."

In 1954 Burlingame published *Henry Ford, a Great Life in Brief.* In it, he discusses what *San Francisco Chronicle* reviewer Jane Voiles referred to as Ford's "two obsessions"—the quest for perfection in the manufacturing of automobiles and "the welfare of the common man." He also presents a portrait of Ford that *Chicago Sunday Tribune* critic Robert Molloy called "friendly" but not necessarily "flattering." In addition, Burlingame questions some of the unexpected ramifications of Ford's accomplishments in the area of mass production. In the *Saturday Review,* S. T. Williamson summarized: "The Burlingame account steers clear of the mythical adulation and equally mythical debunking of Ford." Voiles called the study "short but not without penetration."

Another of Burlingame's biographical studies veers away from science and technology to examine the social and political impact of Benjamin Franklin. The young adult work, *Benjamin Franklin, Envoy Extraordinary,* covers the years that Franklin spent as a diplomat, including his trips to England and France. "The author writes straightforward prose," A. C. Land wrote in the *American Historical Review,* "drawing on recent scholarship and adding a dash of spice from Franklin's endlessly amusing correspondence." *Saturday Review* critic Zena Sutherland was drawn especially to Burlingame's colorful depictions of "the intrigues and counter-intrigues of politicians and statesmen." *Library Journal* reviewer K. T. Willis recommended: "This is easily the first biography of [Franklin] for young Americans to read."

BIOGRAPHICAL/CRITICAL SOURCES:

PERIODICALS

American Historical Review, October, 1967.
Booklist, October 15, 1947; February 1, 1953; December 15, 1953; February 15, 1955; November 1, 1959; September 15, 1960.
Bookmark, January, 1953; March, 1955; November, 1959.
Boston Transcript, August 28, 1926, p. 2.
Chicago Sunday Tribune, December 28, 1952, p. 3; November 15, 1953, p. 34; January 23, 1955, p. 4.
Christian Science Monitor, February 11, 1960, p. 11.
Commonweal, November 21, 1947.
Horn Book, January, 1948; August, 1960.
Kirkus Reviews, September 15, 1947; October 15, 1952; October 15, 1953; November 15, 1954; March 15, 1960.
Library Journal, October 15, 1947; November 15, 1947; February 1, 1953; January 1, 1954; February 15, 1955; October 1, 1959; May 15, 1960; April 15, 1967.
Nation, May 28,2 1955.
New Yorker, April 9, 1955.
New York Herald Tribune Book Review, February 1, 1953, p. 12; November 15, 1953; March 20, 1955, p. 11; October 25, 1959, p. 11; May 8, 1960.
New York New Technical Books, July, 1947.
New York Times, August 15, 1926, p. 6; November 9, 1947, p. 65; January 25, 1953, p. 22; October 25, 1953; February 13, 1955, p. 3.
New York Times Book Review, October 11, 1959, p. 18; May 15, 1960, p. 40.
San Francisco Chronicle, February 8, 1953, p. 16; February 6, 1955, p. 16; November 29, 1959, p. 28.
Saturday Review, March 21, 1953; January 22, 1955; December 12, 1959; March 18, 1967.
Saturday Review of Literature, November 15, 1947.
Springfield Republican, September 26, 1926, p. 7-F; January 11, 1953, p. 4-D; December 13, 1953, p. 40-A; April 3, 1955, p. 8-C; May 1, 1960, p. 5-D.*

BURN, A(ndrew) R(obert) 1902-1991

PERSONAL: Born September 25, 1902, in Kynnersley, Shropshire, England; died in 1991; son of Andrew Ewbank (a clergyman) and Celia Mary (Richardson) Burn; married Mary Wynn Thomas, December 31, 1938. *Education:* Christ Church, Oxford, B.A., 1925, M.A., 1928. *Politics:* Social Democrat. *Religion:* Anglican ("skeptical"). *Avocational interests:* Mountaineering, gliding, travel.

CAREER: Uppingham School, Uppingham, England, senior classical master, 1927-40; British Embassy, Athens, Greece, second secretary, 1944-46; University of Glasgow, Glasgow, Scotland, senior lecturer, 1946-65, reader in ancient history, 1965-69. College of Wooster, Wooster, Ohio, Gillespie Professor, 1958-59; Institute for Advanced Study, Princeton, NJ, member, 1961-62; A College Year in Athens, Inc., professor, 1969-72. *Military service:* Intelligence Corps, 1941-43; became captain.

AWARDS, HONORS: Silver Cross, Order of the Phoenix (Greece), 1975; D. Litt., Oxford University, 1982.

WRITINGS:

Minoans, Philistines, and Greeks, B.C. 1400-900, Knopf (New York City), 1930, reprinted, Greenwood Press (Westport, CT), 1974.
(Translator and author of commentary) *The Romans in Britain: An Anthology of Inscriptions,* Basil Blackwell (Oxford, England), 1932, 2nd edition, University of South Carolina (Columbia), 1968.
The World of Hesiod, Knopf, 1936, reprinted as *The World of Hesiod: A Study of the Greek Middle Ages, c. 900-700 B.C.,* B. Blom (New York City), 1968.
This Scepter'd Isle: An Anthology of English Poetry, Pyros (Athens), 1940.
Philoi toi Vivliou, [Alexandria, Egypt], 1942, translation published as *The Modern Greeks,* Thomas Nelson, 1944.
Alexander the Great and the Hellenistic Empire, Hodder & Stoughton, 1947, Macmillan (New York City), 1948, enlarged edition published as *Alexander the Great and the Hellenistic World,* Collier (New York City), 1962, published as *Alexander the Great and the Middle East,* Penguin (Harmondsworth, England), 1973.
Pericles and Athens, English Universities Press, 1948, Collier, 1962.

Agricola and Roman Britain, English Universities Press, 1953, revised edition, Collier, 1962.

(Contributor) John Bowle, editor, *An Encyclopedia of World History,* Hutchinson, 1958.

The Lyric Age of Greece, Edward Arnold, 1960, Minerva Press (New York City), 1968.

Persia and the Greeks: The Defence of the West, c. 546-478 B.C., St. Martin's (New York City), 1962, revised edition (with D. M. Lewis), Duckworth, 1985.

(Contributor) Michael Grant, editor, *The Birth of Western Civilization,* Thames & Hudson, 1964.

A Traveller's History of Greece, Hodder & Stoughton, 1965, Funk, (New York City), 1967, published as *The Pelican History of Greece,* Pelican, 1966.

The Warring States of Greece from Their Rise to the Roman Conquest, McGraw (New York City), 1968.

(With J. M. B. Edwards) *Greece and Rome, 750 B.C./A.D. 565,* Scott, Foresman (Glenview, IL), 1970.

(With Mary Burn) *The Living Past of Greece: A Time-Traveller's Tour of Historic and Prehistoric Places,* foreword by Lawrence Durrell, illustrated by Bill Hawker, Little, Brown (Boston, MA), 1980.

(Contributor) *The Cambridge History of Iran,* Volume II, Cambridge University Press, 1985.

Contributor to *Civilizations of the Ancient Mediterranean,* edited by M. Grant and Rachel Kitzinger, Scribner (New York City). Contributor to encyclopedias and professional journals.

SIDELIGHTS: Critics praised A. R. Burn's book *The World of Hesiod* when it was published in 1936. The Greek middle ages, described by *New Statesman & Nation* reviewer C. M. Bowra as a "time when a primitive agricultural community began to experiment with its institutions and to change its ideas," encompass the period from 900 to 700 B.C. This was the world of the poet Hesiod, who left behind what may be the only primary source of information about this period of ancient Greece. Bowra pointed out, however, that classical historian Burn supplemented Hesiod's account "with all the material, literary and archaeological, which he can find." Because of the paucity of documentation, contended a reviewer for the *International Journal of Ethics,* a work like *The World of Hesiod* "requires very much of the hypothetical to hold it together." This reviewer particularly appreciated Burn's apparent realization "that he must often outtalk his information." Bowra called the work "[a] chapter of history which is well written, well documented, and composed in an admirably fair and scientific spirit."

Alexander the Great and the Hellenistic Empire is one of dozens that glorify the feats of the Macedonian warrior, but critics elevated Burn's study above the rest. The *San Francisco Chronicle* declared: "It is doubtful that this greatest adventure story of all times has ever been related with greater brilliance, charm and scholarship than in the volume of Burn." In the *Saturday Review of Literature,* Asher Byrnes praised the author for "[a] brilliant performance as thrilling as a novel and yet solid history." A *Times Literary Supplement* critic mentioned minor complaints, but brushed them aside to conclude: "There can be nothing but praise and admiration for a book which is high-spirited, stirring, popular in the best sense, on the one hand, scholarly and judicious on the other."

The book *Pericles and Athens,* which appeared a year later, was also lauded by reviewers. *Nation* critic Joseph Kraft complimented the author for his broad knowledge and "refreshingly sophisticated" mind. "Periclean Athens is a glittering theme," commented Geoffrey Bruun in the *Saturday Review of Literature,* and the author "treats it fittingly, linking the crises of Athenian democracy to our own times [post-World War II] with adroit allusions."

The Lyric Age of Greece examines the nation-state as it came of age in the seventh and sixth centuries B.C. *Canadian Forum* reviewer J. W. Cole "found this an exciting and eminently readable book." Cole predicted that Burn's interpretations, particularly of Greece's colonization phase, "are likely to provide for some years the best and most readily available account of this very important period." In the *Christian Science Monitor,* Zeph Stewart commented that Burn "combines factual presentation with chatty anecdote in a way which recalls some of the ancient authors whom he so freely quotes," but faulted the quality of Burn's "poetic translations." A *Times Literary Supplement* critic also criticized the translations, but countered that "Mr. Burn could not be dull if he tried." The *Times Literary Supplement* praised Burn as "a scholar whose detailed grasp of the minutiae of ancient history is reinforced by wide personal and topographical knowledge, great imaginative insight, and a pleasantly warm style."

This observation was seconded in a *Times Literary Supplement* review of Andrew and Mary Burn's handbook for travelers, *The Living Past of Greece:* "For a book of this kind and size, the topographical description of Athens is masterly, being detailed enough without risking confusion, and by the end of it, the reader has been conducted with affectionate facility through a history of Athenian political institutions."

Persia and the Greeks: The Defence of the West, c. 546-478 B.C. was called a "solidly satisfying . . . achievement" by a *Times Literary Supplement* critic, who described the book as "an excellent example of the new-style approach to Hellenistic antiquities." The critic's definition of this approach seems to apply to Burn's entire body of work: "commonsensical yet by no means over-pragmatic, suspicious of propaganda without ever indulging in knowingly cynical hindsight, not afraid to let rip on occasion with a juicy chunk of narrative or characterization, but as far removed as could be from mere romantic sensationalism." The *Times Literary Supplement* credited Burn for "restor[ing] to their natural clarity waters that have been for too long muddied by fruitless scholarly controversy."

Burn told *CA:* "Why do I write? Believe it or not, to try to make the world better, even if by an amount not visible to the naked eye. It is a matter of earliest influences—I was born in [a] Shropshire rectory, brought up by very good and fairly enlightened, Victorian-educated parents, and destined for the Church—but I could not accept the theology. So I kept the ethics and chucked the dogma.

"*Man: A Brief History* [an unpublished work] contains much thought on Marx, whose works are of major importance to the understanding of modern human society. I conclude that while we cannot do much about changing our genetically-conditioned natures, *social* conditions can do much, for good or ill, about how we channel those natures—producing, for instance, Athenians or Spartans. The book will end, if I live to finish it, with a severe criticism of what Marxist-Leninist parties have done in practice, for they have evolved all the worst characteristics of intolerant churches."

BIOGRAPHICAL/CRITICAL SOURCES:

PERIODICALS

American Political Science Review, December, 1937.
Best Sellers, June 1, 1969.
Boston Transcript, October 23, 1937, p. 2.
Canadian Forum, August, 1961.
Choice, October, 1969.
Christian Science Monitor, June 8, 1961, p. 11.
International Journal of Ethics, January, 1938.
Library Journal, February 1, 1961; July, 1969.
Nation, December 24, 1949.
New Statesman & Nation, July 11, 1936.
New York Times, July 11, 1948, p. 12.
San Francisco Chronicle, July 11, 1948, p. 12.
Saturday Review of Literature, July 3, 1948; December 31, 1949.
Times Educational Supplement, October 24, 1980.
Times Literary Supplement, March 27, 1937, p. 230; January 17, 1948, p. 42; April 21, 1961, p. 248; July 12, 1963, p. 508; March 6, 1969, p. 234; May 9, 1980.
Yale Review, June, 1963.*

* * *

BURNETT, Constance Buel 1893-1975

PERSONAL: Born May 15, 1893, in New York, NY; died in 1975; daughter of Clarence Clough (an editor) and Mary Alice (Snow) Buel; married Vivian Burnett, November 21, 1914 (deceased); children: Verity Chisholm, Dorinda Le Clair. *Education:* Attended Brearley School, New York, NY, and Kent Place School, Summit, NJ.

CAREER: Writer.

WRITINGS:

The Shoemaker's Son (Junior Literary Guild selection), Random House (New York City), 1941.
(Contributor) *Topflight,* Nelson, 1946.
Lucretia Mott, Bobbs-Merrill (New York City), 1951.
Five for Freedom, Abelard-Schuman (New York City), 1953, reprinted as *Five for Freedom: Lucretia Mott, Elizabeth Cady Stanton, Lucy Stone, Susan B. Anthony, Carrie Chapman Cott,* Greenwood Press (Westport, CT), 1968.
The Silver Answer: A Romantic Biography of Elizabeth Barrett Browning, illustrated by Susan Foster, Knopf (New York City), 1955.
Let the Best Boat Win: The Story of America's Greatest Yacht Designer, illustrated by John O'Hara Cosgrave II, Houghton (Boston, MA), 1957.
Captain John Ericsson, Father of the Monitor, Vanguard, 1960.
Happily Ever After: A Portrait of Frances Hodgson Burnett, Vanguard, 1965.

SIDELIGHTS: Constance Buel Burnett published the first of several juvenile biographies in 1941, when she was a widow nearing fifty years of age. *The Shoemaker's Son* is a biography of storyteller Hans Christian Andersen. It is, according to *Books* reviewer M. L. Becker, reminiscent of Andersen's own tale of the ugly duckling. Burnett wrote of Andersen's birth into poverty in early nineteenth-century Denmark and the struggles he endured on the road to fame. A. M. Jordan described the biography in *Horn Book* as an "appealing picture of [Andersen's] childlike nature and awkward person" and praised the author for evoking an image "so animated and spontaneous, so exasperating and lovable." The *Christian Science Monitor* reported: "Miss Burnett has written warmly and with sympathy . . . about the naive, impractical, grotesque yet lovable being whose genius and inordinate ambition won him friends and ridicule, criticism, . . . and popularity." *Library Journal* reviewer Eleanor Kidder found *The Shoemaker's Son* "spontaneous and well-synthesized," noting that Burnett "made the difficult personality . . . neither too grotesque nor too sentimental."

Five for Freedom uses the biographies of five early feminists to paint what *Kirkus Reviews* called "the history of women's rights." The five women that Burnett selected were Lucretia Mott, Elizabeth Cady Stanton, Lucy Stone, Susan B. Anthony, and Carrie Chapman Catt. "One does not read of five separate lives," however, wrote Elizabeth Yates in the *Christian Science Monitor,* "but of the development of a single idea which unified five women over the span of a century and a continent." This was accomplished, Yates suggested, by Burnett's "flowing narrative' and "eager pace . . . matched by earnestness of purpose."

The Silver Answer: A Romantic Biography of Elizabeth Barrett Browning presents Browning's "character and personality through the . . . sharply contrasting periods of her life," reported *Horn Book.* One of these periods was her romance with Robert Browning, a story that Burnett relates "with delicacy and perception," according to *New York Times* reviewer M. C. Scoggin. *Kirkus Reviews* commented that "[their] halting romance and eventual happiness get full and tender treatment here," and *Library Journal* recommended *The Silver Answer* as "completely absorbing."

Let the Best Boat Win: The Story of America's Greatest Yacht Designer reflects Burnett's personal interest in sailing. It is the story of Nathanael Greene Herreshoff, who designed, built, and raced his boats during what *Horn Book* called "the heyday of pleasure sailing." *Kirkus Reviews* reported that Burnett tells the story of triumph and tragedy with "[c]ompassion, enthusiasm, clarity, simplicity and sincerity." *Saturday Review* praised the author for her ability to "[emphasize] Herreshoff's uniqueness without caricaturing him." Another story of success and failure and eccentricity is *Captain John Ericsson, Father of the Monitor.* Once again, the author was praised for her sensitivity in portraying an unusual personality in a sympathetic way. This biography was also commended for its detail about many of Ericsson's mechanical inventions and for what a *Kirkus Review* critic called "a colorful picture of the period [1803-1889] and . . . of the torment and elation of adventure."

Burnett's final book, *Happily Ever After: A Portrait of Frances Hodgson Burnett,* is the biography of her mother-in-law, the writer who created *Little Lord Fauntleroy.* Like some of Burnett's earlier subjects, Frances began her life in poverty and struggled valiantly to achieve success. When she finally arrived at the pinnacle of her career, Frances's success was, according to *Commonweal* reviewer E. M. Graves, nothing short of "phenomenal." *Horn Book* praised the account as simultaneously objective and sympathetic.

BIOGRAPHICAL/CRITICAL SOURCES:

PERIODICALS

Booklist, November 15, 1941; May 1, 1953; May 1, 1955; December 15, 1957; May 15, 1961.

Bookmark, April, 1961.

Books, November 2, 1941, p. 9.

Book Week, July 4, 1965, p. 9.

Chicago Sunday Tribune, November 17, 1957, p. 44; May 14, 1961, Section 2, p. 13.

Christian Science Monitor, November 8, 1941, p. 10; May 28, 1953, p. 11; March 31, 1955, p. 11; November 7, 1957, p. 16; May 11, 1961, p. 4-B.

Commonweal, May 28, 1965.

Horn Book, November, 1941; June, 1955; December, 1957; June, 1965.

Kirkus Reviews, August 15, 1952; February 1, 1955; September 1, 1957; October 1, 1960.

Library Journal, October 15, 1941; April 15, 1955; December 1, 1957; February 15, 1961; July, 1965.

New Yorker, September 20, 1941; November 26, 1955.

New York Herald Tribune Book Review, June 12, 1955, p. 6; November 17, 1957, p. 8.
New York Times, May 22, 1955, p. 26.
New York Times Book Review, March 26, 1961, p. 36; July 11, 1965, p. 34.
San Francisco Chronicle, May 24, 1953, p. 27; May 22, 1955, p. 21.
Saturday Review, November 16, 1957.
Saturday Review of Literature, November 8, 1941.
Springfield Republican, April 26, 1953, p. 7-C.*

* * *

BURNS, E(dward) Bradford 1932-

PERSONAL: Born August 28, 1932, in Muscatine, IA; son of Edward Sylvester (a mayor) and Wanda A. (Schwandke) Burns. *Education:* University of Iowa, B.A., 1954; Tulane University, M.A., 1955; Columbia University, Ph.D., 1964; foreign study at University of San Carlos, Guatemala, 1953, University of Lisbon, 1955-56, and Central University of Caracas, 1959-60. *Religion:* Episcopalian. *Avocational interests:* Competent in Spanish and Portuguese, has been in Brazil on several occasions, and has traveled throughout other Latin America countries and in Europe.

ADDRESSES: Office—Department of History, University of California, Los Angeles, CA 90024.

CAREER: Researcher in Brazil, principally in Historical Archives of Itamaraty, 1962-63; State University of New York at Buffalo, assistant professor of history, 1963-64; University of California, Los Angeles, assistant professor of history, 1964-67; Columbia University, New York City, associate professor of history, 1967-69; University of California, Los Angeles, professor of history, 1969—. Council on Foreign Relations, Portuguese and Spanish language consultant, 1961-64; National Council of Churches, Latin America area lecturer, 1963-66; also lecturer at University of Parana and University of Brazil. *Military service:* U.S. Navy, 1956-59; became lieutenant junior grade.

MEMBER: American Historical Association, Conference on Latin American Studies, Academy of Political Science, Society for the History of Discoveries, Association of Brazilian Historians (executive secretary, 1964-65), Instituto Historico e Geographico Brasilerio, Pacific Coast Council on Latin American Studies (president, 1973-74), Phi Beta Kappa, Phi Sigma Iota.

AWARDS, HONORS: Ford Foundation grant; Rockefeller Foundation fellowship for further research on Brazilian foreign policy (in Brazil), 1966-67; Bolton Prize for *Perspectives on Brazilian History,* 1967; Fulbright fellowship, 1974; other fellowships for study in South and Central America.

WRITINGS:

The Unwritten Alliance, Rio-Branco and Brazilian-American Relations, Columbia University Press (New York City), 1966.
(Editor) *A Documentary History of Brazil,* Knopf (New York City), 1966.
(Editor) *Perspectives on Brazilian History,* Columbia University Press, 1967.
Nationalism in Brazil: A Historical Survey, Praeger (New York City), 1967.
A History of Brazil, Columbia University Press, 1970.
Latin America: A Concise Interpretive History, Prentice-Hall (Englewood Cliffs, NJ), 1972.
Latin American Cinema: Film and History, Latin American Center, University of California, Los Angeles, 1975.
(With Thomas E. Skidmore) *Elites, Masses, and Modernization in Latin America, 1850-1930,* University of Texas Press (Austin, TX), 1979.
The Poverty of Progress: Latin America in the Nineteenth Century, University of California Press (Berkeley, CA), 1980.
Eadweard Muybridge in Guatemala, 1875: The Photographer as Social Recorder, University of California Press, 1986.
At War in Nicaragua: The Reagan Doctrine and the Politics of Nostalgia, Harper (New York City), 1987.
Patriarch and Folk: The Emergence of Nicaragua, 1798-1858, Harvard University Press (Cambridge, MA), 1991.
(Editor) *Latin America: Conflict and Creation; A Historical Reader,* Prentice-Hall, 1993.
Kinship with the Land: Regionalist Thought in Iowa, 1894-1942, University of Iowa Press (Iowa City, IA), 1996.

Contributor of articles on Latin American history to scholarly journals in United States, Panama, Brazil, and Portugal.

SIDELIGHTS: E. Bradford Burns's first book was welcomed by scholars in the field of early twentieth-century Brazilian-American studies, a field that *Choice* claimed "has long needed an exhaustive analysis." C. G. Fenwick described *The Unwritten Alliance: Rio-Branco and Brazilian-American Relations* in the *Annals of the American Academy of Political and Social Science* as "the story of the beginning of a friendship between the two countries which has lasted . . . not so much because of the common material interests of the two countries as because of . . . the statesmen guiding their policies." The *Choice* reviewer remarked: "There is no comparable work in English."

The edited collection, *A Documentary History of Brazil,* was an equally welcome volume. According to *Choice,* "There is no work like it in either English or Portuguese." Burns's collection includes information from a variety of sources: official documents, travel pieces and memoirs, as well as creative works like novels and poems. The editor arranged the pieces according to their historical period and included a variety of themes—"political evolution, territorial expansion, and cultural fusion," as a *Library Journal* contributor reported. *Choice* recommended the work as "further testimony to [Burns's] competence."

Another edited work also earned high praise. In the *Annals of the American Academy of Political and Social Science,* J. M. Young described the selection process that Burns employed for *Perspectives on Brazilian History:* eligible essays "probed Brazil's past, provided wider perspective, served as critical selective guides to the historical literature, and provided some discussion of the major problems posed by the study of the evolution of Brazil." A *Choice* contributor commented: "All of the essays . . . contribute much material toward fuller understanding of Brazil." That reviewer made a point of noting that Burns's introduction "is as valuable a contribution as the writings of the other . . . authors." Young's conclusion was unequivocal: "The impact of this book on Brazilian historiography is what Frederick Jackson Turner's frontier thesis was for American historiography."

Nationalism in Brazil: A Historical Survey was not so widely admired. T. E. Skidmore called it "a weak book on an important subject." In the *American Historical Review,* Skidmore faulted Burns for failing to differentiate various types of nationalism and nationalistic sentiments, for several ostensible omissions, and for "seldom [making] clear whether he is talking about thought or about action." E. E. Godfrey found value in the book, however, reporting in the *Annals of the American Academy of Political and Social Science* that the final chapters "[exhibit] originality." Godfrey also noted Burns's observation "that any Brazilian government will ignore long-established nationalist aspirations at its own peril." A *Choice* reviewer declared: "Burns has the facility to compress great historical areas without losing sight of essential material." *Choice* recommended *Nationalism in Brazil* as a wide-ranging account that covers all perspectives of the topic—not only political, military, and economic, but cultural and social as well.

The book *A History of Brazil* is an interdisciplinary study that ranges from the discovery of Brazil by Europeans through the 1960s. *Choice* reported: "Burns, in an attractive style, manages to include a great deal of basic information." *Library Journal* reviewer Gerald Cole predicted that *A History of Brazil* "is destined to become a standard item for all reading lists on Brazil."

BIOGRAPHICAL/CRITICAL SOURCES:

PERIODICALS

American Historical Review, October, 1966; October, 1969.

American Political Science Review, March, 1968.

Annals of the American Academy of Political and Social Science, September, 1966; July, 1969; September, 1971.

Choice, October, 1966; May, 1968; May, 1969; June, 1971; December, 1972.

Library Journal, June 1, 1966; May 1, 1967; November 1, 1968; January 15, 1971.

Social Studies, November, 1973.

* * *

BURROWS, Millar 1889-1980

PERSONAL: Born October 26, 1889, in Wyoming, OH; died April 29, 1980, in Ann Arbor, MI; son of Edwin Jones (in business) and Katharine (Millar) Burrows; married Irene Gladding, July 6, 1915 (died January 15, 1967); children: Edwin Gladding. *Education:* Cornell University, B.A., 1912; Union Theological Seminary, New York City, M.Div., 1915; Yale University, Ph.D., 1925.

CAREER: Ordained Presbyterian minister, 1915; pastor of Presbyterian churches in rural Texas, 1915-19;

Interchurch World Movement, New York City, rural survey supervisor for Texas, 1919-20; Tusculum College, Greenville, TN, professor of Bible and college pastor, 1920-23; Brown University, Providence, RI, assistant professor, 1925-29, associate professor, 1929-32, professor of Biblical literature and history of religions, 1932-34; Yale University, New Haven, CT, Winckley Professor of Biblical Theology, 1934-58; writer and researcher. American University of Beirut, visiting professor, 1930-31; American School of Oriental Research in Jerusalem, director, 1931-32, 1947-48; American Schools of Oriental Research, president, 1934-48. American Middle East Relief, member, 1954.

WRITINGS:

Founders of Great Religions: Being Personal Sketches of Famous Leaders, Scribner (New York City), 1931.

Bible Religion: Its Growth in the Scriptures, Abingdon (Nashville, TN), 1938.

What Mean These Stones?: The Significance of Archeology for Biblical Studies, American Schools of Oriental Research (Philadelphia, PA), 1941.

Outline of Biblical Theology, Westminster (Philadelphia), 1946.

Palestine Is Our Business, Westminster, 1949.

The Dead Sea Scrolls, with translations by the author, Viking (New York City), 1955.

More Light on the Dead Sea Scrolls: New Scrolls and New Interpretations, with Translations of Important Recent Discoveries, Viking, 1958.

Diligently Compared, Thomas Nelson (Nashville), 1964.

(Contributor) Harry Thomas Frank and William L. Reed, editors, *Translating and Understanding the Old Testament: Essays in Honor of Herbert Gordon May,* Abingdon, 1970.

(Contributor) James L. Crenshaw and John T. Wiles, editors, *Essays in Old Testament Ethics,* Ktav (New York City), 1974.

Jesus in the First Three Gospels, Abingdon, 1977.

Contributor to numerous journals in his field.

SIDELIGHTS: When Millar Burrows published *Founders of Great Religions: Being Personal Sketches of Famous Leaders,* critics accorded the author their respect and admiration. Burrows, a Presbyterian minister, included brief biographies of such religious figures as Lao-tze, Confucius, Mahavira, Buddha, Zoroaster, Moses, Mohammed, Nanak, and Jesus. In addition to biographical detail for each individual, Burrows added what a *Saturday Review of Literature* contributor called "an illuminating study of the historical background and a clear analysis of the main principles of each [religion]." Furthermore, as A. S. Woodburne reported in the *Crozer Quarterly,* Burrows "endeavors to give his readers an insight into the soul of [each] leader. The result is not only an excellent portrait, but one that possesses the added charm of a good literary style." *Christian Century* reviewer A. E. Haydon was particularly impressed with the honesty of the work. Haydon wrote: "The last chapter in which the author makes a summary of the agreement and difference in the ideas and ideals of the religious leaders, reveals not only a genuine understanding of the religions but also, a much rarer thing, an ability to be thoroughly objective in dealing with faiths not his own."

Burrows spent many years engaged in archaeological research in the Holy Land. He directed the American School of Oriental Research in Jerusalem and served as the president of the American Schools of Oriental Research for nearly fifteen years. During that time he wrote *What Mean These Stones? The Significance of Archeology for Biblical Studies,* a survey of archaeological discoveries that have shed light on various parts of the Christian Bible. "The book is just what the general Bible student has long needed," announced the *Christian Century,* a survey that addresses not only the biblical text and language(s) in which it was written, but also "its historic, material, religious and ethical backgrounds." I. G. Matthews commented in the *Crozer Quarterly:* "To understand the Bible is more important than to defend it. We . . . [hope] that this volume will be of value to the many divergent groups interested in a better understanding of the Bible."

Another of Burrows's contributions to the understanding of the Bible is his *Outline of Biblical Theology.* In it, according to *Crozer Quarterly* reviewer E. E. Aubrey, Burrows "seeks first to discover what the Bible says, then whether the conception under study is tenable, and finally [what its relevance is today]." S. V. McCasland commended the author in *Christian Century:* "With fidelity to the most exacting standards of research in the history, archeology, languages and cultures of Hebrew and Christian antiquity, yet with a sympathetic insight into the problems of our time . . . , he has written a survey of the enormous range of biblical ideas whose every sentence is helpful and exciting." Likewise, Aubrey urged, "At a time when so much neoorthodox theology is read into the Bible and made normative as 'the biblical viewpoint,' it is highly important that students of theology should

. . . use Dr. Burrows' book to recover a sound perspective in the exegesis of scriptures."

When the Dead Sea Scrolls were discovered in 1947, Burrows was there, and he remained closely connected with subsequent research on the documents. In 1955 he published *The Dead Sea Scrolls,* the complete account of discovery and research up to the time of publication. In addition, Burrows included his own translations of some of the original scrolls. W. F. Albright wrote in the *New York Herald Tribune Book Review* that Burrows "is better qualified to write this book than perhaps anyone else in the English-speaking world." In addition to his scholarly credentials, Albright explained, the most qualified writer "must also be able to write clearly and . . . [to] show good judgment in distinguishing between fact and fancy, historical probability and tangential speculation. In both these respects, Mr. Burrows stands high." One of the most laudatory commendations was penned by *New York Times* critic Nelson Glueck: "Burrows' book is an invaluable guide both for the uninformed and the deeply initiated attracted to this new wonderland of widened horizons of religious experience and expression in the Holy Land."

The Dead Sea Scrolls became a best-seller in the popular market, despite its scholarly theme. *More Light on the Dead Sea Scrolls* continues the story of discovery and analysis. To the surprise of some critics, the ongoing analysis of the scrolls did not reduce the quantity of disputable issues that had occupied scholars for years; rather, it raised new questions and generated new controversies. The complexities of these issues, examined in the same meticulous detail that characterized Burrows's earlier works, discouraged some critics from recommending the sequel to the general reader, but few dismissed it as unimportant or questioned its value. A *Kirkus Reviews* critic recommended *More Light on the Dead Sea Scrolls* as "an important work with a doubled edged appeal" to readers "drawn by the desire to know more about the life and times of Christ" and to archaeologists and researchers who will appreciate the rigor of Burrows's research and the intellectual restraint that he imposes on his interpretations.

BIOGRAPHICAL/CRITICAL SOURCES:

BOOKS

Burrows, Edwin Gladding, *The Cup and the Unicorn: Episodes from a Life; Millar Burrows, 1889-1980,* privately printed, 1981.

PERIODICALS

Booklist, December, 1931; December 15, 1955; June 1, 1958.
Books, January 3, 1932, p. 10.
Boston Transcript, September 23, 1931, p. 2.
Catholic World, August, 1958.
Christian Century, September 16, 1931; January 7, 1942; March 12, 1947.
Christian Science Monitor, December 8, 1955, p. 9; June 2, 1958, p. 13.
Crozer Quarterly, January, 1932; January, 1942; April, 1947.
Kirkus Reviews, September 1, 1955; March 15, 1958.
Library Journal, December 1, 1955; May 1, 1958.
Manchester Guardian, September 9, 1958, p. 4.
New York Herald Tribune Book Review, December 11, 1955, p. 4; June 15, 1958, p. 6.
New York Times, September 13, 1931, p. 12; November 20, 1955, p. 54.
San Francisco Chronicle, December 11, 1949, p. 26; December 11, 1955, p. 20.
Saturday Review of Literature, October 17, 1931.
Survey, November 1, 1931; February, 1950.

OBITUARIES:

PERIODICALS

New York Times, May 3, 1980.*

* * *

BURT, Nathaniel 1913-

PERSONAL: Born November 21, 1913, in Moose, WY; son of Maxwell Struthers (an author) and Katharine (Newlin) Burt (an author); married Margaret Clinton, August 5, 1942; children: Margery Brooke, Christopher Clinton. *Education:* New York University, B.S. (music education), 1939; Princeton University, M.F.A., 1949. *Politics:* Democrat. *Religion:* Episcopalian.

ADDRESSES: Home—13 Campbelton Cir., Princeton, NJ 08540.

CAREER: Princeton University, Princeton, NJ, teacher in music department, 1939-41, 1950-52; Westminster Choir School, Princeton, teacher in music department, 1950-51; full-time writer, 1954—. Composer, with performed works that include a ballet, "Chanson Innocente," and an orchestral overture, "The Elegy of Lycidas." Princeton Chamber Orchestra, vice-president. *Military service:* U.S. Naval Reserve, active duty, 1942-45; served as communications officer in Pacific theater; became lieutenant.

MEMBER: Authors League of America, PEN, Princeton Historical Society, Friends of Music of Princeton University (chair), Atheneum (Philadelphia; trustee), Franklin Inn (Philadelphia), Rittenhouse Club (Philadelphia); Coffee House Club (New York City), Nassau Club (Princeton), Century Association (New York City).

WRITINGS:

Rooms in a House and Other Poems, 1931-1944, Scribner (New York City), 1947.

Question on a Kite (poetry), Scribner, 1950.

Scotland's Burning (novel), Little, Brown (Boston, MA), 1954.

Make My Bed (novel), Little, Brown, 1957.

The Perennial Philadelphians: The Anatomy of an American Aristocracy, Little, Brown, 1963.

War Cry of the West: The Story of the Powder River (juvenile), illustrated by Brinton Turkle, Holt (New York City), 1964.

Leopards in the Garden (novel), Little, Brown, 1968.

First Families: The Making of an American Aristocracy, Little, Brown, 1970.

Palaces for the People: A Social History of the American Art Museum, Little, Brown, 1977.

Jackson Hole Journal, University of Oklahoma Press (Norman, OK), 1983.

Wyoming, with photographs by Don Pitcher, Compass American Guides (Oakland, CA), 1991.

Also co-author of *Literary Heritage of New Jersey* (Volume 20 of 300th anniversary series), 1964. Contributor to *Musical Quarterly, Town and Country,* and other periodicals.

SIDELIGHTS: Nathaniel Burt has achieved success in a variety of genres. His first poetry collection was well received, as was his first novel and his first work of social history.

Reviewers of *Rooms in a House and Other Poems, 1931-1944* noted a connection between the lyric quality of Burt's poetry and his original profession as a musician and composer. Robert Hillyer commented in the *Saturday Review of Literature:* "When he is at his simplest and most melodic, [Burt's] lyrics are beautiful." The critic then praised his "well-wrought epigram" and likened Burt's sonnets to those of Shakespeare and Petrarch, and concluded: "When we add that such a poem as 'Tower of Roland' has the magic of incantation, we have accorded him an almost Draytonian variety." Elizabeth Johnson informed readers of the *New York Times:* "His verse has the old-fashioned cachet of slight wistfulness and sometimes whimsy. This is not wholly a drawback, for Mr. Burt's imagery is often trenchant and vivid." Calling Burt an author "who probably has a good deal to say," the *Christian Science Monitor* predicted a promising future.

Burt's first novel is *Scotland's Burning,* "a haunting and quite profound story," as G. H. Favre described it in the *Chicago Sunday Tribune,* of a young boy's experiences at a private American preparatory school. Favre and other critics noted that Burt described life at a boys' school accurately and believably, although, as J. H. Jackson observed in the *San Francisco Chronicle,* "Burt chooses not to sensationalize, as so many have done with this background." Jackson found *Scotland's Burning* to be "[w]ritten with great perception and in sensitive, genuinely distinguished prose." *Library Journal* reviewer R. W. Henderson called it "[a] psychological novel . . . of the mental confusion, heartaches and loyalties of prep school life." A *Nation* contributor recommended the novel as an insightful exploration of "evil, fear, and responsibility." "This is an excellent book," stated Gene Baro in the *New York Herald Tribune Book Review;* "here is a microcosm of the great world rendered with restraint and artistry."

Another novel, *Make My Bed,* is a lighter story about a young woman who can't decide which of her admirers to marry. The *San Francisco Chronicle* called it "[a] refreshing novel" in which the author "achieves a gentle suspense." In the *New York Herald Tribune Book Review,* Sylvia Stallings appreciated Burt's sensitive depiction of the woman's dilemma: "It is all described with wit and sympathy, not forgetting the three young people's honest struggles to reach an understanding of themselves while coming to terms with each other." Henry Cavendish of the *New York Times* called *Make My Bed* "a breezy novel of academic sophistication."

In *The Perennial Philadelphians: The Anatomy of an American Aristocracy,* Burt turned his attention to what might be classified as a social history of upper-class Philadelphia. In his foreword, Burt makes it clear that his book is meant to be an introduction, not a comprehensive exploration or a judgment of

Philadelphia's upper crust; nevertheless, critical reception was mixed. J. H. Berg (who happened to be a Philadelphia native) wrote in the *Christian Science Monitor:* "Mr. Burt has painted a vivid portrait aided by a sharp eye, a sharp ear, a sharp wit, and a brush tip sharp enough to draw a few drops of Old Philadelphia blood." Berg found the entire book, "including Appendix, Acknowledgments, Reading List and Index completely fascinating." Carl Bridenbaugh of the *New York Times Book Review* observed the same brush tip at work, though from a markedly different perspective. He commented: "Many members of the gentry in Philadelphia and elsewhere, though willing at once to concede this to be one of the best books ever written about them will, at the same time, have to brand Nathaniel Burt 'a traitor to his class'. . . . This, surely, is not Old Philadelphia Good Taste." A *Reporter* critic suggested: "To someone who is a relative stranger to Philadelphia, so many pages of concern with a small group of families seems odd and quirkish, the social history of an unlikely enclave. . . . Mr. Burt . . . gives the impression that Philadelphia exists only in so far as it is recognized by what he finally calls the gentry."

In recent years, Burt has turned his attention to the American West. *War Cry of the West: The Story of the Powder River* is a retelling for children of the history of Wyoming published in 1938 by his father, author Maxwell Struthers Burt. The newer version, commented Iris Vinton in the *New York Times Book Review,* retains all "of the verve and style of the original." *War Cry of the West* begins in prehistory and brings the young reader to the present day through colonization by Indians and later by white settlers, warfare among Indians and with the white soldiers, and eventually the arrival of the twentieth-century "dude ranch." Vinton commented: "There's a big feast of true adventure in this small book."

BIOGRAPHICAL/CRITICAL SOURCES:

PERIODICALS

Best Sellers, October 15, 1963.
Booklist, February 1, 1954.
Book Week, October 13, 1963, p. 6.
Book World, September 27, 1970, p. 4.
Catholic World, May, 1954.
Chicago Sunday Tribune, January 17, 1954, p. 13.
Christian Science Monitor, June 21, 1947, p. 11; March 25, 1954, p. 11; October 17, 1963, p. 10.
Horn Book, August, 1964.
Kirkus Reviews, November 1, 1953.
Library Journal, December 15, 1953; October 1, 1963; February 15, 1964; August, 1970.
Nation, January 9, 1954.
New Statesman & Nation, October 23, 1954.
New Yorker, February 20, 1954; November 16, 1963.
New York Herald Tribune Book Review, January 17, 1954, p. 1; November 17, 1957, p. 3.
New York Times, August 10, 1947, p. 10; January 17, 1954, p. 5; November 17, 1957, p. 52.
New York Times Book Review, October 13, 1963, p. 1; May 10, 1964, p. 28; September 13, 1970, p. 73.
Reporter, October 24, 1963.
San Francisco Chronicle, January 20, 1954, p. 19; December 15, 1957, p. 21.
Saturday Review, February 27, 1954.
Saturday Review of Literature, June 21, 1947.
Time, February 1, 1954.
Times Literary Supplement, November 5, 1954, p. 701.

* * *

BURTON, (Alice) Elizabeth 1908-
(Susan Alice Kerby)

PERSONAL: Born October 4, 1908, in Cairo, Egypt; daughter of Richard and A. S. G. (Kerby) Burton; married John Theodore Aitken (divorced). *Politics:* Liberal. *Religion:* Church of England.

ADDRESSES: Home—Witney, Oxfordshire OX8 6N2, England. *Agent*—John Farquharson Ltd., 162-168 Regent St., London W1R 5TB, England.

CAREER: Writer. Has also worked in journalism, radio, and advertising.

WRITINGS:

Cling to Her, Waiting (novel), Andrew Dakers, 1939.
The Elizabethans at Home: On Everyday Life in the Time of Elizabeth I, illustrated by Felix Kelly, Secker & Warburg, 1958, published as *The Pageant of Elizabethan England,* Scribner (New York City), 1959.
The Pageant of Stuart England, Scribner, 1962 (published in England as *The Jacobeans at Home,* Secker & Warburg, 1962).
Here Is England (Junior Book of the Month Club selection), Farrar, Straus (New York City), 1965.

The Georgians at Home, 1714-1830, illustrated by Kelly, Longmans, Green (London, England), 1967, published as *The Pageant of Georgian England,* Scribner, 1968.

The Pageant of Early Victorian England, 1837-1861, illustrated by Kelly, Scribner, 1972 (published in England as *The Early Victorians at Home, 1837-1861,* Longman, 1972).

Elizabethans, Georgians, and Early Victorians, Arrow, 1973.

Victorians, Readers Union, 1974.

The Pageant of Early Tudor England: 1485-1558, illustrated by Kelly, Scribner, 1976 (published in England as *The Early Tudors at Home,* Alan Lane, 1976).

Contributor to magazines and newspapers.

NOVELS; UNDER PSEUDONYM SUSAN ALICE KERBY

Fortnight in Frascati, Andrew Dakers, 1940.

Miss Carter and the Ifrit, Hutchinson, 1945, reprinted, Arno Press (New York City), 1978.

Fortune's Gift, Dodd (New York City), 1947 (published in England as *Many Strange Birds,* Hutchinson, 1947).

The Roaring Dove, Dodd, 1948 (published in England as *Gone to Grass,* Hutchinson, 1948).

Mr. Kronion, Werner Laurie, 1949.

Fortune's Gift has been translated into French.

SIDELIGHTS: Elizabeth Burton is the author of several popular histories of everyday life in England during different periods of history. Eschewing the subjects of academic history such as politics, warfare, and economics, Burton focuses on daily household activities. She writes about homes and their furnishings, gardens and food, fashion and adornment, illnesses and medicines. Using a variety of sources, including official documents, letters, diaries, memoirs, and contemporary printed materials, she describes both the vanities of the rich and the miseries of the poor.

The first volume was published in the United States as *The Pageant of Elizabethan England.* "This book could please a wide diversity of people," wrote E. B. Hungerford in the *Chicago Sunday Tribune,* "from cooks to gardeners to historians." It did not please some historians, however, who faulted the author for what *New York Times* critic L. B. Wright called "facile generalizations that are often wide of the mark." The *Times Literary Supplement* also complained about omissions in the bibliography of sources. Reviewers like Paul Kendall of the *New York Herald Tribune Book Review* dismissed such issues: "[If] her recapturing of the past is a trifle on the superficial side, it is, after all, the surfaces of living that she is holding up to our gaze." Hungerford insisted that Burton "writes with charm and a bright wit that thrusts at the vanities of fashion." While the *Manchester Guardian* offered a mixed review, the critic remarked: "It is most refreshing to find one so enthusiastic about these things who can yet keep her head and be severely critical of Elizabethan taste." W. H. Dunham told readers of the *Yale Review:* "The Pageant is . . . lively, and Miss Burton has lifted social history from the slough of antiquarianism."

Burton next published *The Pageant of Stuart England,* which describes both the opulence of the Stuart court and the subsequent austerity of Cromwell and his retinue. "Admirers of the earlier book will enjoy this," reported R. R. Rea in *Library Journal.* Indeed, a *New Yorker* critic was even more impressed with the second volume than with the first, calling it "detailed, precise, charmingly opinionated, funny, and right." Again, the *Times Literary Supplement* criticized the quality of Burton's bibliography and hinted at possible inaccuracies, but even that reviewer characterized *The Pageant of Stuart England* as "a most amusing book about everyday things long ago."

The Pageant of Georgian England covers the years from 1714 to 1830. *Library Journal*'s Paul von Khrum recommended the volume as "[a] thoroughly readable social history" enhanced by the author's "lack of pretention" and enlivened by "her occasional sharp wit." Similarly, *Choice* commended this history "filled with interesting examples drawn from all levels of society, loosely linked with sometimes pungent comment." A later work, *The Pageant of Early Victorian England, 1837-1861,* was described by the *Library Journal* as "an interesting and well-written narrative." A. J. Hamilton remarked in *America* that Burton "catches the spirit of the age" in her "kaleidoscopic journey."

BIOGRAPHICAL/CRITICAL SOURCES:

PERIODICALS

America, November 4, 1972.

Best Sellers, October 1, 1972.

Booklist, February 1, 1959.

Bookmark, March, 1959.

Chicago Sunday Tribune, February 1, 1959, p. 3.

Choice, June, 1969.
Kirkus Reviews, December 1, 1958.
Library Journal, February 1, 1959; January 1, 1963; April 15, 1968; July, 1968; July, 1972.
Manchester Guardian, October 3, 1958, p. 9.
New Statesman, November 8, 1958; August 11, 1972.
New Yorker, January 4, 1959; December 15, 1962.
New York Herald Tribune Book Review, January 25, 1959, p. 4.
New York Times, August 2, 1959, p. 18.
San Francisco Chronicle, March 8, 1959, p. 17.
Times Literary Supplement, October 3, 1958, p. 558; February 22, 1963, p. 122; July 21, 1972, p. 841.
Yale Review, September, 1959.

* * *

BUTLER, Beverly Kathleen 1932-

PERSONAL: Born May 4, 1932, in Fond du Lac, WI; daughter of Leslie Willis (an engineer) and Muriel (Anderson) Butler; married Theodore V. Olson, 1976. *Education:* Mount Mary College, B.A., 1954; Marquette University, M.A., 1961. *Religion:* Episcopalian. *Avocational interests:* Music, reading, travel, outdoor life, animals.

CAREER: Mount Mary College, Milwaukee, WI, teacher, 1962-74. Lecturer at schools, libraries, and clubs.

MEMBER: Allied Authors, Wisconsin Regional Writers Guild.

AWARDS, HONORS: 17th Summer-Dodd Mead prize, 1955, for *Song of the Voyageur;* Woodrow Wilson fellowship, 1960-61; Clara Ingram Judson Award, 1963, for *Light a Single Candle;* Johnson Foundation Award of Council for Wisconsin Writers, 1966, and Award of Merit for distinguished service to history, State Historical Society of Ohio, for *Feather in the Wind.*

WRITINGS:

ALL PUBLISHED BY DODD (NEW YORK CITY), EXCEPT AS NOTED

Song of the Voyageur, 1955.
The Lion and the Otter, 1957.
The Fur Lodge, 1959.
The Silver Key, 1961.
Light a Single Candle, 1962.
Feather in the Wind, 1965.
Captive Thunder, 1969.
The Wind and Me (verse), illustrated by Mircea Vasiliu, 1971.
Gift of Gold, 1972.
A Girl Named Wendy, 1976.
My Sister's Keeper, 1980.
Ghost Cat, 1984.
Maggie by My Side, 1987.
Witch's Fire, Cobblehill Books (New York City), 1994.

SIDELIGHTS: Beverly Butler is a Wisconsin native who lost her eyesight at age fourteen. Despite this challenge, she has established successful careers as a teacher, librarian and freelance writer. Her novels frequently involve themes of displacement, the trials of coming of age, a transforming ordeal, and young love. The love interest is frequently a person of foreign extraction or of Native American ancestry—individuals set apart as outsiders to the established, tight-knit frontier communities.

Song of the Voyageur, Butler's first novel, is set in the 1830s. The young heroine, Diane, leaves her home in Massachusetts, and moves to a lonely cabin outpost near a frontier town in Wisconsin. Following numerous hardships, she finally finds love and happiness with the half-Native American Jean Cormier. M. W. Reid of *Library Journal* praised the book's "fine feeling for human relationships and beauties of the countryside," while a *New York Herald Tribune Book Review* critic noted the "sensitive characterization, a delightful family, and vivid descriptions of sounds, smells, and sights."

In *The Lion and the Otter,* set in the 1760s, Jacques Saint Charles marries a Native American girl and his sister, Emilie, falls in love with an English soldier. In *Fur Lodge,* Jules Bochart, fourteen, accompanies a fur-trading expedition up the Minnesota River to the camp of the fierce Yankton Indians. Jules sustains a fourteen-day ordeal alone on the prairie with only three handfuls of corn for food when he strives to prove his manhood by volunteering to guard the expedition's furs. In *Feather in the Wind,* the year is 1832. With the threat of impending attack on their settlement by the Sauk Indians, a nineteen-year-old girl, Alex Lindsay, tries to convince her father to leave their lonely cabin and seek shelter in Fort Winnebago. She finds a romantic interest in a young Scotsman who is traveling with a blind orphan girl.

My Sister's Keeper is based on the historical events involving the forest fire that destroyed the Wisconsin lumber town of Peshtigo in 1871. Seventeen-year-old Mary James travels to the drought-stricken region to help her sister, Clara, with household duties during the latter half of her fourth pregnancy. The fun-loving, vain and flirtatious Mary is resentful of being summoned away from her own home to aid her dour older sister with the drudgery of her daily chores and the care of three young children. Mary soon finds herself infatuated, though, with Mary's handsome, dashing husband, Ellery. The sisters' already strained relationship is further tested by Mary's insistent vying for Ellery's attention. Their lives are overturned and reshaped by the forest fire that devastates their community. In its aftermath, Mary, disfigured by the fire, achieves a newfound respect for Clara, and an appreciation for the children and the family ties and responsibilities that bind them. Mary also accepts the attentions of their neighbor, Sigvard, whose company she originally had spurned. The book received a number of favorable reviews that commended its historical detail and sense of place and Butler's narrative skill in immersing the reader in the horrors of the forest fire. John Lansingh Bennett, in a *Best Sellers* review noted that "the changes wrought in each of the characters are solid, convincing and moving."

BIOGRAPHICAL/CRITICAL SOURCES:

PERIODICALS

Best Sellers, June, 1980, p. 119.
Booklist, May, 1980, p. 1266.
Book World, May 4, 1969, p. 32.
Chicago Sunday Tribune, November 13, 1955, p. 40; November 17, 1957, p. 48; November 1, 1959, p. 24.
Commonweal, November 5, 1965, p. 158; November 5, 1965, p. 158.
Language Arts, October, 1980, p. 792.
Library Journal, November 15, 1955, p. 2648.
New York Herald Tribune Book Review, November 13, 1955, p. 10; February 16, 1958, p. 10; February 21, 1960, p 10.
New York Herald Tribune Lively Arts, May 14, 1961, p. 31.
New York Times, November 27, 1955, p. 44; December 22, 1957, p. 16.
New York Times Book Review, February 13, 1966, p. 30; November 1, 1959, p. 28; March 19, 1961, p. 42; February 13, 1966, p. 30.
San Francisco Chronicle, November 13, 1955, p. 8.
School Library Journal, April, 1980, p. 120-1.
Springfield Republican, January 22, 1961, p. 4D.
Wisconsin Library Bulletin, January, 1958; May, 1961.*

* * *

BUTLER, Richard
See ALLBEURY, Theodore Edward le Bouthillier

* * *

BYRD, Max (W.) 1942-

PERSONAL: Born in 1942, in Atlanta, GA.

ADDRESSES: *Office*—Department of English, University of California, Davis, CA 95616-5224. *Agent*—Virginia Barber Literary Agency, 101 5th Ave., New York, NY 10011.

CAREER: Yale University, New Haven, CT, assistant professor, 1970-75, associate professor of English, 1975-76; University of California, Davis, associate professor, 1976-81, professor of English, 1981—. Worked on Squaw Valley Writers Conference staff.

AWARDS, HONORS: Shamus Award, Private Eye Writers of America, 1982, for *California Thriller.*

WRITINGS:

MYSTERY NOVELS; PUBLISHED BY BANTAM (NEW YORK CITY)

California Thriller, 1981.
Fly Away, Jill, 1982.
Finders Weepers, 1983.
Target of Opportunity, 1988.
Fuse Time, 1991.

HISTORICAL NOVELS; PUBLISHED BY BANTAM

Jefferson, 1993.
Jackson, 1997.

OTHER

Visits to Bedlam: Madness and Literature in the Eighteenth Century, University of South Carolina Press (Columbia), 1974.

(Editor) *Daniel Defoe: A Collection of Critical Essays,* Prentice-Hall (Englewood Cliffs, NJ), 1976.

London Transformed: Images of the City in the Eighteenth Century, Yale University Press (New Haven, CT), 1978.

Tristram Shandy (nonfiction), Allen & Unwin (Boston), 1985.

Also, contributor to the periodical *The Writer.*

SIDELIGHTS: Max Byrd is an author with diverse talents; he has written scholarly investigations into English literature, historical novels, and contemporary detective novels. Writing about the nonfiction book *London Transformed: Images of the City in the Eighteenth Century* for the *New Republic,* Alan Sillitoe found Byrd "interesting" in his explorations of "recurrent images of London at key points in the eighteenth century" through the poetic works of Daniel Defoe, Alexander Pope, Henry Fielding, James Boswell, Samuel Johnson, William Blake, and William Wordsworth. "It is a book about the way in which reality fails to live up to the noblest possibilities of language," remarked *Times Literary Supplement* contributor Pat Roger. "For Mr. Byrd is above all a critic of primary texts, and a very good one. He explores rather than analyzes, and he searches the metaphoric life of his chosen books for clues to the feeling within. Texture rather than structure dominates his discussion of each work. . . . We can be grateful to Mr. Byrd for his profound and eloquent exploration of the subject."

In a later scholarly volume, Byrd examined a single novel by eighteenth-century British novelist Laurence Sterne. The wit and sense of speech of *Tristram Shandy* are two elements discussed in this study, according to David Profumo in the *Times Literary Supplement.* The critic deemed Byrd "particularly good on the book's style, an area where so many others have been repetitious or dull."

In 1981 Byrd published his first novel, initiating a series featuring West Coast detective Mike Haller. *California Thriller* "set up an interesting and plausible plot situation," reflected Robin W. Winks in a *New Republic* review, but relied on violence for its ending. Winks felt that the book would "fulfill every expectation of those who like, and those who hate, detective fiction." Winks judged the second Haller novel, *Fly Away, Jill,* more successful, commending its tight plotting. Reviews of Byrd's subsequent novels, some of which continued the Haller series, highlighted virtues such as the vividness of his writing and his skill with characterization.

In 1993, Byrd's first historical novel, *Jefferson,* was published. Four years later, Byrd produced another within the genre—*Jackson.* Both books feature early United States presidents, the latter tells of "Andrew Jackson, not in any simple biographical sense," indicated Keith Henderson in a favorable *Christian Science Monitor* review, "but in the broader sense of how America's first great populist created a political and social vortex that drew in all kinds of people." *Library Journal* contributor Dawn Anderson similarly proclaimed that *Jackson* provides "wonderful insights into the people and times of our infant republic."

"Deftly balancing fact and fiction, Byrd invests his tale with color, emotion and grand historical drama," concluded a *Publishers Weekly* reviewer. "*Jackson* is colorfully told through several points of view," explained Gerald Walker in *Wall Street Journal,* primarily through the perspective of David Chase, an expatriate who moves back from Europe to be with family. Chase is commissioned to write an unfavorable biography of Jackson and in order to damage his presidential campaign. In the process of writing the biography, Chase becomes torn between completing the book as instructed or doing what he feels is best for the country. The voice and action of other characters, such as Hogwood, the man originally commissioned to write the negative portrait of Jackson but unable to complete it due to health issues, and Hogwood's daughter, with whom Chase has an affair, also help tell the story of the seventh president. "The gripping narrative reaches back in time to untangle the innuendoes, rumors, and heroic hype that surround and submerge General Jackson," lauded Margaret Flanagan in *Booklist.* "The heart of the book . . . is an enthralling, masterly account of the Battle of New Orleans in 1815," according to Walker, who maintained: "With *Jackson,* Mr. Byrd has vaulted . . . into the front rank of American historical novelists."

BIOGRAPHICAL/CRITICAL SOURCES:

PERIODICALS

Booklist, October 15, 1993, p. 417; March 15, 1997, p. 1224.

Christian Science Monitor, April 4, 1997, p. 15.

Georgia Review, winter, 1993, pp. 814-817.

Library Journal, January, 1997, p. 143.

Los Angeles Times Book Review, April 19, 1981, p. 6; January 31, 1982, p. 11; July 24, 1983, p. 6.

New Republic, May 13, 1978, pp. 29-31; August 22, 1981, p. 39; March 3, 1982, p. 38.
New York Times Book Review, March 19, 1978, p. 16; October 30, 1983, p. 31; November 6, 1988, p. 29; November 23, 1993, p. C20.
Publishers Weekly, December 2, 1996, p. 40.
Times Literary Supplement, March 28, 1975, p. 328; June 23, 1978, p. 689; November 29, 1985, p. 1352; December 27, 1985, p. 1478.
Tribune Books (Chicago), October 9, 1988, p. 7; March 3, 1991, p. 6.
Wall Street Journal, December 8, 1993, p. A12; May 14, 1997, p. 20.
Washington Post Book World, May 15, 1994, p. 4.
Writer, October, 1989; October, 1993.*

C

CADELL, (Violet) Elizabeth 1903-1989 (Harriet Ainsworth)

PERSONAL: Born November 10, 1903, in Calcutta, India; died, October 9, 1989; daughter of Frederick Reginald (a colonial officer) and Elizabeth (Lynch) Vandyke; married Henry Dunlop Raymond Mallock Cadell (a banker), 1928 (deceased); children: one son, one daughter. *Politics:* Conservative. *Religion:* Church of England.

CAREER: Novelist.

WRITINGS:

NOVELS

My Dear Aunt Flora, R. Hale (London), 1946.

Last Straw for Harriet, Morrow (New York City), 1947, published in England as *Fishy, Said the Admiral,* R. Hale, 1948.

River Lodge, R. Hale, 1948.

Gay Pursuit, Morrow, 1948, published in England as *Family Gathering,* R. Hale, 1979, published as *The Marrying Kind,* Morrow, 1980.

Iris in Winter, Morrow, 1949, reprinted, Thorndike Press (Thorndike, ME), 1996.

Brimstone in the Garden, Morrow, 1950.

Sun in the Morning (for young readers; Catholic Children's Book Club selection), Morrow, 1950, reprinted, Thorndike Press, 1996.

The Greenwood Shady, Hodder & Stoughton (London), 1951.

Enter Mrs. Belchamber, Morrow, 1951, reprinted, Thorndike Press, 1996, published in England as *The Frenchman and the Lady,* Hodder & Stoughton, 1952.

Men and Angels, Hodder & Stoughton, 1952.

Crystal Clear, Morrow, 1953, published in England as *Journey's Eve,* Hodder & Stoughton, 1953.

Spring Green, Hodder & Stoughton, 1953, reprinted, White Lion, 1973.

The Cuckoo in Spring, Morrow, 1954, reprinted, Thorndike Press, 1984.

Money to Burn, Hodder & Stoughton, 1954, Morrow, 1955, reprinted, White Lion, 1973.

Around the Rugged Rock, Morrow, 1954, reprinted Thorndike Press, 1995, published in England as *The Gentlemen Go By,* Hodder & Stoughton, 1964.

The Lark Shall Sing, Morrow, 1955, published as *The Singing Heart,* Berkley (New York City), 1959.

The Blue Sky of Spring, Hodder & Stoughton, 1956, reprinted, Coronet, 1973.

I Love a Lass, Morrow, 1956, reprinted, Thorndike Press, 1994.

Bridal Array, Hodder & Stoughton, 1957, reprinted, Corgi (London), 1973.

The Green Empress, Hodder & Stoughton, 1958, reprinted, Corgi, 1973.

Sugar Candy Cottage, Hodder & Stoughton, 1958.

Alice, Where Art Thou?, Hodder & Stoughton, 1959.

The Yellow Brick Road, Morrow, 1960, reprinted, White Lion, 1973.

Honey for Tea, Hodder & Stoughton, 1961, Morrow, 1962, reprinted, Thorndike Press, 1985.

Six Impossible Things, Morrow, 1961.

The Toy Sword, Morrow, 1962, reprinted, Thorndike Press, 1994, published in England as *Language of the Heart,* Hodder & Stoughton, 1962.

Letter to My Love, Hodder & Stoughton, 1963.

Mixed Marriage: The Diary of a Portuguese Bride, Hodder & Stoughton, 1963.

Come Be My Guest, Morrow, 1964, published in England as *Be My Guest,* Hodder & Stoughton, 1964, reprinted, Thorndike Press, 1998.
Canary Yellow, Morrow, 1965.
The Fox from His Lair, Hodder & Stoughton, 1965, Morrow, 1966.
The Corner Shop, Hodder & Stoughton, 1966, Morrow, 1967, reprinted, Thorndike Press, 1997.
The Stratton Story, Hodder & Stoughton, 1967.
Mrs. Westerby Changes Course, Morrow, 1968.
The Golden Collar, Morrow, 1969, reprinted, Thorndike Press, 1985.
The Friendly Air, Hodder & Stoughton, 1970, Morrow, 1971.
The Past Tense of Love, Morrow, 1970.
Home for the Wedding, Hodder & Stoughton, 1971, Morrow, 1972.
The Haymaker, Hodder & Stoughton, 1972.
Deck with Flowers, Hodder & Stoughton, 1973, Morrow and G. K. Hall, 1974, reprinted, Thorndike Press, 1997.
Royal Summons, Morrow and G. K. Hall, 1973.
The Fledgling, Morrow and G. K. Hall, 1975.
Game in Diamonds, Morrow and G. K. Hall, 1976.
Parson's House, Morrow, 1977, Thorndike Press, 1999.
The Round Dozen, Morrow and G. K. Hall, 1978.
River Lodge, R. Hale, 1978.
Return Match, Morrow and G. K. Hall, 1979.
Family Gathering, R. Hale, 1979.
The Marrying Kind, Morrow and G. K. Hall, 1980.
Any Two Can Play, Morrow and G. K. Hall, 1981.
A Lion in the Way, Morrow and G. K. Hall, 1982.
Remains to Be Seen, Morrow, 1983.
The Waiting Game, Morrow, 1985.
The Empty Nest, Morrow, 1986.
Out of the Nest, Morrow, 1987.
Out of the Rain, Morrow and Thorndike Press, 1987.

NOVELS UNDER PSEUDONYM HARRIET AINSWORTH

Consider the Lilies, Hodder & Stoughton, 1955, published under name Elizabeth Cadell, White Lion, 1974.
Shadows on the Water, Hodder & Stoughton, 1958, published under name Elizabeth Cadell, Morrow, 1958, reprinted, Thorndike Press, 1995.
Death among Friends, Hodder & Stoughton, 1964.

SIDELIGHTS: Raised in India, Elizabeth Cadell was educated in England and often travelled to Ireland. As a widow she discovered her talent for writing and went on to produce a prodigious number of light, romantic novels. The essence of Cadell's novels is normality. Her heroines and heroes are nearly always middle class: her basic plot involves two people of like class who must, on some level, meet as equals, as they find one another, overcome obstacles and develop a romantic relationship. The potential obstacles are usually of a nature that the reader, if not the protagonists, finds mildly amusing. Her heroines are noteworthy for their intelligence, their practical and efficient nature, while their weaknesses are frequently the same warm-heartedness and impulsiveness that make them so endearing to their friends, relatives, and romantic interests.

Cadell's novels are often set in Spain or Portugal, drawing upon her familiarity with these locations. The typical supporting cast of a Cadell novel includes a whimsical wealth of bizarre characters—eccentric elderly ladies, impish yet often irresistible nieces, nephews, and other children, as well as playful and lovable animals—many or all of whom in one way or another interfere with the budding courtship. Cadell's gently comedic tone allowed her a greater degree of realism than was generally found in that of her contemporaries in the romance genre. One area this involves is her heroines' minor foibles, for example, in *The Lark Shall Sing,* Lucille's bossiness. Another area is the effort she spent in the realistic character development of the children in her books. Susan Branch, in a *Twentieth-Century Romance and Historical Writers* essay, noted "The eye that Cadell turns on the aged, like the eye she turns on the young, is sympathetic but not sentimental."

Yet another departure from the conventions of the romance genre, particularly in some of Cadell's early novels, the plot focuses upon a middle-aged, attractive woman who is embroiled in family or romantic problems. For example, in *Last Straw for Harriet,* it is not the romantic younger couple on whom the story centers, but on Harriet Ellison, an English widow with four children. The story involves her concerns with keeping her brother, the admiral, from visiting during the spring holidays; a young girl, a volunteer gardener, who may have romantic designs on her oldest son, Charles; the unexpected return of a sister-in-law long absent; as well as numerous other genteel plot twists.

Her *Brimstone in the Garden* is an unusual combination social satire and ghost story set in the tiny English village of Deepwood. Three romances reach satisfactory conclusions, partly through human intervention and partly by supernatural means. Her *Sun in the Morning* tells of three young girls who met in Calcutta at age ten, later were separated during World War I, but then meet again six years later, picking up their mutual friendship where they left off.

Yellow Brick Road is the story of Jody Hern, a young woman whose already complex life is suddenly further complicated when she is found, unconscious and suffering from a concussion, in London. When revived, she claims to remember a young man leading a goat—a memory everyone else thinks is an hallucination. But he turns out to be a very real young naval commander home on leave, who becomes her new romantic interest. The tale involves a chase, adventure, and numerous other complications in its blend of romance and suspense.

BIOGRAPHICAL/CRITICAL SOURCES:

BOOKS

Twentieth-Century Romance and Historical Writers, third edition, St. James Press (Detroit, MI), 1994.

PERIODICALS

Catholic World, September, 1950; August, 1960.
Chicago Sun Book Week, March 9, 1947, p. 11.
Chicago Sunday Tribune, September 10, 1950, p. 17; November 19, 1950, p. 14; June 11, 1961, p. 3; July 29, 1962, p. 5.
Christian Science Monitor, August 5, 1950, p. 9; June 28, 1962, p. 11.
Cleveland Open Shelf, August, 1950, p. 16.
New Yorker, August 19, 1950.
New York Herald Tribune Book Review, March 9, 1947, p. 6; August 6, 1950, p. 6; November 12, 1950, p. 18; July 19, 1960, p. 9; July 16, 1961, p. 15; March 18, 1962, p. 6; June 17, 1962, p. 8.
New York Times, April 6, 1947, p. 20; August 6, 1950, p. 16; September 24, 1950, p. 30.
New York Times Book Review, January 14, 1962, p. 42; August 12, 1962, p. 24; January 22, 1967, p. 40.
San Francisco Chronicle, March 16, 1947, p. 10.
Saturday Review of Literature, April 19, 1947; September 2, 1950; November 11, 1950.
Springfield Republican, August 13, 1950, p. 8B.*

CADY, Jack A(ndrew) 1932-
(Pat Franklin)

PERSONAL: Surname rhymes with "lady"; born March 20, 1932, in Columbus, OH; son of Donald Victor (an auctioneer) and Pauline Lucille (a teacher and businesswoman; maiden name, Schmidt) Cady; married Betty Rex; married Patricia Distlehurst, March, 1966 (divorced January, 1972); married Deborah Robson (a writer and weaver), August, 1973 (divorced, 1976). *Education:* University of Louisville, B.S., 1961. *Politics:* "Every political system and form known is a catastrophe." *Religion:* Quaker ("not a good one").

ADDRESSES: Home—933 Tyler St., Port Townsend, WA 98368.

CAREER: Auctioneer in Louisville, KY, 1956-61; U.S. Department of Health, Education and Welfare, Corbin, KY, Social Security claims representative, 1961-62; truck driver in the southeastern United States, 1962-65; tree high climber in Arlington, MA, 1965-66; landscape foreman in San Francisco, CA, 1966-67; University of Washington, Seattle, assistant professor of English, 1968-72; Knox College, Galesburg, IL, visiting writer, 1973; Clarion State College, Clarion, PA, visiting writer, 1974; Cady-Robson Landscaping, Port Townsend, WA, in landscape construction, beginning 1974; *Port Townsend Journal,* Port Townsend, editor and publisher, 1974-76; Sitka Community College, Sitka, Alaska, visiting writer, 1977-78; freelance writer, 1978—. Has lectured at numerous colleges in the western United States. Landscape consultant. *Military service:* U.S. Coast Guard, 1952-56; became petty officer 2nd class.

AWARDS, HONORS: "First" Award from *Atlantic Monthly,* 1965, for short story "The Burning"; National Literary Award from National Council of the Arts, 1971, for story "The Shark"; Washington Governor's Award and Iowa Award for Short Fiction from University of Iowa Press, both 1972, for *The Burning and Other Stories;* World Fantasy Award, 1993, for collection; Nebula Award, Science Fiction Writers Association, 1994, for short story.

WRITINGS:

STORY COLLECTIONS

The Burning and Other Stories, University of Iowa Press (Iowa City), 1973.

Tattoo and Other Stories, Circinatum, 1978.
The Sons of Noah and Other Stories, Broken Moon Press (Seattle), 1992.

NOVELS

The Well, Arbor House (New York City), 1980.
Singleton, Madrona, 1981.
The Jonah Watch, Arbor House, 1982.
McDowell's Ghost, Arbor House, 1982.
The Man Who Could Make Things Vanish, Arbor House, 1983.
Street, St. Martin's (New York City), 1994.
Imagehi, Broken Moon Press, 1994.
The Off Season: A Victorian Sequel, St. Martin's, 1995.

UNDER PSEUDONYM PAT FRANKLIN

Dark Dreaming, Diamond (New York City), 1991.
Embrace of the Wolf, Diamond, 1993.

OTHER

Work anthologized in *Best American Short Stories,* edited by Martha Foley, Houghton, 1966, 1969, 1970, 1971, and *American Literary Anthology No. 3,* edited by George Plimpton and Peter Ardery, Viking, 1971. Columnist, *Port Angeles Daily News.* Contributor of stories to magazines, including *Atlantic Monthly, Twigs, Omni, Magazine of Fantasy and Science Fiction, Carolina Quarterly, Overdrive,* and *Yale Review.*

SIDELIGHTS: Jack Cady is a literary fiction writer whose work borrows elements from the genres of horror and fantasy. Cady, explains Darrell Schweitzer in the *St. James Guide to Horror, Ghost and Gothic Writers,* "is certainly not a 'horror writer' *per se,* any more than was Joseph Conrad (to whom he is sometimes compared). . . . His lyrical, deeply textured fictions often border on the strange and bizarre, whether they step all the way over the line into the openly fantastic or not."

Among Cady's best known works is the short story "By Reason of Darkness," first published in 1988. "Here," Schweitzer believes, "we see all of Cady's strengths: the intense imagery, the well-realized, off-kilter characters who bond together in something beyond ordinary friendship . . . ; and the poetic language which, in addition to the subject matter . . . has caused this story, especially, to be compared to Conrad's 'The Heart of Darkness.'"

The Off Season has also garnered Cady critical praise. Set in a coastal resort town in the Northwest, similar to Cady's home of Port Townsend, the novel tells of an apocalyptic disturbance of time which causes a revival of the town's dead, including their most evil resident of all. An odd assortment of living and dead characters join together to save the town from this menace. "This battle," writes George Needham in *Booklist,* "and its stunning results are chillingly related. . . . With elements of fantasy, science fiction, and even *Northern Exposure* at its best, this novel has something to appeal to nearly all readers." The critic for *Publishers Weekly* describes *The Off Season* as "a curious pastiche that echoes unequal parts of *The Divine Comedy, Alice in Wonderland, Pilgrim's Progress* and *Don Quixote.*" The critic concludes by calling the novel a "caustic fable" that is "admirable and worthy of note."

Cady once told *CA:* "Art and writing, when it attains to the condition of literature, is non-secular. Politics, religion, economies have nothing to do with good writing. The writer has nothing to sell. All he does is try to discover a true thing and then say it truly. That is the whole job. Art allows humans to be humane in human affairs. It sustains. It seeks not idealism but rather, continues to discover and bring to light the ideal. To do this one must assume the highest standards and pursue them relentlessly. Writing is only one of the arts. It is not greater or substantially different from painting, sculpture, teaching, acting, or the composition of music. The guy who works at it is not an artist. Instead, he works as hard as he can at what he's doing and it may be that the result attains to a condition greater than himself."

BIOGRAPHICAL/CRITICAL SOURCES:

BOOKS

St. James Guide to Horror, Ghost and Gothic Writers, St. James Press (Detroit), 1998.

PERIODICALS

Booklist, April 15, 1994, p. 1517; September 1, 1994, p. 22; October 15, 1995, p. 384.
Publishers Weekly, April 11, 1994, p. 60; September 12, 1994, p. 82; September 25, 1995, p. 43.

* * *

CADY, John Frank 1901-1996

PERSONAL: Born July 14, 1901, in Boonville, IN; died June 17, 1996; son of J. Frank (a photographer) and Katie (Johnson) Cady; married Effie Wright, August 30, 1930 (died 1933); married Vivian Thomas, June 8, 1935; children: John Thomas, Susan Grace Funk, George Franklin. *Education:* DePauw University, A.B., 1923; University of Cincinnati, A.M., 1924; University of Pennsylvania, Ph.D., 1929. *Politics:* Democrat. *Religion:* Methodist. *Avocational interests:* Golf.

CAREER: University of Maine at Orono, instructor, 1925-26; University of Pennsylvania, Philadelphia, instructor, 1926-27; West Virginia State Normal School (now Marshall University), Huntington, associate professor, 1929-30; Franklin College of Indiana, Franklin, professor of history and political science, 1930-35; Judson College (now a part of the University of Rangoon), Rangoon, Burma, lecturer, 1935-38; Franklin College of Indiana, dean and professor of history, 1938-43; Office of Strategic Services, Washington, DC, research analyst, 1943-45; U.S. State Department, Washington, DC, and Rangoon, Burma, foreign service officer and specialist on Burma, 1945-49; Ohio University, Athens, professor of history, 1949-71, distinguished professor of history, 1962, emeritus distinguished professor, 1971-96. Visiting lecturer in Southeast Asia program, at Cornell University, 1953; Rockefeller Foundation lecturer in history, Thammasat University, Bangkok, 1968-69.

MEMBER: Association for Asian Studies (director, program chair, research chair, of Southeast Asia section), American Historical Association, Ohio Academy of History.

AWARDS, HONORS: Carnegie Award of American Historical Association, 1954, and Ohioana Book Award, 1956, for *The Roots of French Imperialism in Eastern Asia;* Guggenheim fellow and Fulbright scholar at University of Rangoon, 1955-56; Ohio Academy of History Award, 1962, for *A History of Modern Burma;* Guggenheim fellow, 1961; L.H.D., Franklin College, 1962; honorary Doctor of Literature, Depauw University, 1963, and Doctor of Humanities, 1981.

WRITINGS:

Western Opinion and the War of 1812, F. J. Heer Printing Co., 1924.

Foreign Intervention in the Rio de la Plata, 1838-1850, University of Pennsylvania Press (Philadelphia, PA), 1929, reprinted, AMS Press (New York City), 1969.

The Centennial History of Franklin College, Franklin College (Franklin, IN), 1934.

The Origin and Development of the Missionary Baptist Church, Franklin College, 1942.

(With Patricia Barnett and Shirley Jenkins) *The Development of Self-Rule and Independence in Burma, Malaya and the Philippines,* American Institute of Pacific Relations, 1948.

The Roots of French Imperialism in Eastern Asia, Cornell University Press (Ithaca, NY), 1954.

Political Institutions of Old Burma, Department of Far East Asia Studies, Cornell University (Ithaca, NY), 1954, reprinted, 1973.

A History of Modern Burma, with supplement, Cornell University Press, 1958.

Southeast Asia: Its Historical Development, McGraw (New York City), 1964.

Thailand, Burma, Laos and Cambodia, Prentice-Hall (Englewood Cliffs, NJ), 1966.

The History of Post-War Southeast Asia, Ohio University Press (Athens, OH), 1974.

The United States and Burma, Harvard University Press (Cambridge, MA), 1976.

The Southeast Asian World, Forum Press (St. Louis, MO), 1977.

Our Burma Experience of 1935-1938, E. J. Brill (Long Island City, NY), 1981.

Contacts with Burma, 1935-1949: A Personal Account, Ohio University Center for International Studies (Athens, OH), 1983.

CONTRIBUTOR

Lennox Mills and others, *The New World of Southeast Asia,* University of Minnesota Press (Minneapolis, MN), 1949.

Charles B. Schleicher, *Introduction to International Relations,* Prentice-Hall, 1954.

Charles B. de Huszar, *Soviet Expansion and Power,* Crowell (New York City), 1954.

Philip W. Thayer, editor, *Nationalism and Progress in Free Asia,* Johns Hopkins Press (Baltimore, MD), 1956.

William Henderson, editor, *Southeast Asia: Problems of United States Policy,* M.I.T. Press (Boston, MA), 1963.

Donald Newton Wilber, *The Nations of Asia,* Hart Publishing, 1966.

Han-Kyo Kim, editor, *Essays on Modern Politics and History,* Ohio University Press, 1969.

OTHER

Contributor to *Contemporary Civilization* and *World Book, Americana, Colliers,* and *Britannica* encyclopedias. Contributor of articles to journals, including *Far*

Eastern Quarterly, Journal of Modern History, Far Eastern Survey, Solidarity, and *Baptist Observer.*

SIDELIGHTS: John Frank Cady was an internationally recognized expert on Southeast Asia in general and the country of Burma in particular. Cady's work on the roots of European imperialism in the region—and his studies on Buddhist resistance to European-style governments—became quite important when the United States entered the Vietnam War. Having spent parts of four different decades in Southeast Asia, Cady also served as a consultant to the U.S. State Department, especially in the years immediately following the Second World War.

Cady published *The Roots of French Imperialism in Eastern Asia* in 1954. While his study concerned the nineteenth century, it held important implications for current events in the region as well. In his *American History Review* piece on the book, J. K. Fairbank declared it an "illuminating and well-organized study of French expansion in China and Indo-China. . . . [Cady] constantly enlivens a clear-cut narrative with revealing detail." Noted W. C. Johnstone in *Annals of the American Academy:* "Throughout [the book], the importance of the prestige of France and the high value which French representatives placed upon the export of French culture is clearly shown. It is hoped that the author may continue his research."

A History of Modern Burma, published in 1958, further extended Cady's professional reputation. "It is quite safe to predict that the bulk of this large and carefully documented book will stand as a valuable guide to others for some years to come," observed F. N. Trager in *Annals of the American Academy.* "The significance of Cady's History consists chiefly in his taking seriously the issue of Burmese nationalism." *Library Journal* contributor William Henderson cited the work for its "admirable objectivity" and deemed it "a major contribution [that] calls attention to the growing maturity of Southeast Asian studies in the United States." In the *American History Review,* Cecil Hobbs wrote: "For many years there has existed the urgent need for a good all-round history of Burma. This volume presents a very important part of that history." Hobbs concluded that Cady, "a student of political science as well as of history, is a good observer of political developments."

Perhaps not surprisingly, Cady's publications during the 1960s and early 1970s concerned Southeast Asia as a region. Drawing upon his scholarly work, Cady sought to explain the history and politics of Southeast Asia for general readers. His results drew mixed reviews. In a *Choice* piece on *Thailand, Burma, Laos, and Cambodia,* the critic faulted Cady for covering too much material, noting that the book "moves lifelessly from event to event." D. G. E. Hall, reviewing the same book for *Pacific Affairs,* maintained that Cady "has arranged his chapters in chronological order of periods in each of which he surveys contemporaneous developments over the whole field. It is the most satisfactory way of treating his subject in so small a compass, and he has shown commendable skill in carrying it out. In the actual process of surveying, however, he tends to run into difficulties, largely one suspects, through not having adequately checked up some of his statements." In a review of *Southeast Asia: Its Historical Development,* Paul Bixler concluded that the book "emphasizes the area's cultural complexities. . . . This substantial volume is something for every library with serious intentions about keeping up with modern information."

BIOGRAPHICAL/CRITICAL SOURCES:

PERIODICALS

American History Review, July, 1955, p. 905; January, 1959, p. 390; January, 1965, p. 558; October, 1967, p. 203.

American Political Science Review, December, 1958, p. 1192.

Annals of the American Academy, July, 1955, p. 178; September, 1958, p. 183.

Choice, May, 1967, p. 332.

Christian Science Monitor, August 13, 1958, p. 9.

Library Journal, August, 1958, p. 2155; March 1, 1964, p. 1084; December 1, 1966, p. 5956.

Pacific Affairs, winter, 1965, p. 459; spring-summer, 1967, p. 160.

Political Science Quarterly, December, 1958, p. 621.*

* * *

CAESAR, (Eu)Gene (Lee) 1927-
(Johnny Laredo, Anthony Sterling)

PERSONAL: Born December 10, 1927, in Saginaw, MI; son of Ernest Thor and Eunice (Lee) Caesar; married Judith May Hall, 1953; children: Cheryl Lee, Craig Arthur. *Education:* Attended Central Michigan College (now University), 1945, Case Institute of Technology (now Case Western Reserve University),

1945-46, and University of Miami, Coral Gables, FL, 1947-49. *Avocational interests:* Wildlife, American history, travel.

ADDRESSES: Agent—Curtis Brown Ltd., 575 Madison Ave., New York, NY 10022.

CAREER: Saginaw Steering Gear, Saginaw, MI, machine operator, 1950-53; Republic Aviation, Farmingdale, Long Island, NY, mechanic, 1954-55; professional writer, 1955—. *Military service:* U.S. Naval Air Corps, 1945-46.

AWARDS, HONORS: Western Heritage Award, 1961, for *King of the Mountain Men.*

WRITINGS:

Mark of the Hunter, William Sloane Associates, 1953.
(Under pseudonym Johnny Laredo) *Come and Get Me,* Popular Library, 1956.
The Wild Hunters: The Wolves, the Bears, and the Big Cats, Putnam (New York City), 1957.
King of the Mountain Men: The Life of Jim Bridger, Dutton (New York City), 1961.
Rifle for Rent, Monarch (New York City), 1963.
Incredible Detective: The Biography of William J. Burns, Prentice-Hall (Englewood Cliffs, NJ), 1968.
(With Robert N. McKerr and James Phelps) *New Equity in Michigan School Finance: The Story of the Bursley Act,* Michigan Senate Committee on Education (Lansing), 1973.

Contributor of articles to *True, Holiday, Saturday Evening Post, Argosy, Virginia Quarterly Review, Field and Stream, Stag,* and *Bluebook.*

SIDELIGHTS: Gene Caesar became interested in writing while studying engineering as a Navy student. "Somehow found myself," he once told *CA,* "in a creative writing course taught by Pulitzer Prize-winning Dr. S. I. Hayakawa." After attempting novels, Caesar found what he calls his "stock in trade," a full-fledged short story with an outdoor background. His writing interest in wild animals has been supplanted more recently by an interest in Western Americana. "America's past is more colorful and exciting than anything the human imagination could conjure up." Caesar states: "This is especially true of the lusty, fast-paced chronicle of the West."

Caesar's debut, *Mark of the Hunter,* received mixed reviews. A story presenting the northern Michigan adventures of one man searching for his purpose in life, "violence and a ceaseless struggle against normal living becomes the pattern of existence for the insatiable hunter who takes his lovemaking as his immediate emotions dictate regardless of consequences," described a *Springfield Republican* critic. "The rough-hewn symbolism of the implacable hunter is accurate, but the author has not set it, correctly proportioned, in a valid social context," faulted Nicholas Monjo in the *Saturday Review,* contending: "When [Caesar] ascribes the dynamics of social dissatisfaction and liberal strivings wholly to sexual motivation in disguise, he robs love and politics alike of their rightful share of will and reason." Although the book's "hunting scenes alone [are] worth while," declared *Library Journal* contributor R. W. Henderson. "[Caesar's] characters, engrossed with sex, prone to fight with little provocation, are little better than animals." A more favorable assessment was given by the *Springfield Republican* critic who declared: "The book is not easily laid aside once opened and the promising young writer wastes little time as he his could from one violent situation to another."

King of the Mountain Men: The Life of Jim Bridger, a "vital and often exciting . . . [piece of] American history at the ground level" according to *Springfield Republican* critic D. B. Bagg, presents the quest of Bridger, a man who lived only in the wilderness from age eighteen to thirty-five and served as a scout and path finder for the army, and struggled to establish and maintain a fur trading company despite established competition and angry Indians. A *Booklist* reviewer applauded the "realistic, authentic details" of the biography. *Library Journal* contributor Clarence Gorchels believed both "scholar" and "non-scholar" will take interest in the book, for it contains "source materials" as well as "all the excitement of Indian fights, pioneering, trapping and trading, and personal and business conflict." *San Francisco Chronicle* reviewer W. H. Hutchinson concluded: "In essence, Gene Caesar has written a popular narrative about the [fascinating] gory, glory days of the American Fur Trade. . . . Caesar has done a good job of organizing his material and making a flowing narrative out of disconnected incidents."

In another biography, *Incredible Detective: The Biography of William J. Burns,* Caesar focuses on a man who established a detective agency whose early-twentieth century escapades seem better than could be imagined in fiction. "Though Mr. Caesar has tried to be objective about his subject, the admiration shows through, and with cause," noted *Library Journal* reviewer D. W. Harrison, who recommended the book, believing it to be enjoyable for readers of biographies as well as "crime or mystery buff[s]." *Saturday Review* critic Sergeant Cuff concluded: "Despite its rather flamboyant title, this work is thoroughly objective and occasionally sharply critical. There are fascinating case histories."

BIOGRAPHICAL/CRITICAL SOURCES:

PERIODICALS

Best Sellers, August 1, 1968.
Booklist, December 15, 1957; July 1, 1961.
Chicago Sunday Tribune, July 2, 1961.
Kirkus, July 1, 1953; September 1, 1957; March 15, 1961.
Library Journal, October 15, 1953; October 15, 1957; June 1, 1961; June 15, 1968.
San Francisco Chronicle, July 4, 1961.
Saturday Review, October 3, 1953; December 7, 1957; September 28, 1968.
Springfield Republican, October 4, 1953; June 18, 1961.*

* * *

CALDER, Ritchie
See RITCHIE-CALDER, Peter Ritchie

* * *

CALDER-MARSHALL, Arthur 1908-1992
(William Drummond)

PERSONAL: Some sources index surname as Marshall; born August 19, 1908, in Wallington, Surrey, England; died April 17, 1992; son of Arthur Grotjan and Alice (Poole) Calder-Marshall; married Violet Nancy Sales, 1934; children: two daughters. *Education:* Hertford College, Oxford, B.A., 1930.

CAREER: Denstone College, Staffordshire, England, schoolmaster, 1931-33; author, biographer, and critic, 1933-92. Scriptwriter for Metro-Goldwyn-Mayer in Hollywood, CA, 1937. *Wartime service:* British Petroleum Warfare Department, 1941; British Ministry of Information, films division, 1942-45.

MEMBER: Royal Society of Literature (fellow), Savile Club, National Liberal Club.

WRITINGS:

About Levy, J. Cape (London), 1933, Scribner (New York City), 1934.
Two of a Kind, J. Cape, 1933.
A Crime Against Cania (short stories), Golden Cockerel Press, 1934.
At Sea, Scribner, 1934.
Dead Centre, J. Cape, 1935.
A Pink Doll (short stories), Grayson Books, 1935.
Pie in the Sky, Scribner, 1937.
A Date with a Duchess and Other Stories, J. Cape, 1937.
The Way to Santiago, Reynal & Hitchcock, 1940.
A Man Reprieved, J. Cape, 1949.
Occasion of Glory, J. Cape, 1955.
The Scarlet Boy, Hart-Davis (London), 1961, Harper (New York City), 1962.
Season of Goodwill (play based on novel *Every Third Thought,* by Dorothea Malm), Samuel French (New York City), 1965.

NONFICTION

(With Edward J. H. O'Brien and J. Davenport) *The Guest Book,* Arthur Barker, 1935, Frederick Stokes, 1936.
Challenge to Schools: A Pamphlet on Public School Education, Hogarth Press, 1935.
The Changing Scene (essays on English society), Chapman & Hall, 1937.
(With others) *Writing in Revolt: Theory and Examples,* Fact, 1937.
Glory Dead (travel), M. Joseph, 1939.
The Book Front, Bodley Head, 1947.
The Watershed (travel), Contact Publications, 1947.
(Editor and author of introduction) Tobias Smollett, *Selected Writings,* Falcon Press (London), 1950.
The Magic of My Youth (autobiography), Hart-Davis, 1951.
No Earthly Command (biography of Alexander Riall Wadham Woods), Hart-Davis, 1957.
Havelock Ellis: A Biography, Hart-Davis, 1959, published as *The Sage of Sex: A Life of Havelock Ellis,* Putnam, 1960.
The Enthusiast (biography of Joseph Leycester Lyne), Faber, 1962.
(Editor) *The Bodley Head Jack London,* four volumes, Bodley Head (London), 1963-66.
The Innocent Eye (biography of Robert Flaherty), W. H. Allen, 1963, Harcourt, 1966.

Wish You Were Here: The Art of Donald McGill, Hutchinson, 1966.

(Editor and author of introduction) *Prepare to Shed Them Now: The Ballads of George R. Sims,* Hutchinson, 1968.

(Editor and author of introduction) Thomas Paine, *The Rights of Man and Other Writings,* Heron Books, 1970.

Lewd, Blasphemous, and Obscene: Being the Trials and Tribulations of Sundry Founding Fathers of Today's Alternative Societies, Hutchinson, 1972.

CHILDREN'S BOOKS

The Man from Devil's Island, Hart-Davis, 1958.

The Fair to Middling: A Mystery, Hart-Davis, 1959.

Lone Wolf: The Story of Jack London, Methuen, 1961, Duell, Sloan & Pearce, 1962.

UNDER PSEUDONYM WILLIAM DRUMMOND

Midnight Lace, Pan Books (London), 1960.

Victim, Corgi (London), 1961.

Life for Ruth, Corgi, 1962.

Night Must Fall, Sugnet (New York City), 1964.

Gaslight, Paperback Library (New York City), 1966.

OTHER

Also author of screenplay, *The World Is Rich,* 1946, and many documentary filmscripts.

SIDELIGHTS: Arthur Calder-Marshall was an author of adult and children's novels, biographies, and other nonfiction who, although widely read and lauded for his originality, wit, and technical skill, did not receive the attention some critics felt was his due. According to Brian Stableford in the *St. James Guide to Horror, Ghost and Gothic Writers,* Calder-Marshall enjoyed a reputation in horror and fantasy circles for *The Fair to Middling,* a novel about a travelling show coming to a small town, and *The Scarlet Boy,* a story of exorcism. Both novels, Stableford noted, "are among the most interesting and most cleverly-constructed examples of reverent Christian fantasy."

Calder-Marshall aspired to be a writer while still in high school. After teaching for two years in the early 1930s, he began his freelance writing career, working first as a scriptwriter for Metro-Goldwyn-Mayer in the late 1930s, then serving during World War II in the film division of the British Ministry of Information.

The Fair to Middling is in the tradition of such fantasy classics as Charles G. Finney's *The Circus of Dr. Lao* and Ray Bradbury's *Something Wicked This Way Comes.* In all of these stories, a circus or travelling show visits a small town and changes the lives of the local inhabitants forever. In Calder-Marshall's novel, the staff and children of Alderman Winterbottome's School for Incapacitated Orphans confront the denizens of a hellish carnival. As Stableford noted, "Although it is a Christian allegory there is nothing particularly pious about *The Fair to Middling;* it offers an intriguingly respectful account of the seductiveness of evil without resorting to undue psychological terrorism in spelling out the penalties of sinful self-indulgence. Even so, its clever wit carefully fails to conceal the darker undercurrent which lurks beneath the surface."

The Scarlet Boy is a disturbing tale of a haunting. Stableford explained: "As the elusive but determinedly unquiet spirit of a boy who committed suicide becomes increasingly troublesome to the living—especially to the sensitive—the plot moves inexorably towards a formal exorcism. The real point of the story, however, is not so much the suspicion that the unsettled dead may return to pester the gifted, as it is the conviction that unsettling memories are far better confronted than repressed."

BIOGRAPHICAL/CRITICAL SOURCES:

BOOKS

St. James Guide to Horror, Ghost and Gothic Writers, St. James Press (Detroit), 1998.

OBITUARIES:

PERIODICALS

Times (London), April 22, 1992.*

* * *

CALKINS, Lucy McCormick

PERSONAL: Born in Boston, MA; daughter of Evan and Virginia Calkins; married John Skorpen; children: Miles Evan. *Education:* Attended Mount Holyoke College, 1969-71; Williams College, B.A., 1973; University of Hartford, M.A., 1974; New York University, Ph.D., 1982.

ADDRESSES: Home—2 Dawn Lane, Ridgefield, CT 06877. *Office*—The Writers Project, P.O. Box 77, Teachers College, Columbia University, 525 West 121st St., New York, NY 10027. *Agent*—John Wright, 112 Shelbank Pl., Rockville Centre, NY 11570.

CAREER: High school English teacher in Hartford, CT, 1973-74; teacher at primary school in Oxfordshire, England, 1974-75; teacher and program leader at junior high school in Durham/Middlefield, CT, 1975-76; co-founder and teacher at public alternative elementary school in Durham/Middlefield, 1976-78; University of New Hampshire, Durham, research associate for National Institute of Education project, "How Children Change as Writers," 1978-80; Columbia University, Teachers College, New York, NY, began as assistant professor, became associate professor of English Education and director of the Writers Project, 1982—. Member of summer writing faculty at University of New Hampshire, 1981-82, and Northeastern University, 1982; speaker in more than one hundred school districts in the United States and Canada; interviewed on radio and television programs; consultant to *Time, Learning,* and *Sesame Street.*

MEMBER: International Reading Association, National Council of Teachers of English, National Conference on Research in English, Commission on Composition.

AWARDS, HONORS: Grants from New York City Board of Education, 1984-88, Morgan Guaranty Trust Co., 1984-85, 1985-86, 1987-88, Hazen Foundation, 1984-85, Conrad Hilton Foundation, 1984-85, Edwin Gould Foundation, 1984-85, 1985-87, 1987-89, New York Times Foundation, 1985-86, 1986-87, and Valentine Perry Snyder Foundation, 1985-86.

WRITINGS:

(Contributor) R. D. Walshe, editor, *Donald Graves in Australia,* Primary English Teaching Association, 1981.

Lessons from a Child: On the Teaching and Learning of Writing, Heinemann Educational (Exeter, NH), 1983.

(Contributor) Angela Jaggar, editor, *Child-Watching: Observing the Language Learner,* International Reading Association (Newark, DE), 1984.

(Contributor) B. McClelland, editor, *New Perspectives on Composition Research,* Modern Language Association of America (New York), 1985.

The Art of Teaching Writing, Heinemann Educational, 1985, second edition, 1994.

The Writing Workshop, Heinemann Educational, 1988.

(With Shelley Harwayne) *Living between the Lines,* Heinemann (Portsmouth, NH), 1991.

Raising Lifelong Learners: A Parent's Guide, Addison-Wesley (Reading, MA), 1997.

Contributor *Classroom Practices in Teaching English,* National Council of Teachers of English, 1980, and education journals.

SIDELIGHTS: In a *New York Times* book review, Fred M. Hechinger wrote that *The Art of Teaching Writing* "is a book for all teachers and parents who cherish writing, reading and children." Lucy McCormick Calkins believes that the successful writing teacher must be a person who loves both reading and writing and focuses on the child rather than the textbook. The writing classroom must become a writing workshop where children can share their work. The teacher must listen to the child and be aware of the ways in which his needs change as he grows older. Calkins's book provides guidelines for accomplishing these objectives, emphasizing the art rather than the skills of teaching.

Calkins favors the "whole-word" approach to reading rather than phonics. She believes children should learn reading as an extension of their speaking skills, instead of focusing on the sounds made by individual letters. To teach writing skills, she asserts in her books, children must be encouraged to think of themselves as authors. To this end, she recommends the use of journals and other tools to help the child's own experiences seem vivid and important. "These scrapbooks of inspiration and experience are the raw material from which student writers draw their inspiration and understand the themes and issues that are central to their own lives," explained Linda Irwin-DeVitis in an *Educational Studies* review of the revised edition of *The Art of Teaching Writing.* The book also offers numerous other suggestions for creating a good learning environment.

A reviewer for *Language Arts* deemed *The Art of Teaching Writing* "an outstanding publication on the latest developments in writing instruction" and added: "[It] can make the process of writing less frightening for the beginning teacher and more empowering for the more experienced." Irwin-DeVitis had a somewhat different opinion, for although she stated that "for the novice teacher, *The Art of Teaching Writing* may be an invitation and an inspiration to growth," she warned that "it may also be threatening. . . . Calkins' devotion to writing and her years of apprenticeship are far from the norm. Beginning and preservice teachers may be somewhat overwhelmed." The reviewer decided that *The Art of Teaching Writing* is "a book whose power and peril lie in the distinctive and poetic voice of its author and the personal focus of the analysis. Because she draws heavily on her own experiences . . . while minimizing reference to the theoretical and research literature that provide the foundation for her vision, *The Art of Teaching Writing* will be easily dismissed by those who are made uncomfortable by its message."

Irwin-DeVitis concluded: "Whatever its shortcomings, Calkins' book is an eloquent glimpse into what writing instruction in our classrooms can be. Teachers of writing will see their work dignified and their expertise affirmed. The poetic fusion of the personal and professional make . . . a refreshing and insightful departure from mainstream and formulaic academic writing. . . . Her assertion that reflective, informed, and caring teachers are constantly growing, learning, and adapting their instruction is both a validation and a challenge."

BIOGRAPHICAL/CRITICAL SOURCES:

PERIODICALS

Educational Studies, fall, 1995, pp. 248-55.
Language Arts, March, 1995, pp. 228-29.
Library Journal, October 1, 1997, p. 97.
New York Times, December 3, 1985.
New York Times Book Review, October 12, 1997, p. 37.
Reference & Research Book News, August, 1994, p. 40.

* * *

CALLAHAN, North 1908-

PERSONAL: Born August 7, 1908, near Sweetwater, TN; son of R. B. and Naomi (North) Callahan; married Jennie Waugh, 1939; children: Mary Alice, North, Jr. *Education:* University of Chattanooga (now University of Tennessee at Chattanooga), A.B., 1930; Columbia University, A.M., 1950; New York University, Ph.D., 1955. *Religion:* Member of Reformed Church in America. *Avocational interests:* Traveling, motion pictures.

ADDRESSES: Home—25 South Germantown Rd., Chattanooga, TN 37411.

CAREER: Teacher and principal in various Tennessee public schools, 1930-35; education advisor for Tennessee Valley Authority and Civilian Conservation Corps, 1935-37; newspaperman in Tennessee and Texas, 1937-39; *Dallas News,* Dallas, TX, New York correspondent, 1939-44; public relations consultant in New York City, 1945-50; Finch College, New York City, professor of history, 1956-57; New York University, New York City, associate professor, 1956-62, professor of history, 1962-73, professor emeritus, 1973—. *Military service:* U.S. Army, Adjutant General's department, 1940-45; became lieutenant colonel.

MEMBER: American Historical Association, Organization of American Historians, American Studies Association, American Academy of Political and Social Science, Authors Guild; Military-Naval Club and Rotary Club (both New York).

AWARDS, HONORS: New York University Founders Day Honor Award, 1956; American Revolutionary Round Table Award, 1958, for *Henry Knox: George Washington's General*; visiting scholar grant from Huntington Library, 1960; grant from American Philosophical Society; L.H.D., University of Chattanooga, 1964.

WRITINGS:

The Armed Forces As a Career, McGraw (New York City), 1947.
Smoky Mountain Country, Duell, 1952, revised edition edited by Erskine Caldwell, Smoky Mountain Historical Society (Sevierville, TN), 1988.
Henry Knox: General Washington's General, Rinehart (New York City), 1958.
Daniel Morgan: Ranger of the Revolution, Holt, Rinehart and Winston (New York City), 1961.
Royal Raiders: The Tories of the American Revolution, Bobbs-Merrill (Indianapolis, IN), 1963.
Flight from the Republic: The Tories of the American Revolution, Bobbs-Merrill, 1967, reprinted, Greenwood Press (Westport, CT), 1976.
Carl Sandburg: The Lincoln of Our Literature, New York University Press (New York City), 1970.
George Washington: Soldier and Man, Morrow (New York City), 1972.
Connecticut's Revolutionary War Leaders, edited by Glenn Weaver, Pequot Press (Chester, CT), 1973.

TVA Bridge over Troubled Waters, A. S. Barnes (South Brunswick, NJ), 1980.
Peggy (novel), Cornwall Books (New York City), 1982.
Daybreak (novel), Cornwall Books, 1985.
Carl Sandburg: His Life and Works, Pennsylvania State University Press (University Park), 1987.
Thanks Mr. President: The Trail-Blazing Second Term of George Washington, Cornwall Books, 1991.

Contributor of articles to newspapers and professional journals. Author of syndicated column, "So This Is New York," 1943-68. Editor, *Army Life,* 1943-46.

SIDELIGHTS: North Callahan once told *CA:* "An honorary degree of mine had a citation which stated, 'He found teaching and writing exciting.' True, and the former seemed the only way I could make a living while engaging in the latter. Writing is a terribly hard job and only for those with a true dedication."

Callahan has written several novels; however, the body of his work has been nonfiction books, a number of which deal with aspects of the American Revolutionary War and its military leaders. Callahan's *Henry Knox: General Washington's General* drew mixed reviews. R. A. Feer of *New England Quarterly* leveled these criticisms at the biography: "If too much space and care are lavished in praise of Knox, too little is spent in asking thoughtful questions and analyzing and explaining him and the problems with which he dealt. . . . The volume would also have benefited from more thorough proofreading, greater accuracy in footnotes, considerably more care in reproducing quotations, and more frequent documentation." Conversely, H. H. Peckham of *American History Review* summarized: "If this is not the definitive biography of Henry Knox, it is easily the best to date."

Mixed reception also greeted other Callahan publications. R. N. Sheridan of *Library Journal* complained that *Daniel Morgan: Ranger of the Revolution* "lacks the feel of the man and his time."

However, other reviews were far more favorable. A *Kirkus* critic said, "Although uneven in style and over-fictionalized, this careful study of a brilliant general is an important addition to American military annals and will appeal to students and teachers of Revolutionary War history." Similarly, C. W. E. Morris lauded in the *Christian Science Monitor:* "Mr. Callahan has made another significant contribution to the literature of the Revolutionary period." And W. M. Wallace wrote in *American History Review,* "On the whole, this is a fine book."

Another title concerning the Revolutionary period, *George Washington: Soldier and Man,* begins with Washington's appointment as the commander-in-chief of the Revolutionary Army. It details his victories in New England, the winters at Valley Forge and Morristown, and various campaigns through Yorktown. A reviewer for *Choice* lauded its accessibility: "[Callahan] presents the general reader with battle history approached through vignettes of officers, a flair for the romantic and dramatic, a breezy style, and an absence of scholarly impedimenta." And J. Q. Feller of *Best Sellers* contended that "Dr. Callahan has ably succeeded in his purpose: he has given us a skillfully drawn portrait of Washington as soldier and man."

An example of a Callahan book of differing subject matter is *Carl Sandburg, Lincoln of Our Literature.* Callahan reportedly was a personal friend of the late Carl Sandburg, and his book was written "with the cooperation of the Sandburg family." T. F. Smith, in a *Library Journal* review, said, "This well-written biography affords an excellent way to become acquainted with Carl Sandburg. . . . The book gives one the feel of the country and of the man, from the roving days of Sandburg's youth to his national success as a poet, biographer, and folksong entertainer."

BIOGRAPHICAL/CRITICAL SOURCES:

PERIODICALS

American History Review, April, 1959; July, 1961.
American Literature, March, 1971.
Best Sellers, July 1, 1967; September 15, 1972.
Booklist, April 1, 1961.
Choice, December, 1972.
Christian Science Monitor, February 20, 1961, p. 9.
Kirkus, January 1, 1961.
Library Journal, March 15, 1961; March 15, 1970.
New England Quarterly, March, 1959.
New York Herald Tribune Books, July 30, 1961, p. 13.
New York Times Book Review, December 10, 1972, p. 48.
San Francisco Chronicle, January 18, 1959, p. 12.*

* * *

CAMERON, Roderick (William) 1913-1985

PERSONAL: Born in 1913 in New York, NY. *Education:* Educated in England, Switzerland, and Germany.

CAREER: Worked for British Intelligence and for the U.S. Office of Strategic Services before devoting himself to travel and writing.

WRITINGS:

Equator Farm, Heinemann (London), 1955.
Time of the Mango Flowers, Heinemann, 1958.
Shadows from India: An Architectural Album, British Book Centre, 1960.
The Golden Haze: With Captain Cook in the South Pacific, World Publishing (New York City), 1964.
The Viceroyalties of the West: The Spanish Empire in Latin America, Little, Brown (Boston), 1968.
Australia: History and Horizons, Columbia University Press (New York City), 1971.
Shells, Octopus Books (London), 1972.
The Golden Riviera, Weidenfeld & Nicolson (London), 1975.
Great Comp and Its Garden: One Couple's Achievement in Seven Acres, Bachman & Turner (Maidstone, England), 1981.

SIDELIGHTS: Roderick Cameron wrote a number of travel books after leaving a career in military intelligence. His travels took him throughout the world, and his books—illustrated with his own photographs—covered such countries as Australia, India, and Mexico.

India is the focus of Cameron's books *Time of the Mango Flowers* and *Shadows from India: An Architectural Album.* In *Time of the Mango Flowers,* Cameron provided what the reviewer for *Kirkus* called "a leisurely tour of India. Stopping off at various temples, monuments, government houses and gardens, he integrates into his architectural discussion, observations on Indian life and anecdotes on Indian history and tradition." According to R. T. K. Archer in *Saturday Review, Time of the Mango Flowers* "is an excellent book by a thoughtful and intelligent observer." While the critic for the *Times Literary Supplement* found that "the book is a mosaic, containing a number of valuable, occasionally even brilliant, descriptions, . . . it fails to amount to an artistic whole," Dorothy Woodman in *New Statesman* believed: "Cameron has the eye of an architect, and a painter. . . . [The book] is an engaging trio of extracts from earlier visitors—chosen, I think, with much skill and sensitivity—of [Cameron's] own lively comments and of photographs, many of which have an unusual beauty."

Shadows from India is a pictorial history of some 1,300 years of Indian architecture, with Cameron supplying both text and photographs for the book. Lincoln Kirstein in the *Nation* praised the effort: "This most brilliant book of architectural photographs . . . is certainly the richest coverage available generally. . . . The most beautiful of this year's photographic collections." The reviewer for the *Times Literary Supplement* noted that Cameron "has a literary sense as well as the artist's eye, interpreting and evoking with his camera and always sustaining the link between past and present. . . . A most civilized and learned guide book." Anne Duchene in the *Manchester Guardian* claimed that Cameron writes a "modest, humane text, pleasantly inclined to anecdote. . . . His sections on Moslem and Rajput building are fascinating, that on Kashmir enchanting, and that on the Palladian glories and bungaloid fantasies of British India worthy to inspire Mr. Betjeman."

BIOGRAPHICAL/CRITICAL SOURCES:

PERIODICALS

Choice, July, 1969.
Kirkus, October 1, 1958.
Library Journal, November 15, 1968; November 15, 1971.
Manchester Guardian, August 22, 1958, p. 4; November 7, 1958, p. 6.
New Statesman, November 29, 1958.
New York Times Book Review, June 14, 1959, p. 28; December 19, 1971.
Saturday Review, January 10, 1959.
Spectator, September 6, 1975.
Times Literary Supplement, July 4, 1958, p. 382; November 14, 1958, p. 659; November 14, 1968, p. 1290; June 16, 1972, p. 690.*

* * *

CAMPBELL, Camilla 1905-1992

PERSONAL: Born April 15, 1905, in Fort Worth, TX; died February 16, 1992; daughter of Stanley (an attorney) and Clota (Terrell) Boykin; married Dan W. Campbell (a testing engineer), June 10, 1929. *Education:* Attended Texas Christian University, 1922-24, and University of Missouri, 1927-28.

CAREER: Elementary teacher in Fort Worth, TX, 1924-27, 1928-29; feature writer for *Fort Worth Star Telegram,* Fort Worth, 1943-44; writer for young people. Member of Girl Scout board, San Antonio,

1954-58, and Friends of the Library, 1959-63; leader of as many as four senior Girl Scout troops at one time.

MEMBER: Texas Historical Association, Texas Institute of Letters (member of executive council, 1959-60), Theta Sigma Phi.

AWARDS, HONORS: *Horn Book* honor selection, 1956, for *Star Mountain and Other Legends of Mexico;* Cokesbury Award, Texas Institute of Letters, 1958, for *Coronado and His Captains.*

WRITINGS:

Galleons Sail Westward, Mathis, Van Nort, 1939.
Star Mountain and Other Legends of Mexico, illustrated by Ena McKinney, Whittlesey House (New York City), 1946, revised edition with new illustrations by Frederic Marvin, McGraw (New York City), 1968.
The Bartletts of Box B Ranch (Junior Literary Guild selection) illustrated by Glenn Chesnut, Whittlesey House, 1949.
Coronado and His Captains, illustrated by Harve Stein, Follett (New York City), 1958.
Viva la Patria, illustrated by Nilo Santiago, Hill & Wang (New York City), 1970.
The Peewit's Cry: A Norfolk Childhood, East Anglian Magazine Limited (Ipswich, England), 1980.

Contributor of stories and plays to children's publications, and adult poetry and articles to magazines.

WORK IN PROGRESS: A biography of William Barrett Travis, commander of the Alamo; a novel on colonial Texas.

SIDELIGHTS: Camilla Campbell's books for children and adolescents generally deal with historical subjects and other cultures because she believes "it is a mistake for young people to be isolated in time (the present) as well as geographically." Campbell's *Star Mountain and Other Legends of Mexico* retells traditional folk legends on a variety of subjects, including nature, the saints, and the origin of street names. M. L. Becker, writing in *Weekly Book Review,* stated: "Mexico has seldom come so pleasantly and persuasively to her young neighbors in the North as in this book." M. A. Herr of *Library Journal* described the collection as "interesting and full of the atmosphere of the country."

The Bartletts of Box B Ranch sets its tale for ages eight to eleven against the backdrop of a large Texas cattle ranch. M. M. Smith of *Library Journal* felt that "the characters are stereotyped," but "the ranch background . . . [is] interesting." E. L. Buell of the *New York Times* observed: "Underneath the easy flow of the story there is an emphasis upon sound human relationships and the upon the fact that youngsters 'need to share in things—both work and play.'"

In *Coronado and His Captains* Campbell tells the story of sixteenth-century Spanish explorer Francisco de Coronado and his search for the Seven Cities of Cibola. A reviewer for *Horn Book* noted: "The reader is never conscious that incidents or situations may have required filling in by the author's imagination, so well integrated is the tremendous research that must have gone into this biography." A reviewer for *Booklist* faulted the book for not being "very exciting reading," but credited it as "useful in connection with the study of explorers and the history of the region."

BIOGRAPHICAL/CRITICAL SOURCES:

PERIODICALS

Booklist, October 1, 1946; June 1, 1949; January 1, 1959, p. 243.
Horn Book, November, 1946; February, 1959, p. 38.
Kirkus, July 1, 1946; March 1, 1949.
Library Journal, October 1, 1946, p. 1334; December 15, 1958; June 1, 1949, p. 895.
New York Herald Tribune Weekly Book Review, June 12, 1949, p. 8.
New York Times, September 1, 1946, p. 11; May 15, 1949, p. 22.
San Antonio Light, March 15, 1959.
San Antonio News, June 15, 1962.
San Francisco Chronicle, November 10, 1946, p. 14.
Saturday Review of Literature, November 9, 1946.
Springfield Republican, August 18, 1946, p. D4; May 15, 1949, p. C8.
Weekly Book Review, August 25, 1946, p. 6.*

* * *

CAMPBELL, Jeffrey
See BLACK, Campbell

* * *

CANDELARIA, Nash 1928-

PERSONAL: Born May 7, 1928, in Los Angeles, CA; son of Ignacio N. (a railway mail clerk) and Flora

(Rivera) Candelaria; married Doranne Godwin (a fashion designer), November 27, 1955; children: David, Alex. *Education:* University of California, Los Angeles, B.S., 1948. *Politics:* "I usually seem to vote for the person who doesn't get elected." *Religion:* "Non-church-going monotheistic and cultural Christian." *Avocational interests:* The arts and family, reading, and the stock market.

ADDRESSES: Home and office—1295 Wilson St., Palo Alto, CA 94301.

CAREER: Don Baxter, Inc. (pharmaceutical firm), Glendale, CA, chemist, 1948-52; Atomics International, Downey, CA, technical editor, 1953-54; Beckman Instruments, Fullerton, CA, promotion supervisor, 1954-59; Northrup-Nortronics, Anaheim, CA, in marketing communications, 1959-65; Hixon & Jorgensen Advertising, Los Angeles, CA, account executive, 1965-67; Varian Associates, Inc. (in scientific instruments), Palo Alto, CA, advertising manager, 1967-82; free-lance writer, 1982-85; Daisy Systems Corp., Mountain View, CA, marketing writer, 1985-87; Hewlett-Packard Co., Palo Alto, marketing writer, 1987—. *Military service:* U.S. Air Force, 1952-53; became second lieutenant.

AWARDS, HONORS: Not by the Sword was a finalist in the Western Writers of America Spur Award competition, 1982, and received the Before Columbus Foundation American Book Award, 1983.

WRITINGS:

Memories of the Alhambra (novel), Cibola Press (Palo Alto, CA), 1977.

(Contributor) Gary D. Keller and Francisco Jimenez, editors, *Hispanics in the United States: An Anthology of Creative Literature,* Bilingual Press (Ypsilanti, MI), Volume 1, 1980, Volume 2, 1982.

Not by the Sword (novel), Bilingual Press, 1982.

(Contributor) Nicholas Kanellos, editor, *A Decade of Hispanic Literature: An Anniversary Anthology* Arte Publico, 1982.

Inheritance of Strangers (novel), Bilingual Press (Binghampton, NY), 1984.

The Day the Cisco Kid Shot John Wayne (short stories), Bilingual Press (Tempe, AZ), 1988.

Leonor Park (novel), Bilingual Press, 1991.

Contributor of short stories to *Bilingual Review;* contributor to *Science.* Editor, *VIA.*

SIDELIGHTS: Nash Candelaria is a historical novelist who writes about the Hispanic people of New Mexico. Himself a descendent of one of the founders of Albuquerque, Candelaria "explores the relationship between historical incident and individual destiny," to quote *Dictionary of Literary Biography* correspondent Paula W. Shirley. Candelaria's works—written in English—have reached a readership beyond the Chicano community in which he was raised, helping to increase awareness of the cultural conflicts and nuances of assimilation among Hispanic Americans.

Although he was born and raised in Los Angeles, Candelaria spent many of his summers in New Mexico with his extended, Spanish-speaking family. These summertime experiences helped him to forge an awareness of the unique aspects of New Mexican Chicano culture—and his immersion in Anglo life gave him a broader perspective on how his family's culture was changing in modern times. According to Shirley, "Participation in Anglo and Hispanic life made [Candelaria] feel part of both cultures yet gave him a certain objectivity that has to a great extent determined the course of his writing." These impulses would simmer many years while the author earned a college degree in chemistry and embarked on a long and fruitful career of science writing, science advertising, and sales promotions.

During his tour of duty in the Korean War, Candelaria began to spend his spare time writing fiction. He continued when he returned to civilian life, and by his own estimate he penned seven novels that never saw print before finally embarking on the project that would become *Memories of the Alhambra* in 1977.

Memories of the Alhambra is the first novel in a tetralogy that explores the links between family and history in New Mexico. The saga that unfolds in *Memories of the Alhambra* is enriched in the subsequent titles, *Not by the Sword, The Inheritance of Strangers,* and *Leonor Park.* All of the works follow the various vicissitudes of the Rafa family, small landowners in the vicinity of Albuquerque. Candelaria is quoted in the *Dictionary of Hispanic Biography* as having said that his Rafa series grew from a desire to reveal to his sons "something of their Hispano-Indian background" as his own pride in his heritage grew.

In *Memories of the Alhambra,* the foundation for the tetralogy is laid in the depiction of "the contemporary conflict of the Hispanic New Mexican who identifies with the Spanish and European past more than with his Indian and mestizo heritage," to quote Shirley. The central character, Jose Rafa, leaves his home and family in search of his genealogical ties to European conquistadors, in a psychological attempt to free himself from what he perceives as an inferior Mexican ancestry. Rafa's travels only serve to illustrate that European and Native American are inexorably tied in Mexico, and he dies disappointed with the discovery. In a review of the book in *De Colores,* Vernon E. Lattin wrote: "Candelaria adds a new page to the Chicano novel, testifying to the fact that Chicano fiction is not limited to certain ideological themes or certain stock answers to questions of identity and ethnicity."

The issues of history, genealogy, and myth are further explored in the subsequent Rafa novels, two of which are set in the nineteenth century in the years encompassing the Mexican War of 1846 to 1848. Shirley declared that the books are concerned with "tradition and the continuing struggle to preserve it," as Yankees overrun New Mexico and proceed to influence its Spanish-speaking inhabitants. "Candelaria's Rafa [tetralogy] is a novelistic representation of his view of culture as steadily evolving," observed Shirley. "Through his work he rejects the notion 'that there is a fixed Chicano culture that we can go back to, like Eden, when in reality it is changing all the time.' This appears to be a repudiation of the myth of Aztlan in favor of acceptance of the inevitability of radical change and assimilation." Despite his assimilationist view, however, Candelaria "vividly depicts the present in which his characters live and their natural resistance to change," noted Shirley. The critic concluded that, as a historical novelist, Candelaria "contributes a view of historical reality which enhances the reader's understanding of the Chicano experience."

Candelaria once told *CA:* "*Memories of the Alhambra* is about the Chicano heritage myth of being descendants of conquistadors, the unsolvable dilemma of Hispanics from the state of New Mexico who acknowledge their European heritage and may not accept their American Indian heritage. . . . *Not by the Sword* is a look at the Mexican War (1846-48) from the point of view of New Mexicans, who became Americans by conquest. *Inheritance of Strangers,* a sequel to *Not by the Sword,* looks at the aftermath of the Mexican War forty years later, and the problems of assimilation; it focuses on the futility of revenge and the difficulty of forgiveness by a conquered people. *The Day the Cisco Kid Shot John Wayne* is a collection of twelve stories that give insight into and understanding of the Hispanic experience in the United States and its interface with the dominant Anglo culture.

"I am a descendant of one of the founding families of Albuquerque, New Mexico, and an ancestor, Juan, authored a history of New Mexico in 1776. Although I was born in California, I consider myself a New Mexican by heritage and sympathy. My writing is primarily about Hispanic Americans, trying, through fiction, to present some of their stories to a wider audience that may only be aware of them as a 'silent minority.'"

BIOGRAPHICAL/CRITICAL SOURCES:

BOOKS

Dictionary of Hispanic Biography, Gale (Detroit, MI), 1996, pp. 159-161.

Dictionary of Literary Biography, Volume 82: *Chicano Writers, First Series,* Gale, 1989, pp. 68-73.

Martinez, Julio A., and Francisco A. Lomeli, editors, *Chicano Literature: A Reference Guide,* Greenwood Press (Westport, CT), 1985.

Meier, Matt S., *Mexican American Biographies: A Historical Dictionary, 1836-1987,* Greenwood Press, 1988.

PERIODICALS

Best Sellers, August, 1977; May, 1983.

Carta Abierta, Number 9, 1977.

De Colores, September, 1980, pp. 102-14, 115-29.

La Opinion, March 31, 1985, pp. 6-7.

New Mexico Magazine, September, 1977.

Western American Literature, summer, 1978, p. 191; spring, 1984.

* * *

CANE, Melville (Henry) 1879-1980

PERSONAL: Born April 15, 1879, in Plattsburg, NY; died March 10, 1980; son of Henry William (a merchant) and Sophia (Goodman) Cane; married Florence Naumbury, December 23, 1909 (died, 1953); children: Katherine Detre, Mary (Mrs. Arthur Robinson). *Education:* Columbia University, A.B., 1900, LL.B., 1903.

CAREER: Lawyer in New York City, 1905-80. Founding partner of law firm of Ernst, Cane, Berner & Gitlin. Member of board of directors of Harcourt Brace Jovanovich, Inc., 1940-80.

MEMBER: Association of the Bar (New York), Poetry Society of America, Columbia University Club.

AWARDS, HONORS: Columbia University medal for conspicuous alumni service, 1933, and medal for excellence in law and literature, 1948; Poetry Society of America annual poetry award established by Harcourt Brace Jovanovich named in his honor, 1960; Poetry Society of America gold medal, 1971.

WRITINGS:

POETRY, EXCEPT AS INDICATED; PUBLISHED BY HARCOURT (NEW YORK CITY)

January Garden, 1926.
Behind Dark Spaces, 1930.
Poems: New and Selected, 1938.
A Wider Arc, 1947.
Making a Poem (prose), 1953.
And Pastures New, 1956.
Bullet-Hunting and Other New Poems, 1960.
To Build a Fire: Recent Poems and a Prose Piece (includes six translations by the author of poetry by Evgeny Vinokurov), 1964.
So That It Flower: A Gathering of Poems, 1966.
All and Sundry: An Oblique Autobiography, 1968.
Eloquent April: New Poems and Prose, 1971.
The First Firefly: New Poems and Prose, 1974.
Snow toward Evening, 1974.

EDITOR

(With Harry E. Maule) *The Man from Main Street: A Sinclair Lewis Reader* (anthology), Random House (New York City), 1953.
(With John Farrar and Louise Townsend Nicholl) *The Golden Year: The Poetry Society of America Anthology, (1910-1960),* foreword by Clarence R. Decker, Books for Libraries (Freeport, NY), 1960.

OTHER

Also author of sound recordings, (contributor) *When in Disgrace with Fortune and Men's Eyes* (poets reading the same Shakespeare sonnet at the City College of New York, between 1938 and 1941), circa 1938-41; *Poems, Selections* (Melville Cane reading his poems at the City College of New York, February 28, 1941), 1941; *Poems, Selections* (Melville Cane reading his poems with comment in the Recording Laboratory, March 25, 1960), 1960.

Contributor of poems, articles, and stories to magazines, including *American Scholar, Atlantic Monthly, Columbia Literary Monthly, McCall's, New York Times, Pages from Tarusa, Poetry in Crystal, Saturday Review, Southwest Review, Sporting News,* and *University Review.*

SIDELIGHTS: Melville Cane first became interested in writing while practicing law. Beginning early in his career, he represented many prominent authors, including Upton Sinclair, Thomas Wolfe, William Saroyan, and Sinclair Lewis. At Columbia University, two of his classmates were Alfred Harcourt and Donald Brace and, in 1919, he drew up incorporation papers for their publishing concern, Harcourt Brace (now Harcourt Brace Jovanovich). As a member of the board of directors of that firm, he often advised on legal matters as well as literary ones.

In addition to his successful legal career, Cane's literary career as a poet spanned some five decades, and twelve collections of his poems were published. He also contributed to numerous anthologies, and, with others, edited two more. His work frequently drew favorable reviews.

His *Poems: New and Selected* was lauded by a *Books* reviewer who praised that, "those who prefer work that is clear and direct, solid in conception yet spare and neatly turned, will enjoy Mr. Cane's nature lyrics." Robert Hillyer, writing about *And Pastures New* in the *New York Times,* stated: "In the finest sections of Cane's book . . . he is spiritually akin to such lyrists as Herrick, Marvell and the old Chinese poets as we read them in Arthur Waley's translations." A *Kirkus* reviewer deemed the title poem of *Bullet-Hunting and Other New Poems,* "an interesting narrative piece of the post Civil War period, based on a real incident, imaginatively expended." And the same reviewer praised: "The short poems, especially the first ten, add considerably to [Cane's] stature as a poet. . . . They have charm, a light touch and a pleasant philosophical animadversion on the nature of things."

X. J. Kennedy, reviewing *To Build a Fire: Recent Poems and a Prose Piece* in the *New York Times Book Review,* termed Cane's translations of Russian writer Evgeny Vinokurov's poems as "vigorous," and lauded

Within the Dark for achieving "a beautifully sustained elegy." *So That It Flower: A Gathering of Poems* prompted a *Choice* critic to describe Cane as a "sensitive romantic poet . . . who is dominated by his own rationality." And E. H. Walden of *Library Journal* noted: "Simplicity is the keynote which is achieved by directness of thought and brevity of words." Walden continued: "Even in his most humorous moments, one senses a keen insight and a sensitivity to hidden and subtle details. There is a spontaneity in his verse, yet when analyzed, constraint and craftsmanship show through."

The relationship between law and literature in Cane's life influenced his ideas on writing. According to a *New York Times* article by Ian T. Macauley, Cane once wrote: "You have to be accurate in law, and you have to be accurate in a poem. . . . In both fields there has to be a precise inspection of the object." This interest in precision was noted by critics, and they praised Cane's poetry for its simplicity. For example, E. H. Walden, in *Library Journal,* noted, "There is a spontaneity in his verse, yet when analyzed, constraint and craftsmanship show through." Although Cane's legal work required a great degree of seriousness and restraint, he felt free to let his sense of humor come to the fore in his poetry. Critics such as L. T. Nicholl and Gorham Munson commended Cane for the lightheartedness evident in his poetry. In the *New York Herald Tribune Book Review,* Nicholl wrote: "Mr. Cane is unique for the technical control which serves deep emotional need and also [for his] mad and merry wit." Munson, reviewing *And Pastures New* in *Saturday Review,* commented: "[Cane] is truly a serious poet, but he is saved from gravity by his playfulness, the playfulness that makes his light verse delightful and his serious verse springy in spirit." He expressed in his poetry, according to Harcourt Brace Jovanovich chair William Jovanovich, as noted by Macauley, "the saving characteristic of finding life too serious to be viewed seriously."

BIOGRAPHICAL/CRITICAL SOURCES:

BOOKS

Cane, Melville, *All and Sundry: An Oblique Autobiography,* Harcourt, Brace & World (New York City), 1968.

PERIODICALS

American Scholar, autumn, 1968.
Books, September 18, 1939, p. 18.
Boston Transcript, September 10, 1938.
Choice, July, 1966.
Christian Century, July 13, 1938.
Christian Science Monitor, August 31, 1938, p. 11; December 24, 1964, p. 5.
Kirkus, December 1, 1959.
Library Journal, March 1, 1966.
New Yorker, May 18, 1968.
New York Herald Tribune Book Review, March 11, 1956, p. 5.
New York Times, October 31, 1938, p. 2; March 4, 1956, p. 10.
New York Times Book Review, April 10, 1960, p. 40; December 20, 1964, 4.
San Francisco Chronicle, August 16, 1953, p. 19; August 19, 1956, p. 20.
Saturday Review, December 26, 1953; June 16, 1956; May 21, 1966.
Saturday Review of Literature, December 17, 1938.
Time, September 19, 1938.

OBITUARIES:

PERIODICALS

Publishers Weekly, March 21, 1980.
Newsweek, March 24, 1980.
New York Times, March 11, 1980.*

* * *

CARTER, Nick
See BRANDNER, Gary (Phil)

* * *

CARVIC, Heron ?-1980

PERSONAL: Born in London, England; died February, 1980; married Phyllis Neilson-Terry (an actress). *Education:* Attended Eton College.

CAREER: Dancer, actor, designer, builder, decorator, and market gardener; novelist.

MEMBER: Writers Guild of Great Britain, Crime Writers Association.

AWARDS, HONORS: Special award from Mystery Writers of America, 1969.

WRITINGS:

MYSTERY NOVELS

Picture Miss Seeton, Harper (New York City), 1968.
Miss Seeton Draws the Line, Bles (London), 1969, Harper, 1970.
Witch Miss Seeton, Harper, 1971.
Miss Seeton Sings, Harper, 1973.
Odds on Miss Seeton, Harper, 1975.

SIDELIGHTS: Heron Carvic's detective character Miss Seeton is drawn from the same cloth as Agatha Christie's Miss Marple, according to several critics. Writing in the *Christian Science Monitor,* Pamela Marsh explained: "Miss Seeton is elderly, English, intrepid and only dimly aware that danger exists at all. . . . Though Mr. Carvic's touch is a shade heavier, nearer caricature than Miss Christie's, his book certainly belongs on the lower shelf of the same bookcase." A. J. Hubin, writing in the *New York Times Book Review,* found Miss Seeton to be "an unqualified joy."

Miss Seeton's adventures, always told with a lightly humorous touch, took the elderly crimefighter into the London underworld of narcotics dealers, into a pursuit of a child murderer, and into the dangerous world of continental art forgery. Speaking of the novel *Miss Seeton Sings,* H. C. Velt in *Library Journal* noted that "one may just as easily hate as adore the charming, ladylike, Miss Marple-ish, para-policewoman Miss Seeton, but there are very funny set pieces, and what an agreeable change it is to have a pleasant and optimistic view of the world." Hubin summed up Miss Seeton as "a most beguiling protagonist with a sublime sense of humor." Since Carvic's death in 1980, the Miss Seeton series has been continued by the authors Hampton Charles and Hamilton Crane.

BIOGRAPHICAL/CRITICAL SOURCES:

PERIODICALS

Best Sellers, August 15, 1968; March 15, 1970; April 15, 1974.
Christian Science Monitor, July 22, 1968, p. 11.
Critic, July/August, 1973.
Harper, September, 1968.
Library Journal, June 1, 1968; January 1, 1970; March 1, 1973.
New York Times Book Review, August 11, 1968, p. 24; March 1, 1970, p. 45; April 1, 1973, p. 34.
Saturday Review, September 14, 1968; February 28, 1970.*

CASE, (Brian) David (Francis) 1937-

PERSONAL: Born December 22, 1937, in Gloversville, NY; son of Francis Daniel and Joyce (Groves) Case; married Valerie Priest; children: Mardou, Jason, Sebastian. *Education:* Received degrees from State University of New York at Albany, 1956, and Endicott College, 1959. *Politics:* "Rightwing." *Religion:* None.

ADDRESSES: *Home*—Kirk Michael, Isle of Man. *Agent*—Dick Curtis, 171 East 74th St., New York, NY 10021.

CAREER: Writer, 1958—.

AWARDS, HONORS: Short story award from *Scholastic,* 1952, for "I Wait on a Hill."

WRITINGS:

The Cell: Three Tales of Horror, Hill & Wang (New York City), 1969, published as *The Cell, and Other Tales of Horror,* Macdonald & Co. (London), 1969.
Fengriffen: A Chilling Tale, Hill & Wang, 1970, published as *And Now the Screaming Starts,* Pan Books (London), 1973.
Fengriffen and Other Stories, Macdonald & Co., 1971.
Plumb Drillin' (western novel), Stein & Day (New York City), 1975, published as *Gold Fever,* Tower Books (New York City), 1982.
The Fighting Breed (western novel), Zebra (New York City), 1979.
Wolf Tracks (horror novel), Tower Books, 1980.
The Third Grave, Arkham (Sauk City, WI), 1981.
Among the Wolves, Arkham, 1982.
Pelican Cay (horror novel), Arkham, 1982.
A Cross to Bear (horror novel), Pan Books, 1982.
Guns of Valentine, Ace Books (New York City), 1982.

Also author of the western novels *Black Hats* and *Fighting Cocks.* Work represented in anthologies. Author of about four hundred pornographic novels, under at least seventeen pseudonyms.

ADAPTATIONS: The story "Fengriffen" was filmed as *And Now the Screaming Starts. . . .*, 1973; the story "The Hunter" was filmed as *Scream of the Wolf,* 1974.

SIDELIGHTS: David Case has written prolifically in several genres, including westerns, horror and adult pornography. With his horror short stories, according to Chris Morgan in the *St. James Guide to Horror, Ghost and Gothic Writers,* Case "quickly established a reputation as a fine and promising horror writer."

Many of Case's horror stories concern werewolves. "The Cell," for example, tells of a seemingly ordinary married man who suffers from lycanthropy, a condition he considers comparable to any other disease. Once a month, he retreats to a prison cell he has constructed to keep himself from harming others during his werewolf phase. "As the story progresses," Morgan writes, "his psychological peculiarities become clear—he feels little or no responsibility for the murders he has committed—and his unpleasant demise seems justified."

Case once told *CA:* "My first book was published while I was still at school. I have been traveling steadily for twenty-four years in the United States, Europe, and Africa. In 1962, on the Yugoslavia-Greece frontier, I think I saw a were-wolf. It's not the sort of thing to which one can swear, and I'm not at all superstitious, but the son of a bitch had yellow eyes and bristling hair and was dressed in rags and if it wasn't a lycanthrope, it was the next best thing. I have been known to back a horse and take a drink. I have the only Cadillac on the Isle of Man."

BIOGRAPHICAL/CRITICAL SOURCES:

BOOKS

St. James Guide to Horror, Ghost and Gothic Writers, St. James Press (Detroit), 1998.

* * *

CAVE, Hugh B(arnett) 1910-

PERSONAL: Born July 11, 1910, in Chester, England; married Margaret P. Long, 1935; children: Kenneth L., Donald H.

ADDRESSES: Home—Oak Harbor, WA.

CAREER: Freelance writer. War correspondent during World War II.

AWARDS, HONORS: World Fantasy Award for best collection/anthology from World Fantasy Convention, 1978, for *Murgunstrumm and Others;* Horror Writers of America Lifetime Achievement Award, 1991.

WRITINGS:

Fishermen Four, Dodd (New York City), 1942.
Long Were the Nights, Dodd, 1944.
The Fightin'est Ship, Dodd, 1944.
We Build, We Fight, Harper (New York City), 1945.
Wings across the World, Dodd, 1945.
I Took the Sky Road, Dodd, 1946.
Haiti: Highroad to Adventure, Holt (New York City), 1952.
The Cross on the Drum, Doubleday (New York City), 1959.
Black Sun, Doubleday, 1960.
The Mission, Doubleday, 1960.
Four Paths to Paradise: A Book about Jamaica, Doubleday, 1961.
The Witching Lands: Tales of the West Indies, Doubleday, 1962.
Run, Shadow, Run, R. Hale (London), 1968.
Larks Will Sing, R. Hale, 1969.
Murgunstrumm and Others (collection), Carcosa (Chapel Hill, NC), 1977.
Legion of the Dead, Avon (New York City), 1979.
The Nebulon Horror, Dell (New York City), 1980.
The Evil, Charter (New York City), 1981.
Shades of Evil, Charter, 1982.
Disciples of Dread, Tor Books (New York City), 1988.
The Corpse Maker (stories), edited by Sheldon Jaffery, Starmont House (Mercer Island, WA), 1988.
The Voyage (children's book), Macmillan (New York City), 1988.
Conquering Kilmarnie, Macmillan, 1989.
The Lower Deep, Tor Books, 1990.
Lucifer's Eye, Tor Books, 1991.
The Sacred Cave and Other Poems, Omega Cat Press (Cupertino, CA), 1992.
Magazines I Remember, Tattered Pages Press (Chicago), 1994.
Death Stalks the Night (stories), Fedogan & Bremer (Minneapolis), 1995.
Bitter/Sweet (stories), Necronomicon Press (West Warwick, RI), 1996.

Also author of *The Witching Lands,* 1962, and *The Wild One.* Contributor of fiction to numerous anthologies, and to *Saturday Evening Post, Cosmopolitan, Good Housekeeping, Redbook, Astounding Stories, Ghost Stories, Strange Tales, Weird Tales, Spicy*

Mystery Stories, Terror Tales, Horror Stories, and many other American and English magazines.

SIDELIGHTS: "Hugh B. Cave's long and distinguished career as a weird-fiction writer spans most of the twentieth century and the enduring appeal of his tales of horror and the supernatural is attributable to his mastery of the fundamentals of good storytelling: plot, atmosphere and character," writes Stefan Dziemianowicz in the *St. James Guide to Horror, Ghost and Gothic Writers.*

Cave began his career as a writer for the pulp magazines of the 1920s and 1930s, creating stories of terror for a wide variety of publications. His stories of the time, Dziemianowicz notes, concerned such staple subjects as "weird scientific experiments . . . , vengeance from beyond the grave . . . , the fatal family curse . . . , shape-shifting . . . , the haunted mansion . . . , and so forth. Cave, however, was adept at finding a new angle or approach to ideas long-mired in cliche."

In the mid-1930s Cave began writing for the shudder pulps, magazines featuring stories in which a mood of supernatural terror was eventually revealed to have a natural explanation. "Cave was one of the writers," Dziemianowicz explains, "most responsible for shaping the shudder-pulp sensibility, which transformed rural American towns into Gothic landscapes, local powerbrokers into megalomaniacal fiends, and ordinary men and women into paragons of imperilled virtue."

Cave once told *CA:* "I have been writing for publication since I was in high school, and that was not yesterday. One thing I have always solidly believed is that a writer must write to be understood by his readers, and I fear this is now becoming an outmoded credo. Many of today's writers seem to think obscurity is a virtue and have apparently decided that a reader who can't understand them will think them 'artistic.'

"I saw this coming when I was for years a judge in the *Scholastic Magazine*'s annual short story contests for high-school students. High-school English teachers were obviously teaching it. Now many of those students are writers with a dangerous contempt for discipline, and others are editors who mistakenly think that prose, to be effective, must be as murky as swamp water. It's a pity. The great writers of the past would not be remembered today had they fallen into this subtle trap."

BIOGRAPHICAL/CRITICAL SOURCES:

BOOKS

Parente, Audrey, *Pulp Man's Odyssey: The Hugh B. Cave Story,* Starmont House, 1988.

St. James Guide to Horror, Ghost and Gothic Writers, St. James Press (Detroit), 1998.

* * *

CECIL, Robert 1913-1994

PERSONAL: Born March 25, 1913, in England; died February 28, 1994, in England; son of Charles and Marjorie (Porteous) Cecil; married Kathleen Marindin, September 17, 1938; children: Veronica, Brigid, Robert. *Education:* Caius College, Cambridge, B.A., 1935, M.A., 1961. *Avocational interests:* Sufism, gardening, chess.

CAREER: Entered British Foreign Service, 1936, served in the Foreign Office, London, 1939-45; British Embassy, Washington, DC, first secretary, 1945-48; Foreign Office, 1948-52, counsellor and head of American Department, 1951; British Embassy, Copenhagen, Denmark, counsellor, 1952-55; consul-general in Hanover, West Germany, 1955-57; British Embassy, Bonn, West Germany, counsellor, 1957-59; British Information Services, New York, NY, director-general, 1959-61; Foreign Office, head of Cultural Relations Department, 1962-67; Reading University, Reading, England, reader in contemporary German history, beginning 1968, chair of the School of Postgraduate Studies.

MEMBER: Institute for Cultural Research (chairman, beginning 1972), Royal Institute of International Affairs.

AWARDS, HONORS: Companion of Order of St. Michael and St. George.

WRITINGS:

Levant and Other Poems, Fortune Press, 1940.

Time and Other Poems, Putnam (London), 1955.

Life in Edwardian England, Putnam, 1969.

The Myth of the Master Race: Alfred Rosenberg and Nazi Ideology, Batsford (London), 1972.

Hitler's Decision to Invade Russia, 1941, Davis-Poynter (London), 1975.

(Editor) *The King's Son: Readings in the Traditional Psychologies and Contemporary Thought on Man,* Octagon Press (London), 1980.

A Divided Life: A Personal Portrait of the Spy Donald Maclean, Morrow (New York City), 1989.

Also author of *The Masks of Death: Changing Attitudes in the 19th Century.* Contributor to *American Heritage, Poetry, Atlantic Monthly,* and *History Today.*

SIDELIGHTS: Robert Cecil was a diplomat and scholar whose written works focused on modern history. His best-received books were *The Myth of the Master Race: Alfred Rosenberg and Nazi Ideology* and *A Divided Life: A Personal Portait of the Spy Donald Maclean.*

In *The Myth of the Master Race* Cecil examined the racial ideology of Nazi theorist Alfred Rosenberg, who was executed at Nuremberg for war crimes following World War II. Cecil's account of Rosenberg's life and thought is "elegantly written," reported F. E. Hirsch in *Library Journal.* The study, according to the *Economist* reviewer, was "the first full biography of Rosenberg in the English language." The critic for the *Times Literary Supplement* found: "Cecil's evaluation of Rosenberg's influence, the reasons for his later decline and the general role of ideology in helping the Nazis to seize and keep power are judicious and full of common sense."

Cecil turned his attention to Soviet spy Donald Maclean in *A Divided Life.* A member of the spy ring surrounding noted British traitor Kim Philby, Maclean worked for British intelligence as a double agent until being forced to flee in 1951. Maclean was to spend the remainder of his life, some thirty years, living in the Soviet Union. "Though Robert Cecil is sympathetic to Maclean, he is not taken in," wrote Robin W. Winks in the *New York Times Book Review,* "Cecil is just the right person to assess Donald Maclean because he is balanced."

BIOGRAPHICAL/CRITICAL SOURCES:

PERIODICALS

Annals of the American Academy, March, 1973.
Best Sellers, April 1, 1970.
Choice, December, 1972.
Economist, May 27, 1972.
Library Journal, September 15, 1970; August, 1972.
New York Times Book Review, October 29, 1972, p. 55; April 16, 1989, p. 1.
Times Literary Supplement, November 17, 1972, p. 1400.

OBITUARIES:

PERIODICALS

Times (London), March 2, 1994, p. 19.*

* * *

CHARLES, Kate 1950-

PERSONAL: Real name, Carol Chase; born July 13, 1950, in Cincinnati, OH; daughter of Elmer Clinton Fosher, Jr. (an investment officer) and Kathryn Lucile Fosher (a homemaker; maiden name, Fancher); married Rory Lee Chase (an administrator), July 14, 1973. *Education:* Illinois State University, B.A., 1972; Indiana University, M.L.S., 1973. *Religion:* Church of England. *Avocational interests:* Visiting churches, traveling, music, and singing.

ADDRESSES: Home—4 St. George's Rd., Bedford MK40 ZL5, England. *Agent*—Carol Heaton, Elaine Greene Ltd., 37 Goldhawk Rd., London W12 8QQ, England.

CAREER: WGUC Radio, Cincinnati, OH, promotion assistant and record librarian, 1981-85; St. Paul's Church, Bedford, England, parish administrator, 1988-91; writer, 1991—. Freelance desktop publisher.

MEMBER: Crime Writers' Association (member of executive committee, 1993—), Sisters in Crime, Society of Authors, PEN.

WRITINGS:

"BOOK OF PSALMS" SERIES

A Drink of Deadly Wine, Headline (London), 1991, Mysterious Press (New York City), 1992.
The Snares of Death, Headline, 1992, Mysterious Press, 1993.
Appointed to Die, Mysterious Press, 1993.
A Dead Man Out of Mind, Mysterious Press, 1994.
Evil Angels Among Them, Headline, 1995, Mysterious Press, 1996.

SIDELIGHTS: Born and raised in the United States, Kate Charles told *CA* she has been "a lifelong Anglophile." In 1986, Charles, whose real name is Carol

Chase, realized her longtime ambition of moving to England, where she began to write mystery novels set in the Anglican church and featuring David Middleton-Brown, a solicitor, and London artist Lucy Kingsley.

The setting of her first work, *A Drink of Deadly Wine,* was largely inspired by her job as parish administrator in a local Anglican church. In the novel, Reverend Gabriel Neville, a vicar soon to be named Area Archdeacon of the Anglican church, is threatened by an anonymous blackmailer that his former homosexual affairs will be revealed unless he resigns. The vicar turns to a previous lover, David Middleton-Brown, asking him to investigate the threat, fearing it may ruin his marriage and career. Marilyn Stasio of the *New York Times Book Review,* who terms the novel an "ecclesiastical mystery," remarks that "*A Drink of Deadly Wine* can add novelty to its other accomplishments. Included among these are characters dotty enough to have wandered in from an Angela Thirkell novel, an Anglican High Church setting resplendent with Gothic pomp and pageantry, and a neatly contained plot that puts a new moral twist on the old whodunit formula." Charles began writing on a full-time basis when the publication of *A Drink of Deadly Wine* caused her to be dismissed from her position at the parish.

In *The Snares of Death,* a village minister who removed candles, statues and other devotional items from the local church—claiming they were signs of idolatry—has been found murdered. Although Stasio finds that Charles has "a jaundiced eye" when speaking of church officials, "there is real tenderness, though, in her detailed portraits of the faithful, from the sensitive student of church architecture who functions as sleuth to the dear old church biddies who arrange the flowers and spread the gossip." The critic for *Publishers Weekly* finds that "Charles entertains with well-drawn characters, a serviceable plot—though no real surprises—and a deftly explored High Church milieu."

Appointed to Die tells of a rivalry over who shall become the new dean of an Anglican cathedral. When one candidate turns up dead, the entire church community is thrown into turmoil and Middleton-Brown and Kingsley must uncover the murderer. Emily Melton in *Booklist* calls *Appointed to Die* "a nicely written, entertaining British novel in the tradition of Charles' compatriot Barbara Pym."

Three murders, a set of valuable ecclesiastical silver, personal scandal, and a robbery figure into the plot of *A Dead Man Out of Mind.* Middleton-Brown and Kingsley must sort through a variety of suspects before uncovering the criminal. The critic for *Publishers Weekly* calls the novel a "continuously absorbing mystery" and praises the "adroitly drawn main characters" and "finely etched supporting cast." Melton finds it to be "a devilishly clever little mystery that's chock-full of intrigue, scandal, greed, evil, and all sorts of other nastiness not normally associated with the Church."

Evil Angels Among Them finds Middleton-Brown and Kingsley helping out a friend who has just been appointed rector of a village church and is receiving a less-than-welcome reception from the locals. When one of the local women is murdered, "suspicions are rampant, and it takes . . . resourcefulness and intuition to find the killer and smooth the troubled waters," as Melton explains. "Charles's characterizations are entertainingly venomous and penetrating, with just enough believable goodness to balance the equally believable evil at play," according to the critic for *Publishers Weekly.*

Noting that critics have compared her novels to those of English novelist Barbara Pym, Charles commented to *CA,* "I like to think of my books as 'Barbara Pym meets [English crime novelist] P. D. James,' so the comparisons with Barbara Pym are always particularly gratifying!"

BIOGRAPHICAL/CRITICAL SOURCES:

PERIODICALS

Booklist, November 1, 1994, p. 480; November 1, 1995, p. 456; October 1, 1996, p. 324.

Guardian Weekly, March 8, 1992, p. 27.

Kirkus Reviews, August 15, 1992, p. 1018.

New York Times Book Review, November 8, 1992, p. 61; December 12, 1993.

Publishers Weekly, August 10, 1992, p. 57; October 18, 1993, p. 65; September 12, 1994, p. 84; August 28, 1995, p. 105; August 19, 1996, p. 54.

* * *

CHESTER, Deborah 1957-
(Jay D. Blakeney, Sean Dalton)

PERSONAL: Born April 25, 1957, in Chicago, IL; daughter of Kern E. (a chiropractor) and Ann (an image consultant; maiden name, Hatcher) Chester. *Education:* University of Oklahoma, B.A. (with honors), 1978, M.A., 1986. *Religion:* Church of Christ. *Avocational interests:* Gardening, needlework.

ADDRESSES: Home—Norman, OK.

CAREER: Writer, 1978—.

AWARDS, HONORS: The Sign of the Owl was named to the Best Books for Young Adults list, American Library Association, 1981; named Oklahoma Writer of the Year, 1985.

WRITINGS:

NOVELS

A Love So Wild, Coward, 1980.
French Slippers, Coward, 1981.
Royal Intrigue, Dell (New York), 1982.
Heart's Desire, Avon (New York), 1983.
Captured Hearts, Harlequin (Tarrytown, NY), 1989.

OTHER

The Sign of the Owl (juvenile), Four Winds Press, 1981.

Also author of other books. Contributor to *Good Housekeeping. A Love So Wild* has been published in German; *Heart's Desire* has been published in Italian.

UNDER PSEUDONYM JAY D. BLAKENEY

The Children of Anthi, Ace Books (New York City), 1985.
The Omcri Matrix, Ace Books, 1986.
The Goda War, Ace Books, 1989.
Requiem for Anthi, Ace Books, 1990.

UNDER PSEUDONYM SEAN DALTON

Space Hawks, Ace Books, 1990.
Code Name Peregrine, Ace Books, 1990.
Beyond the Void, Ace Books, 1990.
The Rostma Lure, Ace Books, 1991.
Destination Mutiny, Ace Books, 1991.
The Salukan Gambit, Ace Books, 1991.
Time Trap, Ace Books, 1992.
Showdown, Ace Books, 1992.
Pieces of Eight, Ace Books, 1992.

WORK IN PROGRESS: A medical thriller; a science fiction novel.

SIDELIGHTS: Deborah Chester has published many romance novels under her own name; she has also written numerous science fiction books under the pseudonyms Jay D. Blakeney and Sean Dalton. Her first published book, *A Love So Wild,* is a romance inspired by the Regency love stories of Georgette Heyer. Chester once told *CA* that Heyer was one of her favorite writers during her youth. She stated that Heyer's romances "opened a whole new world to me, a world of elegance, style, and wit. The first novel I published was . . . written from my fascination with an era brought to life through Heyer's work. So in part, I must attribute that breakthrough in my early career to her influence." She named Alastair Maclean and Andre Norton as two other writers who had a profound influence on her. "They are no longer my favorites, but during my formative years, they provided me with hours of enjoyment, and I credit their work with helping shape my desire to become a writer. Norton's tales of science fiction and fantasy spurred my childhood imagination. Her vivid style and original viewpoint taught me how to look at the world around me through different, even multiple perspectives. Maclean's adventure novels held excitement, danger on every page, riveting suspense, and fast pace. Even to this day, I am happiest writing stories that incorporate as many of those elements as possible."

Chester's science fiction is a satisfying blend of "action, blood and magic," according to *Kliatt* reviewer Susan E. Chmurynsky. Discussing *Reign of Shadows,* Chmurynsky noted that the story got off to a slow start, but "rebounds," thanks in part to intriguing characters that "grow on the reader." The principals are Caelon E'Non, the son of a famous healer, and Elandra, a servant girl who is half-sister to the Emperor's fiancee. Caelon's father forces him to attend a school for healers, but his bad attitude and poor grades finally lead to his expulsion, freeing him to live out his dream of becoming a soldier. But when his family home is attacked, Caelon is sold as a slave and eventually becomes one of the Emperor's gladiators. In the sequel, *Shadow War,* Caelon becomes a member of the Emperor's Imperial Guard and the personal protector of Elandra, who has supplanted her half-sister and become the Empress. Sister Avila Lamb, another *Kliatt* reviewer, deemed *Shadow War* an "exciting" story and "a real page-turner."

Chester commented: "Going to the University of Oklahoma to major in professional writing was the smartest thing I ever did. The intense training in craft which I received there finally enabled me to harness my spark of talent and do something salable with it. The instructors were published novelists who knew what they were talking about. And it was through contacts made at the university that I got my first agent, wrote my first publishable manuscripts, and began to sell at age 21.

"I am not a 'literary' writer in the sense that I attempt to create a heavily thematic book awash in symbolism and designed to be read and understood only by an erudite few. My purpose in writing is to entertain myself and my readers. I want to give people their money's worth by providing them with a story that is fun to read. To me, the highest compliment I can receive from a reader is, 'I stayed up all night to finish your book because I couldn't put it down.'

"My work habits have changed over the years. I used to write one book a year, taking off about three months between projects. Then I started writing on a computer, and my productivity has increased steadily ever since. Writing nine series novels (the 'Operation Starhawks' series and 'Time Trap' series) in three years really forced me to exercise self-discipline. With a book deadline every four months, I couldn't write at a leisurely pace. I set myself a strict daily page quota to be sure I met my deadlines. My ideal schedule, however, is where I produce about 50 pages a week. No matter what, I think it's very important that I always work steadily on a book, because that keeps my momentum going. It also keeps my mind on the novel, and that helps me avoid mistakes with plot or characterization. I prefer to write an entire chapter at a sitting. If that's not possible, then I make sure I at least complete the scene I'm working on before I leave the keyboard. That keeps my emotional involvement with the characters and story at an optimum level.

"Although I have written several books sold on the basis of proposal or outline, I prefer to write on speculation. I have learned the necessity of outlining, but I would rather let a book grow in my mind, taking shape bit by bit. Whenever I get a piece of it grown, I outline that portion to see if the plot is going to hold together, then I let it grow some more. If the book is complex, I may revamp the whole synopsis several times over the course of the project. But to sit down cold and outline a book from start to finish, then stick with that to the letter—no, that's not for me. I'm usually halfway through the book before I begin to feel like I'm definitely on the right track. I figure my subconscious always knows how the book is going to turn out. What's important is for me to catch up with it, stick to story principles, and not get in its way.

"Who can say what motivates me to write? The story idea is the temptress, luring me out into the darkness, step by step, away from familiar ground. But without discipline, pride, professionalism, and the need to earn a living at this business, art alone won't bring it together. For me, writing is a profession, not a hobby."

BIOGRAPHICAL/CRITICAL SOURCES:

PERIODICALS

Bulletin of the Center for Children's Books, December, 1981, p. 66.
Booklist, July 15, 1981, p. 1446.
Horn Book, August, 1981, pp. 430-431.
Kliatt, September, 1996, p. 16; May, 1997, p. 12.

* * *

CHRISTMAS, Joyce 1939-
(Christmas Peterson, a joint pseudonym)

PERSONAL: Surname originally Smith, changed by marriage in 1970; born August 17, 1939, in Hartford, CT; daughter of Wilfred R. (in business) and Anne (a nurse; maiden name, Plumb) Smith. *Education:* Attended Radcliffe College; Harvard University, B.A. (magna cum laude), 1961.

ADDRESSES: Home—21-19 45th Rd., Long Island City, NY 11101. *E-mail*—Christmasj@aol.com; www.writerswrite.com/authors/joycechristmas. *Office*—Chervenak, Keane & Co., 307 East 44th St., New York, NY 10017. *Agent*—Evan Marshall, 6 Tristam Place, Pine Brook, NJ 07058-9445.

CAREER: Writer (magazine), Boston, MA, 1963-68, began as editorial assistant, became associate editor; freelance public relations and advertising writer and copy editor, 1968-76; freelance public relations and advertising writer and copy editor, 1976—. Chervenak, Keane & Co. (hotel consultants), New York City, hotel computer consultant and managing editor of *CKC Report: Hotel Technology Newsletter,* 1981—.

MEMBER: International Association of Hospitality Accountants, International Association of Crime Writers, Authors Guild, Mystery Writers of America (member of national board), Sisters in Crime.

AWARDS, HONORS: Macavity Award nomination for story "Takeout"; fiction guest of honor, Cluefest mystery convention, 1997.

WRITINGS:

(With Jon Peterson, under joint pseudonym Christmas Peterson) *Hidden Assets,* Avon (New York City), 1981.
Blood Child, Signet (New York City), 1982.
Dark Tide, Avon, 1983.

Ghostwriter of numerous nonfiction books. Contributor to *Plays, Ellery Queen's Mystery Magazine, Mystery Readers Journal* and to trade publications for the hotel industry.

"LADY MARGARET PRIAM MYSTERY SERIES"

Suddenly in Her Sorbet, Fawcett (New York City), 1988.
Simply to Die For, Fawcett, 1989.
A Fete Worse Than Death, Fawcett, 1990.
Friend or Faux, Fawcett, 1991.
A Stunning Way to Die, Fawcett, 1991.
It's Her Funeral, Fawcett, 1992.
A Perfect Day for Dying, Fawcett, 1994.
Mourning Gloria, Fawcett, 1996.
Going Out in Style, Fawcett, 1998.

"BETTY TRENKA MYSTERY SERIES"

This Business Is Murder, Fawcett, 1993.
Death at Face Value, Fawcett, 1995.
Downsized to Death, Fawcett, 1997.

SIDELIGHTS: Joyce Christmas writes two ongoing mystery series featuring female detectives. The Lady Margaret Priam series tells of a British society lady now living in America whose sleuthing takes her into the upper echelons of the Manhattan elite. The Betty Trenka series focuses on a retired office manager restless with the free time retirement has brought her.

Usually set in New York City, the Priam stories revolve around charity events, exclusive shops, and the romantic relationship between Priam and police detective Sam De Vere. Speaking to Claire E. White in the *Writer* magazine, Christmas explains that romance and mystery are a difficult combination: "The genre isn't really suited to romance unless it's an integral part of the plot. But I think the protagonist needs an emotional partner to rely on. You know, writing a book means filling up pages with something happening, and it can't always be a murder."

In *Mourning Gloria,* Lady Margaret is participating in a designer show house fund-raising event organized by prominent social matron Gloria Anton. "In this hilarious send-up of high society," writes the critic for *Publishers Weekly,* "Lady Margaret soon sees through the pampered and polished veneer of these society mavens into a tangle of lies and hatreds. . . . An enjoyable, lighthearted immersion into sophisticated society."

"I began my career as an editor," Christmas once told *CA,* "and found the transition to ghosting nonfiction an easy one. It was easier still to move from there to writing my own fiction and anything else that needed to be written."

BIOGRAPHICAL/CRITICAL SOURCES:

PERIODICALS

Publishers Weekly, July 22, 1996, p. 235.
Writer, July, 1998, p. 10.

* * *

CISNEROS, Antonio 1942-1989

PERSONAL: Born December 27, 1942, in Lima, Peru; died in 1989. *Education:* Attended Catholic University, Lima; National University of San Marcos, Ph.D., 1974.

CAREER: Poet and essayist. Teacher of literature at University of Huamanga, Ayacucho, Peru, 1965, University of Southampton, Southampton, England, 1967-70, University of Nice, Nice, France, 1970-72, and University of San Marcos, Lima, Peru, beginning in 1972; University of Budapest, Budapest, Hungary, exchange professor, 1974-75.

AWARDS, HONORS: Peruvian National Poetry Prize, 1965, for *Comentarios reales;* Cuban Casa de las Americas prize, 1968, for *Canto ceremonial contra un oso hormiguero.*

WRITINGS:

POETRY

Destierro, [Lima, Peru], 1961.

David, El Timonel (Lima), 1962.

Comentarios reales (title means "Royal Commentaries"; also see below), Ediciones de la Rama Florida and Ediciones de la Biblioteca Universitaria, 1964.

Canto ceremonial contra un oso hormiguero (title means "Ceremonial Song Against the Anteater"; also see below), Casa de las Americas (Havana), 1968.

The Spider Hangs Too Far from the Ground (contains selections from *Comentarios reales* and *Canto ceremonial contra un oso hormiguero*), translated by Maureen Ahern, William Rowe, and David Tipton, Cape Goliard (London), 1970.

Agua que no has de beber (also see below), CMB Ediciones (Barcelona), 1971.

Como higuera en un campo de golf (also see below), Instituto Nacional de Cultura (Lima), 1972.

El libro de Dios y los hungaros (also see below), illustrations by David Herskovitz, Libra-1 (Lima), 1978.

(Contributor) *Cuatro poetas: Victor Garcia Robles, Antonio Cisneros, Pedro Shimose, Armando Tejada Gomez,* Casa de las Americas, 1979.

At Night the Cats (bilingual text; contains selections from *Comentarios reales, Canto ceremonial contra un oso hormiguero, Agua que no has de beber, Como higuera en un campo de golf, El libro de Dios y los hungaros,* and *La cronica del Nino Jesus;* also see below), edited and translated by Ahern, Rowe, and Tipton, Red Dust (New York City), 1985.

Monologo de la casta Susana y otros poemas, Instituto Nacional de Cultura (Peru), 1986.

Also author of *La cronica del Nino Jesus,* 1981. Contributor to anthologies.

WORK IN PROGRESS: Cisneros was working on *Los hijos de Albion,* a collection of essays on British poetry, at the time of his death.

SIDELIGHTS: An award-winning Peruvian poet, the late Antonio Cisneros was internationally acclaimed for his satirical works challenging the established values and conventions of his native country. The author first attracted literary attention with the poetry volumes *Comentarios reales* and *Canto ceremonial contra un oso hormiguero,* works exploring alternative interpretations of history and myth. Proceeding to produce such collections as *Agua que no has de beber, Como higuera en un campo de golf,* and *At Night the Cats,* Cisneros consistently won critical approval for his precise language, evocative imagery, and irreverent and ironic humor. Deeming the author "the most distinguished poet now writing in Peru," Jack Schmitt in the *Los Angeles Times Book Review* further proclaimed: "Cisneros . . . is today one of the major poets of all Spanish America."

Born in Lima, Peru in 1942, Cisneros grew up with an avid interest in poetry. He studied literature at the Catholic University in Lima, and much later—after having published and taught for years—received a doctorate degree from the National University of San Marcos. He sought to broaden his experiences through travel and, in addition to teaching literature in his native Peru, taught at foreign universities in England, France, and Hungary.

Many critics have attributed Cisneros' fresh perspective on his own country to his multicultural experiences. "Cisneros is the product of over ten years of travel between London, Nice and Budapest; the political unrest of the 60s in his own country and abroad; and a keen sense of literary technique," explained Gloria F. Waldman in *Hispania.* "He brings his own ironic, gently critical voice to the exotic settings he evokes." In the *Dictionary of Hispanic Biography,* James McCarthy noted: "By living in . . . European countries—with their own decidedly different historical perspectives on colonialism—Cisneros came to see those countries and Peru more clearly. His time abroad gave him a sharpened perspective on the world around him as well as a keener view of his own Peruvian culture."

Cisneros produced the poetry collections *Destierro* and *David* in the early 1960s, but it was not until the appearance of *Comentarios reales* that the poet earned international recognition. Published when Cisneros was twenty-two years old, the work offers sardonic views of Peruvian history. In doing so, *Comentarios reales* was considered significant for its departure from traditionally repressive twentieth-century Peruvian poetry, and the work garnered Peru's National Poetry Prize in 1965. Reviewing the poems of *Comentarios reales* when many of them appeared in a 1970 volume titled *The Spider Hangs Too Far From the Ground,* a *Times Literary Supplement* writer thought the pieces "terse and irreverent." The reviewer extolled, for example, such poems as "Dead Conquerors" for not mythologizing past warriors, quoting: "Shat upon by scorpions & spiders few / survived their horses." "As for the nineteenth century," the critic continued, "all that remains are a few grotesque monuments and allegories. . . . Ants, vultures, rocks, red cactus are the elements of [a] pitiless landscape in which neither history nor environment can offer shelter." McCarthy observed of *Comentarios:* "While critics appreciated [Cisneros's] boldness, they perceived that [his] wit served not simply to degrade his nation but to hold it up to gentle, but insistent, scrutiny." McCarthy concluded that the work "established Cisneros as a permanent poetic voice in his nation."

Cisneros enjoyed continued success with his next volume, *Canto ceremonial contra un oso hormiguero,* winner of the Cuban Casa de las Americas prize in 1968. While this volume branches out to embrace Cisneros' remembrances of travels and experiences in Ayacucho and England, it nonetheless casts a critical eye on culture and history. Discussing the poems of *Canto ceremonial* (some of which also appeared in *The Spider Hangs Too Far From the Ground*), the *Times Literary Supplement* critic considered "Chronicle of Lima" one of the volume's finest offerings; in it, "history and organic growth have been halted and distorted. The poet's Lima is a place of accidental, historical fragments, of absurd superimposed modernity, 'the jungle of cars, a sexless snake of no known species'—a city whose seasons have been altered by the cutting down of forests, where the sea is only visible in rust, where rivers have dried up and 'a white furry veil protects you from the open sky.'"

Cisneros' subsequent poetry volumes further destroy myth, legend, history, and culture through his hallmark satirical voice. *Agua que no has de beber,* containing twenty-two poems written between the years 1964 and 1966, was published in 1971, and the poet's *Como higuera en un campo de golf* appeared in 1972. Selections from these two volumes, as well as those from *Comentarios reales* and *Canto ceremonial* and Cisneros' more recent productions, 1978's *El libro de Dios y los hungaros* and 1981's *La cronica del Nino Jesus,* all appear in *At Night the Cats;* this bilingual anthology containing seventy-six poems was published in 1985.

"For those not previously familiar with Antonio Cisneros' original voice, . . . *At Night the Cats* is an excellent introduction," wrote Waldman. Widely praised for its excellent translation and its choice selections that capture the essence of Cisneros' voice and style, the book gave critics another opportunity to extol Cisneros' craftsmanship. "His early poems, characterized by their epigrammatic brevity, are lean and taut, precise in language and ironic in tone," declared Schmitt. Discussing Cisneros' later works, the reviewer praised the author's "intensely poetic imagination; his stunning images and metaphors, often surreal; his incisive irony and droll humor, sometimes wistful, often self-mocking; his personal, confessional tone; his decorum and reserve, so typical of Peruvians, and also his passion and tenderness." Waldman concurred and compared Cisneros to such famed twentieth-century Hispanic poets as the irreverent Nicanor Parra, the historically astute Pablo Neruda, and the melancholic Cesar Vallejo. Waldman concluded by deeming *At Night the Cats* a "highly valuable volume . . . that will surely make new and old readers smile, and sometimes even laugh out loud, cause indignation at ancient and present injustices, and delight, as good poetry does."

Cisneros' poetry has appeared in numerous anthologies in such languages as French, German, Russian, Danish, and Ukrainian. He also wrote a number of scholarly essays for periodicals and anthologies. Cisneros died in 1989.

BIOGRAPHICAL/CRITICAL SOURCES:

BOOKS

Cisneros, Antonio, *The Spider Hangs Too Far from the Ground,* Cape Goliard (London), 1970.
Dictionary of Hispanic Biography, Gale (Detroit, MI), 1996, pp. 225-27.

PERIODICALS

Hispania, September, 1987.
Los Angeles Times Book Review, October 27, 1985.
Times Literary Supplement, August 21, 1970.*

* * *

CLARK, John Pepper
See CLARK BEKEDEREMO, J(ohnson) P(epper)

* * *

CLARK, Stephen R(ichard) L(yster) 1945-

PERSONAL: Born October 30, 1945, in Luton, England; son of David Allen Richard (a teacher of engineering) and Kathleen (Finney) Clark; married Edith Gillian Metford (a researcher), July 1, 1972; children: Samuel, Alexandra, Verity. *Ethnicity:* "British." *Education:* Oxford University, B.A., 1968, M.A. and D.Phil., both 1973. *Politics:* Libertarian. *Religion:* Episcopalian.

ADDRESSES: *Home*—1 Arnside Rd., Oxton, Birkenhead, Merseyside L43 2JU, England. *Office*—Department of Philosophy, University of Liverpool, Liverpool, England.

CAREER: Professor of philosophy, University of Liverpool, Liverpool, England, 1984—; Dean of Arts Faculty, 1995-98; Fellow of All Souls College, Oxford, 1968-75; lecturer Glasgow University, 1974-83.

MEMBER: Aristotelian Society, Vegetarian Society, Royal Society of Arts.

WRITINGS:

Aristotle's Man, Clarendon Press, 1975.

The Moral Status of Animals, Clarendon Press, 1977, second edition, 1983.

The Nature of the Beast: Are Animals Moral?, Oxford University Press, 1982.

From Athens to Jerusalem: The Love of Wisdom and the Love of God, Clarendon Press, 1984.

The Mysteries of Religion, Blackwell, 1986.

Civil Peace and Sacred Order, Clarendon Press, 1989.

A Parliament of Souls, Clarendon Press, 1990.

God's World and the Great Awakening, Clarendon Press, 1991.

How to Think about the Earth, Mowbrays, 1993.

How to Live Forever, Routledge, 1995.

Animals and their Moral Standing, Routledge, 1997.

God, Religion and Reality, SPCK, 1998.

The Political Animal, Routledge, 1998.

Biology and Christian Ethics, Cambridge University Press, 1999.

Contributor to philosophical journals, including *Inquiry*. Editor of *Journal of Applied Philosophy*.

SIDELIGHTS: Stephen R. L. Clark's books admonish members of the philosophical and scientific community to reevaluate some of the cherished notions of various disciplines, particularly as they relate to the humane treatment of animals. Of his *The Nature of the Beast: Are Animals Moral?,* Brigid Brophy writes in the *Times Literary Supplement*: "The burden of this book is to dissuade scientists, and in particular ecologists and sociobiologists, from the notion that they are doing something scientific when, discounting the awareness that goes with perceptions, they try to adopt 'aseptic' attitudes and vocabulary in their accounts of animals' behaviour. . . . What in effect Clark presents is a well-documented survey of present ethological thought in which he points to the places where muddled concepts or concepts adopted without recognition of their implications are making a nonsense of science. . . . Clark's exercise is of practical and moral, as well as academic, value."

Clark also applies himself to the philosophical grounds for morality among human beings. In *From Athens to Jerusalem: The Love of Wisdom and the Love of God,* "Clark's main argument against embracing scepticism," writes *Times Literary Supplement* contributor D. Z. Phillips, "is his invitation to the sceptic to note that, in all human activities, justifications must come to an end somewhere. We act without further reasons. Clark, however, wants us to call such bed-rock responses 'acting on faith.' If this lack of further grounds is true of basic responses, whether religious or not, why should all such responses be called faith, or compared to a religious faith which would naturally belong only to some of the responses?. . . Here, belief appears to be a presupposition entailed by our basic responses, whereas, in fact, it is those basic responses which are the conditions of concept-formation where our beliefs are concerned."

Clark told *CA:* "I wish to keep myself, and others, awake: to avoid the fog of unreason and self-deception which keeps us from appreciating, and revering, the beauty of other creatures, and from making necessary connections between out thought and action. I have been influenced most by Plato, Aristotle, Plotinus, Chesterton and the great poets. In composing, I will usually begin by identifying passages of philosophers and poets relevant to my current concerns, blocking out the main argument and then developing the theme in and around those points. I write on my chosen topics—animals, consciousness, immortality, imagination—because I think these are the points where we most need to wake ourselves up."

BIOGRAPHICAL/CRITICAL SOURCES:

PERIODICALS

Nature, November 11, 1982.

Times Literary Supplement, October 15, 1982; January 25, 1985; June 12, 1987.

**CLARK BEKEDEREMO, J(ohnson) P(epper) 1935-
(John Pepper Clark)**

PERSONAL: Born April 6, 1935, in Kiagbodo, Nigeria; son of Clark Fuludu (an Ijaw tribal leader) and Poro Clark Bekederema; married Ebun Odutola; children: three daughters, one son. *Education:* University of Ibadan, B.A. (with honors), 1960.

ADDRESSES: Office—c/o EC Repertory Theatre, J. K. Randle Hall, King George V Rd., Onikan, Lagos, Nigeria. *Agent*—Andrew Best, Curtis Brown Ltd., 162-168 Regent St., London W1R 5TB, England.

CAREER: Poet, playwright, and filmmaker. Nigerian Federal Government, information officer, 1960-61; *Daily Express,* Lagos, Nigeria, head of features and editorial writer, 1961-62; University of Lagos, Lagos, research fellow, 1964-66, professor of African literature and instructor in English, 1966-85.

MEMBER: Society of Nigerian Authors (founding member).

AWARDS, HONORS: Institute of African Studies research fellow, 1961-62, 1963-64; Parvin fellow, Princeton University, 1962-63.

WRITINGS:

Song of a Goat (play; also see below; produced at Ibadan University, 1961), Mbari Writers Club (Ibadan), 1961.

Poems, Mbari Press (Ibadan), 1962.

(Contributor) Gerald Moore, editor, *Seven African Writers,* Oxford University Press (Oxford), 1962.

Three Plays: Song of a Goat, The Masquerade, The Raft ("Bikoroa" trilogy), Oxford University Press, 1964.

(Contributor) John Reed and Clive Wake, editors, *A Book of African Verse,* Heinemann, 1964.

America, Their America (nonfiction), Deutsch, 1964, Africana Publishing, 1969.

A Reed in the Tide, Longmans, 1965, 2nd edition published as *A Reed in the Tide: A Selection of Poems,* Humanities, 1970.

Ozidi: A Play, Oxford University Press, 1966.

(Contributor) *West African Verse: An Anthology,* Longmans, 1967.

Casualties: Poems, 1966-68, Africana Publishing, 1970.

The Example of Shakespeare: Critical Essays on African Literature, Northwestern University Press, 1970.

(Translator) Okabou Ojobolo, *The Ozidi Saga,* Ibajan University Press, 1977.

A Decade of Tongues: Selected Poems 1958-1968, Longmans, 1981.

Scriptwriter, director, and producer of documentary films *The Ozidi of Atazi* and *The Ghost Town.* Founder and editor, *Horn* (literary magazine); co-editor, *Black Orpheus,* 1968—. Contributor of literary criticism to *Presence Africaine, Nigeria, Transition, African Forum, Black Orpheus,* and other journals. Contributor to anthologies, including *The Example of Shakespeare: Critical Essays on African Literature,* 1970, and *The Philosophical Anachronism of William Godwin,* 1977.

SIDELIGHTS: Nigerian-born J. P. Clark Bekederemo has been called one of the central figures of West African drama, and he is equally well known as one of his country's foremost poets. In both roles he combines classical Western style and structure with stories, characters, and themes rooted in his native Ijaw tradition to create a body of work that is both universal and culturally unique. In a discussion with university students in 1970 included in *Palaver: Interviews with Five African Writers in Texas,* Clark Bekederemo commented on the cross-cultural fusion in his work, noting, "In a new nation like Nigeria which cuts across several groups of people, or rather which brings together several peoples speaking different languages, you've got to have a *lingua franca,* and this is the role that English is playing in the absence of one widely spoken Nigerian language . . . . I belong to the new community of Nigerians who have undergone a new system of education and therefore share a new kind of culture, a synthetic one which exists alongside the traditional one to which fortunately I also belong."

Like the life he has led, the new Nigerian culture Clark Bekederemo references is a bridging of two worlds, African and European. Clark Bekederemo's father was an Ijaw tribal leader in a fishing village in Eastern Nigeria. The author attended local elementary school and the Government College in Ughelli before pursuing a bachelor's degree in English from University College in Ibadan, a branch of the University of London, and a partially completed fellowship at Princeton University in the United States.

Critics have found ample evidence of Clark's bifurcated background in his plays and poetry, noting the presence of Ijaw myths, legends, and religion, masks, pantomimes, drumming, and dancing alongside poetic dialogue that seems distinctly Shakespearean, within epic tragedies styled after Sophocles or Euripides. Commenting in *English Studies in Africa,* T. O. McLoughlin observed, "The interesting point about John Pepper Clark is that his awareness of what he calls 'traditional' and 'native' influences has come to dominate what he has learned from western literature."

Clark Bekederemo's first dramatic work was the 1960 play *Song of a Goat,* about Zifa, a fisherman, whose sexual impotence causes his wife, Ebiere, to seek advice from the village Masseur. The Masseur, a sort of doctor-mystic, suggests that Zifa's younger brother, Tonye, should, as a practical matter, assume the husband's duties. Both husband and wife reject the idea, but eventually Ebiere's frustration drives her to seduce Tonye. Zifa uncovers the truth and attempts to murder his brother. Though Tonye escapes his brother's wrath, his guilt is too heavy and he hangs himself. Zifa walks into the sea to drown and Ebiere is left pregnant, setting the stage for *The Masquerade,* Clark Bekederemo's 1964 sequel to this tragic family drama.

African American playwright LeRoi Jones asserted in *Poetry:* "[*Song of a Goat*] is English, but it is not. The tone, the references . . . belong to what I must consider an African experience. The English is pushed . . . past the immaculate boredom of the recent Victorians to a quality of experience that is non-European, though it is the European tongue which seems to shape it, externally." Acknowledging that cultural background affects how an audience experiences *Song of a Goat,* Clark Bekederemo once told a group of American students, "The idea of sacrifice is a universal one, but the theme of impotence is something that doesn't have the same kind of cultural significance for you as it has for me. The business of reproduction, of fertility, is a life and death matter in my home area. If a man doesn't bear, he has not lived. And when he is dead, nobody will think of him."

The Masquerade is a lyrical, fairy-tale tragedy that has been compared to Shakespeare's *Romeo and Juliet.* In the play Ebiere's son, Tufa, is a grown man who woos Titi, a popular village girl who has refused all other suitors. Through lavish presents and attention he wins the favor of Titi and her father, Diribi, and an extravagant wedding is arranged. Prior to the nuptials, however, the groom's family history is discovered. Everyone, including the innocent Tufa, is surprised to learn he is the son of his father's brother and that his conception caused the deaths of all his parents. As the plot hurtles to a climax Diribi shoots and kills his daughter in a furious rage, then is forced by the despondent Tufa to end his life as well.

Critic William Connor praised *The Masquerade* in *World Literature Written in English,* saying, "I can think of no other modern play which in its compactness, the power of its tragic irony and the neatness of its resolution comes as close to duplicating the achievement of Clark's models, the classical Greek tragedies." Nevertheless, the play was generally dismissed by other critics as second-rate, unbelievable storytelling, and what began in the playwright's mind as a classically modeled tragic trilogy was never completed.

Instead, Clark Bekederemo wrote *The Raft,* a tragedy about four lumbermen attempting to earn money by delivering a load of logs downriver to a wealthy buyer. Although *The Raft* has often been described as a political drama foretelling the fate of Nigeria at the time of its Civil War, the playwright himself insists he was not trying to write a "political thesis," but instead was "trying to create a human condition which I knew existed not only in Nigeria but elsewhere."

Through much of the 1960s Clark Bekederemo continued to write plays, culminating in his 1966 adaptation of the sprawling Ijaw epic, *Ozidi,* one of the tribe's masquerade serial plays which are told in seven days, and which incorporate music, dance, and mime. After *Ozidi,* however, the author turned from drama to poetry and did not write another play for nearly twenty years.

The intervening decades saw the publication of a handful of volumes of poetry, including *A Reed in the Tide* (1965), the first international publication of Clark Bekederemo's verse, *Urhobo Poetry* (1980), *Mandela and Other Poems* (1988), and *Collected Poems, 1958-1988* (1991). Like his drama, Clark Bekederemo's poetry reflects both African and European cultures, describing the author's surroundings and experiences in his native country and abroad in a style that has been likened to the English poet Gerard Manley Hopkins. While he wasn't writing plays Clark Bekederemo also published criticism in magazines, journals, and books, including *The Example of Shakespeare: Critical Essays on African Literature* (1970) and *The Philosophical Anachronism of William Godwin* (1977).

1985's "Bikoroa" plays marked Clark Bekederemo's return to playwriting and his renewed interest in familiar themes. Family conflict, revenge, and hereditary suffering play prominent parts in this epic trilogy about two quarreling brothers who kill each other, and pass their strife along to their sons and their grandsons. This cycle of plays has been called "more relaxed and less relentlessly tragic" than the author's earlier plays, perhaps because the Bikoroa plays, which include *The Boat, The Return Home,* and *Full Circle* are written in prose, not verse. Still, Clark Bekederemo is a writer with a poet's penchant for simile, metaphor and turn-of-phrase, so it is not surprising to hear an angry man in a hurry described as "a whirlwind with a lot of dust in its eye."

When asked about the artist's role in society, Clark Bekederemo's first response is typically a practical one. "I think that the writer—whether African, European or American—is just like a lawyer, a doctor, a carpenter, a janitor, one type of citizen within society," he insisted before a student audience. "He has his work as has everyone with a job to do." And what is the writer's job? Clark Bekederemo suggested, "The commitment to produce something beautiful, and perhaps functional as well—this is the business of the artist as an interpreter, as a maker, as a creator, as a constant renewer of life."

BIOGRAPHICAL/CRITICAL SOURCES:

BOOKS

Black Literature Criticism, Gale (Detroit), 1992.
Contemporary Dramatists, fifth edition, St. James Press (Chicago), 1993.
Contemporary Literary Criticism, Gale, Volume 38, 1986.
Drama Criticism, Gale, Volume 5, 1995.
King, Bruce, editor, *Post-Colonial English Drama,* St. Martin's Press (New York), 1992.
Laurence, Margaret, *Long Drums and Cannons: Nigerian Dramatists and Novelists,* Macmillan (London), 1968.
Lindforth, Bernth, and others, editors, *Palaver: Interviews with Five African Writers,* University of Texas at Austin, 1972.
Pieterse, Cosmo, and Dennis Duerden, editors, *African Writers Talking,* Africana Publishing (New York City), 1972.
Smith, Rowland, editor, *Exile and Tradition: Studies in African And Caribbean Literature,* Longman, 1976.

PERIODICALS

Concerning Poetry, fall, 1984.
English Studies in Africa, March, 1975, pp. 31-40.
Ibadan, June, 1966.
Literature East and West, March, 1968, pp. 56-67.
Modern Drama, May, 1968, pp. 16-26.
Poetry, March, 1964.
World Literature Written in English, November, 1976, pp. 297-304; November, 1979, pp. 278-86; autumn, 1987; spring, 1988.

—Sidelights by Lane A. Glenn

* * *

CLIFF, Michelle 1946-

PERSONAL: Born November 2, 1946, in Kingston, Jamaica; naturalized United States citizen. *Education:* Wagner College, A.B., 1969; Warburg Institute, London, M.Phil., 1974.

ADDRESSES: Agent—Faith Childs Literary Agency, 275 West 96th St., No. 31B, New York, NY 10025.

CAREER: Life, New York City, reporter and researcher, 1969-70; W. W. Norton & Co., Inc. (publisher), New York City, production supervisor of Norton Library, 1970-71, copy editor, 1974-75, manuscript and production editor specializing in history, politics, and women's studies, 1975-79; *Sinister Wisdom,* Amherst, MA, co-publisher and editor, 1981-83; Norwich University, Vermont College Campus, Montpelier, member of cycle faculty for adult degree program, 1983-84; Martin Luther King, Jr., Public Library, Oakland, CA, teacher of creative writing and history, 1984—; writer of Afro-Caribbean (Indian, African, European) heritage literature. Member of editorial board of *Signs: A Journal of Women in Culture and Society,* 1980-89. Member of faculty at New School for Social Research, 1974-76, Hampshire College, 1980, 1981, University of Massachusetts at Amherst, 1980, and Vista College, 1985; visiting faculty at San Jose State, 1986, and University College of Santa Cruz, 1987; visiting lecturer at Stanford University, 1987-1991; visiting writer at Trinity College, 1990; Allan K. Smith Visiting Writer at Trinity College, 1992; speaker at workshops and symposia in United States and abroad.

MEMBER: Authors Guild, Authors League of America, Poets and Writers, PEN, Sisters in Support of Sisters in South Africa (member of the board).

AWARDS, HONORS: MacDowell Fellow at MacDowell College, 1982; National Endowment for the Arts fellow, 1982, 1989; Massachusetts Artists Foundation fellow, 1984; Eli Kantor fellow at Yaddo, 1984; Fulbright Fellowship, New Zealand, 1988; National Endowment for the Arts fellow in fiction, 1989.

WRITINGS:

(Editor) *The Winner Names the Age: A Collection of Writing by Lillian Smith,* Norton (New York City), 1978.
Claiming an Identity They Taught Me to Despise (poems), Persephone Press (Watertown, MA), 1980.
Abeng (novel), Crossing Press (Trumansburg, NY), 1984.
The Land of Look Behind: Prose and Poetry, Firebrand Books (Ithaca, NY), 1985.
No Telephone to Heaven (novel), Dutton (New York City), 1987.
Bodies of Water (short stories), Dutton, 1990.
Free Enterprise (novel), Dutton, 1993.

Work represented in anthologies, including *Extended Outlooks,* Macmillan, 1983; and *Home Girls,* edited by Barbara Smith, Kitchen Table Press, 1983. Author of introduction of *Macht und Sinnlichkeit,* by Audre Lorde and Adrienne Rich, Subrosa Frauenverlag, 1983. Contributor to books, including *Between Women,* edited by Carol Asher, Louise De Salvo, and Sally Ruddick, Beacon Press, 1984; *Early Ripening,* edited by Marge Piercy, Pandora Press, 1987; *Caribbean Women Writers,* edited by Selwyn Cudjoe, Calaloux, 1990; *Critical Fictions,* edited by Philomena Mariani, Bay Press, 1991; *Between Friends,* edited by M. Pearlman, Houghton Mifflin, 1993. Also contributor of articles and reviews to magazines, including *Voice Literary Supplement, Ms., Chrysalis, Conditions, Feminary, Frontiers, Graywolf Annual, Sojourner, Sinister Wisdom, Black Scholar, Heresies,* and *Feminist Review.* Poetry and short fiction pieces have appeared in *Conditions, Sojourner, Iowa Review, American Voice, Ms., Voice Literary Supplement,* and *Parnassus.*

WORK IN PROGRESS: Caliban's Daughter, a book of essays; *The Story of a Million Items,* a second collection of short fiction.

SIDELIGHTS: Michelle Cliff was born in Jamaica and moved with her family to New York City as a child. Her status as a light-skinned creole, a woman, and a lesbian marks her as an outsider, even within her own family, and a member of an oppressed group. In poetry, autobiographical fiction, and nonfiction essays, Cliff explores the varieties of oppression, particularly under the system of colonialism. Simon Gikandi summarized Cliff's project in an essay in his *Writing in Limbo: Modernism and Caribbean Literature:* "The uniqueness of Cliff's aesthetics lies in her realization that the fragmentation, silence and repression that mark the life of the Caribbean subject under colonialism must be confronted not only as a problem to be overcome but also as a condition of possibility—as a license to dissimulate and to affirm difference—in which an identity is created out of the chaotic colonial and postcolonial history."

In her first book, *Claiming an Identity They Taught Me to Despise,* a collection of prose poems, Cliff focuses on intraracial prejudice, delineating how it feels to be urged to pass for white by one's own family members, acknowledging an awareness of both the advantages gained by being light-skinned in a colorist society and the ways in which light-skinned blacks are taught to collaborate with the masters to keep the dark-skinned down. In addition, pieces such as "The Laughing Mulatto (Formerly a Statue) Speaks" conflate passing for white and passing for heterosexual in a racist and homophobic society, "suggesting that one component of identity is intrinsically linked to all others," Annmarie Pinarski proposed in *Gay and Lesbian Literature.*

Like her poems, Cliff's novels "draw conections among the histories and experiences of women and other colonized peoples, including those individuals marginalized because of their sexual orientation," Pinarski remarked. In her first novel, *Abeng,* Cliff introduces Clare Savage, who shares many elements of the author's own history, including being the lightest skinned person in her family. In *Abeng,* Clare's lightness symbolizes a kind of blindness to history, as the author explained to Jacqueline Brice-Finch in *Twentieth-Century Caribbean and Black African Writers.* It is both a source of power within her colorist society and a disguise that allows her to be invisible, but one that keeps her from forming a whole identity. "Clare's quest to make meaning of her life is facilitated through interactions with her mulatto-born mother Kitty, her well-respected grandmother, her first love, a black girl named Zoe, and Miss Beatrice, a white woman who teaches Clare not to 'act like a boy,'" according to Pinarski.

Cliff's second novel, *No Telephone to Heaven,* reintroduces Clare as an adult who returns to Jamaica to acknowledge and absorb its history as her own. Both Brice-Finch and Pinarski note that Cliff herself has affirmed the importance of the grandmother figure as another thread that connects her first two novels. In *No Telephone,* Clare returns to her grandmother's farm, where a group of nascent guerillas is encamped, whom she befriends. Indeed, "throughout the novel Clare encounters people who struggle to come to terms with their pasts," Brice-Finch remarked and the result is "a dystopian novel about the crippling effects of colonialism."

Free Enterprise, Cliff's third novel, is considered her strongest work to date by Brice-Finch. The novel focuses on two African-American women who come together to aid John Brown in his fight against slavery, and contrasts them with two contemporary white women, for whom it is possible to openly acknowledge their support of antislavery efforts. Critic Pinarski sees the overarching theme of Cliff's fiction as "the struggle for identity and wholeness in a fragmented, incomprehensible world shattered by racism, sexism, imperialism, and homophobia." Brice-Finch emphasizes the universality of Cliff's concerns, which opens the way for a more optimistic reading of her works: "Her journeys of discovery crisscross all continents, forging links that bind us inextricably together in one global community."

Michelle Cliff once told *CA:* "I received my education in the United States, Jamaica, and England. I have traveled widely in Europe and lived in London from 1971 through 1974. I am proficient in several languages, including French, Italian, and Spanish, and I have a reading knowledge of Latin. My interests, besides creative writing, are black history, especially the survival of African forms and ideas among Afro-American and Afro-Caribbean people, and visual art, particularly the art of the Italian Renaissance and the art of Afro-American women. Along with my present writing projects, I am engaged in preparing a writing course for young black writers in the Oakland, California, community.

"In my writing I am concerned most of all with social issues and political realities and how they affect the lives of people. Because I am a Jamaican by birth, heritage, and indoctrination, born during the time the island was a British Crown Colony, I have experienced colonialism as a force first-hand. Thus colonialism—and the racism upon which it is based—are subjects I address in most of my writing.

"In my novel *Abeng* I try to show the evils of colonialism, including the brutalities of slavery, the erasure of the history of a colonized people, and the rifts which occur among colonized peoples. The primary relationship in my book, around which the plot pivots, is that between a light-skinned girl named Clare Savage and a darker girl named Zoe. They have between them a past in which lighter-skinned people become the oppressors of darker people—although both groups are comprised of people of color and both groups have their origins in slavery. Generally speaking, the creoles of Jamaica, of mixed racial heritage—African and English for the most part, but also of other groups—were placed higher in the social and economic strata of the island by the colonial overlords. Zoe and Clare meet across this divide, sharing at first an idyllic friendship on the country property of Clare's grandmother, on which Zoe, her mother, and her sister are squatters. Gradually—then suddenly—through an incident of violence in which Clare's indoctrination as a member of the almost-ruling class is shown, the split between the two girls becomes obvious. The novel ends with Clare only barely aware of who she is in this society, but certain that something is wrong in her homeland and with her people.

"While most of the actual events of the book are fiction, emotionally the book is an autobiography. I was a girl similar to Clare and have spent most of my life and most of my work exploring my identity as a light-skinned Jamaican, the privilege and the damage that comes from that identity. For while identification with the status of oppressor can be seen as privilege, and brings with it opportunities denied oppressed people, it also inflicts damage on the privileged person. In my sequel to *Abeng* I will take Clare Savage into her thirties through a journey in which she rejects the privilege offered her and seeks both wholeness as a person of color and a recommitment to her country.

"I am also interested in black women as visual artists, particularly in the survival of African art forms and in African philosophical and religious principles among Afro-American artists. This reflects my continuing interest in history and my growing awareness of how much of history is submerged, how much written history is distorted. I see, for example, that the leadership positions held by many Afro-American women in the abolitionist movement, the civil rights movement, and the anti-lynching movement are similar to the roles that have been assumed by women in West African societies. The book I am writing on this subject will deal with visual art, but also with the larger questions of the historic role of black American women, the values they have conveyed, the social responsibility they have assumed."

BIOGRAPHICAL/CRITICAL SOURCES:

BOOKS

Davies, Carole Boyce, and Elaine Savory Fido, editors, *Out of the Kumbla: Caribbean Women and Literature,* Third World Press, 1990, pp. 111-42.

Dictionary of Literary Biography, Volume 157: *Twentieth-Century Caribbean and Black African Writers, Third Series,* Gale (Detroit), 1996.

Gay and Lesbian Literature, Volume 2, St. James Press, 1998, pp. 91-92.

Gikani, Simon, *Writing in Limbo: Modernism and Caribbean Literature* Cornel University Press, 1992, pp. 231-51.

Smith, Sidonie, editor, *De/Colonizing the Subject: The Politics of Gender in Women's Autobiography,* University of Minnesota Press, 1992, pp. 321-45; pp. 139-68.

PERIODICALS

Ariel, January, 1993, pp. 35-56.

Callaloo, winter, 1993, pp. 180-91.

Conditions, no. 13, 1986, pp. 189-91.

Contemporary Literature, winter, 1993, pp. 595-619; spring, 1995, pp. 82-102

Journal of the Midwest Modern Language Association, spring, 1992, pp. 23-31.

Kenyon Review, winter, 1993, pp. 57-71.

New York Times Book Review, September 23, 1990, p. 22.

Times Literary Supplement, February 23, 1990, p. 203.

Washington Post, June 8, 1993, pp. C1-4.

* * *

COEL, Margaret 1937-

PERSONAL: Born October 11, 1937, in Denver, CO; daughter of Samuel F. (a railroad engineer) and Margaret (McCloskey) Speas; married George W. Coel (a dentist), July 22, 1992; children: William (deceased), Kristin M., Lisa M. *Education:* Marquette University, B.A., 1960; graduate study at University of Colorado; attended Oxford University. *Politics:* Democrat. *Religion:* Roman Catholic. *Avocational interests:* Travel.

ADDRESSES: Home—3155 Lafayette Dr., Boulder, CO 80303.

CAREER: Westminster Journal, Westminster, CO, reporter, 1960-61; *Boulder Daily Camera,* Boulder, CO, feature writer, 1972-75. Member of board of directors of Historic Boulder; guest lecturer to numerous groups and organizations, including Denver Museum of Natural History, Colorado State Historical Society and the National Convention of Questers.

MEMBER: Western Writers of America, Mystery Writers of America, Colorado Authors League (board of directors, 1987-92; president, 1990-91).

AWARDS, HONORS: Fellow at Bread Loaf Writers' Conference, 1981; Best Nonfiction Book of the Year Award, National Association of Press Women, 1981, for *Chief Left Hand;* Top Hand Award for best nonfiction book by a Colorado Author, Colorado Authors League, 1986, for *Goin' Railroading.*

WRITINGS:

Chief Left Hand: Southern Arapahoe, University of Oklahoma Press (Norman), 1981.

The Next 100 Years: A Report, University of Colorado, Medical School, 1983.

(With Jane Barker and Karen Gilleland) *The Tivoli: Bavaria in the Rockies,* Colorado & West (Boulder), 1985.

(With Gladys Doty and Gilleland) *Under the Golden Dome: Colorado's State Capitol,* Colorado & West, 1985.

(With father, Sam Speas) *Goin' Railroading: A Century on the Colorado High Iron,* Pruett (Boulder, CO), 1986, new edition published as *Goin' Railroading: Two Generations of Colorado Stories,* 1992.

450 Best Sales Letters for Every Selling Situation, Prentice-Hall (Englewood Cliffs, NJ), 1991.

The Pride of Our People: The Colorado State Capitol, Colorado General Assembly, 1992.

The Eagle Catcher, University Press of Colorado (Niwot, CO), 1995.

The Ghost Walker, Berkley (New York City), 1996.

The Dream Stalker, Berkley, 1997.

The Story Teller, Berkley, 1998.

Also co-author of *A New Westminster,* 1987. Contributor of articles to newspapers and magazines, including the *New York Times, Christian Science Monitor, National Observer, American Heritage of Invention and Technology, Rendezvous Magazine,* and *Old West Magazine.* Contributor of book reviews to *Denver Post.*

SIDELIGHTS: An accomplished writer of nonfiction and mystery novels, Margaret Coel is best known for her series of mystery novels set on an Arapaho Indian reservation in Wyoming and featuring attorney Vicky Holden and priest John O'Malley.

In *The Eagle Catcher,* the murder of the Wind River Reservation's tribal chief involves O'Malley in an effort to prove that the chief's son is innocent of the crime. O'Malley, a recovering alcoholic assigned to the reservation's St. Francis Mission, must also cope with his strong attraction to Arapaho attorney Holden. The critic for *Publishers Weekly* finds that "likeable, well-drawn characters and a lively pace mark this novel."

The Ghost Walker begins with O'Malley finding a dead body in a roadside ditch; but the body disappears before the authorities arrive. The Arapaho believe the dead man has become a Ghost Walker, one whose soul must wander the earth searching for a way to the afterworld. *The Ghost Walker* is an "excellent mystery," Stuart Miller writes in *Booklist,* while the critic for *Publishers Weekly* calls the novel a "well-crafted adventure."

In *The Dream Stalker,* O'Malley is entangled in a plan to build a nuclear waste disposal site on the reservation, a plan favored by the poverty-stricken Arapaho. Holden receives death threats for opposing the project, and a thirty-year-old murder figures into a murder in the present-day. "Coel enchants and intrigues by presenting uniformly well developed, realistic characters . . . who face difficult moral choices," as John Rowen writes in *Booklist.* Rex E. Klett in *Library Journal* praises the "usual commendable plotting and characterization" in *The Dream Stalker,* while the critic for *Publishers Weekly* notes that "the nicely drawn Wyoming backdrop, capable plotting and engaging characters all add up to another coup for Coel."

The Story Teller concerns a missing ledger book—an Arapaho pictograph record of a nineteenth century massacre of their people. When the book goes missing from a Denver museum, three students end up murdered and O'Malley and Holden must track down the killer. "All the strengths of this fine series are present here: Coel's knowledge of and respect for western history, a solid mystery with a credible premise in Indian lore and the struggles of Holden and O'Malley with their powerful, but so far unconsummated, attraction to each other."

In her nonfiction books, Coel has used her skills to introduce readers to the people who took part in history's greatest events. Coel's first study, *Chief Left Hand,* strives "to convey to the reader a sense that the inhabitants of the plains before the white man arrived were people with hopes and plans, talents and abilities, just like any other group of people," the author once told *CA.*

Coel's interest in "people at work under special circumstances . . . at a special time" led her to write *Goin' Railroading,* she told *CA.* An account of the development of the railroad across America's West, the study features the authentic voice of Sam Speas, the author's father, who spent decades tending the boilers of old steam engines. Through Coel, Speas recalls both the personal and historical aspects of the railroad. Calling Speas "a better storyteller than historian," a *Publishers Weekly* critic observes that the tales "come alive" when Speas focuses on his personal experiences as a railroad worker. Speas's fascinating anecdotes, the critic adds, allow "the romance of the rails [to] slowly charm the reader."

BIOGRAPHICAL/CRITICAL SOURCES:

PERIODICALS

Booklist, October 1, 1996, p. 325; August, 1997, p. 1882.

Library Journal, September 1, 1997, p. 222; June 1, 1998, p. 186.

Publishers Weekly, November 29, 1991, p. 46; April 3, 1995, p. 49; August 19, 1996, p. 54; July 14, 1997, p. 67; August 3, 1998, p. 77.

* * *

COFER, Judith Ortiz 1952-

PERSONAL: Born February 24, 1952, in Hormigueros, P.R.; immigrated to the United States, 1956; daughter of J. M. (in U.S. Navy) and Fanny (Morot) Ortiz; married Charles John Cofer (in business),

November 13, 1971; children: Tanya. *Education:* Augusta College, B.A., 1974; Florida Atlantic University, M.A., 1977; attended Oxford University, 1977.

ADDRESSES: Home—P.O. Box 938, Louisville, GA 30434. *Office*—Department of English and Creative Writing, University of Georgia, Athens, GA 30602. *Agent*—Berenice Hoffman Literary Agency, 215 West 75th St., New York, NY 10023.

CAREER: Bilingual teacher at public schools in Palm Beach County, FL, 1974-75; Broward Community College, Fort Lauderdale, FL, adjunct instructor in English, 1978-80, instructor in Spanish, 1979; University of Miami, Coral Gables, FL, lecturer in English, 1980-84; University of Georgia, Athens, instructor in English, 1984-87, Georgia Center for Continuing Education, instructor in English, 1987-88; Macon College, instructor in English, 1988-89; Mercer University College, Forsyth, GA, special programs coordinator, 1990; University of Georgia, Athens, associate professor of English and Creative Writing, 1992—. Adjunct instructor at Palm Beach Junior College, 1978-80. Visiting professor at numerous colleges and universities, including University of Michigan, Arizona University, and University of Minnesota, Duluth. Conducts poetry workshops and gives poetry readings. Member of regular staff of International Conference on the Fantastic in Literature, 1979-82; member of literature panel of Fine Arts Council of Florida, 1982; member of administrative staff of Bread Loaf Writers' Conference, 1983 and 1984.

MEMBER: Poetry Society of America, Poets and Writers, Associated Writing Programs.

AWARDS, HONORS: Scholar of English Speaking Union at Oxford University, 1977; fellow of Fine Arts Council of Florida, 1980; Bread Loaf Writers' Conference, scholar, 1981, John Atherton Scholar in Poetry, 1982; grant from Witter Bynner Foundation for Poetry, 1988, for *Letters from a Caribbean Island;* National Endowment for the Arts fellowship in poetry, 1989; Pulitzer Prize nomination, 1989, for *The Line of the Sun;* Pushcart Prize for nonfiction, 1990; O. Henry Prize for short story, 1994; Anisfield Wolf Award in Race Relations, 1994, for *The Latin Deli.*

WRITINGS:

Latin Women Pray (chapbook), Florida Arts Gazette Press, 1980.

The Native Dancer (chapbook), Pteranodon Press, 1981.

Among the Ancestors (chapbook), Louisville News Press, 1981.

Latin Women Pray (three-act play), first produced in Atlanta at Georgia State University, June, 1984.

Peregrina (poems), Riverstone Press (Golden, CO), 1986.

Terms of Survival (poems), Arte Publico (Houston, TX), 1987.

(Contributor) *Triple Crown: Chicano, Puerto Rican and Cuban American Poetry* (trilogy; contains Cofer's poetry collection *Reaching for the Mainland*), Bilingual Press (Ypsilanti, MI), 1987.

The Line of the Sun (novel), University of Georgia Press (Athens, GA), 1989.

Silent Dancing: A Partial Remembrance of a Puerto Rican Childhood (personal essays), Arte Publico, 1990.

The Latin Deli, University of Georgia Press, 1993.

An Island Like You: Stories of the Barrio (young adult), Orchard Books (New York City), 1995.

The Year of Our Revolution: New and Selected Stories and Poems, Arte Publico, 1998.

Also author of the poetry collection *Letters from a Caribbean Island.*

OTHER

Contributor to anthologies, including *Hispanics in the U.S.,* Bilingual Review/Press (Tempe, AZ), 1982; *Woman of Her Word,* Arte Publico, 1983; *The Heath Anthology of Modern American Literature,* Heath (Boston, MA), 1990; *Pushcart Prize XV Anthology,* Pushcart Press (Atlanta, GA), 1990; *Puerto Rican Writers at Home in the U.S.A.,* Open Hand (New York City), 1991; and *Literature: Reading, Reacting, Writing,* Holt (New York City), 1991.

Contributor of poems to magazines, including *Southern Humanities Review, Poem, Prairie Schooner, Apalachee Quarterly, Kansas Quarterly,* and *Kalliope.* Poetry editor of *Florida Arts Gazette,* 1978-81; member of editorial board of *Waves.*

SIDELIGHTS: Judith Ortiz Cofer is a highly regarded poet, essayist, and novelist who has written extensively on the experience of being a Puerto Rican in the United States. Cofer was born in Hormingueros, Puerto Rico, but raised and educated primarily in New Jersey. She grew up attempting to reconcile her parents' traditional values with her experiences stateside, eventually producing work that "focuses on the effect on Puerto Rican Americans of living in a world split between the island culture of their homeland and the teeming tenement life of the United States," to quote Marian C. Gonsior in the *Dictionary of Hispanic Biography.*

Cofer left Puerto Rico as a young child, when her father joined the U.S. Navy and was assigned to a post in the Brooklyn Naval Yard. The family lived in Paterson, New Jersey, but undertook extensive visits back to Puerto Rico whenever the father was sent to sea. Back in New Jersey, it was Cofer who learned English in order to help her Spanish-speaking mother run the household and make important decisions. In an interview for *Melus,* the author spoke of reconciling the contradictions in her cultural identity: "I write in English, yet I write obsessively about my Puerto Rican experience. . . . That is how my psyche works. I am a composite of two worlds. . . . I lived with . . . conflictive expectations: the pressures from my father to become very well versed in the English language and the Anglo customs, and from my mother not to forget where we came from. That is something that I deal with in my work all the time."

Trained to be a teacher, Cofer came to creative writing as a graduate student, when she began to craft poems in English about Latina women and their concerns. Her work began to appear in literary periodicals as well as chapbooks and collections by small presses. "I think poetry has made me more disciplined," Cofer observed in *Melus.* "It taught me how to write, because to write a poem takes so much skill. . . . Poetry contains the essence of language. Every word weighs a ton. . . . Poetry taught me about economizing in language and about the power of language. So I will never stop writing poetry."

Branching out from poetry in the late 1980s, Cofer published a well-received novel, *The Line of the Sun,* in 1989, and an essay collection, *Silent Dancing,* in 1990. *The Line of the Sun* was applauded by *New York Times Book Review* contributor Roberto Marquez for the "vigorous elegance" of its language. Marquez called Cofer "a prose writer of evocatively lyrical authority, a novelist of historical compass and sensitivity." The first half of *The Line of the Sun* depicts the poor village of Salud, Puerto Rico, and introduces the characters Rafael Vivente and his wild brother-in-law, Guzman. *Los Angeles Times Book Review* contributor Sonja Bolle noted that the author's eye for detail "brings alive the stifling and magical world of village life." The second part of the novel follows Rafael to Paterson, New Jersey, where his daughter Marisol, the story's narrator, grows up. Marisol's father encourages her to become wholly American, but her mother advises her to adopt the customs and values of Puerto Rico. Marisol learns about her heritage mainly through the stories told by her family, which often focus on her Uncle Guzman, the "demon child"; his arrival at her New Jersey home helps Marisol to balance the American and Puerto Rican aspects of her identity. Though Marquez criticized parts of the plot as contrived, he proclaimed Cofer as "a writer of authentic gifts, with a genuine and important story to tell." *The Line of the Sun* was nominated for a Pulitzer Prize in 1989.

The title of *Silent Dancing* is derived from a home movie of Cofer's parents in their youth. The scene is a New Year's Eve party, and the revelers form a conga line in which each gets a moment of personal attention from the camera. The author uses the film clip as a launching place for a discussion of how her parents' generation—and hers—has responded to the challenge of living between cultures, not wholly comfortable in either.

This theme has been extended into Cofer's volume for young adults, *An Island Like You: Stories of the Barrio.* Set in Paterson, New Jersey, the collection consists of stories about young expatriate Puerto Ricans who live in a tenement building. *Horn Book* contributor Nancy Vasilakis deemed the book "a milestone in multicultural publishing for children," noting: "The Caribbean flavor of the tales gives them their color and freshness, but the narratives have universal resonance in the vitality, the brashness, the self-centered hopefulness, and the angst expressed by the teens as they tell of friendships formed, romances failed, and worries over work, family, and school." In a different *Horn Book* review, Rudine Sims Bishop wrote of *An Island Like You:* "There is humor, and poignancy as well. The voices in these stories ring true, as do the stories themselves. I hope Cofer continues to write for young people." A *Publishers Weekly* reviewer concluded: "This fine collection may draw special attention for its depictions of an ethnic group underserved by YA writers, but Cofer's strong writing warrants a close look no matter what the topic."

Cofer told *CA:* "The 'infinite variety' and power of language interest me. I never cease to experiment with it. As a native Puerto Rican, my first language was Spanish. It was a challenge, not only to learn English, but to master it enough to teach it and—the ultimate goal—to write poetry in it.

"My family is one of the main topics of my poetry; the ones left behind on the island of Puerto Rico, and the ones who came to the United States. In tracing their lives, I discover more about mine. The place of birth itself becomes a metaphor for the things we all must leave behind; the assimilation of a new culture is the coming into maturity by accepting the terms necessary for survival. My poetry is a study of this process of change, assimilation, and transformation."

BIOGRAPHICAL/CRITICAL SOURCES:

BOOKS

Cofer, Judith Ortiz, *Silent Dancing: A Partial Remembrance of a Puerto Rican Childhood,* Arte Publico (Houston, TX), 1990.

Dictionary of Hispanic Biography, Gale (Detroit, MI), 1996, pp. 235-36.

PERIODICALS

Booklist, February 15, 1995, p. 1082.

Georgia Review, spring/summer, 1990, pp. 51-59.

Horn Book Magazine, July-August, 1995, pp. 464-65; September-October, 1995, pp. 581-83.

Library Journal, July, 1998, p. 76.

Los Angeles Times Book Review, August 6, 1989, p. 6.

Melus, fall, 1993, pp. 83-97; fall, 1997, pp. 206-08.

New York Times Book Review, September 24, 1989, pp. 46-47.

Publishers Weekly, April 17, 1995, p. 61; July 27, 1998, p. 78.

Women's Review of Books, December, 1990, p. 9.

* * *

COLON, Jesus 1901-1974

PERSONAL: Born in 1901 in Cayey, Puerto Rico; died in 1974, in New York, NY; came to the United States in 1918.

CAREER: Worked menial jobs while serving as correspondent for such Puerto Rican newspapers as *Justicia* and *Union Obrera;* contributor to English-language communist newspapers, including *The Daily Worker, The Worker,* and *Mainstream;* community activist and candidate for local office in New York City, 1952-69; founder, Editorial Hispanica (small press); writer.

WRITINGS:

A Puerto Rican in New York, and Other Sketches, Mainstream Publishers, 1961, 2nd edition, illustrated by Ernesto Ramos Nieves, International Publishers (New York City), 1982.

(Translator) Kenneth B. Hoyt, *Fundamentos basicos de career education,* U.S. Government Printing Office, Department of Health, Education, and Welfare, Office of Education (Washington, DC), 1979.

Contributor to periodicals, including *El Machete Criollo* and *El Nuevo Mundo.*

SIDELIGHTS: Jesus Colon faced many obstacles to success when he arrived in the United States in 1918: he was a man of color, a Spanish-speaking Puerto Rican, and a socialist. Nevertheless, Colon became a well-known New Yorker, a respected journalist in both Puerto Rico and America, and founder of a small publishing house. His 1961 collection of newspaper sketches, *A Puerto Rican in New York,* "served as inspiration for later Hispanic writers who came to be called Nuyoricans," to quote Jennifer Kramer in the *Dictionary of Hispanic Biography.*

A Puerto Rican in New York was among the first works of Hispanic literature to depict the immigrant experience, and Colon understood this experience perhaps as well as anyone. Of African descent, he was born in Cayey, Puerto Rico, in 1901 and stowed away to America as a teenager in 1918. Arriving in New York City, he supported himself by a series of menial jobs while contributing newspaper articles to periodicals back on the island. His own experiences with discrimination helped to foster an interest in socialism, and by the 1940s he was publishing pieces in English-language journals such as *The Daily Worker* and *Mainstream.* From the outset of his writing career, Colon was most interested in "analysis of the political situation of expatriate Puerto Ricans and their relationships with the Puerto Rican independence movement," according to Kramer.

During the 1950s, when communism was at its most suspect, Colon ran for political office—unsuccessfully—on a communist ticket. He was also deeply involved with the Puerto Rican independence movement as well as labor movements in America. His aims were very serious, but he was nevertheless able to look at his situation with humor, and *A Puerto Rican in New York* reflects that ironic wit. Kramer declared: "The literary output of Colon, his contemporaries, and other Hispanic writers who followed them drew from a folk tradition of oral communication and bicultural adjustment. Colon especially addressed issues of race and class, since as an immigrant of color he suffered discrimination on many fronts. However, . . . [his writings] demonstrate that he could face difficulties with humor and dignity while keeping a foot on each coastline."

Among Colon's accomplishments was the founding of Editoral Hispanica, a small press that published books on history and politics as well as literary efforts in Spanish by Hispanic writers. Colon died in 1974 soon after completing work on his other full-length book, *Fundamentos basicos de career education.*

BIOGRAPHICAL/CRITICAL SOURCES:

BOOKS

Dictionary of Hispanic Biography, Gale (Detroit, MI), 1996, pp. 237-39.

Hispanic-American Almanac, Gale, 1993.

PERIODICALS

New York Times, October 27, 1969, p. 48.*

* * *

COMFORT, B(arbara) 1916-

PERSONAL: Born September 4, 1916, in Nyack, NY; daughter of Walter Rockefeller and Dorothy (Bell) Comfort. *Education:* Attended school in New Jersey. *Religion:* Protestant.

ADDRESSES: Home—39 Charlton St., New York, NY 10014; and R.R.1, Box 219, Londonderry, VT 05148. *Agent*—Peekner Literary Agency, Inc., P.O. Box 3308, Bethlehem, PA 17018.

CAREER: Artist, with solo exhibitions of her work. Comfort, Inc., designer of acrylics; Portraits, Inc., member; Landgrove Press, director. Operator of a welding factory during World War II.

MEMBER: National Arts Club, Southern Vermont Artists.

WRITINGS:

MYSTERY NOVELS

Vermont Village Murder, Landgrove (Landgrove, VT), 1982.

Green Mountain Murder, Landgrove, 1986.

Phoebe's Knee, Landgrove, 1986.

Grave Consequences, Landgrove, 1989.

The Cashmere Kid, Countryman Press (Woodstock, VT), 1993.

Elusive Quarry, Foul Play Press (Woodstock, VT), 1995.

A Pair for the Queen, Foul Play Press, 1998.

ILLUSTRATOR

De Jong, Meindert, *The Tower by the Sea,* Harper (New York City), 1950.

SIDELIGHTS: B. Comfort's mysteries feature seventy-something amateur detective Tish McWhinny, who lives in rural Vermont and whose adventures concern the people and places of her locale. Tish's sleuthing usually includes her close friend, 88-year-old Hilary Oats, and niece Sophie.

In *The Cashmere Kid,* Tish is asked to watch her niece's goat herd while she is away on vacation, a task made more complicated when the herd's prize stud goes missing and the neighboring farmer is found bludgeoned to death. The critic for *Publishers Weekly* explains: "Comfort portrays a delightful and believable cast of characters, especially down-to-earth Tish and her crusty gentleman friend Hilary Oats."

Elusive Quarry begins with the dynamiting of Tish's niece's house, drawing the attention of Treasury Department agents to their rural community. The dynamite is traced to Tish's boyfriend Hilary, while the treasury agents suspect the explosion was an inside job. "Despite a disjointed plot that doesn't quite gel," writes the *Publishers Weekly* reviewer, "Comfort's lovable Tish and Hil easily hold the reader's interest."

A Pair for the Queen finds Tish investigating the murder of Hil's godson at a dog show; she soon finds herself entangled in art forgery, pornography and car theft. Comfort, according to the *Publishers Weekly* critic, "shows once again that her pair of crackerjack sleuths, fragile as they are, can still carry a story."

BIOGRAPHICAL/CRITICAL SOURCES:

PERIODICALS

Publishers Weekly, April 12, 1993, p. 50; April 3, 1995, p. 49; June 1, 1998, p. 48.

* * *

CONANT, Susan

PERSONAL: Married Carter Umbarger (a clinical psychologist), 1968; children: Jessica. *Education:* Radcliffe College, A.B., 1968; Harvard University, Ed.D., 1978.

ADDRESSES: Home—Newton, MA.

CAREER: Educational researcher, 1978-88; writer, 1988—. Alaskan Malamute Protection League, Massachusetts coordinator.

MEMBER: Mystery Writers of America (member of board of directors of New England chapter), American Crime Writers League, Alaskan Malamute Club of America, Dog Writers Association of America, Sisters in Crime, New England Dog Training Club, Charles River Dog Training Club.

AWARDS, HONORS: Maxwell Award, Dog Writers Association of America, 1991, for *A Bite of Death.*

WRITINGS:

MYSTERY NOVELS

A New Leash on Death, Berkley Publishing (New York City), 1990.
Dead and Doggone, Berkley Publishing, 1990.
A Bite of Death, Berkley Publishing, 1991.
Paws before Dying, Berkley Publishing, 1991.
Gone to the Dogs, Doubleday (New York City), 1992.
Bloodlines, Doubleday, 1992.
Ruffly Speaking, Doubleday, 1994.
Black Ribbon, Doubleday, 1995.
Stud Rites, Doubleday, 1996.
Animal Appetite, Doubleday, 1997.
The Barker Street Regulars, Doubleday, 1998.
Evil Breeding, Doubleday, 1998.

OTHER

(With Milton Budoff and Barbara Hecht) *Teaching Language-Disabled Children: A Communication Games Intervention,* Brookline Books (Cambridge, MA), 1983.
Financial Management Course Manual, Life Management Institute (Atlanta), 1987.
Living with Chronic Fatigue: New Strategies for Coping with and Conquering CFS, Taylor Publishing (Dallas), 1990.
(With others) *Managing for Solvency and Profitability in Life and Health Insurance Companies,* Life Management Institute, 1996.

Contributor to *DOGWorld* and *American Kennel Gazette;* editor of *Pawprint.*

SIDELIGHTS: Susan Conant's mystery novels feature Holly Winter, a dog trainer and columnist for *Dog's Life Magazine.* Winter is described by a critic for *Publishers Weekly* as a "witty, independent, yet fallible sleuth with inordinate pride in her two Alaskan Malamutes." Winter's adventures take place in the worlds of dog breeding and dog shows.

In *Stud Rites,* for example, Winter is covering an Alaskan Malamute dog show in Massachusetts when the owner of a prize stud dog is murdered. Soon, one of the show's judges is also found killed, and Winter must track down the killer among the show's participants. The critic for *Publishers Weekly* calls *Stud Rites* "a frisky look at mayhem unleashed."

The Barker Street Regulars takes Winter to a local nursing home where her dog is being trained to be a companion to the elderly. She befriends one of the patients, a Sherlock Holmes buff, and the pair are called upon to investigate a psychic who claims to be able to reunite patients with their deceased pets. "Conant," remarks the critic for *Publishers Weekly,* "cleverly incorporates Holmes and Watson lore into her plot and writes eloquently of what it is like to lose a beloved pet." Once the story is underway, according to Jown Rowen in *Booklist,* "it displays an agreeable mix of appealing characters, well-realized setting, and snappy dialogue."

BIOGRAPHICAL/CRITICAL SOURCES:

PERIODICALS

Booklist, February 1, 1998, p. 902.
Boston Magazine, May, 1997, p. 58.

Library Journal, February 1, 1998, p. 116.
Publishers Weekly, December 12, 1994, p. 53; May 27, 1996, p. 69; February 3, 1997, p. 97; February 23, 1998, p. 55.

* * *

COONTZ, Stephanie

PERSONAL: Born August 31, 1944, in Seattle, WA; daughter of Sydney H. (an economist) and Patricia (McIntosh; present surname, Waddington) Coontz; children: Kristopher. *Education:* University of California, Berkeley, B.A., 1966; University of Washington, Seattle, M.A., 1970.

ADDRESSES: Home—Olympia, WA. *Office*—Department of History and Women's Studies, 3127 Seminar Building, Evergreen State College, Olympia, WA 98505. *Agent*—Sydelle Kramer, Francis Goldin Agency.

CAREER: Evergreen State College, Olympia, WA, faculty member affiliated with department of History and Women's Studies, 1975—. Exchange professor, Kobe University of Commerce, 1986; lecturer, Washington Humanities Commission, 1989-91; visiting scholar, The National Faculty, 1990—; exchange professor, University of Hawaii at Hilo, 1992; visiting associate professor of sociology, University of Hawaii at Hilo, 1994.

MEMBER: Organization of American Historians, American Studies Association, American Historical Association.

AWARDS, HONORS: Woodrow Wilson fellow, 1968-69; Governor's Writers Award, 1988.

WRITINGS:

(With Peta Henderson) *Women's Work, Men's Property: On the Origins of Gender and Class,* Verso (New York City), 1986.
The Social Origins of Private Life: A History of American Families, Verso, 1988.
America's Families: Fables and Facts, Basic Books (New York City), 1991.
The Way We Never Were: American Families and the Nostalgia Trap, Basic Books, 1992.
The Way We Really Are: Coming to Terms with America's Changing Families, Basic Books, 1997.

Also editor of *American Families: A Multicultural Reader,* 1998. Contributor of articles and reviews to journals and newspapers.

SIDELIGHTS: Stephanie Coontz examined the myths and realities of American families in two books: *The Way We Never Were: American Families and the Nostalgia Trap* and *The Way We Really Are: Coming to Terms with America's Changing Families.* In the first volume, Coontz proposed that the popular idea of a typical American family during the 1950s—a breadwinning father, homemaker mother, and two or three children—was never the real societal norm. She examines the reality of family relationships during various eras in American history and probes the reasons that the 1950s myth is held in such high esteem. *New York Times* reviewer Donald Katz called *The Way We Never Were* "often brilliant and invariably provocative." Noting that the book appeared during a time when election campaigns were full of rhetoric about "family values," Katz commented, "Ms. Coontz tries to turn the focus of a tedious public debate away from an idealized image of individual roles and domestic life by using economic and social data to describe an America in which people are struggling every day to make ends meet and raise their children." *New York Review of Books* critic Nicholas Lemann also praised *The Way We Never Were* as "important and useful."

Coontz continued her explorations of American family life in 1997 with *The Way We Really Are: Coming to Terms with America's Changing Families.* The book was a "well-researched, wide-ranging appraisal" and "an engaging experience for nonspecialist readers," according to *Social & Behavioral Sciences* reviewer W. Feigelman. The book offered suggestions on ways to improve social programs to better serve the many unique family situations that exist in America today. *New York Times* reviewer Eden Ross Lipson felt that *The Way We Really Are* "should offer reassurance to people in every kind of family muddling through every stressful stage." Martha Baskin was similarly enthusiastic in *Progressive:* "It is refreshing to find a book that leaps beyond the radical right's slurs against single parents, 'careerist' mothers, and non-traditional families and goes straight to the massive changes needed in the country's attitudes and institutions. Now all we need to know is how to bring those changes about. Considering Coontz's recent books, she's probably not short on ideas."

BIOGRAPHICAL/CRITICAL SOURCES:

PERIODICALS

Book World, October 11, 1992, p. 3.
Business Week, November 23, 1992, p. 15.
Chronicle of Higher Education, November 4, 1992, p. A8.
Choice, February, 1993, p. 1033; September, 1997, p. 224.
Contemporary Sociology, July, 1993, p. 569.
Lear's, July, 1993.
Library Journal, September 15, 1992.
Ms., May, 1997, p. 90.
New Republic, August 16, 1993, pp. 26-32.
New York Review of Books, February 3, 1994, pp. 9-13.
New York Times Book Review, November 8, 1992, p. 21; September 14, 1997, p. 23.
Progressive, September, 1997, p. 44.
Publishers Weekly, August 23, 1993, p. 67.
Times Literary Supplement, September 22, 1989.
Tribune Books (Chicago), August 29, 1993, p. 67.
Voice Literary Supplement, October, 1992, p. 33.
Whole Earth Review, fall, 1993, p. 14.
Women's Review of Books, November, 1997, p. 16.

* * *

COOPER, Dennis 1953-

PERSONAL: Born January 10, 1953, in Pasadena, CA; son of Clifford (an entrepreneur) and Ann (King) Cooper. *Education:* Attended Pasadena City College and Pitzer College. *Politics:* "Anarchist."

ADDRESSES: Home—East Hollywood. *Agent*—Ira Silverberg Communications, 61 Fourth Ave., 3rd Floor, New York, NY 10003.

CAREER: Novelist, poet, and art critic.

AWARDS, HONORS: Nomination for *Los Angeles Times* poetry prize, 1982, for *The Tenderness of the Wolves;* Ferro-Grumley Award from Ferro-Grumley Foundation, 1990.

WRITINGS:

Idols (poetry), Sea Horse, 1979.
The Tenderness of the Wolves (poetry), Crossing Press, 1981.
Safe (novella, novelistic prose poem), Sea Horse, 1984, included in *Wrong: Stories,* Grove (New York City), 1994.
He Cried, Black Star Series, 1984.
Closer (novel), Grove, 1989.
The Undead (play), produced in Los Angeles at Mark Taper Forum, 1989.
Knife/Tape/Rope (play), produced in New York City, 1989.
Frisk (novel), Grove Weidenfeld (New York City), 1991.
(Editor) *Discontents: New Queer Writers,* Amethyst Press (New York City), 1992.
Wrong: Stories, Grove, 1992, contains previously published novella *Safe.*
Jerk (art by Nayland Blake), Artspace Books (San Francisco), 1993.
Try (short stories), Grove, 1994.
The Dream Police: Selected Poems, 1969-1993, Grove, 1995.
(With Keith Mayerson) *Horror Hospital Unplugged,* Juno Books (New York City), 1996.
Guide, Grove, 1997.

Art critic for *Art Forum* and *Art Scribe,* 1987—. Founded *Little Caesar* (literary journal), 1976; published a volume of poetry, *Tiger Beat,* Little Caesar Press, 1978.

SIDELIGHTS: Poet, playwright, novelist, and author of short fiction, Dennis Cooper has earned the reputation of a creative stylist because of his unique prose that incorporates elements of poetry. Critics have categorized his works as disturbing glimpses of a male homosexual subculture filled with despair. "The truth is, Cooper is far better known for his sensationalistic subject matter than for his careful, innovative artistry," remarked John Weir in *The Advocate.* Jonathan Bing described in a 1994 *Publishers Weekly* interview with Cooper: "At once clinical and creepily meditative, Cooper's fiction has been championed by some as a bold, dystopian vision of sexual desire and moral laxity in contemporary life, but it has also proven too unsavory for others. . . . [H]is emotionally drained, gay teen and twenty-something characters are hustlers, punk rockers, artists and loners who fill their time with anonymous sex, horror films, amateurish artistic ventures and random acts of self mutilation." Although "Cooper's characters are often drugged-out L.A. punks and suburban slackers whose sexual confusion makes them vulnerable to predatory adults," reported Weir in a 1994 interview. Cooper and his colleagues adamantly deny notions that Cooper's work condones brutality against youth. According to Weir, Cooper claims: "'My writing depicts a world where all adults are evil and all children are innocent,' Cooper says, adding, "I hate people who abuse young people.'" Cooper's quotes in both interviews proclaim a fascination with violence, death, and uncontrollable desires and a will to stay connected to the teen-age mentality, resist the 'adult' world, and remain a marginal, non-mainstream writer.

Cooper's books have been criticized by some reviewers and gay-rights activist for their political incorrectness and matter-of-fact descriptions of graphic sex and violence. Nonetheless, John Ash, in a *Washington Post Book World* review of *Closer,* declared, "There can be no doubt about the power and originality of his writing." "Because Cooper's writing is deliberately assaultive," noted Weir, "it is often dismissed sarcastically by people who lack the patience to read it." "Cooper contends that . . . literal interpretations [of his work] often fail to grasp the experimental ideas and complex aesthetic effects he seeks to achieve in his books," stated Bing, who quoted Cooper as saying: "I always want them to come from a place that's not conventional and then only get conventional when they absolutely have to make a point of to keep the eye moving down the page." Even though Cooper's subject matter may be offensive, his peers recognize Cooper "not for his disturbing content but for his prose style," wrote Weir. According to Weir, Cooper's contemporaries find inspiration in his "compressed style," and use of "real 'spoken' word." Vince Aletti in his review of *Closer* for the *Village Voice* wrote: "For stories that gravitate toward the nexus of sex and death, alienation and compulsion, he's devised a flat, dry, determinedly unembellished style remarkable both for its poetic compression and its colloquial ease."

Cooper, who at one time was expelled from a private boy's secondary school, began college but stopped after his freshman year. He started a now defunct journal, *Little Caesar,* and began writing and publishing poetry. *Wrong* is a collection of some of Cooper's earliest poetry and includes his 1984 novella *Safe.* According to Bing, the reprinting of Cooper's early writing in *Wrong* has caused some discomfort for Cooper who says the work "just embarrasses me." *Los Angeles Times Book Review* contributor Michael Harris, like Cooper, recognized the mixed quality of *Wrong*'s contents, calling the book "formally adventurous, if uneven in quality." William T. Vollmann concluded in *The New York Times Book Review* that "Mr. Cooper's style and even his grammar occasionally lapse. Nonetheless, parts of 'Wrong' are very, very, good."

One of Cooper's first novels, *Closer,* was published in 1989 and "is an ingenious conceptual study of a circle of solipsistic high school boys centering around the angelic, drugged-out George Miles, who is seduced by an older man whose fetish is to inject his lovers with Novocain and dissect them," described Bing. Thomas R. Edwards, in a review for *New York Review of Books* called *Closer* a "noncommittal, rigorously descriptive, unmoralizing book," and deemed the work as "an attempt to face squarely what Cooper sees as the implications of homosexuality's darkest corners."

Cooper's next novel, *Frisk,* details the imaginary exploits of 13-year-old Dennis, who "encounters some snuff photos of a disemboweled teenager." According to Bing, "[m]ore thoroughly than his previous work, *Frisk* evinces Cooper's fascination with human flesh and with the sexually laden pathological desire to open the body up to explore its sacred interior." C. Carr wrote in *Village Voice: "Frisk* is such a compelling read that we end up implicated in our voyeurism, transfixed like young Dennis at the image of the 'crater.' It's then up to us to decide what it means to imaging the forbidden." Less impressed was David Kauffman who concluded in a review for *The Nation* that "Cooper is most intriguing for the heavy dose of morality he divulges through his perfectly amoral or numb tone, *Frisk* remains less than satisfying as a novel, which may be unavoidable for an author who repeatedly sets out to mock the novel as a form."

When writing *Try,* called "a harrowing, intricately accomplished work of art" by Michael Cunningham in the *Los Angeles Times Book Review,* Cooper was at an emotional peak. Not surprisingly, *Try* includes and considers emotional elements more than past writings. "In *Try,*" wrote Bing, "Cooper avails himself of more traditional narrative techniques, and as a result, [the protagonist] is one of the most nuanced and sympathetic case studies in child abuse in recent fiction." *New York Times Book Review* critic Catherine Texier described *Try* as "a love story, all the more poignant because it is so brutally crushed." "Suffice it to say that I found no trace of poignancy," remarked James Gardner in his article for the *National Review,* directly referencing Texier's description. Gardner stated: "If this work were marketed as pornography, the term being used not in reproach but simply for purposes of description, we should be forced to acknowledge its usefulness to those whose fantasy life comprises the sodomizing of children, necrophilia, and coprophilia. What is entirely unpalatable is the squeamishness of *Try*'s reviewers, squeamish not in the sense of opposing so off-color a work, but in the sense of being too timid to call it by its name."

Guide, Cooper's 1997 novel, "does not meet [the] high standard" of Cooper's best work concluded a *Publishers Weekly* review. This review stated that "Cooper's best work is hypnotic and unsettling in its explorations of the underside of sexual desire." Disagreeing with this analysis, other reviewers, such as Gary Indiana for the *Los Angeles Times Book Review* and Bruce Hainley for *The Nation,* remarked that, indeed, the novel differentiates itself from his past work, but it's uniqueness does not lessen its quality. "With *Guide,* Cooper has provided a handbook to his complex concerns while shattering what too many have come to think of as his only hallmarks," wrote Hainley. He continued, "the daring of *Guide* is how clearly he shows his interests in extremity to be a way of getting at the precariousness of living through language stripped down to its most vulnerable, tender and sweet. Vulnerable, tender and sweet—Dennis Cooper? Yes." Indiana wrote, "'Guide' is a much broader farce than Cooper's previous novels. . . . [it] amplifies the horror that is Cooper's specialty by further breaking down the glass wall between the imaginary and the real. I don't want to take anything away from this book's outrageousness by saying that it's the most seductively frightening, best-written novel of contemporary urban life that anyone has attempted in a long time; it's the funniest, too."

BIOGRAPHICAL/CRITICAL SOURCES:

PERIODICALS

Advocate, March 8, 1994, pp. 59-60.

Los Angeles Times Book Review, March 8, 1992, p. 6; July 3, 1994, pp. 3, 8; June 8, 1997, p. 14.

Nation, July 1, 1991, pp. 21-23; June 16, 1997, pp. 34-35.

National Review, June 17, 1996, pp. 54-57.

New Statesman & Society, September 30, 1994, p. 56.

New York Review of Books, August 17, 1989, pp. 52-53.

New York Times Book Review, May 14, 1989, p. 23; April 26, 1992, p. 13; March 20, 1994, p. 7.

Observer, March 27, 1994, p. 17.

Publishers Weekly, March 22, 1991, p. 72; March 21, 1994, pp. 48-49; May 5, 1997, p. 196.

Times Literary Supplement, May 27, 1994, p. 21.

Village Voice, May, 1989, pp. 28-29; July 16, 1991, p. 67; August, 1992, p. 87.

Washington Post Book World, July 16, 1989, p. 7.*

* * *

COPPER, Basil 1924-
(Lee Falk)

PERSONAL: Born February 5, 1924, in London, England; married Annie Renee Guerin. *Education:* Attended a private college. *Avocational interests:* Old films.

ADDRESSES: *Home*—Stockdoves, South Park, Sevenoaks, Kent TN13 1EN, England.

CAREER: News editor with a Kent county newspaper for thirty years; freelance writer, 1970—.

MEMBER: Society of Authors, Crime Writers Association, British Film Institute, Tunbridge Wells Vintage Film Society (founder), Vintage Film Circle.

AWARDS, HONORS: *From Evil's Pillow* was a "year's best book" runner-up at the First World Fantasy Convention.

WRITINGS:

NOVELS

The Great White Space, R. Hale (London), 1974, St. Martin's (New York City), 1975.

The Curse of the Fleers, Harwood Smart (London), 1976, St. Martin's, 1977.

Necropolis, illustrated by Stephen E. Fabian, Arkham House (Sauk City, WI), 1980.

The House of the Wolf, illustrations by Fabian, Arkham House, 1983.

Into the Silence, Sphere Books (London), 1983.

The Black Death, illustrated by Hawks, Fedogan & Bremer (Minneapolis), 1991.

STORY COLLECTIONS

Not after Nightfall: Stories of the Strange and Terrible, New English Library (London), 1967.

From Evil's Pillow, Arkham House, 1973.

When Footsteps Echo: Tales of Terror and the Unknown, St. Martin's, 1975.

And Afterward, the Dark: Seven Tales, Arkham House, 1977.

Here Be Daemons: Tales of Horror and the Uneasy, St. Martin's, 1978.

The Dossier of Solar Pons, Pinnacle Books (New York City), 1979.

The Further Adventure of Solar Pons, Pinnacle Books, 1979.

The Secret Files of Solar Pons, Pinnacle Books, 1979.

Some Uncollected Cases of Solar Pons, Pinnacle Books, 1980.

Voices of Doom: Tales of Terror and the Uncanny, St. Martin's, 1980.

(Editor) August Derleth, *The Solar Pons Omnibus,* two volumes, Arkham House, 1982.

The Exploits of Solar Pons, illustrated by Hawks, Fedogan & Bremer, 1993.

The Recollections of Solar Pons, illustrated by Stefanie K. Hawks, Fedogan & Bremer, 1996.

"MIKE FARADAY" PRIVATE EYE NOVELS

The Dark Mirror, R. Hale, 1966.

Night Frost, R. Hale, 1966.

No Flowers for the General, R. Hale, 1967.

Scratch on the Dark, R. Hale, 1967.

Die Now, Live Later, R. Hale, 1968.

Don't Bleed on Me, R. Hale, 1968.

The Marble Orchard, R. Hale, 1969.

Dead File, R. Hale, 1970.

No Letters from the Grave, R. Hale, 1971.

The Big Chill, R. Hale, 1972.

Strong-Arm, R. Hale, 1972.

A Great Year for Dying, R. Hale, 1973.

Shock-Wave, R. Hale, 1973.

The Breaking Point, R. Hale, 1973.

A Voice from the Dead, R. Hale, 1974.

Feedback, R. Hale, 1974.

Ricochet, R. Hale, 1974.

The High Wall, R. Hale, 1975.

Impact, R. Hale, 1975.

A Good Place to Die, R. Hale, 1975.

The Lonely Place, R. Hale, 1976.

Crack in the Sidewalk, R. Hale, 1976.

Tight Corner, R. Hale, 1976.

The Year of the Dragon, R. Hale, 1977.

Death Squad, R. Hale, 1977.

Murder One, R. Hale, 1978.

A Quiet Room in Hell, R. Hale, 1979.

The Big Rip-Off, R. Hale, 1979.

The Caligari Complex, R. Hale, 1980.

Flip-Side, R. Hale, 1980.

The Long Rest, R. Hale, 1981.

The Empty Silence, R. Hale, 1981.

Dark Entry, R. Hale, 1981.

Hang Loose, R. Hale, 1982.

Shoot-Out, R. Hale, 1982.

The Far Horizon, R. Hale, 1982.

Trigger-Man, R. Hale, 1983.

Pressure-Point, R. Hale, 1983.

Hard Contract, R. Hale, 1983.

The Narrow Corner, R. Hale, 1983.

The Hook, R. Hale, 1984.

You Only Die Once, R. Hale, 1984.

Tuxedo Park, R. Hale, 1984.

The Far Side of Fear, R. Hale, 1984.

Snow-Job, R. Hale, 1986.

Jet-Lag, R. Hale, 1986.

Blood on the Moon, R. Hale, 1986.

Heavy Iron, R. Hale, 1987.

Turn Down an Empty Glass, R. Hale, 1987.

Bad Scene, R. Hale, 1987.

House-Dick, R. Hale, 1988.

Print-Out, R. Hale, 1988.

NOVELS UNDER PSEUDONYM LEE FALK

The Phantom, Avon (New York City), 1972.

The Phantom and the Scorpia Menace, Avon, 1972.

The Phantom and the Slave Market of Mucar, Avon, 1972.

NONFICTION

The Vampire: In Legend, Fact, and Art (nonfiction), R. Hale, 1973, Citadel (New York City), 1974.

The Werewolf: In Legend, Fact, and Art (nonfiction), St. Martin's, 1977.

SIDELIGHTS: Basil Copper has written prolifically in the mystery and horror genres. He has written over fifty novels featuring Los Angeles private eye Mike Faraday, as well as collections of short stories featuring 1920s detective Solar Pons. But Copper is best known for his horror fiction. As Mike Ashley explains in the *St. James Guide to Horror, Ghost and Gothic Writers,* Copper "remains the most complete traditionalist working in the field of horror fiction today."

Ashley notes that Copper's "soul is in the mist-enshrouded age of the late Victorian and Edwardian era, or a timeless 1920s that nostalgia has created. Copper is a great emulator, rather in the vein of his mentor August Derleth. He is able to reproduce accurately the pace, mood and approach of the work of authors he admires, particularly H. P. Lovecraft, Mickey Spillane, Arthur Conan Doyle, and Derleth himself. This is not to detract from Copper's creative abilities—he can produce excellent original material—rather it is a demonstration of his flexibility within the field. . . . In the horror field, Copper's work falls loosely into three categories. There are his stories which emulate the work of H. P. Lovecraft, there are those which are Victorian gothics, and there are his own individual stories."

Copper's Lovecraftian fiction includes his novels *The Great White Space* and *Into the Silence* which, according to Ashley, are both "similar in structure and development to Lovecraft's major works such as *At the Mountains of Madness.* Copper superbly captures the timelessness of Lovecraft's 1920s and 1930s when individuals, usually university professors, explored little-known parts of the globe. The books start with that apprehension and excitement of entering the unknown checked to some degree by a more leisurely academic pace and reserve until events begin to snowball out of control and menaces from Earth's distant past are unearthed."

Copper's more Victorian fiction is, according to Ashley, "best exemplified by *Necropolis,* a wonderful emporium of a novel in which a private investigator, looking into the death of a client's father, unearths foul deeds in the depths of the massive Brookwood Cemetery. The novel is set in the same atmospheric London as Sherlock Holmes: in fact Inspector Lestrade is one of the characters and there are several cross-references to Holmes's cases. Copper succeeded in recreating this atmosphere in his later novels, *The House of the Wolf* and *The Black Death,* though neither of these had the gothic extravagance of *Necropolis.*"

Copper's more individualistic stories, those drawing upon his vast knowledge of the ghost and horror genre to create wholly original effects, include those works in which "Copper likes to bring the reader into the narrator's mind and follow the gradual mental degradation amidst rising fright," as Ashley writes. Among his best works, and "arguably Copper's best short story," Ashley notes, is "The Janissaries of Emilion," a story in which "a visionary is killed by a product of his own dreams," Ashley explains. Other stand-out stories, Ashley writes, are "The Grey House," "a vivid haunted-house story which presages Stephen King's *The Shining* in its evocation of possession. Another powerful story . . . , one which demonstrates Copper's interest in and knowledge of the cinema, [is] 'Amber Print' in which two collectors discover an unknown and, it transpires, haunted print of *The Cabinet of Dr. Caligari.*" Ashley believes the recent story "Wish You Were Here," another haunted house story, to be among Copper's finest works "because he is able to bring to the story his wide experience of horror fiction and his ability to create an almost Victorian atmosphere . . . to produce a modern-day ghost story which packs the punch of a century of supernatural fiction."

BIOGRAPHICAL/CRITICAL SOURCES:

BOOKS

St. James Guide to Horror, Ghost and Gothic Writers, St. James Press (Detroit), 1998.

PERIODICALS

Publishers Weekly, September 25, 1995, p. 47.

* * *

COUNSELMAN, Mary Elizabeth 1911-1994 (Charles Dubois, Sanders McCrorey, John Starr)

PERSONAL: Born November 19, 1911, in Birmingham, AL; died in 1994; daughter of John Sanders (a professor) and Netti Young (an art teacher; maiden name, McCrorey) Counselman; married Horace Benton Vinyard, November 13, 1941 (died, 1978); children: William Sanders. *Education:* Attended Alabama College and University of Alabama. *Politics:* "Citizen of the world." *Religion:* "Universalist (inherited Methodist)."

CAREER: Reporter for *Birmingham News,* Birmingham, AL; instructor in creative writing at Gadsden State Junior College, Gadsden, AL; instructor in creative writing at University of Alabama; founder, publisher, and editor of Verity Publishing Co., Gadsden, beginning in 1976. Lecturer at writer's conclaves and colonies throughout southern United States, including Venice Writer's Colony, Birmingham Penwomen, and Biloxi Writer's Colony.

MEMBER: American Penwomen (Birmingham chapter), National Fantasy Fan Federation, Chi Delta Phi, Dinosaurs.

AWARDS, HONORS: National Endowment for the Arts fellow, 1976-77; award from the National Fantasy Fan Federation, for short story, "Overture."

WRITINGS:

Half in Shadow (young adult short stories), Consul (London), 1964, Arkham House (Sauk City, WI), 1978.

African Yesterdays (young adult short stories), Verity Publishing (Gadsden, AL), 1975, revised and enlarged edition, 1977.

Move Over—It's Only Me (poetry), Verity Publishing, 1976.

The Fifth Door (a textbook on the subgenre of science fiction), Strange Books, 1982.

The Face of Fear and Other Poems, Depot Press, 1982.

Also author of *Everything You Want To Know About the Supernatural,* Verity Publishing, and *The Eye and the Hand* (poetry), Verity Publishing. Editor, *Year at the Spring* magazine, 1977-80. Short stories have appeared in anthologies, including *Ghostly Gentlewomen, Far Below and Other Horrors,* and *The Roots of Evil,* and in school textbook anthologies. Contributor (sometimes under pseudonyms Charles Dubois, Sanders McCrorey, and John Starr) of short stories and poetry to periodicals, including *Collier's, Saturday Evening Post, Weird Tales, Jungle Stories* and *Ladies' Home Journal.*

ADAPTATIONS: Some of Counselman's short stories were adapted for television and appeared on *G.E. Theatre* and other programs; they have been televised in fifteen different countries. Her televised stories include "The Three Marked Pennies," "Parasite Mansion," and "Gleason's Calendar."

SIDELIGHTS: Mary Elizabeth Counselman wrote short stories for the pulp magazines of the 1930s and 1940s, especially *Weird Tales,* the preeminent American horror magazine of the twentieth century. "Counselman's fiction," explained Stefan Dziemianowicz in the *St. James Guide to Horror, Ghost and Gothic Writers,* "began appearing in *Weird Tales* in 1933, where she would publish sporadically for almost 20 years." Counselman's characters, Dziemianowicz maintained, "are invariably just plain folk whose mundane lives do not admit the possibility of the fantastic." Many of her stories first published in *Weird Tales* have continued to enjoy reprinting in anthologies of horror stories ever since.

Among Counselman's most enduring tales is "The Three Marked Pennies," first published in *Weird Tales* in 1934. In a small rural town an anonymous contest is announced: three marked pennies—one each with a triangle, a square and a circle—will be circulated in the town's money. Those citizens who find the marked pennies will receive prizes, one will be given money, another a cruise around the world, and the third death. But which prize will be rewarded for which marked coin is a mystery. The speculations aroused by the odd contest, Dziemianowicz noted, reveals to the townspeople "that they are not the community united by common beliefs and values that they once thought they were. Terse and sardonic, 'The Three Marked Pennies' proved one of the most popular stories ever published in *Weird Tales* and has since become Counselman's most reprinted work."

Counselman once told *CA:* "I have always been interested in the parable as an oblique method of 'counseling' the readers who object to 'stuffy preaching.' The symbol has been used from the Greek, Egyptian, and Mesopotamian myths through current fantasies to explore the subconscious drives and rationales of mankind—as groups and as individuals. I feel that our basic sense of values can be regained through the in-depth study of old myths and legends, as well as modern fiction based on these. Judging from reader response to my stories (which have been translated into languages I do not even know) this use of symbol has universal appeal."

BIOGRAPHICAL/CRITICAL SOURCES:

BOOKS

St. James Guide to Horror, Ghost and Gothic Writers, St. James Press (Detroit), 1998.*

* * *

CRAIG, Philip R. 1933-

PERSONAL: Born December 10, 1933, in Santa Monica, CA; son of Platt Perry (a rancher) and Grace (Kiefer) Craig; married Shirley Jane Prada, December 10, 1957; children: Kimberlie Anne, James Stuart. *Education:* Boston University, B.A., 1957; University of Iowa, M.F.A., 1962. *Politics:* Independent. *Religion:* "Erratic."

ADDRESSES: Home—36 Orchard Rd., Hamilton, MA 01936. *Office*—Department of English, Wheelock College, 200 Riverway, Boston, MA 02215. *Agent*—Elizabeth Otis, McIntosh & Otis, Inc., 475 Fifth Ave., New York, NY 10017.

CAREER: Wheelock College, Boston, MA, assistant professor of English, 1964—. Member of communications curriculum team for the planned community college, Boston Model Cities Program.

MEMBER: American Association of University Professors.

AWARDS, HONORS: About three dozen fencing awards, including being named to the all-American team.

WRITINGS:

MYSTERY NOVELS

Gate of Ivory, Gate of Horn, Doubleday (New York City), 1969.
A Beautiful Place to Die, Scribner (New York City), 1989.
The Woman Who Walked into the Sea, Scribner, 1991.
The Double Minded Men, Scribner, 1992.
Cliff Hanger, Scribner, 1993.
Off Season, Scribner, 1994.
A Case of Vineyard Poison, Scribner, 1995.
Death on a Vineyard Beach, Scribner, 1996.
A Deadly Vineyard Holiday, Scribner, 1997.
A Shoot on Martha's Vineyard, Scribner, 1998.

OTHER

Contributor of articles and play reviews to *New Bedford Standard Times.*

SIDELIGHTS: "Most readers of mysteries . . . ," writes Philip R. Craig in an article for the *Writer* magazine, "are actually more interested in characters and locale than in plot, puzzle solving, or other traditional aspects of crime stories." Craig's own mysteries are set on Martha's Vineyard and feature J. W. Jackson, a retired Boston policeman, and Zee Madieras, Jeff's beautiful love interest.

Jackson works as a guide for tourists who visit Martha's Vineyard. He enjoys fishing the local waters and cooking his catch. Jackson's profession allows readers to take a tour of the island themselves with every adventure. In this way, according to a critic for *Publishers Weekly,* "Craig shows off his affectionate knowledge of Martha's Vineyard, from the touristy towns to the locals' favorite fishing spots." Speaking of the novel *Death on a Vineyard Beach,* Stuart Miller in *Booklist* notes that, "as usual, Craig offers up a corking good mystery with many interludes devoted to catching and cooking clams, bluefish, and other fruits of the sea."

BIOGRAPHICAL/CRITICAL SOURCES:

PERIODICALS

Booklist, May 15, 1996, p. 1571.
Library Journal, May 1, 1997, p. 144; May 1, 1998, p. 143.
New York Times Book Review, July 16, 1969.
Publishers Weekly, April 26, 1993, p. 60; March 30, 1994, p. 38; April 24, 1995, p. 63; April 14, 1997, p. 59; April 20, 1998, p. 50.
Writer, May, 1998, p. 13.

* * *

CROSS, John Keir 1914-1967
(Stephen MacFarlane, Susan Morley)

PERSONAL: Born August 19, 1914, in Carluke, Scotland; died January 22, 1967; married; children: one son.

CAREER: Writer. Former insurance clerk, hobo, and traveling busker/ventriloquist; British Broadcasting Corp., London, England, worked in the drama, variety, features, and Children's Hour departments writing and producing radio plays and features, as well as adapting stories and books for broadcast, 1937-46, co-writer of daily radio series, *The Archers,* 1962-67.

WRITINGS:

JUVENILES

Studio J Investigates: Spy Story for Children (illustrated by Joseph Avrach), P. Lunn (London), 1944.
Jack Robinson (illustrated by John R. Parsons), P. Lunn, 1945.
The Angry Planet: An Authentic First-Hand Account of a Journey to Mars in the Spaceship Albatross

(illustrated by Robin Jacques), P. Lunn, 1945, Coward-McCann (New York City), 1946.

The Owl and the Pussycat (illustrated by Jacques), P. Lunn, 1946, published as *The Other Side of Green Hills,* Coward-McCann, 1947.

The Man in Moonlight (illustrated by Jacques), J. Westhouse (London), 1947.

The White Magic, J. Westhouse, 1947.

(Editor) *The Children's Omnibus* (illustrated by H. M. Brock), P. Lunn, 1948.

Blackadder: A Tale of the Days of Nelson (illustrated by Jacques), F. Muller (London), 1950, Dutton (New York City), 1951.

The Flying Fortunes in an Encounter with Rubberface!, F. Muller, 1952, published as *The Stolen Sphere: An Adventure and a Mystery,* Dutton, 1953.

The Red Journey Back: A First-Hand Account of the Second and Third Martian Expeditions by the Spaceships Albatross and Comet (illustrated by Jacques), Coward-McCann, 1954, published as *SOS from Mars,* Hutchinson (London), 1954.

The Dancing Tree, Hutchinson, 1955, reprinted, World Distributors, 1963.

(Editor) *Best Horror Stories,* Faber (London), 1957, reprinted, 1962.

The Sixpenny Year: A Country Adventure, Hutchinson, 1957.

Elizabeth in Broadcasting, Hutchinson, 1957.

(Editor) *Best Black Magic Stories,* Faber, 1960.

(Editor) *Best Horror Stories 2,* Faber, 1965.

UNDER PSEUDONYM STEPHEN MACFARLANE

Detectives in Greasepaint (illustrated by Avrach), P. Lunn, 1944.

Lucy Maroon: The Car that Loved a Policeman (illustrated by Bruce Angrave), P. Lunn, 1944.

Mr. Bosanko, and Other Stories (illustrated by Angrave), P. Lunn, 1944.

The Strange Tale of Sally and Arnold, P. Lunn, 1944.

The Blue Egg, P. Lunn, 1944.

The Story of a Tree (illustrated by R. A. Brandt), P. Lunn, 1946.

RADIO PLAYS

The Brockenstein Affair, British Broadcasting Corp. (BBC), 1962.

The Free Fishers, BBC, 1964.

Bird of Dawning, BBC, 1965.

Be Thou My Judge, BBC, 1967.

The Green Isle of the Great Deep, BBC, 1986.

Also author of *The Kraken Wakes,* BBC, and of scripts for *The Archers* radio series, 1962-67.

OTHER

Aspect of Life: An Autobiography of Youth, Selwyn & Blount (London), 1937.

The Other Passenger: Eighteen Strange Stories (illustrated by B. Angrave), J. Westhouse, 1944, Lippincott (Philadelphia), 1946, abridged edition published as *Stories from 'The Other Passanger,'* Ballantine (New York City), 1961.

(Under pseudonym Susan Morley) *Mistress Glory,* Dial Press (New York City), 1948 (published under name John Keir Cross as *Glory,* W. Laurie [London], 1951).

(Under pseudonym Susan Morley) *Juniper Green,* Dial Press, 1953 (published under name John Keir Cross, W. Laurie, 1952).

She Died Young (television play), BBC, 1961.

SIDELIGHTS: "To modern readers," Gary Westfahl wrote in the *St. James Guide to Horror, Ghost and Gothic Writers,* "especially those on the western side of the Atlantic, John Keir Cross is a distant, elusive figure. His extensive work for the BBC radio network is forgotten and essentially untraceable; his books are all long out of print and difficult to locate; his best-remembered works in America—the science-fiction novels for children *The Angry Planet, The Stolen Sphere,* and *The Red Journey Back*—are undistinguished." According to Westfahl, Cross's story collection *The Other Passenger* is "the major reason why he should be remembered today."

The stories gathered in *The Other Passenger* concern characters, Westfahl noted, from "various levels of British society—aristocrats, working-class merchants and teachers, artists and musicians—Cross finds them filled with their own quiet frustrations, suppressed longings and unanswered questions. They are usually impelled to some bold action to satisfy their desires, yet the resulting events or revelations are invariably unpleasant. Thus, while stories often lack an overt horrific element or atmosphere, they present and endorse the underlying ethos of horror: stay where you are, ask no questions, make no changes, or suffer the consequences."

Cross presents his stories with what Westfahl called a "deliberate and self-conscious artlessness; narrators regularly apologize for rambling on about unimportant things, not stating things clearly, and not being able to fully explain the events they recount. Through this style, more than his statements, Cross conveys the message that life is full of unknowns and uncertainties, making all of our lives like little horror stories."

Critical reaction to *The Other Passenger* was generally favorable. Anthony Boucher, reviewing the collection in the *San Francisco Chronicle,* compared Cross to John Collier and concluded that he should "be welcomed gladly to the macabre field in which he has so lamentably few competitors." B. V. Winebaum in the *New York Times* cited the story "Esmeralda" as a particular stand-out, praising how Cross "mixes understandable frustration with bloody horror, [and] creates a ghostish character who is ephemeral enough, together with being convincingly evil, to provoke the disastrous collapse of the sinning mortal of the story." Writing in the *Library Journal,* H. S. Taylor called Cross "a master of characterization" who "selects with unerring discrimination the emotions, incidents and inevitabilities calculated to produce enjoyment for his readers." "Most of the stories," wrote Edwin Fadiman, Jr. in the *Weekly Book Review,* "leave you strangely disturbed, slightly at odds with normality. . . . You suddenly feel beyond the yellow circle of your reading lamp there's something waiting, waiting to pounce. The bristles on the back of your neck rise up, a shiver runs down your spine and the author has achieved his purpose."

BIOGRAPHICAL/CRITICAL SOURCES:

BOOKS

St. James Guide to Horror, Ghost and Gothic Writers, St. James Press (Detroit), 1998.

PERIODICALS

Atlantic, December, 1946.
Booklist, February 1, 1947; January 15, 1948; September 15, 1951.
Book Week, July 28, 1946, p. 7; November 10, 1946, p. 3.
Chicago Sun Book Week, December 3, 1947, p. A15.
Chicago Sunday Tribune, September 30, 1951, p. 10.
Horn Book, December, 1953.
Kirkus, June 1, 1946; November 1, 1947; August 1, 1951; May 15, 1953; January 15, 1954.
Library Journal, July, 1946; November 1, 1946; September 1, 1951; September 1, 1953; April 15, 1954.
New Republic, September 9, 1946.
New York Herald Tribune Book Review, November 15, 1953, p. 30; May 23, 1954, p. 8.
New York Times, July 28, 1946, p. 16; November 10, 1946, p. 2; December 28, 1947, p. 9; August 26, 1951, p. 18; August 23, 1953, p. 20; August 8, 1954, p. 16.
San Francisco Chronicle, September 22, 1946, p. 18.
Saturday Review of Literature, August 10, 1946; November 9, 1946; May 15, 1954.
Weekly Book Review, August 18, 1946, p. 6; November 10, 1946, p. 36.*

* * *

CROWTHER, Peter 1949-
(Nick Hassam)

PERSONAL: Born July 4, 1949, in Leeds, England; son of Percival (an engineer) and Kathleen (Bowling) Crowther; married Nichola Hassam (a teacher), October 23, 1976; children: Oliver James, Timothy Nicholas. *Education:* Attended Leeds Metropolitan University. *Politics:* Socialist. *Religion:* "Lapsed Protestant."

ADDRESSES: *Home and office*—Bridgewood, 22 South Dr., Harrogate HG2 8AU, England. *Agent*—Susan Gleason, 325 Riverside Dr., New York, NY 10025.

CAREER: Leeds Permanent Building Society, Leeds, England, communications manager, 1980-95; freelance writer and consulting editor, 1995—.

MEMBER: Horror Writers of America, Science Fiction and Fantasy Writers of America, Mystery Writers of America.

WRITINGS:

EDITOR

Narrow Houses: Tales of Superstition, Suspense and Fear, Little, Brown (London), 1992, Warner Books (New York City), 1994.
Touch Wood: Narrow Houses, Volume 2, Little, Brown, 1993, Warner Books (New York City), 1996.
Blue Motel: Narrow Houses, Volume 3, Little, Brown, 1994, White Wolf (Atlanta, GA), 1996.
Heaven Sent: An Anthology of Angel Stories, DAW Books (New York City), 1995.
(With Edward E. Kramer) *Tombs,* White Wolf, 1995.
(With Kramer) *Dante's Disciples,* White Wolf, 1996.

Destination Unknown, White Wolf, 1997.
Tales in Time, White Wolf, 1997.

OTHER

(With James Lovegrove) *Escardy Gap* (novel), Tor Books (New York City), 1996.
Forest Plains (story collection), Hypatia Press (Eugene, OR), 1996.
The Longest Single Note and Other Strange Compositions (story collection), CD Publications (Baltimore), 1998.

Contributor to periodicals, sometimes under pseudonym Nick Hassam.

SIDELIGHTS: Peter Crowther has edited a number of popular anthologies of horror fiction, written a critically praised horror novel, and has published a number of short stories in the genre as well.

As an anthologist, Crowther edited the *Narrow Houses* series of anthologies. The series title comes from a traditional description of coffins as being "narrow houses for the dead." The critic for *Publishers Weekly* describes the first volume in the *Narrow Houses* series as "an impressive variety of superb fiction." The anthology *Tombs,* co-edited by Crowther and Edward E. Kramer, focuses on stories involving some sort of entombment, either in a literal or metaphoric sense. The collection includes works from such diverse writers as William F. Buckley, Jr., and Michael Moorcock. The *Publishers Weekly* reviewer dubs *Tombs* an "agreeable grab bag of claustrophobic, mortifying pleasures." Writing in the *St. James Guide to Horror, Ghost and Gothic Writers,* Chris Gilmore calls Crowther "a notable anthologist in the horror and dark fantasy fields."

Crowther's novel *Escardy Gap,* co-written with James Lovegrove, concerns a visit to a small town by Jeremiah Rackstraw and the Company, a bizarre group of sideshow performers. The town is, according to Gilmore, "the sort of smug, ultra-folksy Midwestern rural community where everyone knows everyone else." Once Jeremiah and his performers gain the townspeople's confidence, they "set about the predictable mayhem, each in his/her own special way," writes Gilmore. "It's handled as more than usually imaginative black farce with some fine bravura passages. . . Most importantly the authors address a nagging wrongness found in almost all genre horror but very little fantasy, however dark: that the evil incursion is unsought and unearned. Horrid as the folk are, with their cracker-barrel wisdom, Mom's pie, regular churchgoing and long evenings gossiping on the porch, they deserve nothing than to be left to get on with it. While the real world is full of injustice, the supernatural should effect a certain symmetry between what is sown and what is reaped. The [town's] Mayor expresses this forcefully enough to Rackstraw, only to be told that for all the torture and murder there is neither rationale nor justice, only the exercise of malign whimsy."

BIOGRAPHICAL/CRITICAL SOURCES:

BOOKS

St. James Guide to Horror, Ghost and Gothic Writers, St. James Press (Detroit), 1998.

PERIODICALS

Library Journal, August, 1997, p. 141.
Publishers Weekly, September 12, 1994, p. 86; May 15, 1995, p. 61; July 29, 1996, p. 72.

* * *

CUNNINGHAM, J(ames) V(incent) 1911-1985

PERSONAL: Born August 23, 1911, in Cumberland, MD; died of heart failure, March 30, 1985, in Waltham (one source says Marlboro), MA; son of James Joseph and Anna (Finan) Cunningham; married Barbara Gibbs (a poet), 1937 (divorced, 1942); married Dolora Gallagher, 1945 (divorced, 1949); married Jessie Campbell, 1950; children: Marjorie Lupien. *Education:* Stanford University, A.B., 1934, Ph.D., 1945.

CAREER: Stanford University, Stanford, CA, instructor, 1937-45; University of Hawaii, Honolulu, assistant professor, 1945-46; University of Chicago, Chicago, assistant professor, 1946-52; University of Virginia, Charlottesville, assistant professor, 1952-53; Brandeis University, Waltham, MA, professor of English, 1953-80, University Professor, 1976-80, professor emeritus, 1980-85. Visiting professor at Harvard University, 1952, University of Washington, 1956, Indiana University at Bloomington, 1961, University of California, Santa Barbara, 1963, and Washington University, 1976. *Wartime service:* Mathematics teacher at an Air Force base in southern CA.

AWARDS, HONORS: Guggenheim fellowship in poetry, 1959-60, 1966-67; National Institute of Arts and Letters grant, 1965; National Endowment for the Arts grant, 1966; Academy of American Poets fellowship, 1976.

WRITINGS:

POETRY

The Helmsman, Colt (San Francisco), 1942.
The Judge Is Fury, Morrow (New York City), 1947.
Doctor Drink, Cummington (Cummington, MA), 1950.
Trivial, Vulgar, and Exalted: Epigrams, Poems in Folio (San Francisco), 1957.
The Exclusions of a Rhyme, Swallow Press (Denver), 1960.
To What Strangers, What Welcome, Swallow Press, 1964.
Some Salt: Poems and Epigrams, Perishable Press (Mount Horeb, WI), 1967.
Selected Poems, Perishable Press, 1971.
The Collected Poems and Epigrams of J. V. Cunningham, Swallow Press, 1971.
Let Thy Words Be Few, Symposium Press (Los Angeles), 1986.
The Poems of J. V. Cunningham, edited and with an introduction by Timothy Steele, Swallow Press/Ohio University Press (Athens), 1997.

OTHER

(Translator) P. Nicole, *Essay on True and Apparent Beauty. . . . ,* Augustan Reprint, 1950.
Woe or Wonder, University of Denver Press (Denver), 1951.
Tradition and Poetic Structure, Swallow Press, 1960.
The Journal of John Cardan, [with] *The Quest of the Opal* [and] *The Problem of Form,* Swallow Press, 1964.
(Editor) *The Renaissance in England,* Harcourt (New York City), 1966.
(Editor) *Problem of Style,* Fawcett (New York City), 1966.
(Editor) *In Shakespeare's Day,* Fawcett, 1970.
The Collected Essays of J. V. Cunningham, Swallow Press, 1976.

Contributor to *Poets on Poetry,* edited by Howard Nemerov, Basic Books, 1966, and *Brandeis Essays in Literature,* edited by John Hazel Smith, 1983.

ADAPTATIONS: Several of Cunningham's poems were set to music in the song cycle "In the Thirtieth Year" by Robin Holloway.

SIDELIGHTS: J. V. Cunningham, poet, critic, editor, and general man of letters, gained the high regard of his literary colleagues for his concise, witty, epigrammatic poetry. In a 1961 study, *The Poetry of J. V. Cunningham,* his mentor Yvor Winters called him "the most consistently distinguished poet writing in English today, and one of the finest in the language." About the same time, Thom Gunn wrote in a *Yale Review* article on *The Exclusions of a Rhyme* that Cunningham "must be one of the most accomplished poets alive, and one of the few of whom it can be said that he will still be worth reading in fifty years' time." In 1998, thirteen years after Cunningham's death, *Weekly Standard* contributor J. Bottum, reviewing the comprehensive collection *The Poems of J. V. Cunningham,* opined that Cunningham "may have been the most talented poet of his generation, one of only three or four masters of a particular poetic form in the history of English poetry, and a genuine American original." That form is the epigram, a term generally reserved for short, pithy poems (or sometimes, bits of prose). According to Bottum, many of Cunningham's poems are true epigrams, but even "his longer poems tended toward the epigrammatic—little quotable bits that express a thought with exceptional neatness." Cunningham's epigrammatic lines range from the solemn—"Life flows to death as rivers to the sea / And life is fresh and death is salt to me"—to the humorous—noting that a reader "Dislikes my book; calls it, to my discredit / A book you can't put down before you've read it."

Cunningham's poetry did not bring him great fame, but this unfortunate state of affairs can be explained. Early in his career, Cunningham tried some modernist techniques, but most of his poetry was in a formal, classic style, with emphasis on meter, rhyme, and precise use of language. This may have led some readers to consider his poems old-fashioned, and Cunningham was certainly never trendy. "Although he lived through a number of poetic fads, he managed to remain unfashionable during them all," Bottum observed. Also, Cunningham's output of poetry was not large. He produced, Bottum noted, "fewer than two hundred poems—several only two lines long." While these factors kept Cunningham from reaching a large reading public, his admirers have contended that readers will find it worthwhile to seek out Cunningham's work.

In a review of Cunningham's first poetry collection, *The Helmsman,* for *Poetry* magazine, Edward Weismiller wrote that the poems, "difficult as they are to place in the stream of American and English poetry, are of unusual interest. They are the products of a talent which is emphatically and avowedly not modern, but which, though it operates within quite narrow bounds, and intentionally so, is none the less expert and sensitive." Gunn commented that the poems in *The Exclusions of a Rhyme* use none of the forms popular in the mid-twentieth century; the verses "are stylistically as much of the seventeenth century as of the twentieth." This could prove off-putting to some readers, Gunn allowed, but added that no one should assume that a writer, such as Cunningham, "who scans, rhymes, and writes syntactically is less passionate than one who uses sentence fragments and free verse." Indeed, Cunningham shows great passion about a variety of topics in his poetry, Gunn asserted. In an essay for the *Dictionary of Literary Biography,* Steven Helmling remarked that Cunningham was suspicious of much of modern poetry's reliance on imagery. "For him, poetry must engage some outer reality not simply by pointing at it with an image or expressing a mood in relation to it; the poem must treat experience, make something of it," Helmling observed. Experiences treated in Cunningham's poetry include love, sex, his boyhood home of Montana, and the quest to understand the universe. Helmling pointed out that Cunningham's title for one of his collections, *Trivial, Vulgar and Exalted: Epigrams,* "suggests the extraordinary range" of the poet's subject matter.

Alongside the acclaim for Cunningham's verse stood some reservations about it. Weismiller, while finding much to praise, also found signs of emotional detachment in the poet's work. He opined that "there is something cold about Cunningham's poetry which seldom permits the reader to do more than admire; he regards the poet's experience, but does not enter in. . . . [Cunningham] remains, of course, an admirable poet, whose technique is superb, but whose chosen austerity often puts a wall of clear ice between him and the reader." Louis Simpson, discussing *The Exclusions of a Rhyme* in the *Hudson Review,* saw Cunningham's work as excessively constrained. "I admire Mr. Cunningham . . . and I am glad that there is one of him in America," Simpson wrote. "But there are other ways of poetry which, I am afraid, Mr. Cunningham would exclude, and this brings me to my main criticism of his verse. It is simply that you cannot show the triumph of discipline over disorder unless you also show the disorder." Bottum, while holding Cunningham in high esteem, argued that "it is worth asking why Cunningham is not an even better poet—why the reader feels at last a narrowness in his verse, a poetic gift greater than his poetic output." Bottum believed he knew the answer: "Cunningham had nowhere to go once he mastered the epigram and the epigrammatical turn. His poems contain everything the epigram can do, but the epigram does not contain everything his poems could have done—and consequently, much of his best poetry was never written and much of his greatest poetic impulse fell away unused." Despite these criticisms, though, many reviewers have proclaimed Cunningham's poetry to be work of lasting importance. Winters, who had some differences with his friend Cunningham, nevertheless asserted that while the output of some popular twentieth-century poets will not age well, "the style of Cunningham . . . will not be dated."

Cunningham put himself in the position of critiquing his poetry in an essay, *The Quest of the Opal: A Commentary on 'The Helmsman.'* Winters took issue with some of the ideas Cunningham expressed—such as a disdain for the use of sensory perception in poetry—and went so far as to wish Cunningham had never written the essay. Some other scholars, though, have found much of value in *The Quest of the Opal.* "As an exposition of his beliefs about poetry and as a commentary on several of his greatest poems, [it] is unsurpassable, the single most important prose text a student of Cunningham can read," Helmling wrote. Because the work is "so brilliant and so quotable," he added, "it seems unlikely that any critic will ever discuss Cunningham's poetry in any terms except Cunningham's."

Cunningham's prose efforts also include *Woe or Wonder,* which *Spectator* contributor Patrick Cosgrave described as "one of the few great (I chose the word very carefully) volumes of Shakespearian criticism." Geoffrey H. Hartman, in a piece for *Poetry* magazine, praised *Woe or Wonder* for looking realistically at Shakespeare's plays rather than trying to find hidden meanings in them. "To keep the truly old from misuse is surely as important as to recognize the genuinely new," Hartman remarked. Denis Donoghue, writing in *Sewanee Review,* called *Woe or Wonder* "the best introduction to Shakespeare's tragedies which I have read." This and several of Cunningham's other essays, on subjects such as literary style, were reprinted in *The Collected Essays of J. V. Cunningham.* This publication led Donoghue to observe in the *New York Times Book Review* that Cunningham had "limitations" as a critic:

"Cunningham's mind is remarkably powerful, but it is always already made up, and it only receives such new experience as will confirm its judgment." At the same time, Donoghue declared, "The merit of Cunningham's criticism is indisputable. He is in touch with crucial themes, perennial rather than novel. He is relentless in his search for lucidity. . . . He speaks only when he has something to say and when he has taken pains to discover the facts of the case."

BIOGRAPHICAL/CRITICAL SOURCES:

BOOKS

Contemporary Literary Criticism, Gale (Detroit), Volume 3, 1975, Volume 31, 1985.

Dictionary of Literary Biography, Volume 5: *American Poets since World War II,* Gale, 1980.

Donoghue, Denis, *Connoisseurs of Chaos,* Macmillan (New York City), 1965.

Gullans, Charles B., *A Bibliography of the Published Works of J. V. Cunningham,* University of California Library, Los Angeles, 1973.

Hungerford, Edward, editor, *Poets in Progress,* Northwestern University Press (Evanston, IL), 1962.

Winters, Yvor, *The Poetry of J. V. Cunningham,* Swallow Press (Denver), 1961.

PERIODICALS

Chicago Tribune, April 4, 1985.

Detroit Free Press, April 3, 1985.

Hudson Review, summer, 1960, pp. 284-93.

Michigan Quarterly Review, spring, 1972.

New Republic, January 28, 1978, pp. 25-26, 28-29.

New York Times, April 3, 1985.

New York Times Book Review, November 13, 1960; August 7, 1977, p. 12.

Poetry, August, 1942, pp. 279-82; December, 1960, pp. 181-85; August, 1961, pp. 332-36.

Publishers Weekly, June 30, 1997, p. 72.

Saturday Review, October 29, 1960.

Sewanee Review, summer, 1961, pp. 476-84.

Southern Review, spring, 1979, pp. 545-59.

Spectator, October 23, 1971, pp. 588-89.

Times Literary Supplement, September 23, 1960.

TriQuarterly, winter, 1961, pp. 20-26.

Washington Post, April 5, 1985.

Washington Post Book World, December 7, 1997, p. 10.

Western Humanities Review, winter, 1973.

Weekly Standard, February 16, 1998, pp. 31-35.

Yale Review, September, 1960, pp. 125-35.*

—Sketch by Trudy Ring

* * *

CURZON, Clare

See BUCHANAN, Marie

D

DALTON, (John) David 1944-

PERSONAL: Born January 15, 1944, in London, England; son of John E. (a surgeon) and Kathleen (an actress; maiden name, Tremaine) Dalton. *Education:* Attended Columbia University, 1960-64.

ADDRESSES: Home—78 Bank St., New York, NY 10014. *Agent*—Clyde Taylor, 34 Perry, New York, NY 10014.

CAREER: Author.

WRITINGS:

(With Jonathan Cott) *Get Back,* Apple, 1970.
Janis, Simon & Schuster (New York City), 1971.
(Editor) *Rolling Stones,* Amsco Music (New York City), 1971.
(With David Felton) *Mindfuckers: A Source Book on the Rise of Acid Fascism in America, including Material on Charles Manson, Mel Lyman, Victor Baranco, and Their Followers,* Straight Arrow Books (San Francisco), 1972.
James Dean, the Mutant King, Straight Arrow Books, 1974.
(With Lenny Kaye) *Rock 100,* Grosset (New York City), 1977.
The Rolling Stones: The First Twenty Years, Knopf (New York City), 1981.
(Compiler with Mick Farren) *The Rolling Stones in Their Own Words,* Putnam (New York City), 1983.
(Author of text) *James Dean: American Icon,* St. Martin's (New York City), 1984.
Piece of My Heart: The Life, Times and Legend of Janis Joplin, St. Martin's, 1985, published as *Piece of My Heart: A Portrait of Janis Joplin,* Da Capo Press (New York City), 1991.
(Author of introduction) *James Dean Revealed!: James Dean's Sexational Lurid Afterlife from the Scandal and Movie Magazines of the Fifties,* Delta (New York City), 1991.
Mr. Mojo Risin': Jim Morrison, the Last Holy Fool, St. Martin's, 1991.
(With Marianne Faithfull) *Faithfull: An Autobiography,* Little, Brown (Boston), 1994.
(With Rock Scully) *Living with the Dead: Twenty Years on the Bus with Garcia and the Grateful Dead,* Little, Brown, 1996.
El Sid: Saint Vicious, St. Martin's, 1997.

Contributing editor of *Rolling Stone,* 1968-75.

SIDELIGHTS: David Dalton has written biographies of rock music icons such as Janis Joplin, Jim Morrison, Jerry Garcia and Sid Vicious, as well as film star James Dean. He has also collaborated with singer Marianne Faithfull on her autobiography.

In 1972's *Janis,* Dalton presents an overview of the rock singer's life from her days in high school in Texas to her tragic early death at the age of 27 from a drug overdose in a Los Angeles motel room. Accompanied by many photographs of the star, Dalton's text is fragmentary and elusive, sometimes presenting written accounts of her life and sometimes transcripts of brief interviews with Joplin. The critic for the *New York Review of Books* admits that Dalton's book "cannot get past the myth of Janis precisely because she spent her whole life erasing historical reality and replacing it with myth." Peter Martin, writing in the *New York Times Book Review,* criticizes the book for being "written with the reverence and rhetoric ordinarily reserved for the Buddha's life." But J. A. Avant in *Library Journal* writes: "This formless, fascinating account seems like a weird odyssey, written in that wordy *Rolling Stone* style justly disliked by some readers, but which the Janis presented here would probably have loved."

James Dean: The Mutant King is Dalton's biography of the famed film star who died in a car crash at an early age. Leo Braudy in the *New York Times Book Review* notes that "Dalton's effort to make Dean into a cult figure for the present cuts Dean off from the roots of history and humanity that nourished the myth to begin with." "Dalton writes somewhat breathless prose, even a but gushy here and there," the *Choice* critic believes, but Sammy Staggs in *Library Journal* finds that, "as movie star biographies go, it is better than most."

Dalton collaborated with rock singer Marianne Faithfull to write *Faithfull: An Autobiography*. A singer whose career took off at the age of seventeen when her song "As Tears Go By" made her an overnight sensation, and who then was known as the girlfriend of Mick Jagger of the Rolling Stones, Marianne Faithfull reveals in her autobiography how she has overcome early problems, including a heroin addiction, to continue working as a nightclub singer in the 1990s. While several critics deplore the book's emphasis on sexual conquests and drug use, they praise Faithfull's descriptions of the milieu from which she emerged. K. Kaufmann in the *Lambda Book Report* writes: "Faithfull is at her best when discussing the artistic pretensions and sexism of the rock culture of the sixties." The critic for *Publishers Weekly* finds that, "writing with Dalton . . . , she depicts with penetrating insight the world of 'free love, psychedelic drugs, fashion, Zen, Nietzsche, tribal trinkets, customized Existentialism, hedonism and rock 'n' roll' that absorbed her energies from the beginning of her singing career."

Dalton collaborated with Grateful Dead band manager Rock Scully to write *Living with the Dead.* Both a biography of Jerry Garcia, the band's driving force, as well as an account of the band itself, the book is, according to Mike Tribby in *Booklist,* "a significant hunk of rock and pop culture history." After a quick rise during the Haight-Ashbury days of 1960s San Francisco, the Grateful Dead began a twenty-year stint as a band continuously touring the United States and Europe whose concerts drew devoted fans and attracted countless hangers-on. The critic for *Publishers Weekly* notes that the book treats the Grateful Dead "as a social phenomenon."

Punk rock star Sid Vicious is the subject of Dalton's *El Sid: Saint Vicious.* Lead singer for the band Sex Pistols, a concoction of rock impresario Malcolm McLaren, Sid Vicious (real name John Ritchie) found himself cast in a bad boy role for public consumption. Dalton's account of Sid's short life, cut short by a heroin overdose at the age of 21, is, Tribby reports, an "illuminating look at punk rock's crassest commercial manifestation." "Dalton's aim," notes the critic for *Publishers Weekly,* "is not so much to write a biography as to capture the punk milieu and to parse Vicious's larger-than-life persona; but he stumbles in both attempts. . . . But Dalton dearly has a feel for punk and there's some lively writing in the book."

BIOGRAPHICAL/CRITICAL SOURCES:

PERIODICALS

Artforum, November, 1994.
Booklist, July 1, 1977; January 1, 1996, p. 775; August, 1997, p. 1866.
Book World, February 27, 1972, p. 11.
Choice, October, 1974.
Lambda Book Report, January-February, 1995, p. 42.
Library Journal, December 15, 1971; April 15, 1972; November 15, 1974; February 1, 1977.
New York Review of Books, January 27, 1972.
New York Times Book Review, February 20, 1972, p. 4; September 22, 1974, p. 6.
Publishers Weekly, July 11, 1994, p. 71; November 20, 1995, p. 62; January 1, 1996, p. 39; July 7, 1997, p. 62.
School Library Journal, April, 1977.

* * *

DALTON, Sean
See CHESTER, Deborah

* * *

DAUBE, David 1909-

PERSONAL: Born February 8, 1909, in Freiburg im Breisgau, Germany; son of Jakob and Selma (Ascher) Daube; married Herta Babette Aufseesser, 1936 (divorced, 1964); children: Jonathan Mahram, Benjamin Jeremy, Michael Matthew. *Education:* University of Freiburg im Breisgau, Referendar, 1930; University of Goettingen, Dr.Jur. (with distinction), 1932; Cambridge University, Ph.D., 1936; Oxford University, M.A., DCL., both 1955.

ADDRESSES: Office—School of Law, 225 Boalt Hall, University of California, Berkeley, CA 94720.

CAREER: Cambridge University, Cambridge, England, fellow of Caius College, 1938-46, university lecturer in law, 1946-51; Aberdeen University, Aberdeen, Scotland, professor of jurisprudence, 1951-55; Oxford University, Oxford, England, Regius Professor of Civil Law, 1955-70, Regius Professor Emeritus, 1970—, fellow of All Souls College, 1955-70, fellow emeritus, 1980—; University of California, Berkeley, professor of law and director of Robbins Collection, 1970-81, professor emeritus, 1981—. Member of academic board, Institute of Jewish Study, London, 1953—; senior fellow, Yale University, 1962; Delitzsch Lecturer, University of Muenster, 1962; Gifford Lecturer, Edinburgh University, 1962-63; Olaus Petri Lecturer, Uppsala University, 1963; Ford Professor of Political Science, University of California, Berkeley, 1964; Riddell Lecturer, University of Newcastle, 1965; Gray Lecturer, Cambridge University, 1966; Lionel Cohen Lecturer, University of Jerusalem, 1970; Messenger Lecturer, Cornell University, 1971. Honorary professor of history, University of Konstanz, 1966—; honorary fellow, Caius College, Cambridge University, 1974—.

MEMBER: Classical Association of Great Britain (president, 1976-77), British Academy (fellow), American Academy of Arts and Sciences (fellow), World Academy of Art and Sciences (fellow), Royal Irish Academy (corresponding fellow), Akademie der Wissenschaften (Goettingen; corresponding fellow), Akademie der Wissenschaften (Munich; corresponding fellow).

AWARDS, HONORS: LL.D., Edinburgh University, 1958, and University of Leicester, 1964; Doctorat, University of Paris, 1963; D.H.L., Hebrew Union College, 1971; Dr.Jur., University of Munich, 1972; Oxford Centre for Postgraduate Hebrew Studies fellow, 1973.

WRITINGS:

Studies in Biblical Law, Cambridge University Press (New York City), 1947, reprinted, Ktav (New York City), 1969.

The New Testament and Rabbinic Judaism, Athlone Press, 1956, reprinted, Arno (New York City), 1973.

Forms of Roman Legislation, Clarendon Press, 1956, reprinted, Greenwood Press, 1979.

(Editor with William D. Davies) *The Background of the New Testament and Its Eschatology,* Cambridge University Press, 1956.

(Editor) *Studies in the Roman Law of Sale,* Clarendon Press, 1959.

The Exodus Pattern in the Bible, Faber, 1963, reprinted, Greenwood Press (Westport, CT), 1979.

The Sudden in the Scriptures, E. J. Brill, 1964.

Collaboration with Tryanny in Rabbinic Law: The Riddell Memorial Lectures, Oxford University Press, 1965.

Roman Law: Linguistic, Social, and Philosophical Aspects, Aldine, 1969.

Legal Problems in Medical Advance, Magnes Press (Jerusalem), 1971.

Civil Disobedience in Antiquity, Edinburgh University Press (Edinburgh, Scotland), 1972.

The Duty of Procreation, Edinburgh University Press, 1977.

Typologie im Werk des Flavius Josephus, Verlag der Bayerischen Akademie der Wissenschaften, 1977.

Die Geburt der Detektivgeschichte aus dem Geiste der Rhetorik, Universitatscerlag Kontanz, 1983.

Appeasement or Resistance, and Other Essays on New Testament Judaism, University of California Press (Berkeley), 1987.

Collected Works of David Daube, edited by Calum M. Carmichael, Robbins Collection (Berkeley), 1992.

SIDELIGHTS: David Daube is a highly respected biblical and legal scholar. As a critic for the *Times Literary Supplement* notes: "Of all the brilliant legal historians who have contributed beyond the strict bounds of their own subject David Daube is one of the most learned, humane and original."

Of *Roman Law: Linguistic, Social and Philosophical Aspects,* the *Times Literary Supplement* reviewer writes: "Professor Daube fully displays his many talents and his great learning in a style both lively and humorous. . . . [He] enjoys himself and delights the reader with a miscellany of ideas . . . brought together to give a fresh slant on institutions normally dealt with separately and from a very staid standpoint." The reviewer for *Choice* calls the same title "an unusual book, learned, wise, and filled with Oxfordian humor."

In his study *Civil Disobedience in Antiquity,* Daube examines the nonviolent protests of many different groups of people in ancient Rome, Israel, and Greece. Intending to present little-known information in a nonacademic manner, Daube's "wit and erudition are evident on every page of these rambling lectures," writes the *Choice* critic. R. J. Lenardon in *Library Journal* finds that "Daube's personal selection of examples is fascinating, and he offers new insights into the reasons for individual actions. He is especially perceptive in his treatment of the Biblical period."

BIOGRAPHICAL/CRITICAL SOURCES:

BOOKS

Bammel, E., editor, *Donum Gentilicium: New Testament Studies in Honor of David Daube,* Clarendon Press, 1978.

Carmichael, Calum M., editor, *Essays on Law and Religion: The Berkeley and Oxford Symposia in Honour of David Daube,* Robbins Collection, 1993.

Jackson, Bernard S., editor, *Studies in Jewish Legal History: Essays in Honour of David Daube,* Jewish Chronicle Publications, 1974.

Watson, Alan, editor, *Daube Noster: Essays in Legal History for David Daube,* Scottish Academic Press (Edinburgh), 1974.

PERIODICALS

American History Review, June, 1970.

Choice, November, 1969; December, 1973.

Library Journal, October 1, 1973.

Times Literary Supplement, June 26, 1969, p. 708; March 30, 1973, p. 356.

* * *

DAVIDSON, Chalmers Gaston 1907-1994

PERSONAL: Born June 6, 1907, in Chester, SC; died June 25, 1994; son of Zeb Vance (a mayor and probate judge) and Kate (Gaston) Davidson; married Alice Graham Gage, March 20, 1937; children: Robert Gage, Alice Graham (Mrs. William H. Sims III), Mary Gage. *Education:* Davidson College, B.A., 1928; Harvard University, M.A., 1930, Ph.D., 1942; University of Chicago, M.A., 1936.

CAREER: Instructor in history at Chamberlain Hunt Military Academy, Port Gibson, MS, 1928-29, Blue Ridge School for Boys, Hendersonville, NC, 1933-34, and The Citadel, Charleston, SC, 1934-35; Davidson College, Davidson, NC, professor of history and director of library, 1936-76. Lecturer, Piedmont University Center, 1967-68. Member, North Carolina Governor's Carolina Tercentenary Commission, beginning 1963. *Military service:* U.S. Naval Reserve, 1944-46; served in Pacific; became lieutenant junior grade.

MEMBER: North Carolina Literary and Historical Association (president, 1961-62), Historical Society of North Carolina (president, 1966-67), Mecklenburg County Historical Association (president, 1956-57), Phi Beta Kappa, Omicron Delta Kappa, Beta Theta Pi, Society of the Cincinnati.

AWARDS, HONORS: Charles A. Canon Award, 1951, for contribution to North Carolina history.

WRITINGS:

Major John Davidson of "Rural Hill," Mecklenburg County, NC: Pioneer, Industrialist, Planter, Lassiter Press (Charlotte, NC), 1943.

(With William P. Cumming) *Davidson College Library Handbook,* Davidson College (Davidson, NC), 1948.

Cloud over Catawba, Mecklenburg Historical Society, 1949.

Friend of the People: The Life of Dr. Peter Fayssoux of Charleston, South Carolina, Medical Association of South Carolina (Columbia, SC), 1950.

Piedmont Partisan: The Life and Times of Brigadier-General William Lee Davidson, Davidson College, 1951.

Mid-Point for '28 (class history), Davidson College, 1953.

Gaston of Chester, privately printed, 1956.

The Plantation World Around Davidson: The Story of North Mecklenburg "Before the War," Mecklenburg Historical Association (Davidson, NC), 1969.

The Last Foray: The South Carolina Planters of 1860, University of South Carolina Press (Columbia), 1971.

High-point for '28: The Fiftieth Anniversary of the Davidson College Class of 1928, Compiled from Questionaires Returned by Members of the Class and Records in the Alumni Office of the College, Davidson College, 1978.

The Colonial Scotch-Irish of the Carolina Piedmont, Chester County Historical Society (Chester, SC), 1979.

The Generations of Davidson College: A Study of Three-Generation Families, privately printed, 1980.

Contributor to *Dictionary of American Biography* and to scholarly and popular periodicals.

SIDELIGHTS: Chalmers Gaston Davidson wrote histories and biographies focusing on the events and people of the Carolinas. His biography *Friend of the People: The Life of Dr. Peter Fayssoux of Charleston, South Carolina,* details the life of a medical doctor well-known in South Carolina at the time of the American Revolution, serving as chief physician at Charleston Hospital for many years. The critic for the *Saturday Review of Literature* stated that Davidson calls Fayssoux "the father of medicine in his native state, and the record justifies his claim to distinction alike in science and in public affairs." C. G. Singer in the *American History Review* claimed that "Davidson has handled a difficult study with proficiency and has made a definite contribution to our knowledge."

Davidson tells of another Carolinian who achieved prominence during the American Revolution in *Piedmont Partisan: The Life and Times of Brigadier-General William Lee Davidson.* Davidson's account is, according to H. T. Lefler in *American History Review,* "a well-organized, beautifully written, and heavily documented account of one of North Carolina's most successful Revolutionary leaders." The critic for *U. S. Quarterly Book Review* believed that Davidson succeeds in this study "in adding to an understanding of Scotch-Irish pioneering, of Presbyterianism in the old West, and of the nature and extent of the Revolution in North Carolina."

The campus of Davidson College was originally part of the plantation owned by Davidson's great-great uncle. About once every ten years Davidson gets out a booklet, *The Generations of Davidson College,* which lists those families represented in the student body for three or more generations.

BIOGRAPHICAL/CRITICAL SOURCES:

PERIODICALS

American History Review, April, 1951; July, 1952.
American Political Science Review, June, 1951.
Raleigh News and Observer, December 14, 1952.
Saturday Review of Literature, October 21, 1950.
U. S. Quarterly Book Review, June, 1952.*

* * *

DAVIDSON, Eugene (Arthur) 1902-

PERSONAL: Born September 22, 1902, in New York, NY; son of William and Bertha (Passarge) Davidson; married Louise Keil, April 6, 1928 (divorced); married Suzette M. Zurcher, November, 1968; children: (first marriage) Eugene, Lisa. *Education:* Yale University, B.A., 1927, graduate study, 1927-28.

CAREER: Yale University Press, New Haven, CT, editor, 1929-59; *Modern Age,* Chicago, IL, editor, 1960-70. President, Foundation for Foreign Affairs, 1957-70; chairman, Committee on European Problems. Lecturer in Germany and at U. S. colleges, 1947, and 1962.

MEMBER: PEN, Arts Club (Chicago), Graduates Club and Elizabethan Club (both New Haven).

AWARDS, HONORS: Litt.D., Park College, 1977.

WRITINGS:

The Death and Life of Germany: An Account of the American Occupation, Knopf (New York City), 1959.

The Trial of the Germans: An Account of the Twenty-Two Defendants before the International Military Tribunal at Nuremberg, Macmillan (New York City), 1966.

The Nuremberg Fallacy: Wars and War Crimes since World War II, Macmillan, 1973.

The Making of Adolf Hitler, Macmillan, 1977, published as *The Making of Adolf Hitler: The Birth and Rise of Nazism,* University of Missouri Press (Columbia), 1997.

The Unmaking of Adolf Hitler, University of Missouri Press, 1996.

Contributor of book reviews, articles, and poetry to magazines, including the *Yale Review, Freeman, Saturday Review of Literature,* and *Progressive.*

SIDELIGHTS: Eugene Davidson has written several scholarly studies about Nazi Germany, Adolf Hitler and the Nuremberg war crimes trials of World War II. Davidson was a reporter at the 1961 Adolf Eichmann trial in Jerusalem, in which the Nazi war criminal was tried and executed for participation in the Jewish Holocaust of World War II.

In *The Death and Life of Germany: An Account of the American Occupation,* Davidson chronicles the primary events in post-war German history. Calling the study "a very thorough and judicious assortment of revealing data on every aspect of the occupation," J. K. Pollock in the *Annals of the American Academy* concludes that "the thorough and careful research which [Davidson] has done in this vast field deserves nothing but commendation." Edith Lenel in *Library Journal* notes that Davidson's "fairness and psychological insight have enabled him to present the essential events, the gradual and subtle changes in the relations between the former adversaries in the larger context of world politics so as to form a convincing, well-rounded summary." While E. S. Pisko in the *Christian Science Monitor* calls Davidson's coverage of the early post-war years "a colorful and often poignant re-creation of an era that had the haunting strangeness of a surrealistic painting," E. A. Mowrer in the *Springfield Republican* praises the study as "smoothly written and quietly dramatic, fascinating from end to end."

Davidson focused on the Nuremberg war crimes trials in *The Trial of the Germans: An Account of the Twenty-Two Defendants before the International Military Tribunal at Nuremberg* and looked at the effects the trials had on later political events in *The Nuremberg Fallacy: Wars and War Crimes since World War II.* Several critics found that *The Trial of the Germans* brought up questions about the validity and fairness of the original trials, in which the Allied nations arrested, tried and convicted leading German officials for alleged criminal behavior during World War II. A. J. P. Taylor, writing in the *New York Review of Books,* finds that "the hypocrisy of Nuremberg was revolting enough in 1945. It exceeds all bounds when it is maintained in 1967." L. L. Snyder in *Saturday Review* notes that Davidson does concede "that Nuremberg was not the best forum to establish the rules for a new order: the victors were judging the vanquished. There was demonstrated a remarkable fairness and a fine show of legal form, but some of the individual cases left room for doubt." Calling *The Trial of the Germans* a "significant accomplishment," F. E. Hirsch in *Library Journal* contends that "Davidson catches the court atmosphere quite well."

In *The Nuremberg Fallacy* Davidson examines the lasting effects of the Nuremberg trials and the laws of war established at that time. He finds that wartime behavior since the trials has not improved much, despite international agreements about proper military procedures. Davidson draws on examples from such conflicts as the wars in Southeast Asia, the Six-Day War between Israel and the Arab states, and the Russian invasions of Hungary and Czechoslovakia. While J. S. Wozniak in the *Annals of the American Academy* finds that *The Nuremberg Fallacy* is "a rather disappointing monograph," he nonetheless believes it to "provide a wealth of detail about five highly significant cases of aggression in the contemporary era, and it does raise questions about the nature and causes of modern aggression."

BIOGRAPHICAL/CRITICAL SOURCES:

PERIODICALS

American Historical Review, January, 1960.
Annals of the American Academy, November, 1959; September, 1973.
Booklist, July 1, 1959.
Choice, September, 1973.
Christian Science Monitor, June 3, 1959, p. 13; January 30, 1967, p. 9.
Foreign Affairs, October, 1959.
Library Journal, May 15, 1959; December 15, 1966; June 15, 1973.
Nation, September 19, 1959.
National Review, March 21, 1967.
Newsweek, January 9, 1967.
New York Herald Tribune Book Review, September 6, 1959, p. 10.
New York Review of Books, February 23, 1967.
New York Times, May 24, 1959, p. 3.
New York Times Book Review, November 20, 1977.
Saturday Review, May 30, 1959; February 4, 1967.
Springfield Republican, June 7, 1959, p. D4.*

* * *

DAVIDSON, Morris 1898-1979

PERSONAL: Born December 16, 1898, in Rochester, NY; died April 13, 1979, in Piermont, NY.

CAREER: Artist. Director of Morris Davidson School of Art, New York City; had thirty one-man exhibitions of his paintings. Work included in museum collections at the Jerusalem Museum, the Baltimore Museum, and the Schenectady Museum of Art.

MEMBER: American Federation of Modern Painters and Sculptors (founder).

WRITINGS:

Understanding Modern Art, Coward (New York City), 1932.
Painting for Pleasure, R. Hale (London), 1938.
Approach to Modern Painting, Coward, 1948.

SIDELIGHTS: Morris Davidson was an artist whose paintings were displayed in thirty one-man shows throughout the United States and are included among the collections of several museums. Davidson also ran the Morris Davidson School of Art in New York City for many years, and was a founder of the American Federation of Modern Painters and Sculptors. His books on art seek to explain the modern movement in a straightforward and sensible manner.

In *Understanding Modern Art* Davidson outlines first an approach to understanding the art of any historical period, then gives a brief history of European painting over the past few centuries, then concludes with descriptions of the modern art schools of the twentieth century, including Cubism, Expressionism and Impressionism. Although E. A. Jewell in the *New York Times* felt that Davidson had not completely explained modern art to the uninformed reader, he had provided a study that was "written lucidly and with real earnestness. . . . The author has produced a readable, a not infrequently very illuminating and signally helpful essay." Davidson, according to Thomas Craven in *Books,* "has written a concise, conscientious and, for the most part, excellent introduction to Modernist painting. He avoids showy language and the forbidding terminology employed by most writers on esthetics. . . . His opinions are put forward in a sensible orderly fashion." While the critic for the *Saturday Review of Literature* found *Understanding Modern Art* to be "pretty light weight," he nonetheless concluded: "The point of view is that of a tempered radicalism, and many of the individual estimates are perceptive."

Davidson again wrote an introduction to the basics of modern art in his *Approach to Modern Painting.* In this study, he presented an overview of the sources of modern art and evaluated the works of specific artists working in the modernist schools. Stuart Preston in the *Saturday Review of Literature* lauded Davidson who, Preston believed, "is at his best when analyzing actual works of art; about them he has interesting, felicitous things to say; his judgment is of value." The reviewer for *Kirkus* noted Davidson's approach to art was "sane rather than faddish in its treatment" and his study would "prove a worthwhile addition to the art book shelves."

BIOGRAPHICAL/CRITICAL SOURCES:

PERIODICALS

Booklist, January, 1932; November 15, 1938; June 1, 1948.
Books, January 10, 1932, p. 13.
Kirkus, November 1, 1947.
Library Journal, June 1, 1948.
New Yorker, October 15, 1938.
New York Times, December 27, 1931, p. 15.
Pittsburgh Monthly Bulletin, January, 1932.
Saturday Review of Literature, December 12, 1931; August 7, 1948.

OBITUARIES:

PERIODICALS

New York Times, April 16, 1979.*

* * *

DAVIES, John Paton, Jr. 1908-

PERSONAL: Born April 6, 1908, in Kiating, China; son of John Paton and Helen (MacNeil) Davies; married Patricia Grady, August 24, 1942; children: Alexandra, Patricia, John, Susan, Jennifer, Deborah, Megan. *Education:* Attended University of Wisconsin, 1928 and 1929, Yenching University, 1930; Columbia University, B.S., 1931.

ADDRESSES: Home—3646 Cumberland St. N.W., Washington, DC 20008.

CAREER: U.S. Department of State, Foreign Service officer, 1932-54, serving in Canada, China, Burma, India, U.S.S.R., Germany, and Peru; Estilo S.A. (furniture manufacturers), Lima, Peru, president 1956-64.

AWARDS, HONORS: Two awards from American Institute of Interior Designers for furniture design.

WRITINGS:

Foreign and Other Affairs, Norton (New York City), 1964, new edition, with an introduction by Hans J. Morgenthau, 1966.
Dragon by the Tail: American, British, Japanese, and Russian Encounters with China and One Another, Norton, 1972.

Contributor of articles to *New York Times Magazine, Reporter,* and *Harper's.*

SIDELIGHTS: John Paton Davies has written two books on American foreign policy which draw on his many years of experience as a diplomat. Davies's career with the U. S. Department of State was cut short in the 1950s during the McCarthy era, when those of the political far-left were removed from governmental office.

Foreign and Other Affairs examines such issues as foreign aid, the United Nations, nuclear strategy, and intervention. Robert Murphy in *Book Week* describes the book as "a brilliant analysis of the political and diplomatic problems of our day. . . . A most profitable report for any one even vaguely interested in America's world position." According to C. B. Marshall in *Reporter,* Davies's book "is a winning combination of candor and good prose." "This," writes H. J. Morgenthau in the *New York Review of Books,* "is the book of a professional who knows the world and has a sense of history. It is full of profound insights."

In *Dragon by the Tail: American, British, Japanese, and Russian Encounters with China and One Another,* Davies presents an overview of the interrelations of several of the world's leading political powers. Davies particularly focuses on America's China policy of the 1940s, a time when Davies himself was active in the diplomatic service in China and the fate of post-war China was determined. A. S. Whiting in *New Republic* calls the study "a many-splendored volume, long in perspective, rich in detail and superlative in its prose." "This is a book of many excellences," writes A. J. Nathan in *Library Journal.* "It is first of all the useful memoir of a fascinating career. . . . All this is delivered in a style that is urbane and ironic, precise and brief. No one interested in China will fail to profit from this book, and no one who reads it will fail to enjoy it."

BIOGRAPHICAL/CRITICAL SOURCES:

PERIODICALS

America, September 19, 1964; December 9, 1972.
Best Sellers, October 1, 1972.
Book Week, August 2, 1964, p. 3.
Library Journal, November 15, 1964; August, 1972.
New Republic, October 24, 1964; October 21, 1972.
Newsweek, August 24, 1964.
New Yorker, September 23, 1972.
New York Review of Books, July 30, 1964; November 16, 1972.
New York Times Book Review, Ocrober 29, 1972, p. 3.
Reporter, September 10, 1964.
Saturday Review, September 5, 1964.
Virginia Quarterly Review, winter, 1965.*

* * *

DAVIES, Laurence 1926-

PERSONAL: Born in 1926, in Merthyr Tydfil, Glamorganshire, Wales; married Menna Morgan. *Education:* Studied at University of Wales and University of London; studied piano with Mark Hambourg, 1943-44.

ADDRESSES: Home—103 Minehead Ave., Sully, Glamorganshire, Wales.

CAREER: Monmouthshire, Wales, education officer, 1957-59; University of Wales, Cardiff, senior lecturer in psychology, 1966—; freelance music critic. *Military service:* Royal Air Force, 1945.

WRITINGS:

Liberal Studies and Higher Technology, University of Wales Press, 1965.
The Gallic Muse, Dent (London), 1967, A. S. Barnes (New York City), 1969.
Cesar Franck and His Circle, Houghton (Boston), 1970.
Ravel Orchestral Music, British Broadcasting Corp. (London), 1970, University of Washington Press (Seattle), 1971.
Paths to Modern Music: Aspects of Music from Wagner to the Present Day, Scribner (New York City), 1971.
Franck, Octagon Books (New York City), 1973.

(With Cedric Watts) *Cunninghame Graham: A Critical Biography,* Cambridge University Press (New York City), 1979.

(Editor with Frederick R. Karl) *The Collected Letters of Joseph Conrad,* Cambridge University Press, 1983.

Contributor of articles to *Music and Letters, Music, Opera, Music and Musicians, Journal of Liberal Education,* and *Cambridge Review.*

SIDELIGHTS: Laurence Davies has earned critical praise for his scholarly works on music. In *The Gallic Muse,* for example, Davies gathers several essays on such leading French composers as Satie and Debussy and seeks to find the musical commonalities between them. The critic for the *Times Literary Supplement* finds that "a constant interaction of ideas is traced, springing from the wide artistic world normally inhabited by these composers." "The book is excellent," writes *Library Journal* contributor A. B. Skei. "Davies writes well, and the book should appeal to a broad range of readers."

In *Cesar Francke and His Circle* Davies wrote a history of the famed nineteenth-century Belgian composer and the many influential composers who studied under him. P. L. Miller in *Library Journal* explains: "Davies has undertaken a formidable task. He discusses the most important Franckians in detail, giving biographical facts, analyses of their chief compositions, and even the plots of their forgotten operas." "Davies has written a monumental work," judges the critic for the *Times Literary Supplement.* The critic goes on to state: "A comprehensive study of Franck and his circle in English was certainly needed, and Dr. Davies has every qualification to write it. . . . Likely to long remain a standard work."

Davies traces the beginnings of modern music in his *Paths to Modern Music,* a collection of essays that the reviewer for the *Times Literary Supplement* calls "learned, critical, racily written, well-researched and wide-visioned." While Dika Newlin in *Library Journal* finds that "Davies has moments of insight, on the whole the book seems dated and provincial," the *Choice* critic describes Davies's musical criticism as being "after the method of G. B. Shaw. . . . Music listeners will appreciate the sort of down-to-earth background that should be given in program notes. Students will value this British university tutor's graceful attempt to lift them above the technical side of music."

BIOGRAPHICAL/CRITICAL SOURCES:

PERIODICALS

Choice, September, 1966; March, 1971; January, 1972.

Library Journal, May 15, 1969; December 15, 1970; November 1, 1971.

Times Literary Supplement, February 3, 1966, p. 78; June 1, 1967, p. 480; September 4, 1970, p. 969; June 4, 1971, p. 645.

* * *

DAVIS, Clive E(dward) 1914-

PERSONAL: Born October 19, 1914, in South New Berlin, NY; son of Clyde Seymour (a civil engineer) and Eva (Bird) Davis; married Maxine Peterson (a secretary); children: Douglas Michael, Bruce Edward. *Education:* Attended Syracuse University, 1932-36. *Politics:* Democratic. *Religion:* Episcopalian.

ADDRESSES: Home—3309 Bristol Rd., Sacramento 25, CA 95825.

CAREER: Announcer and program assistant at radio stations in Philadelphia, PA, Worchester, MA, New York, NY, Great Falls, MT, and Sacramento, CA, 1937-62; freelance writer. Licensed commercial pilot, 1947—. *Military service:* U.S. Army Air Forces, World War II; served in Asia, Africa, Europe, and with armies of occupation in Italy and Philippines; became first lieutenant; received Silver Star, Bronze Star (twice), Distinguished Unit Citation with oak leaf cluster. U.S. Air Force Reserve; now lieutenant colonel (retired).

MEMBER: Air Force Association.

AWARDS, HONORS: Air Force Association Medal of Merit, 1956, and citations, 1957 and 1958; Arts and Letters Award of California wing of Air Force Association.

WRITINGS:

The Junior Airman's Book of Airplanes, Dodd (New York City), 1958.

The Book of Missiles, Dodd, 1959.

Man and Space, Dodd, 1960.

Message From Space, Dodd, 1961.

The Book of Air Force Airplanes and Helicopters, Dodd, 1967.

SIDELIGHTS: Clive Edward Davis's books on aerospace topics have earned critical praise as introductory texts for teenaged readers who desire to learn more about space flight. *The Book of Missiles,* for example, is described by Albert Monheit in *Library Journal* as "a descriptive introduction to missiles, dealing almost exclusively with U. S. rocket devices." According to the critic for *Booklist,* the book's "informative, nontechnical treatment . . . is suitable for the general reader but will probably appeal most to teen-age boys."

Davis's *Man and Space* outlines the plans of the American space program as of the early-1960s, when the original seven astronauts had just been chosen. Ruth Handel in *Library Journal* explains that the book contains "brief biographies of the seven men chosen to be the first astronauts and a sampling of the testing used to choose them." The *Booklist* reviewer calls *Man and Space* "a concise and clearly written resume of America's space exploration program."

Messages from Space explains the methods used by scientists to maintain communication with distant missiles and satellites in outer space, as well as how space devices are tracked in flight. T. C. Hines in *Library Journal* notes that Davis's book provides "substantive information in concentrated form." The *Booklist* contributor concludes that *Messages from Space* is "a compact, authoritative account."

BIOGRAPHICAL/CRITICAL SOURCES:

PERIODICALS

Booklist, March 1, 1958; May 1, 1959; December 1, 1960; July 15, 1961.

Chicago Sunday Tribune, November 6, 1960, p. 50; May 14, 1961, p. 16.

Library Journal, April 15, 1958; May 15, 1959; October 15, 1960; April 15, 1961.

New York Herald Tribune Lively Arts, May 14, 1961, p. 35.

Springfield Republican, February 5, 1961, p. D4.

* * *

DAVIS, Curtis Carroll 1916-1997

PERSONAL: Born February 18, 1916, in Baltimore, MD; died February 1, 1997; son of Hoagland Cook (a medical doctor) and Katharine (Carroll) Davis; married G. Margarete Wenderoth, October 11, 1969. *Education:* Yale University, A.B., 1938; Columbia University, M.A., 1939; Duke University, Ph.D., 1947. *Politics:* Independent. *Religion:* Roman Catholic. *Avocational interests:* Collecting rare beer mugs and military miniatures, travel (has gone "round the world").

CAREER: Writer. U.S. Central Intelligence Agency, Washington, DC, desk chief, 1947-49; Star-Spangled Banner Flag House Association, Baltimore, MD, member of directorate, beginning 1962. *Military service:* U.S. Army Air Corps, 1942-46; became captain; received Bronze Star and Presidential Unit Citation. U.S. Army Reserve, Intelligence, 1946-76; lieutenant colonel (retired).

MEMBER: American Association of State and Local History, American Historical Association, United States Commission on Military History, Authors Guild, Authors League of America, National Book Critics Circle, Maryland Historical Society (life member; library committee, member, 1965-97, chair, 1973-77), Society for the Preservation of Maryland Antiquities, North Carolina Historical and Literary Association, Virginia Historical Society, Baltimore Bibliophiles, St. George's Society of Baltimore (life member), Manuscript Society, Edgar Allan Poe Society (member of executive committee), Association of Former Intelligence Officers (life member), Council on Abandoned Military Posts, Reserve Officers Association (life member), Circumnavigators Club.

AWARDS, HONORS: Awarded Sterling Trophy by North Carolina Society of the Cincinnati, for *Revolution's Godchild: The Birth, Death, and Regeneration of the Society of the Cincinnati in North Carolina.*

WRITINGS:

Chronicler of the Cavaliers: A Life of the Virginia Novelist, Dr. William A. Caruthers, Dietz, 1953.

The King's Chevalier: A Biography of Lewis Littlepage, Bobbs-Merrill (Indianapolis), 1961.

(Editor) John Sergeant Wise, *The End of an Era,* Thomas Yoseloff (New York City), 1965.

(Editor) Belle Boyd, *Belle Boyd in Camp and Prison,* Thomas Yoseloff, 1968.

(Editor) William A. Caruthers, *The Knights of the Golden Horse-Shoe,* revised edition, University of North Carolina Press, 1970.

That Ambitious Mr. Legare: The Life of James M. Legare of South Carolina, Including a Collected Edition of His Verse, University of South Carolina Press (Columbia), 1971.

(Contributor) James S. Presgraves, editor, *Wythe County Chapters,* privately printed, 1972.

Revolution's Godchild: The Birth, Death, and Regeneration of the Society of the Cincinnati in North Carolina, University of North Carolina Press (Chapel Hill), 1976.

Contributor to *Proceedings of the American Philosophical Society* and *A Bibliographical Guide to the Study of Southern Literature,* Louisiana State University Press, 1969. Contributor to *Biographical Dictionary of Southern Literature, Concise Dictionary of American Biography, Dictionary of North Carolina Biography, New-York Historical Society's Dictionary of Artists in America, Dictionary of Literary Biography,* and *World Book Encyclopedia.* Contributor of more than sixty articles on historical topics to periodicals, including *American Heritage, Virginia Cavalcade, William & Mary Quarterly,* and *Civil War History*. Editor, annual brochure, "Society of the War of 1812 in the State of Maryland"; member of editorial board, *Maryland Historical Magazine.*

SIDELIGHTS: Curtis Carroll Davis wrote two biographies that earned critical praise. *The King's Chevalier: A Biography of Lewis Littlepage* is the story of an eighteenth- century Virginian who served as assistant to America's Minister to Spain and then as confidential secretary to King Stanislaus II of Poland. Littlepage, according to the critic for *Kirkus,* was a "brilliant and devious American diplomat." Because his personal papers were destroyed after his death, much of Littlepage's remarkable career had to be painstakingly reconstructed from secondary sources scattered throughout Europe. "The research required," noted W. C. Kiessel in *Saturday Review,* "was prodigious." As R. R. Rea wrote in *Library Journal,* "Davis' fascinating biography overshadows wildest fiction with exemplary research brilliantly presented." Kiessel concluded that "Davis has performed the difficult task of converting a footnote in history into a credible biography. Readers with patience and time thoroughly to masticate this kaleidoscopic, stranger-than-fiction career of a soldier of fortune will be well rewarded."

In *That Ambitious Mr. Legare: The Life of James M. Legare of South Carolina,* Davis profiled a Southern poet whose works have not gained a lasting reputation in American literature. His biography, in fact, prints many of the author's poems for the first time since their original publication in nineteenth-century magazines. As B. C. Bach noted in *Library Journal,* "though his poems are imitative, stilted, and obviously fourth rate, the record of a Southerner's struggle . . . to receive literary recognition in mid-19th-Century America is informative." Writing in *American Literature,* J. O. Eidson stated: "Davis has definitely brought [Legare] to life. We may not in the future do much reading of his poems, but 'his slender yet solid claim to lasting reputation' is well documented."

BIOGRAPHICAL/CRITICAL SOURCES:

PERIODICALS

American History Review, April, 1962.
American Literature, January, 1973.
Baltimore Sun, January 15, 1979.
Booklist, November 15, 1961.
Christian Science Monitor, September 15, 1961, p. 9.
Kirkus, June 1, 1961.
Library Journal, August, 1961; September 1, 1971.
News & Courier (Charleston, SC), June 6, 1971.
Saturday Review, October 7, 1961.*

* * *

DAVIS, Earle (Rosco) 1905-1991

PERSONAL: Born January 3, 1905, in Coin, Iowa; died August 28, 1991; son of David Milton and Mary Isabel (Watterson) Davis; married Kathrine K. Laurie, August 4, 1938; children: Nina Virginia, Joseph Scott L., Earle Rosco, Sallie K., Charles W. *Education:* Monmouth College, A.B. and B.Mus., 1927; University of Illinois, M.A., 1928; Princeton University, Ph.D., 1935. *Religion:* Episcopal.

CAREER: Monmouth College, Monmouth, IL, instructor in English, 1928-33; Wichita State University, Wichita, KS, professor of English and chair of department, 1935-49; Kansas State University, Manhattan, professor of English, beginning 1949, head of department, beginning 1950. Fulbright lecturer at University of Adelaide, 1962, and at University College of National University of Ireland, 1969-70.

MEMBER: Modern Language Association of America.

WRITINGS:

An American in Sicily (poetry), Margent Press, 1944.
(Editor with William C. Hummel) *Readings for Opinion: From Literary Ideas and Attitudes,* Prentice-Hall (Englewood Cliffs, NJ), 1952, second edition, 1960.
(Editor with Hummel) *Readings for Enjoyment,* Prentice-Hall, 1959.
The Flint and the Flame: The Artistry of Charles Dickens, University of Missouri Press, 1963.
Vision Fugitive: Ezra Pound and Economics, University Press of Kansas (Lawrence), 1969.
I Sing of America: A Folklore Epic, privately printed, 1981.

Author of articles published in University of Wichita bulletins; contributor of poems and articles to magazines.

SIDELIGHTS: Earle Davis wrote two highly acclaimed studies of literary figures. In *The Flint and the Flame: The Artistry of Charles Dickens,* Davis argues that the career of Charles Dickens shows a definite increase in the author's control of narrative over time. Davis's thesis, then, is that Dickens' last novels are his most accomplished. "Certainly the specialist in Victorian literature will welcome Professor Davis's sturdy refutation of some of the critical nonsense about Dickens's work," wrote J. R. Willingham in *Library Journal.* The reviewer for the *Times Literary Supplement* believed that Davis "gives an excellent analysis of the development of Dickens's craftsmanship and offers much original scholarship on the theatrical and fictional origins of various characters, incidents and narrative devices."

In *Vision Fugitive: Ezra Pound and Economics,* Davis focused his critical attention on a more recent literary figure. Examining Pound's theory of economics, and how the author applied this theory to history, Davis then examined how Pound makes use of his economic ideas in his poems, particularly "The Cantos." In fact, as H. H. Waggoner wrote in *American Literature,* Davis argues that "The Cantos" "cannot be understood or appreciated unless the economic theory at their center is grasped." Joan Kelley, writing in the *Library Journal,* noted that Davis sees Pound as "a flawed and embittered idealist vainly pursuing his fugitive vision of economic utopia." A critic for *Choice* found that Davis's "book is valid as a 'reading' of The Cantos, factual and doggedly comprehensive." Kelly concluded that *Vision Fugitive* "is potentially one of the most important critical considerations of The Cantos to be published in a long time."

BIOGRAPHICAL/CRITICAL SOURCES:

PERIODICALS

American Literature, January, 1970.
Choice, January, 1970.
Library Journal, January 15, 1964; November 15, 1968.
Times Literary Supplement, January 15, 1964, p. 48; August 21, 1970, p. 925.
Virginia Quarterly Review, winter, 1964.*

* * *

DAVIS, James W(arren, Jr.) 1935-

PERSONAL: Born September 14, 1935, in Chillicothe, MO; son of James Warren (a lawyer) and Jennie (Cox) Davis; married Jean Ludwig, June 29, 1963; children: Warren, Clare. *Education:* Harvard University, A.B. (cum laude), 1957; University of Michigan, M.P.A., 1962, Ph.D., 1964.

ADDRESSES: Home—600 West Polo, St. Louis, MO 63105. *Office*—Department of Political Science, Washington University, St. Louis, MO 63130.

CAREER: Worked in Washington, DC, with Washington Metropolitan Regional Conference, summer, 1961, and U.S. Bureau of the Budget, summer, 1962; University of Wisconsin—Madison, assistant professor of political science, 1964-68; Washington University, St. Louis, MO, associate professor, 1968-74, professor of political science, 1974—. Consultant, National Advisory Commission on Selective Service, 1966; adviser in School of Public Administration, National Institute of Development Administration, Bangkok, Thailand, 1968-69. Visiting lecturer, University of Wisconsin, 1970. *Military service:* U.S. Army, Security Agency, 1957-60.

MEMBER: American Political Science Association, American Association for the Advancement of Science, American Society for Public Administration, Midwest Political Science Association, Phi Kappa Phi, Pi Sigma Alpha.

WRITINGS:

(With Kenneth M. Dolbeare) *Little Groups of Neighbors: The Selective Service System,* Markham, 1968.

Springboard to the White House: Presidential Primaries, How They Are Fought and Won, Crowell (New York City), 1968.

(Editor) *Politics, Programs, and Budgets: A Reader in Government Budgeting,* Prentice-Hall (Englewood Cliffs, NJ), 1969.

The National Executive Branch: An Introduction, Free Press (New York City), 1970.

An Introduction to Public Administration, Free Press, 1974.

Contributor to *Political Science and Public Policy,* Markham, 1968, and *Selective Service and American Society,* Russell Sage, 1969. Contributor to political science and public administration journals.

SIDELIGHTS: James W. Davis has written several books examining aspects of the American political system. His *Little Groups of Neighbors: The Selective Service System,* for example, is a study of the draft used to recruit new members of the armed forces. The book examines the structure of the selective service system, its personnel, and the impact the draft had on the larger society of which it was a part. H. A. Marmion in the *Annals of the American Academy* finds that "the book is thoroughly documented and scholarly in approach. . . . A valuable addition to the literature in the field." K. A. Hinckley, writing in the *American political Science Review,* calls *Little Groups of Neighbors* "an ambitious undertaking marked by a reasonably high level of success."

In *Springboard to the White House: Presidential Primaries, How They Are Fought and Won,* Davis used voting statistics from presidential primaries from 1912 to the 1960s to examine such issues as delegate loyalty and opinion poll ratings. Describing the study as "the kind of book one reads comfortably at home over a long evening," D. W. Rae in the *American Political Science Review* concludes that the book's strongest feature "is its author's rapport with politics and his interesting writing."

The National Executive Branch describes the several agencies and offices which comprise the executive branch of the American government. Davis, according to T. E. Cronin in the *American Political Science Review,* "brings together an informative collection of fact, description, and commonsense observations in a readable and compact slim essay-text. . . . He captures much of the ambiguity, complexity, and diversity that are so characteristic of the practices of the executive branch."

BIOGRAPHICAL/CRITICAL SOURCES:

PERIODICALS

American Political Science Review, March, 1968; June, 1969; September, 1971.

Annals of the American Academy, May, 1969.

Choice, May, 1971.

Library Journal, August, 1967.*

* * *

DAVIS, L(awrence) J(ames) 1940-

PERSONAL: Born July 2, 1940, in Seattle, WA; son of Maurice Nelson and Eula Jane (Randall) Davis; married Barbara Frances Ball (a social worker), September 21, 1961; children: Jeremy Randall, Gabriel Sprague, Barbara Victoria, Tina Rose. *Education:* Stanford University, A.B., 1962; Columbia University, graduate study, 1962. *Politics:* Democratic.

ADDRESSES: Home—138A Dean St., Brooklyn, NY 11217. *Agent*—Sterling Lord, Sterling Lord Agency, 660 Madison Ave., New York, NY 10021.

CAREER: Restoration Realty, Brooklyn, NY, salesperson, 1966-69; Sterling Wine and Liquor Co., Brooklyn, morning manager, 1969-70; University of Rochester, Rochester, NY, Writers' Workshop, faculty member, 1970-73, and program director, 1974—, university instructor, summers, 1974-78. Lecturer, New York University, 1972-75; instructor, Hofstra University, 1972-75. Boerum Hill Association, chair of community planning committee, 1965-66, vice-president, 1968-71; chair, United Neighborhood Playground Committee; member, Mayor's Task Force for South Brooklyn. *Military service:* Idaho Air National Guard, 1957-59. U.S. Army Reserve, 1959-64; became sergeant.

AWARDS, HONORS: Wallace Stegner fellowship in creative writing at Stanford University, 1964-65; Guggenheim fellowship, 1975-76; Gerald Loeb Award for distinguished business and financial journalism, 1982.

WRITINGS:

NOVELS

Whence All But He Had Fled, Viking (New York City), 1968.
Cowboys Don't Cry, Viking, 1969.
A Meaningful Life, Viking, 1971.
Walking Small, Braziller (New York City), 1974.

OTHER

Bad Money (nonfiction), St. Martin's (New York City), 1982.
Christina Onassis: A Modern Greek Tragedy (biography), Empire Books, 1983.

Columnist, *Penthouse,* 1972, *National Observer,* 1974-78. Contributor of articles and reviews to newspapers and periodicals. Contributing editor, *Harper's,* 1980-82.

SIDELIGHTS: In his serio-comic novels, L. J. Davis has written of young men overwhelmed with the world around them. *Whence All But He Had Fled* concerns a young artist who cannot help but provoke anger from those he meets. Martin Levin in the *New York Times Book Review* comments that Davis weaves his character's "hapless interludes into an East Village *bildungsroman* that has a nice comic flair." "Along the way," notes Granville Hicks in *Saturday Review,* "there are some comic scenes and a good deal of witty writing." R. F. Cayton of *Library Journal* finds that Davis presents his story in "a comic, crude style which gives the novel some substance. The comedy, while grotesque and grubby, tells me that Mr. Davis has writing talent."

Cowboys Don't Cry follows a young teacher as he flees his empty job and troubled marriage for a series of wild misadventures in New York City. While J. D. Foreman in *Best Sellers* dubbed Davis's effort a "lightweight second novel," R. V. Cassill in *Book World* calls *Cowboys Don't Cry* "a juicy, delectable, stylish, funny, frightening and wise novel."

A Meaningful Life traces the effort of Lowell Lake to restore an old house in the Brooklyn ghetto, an effort that eventually becomes an impossible obsession. Richard Freedman in *Book World* finds that David "keeps you laughing to keep you from crying or blowing out your brains. The continuous, hebephrenic laughter . . . is as restorative as it is nihilistic or hysterical, and it has the authentically crazy tintinnabulation of our times." Although finding parts of the novel to be flat, C. D. B. Bryan in the *New York Times Book Review* states: "One reads it through out of appreciation for an author who is clearly capable, funny at the proper times, both brutally and cheerfully perceptive."

Davis writes about banking and finance in his book *Bad Money.* R. C. Longworth asserts in the *Chicago Tribune Book World* that "Davis is a prize-winning financial reporter who understands the system he writes about: unlike most financial reporters, he writes in straight-forward prose." In the *Washington Post Book World,* Robert Lekachman describes the book as "exceedingly well-written and researched" and concludes, "Among popular financial and business writers, L. J. Davis belongs in the company of Adam Smith and Anthony Sampson—the best in the trade."

Davis once told *CA:* "My principal interests, outside of writing, are in community planning, inter-ethnic relations, and Victorian architecture. I love Brooklyn and Manhattan, have the Bronx and Queens, and am cool to Staten Island. I am fond of French and East Indian food, the street life of the Lower East Side, and Italian grocery stores with cheese.

"I used to think that the writing of fiction was high art and that nonfiction was hackwork, a mug's game; I was wrong about that. The trouble with *Harper's* Lewis Lapham said recently, was that we always predicted everything too soon: the fall of the Shah, the debt crisis in the Third World, the collapse of the OPEC pricing structure. Still, there's a certain amount of satisfaction in the realization that the world is a knowable place, that mysterious forces are not at work, and nothing happens in a vacuum. We may have rung our tocsins too soon, but it was better than never having rung them at all."

BIOGRAPHICAL/CRITICAL SOURCES:

PERIODICALS

Atlantic, July, 1969.
Best Sellers, January 15, 1968; July 1, 1969; October 1, 1971.
Books, January, 1968.
Book World, March 24, 1968, p. 16; June 22, 1969, p. 5; September 26, 1971, p. 3.
Chicago Tribune Book World, January 16, 1983.
Commonweal, May 10, 1968.
Harper's, May, 1968; July, 1969.

Library Journal, January 1, 1968; October 1, 1969; August, 1971.
Los Angeles Times Book Review, December 12, 1982.
New Leader, April 22, 1969.
New Yorker, April 20, 1968.
New York Times Book Review, January 14, 1968, p. 40; June 15, 1969, p. 34; October 10, 1971, p. 44.
Saturday Review, January 20, 1968.
Virginia Quarterly Review, spring, 1968.
Washington Post Book World, October 17, 1982.

* * *

de BERNIERES, Louis 1954-

PERSONAL: Born December 8, 1954, in London, England; son of Reginald Piers Alexander (a charity director) and Jean (a homemaker; maiden name, Ashton) de Berniere-Smart. *Education:* Victoria University of Manchester, B.A. (with honors), 1977; Leicester Polytechnic, postgraduate certificate in education, 1981; University of London, M.A. (with distinction), 1985. *Politics:* Liberal. *Religion:* None. *Avocational interests:* Playing classical and flamenco guitar.

ADDRESSES: Home—London, England. *Agent*—William Morris Ltd., 31/32 Soho Sq., London W1V 5DG, England.

CAREER: Landscape gardener in Surrey, England, 1972-73; schoolteacher and cowboy in Colombia, 1974; mechanic, 1980; teacher in London, England, 1981—. *Military service:* British Army, officer cadet at Sandhurst, 1973-74.

WRITINGS:

NOVELS

The War of Don Emmanuel's Nether Parts, Secker & Warburg (London), 1990, Morrow (New York City), 1991.
Senor Vivo and the Coca Lord, Morrow, 1991.
The Troublesome Offspring of Cardinal Guzman: A Novel, Morrow, 1994.
Corelli's Mandolin, Pantheon Books (New York City), 1994, published in England as *Captain Corelli's Mandolin,* Secker & Warburg, 1994.

WORK IN PROGRESS: Research on the Cathar heresy and the Albigensian crusade, medieval movements in southern France that declared matter evil and proclaimed Jesus' divinity, denying his human aspect.

SIDELIGHTS: In his novels, Englishman Louis de Bernieres has developed his own brand of magical realism—with little known historical incidents and locations far from the mainstream—to explore, as he told *CA,* "issues of freedom, power, and ideology." This magical realism moves "between vividly rendered incidents that stay within the confines of credibility, pastiches of anthropological and travel writing, and evocations of preternatural events and entities," observes Nicolas Tredell in *Contemporary Novelists.* The people of villages that do not appear on any maps of unnamed South American countries or of Greek islands overrun by Mussolini's Italians and Nazis—wealthy landowners, peasants, the military, guerrillas, drug lords, priests and defrocked priests, saints and sinners—mingle with ghosts, resurrected conquistadors, and frolicking dolphins. This approach enables de Bernieres "to engage with major issues of the 20th century—in particular, political and religious corruption and oppression—while retaining a keen perception of the pleasures of life, a sense of humor, a tempered anger, and a graceful utopianism," Tredell notes. And, although the magical realistic style is not typically associated with mainstream English literature, de Bernieres's version is not a pale imitation. Tredell writes, "His actual knowledge of the area whose literature, in its magical-realistic incarnation, he was colonising so assiduously prevented this work from ever quite becoming cheap."

The War of Don Emmanuel's Nether Parts relates how a conflict in an unnamed South American country between wealthy Dona Constanza Evans and some villagers—represented by British landowner Don Emmanuel—becomes a minor revolution. Dona Constanza Evans wants to divert a river critical to the villagers, one which Don Emmanuel uses to wash his nether parts, so that she can keep her swimming pool filled. "The novel's pace is brisk," writes Susan Lowell in the *New York Times Book Review,* "its prose epigrammatic. . . . Farcical incidents alternate with graphic descriptions of torture, ribald sex scenes with tender love stories, political satire with supernatural events." The strong farcical elements set de Bernieres apart from others writing in the same genre. As Lowell suggests, "He is funnier than most magical realists, and more hopeful—perhaps too optimistic, in spite of the grimness of his political and military satire."

In *The Troublesome Offspring of Cardinal Guzman,* a self-absorbed president and a laissez-faire military have left a power vacuum in de Bernieres's unnamed South American country. The vacuum is filled by Cardinal Guzman. Guzman "is a once-decent man corrupted my money and power, whose uncharacteristic attempt to reform national morality produces a crusade led by a pious fanatic and conducted by loot-happy brutes," explains Phoebe-Lou Adams in the *Atlantic Monthly.* "As in its predecessors . . . the improbable characters populating 'The Troublesome Offspring of Cardinal Guzman' interact in ways that are never predictable and are often truly weird," James Polk observes in the *New York Times Book Review.* Yet, Adams points out, while "the details of the action are wildly fanciful, comically grotesque, mercilessly savage, and altogether unpredictable," she believes that "the author's satirical commentary hits targets well beyond the confines of South America." In Polk's estimation, de Bernieres's weird story just takes on a classic theme in a new way. "What we have here is the age-old fight between good and evil. . . . Taking more than a page from Gabriel Garcia Marquez (who has obviously taught him a great deal)," comments the reviewer, "Mr. de Bernieres . . . comes down hard on the side of good times and fornication." And, according to a reviewer for *Publishers Weekly,* "As the novel works to a dramatic climax, readers will join the author in rooting for the life affirming joyousness of [the village of] Cochadebajo, which is skillfully contrasted with the Cardinal's evil nature."

"Eccentric and larger-than-life characters, scenes of bloody horror and grotesque comedy" also characterize *Corelli's Mandolin,* according to Phoebe-Lou Adams in the *Atlantic Monthly.* Yet, in this case, de Bernieres sets his novel in a real place during an actual historical event. During World War II, the Greek island of Cephallonia was occupied by Mussolini's Italians and Hitler's Nazis. The occupation and the tragic events that took place because of it have had lasting effects on the people of Cephallonia. The author explores these effects through the lives of Dr. Iannis, his daughter Pelagia, her fisherman fiance, and the Italian captain, Antonio Corelli, with whom she has an affair. Tredell explains in *Contemporary Novelists,* "De Bernieres dramatizes both the cruelties of the conflict and the possibilities of transcending them through love."

In what *New York Times Book Review* contributor W. S. Di Piero calls "a high-spirited historical romance," de Bernieres demonstrates that he "understands that history is not only a set of actions but also a style of reporting actions." Di Piero explains, "He builds 'Corelli's Mandolin' out of different kinds of reports, composing entire chapters from letters, monologues, memoirs, speeches, excerpts from Dr. Iannis's history, imaginary dialogues, bits of mythography and, in one instance, a propaganda pamphlet." The love story unfolds against a backdrop of these reports, reports of almost tolerable Italian occupation giving way to brutal Nazi domination that includes a German massacre of its Italian allies.

The novel continues the story of the island and the lovers long after the war has ended, but according to Di Piero, after the World War II years, "the novel loses its momentum. . . . The set pieces can be stunning, but the narrative tissue binding them becomes increasingly lumpy or thinned out." Even so, the reviewer finds de Bernieres work is often "remarkable." He concludes, "'Corelli's Mandolin' has at times the rangy, expansive feeling of legend or saga, at other times the cozy intensities of chamber drama. The piece of Greek history it represents is composed of sufferings large and small, of national catastrophes and household agonies." And, in the opinion of a *Publishers Weekly* contributor, "Swinging between antic ribaldry and criminal horror, between corrosive satire and infinite sorrow, this soaring novel glows with a wise humanity that is rare in contemporary fiction."

In his *Contemporary Novelists* profile, Nicholas Tredell sums up the author's appeal: "A novel by Louis de Bernieres is like a series of brightly colored and boldly drawn murals that combine into an exotic epic of life, love, and struggle."

BIOGRAPHICAL/CRITICAL SOURCES:

BOOKS

Contemporary Novelists, 6th edition, St. James Press (Detroit), 1996.

PERIODICALS

Atlantic Monthly, March, 1994, p. 128; October, 1994, p. 132.

New Statesman, April 22, 1994, p. 45.

New York Times Book Review, March 1, 1992; May 8, 1994; November 13, 1994.

Publishers Weekly, December 20, 1993, p. 51; June 27, 1994, p. 54.*

DEE, Ed(ward J., Jr.) 1940-

PERSONAL: Born February 3, 1940, in Yonkers, NY; son of Edward J., Sr. (a highway toll collector) and Ethel (a waiter and teletype operator; maiden name, Lawton) Dee; married Nancy Lee Hazzard, October 1, 1962; children: Brenda Sue Dee Crawford, Patricia Ann Dee Flanagan. *Education:* Rockland Community College, A.A.S., 1974; Fordham University, B.A., 1976, law student, 1977-78; Arizona State University, M.F.A., 1992. *Politics:* Independent. *Religion:* Roman Catholic.

ADDRESSES: *Home*—69 Henlopen Gardens, Lewes, DE 19958. *Agent*—Gail Hochman, Brandt & Brandt, 1501 Broadway, New York, NY 10036.

CAREER: New York Police Department, New York City, police officer, 1962-82, retiring as lieutenant; writer. *Military service:* U.S. Army, 1958-60; U.S. Army Reserve, 1960-64.

MEMBER: Mystery Writers of America, Superior Officers Association for Retirees.

WRITINGS:

14 Peck Slip, Warner Books (New York City), 1994.
Bronx Angel, Warner Books, 1995.
Little Boy Blue, Warner Books, 1997.

SIDELIGHTS: Ed Dee's background as a twenty-year veteran of the New York Police Department lends a great deal of authenticity to his crime novels about NYPD detective Anthony Ryan and his partner, Joe Gregory. In the series opener, *14 Peck Slip,* the two men find a body floating in a barrel on the city's waterfront. It turns out to be that of a policeman who has been missing for ten years. Ryan and Anthony's investigations lead them to some shocking truths about corruption among their peers. Their story is told "in an authentic and powerful voice," asserted a *Publishers Weekly* reviewer. "Any writer who can sing NYPD blues like that is worth keeping an eye on." Marilyn Stasio of the *New York Times* also called attention to Dee's "drop-dead style and authenticity," and further commented that the author has "the eyes, the ears and especially the nose of a cop. You can see one character's fear in his jumpy movement, hear another's anger in his dirty talk. But you can smell the moral decay of the whole city."

Dee won further praise for his next novel, *Bronx Angel.* The story again concerns the murder of a policeman, apparently by a prostitute. On the trail of the killer, "Mr. Dee takes us on a grand tour of the city the way it looks through Ryan's eyes," wrote Stasio in another *New York Times* review, "dirty, dangerous and so sad you wish you could look away. But you can't because you might miss something beautiful, or funny, or just plain nuts." *Booklist* contributor George Needham commented that Dee's "cops are tired and wary but not burned out. They still care about nailing the bad guys; they've just surrendered some of their quixotic notions to the realities of the street."

Dee's third effort, *Little Boy Blue,* is lauded as an "outstanding crime novel" by Wes Lukowsky in *Booklist.* The reviewer praised the author's "intelligent examination of modern families, . . . the extended family of cops; the loyalties exhibited by the Mafia; and the many unrelated groups who band together for companionship and support in an increasingly hostile, indifferent world." A *Publishers Weekly* writer also found that *Little Boy Blue* "crackles with authenticity," and declared: "There's a hard edge to everything and nearly everyone in this gripping novel, which plays some subtle improvisations on the theme of fathers and sons, and family and its obligations, even as Dee creates a tight mystery that emanates a gritty, world-weary air."

Dee once told *CA:* "After retiring from the New York Police Department, I wanted to write about the department in a way that no one had done before. After receiving my M.F.A. in creative writing, I submitted my first book. *Bronx Angel* is a sequel. I intend to use the same characters in a series of books that, I hope, get to the heart of the experience of being a cop in a city like New York. I hope they get at the *truth.*"

BIOGRAPHICAL/CRITICAL SOURCES:

PERIODICALS

Booklist, July, 1994, p. 1925; July, 1995, p. 1863; December 1, 1996, p. 619.
New York Times, July 17, 1994; August 20, 1995.
Publishers Weekly, May 23, 1994, p. 78; June 5, 1995, p. 49; November 11, 1996, p. 54.

* * *

de las LUNAS, Carmencita
See TROCCHI, Alexander

DeLYNN, Jane 1946-

PERSONAL: Born July 18, 1946, in New York, NY; daughter of Wilson (a paper bag manufacturer) and Bernice (a school teacher; maiden name, Deutsch) DeLynn. *Education:* Barnard College, B.A. (cum laude), 1968; University of Iowa, M.F.A. (honors), 1970. *Avocational interests:* Travel (Europe and Mexico), plays, movies, dance, music, books (novels, science, mathematics, history), sports (watching baseball, football, and tennis; swimming).

ADDRESSES: Home—395 Broadway, Apt. 7E, New York, NY 10013-3540.

CAREER: University of Iowa, Ames, teaching assistant, 1969-70; *Kirkus Reviews,* New York City, book reviewer, 1971-76; freelance writer, 1971—; Lehman College, City University of New York, New York City, adjunct assistant professor, 1989-90, substitute assistant professor, 1991-92. Founding managing editor of *Fiction,* 1971-72.

MEMBER: Phi Beta Kappa.

AWARDS, HONORS: Elizabeth Janeway Prize from Barnard College, 1967, for "Variations on an Obituary," and 1968, for "Collected Stories"; Book of the Month Club writing fellowship, 1968, for "Variations on an Obituary"; grant from International PEN, 1975; New York Foundation for the Arts Award, 1978; MacDowell Foundation fellowship, 1980; Edward Albee Foundation Award, William Flanagan Memorial Creative Persons Center, 1981; *New York Times* Notable Book Award, 1988; Yaddo fellowship, 1988 and 1990.

WRITINGS:

Hoosick Falls (play), produced in New York City, 1974.

Some Do, Macmillan (New York City), 1978.

In Thrall, C. N. Potter (New York City), 1982.

(Author of libretto) *The Monkey Opera; or, The Making of a Soliloquy,* Peer Southern Concert Music (New York City), 1982.

Real Estate, Poseidon (New York City), 1988.

Don Juan in the Village, Pantheon (New York City), 1990.

Bad Sex Is Good, Painted Leaf Press (New York City), 1998.

(Editor) *New York Sex: Stories,* Painted Leaf Press, 1998.

Work represented in anthologies, including *The Stone Wall Book of Short Fictions,* edited by Robert Coover and Kent Dixon, Stone Wall Press, 1973. Contributor of articles and reviews to *Redbook, Viva, New Dawn, New York Times Book Review, Advocate, Rolling Stone, Harper's Bazaar, Los Angeles Times Book Review, World, Christopher Street* and other publications.

SIDELIGHTS: Jane DeLynn writes fiction in which the "exigent and explicit writing is mesmerizing," as Judith P. Stelboum states in the *Lambda Book Report.* "The precision of the delicately balanced, cadenced sentence lures us in. The reader is unable to pull herself away from the scene. The word is captivating, and if we follow the word, which we do sometimes hesitantly, sometimes fearfully, angrily, excitedly, we allow ourselves to enter one of DeLynn's stories with voyeuristic embarrassment."

Among DeLynn's most noted works is *Don Juan in the Village,* according to Tina Gianoulis in *Gay and Lesbian Literature,* "a loosely constructed novel consisting of 14 chapters, each of which is a story in the life of Don Juan, an intellectually and emotionally jaded but sexually athletic butch dyke. Each chapter recounts a separate sexual adventure of the rakish Don Juan. . . . The sexuality in *Don Juan in the Village* is explicit. Some parts of the descriptions of s/m sex are so graphic that *Playboy,* a magazine whose content is largely sexual, declined to print it. Some lesbians have been angered by *Don Juan,* some by its sexual content, but others by the venom DeLynn expresses toward the lesbian community." Writing in the *New York Times Book Review,* Bertha Harris claims that in *Don Juan in the Village,* DeLynn "far too often abandons her particular gift for deadpan irony to go wandering amid portentuousness, tough-guy mannerisms and banal philosophizing. Again and again it made me feel like a bartender with a single customer and a long night ahead."

DeLynn once told *CA:* "I have always been interested in the space *between* sentences, that gap in which the 'zing' of life can be heard. I am pulled two ways in my work: toward minimalist formal experiments in which predetermined 'rules' for sentence or paragraph construction force patterns which would not occur in writing unrestricted by such (admittedly arbitrary) rules, and toward looser works of greater richness, complexity, humor.

"Politically, I am a leftist and don't understand how anyone can fail to be. I consider myself a gay feminist, but I despise the superficiality and smug insularity of most Movement-inspired writings. Temperamentally I am a skeptic, and lazy. I engage in no political actions: finding the action and discussion tedious and the possibility of success nil. I am unable to determine whether, like most people in most eras of human history, I simply believe things are getting (and have for some time been getting) worse, or whether, in fact, things *are* worse, and always will be. (I believe the latter.)"

BIOGRAPHICAL/CRITICAL SOURCES:

BOOKS

Gay and Lesbian Literature, Volume 2, St. James Press (Detroit), 1998.

PERIODICALS

Advocate, January 29, 1991.
Lambda Book Report, July, 1998, p. 12.
Library Journal, July, 1982; March 1, 1988.
Nation, October 23, 1982.
New York Times Book Review, March 20, 1988, p. 12; October 21, 1990, p. 15.
Playboy, May, 1988.
Publishers Weekly, January, 1988.

* * *

DIFUSA, Pati
See ALMODOVAR, Pedro

* * *

DIPHUSA, Patty
See ALMODOVAR, Pedro

* * *

DOUGLAS, Marjory Stoneman 1890-1998

PERSONAL: Born April 7, 1890, in Minneapolis, MN; died in 1998, in Miami, FL; daughter of Frank Bryant (a judge and editor) and Lilian (Trefethen) Stoneman; divorced. *Education:* Wellesley College, B.A., 1912.

CAREER: Miami Herald, Miami, FL, reporter and editor, 1915-22; University of Miami, Coral Gables, FL, instructor in English, 1925-29; *Miami Herald,* book editor, 1941-47; University of Miami Press, Baltimore, MD, editor, 1960-63, director emeritus, beginning in 1963. American Red Cross, member of publicity department in France, 1917-20. Speaker on conservation topics. *Military service:* U.S. Naval Reserve, 1917-18.

AWARDS, HONORS: Wellesley College, Horton Hollowell fellowship, 1966-67, Alumnae Achievement Award, 1977; named Conservationist of the Year, Florida Audubon Society, 1975, and Florida Wildlife Federation, 1976; National Conservation Award, American Motors Corp., 1977; achievement award, National Association for State and Local History and Florida Historical Association, 1978; Presidential Medal of Freedom, 1993; Barbour Medal for Conservation; Litt.D., University of Miami; D.H.L., Florida Atlantic University.

WRITINGS:

The Gallows Gate (play), Walter H. Baker (Boston, MA), 1928.
The Everglades: River of Grass, illustrated by Robert Fink, Rinehart, 1947, revised edition, Banyan Books (Miami, FL), 1978.
Road to the Sun (novel), Rinehart, 1951.
Freedom River (junior novel), Scribner (New York City), 1953.
Hurricane, Rinehart, 1958, revised edition, Mockingbird Books (Simons Island, GA), 1976.
Alligator Crossing (junior novel), John Day (New York City), 1959.
The Key to Paris (junior history), Lippincott (Philadelphia, PA), 1960.
Florida: The Long Frontier, Harper (New York City), 1967.

Contributor to *Saturday Evening Post* and other national magazines.

SIDELIGHTS: Marjory Stoneman Douglas was an active force among Florida environmentalists. Through both her lectures and her work with the Friends of the Everglades, she rallied support to maintain the natural state of the Everglades and to preserve and restore the South Florida water supply. Her commitment earned the author a Presidential Medal of Freedom in 1993. "I've seen the ruin [of the environment]," she told the *Miami Herald,* "but now I see hope for the restoration."

When she died in Miami at the age of 108, Douglas had traveled far from her native midwest. Born in Minneapolis in 1890 and educated in New England, Douglas made her way to South Florida prior to World War I. She joined the *Miami Herald* as a journalist in 1915 (some sources say 1914) and succeeded in a field that was not yet open to many women. During World War I, she worked in Europe for the American Red Cross, returning to Florida after the war to promote the right of women to vote.

Douglas remained in South Florida for the rest of her life. She dedicated herself to the monumental task, in the face of land developers and promoters of tourist attractions, to preserve the beauty and future of the Everglades. Using her experience as a journalist and researcher, Douglas wrote *The Everglades: River of Grass,* "[a] fabulous book of fabulous Florida," according to M. K. Rawlings, writing in the *New York Herald Tribune Weekly Book Review.* Calling the book "the first comprehensive study of one of the strangest, most blood-stained regions of our continent," Rawlings praised Douglas for "her rich and sensitive style, her gift for scholarly research, [and] her knowledge."

Everglades is indeed a comprehensive account, more than 400 pages in length, with illustrations by artist Robert Fink. Douglas began with a geological overview of the area's prehistory and proceeded with a detailed historical account of the vast wetlands that she called a "river of grass." "Mrs. Douglas tells the story straight," James Lyons reported in the *New York Times,* "from the coming of the white man and the Spaniard and the Indian before him. The whole fascinating and intricate yarn which is the Everglades she unravels carefully and succinctly." Paul Flowers praised the book for its wealth of folklore and history, writing in the *Saturday Review of Literature:* "[T]here is [also] a delightful vein of wit and humor brightening [Douglas's] skill as narrator, heightening her stature as a prophet; securing her place as an American fighting for preservation of this country's material, human, and spiritual values."

Douglas taught English at the University of Miami in Coral Gables. She published a play, a novel, and a handful of children's books. In the 1940s she worked as a book editor for the *Miami Herald* and, in 1960, Douglas became the editor of the University of Miami Press, a position she held until her retirement in 1963.

In 1967 Douglas published her last major work, *Florida: The Long Frontier.* Similar to *The Everglades* in scope, this historical account begins with the geological origin of what is now the state of Florida and lays out the history of the area through the year 1912. Douglas added her own impressions of the state when she arrived there in 1915 and when she returned to Florida from Europe in 1920. Some critics faulted the author for trying to squeeze too much history into a mere 300 pages, and a reviewer for *Choice* observed an overlapping of lore and fact. However, *Library Journal* reviewer Elizabeth Thalman recommended *Florida* to young adult readers, commenting that "the book gives a vivid impression of the area and brings out the color and excitement of its history."

BIOGRAPHICAL/CRITICAL SOURCES:

PERIODICALS

Choice, June, 1968.
Family Circle, September 1, 1996, pp. 15-18.
Library Journal, November 1, 1967.
Miami Herald, April 6, 1975.
New York Herald Tribune Weekly Book Review, November 30, 1947, p. 4.
New York Times, November 23, 1947, p. 38.
Saturday Review of Literature, December 20, 1947.
Writer's Digest, January, 1969.

OBITUARIES:

PERIODICALS

Independent, May 25, 1998, p. 16.
Maclean's, May 25, 1998, p. 13.*

* * *

DRUMMOND, June 1923-

PERSONAL: Born November 15, 1923, in Durban, South Africa; daughter of John (a physician) and Florence (Green) Drummond. *Education:* University of Cape Town, B.A., 1944. *Politics:* Progressive Federal Party of South Africa. *Religion:* Anglican. *Avocational interests:* Skiing, reading, politics, playing "bad bridge," idling.

ADDRESSES: Home—22 Barrington, 60 South Ridge Rd., Durban 4001, Republic of South Africa.

CAREER: Journalist for *Woman's Weekly* and *Natal Mercury,* Durban, South Africa, 1946-48; secretary in London, England, 1948-50, and with Durban Civic Orchestra, Durban, South Africa, 1950-53; Church Adoption Society, London, assistant secretary, 1954-60; full-time writer, 1960—. Chair of Durban adoption committee, Indian Child Welfare Society, 1963-74. Provincial candidate of Progressive Party in Durban, 1974.

MEMBER: Durban Writers Circle, Soroptimists International, Durban Country Club.

WRITINGS:

The Black Unicorn, Gollancz (London), 1959.
Thursday's Child, Gollancz, 1961.
A Time to Speak, Gollancz, 1962, World Publishing (Cleveland), 1963.
A Cage of Humming-Birds, Gollancz, 1964.
Welcome, Proud Lady, Gollancz, 1964, Holt (New York City), 1968.
Cable Car, Gollancz, 1965, Holt, 1967.
The Saboteurs, Gollancz, 1967, Holt, 1969.
Murder on a Bad Trip, Holt, 1968 (published in England as *The Gantry Episode,* Gollancz, 1968).
The People in Glass House, Gollancz, 1969, Simon & Schuster (New York City), 1970.
Farewell Party, Gollancz, 1971, Dodd (New York City), 1973.
Bang! Bang! You're Dead, Gollancz, 1973.
The Boon Companions, Gollancz, 1974, published as *Drop Dead,* Walker & Co. (New York City), 1976.
Slowly the Poison, Gollancz, 1975, Walker & Co., 1976.
Funeral Urn, Gollancz, 1976, Walker & Co., 1977.
The Patriots, Gollancz, 1979.
I Saw Him Die, Gollancz, 1979.
Such a Nice Family, Gollancz, 1980.
The Trojan Mule, Gollancz, 1982.
The Bluestocking, Gollancz, 1985.
Junta, Gollancz, 1989.
The Unsuitable Miss Pelham, Gollancz, 1990.
Burden of Guilt, Gollancz, 1991.
The Impostor, Gollancz, 1992, St. Martin's (New York City), 1993.
Hidden Agenda, Gollancz, 1993.

SIDELIGHTS: June Drummond "works best telling a tale of the personal past of her protagonists," writes Carol Simpson Stern in the *St. James Guide to Crime and Mystery Writers.* "Generally, these tales are convoluted, full of false identities and moments of discovery." Drummond often sets her novels in her native South Africa, alternating between mysteries and straight novels.

In *A Time to Speak,* Drummond tells the story of two old friends, both medical doctors, who are reunited after many years separation. Their differing views of the racial situation in South Africa eventually tears their friendship apart. John Barkham in the *New York Times Book Review* calls the novel "a minatory tale, surprisingly mature and clear-eyed. Though it is fair to all sides, its implied warning is nonetheless unmistakable." The critic for the *Times Literary Supplement* concludes: "Drummond examines the tragic divisions in South Africa with an admirable impartiality, and in doing so delights the reader with a number of sharp character-studies."

Drummond has sometimes combined elements of the mystery and historical romance genres. In *The Bluestocking,* Drummond included "scandal, rape, contested inheritances, and other material often found in gothic novels," explains Stern, in a mystery story set in the nineteenth century. Stern notes that the novel allows Drummond to "show her skill at recreating the costumes, the spectacle, the masquerades, fashions, and punctilios of an earlier time." *The Imposter,* a novel set during the Regency period, "has the razzle-dazzle plotting of a good mystery and the taut pacing of a good thriller," according to the critic for *Publishers Weekly.*

Drummond once told *CA:* "[I am] unsure of competence in my own language, let alone others, but can read French. [I] like travel if it is not organized, and have visited a number of European countries in a highly disorganized way."

BIOGRAPHICAL/CRITICAL SOURCES:

BOOKS

St. James Guide to Crime and Mystery Writers, 4th edition, St. James Press (Detroit), 1996.

PERIODICALS

Best Sellers, September 15, 1963; August 1, 1970.
Christian Science Monitor, December 28, 1963, p. 9.
Library Journal, October 1, 1963; August, 1970.
New Yorker, September 26, 1970.
New York Times Book Review, September 29, 1963, p. 49; August 9, 1970, p. 14.

Publishers Weekly, April 5, 1993, p. 64; July 18, 1994, p. 236.
Times Literary Supplement, December 7, 1962, p. 949; August 7, 1969, p. 887.

* * *

DRUMMOND, William
See CALDER-MARSHALL, Arthur

* * *

DUBOIS, Charles
See COUNSELMAN, Mary Elizabeth

* * *

DUNN, Katherine (Karen) 1945-

PERSONAL: Born October 24, 1945, in Garden City, KS; daughter of Jack (a linotype operator) and Velma (Golly) Dunn; children: Eli Malachy Dunn Dapolonia. *Education:* Attended Portland State College (now University) and Reed College. *Religion:* None.

ADDRESSES: Home—1603 Northwest 23rd, Portland, OR 97210.

AWARDS, HONORS: Music Corporation of America writing grant; Rockefeller writing grant.

WRITINGS:

NOVELS

Attic, Harper (New York City), 1970.
Truck, Harper, 1971.
Geek Love, Knopf (New York City), 1989.

OTHER

Also author of film script of *Truck.*

SIDELIGHTS: Katherine Dunn's novel *Geek Love* is, according to Jeff VanderMeer in the *St. James Guide to Horror, Ghost and Gothic Writers,* "a modern Gothic classic." VanderMeer explains that "the book's artistic success depends upon its risky structure: two strands (past and present) that alternate chapters, each strand offering insight into the other. Much like the novel's Siamese twins, the two stories intertwine to form one cohesive narrative. This double story-line forces the reader to continually reevaluate the characters and to reassess Dunn's slant on morality."

Both story strands are narrated by the same character, Olympia Binewski, "an albino hunchback dwarf," as VanderMeer describes her. In the present-day narrative, Olympia tells of her attempts to keep her daughter out of the clutches of a wealthy, sadistic woman. The past narrative describes Olympia's childhood among carnival performers, one of whom has created a cult in which people without deformities purposely mutilate themselves to become "freaks." *Geek Love,* VanderMeer notes, contains "commentaries on society [which] run like a hidden vein of satire throughout the book. Dunn's explorations of the utter mercilessness of science when applied by human beings provides a needed counterpoint to her sometimes repetitive lesson that the true monsters are often hidden behind handsome faces with charming smiles."

Dunn once told *CA:* "I have been a believer in the magic of language since, at a very early age, I discovered that some words got me into trouble and others got me out. The revelations since then have been practically continuous.

"There are other inclinations that have shaped the form and direction of my work: rampant curiosity, a cynical inability to accept face-values balanced by lunatic optimism, and the preoccupation with the effervescing qualities of truth that is probably common to those afflicted by absent-mindedness, prevarication, and general unease in the presence of facts. But the miraculous nature of words themselves contains the discipline.

"Writing is, increasingly, a moral issue for me. The evasion of inexpensive facility, the rejection of the flying bridges built so seductively into the language, require a constant effort of will. The determination required for honest exploration and analysis of the human terrain is often greater than I command. But the fruits of that determination seem worthy of all my efforts."

BIOGRAPHICAL/CRITICAL SOURCES:

BOOKS

St. James Guide to Horror, Ghost and Gothic Writers, St. James Press (Detroit), 1998.

PERIODICALS

Life, October 24, 1969.
Nation, August 3, 1970.
New York Times, July 1, 1970.
New York Times Book Review, June 21, 1970.

E

EAMES, David
See BAKER, Denys Val

* * *

EBERLE, Gary 1951-

PERSONAL: Born June 7, 1951, in Toledo, OH; son of Herman (a milk deliverer and letter carrier) and Audrey (a school secretary; maiden name, Morrissey) Eberle; married, May 1, 1976; wife's name Suzanne (an art historian); children: William. *Ethnicity:* "German-Irish American." *Education:* University of Detroit, B.A. (summa cum laude), 1973, M.A. and doctoral study, 1974-78. *Politics:* Democrat. *Religion:* Roman Catholic. *Avocational interests:* Renaissance music performance, fly fishing.

ADDRESSES: Home—Grand Rapids, MI. *Office*—Department of English, Aquinas College, 1607 Robinson Rd. S.E., Grand Rapids, MI 49506.

CAREER: Aquinas College, Grand Rapids, MI, associate professor of English, 1981—. Urban Institute for Contemporary Arts, member of board of directors, 1987-91, member of executive committee, 1989-91; judge of poetry competitions.

MEMBER: Michigan Honors Association (vice-president, 1990-91; president, 1991-93), C. G. Jung Society of Western Michigan (member of executive steering committee, 1979-83), East Grand Rapids Friends of the Library (member of executive board, 1990-93).

AWARDS, HONORS: Scholar, Cranbrook Writers Conference, 1977; grant from Michigan Council for the Arts and Cultural Affairs, 1993.

WRITINGS:

The Geography of Nowhere: Finding One's Self in the Postmodern World, Sheed & Ward (Kansas City, MO), 1994.

Angel Strings (novel), Coffee House Press (Minneapolis, MN), 1995.

Work represented in anthologies, including *PrePress Awards: A Michigan Sampler,* PrePress Publishing (Kalamazoo, MI), 1993. Contributor of stories, poems, and articles to periodicals, including *MacGuffin, Voices, Nexus, Modern Haiku, Common Wages,* and *Crosscurrents: A Quarterly.*

WORK IN PROGRESS: Progeria, a novel; a nonfiction book on sacred time; research on the psychological and social aspects of temporality.

SIDELIGHTS: Gary Eberle's first novel, *Angel Strings,* is successful both as an adventure story and a pointed satire of spiritual life in modern America, according to numerous critics. The story concerns Joe Findlay, a small-time musician who plays backup music for Elvis impersonators in Las Vegas. Findlay's father was a professional magician, and a lifetime of seeing the cheap tricks behind spectacular illusions has given him a cynical outlook. During the course of the story, he teams up with Violet Tans, whose naive credulity counters his jaded nature. A *Publishers Weekly* critic declared that "their adventure resembles a madcap buddy movie, but the territory they explore is a dead-on satirical rendering of the American spiritual landscape: Bible believers, neo-Pagans and New Agers pick and choose among the remains of religions in search of something to believe." The reviewer found the conclusion of the book "unconvincing," but noted that Eberle "writes deftly enough that the result is funny and mostly delightful."

New York Times Book Review critic Robert Plunket declared his aversion to books that focus on the nature of magic, but admitted that even though Eberle's book falls into that category, it was "all bearable and sometimes much more than that" due to the author's "skill as a comic writer. He's trying to be a nice guy . . . but sometimes the wicked satirist in him wrestles the pen away and what comes out can be very amusing indeed." Noting that the characters in the book were a collection of wild caricatures, Plunket added: "When you're writing about a crew like this, the trick is to make the humor seem natural and unforced, and I must say that Mr. Eberle pulls it off quite credibly." With its metaphysical themes, unlikely plot twists, and colorful writing style, *Angel Strings* is "reminiscent of Richard Brautigan and Tom Robbins at their best," asserted George Needham in *Booklist.* "This picaresque adventure is full of unexpected pleasures and packed with larger-than-life characters, wonderful vignettes, and an aura of magic."

Eberle told *CA:* "My primary concern, as an individual, writer, and teacher, has been the loss of the sense of sacred time and sacred space in our daily lives. Everyone is born into our species' long cultural conversation. This conversation ebbs and flows, and vast pieces of it may be lost (as when over one hundred plays by Sophocles disappeared from the western tradition). Parts may be refound (as when seven of those plays were 'rescued') and passed on to new generations or rejected (as Sophocles now may be, along with other 'dead white European males').

"As a teacher for twenty years, I have attempted to preserve the voices of the past before they disappear beneath the electronic tide of virtual realities like television, radio, and the Internet, all of which, I believe, threaten to rob us of a sacred past and leave us afloat in a continuous profane present.

"As a writer, I am trying to join in the fractious conversation of our time, trying to clarify for myself, and I hope others, its terms. This calls for nontraditional thinking and, especially, humor. This is most difficult in a time that is turning increasingly humorless.

"I think there are many similarities among humor, profound philosophical thought, and the sacred. Like good jokes, good philosophy and encounters with the divine need the whole self—body, mind, and spirit—if they are to be fully understood. New thinking (in philosophy, religion, or fiction) requires fracturing and recombining old categories, reassembling them in new ways so that nothing is lost and a new, more complete synthesis comes into being.

"Therefore, I do two kinds of writing. The first I call 'shoes on' writing, which is nonfiction. It is orderly, attempts to be logical, and has as its goal analysis. When that is done, I turn to 'shoes off' writing, which is fictional, chaotic, barefoot, free-floating and, with luck, creative. Through this, I hope to move the conversation of our time along, so that we can recover a sense of the sacred in our daily lives and a sense of wonder in this age of wonders.

"I am influenced by Shakespeare, Wordsworth, and Blake among the honored dead; I[saac] B. Singer, Samuel Beckett, Robertson Davies, and Yasunari Kawabata among the recently passed; and Alice Munro, Guenter Grass, and Gabriel Garcia Marquez among the still living. For some reason I do not understand, none of these is an American writer."

BIOGRAPHICAL/CRITICAL SOURCES:

PERIODICALS

Booklist, September 15, 1995, p. 140.
Kirkus Reviews, July 1, 1995, p. 876-77.
National Catholic Reporter, March 24, 1995, p. 13.
New York Times Book Review, March 17, 1996, p. 11.
Publishers Weekly, August 21, 1995, p. 58.

* * *

EHRLICH, Max 1909-1983

PERSONAL: Born October 10, 1909, in Springfield, MA; died in February, 1983; son of Simon (an accountant) and Sarah (Siegel) Ehrlich; married Doris Rubinstein, 1940 (divorced); married Margaret Druckman, 1980; children: (first marriage) Amy,

Jane (Mrs. Carl Baver). *Education:* University of Michigan, B.A., 1933. *Avocational interests:* Golf, swimming, bridge, travel (travelled extensively in Europe, the Near East, and the Caribbean).

CAREER: Worked in machine shops and tobacco fields, sold magazines, and caddied at golf courses; reporter for *Knickerbocker Press* and *Evening News,* Albany, NY, and for *Republican* and *Daily News,* Springfield, MA; writer, 1949-83. Guest lecturer in creative writing at various universities, including New York University and Columbia University.

MEMBER: Authors Guild, Authors League of America, Writers Guild of America West, Radio Writers Guild.

AWARDS, HONORS: Huntington Hartford Foundation fellow.

WRITINGS:

NOVELS

The Big Eye (Dollar Book Club selection), Doubleday (New York City), 1947.
Spin the Glass Web, Harper (New York City), 1951.
First Train to Babylon (*Readers' Digest* Book Club selection), Harper, 1955, published as *Dead Letter,* Corgi (London), 1958, published as *The Naked Edge,* Corgi, 1961.
The Takers, Harper, 1961.
Deep Is the Blue, Doubleday, 1964.
The High Side, Fawcett (New York City), 1970.
The Edict (based on his screenplay of the same title; also see below), Doubleday, 1971.
The Savage Is Loose, Bantam (New York City), 1974.
The Reincarnation of Peter Proud, Bobbs-Merrill (Indianapolis), 1974.
The Cult, Simon & Schuster (New York City), 1978.
Reincarnation in Venice, Simon & Schuster, 1979.
Naked Beach, Playboy Press (Chicago), 1979.
The Big Boys, Houghton (Boston), 1981.
Shaitan, Arbor House (New York City), 1981.

SCREENPLAYS

(With Frank De Felitta) *Z.P.G.,* Sagittarius Productions, 1972.
(With De Felitta) *The Savage Is Loose,* United Artists, 1972.
(With Gerald Schnitzer) *Waldo,* American International, 1972.
The Reincarnation of Peter Proud (based on his novel of the same title), American International, 1975.

Also author of *The Liar* for Princess Pictures, and *Sail to Glory,* a feature-length documentary, for Schnitzer Productions; author of documentary film scripts for various organizations, including American Red Cross, Boys Club of America, and U.S. Department of Defense. Author of scripts for numerous television series, including *Studio One, The Defenders, G.E. Theatre, Arrest and Trail, Dick Powell Show, Wild Wild West,* and *Star Trek.* Author of scripts for radio series, including *The Shadow, Mr. and Mrs. North, Sherlock Holmes, Nick Carter, The Big Story,* and *Big Town.* Contributor of articles to periodicals. Ehrlich's novels have been translated into several foreign languages.

ADAPTATIONS: First Train to Babylon was filmed as *The Naked Edge,* 1961; *Spin the Glass Web* was filmed starring Edward G. Robinson and John Forsythe; film rights to *The Big Eye, The Takers,* and *Deep Is the Blue* have been purchased by major motion picture studios.

SIDELIGHTS: According to Chris Morgan in the *St. James Guide to Horror, Ghost and Gothic Writers,* Max Ehrlich specialized "in showing how the ordinary well-off American citizen reacts to extraordinary circumstances—which are made to seem plausible and even commonplace. The horror is subtle and understated; the message is: this could happen to you."

Perhaps Ehrlich's most popular novel was *The Reincarnation of Peter Proud,* the story of a young man plagued by disturbing dreams in which he dies. Seeking to find the source of the dreams which are disrupting his life, Peter Proud turns to hypnosis and dream therapy. Research uncovers the fact that he is not having dreams at all; he is reliving memories of a past life. Tracking down this previous life, in which he had been murdered by his wife, Peter becomes entangled with the dangerous woman again and suffers tragic consequences. Morgan called *The Reincarnation of Peter Proud* "an exciting thriller with entertaining supernatural elements."

Ehrlich once told *CA:* "I love to write. Have been a professional author for thirty-five years, and still find it tremendously exciting. If you can make your way in it, earn your bread, then it is the aristocrat of all professions. Where else can you make your fantasies, or dreams, come true?

"I tend to shy away from rigid classification. Yet, in a loose sort of way, I suppose I could be called an author of suspense. The essence of my craft is to make the reader turn the page, by goading him into the question: 'What happens next?' Note that I use the word 'author' and not writer. There is a difference. An author is a creator, an orginator, an innovator. In a broad sense, he writes the novel or the play. But a 'writer' can write anything. Classified ads, articles, publicity, newspaper stories, pornography.

"To any author or dramatist, reality is an enemy. It is useful in the sense that you need reference points on which to hang your story. But the art is an exaggeration, making it all larger than life. Making it *seem* like reality, and making the reader believe in it, because he becomes absorbed in it. I am a story teller. Whatever I write has a beginning, middle and end, and I only hope that it entertains. But I always make some kind of important statement somewhere in the work, something in which I sincerely believe. Not necessarily to uplift the reader; but to uplift myself."

BIOGRAPHICAL/CRITICAL SOURCES:

BOOKS

St. James Guide to Horror, Ghost and Gothic Writers, St. James Press (Detroit), 1998.*

* * *

ENDORE, (Samuel) Guy 1900-1970
(Harry Relis)

PERSONAL: Born July 4, 1900, in New York, NY; died February 12, 1970, in Los Angeles, CA; married Henrietta Portugal, 1927; children: Marcia, Gita. *Education:* Attended Carnegie Institute of Technology (now Carnegie-Mellon University); Columbia University, A.B., 1923, M.A., 1925.

CAREER: Writer and novelist.

MEMBER: Academy of Motion Picture Arts and Sciences, Screen Writers Guild, Authors League of America.

AWARDS, HONORS: Oscar nomination, 1945, for screenplay, *G. I. Joe.*

WRITINGS:

Casanova: His Known and Unknown Life, John Day (New York City), 1929.

The Man from Limbo, Farrar & Rinehart (New York City), 1930.

(Translator) Julien Viand, *An Iceland Fisherman,* P. A. Norstedt, 1931.

The Werewolf of Paris, Farrar & Rinehart, 1933, reprinted, Pocket Books (New York City), 1976.

The Sword of God: Joan of Arc, Garden City Publishing Co. (New York City), 1933.

Babouk, Vanguard (New York City), 1934.

The Crime at Scottsboro, Hollywood Scottsboro Committee, 1938.

The Sleepy Lagoon Mystery, Sleepy Lagoon Defense Committee, 1944, reprinted, R & E Research Associates, 1972.

Methinks the Lady, Duell (New York City), 1946, published as *Nightmare,* Dell (New York City), 1956.

King of Paris (Book-of-the-Month Club selection), Simon & Schuster (New York City), 1956.

Detour at Night, Simon & Schuster, 1958, published as *Detour through Devon,* Gollancz (London), 1959.

Voltaire! Voltaire!, Simon & Schuster, 1961 (published in England as *The Heart and the Mind,* W. H. Allen, 1962).

Satan's Saint, Crown (New York City), 1965.

Call Me Shakespeare: A Play in Two Acts, Dramatists Play Service, 1966.

Synanon, Doubleday (New York City), 1968.

(Translator) Hanns H. Ewers, *Alraune,* edited by R. Reginald and Douglas Menville, Arno, 1976.

SCREENPLAYS

(With Tod Browning, Garrett Fort, and Erich von Stroheim) *The Devil Doll,* Metro-Goldwyn-Mayer, 1936.

The League of Frightened Men, Columbia, 1937.

Carefree, RKO, 1938.

Song of Russia, Metro-Goldwyn-Mayer, 1944.

G. I. Joe, United Artists, 1945.

The Vicious Circle, United Artists, 1948.

Johnny Allegro, Columbia, 1949.

Tomorrow Is Another Day, Warner Brothers, 1951.

He Ran All the Way, United Artists, 1951.

Captain Sindbad, Metro-Goldwyn-Mayer, 1963.

Also author of, with Bernard Schubert, *Mark of the Vampire,* 1935, with P. J. Wolfson and John L. Balderston, *Mad Love,* 1935, and, with David Boehm, *The Raven,* 1935.

ADAPTATIONS: *Methinks the Lady* was filmed as *Whirlpool,* 1949; *The Werewolf of Paris* was filmed as *The Curse of the Werewolf,* 1961.

SIDELIGHTS: Guy Endore was a prolific writer of novels and screenplays, especially works in the horror genre. Although Brian Stableford in the *St. James Guide to Horror, Ghost and Gothic Writers* dismissed Endore's screenplays as "schlock-horror films," he ranked the novel *The Werewolf of Paris* highly. *The Werewolf of Paris,* Stableford believed, "is perhaps entitled to be considered *the* werewolf novel, just as *Dracula* is *the* vampire novel, although it assertively inverts the underlying assumption of formulaic monster stories by preserving the essential innocence of its central character and indicting the world which contains him for its intolerable monstrousness."

Set in Paris of the late 19th century, *The Werewolf of Paris* tells the story of Bertrand Caillet, who has discovered that he has werewolf tendencies beyond his power to control. For a time it seems as if the love of an understanding woman will help him overcome his problem. But when war breaks out and Bertrand is called to serve, he has too many opportunities on the battlefield to indulge his indecent blood urges.

"Purist fans of supernatural horror fiction," noted Stableford, "may complain that *The Werewolf of Paris* is neither supernatural enough nor horrific enough, because Bertrand's condition is too suffocatingly cloaked in ambiguity. The whole point of the exercise is, however, to blur the boundaries between the human and the inhuman, the natural and the unnatural."

In the late forties, Endore, long active in leftist causes, came to the attention of the House Committee on Un-American Activities which was investigating alleged Communist infiltration of the film industry. He was reputedly blacklisted by some film studios because of this investigation and was forced to use the pseudonym Harry Relis for a time in order to sell his screenplays. Despite the restrictions put upon his writing career, Endore stood by his beliefs. "I feel I failed to make the grade as a human being and as a writer," he said at the time, "if I am not known as subversive to everything the investigating committee stands for."

BIOGRAPHICAL/CRITICAL SOURCES:

BOOKS

St. James Guide to Horror, Ghost and Gothic Writers, St. James Press (Detroit), 1998.

PERIODICALS

Christian Science Monitor, August 10, 1968.
New Statesman, February 11, 1966.
New York Times, February 21, 1970.
Rolling Stone, October 7, 1976.
Washington Post Book World, November 28, 1976.*

* * *

EULO, Ken 1939-

PERSONAL: Born November 17, 1939, in Newark, NJ; son of Raymond and Therresa Eulo; married; children: Joey, Donald, Ken. *Education:* Attended University of Heidelberg, 1961-64. *Avocational interests:* Writing poetry.

ADDRESSES: *Home and office*—14633 Valley Vista Blvd., Sherman Oaks, CA 91403. *Agent*—Mitch Douglas, International Creative Management, 40 West 57th St., New York, NY 10019.

CAREER: Playwright, director, and novelist. Director of Playwrights Forum and O'Neill Playwrights; artistic director of Courtyard Playhouse, New York, NY; member of Actors Studio Playwriting Workshop; staff writer for Paramount, 1988—.

MEMBER: Italian Playwrights of America—The Forum, Writers Guild of America, Dramatists Guild.

AWARDS, HONORS: Prize from O'Neill Summer Conference, 1971, for *S.R.O.;* grant from Howard P. Foster Memorial Fund, 1972; fellowship from Arken Industries and J. & L. Tanner, 1973-74; winner of children's theater contest sponsored by Children's Theatre of Richmond, 1974, for *Aladdin.*

WRITINGS:

PLAYS

Bang? An Event in Boxes (one-act), first produced in New York City at Courtyard Playhouse, March 19, 1969.

Zarf, I Love You (two-act), first produced in New York City at Courtyard Playhouse, June 12, 1969.

S.R.O. (two-act), first produced in Waterford, CT, at O'Neill Theater Center, July 5, 1970.

Puritan Night (two-act), first produced in Hartford, CT, March 11, 1971.

Billy Hofer and the Quarterback Sneak (two-act), first produced in New York City at Courtyard Playhouse, December 3, 1971.

Black Jesus (two-act), first produced in New York City at Lincoln Center, February 12, 1972.

The Elevator (one-act), first produced in New York City at Gate Theatre, March 11, 1972.

48 Spring Street (one-act; first produced in New Jersey at Ocean County College Theatre-in-the-Round, October 5, 1973), published in *Off-Off Broadway Theatre Collection,* Volume 1, Galaxie, 1977.

Final Exams (three-act), first produced in New York City at Courtyard Playhouse, November 17, 1975.

The Frankenstein Affair (three-act), first produced in New York City at Courtyard Playhouse, March 22, 1979.

Say Hello to Daddy (two-act), first produced in Chicago, IL, at Pheasant Run Playhouse, June 1, 1979.

Also author of *That's the Way a Champ Should Go,* 1971, *The Rise and Fall of Cris Cowlin* (three-act), and *Stationary Wave* (three-act). Author of scripts for television series, including *Small Wonder, Benson,* and *Marblehead Manor.*

HORROR NOVELS

The Brownstone, Pocket Books, 1980.

The Bloodstone, Pocket Books (New York City), 1981.

The Deathstone, Pocket Books, 1982.

Nocturnal, Pocket Books, 1983.

The Ghost of Veronica Gray, Pocket Books, 1985.

The House of Caine, Tor Books (New York City), 1988.

Also co-author of *Claw,* 1994.

OTHER

Contributor to periodicals, including *Back Stage, Janus, New York Post, New York Times, Off-Off Broadway, Show Business,* and *Village Voice.*

SIDELIGHTS: Ken Eulo's first three horror novels feature the character Chandal, a young woman who must battle an evil cult trying to use her for their own horrific ends.

In *The Brownstone* Chandal discovers that her young husband has been seduced by the cult into working to use her to house an evil spirit. "The novel stands out because of its intensity," writes Don D'Ammassa in the *St. James Guide to Horror, Ghost and Gothic Writers,* "and Eulo's talent for gruesome description."

The Bloodstone finds Chandal under psychiatric care, trying to free herself of the painful memories involving the cult. But the cult again seeks to control her, this time by using a powerful amulet which allows Chandal to change physical shape and gain knowledge of the past. *The Deathstone* resolves the story of Chandal, this time focusing on a battle for her daughter's soul.

In *The House of Caine,* Eulo writes a vampire novel in which Vietnam veteran Robert Martin returns to his hometown to find it overrun by a vampire clan. Martin soon enlists allies in his battle to destroy the creatures. "Eulo's vampires aren't the troubled or sympathetic creatures that dominate much of modern horror fiction," writes D'Ammassa, "they're the old fashioned, thoroughly evil and repulsive variety, and they dissolve spectacularly when finally staked or exposed to the sunlight. There's nothing particularly surprising in this novel . . . , but this is the best-paced and most exciting of [Eulo's] plots, the characters are well drawn, and the suspense is almost unbroken."

Eulo once told *CA:* "I believe very strongly in writing for all media and that the *story* is the most important aspect of writing. A good story with characters that people can care about is what good writing is all about."

BIOGRAPHICAL/CRITICAL SOURCES:

BOOKS

St. James Guide to Horror, Ghost and Gothic Writers, St. James Press (Detroit), 1998.

PERIODICALS

Publishers Weekly, June 6, 1994, p. 57.

F

FALK, Lee
See COPPER, Basil

* * *

FARRIS, John 1936-
(Steve Brackeen)

PERSONAL: Born in 1936 in Missouri; married, wife's name Mary Ann; children: one son.

ADDRESSES: Home—Atlanta, GA. *Office*—c/o Tor Books, 175 Fifth Ave., New York, NY 10010.

CAREER: Novelist, playwright, and screenwriter.

WRITINGS:

NOVELS

The Corpse Next Door, Graphic (New York City), 1956.
Harrison High, Rinehart (New York City), 1959.
The Long Light of Dawn, Putnam (New York City), 1962.
King Windom, Trident (New York City), 1967.
When Michael Calls, Trident, 1967.
The Captors, Trident, 1969.
The Trouble at Harrison High, Pocket Books (New York City), 1972.
Sharp Practice, Simon & Schuster (New York City), 1974.
The Fury, Playboy Press (Chicago), 1976.
All Heads Turn When the Hunt Goes By, Playboy Press, 1978, published as *Bad Blood,* Gollancz (London), 1989.
Shatter, Allen (London), 1980.
Catacombs, Delacorte (New York City), 1981.
The Uninvited, Delacorte, 1982.
Son of the Endless Night, St. Martin's (New York City), 1985.
Minotaur, Tor Books (New York City), 1985.
Wildwood, Tor Books, 1986.
Nightfall, Tor Books, 1987.
The Axman Cometh, Tor Books, 1989.
Fiends, Dark Harvest (Arlington Heights, IL), 1990.
Sacrifice, Tor Books, 1994.
Dragonfly, Tor Books, 1995.
Soon She Will Be Gone, Forge (New York City), 1997.

OTHER

The Death of the Well-Loved Boy (two-act play), first produced Off-Broadway at St. Mark's Playhouse, May 15, 1967.
The Fury (screenplay; adapted from his novel of same title), Twentieth Century-Fox, 1978.
Scare Tactics (story collection), Tor Books, 1988, expanded edition, 1989.

Also author of screenplay *Dear Dead Deliah,* 1972. Contributor of articles to magazines.

UNDER PSEUDONYM STEVE BRACKEEN

The Body on the Beach, Mystery House, 1957.
Baby Moll, Crest (New York City), 1958.
Danger in My Blood, Crest, 1959.

Delfina, Gold Medal (New York City), 1962.
The Guardians, Holt (New York City), 1964.

SIDELIGHTS: Perhaps John Farris's best known novel is *The Fury,* first published in 1976 and later adapted by the author as a screenplay. The story "concerns two siblings who have psychic powers," notes Don D'Ammassa in the *St. James Guide to Horror, Ghost and Gothic Writers,* "and who are ruthlessly exploited by an evil man who sees them as a tool to securing personal power for himself." In this and his other horror novels, Farris, D'Ammassa observes, "has proved himself capable of writing gripping, often unusual stories which took familiar themes in unfamiliar directions."

Among Farris's most popular novels are *All Heads Turn When the Hunt Goes By, The Uninvited,* and *Wildwood.* The first of these novels concerns a family in the Old South who have become entangled in black magic. D'Ammassa points out that the novel was "one of the first modern horror novels to explicitly examine the sexuality implicit in most horror themes." *The Uninvited* tells of a young woman whose fiance has died. But when he returns from the dead to console her in her time of sorrow, the situation soon becomes far more than either of them can handle. D'Ammassa calls *The Uninvited* "an excellent, chilling story of the supernatural." *Wildwood* concerns a family estate which seems to be haunted by unholy creatures from the nearby woods. "Monsters and magic notwithstanding," writes D'Ammassa, "the most terrifying sequences are those in which we begin to question the sanity of the protagonist in this fine blend of psychological and supernatural horror."

Farris's recent *Dragonfly* is the story of a conman who specializes in swindling marriage-minded wealthy women. He meets his match when he romances a wheelchair-bound Georgia writer with a shady family. "Never letting up on the suspense," notes the critic for *Publishers Weekly,* "Farris piles one Grand Guignol moment on top of another with unerring dexterity, a keen knowledge of human nature and a wicked sense of humor."

BIOGRAPHICAL/CRITICAL SOURCES:

BOOKS

St. James Guide to Horror, Ghost and Gothic Writers, St. James Press (Detroit), 1998.

PERIODICALS

Best Sellers, May, 1967; November, 1967; October 1, 1969; July, 1978.
Kirkus Reviews, August 1, 1974; April 15, 1976.
New Yorker, March 20, 1978.
New York Times Book Review, December 17, 1967; November 9, 1969; December 29, 1974.
Psychology Today, October, 1974.
Publishers Weekly, August 8, 1994, p. 380; August 28, 1995, p. 103; June 16, 1997, p. 47.
Washington Post Book World, October 12, 1969.

* * *

FEKETE, John 1946-

PERSONAL: Born August 7, 1946, in Budapest, Hungary; son of Stephen and Lily (Jozefovics) Fekete. *Education:* McGill University, B.A. (with honors), 1968, M.A., 1969; Cambridge University, Ph.D., 1973.

ADDRESSES: Home—181 Wallis Dr., Peterborough, Ontario, Canada K9J 6C4. *Office*—Department of English Literature and Cultural Studies, Trent University, Box 4800, Peterborough, Ontario, Canada K9J 7B8; fax: 705-748-1826. *E-mail*—jfekete@trentu.ca.

CAREER: McGill University, Montreal, Quebec, visiting assistant professor of English, 1973-74; York University, Toronto, Ontario, visiting assistant professor of humanities, 1975-76; Trent University, Peterborough, Ontario, assistant professor, 1976-78, associate professor, 1978-84, professor of English and cultural studies, 1984—, chair of cultural studies department, 1987-90, president of faculty association, 1995-98. Member of board of directors of Canadian Images Film Festival, 1982-84, and Trent Institute for the Study of Popular Culture, 1987-90; chair of the board of directors of the Ontario Confederation of University Faculty Associations, 1996-98.

MEMBER: Modern Language Association, Canadian Association of University Teachers, Canadian Communication Association, Canadian University Teachers of English, Science Fiction Research Association.

AWARDS, HONORS: Social Science and Humanities Research Council of Canada, fellowship, 1979; research grant, 1980, 1991-94; distinguished research professor, Trent University, 1990.

WRITINGS:

The Critical Twilight: Explorations in the Ideology of Anglo-American Literary Theory from Eliot to McLuhan, Routledge & Kegan Paul, 1978.
The Structural Allegory: Reconstructive Encounters with the New French Thought, University of Minnesota Press, 1983.
Life after Postmodernism: Essays on Culture and Value, St. Martin's (New York City), 1988.
Moral Panic: Biopolitics Rising, Robert Davies Publishing, 1994.

Contributor to *Canadian Journal of Political and Social Theory, Philosophy of the Social Sciences, Canadian Journal of Communications,* and *Science-Fiction Studies*. Associate editor of *Telos,* 1974-84.

WORK IN PROGRESS: Science Fiction in Hungary and *Value and Postmodernity.*

SIDELIGHTS: John Fekete told *CA:* "My books are addressed to academic readers in the humanities and social sciences and aim to make some sense of—and to provide some direction to—contemporary debates in the literary institution. Recently, my writing on censorship, gender panic, and the pathologies of everyday culture has reached a wider audience. But my writings and media appearances are really all concerned with the meanings and values that we live by and contest in our everyday lives as well as in our specialized professional practices, and they are all motivated by dreaming forward to a vision of a wiser and happier culture that is not yet in place but only playfully hinted at."

BIOGRAPHICAL/CRITICAL SOURCES:

PERIODICALS

Times Literary Supplement, October 13, 1978.

* * *

FISHER, Philip 1941-

PERSONAL: Born October 11, 1941, in Pittsburgh, PA; son of Leo (a federal government employee) and Anna (a nurse; maiden name, Walker) Fisher; children: Mark. *Education:* University of Pittsburgh, B.A. (magna cum laude), 1963; Harvard University, M.A., 1966, Ph.D., 1970.

ADDRESSES: Home—82 Irving St., Cambridge, MA 02138. *Office*—Department of English, Barker Center, Harvard University, Cambridge, MA 02138.

CAREER: University of Virginia, Charlottesville, assistant professor of English, 1970-72; Brandeis University, Waltham, MA, assistant professor, 1972-79, associate professor, 1979-84, professor of English, beginning 1984; professor of English, Harvard University, Cambridge, MA, c. 1990s. Visiting Andrew Mellon Assistant Professor, Harvard University, 1976-77; visiting professor, Free University of Berlin, 1981, University of Konstanz, 1986, and Yale University, 1986. Fellow, Wissenschafts-Kolleg (Institute for Advanced Study), Berlin, 1987-88; Guggenheim fellowship, 1996-97; Getty scholar, 1998-99.

MEMBER: Phi Beta Kappa.

AWARDS, HONORS: Nomination for National Book Critics Circle Award in criticism, 1985, for *Hard Facts: Setting and Form in the American Novel.*

WRITINGS:

Making up Society: The Novels of George Eliot, University of Pittsburgh Press, 1981.
Hard Facts: Setting and Form in the American Novel, Oxford University Press, 1984.
Making and Effacing Art, Oxford University Press, 1990.
Wonder, the Rainbow: The Aesthetics of Rare Experiences, Harvard University Press, 1998.
Still the New World, Harvard University Press, 1998.

WORK IN PROGRESS: A study of the passions in literature and philosophy, *Vehemence and Wonder; New Cambridge History of American Literature.*

BIOGRAPHICAL/CRITICAL SOURCES:

PERIODICALS

Times Literary Supplement, November 22, 1985.

FORD, G. M. 1945-

PERSONAL: Born July 9, 1945, in Everett, MA; son of Gerald Manson (a contractor) and Elizabeth Clara (a secretary) Ford; children: Jedediah Castiglione. *Education:* Hawthorne College, B.A.; Adelphi University, M.A. (English); University of Washington, Seattle, M.A. (political science). *Politics:* "Left of Ho Chi Minh." *Religion:* "Heathen." *Avocational interests:* Fishing, boating.

ADDRESSES: Home—Seattle, WA. *E-mail*—JXXF@eskimo.com.

CAREER: Rogue Community College, Grants Pass, OR, English teacher, 1972-85; City University, Bellevue, WA, communications teacher, 1986-92.

AWARDS, HONORS: Nominated for Anthony Award, Shamus Award, and Lefty Dilys Award.

WRITINGS:

"LEO WATERMAN" MYSTERY NOVELS

Who in Hell Is Wanda Fuca?, Walker (New York City), 1995.
Cast in Stone, Walker, 1996.
The Bum's Rush, Walker, 1997.
Slow Burn, Avon (New York City), 1998.
Last Ditch, Avon, 1999.

SIDELIGHTS: G. M. Ford is known for creating the character of Leo Waterman, a wisecracking private investigator based in Seattle. Waterman's father was a long-time city councilman, so Leo has connections everywhere in the city. He even has allies among the homeless population; a group he calls "the Boys" who help him out in many ways.

The Waterman series began with *Who in Hell is Wanda Fuca?,* nominated for Anthony and Shamus awards. Dennis Dodge, a reviewer for *Booklist,* called it a "clever, funny mystery" that would appeal especially to readers in the Pacific Northwest, but could be enjoyed by anyone. Dodge described Leo Waterman as the kind of character who "trips into tin walls when he's trying to sneak up on the bad guys and loses the ensuing fistfight but is never at a loss for a wisecrack." Dodge added that "Ford doesn't stint on suspense despite his bent for humor, and readers will likely chase this tale to its surprising conclusion as avidly as Waterman."

Ford's next book, *Cast in Stone,* offered "the same bang-on Seattle settings, the same irreverent humor and addictive suspense, and much more, thankfully, of private eye Leo Waterman," endorsed Dodge in *Booklist.* In this story, a childhood friend of Waterman's is critically hurt in an accident in one of Seattle's seamier districts. The detective's gang of homeless alcoholics help him find out the real story. "Ford keeps the menace growing, while his large cast of colorful characters supplies laughs in some of the best dialogue around," approved a *Publisher's Weekly* reviewer.

Another *Publishers Weekly* writer praised Ford's handling of the homeless characters in *The Bum's Rush,* writing: "Leo exhibits just the right mix of grit and wit, surviving two murder attempts and the unpredictable antics of his offbeat pals. . . . Ford demonstrates real skill with Leo and his 'residentially challenged' cronies in this fast-moving tale, portraying them sympathetically but without sentimentality." Bill Ott also gave high marks to *The Bum's Rush,* commenting in *Booklist:* "Waterman's supporting cast not only adds humor to the proceedings but also offers ironic commentary on the lead characters and their mainstream world, undercutting pretentiousness while displaying their own character flaws with a believable mixture of panache and melancholy."

Slow Burn, Ford's fourth Waterman book, is "a hugely entertaining, over-the-top caper," according to a *Publishers Weekly* critic, who particularly enjoyed the "thoroughly wacky climax in the center of the city involving helicopters, a bull on a pallet, a mammoth barbecue pit and thermodynamics." *Booklist*'s Dodge asserted that "Ford certainly succeeds in entertaining readers who appreciate memorable characters, witty dialogue, and outrageous situations."

Ford once told *CA:* "I have read detective novels since childhood. I simply had to write one before I died. The rest, as they say, is history. I am most influenced by Rex Stout, John D. MacDonald, Ross Macdonald, and Robert B. Parker. I have, at one time or another, included little homages to each in my books. I write from six o'clock in the morning until two o'clock in the afternoon, five days a week. I do not outline. I make it up as I go along."

BIOGRAPHICAL/CRITICAL SOURCES:

PERIODICALS

Booklist, April 15, 1995, p. 1482; April 1, 1996, p. 1345; April 15, 1997, p. 1400; February 1, 1998, p. 902.

Library Journal, February 1, 1998, p. 115.

Publishers Weekly, March 27, 1995, p. 78; March 4, 1996, p. 56; March 10, 1997, p. 53; January 5, 1997, p. 61.

* * *

FRANKLIN, Pat
See CADY, Jack A(ndrew)

* * *

FRIEDLAENDER, Pavel
See FRIEDLANDER, Saul

* * *

FRIEDLANDER, Saul 1932-
(Pavel Friedlander)

PERSONAL: Born Pavel Friedlander October 11, 1932, in Prague, Czechoslovakia; son of Hans (a lawyer) and Ellie (Glaser) Friedlander; married Meiry Hagith, August 20, 1959; children: three. *Education:* Institut d'etudes Politiques, Paris, graduated, 1955; Graduate Institute of International Studies, Geneva, Ph.D., 1963. *Religion:* Jewish.

ADDRESSES: Home—50 rue de Moillebeau, Geneva, Switzerland; Jerusalem, Israel. *Office*—Graduate Institute of International Studies, Geneva, Switzerland.

CAREER: Secretary to the president of the World Zionist Organization, 1958-60; Israeli Ministry of Defense, head of scientific department, 1960-61; Graduate Institute of International Studies, Geneva, Switzerland, associate professor, then professor of contemporary history, 1963—; Hebrew University of Jerusalem, professor and chairman of department of international relations; University of Tel Aviv, Israel, professor; University of California at Los Angeles, professor in endowed Holocaust Studies chair. *Military service:* Israel Defense Forces, 1951-53.

WRITINGS:

Le Role du facteur americain dans la politique etrangere et militaire de l'Allemagne, Septembre 1939-Decembre 1941, Droz, 1963.

Hitler et les Etats-Unis, 1938-1941, Droz, 1963, translated by Aline B. Werth and Alexander Werth as *Prelude to Downfall: Hitler and the United States, 1939-1941,* Knopf (New York City), 1967.

Pie XII et le IIIe Reich Documents, Editions du Seuil (Paris), 1964, translated by Charles Fullman as *Pius XII and the Third Reich: A Documentation,* Knopf, 1966.

Kurt Gerstein ou l'Ambiguite du bien, Casterman, 1967, translated by C. Fullman as *Kurt Gerstein: The Ambiguity of Good,* Knopf, 1969, published as *Counterfeit Nazi: The Ambiguity of Good,* Weidenfeld & Nicolson (London), 1969.

Reflexions sur l'avenir d'Israel, Editions du Seuil, 1969.

L'Antisemitisme nazi: Histoire d'une psychose collective, Editions du Seuil, 1971.

(With Mahmoud Hussein) *Arabes et Israeliens,* translated by Paul Auster and Lydia Davis as *Arabs and Israelis: A Dialogue,* Holmes & Meier (New York City), 1975.

Histoire et psychoanalyse: Essai sur les possibilites et les limites de la psychohistoire, Editions du Seuil, 1975, translated by Susan Suleiman as *History and Psychoanalysis: An Inquiry into the Possibilities and Limits of Psychohistory,* Holmes & Meier, 1978.

Some Aspects of the Historical Significance of the Holocaust, Institute of Contemporary Jewry, Hebrew University of Jerusalem, 1977.

Quand vient le souvenir, Editions du Seuil, 1978, translated by Helen R. Lane as *When Memory Comes,* Farrar, Straus (New York City), 1979.

Reflections on Nazism: An Essay on Death and Kitsch, Harper (New York City), 1984.

(Co-editor) *Visions of Apocalypse: End or Rebirth?,* Holmes & Meier, 1984.

A Conflict of Memories?: The New German Debates about the "Final Solution," Leo Baeck Institute (New York City), 1987.

(Editor) *Probing the Limits of Representation: Nazism and the "Final Solution,"* Harvard University Press (Cambridge, MA), 1992.

Memory, History, and the Extermination of the Jews of Europe, Indiana University Press (Bloomington), 1993.

(With others) *The Jews in European History: Seven Lectures,* introduction by Christian Meier, edited by Wolfgang Beck, Hebrew Union College Press (Cincinnati), 1994.

Nazi Germany and the Jews, Volume 1: *The Years of Persecution, 1933-1939,* HarperCollins (New York City), 1997.

Contributor to *Breaking Crystal: Writing and Memory after Auschwitz,* edited by Efraim Sicher, University of Illinois Press (Urbana), 1998.

WORK IN PROGRESS: Nazi Germany and the Jews, Volume 2: *1939-1945.*

SIDELIGHTS: Born in Prague, Czechoslovakia, on the eve of Adolf Hitler's accession to power in neighboring Germany, Saul Friedlander came from a family of upper-middle-class assimilated Jews. When World War II began—and with it the Holocaust in which the Nazis killed some six million Jews—Friedlander's parents went into hiding, sending their son to France, where he attended a Catholic boys' school under the name Paul-Henri Ferland. Only in 1946, while preparing to enter a Jesuit seminary, did he learn that his parents had died in the Auschwitz death camp. At that point he decided to embrace Judaism. Travelling as a teenager to Israel, Friedlander became an ardent Zionist, but by his early twenties had grown disillusioned with the cause. At that point he left Israel for Europe, where he studied for a number of years, receiving his Ph.D. in history from the Graduate Institute of International Studies in Geneva, Switzerland, in 1963. In subsequent years, Friedlander would teach at the Institute and at various other schools in Europe, Israel, and the United States. Whether in his lectures or his many books, his subject has been the same: the Holocaust, or more specifically the means by which this era in world history is represented by historians.

In one of his most notable works, the autobiographical *When Memory Comes* (1978), Friedlander presents history in a highly personal way. John Burt Foster Jr., in a *Southern Humanities Review* article comparing Friedlander's book with Isak Dinesen's *Out of Africa,* noted what he described as a deceptive quality to the apparent straightforwardness of Friedlander's narrative—a deliberate deceptiveness, to be sure, given the author's situation of having to survive by his wits in postwar Europe and Israel. The young Friedlander makes "radical" changes at each stage of his life, indicated by his changing first name: "the Czech Pavel, the French Paul, and finally (though Friedlander does not explicitly flag the religious significance of the change) the Hebrew Saul." He is ultimately forced to confront the duality of his identity, with his true Jewishness on the one hand, and his adopted Catholicism on the other.

Perhaps with this background, it is not surprising that Friedlander has devoted much of his work to the historic representation of Nazism and the Holocaust, his aim being to circumvent the mythologizing of the one and the marginalizing of the other. The first of these themes found expression in *Reflections on Nazism: An Essay on Kitsch and Death* (1984), and the second in a number of works. *Probing the Limits of Representation* (1992), for instance, arose from a 1990 University of California at Los Angeles symposium on a subject that Bryan Cheyette of the *Times Literary Supplement* described as "the implications of a historical relativism which reduces history to opinion and rejects the testimony even of those who witnessed Nazi atrocities." In other words, there are scholars who, in Friedlander's view, minimize the Holocaust, either by claiming it was not as widespread as is believed, or more often by explaining it as largely accidental rather than a planned act of genocide. The book brings together Hayden White and other noted historians—few of them Holocaust scholars as such—to explore the topic. "[T]his kind of writing," concluded James E. Young in the *Partisan Review,* "suggests that we, and no one else, are also accountable for both the histories we write and the conclusions we draw from them." Sander L. Gilman of *American Historical Review* called it "a handbook for historians—not just those who are interested in the Shoah [Holocaust] but all historians who are interested in the meaning of their craft at the close of the century."

Friedlander explores similar themes in *Memory, History, and the Extermination of the Jews of Europe* (1993), a collection of essays written over a period of years. With *Nazi Germany and the Jews,* the first volume of which appeared in 1997, he approaches his subject head-on: no longer writing about how history should be written, he is writing history itself. Friedlander begins with an examination of the prewar years of Nazi power (1933-39), when Jews were more often persecuted than killed; a second volume was planned that will cover the war years (1939-45), when the systematic extermination went into full effect. *Nazi Germany and the Jews* received the praise of Walter Laqueur, one of the foremost writers on the subject, who in the *Los Angeles Times* called it "a very good, very important book" that he suggested would become "a definitive work."

Istvan Deak, in a review for the *New Republic,* noted that Friedlander has found himself at odds with Daniel Jonah Goldhagen, whose controversial 1996 *Hitler's Willing Executioners* takes a different approach to the subject. In mid-1997 the *New York Times* reported a disagreement between Harvard University and financier Ken Lipper, the latter who proposed endowing a Holocaust studies chair at the university. Lipper's choice was Goldhagen; Harvard's was Friedlander. The decision would be important, Dinitia Smith of the *Times* noted, "because of Harvard's reach and intellectual might," and thus it "could define Holocaust scholarship for years to come." At that point, there was only one other Holocaust studies chair at a major university in the United States: at the University of California, where it was held by Friedlander.

BIOGRAPHICAL/CRITICAL SOURCES:

BOOKS

Contemporary Literary Criticism, Volume 90, Gale (Detroit), 1996.

Friedlander, Saul, *When Memory Comes,* translated by Helen R. Lane, Farrar, Straus, 1979.

PERIODICALS

American Historical Review, October, 1976; April, 1993, pp. 521-22.

Antioch Review, winter 1985, pp. 118-19.

Commentary, January, 1976.

Criticism, winter 1996, pp. 173-79.

German Quarterly, winter 1995, pp. 87-89.

Jewish Social Studies, spring 1995, pp. 161-73.

Los Angeles Times Book Review, February 23, 1997, p. 8.

New Republic, August 11, 1997, pp. 42-43.

Newsweek, August 13, 1979.

New York Review of Books, October 25, 1979, pp. 7-10.

New York Times, August 1, 1979, May 28, 1984; July 19, 1997, p. A11.

New York Times Book Review, October 1, 1976, July 15, 1979; February 23, 1997, p. 12.

Partisan Review, April, 1994, pp. 700-04.

Sewanee Review, January, 1988, pp. 158-68.

Southern Humanities Review, summer 1995, pp. 205-18.

Spectator, May 31, 1997, p. 40.

Time, August 20, 1979.

Times Literary Supplement, March 6, 1981; October 16, 1992, p. 10.

Virginia Quarterly Review, winter, 1980.

* * *

FUKUYAMA, Francis 1952-

PERSONAL: Born October 27, 1952, in Chicago, IL; son of Yoshio (a Congregationalist minister and educator) and Toshiko (a potter; maiden name, Kawata) Fukuyama; married Laura Holmgren (a homemaker), September 8, 1986; children: Julia, David, John. *Education:* Cornell University, B.A., 1974; graduate studies at Yale University, 1974-75; Harvard University, Ph.D. (political science), 1981. *Religion:* Protestant.

ADDRESSES: Home—McLean, VA. *Office*—c/o RAND Corporation, 2100 M St. N.W., Washington, DC 20037. *Agent*—Esther Newberg, International Creative Management, 40 West 57th St., New York, NY 10019.

CAREER: Pan Heuristics, Inc., Los Angeles, CA, consultant, 1978-79; RAND Corporation, Santa Monica, CA, associate social scientist, 1979-81, senior staff member of political science department, 1983-89, consultant, 1990—; U.S. Department of State, Policy Planning Staff, Washington, DC, member of U.S. delegation to Egyptian-Israeli talks on Palestinian autonomy, 1981-82, deputy director, 1989-90, consultant, 1990—. University of California, Los Angeles, visiting lecturer in political science, 1986 and 1989. Member of Council on Foreign Relations.

MEMBER: Sierra Club, American Association for the Advancement of Slavic Studies.

AWARDS, HONORS: Premio Capri International Award and *Los Angeles Times* Book Critics Award in current interest category, both 1992, both for *The End of History and the Last Man.*

WRITINGS:

(Editor, with Andrzej Korbonski) *The Soviet Union and the Third World: The Last Three Decades,* Cornell University Press (Ithaca), 1987.

A Look at "The End of History?," edited by Kenneth M. Jensen, U.S. Institute of Peace (Washington, DC), 1990.

The End of History and the Last Man, Free Press (New York City), 1992.

Trust: The Social Virtues and the Creation of Prosperity, Free Press, 1995.

Author of numerous documents for the RAND Corporation, including *Soviet Threats to Intervene in the Middle East, 1956-1973,* 1980; *Escalation in the Middle East and Persian Gulf,* 1984; *Moscow's Post-Brezhnev Reassessment of the Third World,* 1986; *Gorbachev and the New Soviet Agenda in the Third World,* 1989; and (with Abram N. Shulsky) *The "Virtual Corporation" and Army Organization,* 1997. Contributor to books, including *U.S. Strategic Interests in Southwest Asia,* edited by Shirin Tahir-Kheli, Praeger, 1982; *Hawks, Doves, and Owls,* edited by Graham Allison, Albert Carnesale, and Joseph Nye, Norton, 1985; and *The Future of the Soviet Empire,* edited by Henry Rowen and Charles Wolf, St. Martin's Press, 1987. Contributor to periodicals, including *American Spectator, Commentary, Current History, Foreign Affairs, Guardian, Journal of Democracy, Middle East Contemporary Survey, National Interest, New Republic, Orbis,* and *Political Science Quarterly.*

The End of History and the Last Man has been translated into Brazilian, Danish, Dutch, Finnish, French, German, Greek, Hebrew, Italian, Japanese, Korean, Portuguese, Spanish, and Swedish.

SIDELIGHTS: Following a stint as senior staff member of the political science department of the RAND Corporation, Francis Fukuyama captured attention worldwide in 1989 after penning an essay on the current state of history. Called "The End of History?," the sixteen-page article appeared in the foreign policy journal *National Interest* and became the topic of considerable debate. In his thesis, Fukuyama, who was then working as deputy director of the U.S. State Department's policy planning staff, contended that history had evolved to its logical end: that of liberal democracy. Fukuyama's notion of "history," as explained by Toronto *Globe and Mail* contributor Jeffrey Simpson, is "the struggle for universal acceptance of the most effective and just organization of human society."

Based in part on the ideologies of German philosopher Georg Wilhelm Friedrich Hegel, Fukuyama's argument centers around the fact that one form of government will ultimately win out over all others. Fukuyama maintains that his assertion that liberal democracy has been victorious has been validated by the reunification of Germany and the collapse of Communism. According to James Atlas in the *New York Times,* Fukuyama suggests that "history is a protracted struggle to realize the idea of freedom latent in human consciousness. In the 20th century, the forces of totalitarianism have been decisively conquered by the United States and its allies, which represent the final embodiment of this idea." The end result, predicts Fukuyama, will be "a very sad time," as people turn to solving technological troubles rather than fighting ideological battles.

Fukuyama's essay, which he later expanded into the 1992 book *The End of History and the Last Man,* would continue to be the subject of much debate in the years following its hardbound publication. While some commentators have agreed with the author's delineations, others argue that liberal democracy certainly will be challenged by Third World countries and religious fundamentalists. Some critics pointed to the problems of drugs and poverty in U.S. society as further evidence that liberal democracy may not be the key ideology. In response to such debate, Fukuyama told Atlas: "The last thing I want to be interpreted as saying is that our society is a utopia, or that there are no more problems." He added, "I simply don't see any competitors to modern democracy."

In his 1995 book *Trust: The Social Virtue and the Creation of Prosperity,* Fukuyama argues that "economical success depends only partly on the factors customarily emphasized by economists: Markets, competition, technology and skills," according to a contributor to *The Economist.* George Weigel explained in *Commentary* that "Fukuyama has come to agree that there is life after history," and that the results of this "post-historical" period will be determined by civil society; "'a complex welter of intermediate institutions, including businesses, voluntary associations, educational institutions, clubs, unions, media, charities, and churches,' of which the most crucial is the family," according to Weigel. The detailed case studies in *Trust* illustrate how the level of 'trust' in a society or nation is the key variable determining its capacity to compete in the modern world.

Many critics praised *Trust* for its interesting thesis and engaging style, but faulted Fukuyama for his book's omissions and for failing to prove his thesis.

An *Economist* contributor remarked that, "despite the plausibility of its opening argument, despite Mr. Fukuyama's clear writing and hard work, *Trust* is not convincing." According to Norman Stone in *Management Today,* the book has serious "mis-statements" and "several . . . huge omissions." In *New Republic,* Robert M. Solow called the book's central thesis "interesting, even plausible, but not very original." Within the book's argument, Solow maintained, "there are too many escape hatches, too many spineless terms, too many ways to rationalize exceptions," and concluded that while "the sorts of things that Fukuyama wants to talk about are more important than my colleagues in economics are willing to admit. . . . I would rather they were discussed imprecisely than not discussed at all." "But imprecision is not a virtue," Solow concluded, "a 'for example' is not an argument."

In *New Statesman,* Anthony Giddens echoed Solow's belief that *Trust* lacked a convincing argument for its thesis, however, Giddens described the book as "a work of considerable intellectual substance, engagingly written and ambitious in content." In a *Forbes* review, Steve Forbes described the book as "fascinating, disturbing, well-researched . . . [and] timely." "Fukuyama is not particularly alarmist in his book," summarized Perry Pascarella in *Industry Week:* "The quiet man leads us to see that unrestrained individualism harms society, the economy, and ultimately, the individual. He convinces us that we will have to settle for a less viable society and less productive economy until we find a way to rebalance individualism with community."

BIOGRAPHICAL/CRITICAL SOURCES:

BOOKS

Bertram, Christopher, and Andrew Chitty, *Has History Ended?: Fukuyama, Marx, Modernity,* Avebury (Brookfield, VT), 1994.

Burns, Timothy, *After History?: Francis Fukuyama and His Critics,* Rowman & Littlefield (Lanham, MD), 1994.

PERIODICALS

Commentary, October, 1995, pp. 34-38.

Commonweal, June 19, 1992, pp. 25-26.

Economist, September 2, 1995, pp. 79-80.

Forbes, September 25, 1995, p. 24.

Globe and Mail (Toronto), April 4, 1992, p. C6.

Industry Week, November 6, 1995, pp. 32-36.

Management Today, January, 1996, p. 25.

National Review, November 24, 1989, p. 62.

New Republic, September 11, 1995, pp. 36-39.

New Statesman, October 13, 1995, p. 30.

New York Times, October 22, 1989, p. 38; January 24, 1990.

Time, September 4, 1989, p. 57.

Times (London), February 20, 1992, p. 4.*

G

GABALDON, Diana 1950(?)-

PERSONAL: Born c. 1950; daughter of Jacqueline (Sykes) Gabaldon; married Doug Watkins; children: Laura Juliet, Samuel Gordon, Jennifer Rose. *Education:* Arizona State University, M.S. (marine biology), and Ph.D. (behavioral ecology).

ADDRESSES: *Home*—P.O. Box 584, Scottsdale, AZ 85252.

CAREER: Assistant professor of research, Center for Environmental Studies, Arizona State University, Tempe, until 1992; freelance writer.

AWARDS, HONORS: Best First Novel Award from B. Dalton bookstores, and Best Book of the Year Award from the Romance Writers of America, both 1991, for *Outlander; Voyager* chosen as a main selection of both the Literary Guild and the Doubleday Book Club, 1994.

WRITINGS:

HISTORICAL ROMANCE NOVELS; "OUTLANDER" SERIES

Outlander, Delacorte Press (New York City), 1991.
Dragonfly in Amber, Delacorte Press, 1992.
Voyager, Delacorte Press, 1994.
Drums of Autumn, Delacorte Press, 1997.

Also author of software reviews for *Byte* magazine; contributor of articles to scholarly journals; author of comic book scripts for Disney.

WORK IN PROGRESS: *The Fiery Cross, The Outlandish Companion, King Farewell,* and an untitled mystery.

SIDELIGHTS: Diana Gabaldon's first novel, *Outlander,* was published in 1991. Its protagonist, English nurse Claire Randall, visits Scotland in 1945, hoping to rekindle a marriage stressed by separation during World War II. Occupying herself collecting plant samples while her husband studies history, she accidentally touches a stone in an ancient circle similar to Stonehenge, and she is transported to the year 1743. The novel then recounts events leading to the Second Jacobite Rising through her modern eyes. While in the past, Claire marries Jamie Fraser, an outlaw Scotsman, and eventually must choose between returning to her husband in the twentieth century and remaining in the eighteenth with Jamie. *Outlander* garnered awards from both the Romance Writers of America and B. Dalton bookstores in the year of its publication. A *Publishers Weekly* reviewer hailed *Outlander* as "absorbing and heartwarming"; Cynthia Johnson in *Library Journal* lauded the book as "a richly textured historical novel with an unusual and compelling love story."

Gabaldon followed *Outlander* with a sequel, *Dragonfly in Amber,* in 1992. This novel recounts Claire and Jamie's desperate attempt to alter history by preventing Charles Stuart from actually starting the Jacobite uprising that led to a slaughter of the Scots at the battle of Culloden. When they fail at this, they use Claire's knowledge of history to prepare Jamie's family and clan for this disaster as best they can. However, *Dragonfly in Amber* also deals with a second story in a different timeline—Claire's trip to Scotland with her daughter Brianna in 1968 to tell her about her real father, the eighteenth century Scot, Jamie Fraser. A *Publishers Weekly* critique of this second novel commended Gabaldon's "fresh and offbeat historical view" and asserted that *Dragonfly in Amber* is "compulsively readable."

The third volume in the saga, *Voyager,* appeared on the *Publishers Weekly* hardcover bestsellers list in January, 1994. In this installment, having discovered that Jamie did not die at the battle of Culloden, Claire returns to the eighteenth century to be with him. The years spent apart are recounted, and adventures lead the couple to America in pursuit of Jamie's kidnapped nephew. Roland Green, reviewing *Voyager* in *Booklist,* praised its "highly appealing characters" and "authentic feel." *Locus* contributor Carolyn Cushman opined that Gabaldon "masterfully interweaves" plot elements separated by two centuries, "crossing time periods with abandon but never losing track of the story."

Though *Publishers Weekly* labeled *Voyager* a "triumphant conclusion" to the story of Claire and Jamie, Gabaldon was preparing a fourth book that would carry the characters through the American Revolution. *Drums of Autumn* leapt onto the bestseller lists as soon as it appeared in 1997. Set in the New World, the novel finds the two lovers building a life as the Americans set about building a nation. Jamie and Claire first arrive at Charlston, then join other Scottish exiles along the Cape Fear River in North Carolina. Troubled by events there, the couple moves inland to the mountains in search of tranquility. The couple's attempts at avoiding conflict and an impending war gives the book an epic quality. In the view of a *Booklist* contributor, "Gabaldon is clearly trying to write on the same scale as Margaret Mitchell, and in terms of length and of thoroughness of research, largely succeeds." A reviewer for *Maclean's* notes, "The meticulous period detail is in contrast to the serendipitous development of the central premise: the love story of a modern woman somehow flung into the past."

This quality of *Drums of Autumn* reflects its author's approach to all of the books in the series. In an interview published in *Heart to Heart,* Gabaldon discussed some of her feelings about the series she began with *Outlander:* "Part of my purpose in my books has been to tell the complete story of a relationship and a marriage; not just to end with 'happily ever after,' leaving the protagonists at the altar or in bed. . . . I wanted to show some of the complicated business of actually *living* a successful marriage." Concerning the history depicted in the first three novels and the prospective fourth, Gabaldon revealed that she "wanted to show the changing face of the world at that time, moving from the ancient feudal system of Highland clans to the violent upheavals of democracy in the New World." She further noted that with "Claire's perspective as a time-traveler, we see the events of that time through a modern eye, and can fully appreciate their significance to the future that will come."

Gabaldon's writing career and her books have followed a unique course. While working as a scientist at Arizona State University and raising a family, she also began writing freelance. She joined in discussion forums online on CompuServe, where she eventually found an encouraging audience for her forays into fiction. She also made contacts online that helped her finish her first novel, *Outlander,* and find an agent and publisher. That book and its sequels have enough romantic elements to appeal to more traditional historical romance readers, but Gabaldon's use of a modern heroine, time travel, and other unique characters have allowed her a broader appeal. Anne Stephenson notes in a *Publishers Weekly* profile, "Delacorte . . . now treats her books as general nonfiction." The author told Stephenson that she has come to call her books "historical fantasies."

BIOGRAPHICAL/CRITICAL SOURCES:

PERIODICALS

Booklist, November 15, 1993; November 15, 1996.
Heart to Heart, September/October, 1994, pp. 3, 8-9.
Library Journal, July, 1991, p. 134.
Locus, January, 1994, p. 29.
Maclean's, February 17, 1997, p. 71.
People Weekly, April 14, 1997, p. 64.
Publishers Weekly, May 31, 1991, p. 59; June 22, 1992, p. 49; December 20, 1993, p. 52; January 17, 1994, p. 2; January 6, 1997, p. 50; January 13, 1997, p. 18.
Time, January 20, 1997, p. 79.*

* * *

GARRISON, Phil
See BRANDNER, Gary

GELLES, Richard J(ames) 1946-

PERSONAL: Born July 7, 1946, in Newton, MA; son of Sidney S. (a neckwear manufacturer) and Clara (Goldberg) Gelles; married Judy S. Isacoff (a research assistant), July 4, 1971; children: Jason Charles, David Philip. *Education:* Bates College, B.A., 1968; University of Rochester, M.A., 1970; University of New Hampshire, Ph.D., 1973. *Politics:* "Independent pragmatist." *Religion:* Jewish.

ADDRESSES: Home—155 Stonehenge Rd., Kingston, RI 02881. *Office*—Family Violence Research Program, University of Rhode Island, Kingston, RI 02881.

CAREER: University of New Hampshire, Durham, instructor in sociology, 1970-73; University of Rhode Island, Kingston, assistant professor, 1973-76, director of Family Violence Research Program, 1973—, associate professor, 1976-82, professor of sociology, 1982—, dean of College of Arts and Sciences, 1984-90. Louis Harris & Associates, research director, 1981-90; University of Rochester, lecturer, summer, 1970 and 1971; Harvard University Medical School, lecturer on pediatrics, 1979—. Consultant to various agencies and organizations, including Family Development Study of Children's Hospital Medical Center, Emma Pendleton Bradley Hospital, and Child and Family Services of Newport. Presenter of more than 75 papers on family issues; conference organizer and facilitator; advisory board member for numerous organizations for families and children.

MEMBER: American Association of University Professors, American Federation of Television and Radio Artists, International Society for Research on Aggression, American Sociological Association (chair of Family Section, 1985; chair of William J. Goode Book Award Committee, 1986-87), National Council on Family Relations (chaired Research and Theory Section, 1989-92), Eastern Sociological Society (chair of program committee, 1990-91), Society for the Study of Social Problems (chair of Committee on Media Relations, 1989-90).

AWARDS, HONORS: Grants from various institutions, including National Institute of Mental Health, 1973-82, 1985-90, U.S. Department of Health, Education and Welfare, 1975-80, U.S. Department of Health and Human Services and Department of Defense, 1980-82, National Institute of Justice, 1980, 1982, National Committee for Prevention of Child Abuse and Neglect, 1982, National Science Foundation, 1984-85, Guggenheim Foundation, 1991-94, and Connecticut Superior Court, 1993-94; Distinguished Contribution to Teaching Award, American Sociological Association (Section on Undergraduate Education), 1979.

WRITINGS:

The Violent Home: A Study of Physical Aggression between Husbands and Wives, Sage Publications (Thousand Oaks, CA), 1974.

Family Violence, Sage Publications, 1979, revised edition, 1987.

(With Murray A. Straus and Suzanne K. Steinmetz) *Behind Closed Doors: Violence in the American Family,* Doubleday-Anchor (New York City), 1980.

(With Michael S. Bassis and Ann Levine) *Sociology: An Introduction,* Random House (New York City), 1980; 5th edition, with Levine, McGraw-Hill (New York City), 1995.

(With Bassis and Levine) *Social Problems,* Harcourt (New York City), 1982.

(Editor with David Finkelhor, Gerald Hotaling, and Straus) *The Dark Side of Families: Current Family Violence Research,* Sage Publications, 1983.

(Editor with Claire P. Cornell) *International Perspectives on Family Violence,* Lexington Books (Lexington, MA), 1983.

(With Cornell) *Intimate Violence in Families,* Sage Publications, 1985, revised edition, 1990.

(Editor with Jane B. Lancaster) *Child Abuse and Neglect: Biosocial Dimensions,* Aldine (Hawthorne, NY), 1987.

(With Straus) *Intimate Violence,* Simon and Schuster (New York City), 1988, revised, 1990.

(With Straus) *Physical Violence in American Families: Risk Factors and Adaptations to Violence in 8,145 Families,* Transaction Books (New Brunswick, NJ), 1990.

(Editor with Donileen R. Loseke) *Current Controversies on Family Violence,* Sage Publications, 1993.

Contemporary Families: A Sociological View, with photographs by Judy S. Gelles, Sage Publications, 1995.

The Book of David: How Preserving Families Can Cost Children's Lives, Basic Books (New York City), 1996.

Contributor to numerous books, including *Annual Progress in Child Psychology and Child Development,* edited by Stella Chess and Alexander Thomas, editors, Brunner, 1974; *Child Abuse: An Agenda for*

Action, edited by George Gerbner, Catherine J. Ross, and Edward Zigler, Oxford University Press, 1980; *Marriage and Family: Coping with Change,* edited by Leonard Cargan, Wadsworth, 1985; *The Encyclopedia of Child Abuse,* edited by Robin E. Clark and Judith Clark, Facts on File, 1990; and *One World, Many Families,* edited by Karen Altergott, National Council on Family Relations, 1993.

Contributor to professional journals. Editor of "Family Texts" series, Sage Publications, 1982—. Associate editor, *Journal of Applied Communications Research,* 1974-80, *Journal of Marriage and the Family,* 1977—, *Child Abuse and Neglect: The International Journal,* 1978-90, *Sage Family Studies Abstracts,* 1979—, *Focus on Women,* 1980-83, *Family Studies Review Yearbook,* 1982-85, *Journal of Family Issues* and *Victimology,* 1984—, *Journal of Family Violence* and *Journal of Interpersonal Violence,* 1985—, *International Journal of Law and the Family,* 1987—, *Marriage and Family Review,* 1987-92. Contributing editor, *Brown University Family Therapy Letter,* 1989—. Board of governors, *Violence Update,* 1989—. Editorial board member, *Harry Frank Guggenheim Review of Violence, Aggression, and Dominance,* 1991—.

SIDELIGHTS: Sociologist Richard J. Gelles has gained a reputation as an expert on family violence through his academic career, activism, and numerous textbooks and general-interest books on the topic. He has shown a willingness to question the conventional wisdom surrounding this subject—as he did in *The Book of David: How Preserving Families Can Cost Children's Lives.* In this volume Gelles found fault with a concept that has become accepted by many social service professionals: that preserving or reuniting families is usually a desirable outcome in child abuse cases. Gelles expressed his belief that by focusing on family reunification, the social welfare system is putting children in grave danger. The system, he said, has left children in families where the abuse is certain to continue.

He made his case by concentrating on one child, David, who was born to parents who already had lost custody of a daughter whom they had abused. Social workers largely ignored what had happened to David's sister, however, and let him stay with his parents even when it was reported that he was being abused as well. Finally, David suffered a fatal injury at the hands of his mother at the age of 15 months. Gelles told the child's story "without painting David's parents as malicious or blatantly psychotic," noted Michael E. Lamb in the *Journal of Marriage and the Family.* "Indeed, it is their ordinariness that makes David's fate so sad and the dilemmas so compelling."

Lamb also commented that "rhetorically, the focus on a single child, rather than on anonymous children, proves an effective device for illustrating the many ways in which maltreated children are failed by the social systems and agencies that are ostensibly designed for their protection." Gelles provided substantial information on how these agencies' policies came about. The emphasis on family preservation, he explained, grew out of a 1980 federal law, designed to relieve an overburdened foster care system, that mandated state child protection agencies to make "reasonable efforts" to keep families intact if the agencies were to remain eligible for federal funding. Also, private foundations have poured money into family preservation efforts. "The vast sums of money backing family preservation, Mr. Gelles notes, have resulted in the gross overselling of a policy that can be effective when applied selectively and with great discretion," related Heather Mac Donald in the *Wall Street Journal.* She also observed that Gelles was once a strong proponent of family preservation.

New York Times Book Review critic Celia Dugger also thought Gelles had made a compelling argument that this policy had been overemphasized at the expense of children. But she contended that "it seems entirely possible that Mr. Gelles's approach could produce a different kind of horror story . . . of children wrongly snatched from parents by caseworkers who were so concerned with protecting children physically that they were unwilling to take any risk to keep them with their parents, thus breaking up homes that could hang together with a little help." Lamb voiced doubts about some of Gelles's recommendations for reform: elimination of mandatory reporting of child abuse is bound to be controversial, the critic contended, while a suggestion for improved training of case workers is so nebulous as to have little effect in the near future.

Dugger, Mac Donald, and some other reviewers deemed the book weakened by the fact that, while David was a real child, Gelles intermingled facts of other child abuse cases with David's, effectively making David a composite. "The decision to tamper with the facts effectively denies his readers the ability to evaluate the case on which he has built the 'children first' policies he promotes," Dugger declared. Anthony N. Maluccio, writing in *Social Ser-*

vice Review, asserted that "it would be just as possible—and logical—to create a totally different composite case that would show the presumed virtues of family preservation and its effectiveness in protecting children and promoting their development as well as safety." He saw Gelles's book as marred by "exaggeration, hyperbole, and polemics." The book, he said, fails to mention studies that have reached far more positive conclusions about family preservation, or that many families have overcome their problems with the help of social services. Maluccio also noted that many promoters of family preservation do not see it as appropriate in every case, and urged the development of policies that balance child protection and family preservation. But Mac Donald concluded that decision-makers should answer Gelles's call for "a child-centered welfare policy that places the safety of children ahead of the preservation of the family unit."

The divergent ideas about how to deal with abuse in families are highlighted in *Current Controversies on Family Violence,* which Gelles edited with Donileen R. Loseke. The volume collects the work of numerous expert researchers, representing a variety of viewpoints. In the *Journal of Marriage and the Family,* reviewer John C. Kilburn opined that the book "does the best job I have seen at presenting the spectrum of approaches to the problem in a fair and objective manner." *Family Relations* contributor Teresa Julian pronounced the book "very readable and enjoyable" but thought it was sometimes too elementary, "read[ing] like an undergraduate sociology textbook." She added, though, that "such a presentation may be important to establishing a foundation for readers interested in the specific controversies in the field."

BIOGRAPHICAL/CRITICAL SOURCES:

PERIODICALS

Family Relations, July, 1995, p. 329; April, 1996, p. 243.
Journal of Marriage and the Family, February, 1995, pp. 251-52; February, 1997, pp. 235-36.
New York Times Book Review, April 6, 1980; April 14, 1996, p. 29.
Social Service Review, March, 1997, pp. 135-42.
Wall Street Journal, May 2, 1996, section A, p. 13.
Washington Post, February 9, 1997, section C, pp. 1, 5.
Washington Post Book World, March 23, 1980.*

—*Sketch by Trudy Ring*

GIARDINA, Denise 1951-

PERSONAL: Surname is pronounced Jahr-*dee*-na; born October 25, 1951, in Bluefield, WV; daughter of Dennis (an accountant) and Leona (a nurse; maiden name, Whitt) Giardina. *Education:* West Virginia Wesleyan College, B.A., 1973; Virginia Theological Seminary, M.Div., 1979. *Politics:* "Populist."

ADDRESSES: Home—Charleston, WV.

CAREER: Clerk, typist, and computer operator, beginning in 1974; writer, 1984—. Licensed lay Episcopal preacher; also teacher at West Virginia State College.

MEMBER: Authors Guild.

WRITINGS:

Good King Harry (historical novel), Harper (New York City), 1984.
Storming Heaven (novel), Norton (New York City), 1987.
The Unquiet Earth (novel), Norton, 1992.
Saints and Villains (historical novel), Norton, 1998.

SIDELIGHTS: Denise Giardina was born in West Virginia and raised among the coal mines of Appalachia. Two of her historical novels draw heavily on the author's personal observations of the place and its people. It is a place where the generations-old conflict between the miners and labor unions on one hand, and the mine owners and the government on the other, exists to this day. The bitterness of the ongoing struggle flavors the lives of all the characters in Giardina's novels *Storming Heaven* and *The Unquiet Earth.*

Storming Heaven is a fictional treatment of the Battle of Blair Mountain, which erupted into violence in the summer of 1921. The seeds of violence had been sown over a twenty-year period of land acquisition by the mining companies, a period in which land owners had been persuaded, by trickery according to Giardina, to part with their holdings, leaving them with only one source of income—the mines that had replaced their homes. Faced with lives of backbreaking and dangerous labor at the whim of the tight-fisted mine operators, miners sought protection from labor unions. The mine owners resisted, and the violence escalated until the United States Army was called in to restore order. Relating her story through four narrators, Giardina "has drawn authoritatively on the facts of the period and a store of inherited and first-hand knowledge," wrote Douglas Bauer in the *New York Times*. Her narrators included the wife of a coal miner, a nurse, a union organizer, and a socialist whose grandfather had been killed trying to preserve his rights to his land. In her choice of narrators, Giardina revealed where her own sympathies lay. Bauer criticized the author's intensity in this regard: "One senses in the prose such an urgency to draw, in black and white, the operators' villainy and the miners' heroism, that each side becomes a caricature." In *Publishers Weekly,* Giardina responded by telling interviewer Norman Oder that "she actually tamed down the mine wars."

The Unquiet Earth follows the miners of Justice County from the 1930s to recent times. "[I]t has epic scope and ambition," commented Danny Duncan Collum in the *National Catholic Reporter,* "and it delivers on both counts." The novel traces the miners and their descendants from World War II through President Kennedy's "war on poverty." Love binds them to the land and to each other, and their struggle for dignity and independence continues—through poverty and despair, but not without a vein of determination and an occasional glimmer of hope. Oder described *The Unquiet Earth* and its predecessor as "wrenching stories about families caught up in fighting or accommodating King Coal."

Saints and Villains takes the reader far from the mountains of West Virginia. This is a historical novel about the life and death of German theologian and philosopher Dietrich Bonhoeffer. In it, according to *New York Times* reviewer Paul Baumann, Giardina "displays a thorough knowledge of the historical and theological record." Bonhoeffer was raised in Berlin, a child of privilege with the means to study abroad, including a stint at Union Theological Seminary in New York City in the early 1930s. When he returned to Germany, he was greatly disturbed by his observations of Nazi rule. His vocal opposition to Nazi power eventually drew Bonhoeffer into a plot against Hitler's life. The plan failed, and Bonhoeffer spent his remaining days in prison, where he was executed at the age of thirty-nine.

Giardina was attracted to the study of this martyr, she told Oder, because of "his faith, his patriotism and his loyalty to friends and family," but also because "'he wasn't this plaster saint.'" In the *Publishers Weekly* interview, Giardina stressed that she wanted her book to reach the general reader—including the coal miner—without losing the depth resulting from her research and her own theological education. Giardina supplemented the historical record by creating fictional characters, such as the interrogator Alois Bauer, a black minister who Bonhoeffer could have encountered during his travels in the United States, and a Jewish woman who became the philosopher's love interest. It was the fictional characters who disturbed some critics, like Baumann, who reported that they "seem like phantoms awkwardly interposed in a series of documentary photographs." Other critics focused instead on Giardina's treatment of Bonhoeffer as a man of both commitment and ambiguity. Bonnie Johnston wrote in *Booklist:* "Giardina . . . illuminates the web of moral decisions within which we all exist." Johnston recommended *Saints and Villains* as "compelling."

Giardina told *CA:* "I am an Appalachian writer, interested in the affinities between Appalachia and other exploited places like Poland and Central America. I am also interested in writing that includes the political and spiritual dimensions of life and am not much interested in fiction that pretends these areas do not exist.

"I like to write in first person. I want the reader to live inside the skin of the characters. This is especially important since we live in a time when it is fashionable to be uninvolved in the lives and problems of other people."

BIOGRAPHICAL/CRITICAL SOURCES:

PERIODICALS

Booklist, February 15, 1998, p. 981.
Library Journal, March 1, 1998, p. 127.
National Catholic Reporter, November 19, 1993, p. 33.
New York Times, July 29, 1984, section 7, p. 20; September 20, 1987, section 7, p. 39; August 30, 1992; April 19, 1998.
Publishers Weekly, February 9, 1998, pp. 69-71; December 22, 1997.

* * *

GIBBS, Tony
See GIBBS, Wolcott, Jr.

GIBBS, Wolcott, Jr. 1935-
(Tony Gibbs)

PERSONAL: Born April 5, 1935, in New York, NY; son of Wolcott (a writer) and Elinor (a writer; maiden name, Sherwin) Gibbs; married Elizabeth Villa, January 4, 1958 (divorced); married Elaine St. James (an entrepreneur and writer), April 22, 1978; children: William, Eric. *Education:* Princeton University, B.A., 1957. *Religion:* None.

ADDRESSES: *Home*—Santa Barbara, CA. *Office*—*Yachting,* 50 West 44th St., New York, NY 10036.

CAREER: Doubleday & Co., Inc., New York City, publicity manager, 1958-63, editorial assistant, 1963-64; J. B. Lippincott Co., New York City, editor, 1966-68; *Motor Boating,* New York City, book editor, 1968-75; *Motor Boating and Sailing,* New York City, executive editor, 1975; *Yachting,* New York City, editor, 1975—. Member of Rules of the Road Advisory Commission. *Military service:* U.S. Army National Guard, 1957-63; U.S. Coast Guard Auxiliary.

WRITINGS:

NONFICTION; UNDER NAME TONY GIBBS

Practical Sailing, Hearst Books (New York City), 1971.
Pilot's Work Book, Seven-Seas Press (Newport, RI), 1972.
Pilot's Log Book, Seven-Seas Press, 1972.
Sports Illustrated Powerboating, Lippincott (Philadelphia), 1973.
Sailing: A First Book (juvenile), F. Watts (New York City), 1974.
Backpacking (juvenile), F. Watts, 1975.
Navigation: Finding Your Way on Sea and Land (juvenile), F. Watts, 1975.
Advanced Sailing: the Design, Rigging, Handling, Trailering, Equipping and Maintenance of Modern Sailboats, St. Martin's (New York City), 1975.
The Coastal Cruiser: A Complete Guide to the Design, Selection, Purchase, and Outfitting of Auxiliary Sailboats under 30 Feet, Norton (New York City), 1981.
The Coastal Navigator's Notebook, International Marine Publishing (Camden, ME), 1982.
Cruising in a Nutshell: The Art and Science of Enjoyable Coastwise Voyaging in Small Auxiliary Yachts, Norton, 1983.

MYSTERY NOVELS; UNDER NAME TONY GIBB

Dead Run, Random House (New York City), 1988.
Running Fix, Random House, 1990.
Shadow Queen, Mysterious Press (New York City), 1992.
Landfall, Morrow (New York City), 1992.
Capitol Offense, Mysterious Press, 1995.
Shot in the Dark, Mysterious Press, 1996.
Fade to Black, Mysterious Press, 1997.

OTHER

Author of editor's page, and of "Rough Log," a column in *Yachting,* 1976-78. Contributor to boating magazines.

SIDELIGHTS: Wolcott Gibbs, Jr., who writes under the name Tony Gibbs, published numerous nonfiction books about sailing before going on to establish himself as a mystery author. Gibbs's thrillers reflect his own background in publishing and the nautical world. In *Dead Run, Running Fix,* and *Land Fall,* Gibbs relates the adventures of the owner and crew of the racing yacht *Glory.* Gillian Verdean is the bold, resourceful owner; Jeremy Barr is her wise and stubborn captain; and Patrick O'Mara is the tough first mate. In *Running Fix,* the crew is hired to find a young woman thought to have drowned off the coast of Bermuda. The mystery leads them from Bermuda to the Bronx, to Manhattan and beyond. It is a "suspenseful and adeptly written novel," in the opinion of John Ellsworth in the *New York Times.* "Mr. Gibbs . . . has created a clever and vivid mystery. His book is balanced and well-trimmed, and it sustains its authenticity throughout." Reviewing *Land Fall,* Newgate Callendar remarked in the *New York Times* that Gibbs has "an ability to get inside his characters, a smooth style and dialogue that actually sounds real."

Gibbs featured Diana Speed in the books *Shadow Queen* and *Capitol Offense.* Tall, blond Diana is the chief financial officer of a New York publishing house. In *Capitol Offense,* Speed is asked by her employer, billionaire Roger Charming, to follow a woman who has been threatening his business. Diana's adventure takes her through seedy Times Square porno theaters and into the world of black-market arms deals and corrupt South American officers. *Booklist* contributor George Needham characterized *Capitol Offense* as "a story that goes nowhere while trying to go everywhere," but added that "if you don't stop to think about it, this wild mess can be fun." A *Publisher's Weekly* reviewer thought the book had "promise" but was ultimately overwhelmed by an "overly complex plot." The writer praised Diana and her leading man, Eric Szabo, as "a tough yet vulnerable duo."

Gibbs's nautical background is strongly in evidence in *Shot in the Dark* and *Fade to Black,* a pair of books about a Santa Barbara harbor policeman, Neal Donahoe, and Coast Guard Lt. Victoria "Tory" Lennox. "Even hardcore landlubbers will love this smooth-sailing adventure, a smart, sexy series launch chock-full of boating lore and lingo," enthused a *Publishers Weekly* reviewer. "The action proceeds nonstop. . . . Neal and Tory are fully realized characters with powerful personality differences that work against their mutual physical attraction; there's nothing cozy or cute about their relationship." The sequel, *Fade to Black,* was praised by another *Publishers Weekly* contributor, who found that "Gibbs writes with ease and confidence. . . . [His] nautical knowledge provides a solidly entertaining underpinning to this smooth and swift-sailing adventure story."

BIOGRAPHICAL/CRITICAL SOURCES:

PERIODICALS

Booklist, December 1, 1994, p. 656.

New York Times, August 5, 1990, section 7, p. 18; December 13, 1992.

Publishers Weekly, November 28, 1994, p. 46; May 20, 1996, p. 242; May 19, 1997, p. 70.

* * *

GIRODIAS, Maurice 1919-1990

PERSONAL: Name originally Maurice Kahane; born in 1919 in Paris, France; died of a heart attack, July 3, 1990, in Paris, France; son of Jack Kahane (a publisher); married first wife (divorced); married second wife; children: two daughters. *Education:* Attended Lycee Pasteur, Neuilly-sur-Seine, France.

CAREER: Les Editions du Chene (publisher of art books), Paris, France, founder and editor, 1939-51; Olympia Press (avant-garde publisher), Paris, founder and editor, 1953-64, founder of New York office, 1967; founder of Freeway Press; writer. Founder of Galerie Vendome, 1945, and La Grande Severine, a restaurant and club, 1959.

WRITINGS:

(With Peter Singleton-Gates) *The Black Diaries: An Account of Roger Casement's Life and Times, with a Collection of His Diaries and Public Writings,* Grove (New York City), 1959, special edition, Olympia Press (Paris), 1959.

(Editor) *The Olympia Reader* (selection of erotic stories from "Traveller's" companion series), some stories translated by S. d'Estree and others, illustrated by Norman Rubington, Grove, 1965.

(Editor) *The Best of Olympia: An Anthology of Tales, Poems, Scientific Documents, and Tricks Which Appeared in the Short-lived and Much-lamented Olympia Magazine,* New English Library (London), 1966.

(Editor) *The New Olympia Reader* (selection of erotic stories by American authors from "Traveller's" companion series), illustrated by Kasoundra, Olympia Press, 1970.

(Author of preface) *The Obscenity Report* (contains an edited version of the findings of the U.S. Presidential Commission on Obscenity and Pornography, the Arts Council of Great Britain, and the Danish Forensic Medical Council), Olympia Press, 1971.

Une Journee sur la terre (autobiography), Volume 1: *J'arrive,* Stock (Paris), 1977, translation of *J'arrive* published as *The Frog Prince,* Crown (New York City), 1980.

SIDELIGHTS: French editor and writer Maurice Girodias was credited with bringing about a sexual revolution in both England and America. He was best known as the founding father of the Olympia Press, the avant-garde publisher of erotica and banned literary classics. As a leader in the fight to overcome literary censorship of sexually-explicit material worldwide, Girodias was steadfast in his conviction that the publication of erotica and similar material is a defensible business that secures both an artist's and a reader's right to free thought and expression. As quoted by Henry Popkin in the *New York Times Book Review,* the publisher said of his work, "It would not occur to me to apologize for it."

Girodias's father, Jack Kahane, was a pioneer in the publication of erotic and unconventional literature in English, establishing the Obelisk Press in the 1930s. Several classic works were released under the Obelisk name, most notably Frank Harris's sexually explicit autobiography *My Life and Loves* and Henry Miller's controversial *Tropic of Cancer,* a first-person autobiographical narrative that graphically depicts the carnal exploits of a bisexual American expatriate in France. Sixteen-year-old Girodias designed the cover for *Tropic of Cancer* at his father's request; it features a huge black crab sitting atop a globe, holding a lifeless, reclining human form in its claws.

In 1939, upon his father's death, Girodias inherited the press and eventually built a new publishing company, Les Editions du Chene. At the age of twenty-one, he had become the youngest publisher in the world. Throughout the German occupation of France during World War II—at which time he dropped Kahane, his father's Jewish surname, and assumed Girodias, his mother's maiden name—Girodias dealt mainly in art books, releasing volumes devoted to contemporary European painters, such as Henri Matisse and Pablo Picasso. The publisher soon met with financial difficulties and relinquished his interests in Les Editions du Chene to a leading French publishing house in 1951. Two years later, he founded the Olympia Press, "with a view," he told Roy Newquist in *Conversations,* "of making money and also of publishing books by authors I liked." Olympia earned a reputation for publishing sexually explicit and experimental literary works. Among the titles released by Girodias in the 1950s were Samuel Beckett's *Watt,* Vladimir Nabokov's *Lolita,* J. P. Donleavy's *Ginger Man,* and William Burroughs's *Naked Lunch.*

While headquartered in France, the Olympia Press served as a worldwide publisher of censored books that otherwise would not have been published in the United States, England, or other English-speaking countries. Prior to the late 1940s, literary censorship was virtually nonexistent in France. Yet, a little more than a year after the 1955 release of *Lolita* in France, the French government ordered that its publication be stopped. While the ban was soon lifted, the end of Girodias's publishing career—at least within his native country—was imminent. In an article by Stephanie Harrington for the *Village Voice,* Girodias described the French government under Charles de Gaulle in the 1960s as an outgrowth of the country's delayed industrial revolution: "A new industrial bourgeoisie [had] come into power," the publisher commented, "and . . . created a regime which I can only describe as a soft fascism."

By 1964 sixty of the books Girodias had published were banned by the French government. Fined thousands of dollars and sentenced to several jail terms that were eventually suspended, he saw his publishing activities in France come to a virtual halt. In addition, with a decline in censorship in the United States, the need for an avant-garde publisher like Olympia diminished as well. As Girodias put it in his interview with Newquist, "Censorship always helps sell a book." In 1967 Girodias relocated to New York in order to publish books directly in the States. At this time he established Freeway Press.

Girodias's writings reflect the ideals embraced by his work as a publisher. His penchant for justice and freedom of expression led him to co-author the 1959 volume *The Black Diaries,* an account of Irish insurgent Roger Casement's execution by the British in 1916. Appointed a British consul in the Congo and in South America during the early 1900s, Casement openly denounced the colonial system that had been established in those regions by Belgium and England. Initiated under the guise of progress and humanitarianism, colonialism brought prosperity to the British and Belgian economies at the expense of African and South American natives who were forced to work under inhuman conditions for the European imperialists. Casement documented his findings in two papers, thereby exposing the system of exploitation and, as Girodias related to Newquist, "caus[ing] the world to realize clearly, for the first time, what crimes were being committed in the name of civilization."

After resigning from his position as British consul, Casement joined the Irish Nationalist movement in 1913. Three years later, while trying to persuade Irish leaders to terminate plans for their Easter Sunday rebellion, Casement was arrested and indicted by the British government as a conspirator in the uprising. The introduction of Casement's private diaries into the ensuing trial revealed his homosexuality, a factor that Girodias believes squelched any chances for a reprieve. Casement was hanged in 1916.

Reflecting on his interest in the Casement affair and his presentation of the facts surrounding the case in *The Black Diaries,* Girodias proclaimed in *Conversations:* "There is something frightening in the fact that a superlatively virtuous society, like the post-Victorian, can destroy a man so easily just because his sexual patterns vary from the average."

In the late 1960s, when Girodias was in need of money, he was able to raise fifteen thousand dollars in a single day by promising to write his memoirs.

The resulting manuscript, published in English translation as *The Frog Prince* in 1980, was projected to be the first of three volumes of autobiography to be collected in *Une Journee sur la terre.* Chronicling the first twenty-one years of his life, Girodias sets his journey towards manhood against the political turbulence in France that ended with the occupation of the country by the Germans in 1940. Most critics found the book to be a candid, well-written, insightful, and sometimes comical document, not the explicit account of past sexual exploits that might be expected of an alleged pornographer. In fact, Girodias admits in the book to falling hopelessly in love with a resolute theosophist committed to celibacy. When he finally did lose his virginity—at the age of twenty to an earthy Parisian waitress—the inexperienced author put into practice what he had vicariously learned about sexual technique from censored literature.

In an article for the *New York Times,* Christopher Lehmann-Haupt asserted, "There's a lot more to *The Frog Prince* than sexual frustration," and added that Girodias "comes across as a happy mixture of mooncalf and confidence man, of misfit and boulevardier." But *The Frog Prince* is also a testament to a troubled young life: it depicts the author's strained relationship with his parents, his rebellious years in school, his world travels, the stifling effects of totalitarian rule, and his failed suicide attempt. Richard Kuczkowski in *Library Journal* found the book to be "merely a loose cluster of events, pedestrian reflections, and refrains (his opposition to the state and all bourgeois institutions, developing erotic life, attraction to esoteric movements). It does not sparkle with insight into the people and events of the time." James R. Mellows, writing in the *New York Times Book Review,* suggested that the book "is full of redeeming social significance" and is, "in its way, a sharp indictment of French politics between the two World Wars."

While Girodias was quoted by Popkin as stating, "I am an active and conscious pornographer," he later told Newquist that he objects to the term "pornography . . . because it has a purely emotional meaning." Girodias viewed eroticism as a distinctly human power, "perhaps the only force of evolution in man," he asserted in *Conversations.* In the same interview, he further explained: "What distinguishes the amoeba's way of life from our own . . . is that the energies of the amoeba are directed toward the survival of the species, whereas our outlook includes desire, ambition, art, conquest; we want to absorb the universe, to make it our own. Sexual eroticism is an elementary expression of that drive."

BIOGRAPHICAL/CRITICAL SOURCES:

BOOKS

De St. Jorre, John, *Venus Bound: The Erotic Voyage of the Olympia Press and Its Writers,* Random House (New York City), 1996.

Kearney, Patrick J., *The Paris Olympia Press,* Black Spring Press (London), 1987.

Newquist, Roy, *Conversations,* Rand McNally, 1967.

PERIODICALS

Book World, January 11, 1981.

Library Journal, November 15, 1980.

Los Angeles Times, December 2, 1980; December 11, 1980.

Los Angeles Times Book Review, December 21, 1980.

New York Times, August 24, 1967.

New York Times Book Review, December 21, 1980, p. 8.

Village Voice, May 4, 1967.

OBITUARIES:

PERIODICALS

Los Angeles Times, July 5, 1990.

New York Times, July 5, 1990.

Publishers Weekly, July 27, 1990.

Washington Post, July 6, 1990.*

* * *

GODDARD, Kenneth (William) 1946-

PERSONAL: Born July 6, 1946, in San Diego, CA; son of Joseph William (a vocational education director) and Bernice Elizabeth (Cahoon) Goddard; married Gena Shitara (a laboratory technician), June 22, 1968; children: Michelle Suni. *Education:* Attended University of California at San Diego, 1964-65; University of California, Riverside, B.S., 1968; California State University, Los Angeles, M.A., 1971.

ADDRESSES: *Home*—Oakton, VA. *Office*—Division of Law Enforcement, U.S. Fish and Wildlife Service, P.O. Box 28006, Washington, DC 20005.

CAREER: Riverside County Sheriff's Office Crime Laboratory, Riverside County, CA, criminalist I (forensic scientist), 1968-69; San Bernardino County Sheriff's Office Crime Laboratory, San Bernardino County, CA, criminalist II (deputy sheriff), 1969-72; Huntington Beach Police Department, Huntington Beach, CA, chief criminalist and supervisor of scientific investigation bureau, 1972-79; U.S. Fish and Wildlife Service, Washington, DC, chief of forensic science, 1979—. Technical consultant to and writer for the Police Sciences Institute in Newport Beach, CA, 1975—.

MEMBER: American Academy of Forensic Sciences (fellow), American Society of Crime Laboratory Directors (charter member).

WRITINGS:

NOVELS

Balefire, Bantam (New York City), 1983.
Alchemist, Bantam, 1984.
Prey, Tor Books (New York City), 1992.
Wildfire, Forge (New York City), 1994.
Cheater, Forge, 1996.
Double Blind, Forge, 1997.

NONFICTION

Crime Scene Investigation (nonfiction), Reston (Reston, VA), 1977.
(With Jeff Cope) *Weaponless Control* (nonfiction), C. C Thomas (Springfield, IL), 1979.

OTHER

Contributor to *Police Chief* magazine.

SIDELIGHTS: Termed a "carnage-sodden thriller" by reviewer Curt Suplee in the *Washington Post, Balefire,* Kenneth Goddard's first novel, deals with an international cabal's scheme to sabotage the 1984 Olympics in Los Angeles. The plot is code-named Balefire, and it is set in motion when a terrorist named Thanatos begins committing random butcheries in the city of Huntington Beach, California, not far from Los Angeles. Critics contend that he single-handedly nearly paralyzes the police force before detective sergeant Walter Anderson, obsessed with stopping Thanatos, organizes a group of likeminded colleagues to eliminate the terrorist, even if it means breaking the law themselves. Goddard told the *Washington Post* that he wrote the pro-police story "for the citizen to read and understand why cops get so heavy sometimes, how basically good people can be driven beyond their normal limits."

Goddard created a fictional alter ego with Henry Lightstone, the protagonist of *Prey, Wildfire,* and *Double Blind.* Goddard is the head of a unique wildlife forensics laboratory run by the U.S. Fish and Wildlife Service in Ashland, Oregon; he and his staff work to enforce international, federal, and state laws regarding wildlife. Henry Lightstone is also a member of the Fish and Wildlife Service. Once a homicide detective in San Diego, he now works undercover in Anchorage, Alaska. In his first adventure, *Prey,* Lightstone copes with hunters who believe it is their right to go after endangered animals. Newgate Callendar, reviewing the book in the *New York Times,* noted that it was "a rather unbelievable plot" featuring a cartoonishly heroic team of "good guys" pitted against an international group of hit men. Callendar called the story "fun in an idiotic kind of way" and advised that the author "supplies enough heavy action from beginning to end to keep the reader amused."

In *Wildfire,* Goddard matches Lightstone against a sinister gang of international industrialists, the real-life, ultraradical environmentalist group Earth First!, and a band of eco-terrorists known as the Wildfire Conspiracy, which plots to set huge wildfires in the Sequoia and Yellowstone National Parks. A *Publishers Weekly* writer found this thriller "overblown" and stated that it resembles "both a weapons catalogue and an oversized comic strip." Still, the reviewer concluded, "the tale has a blow-'er-all-to-hell kind of liveliness." *Double Blind,* Lightstone's next adventure, featured "nonstop antics" played out by "industrialist archvillains, congressional caricatures, potbellied militiamen, rogue Army Ranger-Killers-for-hire, undercover FBI agents, Bigfoot and wisecracking Fish and Wildlife swat teams," related another *Publishers Weekly* contributor. A seductive witch with a pet panther, some mythical beasts and a blind fortune-teller who rides a moped round out the cast. Melissa Kuzma Rockicki, reviewing the book for *Library Journal,* termed it an "amusing, fast-paced thriller replete with bizarre characters and outrageous situations."

Goddard once told *CA:* "My primary interests, aside from enjoying life in Virginia with my wife and daughter, involve the direct application of scientific principles and technologies to problems of law enforcement; that is, putting criminal types who prey on others out of commission. I suspect that my writing will continue to reflect this interest for some considerable time period.

"In terms of reading and writing fiction, I most enjoy reading authors who make an effort to place their characters in realistic situations and to provide them with real-life personalities, vocabularies, tools, weapons, and the like. When I am reading an otherwise thoroughly intriguing book, nothing disappoints me more than to suddenly come across a piece of technology (for example, weaponry) that simply does not or could not work or exist in the manner described. As such, I hope to make my fiction enticingly believable, even if the technology is derived solely from imagination."

BIOGRAPHICAL/CRITICAL SOURCES:

PERIODICALS

Library Journal, August, 1997, p. 128.
New York Times, October 11, 1992.
Publishers Weekly, October 24, 1994, p. 53; April 15, 1996, p. 50; September 22, 1997, p. 68.
Washington Post, May 19, 1983.

* * *

GODDARD, Robert (William) 1954-

PERSONAL: Born November 13, 1954, in Fareham, Hampshire, England; son of William James (a civil servant) and Lilian Margaret (Street) Goddard; married Vaunda North (a local government officer), September 14, 1984. *Education:* Peterhouse, Cambridge, B.A., 1976, M.A., 1980; University of Exeter, Postgraduate Certificate in Education, 1977. *Religion:* Anglican.

ADDRESSES: Home—Winchester, England. *Agent*—The Chambers, Chelsea Harbour, London SW10 0XF, England.

CAREER: Devon County Council, Devon, England, educational administrator, 1978-87; full-time writer, 1987—.

AWARDS, HONORS: Booker Prize nomination, 1986, for *Past Caring.*

WRITINGS:

NOVELS

Past Caring, R. Hale (London), 1986, St. Martin's (New York City), 1987.
In Pale Battalions (Literary Guild alternate selection), Poseidon (New York City), 1988.
Painting the Darkness, Poseidon, 1989.
Into the Blue, Poseidon, 1991.
Debt of Dishonour, Poseidon, 1992.
Out of the Sun, Holt (New York City), 1996.
Beyond Recall, Holt, 1998.

OTHER

Contributor of articles to *Illustrated London News, Hampshire Magazine,* and *Writer's Monthly.*

ADAPTATIONS: Into the Blue was adapted for film in the United Kingdom.

SIDELIGHTS: British writer Robert Goddard is esteemed for his skill in creating intriguing and suspenseful narratives. Noted for their richly textured plots, enigmatic characters, and shadowy English settings, Goddard's novels have been compared to those of revered modern romance author Daphne du Maurier.

Goddard's first book, *Past Caring,* depicts the efforts of Martin Radford, a young history graduate, to uncover information on the life of Edwin Strafford, a controversial political figure of Edwardian England. Martin's research is funded by a wealthy South African who, after stumbling upon Strafford's memoirs, wishes to know more about his abrupt resignation from the British cabinet and his truncated romance with Elizabeth Latimer, an English suffragist. Martin eventually uncovers a morass of intrigue, corruption, and murder in Strafford's past and discovers that he himself is remotely connected to the man; Martin's estranged wife is Elizabeth's granddaughter. The interweaving of plots prompted reviewer Alan Bell in the *Los Angeles Times Book Review* to criticize *Past Caring* for being "rather overambitiously conceived. It falls between being a straight novel in which character and motive are the prime target, and a mystery in which the conundrum and its unraveling mean that plot increasingly takes over from the niceties of individual character delineation." Alan Ryan in the *Washington Post Book World,* though, called the novel "an immensely complex tale, with mysteries and suspense in both past and present, but Goddard has remarkable narrative skill and the story never becomes unwieldy." Further applauding the novel's subtle cynicism about the truth of recorded history, Ryan proclaimed *Past Caring* "one of the best novels I've read in a long, long time. . . . The ideas are challenging, and the emotions tug at the heart. I loved every one of its 500 pages."

In his second and third novels Goddard again chooses historical England as a backdrop for stories of mystery and suspense. Set during and after World War I, *In Pale Battalions* chronicles three generations of the Hallows family. The Hallows's history is related to Penelope of the third generation by her mother who, as a result of the family's improprieties, was raised as an orphan by her malicious step-grandmother. The book was praised for its complex plot, multiple narrative voices, and its ability to shock and surprise the reader. In *Painting the Darkness,* Goddard's third novel, Victorian England is the setting for the Davenall family saga. The family is troubled by a suspicious character named James Norton who claims he is the missing Sir James Davenall, a man whose disappearance eleven years earlier was designated a suicide. The plot is complicated by the conflicting opinions of those who knew Sir James Davenall; Davenall's mother, brother, and cousin call Norton an imposter, but the woman Davenall was to marry before his disappearance believes Norton's assertions. Although Julian Symons in the *Washington Post Book World* complained that "less than a quarter of the way through the book, . . . Goddard abandons near-fact for complete fiction, and a Victorian sobriety of style for high Gothic," the reviewer noted that "the Victorian background is solidly and carefully rendered" and "the case of Norton versus Davenall, by which Norton seeks to have his claim accepted, has very clever turns in it." Philippa Toomey in the London *Times* thought *Painting the Darkness* to have "all the ingredients of a first-class melodrama" and deemed it an "engaging and satisfying novel."

Into the Blue, Goddard's fourth book, was well-received by *Los Angeles Times* contributor Carolyn See who described it as "a suspenseful romance, with clue after clue after clue, and hidden pasts, and strings of murders, but all of it is very smart, very complex—profound without being pretentious." The story focuses on Harry Barnett, a middle-aged Englishman whose dull existence is enlivened when the beautiful young Heather Mallender comes to vacation on the Greek island where Harry works as a caretaker. Shortly after the two become friends, Heather mysteriously vanishes while sight-seeing; the rest of the novel deals with Harry's search for clues to her whereabouts. As in Goddard's other stories, the plot eventually reveals numerous twists and turns and an intricate network of connections among the characters. The complexity of *Into the Blue* elicited praise from See who suggested that the book is "fun to read as an intellectual puzzle."

Harry Barnett was again the lead character in Goddard's 1996 novel, *Out of the Sun.* A *Publishers Weekly* reviewer reported: "Using booze to shut out the pain of personal failure, the ineptly idealistic and ever-chivalrous antihero is stunned back into reality" when an anonymous phone caller informs him that he is the father of a nationally known, 33-year-old mathematical genius. This long-lost son is in an apparently irreversible coma, however, following an insulin overdose. Barnett's efforts to save his child lead him through a maze of sinister schemes in the corporate and academic worlds, in what the *Publishers Weekly* writer called "a harrowing odyssey" that ends with "a heartstopping climactic confrontation." *Booklist* contributor Joanne Wilkinson approved: "This well-written thriller offers off-beat subject matter and a finely etched portrait of Harry, a tough old bird whose hands are never quite steady but whose mind is lightning quick." Edwin B. Burgess in *Library Journal* deemed it "by turns scary and intelligent."

Goddard again drew positive reviews with his 1998 offering, *Beyond Recall.* In this novel, the author uses the elements of the classic English mystery—the grand old estate, a disputed family fortune, blackmail, and murder—to create what a *Publishers Weekly* writer termed "an absorbing suspense novel with a modern sensibility." The plot concerns Chris Napier, who returns to his family's ancestral home after years of estrangement. Once there, he begins investigating a 34-year-old murder case. "Goddard intricately interweaves the life stories of three generations," noted the reviewer, and "is meticulous with background details and local color. . . . His characters, with their good manners and dark secrets, seem to have stepped out of a Daphne Du Maurier novel." Marilyn Stasio of the *New York Times* found *Beyond Recall* "evocative," and noted: "There's an elegant arc to Goddard's fluid style, which gracefully orchestrates the story over its broad time span and through the ambiguous testimony of its complex characters."

Goddard once told *CA:* "I find the roots for my writing in my preoccupation with the impact of the past on the present. I was inspired to take up writing by a growing dissatisfaction with much contemporary literature in which I detect a growing rift between technique and meaning. By wedding richness of language and intricacy of plot to narrative drive and dense imagery, I seek to heal that rift."

BIOGRAPHICAL/CRITICAL SOURCES:

PERIODICALS

Booklist, April 15, 1997, p. 1404; April 15, 1998, p. 1381.
Library Journal, May 1, 1997, p. 139; April 15, 1998, p. 112.
Los Angeles Times, January 28, 1991.
Los Angeles Times Book Review, January 25, 1987.
New York Times, January 14, 1987, section C, p. 24; November 13, 1988, section 7, p. 34; May 10, 1992; June 21, 1998.
Publishers Weekly, May 5, 1997, p. 197; April 20, 1998, p. 48.
Times (London), August 19, 1989.
Washington Post Book World, February 1, 1987; August 27, 1989.

* * *

GOLDBERG, Lee 1962-

PERSONAL: Born in 1962.

ADDRESSES: *Agent*—c/o St. Martin's Press, Inc., 175 Fifth Ave., New York, NY 10010.

CAREER: Writer. Television scriptwriter and producer.

WRITINGS:

Unsold Television Pilots: 1955 through 1988, McFarland & Company (Jefferson, NC), 1990.
Unsold TV Pilots: The Almost Complete Guide to Everything You Never Saw on TV, 1955-1990, Carol Publications Group (Secaucus, NJ), 1991.
Television Series Revivals: Sequels or Remakes of Cancelled Shows, McFarland & Company, 1993.
(With others) *Science Fiction Filmmaking in the 1980s: Interviews with Actors, Directors, Producers, and Writers,* McFarland & Company, 1995.
The Dreamweavers: Interviews with Fantasy Filmmakers of the 1980s, McFarland & Company, 1995.
My Gun Has Bullets (fiction), St. Martin's (New York City), 1995.
Beyond the Beyond (fiction), St. Martin's, 1997.

Also author of *The Jewish Student's Guide to American Colleges* and *The New Jewish Student's Guide to American Colleges.* Contributor of novels, under pseudonym Ian Ludlow, to men's adventure series ".357 Vigilante," published by Pinnacle. Author of scripts for *Baywatch, SeaQuest, Spenser: For Hire, Cosby Mysteries,* and other television series.

SIDELIGHTS: Television scriptwriter and producer Lee Goldberg's first novel, *My Gun Has Bullets,* relies on the author's intimate knowledge of behind-the-scenes Hollywood garnered from his years writing scripts for *Baywatch* and other popular television series. When Los Angeles police officer Charlie Willis pulls over for speeding the aging star of a beloved, long-running television series about a grandmotherly type who solves mysteries, the actress shoots him in a blind rage. The network bribes Charlie with the starring role in a series of his own in exchange for his silence, but soon the dead bodies begin to mount as someone plants real bullets in Charlie's prop gun and he accidentally kills a fellow cast member. In the meantime, the production company that owns his show is taken over by the mob, which decides that one way to ensure good ratings is to kill off the competition. Charlie must perform some real detective work in order to keep his newfound career as a TV star alive.

Reviews of *My Gun Has Bullets* were mixed, with critics noting that Goldberg populates the story with broadly-drawn caricatures of such Hollywood stars as Angela Lansbury, whose mystery series garnered the highest ratings for its Sunday-night time slot for nearly a decade, and Bruce Willis, whose heroes have brought in hundreds of millions of dollars for the studios that hire him. However, the effectiveness of the resulting satire was questioned by some as too broadly drawn. "This brash satire of television fare is as empty as the idiocy it aims to prick," complained the reviewer for *Publishers Weekly.* Others were less difficult to please on this score. While *Entertainment Weekly* reviewer Gene Lyons admitted that it may be impossible to lampoon the world of television without "sinking to an unbelievable level of crassness," he also observed that "*My Gun Has Bullets* is apt to make you cackle like a sitcom laugh track." *Booklist* contributor Thomas Gaughan was also enthusiastic, calling *My Gun Has Bullets* "a very funny novel" that is "a pinch of Carl Hiaasen, a dash of Donald Westlake, and a heaping portion of avarice and inanity Hollywood style. It's boffo!"

Goldberg's next novel, *Beyond the Beyond,* drew rave reviews from another *Publishers Weekly* critic, who also expressed appreciation for the author's earlier novel: "As in his riotous . . . *My Gun Has Bullets,* TV writer/producer Goldberg . . . once again bites the hand that feeds him, laughing all the while." The title refers to a space adventure show which, much like the real-life television program *Star Trek,* failed during its network run only to become a huge success in syndication. When a British billionaire who runs a pornography empire launches a new television network, he decides to revive the *Beyond the Beyond* with a new cast. But those involved with the new series are soon targeted for a series of murders. Charlie Willis is again called in to work on the case, and his suspects include rabid fans, a flesh-eating Hollywood agent, and the actor who portrayed the starship captain in the original series. "Everyone betrays everyone, and most are mowed down like crabgrass in this lunatic send-up," stated the *Publishers Weekly* reviewer. "Goldberg knows the biz and has slapped his large, exotic cast of characters into scenes that read like transcripts of network development meetings." The reviewer further praised Goldberg's "spunk and inspired silliness." Benjamin Svetkey commented in *Entertainment Weekly:* "This sharp roman a clef goes where no Hollywood satire has gone before . . . smacking of a certain je ne sais Trek. . . . It's a stingingly funny novel."

BIOGRAPHICAL/CRITICAL SOURCES:

PERIODICALS

Booklist, March 1, 1995, p. 1178.

Entertainment Weekly, March 31, 1995, p. 57; April 25, 1997, p. 65.

Publishers Weekly, February 6, 1995, p. 78; February 24, 1997, p. 65.

* * *

GOLDEN, Arthur 1924-

PERSONAL: Born August 22, 1924, in New York, NY; son of Harry and Gussie (Leavitt) Golden; married Bernice P. Landau, June 3, 1956; children: Susan. *Education:* New York University, B.A., 1947, Ph.D., 1962; Columbia University, M.A., 1948.

ADDRESSES: *Home*—5 Stockbridge Ave., Suffern, NY 10901. *Office*—Department of English, City College of the City University of New York, New York, NY 10031.

CAREER: New York University, New York City, instructor in English, 1959-63; City College of the City University of New York, New York City, instructor, 1963-64, assistant professor, 1965-69, associate professor, 1970-73, professor of English, 1974—. Trustee, Walt Whitman Birthplace Association, Huntington, NY 1967—.

MEMBER: American Studies Association, Bibliographical Society of America, Modern Language Association of America, Long Island Historical Society, Bibliographical Society of University of Virginia.

AWARDS, HONORS: National Endowment for the Humanities grant, 1970-71; Faculty Research Foundation Award, City University of New York, 1970-71.

WRITINGS:

(Editor) *Walt Whitman's Blue Book: The 1860-61 "Leaves of Grass" Containing His Manuscript Additions and Revisions,* New York Public Library (New York City), Volume I: *Facsimile,* 1968, Volume II: *Textual Analysis,* 1968.

(Editor) *Walt Whitman: A Collection of Criticism,* McGraw (New York City), 1974.

Memoirs of a Geisha (novel), Knopf (New York City), 1997.

Contributor of articles and reviews to *PMLA, Bulletin of the New York Public Library, Literature and Psychology, Papers of the Bibliographical Society of America, McGraw-Hill Encyclopedia of World Biography,* and to other publications. Member of editorial board, *Literature and Psychology.*

SIDELIGHTS: Arthur Golden's novel *Memoirs of a Geisha* is a fictionalized autobiography of a famous Japanese geisha. Beginning life in a poor fishing village in the 1920s, Sayuri is eventually sold by her desperate, impoverished father to a training school for geishas—professional "escorts" who learn to please their high-class clients in many ways. Over the years, she endures the cruelty of the head geisha and the humiliations of a life with few choices; she also enjoys the rarefied world inhabited by the women of her class. Eventually, in a traditionally happy ending, she even becomes the mistress of a man she truly loves.

Many commentators noted that one of the most remarkable things about *Memoirs of a Geisha* is the way that Golden, a man raised in a completely alien time and place, was able to capture so convincingly the voice and outlook of his subject in this, his first novel. Michiko Kakutani in the *New York Times* asserted that the book "holds the readers attention, so intimate and knowing is its portrayal of Sayuri's inner life. In recounting her story, Mr. Golden gives us not only a richly sympathetic portrait of a woman, but also a finely observed picture of an anomalous and largely vanished world. He has made an impressive and unusual debut." Joanne Wilkinson concurred in *Booklist:* "Revealing both the aesthetic delights and the unending cruelty that underlie the exotic world of the geisha, Golden melds sparkling historical fiction with a compelling coming-of-age story. Popular fiction at its best."

BIOGRAPHICAL/CRITICAL SOURCES:

PERIODICALS

Booklist, September 1, 1997, p. 7.
Kirkus Reviews, August 15, 1997, p. 1240.
Library Journal, August, 1997, p. 128.
New York Times Book Review, October 5, 1997; October 14, 1997.
Publishers Weekly, July 28, 1997, p. 49.

* * *

GRAHAM, Robert
See HALDEMAN, Joe (William)

* * *

GREENGROIN, Artie
See BROWN, Harry (Peter McNab, Jr.)

GRIMSON, Todd 1952-

PERSONAL: Born February 2, 1952, in Seattle, WA. *Education:* Attended School of Visual Arts.

ADDRESSES: *Agent*—Aaron M. Priest, 122 East 42nd St., Suite 3902, New York, NY 10168.

CAREER: Writer.

AWARDS, HONORS: Grant from Oregon Institute of Literary Arts.

WRITINGS:

NOVELS

Within Normal Limits, Random House (New York City), 1987.
Stainless, HarperPrism (New York City), 1996.
Brand New Cherry Flavor, HarperPrism, 1996.

Contributor of stories to periodicals, including *Quarterly, Bomb, Between C & D,* and *Splash.*

SIDELIGHTS: With *Stainless* and *Brand New Cherry Flavor,* Todd Grimson has positioned himself as a writer of unusual horror stories, marked by a knowing, jaundiced tone that has led some reviewers to describe him as the Bret Easton Ellis of the macabre. Joe Queenan, writing in the *New York Times Book Review,* calls *Stainless* "perhaps the first mass-market Generation X vampire thriller," while *New Statesman* critic Charles Shaar Murray pronounces *Brand New Cherry Flavor* "pierced, tattooed, mirror-shaded." A *Publishers Weekly* contributor, also discussing *Brand New Cherry Flavor,* proclaims Grimson "one of the more inventive new writers probing the dark side of contemporary America."

Grimson's first novel, *Within Normal Limits,* draws on the author's experience as an interviewer in an emergency room. Darrell Patterson, the main character, is an emergency room physician addicted to a variety of pills and the sensation of control they help him to maintain in a stressful atmosphere. A man of practical action, Patterson likes to imagine himself at his best, even in the worst of situations. In a *Chicago Tribune* excerpt of the book, for instance, he says: "I might actually enjoy a war or some other big disaster. . . . Certainly I'd be really, fully alive in my station, my function." When Patterson temporarily gives up the drugs that numb him, he must face his personal problems, such as his wife's unfaithfulness and his dislike for his young son. Eventually, however, he returns to his habit and his falsely capable, robotic behavior, leading *Chicago Tribune* contributor Joseph Coates to characterize *Within Normal Limits* as "a coolly brilliant casebook of a man in despair whose principal, most hopeless patient is himself."

Stainless is an unconventional novel about a subject that has long fascinated writers and readers—vampires. Set in Los Angeles, it centers on an oddly gentle vampire named Justine, who kills only reluctantly, and her relationship with a former rock musician, Keith, who serves as her caretaker and errand boy. The two are gradually falling in love, but their world is disrupted by David, a brutal vampire with a vendetta against Justine. *Los Angeles Times Book Review* critic David L. Ulin describes *Stainless* as a "post-modern vampire story" but also much more. He deems it "a vibrant, edgy love story that takes the conventions of vampire fiction and subtly transforms them . . . Grimson tweaks our preconceptions with the literary equivalent of a knowing wink." For instance, his vampires are not afraid of crosses, and they enjoy watching old horror films on TV. What Ulin finds most interesting about the book is the portrait of Justine, "the vampire with a soul and a conscience." He observes, "The notion of a vampire with a conscience is not a new one, but by making it so essential to his story Grimson humanizes Justine in a unique and startling way." Queenan, though, voices reservations about this "Gothic slacker novel"; he notes that it can be read as a satire of the entertainment industry or of modern American life in general, but considers it marred by cliches. Ultimately, he concludes, *Stainless* is "all sizzle, no stake."

The supernatural and the L.A. showbiz scene mix again in *Brand New Cherry Flavor.* This novel's protagonist is a struggling young actress, Lisa, who engages the services of a witch doctor to gain revenge on a producer who broke his promise to make her an assistant director. There are complications, however: Lisa develops magical powers, but becomes implicated in several murders. There is much more to the book than this, though, according to some critics. "Any horror hack could take that outline and generate a thoroughly unmemorable novel," remarks Murray. "However, Grimson is made of sterner stuff. He ignites this ho-hum plot with the parodic verve of his writing, the gimlet-eyed savagery of his observation, an engaging flair for both social farce and toe-curling splatter, and a formidable gift for juggling the two when they blur." Murray particularly praises Grimson's hip, satirical view of the film business, noting that the book "is a welter of killer zombies, S&M sex, designer drugs . . . and post-punk movie-world gossip-*a-clef.*" A *Times Literary Supplement* reviewer thinks Grimson spends too much time on minor characters and leaves a few loose ends in his story, but on the whole "has produced a novel of vitality and promise."

BIOGRAPHICAL/CRITICAL SOURCES:

PERIODICALS

Chicago Tribune, August 27, 1987.

Los Angeles Times Book Review, August 2, 1987; April 28, 1996, p. 8.

New Statesman, December, 1996, p. 55.

New Yorker, August 10, 1987.

New York Times Book Review, July 19, 1987; April 28, 1996, p. 38.

Observer (London), November 10, 1996, p. 18.

Publishers Weekly, October 7, 1996, p. 63.

Times Literary Supplement, December 20, 1996, p. 24.

Washington Post, April 15, 1996, p. C2.*

H

HALDEMAN, Joe (William) 1943-
(Robert Graham)

PERSONAL: Born June 9, 1943, in Oklahoma City, OK; son of Jack Carroll (a hospital administrator) and Lorena (Spivey) Haldeman; married Mary Gay Potter (a teacher), August 21, 1965. *Education:* University of Maryland, B.S., 1967; University of Iowa, M.F.A., 1975; also attended American University and University of Oklahoma. *Politics:* "Skeptic." *Religion:* "Skeptic." *Avocational interests:* Classical guitar, bicycling, woolgathering, strong drink, travel, gardening, astronomy, painting.

ADDRESSES: *Home and office*—5412 Northwest 14th Ave., Gainesville, FL 32605. *E-mail*—haldeman@mit.edu. *Agent*—Ralph Vicinanza, 111 Eighth Ave., #1501, New York, NY 10011.

CAREER: Freelance writer, 1970—. University of Iowa, teaching assistant, 1975; former editor of *Astronomy;* has taught writing at University of North Florida and other schools; Massachusetts Institute of Technology, adjunct professor, 1983—. *Military service:* U.S. Army, 1967-69; became combat engineer; served in Vietnam; wounded in combat; received Purple Heart and other medals.

MEMBER: Authors Guild, Science Fiction Writers of America (treasurer, 1970-72; chair of Grievance Committee, 1979-80; president, 1992-94), National Space Society, Writers Guild, Poets and Writers.

AWARDS, HONORS: Hugo Award, World Science Fiction Convention, 1975, Nebula Award, Science Fiction Writers of America, 1975, and Locus Award, *Locus* magazine, 1975, all for *The Forever War;* Hugo Award, World Science Fiction Convention, 1976, and Locus Award, *Locus* magazine, 1976, both for best short story, for "Tricentennial"; Ditmar Award, 1976; Galaxy Award, 1978, for *Mindbridge;* Rhysling Award, Science Fiction Poetry Association, 1984, 1990; Hugo Award, World Science Fiction Convention, 1991, for the novella *The Hemingway Hoax;* Nebula Award, Science Fiction Writers of America, 1993, and World Fantasy Award, World Fantasy Convention, 1993, both for "Graves"; Hugo Award, World Science Fiction Convention, 1995, Nebula Award, Science Fiction Writers of America, 1995, and Locus Award, *Locus* magazine, 1995, all for "None So Blind"; Homer Award, 1995; Hugo Award, World Science Fiction Convention, 1998, and Campbell Award, University of Kansas, for *Forever Peace.*

WRITINGS:

SCIENCE FICTION NOVELS

The Forever War, St. Martin's (New York City), 1974.
Mindbridge, St. Martin's, 1976.
Planet of Judgment (a Star Trek novel), Bantam (New York City), 1977.
All My Sins Remembered, St. Martin's, 1977.
(Author of introduction) Robert A. Heinlein, *Double Star,* Gregg (Boston, MA), 1978.
World without End: A Star Trek Novel, Bantam, 1979.
(With brother, Jack C. Haldeman) *There Is No Darkness,* Ace (New York City), 1983.
Tool of the Trade, Morrow (New York City), 1987.
Buying Time, introduction by James Gunn, illustrated by Bryn Barnard, Easton Press (Norwalk, CT), 1989, published in Britain as *The Long Habit of Living,* New English Library (London).

The Hemingway Hoax (novella), Morrow, 1990.
Forever Peace, Ace Books, 1997.

"WORLDS" TRILOGY; SCIENCE FICTION NOVELS

Worlds: A Novel of the Near Future, Viking (New York City), 1981.
Worlds Apart, Viking, 1983.
Worlds Enough and Time: The Conclusion of the Worlds Trilogy, Morrow, 1992.

ADVENTURE NOVELS; UNDER PSEUDONYM ROBERT GRAHAM

Attar's Revenge, Pocket Books (New York City), 1975.
War of Nerves, Pocket Books, 1975.

WAR NOVELS

War Year, Holt Reinhart (New York City), 1972, original version, Pocket Books, 1978.
1968: A Novel, Hodder and Stoughton (London, England), 1994, Morrow, 1995.

SHORT STORY COLLECTIONS

Infinite Dreams, St. Martin's, 1978.
Dealing in Futures: Stories, Viking Press, 1985.
More than the Sum of His Parts, Pulphouse (Eugene, WA), 1991.
Vietnam and Other Alien Worlds (with essays and poetry), New England Science Fiction Association Press (Framingham, MA), 1993.
None So Blind, Morrow, 1996.

PLAYS

The Devil His Due (produced at the University of Iowa Film Workshop), published in *Fantastic* (New York City), August, 1974.
The Moon and Marcek, published in *Vertex* (Los Angeles), August, 1974.
The Forever War, produced in Chicago, 1983.

EDITOR

Cosmic Laughter: Science Fiction for the Fun of It, Holt Reinhart, 1974.
Study War No More: A Selection of Alternatives, St. Martin's, 1977.
Nebula Award Stories 17, Holt Reinhart, 1983.
(With Martin H. Greenberg and Charles G. Waugh) *Body Armor: 2000,* Ace, 1986.
(With Greenberg and Waugh) *Supertanks,* Ace, 1987.
The Best of John Brunner, Ballantine (New York City), 1988.
(With Greenberg and Waugh) *Spacefighters,* Ace, 1988.

OTHER

Work included in numerous "best of" anthologies, including *The Best from Galaxy,* edited by Ejler Jakobbsen, Universal-Award, 1972; *Best SF: 1972,* edited by Harry Harrison and Brian Aldiss, Putnam, 1973; *The Best Science Fiction of the Year—1972,* edited by Terry Carr, Ballantine, 1973; *Best SF: 1973,* edited by Harrison and Aldiss, Putnam, 1974; *The Best from Galaxy,* Volume 3, Award, 1975; *Nebula Award Stories 11,* Harper, 1975; *Best Science Fiction Stories,* Dutton, 1977; *Nebula Award Stories XII,* Harper, 1977; *Annual World's Best SF,* DAW, 1978; *The Best of Destinies,* Ace, 1981; *Best SF Stories of the Year,* Dutton, 1980; *Best of OMNI Science Fiction,* 1980; *Vicious Circles: The Best Modern Sestinas,* 1994; *The Year's Best Science Fiction, Eleventh Annual,* St. Martin's Press, 1994; and *Year's Best Science Fiction,* edited by David Hartwell, HarperPrism, 1996.

Contributor to major science fiction anthologies, including *Orbit Eleven,* edited by Damon Knight, Putnam, 1971; *Showcase,* edited by Roger Elwood, Harper, 1973; *Analog 9,* edited by Ben Bova, Doubleday, 1973; *Combat SF,* edited by Gordon Dickson, Doubleday, 1975; *Frights,* edited by Kirby McCauley, St. Martin's, 1976; *Close Up: New Worlds,* St. Martin's, 1977; *Time of Passage,* Taplinger, 1978; *The Endless Frontier,* Ace Books, 1979; *The Road to SF 3,* Mentor, 1979; *Thieve's World,* edited by Robert Asprin, Ace Books, 1979; *The Future at War,* Ace Books, 1980; and *Dark Forces,* edited by McCauley, Viking, 1980.

Contributor of numerous short stories and articles to *Analog, Galaxy, Isaac Asimov's SF Adventures, Magazine of Fantasy and Science Fiction, Omni, Playboy,* and other publications.

Haldeman's novels have been translated into numerous languages, including French, Italian, German, Dutch, Japanese, Hebrew, Spanish, Swedish, Russian, Greek, Czech, Bulgarian, and Korean.

SIDELIGHTS: In his award-winning science fiction novel *The Forever War,* Joe Haldeman combines his experiences as a soldier during the Vietnam War, in which he was severely wounded, with a realistic, scientifically-accurate presentation. The novel tells of a war that stretches across intergalactic distances and long periods of time, the soldiers involved traveling to remote battlefields via black holes. Because the soldiers travel at faster-than-light speeds, they age far slower than the civilians for whom they fight. This difference in relative age—the soldiers a few years older, their society centuries older—results in an alienation between the soldiers and the people they defend.

"Haldeman exercises his literary license," James Scott Hicks writes in the *Dictionary of Literary Biography,* "to comment on, and ultimately to expunge from his memory, America's last ground war [Vietnam]." Hicks points out that Haldeman's first novel, *War Year,* based on his army diaries, deals with the Vietnam fighting directly. "But the demon of Vietnam," Hicks writes, "was not exorcised from Haldeman's soul by writing [*War Year*], and front-line combat became the subject of . . . *The Forever War.*" Haldeman, Hicks believes, is particularly adept at presenting his "theme of quiet resentment felt by those waging war."

Because of his scientific training in physics and astronomy, Haldeman is particularly careful to present *The Forever War* as realistically and accurately as possible. "The technology involved in this interplanetary campaign," Martin Levin of the *New York Times Book Review* notes in his review of *The Forever War,* "is so sophisticated that the book might well have been accompanied by an operator's manual. But then, all the futuristic mayhem is plugged into human situations that help keep the extraterrestrial activity on a warm and even witty plane."

Among newer novelists in the field, Haldeman, Richard Geis of *Science Fiction Review* believes, "is one of the best realistic science fiction writers going; maybe *the* best." Hicks finds that "Haldeman confronts his readers with painful questions, but he asks them with no small literary skill and with careful attention to scientific credibility." "It's comforting to know," writes Algis Budrys of the *Magazine of Fantasy and Science Fiction,* "that the cadre of impressive talent among younger writers is not diminishing, and to think that people like Haldeman will be around for a long time to set high standards."

Haldeman's "Worlds" trilogy, published over a span of a dozen years, follows the exploits of Marianne O'Hara, who is, summarizes Michael Pavese in *Best Sellers,* "an intelligent, promiscuous (in space promiscuity is encouraged) New New York citizen." Born in space, she travels from her orbiting, manmade world to Earth, to engage in post-graduate studies at N.Y.U., in the first book, *Worlds: A Novel of the Near Future.* It details her adventures and misadventures on Twenty-second century Earth, a far poorer, more decadent, chaotic, and dangerous extension of contemporary society. It is a society rapidly nearing a total breakdown—which, by the denouement, it indeed has, with Marianne's space ship veritably riding the shockwave of nuclear devastation home to New New York. *Worlds Apart* details Marianne's career as an ambitious politician of the orbital worlds, who, thinking her former lover, Jeff Hawkings, is dead (he isn't) from the nuclear holocaust, takes a pair of husbands. In addition, the book not only tracks Jeff's career, now peddling medications to devolved Earth tribes, it includes, notes Charles Platt in *Washington Post,* "a grab-bag of extraneous notions in between: a Manson-worshipping death cult, a starship with an anti-matter drive, a formalized menage-a-trois, a hijacked space shuttle, an expedition into regressed Florida, a new science of behavioral conditioning, and more." In the final book, *Worlds Enough and Time,* Marianne, her two husbands and her cybernetic "twin sister," along with 10,000 other would-be colonists, venture forth in the starship *Newhome* to seek their destinies on an Earth-like planet in the Epsilon Eridani system. A *Publishers Weekly* reviewer lauded: "Haldeman shows his strengths here: the workings of *Newhome* are believably complex, the novel's scientific background is neither strained nor especially complicated, and the reader's attention is focused on O'Hara's character, her inner life and her interpersonal relationships."

In addition to the obvious recurring theme of war—both real and imagined—in many Haldeman's books, essayist Duncan Lunan notes another theme in the *St. James Guide to Science Fiction Writers.* Referring back to *The Forever War,* where the enemy aliens are controlled by a hive-mind, Lunan says, "*Mindbridge* was another examination of human contact with a hive-mind, while *All My Sins Remembered* was a damning indictment not merely of big government but also of the standard SF attitude toward individuality. SF used to be full of people who find out that they're really someone else (usually someone more powerful), and part of the problem in identifying with central characters is often they lack individuality." Says Lunan, "McGavin in *All My Sins Remembered* is a government agent, repeatedly given new identities through psychological conditioning and plastic surgery." Lunan adds, "he is an individual moved and controlled by an organisation which commands his loyalty but is beyond his control." The theme of individuals preyed upon and controlled by ultra-powerful agencies or corporate entities is also central to Haldeman's "Worlds" trilogy, as with the CIA and KGB in *Tool of the Trade,* and by the wealthy in *Buying Time.* And Sybil S. Steinberg says in *Publishers Weekly,* "Evoking painful nostalgia, . . . Haldeman uses bold language, powerful images and a graphic style to tell his emotional tale, in which concentrated, diary-like entries intensify the drama and despair."

Sue Martin, writing in *Los Angeles Times,* terms *The Hemingway Hoax* "A bright, short science fiction novel, . . . [this] quirky effort offers a unique solution to one of the enduring literary mysteries of our time: Just what DID happen to Ernest Hemingway's missing manuscripts, lost in 1922 at the Gare de Lyon in Paris?" She continues, "For Hemingway fans, Haldeman's answer is a hoot, and as different a theory as you can find." Marc Leepson, in a *Book World* review, described Haldeman's fictionalized but largely autobiographical *1968* as "a well-crafted, biting novel set in Vietnam."

Forever Peace is a followup novel to the problems raised in Haldeman's acclaimed *Forever War.* In 2043, an American-led alliance has been battling with the third-world, Ngumi confederation, primarily, on the alliance's part, with "soldierboys"—killing machines controlled by brain-linked "mechanics", among them, the protagonist, physicist Julian Class. Meanwhile, the Jupiter Project, the most ambitious scientific experiment of all time, circles Jupiter—Julian's lover, Amelia, discovers it may endanger not only our solar system, but the universe, in a new "Big Bang." Among other complications, their attempt to stop the disaster runs afoul of an influential Christian cult, the Hammer of God, dedicated to bringing on the Endtime. A *Publishers Weekly* reviewer concludes: "As always, Haldeman, a Vietnam vet, writes with intelligence and power about the horrors of war, and about humanity's seeming inability to overcome its violent tendencies."

A full interview with Haldeman appears in *Contemporary Authors New Revision Series,* Volume 6.

BIOGRAPHICAL/CRITICAL SOURCES:

BOOKS

Dictionary of Literary Biography, Volume 7: *Twentieth-Century American Science Fiction Writers,* Gale (Detroit, MI), 1981.

Gordon, Joan, *The Fiction of Joe Haldeman* (unpublished dissertation), 1981.

Gordon, Joan, *Joe Haldeman,* Starmont House (Mercer Island, WA), 1980.

St. James Guide to Science Fiction Writers, St. James Press (Detroit, MI), 1996.

PERIODICALS

Algol, summer-fall, 1977; summer-fall, 1978.

Analog, March, 1978; September, 1978; July, 1979; November, 1982, pp. 164-65; September, 1983, p. 164; March, 1984, p. 168; February, 1986, p. 182; December, 1986, p. 182; January, 1990, pp. 308-09.

Best Sellers, December, 1976; February, 1978.

Bloomsbury Review, January/February, 1996, pp. 3, 20.

Booklist, June 1, 1975.

Book World, July 2, 1995, p. C95.

Chicago Tribune, September 26, 1976; September 2, 1991, p. 10.

Chicago Tribune Book World, June 14, 1981.

Commonweal, October 27, 1972.

Destinies, November/December, 1978.

Foundation, May, 1978.

Futures, June, 1975.

Galaxy, December, 1976; March, 1978.

Library Journal, October 15, 1997, p. 97.

Los Angeles Times Book Review, October 30, 1983, p. 4; July 8, 1990, p. 9.

Magazine of Fantasy and Science Fiction, May, 1975; October, 1975; April, 1977; September, 1979; August, 1981, pp. 55-56; March, 1984, pp. 43-45.

New Republic, November 26, 1977.

New York Times Book Review, May 21, 1972; March 23, 1975; February 27, 1977; January 15, 1984, p. 29; February 10, 1985, p. 40; June 7, 1987, p. 18; July 2, 1989, p. 15; June 14, 1992, p. 24.

Observer (London), May 8, 1977.

Publishers Weekly, March 13, 1987, p. 70; December 7, 1990, p. 78; April 6, 1992, p. 54; April 17, 1995, p. 38; April 22, 1996, p. 64; August 25, 1997, p. 49.

Science Fiction Review, August, 1976; February, 1977; February, 1978.

Science Fiction Studies, vol. 21, 1994, pp. 238-40.
Starlog, vol. 17, 1978.
Thrust, summer, 1979.
Times Literary Supplement, July 8, 1977.
Washington Post Book World, April 26, 1981; May 13, 1990, p. 8; May 31, 1992, p. 6; July 2, 1995, p. 4.

* * *

HALL, Stephen S. 1951-

PERSONAL: Born October 28, 1951, in Cleveland, OH; son of Robert S. (in business) and Delores (a college administrator; maiden name, Albanese) Hall. *Education:* Beloit College, B.A. (with honors), 1973.

ADDRESSES: *Agent*—Melanie Jackson, Suite 1119, 250 West 57th Street, New York, NY 10107.

CAREER: *Washington Post,* Washington, DC, 1973-75, began as national desk news assistant, became sports reporter; *San Francisco Chronicle,* San Francisco, CA, general assignment reporter, 1978-79; *Science '86,* Washington, DC, contributing editor, 1983-86; *Hippocrates,* Sausalito, CA, contributing editor, 1986—. Freelance writer in Rome, Italy, 1975-77, and New York City, 1980—.

MEMBER: PEN American Center.

AWARDS, HONORS: Lowell Thomas Award, Society of American Travel Writers, 1988.

WRITINGS:

Invisible Frontiers: The Race to Synthesize a Human Gene, Atlantic Monthly Press, 1987.
Mapping the Next Millennium: The Discovery of New Geographies, Random House (New York City), 1992.
A Commotion in the Blood: Life, Death, and the Immune System, Holt (New York City), 1997.

Contributor of chapters to *Newton at the Bat,* Scribner, 1983; *Italian Americans: New Perspectives in Italian Immigration and Ethnicity,* Center for Migration Studies, 1984; and *The Armchair Book of Baseball II,* Scribner, 1987.

WORK IN PROGRESS: Research on gene mapping, AIDS, biotechnology, and baseball.

SIDELIGHTS: Stephen S. Hall writes on scientific matters in a clear and imaginative style, according to critics. His accounts of biological research in *Invisible Frontiers: The Race to Synthesize a Human Gene* and computer cartography in *Mapping the Next Millennium: The Discoveries of New Geographies* are intended for general readers and have been praised by reviewers for their accessibility to the non-scientist. Edward Yoxen commented in the *Times Literary Supplement* that *"Invisible Frontiers* is written as a popular book—there are no footnotes, no references to scholarly literature in the history of science—but it is very far from being superficial. It represents a significant achievement, in gathering and interpreting data."

In describing the competition among three teams of scientists to synthesize the human insulin gene in *Invisible Frontiers,* Hall reveals the extent to which research biology has become a huge commercial venture. The ultimate goal of the scientific teams was to be the first to genetically engineer the production of human insulin. Genentech, a private engineering firm which sponsored the group of scientists that proved most successful with the task, went on to realize substantial profits from the project. Basing his work on more than one hundred interviews, Hall did not avoid the delicate issues that surrounded the enterprise. "This, then, is very much more than a classic story of scientific discovery," Yoxen remarked, pointing out such sensitive areas covered in *Invisible Frontiers* as the effects of industry on an "already highly competitive research culture" and the intense political debates over the safety of recombinant DNA research, in which genetic material from one organism is transferred to another. The book depicts the resentment on the part of scientists over regulatory interference by municipal and federal authorities, as well the frustration felt by junior team members, who often did not receive credit for their contributions to the endeavor. In the *Washington Post Book World,* Wray Herbert observed: "Hall describes not only the science itself, but the scientists—their ambitions, jealousies, frustrations, paranoia, pride—and as a result the laboratories come alive." Writing for the *New York Times Book Review,* Daniel J. Kevles summarized *Invisible Frontiers* as "an illuminating rendition of the technical and the entrepreneurial beginnings of Genentech, now one of the country's leading biotechnology companies, and, by extension, of the birth of the biotechnology industry from the academic womb of molecular biology."

In his second book, *Mapping the Next Millennium,* Hall reveals how scientific researchers in many fields use forms of map-making to arrive at new discoveries. "Hall finds counterparts to intrepid explorers such as Columbus and Magellan not in today's financially embattled geography departments but among the scientists and mathematicians who are using computer graphics to represent and analyze the frontiers of knowledge," noted Edward Tenner in the *Los Angeles Times Book Review.* Full-color illustrations, such as the image of a guinea-pig brain produced by photographing radiation that was introduced into the tissue, accompany Hall's essays on the modern cartographers who chart virtually unseen territory with computers and satellites. James Trefil, writing for the *New York Times Book Review,* found most of Hall's essays full of historical detail, but he noticed certain "distortions." Trefil wrote, "In a chapter devoted to the DNA molecule, for example, he gives wonderful explanations of early genetic work on fruit flies and the development of gene splicing in the 1970s, but then devotes less than a page to the Human Genome Project, which is surely one of the great mapping enterprises of our era." Researchers involved with the Human Genome Project, a contemporary endeavor to catalog the genetic code for every human gene, use a mapping technique to determine where certain traits occur. Tenner, of the *Los Angeles Times Book Review,* expressed some reservations about Hall's presentation of history, noting that the book would have benefited from a more comprehensive look at the people who have helped science develop in a cartographic fashion—most notably such nineteenth-century figures as Lambert-Adolphe Quetelet and Etienne-Jules Marey. Despite such misgivings, Tenner acknowledged the author's eloquence, stating, "Throughout *Mapping,* Hall sustains a string of vivid, concise, often witty metaphors that make him one of the best scientific explainers at work."

A Commotion in the Blood tackles the complicated and potentially confusing history of research into immune therapy treatment for cancer over the past hundred-odd years. Dr. Robert S. Schwartz, in a *New England Journal of Medicine* review, states: "Hall's absorbing, often gripping account of the development of immunotherapy begins with the story of William B. Coley, the inventor of Coley's toxin (a crude mixture of supernatants from bacterial cultures). Coley stumbled on his toxin around 1890 in his search for a factor in hemolytic streptococci that he thought caused regressions, and even cures, of inoperable sarcomas. Helped by the Rockefeller family, Coley produced spectacular results. Others, however, could not reproduce them." Sadly, as a result, Coley ended his career scorned by his medical peers. And Jerome E. Groopman writes in *Wall Street Journal,* "Mr. Hall charts the forces that sweep cancer immunology along in waves of hope and hype." He adds, "Indeed, the story of immune therapy for cancer . . . is rooted in human psychology, which Mr. Hall conveys in a series of fascinating biographies. Rarely is one privileged with such a view—neither jaundiced nor wide-eyed but clear and insightful, reaching deeply into the mind of the modern medical scientist."

A good deal of human drama unfolds as *A Commotion in the Blood* traces the discovery of interferon by Jean Lindenmann and Aleck Isaacs in 1956, while studying viral interference and potential antiviral agents—a purpose for which it proved largely ineffective—followed by Ion Gresser's 1968 findings it caused cancer regression in mice. At that time, the world's supply of interferon was painstakingly produced by extracting it from liters of human leukocytes, and greed on the part of the Biogen company diverted research into interferon cloning for its own profits. Then, in 1975, Doris Morgan discovered interleukin-2 while working in Robert Gallo's laboratory at the National Cancer Institute. However, her discovery did not match his own preconceptions of what the laboratory's goals should be—finding the growth factor for the human myeloid leukemia virus. Her findings were largely buried and she was dismissed from her position with the National Cancer Institute only three years after making her landmark discovery. Meanwhile, in 1975, Steven Rosenberg, also of N.C.I., was testing the infusion of pig lymphocytes into terminally ill cancer patients—a practice that has been termed "dubious" and "pathetic." Rosenberg did, however, recognize the clinical potential of interleukin-2, but, according to Hall, his inept scientific practices actually stalled research into cancer treatment.

Carole Horn, writing in *Washington Post Book World,* lauds *A Commotion in the Blood:* "Hall has scrupulously documented the gains and the price [of cancer research]. He has searched the archives, interviewed scores of scientists, sat with people who have survived their cancers and talked with those who have subsequently died. He opens windows for readers into the laboratories where this highly exacting, tedious work is done and notes the fits and quirks of the sometimes haphazard process of discovery." Horn further praises Hall for his ability to "construct a clear, engaging, carefully documented chronicle of the investigations and discoveries that have begun to delineate the science [of cancer immunology]. . . , and to do so evenhandedly and with great empathy for the scientists, patients and doctors involved."

BIOGRAPHICAL/CRITICAL SOURCES:

PERIODICALS

Booklist, May 15, 1997, p. 1551.
Library Journal, May 15, 1997, p. 97.
Los Angeles Times Book Review, August 9, 1987, p. 13; December 29, 1991, p. 2.
New England Journal of Medicine, October 16, 1997, pp. 1178-79.
New Scientist, August 9, 1997, pp. 42-43.
New York Times Book Review, September 27, 1987, p. 41; March 15, 1992, p. 20; June 29, 1997, p. 9.
Publishers Weekly, May 12, 1997, p. 70.
Science, October 10, 1997, p. 235.
Times Literary Supplement, June 3-9, 1988, p. 605.
Wall Street Journal, July 8, 1997, p. A12.
Washington Post Book World, November 8, 1987, p. 6; May 24, 1992, p. 13; August 24, 1997, p. 3.

* * *

HAMM, Charles Edward 1925-

PERSONAL: Born April 21, 1925, in Charlottesville, VA; married, 1949; children: three. *Education:* University of Virginia, B.A., 1947; Princeton University, M.F.A., 1950, Ph.D., 1960.

ADDRESSES: *Office*—Department of Music, Dartmouth College, Hanover, NH 03755.

CAREER: Cincinnati Conservatory of Music, Cincinnati, OH, instructor in music theory and music history, 1950-57; Tulane University, New Orleans, LA, associate professor of composition and musicology at Newcomb College, 1959-63; University of Illinois, Urbana, IL, professor of musicology, 1963-76; Dartmouth College, Hanover, NH, professor of musicology and head of department, 1976—. Director of musicological archive for Renaissance manuscript studies, University of Illinois, 1963-74.

MEMBER: International Musicological Society, American Musicological Society (president), Italian Society Musical.

AWARDS, HONORS: American Council of Learned Societies grant-in-aid, 1961; Center for International Composition Studies, research grant, Poland, 1966; Guggenheim fellowship, 1967-68; Fulbright research grant, Italy, 1967-68.

WRITINGS:

A Chronology of the Works of Guillaume Dufay, Princeton University Press (Princeton, NJ), 1964.
Opera, Allyn & Bacon, 1966.
(Editor) Igor Fedorovich Stravinskii, *Petrushka,* Norton (New York City), 1967.
(With Bruno Nettl and Ronald Byrnside) *Contemporary Music and Music Cultures,* Prentice-Hall (Englewood Cliffs, NJ), 1975.
Yesterdays: Popular Song in America, Norton, 1979.
Music in the New World, Norton, 1983.
A Chronology of the Works of Guillaume Dufay: Based on a Study of Mensural Practice, Da Capo Press (New York City), 1986.
Afro-American Music, South Africa, and Apartheid, Institute for Studies in American Music, Conservatory of Music, Brooklyn College of the City University of New York (Brooklyln, NY), 1988.
Putting Popular Music in Its Place, Cambridge University Press (New York City), 1995.
Irving Berlin: Songs from the Melting Pot: The Formative Years, 1907-1914, Oxford University Press (New York City), 1997.

Contributor of articles to music journals. Composer of musical compositions, including *Sinfonia,* 1954, *Canto,* 1963, *Mobile for Piano and Tape, Portrait of John Cage, Round,* and *Anyone Lived in a Pretty How Town;* also composer of six operas and several chamber, piano, and vocal works.

SIDELIGHTS: Charles Edward Hamm's books about the history and social significance of music have been widely praised by critics for being insightful and readable. His discussions cover a wide range of music, including opera, popular songs from many eras, and African music. *Yesterdays: Popular Song in America,* is a history of American song from its origins to the present. Robert Palmer of the *New York Times Book Review* conceded that Hamm "has amassed impressive documentation, and he spins an engaging, readable yarn," but contended that Hamm's definition of popular song is too narrow. Palmer also pointed out that Hamm neglects to consider the influence that African American music and popular instrumental music such as ragtime have had on American song. He concluded that "while *Yesterdays* is an interesting and worthwhile book, it isn't a holistic history of American pop and shouldn't be taken as such."

In *Putting Popular Music in Its Place,* Hamm again considered the social significance of popular songs. The book is a collection of twenty essays, originally published in a variety of periodicals. The subjects range from the composer Dvorak to the political uses of music to a report on the fate of the minstrel show. Reviewing the book in *Notes,* Chris Goertzen commented: "I found some of these essays a bit on the short side for what Hamm intended them to accomplish, though this is a flaw so rare in academic writing that it becomes a virtue. . . . This is a strong and stimulating book, one that ought to be read not just for the information presented, but for sheer enjoyment of that rare commodity." Another book, *Music in the New World,* was lauded by Carleton Sprague Smith as "a challenging book which provides a generous amount of new information, a point of view, and a detailed summary of the popular field. We recommend that students of musical Americana read it carefully."

One of the greatest composers of American popular music, Irving Berlin, inspired Hamm's book *Irving Berlin: Songs from the Melting Pot.* R. D. Cohen, a reviewer for *Choice,* deemed the book "a fascinating, insightful, detailed study of Berlin's early years." Noting the many different genres in which Berlin wrote, the reviewer commented, "the author makes a strong case for Berlin's creativity and uniqueness."

Several of the essays in *Putting Popular Music in Its Place* discussed South African music—a subject to which Hamm would later devote a whole book, *Afro-American Music, South Africa, and Apartheid.* Christopher Ballantine, a contributor to *Notes,* called *Afro-American Music, South Africa, and Apartheid* a "lucid and spirited little monograph" and "a valuable contribution to the growing volume of research into the history of urban black music in South Africa."

BIOGRAPHICAL/CRITICAL SOURCES:

PERIODICALS

Best Sellers, March, 1980.
Booklist, April 1, 1997.
Choice, January, 1967, p. 1023; March, 1989, p. 1174; September, 1997, pp. 137-38.
Kirkus Reviews, February 15, 1997, p. 271.
Library Journal, April 1, 1997, p. 93.
Los Angeles Times Book Review, May 20, 1984, p. 12.
Music Educators Journal, April, 1975.
New York Times Book Review, November 11, 1979; April 27, 1997, p. 23.
Notes: The Quarterly Journal of the Music Library Association, March, 1976; September, 1984, pp. 43-45; September, 1991, pp. 133-35; June, 1997, pp. 1175-78.
Village Voice, November 5, 1985, p. 58.
West Coast Review of Books, January, 1980.

* * *

HANDLER, David 1952-

PERSONAL: Born September 14, 1952, in Los Angeles, CA; son of Chester (a salesperson) and Ruth (a homemaker; maiden name, Koffman) Handler. *Education:* University of California, Santa Barbara, B.A., 1974; Columbia University, M.S., 1975.

ADDRESSES: Home—7 Library Lane, Old Lyme, CT. *Agent*—Dominick Abel Literary Agency, 146 West 82nd St., New York, NY 10024.

CAREER: Writer, ghostwriter, screenwriter, and producer. Also worked as syndicated columnist and Broadway critic.

MEMBER: International Association of Crime Writers, Mystery Writers of America, Writers Guild of America.

AWARDS, HONORS: Edgar Allan Poe Award for best original paperback, Mystery Writers of America, and American Mystery Award, both 1991, both for *The Man Who Would Be F. Scott Fitzgerald.*

WRITINGS:

NOVELS

Kiddo, Ballantine (New York City), 1987.
Boss, Available Press (New York City), 1988.

"STEWART HOAG" MYSTERY NOVELS

The Man Who Died Laughing, Bantam (New York City), 1988.

The Man Who Lived by Night, Bantam, 1989.
The Man Who Would Be F. Scott Fitzgerald, Bantam, 1990.
The Woman Who Fell from Grace, Doubleday (New York City), 1991.
The Boy Who Never Grew Up, Doubleday, 1992.
The Man Who Cancelled Himself, Doubleday, 1995.
The Girl Who Ran off with Daddy, Doubleday, 1996.
The Man Who Loved Women to Death, Doubleday, 1997.

OTHER

Also author of screenplays, including scripts for television series *Kate and Allie,* and *The Saint;* contributor to *TV Guide.*

SIDELIGHTS: David Handler's earliest novels are coming-of-age stories set in the author's native Los Angeles, California. His first novel, *Kiddo,* takes place in 1962 and records the adolescent tribulations of Danny Levine, a confused thirteen-year-old who struggles with his Jewish identity, his weight, and his relationships with girls. He latches on to another thirteen-year-old, Newt Biddle, an anti-Semitic preppie who teaches Danny the joys of smoking, shoplifting, and frustrating his parents' efforts to make him learn to play the violin. Eventually Danny makes decisions about his own character and his friends and gives up his rebellious ways, even resuming his violin lessons. David Freeman, writing in the *New York Times Book Review,* concluded that Handler "has great affection for his characters." Danny reappears as the protagonist of Handler's second novel, *Boss,* which is set not in the rebellious 1960s of *Kiddo* but in the more cautious 1970s. Danny is still confused, bumbling, and fighting his waistline; however, a year in Europe has endowed him with a newfound wisdom that allows him to marry and begin working at his father's business.

In his third novel, *The Man Who Died Laughing,* Handler introduces Stewart "Hoagy" Hoag, who is also the protagonist of Handler's later novels. Hoag is a writer whose career has gone flat, so he becomes a ghostwriter and is hired to pen the memoirs of Sonny Day, a famous comic. Soon, however, he is caught in the middle of a murder and begins investigating—with the help of his dog, Lulu—the mysterious break-up of Knight and Day, the most famous comedy team of the fifties, which occurred years before the novel begins. The transcripts of his interviews with family, friends, and enemies provide a nostalgic tour through Hollywood, Las Vegas, and the Jewish resort area in the Catskill Mountains known as the Borscht Belt.

In Handler's 1990 book, *The Man Who Would Be F. Scott Fitzgerald,* Hoag is hired by the literary agent of Cameron Sheffield Noyes, a bratty young New York author with writer's block, to help Noyes write a best-selling autobiography. But what Noyes dictates under Hoag's coaching is instead an expose of the New York celebrity publishing scene. The work in progress prompts anonymous threats that could have come from a variety of unscrupulous characters, each with a motive for wanting to see the project halted. When both Noyes's publisher and ex-lover are murdered and Noyes disappears, Hoag again turns from writer to sleuth. A *Wall Street Journal* contributor wrote of *The Man Who Would Be F. Scott Fitzgerald:* "Charming lead characters and good breezy writing are among this book's strong suits."

In *The Woman Who Fell from Grace* Handler spoofs the real-life sensation aroused by the publication of the sequel to Margaret Mitchell's landmark novel *Gone with the Wind. Oh, Shenandoah* is Alma Glaze's sweeping romantic saga of the American Revolution that has sold over thirty million copies since its publication in 1940. When the heirs to her estate negotiate a deal for what Handler calls "the most eagerly awaited literary sequel of all time," they hire Hoag to take over the writing duties from Glaze's daughter. Hoag quickly finds himself tangled in a mystery. It is well known that Alma Glaze had been accidentally killed right after the film version of *Oh, Shenandoah* was completed. But the housekeeper turns up dead after suggesting that the death of one of the film's stars at the same time was murder. Hoag investigates while preparations for a gala anniversary celebration of the novel go on around him. Sybil Steinberg, writing in *Publishers Weekly,* commented: "Handler's breezy, unpretentious and warmhearted hero provides a breath of fresh air in a world of investigative angst." *New York Times Book Review* contributor Marilyn Stasio noted that Handler "writes a mean plot, full of crises that ingeniously spoof the melodramatic events of the original potboiler saga."

In *The Boy Who Never Grew Up,* Hoag finds himself in Hollywood, where he is hired by director Matthew Wax to ghostwrite a memoir that will preempt the book Wax's estranged actor wife, Pennyroyal Brim, is writing. Hoag finds himself in the middle of a messy divorce battle, one that quickly takes a murderous turn. Steinberg wrote in *Publishers Weekly:* "On the way to a brisk finale, Handler sharply skewers and spoofs La-La Land."

In *The Man Who Cancelled Himself,* Hoag is hired to ghostwrite a memoir of Uncle Chubby, a television comedy star whose career takes a nosedive after he is arrested for public indecency in a Times Square pornography theater. But Uncle Chubby, whose real name is Lyle Hudnut, proves to be a difficult subject—possibly even psychotic. Hoag's research for the book leads to a bombing on the set of Hudnut's television show, a poisoning of the program's cast and crew, and eventually, murder. Handler's own background in the television industry gave the ring of authenticity to his novel, in the estimation of *Booklist* reviewer George Needham. He called *The Man Who Cancelled Himself* "a thoroughly satisfying mystery that offers a cynical look at the economics, politics, and sociology of a TV sitcom. . . . Highly recommended." A *Publishers Weekly* critic concurred that the book is "great fun," largely because of the "gimlet-eyed observations of the fierce, delicious and dizzy infighting in Sitcom Land."

The Girl Who Ran off with Daddy "satisfies both as a mystery and as light comedy," judged Emily Melton in *Booklist.* In this adventure, Hoag's ghostwriting career is floundering, but he hardly cares, as he has plenty of money in savings and the rest of his life is working out nicely. He has a new baby with his live-in ex-wife and a comfortable life as a gentleman farmer in Connecticut. This peaceful interlude is disturbed when an old friend, Thor Gibbs, turns up on Hoag's doorstep. With Gibbs is his new girlfriend, who is young enough to be Thor's granddaughter; and she is, in fact, his stepdaughter. When Thor is murdered, the suspects include his rejected wife, his girlfriend's father, the father's gay lover, and the girlfriend's ex-boyfriends. "Handler controls his material masterfully, delivering newsy verisimilitude and domestic repartee worthy of Nick and Nora Charles," approved a *Publishers Weekly* contributor. Melton further described the book as "breezy, funny, and debonair." Melton also gave her approval to *The Man Who Loved Women to Death,* in which Hoag chases a serial killer who may in fact be one of his old friends. Reviewing that book, she declared: "Handler has written a sleek, sophisticated, over-the-top story that's filled with red herrings, laugh-aloud humor, and plenty of suspense."

BIOGRAPHICAL/CRITICAL SOURCES:

PERIODICALS

Booklist, January 15, 1995, p. 899; April 1, 1996, p. 1346; May 1, 1997, p. 1483.

Library Journal, April 1, 1997, p. 133.

Los Angeles Times, March 5, 1987.

New York Times Book Review, May 3, 1987, p. 37; November 3, 1991, p. 27.

Publishers Weekly, September 21, 1990, p. 69; August 2, 1991, p. 66; July 13, 1992, p. 48; December 5, 1994, p. 68; March 24, 1997, p. 62; January 15, 1996, p. 447.

Wall Street Journal, November 5, 1990, p. A13.

* * *

HARBINSON, Allen
See HARBINSON, W(illiam) A(llen)

* * *

HARBINSON, W(illiam) A(llen) 1941-
(Allen Harbinson)

PERSONAL: Born September 9, 1941, in Northern Ireland; son of Alfred (a welder) and Martha (a stitcher; maiden name, Allen) Harbinson; married Ursula Mayer, November 5, 1969; children: Shaun, Tanya. *Education:* Attended Belfast College of Technology, 1956-57, and Liverpool College of Building, 1958-61.

ADDRESSES: Office—c/o New English Library, Hodder Headline, 338 Euston Rd., London NW1 3BH, England.

CAREER: Writer. Apprentice textile engineer in Belfast, Northern Ireland, 1955-57; apprentice gas fitter in Liverpool, England, 1958-61; freelance writer in London, England, 1967-68; Stonehart Publications, London, subscriptions clerk, 1968-69; *Knave and Fiesta,* London, assistant editor, 1970-71; *Scorpio,* London, assistant editor, 1971-72; chief associate editor in London of *Men Only* and *Club International,* and London office of *Club U.S.A.,* 1972-76. *Military service:* Royal Australian Air Force, medical clerk, 1961-67.

MEMBER: International PEN, British Film Institute, Society of Authors, Royal Overseas League.

AWARDS, HONORS: Critic's Choice Fiction designation, 1986, for *Stryker's Kingdom.*

WRITINGS:

NOVELS

Two Gentlemen of Pleasure, Horwitz (Sydney, Australia), 1967.
The Gentlemen Rogues, Horwitz, 1967.
The Running Man, Horwitz, 1967, Award Books (New York City), 1970.
Guide for the Single Man, Horwitz, 1968.
Death of an Idol, Horwitz, 1969.
Our Girl Friday, Horwitz, 1969.
Instruments of Death, Corgi Books (London), 1973, published as *None But the Damned,* Pinnacle Books (New York City), 1974.
Knock, Intergroup, 1975.
Meat, Panther Books (London), 1975.
(With Lindsay Galloway) *The MacKinnons* (novelization of television series), Panther Books, 1977.
No Limit for Charlie, Panther Books, 1977.
The Oil Heist, Corgi Books, 1978.
Stryker's Kingdom, Corgi Books, 1979.
Revelation, Corgi Books, 1982, Dell (New York City), 1983.
Otherworld, Dell, 1984.
The Light of Eden, Corgi Books, 1987, published as *Eden,* Dell, 1987.
(Under name Allen Harbinson) *The Lodestone,* Sphere (London), 1989.
Dream Maker, Sphere, 1991, Walker (New York City), 1992.

"PROJEKT SAUCER" SERIES

Genesis, Corgi Books, 1979, Dell, 1982.
Inception, Dell, 1991.
Phoenix, New English Library (London), 1995.
Millennium, New English Library, 1995.

BIOGRAPHIES

Bronson!, Pinnacle Books, 1975.
Elvis Presley: An Illustrated Biography, M. Joseph, 1975, Grosset, 1976, revised edition published as *The Life and Death of Elvis Presley,* M. Joseph, 1977, published as *The Illustrated Elvis,* Perigee Books, 1987.
(Editor and compiler of photographs) Colin Wilson, *Ken Russell: A Director in Search of a Hero,* Intergroup, 1975.
George C. Scott: The Man, the Actor, and the Legend, Pinnacle Books, 1977.
Evita: A Legend for the Seventies, Star Publishing (London), 1977.

Also author of *Beauty and the Beast: An Illustrated Biography of Klaus and Nastassja Kinski.*

OTHER

Astronaut (radio play) BBC, 1972.
Projekt UFO: The Case for Man-Made Flying Saucers, Boxtree (London), 1995.

Author of script material for television series *The Explorers,* for BBC-TV, 1974. Contributor of stories and articles to men's magazines in the United States, England, and Australia.

SIDELIGHTS: In his "Projekt Saucer" books, W. A. Harbinson draws on the modern mythology of flying saucers to create a massive fictional speculation concerning man-made saucer craft developed and run by a vast conspiratorial network. As Peter T. Garratt writes in the *St. James Guide to Horror, Ghost and Gothic Writers,* in Harbinson's books there exists a "vast, weird, but not alien or unnatural conspiracy, originating right here on Earth."

As Garratt explains, Harbinson delineates his flying saucer saga by using "the full range of recently described saucer experiences: abductions, experiments with abductees, strange sexual aspects, and of course secret conspiracies going all the way to the top. Indeed, at times it seems that anyone who knows too much is likely to be stopped by interference with his car electrics on a lonely road, whisked away, and unlike run-of-the-mill abductees, never see again."

BIOGRAPHICAL/CRITICAL SOURCES:

BOOKS

St. James Guide to Horror, Ghost and Gothic Writers, St. James Press (Detroit, MI), 1998.

HASSAM, Nick
See CROWTHER, Peter

* * *

HAUTMAN, Pete(r Murray) 1952-
(Peter Murray)

PERSONAL: Born September 29, 1952, in Berkeley, CA; son of Thomas R. (a lawyer) and Elaine (a painter) Hautman; married Mary Logue (a writer). *Education:* Attended Minneapolis College of Art & Design, 1970-72, and University of Minnesota, 1972-77.

ADDRESSES: *Home*—Minneapolis, MN. *Agent*—Jonathon Lazear, 430 1st Ave., No. 416, Minneapolis, MN 55401.

CAREER: Worked at various jobs, usually involving illustration and graphic design, 1972-81; Crowd Caps Inc. (now Crowd Specialties), Minneapolis, MN, vice-president of marketing, 1981-88; Hautman Marketing Services, Minneapolis, MN, owner and operator, 1988-91; writer, 1991—.

MEMBER: Mystery Writers of America, International Association of Crime Writers.

WRITINGS:

NOVELS

Drawing Dead, Simon & Schuster (New York City), 1993.
Short Money, Simon & Schuster, 1995.
The Mortal Nuts, Simon & Schuster, 1996.
Ring Game, Simon & Schuster, 1997.

JUVENILE FICTION

Mr. Was, Simon & Schuster, 1996.
Stone Cold, Simon & Schuster, 1998.

JUVENILE NONFICTION; UNDER NAME PETER MURRAY

You Can Juggle, Child's World (Plymouth, MN), 1992.
The World's Greatest Chocolate Chip Cookie, Child's World, 1992.
The World's Greatest Paper Airplanes, Child's World, 1992.
Silly Science Tricks, Child's World, 1992.
Your Bones, Child's World, 1992.
The Planets, Child's World, 1992.
Rhinos, Child's World, 1992.
Black Widows, Child's World, 1992.
Snakes, Child's World, 1992.
Spiders, Child's World, 1992.
Beavers, Child's World, 1992.
Dogs, Child's World, 1992.
Planet Earth, Child's World, 1992.
The Everglades, Child's World, 1993.
Saturn, Child's World, 1993.
Tarantulas, Child's World, 1993.
The Space Shuttle, Child's World, 1993.
The Amazon, Child's World, 1993.
Frogs, Child's World, 1993.
Hummingbirds, Child's World, 1993.
Beetles, Child's World, 1993.
Chameleons, Child's World, 1993.
Parrots, Child's World, 1993.
Porcupines, Child's World, 1993.
Gorillas, Child's World, 1993.
Sea Otters, Child's World, 1993.
The Sahara, Child's World, 1993.
Dirt, Child's World, 1994.
Kites, Child's World, 1994.
The World's Greatest Pizza, Child's World, 1994.
Science Tricks with Water, Child's World, 1994.
Science Tricks with Light, Child's World, 1994.
Science Tricks with Air, Child's World, 1994.

Also author of numerous other books for children.

SIDELIGHTS: Pete Hautman is the author of more than fifty nonfiction books for children, published under the name Peter Murray, and of several successful adult crime novels. His first foray into adult writing, *Drawing Dead,* described as a "rollicking crime caper" by Marilyn Stasio in the *New York Times,* is about a gang of con artists in pursuit of a cache of vintage comic books. The larger-than-life schemes conceived by these characters "are brilliant enough to dazzle the players in novels by the likes of Joe Gores and Elmore Leonard," judged Stasio. "Whatever Pete Hautman was doing before he wrote *Drawing Dead,* he was wasting his time. He's got those good old writing genes, and the proof is in this first novel." A *Publishers Weekly* reviewer concurred that Hautman had written a "first-class caper novel. . . . A wonderful story, tartly told." Hautman expanded on the adventures of the gang in *Drawing Dead* with his 1995 book *Short Money,* set a few years before the events in the first book. A *Publishers Weekly* writer called it "exhilarating . . . by turns funny and soulful and always unpredictable. . . . Hautman's dialogue sparkles, his plot hums, he's got a nicely complex sense of morality and he's a virtuoso when it comes to describing what it feels like to get punched."

In *The Mortal Nuts,* Hautman again showed his kinship with Elmore Leonard, creating an over-the-top story about a quarter of a million dollars stashed in coffee cans, a tough old man who made the fortune selling tacos, and the scheming young punks who will try to take it from him. Axel Speeter is the chef who makes his yearly income during two weeks at the Minnesota State Fair, and "for a 73-year-old geezer who doesn't talk about anything but tacos, he is one helluva fine character," commented Marilyn Stasio in the *New York Times. Booklist* critic Thomas Gaughan also gave his approval to *The Mortal Nuts.* He noted that "after a hilarious start," the book "takes a grim and jarring turn." He found that "Hautman has a wonderful ear for low-rent dialogue and powers of description that make the sensory welter of a gargantuan midwestern state fair come alive."

Hautman told *CA:* "When I was going through that wondrous horrorshow we call adolescence I realized, as do all adolescents, that I was different from everybody else. My obnoxiously adolescent way of dealing with this alarming situation was to try to convince everyone I met to be more like me. They needed to be shown the *right* way to look at things. Other people simply did not understand, and it was my job to explain it to them.

"I quickly learned that the direct verbal approach was both ineffective and dangerous, so I decided to become a writer. Those who read my books, I believed, would become more like me. Soon the world would be filled with people who understood and agreed with my point of view.

"I no longer see myself as this pied piper character. I feel more like a jester whose mission is to prevent anyone from taking themselves too seriously. I'm no longer out to persuade readers to share my world view. I'm trying to make them laugh. It took me over twenty years to figure that this is what I do best, and that it is what I want to do.

"I hear a lot of authors who didn't publish until their middle ages say that they didn't have the 'life experience' or 'perspective' to write when they were younger. In my opinion, that's not the problem. The real problem most of us have when trying to write at the age of, say, twenty-five, is we're filled with all those nasty hormones, and the idea of pursuing one story idea for days or weeks or months on end is frankly ridiculous. When we are younger we are erupting with ideas, and today's new thought is infinitely more interesting than yesterday's. In my case, at least, I was thirty-eight-years old before I slowed down enough to keep working on the same story idea long enough to make it happen.

"In 1993, I retired from a freelance marketing and design practice to devote myself full time to writing. I live in a large house in south Minneapolis with mystery writer and poet Mary Logue and a cat named Ubik. We spend a lot of time at our second home, an old farmhouse in Stockholm, Wisconsin. Both Mary and I write every day, and we like it. We are each other's editor, audience, critic, and cheerleader."

BIOGRAPHICAL/CRITICAL SOURCES:

PERIODICALS

Booklist, October 1, 1993, p. 253; March 27, 1995, p. 78; April 1, 1996, p. 1346; October 1, 1997, p. 310.

Entertainment Weekly, July 26, 1996, p. 51.

Library Journal, October 1, 1997, p. 122.

Los Angeles Times, February 3, 1994, p. E8.

New York Times, November 7, 1993; June 23, 1996.

New York Times Book Review, November 7, 1993, p. 24.

People, August 5, 1996, p. 32.

Publishers Weekly, August 30, 1993, p. 74; October 28, 1996, p. 83; September 1, 1997, p. 94.

Wall Street Journal, November 22, 1993, p. A12.

* * *

HAVILL, Steven 1945-

PERSONAL: Born June 22, 1945, in Penn Yan, NY; son of Edward (a writer) and Margaret (Nasset) Havill; married Kathleen Murphey (an indexer), February 4, 1969. *Education:* University of New Mexico, B.A., 1969, M.A., 1982.

ADDRESSES: Home—P.O. Box 3253, Milan, NM 87021.

CAREER: Greenhow Newspapers, Inc., Penn Yan, NY, reporter and editor, 1973-76; Grants High School, Grants, NM, teacher of biology and English, 1979—.

AWARDS, HONORS: Finalist for Medicine Pipe Bearers Award from Western Writers of America, 1982, for *The Killer.*

WRITINGS:

WESTERN NOVELS

The Killer, Doubleday (New York City), 1981.
The Worst Enemy, Doubleday, 1982.
Leadfire, Doubleday, 1984.
Timber Blood, Doubleday, 1986.

"BILL GASTNER" DETECTIVE NOVELS

Heartshot, St. Martin's (New York City), 1991.
Bitter Recoil, St. Martin's, 1992.
Twice Buried, St. Martin's, 1994.
Before She Dies, St. Martin's, 1996.
Privileged to Kill, St. Martin's, 1997.
Prolonged Exposure, St. Martin's, 1998.

SIDELIGHTS: Steven Havill began his fiction career with such unconventional westerns as *The Killer* and *Leadfire;* later, the author cemented his success with his "Bill Gastner" mystery series. Gastner is a portly insomniac who serves as undersheriff of Posadas County, New Mexico. *Booklist* contributor Wes Lukowsky found that the first Gastner novel set a "high standard," which was successfully met in later books. "Gastner is an incisive investigator," mused Lukowsky. "Unlike other fictional detectives who approach murder as personal affront, Gastner sees himself as the victims' advocate, striving to even the scales of justice for those no longer able to do it themselves." A *Publishers Weekly* critic also judged the series "estimable" and noted that the author "sensitively explores the area's Mexican-American culture."

Reviewing *Before She Dies,* the fourth Gastner book, Lukowsky called it the best thus far, "no small feat in a series as strong as this one. Gastner is compassionate, intelligent, bulldog tough, and painfully aware of all his limitations, both physical and emotional. The same inward eye that provides insights into his own soul can quickly swivel outward to discern others' hidden traits." A unique feature of the series is the ongoing subplot of Gastner's health. Overweight, seemingly addicted to chili, and apparently unwilling to do anything about his unhealthy habits, Gastner is constantly badgered by his deputy Estelle and her physician spouse to take better care of himself. *Prolonged Exposure,* the fifth title in the series, finds Gastner in Michigan recuperating from heart surgery at his daughter Camille's. His wish to return home is answered when he is notified that his house has been burglarized. He is soon drawn into a much more serious problem—the kidnapping of small children and the discovery of a black-market child exploitation ring. Lukowsky called this book "another small-town caper in which common sense, compassion, loyalty, and decency are law enforcement's primary tools against an increasingly brutal world. It's a good thing Gastner has had his heart mended because it may be the biggest in contemporary crime fiction."

Havill once commented to *CA:* "I believe there must be a market for slightly off-genre westerns, where characters use their heads, and not every hero is flinty-eyed and steely-nerved, with speed-of-light reflexes. I enjoy writing stories where physicians are dominant characters. Medicine played a critical part on the frontier. *The Killer* was prompted by my love of writing for storytelling's sake. The main character is a basically good person who must face the consequences of a grave mistake—a mistake prompted more by immaturity than anything else."

BIOGRAPHICAL/CRITICAL SOURCES:

PERIODICALS

Booklist, March 1, 1994, p. 1184; March 1, 1996, p. 1125; February 15, 1997, p. 1006; February 15, 1998, p. 988.
Library Journal, February 1, 1981; February 1, 1997, p. 111; March 1, 1998, p. 131.
Publishers Weekly, March 7, 1994, p. 57; December 16, 1996, p. 45; February 9, 1998, p. 78.

* * *

HAYS, Peter L. 1938-

PERSONAL: Born April 18, 1938, in Bremerhaven, Germany; son of Eric (a grocer) and Elsa (Nussbaum) Hays; married Myrna Mantel (a teacher), September 14, 1963; children: Melissa Anne, Eric Lee, Jeffrey Michael. *Education:* University of Rochester, A.B., 1959; New York University, M.A., 1961; Ohio State University, Ph.D., 1965.

ADDRESSES: Home—Davis, CA. *Office*—Department of English, University of California, Davis, CA 95616.

CAREER: Ohio State University, Columbus, instructor in English, 1965-66; University of California, Davis, assistant professor, 1966-72, associate professor, 1972-77, professor of English and comparative literature, 1977—, chairman of English department, 1974-77. Fulbright lecturer in Mainz, Germany, 1977-78. Instructor in department of independent instruction, University of California, Berkeley. *Military service:* U.S. Army, 1959-60. U.S. Army Reserve, 1960-66.

MEMBER: Modern Language Association of America, Philological Association of the Pacific Coast, Society for the Study of Southern Literature.

WRITINGS:

The Limping Hero, New York University Press (New York City), 1971.
A Concordance to Hemingway's "In Our Time," G. K. Hall (Boston), 1990.
Ernest Hemingway, Continuum (New York City), 1990.

Contributor of numerous articles to literature journals.

WORK IN PROGRESS: Research on folklore and literature.

SIDELIGHTS: Peter L. Hays's book *Ernest Hemingway* was lauded by several reviewers as a concise, insightful introduction to the life and work of the man many people consider one of the greatest American authors. Hemingway's life was full and complicated and his writing moved through several distinct stages. Hays divided his study of the author into seven sections. One focused on biographical facts; another presented a description of Hemingway's style and its influence on the writing that followed it; and there were also notes on his greatest successes, a chronology of his publishing history, and an extensive bibliography. His remarks covered classics such as *To Have and Have Not* and *Green Hills of Africa;* later efforts including *Men at War, Over the River and into the Trees,* and *The Old Man and the Sea;* and works published posthumously, such as *The Garden of Eden, The Dangerous Summer,* and *A Moveable Feast.*

Roland Wulbert, a reviewer for *Booklist,* noted that the book broke no new critical ground and commented that the historical portion of the book was "sketchy," but he concluded that "all in all," it was "a concise and serviceable introduction to Hemingway's crowded life and oeuvre." *Choice* contributor F. L. Ryan concurred that "there is not much that is new for the Hemingway scholar or the veteran reader," but he approved of Hays's commentary as "refreshingly brief but provocative." Ryan concluded: "Strongly recommended for anyone, particularly the undergraduate or community college student who needs a handbook that is both informative and lively."

Hays once told *CA,* "Although faculty may be paid only for their teaching and promoted . . . largely for their publications, publication, for me, is not separate from teaching, but rather, extends the podium offered in the classroom and allows professors further scope 'to profess' their views, to educate more widely."

BIOGRAPHICAL/CRITICAL SOURCES:

PERIODICALS

American Literature, March, 1991, p. 176.
American Reference Books Annual, 1991, p. 468.
Booklist, April 15, 1990, p. 1602.
Choice, December, 1990, p. 628.

* * *

HEARD, (Henry Fitz) Gerald 1889-1971
(H. F. Heard)

PERSONAL: Born October 6, 1889, in London, England; came to the United States in 1937; died August 14, 1971; son of Henry James (a prebendary of the Church of England) and Maude (Bannatyne) Heard. *Education:* Gonville and Caius College, Cambridge, honors in history, 1911, graduate work, 1911-12.

CAREER: Author, lecturer, researcher. Worked with Agricultural Co-op Movement in Ireland, 1919-23, in England, 1923-27. Radio lecturer, 1929-71; science commentator, British Broadcasting Corp., 1930-

34; lecturer, Oxford University, 1929-31; visiting lecturer, Washington University, St. Louis, MO, 1951-52, 1955-56; Haskell Foundation Lecturer at Oberlin College and Macliesh Lecturer at Rockford College, both 1958.

AWARDS, HONORS: Bollingen Foundation grant, 1955-56; Henrietta Hertz Award of the British Academy, for *The Ascent of Humanity.*

WRITINGS:

Narcissus: An Anatomy of Clothes, Dutton (New York City), 1924.
The Ascent of Humanity: An Essay on the Evolution of Civilization, Harcourt (New York City), 1929.
Social Substance of Religion: An Essay on the Evolution of Religion, Harcourt, 1931.
The Emergence of Man, J. Cape (London), 1931, Harcourt, 1932.
This Surprising World: A Journalist Looks at Science, Cobden-Sanderson (London), 1932.
These Hurrying Years: An Historical Outline, 1900-1933, Oxford University Press (New York City), 1934.
The Source of Civilisation, J. Cape, 1935.
Science in the Making, Faber (London), 1935.
Exploring the Stratosphere, Thomas Nelson (London), 1936.
Science Front 1936, Cassell (New York City), 1937.
The Third Morality, Morrow (New York City), 1937.
Pain, Sex, and Time: A New Hypothesis of Evolution, Harper (New York City), 1939.
A Quaker Mutation, Pendle Hill (Wallingford, PA), 1940.
Man the Master, Harper, 1941.
The Creed of Christ: An Interpretation of the Lord's Prayer, Harper, 1941.
The Code of Christ, Harper, 1941.
Training for the Life of the Spirit, two volumes, Cassell, 1941-44.
A Dialogue in the Desert, Harper, 1942.
A Preface to Prayer, Harper, 1944.
The Recollection, James Delkin (Stanford, CA), 1944.
The Gospel According to Gamaliel, Harper, 1945.
The Eternal Gospel, Harper, 1946.
Militarism's Post-Mortem, P. P. U. (London), 1946.
Is God Evident?: An Essay toward a Natural Theology, Harper, 1948.
(Editor) *Prayers and Meditations,* Harper, 1949.
The Riddle of the Flying Saucers: Is Another World Watching?, Carroll & Nicholson (London), 1950, published as *Is Another World Watching?: The Riddle of the Flying Saucers,* Harper, 1951.
Is God in History?: An Inquiry into Human and Prehuman History in Terms of the Doctrine of Creation, Fall and Redemption, Harper, 1950.
Morals since 1900, Harper, 1950.
The Black Fox: A Novel of the Seventies, Harper, 1951.
Ten Questions on Prayer (pamphlet), Pendle Hill, 1951.
Gabriel and the Creatures, Harper, 1952, published in England as *Wishing Well: An Outline of the Evolution of the Mammals Told as a Series of Stories about How the Animals Got Their Wishes,* Faber, 1953.
The Human Venture, Harper, 1955.
(With others) *Kingdom without God: Road's End for the Social Gospel,* Foundation for Social Research (Los Angeles), 1956.
Training for a Life of Growth, Wayfarer Press (Santa Monica, CA), 1959.
The Five Ages of Man: The Psychology of Human History, Julian Press (New York City), 1963.

UNDER NAME H. F. HEARD

A Taste for Honey, Vanguard (New York City), 1941, reprinted, Lancer Books (New York City), 1964.
Reply Paid: A Mystery, Vanguard, 1942.
Murder by Reflection, Vanguard, 1942.
The Great Fog, and Other Weird Tales, Vanguard, 1944, revised edition published as *The Great Fog: Weird Tales of Terror and Detection,* Sun Dial Press (New York City), 1946.
Dopplegangers: An Episode of the Fourth, the Psychological, Revolution, 1997, Vanguard, 1947.
The Lost Cavern, and Other Tales of the Fantastic, Vanguard, 1948.
The Notched Hairpin, Vanguard, 1949.
The Amazing Mycroft Mysteries: Three Novels, Vanguard Press (New York City), 1980.

SIDELIGHTS: Gerald Heard wrote prolifically in the fields of theology, supernatural fiction, and science. A radio broadcaster and newspaper journalist during the 1930s, Heard became a popular philosopher upon his move to California in 1937. At this time he published many works speculating about the connections between evolutionary science and mystical theology. Brian Stableford, writing in the *St. James Guide to Horror, Ghost and Gothic Writers,* noted that Heard "brought a distinctively dogged philosophical adventurousness to all of his work." Heard published a number of works that have kept his reputation alive as a writer of horror fiction. Eudora Welty, speaking of Heard's short stories in an essay for the *New York Times,* described them as "good supernatural stories of science and idea."

The Black Fox: A Novel of the Seventies tells the story of an Anglican priest who resorts to black magic against a rival, only to be haunted by the demons he has called forth. Stableford called *The Black Fox* "Heard's purest and most traditional horror story. . . . Although the novel is wordy and perhaps overly pretentious it builds up considerable tension by virtue of its implacably earnest treatment of its central theme and the serious attention it pays to fundamental issues of theology." The novel is, according to E. F. Walbridge in *Library Journal,* "one of the most distinguished novels of the supernatural since *The Turn of the Screw.*" Villiers Gerson in the *New York Times* dubbed the novel a "subtle, beautifully written fantasy," while H. H. Holmes in the *New York Herald Tribune Book Review* concluded that *The Black Fox* was "one of the few distinguished supernatural novels of the last decade."

While Heard's short stories range from the supernatural to science fiction and mystery, they often involve clergy as main characters and churches as settings. Stableford cited the story "Dromenon," the tale of a strange antiquarian who discovers the disturbing true nature of an early church, as "the most significant horror story in *The Great Fog and Other Weird Tales.*" Likewise using a religious setting is Heard's "The Cup," the story of the Holy Grail, found accidently at a little church in England and the focus of an intense battle between good and evil. Stableford concluded that when Heard "deployed his talents to best effect . . . , he produced first-rate stories that are markedly unlike the standard products of their genres. An eclectic collection of his best short fiction could bring together some extraordinary and fascinating works."

BIOGRAPHICAL/CRITICAL SOURCES:

BOOKS

St. James Guide to Horror, Ghost and Gothic Writers, St. James Press (Detroit, MI), 1998.

Savage, D. S., *Mysticism and Aldous Huxley: An Examination of Heard-Huxley Theories,* Folcroft Library Editions (Folcroft, PA), 1977.

PERIODICALS

Booklist, July 15, 1944.

Bookmark, December, 1951.

Book Week, May 28, 1944, p. 2.

Chicago Sun, March 12, 1948.

Christian Century, December 25, 1940; June 7, 1944; December 19, 1945; November 6, 1946; September 8, 1948; April 4, 1951.

Christian Science Monitor, May 16, 1951, p. 9.

Churchman, May 1, 1944.

Cleveland Open Shelf, September, 1951, p. 17.

Commonweal, March 5, 1937; July 30, 1948.

Crozer Quarterly, January, 1945; January, 1949; July, 1951.

Hibbert Journal, January, 1951.

Kirkus, February 1, 1944; May 1, 1944; June 15, 1944; February 1, 1948; June 15, 1948; February 1, 1951; March 1, 1951; November 1, 1951.

Library Journal, August, 1944; February 15, 1948; May 1, 1951; November 1, 1951.

Manchester Guardian, July 7, 1950, p. 4.

Nation, October 16, 1929; September 26, 1934.

New Republic, August 21, 1929; February 24, 1932.

New Statesman, December 7, 1929; April 14, 1934; February 22, 1936.

New Statesman & Nation, September 30, 1950; December 30, 1950.

New Yorker, June 17, 1944; September 16, 1944; March 13, 1948; January 20, 1951.

New York Herald Tribune Book Review, April 15, 1951, p. 5; November 11, 1951, p. 12.

New York Times, October 13, 1929; January 17, 1932; September 9, 1934; May 9, 1937; September 19, 1937; May 7, 1944, p. 6; July 9, 1944, p. 24; September 3, 1944, p. 5; January 6, 1946; September 15, 1946; March 7, 1948; April 29, 1951, p. 18; December 9, 1951, p. 30.

New York Times Book Review, January 5, 1964.

San Francisco Chronicle, October 20, 1946; March 9, 1947; March 21, 1948, p. 24; August 15, 1948, p. 12; April 29, 1951, p. 24.

Saturday Review, August 17, 1929; January 30, 1932; September 8, 1934; March 15, 1947; May 15, 1948; April 28, 1951; July 28, 1951; November 17, 1951; February 29, 1964.

Spectator, November 21, 1931; April 27, 1934; January 15, 1937; July 28, 1950.

Springfield Republican, April 29, 1951, p. C8.

Times Literary Supplement, December 21, 1935; October 20, 1950, p. 659; January 26, 1951, p. 49.

Weekly Book Review, May 28, 1944, p. 23; September 3, 1944; November 19, 1944, p. 20.*

HEARD, H. F.
See HEARD, (Henry Fitz) Gerald

* * *

HENDERSON, William McCranor 1943-

PERSONAL: Born August 4, 1943, in Charlotte, NC; son of William (an anthropologist) and Nancy (a playwright; maiden name, Wallace) Henderson; married Carol Douglas (a journalist), 1975; children: Olivia, Colette. *Education:* Oberlin College, B.A., 1965; attended University of Iowa, 1965-66. *Politics:* Independent. *Religion:* "Non-affiliated."

ADDRESSES: *Office*—CB #3520, Greenlaw Hall, University of North Carolina—Chapel Hill, Chapel Hill, NC 27599-3520. *Agent*—Russell & Volkening, Inc., 50 West 29th St., New York, NY 10001.

CAREER: Freelance editor and sound recordist for documentary films, New York City, 1966-68; producer of the short film *Zelenka,* late 1960s; WBAI-FM, New York City, staff producer and host of free-form *Medicine Hat* program, 1969-70; musician, Boston, MA, 1970-75; freelance audio-visual writer and producer, Boston and New York City, 1977-88; screenwriter, Los Angeles, CA, 1979-81; University of North Carolina at Chapel Hill, teacher of creative writing, 1989—.

AWARDS, HONORS: CINE Golden Eagle award, 1968, for film *Zelenka.*

WRITINGS:

Stark Raving Elvis, Dutton (New York City), 1984.
I Killed Hemingway, St. Martin's (New York City), 1993.
I, Elvis: Confessions of a Counterfeit King, Boulevard Books (New York City), 1997.

WORK IN PROGRESS: *Applestock Nation,* a novel about the 1960s.

SIDELIGHTS: William McCranor Henderson has combined popular culture and satire in his three books, *Stark Raving Elvis, I Killed Hemingway,* and *I, Elvis: Confessions of a Counterfeit King.* Henderson has a diversified resume that includes a stint at the prestigious University of Iowa Writer's Workshop, behind-the-scenes work on documentary films, and playing guitar and electric violin for various Boston-area rock bands.

Henderson had produced radio plays and an acclaimed short film in the late 1960s and early 1970s, but *Stark Raving Elvis* was his first foray into the novel form. The work met with favorable reviews upon publication in 1984, and was followed nearly a decade later by Henderson's second novel, *I Killed Hemingway.* His third book, *I, Elvis,* is a journalistic account of his foray into the world of Elvis impersonators.

Stark Raving Elvis is a parody of the gargantuan mythos surrounding Elvis Presley, the so-called "King of Rock and Roll," whose popularity has endured since his 1977 death. Henderson's novel weaves together various facets of the King's legend and legacy as the book's protagonist, Byron "Blue Suede" Bluford, makes almost the same fateful life journey as his idol. Bluford discovers he has a talent for imitating Presley in a 1958 talent contest in his hometown of Portland, Maine. He then becomes obsessed with Elvis, first as a devoted fan, then as a first-rate imitator. His fixation on the singer culminates in a 1976 meeting with Presley, a year before the King's death. At that fateful encounter, the bloated and catatonic Elvis presents Bluford with one of his prized revolvers as a gift.

When Presley expires the following year, Bluford is ready to step into his shoes and joins the legions of Elvis impersonators on the road to stardom in Las Vegas. Yet Bluford soon learns that his act, that of the young, lean, and rebellious Elvis of the 1950s, does not play as well in Vegas as the overweight, sequinned King of later years. He adjusts his stage persona accordingly, then flirts with the same self-destruction that claimed Presley.

In reviewing *Stark Raving Elvis* for the *New York Times Book Review,* critic Nikki Giovanni described it as "a funny, revealing novel that shows what happens to those who refuse to let youth go." *Village Voice* writer Ed Ward commented that "*Stark Raving Elvis* tells a story that's simultaneously preposterous and profoundly concerned with contemporary American culture and its myths." Ward summarized Henderson's first attempt at the novel form by asserting that the author "has a fine ear for dialogue and a way of writing that doesn't condescend to his characters or ring false."

Henderson's second novel, 1993's *I Killed Hemingway,* is another humorous and satirical look at a celebrity, author Ernest Hemingway, whose posthumous fame has extreme consequences for a number of the novel's characters. The plot is set in motion when a publishing firm receives a portion of an autobiography written by a ninety-three-year-old man in Key West, Florida, who claims to have murdered Hemingway. Eric "Pappy" Markham, the author of the memoir, alleges that he was the macho man that Hemingway idolized, imitated, and eventually plagiarized, robbing Pappy of the fame he deserved. As revenge, Markham killed Hemingway in 1961, making it appear to be a suicide, and he now wants to reveal the true story to the world.

Sensing that the memoir could be a sensational best-seller, the publishing company dispatches Elliot McGuire to investigate Pappy's claims. To this point in his life McGuire has, like Pappy Markham, been obsessed with Hemingway. As a boy, McGuire sent an angry letter to Hemingway, and the author's suicide a few days later has haunted McGuire for years. He later became a renowned Hemingway scholar, but his career faltered when he was ostracized by his intellectual peers for a drunken statement made at a literary event. Now he has become a hack biographer for wealthy customers, a job he despises. He is in the midst of developing his own biography-based self-help system, Life Forms, when a friend lands him the job of sizing up Pappy Markham's memoir. Though the assignment is a lucrative change for McGuire, he finds Markham's claims ludicrous.

Once in Key West, McGuire discovers that Pappy has no memoir, but when the old man offers him a large portion of the advance to ghost-write a manuscript, McGuire agrees. Pappy's tales of boozing and womanizing in 1920s Paris are compelling, portraying Markham as even more Hemingway-esque than the writer himself. When the finished book becomes a best-seller, McGuire is consumed with guilt, and he resolves to clear Hemingway's name by revealing Pappy as a fraud. The resulting intrigue allows Henderson to satirize print media, television talk shows, and other elements of popular culture while paving the way for a final showdown between Pappy and McGuire.

I Killed Hemingway met with favor from reviewers for its biting look at the mythology of extinct celebrities. "His ability to shatter an icon," a *Publishers Weekly* reviewer noted, "then glue the pieces back together, unnerves his readers as surely as it does his exhausted, desperate characters." Robert Grudin of the *New York Times Book Review* was also enthusiastic. He found that Henderson's theme evoked some very real complexities of literary success and reputation and lauded the work as "complex, amusing and palpably symbolic."

Henderson took another approach to the Elvis Presley legend with his third book, *I, Elvis: Confessions of a Counterfeit King*. The book arose from a challenge from one of Henderson's editors, who dared him to try making himself into a decent Elvis impersonator. And so, at the age of 52, the author plunged into the bizarre world of Elvis fans and celebrity impersonators. He studied other Elvis performers; bought himself appropriate costumes and wigs; practiced with a karaoke machine and Presley recordings; and struggled to perfect his stage moves. This all makes for reading that is "hilarious, informative, and touching in turn," approved *Library Journal* contributor Carol J. Binkowski. "His tale and astute observations make this a page-turner."

After honing his act, Henderson convinced a musician friend to let him perform at an outdoor concert. From there, he moved on to an Elvis competition in New Hampshire (in which he finished in last place), then another Elvis showcase in Jacksonville, Florida, and finally the pinnacle of Elvis impersonation: the annual "Images of Elvis" competition in Memphis, Tennessee. A *Kirkus Reviews* contributor enthusiastically endorsed *I, Elvis* as "a rollicking piece of gonzo journalism" and "a jolly, sparkling trip through Elvis country." The critic continued: "Henderson captures without fuss or condescension the gut-level fandom that makes people, including himself, want to impersonate Elvis, and he is dead-on about the cultural divide, largely along class lines, that separates Elvis fans from those who have never really gotten it. . . . But Henderson's great achievement is to convey, in elegantly droll prose, what it's like to imagine being a great performer—'the Elvis equivalent of flying dreams'—in the face of real-world evidence to the contrary."

Henderson once told *CA:* "I was born in Charlotte, North Carolina, in 1943, and grew up in Chapel Hill. As a boy I was musical and seemed to be headed, if anywhere, in that direction. In high school I led a double life: secret reader and symphony violinist, and rock 'n' roll guitarist. During the school year my bands worked the fraternity circuit. When school was out I disappeared to play in classical summer festival orchestras, accompanying festival-hopping soloists like Isaac Stern, Beverly Sills, and Grant Johannesen.

"I didn't write anything until late in my college years, and when I did, it was poetry. Senior year at Oberlin, I won the Plum Creek Review poetry prize, and after graduation went on to the University of Iowa's Writer's Workshop. Accepted as a poet, I decided (in an act of prophecy and idiocy) to switch, if I could, into the fiction program. It was easy: I simply talked the program secretary into making the necessary changes and—presto, I was a fiction writer. I had never actually written fiction, but that seemed only a minor obstacle. It was a good time for fiction at Iowa. Kurt Vonnegut was there, along with Nelson Algren, Jose Donoso, and Vance Bourjailly. But, unprepared as I was, I spooked myself by doing so poorly that I withdrew from the program, and it was a good fifteen years before I would try fiction again.

"In the meantime I went to New York and got into the technical side of documentary filmmaking, ending up a freelance film editor and location sound recordist. My short film *Zelenka* won a CINE Golden Eagle award and was seen in festivals around the world. In 1969 I made a sideways move into radio where I managed to write and produce a number of radio plays for WBAI-FM in New York where I was a staff producer and had my own live free-form magazine show, '*Medicine Hat*.' This was the 'psychedelic' era at WBAI and the on-air personalities were young, mischievous, and unpredictable. The station maintained a marvelous pop music collection, and I filled my show with curious and esoteric word-tapes and collages of album cuts. Little by little, my delight with the explosion of new music was drawing me back into rock 'n' roll. One day, on impulse, I bought not one but two guitars, a vintage Fender Stratocaster and a beat-up Gibson Les Paul. I had my mother ship me my old Fender Twin Reverb amplifier, and I walked into the station manager's office and resigned from WBAI.

"After a summer in Berkeley, California, I moved to Boston and spent the next five years making my living in various rock 'n' roll road bands, including two years with Cambridge bar legend John Lincoln Wright. Marriage and old age (I was over thirty!) ended this phase of my life. Settling down in Cambridge, I got work as a freelance audio-visual writer and producer while my wife plied her trade as a modern dancer. I specialized in soundtracks, music editing, and jingle writing. We moved back to New York for two years, then out to Los Angeles, where I took a crack at learning the screenwriting trade. After two years, I had absorbed quite a bit of screenplay technique (valuable lessons, especially in plot structure, or as they call it out there, 'story'), but my wife and I began to realize we were not cut out for endless summer, or the entertainment 'company town' character of Los Angeles. We bolted for Calais, Maine, near the Canadian border, where we took work as a gardener-handyman team for some rich summer folks with a mansion and twelve acres. Here I finally faced up to my long-buried ambition to write fiction and banged out the first draft of *Stark Raving Elvis*.

"Two years later, *Stark Raving Elvis* was published. Not long after that, I began the early work on *I Killed Hemingway*. Today I have a teaching job at the University of North Carolina at Chapel Hill. My wife (same one) is now a freelance magazine journalist, and my daughters are seven and ten. When I look back it's hard to believe how long and tortuous a route I took to get where I knew I'd end up all along. But it's been a life, and not a bad one at that."

BIOGRAPHICAL/CRITICAL SOURCES:

PERIODICALS

Booklist, July, 1997, p. 1789.
Boston Globe, December 30, 1984.
Boston Herald, November 18, 1984.
Kirkus Reviews, June 1, 1997, p. 852.
Library Journal, February 15, 1993, p. 192; July, 1997, p. 85.
New York Times, August 30, 1987, p. 34.
New York Times Book Review, December 9, 1984, p. 26; May 9, 1993, p. 9; December 5, 1993, p. 62; April 9, 1995, p. 32.
Philadelphia Inquirer, October 14, 1984.
Publishers Weekly, January 25, 1993, p. 77; February 27, 1995, p. 101; June 16, 1997, p. 52.
San Francisco Chronicle, April 18, 1993.
Village Voice, January 29, 1985, pp. 47-48, 57.

* * *

HINES, Thomas S(pight) 1936-

PERSONAL: Born October 28, 1936, in Oxford, MS; son of Thomas S. (a college administrator and teacher) and Polly (a teacher; maiden name, Moore)

Hines; married Dorothy Taylor (a teacher), June 9, 1967; children: Tracy Odessa, Taylor Spight. *Education:* University of Mississippi, B.A., 1958, M.A., 1960; University of Wisconsin, Ph.D., 1971. *Politics:* Democrat. *Religion:* Episcopalian.

ADDRESSES: *Home*—2207 Selby Ave., Los Angeles, CA 90064. *Office*—Department of History, 6265 Bunche Hall, University of California, Los Angeles, CA 90024.

CAREER: University of California, Los Angeles, assistant professor, 1968-74, associate professor of history, 1974—, joint appointment in the School of Architecture. Visiting professor at University of Texas, 1974-75. *Military service:* U.S. Army, 1960-63; became first lieutenant.

MEMBER: American Studies Association, Society of Architectural Historians.

AWARDS, HONORS: Pacific Coast Prize, 1975, and John H. Dunning Prize, 1976, both from American Historical Association for *Burnham of Chicago.*

WRITINGS:

Burnham of Chicago: Architect and Planner, Oxford University Press (New York City), 1974, 2nd edition, University of Chicago Press (Chicago), 1979.

Richard Neutra and the Search for Modern Architecture: A Biography and History, Oxford University Press (New York City), 1981, University of California (Berkeley), 1994.

The Architecture of Richard Neutra: From International Style to California Modern, Museum of Modern Art (New York City), 1982.

(With Robert Judson Clark) *Los Angeles Transfer: Architecture in Southern California, 1880-1980: Papers Read at a Clark Library Seminar, 25 April 1981, in the Bicentennial Year of the City of Los Angeles,* University of California (Los Angeles), 1983.

(With Franklin D. Israel) *Franklin D. Israel: Buildings and Projects,* Rizzoli (New York City), 1992.

William Faulkner and The Tangible Past: The Architecture of Yoknapatawpha, University of California Press (Berkeley), 1996.

Contributor to books including *The Final Official Report of the Director of Works of the World's Columbian Exposition/World's Columbian Exposition,* by Daniel Burnham, Garland Publications, 1989; and *Sex, Death, and God in L. A.,* edited by David Reid, Pantheon, 1992, University of California, 1994. Contributor of articles to journals, including *American Quarterly, Pacific Historical Review, Journal of the Society of Architectural Historians, Progressive Architecture, Oppositions,* and *Los Angeles Architect.*

SIDELIGHTS: In 1974 Thomas S. Hines took on quite a task when he chose to write about Chicago architect Daniel H. Burnham. Known to his contemporaries of architectural design as "The Betrayer" in 1893 for his design of that year's Chicago World's Fair, Burnham broke Midwest and Chicago School architectural traditions. In this in-depth biography *Burnham of Chicago: Architect and Planner,* Hines addresses the life story of a man who, by 1912 when he died, was also known, according to *American Historical Review* contributor Kenneth Jackson, as "the most famous architect in America and a city planner of international renown." A complex, controversial, and influential architect, Burnham's work, not completely without error, was not easy to present since the likes of Frank Lloyd Wright and Louis Sullivan gave Burnham much to measure against. Hines highlights several of Burnham's planning projects including the aforementioned Chicago World's Fair, the monumental Plan for Chicago of 1909, the "City Beautiful" movement including Cleveland, San Fransisco, and ultimately the culmination and completion of L'Enfant's plans for Washington, DC.

Critics praise Hines in reviewing *Burnham of Chicago* and give him full marks for his scholarship and objectivity on such a volatile subject. As Jackson asserts, "*Burnham of Chicago* is an excellent book and a model of scholarship, good judgment, and literary grace." Reyner Banham of *Architecture and Planning* discusses the dichotomy of Chicago's architecture between the Chicago School and Burnham's maverick ideas as a sore subject not easily analyzed, but that Hines, "though not entirely above the battle, nevertheless has more balance and intellectual curiosity than most of the partisans. . . . Professor Hines recounts without polemic, balancing achievements against inadequacies, in a nicely paced narrative." *New York Times Book Review* analyst Paul Goldberger comments on Hines' reproductions: "Unfortunately, the quality of the photographs here is way below par." But Goldberger joins the others in praising Hines' ability to objectively tell Burnham's story: "in his readable and excellent new biography . . . the sensitivity with which [Hines] discusses it is indicative of his general approach. . . . [The] book as a whole is a model of the balanced portrait, sure of Burnham's importance but always conscious of his failings."

Nearly ten years later Hines, in his 1982 book *Richard Neutra and the Search for Modern Architecture,* again tells a biographical story of yet another controversial figure in architecture. Seemingly more egotistical than Burnham, Neutra himself stands out in his field as much more published author of articles, books, and exhibitions of his prolific work and ideas. Very much in the public eye with so much written about Neutra, Hines' attempt here is to pigeon-hole the architect within the Modern Movement of the 1920s and 1930s. With contemporaries such as Le Corbusier, Gropius, Mies van Rohe, and Saarinen, Neutra's work was challenged to rise to their level. Critics give Hines laudatory though reserved comments. In the *New York Times Book Review,* Goldberger champions Hines' work on Neutra as equally challenging to his work on Burnham: "Hines . . . has brought to *Neutra* a balanced understanding. He is neither worshipful nor harsh, and his superb book is not only the story of a single life but a sensitive examination of a wide range of issues that have confronted architects in the mid-20th century." David Gebhard in *Architecture* challenges Hines for holding back. While Gebhard believes "Hines has provided an excellent social history of Neutra and his times," he views Hines' objectivity as a detriment, "Hines has not been critical enough of Neutra's egocentrism." Even still, *Choice* magazine praises Hines for "an admirable book about a California-based architect. . . . It is a thoroughly researched, fair, well-illustrated, and clear and readable description of the forces that shaped the career and life of a successful and difficult man."

Joining briefly with contemporary Franklin D. Israel in 1992, Thomas Hines contributes his expertise in an essay for Israel's work *Franklin D. Israel: Buildings and Projects.* Here Israel explores his oeuvre as reaction to the avant-garde and bold innovations of contemporary architects, such as himself, based out of Los Angeles, California. Hines, colleague and collaborator with Israel, offers closing comments to this, Israel's autobiographical-in-nature monograph. *Art in America* contributor Jayne Merkel views Hines' essay thusly: "[*Franklin D. Israel: Buildings and Projects*] begins with a clear, explanatory essay by Israel himself and ends with a fine traditional art-historical summary of his career, with his strengths, sources and influences intelligently considered by Thomas Hines."

In *William Faulkner and the Tangible Past: The Architecture of Yoknapatawpha,* Hines provides over 100 photographs, some twenty-five of buildings no longer standing, with brief, yet aesthetic, text on the Mississippi Faulkner carefully, and perhaps even lovingly, used as more than a backdrop to his most famous stories. Hines writes of Faulkner's "architectural consciousness," using Faulkner's letters and works as proof. Hines examines this region's landscape, Indian mounds, and the influence of the Greek Revival, Gothic Revival, Postbellum Victorian and Modernist architectural movements of the last two centuries on northern Mississippi and Faulkner's view of it. Writing for *The New York Times Book Review,* Henry Taylor presents his view of Hines' *Yoknapatawpha* as a very learned piece representing not only Hines' scholarly nature, but his ability to make the endearment of such a place accessible to the reader, as Mississippi's welcoming nature would have it: "This expertise is the beneficiary of a clear and graceful style. Very rarely, Mr. Hines will send the novice to the dictionary. . . . Most of the time the book is informative, even at an elementary level, without being patronizing." Taylor's one criticism addresses the seemingly unnecessary delineation of the Hines and Faulkner genealogical connections embodied in a letter from Hines to his son, arguing that Hines treats the subject "more thoroughly than some readers will appreciate." But Taylor does claim that one of the successful elements to this treatment of the Mississippi architecture, through the eyes of literary genius Faulkner, is the providing of color plates and photographs, some of which Hines shot himself. Taylor asserts, "The balance between text and illustration is in the hands of a resourceful teacher."

Hines once told *CA:* "All good historians have to be voyeurs, inordinately curious about other peoples' lives. Reconstructing the past and creating 'history' allows me to explicate (and attempt to make convincing) situations that novelists could hardly get by with 'perpetrating.' Even in dealing with the most recent events, I try to remember L. P. Hartley's line, 'The past is a foreign country; they do things differently there.'"

BIOGRAPHICAL/CRITICAL SOURCES:

PERIODICALS

American Historical Review, February, 1976, p. 215.
Architectural Digest, February, 1991, p. 58.
Art in America, February, 1994, p. 33.
Booklist, October 1, 1982, p. 178.

Book World, November 28, 1982, p. 13.
California, February, 1983, p. 110.
Choice, November, 1982, p. 417.
Christian Century, November 13, 1974, p. 1072.
Journal of American History, December, 1979, p. 687.
Library Journal, February 15, 1975, p. 387; November 1, 1982, p. 2088.
Newsweek, December 7, 1992, p. 74.
New York Times Book Review, November 10, 1974, p. 7; June 24, 1979, p. 41; December 12, 1982, p. 12; February 9, 1997, p. 7.
Pacific Historical Review, February, 1984, p. 97.
Reviews in American History, September, 1975, p. 348; December, 1983, p. 582.
Times Literary Supplement, June 13, 1975, p. 652; May 4, 1984, p. 485.
Virginia Quarterly Review, spring, 1975, p. R48.*

—Sketch by Mari Artzner Wolf

* * *

HJORTSBERG, William (Reinhold) 1941-

PERSONAL: Surname is pronounced Yorts-berg; born February 23, 1941, in New York, NY; son of Helge (a restaurateur) and Ida (Welti) Hjortsberg; married Marian Souidee Renken, June 2, 1962; children: Lorca Isabel, Max William. *Education:* Dartmouth College, B.A., 1962; graduate study at Yale University, 1962-63, and Stanford University, 1967-68.

ADDRESSES: Home—Main Boulder Rte., McLeod, MT 59052. *Agent*—Robert Dattila, Phoenix Literary Agency, 150 East 74th St., New York, NY 10021.

CAREER: Writer. Teacher in St. Croix, Virgin Islands, 1963-64, 1966-67, draughtsman in New Haven, CT, 1965, and stock boy in a grocery in Bolinas, CA, for three months of 1968.

AWARDS, HONORS: Wallace Stegner creative writing fellowship, 1967; *Playboy* Editorial Award for best new fiction contributor, 1971, for short version of *Gray Matters;* National Endowment for the Arts, creative writing fellowship grant, 1976.

WRITINGS:

Alp, Simon & Schuster (New York City), 1969.
Gray Matters, Simon & Schuster, 1971.
Symbiography, Sumac Press (Fremont, MI), 1973.
Toro! Toro! Toro!, Simon & Schuster, 1974.
Falling Angel, Harcourt (New York City), 1978.
Tales & Fables, Sylvester & Orphanos (Los Angeles), 1985.
Nevermore, Atlantic Monthly Press (New York City), 1994.

Also author of filmscript, *Thunder and Lightning,* for Twentieth-Century Fox. Contributor to *Prize College Stories,* Random House, 1963. Contributor to *Look, Sports Illustrated, Playboy, Last Supplement of the Whole Earth Catalog, New York Times Book Review, Catholic World,* and other periodicals. *Gray Matters* has been translated into several European languages and Japanese.

SIDELIGHTS: William Hjortsberg has written two novels which combine elements of the supernatural with the crime novel genre. In *Falling Angel,* set in 1959, private eye Harry Angel is hired by Louis Cyphre to locate a nightclub singer named Johnny Favorite. Favorite was popular during the Second World War but was injured while performing overseas for the troops. He was sent to a hospital stateside and Cyphre, who claims to have helped the singer early in his career, cannot find him. Angel begins his investigation but soon finds that people he interviews wind up dead, and uncovers disturbing suggestions that Favorite may have sold his soul to the devil for show business success. S. T. Joshi, writing in the *St. James Guide to Horror, Ghost and Gothic Writers,* calls *Falling Angel* "as clever a fusion of the hard-boiled crime story with the tale of supernatural horror as any novel in recent years."

In *Nevermore,* Hjortsberg sets his story in 1920s New York City and teams Harry Houdini with Arthur Conan Doyle in tracking down a serial killer whose crimes are imitations of deaths found in the stories of Edgar Allan Poe. Although Joshi believes that the novel "strains credulity, failing to produce either a satisfying mystery story or an engaging tale of the supernatural," the critic for *Publishers Weekly* dubs it a "droll and captivating fantasy—part gothic mystery, part Who's Who of the Jazz Age, part Perils of Pauline." Wes Lukowsky in *Booklist* concludes that *Nevermore* is "an entertaining historical mystery."

Before settling in Montana in 1971, Hjortsberg spent almost nine years abroad—mainly in Mexico, St. Croix, on the island of Formentera in Spain, and in

Puerto Limon, Costa Rica. He writes: "I enjoy fly fishing, both for trout and in salt water; upland game shooting, skiing, riding horses, body surfing, sketching, exploring unfamiliar places, and conversation. Although born in New York, I tend now to avoid cities. As a boy, I wanted to be a painter. I believe that the land and sky and water belong to the people and are not the exclusive property of industry and commerce . . . I don't believe in nationalism, flags, boundary lines, systems, or nineteenth-century technology. I like the Apollo Project photos of earth; one world, alive and green."

BIOGRAPHICAL/CRITICAL SOURCES:

BOOKS

St. James Guide to Horror, Ghost and Gothic Writers, St. James Press (Detroit, MI), 1998.

PERIODICALS

Booklist, October 1, 1994, p. 242.
Life, October 24, 1969.
Los Angeles Times, October 17, 1971.
New Republic, September 13, 1974.
New York Times, December 16, 1969.
New York Times Book Review, October 31, 1971, August 25, 1974.
Publishers Weekly, August 1, 1994, p. 70.

* * *

HOAG, Tami 1959-

PERSONAL: Born January 20, 1959, in Cresco, IA; daughter of Melanor (in insurance sales) and Joyce (a homemaker; maiden name, LaPointe) Mikkelson; married Daniel Hoag (a computer programmer and business manager), September 24, 1977. *Avocational interests:* Collecting and restoring antique furniture, studying regional American dialects, horseback riding.

ADDRESSES: Home—Goodhue, MN. *Agent*—Andrea Cirillo, Jane Rotrosen Agency, 318 East 51st St., New York, NY 10022.

CAREER: Former trainer and rider of show horses and salesperson of bathroom accessories; writer, 1987—.

AWARDS, HONORS: Career Achievement Award, *Romantic Times.*

WRITINGS:

ROMANCE NOVELS

McKnight in Shining Armor, Bantam (New York City), 1988.
The Trouble with J. J., Bantam, 1988.
Straight from the Heart, Bantam, 1989.
Mismatch, Bantam, 1989.
Man of Her Dreams, Bantam, 1989.
Rumor Has It, Bantam, 1989.
Magic, Doubleday (New York City), 1990.
Tempestuous, Bantam, 1990.
The Rainbow Chasers: Heart of Gold, Bantam, 1990.
The Rainbow Chasers: Keeping Company, Bantam, 1990.
The Rainbow Chasers: Reilly's Return, Bantam, 1990.
Heart of Dixie, Bantam, 1991.
Sarah's Sin, Bantam, 1991.
The Restless Heart, Bantam, 1991.
Still Waters, Bantam, 1992.
The Last White Knight, Bantam, 1992.
Taken by Storm, Bantam, 1992.
Lucky's Lady, Doubleday, 1992.

SUSPENSE NOVELS

Night Sins, G.K. Hall (Thorndike, ME), 1995.
Guilty as Sin, G.K. Hall, 1996.
Cry Wolf, Thorndike Press (Thorndike, ME), 1996.
A Thin Dark Line, Bantam, 1997.

ADAPTATIONS: Night Sins was adapted into a four-hour television mini-series starring Valerie Bertinelli and Harry Hamlin and was first broadcast by CBS-TV in February, 1997; the television rights for *Guilty as Sin* and *A Thin Dark Line* have both been sold.

WORK IN PROGRESS: A reworking of *Dark Paradise* as a suspense novel; a novel about a female FBI agent who leaves behind the agency to work as a victim's rights advocate in Minnesota.

SIDELIGHTS: After achieving significant success as a romance writer, Tami Hoag found more and more of the dark elements of suspense novels creeping into her writing. So, in the mid-1990s, she turned her talents to writing straightforward suspense novels.

Her success continued and actually grew. *Night Sins,* 1995, *Guilty as Sin,* 1996, a darker revision of *Cry Wolf,* 1997, and *A Thin Dark Line,* also 1997, all reached bestseller lists.

Hoag's suspense novels typically take on the kind of dark tragedies that sometimes strike average communities in Minnesota and across the nation. A terrible crime or series of crimes has the community fearing a monster in its midst. Yet, as Allison Lynn and Joanne Fowler observe in *People Weekly,* "She stands apart for writing about her sensational subjects in a levelheaded way." Part of this levelheadedness comes from the author's attention to the details. As Bridget Kinsella comments in a *Publishers Weekly* profile, "Considerable background research is another component of Hoag's work, and she says her compulsion for real details has increased with each title." But Hoag goes beyond the details, believes reviewer Joyce Slater, quoted in *People:* "Even though her books deal with gruesome crimes, her sense of morality really comes through. . . . You actually care about the characters." In fact, according to Kinsella, "Her stories always seem to emerge from her characters." And, her characters have a well developed complexity, Kinsella comments: "To facilitate character development, Hoag composes comprehensive psychological profiles of her main characters, complete with details of their childhoods and relationships with others. Many of her protagonists are plucky, determined but vulnerable women attracted to strong, opinionated men."

In *Night Sins* and *Guilty as Sin,* Hoag spins the story of the kidnapping of an eight-year-old boy and its affect on a small town outside Minneapolis. "The Norman Rockwell-esque community of Deer Lake, Minn., takes a turn toward Stephen King territory when the local lady doctor's son is snatched by a fiend who leaves enigmatic notes," points out a contributor to *Publishers Weekly.* Megan O'Malley, of the state police, arrives to help the local authorities with the case. "Though Hoag provides occasional passages of genuine suspense," continues the reviewer, "the intrigue here is never fully realized." In the sequel, O'Malley is in the hospital, but prosecutor Ellen North takes up the effort to put the prime suspect and any accomplices behind bars. "Those unfamiliar with *Night Sins* will need some time to sort out the characters' Peyton Place-like involvements," notes a *Publishers Weekly* review. "Readers new and old, however will enjoy the political infighting, the legal jockeying and the several jolts of Grand Guignol violence. Hoag, who knows how to push the right buttons, is a suspense writer to watch."

A Thin Dark Line takes place in a small Louisiana parish where a string of rapes and murders has the residents in a state of panic. The main suspect eludes trial because of a legal technicality. Annie Broussard, a deputy for the sheriff's department, takes up the case. "This latest thriller wastes no time," states a *Publishers Weekly* reviewer; "it's creepy from the prologue, a tortured poem written by the murderer, which both establishes the tone and cleverly sets up the ending." Even though Hoag has stepped beyond the familiar confines of her home state of Minnesota, she "displays a firm grasp on locale," the reviewer adds. She also shows, in the opinion of Gene Lyons of *Entertainment Weekly,* a grasp for the genre. "Romance novelist Hoag handles the novel's police procedural aspects smoothly," he writes. *Library Journal* contributor Laurel A. Wilson finds the story uneven, maintaining "Hoag almost scuttles her own story by making the first 200 pages dull and repetitive before finally settling down to let the character evolve and the story take its own dark, satisfying turns." Yet, in the *Publishers Weekly* reviewer's estimation, "There's plenty of suspense in waiting to see how it will all be resolved. Psychopathic villains are common enough, but Hoag has managed to endow hers with a scarred entourage that provides a tragic note."

For Kinsella, "The two faces of Tami Hoag—the practical, upbeat Minnesotan and the subversive crime writer, fascinated by the darker currents of the criminal mind—seem to coexist harmoniously." The reviewer concludes, "In integrating them in her work, Hoag has clearly come into her own."

BIOGRAPHICAL/CRITICAL SOURCES:

PERIODICALS

Detroit News, February 21, 1997.

Entertainment Weekly, January 31, 1997, p. 55; March 28, 1997, p. 62.

Library Journal, February 15, 1997, p. 162.

Maclean's, May 19, 1997, p. 41.

People Weekly, February 24, 1997, pp. 15, 75.

Publishers Weekly, December 19, 1994, p. 44; January 8, 1996, p. 55; April 8, 1996, p. 33; January 13, 1997, p. 52; April 21, 1997, p. 47.*

HOCHSCHILD, Arlie Russell 1940-

PERSONAL: Born January 15, 1940, in Boston, MA; daughter of Francis Henry (a diplomat) and Ruth (Libbey) Russell; married Adam Marquand Hochschild (a magazine editor), June 26, 1965; children: David Russell, Gabriel Russell. *Education:* Swarthmore College, B.A., 1962; University of California, Berkeley, M.A., 1965, Ph.D., 1969. *Politics:* "Left/Liberal." *Religion:* Agnostic.

ADDRESSES: Home—84 Seward St., San Francisco, CA 94114. *Office*—Department of Sociology, University of California, Berkeley, CA 94720.

CAREER: University of California, Santa Cruz, assistant professor of sociology, 1969-71; University of California, Berkeley, assistant professor, 1971-75, associate professor, 1975-84, professor of sociology, 1984—, acting chair of sociology department, 1979-80. Swarthmore College, E. M. Lang visiting professor, fall, 1992; Ford Foundation Work Family Collaborative Research Project, advisor, 1991—; Institute for Social Change at the University of California-Berkeley, member of advisory committee, 1984-86, 1993-94; *American Prospect* and *Gender and Society,* member of board of editors.

MEMBER: American Sociological Association, Sociologists for Women in Society, American Gerontological Society, American Federation of Teachers.

AWARDS, HONORS: Guggenheim fellowship, 1976-77; Charles Cooley Award for *The Managed Heart: Commercialization of Human Feeling;* Notable Book of the Year in Social Sciences awards, *New York Times Book Review,* 1983, 1989; *The Second Shift: Working Parents and the Revolution at Home* was selected by the *New York Times* as a book "of particular interest," 1989; Ford Foundation grantee, 1990-91; Sloan Foundation fellowship to study family-friendly reforms in the workplace, 1993-95; fellow, Center for Advanced Study in Behavioral Studies, Stanford University.

WRITINGS:

The Unexpected Community: Portrait of an Old Age Subculture, Prentice-Hall, 1973, 2nd edition, 1978.

Coleen, the Question Girl (children's story), Feminist Press, 1973.

The Managed Heart: Commercialization of Human Feeling, University of California Press, 1983.

(With Anne Machung) *The Second Shift: Working Parents and the Revolution at Home,* Viking (New York City), 1989.

The Time Bind: When Work Becomes Home and Home Becomes Work, Holt (New York City), 1997.

Contributor to professional journals.

SIDELIGHTS: Sociologist Arlie Russell Hochschild gave the world an illuminating and sometimes disturbing picture of the heavy workload shouldered by modern women in her study *The Second Shift: Working Parents and the Revolution at Home.* Through careful study and analysis of fifty couples, she showed that—in addition to maintaining the demanding careers they started before becoming mothers—most women do about 75 percent of the housework in their homes and 80 percent of the child-care tasks in their families. In other words, after putting in a full day at the office, they also come home to work a "second shift" that adds up to an entire month of 24-hour work days each year. Hochschild's book, "well-researched and well-written," is "a sad testimony to what little distance has been covered since the early 1970s, when women began entering the work force in droves," commented *Detroit Free Press* contributor Ruth Bayard Smith.

Hochschild's study had its genesis years before its publication, when the author was working as an untenured assistant professor at the University of California, Berkeley. In order to hold on to her position at the school and continue to nurse her infant son, she began bringing the child to her office. Although those around her were mostly supportive of the arrangement, Hochschild felt unsure of her ability to maintain her professional image under those circumstances. She questioned why she should feel that way, and why her male colleagues never seemed to have to struggle to balance career and family responsibilities.

While pondering these issues, Hochschild was working on her first book, *The Unexpected Community: Portrait of an Old Age Subculture.* Based on data gathered in 1969 for her Ph.D. thesis, the book examined the lives of forty-three elderly people living in a lower-income housing project. Facing rejection from a youth-oriented society, these people banded together to help each other through the difficulties of their daily lives. Though it was an academic study, *The Unexpected Community* was characterized by reviewers as a straightforward book suitable for reading by general audiences.

Hochschild's writing was again praised with her second publication, *The Managed Heart: Commercialization of Human Feeling,* which was called "lively and stimulating" by *Nation* reviewer Marcia Millman. In this book, the author presents the concept of "emotional labor," in which people are paid to suppress their authentic feelings and sell synthetic emotions as commodities. The basis for her book was a study she conducted on airline attendants, both at work and in their training classes. At the time of the study, airlines were freer to recruit distinct types of women and use them as emblems of the sexualized images they wished their companies to project. Thus United Airlines hired women who looked like the "girl next door"; Pan Am looked for those who could portray a sophisticated, upper-class type; and Pacific Southwest sought out candidates who appeared to be brassy, sexy, and fun-loving. The stress of fitting into these artificial roles caused many attendants to experience emotional numbness and dissociation. In *The Managed Heart,* Hochschild proposed that teachers, nurses, and many other workers were also paid to play out roles requiring them to suppress their true feelings and do a considerable amount of acting.

"Hochschild's book is interesting on a number of levels," reported Millman. "Its greatest value lies in its complex exploration of the nature of emotion. . . . Hochschild plays with a wide range of approaches to understanding emotion, and adds an important dimension by showing how feeling has become another form of work." Like *The Unexpected Community, The Managed Heart* was widely praised for its readability; Gail Sheehy commented in the *New York Times Book Review* that it "is written so accessibly that it appeals to both the academic and the general reader."

Hochschild proved her ability to attract mainstream audiences when *The Second Shift* was published in 1989. The book, which was praised by *Newsweek* reviewer Jim Miller as having "some of the detail and texture of a good novel," provoked a great deal of media attention with its claim that the women's revolution had actually increased inequity for women. Some reviewers pointed out that even though Hochschild is a declared feminist, she had actually supplied ammunition for conservative traditionalists who believe that women should never have entered the workplace. Her studies showed that even in couples who thought they shared domestic duties fairly, the women almost always carried a disproportionately large share of the burden. In one family that Hochschild observed, the wife was responsible for the household, finances, and children; the husband, in contrast, took care of the car and the dog, and believed that he was contributing equally to their domestic life. Hochschild noted that even when the women were aware of the disparity, they tended to hold their tongues and live with it rather than increase tensions with their mates by fighting to strike a better balance.

"What Hochschild describes . . . is so gloomy, at least for two-career couples who are trying to raise children, that the information should be withheld from the young, or the race may not reproduce," declared John Skow in *Time.* As quoted in the *Ann Arbor News,* Hochschild agreed that the facts presented in her book are "serious and consequential . . . in an age of easy divorce, this is a principal cause of strain for couples." Her primary purpose for writing the book, she told *Chicago Tribune* interviewer Nina Burleigh, was to create "a sense of urgency" about the situation. "I am trying to take the veil off a certain cultural myth that prevents us from appreciating the seriousness of the issue. This is the myth of the strainless women with the flying hair, the one with a briefcase in one hand, a child in the other and a look of confidence and control. Implicitly we are made to think, 'If only I could be that confident, energetic, well-organized, I could resolve the contradicting demands of work and family.'" Despite the deep roots of the problems she described, Hochschild voiced optimism about finding resolutions to those problems. As she told the *Ann Arbor News:* "I am in no way pessimistic about working them out. There should be a new form of discourse that could bring to light the deeper emotional meanings of common contributions at home. And if people had conversations about that, a lot might change."

Like *The Second Shift, The Time Bind: When Work Becomes Home and Home Becomes Work,* Hochschild's next book, was considered a provocative analysis of a problem felt to be increasingly experienced in late-twentieth-century American lives, in this case the imbalance of time allotted to work and family. Based on three summers' research with employees at all levels of a Midwestern company touted as one of the most family-friendly in the nation, *The Time Bind* found that men and women at all levels of employment generally failed to take advantage of the company's lenient policies intended to ease the strain of work on family. Most controversial of all was Hochschild's contention that rather than a consequence of economic need, people were actually extending their work days at the expense of time spent with spouses, and most of all with children, out of choice. With the advent of team work and improved work environments, work can be a pleasurable respite from the emotional demands of a messy homelife complicated by divorce and blended families, according to the author. "Her conclusion is that, even here, children are becoming the ultimate victims of a society that values economic output above all else," explained Kirstin Downey Grimsley in the *Washington Post.*

The response to Hochschild's thesis was intense, generating praise and censure from both ends of the political spectrum. "Work/family balance has emerged as one of the most fiercely contested terrains in the culture wars between liberals and conservatives over where the country is headed," observed Peter G. Gosselin in the *Boston Globe.* "And—Hochschild insists, to her surprise—she has weighed in with a bombshell." While some conservatives applauded Hochschild's research, claiming that it provided concrete evidence that the influx of women into the marketplace, often seen as one of the gains of modern feminism, is detrimental to children and the family, other, equally conservative, commentators, denigrated the author's call for a shorter work week and pointed out that her sample group is not representative of society as a whole. "Men and (especially) women with MBAs doing well at a high-powered company are, for self-selecting reasons, among society's least likely candidates to curtail careers for family life," noted Lisa Schiffren in the *Wall Street Journal.* A number of reviewers, on the other hand, including those who faulted *The Time Bind* for various reasons, admitted that there was a kernel of truth to her argument. "Ms. Hochschild has exposed something that feels like an unacknowledged home truth, America's clean little secret," wrote Nicholas Lemann in the *New York Times:* "work, not even the substance of it but the buzzy surface feeling of office life, is for many of us a source of intense pleasure."

"Sociologist Arlie Russell Hochschild is one of a privileged breed, an academic with a popular following," wrote Suzanne Mantell in *Publishers Weekly.* Mantell noted that the concept "second shift," which Hochschild invented in a book of the same title to describe the work that American women do at home *after* they leave their paying jobs, has entered the language as a truism about American life. "If Hochschild's time bind—meaning the crushing lack of time we collectively experience at home—becomes a term as familiar, it will be a tribute to her meticulous description of the situation," Mantell continued.

Not all of Hochschild's reviewers agreed with this description of the merits of the author's prose—Schiffren dubbed Hochschild's language "overwrought"—nor would they all proclaim the universal applicability of the author's diagnosis of what is wrong with this corporation, and by extension, with this country. Nevertheless, "as *The Time Bind* helpfully documents, the notion that men and women can easily balance the demanding responsibilities of job and family has proved, at least for a good many people, a damaging myth," concluded Leslie Lenkowsky in *Commentary.*

BIOGRAPHICAL/CRITICAL SOURCES:

BOOKS

Best Sellers, Volume 4, Gale (Detroit, MI), 1989.

PERIODICALS

Ann Arbor News, August 6, 1989.
Booklist, May 1, 1997, p. 1467.
Boston Globe, May 25, 1997, p. N13; May 28, 1997, p. F1.
Business Week, July 21, 1997, p. 93.
Chicago Tribune, November 5, 1989; June 2, 1997, sec. 1, p. 17.
Choice, April, 1979, pp. 297-98.
Commentary, September, 1997, p. 71.
Detroit Free Press, August 6, 1989.
Fortune, June 9, 1997, p. 160.
Harper's Magazine, December, 1997, p. 47.
Kirkus Reviews, March 15, 1997, p. 439.
Library Journal, May 1, 1997, p. 118.
Los Angeles Times, August 1, 1989.
Los Angeles Times Book Review, June 1, 1997, p. 6.
Ms., July, 1997, p. 89.
Nation, December 31, 1983, pp. 703-06.
Newsweek, July 31, 1989, p. 65; April 28, 1997, p. 64.
New York Times Book Review, October 23, 1983, pp. 7, 36; June 25, 1989; May 11, 1997, p. 8; June 1, 1997, p. 40.
Publishers Weekly, March 24, 1997, p. 69; May 5, 1997, p. 182.
Time, August 7, 1989, p. 62.

Utne Reader, July, 1997, p. 95.
Wall Street Journal, July 2, 1997, p. A12.
Washington Post, May 18, 1997, p. H4.
Washington Post Book World, June 4, 1989.

* * *

HONEYCOMBE, Gordon 1936-

PERSONAL: Born September 27, 1936, in Karachi, India; son of Gordon Samuel (a sales manager) and Dorothy Louise (Fraser) Honeycombe. *Education:* University College, Oxford, M.A. (with honors), 1961. *Avocational interests:* Brass-rubbing, bridge, genealogy, curry, crosswords, pigs, mountains, the sea.

ADDRESSES: *Agent*—Peters, Fraser and Dunlop, The Chambers, Chelsea Harbour, Lots Rd., London SW10 0XF, England.

CAREER: Radio Hong Kong, Hong Kong, announcer, 1956-57; Scottish Home Service, Glasgow, radio announcer, 1958; Royal Shakespeare Co., Stratford-on-Avon, England, actor, 1962-63; television actor, 1964; Independent Television News, London, England, newscaster, 1965-77; author, playwright, and lecturer, 1978—; news presenter on *TV-AM,* England, 1984-89; actor, director, and television presenter, 1989—. Directed his play *The Redemption* in Western Australia, March, 1990. Performer in television series, including *That Was the Week That Was, The Foundation,* and *First among Equals;* has appeared in films, including *The Medusa Touch, Ransom,* and *The Fourth Protocol;* has presented television series, including *Family History* and *Arthur C. Clarke's Mysterious World;* has appeared in plays, including *The Prisoners, Playback 625,* and *Run for Your Wife. Military service:* British Army, Royal Artillery, 1955-57; served in Hong Kong.

AWARDS, HONORS: Silver Medal, New York Film and Television Festival, 1975, for *Time and Again.*

WRITINGS:

The Miracles (two-act play), produced in Oxford, England, at Pusey House Chapel, 1960.
The Redemption (two-act play; produced in Consett, England, at Consett Civic Theatre, 1970), Methuen, 1964.
The Golden Vision (television play), broadcast by British Broadcasting Corp. (BBC), 1968.
Neither the Sea nor the Sand (novel), Hutchinson (London), 1969, Weybright (New York City), 1970.
Dragon under the Hill (novel), Hutchinson, 1972, Simon & Schuster (New York City), 1973.
Adam's Tale (novel), Hutchinson, 1974.
Time and Again (television play), broadcast by Westward Television (England), 1975.
Red Watch (nonfiction), Hutchinson, 1976.
The Princess and the Goblins (two-act musical play), produced in Great Ayton, England, at Rosehill Theatre, 1976.
Waltz of My Heart (two-act musical biography of Ivor Novello), produced in Bournemouth, England, at Winter Garden, 1980.
(Editor and author of introduction) Tatsuichiro Akizuki, *Nagasaki 1945* (nonfiction), Quartet Books (London), 1981.
Royal Wedding (nonfiction), M. Joseph (London), 1981.
The Edge of Heaven (fiction), Hutchinson, 1981.
The Murders of the Black Museum (nonfiction), Hutchinson, 1982.
The Year of the Princess (nonfiction), Hutchinson, 1982.
Selfridges: Seventy-Five Years (nonfiction), Park Lane (London), 1984.
TV-AM's Official Celebration of the Royal Wedding (nonfiction), Weidenfeld & Nicolson (London), 1986.
The Thirteenth Day of Christmas (television play), broadcast by Granada Television (England), 1986.

Also author, with Rosemary Davies, of screenplay adaptation of *Neither the Sea Nor the Sand,* 1972.

DRAMATIZATIONS

Paradise Lost, broadcast by BBC-Radio 4, 1974.
God Save the Queen (two-act dramatized anthology), produced in Chichester, England, at Chichester Festival Theatre, 1977.
A King Shall Have a Kingdom (two-act dramatized anthology), produced in York, England, at Theatre Royal, 1977.
Lancelot and Guinevere, broadcast by BBC-Radio 4, 1977, produced on the West End at the Old Vic, 1980.

SIDELIGHTS: Gordon Honeycombe's novel *Neither the Sea Nor the Sand* concerns a young man who, shortly after meeting the love of his life, dies unexpectedly of a heart attack. His girlfriend's love brings him back from the dead; but he lives a kind of zombie-like existence in which he is not in complete control of his actions. Worse, his body is decaying as would any other dead body. "So an unsentimental love story," remarks Chris Morgan in the *St. James Guide to Horror, Ghost and Gothic Writers,* "becomes a grotesque tragedy. The gradual deterioration of Hugh's body is not avoided. The novel includes some grossly unpleasant scenes. . . . For a first novel this is competent and remarkably accomplished."

Honeycombe's *Red Watch* is the true story of a fatal fire and the men who fought it. Its publication coincided with the first national fireman's strike in Britain and, according to Honeycombe, in conjunction with an article he wrote supporting the fireman in the *Daily Mail,* indirectly led to his resignation as a television newscaster. About the experience, Honeycombe told *CA:* "I happened to get to know this particular Watch at this particular fire station in London through a charity event. Six months later they had to deal with the worst fire in central London that year (1974). I was not at the fire, but afterwards I heard the firsthand accounts of the men who had fought the blaze. Seven people, including one Red Watch fireman, died. I thought it was a story well worth telling, for no one then knew or cared about what a fireman's job entailed, and it was a story never told before. Strangely, it was while I was writing the book that I learned that my great-grandfather, Samuel Honeycombe, had been the first captain and founder of the Northfleet Fire Brigade in Kent in 1885."

BIOGRAPHICAL/CRITICAL SOURCES:

BOOKS

St. James Guide to Horror, Ghost and Gothic Writers, St. James Press (Detroit, MI), 1998.

PERIODICALS

Times (London), December 11, 1986.
Times Literary Supplement, January 1, 1982.
Washington Post Book World, November 28, 1982.

* * *

HOPKINSON, Deborah 1952-

PERSONAL: Born February 4, 1952, in Lowell, MA; daughter of Russell W. (a machinist) and Gloria D. Hopkinson; married Andrew D. Thomas (a teacher); children: Rebekah, Dimitri. *Education:* University of Massachusetts—Amherst, B.A., 1973; University of Hawaii, M.A., 1978. *Avocational interests:* Reading, hiking, swimming, history.

ADDRESSES: Home—3561-D Pinao St., Honolulu, HI 96822. *Office*—East-West Center, 1777 East-West Rd., Honolulu, HI 96848.

CAREER: Manoa Valley Theater, Honolulu, HI, marketing director, 1981-84; University of Hawaii Foundation, Honolulu, development director, 1985-89; East-West Center, Honolulu, development director, 1989—. Creative Fund Raising Associates, Honolulu, consultant, 1991—. Board member of the National Society of Fund Raising Executives, Aloha Chapter, 1985-91.

MEMBER: Society of Children's Book Writers and Illustrators, National League of American Pen Women.

AWARDS, HONORS: Merit award, Society of Children's Book Writers and Illustrators, 1991; work-in-progress grant recipient, Society of Children's Book Writers and Illustrators, 1993.

WRITINGS:

JUVENILES

Pearl Harbor, Dillon Press/Macmillan (New York City), 1991.
Sweet Clara and the Freedom Quilt, illustrated by James Ransome, Knopf (New York City), 1993.
Birdie's Lighthouse, Atheneum (New York City), 1996.
The Brightest Day: the Story of the Jubilee Singers, Atheneum, 1998.

Contributor of short stories to periodicals, including *Cricket.*

SIDELIGHTS: "As a girl, I always wanted to be a writer," Deborah Hopkinson commented. "But I never knew what I wanted to write. Then, when my daughter Rebekah was about three, we were reading a lot of children's books. Having a full-time career and a child, I was very busy. But I thought, 'Maybe I'll try writing for children. At least the books are short!' I have since found out that simply because a story is short, that doesn't mean that it is easy to write!"

Hopkinson's first book, *Pearl Harbor,* was published in 1991 as part of Dillon Press's "Places in American History" series. Aimed at older children, the book tells the story of the surprise Japanese bombing of Pearl Harbor during World War II and includes photographs showing Pearl Harbor both during the war and today.

For her second book, Hopkinson decided to try her hand at fiction. *Sweet Clara and the Freedom Quilt* is about a slave girl who is separated from her mother and sent to work in the fields. She lives with an elderly woman named Aunt Rachel, who teaches her to sew. Clara becomes a seamstress, but she is always preoccupied with thoughts of her mother and freedom. Clara overhears other slaves discussing the "underground railroad," and decides to use her sewing skills to help herself and other slaves escape. In her spare time, she sews a quilt; but instead of patchwork, Clara's quilt is a map detailing an escape route. When she finally does escape the plantation, she leaves the quilt for other slaves.

Hopkinson commented: "The idea for *Sweet Clara and the Freedom Quilt* came to me while listening to a radio story about African American quilts. I consider this story a wonderful gift, and feel very happy that I was able to tell it." The story "brings power and substance to this noteworthy picture book," writes a reviewer for *Publishers Weekly* who concludes: "This first-rate book is a triumph of the heart."

Hopkinson gave her readers another exciting story about a brave young girl with *Birdie's Lighthouse.* Set in the mid-nineteenth century, the book takes the form of a ten-year-old girl's diary. Bertha "Birdie" Holland, the main character, moves to a lighthouse island in Maine with her father after he gives up his life as a sailor. Birdie's brother is more interested in fishing than in the workings of the beacon light, but Birdie herself becomes fascinated with the job. Eventually, she learns enough about the lighthouse to man it herself when her father falls gravely ill.

Although Birdie is a fictional character, she is closely based on real-life girls whose heroic lighthouse adventures are well-documented. The book is illustrated with watercolor and pen-and-ink, and these pictures were remarked upon by several reviewers as an important part of the book. Praising the work as a whole, Mary M. Burns wrote in *Horn Book:* "With an exemplary assemblage of genre paintings perfectly attuned to the flow of the text, the whole is restrained yet charged with emotion." A *Kirkus Reviews* contributor enthused: "Period details and a spirited heroine with a clear voice make this book a genuine delight." A *Publishers Weekly* reviewer found *Birdie's Lighthouse* "atmospheric" and Birdie herself "brave and likable." The reviewer believed that "the text is unlikely to be mistaken for the voice of an actual young girl," but praised "Hopkinson's narrative and its careful attention to period and setting" and concluded that "its nuances of feeling and historical detail shine through." And Anne Parker in *School Library Journal* called *Birdie's Lighthouse* "a shining bit of historical fiction."

In addition to her books, Hopkinson also writes short stories, especially for *Cricket* magazine. While her main interest "is stories that also tell about history," she adds, "I also like to write about girls, because when I was a girl, there weren't many stories about the exciting things that girls can do!"

BIOGRAPHICAL/CRITICAL SOURCES:

PERIODICALS

Booklist, June 1, 1997, p. 1718.

Bulletin of the Center for Children's Books, July/August 1993, p. 346.

Horn Book, July-August, 1997, p. 443.

Kirkus Reviews, May 1, 1997, p. 722.

Publishers Weekly, February 8, 1993, p. 87; July 12, 1993, pp. 25-26; April 14, 1997, p. 74.

School Library Journal, June 1993, p. 76; June, 1997, pp. 90-92.

* * *

HOVING, Thomas 1931-

PERSONAL: Born January 15, 1931, in New York, NY; son of Walter (in business) and Mary Osgood (Field) Hoving; married Nancy Melissa Bell (a management consultant), October 3, 1953; children: Petrea Bell. *Education:* Princeton University, B.A. (summa cum laude), 1953, M.F.A., 1958, Ph.D., 1959.

ADDRESSES: Home—150 East 73rd St., New York, NY 10021.

CAREER: Metropolitan Museum of Art, Department of Medieval Art and the Cloisters, New York City, curatorial assistant, 1959-60, assistant curator, 1960-63, associate curator, 1963-65, curator, 1965-66; New York City, commissioner of parks, 1966-67, administrator of recreation and cultural affairs, 1967; Metropolitan Museum of Art, director, 1967-77; management consultant, 1977—. Correspondent and interviewer for American Broadcasting Co. (ABC-TV) feature news program *20/20.* Director of International Business Machines (IBM) Americas, H. S. Stuttman Co., and Manhattan Industries. *Military service:* U.S. Marine Corps, 1953-55; became first lieutenant.

MEMBER: American Institute of Architects (honorary member).

AWARDS, HONORS: National Council of the Humanities fellowship, 1955; Kienbusch and Haring fellowship, 1957; distinguished citizen award from Citizens Budget Committee, 1966; award from *Cue* magazine, 1966; LL.D. from Pratt Institute, 1967; distinguished achievement award from Advertising Club of America, 1968; LL.D. from Princeton University, 1968; D.F.A. from New York University, 1968; Litt.D. from Middlebury College, 1968.

WRITINGS:

The Sources of the Ivories of the Ada School (Ph.D. thesis), Princeton University Press (Princeton, NJ), 1960.

(Editor) *The Chase, the Capture: Collecting at the Metropolitan,* Metropolitan Museum of Art (New York City), 1975.

Two Worlds of Andrew Wyeth: Kuerners and Olsons, Metropolitan Museum of Art, 1976.

Tutankhamun: The Untold Story, Simon & Schuster (New York City), 1978.

King of the Confessors, Simon & Schuster, 1981.

Masterpiece (novel), Simon & Schuster, 1986.

Discovery! (novel), Simon & Schuster, 1989.

Making the Mummies Dance: Inside the Metropolitan Museum of Art, Simon & Schuster, 1993.

(With Andrew Wyeth) *Andrew Wyeth: Autobiography, as Told to Thomas Hoving,* Bulfinch, 1995.

False Impressions: The Hunt for Big-Time Art Fakes, Simon & Schuster, 1996.

Greatest Works of Art of Western Civilization, Artisan/Workman (New York City), 1997.

Author of Metropolitan Museum of Art guidebooks and art calendars. Consultant to *Museums, New York* and author of its column "Happenings." Contributor of articles to *Apollo* magazine, *House Beautiful,* and *Metropolitan Museum of Art Bulletin.* Editor for *Connoisseur* magazine.

SIDELIGHTS: Thomas Hoving joined the curatorial staff of the Metropolitan Museum of Art in New York City in 1959 after James J. Rorimer, the museum director at that time, heard Hoving lecture at New York's Frick Collection on the Annibale Carracci frescoes of the Farnese Gallery in Rome. Hoving started as a curatorial assistant in the Cloisters, the Metropolitan's collection of medieval art, which includes a number of intact medieval cloisters, or enclosed colonades, brought over from Europe. Hoving quickly moved up to curator of the Met's Cloisters, in part because of his discovery of the twelfth-century medieval ivory the Bury St. Edmunds Cross. Following that, Hoving took a brief respite from the art world joining the New York City Parks Department as commissioner under the auspices of 1966 mayor John Lindsay. Building a reputation for himself as a great public relations man for the parks system, Hoving was soon romanced back to the Metropolitan when, in 1967, his former mentor Rorimer died and Hoving was appointed the new director of the largest art museum in the world.

Hoving spent ten years at the Met, striving to change the museum's operations and attempting to make art more accessible to all people, which at times rattled many a cage in the New York art community. Following his departure from the Met, Hoving has been writing about his many adventures in the art world, particularly about his tenure at the Met. His writing has shattered myths, reputations, and pretenses of the world art community. Though critics have considered his work controversial, claiming his sense of detail too sketchy or too embellished, or Hoving's truths to be his truths alone, Hoving's books have been very popular with the public as the books have spent many weeks on *The New York Times* "Best Seller" lists.

In 1977, after Hoving's departure from the Metropolitan, and appearing in bookstores at the same time as the Met's premiere showing of treasures of King Tutankhamun, Hoving's first book *Tutankhamun: The Untold Story* joined the "King Tut" craze, but with a twist. In this volume Hoving discusses the fascinating and controversial tale of Howard Carter's discovery of King Tutankhamun's tomb in 1922 and his celebratory, and clandestine, "pilfering" of the archaeological site. Though some critics were unimpressed with Hoving's story-telling, Barbara G.

Mertz was of the mind that the book somewhat clarified the real picture of archaeology and Egyptology, commenting that *Tutankhamun* "gives considerable insight into the sometimes sordid, sometimes amusing complications that affect all human activities, even archaeology."

In Hoving's *King of the Confessors,* the history and capture of the Bury St. Edmund's cross, a twelfth century medieval ivory, is revealed. Here the reader discovers Hoving's obsessive involvement, and pursuit, on an international scale, of the controversial acquisition of this damaged, incomplete, yet highly valuable medieval artifact, costing the Met $600,000, a very large sum by 1960s standards. In a 1980 interview with *CA,* Hoving explained, "That twelfth-century cross, which I consider to be one of the greatest works of art ever created . . . changed my life. . . . It is owing to that cross that I became director of the Metropolitan." Critics of *King* tried to hold back praise. Accusing Hoving of self-aggrandizement, Walter Goodman, writing for the *New York Times Book Review,* states that "The promotional pizazz that marked Mr. Hoving's reign at the Met is here devoted to himself. He concedes that ambition generally overcame his scruples." But Goodman also admits that "to appreciate Thomas Hoving's tale, we must scrape away the self-celebration and the questionable passages in order to enjoy a remarkable tale of international espionage, art history and museum one-upmanship." Long time art critic and philosopher Arthur Danto, writing for *Nation,* cheers Hoving's tale as though Hoving were a knight, adding, "I liked the cheerful amorality of the quest, and the glimpse into the underside of the museum world, full of monsters."

Thomas Hoving's next two works were fiction and the critics were harsh. In his 1986 novel *Masterpiece,* Hoving introduces a woman and a man bent on professional advancement, creating an acquisition competition between the Metropolitan Museum of Art in New York and the National Gallery in Washington DC. Their chemistry clashes as well in their attempts to attain a rare and valuable Velasquez painting for their own museum. Potentially reading like pulp, critics felt the narrative, descriptions, and voice unrealistic. Finding some of Hoving's text embarrassingly laughable, critic for *The New York Times Book Review* Lawrence Weschler asks, "Does anyone really sound like that?" He muses that Hoving may have been "simply lampooning the entire blockbuster genre—but parody has to be at least as well written as the genre it upends, and *Masterpiece* isn't." *Kirkus Reviews* claims the work "As styleless as any middlebrow thrill," but conceding that *Masterpiece* "cries out for celluloid." Hoving's second attempt at fiction, *Discovery!,* is a sequel to *Masterpiece* revisiting Foster and Cartwright, now married. The couple find themselves on an archaeological dig in Italy and knee-deep in underworld intrigue and corruption. Again, the critics were disappointed. But *Kirkus Reviews* suggested that "the hundred pages or so of connoisseurship (much of it erotic) are worth the novel's failings."

Probably Hoving's most popular work came in 1993 with his best-selling publication *Making the Mummies Dance: Inside the Metropolitan Museum of Art.* Abandoning fiction, Hoving discusses how he achieved greatness by gaining and inventing the avant-garde directorship of the Metropolitan Museum of Art in New York for the ten years between 1967 and 1977. Beginning his career after college at the Met in 1959 as a curatorial assistant, Hoving put his Princeton doctorate in art and archaeology to the test. But he also liked politics, in particular, John Lindsay, the 1966 mayor of New York. When asked by Lindsay to head the New York City Parks Department, Hoving walked away from art and the museum and learned what power and publicity in politics could do for one's passion to make changes in a staid world. Learning well by changing the face and policies of the NYC Parks, in particular Central Park with it's building-sized banners for the public to paint on and Hoving's famous "Happenings" as a few of his achievements under Lindsay, Hoving was soon asked to return to the Met in 1967, this time as museum director. When Hoving spoke with Lindsay to tell him he would accept, Hoving quotes Lindsay in *Mummies,* "Leaving so soon? . . . you've barely begun. Well, it's a great opportunity. Best of its kind in the country. I can see that. But . . . have you considered the boredom? Seems to me the place is dead. But, Hoving, you'll make the mummies dance." Not afraid to step on toes and rattle cages, Hoving tells of the cavalier, yet focused, wit he used to break rules, precedents, to improve things and make a difference in what Lindsay referred to as a "dead" place.

In spite of some mistakes and failures, when considering whether Hoving brought the Met back to life, "success" could sum it all up, if one takes Hoving's word in *Mummies.* Many critics did not, accusing Hoving not only of embellishing his stories of his ten-year tenure, but outright lying. Contributor to *Art History* Hilton Kramer asserts that Hoving's one self-laudatory tale about an alleged investigation into the hiring practices at the Met just prior to his being given the directorship is full of error, miscalculations of dates, details, names, and titles. In his review of *Mummies,* Kramer quotes Michael Kimmelman of the *New York Times,* "'This anecdote . . . is vintage Hoving for its combination of skulduggery, one-upmanship, bravado and unreliability.'" James Gardner in the *National Review* begins his review "If this were a better book, it would probably be far less enjoyable," calling the book "a vulgar crowdpleaser."

Jo Ann Lewis of the *Washington Post* praised Hoving's *Mummies* as a "riveting, revealing and outrageously nasty social document about the '70s art world that has set phone lines buzzing, faxes humming and—not incidentally—the book climbing up the *New York Times* bestseller list." Hoving's honesty made many people nervous as he discussed such things as his own and his staff administrators' characters, infidelities, and failed exhibits. But he self-lauded the grand achievements such as developing small installation shows and blockbuster exhibits of dead and living artists, face-lifting the building itself, increasing the permanent collection, and turning the little bookstore into a spacious first floor adventure-in-shopping for art books, gifts, and even moderate market reproductions. Hoving's thick-skinned aggressive business-like approach and trail-blazing has been seen as the prototype and catalyst for change in the way museums are managed now and how people in America approach art today. In an interview with Lewis, Hoving explains, "When I went back to the Met, I was no longer a curator: I was a politician who'd learned how the city worked, and how businesses worked, and I wanted to get things done."

Eric Gibson, contributor to *Insight on the News,* offers two reasons for *Mummies*'s importance. The first is that "Hoving's career ushered in the 'modern' museum. . . . His book provides the most detailed chronicle yet of this fateful transformation of our museums." The second reason for *Mummies*'s significance is that "it provides a sobering glimpse of just what a museum director is prepared to do to secure a treasured acquisition. . . . Whether we like it or not, Hoving is the first of an entirely new breed of museum director." Gibson views this story and the attitude of the man who tells it as "the unrepentant, wink-at-the-audience pride of an inveterate seducer." Defending Hoving's controversial tactics, Gibson states that "Hoving at least possessed a knowledge and a love of art," adding, "this book is necessary reading for anyone who wants to understand how we have gotten where we are today, and what has been lost along the way."

A brief break in style, Hoving wrote a catalog meant to accompany a retrospective art exhibit of Andrew Wyeth in 1995 at the Nelson-Atkins Museum of Art in Kansas City. Having interviewed the much-loved and respected American watercolorist Andrew Wyeth in 1976, Hoving gleaned comments made by Wyeth about each of the over four thousand pieces he had painted down to just those that would appear in the 1995 Kansas City exhibit. He titled the show's catalog *Andrew Wyeth: Autobiography.* Though his initial publication of the Wyeth interview did not sell as well as Hoving would have liked, he is proud of it and asserts: "The artist was very cooperative. The book marks the first time an art historian ever interviewed Wyeth."

But Hoving could not be muzzled for long. In his 1996 book *False Impressions: The Hunt for the Big-Time Art Fakes,* Hoving again boldly tells art tales, but this time blasting away at forgers and the dupes who have been taken in by them. After at least three decades in the art-buying and museum business, Hoving shows how some of the world famous art forgers have wielded their craft. He discusses how colleagues from other major museums have been taken in by these forgers. Though hoodwinked himself on at least three occasions, still Hoving names himself as one "fakebuster" who can sniff out any forgery. Critics were split in their responses. Contributing to the *Sewanee Review,* Malcolm Goldstein accuses Hoving of feeling "obvious pleasure" when "recounting the mistakes of his colleagues in the museum world. . . . One would expect greater charity, or at least greater restraint, from so intelligent and learned a man." Writing in *Business Week,* Thane Peterson takes a swipe at Hoving as well: "Fascinating as it is *False Impressions* shares many of the weaknesses of *Mummies.* Hoving can't resist the unkind rumor." But in the Lewis interview Hoving's wife Nancy defends her husband: "Stepping on toes has never been a problem for him: He doesn't feel it, so he doesn't think anybody else does either."

Jay Rayner of the London *Observer* gives Hoving credit for a story well told: "The book is at its most enjoyable when he is recounting the detective work that led to the uncovering of great fakes." Philip Kopper in the *Washington Post* heralds *False Impressions* as fascinating: "Hoving is best when writing about things and people he knows and likes. Consequently there is gold here." Kopper goes even farther to wryly suggest its validity as an excellent reference book for art collectors and art students but adds, "When [*False Impressions*] finds its place on the shelf as the text for Art Fakes 101, let it be without the jacket's clowning pictures that telegraph the author's posturing prose inside. For that is not where this informing book's value lies."

Hoving's most recent work is *Greatest Works of Art of Western Civilization,* published in 1997. What makes this standard oversized coffee-table book of art different is that the artworks featured are handpicked by Hoving himself, presenting them as "the ones that changed my life. . . . All I cared about were my reactions and whether they mirrored the power, the mystery, and the magnetism of the works themselves." Eric Bryant in *Library Journal* asserts that Hoving's annotations accompanying each work of art, outside of a one-page introduction, are "brief, often gossipy commentaries." But Jo Ann Lewis' conclusion in her review for *Mummies* could also stand for *Greatest Works:* "the story was more fun the way Hoving told it." Bryant also claims that while many of the 111 works have been featured in other books, many are surprises, and further implies that Hoving's name as the former director of the Metropolitan Museum of Art in New York should be ample justification for examining *Greatest Works.*

In a 1980 *Contemporary Authors* interview Hoving gave candid and insightful responses to Barbara Braun's questions. When asked how he writes he responded: "very fast. . . . I write in longhand—anywhere, on planes, in cars. Then a secretary types it up. *Tutankhamun* took just two drafts, whereas letters can sometimes take up to twelve drafts." Braun asked Hoving what art writers he admired and his answer was sure and succinct, "Longhi, Max Friedlaender, Krautheimer, and Panofsky." While he felt Kenneth Clark's *Civilisation* admirable, Hoving held back accusing Clark of omitting Germany "almost entirely." Since his departure from the Met, Hoving has certainly kept busy as editor of *Connoisseur* magazine, performing management consulting with his business partner wife Nancy, sitting in as columnist of "Happenings" for *Museums, New York,* and reporting and interviewing on the American Broadcasting Company's news program *20/20.* Braun quotes Hoving, "I thoroughly enjoy it. . . . [All] these activities go to support my writing, which I like better than anything."

An interview with Hoving appears in *CA,* Volume 101.

BIOGRAPHICAL/CRITICAL SOURCES:

PERIODICALS

America, May 15, 1982, p. 387.
American History Illustrated, November, 1987, p. 10.
Art in America, June, 1986, p. 18; June, 1986, p. 28; January, 1987, p. 19.
ARTnews, March, 1993, p. 60.
Atlantic, January, 1982, p. 88.
Atlantic Monthly, June, 1996, p. 126.
Booklist, November 1, 1992, p. 466; May 1, 1996, p. 1481.
Business Week, February 1, 1993, p. 13; June 3, 1996, p. 15.
Chicago Tribune Book World, October 22, 1978.
Connoisseur, January, 1982, p. 1.
Cosmopolitan, December, 1981, p. 22.
Economist, January 23, 1993, p. 83.
House Beautiful, January, 1982, p. 33.
Insight on the News, February 8, 1993, p. 22.
Library Journal, November 1, 1992, p. 83; October 15, 1997, p. 58; May 15, 1996, p. 57.
Nation, February 8, 1993, p. 166.
National Review, December 11, 1981, p. 1496; March 1, 1993, p. 65.
New Republic, April 12, 1993, p. 36.
New York, December 7, 1981, p. 61.
New Yorker, February 8, 1993, p. 106.
New York Review of Books, March 4, 1993, p. 8.
New York Times, December 26, 1978.
New York Times Book Review, November 12, 1978; January 3, 1993, p. 1; May 19, 1996, p. 20.
People Weekly, October 26, 1981, p. 32; December 1, 1986, p. 20.
Publishers Weekly, May 8, 1987, p. 60; June 16, 1989, p. 57; June 21, 1989, p. 58; November 23, 1992, p. 45; February 26, 1996, p. 90.
Time, November 16, 1981, p. 141; September 1, 1986, p. 85.
Washington Post Book World, November 26, 1978.
Wilson Library Bulletin, January, 1982, p. 385.*

— Sketch by Mari Artzner Wolf

K

KAPLAN, Anne Bernays 1930-
(Anne Bernays)

PERSONAL: Born September 14, 1930, in New York, NY; daughter of Edward L. and Doris (Fleischman) Bernays; married Justin D. Kaplan (a writer/ biographer), 1954; children: Susanna Bernays, Hester Margaret, Polly Anne. *Education:* Attended Wellesley College, 1948-50; Barnard College, B.A., 1952.

ADDRESSES: *Home and office*—16 Francis Ave., Cambridge, MA 02138.

CAREER: *Discovery,* New York City, managing editor, 1952-54; Houghton Mifflin Co., New York City, editorial assistant, 1955-57; Emerson College, Boston, MA, prose writer-in-residence, 1976-77, 1980-81; teacher, Harvard Extension Program, 1977-82.

WRITINGS:

NOVELS; UNDER NAME ANNE BERNAYS

The New York Ride, Trident, 1965.
Prudence, Indeed, Trident, 1966.
The First to Know, Popular Library (New York City), 1975.
Growing Up Rich, Little, Brown (Boston), 1975, Scribner's (New York City), 1986.
The School Book, Harper (New York City), 1980.
The Address Book, Little, Brown, 1983.
Professor Romeo, Weidenfeld & Nicolson (New York City), 1989.

OTHER; UNDER NAME ANNE BERNAYS

Short Pleasures (short stories), Doubleday (New York City), 1962.
(With Pamela Painter) *What If?: Writing Exercises for Fiction Writers,* HarperCollins Publishers (New York City), 1990.
(Author of Introduction) Mark Twain, *Merry Tales,* Oxford University Press, (New York City), 1996.
(With Justin Kaplan) *The Language of Names,* Simon & Schuster (New York City), 1997.

Contributor of articles to journals.

SIDELIGHTS: Reviews frequently remark on the wit, irony, and entertaining quality present in novelist Anne Bernays Kaplan's work. Published under the name Anne Bernays, her novels center around female protagonists, or women's concerns, and repeatedly contain elements of a collegiate environment.

Bernays's first novel, *The New York Ride,* is a "witty, sophisticated and sardonic look" at young people in the 1960s, described a *Publishers Weekly* critic in 1966. *New York Ride* features Mary, the "heroine" and her friend Betsy, following them throughout their collegiate travels abroad, postgraduate life, and in marriage "searching for happiness thereafter," recounted *New York Times* contributor Charles Poore. Poore noted: the "novel has a special interest, an unusual perspective. . . . Bernays has a good gift for phrasing. . . . Granted that post-Gatsby revels have been done to death in our literature. Nevertheless, Miss Bernays can still revive their gruesome lividness." Martin Levin stated in the *New York Times Book Review* that the novel is written in a "diaristic, descriptive style" but faulted the character of Besty's for a lack of depth. According to Levin, "we see Betsy's compulsive behavior, her contrariness, [and] her suicidal bent" through Mary, but these descriptions are not enough to reveal a psychological portrait of Betsy. In contrast, characterization was chief among the praises given to Bernays's second novel, *Prudence, Indeed,* which focuses on social worker/psychologist Sophie and her marriage. Similar to other reviews, Thomas Lask wrote in the *New York Times* that *Prudence, Indeed* is interesting, contains irony and humor, and praised: "Miss Bernays has a bright, perky style, a sharp eye for locating the weakness in her people and a knack for letting them reveal those weaknesses."

Growing Up Rich describes the life change of a 14 year old girl who moves from an affluent lifestyle to the home of middle class foster parents after her parents die in a plane crash. Although *Kirkus Reviews* called Bernays "an entertaining writer," in this "almost . . . period piece of the '40's. . . . not much happens." However, a critic for *Time* called the story a "brilliantly written, hard-edged novel of adolescence with. . . . an oddly sentimental conclusion to a bitter book, and precisely the kind that Dickens would have approved."

"*Professor Romeo,* a tale of sexual harassment on a university campus, is a novel with a topical subject and a provocative twist," opened Eva Hoffman's *New York Times* review of the book. The male protagonist, Harvard professor Jacob Barker, is unique to the traditionally female perspectives of both Bernays's novels and harassment discussions. According to Molly Hite in *Women's Review of Books:* "[*Professor Romeo*] attempts the delicate balancing act of conveying the attitudes that allow the harasser to believe he is engaged in a fundamentally consensual and indeed contractual exchange, while at the same time allowing the reader to apprehend the mechanisms of power and gendered blindness that make the equality necessary for consent and contract an impossibility." Hite applauded Bernays's "daring" efforts, but concluded that "the balance is not always sustained." "Unfortunately, in Jacob," summarized Hoffman, "[Bernay] has created a protagonist so charmless, fatuous and self-deceived that he strains suspension of disbelief and the novel's perspective, closely identified with him, flounders between a rather puzzling case study and simple farce." Arthur Schlesinger, Jr. similarly faulted the believability of Jake's character and ended his review in the *New York Times Book Review:* It "is vivid in academic flavor, strong in theme, sharp in its perceptions, alert to emotional contradictions. . . . above all, a work of sharp irony, standing back from making simple or fashionable judgments and taking a nicely jaundiced view of our contemporary sexual skirmishes."

Bernays collaborated with her husband, Justin Kaplan, to write *The Language of Names,* a book which "covers such topics as movie star names, maiden names, ethnic-group names, androgynous names, corporate names, name changes, name etiquette and literary names," reported Adam Goodheart in the *Washington Post.* Reviewers commonly recognized the book as entertaining. "Rarely has the fundamental human function of naming received such an energetic, enlightening and engaging treatment," noted *Publishers Weekly.* Despite presenting "all sorts of unexpected things" about names, Goodheart believed that *The Language of Names* "offers its readers both too much and too little. The text is often sidetracked by [unnecessary] historical and biographical details. . . . At the same time, some big questions go unanswered: What are the origins of the Western naming system?. . . . The authors also exaggerate the importance of names in shaping their owners' identities." "Mr. Kaplan and Ms. Bernays's approach is genial, light-handed, as if engaging the reader in party conversation," remarked Marina Warner in the *New York Times Book Review,* "the effect, however, is a little desultory. Faced with the intrinsic philosophical nature of this tough subject, they prefer to treat linguistics, structuralism and other approaches with amused detachment; instead they introduce anecdotes, tell jokes, linger on favorite figures like Mark Twain and Walt Whitman."

BIOGRAPHICAL/CRITICAL SOURCES:

PERIODICALS

Bloomsbury Review, March 1991, p. 15.

Chicago Tribune, March 17, 1997, p. 3.

Kirkus Reviews, May 15, 1965, p. 508; September 1, 1966, p. 925; July 15, 1975, p. 790.

Los Angeles Times Book Review, March 23, 1997, p. 10.

New York Times, June 20, 1965, p. 31; June 26, 1965, p. 27; February 18, 1967, p. 27; July 19, 1989, p. C19.

New York Times Book Review, November 13, 1966, p. 70; October 5, 1975, p. 48; August 3, 1980, p. 14; July 23, 1989, pp. 1, 26; February 16, 1997, p. 7.

Publishers Weekly, May 9, 1966, p. 81; December 9, 1996, pp. 52-54.
Time, October 20, 1975, pp. 93-94.
Village Voice, October 8, 1980, p. 47.
Washington Post, February 3, 1997.
Women's Review of Books, July, 1989, pp. 6-7.*

* * *

KELLY, Patrick
See ALLBEURY, Theodore Edward le Bouthillier

* * *

KELLY, Richard (Michael) 1937-

PERSONAL: Born March 16, 1937, in New York City; son of Bernard (in police work) and Anna (Kaufman) Kelly; married Barbara Hunter (a social worker), June 6, 1961. *Education:* City College (now of the City University of New York), B.A., 1959; Duke University, M.A., 1960, Ph.D., 1965.

ADDRESSES: Home—136 Sunrise Dr., Knoxville, TN 37919. *Office*—Department of English, University of Tennessee, Knoxville, TN 37996. *E-mail*—rmkelly@bellsouth.net.

CAREER: University of Tennessee, Knoxville, assistant professor, 1965-69, associate professor, 1969-75, professor of English, 1975—, Lindsay Young Professor, 1998—, director of graduate studies in English, 1981-84. Guest on television programs, including "The Today Show," "PM Magazine," and "CBS Evening News with Dan Rather."

MEMBER: Lewis Carroll Society of North America, Phi Beta Kappa.

AWARDS, HONORS: Fellowships from Woodrow Wilson Foundation, 1960, 1965, Carnegie Foundation, and National Defense Education Act.

WRITINGS:

(Editor) *The Best of Mr. Punch: The Humorous Writings of Douglas Jerrold,* University of Tennessee Press, 1970.
Douglas Jerrold, G. K. Hall (Boston), 1972.
Lewis Carroll, G. K. Hall, 1977, revised edition, 1990.
(Editor with Stanley Appelbaum) *Great Cartoonists of Nineteenth-Century Punch,* Dover (New York City), 1981.
The Andy Griffith Show, John Blair, 1981, revised edition, 1984.
George du Maurier, G. K. Hall, 1983.
Graham Greene, Ungar, 1984.
Daphne du Maurier, G. K. Hall, 1987.
V. S. Naipaul, Continuum, 1989.
Graham Greene: A Study of the Short Fiction, Twayne (Boston), 1992.
The Art of George du Maurier, Scholar, 1996.
(With Barbara Kelly) *The Carolina Watermen: Bug Hunters and Boatbuilders,* Blair, 1993.

Contributor of essays and chapters to publications, including *Victorian Newsletter, Studies in Short Fiction, Studies in Browning,* and *Studies in English Literature.*

WORK IN PROGRESS: A critical edition of *Alice's Adventures in Wonderland* for Broadview Press.

SIDELIGHTS: Richard Kelly once told *CA:* "My interest in popular comic writers such as Jerrold and Carroll led me to study the popular cartoons and drawings of Victorian *Punch.* From there it was a small leap to the visual and verbal comedy of the 'Andy Griffith Show,' which I think is every bit as carefully orchestrated as the early Dickens—both being serialized humor, both presenting pictures and text. Du Maurier, as artist and novelist, was an obvious extension of my interest in high quality popular culture. As an antidote to all that mirth, I have now written a book about V. S. Naipaul and rarely laugh anymore."

BIOGRAPHICAL/CRITICAL SOURCES:

PERIODICALS

Los Angeles Times Book Review, November 1, 1981.

* * *

KENT, Allegra 1938(?)-

PERSONAL: Born August 11, 1938 (some sources say 1937), in Los Angeles (some sources say Santa Monica), CA; married Bert Stern (a photographer),

February 28, 1959; children: Tristiana, Susannah, Bret. *Education:* Studied dance with Bronislava Nijinska; attended School of American Ballet and University of California, Los Angeles.

ADDRESSES: Office—c/o New York City Ballet Company, Lincoln Center Plaza, New York, NY 10023.

CAREER: New York City Ballet Company, New York, NY, dancer, 1953-83, principal dancer, 1957-66; appeared as guest artist at ballet companies, including Bavarian State Opera Ballet and the Ballet of Los Angeles; worked as freelance ballet coach and teacher; director, Stamford City Ballet, Stamford, CT.

WRITINGS:

Allegra Kent's Water Beauty Book, St. Martin's (New York City), 1976.

(With James Camner and Constance Camner) *The Dancer's Body Book,* Morrow (New York City), 1984.

Once a Dancer. . . An Autobiography, St. Martin's, 1997.

SIDELIGHTS: In her autobiography *Once a Dancer* celebrated ballerina Allegra Kent has portrayed a life as quixotic and turbulent as her controversial thirty-year career with the New York City Ballet. Reviewing *Once a Dancer* for *Dance Magazine* Harris Green states: "Everything about Kent's life was as unique as her fluid, haunting dancing." Green goes on to observe that "readers should find Allegra Kent in print as distinctively riveting as she ever was on stage." According to Heather Watts in *Vanity Fair:* "Through Kent's wise and courageous reflections . . . we see her unique spirit, and almost see again her glorious dancing."

Laura Jabobs in the *Washington Post* characterizes the childhood related in *Once A Dancer* as "the crazy kind you might find in the fiction of Flannery O'Connor," and Jennifer Dunning in *The New York Times Book Review* sees Kent's early years as "monstrous." Kent's father emerges as an affable no-account, a gambler and oil-well speculator who soon deserted his family. Her mother, Shirley, appears as an erratic tyrant, embracing one philosophy or religion after another (from Christian Science to Krishnamurti) and imposing an itinerant and indigent life upon her young daughter.

At the age of 11 Kent discovered she had a talent for jumping and decided to take up ballet, primarily to gain her mother's attention. Turning her daughter into a prima ballerina soon became Shirley's obsession. After intensive instruction in dance, Kent was accepted into the New York City Ballet at the age of 15, where her mother's influence was gradually superseded by that of legendary choreographer George Balanchine. Within four years Balanchine promoted Kent to the role of principal dancer. Shirley now rebelled against her daughter's success, trying to get her to abandon ballet and go back to school, forcing her into a plastic surgery that misfired before her first starring role. According to Joan Acocella in *The New York Times:* "This childhood section is the best part of the book: witty, fast-paced, full of deft omissions, wonderful catchings-up. . . . For Ms. Kent, as for so many autobiographers, childhood, because its circumstances were arranged by others, has a special poetry, on which they can report with disinterestedness and clarity. Only with later life . . . does the confusion set in."

Kent's adult years as related in *Once a Dancer* include her tumultuous marriage to photographer Bert Stern, the births of her three children, and her tenure under Balanchine at the New York City Ballet, a tenure marked by illnesses, depression, unexplained absences, and ongoing controversy. Kent portrays herself as an eccentric, breaking all the rules Balanchine had established for his dancers, and often unconsciously trying to sabotage her own achievements. Acocella observes: "This later period makes for grim reading at times." Nevertheless, throughout the fifties and early sixties, Kent became the premier American ballerina, fashioning a unique stage persona that was acclaimed as mysterious, poetic, and sensual.

On the whole, reviewers find little to fault in *Once a Dancer.* Dunning notes that Kent often "hides behind a veil of drama, sometimes with exasperating silliness," yet goes on to call her a "witty evocative writer" and also feels that her autobiography "is the rare dance book that communicates the pure joy of dancing and moving to music." Chris Ledbetter of the *Chicago Tribune* concludes: "Allegra Kent comes through it all with insight and humor. She never whines or blames others—not even her mother—for what she has endured. She has lived as gracefully as she danced."

BIOGRAPHICAL/CRITICAL SOURCES:

BOOKS

International Directory of Ballet, Volume 1, St. James Press (Detroit, MI), 1993, pp. 753-55.

PERIODICALS

Chicago Tribune, February 25, 1997, p. 3.
Dance Magazine, January, 1997, p. 98.
Interview, March, 1997, p. 106.
New York Times, April 22, 1997, p. C14.
New York Times Book Review, January 19, 1997, p. 6.
Vanity Fair, February, 1997, pp. 108-09.
Wall Street Journal, January 16, 1997, p. A16.
Washington Post Book World, April 20, 1997, p. 5.*

* * *

KERBY, Susan Alice
See BURTON, (Alice) Elizabeth

* * *

KERR, Ben
See ARD, William (Thomas)

* * *

KEVLES, Bettyann Holtzmann 1938-

PERSONAL: Surname is pronounced *Kev*-less; born August 20, 1938, in New York, NY; daughter of David Marshal (a lawyer) and Sondra (a theatrical producer; maiden name, Alosoroff) Holtzmann; married Daniel Jerome Kevles (a historian), May 18, 1961; children: Beth, Jonathan. *Education:* Vassar College, B.A., 1959; Columbia University, M.A., 1961.

ADDRESSES: Home—575 La Loma Rd., Pasadena, CA 91108.

CAREER: Sunbeam, Northridge, CA, editor and writer, 1967-69; Westridge School, Pasadena, CA, history instructor, 1970-76; *Los Angeles Times,* Los Angeles, CA, columnist, 1982-88. University of California Press, sponsoring editor, 1984-87; Stanford University Press, consulting editor, 1988—.

AWARDS, HONORS: Award for best older juvenile book, New York Academy of Sciences, 1977, and for best nonfiction book, *Boston Globe/Horn Book,* 1978, both for *Watching the Wild Apes: The Primate Studies of Goodall, Fossey, and Galdikas.*

WRITINGS:

Watching the Wild Apes: The Primate Studies of Goodall, Fossey, and Galdikas, Dutton (New York City), 1976.
(Contributor) Alice Lawrance, editor, *Cassandra Rising: Science Fiction by Women,* Doubleday (New York City), 1978.
Thinking Gorillas: Testing and Teaching the Greatest Ape, Dutton, 1980.
Listening In, Scholastic Book Services (New York City), 1981.
Females of the Species: Sex and Survival in the Animal Kingdom, Harvard University Press (Cambridge, MA), 1986.
Naked to the Bone: Medical Imaging in the Twentieth Century, Rutgers University Press (New Brunswick, NJ), 1997.

Contributor of science fiction and spy stories to anthologies.

SIDELIGHTS: Bettyann Kevles's *Females of the Species: Sex and Survival in the Animal Kingdom* has been praised for its detailed account of the contributions female animals make to the evolutionary process—an area obscured for many years by science's focus on male animals. "*Females of the Species* is a survey of how female animals in nature play the Darwinian game of struggle for personal reproductive success," noted Stephen Jay Gould in the *New York Review of Books,* adding: "This work concentrates on demolishing a reverse fallacy—the long tradition, now thankfully fading (with a substantial push to oblivion from this book), for interpreting what female animals do in the light of supposed role models imposed by sexist societies upon human females." Sara Neustadtl commented in the *Women's Review of Books* that "[Kevles's] purpose, which she presents in a fluid and graceful style that will encourage reading by non-biologists, is to provide a compendium of the female behaviors biologists discovered once they opened their eyes, and the conclusions they have chosen to draw from their results."

Gould went on to praise *Females of the Species* as an "unrelenting bestiary of examples from beetles to baboons—hundreds and hundreds of tales about female behavior, organized in sections on courtship, mating, motherhood, and sisterhood, and all aimed to reinforce the point that females participate in the Darwinian struggle for reproductive success as actively and as assiduously as males, only differently." He added: "Anyone can wax eloquent about diversity as nature's theme; Kevles has sunk years of work into its documentation."

With the publication of *Naked to the Bone: Medical Imaging in the Twentieth Century,* Kevles earned critical acclaim at several levels. The foundation of the book is a historical account of the development of medical imaging technology, beginning with the unexpected discovery of x-rays by Wilhelm Conrad Roentgen in 1895. Kevles writes, according to *New Scientist* reviewer John E. Harrison, "with an engaging, easy style that takes the reader on a fascinating journey." The second part of the book is devoted to the technological advances of the twentieth century, including ultrasound, computerized tomography scanning (CT or CAT), magnetic resonance imaging (MRI), positron emission tomography (PET), and mammography. Kevles demystifies the scientific terminology by using supporting anecdotes, comparing, for example, the sophistication of medical diagnostic techniques available at the time of President James A. Garfield's assassination in 1881 with available knowledge when President William McKinley was assassinated in 1901 and later when President Ronald Reagan was shot in 1981. She "has been successful in making technological history absorbing," wrote Christopher Lehmann-Haupt in the *New York Times.*

Some critics also lauded Kevles for the value of her commentary that transcends the mere historical account. *Science* reviewer Paul Boyer pointed out: "This deeply researched work firmly embeds its inherently fascinating story within a larger cultural matrix." Kevles discusses the debt that medical imaging technology owes to non-medical inventions, such as innovations that emerged as a result of World War II and the continued evolution of computer systems. She explains the impact that medical imaging advances have had in other fields, including forensic investigation and criminal trial proceedings. Kevles describes the deadly toll that early x-ray research extracted from radiologists unaware of danger and, according to Harrison, "gives considerable attention to the ethical issues that arise from imaging the human body, particularly the risks." She addresses political and economic concerns, as well, weighing the immense cost of research and the diagnostic machines themselves against the magnitude of patients' and doctors' needs. As Peter Campbell summarized Kevles's explanation in the *London Review of Books:* "[The machines] . . . are wonderful . . . [b]ecause . . . they have made non-invasive intervention as well as exploration possible. On the other hand, they may have encouraged an indulgence in, and reliance on, expensive tests in an environment where resources are finite." At times, Lehmann-Haupt reported, "she tells her story from a feminist perspective, noting how ultrasound has helped women to gain control over their bodies," but at the same time, according to Boyer, pointing out that ultrasound has "added powerful emotional resonance to the abortion debate."

To Lehmann-Haupt, "the most exciting chapter [of *Naked to the Bone*] concerns how X-rays revolutionized the way people saw reality." Kevles relates the advances in medical imagery to the arts and popular culture. In literature, she cites *The Invisible Man,* written by H. G. Wells in 1897; in comic books and film, there was Superman and his x-ray vision. She links the x-ray to the development of surrealist and cubist movements in art, and describes a 1994 ballet titled *MRI.* Some critics faulted Kevles for overemphasizing this impact on the arts and for neglecting European contributions to the field of medical imaging but, as Boyer summarized: "*Naked to the Bone* brilliantly explores that liminal frontier terrain where medicine, technology, economics, and culture converge and interact."

Although primarily a science writer, Kevles has also written science fiction and spy stories. She commented to *CA* on the overlap among these venues: "Writing about science has led me into writing fiction again. There's just a thin line, and the real becomes preposterous."

BIOGRAPHICAL/CRITICAL SOURCES:

PERIODICALS

Booklist, November 1, 1996, p. 470.
Choice, June, 1997, p. 1697.
Discover, December, 1997, p. 73.
Library Journal, January, 1997, p. 140.
London Review of Books, May 22, 1986; July 31, 1997, pp. 30-31.
Los Angeles Times Book Review, April 20, 1986.
Nature, April 10, 1997, pp. 567-68.

New Scientist, January 18, 1997, pp. 38-39.
New Yorker, July 21, 1986.
New York Review of Books, September 25, 1986.
New York Times Book Review, October 5, 1986; August 25, 1991, p. 11; May 5, 1997, p. C-16; June 29, 1997, p. 7-31.
Publishers Weekly, November 25, 1996, p. 63.
Science, June 27, 1997, pp. 1996-97.
Times Literary Supplement, January 16, 1987; March 14, 1997, pp. 4-6.
Washington Post Book World, February 9, 1997, p. 13.
Women's Review of Books, August, 1986.

L

LANGER, Ellen J(ane) 1947-

PERSONAL: Born March 25, 1947, in New York, NY; daughter of Norman J. (a pharmacist) and Sylvia (Tobias) Langer. *Education:* New York University, B.A., 1970; Yale University, Ph.D., 1974. *Politics:* Democrat. *Religion:* Jewish. *Avocational interests:* Theater, horseback riding, tennis.

ADDRESSES: Home—Cambridge, MA. *Office*—Department of Psychology, Harvard University, 3 Kirkland St., Cambridge, MA 02138-2044.

CAREER: New Century Publishing Co., New York City, freelance writer, 1969-70; Graduate School and University Center of the City University of New York, New York City, assistant professor of psychology, 1974-77; Harvard University, Cambridge, MA, associate professor, 1977-81, professor of psychology, 1981—. Associated with Harvard University Medical School division on aging, 1979—; chair of social psychology program, Harvard University, 1982—; chairman of Faculty Arts and Sciences Committee of Women, 1984-88.

MEMBER: American Psychological Association, American Association for the Advancement of Science, Society of Experimental Social Psychologists, Phi Beta Kappa, Psi Chi, Sigma Xi.

AWARDS, HONORS: Grant from the Sloan Foundation, 1982; award for distinguished contributions of psychology in the public interest, American Psychological Society, 1988; Guggenheim fellow; grants from NIMH, National Science Foundation, Society for Psychological Study of Social Issues, and Milton Fund; award for distinguished contribution of basic science to applied psychology, American Psychological Society, 1995.

WRITINGS:

(With Carol S. Dweck) *Personal Politics: The Psychology of Making It,* Prentice-Hall (Englewood Cliffs, NJ), 1973.

The Psychology of Control, Sage Publications, 1983.

Mindfulness, Addison-Wesley (Reading, MA), 1989.

(Editor with Charles Alexander) *Higher Stages of Development,* Oxford University Press (New York City), 1989.

The Power of Mindful Learning, Addison-Wesley, 1997.

Also author, with Roger Shank, of *Beliefs, Reasoning and Decision-Making,* 1994. Contributor of articles to periodicals.

WORK IN PROGRESS: Research articles dealing with the elderly, deviance, health, and competence.

SIDELIGHTS: Ellen Langer examines the optimum workings of the human mind in her books *Mindfulness* and *The Power of Mindful Learning*. Langer, a professor of psychology at Harvard University, believes that "mindlessness" is pervasive in our society—in other words, that people tend to respond with the most routine reaction instead of really experiencing and responding appropriately in various situations. A key culprit in the spread of mindlessness, she believes, is the educational system. By placing too much emphasis on facts as sacred truths, it discourages open-mindedness and creativity. Langer also criticizes the "outcome orientation" of the educational system, which teaches that there is one right way to do things and one correct solution. A "process orientation" system, she says, would yield more flexible, adaptable people who could function more efficiently in changing circumstances. Reviewing *Mindfulness* in *Bloomsbury Review,* Richard J. Holmes noted that "experiments conducted by Langer and her colleagues seem to indicate that creativity, intuition, insight, and other psychological qualities conducive to mindfulness lead to a balanced state of body and mind." Holmes cautioned that the book was not a "how-to" manual, but rather a challenging exercise in seeing things from multiple perspectives. He concluded: "In its overall effect, the book can also literally *change your mind* from mindless acceptance of life, based on consensus that you never (or seldom) question, to a mindful exploration of life, based on perceptions that are closer to your own personal experiences. Persons who can develop this 'ever-ready-state-of-mind' will be more likely to design creative strategies for change, which, in turn, will heighten the chances not only of survival on this planet, but will exert considerable pressures on its citizens to evolve . . . mindfully."

Langer enlarged her comments on mindlessness in the educational system in *The Power of Mindful Learning,* described by a *Kirkus Reviews* contributor as "a wonderfully thoughtful and thought-provoking" sequel to the earlier volume. Langer simplified the philosophy of the current educational system into seven myths, including the ideas that basic skills and ideas must be drilled into students until they are second nature; that forgetting is a problem; that focusing on one thing at a time is the proper way to learn; and that delaying gratification is important. It would be better, she suggests, to promote "openness to novelty; alertness to distinction; sensitivity to different contexts; implicit, if not explicit, awareness of multiple perspectives; and orientation in the present," as the *Kirkus Reviews* writer put it. The critic concluded: "Langer's arguments are extremely persuasive and supported with meticulous research. . . . An excellent introduction to what might be (and certainly should be) the next paradigm shift in education."

BIOGRAPHICAL/CRITICAL SOURCES:

PERIODICALS

American Journal of Psychology, summer, 1997, pp. 309-13.

Bloomsbury Review, January/February, 1991, p. 14-15.

Kirkus Reviews, February 1, 1997, p. 201.

New York Times, September 23, 1997, p. F1.

New York Times Book Review, May 18, 1997, p. 17.

* * *

LAREDO, Johnny
See CAESAR, (Eu)Gene (Lee)

* * *

LEHANE, Dennis 1965-

PERSONAL: Born August 4, 1965, in Dorchester, MA; son of Michael (a foreman) and Ann (a school cafeteria worker) Lehane. *Ethnicity:* "Caucasian." *Education:* Eckerd College, B.A.S., 1988; Florida International University, M.F.A., 1993. *Politics:* "Relatively apolitical." *Avocational interests:* Directing films.

ADDRESSES: *Agent*—Ann Rittenberg, Ann Rittenberg Literary Agency, Brooklyn, NY 11215.

CAREER: Writer. Therapeutic counselor for mentally handicapped, emotionally disturbed children, 1986-91; Florida International University, Miami, instructor in English, 1991-93; Ritz-Carlton Hotel, Boston, MA, chauffeur, 1993-95.

AWARDS, HONORS: Shamus Award, best first novel, 1994, for *A Drink before the War.*

WRITINGS:

MYSTERY NOVELS

A Drink before the War, Harcourt (Orlando, FL), 1994.

Darkness, Take My Hand, Morrow (New York City), 1996.

Sacred, Morrow, 1997.

Gone, Baby, Gone, Morrow, 1998.

OTHER

Writer, director, and producer of the film *Neighborhoods.*

SIDELIGHTS: Dennis Lehane's "voice, original, haunting and straight from the heart, places him among that top rank of stylists who enrich the modern mystery novel," declared a *Publishers Weekly* writer. Numerous other critics concur that Lehane's hard-edged style, ambiguous characters, and unresolved endings combine to create some of the best in modern mystery writing. His main characters are Patrick Kenzie and Angela Gennaro—two young, cynical detectives based in Boston, where they grew up together. Their debut in *A Drink before the War* showed "plenty of promise," according to Emily Melton in *Booklist. New York Times* reviewer Marilyn Stasio warned that the novel was marred by "a lot of cornball cliches and puerile private-eye humor," but she admitted that Lehane "has some honest things to say about racial and class warfare in working-class neighborhoods. . . . This is good, serious stuff, but it's not easy to reconcile it with the flippant style."

Darkness, Take My Hand was the next novel featuring Patrick and Angie, and it drew rave reviews from numerous critics. In this story, the detectives search for a brutal rapist and killer with connections to their own past. Melton described it in *Booklist* as "an explosive story that is at once gut-wrenchingly violent and achingly melancholy. . . . In a series of heart-stopping climaxes that grow ever more terrifying and bloody, Patrick and Angie lose nearly everything. Lehane's perfectly crafted plot leers, teases, taunts, and lulls, scattering bits of humor and heartbreak among the soul-chilling episodes of death and destruction. A tour de force from a truly gifted writer." Pam Lambert was also enthusiastic, calling the book a "crackling thriller." She went on in her *People* review: "Lehane's plotting is heart-poundingly suspenseful. However, even it is topped by the novels' subtler attractions: a sense of place as palpable as the pungent tang of garlic in the North End air, haunting characters and a gracefully elegiac style that lingers long after you've closed the covers."

Sacred was "another gritty and surpassingly entertaining mystery" that proved Lehane "belongs in the big leagues," in the opinion of *Publishers Weekly*'s reviewer. That writer pointed out Patrick's "smart and often funny narration" as one of the strengths of the book and commented that "for most of the novel, the punishing pace and internal plot logic perform in perfect tandem." Lambert gave her approval to *Sacred* in her *People* review, calling the book a "dark maelstrom of a mystery." She admitted that in her opinion, the book lacked the "terrible beauty" of *Darkness Take My Hand,* but concluded that it "still crackles with enough suspense to make for many a midsummer night's screams." The detectives search for a little girl kidnapped by a child pornography ring in Lehane's fourth novel, *Gone, Baby, Gone.* Karen Anderson, a reviewer for *Library Journal,* described it as "a tense, edge-of-your-seat story about a world that is astoundingly cruel and unbearably violent to its most innocent members." And Lambert, in another *People* assessment, called *Gone, Baby, Gone* a "chilling, masterfully plotted tale into that dark place where men try to play God and everyone gets hurt."

Lehane once told *CA:* "My primary motivation for writing is that I'm not much good at anything else. Plus, if you choose a career in the arts, it's socially acceptable to sleep 'til noon and not groom yourself until dinner. In all seriousness, I'm not sure I have a primary motivation. I write because I enjoy it. I would do it whether I was being paid or not. I like telling stories. I like the way words look and the way they sound; I love their rhythm when they are strung together with precision.

"It's hard for me to point to particular influences on my work. I have been compared to Raymond Chandler on occasion, which I find odd, if only because I haven't read Chandler's work since I was nine or ten, and I don't remember much of it. While I write mysteries, I very rarely read them anymore, so I'm not sure anyone in that genre affects my own writing in any significant way. The summer I turned fourteen, I read *The Wanderers* by Richard Price, saw Martin Scorsese's *Mean Streets,* and heard Springsteen's 'Born to Run' for the first time, and I remember it all had a strong effect on me. For the first time in my life, I was exposed to literature, film, and music about the kind of people I grew up with, the kind of people I was interested in writing about.

"Otherwise, in terms of literature in general, I have been deeply impressed by the writings of Walker Percy, Don Delillo, Graham Greene, William Kennedy, Gabriel Garcia Marquez, Pete Dexter, Toni Morrison, and Andre Dubus, to name a few. I guess you can see some of their influences in the thematic concerns of my novels, though not really in the execution of the plot or in the tone of my 'voice.'

"I barely have a writing process. I have tried to force myself to write every day, keep a journal, and so on, but all that seems to do is make me self-conscious. I tend to write best in big bursts after long periods of silence. During those bursts, I usually write sixteen hours a day, day in and day out, until the battery runs dry. I don't recommend this process, but it's the only one that's ever worked for me.

"I'm not entirely sure what inspired me to write on the subjects I've chosen. I never intended to be a mystery novelist. Before I wrote my first mystery novel, I was writing a lot of very dark, esoteric short stories, heavily influenced by Dostoevsky and Raymond Carver, Walker Percy, too, probably. I felt like I needed a break, and I decided to try something 'fun.' This turned out to be *A Drink before the War,* my first book. Because I set it in Boston, I tried to tackle the subject of race relations. If you are going to set books in Boston, sooner or later you have to deal with it; it's so intrinsic to the character of the city.

"For my second book *Darkness Take My Hand,* I took an everything-and-the-kitchen-sink approach to it. I wanted to pay homage to the sort of moral murkiness that exists in the writings of Conrad and Greene and Delillo, to create a world in which you're never sure where anyone stands, where all motives are questionable, where the hero himself is very much in danger of becoming what he beholds as he chases some very twisted, evil characters around.

"To a large extent that's what interests me most. What is the hero's culpability in the events in which he's involved? When does the evil from 'without' threaten to become the evil 'within'? There's a popular idea in a lot of mysteries I've read that the hero must be the white knight, the upstanding man in an amoral world. It's a continuation of the Hemingway idea that a man must live by his code, and that code will see him through.

"Maybe because I'm a post-Watergate, post-Vietnam Gen Xer or whatever the current label is for people my age, I just never bought that good-will-out theory. It seems far more interesting to me to write about very flawed men and women in a very flawed world, trying to do the best they can to get along. Good doesn't always win out, but the *attempt* to do good matters a bit."

BIOGRAPHICAL/CRITICAL SOURCES:

PERIODICALS

Booklist, November 15, 1994, p. 582; July, 1996, p. 1809.

Library Journal, June 15, 1997, p. 98; July, 1998, p. 137.

New York Times, December 11, 1994.

People, July 22, 1996, p. 30; August 25, 1997, p. 38; August 10, 1998, p. 43.

Publishers Weekly, October 10, 1994, p. 65; May 27, 1996, p. 67; May 26, 1997, p. 69.

* * *

LEIDER, Emily Wortis 1937-

PERSONAL: Surname pronounced *Ly*-der; born December 23, 1937, in New York, NY; daughter of Joseph (a psychiatrist) and Helen (a social worker; maiden name, Zunser) Wortis; married William Leider (a pediatrician), December 22, 1957; children: Jean, Richard. *Education:* Barnard College, B.A., 1959; Columbia University, M.A., 1961. *Religion:* Jewish.

ADDRESSES: Home—P. O. Box 210105, San Francisco, CA 94121. *Office—San Francisco Review of Books,* 2140 Vallejo, San Francisco, CA 94123.

CAREER: Northwestern University, Evanston, IL, instructor in English literature and writing, 1964-66; Antioch College West, San Francisco, CA, instructor in poetry and women's studies, 1973-76; *San Francisco Review of Books,* San Francisco, associate editor, 1977—.

MEMBER: Poets and Writers.

WRITINGS:

Rapid Eye Movement and Other Poems, Bay Books, 1976.

(Editor and author of postscript) Miriam Shomer Zunser, *Yesterday: The Memoir of a Russian Jewish Family,* Harper (New York City), 1978.

California's Daughter: Gertrude Atherton and Her Times, Stanford University Press (Stanford, CA), 1991.

Becoming Mae West: The Shaping of an Icon, Farrar, Straus (New York City), 1997.

WORK IN PROGRESS: Poems.

SIDELIGHTS: In *Becoming Mae West* Emily Leider not only paints a detailed portrait of the notorious stage and screen legend, but also portrays West's career in its historical context as a reflection of the changing face of American moral values from the early 1900s to the late 1930s, from a period that was uniformly Victorian to one where libertinism had gained a strong foothold. The daughter of a German mother and a drunken prizefighter father, the Brooklyn-born West went on to a highly successful career in vaudeville and film that made her one of the best-known sexual icons of the twentieth century. According to Martha McPhee, writing in the *New York Times,* most people remember West as "a pneumatic blonde, part siren, part caricature, strutting slowly across the screen, all hips and bosom, her famous one-liners sliding out of the corner of her mouth." Leider's stated aim in her biography is "to penetrate the layers of makeup to probe the elusive singular woman" beneath. Detailing West's career, the plots of her films, her family life, her numerous love affairs, her financial dealings, her relationships with other stars such as Cary Grant and Marlene Dietrich, even her experiments in spiritualism, Leider depicts West as an independent and strong-willed woman who created her own legend, a feminist forerunner of such later performers as Roseanne and Madonna.

Reviewing *Becoming Mae West* for *Booklist,* Donna Seaman praises the book as an "eye-opening, candid, lushly detailed and immensely entertaining biography," and also notes that West emerges as "a pioneering woman artist who challenged the hypocritical sexual mores of her times." A reviewer for *Publisher's Weekly* states: "Exhaustive research, fine writing and a keen appreciation of Mae West's own bawdy wit inform this energetic and erudite biography." In contrast, M. G. Lord of the *Voice Literary Supplement* presents a more critical view both of West and of Leider's evaluation of her life. Lord sees West as "backward and obnoxious," a "hollow" icon, contending that she was both racist and anti-lesbian, and "did little to enhance the lives of her fellow women" other than "her pioneering rejection of the social pressure to become a mother." While granting that Leider "has written a graceful, meticulously documented biography," the reviewer goes on to state that it is "probably more than her tedious subject deserved."

Leider is also the author of a book of poems and a biography of turn-of-the-century California author Gertrude Atherton. Like Mae West, Atherton was an independent woman who challenged contemporary values. Her steamy novels were often banned and her flamboyant public persona defied the accepted behavior for women of her time. Reviewing *California's Daughter: Gertrude Atherton and Her Times* for *Canadian Literature,* Michele O'Flynn describes it as "a very carefully researched biography which examines important issues, works and events that played a role in . . . Atherton's day."

Leider told *CA:* "My poems tend to be concise and imagistic lyrics with narrative and dramatic leanings. *Rapid Eye Movement* contains a sequence of poems based on characters and events in my grandmother's memoir, *Yesterday.*"

BIOGRAPHICAL/CRITICAL SOURCES:

PERIODICALS

Booklist, May 1, 1997, p. 1473.
Canadian Literature, spring, 1993, pp. 155-56.
Entertainment Weekly, June 20, 1997, p. 68.
Interview, May, 1997, p. 30.
Library Journal, April 1, 1997, p. 96.
New York Times, June 27, 1997, p. G11.
New York Times Book Review, April 14, 1991, p. 20; July 27, 1997, p. 11.
Publishers Weekly, May 5, 1997, p. 189.
Voice Literary Supplement, summer, 1997, p. 14.
Washington Post, June 29, 1997, p. 3.*

* * *

LENGEL, Frances
See TROCCHI, Alexander

* * *

LEVINE, Paul (J.) 1948-

PERSONAL: Born January 9, 1948, in Williamsport, PA; son of Stanley (a retail merchant) and Sally (a retail merchant) Levine, married Alice Holmstrom, August 22, 1975 (divorced July 27, 1992); children: Wendy, Michael. *Education:* Pennsylvania State University, B.A., 1969; University of Miami, J.D. (cum laude), 1973. *Politics:* Democrat. *Religion:* Jewish.

ADDRESSES: Home—Coconut Grove, FL. *Agent*—Kristine Dahl, International Creative Management, 40 West 57th St., New York, NY 10019.

CAREER: Writer. *Miami Herald,* Miami, FL, reporter, 1969-70; *Los Angeles Times,* Los Angeles, CA, stringer, 1972; admitted to the Bar of Florida State, 1973, the Bar of U.S. Supreme Court, 1977, the Bar of the District of Columbia, 1978, and the Bar of the Commonwealth of Pennsylvania, 1989; attorney at law firms in Florida, 1973-77; Bartel, Levine & Shuford, FL, trial and appellate attorney and partner, 1977-78; Morgan, Lewis & Bockius, Miami, attorney and partner, 1978-87; Spence, Payne, Masington, Grossman & Needle, Miami, counsellor, 1987-88; Grossman & Roth, Miami, counsellor, 1988-91. University of Miami School of Law, adjunct faculty of communications law, 1978-80; creator, writer, and talent for nationally syndicated show, *You & The Law,* 1978-82; previously legal commentator for *WPLG-TV News* and *AM South Florida;* serves on the Pennsylvania State University School of Communications alumni board of directors and Pennsylvania State University Libraries advisory board; speaker on various law issues.

MEMBER: Sigma Delta Chi Journalism Society, American Bar Association, American Trial Lawyers Association, Academy of Florida Trial Lawyers, Florida Bar Media Relations Committee (vice chair, 1985), Authors Guild, Kappa Tau Alpha, Phi Kappa Phi, Omicron Delta Kappa, Phi Eta Sigma.

AWARDS, HONORS: William Randolph Hearst National Writing Competition, third place, 1968, first place, 1969; Society of Professional Journalists/ Sigma Delta Chi Award, 1968, for newspaper writing; first place, National Moot Court Competition, Atlanta and New York, both 1971; grand prize and first place, Florida Bar Media Awards Competition, 1979, for television show *You & The Law.*

WRITINGS:

"JAKE LASSITER" DETECTIVE NOVELS

To Speak for the Dead, Bantam (New York City), 1990.
Night Vision, Bantam, 1991.
False Dawn, Bantam, 1993.
Mortal Sin, Morrow (New York City), 1994.
Slashback, Morrow, 1995.
Fool Me Twice, Morrow, 1996.
Flesh and Bones, Morrow, 1997.
9 Scorpions, Pocket Books (New York City), 1998.

OTHER

What's Your Verdict?, Dell (New York City), 1980.

Contributor to periodicals, including *Reporters' Handbook, University of Miami Law Review, Lawyers Monthly, Newsweek, Editor and Publisher, Sun Sentinel, New York Times, Miami Review, Miami Herald, Palm Beach Post,* and *St. Petersburg Times.* Author of a nationally-syndicated newspaper column.

ADAPTATIONS: *To Speak for the Dead* was adapted for television as *Lassiter: Justice on the Bayou,* National Broadcasting Company, 1995.

SIDELIGHTS: Former trial lawyer Paul Levine uses his courtroom experiences to produce mystery novels featuring Jake Lassiter, a football player turned defense attorney who becomes embroiled in murder cases. In Levine's first novel, *To Speak for the Dead,* Lassiter defends Roger Salisbury, a surgeon charged with malpractice in the death of his patient Philip Corrigan. Melanie Corrigan believes that Salisbury fatally cut her husband's aorta during surgery. Although the surgeon is acquitted, Philip's daughter, Susan, is not satisfied and tries to prove that the death was a conspiracy between Salisbury and his lover, Melanie. Jake and Susan team up with retired coroner Charlie Riggs and exhume Philip's body to find clues, but discover two bodies in the grave. Richard North Patterson, in *Washington Post,* deemed that the novel's "climax is genuinely chilling and, in its abruptness, just right." Patterson also added that Levine's courtroom scenes have a "real bite and authority."

Jake Lassiter reappears as the protagonist in Levine's second novel, *Night Vision.* As special prosecutor for a serial murder case, Lassiter again seeks the help of Charlie Riggs. The first murder victim is television newscaster Michelle Diamond, who is strangled to death after questioning her occasional lover and state attorney, Nick Wolf, about a suspected Vietnam conspiracy. The next two victims—like Diamond—were members of Compu-Mate, an electronic sex hotline. While investigating the deaths, Jake uncovers political corruption and a complex scenario pointing to several suspects, including Wolf, a detective, a professor, an actor, and the owners of Compu-Mate. With help from a British serial-killer expert, Jake and Charlie close in on the murderer. Critics once again lauded Levine's ingenious conclusion but felt *Night Vision* suffered from heavy plotting.

In *False Dawn,* the third entry in the Lassiter series, Jake takes on a beautiful Finnish spy, Japanese art smugglers, CIA double agents, and Cuban exiles. A *Publishers Weekly* reviewer found the plot overly complicated, complaining that the "double-, triple- and quadruple-crosses" pile up "to the point of self-parody." Nevertheless, allowed the reviewer, "the silliness is redeemed only by the character of Levine's hero and narrator. Lassiter is like the sole halfback in a field full of quarterback: he just takes the ball and runs." The critic concluded that *False Dawn* is "a quirky little mystery with enough twists and turns to satisfy Robert Ludlum fans and a unique hero."

Mortal Sin finds Lassiter becoming involved with his former lover, Gina, even though she is engaged to land developer Nicky Florio. Florio's latest project, on a Native American reservation in the Everglades, has upset ecologists. When one conservationist opposing the project dies under mysterious circumstances, Lassiter reluctantly agrees to defend Nicky in court. Before long, Lassiter finds himself framed for murder and in danger of losing his own life. Reviewing *Mortal Sin* in *Booklist,* Wes Lukowsky noted that the Lassiter series is "continually improving," and described the book as "a violent, sexy thriller with a brutal, almost operatic conclusion."

Lukowsky also gave high marks to *Flesh and Bones,* in which Lassiter defends a woman charged with murdering the father who abused her as a child. The *Booklist* contributor stated that "Lassiter is smart, tough, funny, and very human. He's coming on fast as one of the most entertaining series characters in contemporary crime fiction." The *Publishers Weekly* critic who reviewed *Flesh and Bones* concurred that the Lassiter series is "refreshingly unpretentious" and named Levine "a wily and spirited practitioner of ripe plotting and big-time narrative excess."

Levine once told *CA:* "My background as a trial lawyer (seventeen years) forms the basis for my series of Jake Lassiter novels. Jake is the 'ex- football player, ex-public defender, ex-a-lot-of-things' who does the best he can in and out of court. He doesn't play by any rules but his own. He believes that codes of ethics are invented by lawyers from deep-carpet law firms to favor the side with the most money. As he says in *False Dawn,* Jake prefers cases he believes in. 'Best is to have a client you like, a cause that is just, and a check that doesn't bounce. Two out of three and you're ahead of the game.'"

BIOGRAPHICAL/CRITICAL SOURCES:

PERIODICALS

Booklist, January 1, 1994, p. 810; June 1, 1994, p. 1779; January 15, 1995, p. 899; January 1, 1996, p. 796; November 15, 1996, p. 574.

New York Times, May 23, 1993.

Publishers Weekly, February 22, 1993, p. 84; April 3, 1995, p. 30; October 9, 1995, p. 79; January 13, 1997, p. 59.

Washington Post, September 4, 1990.

* * *

LLOYD, Charles
See BIRKIN, Charles (Lloyd)

* * *

LOVELACE, Earl 1935-

PERSONAL: Born July 13, 1935, in Toco, Trinidad; mother's name, Jean Watley Lovelace; married, wife's name Jean; children: Walt, Che (son), Lulu. *Education:* Studied at Eastern Caribbean Institute of Agriculture and Forestry, 1961-62, and Howard University, 1966-67; Johns Hopkins University, M.A., 1974.

CAREER: Novelist, journalist, playwright, and short story writer. *Trinidad Guardian,* proofreader, 1953-54; Jamaica Civil Service, forest ranger for Department of Forestry and agricultural assistant for Department of Agriculture, 1956-66; Federal City College (now University of the District of Columbia), Washington, DC, instructor, 1971-73; University of the West Indies, St. Augustine, Trinidad, lecturer in literature and creative writing, 1977—. Johns Hopkins University, visiting novelist-in-residence; University of Iowa, writer-in-residence, 1980; Hartwick College, writer-in- residence, 1986. Dragon Productions, producer.

AWARDS, HONORS: British Petroleum Independence Award, 1964, for *While Gods Are Falling;* Pegasus Literary Award, outstanding contributions to the arts in Trinidad & Tobago, 1966; awards for best play and best music, 1977, for *Pierrot Ginnard;*

Guggenheim fellowship, 1980; grant from National Endowment for the Humanities, 1986.

WRITINGS:

While Gods Are Falling (novel), Collins (London, England), 1965, Regnery (Chicago, IL), 1966.

The Schoolmaster (novel), Regnery, 1968.

(And director) *My Name Is Village* (musical), produced in Port of Spain, Trinidad, at Queen's Hall, 1976.

Pierrot Ginnard (musical), produced at Queen's Hall, 1977.

Jestina's Calypso (play), produced in St. Augustine, Trinidad, at University of the West Indies, 1978, then in Northampton, MA, at Mendenhall Center for the Performing Arts, Smith College, 1988.

The Dragon Can't Dance (novel), Deutsch (London), 1979, Three Continents (Washington, DC), 1981.

The New Hardware Store (play), produced at University of the West Indies, 1980, then in London, England, at Camden Arts Theatre, 1985.

The Wine of Astonishment (novel), Heinemann (London; some sources say Deutsch), 1982, Vintage (New York City), 1984.

Jestina's Calypso and Other Plays (includes *The New Hardware Store, My Name Is Village, and Jestina's Calypso*), Heinemann, 1984.

The Dragon Can't Dance (stage adaptation of his novel; produced at Queen's Hall, 1986), published in *Black Plays 2,* edited by Yvonne Brewster, Methuen (London), 1989.

The Wine of Astonishment (play), produced at Queen's Hall, 1987 (some sources say 1988).

A Brief Conversion and Other Stories, Heinemann (Oxford, England), 1988.

Salt (novel), Persea Books (New York City), 1997.

Author of the play *The New Boss,* 1962. Columnist and editorial writer, *Trinidad & Tobago Express.* Contributor to periodicals, including *Voices, South,* and *Wasafiri.*

SIDELIGHTS: Born in Toco, Trinidad, Earl Lovelace has been hailed by numerous critics as one of the Caribbean's more gifted and talented writers. "Earl Lovelace is primarily a wonderful storyteller," stated John J. Figueroa in *Contemporary Novelists.* "He holds one's interest whether through exciting dialogue which rings true, or by his descriptive ability and his portrayal of the inner conflicts which puzzle his characters."

For the most part, Lovelace sets his writings in his homeland of Trinidad or in one of the neighboring Caribbean islands. Julius Lester commented in the *New York Times Book Review* that Lovelace is "a writer of consummate skill. A native of Trinidad, Mr. Lovelace writes about his homeland from the inside, creating characters with whom the reader quickly identifies despite differences of race, place and time."

According to Daryl Cumber Dance in his book, *Fifty Caribbean Writers: A Bio-Bibliographical Critical Sourcebook:* "The major theme in Earl Lovelace's work is the quest for presented, a term which he prefers to *manhood* or *identity* and which he describes as 'man's view of himself, the search as it were for his integrity'. . . . Frequently, however, this quest is threatened as his characters encounter the impersonal, dehumanizing urban world."

In his first novel, *While Gods Are Falling,* Lovelace tells the story of Walter Castle, who, as Chezia Thompson-Cager wrote in the *Dictionary of Literary Biography,* "feels imprisoned by his identity and stifled by the poverty into which his father's misfortune has cast the family." He "feels compelled to fortify himself against failure and mediocrity by cutting himself off from his community."

Thompson-Cager identified another element of *While Gods Are Falling* that appears throughout much of Lovelace's work: "The novel is narrated by alternating a chronicle of present events with the past." In a similar vein, Figueroa referred to the author's "concern with the ambiguous relationship between change and progress" and "the relationship between the rural and urban styles of living." In *While Gods Are Falling,* Walter wants to leave the poverty, crime, and confusion of urban Port of Spain and return to the countryside of his childhood, where he hopes to rediscover his identity.

The Schoolmaster is a novel about the building of a school in the remote Trinidad village of Kumaca. "Lovelace's *The Schoolmaster* is set in Trinidad and is a real story-teller's novel, moving with grace from a gently sentimental beginning to a tragic climax," declared A. S. Byatt in the *New Statesman.* Martin Levin remarked in the *New York Times Book Review* that "*The Schoolmaster* is a folk fable with the clean, elemental structure of Steinbeck's *The Pearl.* But unlike *The Pearl,* Mr. Lovelace tells his story from the inside looking out, using the unsophisticated accents of everyday speech to lead to a Homeric conclusion." Levin added that Lovelace is a "writer of elegant skills, with an infectious sensitivity to the heady Caribbean atmosphere."

The Dragon Can't Dance tells the story of the poor and discouraged people of Calvary Hill as they attempt to renew their heritage, culture, and sense of community by participating in Carnival, an annual celebration commemorating the crucifixion and resurrection of Jesus Christ. Dance suggested that "Lovelace's most successful treatment of the quest for personhood comes in *The Dragon Can't Dance.*" Dance went on to note that Lovelace "has powerfully revealed the folk of Calvary Hill and involved us in their lives in such a meaningful and moving manner that we appreciate their traditions, applaud their victories, suffer their defeats, rejoice in their growth, and acknowledge their personhood. Here too, as in all of his previous works, he has successfully captured the sights and sounds and rhythms of Trinidad in a captivating tale, often tragic, but also often relieved by the comic tone, style, language, and interludes that are vintage Lovelace." Lovelace's next novel, *The Wine of Astonishment,* is perhaps the most well-known work to readers living outside the Caribbean. This novel follows a Bonasse peasant woman as she witnesses the repercussions that result after the government denies members of the Spiritual Baptists the right to worship their religion.

"The novel's basic theme is the clash between the tradition and the modern, between cultural integrity and assimilation, in the village of Bonasse," explained Lester in the *New York Times Book Review.* "In *The Wine of Astonishment*—written entirely in the soft sibilance of Trinidadian speech—Mr. Lovelace sensitively and perceptively explores ancient conflicts, both personal and political."

Writing in the *Washington Post Book World,* Donald McCaig noted that *The Wine of Astonishment* "is written in patois, a musical dialect, full of sweet metaphors. It's lovely stuff to read aloud. And it can put the reader where he's never been before." McCaig also remarked that "Lovelace's idiomatic prose forces his reader to understand another people from the inside out. That's a good trick, and only the best novelists can do it."

"The argument for the enlightenment of the West Indian community is the hallmark of Lovelace's work," wrote Thompson-Cager. His writing "displays an uncommon love for himself as a black man, for his language, for his people, and for their potential greatness." Figueroa commented: "[Lovelace] takes his ability to enshrine the full Trinidadian—and Caribbean—experience . . . to further levels of perfection in his short story collection *A Brief Conversation [and Other stories].* In doing so he fulfills one of the oldest desires of writers of fiction: to mix the useful with the pleasurable." Thompson-Cager cited the title story as one in which a young man acquires "respect for life and a willingness to fight to preserve dignity." Figueroa recommended the *story Call Me 'Miss Ross' for Now:* "[T]he portrayal of Miss Ross . . . confirms what we knew of this writer before, that he has the master's touch, and in being hilarious at times he is in no way frivolous but deeply serious."

Several years elapsed before Lovelace produced his next major work of fiction, *Salt.* Some years earlier Thompson-Cager had commented: "The climaxes of Lovelace's [works] usually depend on two elements: the decision of one individual to be the person who makes the sacrifice that facilitates positive change within the community; and the emergence of a partnership or love relationship that strengthens or affirms familial and communal bonds." In *Salt* these elements appear to be blended into the characters of Bango and Alford George. William Ferguson wrote in the *New York Times Book Review:* "Bango, with his folk tales, his charm . . . represents the indigenous values of Trinidad." He is a worker and political activist whose conscious goal in life is to organize a holiday parade that includes representatives of every racial group in Trinidad. As Andrea Henry explained in the *Times Literary Supplement,* the emancipation of African slaves had caused a worker shortage that was filled by Chinese and Indian laborers, and Bango's village had become "a synthetic community, now struggling to hold itself together." "[N]ot entirely conscious of it himself," Henry wrote, Bango "is on a journey to seek reparation for the wrongs committed against his people." "His opposite number," Ferguson declared, "is Alford George, a Trinidadian whose ideals are European and who therefore lives in perpetual disillusionment." After failing at a career opportunity in England, failing at teaching, and failing as a political reformer, "Alford has a much-delayed epiphany," as Ferguson put it. Inspired by Bango, Alford discovers a new reality within himself.

Henry concluded that "one of the key achievements of *Salt* is [the] balancing of stories from black slave history with current ideas about racial issues. The past is inextricably bound to the present." She called the novel "a rich voyage of discovery" but was troubled by shifts of narrator from one chapter to the next and shifts of voice from one race or time period to another. *Washington Post Book World* reviewer Kwame Dawes reported that *Salt* "lack[ed] urgency" and the "currency of vision" of *The Dragon Can't Dance* or *The Wine of Astonishment,* but determined that *Salt* is Lovelace's "most assured work to date, and it allows him to display his remarkable capacity as a poetic and innovative fiction writer."

BIOGRAPHICAL/CRITICAL SOURCES:

BOOKS

Contemporary Literary Criticism, Volume 51, Gale (Detroit, MI), 1989.

Contemporary Novelists, sixth edition, St. James Press, 1996.

Dance, Daryl Cumber, editor, *Fifty Caribbean Writers: A Bio-Bibliographical Critical Sourcebook,* Greenwood Press (Westport, CT), 1986.

Dictionary of Literary Biography, Volume 125, Gale, 1993.

PERIODICALS

Kirkus Reviews, January 1, 1997, p. 14.

New Statesman, January 5, 1968, p. 15; September 27, 1996, p. 60.

New York Times Book Review, October 30, 1966, p. 76; November 24, 1968, pp. 68-69; January 6, 1985, p. 9; April 20, 1997, section 7, p. 19.

Observer, August 25, 1996, p. 16.

Times (London), March 12, 1985.

Times Literary Supplement, September 20, 1996, p. 24.

Tribune Books (Chicago), March 23, 1997, pp. 4-5.

Washington Post Book World, March 6, 1988, p. 7; March 30, 1997, p. 11.*

* * *

LUBBOCK, Percy 1879-1965

PERSONAL: Born June 4, 1879, in London, England; died August 1 (some sources say August 2), 1965; son of Frederic and Catherine (Gurney) Lubbock; married Sybil Cuffe, 1926 (died, 1943). *Education:* Attended Eton College and King's College, Cambridge.

CAREER: Writer. Cambridge University, Magdalene College, Cambridge, England, curator of Pepys Library, 1906-08. *Military service:* Served with British Red Cross during World War I.

AWARDS, HONORS: James Tait Black Prize for biography, 1922, for *Earlham. Reminiscences of the Author's Early Life at Earlham Hall, Norfolk; Femina-Vie Heureuse* Prize, 1923; Royal Society of Literature Benson Medal, 1926; named Commander, Order of the British Empire, 1952.

WRITINGS:

Elizabeth Barrett Browning in Her Letters, Smith & Elder (London), 1906, AMS Press, 1974.

Samuel Pepys, Scribner (New York City), 1909.

The Craft of Fiction (criticism), Scribner, 1921.

George Calderon: A Sketch from Memory, Grant Richards Press (London), 1921.

Earlham. Reminiscences of the Author's Early Life at Earlham Hall, Norfolk (history and biography), Scribner, 1922.

Roman Pictures (novel), Scribner, 1923.

The Region Cloud (novel), Scribner, 1925.

Mary Cholmondeley: A Sketch from Memory, J. Cape (London), 1928.

Shades of Eton (autobiography), Scribner, 1929.

Portrait of Edith Wharton, Appleton Century (New York City), 1947.

Marjory Gane Harkness, editor, *Percy Lubbock Reader,* Boni Liveright, 1957.

EDITOR

A Book of English Prose, two volumes, Cambridge University Press (Cambridge), 1913.

(And author of preface) Henry James, *The Ivory Tower,* Scribner, 1917.

H. James, *The Middle Years,* Scribner, 1917.

(And author of preface) James, *The Sense of the Past,* Scribner, 1917.

The Letters of Henry James, two volumes, Scribner, 1920.

The Novels and Stories of Henry James, thirty-five volumes, Scribner, 1921-23.

The Diary of Arthur Christopher Benson, Longmans, Green (New York City), 1926.

OTHER

Also contributor to periodicals, including *Quarterly Review.*

SIDELIGHTS: Writer Percy Lubbock was descended from a long line of bankers, scientists, and mathematicians. Born into a well-known Quaker family, he resided at Earlham Hall, near Norwich, England. Lubbock's "best book," according to *Dictionary of Literary Biography* contributor D. W. Jefferson, "is that in which he remembers his childhood." *Earlham. Reminiscences of the Author's Early Life at Earlham Hall, Norfolk* is a "sustained meditation on a much-loved place, every aspect and part of which, with its human associations, are cherished and preserved." Not surprisingly, Lubbock's acquaintances and experiences are visible throughout his writings, among them his friendships with Henry James and Edith Wharton. James was a prominent focus in Lubbock's work, and Lubbock's 1916 obituary on James, which appeared in the *Quarterly Review,* was hailed by Jefferson as "a remarkable appreciation of [James'] art as a novelist [that] establishes Lubbock as one of the most perceptive of his admirers, perhaps the critic who did most to create an atmosphere of recognition of James's special qualities." Unlike his friend James, Lubbock's own novels, *Roman Pictures* and *The Region Cloud* were not overwhelmingly well received by critics; as Jefferson stated, "Lubbock was not successful in fiction, and he did well to return to writing about authors."

Earlham is one of many biographical books Lubbock produced, and it is exemplary of his distinctive style of biography. Describing two of Lubbock's books—on George Calderson (1921) and Mary Cholmondeley (1928), which are both subtitled *A Sketch from Memory*—Jefferson noted that both "are personal memoirs with the central emphasis on qualities of characters as experienced by the author, nuances of personality carefully pondered and described. There is a certain amount of information about their lives but no systematic record such as a professional biographer would provide. There are brief comments on their literary works but no attempt to trace a literary career." Jefferson specified: "In assessing the worth of the person he is concerned with such virtues as integrity and genuineness, moral and social qualities, not with the techniques and methods of an artist. . . . Lubbock of course was an accomplished critic of novels, but the combination of the two functions, the appraisal in one book of an author as a persona and also as an artist, was to him antipathetic."

In writing *Portrait of Edith Wharton,* Lubbock determined that Wharton's letters would not adequately reveal her personality. Indeed, R. W. B. Lewis, in *Edith Wharton: A Biography,* expressed surprise that Lubbock was asked to write a biography of Wharton at all, for he was not knowledgeable about some portions of her life, such as her childhood. And although once friendly with Wharton, more than a decade prior to her death Wharton and Lubbock had had a "falling out" that was never reconciled. In writing her biography, Lubbock therefore requested assistance from the novelist's friends and acquaintances of Wharton, who provided the book with its "good stories and humorous touches," in the opinion of Jefferson.

Shades of Eton describes Lubbock's education at Eton. "Much of it is in celebration of notable schoolmasters of who the headmaster, Edmund Warre, is preeminent," according to Jefferson, who recognized in the book one of Lubbock's "idiosyncrasies . . . a tendency to be rather selective in his use of particular details, sometimes eschewing them altogether in a way that has its own rhetorical effect." Such an effect is evident when Lubbock writes of Warre's "genial talk" with the boys about proper behavior, but fails to recall the headmaster's exact words. "It is not memory that fails me, only the face to do so," Lubbock would write by way of explaining his lapse. Jefferson expounded on this characteristic of Lubbock's writing, noting that "Studied omission of certain elements of his subject are . . . characteristic of his policy in literary biography to such an extent as to raise questions about his relation to that genre. In presenting an imaginative portrait of an author he avoided the facts and documentary items that might obtrude and not harmonize with the delicate impression that he sought to convey."

One of Lubbock's best known works is *The Craft of Fiction,* which Jefferson called "a pioneer work" that belongs "in a category by itself." For *The Craft of Fiction,* Lubbock borrowed from the literary concepts of Henry James. James claimed that a novelist must possess a sense of reality and then complement that with the ability to discern a unique subject from life. Lubbock assessed this ability as "the power that recognizes the fruitful idea and seizes it as a thing apart." After choosing a subject, the novelist, according to James, must define the form of the novel. James insisted that the form of the novel must be that the illusion of reality is obtained.

Lubbock pursued James' "novel as reality" concept still further. He suggested that an ideal shape existed by which the novel best lent itself to the illusion of reality. Lubbock proposed that the best way for a novelist to achieve this illusion in the work was with the dramatic (as opposed to narrative) form. In short, Lubbock favored enactment over description. "As for intensity of life . . . ," he wrote, "the novelist has recourse to his other arm, the one that corresponds with the single arm of the dramatist. Inevitably, as the plot thickens and the climax approaches—inevitably, whenever an impression is to be emphasized and driven home—narration gives place to enactment, the train of events to the particular episode, the broad picture to the dramatic scene."

Lubbock also refuted the first-person narrative style. Referring to the narrator, he wrote that "he can only recall the past and tell us what he was, only *describe* his emotion; and he may describe very vividly . . . but it would necessarily be more convincing if we could get behind this description and judge for ourselves." In support of his earlier case for "enactment," Lubbock concluded, "Drama we want, always drama, for the central, paramount affair, whatever it is." However, Lubbock does not insist that all novelists should ascribe to his own preference for drama without regard for subject or theme. "Such is the progress of the writer towards drama," he noted; "such is his method of evading the drawbacks of a mere reporter and assuming the advantages, as far as possible, of a dramatist. How far he may choose to push the process in his book—that is a matter to be decided by the subject; it entirely depends upon the kind of effect that the theme demands. It may respond to all the dramatization it can get, it may give all that it has to give for less. The subject dictates the method."

Critical assessments of *The Craft of Fiction* have been mixed. A reviewer for *Outlook* was unimpressed with Lubbock's criticism, writing that "if there are any who desire to be called critics without exercising a critical judgment, they should study Mr. Lubbock carefully." The same critic noted sarcastically, "It only remained to invent a jargon and turn literary criticism into studio gossip." Taking offense with Lubbock's obsession with form, the *Outlook* critic mused, "The time may yet come when even a Tolstoy will be superciliously challenged: 'Are you crystallized?'"

BIOGRAPHICAL/CRITICAL SOURCES:

BOOKS

Bell, Millicent, *Edith Wharton and Henry James: The Story of Their Friendship,* Braziller (New York City), 1965.

Grosse, Edmund, *More Books on the Table,* Heinemann (London), 1923.

Dictionary of Literary Biography, Volume 149: *Late Nineteenth- and Early Twentieth-Century British Literary Biographers,* Gale (Detroit), 1995.

Lewis, R. W. B., *Edith Wharton: A Biography,* Harper (New York City), 1975.

Lubbock, Percy, *The Craft of Fiction,* Scribner, 1921.

Lubbock, Percy, *Shades of Eton,* Scribner, 1929.

PERIODICALS

Dial, March, 1922.

London Mercury, February, 1923.

Month, December, 1952.

Outlook, March 4, 1922.

Yale Review, December, 1947.*

* * *

LUDLAM, Charles 1943-1987

PERSONAL: Born April 12, 1943, in Floral Park, NY; died of pneumonia as a complication of acquired immune deficiency syndrome (AIDS), May 28, 1987. *Education:* Hofstra University, degree in dramatic literature, 1965.

CAREER: Actor in plays, including *Big Hotel,* 1967, and *Eunuchs of the Forbidden City,* 1972; actor in motion pictures, including *Lupe,* 1966, and *The Big Easy;* co-founder of Play-House of the Ridiculous, Greenwich Village, 1966, and Ridiculous Theatrical Company (off-Broadway), New York City, 1967. Worked as a producer; taught at colleges and universities, including one year at Yale University as associate adjunct professor and playwright-in-residence; was associated with Carnegie-Mellon University, New York University, and Connecticut College for Women.

AWARDS, HONORS: Four Obie Awards, *Village Voice,* including 1973 for acting, and 1987, for distinguished achievement; Drama Desk Award, and Rosamond Gilder Award for distinguished achievement in theatre, both 1986; grants from National Endowment for the Arts and New York State Council on the Arts; fellowships from Ford Foundation,

Rockefeller Foundation, and Guggenheim Foundation.

WRITINGS:

PLAYS

Big Hotel, produced in New York City, 1967.

Conquest of the Universe, produced in New York City, 1967, revised edition produced in New York City as *When Queens Collide,* 1967.

The Grand Tarot, produced in New York City, 1969.

(And director) *Bluebird* (produced in New York City, 1970, revised version produced in New York City, 1975), in *More Plays from Off-Off Broadway,* edited by Michael Smith, Bobbs-Merrill (Indianapolis), 1972.

(And director) *Corn,* produced in New York City, 1972.

(And director) *Eunuchs of the Forbidden City* (five-act), produced in New York City at the Theater for the New City, 1972.

(And director) *Camille: A Tear Jerker* (adapted from the play by Alexander Dumas), produced in New York City, 1973.

(And director) *Hot Ice* (satire of Hollywood gangster films), produced in New York City, 1974.

(And director) *Stage Blood* (produced in New York City, 1974), Samuel French (New York City), 1979.

(And director) *The Ventriloquist's Wife* (adapted from the film *Dead of Night*), produced in New York City, 1977.

(And director) *Utopia Inc.,* produced in New York City at Ridiculous Theater, 1978.

The Enchanted Pig (children's play; produced off-Broadway, 1979), Samuel French, 1989.

Theatre of the Ridiculous, edited by Bonnie Marranca and Gautam Dasgupta, Performing Arts Journal Publications (New York City), 1979.

Reverse Psychology (produced in 1980), Samuel French, 1989.

The Mystery of Irma Vep: A Penny Dreadful (produced in 1984), Samuel French, 1987.

Bluebeard: A Melodrama in Three Acts, Samuel French, 1987.

The Artificial Jungle: A Suspense Thriller, Samuel French, 1987.

The Ridiculous Theatrical Company Presents Medea: A Tragedy (adapted from the play by Euripides), Samuel French, 1988.

The Complete Plays of Charles Ludlam, Perennial Library (New York City), 1989.

Love's Tangled Web, Samuel French, 1989.

Ridiculous Theatre: Scourge of Human Folly: The Essays and Opinions of Charles Ludlam, edited by Steven Samuels, Theatre Communications Group (New York City), 1992.

Also author of theatrical works *Professor Bedlam's Educational Punch and Judy Show* (puppet drama), 1975; *Der Ring Gott Farblonjet* (a farce of Richard Wagner's opera of the same title), 1977; *Le bourgeois avant-garde* (based on the Moliere play *The Bourgeois Gentleman*), 1983; *Galas: A Modern Tragedy,* 1983; *The Artificial Jungle* (spoof of film adaptation of James M. Cain's novel *Double Indemnity*), 1986; and *Salammbo,* 1986. Adaptor, *Jack and the Beanstalk* (children's play); co-contributor, with Bill Vehr, to *Turds in Hell* (produced, 1979), published in *Drama Review.*

SIDELIGHTS: Educator, actor, producer, director, and playwright Charles Ludlam, co-founder of New York's Ridiculous Theatrical Company, was known as the author of innovative and sometimes outrageous stage productions characterized by his own blend of satire, camp, and parody. Many critics roundly praised him for bringing new life to the theatre. Leaving the Playhouse of the Ridiculous due to internal disagreements, he co-founded the Off-Broadway Ridiculous Theatrical Company in 1967 and wrote, directed, and acted in all of the troupe's plays, winning several Obie Awards, a Drama Desk Award, and the Rosamond Gilder Award. In addition to his stage work both outside and within his theatre troupe, where he occasional impersonated females, Ludlam directed operas, acted in the feature film *The Big Easy,* and taught at colleges and universities, including one year as associate adjunct professor and playwright-in-residence at Yale University. Among his best-known plays are *The Mystery of Irma Vep: A Penny Dreadful, Conquest of the Universe, Camille: A Tearjerker,* and the satiric *The Artificial Jungle.*

Ludlam took dialogue, characters, and scenes from a wide variety of sources: from popular songs to classical drama. Ludlam's scripts allow actors the freedom to improvise and directly speak with their audience. His first play, 1967's *Big Hotel,* is almost empty of plot, thereby allowing ample room for improv. However, such freedom was not always positive. Reviewing the performances, critics noted their chaotic disorder and unevenness from night to night. Ludlam's later works would be more disciplined than were his earlier works.

"If Charles Ludlam had lived fifty years ago," wrote Mel Gussow in the *New York Times,* "he might have been a vaudeville headliner, but he would have never lost his sense of the Ridiculous." This "sense of the Ridiculous" is readily evident in most of Ludlam's work. *Bluebeard,* the first of the Ridiculous Theatrical Company's plays to be widely reviewed, is about a mad scientist bent on creating a third genital. *Ventriloquist's Wife* concerns an actor who is upstaged and dominated by his dummy, and *Eunuchs of the Forbidden City* embraces a host of bizarre characters, including an empress who kills her son and triggers the Boxer Rebellion, an emperor who impregnates a concubine, and numerous eunuchs mouthing lines like "We have no power to love. . . . We must love power."

Ludlam's dialogue is punctuated with numerous puns and sincerely delivered cliches. Some of his more notorious lines are referred to as "Ludlamisms." "Boredom is absence of yumyum," declares a character in *Eunuchs of the Forbidden City.* Another announces, "I don't think of myself as being castrated—I think of myself as being extremely well circumcised." In *The Ventriloquist's Wife,* a performer preparing to saw a woman in half remarks, "The last woman I sawed in half is living in Paris and London."

Ludlam's later works for the stage were praised by Gussow: *Eunuchs of the Forbidden City* was dubbed "an exuberant and robust work, one of Ludlam's most polished and comic inventions." Gussow also observed, "*The Ventriloquist's Wife* raises ventriloquism to a high comic art." He was less impressed with *Utopia Inc.* "It lacks the monstrous lunacy of . . . *Bluebeard,* " claimed Gussow, who also noted the absence of "the blissful virtuosity of *The Ventriloquist's Wife.*" Gussow suggested that Ludlam, who acted in his plays, was also less impressive. "The role straitjackets his comic impulse," Gussow lamented, "and cheats the audience of a prime Ridiculous delectation."

"With *The Mystery of Irma Vep* and *The Artificial Jungle,* Mr. Ludlam undoubtedly found his widest audience," concluded *New York Times* critic Jeremy Gerard. First performed in 1984, *The Mystery of Irma Vep* was described by David Sterritt in *Christian Science Monitor* as a very funny, "ridiculous . . . sly . . . silly" play by "a solid and experienced company," the Ridiculous Theatrical Company, and its "versatile" "backbone," Ludlam. Although Don Nelson faulted the play in his *New York Daily News* review as having "stretches . . . when yawns rather than laughs were the proper reaction because Ludlam tends to over-write," he recognized the production as "one of the best performances [for inspired parody] . . . in some time." Frank Rick, chief drama critic of the *New York Times,* cited *The Mystery of Irma Vep* as one of the best plays of 1984.

In articles immediately following his death, critics recognized Ludlam's life's work. The sentiments of *Village Voice* contributor Michael Feingold were echoed in such periodicals as *New York Times, Drama Review,* and *Pittsburgh Post-Gazette.* Feingold wrote: "There was so much substance to Charles Ludlam's art, so much intelligence and such a variety of gifts in him as a person, that his loss seems at the moment to have crumbled our theatre with one blow, as if the keystone had suddenly been pulled out of an arch. The descriptions that are starting to fly about, of him as playwright, director, actor, are already a diminution of his stature. They leave out, for instance, his skills as a puppeteer and a ventriloquist, and as a designer for the stage. . . . The variety of Charles's talents was simply a sign of what made his work so rich and so far-reaching in importance."

Ludlam seems to have summed up his attitude towards his art when he spoke before a presentation of Utopia Inc. "Don't look for deeper meaning," he warned. "Just take it at face value."

BIOGRAPHICAL/CRITICAL SOURCES:

BOOKS

Contemporary Literary Criticism, Gale (Detroit), Volume 46, 1988, Volume 50, 1988.

Ludlam, Charles, *Theatre of the Ridiculous,* edited by Bonnie Marranca and Gautam Dasgupta, Performing Arts Journal Publications, 1979.

Ludlam, Charles, *Ridiculous Theatre: Scourge of Human Folly: The Essays and Opinions of Charles Ludlam,* edited by Steven Samuels, Theatre Communications Group, 1992.

Roemer, Rick, *Charles Ludlam and the Ridiculous Theatrical Company: Critical Analyses of Twenty-nine Plays,* McFarland (Jefferson, NC), 1998.

PERIODICALS

Christian Science Monitor, November 13, 1984, p. 50.

Daily News (New York City), October 8, 1984.
Nation, October 11, 1980, pp. 354-56; November 29, 1986, p. 618-19.
New York Post, September 26, 1983.
New York Theatre Critics' Reviews, December 12, 1983; November 19, 1984.
New York Times November 27, 1967, p. 60; May 5, 1970, p. 58; March 4, 1971, p. 28; April 7, 1972, p. 27; November 24, 1972, p. 43; May 4, 1973, p. 24; March 10, 1974, p. 3; May 14, 1974, p. 31; December 9, 1974, p. 54; December 28, 1977; December 5, 1978, p. C7; April 24, 1979, p. C10; September 16, 1983, p. C3; September 23, 1986, p. 13.
Opera News, April 10, 1993, p. 8.
Theatre Journal, March, 1984, pp. 103-05.

OBITUARIES:

PERIODICALS

Chicago Tribune, May 31, 1987.
Dallas Morning News, June 7, 1987.
Drama Review, winter, 1987, pp. 8-9.
Globe and Mail (Toronto), May 30, 1987.
Los Angeles Times, May 30, 1987.
Newsweek, June 8, 1987.
New York Times, May 29, 1987, p. A1; June 7, 1987, p. 6.
Pittsburgh Post-Gazette, May 30, 1987.
Village Voice, June 9, 1987, p. 88; August 4, 1987, pp. 87-88.*

* * *

LUDWIG, Jack 1922-

PERSONAL: Born August 30, 1922, in Winnipeg, Manitoba, Canada; son of Misha and Fanny (Dolgin) Ludwig; married Leya Lauer, 1946; children: Susan, Brina. *Education:* University of Manitoba, B.A., 1944; University of California, Los Angeles, Ph.D., 1953. *Avocational interests:* Singing.

ADDRESSES: Home—P.O. Box "A," Setauket, NY 11733. *Office*—268 Humanities Bldg., State University of New York, Stony Brook, NY 11733.

CAREER: Williams College, Williamstown, MA, instructor, 1949-53; Bard College, Annandale, NY, assistant professor, then associate professor and chairman of Division of Language and Literature, 1953-58; State University of New York at Stony Brook, professor of English, 1961—. Chair of humanities group, Harvard International Seminar, Cambridge, MA, summers, 1963-66. Writer-in-residence, University of Toronto, 1968-69; resident playwright, Stratford (Ontario) Shakespeare Festival, 1970; senior writer-in-residence, Banff Centre, 1974; visiting professor, University of California, Los Angeles, 1976. Consultant, Commission on College Physics film project, 1965-66, Canadian Broadcasting Corp. prison film, 1970, and Stratford Shakespeare Festival National Arts Centre theater project, 1970. Also has taught at the University of Minnesota.

AWARDS, HONORS: Atlantic First Award for fiction, *Atlantic Monthly,* 1960; Longview Foundation fiction award, 1960; Martha Foley Best American Short Story Award, 1961; O. Henry Short Story Award, 1961 and 1965; Canada Council Senior Arts Fellowship Awards in Fiction, 1962, 1967-68, and 1975-76.

WRITINGS:

Recent American Novelists, University of Minnesota Press (Minneapolis), 1962.
Confusions (novel), New York Graphic Society (Greenwich, CT), 1963.
Requiem for Bibul, Clarke, Irwin (Toronto), 1967.
Above Ground (novel), Little, Brown (Boston), 1968.
Hockey Night in Moscow, original drawings by Aislin, Simon & Schuster (Richmond Hill, Ontario), 1972, enlarged edition published as *The Great Hockey Thaw; or, The Russians Are Here!,* Doubleday (Garden City, NY), 1974.
A Woman of Her Age (novel), McClelland & Stewart, (Toronto), 1973.
Homage to Zolotova, Banff Press, 1974.
Five Ring Circus: The Montreal Olympics, Doubleday, 1976.
Games of Fear and Winning: Sports with an Inside View, Doubleday, 1976.
The Great American Spectaculars: The Kentucky Derby, Mardi Gras, and Other Days of Celebration, Doubleday, 1976.

CONTRIBUTOR

James Baker and Thomas Staley, editors, *James Joyce's "Dubliners,"* Wadsworth, 1969.
William Kilbourn, editor, *Canada: A Guide to the Peaceable Kingdom,* St. Martin's Press (New York City), 1971.

George Woodcock, editor, *The Canadian Novel in the Twentieth Century,* McClelland & Stewart, 1975.

Terry Angus, editor, *The Prairie Experience,* Macmillan (New York City), 1975.

Kilbourn, editor, *The Toronto Book,* Macmillan, 1976.

Work represented in anthologies, including *Best American Short Stories,* edited by Martha Foley and David Burnett; *Prize Stories: The O. Henry Awards,* edited by Richard Poirier; *Contemporary American Short Stories,* edited by Douglas and Sylvia Angus; *A Book of Canadian Stories,* edited by Desmond Pacey; *The Urban Experience,* edited by John Stevens; *The Canadian Century,* edited by A. J. M. Smith; and *Canadian Short Stories,* edited by Robert Weaver. Contributor of numerous short stories, articles, and reviews to magazines and newspapers in the United States, Canada, and Europe, including *Tamarack Review.*

OTHER

(Editor with W. Richard Poirier) *Stories: British and American,* Houghton (Boston), 1953.

(Editor with Andy Wainwright) *Soundings: New Canadian Poets,* Anansi (Toronto), 1970.

Adapter of several plays, including *The Alchemist,* by Ben Jonson, for Stratford Shakespeare Festival, *Hedda Gabler,* by Henrik Ibsen, for CBC-TV, and *Ubu Roi,* by Alfred Jarry, for Stratford Workshop. Co-editor, *Noble Savage.*

WORK IN PROGRESS: Two novels, *The Rites of Leo Spring* and *The November May Day of Doba Montreal,* and a novella, *Meesh;* a play, *General Agamemnon;* a contemporary version of *Ubu Roi* titled *Ubu Rex;* short stories for inclusion in a collection; criticism on the novel of the 1960s and 1970s, on Joyce, Yeats, and the poetry of John Berryman, and on technology, values, and society.

SIDELIGHTS: Professor and author Jack Ludwig has edited several anthologies, published nonfiction works focusing primarily on sports, contributed to periodicals, and written numerous essays, short stories, and novels. "Ludwig enjoys a reputation as a writer of vitality and versatility," in the opinion of Hallvard Dahlie in *Dictionary of Literary Biography.* Noting that Ludwig has "established himself as something of a literary phenomenon in both Canada and the United States," Dahlie further explains that Ludwig's "major fictional concerns and characterizations" ascribe "to the North American Jewish literary tradition." "Ludwig's incisive wit and his ability to cut through the hypocrisy and pretense of his worlds are his strong features," Dahlie added, "but a problem that recurs for the reader is to find a character drawn with sufficient compassion against who he can measure the shortcomings that Ludwig quite appropriately brings into focus. . . . Ludwig's posture of detachment from the worlds he depicts relegates his fiction at times closer to artifice than to art, with his protagonists emerging as caricatures rather than credible representatives of a confused world."

Although Ludwig won a number of awards in the early and mid-1960s, his subsequent work has not brought him similar acclaim. Overall, he is perhaps best regarded for his short stories and journalism. In general, his novels have been given mixed reviews. In Ludwig's debut novel, *Confusions,* a story depicting "the morally, racially, and sexually confusing world of a schizophrenic protagonist" in Dahlie's opinion, wordplay, jokes, and witty banter "constitute the basis of Ludwig's prose, and their brilliance can be offset by tedium and predictability," according to the critic. In *Above Ground,* Ludwig's semi-autobiographical novel, "Jack Ludwig assumes the persona of an engaging narrator, Joshua, who again offers no more plot than the random events of his life sorted out in striking scenes," maintains a *Partisan Review* critic. "This puts a great strain on Ludwig's performance and turns his novel into a concert program," the critic added. "We want to be held, not merely entertained, by his range and depth of feeling. Much of the time he can sustain it . . . . [Yet] if at times the material is weak, the performance in *Above Ground* is grand; the design enriches a mode which might be labeled American existential. The novel is immensely entertaining, never frivolous." Less enthusiastic, a *Kenyon Review* contributor called the book "exceedingly hard to get through and not yielding much pleasure." While noting that "Ludwig has a good ear, the passage develops a rhythm, and some of the sensations are fine," the critic found the author's use of compound words—"tarpaperpatched", "springsprung", "chalkygreen"—"a stylistic indulgence." "Too often the 'poetry' of his insistent voice overwhelms the possibilities for any modulation, variations of intensity," the *Kenyon* critic concluded.

"For a novel about survival, *Above Ground* as a curiously lifeless quality," in the opinion of a *New York Times Book Review* critic. "It is a book that yearns after a sense of language and, pursuing it, ends tangled in clumsy word constructions, strained metaphors, and images weighted with echoes from other, better writers. . . . [Furthermore,] it is hard to tell the characters apart. . . . The girls are all equally bosomy and equally addicted to literary allusions. If Joshua is finally their victim, he is drawn so abstractly that it is hard to care."

A reviewer in *Fiddlehead* concluded of Ludwig's *Above Ground* that it is "not a bad novel. There is a picaresque comic element about it which is often amusing. There are certain scenes which approach pathos." But the reviewer strongly criticized Ludwig for limiting himself to the image of female breasts as a means of expressing his central theme—that of woman-as-wet-nurse who tends to man's needs with love in order to keep him alive (i.e., "above ground"). As a result of this preoccupation, "the characterization of the women had all the individuality of a *Playboy* fold-out. . . . And inasmuch as the novel appears to be very autobiographical, the result is embarrassing."

Finally, a *Canadian Forum* reviewer was bothered by *Above Ground,* noting that while Ludwig is capable of writing sophisticated prose, "the total impact is less than that of his best stories. . . . The feeling I'm finally left with is one of exposure to brilliant triviality. . . . In [the novel], Ludwig offers bits of learning, hints of mythic parallels, and a good deal of fugitive insight. But his central concern seems to me basically sentimental, in the sense that the world he offers us is not the one that exists, but the one that he wants to exist. . . . He has given us a novel that does not suggest as much about humanity and its situation as it does about the situation of the novelist himself."

In Ludwig's third novel, *A Woman of Her Age,* the author achieves his greatest character triumph in Doba Goffman, a woman he had first created in a 1959 story published in the *Tamarack Review.* "Unlike many of Ludwig's earlier characters, Doba is compassionately drawn," maintains Dahlie, "and she emerges ultimately as a proud and almost tragic figure. . . . She sustains the half dozen other characters of the novel. . . . The dramatic strength here resides in the fact that what is depicted is not merely one day in the life of Doba Goffman, but the last day of her life."

Ludwig's significance in the North American literary community has decreased since the early years of his career, opines Dahlie: "On the whole it seems that Ludwig has not been as successful with the novel as he has been with the short story, and he has made his mark, too, in his controversial nonfiction books about the sports worlds that he knows intimately. What is missing in his full-length fiction are a sustained compassion and a consistent point of view; where incisive wit and brilliant expose will satisfy journalistic requirements and the conventions of the shorter sketch, they are not in themselves sufficient for the novels of the first order. "His problem," writes Lila Stonehewer, "is how to sustain a heighten prose style without becoming tiresome, how to achieve variety without bathos."

BIOGRAPHICAL/CRITICAL SOURCES:

BOOKS

Cameron, Donald, *Conversations with Canadian Novelists,* Macmillan (Toronto), 1973.

Dictionary of Literary Biography, Volume 60: *Canadian Writers since 1960, Second Series,* Gale (Detroit), 1987.

Gibson, Graeme, *Eleven Canadian Novelists,* Anansi (Toronto), 1973.

Parr, John, *Speaking of Winnipeg,* Queenston House (Winnipeg), 1974.

Davey, Frank, *From There to Here: A Guide to English-Canadian Literature since 1960,* Press Porcepic (Erin, Ontario), 1974.

PERIODICALS

Books in Canada, January-February, 1974.

Canadian Forum, January, 1969.

Canadian Literature, winter, 1964; summer, 1966, pp. 34-42; spring, 1969, pp. 49-53; summer, 1974.

Fiddlehead, summer, 1968.

Kenyon Review, number 5, 1968.

National Observer, July 15, 1968.

New Yorker, July 6, 1968.

New York Times Book Review, July 28, 1968.

Partisan Review, fall, 1968.

Tamarack Review, autumn, 1963; November, 1973.

Virginia Quarterly Review, summer, 1968.*

* * *

LUKE, Peter (Ambrose Cyprian) 1919-1995

PERSONAL: Born August 12, 1919, in St. Albans, Hertfordshire, England; died January 23, 1995, in

Cadiz; son of (Sir) Harry (a writer) and Joyce (Fremlin) Luke; married Carola Peyton-Jones (died); married Lettice Crawshaw (divorced); married June Tobin (an actress), 1963; children: (second marriage) one daughter, one son; (third marriage) three daughters, two sons. *Education:* Attended Byam Shaw School of Art, London, and Atelier Andre Lhote Studio, Paris. *Avocational interests:* Andalusian horses, country life, tauromachia.

CAREER: Reuters Ltd., London, England, sub-editor, 1946-47; worked in wine trade in Portugal, Spain, and France, 1947-57; *Queen* magazine, London, book critic, 1957-58; American Broadcasting Companies (ABC-TV), London, drama and story editor, 1958-60, *Bookman* editor, 1960-61, *Tempo* (arts program) editor, 1961-63; British Broadcasting Corp. (BBC-TV), London, drama producer, 1963-67; freelance writer, 1967-95. Dublin Gate Theatre, Dublin, Ireland, director, 1977-95. Also worked as a diamond-point glass engraver. *Military service:* Royal Rifle Brigade, 1940-46; served in Middle East, North Africa, Italy, Germany, and second front in France; received Military Cross.

MEMBER: Writers Guild of Great Britain, Society of Authors, Eton Viking Rowing Club, Kildare Street and University Club.

AWARDS, HONORS: Italia Prize, 1967, for "Silent Song"; Antoinette Perry Award nomination for best play, 1969, for *Hadrian VII.*

WRITINGS:

The Play of Hadrian VII (based on *Hadrian the Seventh* and other works by Frederick Rolfe, also known as Baron Corvo; produced at Birmingham Repertory Theatre, 1967; revision produced in London in 1968; produced on Broadway at Helen Hayes Theatre, 1969), Deutsch (London), 1968, Knopf (New York City), 1969.

Sisyphus and Reilly: An Autobiography, Deutsch, 1972.

Bloomsbury (produced in London's West End, 1974), Samuel French, 1976.

(Editor) *Enter Certain Players: Edwards-MacLiammoir and the Gate* (festschrift), Dolmen (Dublin), 1978.

Collected Short Stories, Goldsmith Press (Kildare), 1979.

Under the Moorish Wall: Adventures in Andalusia, Dolmen, 1980.

Telling Tales: Collected Short Stories, Goldsmith Press, 1981.

Also author of *The Other Side of the Hill* (novel), 1984; and *The Mad Pomegranate and the Praying Mantis: An Andalusian Adventure* (memoirs), 1985. Author of teleplays, including *Small Fish Are Sweet,* 1959; *Pig's Ear with Flowers,* 1960; *Roll on, Bloomin' Death,* 1961; (with William Sansom) *A Man on Her Back,* 1966; *The Devil a Monk Wou'd Be,* 1967; (and director) *Anach Cuan: The Music of Sean O'Riada,* BBC-TV, 1967; and (also director) *Black Sound—Deep Song: The Andalusian Poetry of Federico Garcia Lorca,* BBC-TV, 1968.

Contributor to periodicals, including *Envoy, Cornhill, Vogue, Queen, New Statesman, Times Literary Supplement,* and *Listener.* Also translator of works from the Spanish.

SIDELIGHTS: English scriptwriter, producer, director, book critic, novelist, short story writer, autobiographer, editor, and dramatist Peter Luke was educated at Eton, attended the Byam Shaw School of Art, then studied under the cubist painter Andre Lhote in Paris. Luke had planned a career as an artist, but his studies were halted by the onset of World War II and his service in the British Army. After leaving the military, Luke worked as a journalist before assuming an apprenticeship in the wine trade which took him to Portugal, France, and Spain. "The brush, the diamond-point, the typewriter have been the tools of my trade to date," Luke once told *Listener.* "Tomorrow they may be a hammer and chisel or a pick and shovel. But it was the former ones—or rather the attitudes engendered by them—that I have brought with me to television. Once within, I learned, more or less by accident, something of the craft of creating drama."

Luke wrote teleplays while working in the wine trade industry. Then, in 1958, he became story editor of the television program *Armchair Theatre.* He worked as editor of *The Bookman* from 1962 to 1963, and as producer of the arts program *Tempo* from 1963 to 1964. The British Broadcasting Company (BBC-TV) employed Luke as drama producer between 1963 and 1967 for their *Play of the Week* and *Wednesday Play* programs; also for the BBC, Luke wrote and directed the films *Anach Cuan* and *Black Sound—Deep Song,* as well as numerous radio plays. His other writings include the stage play *Hadrian VII,* the historical novel *The Other Side of the Hill,* and two autobiographical books, *Sisyphus and Reilly* and *The Mad*

Pomegranate & the Praying Mantis: An Andalusian Adventure.

"Hungarian chromosomes, of which Luke has plenty, are supposed to make for success in show business," reported a contributor to the *Observer Review.* Yet Luke's tutors at Eton never expected success from their wayward pupil in spite of his Hungarian grandfather from Detroit. Luke's school reports, some of which were quoted in a *Times Literary Supplement* review of *Sisyphus and Reilly,* show the unanimous disapprobation of his tutors: "Many of my pupils are incompetent at managing their own affairs but Luke is far the most incompetent. . . . He has the ability to appear awake and actually to be asleep." Luke's reputation as "dreadfully backward," "lazy," and "naturally idle" provoked one tutor to say, "I cannot prophesy anything but failure."

Despite these less than encouraging reports, Luke's tutors admitted, "He is quite willing and cheerful in spite of misfortunes." That virtue remained an obvious part of Luke's philosophy even after his stage success spared him from depending on his cheerful disposition to live. "So, looking back (from a mountain in Spain) I see that I've been rather lucky. I've been in the right place at the right time," Luke wrote in *Listener.* When a television drama editor told Luke that he would no longer assign work to someone living so far away, Luke had an answer typical of his attitude: "I replied that I would rather die of starvation in Spain than of bronchitis in London."

In 1959, while in charge of scripts for ABC's London-based *Armchair Theatre* program, Luke was approached by director James Roose-Evans to adapt Frederick Rolfe's 1904 work *Hadrian the Seventh.* Luke, whose father was once associated with Rolfe, agreed to the difficult challenge. *Hadrian the Seventh,* an autobiographical fantasy, finds Rolfe's alter ego, George Arthur Rose, denied entry into the priesthood. Then, through a series of unexpected events, Rose suddenly believes himself elected pope. In his revision, Luke dispensed with the character of Rose, focusing instead on Rolfe, whose eccentric personality and quirky behavior while discharging his papal duties is the source of the play's humor. Luke has Rolfe fantasize that the "two bailiffs who come to seize [his] possessions turn into . . . the two ecclesiastics . . . [who] offer him ordination as a priest," explained *Dictionary of Literary Biography* contributor Robert Coskren. As such, Hadrian emerges from the delusion of Rolfe, becomes pope, performs his papal duties, and eventually dies. Rolfe then emerges, to witness the bailiffs removing the last of his possessions before leaving Rolfe in a completely empty room.

Once written the script went unproduced for four years, as many thought the lead role too difficult and the play not commercial enough. Originally a three act play, Alec McCowen, who eventually acted in the lead role, convincingly argued that the second act be removed, adding any necessary material to the other two acts. "For Luke it was a painful procedure, but it meant a production," recounted Coskren. Critics who viewed the opening-night production were unimpressed; London *Times* contributor Irving Wardle concluded that Rolfe's novel was unadaptable, and Luke's dramatic devices unworkable. Despite the lackluster response to its Birmingham run, *Hadrian VII* was again revised, with an eye to quickening the pace and strengthening its character's motivations.

The play's West End run was a much greater success. Luke's revised adaptation of Rolfe's *Hadrian the Seventh* brought the playwright international kudos, not to mention rave reviews from London critics. In the London *Sunday Times,* Harold Hobson called it a "splendid, colourful, recklessly melodramatic and vituperatively brilliant drama." A *National Observer* contributor declared: "Mr. Luke's play is good, at times fascinating. But it is essentially a one-character evening, though its author does go at that one character as a surgeon doing very delicate work. Carefully he peels away Rolfe's facade to reveal the confused, tortured dreamer at the core." Several critics noted that, to Luke's credit, actors playing the title role of Hadrian were critically acclaimed for their performances. When the play production crossed the Atlantic and opened in New York, the reviews were equally positive. *Show Business* observed, "Without any gimmicks, courting of the sensational, or attempts at innovation, *Hadrian VII* is quite simply the best play on Broadway this season."

Following the success of *Hadrian VII,* when he was about fifty years old, Luke moved to Spain and worked as a freelance writer for the remaining years of his life. During this period he wrote, among other things, several television plays and another theatrical production, *Bloomsbury.* Structured by the thoughts and detached narration of writer Virginia Woolf, *Bloomsbury* involves Woolf's Bloomsbury circle of writers and artists. However, the play "was pat," according to Coskren, who indicated that *Bloomsbury* "fails, both to history and to personality." In *Plays and Players,* Sandy Wilson acknowledged that when this "ambitious" play "works, it works very well; but it tends to leave one at the end with a slight feeling of indigestion and a suspicion that much of the depth and significance of the events we have witnesses has been sacrificed for the sake of a jolly Evening in the Theatre." And *Drama* critic J. W. Lambert judged *Bloomsbury* to be primarily "a shoddy piece of work to have come from the author of *Hadrian VII.*"

Luke's autobiographical *Sisyphus and Reilly* was recognized by a *Times* contributor as a "beautifully written book" containing "a diverting series of autobiographical remembrances of things past." A reviewer for the *Times Literary Supplement* discussed the common life patterns that run through Luke's autobiography, concluding: "Familiar this may be: but Mr. Luke has an original talent for writing of the blank spaces between the incidents of life, the grey times of waiting and inertia. He can write gaily of unhappiness, ironically of success, shyly of his own courage, bravely of his fears. Perhaps only another Etonian will understand how typically Etonian is his attitude to everything that ought to be taken seriously."

BIOGRAPHICAL/CRITICAL SOURCES:

BOOKS

Contemporary Literary Criticism, Volume 38, Gale (Detroit), 1986.
Dictionary of Literary Biography, Volume 13: *British Dramatists since World War II,* Gale, 1982.
Luke, Peter, *Sisyphus and Reilly: An Autobiography,* Deutsch, 1972.
McCowen, Alec, *Double Bill,* Elm Tree (London), 1980.

PERIODICALS

Books and Bookmen, May, 1970.
British Book News, April, 1985.
Commonweal, February 7, 1969, pp. 588-89.
Drama, autumn, 1974, p. 48.
Listener, September 12, 1968.
Nation, January 27, 1969, pp. 124-25.
National Observer, January 20, 1969.
New York, September 23, 1974, p. 67.
New York Theater Critic's Reviews, January 13, 1969, p. 393.
New York Times, January 9, 1969, p. 22; January 19, 1969, pp. 1, 22.
Observer Review, January 16, 1972.
Players Magazine, December, 1970-January, 1971, pp. 68-71.
Plays and Players, August, 1974, pp. 40-41.
Show Business, January 25, 1969.
Times (London), November 6, 1961, p. 14; July 13, 1972; August 23, 1984, p. 9.
Times Literary Supplement, September 29, 1972.
Variety, January 15, 1969.
Washington Post, March 4, 1970.
Women's Wear Daily, January 9, 1969.

OBITUARIES:

PERIODICALS

Times (London), January 24, 1995, p. 21.*

M-O

MACFARLANE, Stephen
See CROSS, John Keir

* * *

MAIMAN, Jaye 1957-

PERSONAL: Born October 31, 1957, in Brooklyn, NY; daughter of Ira Raymond and Sylvia Maiman. *Education:* Brooklyn College of the City University of New York, B.A.; graduate study at University of Virginia. *Religion:* Jewish.

ADDRESSES: Home—Brooklyn, NY.

CAREER: Writer.

MEMBER: Mystery Writers of America, Sisters in Crime, Public Relations Society of America.

AWARDS, HONORS: Lambda Literary Award for best lesbian mystery, 1992, for *Crazy for Loving.*

WRITINGS:

I Left My Heart, Naiad Press (Tallahassee), 1991.
Crazy for Loving, Naiad Press, 1992.
Under My Skin, Naiad Press, 1993.
Someone to Watch, Naiad Press, 1995.

SIDELIGHTS: Jaye Maiman's mystery novels feature a former romance novelist turned detective named Robin Miller in cases which involve members of the lesbian community. Miller's adventures, which have earned Maiman a Lambda Award, combine detective sleuthing with poignant looks at lesbian life.

In *Under My Skin,* Miller investigates the death of a close friend. The sheriff and undertaker call it a heart attack, but Robin has her suspicions, especially because her friend was being investigated by unknown parties. The critic for *Publishers Weekly* claims that "Robin's sleuthing is as sharp as always." In *Someone to Watch,* Miller must prove a friend innocent of murder when a fashion photographer is found dead. Ties to a politician and the gay activist community only complicate matters, as does Miller's guilt over accidently killing her sister as a child. Whitney Scott in *Booklist* finds that *Someone to Watch* is "sure to excite current fans and win many new ones."

BIOGRAPHICAL/CRITICAL SOURCES:

PERIODICALS

Booklist, July, 1995, p. 1864.
Publishers Weekly, December 6, 1993, p. 69.

* * *

MAMET, David (Alan) 1947-

PERSONAL: Surname is pronounced "*Mam*-et"; born November 30, 1947, in Chicago, IL; son of Bernard Morris (an attorney) and Lenore June (a teacher; maiden name, Silver) Mamet; married Lindsay Crouse (an actress), December 21, 1977 (divorced); married Rebecca Pidgeon (an actress), 1991; children: Willa, Zosia, Clara. *Education:* Attended Neighborhood Playhouse School of the Theater, 1968-69; Goddard College, B.A., 1969. *Politics:* "The last refuge of the unimaginative." *Religion:* "The second-to-last."

ADDRESSES: Home—Chicago, IL. *Agent*—Howard Rosenstone, Rosenstone/Wender, 3 East 48th St., New York, NY 10017.

CAREER: Playwright, screenwriter, director, and producer. St. Nicholas Theater Company, Chicago, IL, founder, 1973, artistic director, 1973-76, member of board of directors, beginning 1973; Goodman Theater, Chicago, associate artistic director, 1978-79. Producer of motion pictures, including *Lip Service,* 1988, *Hoffa,* 1992, and *A Life in the Theater,* 1993. Actor in motion pictures, including *Black Widow,* 1986, and *The Water Engine,* 1992. Special lecturer in drama, Marlboro College, 1970; artist-in-residence in drama, Goddard College, 1971-73; faculty member, Illinois Arts Council, 1974; visiting lecturer in drama, University of Chicago, 1975-76 and 1979; teaching fellow, School of Drama, Yale University, 1976-77; guest lecturer, New York University, 1981; associate professor of film, Columbia University, 1988. Has also worked in a canning plant, a truck factory, at a real estate agency, and as a window washer, office cleaner, and taxi driver.

MEMBER: Dramatists Guild, Writers Guild of America, Actors Equity Association, PEN, United Steelworkers of America, Randolph A. Hollister Association, Atlantic Theater Company (chair of the board).

AWARDS, HONORS: Joseph Jefferson Award, 1975, for *Sexual Perversity in Chicago,* and 1976, for *American Buffalo;* Obie Awards, *Village Voice,* for best new American play, 1976, for *Sexual Perversity in Chicago* and *American Buffalo,* for best American play, 1983, for *Edmond,* and for best play, 1995, for *The Cryptogram;* Children's Theater grant, New York State Council on the Arts, 1976; Rockefeller grant, 1976; Columbia Broadcasting System fellowship in creative writing, 1976; New York Drama Critics' Circle Award for best American play, 1977, for *American Buffalo,* and 1984, for *Glengarry Glen Ross;* Outer Critics Circle Award, 1978, for contributions to the American theater; Academy Award ("Oscar") nomination for best adapted screenplay, Academy of Motion Picture Arts and Sciences, 1983, for *The Verdict,* and 1997, for *Wag the Dog;* Society for West End Theatre Award, 1983; Pulitzer Prize for drama, Joseph Dintenfass Award, Elizabeth Hull-Warriner Award, Dramatists Guild, Antoinette Perry ("Tony") Award nomination, American Theater Wing, for best play, all 1984, all for *Glengarry Glen Ross,* Antoinette Perry ("Tony") Award nomination for best reproduction of a play, 1984, for *American Buffalo;* Antoinette Perry ("Tony") Award for best play, 1988, for *Speed-the-Plow;* American Academy and Institute of Arts and Letters Award for Literature, 1986; Golden Globe Award nomination for best screenplay, 1988, for *House of Games;* Writers Guild Award nomination for best screenplay based on material from another medium, 1988, for *The Untouchables.*

WRITINGS:

PLAYS

Lakeboat (one-act; produced in Marlboro, VT, 1970; revised version produced in Milwaukee, WI, 1980), Grove (New York City), 1981.

Duck Variations (one-act; produced in Plainfield, VT, 1972; produced Off-Off-Broadway, 1975), published in *Sexual Perversity in Chicago and Duck Variations: Two Plays,* Grove, 1978.

Sexual Perversity in Chicago (one-act; produced in Chicago, 1974; produced Off-Off-Broadway, 1975), published in *Sexual Perversity in Chicago and Duck Variations: Two Plays,* Grove, 1978.

Squirrels (one-act), produced in Chicago, 1974.

The Poet and the Rent: A Play for Kids from Seven to 8:15, produced in Chicago, 1974, published in *Three Children's Plays,* 1986.

American Buffalo (two-act; produced in Chicago, 1975; produced on Broadway, 1977), Grove, 1977.

Reunion (one-act; produced with *Sexual Perversity in Chicago,* Louisville, KY, 1976; produced Off-Broadway with *Dark Pony* and *The Sanctity of Marriage,* 1979), published with *Dark Pony* in *Reunion and Dark Pony: Two Plays,* Grove, 1979, also published with *Dark Pony* and *The Sanctity of Marriage* in *Reunion, Dark Pony, and The Sanctity of Marriage: Three Plays,* Samuel French (New York City), 1982.

Dark Pony (one-act; produced with *Reunion,* New Haven, CT, 1977; produced Off-Broadway with *Reunion* and *The Sanctity of Marriage,* 1979), published with *Reunion* in *Reunion and Dark Pony: Two Plays,* Grove, 1979, also published with *Reunion* and *The Sanctity of Marriage* in *Reunion, Dark Pony, and The Sanctity of Marriage: Three Plays,* Samuel French, 1982.

All Men Are Whores (produced in New Haven, 1977), published in *Short Plays and Monologues,* Dramatists Play Service, 1981.

A Life in the Theatre (one-act; produced in Chicago, 1977; produced Off-Broadway, 1977), Grove, 1978.

The Revenge of the Space Pandas; or, Binky Rudich and the Two Speed-Clock (produced in Queens, NY, 1977), Sergel, 1978.

(And director) *The Woods* (two-act; produced in Chicago, 1977; produced Off-Broadway, 1979), Grove, 1979.

The Water Engine: An American Fable (two-act; produced as a radio play on the program *Earplay,* Minnesota Public Radio, 1977; stage adaptation produced in Chicago, 1977; produced Off-Broadway, 1977), published with *Mr. Happiness* in *The Water Engine: An American Fable and Mr. Happiness: Two Plays,* Grove, 1978.

Mr. Happiness (produced with *The Water Engine,* on Broadway, 1978), published with *The Water Engine: An American Fable* in *The Water Engine: An American Fable and Mr. Happiness: Two Plays,* Grove, 1978.

Lone Canoe; or, The Explorer (musical), music and lyrics by Alaric Jans, produced in Chicago, 1979.

The Sanctity of Marriage (one-act; produced Off-Broadway with *Reunion* and *Dark Pony,* 1979), published in *Reunion, Dark Pony, and The Sanctity of Marriage: Three Plays,* Samuel French, 1982.

Shoeshine (one-act; produced Off-Off-Broadway, 1979), published in *Short Plays and Monologues,* Dramatists Play Service, 1981.

Short Plays and Monologues, Dramatist Play Service, 1981.

A Sermon (one-act), produced Off-Off-Broadway, 1981.

Donny March, produced 1981.

Litko (produced in New York City, 1984), published in *Short Plays and Monologues,* Dramatists Play Service, 1981.

Edmond (produced in Chicago, 1982; produced Off-Broadway, 1982), Grove, 1983.

The Disappearance of the Jews (one-act), produced in Chicago, 1983.

The Dog, produced 1983.

Film Crew, produced 1983.

4 A.M., produced 1983.

Glengarry Glen Ross (two-act; produced on the West End, 1983; produced on Broadway, 1984), Grove, 1984.

Five Unrelated Pieces (produced Off-Off-Broadway, 1983; includes *Two Conversations, Two Scenes,* and *Yes, but so What*), published in *A Collection of Dramatic Sketches and Monologues,* Samuel French, 1985.

Vermont Sketches (contains *Pint's a Pound the World Around, Deer Dogs, Conversations with the Spirit World* and *Dowsing;* produced in New York City, 1984), published in *A Collection of Dramatic Sketches and Monologues,* Samuel French, 1985.

The Shawl [and] *Prairie du Chien* (one-acts; produced together at the Lincoln Center, 1985), Grove, 1985.

A Collection of Dramatic Sketches and Monologues, Samuel French, 1985.

Vint (one-act; based on Anton Chekov's short story; produced in New York City with six other one-act plays based on Chekov's short works, under the collective title *Orchards,* 1985), published in *Orchards,* Grove, 1986.

(Adaptor) Chekov, *The Cherry Orchard* (produced at Goodman Theatre, 1985), Grove, 1987.

Three Children's Plays (includes *The Poet and the Rent: A Play for Kids from Seven to 8:15, The Revenge of the Space Pandas; or, Binky Rudich and the Two Speed-Clock,* and *The Frog Prince*), Grove, 1986.

The Woods, Lakeboat, Edmond, Grove, 1987.

Speed-the-Plow (produced on Broadway, 1988), Grove, 1988.

Where Were You When It Went Down?, produced in New York City, 1988.

(Adaptor and editor) Chekov, *Uncle Vanya,* Grove, 1989.

Goldberg Street (short plays and monologues), Grove, 1989.

Bobby Gould in Hell, produced with *The Devil and Billy Markham* by Shel Silverstein, New York City, 1989.

Five Television Plays: A Waitress in Yellowstone; Bradford; The Museum of Science and Industry Story; A Wasted Weekend; We Will Take You There, Grove, 1990.

Oleanna (produced, 1991), Pantheon (New York City), 1992, Dramatists Play Service, 1993.

(Adaptor) Anton Chekov, *The Three Sisters: A Play,* Samuel French, 1992.

A Life with No Joy in It, and Other Plays and Pieces (contains *Almost Done, Monologue, Two Enthusiasts, Sunday Afternoon, The Joke Code, A Scene, Fish, A Perfect Mermaid, Dodge, L.A. Sketches, A Life with No Joy in It, Joseph Dintenfass,* and *No One will Be Immune*), Dramatists Play Service, 1994.

Plays—One (collection; includes *Duck Variations, Sexual Perversity in Chicago, Squirrels, American Buffalo, The Water Engine,* and *Mr. Happiness*), Methuen (New York City), 1994.

(And director) *The Cryptogram* (produced in London, 1994; produced Off-Broadway, 1995), Dramatists Play Service, 1995, Vintage (New York City), 1995.

The Old Neighborhood: Three Plays (includes *The Disappearance of the Jews, Jolly,* and *Deeny*), Vintage, 1998.

Also author of *No One Will Be Immune and Other Plays and Pieces,* and *Oh Hell.*

SCREENPLAYS

The Postman Always Rings Twice (adaptation of the novel by James M. Cain), Paramount, 1981.

The Verdict (adaptation of the novel by Barry Reed), Columbia, 1982.

(And director) *House of Games* (based on a story by Mamet; produced by Orion Pictures, 1987), Grove, 1987.

The Untouchables (based on the television series), Paramount, 1987.

(With Shel Silverstein; and director) *Things Change* (produced by Columbia Pictures, 1988), Grove, 1988.

We're No Angels (adaptation of the 1955 film of the same name; produced by Paramount, 1989), Grove, 1990.

(And director) *Homicide* (produced by Columbia, 1991), Grove, 1992.

Glengary Glen Ross (based on Mamet's play of the same title), New Line Cinema, 1992.

The Water Engine (teleplay; based on Mamet's play of the same title), Amblin Television, 1992.

Hoffa, 20th-Century Fox, 1992.

Texan (film short), Chanticleer Films, 1994.

(And director) *Oleanna* (based on Mamet's play of the same title), Samuel Goldwyn, 1994.

Vanya on 42nd Street (adapted from the play *Uncle Vanya* by Anton Chekhov), Film Four International, 1994.

American Buffalo (based on Mamet's play of the same title), Samuel Goldwyn, 1996.

(And director) *The Spanish Prisoner,* Sweetland Films, 1997.

The Edge, 20th-Century Fox, 1997.

Wag the Dog (based on the novel *American Hero* by Larry Beinhart), New Line Cinema, 1997.

Also author of the teleplay *A Life in the Theater,* based on Mamet's play of the same title.

NOVELS

The Village, Little, Brown, 1994.

The Old Religion: A Novel (historical fiction), Free Press, 1997.

OTHER

Warm and Cold (children's picturebook), illustrations by Donald Sultan, Solo Press, 1984.

(With wife, Lindsay Crouse) *The Owl* (children's book), Kipling Press, 1987.

Writing in Restaurants (essays, speeches, and articles), Penguin (New York City), 1987.

Some Freaks (essays), Viking, 1989.

(With Donald Sultan and Ricky Jay) *Donald Sultan: Playing Cards,* edited by Edit deAk, Kyoto Shoin (Kyoto, Japan), 1989.

The Hero Pony: Poems, Grove Weidenfeld (New York City), 1990.

On Directing Film, Viking, 1992.

The Cabin: Reminiscence and Diversions, Random House (New York City), 1992.

A Whore's Profession: Notes and Essays (includes *Writing in Restaurants, Some Freaks, On Directing Film,* and *The Cabin*), Faber (New York City), 1994.

Passover (children's picturebook), illustrated by Michael McCurdy, St. Martin's Press (New York City), 1995.

The Duck and the Goat (children's picturebook), illustrated by Maya Kennedy, St. Martin's Press, 1996.

Make-Believe Town: Essays and Remembrances, Little, Brown (Boston), 1996.

True and False: Heresy and Common Sense for the Actor (essays), Pantheon (New York City), 1997.

3 Uses of the Knife: On the Nature and Purpose of Drama (part of the "Columbia Lectures on American Culture" series), Columbia University Press (New York City), 1998.

On Acting, Viking, 1999.

Also author of episodes of *Hill Street Blues,* NBC, 1987, and *L.A. Law,* NBC. Contributing editor, *Oui,* 1975-76.

ADAPTATIONS: The film *About Last Night. . . ,* released by Tri-Star Pictures in 1986, was based on Mamet's *Sexual Perversity in Chicago.*

WORK IN PROGRESS: Writing and directing two films: *The Winslow Boy* and *State and Maine,* both in production.

SIDELIGHTS: David Mamet has acquired a great deal of critical recognition for his plays, each one a microcosmic view of the American experience. "He's that rarity, a pure writer," noted Jack Kroll in *Newsweek,* "and the synthesis he appears to be making, with echoes from voices as diverse as Beckett, Pinter, and Hemingway, is unique and exciting." Since 1976, Mamet's plays have been widely produced in regional theaters and in New York City. One of Mamet's most successful plays, *Glengarry Glen Ross,* earned the New York Drama Critics' Circle Award for best American play and the Pulitzer Prize in drama, both in 1984. Critics have also praised Mamet's screenwriting; he received Academy Award nominations for best adapted screenplay for *The Verdict* in 1983, and for *Wag the Dog* in 1997.

Mamet "has carved out a career as one of America's most creative young playwrights," observed Mel Gussow in the *New York Times,* "with a particular affinity for working-class characters." These characters and their language give Mamet's work its distinct flavor. Mamet is, according to Kroll, "that rare bird, an American playwright who's a language playwright." "Playwriting is simply showing how words influence actions and vice versa," Mamet explained to *People Weekly* contributor Linda Witt. "All my plays attempt to bring out the poetry in the plain, everyday language people use. That's the only way to put art back into the theater." Mamet has been accused of eavesdropping, simply recording the insignificant conversations of which everyone is aware; yet, many reviewers recognize the playwright's artistic intent. Jean M. White commented in the *Washington Post* that "Mamet has an ear for vernacular speech and uses cliche with telling effect." Furthermore, added Kroll, "Mamet is the first playwright to create a formal and moral shape out of the undeleted expletives of our foul-mouthed time."

In his personal and creative life, Mamet has resisted the lure of Broadway, its establishment, and its formulas for success. He was born and raised in Chicago—his father was a labor lawyer—and he still lives there part of the year, spending the remainder of his time in Boston. The Windy City serves not only as inspiration for much of his work, but it has also provided an accepting audience for Mamet's brand of drama, especially in the early days of his career, when he worked nights as a busboy at The Second City and spent his days with the theater crowd and writing his plays. "Regional theaters are where the life is," he told Robin Reeves in *Us.* "They're the only new force in American theater since the 30s." Yet, despite Mamet's seeming indifference to Broadway and the fact that the language and subject matter of his plays make them of questionable commercial value, several of his plays have been featured on Broadway.

The first of Mamet's plays to be commercially produced were *Sexual Perversity in Chicago* and *Duck Variations.* 1974's *Sexual Perversity* portrays the failed love affair between a young man and woman, each trying to leave behind a relationship with a homosexual roommate. The dialogue between the lovers and their same-sex roommates reveals how each gender can brutally characterize the other. Yet, "the play itself is not another aspect of the so-called battle of the sexes," observed C. Gerald Fraser in the *New York Times.* "It concerns the confusion and emptiness of human relationships on a purely physical level." *New Yorker* reviewer Edith Oliver maintained that "The piece is written with grace," and found it "one of the saddest comedies I can remember." In *Duck Variations,* two old Jewish men sit on a bench in Chicago looking out on Lake Michigan. Their observation of the nearby ducks leads them into discussions of several topics. "There is a marvelous ring of truth in the meandering, speculative talk of these old men," maintained Oliver, "the comic, obsessive talk of men who spend most of their time alone, nurturing and indulging their preposterous notions." In the conversation of these men, wrote T. E. Kalem in *Time,* "[Mamet] displays the Pinter trait of wearing word masks to shield feelings and of defying communication in the act of communicating." *Duck Variations* reveals, according to Oliver, that Mamet is an "original writer, who cherishes words and, on the evidence at hand, cherishes character even more." "What emerges is a vivid sense of [the old men's] friendship, the fear of solitude, the inexorable toll of expiring lives," concluded Kalem.

Mamet emerged as a nationally acclaimed playwright with his 1975 two-act *American Buffalo.* "America has few comedies in its repertory as ironic or as audacious as *American Buffalo,*" proclaimed John Lahr in the *Nation.* Set in a junk shop, the play features the shop's owner, an employee, and a friend engaged in plotting a theft; they hope to steal the coin collection of a customer who, earlier in the week, had bought an old nickel at the shop. When the employee fails to tail the mark to his home, the plot falls into disarray and "the play ends in confused weariness," explained Elizabeth Kastor in the *Washington Post*. Although little takes place, Oliver commented in the *New Yorker,* "What makes [the play] fascinating are its characters and the sudden spurts of feeling and shifts of mood—the mounting tension under the seemingly aimless surface, which gives the play its momentum."

American Buffalo confirmed Mamet's standing as a language playwright. Reviewing the play in the *Nation,* Lahr observed, "Mamet's use of the sludge in American language is completely original. He hears panic and poetry in the convoluted syntax of his beleaguered characters." And, even though the language is uncultivated, David Richards contended in the *Washington Post* that "the dialogue [is] ripe with unsettling resonance." As Frank Rich of the *New York Times* remarked, "Working with the tiniest imaginable vocabulary . . . Mamet creates a subterranean world with its own nonliterate comic beat, life-and-death struggles, pathos and even affection."

In this play, critics also see Mamet's vision of America, "a restless, rootless, insecure society which has no faith in the peace it seeks or the pleasure it finds," interpreted Lahr. "*American Buffalo* superbly evokes this anxious and impoverished world." Its characters, though seemingly insignificant, reflect the inhabitants of this world and their way of life. "In these bumbling and inarticulate meatheads," believed Lahr, "Mamet has found a metaphor for the spiritual failure of entrepreneurial capitalism."

Since its first Chicago production in 1975, *American Buffalo* has been produced in several regional theaters and has had three New York productions. In Mamet's management of the elements of this play, *New York Times* reviewer Benedict Nightingale highlighted the key to its success: "Its idiom is precise enough to evoke a city, a class, a subculture; it is imprecise enough to allow variation of mood and feeling from production to production." Nightingale added in another article, "*Buffalo* is as accomplished as anything written for the American stage over . . . the last 20 years."

In 1979 Mamet was given his first opportunity to write a screenplay. As he told Don Shewey in the *New York Times,* working on the screenplay for the 1981 film version of James M. Cain's novel *The Postman Always Rings Twice* was a learning experience. "[Director Bob Rafelson] taught me that the purpose of a screenplay is to tell the story so the audience wants to know what happens next," Mamet maintained, "and to tell it in pictures." He elaborated, "I always thought I had a talent for dialogue and not for plot, but it's a skill that can be learned. Writing for the movies is teaching me not to be so scared about plots." Mamet's screenplay for *The Postman Always Rings Twice* has received mixed reviews. Its critics often point, as Gene Siskel did in the *Chicago Tribune,* to Mamet's "ill-conceived editing of the book's original ending." Yet, except for the ending, suggested Vincent Canby in the *New York Times,* "Mr. Mamet's screenplay is far more faithful to the novel than was the screenplay for Tay Garnett's 1946 version." Thus, Robert Hatch noted in the *Nation,* "Mamet and Rafelson recapture the prevailing insanity of the Depression, when steadiness of gaze was paying no bills and double or nothing was the game in vogue."

In the 1982 film *The Verdict,* screenwriter Mamet and director Sydney Lumet "have dealt powerfully and unsentimentally with the shadowy state that ideas like good and evil find themselves in today," observed Jack Kroll in *Newsweek.* The film stars Paul Newman as a washed-up lawyer caught in a personal, legal, and moral battle. "David Mamet's terse screenplay for *The Verdict* is . . . full of surprises," contended Janet Maslin in the *New York Times;* "Mamet has supplied twists and obstacles of all sorts." "Except for a few lapses of logic and some melodramatic moments in the courtroom," proclaimed a *People Weekly* reviewer, "[this] script from Barry Reed's novel is unusually incisive." Kroll detailed the screenplay's strong points, calling it "strong on character, on sharp and edgy dialogue, on the detective-story suspense of a potent narrative." In a *New Republic* article, Stanley Kauffmann concluded, "It comes through when it absolutely must deliver: Newman's summation to the jury. This speech is terse and pungent: the powerful have the power to convert all the rest of us into victims and that condition probably cannot be changed, but must it always prevail?"

After writing *The Verdict,* Mamet began working on his next play, *Glengarry Glen Ross*. Mamet's Pulitzer Prize-winning play is "so precise in its realism that it transcends itself," observed Robert Brustein in the *New Republic,* "and takes on reverberant ethical meanings. It is biting, . . . showing life stripped of all idealistic pretenses and liberal pieties." The play is set in and around a Chicago real estate office whose agents are embroiled in a competition to sell the most parcels in the Florida developments Glengarry Highlands and Glen Ross Farms. "Craftily constructed, so that there is laughter, as well as rage, in its dialogue, the play has a payoff in each scene and a cleverly plotted mystery that kicks in with a surprise hook at its ending," wrote Richard Christiansen in the *Chicago Tribune.*

As in Mamet's earlier plays, the characters and their language are very important to *Glengarry Glen Ross.* In the *Nation,* Stephen Harvey commented on Mamet's ability to create characters who take on a life of their own within the framework of the play: In *Glengarry,* "he adjusts his angle of vision to suit the contours of his characters, rather than using them to illustrate an idea." Mamet told Kastor of the *Washington Post,* "I think that people are generally more happy with a mystery than with an explanation. So the less that you say about a character the more interesting he becomes." Mamet uses language in a similar manner. Harvey noted, "The pungency of Glengarry's language comes from economy: if these characters have fifty-word vocabularies, Mamet makes sure that every monosyllable counts." And as Kroll remarked, "His antiphonal exchanges, which dwindle to single words or even fragments of words and then explode into a crossfire of scatological buckshot, make him the Aristophanes of the inarticulate." Mamet is, according to *New York Times* reviewer Benedict Nightingale, "the bard of modern-day barbarism, the laureate of the four-letter word."

For the real estate agents in *Glengarry Glen Ross,* the bottom line is sales. And, as Robert Brustein noted, "Without a single tendentious line, without any polemical intention, without a trace of pity or sentiment, Mamet has launched an assault on the American way of making a living." Nightingale called the play "as scathing a study of unscrupulous dealing as the American theater has ever produced." The Pulitzer Prize awarded to Mamet for *Glengarry Glen Ross* not only helped increase its critical standing, but it also helped to make the play a commercial success. However, unlike his real estate agents, Mamet is driven by more than money. He told Kastor, "In our interaction in our daily lives we tell stories to each other, we gossip, we complain to each other, we exhort. These are means of defining what our life is. The theater is a way of doing it continually, of sharing that experience, and it's absolutely essential."

The Cryptogram, Mamet's 1994 play, "dramatizes a child's emotional abuse in a way that no other American play has ever attempted: from the child's point of view," according to *New Yorker* critic John Lahr. The playwright draws on his personal experiences of violent outbreaks, mistrust, and betrayal that he encountered in his own family, but the play blurs such autobiographical elements between its author's fictions. Taking place in Chicago over the span of a single month during the late 1950s, the play's main character, ten-year-old John, is trying to make sense of the double message dispensed by his parents and family friends: lies and unkept promises are commonplace, yet he is expected to trust those who deceive him. "People may or may not say what they mean," Mamet explained to Lahr, "but they *always* say something designed to get what they want." Characteristically, language plays an important role in *The Cryptogram:* as its author noted, "The language of love is . . . fairly limited. 'You're beautiful,' 'I need you,' 'I love you,' 'I want you.' Love expresses itself, so it doesn't need a lot of words. On the other hand, aggression has an unlimited vocabulary."

While Mamet's own directorship of *The Cryptogram* received the traditional mixed reviews from critics due to his fractured language, *New York Times* reviewer Vincent Canby found much to praise. Calling the play "a horror story that also appears to be one of Mr. Mamet's most personal plays," Canby noted that "It's not about the sort of physical abuse we see in television docudramas, but about the high cost of the emotional games played in what are otherwise considered to be fairly well-adjusted families." *The Cryptogram* received the Obie Award from the *Village Voice* for best play in 1995.

In 1994, on the heels of *The Cryptogram,* Mamet published his first novel, *The Village.* Taking place in a small, once-thriving town in New England, the novel reveals the emotional complexity of the lives of its characters. From Dick, the hardware-store owner fighting to stay in business, Manis, a local prostitute, and especially Henry, an "outsider" retired and escaping a failed marriage who wants to recapture the macho lifestyle of a century ago, Mamet captures "the flat, dark underside of the flapjack of small town life that Thorton Wilder's 'Our Town' served as the fluffy, arcing top to," according to *Tribune Books* reviewer Ross Field. While reviewers noted that the novel's characters and central idea are well conceived, the novel's dialogue caused some critics to water down their enthusiasm for the book. James McManus contended in the *New York Times Book Review* that, "because of the novel's design and mechanical problems, the potency of [some] scenes tends not to accumulate. For a playwright of such muscular succinctness, Mr. Mamet has a narrative prose that turns out to be weirdly precious." However, in his review for the *Washington Post Book World,* Douglas Glover praised *The Village.* "Mamet's novel explores a community with its own laws, language, codes, habits and sense of honor," noted Glover. "It does so with a deft reverence for the real—Mamet's eye for detail and his ear for the rhythms of vernacular speech are incomparable—coupled with a certain difficulty of approach, an avant-garde edge."

In addition to plays and screenplays, Mamet has published several collections of essays, including *Writing in Restaurants, Some Freaks, On Directing Film, The Cabin,* and *Make-Believe Town,* the first four volumes later collected as *A Whore's Profession: Notes and Essays.* These revealing collections are packed with Mamet's fascinating thoughts, opinions, recollections, musings, and reports on a variety of topics such as friendship, religion, politics, morals, society, and of course, the American theater. "The 30 pieces collected in David Mamet's first book of essays contain everything from random thoughts to firmly held convictions," stated Richard Christiansen in his review of *Writing in Restaurants* for Chicago's *Tribune Books,* "but they all exhibit the author's singular insights and moral bearing." Christiansen pointed out that "many of the essays have to do with drama, naturally, but whether he is talking to a group of critics or to fellow workers in the theater, Mamet is always urging his audience to go beyond craft and into a proud, dignified, loving commitment to their art and to the people with whom they work."

Writing for the *Times Literary Supplement,* Andrew Hislop declared that "Mamet has been rightly acclaimed as a great dialoguist and a dramatist who most effectively expresses the rhythms of modern urban American (though the poetic rather than mimetic qualities of his dialogue are often underestimated). The best writing in [*Writing in Restaurants*] comes when he muses on the details of America—and his own life." Hislop continued, "Running through the book is the idea that the purpose of theatre is truth but that the decadence of American society, television and the materialism of Broadway are undermining not just the economic basis but the disciplines and dedication necessary for true theatre."

The Cabin, published in 1992, contains twenty essays that reflect their author's macho concerns—guns, cigars, beautiful women—as well as his life as a writer. The work's structure was characterized by *Los Angeles Times Book Review* critic Charles Solomon as "a succession of scenes illuminated by an erratic strobe light: A single moment appears in harsh focus, then vanishes." We follow the author from his tumultuous childhood in "The Rake" to a description of his New Hampshire haven where he does his writing in the title essay. The two dozen essays in *Make-Believe Town* recall Mamet's love of the theater and his respect for his Jewish heritage and introduce those "appalled" by the language of his stage plays to "Mamet the thoughtful learner, teacher, the friend, the literary critic, the hunger-nature writer, the culture, press and film critic, the political commentator, the moralist and, most delightfully, the memoirist," according to *Tribune Books* critic John D. Callaway.

BIOGRAPHICAL/CRITICAL SOURCES:

BOOKS

Bigsby, C. W. E., *David Mamet,* Metheun, 1985.

Bock, Hedwig, and Albert Wertheim, editors, *Essays on Contemporary American Drama,* Max Hueber (Munich), 1981, pp. 207-23.

Brewer, Gay, *David Mamet and Film: Illusion/Disillusion in a Wounded Land,* McFarland (Jefferson, NC), 1993.

Carroll, Dennis, *David Mamet,* St. Martin's Press, 1987.

Contemporary Authors Bibliographical Series, Volume 3, Gale (Detroit), 1986.

Contemporary Literary Criticism, Gale, Volume 9, 1978, pp. 360-61; Volume 15, 1980, pp. 355-58; Volume 34, 1985, pp. 217-24; Volume 46, 1988, pp. 245-56; Volume 91, 1996, pp. 143-55.

Dean, Anne, *David Mamet: Language as Dramatic Action,* Fairleigh Dickinson University Press, 1990.

Drama Criticism, Volume 4, Gale, 1994.

Kane, Leslie, editor, *David Mamet: A Casebook,* Garland, 1991.

Kane, Leslie, *David Mamet's Glengarry Glen Ross: Text and Performance,* Garland (New York City), 1996.

Kane, Leslie, *Weasels and Wisemen: Education, Ethics, and Ethnicity in David Mamet,* St. Martin's Press, 1999.

King, Kimball, *Ten Modern American Playwrights,* Garland, 1982.

PERIODICALS

America, May 15, 1993, p. 16; September 23, 1995, p. 26.

Booklist, December 1, 1992; June 1, 1994.

Chicago, January, 1990, p. 65.

Chicago Tribune, January 18, 1987, p. 7; October 11, 1987; May 4, 1988; February 19, 1989; December 10, 1989.

Commonweal, December 4, 1992, p. 15.

Daily News, March 26, 1984.

Entertainment Weekly, August 21, 1992, pp. 50-51; June 9, 1995, p. 68.

Gentlemen's Quarterly, October, 1994, p. 110.

Georgia Review, fall, 1983, pp. 601-11.

Harper's, May, 1978, pp. 79-80, 83-87.

Insight on the News, January 9, 1995, p. 26.

Kirkus Reviews, April 15, 1996, p. 580.

Library Journal, January, 1991, p. 106; June 1, 1996, p. 106.

London Review of Books, July 7, 1994, p. 7.

Los Angeles Times, November 27, 1979; June 25, 1984; July 7, 1987; October 11, 1987.

Los Angeles Times Book Review, December 13, 1992, p. 3; March 6, 1994, p. 8; June 30, 1996, p. 10; July 28, 1996, p. 11.

Nation, May 19, 1979, pp. 581-82; April 14, 1981; October 10, 1981; April 28, 1984, pp. 522-23; June 27, 1987, pp. 900-02.

National Review, January 18, 1993, p. 28.

New Leader, April 16, 1984, pp. 20-21; December 14, 1992, p. 26.

New Republic, July 12, 1982, pp. 23-24; February 10, 1986, pp. 25-26, 28; October 29, 1990, pp. 32-37; April 24, 1995, p. 46.

New Statesman & Society, September 30, 1983, pp. 33, 36; July 2, 1993, p. 34.

Newsweek, February 28, 1977, p. 79; March 23, 1981; November 8, 1982; December 6, 1982; April 9, 1984, p. 109; October 19, 1987; November 9, 1992, p. 65.

New York, December 20, 1982, pp. 62, 64; June 8, 1987, pp. 68-69; March 9, 1992, p. 77; November 9, 1992, p. 72; November 30, 1992, p. 129; August 2, 1993, p. 50; October 11, 1993, p. 79; February 21, 1994, p. 52.

New Yorker, November 10, 1975; October 31, 1977, pp. 115-16; January 16, 1978; October 29, 1979, p. 81; June 15, 1981; November 7, 1983; June 29, 1987, pp. 70-72; November 16, 1992, pp. 121-26; August 1, 1994, p. 70; April 10, 1995, pp. 33-34.

New York Post, December 24, 1985; March 26, 1984.

New York Times, July 5, 1976; March 18, 1979; April 26, 1979; May 26, 1979; June 3, 1979; October 19, 1979; March 20, 1981; May 29, 1981; June 5, 1981; February 17, 1982; May 17, 1982; June 17, 1982; October 24, 1982; October 28, 1982, p. C20; December 8, 1982; May 13, 1983; October 9, 1983, pp. 6, 19; November 6, 1983; March 26, 1984, p. C17; March 28, 1984; April 1, 1984; April 18, 1984; April 24, 1984; September 30, 1984; February 9, 1986; April 23, 1986; January 1, 1987; March 15, 1987; June 3, 1987; October 11, 1987; May 4, 1988; December 4, 1989; April 14, 1995, p. C3.

New York Times Book Review, December 17, 1989; January 17, 1993, p. 24; November 20, 1994, p. 24; April 9, 1995, p. 20; July 14, 1996, p. 17.

People Weekly, November 12, 1979; December 20, 1982; May 4, 1987.

Playboy, September, 1994, p. 78; April, 1995, p. 51.

Premiere, January, 1990, p. 108.

Publishers Weekly, November 16, 1992, p. 55; July 4, 1994, p. 52; April 8, 1996, p. 46.

Saturday Review, April 2, 1977, p. 37.

Time, July 12, 1976; April 9, 1984, p. 105; December 25, 1989, pp. 87-90; August 24, 1992, p. 69; November 2, 1992, p. 69; October 18, 1993, p. 109; August 29, 1994, p. 71.

Times Literary Supplement, January 29, 1988; July 15, 1994, p. 21; February 16, 1996, p. 23.

Tribune Books (Chicago), January 18, 1987; December 13, 1992, p. 7; May 5, 1996, p. 3.

Us, January 10, 1978.

Variety, February 24, 1992, p. 257; May 11, 1992, p. 127; August 24, 1992, p. 65; April 5, 1993, p. 185; February 7, 1994, p. 60.

Village Voice, July, 1976, pp. 101, 103-04.

Washington Post, May 4, 1988.

World Literature Today, summer, 1982, p. 518.

OTHER

DM: The David Mamet Review (newsletter of the David Mamet Society), 1994—.

* * *

McCROREY, Sanders

See COUNSELMAN, Mary Elizabeth

McWILLIAMS, Peter 1949-

PERSONAL: Born August 5, 1949, in Detroit, MI; son of Henry G. and Mary (Toarmina) McWilliams. *Education:* Attended Eastern Michigan University; studied under Maharishi Mahesh Yogi at Maharishi International University. *Avocational interests:* Beethoven and Mozart, making color sound films, driving a Volkswagen.

ADDRESSES: Home—Los Angeles, CA. *Office*—Prelude Press, P.O. Box 69773, Los Angeles, CA 90069.

CAREER: Teacher of transcendental meditation, International Meditation Society, Los Angeles, CA; co-founder, Three Rivers Press; publisher, Versemonger Press and Lion Press; former owner of Leo Press, Hoboken, NJ; currently owner of Prelude Press, Los Angeles. Founder of *Medical Marijuana Magazine Online.* Poet laureate, Maharishi International University.

WRITINGS:

POETRY

Come Love with Me and Be My Life, Versemonger Press (Allen Park, MI), 1967.
I Have Loved (formerly entitled *"Love Two"*), Versemonger Press, 1968.
For Lovers and No Others, Versemonger Press, 1968.
I Love Therefore I Am, Versemonger Press, 1969.
The Hard Stuff: Love, Versemonger Press, 1969.
Evolving at the Speed of Love, Versemonger Press, 1971.
Surviving the Loss of a Love, Versemonger Press, 1971.
Love Y An Experience Of, Doubleday (New York City), 1972.
Love and All the Other Verbs of Life, Doubleday, 1973.
Love Is Yes, Versemonger Press, 1973.
This Longing May Shorten My Life, Versemonger Press, 1974.
Catch Me with Your Smile, edited by Susan Polis Schutz, Blue Mountain Press (Boulder, CO), 1976.
Come Love With Me & Be My Life: The Complete Romantic Poetry of Peter McWilliams, Prelude, 1991.
I Marry You Because, Prelude, 1993.

NONFICTION

(With Denise Denniston) *The TM Book: How to Enjoy the Rest of Your Life,* Warner (New York City), 1975.
(With Melba Colgrove and Harold Bloomfield) *How to Survive the Loss of a Love: Fifty-eight Things to Do When There Is Nothing to Be Done,* Leo Press (Hoboken, NJ), 1976.
The Word Processing Book: A Short Course in Computer Literacy, Prelude (Los Angeles), 1982.
The Personal Computer Book, Prelude, 1982.
Word Processing on the KayPro, Prelude, 1983.
The Personal Computer in Business Book, Prelude, 1983.
Questions & Answers on Word Processing, Prelude, 1983.
Personal Computers and the Disabled, Quantum Press/Doubleday (New York City), 1984.
The Peter McWilliams Personal Computer Buying Guide, Quantum Press, 1985.
Personal Electronics Book, Prentice Hall (New York City), 1987.
(With John-Roger) *Life 101: Everything We Wish We Had Learned about Life in School—But Didn't,* Prelude, 1990.
(With John-Roger) *Do It! Let's Get Off Our Buts,* Prelude, 1991, revised edition, 1994.
Ain't Nobody's Business If You Do: The Absurdity of Consensual Crimes in a Free Society, Prelude, 1993.
(With John-Roger) *The Portable Do It! 172 Essential Excerpts Plus 190 Quotations from the Number One New York Times Bestseller "Do It! Let's Get Off Our Buts,"* Prelude, 1993.
(With John-Roger) *We Give to Love: Giving Is Such a Selfish Thing: Notes and Quotes on the Joys of Heartfelt Service,* Prelude, 1993.
(With John-Roger) *Wealth 101: Wealth Is Much More than Money,* Prelude, 1993.
The Book about Drugs, Prelude, 1994.
(With Colgrove and Bloomfield) *How to Heal Depression,* Prelude, 1994.
Life 102: What to Do When Your Guru Sues You, Prelude, 1994.
You Can't Afford the Luxury of a Negative Thought, Prelude, 1995.
(With Harold Bloomfield and Mikael Nordfors) *Hypericum & Depression: Can Depression Be Successfully Treated with a Safe, Inexpensive, Medically Proven Herb Available without a Prescription?,* Prelude, 1996.
The Life 101 Quote Book, Prelude, 1997.
Love 101: To Love Oneself Is the Beginning of a Lifelong Romance, Prelude, 1997.

OTHER

Portraits (photographs), Prelude, 1992.

Also author of *It's Nice to Know Someone like You: A Collection of Poems,* 1981; *Word Processing on the IBM,* 1983; and numerous other volumes; co-author of *Take-Charge-of-Your-Life Therapy,* 1995.

WORK IN PROGRESS: Two nonfiction works, *A Question of Compassion: An AIDS-Cancer Patient Explores Medical Marijuana* and *The Big Lie: Deceiving America about Medical Marijuana.*

SIDELIGHTS: Peter McWilliams is a poet and an author of self-help and computer books who has also attracted attention for his involvement with a spiritual adviser who he says "brainwashed" him and for his marijuana-related arrests. An advocate of marijuana legalization, McWilliams has used the drug to relieve the side effects of his treatment for AIDS and cancer. He has made the case for marijuana decriminalization and other libertarian measures in his book *Ain't Nobody's Business If You Do: The Absurdity of Consensual Crimes in a Free Society.* He also disseminates his views on this subject through the World Wide Web-based *Medical Marijuana Magazine Online,* which he founded. Among his other ventures, he has published most of his own books through a series of companies, the latest of which is Prelude Press.

McWilliams began writing and publishing poetry while still in high school. A few years later, his interest in transcendental meditation and other self-help philosophies led to his writing books on these subjects. By the time he was twenty-nine, he had, as Bob Sipchen put it in an article for *Playboy,* "written and published several books, made a fortune and lost it on a greeting card company, experimented with a panoply of enlightenment peddlers and several times sunk into despair." In 1978 his quest for self-esteem and spiritual knowledge brought him to a session of the Insight Transformational Seminars offered by the Church of the Movement of Spiritual Inner Awareness (MSIA). The head of the church was a former high school teacher, Roger Delano Hinkins, known to his followers as John-Roger. McWilliams was a devoted convert, becoming an MSIA minister and John-Roger's co-author on books including *Life 101: Everything We Wish We Had Learned about Life in School—But Didn't* and *We Give to Love: Giving Is Such a Selfish Thing: Notes and Quotes On the Joys of Heartfelt Service.*

By the mid-1980s, MSIA was enjoying a wave of popularity, but there were hints that all was not well: John-Roger was rumored to have mishandled funds and to have coerced associates into sex, charges that he denied. People who left the church complained they received threats. McWilliams stood solidly by John-Roger for several years, but says that in the early 1990s, when he began taking Prozac to relieve chronic depression, he realized John-Roger had brainwashed him. He no longer believed John-Roger had great mystic powers, and he repudiated his former spiritual leader. John-Roger and MSIA soon sued McWilliams for what they said was their share of the royalties on the books on which John-Roger and McWilliams had collaborated. McWilliams countersued, contending the money he had already paid John-Roger amounted to stolen funds. This episode led to McWilliams' book *Life 102: What to Do When Your Guru Sues You,* which had political repercussions. Among other things, the book mentioned writer Arianna Huffington's involvement with MSIA, and this became an issue when her husband, Michael, ran (unsuccessfully) against Dianne Feinstein for a U.S. Senate seat in California in 1994.

Amid all this, McWilliams produced *Ain't Nobody's Business If You Do,* in which he argues that drug use, gambling, and unorthodox sexual and religious practices should be legal as they do no harm to other people or their property. In a review for *Reason,* Brian Doherty found the book marred by its length—815 pages—and McWilliams's tendency "to believe almost anything he hears or reads." The book is full of undocumented statistics, Doherty complained. He also thought McWilliams too simplistic in blaming Christianity for repressive laws and had a quibble about his writing style, saying the author "deals in advice bestowed with bold strokes and emphatic insistence." In the publication *Whole Earth,* Patrizia DeLucchio voiced a similar charge, saying the book "shares the tendency to confuse rant with logic as the society it criticizes." Still, she found the book worthwhile, and Doherty allowed that there was a germ of value in it. "McWilliams proves he has in him a snappy and informative 200-to-300 page book on the fiscal, moral, and constitutional horrors of laws against consensual crime," he remarked. "Too bad he wrote this one instead."

McWilliams was at the center of controversy over "consensual crime" in the late 1990s. The Michigan State Police arrested him for marijuana possession while he was visiting Detroit in December 1996, and a year later, when he was working on a book titled *A Question of Compassion: An AIDS-Cancer Patient Explores Medical Marijuana,* agents from the federal Drug Enforcement Agency (DEA) raided his home in Los Angeles and seized a small amount of marijuana, as well as a computer that contained information for his book. McWilliams contended he was targeted by the DEA because the upcoming book criticizes the agency. Eventually, the DEA returned the computer, albeit with a virus that had scrambled some of the files for the book. He did not blame the DEA for the virus, however, and he vowed to reconstruct that book and to write another one, *The Big Lie: Deceiving America about Medical Marijuana.*

BIOGRAPHICAL/CRITICAL SOURCES:

PERIODICALS

Detroit News, June 6, 1997; November 6, 1997.
Los Angeles Times, December 18, 1997.
People, October 31, 1994, p. 69.
Playboy, March, 1995, p. 104.
Publishers Weekly, September 6, 1993, p. 75; January 19, 1998.
Reason, February, 1994, p. 63.
Whole Earth, winter, 1997, p. 67.*

—Sketch by Trudy Ring

* * *

MOORE, Clayton
See BRANDNER, Gary

* * *

MORAN, Mike
See ARD, William (Thomas)

* * *

MORLEY, Susan
See CROSS, John Keir

MUKHERJEE, Bharati 1940-

PERSONAL: Born July 27, 1940, in Calcutta, India; came to the United States, 1961; moved to Canada, 1968; became Canadian citizen in 1972; became permanent U.S. resident in 1980; daughter of Sudhir Lal (a chemist) and Bina (Barrerjee) Mukherjee; married Clark Blaise (a writer and professor), September 19, 1963; children: Bart Anand, Bernard Sudhir. *Education:* University of Calcutta, B.A., 1959; University of Baroda, M.A., 1961; University of Iowa, M.F.A., 1963, Ph.D., 1969. *Religion:* Hindu.

ADDRESSES: Office—c/o Elaine Markson, 44 Greenwich Ave., New York, NY 10011; and University of California, Department of English, 322 Wheeler Hall, Berkeley, CA 94720-4714. *Agent*—Grove Weidenfeld, 841 Broadway, New York, NY 10003.

CAREER: Marquette University, Milwaukee, WI, instructor in English, 1964-65; University of Wisconsin (now University of Wisconsin—Madison), Madison, instructor, 1965; McGill University, Montreal, Quebec, lecturer, 1966-69, assistant professor, 1969-73, associate professor, 1973-78, professor, 1978; Skidmore College, Saratoga Springs, NY, visiting assistant professor of English, 1979-80, 1981-82; Emory University, visiting assistant professor of English, 1983; Montclair State College, associate professor of English, 1984; City University of New York, professor, 1987-89; University of California, Berkeley, professor, 1987—.

MEMBER: PEN.

AWARDS, HONORS: Grants from McGill University, 1968 and 1970, Canada Arts Council, 1973-74 and 1977, Shastri Indo-Canadian Institute, 1976-77, Guggenheim Foundation, 1978-79, and Canadian Government, 1982; first prize from Periodical Distribution Association, 1980, for short story "Isolated Incidents"; National Magazine Awards second prize, 1981, for essay "An Invisible Woman"; National Endowment for the Arts award, 1986; National Book Critics Circle Award for best fiction, 1988, for *The Middleman and Other Stories.*

WRITINGS:

NOVELS

The Tiger's Daughter, Houghton (Boston), 1972.
Wife, Houghton, 1975.

Jasmine, Grove (New York City), 1989.
The Holder of the World, Knopf (New York City), 1993.
Leave It to Me, Knopf, 1997.

SHORT STORY COLLECTIONS

Darkness, Penguin (New York City), 1985.
The Middleman and Other Stories, Grove, 1988.

OTHER

Kautilya's Concept of Diplomacy: A New Interpretation, Minerva, 1976.
(With husband, Clark Blaise) *Days and Nights in Calcutta* (nonfiction), Doubleday (New York City), 1977.
(With Blaise) *The Sorrow and the Terror: The Haunting Legacy of the Air India Tragedy,* Viking (New York City), 1987.
Political Culture and Leadership in India (nonfiction), South Asia, 1991.
Regionalism in Indian Perspective (nonfiction), South Asia, 1992.

Contributor to periodicals, including *Mother Jones, New York Times Book Review, Village Voice Literary Supplement, Salmagundi,* and *Saturday Night.*

WORK IN PROGRESS: A Different Canadian: The East Indian Experience of Canada, an expansion of the essay "An Invisible Woman," for McClelland & Stewart; a novel.

SIDELIGHTS: Bharati Mukherjee's writings largely reflect her personal experiences in crossing cultural boundaries. In novels such as *Jasmine, The Tiger's Daughter,* and *The Holder of the World,* as well as in her award-winning short stories, Indian-born Mukherjee "adds to the authority of her [multicultural] background an acute sense of the violence and chaos, however restrained, which can lie beneath the surface of a society, old or new, or of a person," explains Ann Mandel in the *Dictionary of Literary Biography.* A "request for recognition—the desire to be 'visible' . . . to be recognized as person rather than as ethnic stereotype—characterizes much of Mukherjee's writing," Mandel adds. "Her characters sometimes cry out to be seen for who they really are; and sometimes, weak or tired, they surrender to taking on the identity of the 'type' that others see them to be."

Born to wealthy parents in Calcutta, Mukherjee first moved to the United States to pursue her studies in English at the University of Iowa. While at the university's writing workshop, she met and married Canadian novelist Clark Blaise. Although the couple settled in Canada for several years, they eventually moved back to the United States because of the racism she experienced. As Mukherjee would write in the introduction to her 1985 short story collection, *Darkness:* "If I may put it in its harshest terms, in Canada, I was frequently taken for a prostitute or shoplifter." She now teaches at the University of California at Berkeley.

In *The Tiger's Daughter,* published in 1972, Mukherjee creates a heroine, Tara, who, like herself, returns to India after several years in the West to discover a country quite unlike the one she remembered. Memories of a genteel Brahmin lifestyle are usurped by new impressions of poverty, hungry children, and political unrest. "In other words," a *Times Literary Supplement* reviewer notes, "Tara's westernization has opened her eyes to the gulf between two worlds that still makes India the despair of those who govern it."

"Miss Mukherjee writes entertainingly and with a sort of fluid prose that is very good to read," critic Roger Baker writes in his review of *The Tiger's Daughter* for *Books and Bookmen.* "She can make her characters spring to life with a word and has what seems to be an acute ear for dialogue." The *Times Literary Supplement* critic adds that Mukherjee's "elegant first novel" is skillfully wrought, with lively dialogue and full, descriptive passages. Yet he finds the novel's heroine oddly lacking: "Because [Mukherjee] controls her emotions with such a skilled balance of irony and colorful nostalgia her novel is charming and intelligent—and curiously unmoving. . . . Tara herself remains so ineffectual a focus . . . it is hard to care whether or not she will be able to return."

Mukherjee's second novel, *Wife,* is the story of a young Indian woman, Dimple, who attempts to reconcile the Bengali ideal of the perfect passive wife with the demands of real life. Dimple's arranged marriage to an engineer is followed by the couple's immigration to a New York City neighborhood. There she "watches television, sleeps, studies *Better Homes and Gardens,* and timorously meets people," Rosanne Klass details in *Ms.* "She is afraid to go out alone, and well she might be, since nobody—on TV or off—seems to talk about anything but murders and muggings." This alien environment, along with Dimple's inherent instability, prompts her to contemplate suicide or murder (she eventually chooses the latter, killing her husband). "Underneath the passivity lives rage which the heroine is hardly conscious of until it fully extends itself from fantasy to reality," Willa Swanson remarks in the *Antioch Review*.

Swanson finds *Wife* a moving study of an individual whom society sees as a trivial object. "There is much wit, a good ear for dialogue, and above all the creation of a character that gives an insight into the sudden, seemingly inexplicable, explosion of a docile, passive person into violence," Swanson relates. Yet other reviewers have not been as comfortable with the motive behind Dimple's violent outburst. Klass notes that "possibly Dimple is supposed to be schizophrenic, but . . . it isn't indicated. The book seems to suggest that she goes bonkers from . . . a surfeit of . . . liberated women, Americanized men, and wilting houseplants. I have known a few Indian women in New York. Many had adjustment problems, . . . but none . . . felt that knifing their husbands would really help." And Martin Levin of the *New York Times Book Review* reiterates this sentiment: "The title and the drift of the book imply that the protagonist is in some way a victim of her social status. . . . However oppressed Dimple may be, she is also very crazy, a fact about which the author is amusing but ambiguous. You could raise Dimple's consciousness by ninety degrees and still have a zombie."

The gradual merger of the First and Third Worlds is the topic underlying *Jasmine,* Mukherjee's third novel. Jasmine, a poor but independent young Hindu woman, leaves her native country after her husband is killed in a terrorist bombing, gaining passage to Florida via ship. Brutally raped by the ship's captain—whom she kills in self-defense—Jasmine travels to New York City to work as an *au pair* for a Yuppie couple and as a language tutor at Columbia University. After the couple's relationship goes sour, the Indian woman moves to Iowa, where she hopes to escape the flux of modern society. As Eric Larsen notes in the *Los Angeles Times Book Review,* Jasmine "is devastating in Iowa. Her level voice delicately but relentlessly brings out the contradictions of a world trying in vain to resist or ignore the passing of its self-confidence." Reduced to the level of caregiver that she sought to escape in her native India, Jasmine has come full circle; the First and Third worlds travel the same course.

Framed by the narrative of Beigh Masters, a self-styled "asset searcher" on a client-directed quest for a large diamond known as the "Emperor's Tear" until she is sidetracked by one of the diamond's former owners, *The Holder of the World* takes readers three centuries into the past of both the United States and India. The novel's heroine, Hannah Easton, is a rebellious young woman born in Massachusetts in 1670. The daughter of a Puritan woman and her Native American lover, Hannah is abandoned by her mother, whose defiance of Western culture will serve as an example to her daughter. Hannah's life progresses unconventionally; she marries an East India Company trader and travels to India. There, after being abandoned by her husband, who has become a pirate, she takes Indian lovers, eventually becoming the wife of a prince. "Told in Mukherjee's wonderful prose, whose economy allows for lyricism without clutter, Hannah's life is the same sort of cross-cultural fairy tale that captivated readers of . . . 'Jasmine,'" notes Kathryn Harrison in the Chicago *Tribune Books.*

In addition to novels, Mukherjee has written several collections of well-received short stories. *Darkness,* published in 1985, contains a dozen tales, most of which were written shortly after the author moved from Canada to the United States. All of the stories feature immigrants—newcomers who attempt to transcend either their cultural past or the unpleasant circumstances of their present. "Mukherjee's characters encounter society in ways that are either marginal or confrontational," explains *Books in Canada* reviewer Neil Bissoondath. "They are challenged by its norms, often fail to understand its mechanics, misinterpret its values; their vision becomes twisted." Particularly in the stories that take place in Canada, racial oppression predominates. In "The World According to Hsu," for example, the title character becomes almost paranoid due to the overt contempt for Indians exhibited by those she seeks to call her fellow countrymen. As Mukherjee writes: "In Toronto, she was not Canadian, not even Indian. She was something called, after the imported idiom of London, a Paki. And for Pakis, Toronto was hell." However, the effect of *Darkness* is not totally bleak; as Patricia Bradbury concludes in *Quill & Quire,* Mukherjee "is showing identities slowly breaking into pieces, cracked open by raw and totally alien dreams. But she always shows this with artistic grace and with the unstated promise that identities, in new and unimaginable moulds, will soon be rebuilt again."

Mukherjee's second story collection, 1988's *The Middleman and Other Stories* won the National Book Critics Circle Award for best fiction. Focusing on Mukherjee's characteristic theme, Third World immigrant experiences in the United States and Canada, *The Middleman* continues to examine the intimate commingling between East and West. Through narrators that include a Smyrnan mercenary, an investment banker based in Atlanta, and, particularly, Indian women attempting to redefine their traditional Hindu upbringing within a far more liberal American culture, Mukherjee's stories remain unsentimental yet affecting in their approach. "The stories in 'The Middleman' are streets ahead of those in 'Darkness,'" contends *New York Times Book Review* critic Jonathan Raban. "Not only has Ms. Mukherjee vastly enlarged her geographical and social range . . . , but she has greatly sharpened her style. Her writing here is far quicker in tempo, more confident and more sly than it used to be." Joseph Coates maintains in Chicago's *Tribune Books* that, in *The Middleman,* the author illuminates not only the world of the immigrant to the great melting pot of culture promised by a move to North America, but also the "definitive measure of our collective character" as multi-generational Americans. "By focusing on the most authentic Americans, the ones who just got here," Coates writes, "Mukherjee makes us see that the reason we persecute and then sentimentalize our newest compatriots is that they too accurately reflect us, the values, priorities and brutalities we'd rather not admit."

After a ten-year sojourn in Canada, Mukherjee returned to her native country in 1973, accompanied by her husband, Clark Blaise, who was visiting for the first time and eager to embrace his wife's former culture. Both encountered an India that neither anticipated: she found a world far less innocent than the one she remembered, and he met a people more enigmatic than he had ever imagined. Together, the couple collaborated on *Days and Nights in Calcutta,* a journal of their visit. James Sloan Allen writes in the *Saturday Review* of the couple's polar reactions: "Blaise, at first blinded by the squalor and the terrors, discovers a magic that enfolds reality in myth and ennobles Bengali life through a love of culture. His journal glows with the enthusiasm of discovery . . . and he turns against 'the whole bloated, dropsical giant called the West.' Mukherjee, by contrast, becomes angry and sad. For her fondly recalled traditions now mask fear and oppression—especially of women." Rather than examine the culture broadly, as her foreign husband can do, Mukherjee cannot help but see individuals, particularly those upper class women with whom she grew up and who she would have become. Her visit is filled with love and hate, sympathy and an unwillingness to forgive; she is in exile by choice but, in her words, "while changing citizenship is easy, swapping cultures is not." "It is that sort of honesty, turned by Mukherjee and Blaise upon themselves and their surroundings, that makes this book so distinctive and affecting a chronicle of voyages and discoveries," Margo Jefferson of *Newsweek* concludes.

Mukherjee returned to the novel form in 1997 with *Leave It to Me,* a story that, according to Michiko Kakutani of the *New York Times,* encompasses all of the author's "trademark preoccupations: exiles, emigres and outsiders tirelessly reinventing themselves, as they shed old lives, old lovers, old selves; and an America reeling from violence and nonstop change, a country in which freedom has translated into rootlessness, possibility into dislocation." The plot revolves around Debby DiMartino, the adopted daughter of an Italian-American family in upstate New York. Debby eventually begins a search for her birth parents, knowing only that her mother was a California hippie who abandoned her in Southeast Asia. Her search takes her down some violent roads, leading Marni Jackson in *Maclean's* to describe her as "part Electra, part avenging goddess from an Indian fairy tale, and part all-American Tarantino waif on a killing spree."

When Debby reaches California, she sheds her old name and identity to become Devi Di and settles into San Francisco's Haight-Ashbury district. There she continues to manipulate and harm people, driven by a horrible resentment of her biological parents' lack of responsibility toward her. Many reviewers found Devi's fury hard to believe. States Kakutani, "No doubt the increasingly disturbing events that transpire in *Leave It to Me* are supposed to underscore Ms. Mukherjee's dark view of an America on the brink of the millennium. Unfortunately, the reader doesn't buy it. Instead of believing that a blood-dimmed tide of random violence has been unleashed upon the land, one simply finishes the book convinced that randomness has infected Ms. Mukherjee's writing and her story." Susan Dooley concurs in *Washington Post Book World* that "Mukherjee writes vivid prose, but she has failed to give her novel a unity or to explain Debbie/Devi in ways that provide the reader a clue as to why the product of middle-class

Schenectady would turn herself into a warrior goddess, vengeful and violent."

Other critics find the book to be a powerful statement on American life, however. Lorna Sage states in her *New York Times Book Review* assessment, "Some readers will see in it visionary vengeance on American hubris, a triumph of alien genes, Devi as a force of nature. Yet it also seems to contain a mocking attack on the very notion of speaking for outsiders. . . . Devi is a brilliant creation—hilarious, horribly knowing and even more horribly oblivious—through whom Bharati Mukherjee, with characteristic and shameless ingenuity, is laying claim to speak for an America that isn't 'other' at all."

BIOGRAPHICAL/CRITICAL SOURCES:

BOOKS

Alam, Fakrul, *Bharati Mukherjee,* Twayne (New York City), 1996.

Bestsellers 89, Issue 2, Gale (Detroit), 1989.

Contemporary Literary Criticism, Volume 53, Gale, 1989.

Dhawan, R. K., *The Fiction of Bharati Mukherjee: A Critical Symposium,* Prestige (New Delhi, India), 1996.

Dictionary of Literary Biography, Volume 60: *Canadian Writers since 1960,* Gale, 1986.

PERIODICALS

Amerasia Journal, fall, 1993, p. 103; winter, 1994, p. 188.

Antioch Review, spring, 1976.

Booklist, April 15, 1997, p. 1365.

Books and Bookmen, November, 1973.

Books in Canada, August, 1985, pp. 21-22.

Chicago Tribune, November 13, 1994, section 14, p. 8.

Christian Science Monitor, February 2, 1977.

Connoisseur, August, 1990, p. 84.

Glamour, September, 1989, p. 212.

Library Journal, May 1, 1997, p. 152; June 15, 1997, p. 98.

Los Angeles Times Book Review, September 17, 1989, pp. 3, 10; October 10, 1993, pp. 3, 11; August 28, 1994, p. 11; January 14, 1996, p. 11.

Maclean's, August 19, 1985, p. 51; October 23, 1989, p. 72; July 21, 1997, p. 55.

Mother Jones, December, 1989, p. 43.

Ms., October, 1975.

New Statesman & Society, November 19, 1993, p. 45.

Newsweek, February 7, 1977.

New York, September 25, 1989, p. 132.

New Yorker, November 15, 1993, p. 127.

New York Times, January 25, 1977; November 12, 1993, p. C31; June 24, 1997, p. C18.

New York Times Book Review, June 8, 1975; January 12, 1986, p. 14; June 19, 1988, pp. 1, 22; September 10, 1989, p. 9; October 10, 1993, p. 7; January 8, 1995, p. 12; December 3, 1995, p. 49; July 20, 1997, p. 33.

People, October 25, 1993, p. 51; September 8, 1997, p. 36.

Publishers Weekly, April 21, 1997, p. 59.

Quill & Quire, August, 1985, p. 43.

Saturday Review, February 5, 1977.

Time, September 11, 1989, p. 84.

Times Literary Supplement, June 29, 1973; July 18, 1997, p. 22.

Tribune Books (Chicago), July 17, 1988, p. 14; October 24, 1993, p. 5.

USA Today Magazine, May, 1990, p. 96.

Vogue, September, 1989, p. 512.

Washington Post Book World, August 27, 1989, p. 2; October 24, 1993, pp. 1, 11; September 4, 1994, p. 5; August 10, 1997, p. 4.

World Literature Today, summer, 1986, pp. 520-21.

* * *

MURRAY, Peter
See HAUTMAN, Pete(r Murray)

* * *

NEWELL, Crosby
See BONSALL, Crosby Barbara (Newell)

* * *

NORDAN, Lewis (Alonzo) 1939-

PERSONAL: Born August 23, 1939, in Jackson, MS; son of Lemuel Alonzo and Sara (a teacher; maiden name, Hightower) Bayles; married Mary Mitman, April 28, 1962 (divorced January, 1983); married Alicia Blessing, July 3, 1986; children (first marriage): Russell Ammon (deceased), Lewis Eric, John Robert (deceased). *Education:* Millsaps College, B.A., 1963; Mississippi State University, M.A., 1966; Auburn University, Ph.D., 1973. *Politics:* Democrat. *Religion:* Episcopalian.

ADDRESSES: Home—Pittsburgh, PA. *Office*—Department of English, University of Pittsburgh, Pittsburgh, PA 15260.

CAREER: Teacher at public schools in Titusville, FL, 1963-65; Auburn University, Auburn, AL, instructor in English, 1966-71; University of Georgia, Athens, instructor in English, 1971-74; worked variously as an orderly, nightwatchman, and clerk, 1975-81; University of Arkansas, Fayetteville, assistant professor of English, 1981-83; University of Pittsburgh, Pittsburgh, PA, assistant professor of English, 1983—. *Military service:* U.S. Navy, 1958-60.

AWARDS, HONORS: John Gould Fletcher Award for fiction, University of Arkansas, 1977, for short story "Rat Song"; National Endowment for the Arts grant, 1978-79; Porter Fund Prize, 1987; Notable Book Award, American Library Association, 1992; Best Fiction Award, Mississippi Institute of Arts and Letters, 1992.

WRITINGS:

Welcome to the Arrow-Catcher Fair (short stories; also see below), Louisiana State University Press (Baton Rouge), 1983.
The All-Girl Football Team (short stories; also see below), Louisiana State University Press, 1986.
Music of the Swamp, Algonquin (Chapel Hill, NC), 1991.
Wolf Whistle: A Novel, Algonquin, 1993.
The Sharpshooter Blues: A Novel, Algonquin, 1995.
Sugar among the Freaks: Selected Stories (selections from *Welcome to the Arrow-Catcher Fair* and *The All-Girl Football Team*), Algonquin, 1996.
Lightning Song, Algonquin, 1997.

Contributor to *Harper's, Redbook, Playgirl,* and small literary magazines.

SIDELIGHTS: Welcome to the Arrow-Catcher Fair is Lewis Nordan's first published collection of short fiction. Critiquing the volume for the *New York Times Book Review,* Edith Milton pronounced its stories "splendid," an illustration of the diversity that the short story form can take. While the reviewer commented that the stories' variety worked against the book as a collection, she did note as a recurrent theme "the juxtaposition of an unglamorous *modern* reality, comically reduced, against an equally comic but larger-than-life mythology about the past that surrounds it."

Most of the stories included in *Welcome to the Arrow-Catcher Fair* and *The All-Girl Football Team,* Nordan's second collection of short fiction, are reprinted in *Sugar among the Freaks.* The collection exhibits Nordan's characteristically outrageous humor based on the often unpalatable doings of the eccentric characters who inhabit the fictional town of Arrow-Catcher, Mississippi, and its environs. In "The Storyteller," a retired football coach sipping spiked coffee in a local diner recounts the story of a renegade circus elephant who was executed by hanging. In "John Thomas Bird," an unattractive high school girl goes swimming with a handsome boy and saves him from drowning, though she realizes why he may be sorry she has. Reviewers familiar with Nordan's novels remarked that the stories contain the author's signature blend of immoderate humor with bleak tragedy and sincere emotion, held together by a style Brad Hooper in *Booklist* characterized as "Nordan's back-porch-and-grits kind of magic realism."

Nordan's short story collections introduce a recurring character named Sugar, who appears in his first novel, *Music of the Swamp,* and a town, Arrow-Catcher, that reappears in several of his later novels, including *Wolf Whistle.* In this critically acclaimed work, Nordan fictionalizes the 1955 murder of Emmett Till, a fourteen-year-old black boy who was lynched for whistling at a white woman, and whose death ignited the civil rights movement. "Though the subject would seem to demand almost religious gravity, Nordan's version is astonishing: he conveys the horror of the murder and the injustice of the killers' acquittal in scenes that recall Gabriel Garcia Marquez and other magical realists," remarked Sam Staggs in *Publishers Weekly.* Nordan's treatment of the well-known historical event was widely considered audacious—he includes the point-of-view of some local buzzards, among numerous others—and remarkably successful. "Truly, Lewis Nordan has written an outrageous, audacious book that should be applauded not only as a brave social act but as an extraordinary aesthetic achievement," exclaimed *Nation* contributor Randall Kenan. Though Kenan complained that Nordan ultimately withdraws, out of apparent timidity, from the sorrowing hearts and minds of the murdered boy and his family, this flaw "does not obscure what is an immense and wall-shattering display of talent," he added. Nordan was irresistibly drawn to the story, the author told Staggs in a *Publishers Weekly* interview, because of his proximity to the historical event and what it taught him about his own unthinking racism. Nordan was fifteen years old and living in a town nearby when the lynching occurred, and he and his friends even joked about it until another boy told them to stop. "He said, 'That's not right. I don't like that kind of joke. That boy they killed was just a boy like anybody, I don't care if he was colored.'" That sequence of events "changed my life so abruptly, so profoundly, that I have a hard time even telling about it," Nordan told Staggs. "Almost no other event has had such an effect on me."

Nordan created a llama farm just outside Arrow-Catcher for the setting of *Lightning Song,* a coming-of-age story as Southern gothic tragi-comedy. Leroy is twelve years old and just discovering the trials of romantic love and sexuality courtesy of a local baton twirler when his uncle moves in and begins wooing his mother. "In plot summary, [*Lightning Song*] might sound like one of those depressingly perky and eccentric white Southern stories, but it isn't: it's deeper and richer and more complex," averred Valerie Sayers in the *New York Times.*

Sharpshooter Blues features another cast of Southern misfits located just outside Arrow-Catcher in a small store surrounded by swamp where an encephalitic boy of about twenty sells gas and bootleg whiskey. Hydro, as the boy is called, enjoys comic books and hanging with his friends, ten-year-old Louis, and Morgan, the midget sharpshooter of the title, until the day two teenagers attempt to rob the store and have a little sexual fun with Hydro before killing him. Hydro ends up killing the thieves and though no one believes he did it, everyone's life is changed. "The characters' rhythmic dialogue and their striving for redemption set a biblical tone, lightened by infusions of quirky humor," wrote Karen Angel in the *Washington Post Book World.*

Nordan once told *CA:* "I was a storyteller a long time before I became a writer. Everyone in my family is a storyteller, though none of the others are writers. For a long time I thought I was somehow defective for not being able to tell the truth—the 'truth,' I should say—without changing it, amplifying it, or romanticizing it. This seemed to be a flaw in my character. Now I think that it may be a flaw, but it is also a gift for which I am grateful."

Nordan is a storyteller in the Southern tradition, utilizing the magical realism and grotesque characters that became associated with the genre with William Faulkner and Flannery O'Connor. On this subject Nordan told Staggs in a *Publishers Weekly* interview, "My theory about the grotesque in my own work, and in storytelling generally, is that it's a way of saying, 'This is more remarkable than anything you've seen today; this is even more remarkable than your own crazy family!'" Still, as reviewers have noted, Nordan's humor does not disguise the deep, often painful, emotional lives of his characters, making human even the least likable of them. "Nordan is a very funny writer, and his stories are moving in a way that summary cannot convey," wrote Mark Childress in the *Los Angeles Times Book Review.* But Nordan is also, Childress continued, "not the kind of writer to forget that people tend to laugh when the pain is greatest."

BIOGRAPHICAL/CRITICAL SOURCES:

PERIODICALS

Atlanta Journal and Constitution, November 28, 1993, p. K8.

Bloomsbury Review, July, 1996, p. 25.

Booklist, October 1, 1993, p. 254; March 15, 1994, p. 1350; July, 1995, p. 1836; January 1, 1996, p. 737; March 15, 1996, pp. 1241, 1272; March 1, 1997, p. 1068.

Book World, October 3, 1993, p. 4; February 4, 1996, p. 8.

Carolina Quarterly, summer, 1994, pp. 79-81.

Chicago Tribune, October 28, 1993, sec. 5, p. 3.

Entertainment Weekly, May 24, 1996, p. 89; May 23, 1997, p. 61.

Kirkus Reviews, July 15, 1993, p. 885; June 15, 1995, p. 806; April 1, 1997, p. 493.

Kliatt, November, 1992, p. 10.

Library Journal, September 1, 1993, p. 223; April 15, 1994, p. 140; August, 1995, p. 119; April 1, 1996, p. 121; April 1, 1997, p. 128.

Los Angeles Times, November 1, 1993, p. E3.

Los Angeles Times Book Review, August 6, 1995, p. 6; October 29, 1995, p. 2.

Nation, November 15, 1993, p. 592.

Newsweek, November 29, 1993, p. E78.

New York Times Book Review, January 15, 1984; January 2, 1994, p. 14; November 5, 1995, p. 23; May 25, 1997, p. 9; June 1, 1997, p. 35.

People Weekly, January 15, 1996, p. 36.

Publishers Weekly, August 2, 1993, p. 61; October 18, 1993, p. 50; July 10, 1995, p. 43; March 10, 1997, p. 47.
Southern Living, December, 1993, p. 89; November, 1995, p. 23; June, 1997, p. 60.
Voice Literary Supplement, October, 1995, p. 14.
Voice of Youth Advocates, June, 1994, p. 88.
Washington Post, October 3, 1993, p. 4; February 4, 1996, p. 8.
World & I, December, 1995, pp. 233, 245, 253.

* * *

OWEN, Philip
See PHILIPS, Judson (Pentecost)

P-R

PAGLIA, Camille (Anna) 1947-

PERSONAL: Born April 2, 1947, in Endicott, NY; daughter of Pasquale (a professor of Romance languages) and Lydia Paglia. *Education:* State University of New York, Binghamton, B.A., 1968; Yale University, M.Phil., 1971, Ph.D., 1974.

ADDRESSES: *Home*—Swarthmore, PA. *Office*—Department of Humanities, University of the Arts, 320 South Broad St., Philadelphia, PA 19102. *Agent*—Lynn Nesbit, Janklow and Nesbit, 598 Madison Ave., New York, NY 10022.

CAREER: Bennington College, Bennington, VT, faculty member in Literature and Languages Division, 1972-80; Wesleyan University, Middletown, CT, visiting lecturer in English, 1980; Yale University, New Haven, CT, fellow of Ezra Stiles College, 1981, visiting lecturer in comparative literature, 1981 and 1984, visiting lecturer in English, 1981-83, fellow of Silliman College, 1984; University of the Arts, Philadelphia, PA, assistant professor, 1984-86, associate professor, 1987-91, professor of humanities, 1991—.

AWARDS, HONORS: National Book Critics Circle Award nomination for criticism, 1991, for *Sexual Personae: Art and Decadence from Nefertiti to Emily Dickinson.*

WRITINGS:

Sexual Personae: Art and Decadence from Nefertiti to Emily Dickinson, Yale University Press (New Haven, CT), 1990.

Sex, Art, and American Culture: Essays, Vintage Books (New York City), 1992.

Vamps & Tramps: New Essays, Vintage Books, 1994.

SIDELIGHTS: Camille Paglia's unorthodox feminist views on the role of sexuality in the development of art and culture in Western civilization became the subject of heated debate with the publication of her first book, *Sexual Personae: Art and Decadence from Nefertiti to Emily Dickinson,* in 1990. In the book, and in her subsequent media statements and campus appearances across the country, Paglia has aroused controversy by accusing the contemporary feminist establishment of suppressing the aesthetics of art and beauty and the dangers of sexuality; she warns that historical reality is being ignored in the push for change. Paglia has in turn been criticized by some for her statements on issues such as date rape, pornography, and educational reform. A selection of her many articles, interviews, and lectures appears in the 1992 publication, *Sex, Art, and American Culture.*

Paglia posits in *Sexual Personae* that "the amorality, aggression, sadism, voyeurism, and pornography in great art have been ignored or glossed over by most academic critics." She highlights the appearances of such themes in order "to demonstrate the unity and continuity of Western culture" and disprove the modernist idea that culture is fragmented and meaningless. Terry Teachout in the *New York Times Book Review* stated that "to this end, *Sexual Personae* serves as an illustrated catalogue of the pagan sexual symbolism that Ms. Paglia believes to be omnipresent in Western art." Paglia outlines a number of sexually-charged figures which she calls "sexual personae," a term that *Nation* contributor Mark

Edmundson defined as "erotic archetypes, figures that compel sexual fascination from all perceivers, whatever their professed erotic preferences." These archetypes include the femme fatale, the Great Mother, the vampire, and the hermaphrodite.

Paglia's application of her theory to authors such as the Marquis de Sade, Samuel Taylor Coleridge, and Emily Dickinson proved interesting to many reviewers. "Her fascination with 'perversity' in literature brings her to some startling interpretations," acknowledged Lillian Faderman in the *Washington Post Book World.* The reviewer also observed that Paglia's "discussion of the sexual ambiguities and obsessions that critics have ignored or minimized in major American writers is especially compelling." Walter Kendrick, in his *Voice Literary Supplement* assessment, applauded Paglia's "detailed, subtle readings of [Oscar Wilde's] *The Picture of Dorian Gray* and *The Importance of Being Earnest* and a delicious hatchet job on Emily Dickinson, whom Paglia reads as 'that autocratic sadist,' 'Amherst's Madame de Sade.'"

The author's interest in the sexual element throughout Western history is based on the basic duality or struggle she sees underlying this culture. Using a comparison based on Greek mythology, Paglia comments that the rational, Apollonian force of humanity that creates the order of society is constantly striving to protect itself from the Dionysian, or dark, chaotic forces of nature. She describes the Dionysian element as "the chthonian [earth-bound] realities which Apollo evades, the blind grinding of subterranean force, the long slow suck, the murk and ooze." And despite all the grand scientific and philosophical achievements of Western logic, this irrational pagan force of nature continually wells up, revealing itself in sex, art, and other aspects of popular culture, theorizes Paglia. Sex, especially, reveals these tensions: "Sex is the point of contact between man and nature, where morality and good intentions fall to primitive urges."

This unwieldy instinct unleashes the darker forces that Paglia claims are ignored by mainstream feminists and others who idealize sex as inherently pure, positive, and safe. The perversities that occur in sexual behavior are not caused by social injustice, maintains Paglia, but by natural forces that have not been properly contained by society's defenses. The artifice of society, which is exemplified in the classic works of art, literature, and philosophy of Western culture, is given the highest status by Paglia for this role of protecting and advancing humanity. "Much of western culture is a distortion of reality," she says in *Sexual Personae.* "But reality *should* be distorted; that is, imaginatively amended." Mark Edmundson summarized Paglia's idea that "the glory of art lies in its power to extemporize fictive identities—the personae—that swerve away from biology's literal insistence on what we are. . . . Decadence ritualizes, and thus subdues, erotic violence."

This favorable view of decadence and pornography has set Paglia in direct opposition to the opinions of many in academic and feminist circles. Feminist thought that condemns pornography as the imposition of social prejudice on the inherent goodness of sexuality is decried by Paglia as naive. She accuses feminists with these beliefs of uncritically accepting the ideals of eighteenth-century French philosopher Jean-Jacques Rousseau, who paired nature with freedom and nobility and considered the structures of society oppressive. Paglia's view is that "feminism has exceeded its proper mission of seeking political equality for women and has ended by rejecting contingency, that is, human limitation by nature or fate." Paglia's own brand of feminism, which she outlined in a lecture given at the Massachusetts Institute of Technology, as published in *Sex, Art, and American Culture,* is not based on the Rousseauian idealism which she says was revived in the 1960s, but on the practical realities of sex and culture. She cites as her formative feminist heroes pilot Amelia Earhart, actress Katharine Hepburn, and French theorist Simone de Beauvoir.

Paglia also asserts that "nature's burden falls more heavily on one [the female] sex," that women's natural identity does not create the same type of tension that is found in men. Overwhelmed by the powerful psychological domination of the mother and her relationship with the life and death forces of the earth, men turn to cerebral achievement in an attempt to establish a separate identity from the female and protect themselves from the primal elements, posits Paglia. Statements such as Paglia's widely quoted line, "If civilization had been left in female hands, we would still be living in grass huts," were interpreted by some reviewers to be a rationalization for limiting women's role in society to that of a passive object. Lillian Faderman, in her review of *Sexual Personae* suggested, "Paglia believes that there is indeed a basis for sexual stereotypes that is biological and firmly rooted in the unconscious." Helen Vendler was also concerned that Paglia's theory does not allow for women to participate in cultural achievement equally with men: "To Paglia, women writers remain 'chthonic,' earthbound, and swamplike, unable to rise to such inventive Apollonian designs," she declared in *New York Review of Books.*

Anticipating such reactions in her introduction to *Sexual Personae,* Paglia asserts that women actually hold a privileged status of power in relation to men: "I reaffirm and celebrate woman's ancient mystery and glamour. I see the mother as an overwhelming force who condemns men to lifelong sexual anxiety, from which they escape through rationalism and physical achievement." In addition, she argues that the power of Apollonian society is, or should be, just as accessible to women as to men. Responding to Vendler, Paglia claimed in the *New York Review of Books* that *Sexual Personae* had been misread and misunderstood by Vendler and others. "From first chapter to last, my thesis is that all writing, all art is Apollonian. Every woman who takes pen or brush in hand is making an Apollonian swerve away from nature, even when nature is her subject."

The untraditional subject and style of the *Sexual Personae,* despite the reservations of some critics, was widely praised. Faderman called *Sexual Personae* "a remarkable book, at once outrageous and compelling, fanatical and brilliant. As infuriating as Paglia often is, one must be awed by her vast energy, erudition and wit." Teachout commented that Paglia "is an exciting (if purple) stylist and an admirably close reader with a hard core of common sense. For all its flaws, her first book is every bit as intellectually stimulating as it is exasperating." Edmundson concluded that in exploring the issue of sexuality and sexual personae in culture Paglia "has found a part of the story that no one is telling. It's a splendid and exhilarating find, and makes for a brilliant book." In *Sexual Personae,* Paglia promised a second volume that will focus on similar themes in popular culture since the turn of the century, particularly Hollywood films and rock music.

In addition to pursuing this work, in 1992 Paglia published *Sex, Art, and American Culture,* a collection of her articles, interviews, and lectures. Included are commentaries on pop-star Madonna, whom Paglia considers "the true feminist" for the street-smart brand of sexuality that fills her rock songs and music videos. "Madonna has taught young women to be fully female and sexual while still exercising control over their lives," Paglia asserts in "Madonna I: Animality and Artifice." In other essays she discusses actress Elizabeth Taylor, artist Robert Mapplethorpe, professor Milton Kessler, and others in the public eye. Also included are Paglia's further indictments of certain academic trends, particularly women's studies and French deconstructionist theory, as found in the essays "Junk Bonds and Corporate Raiders" and "The M.I.T. Lecture."

Two chapters of *Sex, Art, and Modern Culture* are devoted to date rape, which Paglia contends is an ethical violation that contemporary feminists do little to prevent. "Rape is an outrage that cannot be tolerated in civilized society," she posits in "Rape and Modern Sex War." "Yet feminism, which has waged a crusade for rape to be taken more seriously, has put young women in danger by hiding the truth about sex from them." Rather than relying on grievance committees to solve the problem of rape on campuses and elsewhere, Paglia feels the solution lies in informing women about the "what is for men the eroticism or fun element in rape" so that by understanding rape, women can learn to protect themselves from it by using "common sense." In other essays, Paglia, a libertarian, outlines her beliefs that the state should not intrude into the private realm; she is prochoice and supports decriminalization of prostitution and legalization of drugs. Arguing that Paglia's is an unconventional but important voice, a *Publishers Weekly* reviewer concluded that in *Sex, Art, and Culture* the author presents "an ambitious range of art and ideas, her invocation of primal sexuality adding a missing element to critical debates."

Vamps & Tramps: New Essays is "a hodgepodge of just about everything [Paglia] has written, filmed and said in magazines, newspapers, movies and television" since the publication of *Sex, Art, and Culture* two years earlier, states Suzanne Fields in *Insight on the News.* The book "is paradoxically dazzling and dull, sensuous and senseless, reactive and repetitious," according to Fields. Mary Beard notes in *New Statesman & Society* that the book is "generously subtitled 'new essays.'" Beard explains that there is "nothing remotely new about the ideas" and "very few of the pieces are what most readers would call 'essays' either." Instead, Beard believes the book is "an ill-stitched compilation of book reviews, some (lusty but thin) bits of journalism plus a routine encyclopedia article on the history of love poetry. . . . This is megalomania on a lunatic scale." Beard continues: "Had [Paglia] listened to Carol Gilligan, Marilyn French, Elaine Showalter and the others, she might have learned that she was not the first to wonder about these problems, and that the issues are a good deal more complex than her monomania allows." In a similar vein, *Commentary*'s Elizabeth Kristol writes: "The challenge in reading so melodramatic a writer is figuring out which ideas are genuinely new (and not just unexpected departures from an otherwise predictable ideological platform), which are genuinely original (and not simply designed to shock), and which are sufficiently valuable as to make all the other stuff worth wading through."

Critics noted that *Vamps & Tramps* is a "hodgepodge" in several ways: content, tone, and quality. According to Fields, *Vamps & Tramps* is "a gold mine of theory and intelligent criticism, but be warned. Reading it requires sifting and sorting amid water, dirt and gravel to get to the shining mettle." Steve Sailer remarks in the *National Review:* "Unfortunately *Vamps & Tramps* suffers from the mixing of its author's three discordant personae: scholar, polemicist, and celebrity role model. While never dull, this unabridged compilation can be repetitious. Because Miss Paglia ties every topic into The Theory, most of her op-eds include a rushed recap of the tragicomic world view she elucidated with supreme clarity in *Sexual Personae*'s first chapter." "On the whole, *Vamps & Tramps* is a carnival. We see Paglia here in all her guises, from the highly serious to the completely loopy," writes David Link in *Reason.*

Several critics remarked that a "quieter," less "self-centered" side to Paglia briefly surfaced in *Vamps & Tramps*. "Paglia dispenses her wisdom like Dear Abby on speed," writes Link. "In fact, her prose is consistently among the most colorful and effective today. No one in the chattering classes can match her when it comes to the punishing reproach." However, Link continues, "*Vamps & Tramps* shows a personal side of Paglia that I don't recall having seen before, and it's a welcome departure." As an example of Paglia's softer side, Link cites an essay on four gay men whom Paglia claims have been central to her life. "For once," Link argues, "the writing is not self-centered. In giving the spotlight to others, Paglia demonstrates a grace and generosity few might suspect her of." In *Time,* Richard Corliss comments: "There are also quieter pieces, notably a loving memoir of four homosexual friends who helped her shape her sensibility. But it's silly to ask this brainy pipshriek to calm down; shouting is her form of conversation."

"A book by Paglia is a lot like sex itself," remarks Link, "when it's good, it's very, very good. And when it's bad, it's still pretty good. *Vamps & Tramps* is a step above pretty good." Fields concurs, "*Vamps & Tramps* is not a book for the squeamish or smug, but it's fun to read and watch the author scorch her enemies with the concentrated power of a white-hot mind."

BIOGRAPHICAL/CRITICAL SOURCES:

BOOKS

Contemporary Literary Criticism, Volume 68, Gale, 1991, pp. 303-20.

Paglia, Camille, *Sex, Art, and American Culture: Essays,* Vintage Books, 1992.

Paglia, *Sexual Personae: Art and Decadence from Nefertiti to Emily Dickinson,* Yale University Press, 1990.

PERIODICALS

Commentary, February 1995, pp. 68-71.

Insight on the News, November 21, 1994, p. 28.

Nation, June 25, 1990, pp. 897-99.

National Review, December 31, 1994, pp. 58-59.

New Statesman & Society, April 14, 1995, p. 43.

Newsweek, September 21, 1992, p. 82.

New York, March 4, 1991, pp. 22-30.

New York Review of Books, May 31, 1990, pp. 19-25; August 16, 1990, p. 59.

New York Times Book Review, July 22, 1990, p. 7.

Publishers Weekly, August 17, 1992.

Reason, February, 1995, pp. 60-63.

Time, January 13, 1992, pp. 62-63, December 12, 1994, p. 90.

Times (London), April 13, 1991, pp. 10-11.

Times Literary Supplement, April 20, 1990, p. 414.

Village Voice, September 29, 1992, pp. 92-94.

Voice Literary Supplement, March, 1990, p. 7.

Washington Post Book World, February 18, 1990, p. 5.*

* * *

PALMER, William J. 1943-

PERSONAL: Born August 7, 1943, in Charlotte, NC; son of William J. (in sales) and Ellen Jane (a homemaker; maiden name, Lemmon) Palmer; married Maryann McShaffrey (a registered nurse and health care administrator), August 28, 1965; children: Christine, Nancy, Jill. *Education:* University of Notre Dame, B.A., 1965, Ph.D., 1969; Ohio State

University, M.A., 1966. *Politics:* Democrat. *Religion:* Roman Catholic.

ADDRESSES: Home—723 North Salisbury St., West Lafayette, IN 47906. *Office*—Department of English, Purdue University, West Lafayette, IN 47907. *Agent*—Jane Jordan Browne, Multi-Media Product Development, Inc., 410 South Michigan Ave., Chicago, IL 60605.

CAREER: Purdue University, West Lafayette, IN, professor of English, 1969—. Member of West Lafayette City Council.

MEMBER: Modern Language Association of America, National Council of Teachers of English, Dickens Society, American Film Institute, American Studies Association.

AWARDS, HONORS: Grant from National Endowment for the Humanities, 1981-82; winner of several Excellence in Teaching awards, Department of English, Purdue University.

WRITINGS:

MYSTERY NOVELS

The Detective and Mr. Dickens: Being an Account of the Macbeth Murders and the Strange Events Surrounding Them (Literary Guild selection), St. Martin's (New York City), 1990.

The Highwayman and Mr. Dickens: An Account of the Strange Events of the Medusa Murders, St. Martin's, 1992.

The Hoydens and Mr. Dickens: The Strange Affair of the Feminist Phantom, St. Martin's, 1997.

OTHER

The Fiction of John Fowles, University of Missouri Press, 1975.

The Films of the Seventies: A Social History, Scarecrow (Metuchen, NJ), 1987.

The Films of the Eighties: A Social History, Southern Illinois University Press (Carbondale), 1994.

Dickens and New Historicism, St. Martin's, 1997.

Contributor to books, including *Dickens Studies Annual,* edited by Robert B. Partlow, Jr., Southern Illinois University Press, 1977; and *Rediscovering America: Critical Essays on the Literature and Film of the Vietnam War,* edited by Owen Gilman and Lorrie Smith, Garland Publishing, 1990. Contributor of articles and reviews to journals and newspapers. Film reviewer, *Journal and Courier* (Lafayette, IN). Editor, *Modern Fiction Studies,* spring, 1985, and spring, 1987.

SIDELIGHTS: William J. Palmer, a professor of English at Purdue University, has written several mystery novels featuring the nineteenth-century British novelist Charles Dickens. These novels, Palmer explains, were actually written by Wilkie Collins, another nineteenth-century novelist and a close friend of Dickens, and Palmer has only rediscovered, edited and published them. The Dickens novels concern real-life historical figures of the time and are written in the style of the period.

Palmer's debut novel, *The Detective and Mr. Dickens,* is set in London of the 1850s and draws its characters from both English history and literature. Dickens' real-life friend, novelist Wilkie Collins, is the narrator who, after the recent funeral of Dickens, recalls in his journal a murder case that the two friends were asked to help solve ten years before. As the investigation into the killing of a wealthy lawyer unfolds, Palmer introduces characters from such well-known Dickens' novels as *Bleak House, David Copperfield,* and *Great Expectations* in order to create a seedy, Dickensian London that *Los Angeles Times Book Review* contributor Laura Kalpakian calls "grisly" but "less horrifying, less lurid than the London of, say, *Bleak House.*" The reviewer also relates that "Palmer's book, in short, takes place in that marshy bog where literature and history meet, and he has mapped his way here creditably." Margaret Cannon comments in the Toronto *Globe and Mail* that "Palmer knows his subjects and his times intimately, and so there is scarcely a false step in this masterful pastiche. . . . Few first novels can boast a cast [of characters] as well-drawn as this, and a 'what-if' plot that works as well."

In *The Highwayman and Mr. Dickens,* Palmer again borrows elements from Dickens' fiction to write the story of a young actress accused of murder. Along with Inspector Bucket of Scotland Yard, a character introduced by Dickens in his novel *Bleak House,* Dickens and Collins work as a Holmes-and-Watson detective team to solve the case. "There are plenty of Victorian touches and Dickensiana," notes Frederick Busch in the *New York Times Book Review.*

The Hoydens and Mr. Dickens takes Dickens and Collins into a murder mystery surrounding London's feminist movement. "The story offers," notes Ilene

Cooper in *Booklist,* "not only a mystery but also a look at some of the more prurient aspects of nineteenth-century London society, including voyeurism and lesbianism." The critic for *Publishers Weekly* finds *The Hoydens and Mr. Dickens* to be a "well-crafted adventure" in which "Palmer exposes the era's sexual double standards." Cooper concludes: "Atmospheric and cunningly plotted, this is an absorbing entry in the celebrity-as-detective genre."

Palmer once told *CA:* "My first rule is that every work of art is participated in by every other work of art which has gone before. My second rule is that every fiction is somehow about the creation of fiction. That is one reason why the fiction of John Fowles is such an important influence upon me.

"My avocation is acting. My 'Mr. Dickens' novels are all about actors."

BIOGRAPHICAL/CRITICAL SOURCES:

PERIODICALS

Booklist, February 15, 1997, p. 1007.
Film Quarterly, summer, 1994, p. 41.
Globe and Mail (Toronto), December 8, 1990.
Journal of Popular Film and Television, spring, 1996, p. 48.
Library Journal, March 15, 1998, p. 66.
Los Angeles Times Book Review, January 20, 1991.
New York Times Book Review, December 16, 1990; October 18, 1992.
Publishers Weekly, December 30, 1996, p. 58.

* * *

PATTERSON, James (B.) 1947-

PERSONAL: Born March 22, 1947, in Newburgh, NY; son of Charles (an insurance broker) and Isabelle (a teacher and homemaker; maiden name, Morris) Patterson. *Education:*Manhattan College, B.A., 1969; Vanderbilt University, M.A., 1970.

ADDRESSES: Home—760 West End Ave., New York, NY 10025. *Office*—J. Walter Thompson Co., 466 Lexington Ave., New York, NY 10017. *Agent*—Arthur Pine Associates, Inc., 250 West 57th St., Suite 417, New York, NY 10019.

CAREER: J. Walter Thompson Co., New York City, junior copywriter, beginning in 1971, vice president and associate creative supervisor of JWT/U.S.A. Co., 1976, senior vice president and creative director of JWT/New York, 1980, executive creative director and member of board of directors, 1984, chairman and creative director, 1987, and chief executive officer, 1988, chairman of JWT/North America, 1990.

AWARDS, HONORS: Edgar Award, Mystery Writers of America, 1977, for *The Thomas Berryman Number.*

WRITINGS:

The Thomas Berryman Number, Little, Brown (Boston), 1976.
The Season of the Machete, Ballantine (New York City), 1977.
The Jericho Commandment, Crown (New York City), 1979.
Virgin, McGraw (New York City), 1980.
Black Market, Simon & Schuster (New York City), 1986.
The Midnight Club, Little, Brown, 1989.
(With Peter Kim) *The Day America Told the Truth: What People Really Believe about Everything That Matters* (nonfiction), Prentice-Hall, 1991.
Along Came a Spider, Little, Brown, 1993.
Kiss the Girls, Little, Brown, 1995.
Jack and Jill, Little, Brown, 1996.
(With Peter de Jonge) *Miracle on the 17th Green,* Little, Brown, 1996.
See How They Run, Warner, 1997.
Cat and Mouse, Little, Brown, 1997.
When the Wind Blows, Little, Brown, 1998.

ADAPTATIONS: Along Came a Spider was filmed by Paramount in 1997; *Kiss the Girls* was also filmed by Paramount in 1997.

SIDELIGHTS: James Patterson, chairman of the J. Walter Thompson advertising agency, also writes bestselling mystery novels in his spare time. Writing in *Publishers Weekly,* Andre Bernard and Jeff Zaleski describe Patterson as "a novelist who has achieved fame and great fortune through violence-splashed, suspense-pumped crime thrillers."

After writing five novels with modest sales, including the Edgar Award-winning *The Thomas Berryman Number,* Patterson found overnight success with *Along Came a Spider.* The story of a crazed math teacher who kidnaps two of his students, the novel, according to Marilyn Stasio in the *New York Times Book Review,* "does everything but stick our finger in a light socket to give us a buzz."

Along Came a Spider introduced Alex Cross, a black police psychologist who figures into Patterson's subsequent thrillers as well. Cross, writes Cynthia Sanz in *People,* "is known for his obsessive investigations and his ability to get inside the minds of the most deranged killers." Patterson explains to Bernard and Zaleski why a white author chose a black lead character for his mysteries: "It struck me that a black male who does the things that Alex does—who succeeds in a couple of ways, tries to bring up his kids in a good way, who tries to continue to live in his neighborhood and who has enormous problems with evil in the world—he's a hero."

A critic for *Publishers Weekly* calls Patterson "always a generous author (lots of plot and intrigue) if not a stylish one." Patterson tells Bernard and Zaleski that in his early books "I was writing sentences, and some of the sentences were good. What I've learned over time is telling stories. . . . Ideally, somewhere along the line, I'd like to write sentences that tell a story." Speaking of *Cat and Mouse,* Emily Melton finds that "suspense, terror, in-your-face action, strange (and sometimes confusing) plot twists, and a darkly explosive ending will have readers lining up, eager to claim their copy of Patterson's latest sure-to-be-a-hit page-turner."

BIOGRAPHICAL/CRITICAL SOURCES:

PERIODICALS

Booklist, September 1, 1996, p. 30; September 1, 1997, p. 8.
Economist, December 13, 1997, p. 14.
Entertainment Weekly, September 6, 1996, p. 68; September 27, 1996, p. 75.
Library Journal, October 1, 1997, p. 124.
Los Angeles Times, April 10, 1989.
New York Times, January 17, 1989, p. D19.
New York Times Book Review, May 14, 1989, p. 22; February 7, 1993.
People, October 7, 1996, p. 38; November 17, 1997, p. 38.
Publishers Weekly, September 16, 1996, p. 68; October 21, 1996, p. 58; October 13, 1997, p. 56; January 5, 1998, p. 28.

PECK, Dale 1967-

PERSONAL: Born July 13, 1967, in Bay Shore, NY; son of Dale (a plumber) and Eileen (Staplin) Peck. *Education:* Drew University, B.A., 1989.

ADDRESSES: Agent—Irene Skolnick, 121 West 27th St., Suite 601, New York, NY 10001.

CAREER: Novelist. Former staff member, *Out Magazine.*

MEMBER: AIDS Coalition to Unleash Power (ACT UP).

AWARDS, HONORS: Guggenheim fellow, 1994.

WRITINGS:

Martin and John: A Novel, Farrar (New York City), 1993, published as *Fucking Martin,* Chatto & Windus (London), 1993.
The Law of Enclosures, Farrar, 1996.
Now It's Time to Say Goodbye, Farrar, 1998.

SIDELIGHTS: The 1993 appearance of *Martin and John: A Novel* catapulted young writer Dale Peck to the forefront of contemporary American gay fiction. Before the publication of his first novel, Peck was a member of ACT UP in New York City, an AIDS activist group known for their controversial tactics—Peck was the man who disrupted an on-air CBS newscast in 1990. *Martin and John* developed in part out of Peck's own experiences and relationships, and many reviews of the book discussed its intensely confessional tone, part autobiography, part anti-autobiography. *Los Angeles Times Book Review* critic Richard Eder termed it "a dazzling explosion of voices and stories that hide behind and emerge out of each other. It is a book of theatrical quick changes."

Because of its layers, its hidden corners, its repetitiveness, *Martin and John* resists an easy description of plot. It is narrated by John, a young man who has fled an abusive household. His lover is Martin, who eventually becomes ill with AIDS, and the sequence of events between them takes place primarily in New York City and Kansas. Interspersed into the sparse narrative action are a legion of smaller stories, each one also involving characters named Martin and John. Sometimes Martin is a rich man who showers young John with love, jewelry, and affection; in other instances he is a fellow security guard in Kansas, a teenage runaway found in a barn, or a sadistic

New York pimp. John changes character as well as he recounts an upbringing fraught with conflict and abuse. Most of his recollections involve a widowed father with a drinking problem who savagely beats John when the teenager admits his homosexuality; other vignettes recount his father dressing up in his dead wife's clothes. In some stories the death of John's mother occurred when he was still young, in other instances she lingers in a nursing home for years or is perfectly healthy, happy, and divorced—but then one of her boyfriends is a man named Martin who seduces the teenage John. "It can be hard to make out, and I had to go back over it a second time," wrote Eder of *Martin and John*'s complicated structure; "and it changed color and shape somewhat when I did. But the darkness, glitteringly backlit or spotlit . . . prevails almost entirely."

In an interview published in *Contemporary Literary Criticism Yearbook,* Peck explained the genesis of *Martin and John:* "There are autobiographical themes in the book but no autobiography. The only 'real life' aspects of the novel are the settings based on places I've lived. . . . There are similarities in the character of the father to my father, there are similarities in the character of John to my own character, and there are similarities in the female characters to my stepmothers. . . . None of them, however, are actually based on real people." Later in the interview, Peck explained how the structure developed: "The novel originally began with a short story—the story 'Transformations' was the first Martin and John story I wrote. Then, when I wrote another story dealing with the same issues, I couldn't think of character names and so I used the [names Martin and John again]. After writing those two stories, I conceived of the whole project of *Martin and John.* I worked on the book for about four years, and when it was finished I had five hundred pages of manuscript from which I cut 300 pages of stories."

Voice Literary Supplement writer Vince Aletti discussed the novel's spiraling effect between Martin and John's real relationship in the traditional narrative and the fantasy episodes that John writes of in the parallel text, comparing it to a puzzle. "Attempting to transform his history into fiction—something healing, revealing, and 'true'—John can only shuffle things around. And no matter how many times he reinvents his story, he keeps coming back to a few ugly, sad facts: abuse, abandonment, lost love, death." Aletti faulted this approach that Peck undertook, opining that by "teasing his story every which way—whipping up raw tragedy, offhand comedy, and lots of hallucinated melodrama with a very small constellation of characters—he's playing author in a showy, postmodern way." In the end Martin dies of AIDS, cared for by John until a terrible demise in a bathtub. The reader next finds the surviving John in his room, writing, and waiting for his own illness to develop.

Many critics praised the first-time novelist and his tour-de-force work. *New York Times* reviewer Michiko Kakutani noted that "if this fiercely written novel offers an indelible portrait of gay life during the plague years, it also opens out to become a universal story about love and loss and the redemptive powers of fiction. It is a story about the cycles of pain and grief that spiral through people's lives, and the efforts an artist makes to reorder and transcend that hurt." Kakutani commended the young author's level of compassion and insight, concluding that "his wisdom about human feelings, his talent for translating those feelings into prose and his sophisticated mastery of literary form all speak to a maturity that belies his 25 years. In short, a stunning debut." *Times Literary Supplement* reviewer Gregory Woods faulted Peck for "at times sounding as if he had just been given a thesaurus," yet termed the instances "minor faults in a fascinating first novel." In the *Los Angeles Times Book Review* piece, Eder asserted that "Peck's first novel has a dark brilliance and moments of real beauty, but it is a book that is shocking, hard to accept fully, and hard to ignore. It is impassioned in its identification with the gay condition, yet it rides fiercely athwart any common notion of political correctness."

Peck's 1996 novel *The Law of Enclosures,* according to Victoria Stagg Elliott in *Gay and Lesbian Literature,* consists of "two novellas about heterosexual couples. . . . Their stories of marriage gone bad are told in alternating chapters interrupted by an autobiographical interlude about Peck's mother and the three stepmothers he acquired as a result of his father's frequent marrying." John Brenkman in the *Nation* notes: "There is an extraordinary sense of the risk and adventure of writing in every page of this novel." "Peck's talent," writes Nancy Pearl in *Booklist,* "is undeniable, and readers willing to take on an unconventional novel will find much to admire. It is filled with powerful writing, unforgettable sentences . . . , and perceptions on love and betrayal that are so painfully acute it is hard to believe Peck is only in his late twenties." The critic for *Publishers Weekly* calls *The Law of Enclosures* a "lyrical and boldly constructed novel" and "not only an unblinking look at the dark chambers of the human heart, [but] a brave artistic gamble—one that, ultimately, comes up spades."

Now It's Time to Say Goodbye is set in a small Kansas town where Colin Newman and his boyfriend Justin Time have decided, after they realize they know 500 fellow New Yorkers who have died of AIDS, to settle. As Vanessa Bush states in *Booklist,* "The pair brings with them a conceit that their complicated lives of wealth, betrayal, and cruelty are beyond the comprehension of the rural town." "They soon discover, however, that even here human passions and prejudice run deep," notes David W. Henderson in *Library Journal.* When a local girl is abducted and killed, and Justin is attacked, Colin uncovers dark motives and racial antagonisms among the town's social elite. "Peck," writes the critic for *Publishers Weekly,* "is a powerful stylist, capable of incandescent descriptions of the unforgiving flatlands from which the town emerged." "Peck's novel," concludes Bush, "is a compelling thriller with subtle and informed knowledge of race relations in the U.S."

BIOGRAPHICAL/CRITICAL SOURCES:

BOOKS

Contemporary Literary Criticism, Volume 81, Gale (Detroit), 1993.

Gay and Lesbian Literature, Volume 2, St. James Press (Detroit), 1998.

PERIODICALS

Advocate, May 26, 1998, p. 78.

Booklist, December 15, 1995, p. 686; February 15, 1998, p. 948.

Boston Phoenix, December, 1995.

Entertainment Weekly, April 16, 1993, p. 49.

Gay Times, February, 1996, pp. 54-56.

JAMA: The Journal of the American Medical Association, March 2, 1994, p. 717.

Lambda Book Report, June, 1998, p. 21.

Library Journal, April 15, 1998, p. 115.

Los Angeles Times Book Review, January 24, 1993, pp. 3, 7.

Nation, January 29, 1996, p. 31.

New Yorker, February 1, 1993, p. 107.

New York Times, February 9, 1993, p. C15.

Observer, May 23, 1993, p. 71.

Publishers Weekly, October 16, 1995, p. 40; March 16, 1998, p. 51.

Times Literary Supplement, March 26, 1993, p. 20.

Tribune Books (Chicago), January 16, 1994, p. 8.

Voice Literary Supplement, February, 1993, pp. 5-6.

* * *

PENTECOST, Hugh
See PHILIPS, Judson (Pentecost)

* * *

PETERSON, Christmas
See CHRISTMAS, Joyce

* * *

PETRIE, Rhona
See BUCHANAN, Marie

* * *

PHILIPS, Judson (Pentecost) 1903-1989
(Philip Owen, Hugh Pentecost)

PERSONAL: Born August 10, 1903, in Northfield, MA; died of complications from emphysema, March 7, 1989, in Sharon, CT; son of Arthur (an opera singer) and Frederikco (an actress; maiden name, Pentecost) Philips; married Norma Burton (an actress), 1951; children: David, Caroline, John, Daniel. *Education:* Columbia University, B.A., 1925.

CAREER: Writer. *New York Tribune,* New York City, high school sports reporter, beginning 1926; *Harlem Valley Times,* Amenia, NY, co-owner and editor, 1949-56; *Lakeville Journal,* Lakeville, CT, political columnist and book reviewer, beginning 1951; Sharon Playhouse, Sharon, CT, founder and director, 1951-72; WTOR-Radio, Torrington, CT, talkshow host, 1970-76.

MEMBER: Mystery Writers of America (founding member and past president).

AWARDS, HONORS: First prize in Dodd, Mead's mystery competition, 1939, for *Cancelled in Red;* Mystery Writers of America Grand Master Award, 1973; Nero Wolfe Award, 1982.

WRITINGS:

(With Robert W. Wood, Jr.) *Hold 'Em Girls! The Intelligent Woman's Guide to Men and Football,* Putnam (New York City), 1936.
(With Thomas M. Johnson) *Red War,* Doubleday (New York City), 1936.
Murder in Marble, Dodd, Mead (New York City), 1940.
Killer on the Catwalk, Dodd, Mead, 1959.
Whisper Town, Dodd, Mead, 1960.
Murder Clear, Track Fast, Dodd, Mead, 1961.
A Dead Ending, Dodd, Mead, 1962.
(Editor) *Cream of the Crime,* Holt (New York City), 1962.
The Dead Can't Love, Dodd, Mead, 1963.
(Under pseudonym Philip Owen) *Mystery at a Country Inn,* Berkshire Traveller Press (Pittsfield, MA), 1979.

"COYLE AND DONOVAN" SERIES; NOVELS

Odds on the Hot Seat, Dodd, Mead, 1941.
The Fourteenth Trump, Dodd, Mead, 1942.

"PETER STYLES" SERIES; NOVELS

The Laughter Trap, Dodd, Mead, 1964.
The Black Glass City, Dodd, Mead, 1965.
The Twisted People, Dodd, Mead, 1965.
The Wings of Madness, Dodd, Mead, 1966.
Thursday's Folly, Dodd, Mead, 1967.
Hot Summer Killing, Dodd, Mead, 1968.
Nightmare at Dawn, Dodd, Mead, 1970.
Escape a Killer, Dodd, Mead, 1971.
The Vanishing Senator, Dodd, Mead, 1972.
The Larkspur Conspiracy, Dodd, Mead, 1973.
The Power Killers, Dodd, Mead, 1974.
Walk a Crooked Mile, Dodd, Mead, 1975.
Backlash, Dodd, Mead, 1976.
Five Roads to Death, Dodd, Mead, 1977.
A Murder Arranged, Dodd, Mead, 1978.
Why Murder?, Dodd, Mead, 1979.
Death Is a Dirty Trick, Dodd, Mead, 1980.
Death as the Curtain Rises, Dodd, Mead, 1981.
Target for Tragedy, Dodd, Mead, 1982.

"CAROLE TREVOR AND MAX BLYTHE" SERIES; NOVELS

The Death Syndicate, I. Washburn (New York City), 1938.
Death Delivers a Postcard, I. Washburn, 1939.

UNDER PSEUDONYM HUGH PENTECOST

Cat and Mouse, Royce (New York City), 1945.
The Dead Man's Tale, Royce, 1945.
Chinese Nightmare, Dell (New York City), 1951.
The Assassins, Dodd, Mead, 1955.
The Kingdom of Death, Dodd, Mead, 1960.
The Deadly Friend, Dodd, Mead, 1961.
The Tarnished Angel, Dodd, Mead, 1963.
The Day the Children Vanished, Pocket Books (New York City), 1976.
Murder as Usual, Dodd, Mead, 1977.

UNDER PSEUDONYM HUGH PENTECOST; "LUKE BRADLEY" SERIES; CRIME NOVELS

Cancelled in Red, Dodd, Mead, 1939.
The 24th Horse, Dodd, Mead, 1940.
I'll Sing at Your Funeral, Dodd, Mead, 1942.
The Brass Chills, Dodd, Mead, 1943.

UNDER PSEUDONYM HUGH PENTECOST; "PIERRE CHAMBRUN" SERIES; CRIME NOVELS

The Cannibal Who Overate, Dodd, Mead, 1962.
The Shape of Fear, Dodd, Mead, 1964.
The Evil That Men Do, Dodd, Mead, 1966.
The Golden Trap, Dodd, Mead, 1967.
The Gilded Nightmare, Dodd, Mead, 1968.
Girl Watcher's Funeral, Dodd, Mead, 1969.
The Deadly Joke, Dodd, Mead, 1971.
Birthday, Deathday, Dodd, Mead, 1972.
Walking Dead Man, Dodd, Mead, 1973.
Bargain with Death, Dodd, Mead, 1974.
Time of Terror, Dodd, Mead, 1975.
The Fourteen Dilemma, Dodd, Mead, 1976.
Death after Breakfast, Dodd, Mead, 1978.
Random Killer, Dodd, Mead, 1979.
Beware Young Lovers, Dodd, Mead, 1980.
Murder in Luxury, Dodd, Mead, 1981.
With Intent to Kill, Dodd, Mead, 1982.
Murder in High Places, Dodd, Mead, 1983.
Remember to Kill Me, Dodd, Mead, 1984.
Murder Round the Clock: Pierre Chambrun's Crime File (short stories), Dodd, Mead, 1985.
Nightmare Time, Dodd, Mead, 1986.
Murder Goes Round and Round, Dodd, Mead, 1988.

UNDER PSEUDONYM HUGH PENTECOST; "GEORGE CROWDER" SERIES; CRIME NOVELS

Choice of Violence, Dodd, Mead, 1961.
Around Dark Corners (short stories), Dodd, Mead, 1970.
The Copycat Killers, Dodd, Mead, 1983.
The Price of Silence, Dodd, Mead, 1984.
Murder Sweet and Sour, Dodd, Mead, 1985.
Death by Fire, Dodd, Mead, 1986.
Pattern for Terror, Carroll & Graf (New York City), 1990.

UNDER PSEUDONYM HUGH PENTECOST; "JOHN JERICHO" SERIES; CRIME NOVELS

Sniper, Dodd, Mead, 1965.
Hide Her from Every Eye, Dodd, Mead, 1966.
The Creeping Hours, Dodd, Mead, 1966.
Dead Woman of the Year, Dodd, Mead, 1967.
The Girl with Six Fingers, Dodd, Mead, 1969.
A Plague of Violence, Dodd, Mead, 1970.

UNDER PSEUDONYM HUGH PENTECOST; "LIEUTENANT PASCAL" SERIES; CRIME NOVELS

Lieutenant Pascal's Tastes in Homicide (novellas), Dodd, Mead, 1954.
Only the Rich Die Young, Dodd, Mead, 1964.

UNDER PSEUDONYM HUGH PENTECOST; "JULIAN QUIST" SERIES; CRIME NOVELS

Don't Drop Dead Tomorrow, Dodd, Mead, 1971.
The Champagne Killer, Dodd, Mead, 1972.
The Beautiful Dead, Dodd, Mead, 1973.
The Judas Freak, Dodd, Mead, 1974.
Honeymoon with Death, Dodd, Mead, 1975.
Die After Dark, Dodd, Mead, 1976.
The Steel Palace, Dodd, Mead, 1977.
Deadly Trap, Dodd, Mead, 1978.
The Homicidal Horse, Dodd, Mead, 1979.
Death Mask, Dodd, Mead, 1980.
Sow Death, Reap Death, Dodd, Mead, 1981.
Past, Present, and Murder, Dodd, Mead, 1982.
Murder Out of Wedlock, Dodd, Mead, 1983.
Substitute Victim, Dodd, Mead, 1984.
The Party Killer, Dodd, Mead, 1985.
Kill and Kill Again, Dodd, Mead, 1987.

UNDER PSEUDONYM HUGH PENTECOST; "GRANT SIMON" SERIES; CRIME NOVELS

The Obituary Club, Dodd, Mead, 1958.
The Lonely Target, Dodd, Mead, 1959.

UNDER PSEUDONYM HUGH PENTECOST; "DR. JOHN SMITH" SERIES; CRIME NOVELS

Memory of Murder (novellas), Ziff Davis (New York City), 1947.
Where the Snow Was Red, Dodd, Mead, 1949.
Shadow of Madness, Dodd, Mead, 1950.

SHORT STORIES; UNDER PSEUDONYM HUGH PENTECOST

Secret Corridors, Century (New York City), 1945.
Death Wears a Copper Necktie and Other Stories, Edwards (London), 1946.

Also author of numerous uncollected short stories, including "Lonely Boy," in *Ellery Queen's Mystery Magazine,* August, 1952; "The Day the Children Vanished," in *Best Detective Stories of the Year,* edited by David C. Cooke, New York, Dutton, 1959; "The Lame Duck House Party," in *Ellery Queen's Mystery Magazine,* November, 1959; "A Kind of Murder," in *Ellery Queen's Mystery Magazine,* August, 1962; "Jericho and the Silent Witnesses," in *Ellery Queen's Mystery Magazine,* November, 1965; "The Show Must Go On," in *Ellery Queen's Mystery Magazine,* July, 1977.

PLAYS

Lonely Boy, first produced in Sharon, Connecticut, 1954.
The Lame Duck Party, first produced in Sharon, Connecticut, 1977.

Also author of radio plays *Suspense, Father Brown,* and *The Whisper Men;* author of television plays *The Web, The Ray Milland Show, Studio One,* and *Hallmark Hall of Fame.*

SIDELIGHTS: Judson Philips, better known to mystery fans as Hugh Pentecost, was one of America's most prolific authors of detective fiction. In his fifty-year career he produced more than a hundred novels and countless short stories, making him an acknowledged "old pro" of whodunit fiction. His career, wrote *St. James Guide to Crime and Mystery Writers* contributor Marvin Lachman, "began in 1925 when, still a junior at Columbia University, he sold 'Room Number Twenty-Three,' a locked room mystery, his very first story, to *Flynn's*" magazine. "He became a steady contributor to many magazines and even outlasted two markets for his work, 'pulps' like *Black Mask* and the 'slicks,' e.g., *Collier's.* Philips remained a leading contributor to digest-sized magazines such as *Ellery Queen's Mystery Magazine* until his death."

"I set out in life wanting to be an actor," Judson Philips explained to Jean Ross in a *Contemporary Authors* interview. "My mother was an actress; my father was an opera singer. I got a job when I was eighteen years old in a silent movie with a star named Elaine Hammerstein, who I suppose was the grandniece of Oscar Hammerstein. There weren't very many parts for eighteen-year-old kids, and while this was a good one and it all went very well, I never could get any jobs again." Instead, he turned to writing, quickly earning a reputation as a rapid and lucid wordsmith. In 1929, Philips left New England briefly for Hollywood, where he wrote dialogue for a former student of his father's, John Barrymore. "Barrymore got me the job to go out to Hollywood because he was sure there was nobody literate enough there to write dialogue for him," Philips told Ross, "so I went out and wrote the dialogue for him in 'General Crack.'" "I got involved with most of the mediums that were available for moneymaking," the writer continued to Ross. "Finally, so many people got in the act in some of these public mediums like films and television, there were so many fingers in the pie, that I got sick of it." Philips maintained an interest in theater, and in 1951 he founded the Sharon Playhouse in Sharon, Connecticut. He later wrote two plays specifically for the Sharon Playhouse, *Lonely Boy* (1954) and *The Lame Duck Party* (1977).

Among Philips's most popular works were the series featuring characters Peter Styles, John Jericho, Pierre Chambrun, and Julian Quist. Styles, the one investigator whose adventures Philips chronicled under his own name, is a one-legged magazine columnist presented as a crusader for justice and the American way of life. "Styles not only lost his leg in an accident caused by a driver on drugs, but he later lost his wife who was killed by terrorists," explained Lachman. The journalist-turned-detective has battled a small-town fascistic army, confronted a gang of young psychopaths, and fought a terrorist group operating amid an atmosphere of racial tension. "Julian Quist, head of one of New York's leading public relations firms," stated Lachman, "is blond and handsome, with 'a profile that might have been carved on an ancient Greek coin." Newgate Callendar, writing in the *New York Times Book Review,* called Julian Quist "a wish-fulfillment of our times . . . tall, lean, handsome." Head of a public relations firm, the decisive Quist usually moves through the world of entertainers or the super rich. Often accompanied by an assortment of beautiful women, "Quist may be all slick invention, but he's fun to have around," concluded Haskel Frankel in *Saturday Review.*

The Jericho novels, like the Styles books, "peer over and again at the prejudices and violence of our society," noted a *New York Times Book Review* critic. Jericho is a talented artist, and this position allows the author to sketch views of the seamier side of the artistic community and its wealthy supporters. Jericho himself is a larger than life figure, "whose stature (6'6" and 240 pounds), flaming red beard, and Viking-like appearance made him stand out," stated Lachman. "I was very fond of . . . Jericho who was an artist, a painter, traveled all over the world, crusaded against violence," Philips revealed to Ross. "But he didn't do well in books and I keep him alive now by writing an occasional short story about him for *Ellery Queen's Mystery Magazine.*"

Chambrun, the managing director of Manhattan's Hotel Beaumont, may be Philips's best-known investigator—and, the author added in his *Contemporary Authors* interview, "the most popular one from the public's point of view." Although confined to the posh hostelry, Chambrun sees an assortment of characters—including numerous celebrities—come and go, bringing with them the complications of crime that allow him to do his sleuthing. A veteran of the French Resistance during World War II, Chambrun is often forced into dealing with terrorist situations. "In *Remember to Kill Me,* in the confusion of an urban riot, terrorists seize four V.I.P.'s as hostages, demanding the release of a Central American political prisoner," stated Lachman. "An Army officer who once saved Chambrun's life is kidnapped in *Nightmare Time,* and then the person closest to Chambrun, his secretary and lover, Betsy Ruysdale, is abducted."

Critics generally cite Philips's fast pacing, straightforward yet forceful language, and his feel for timely subjects as reasons for his popularity. As Newgate Callendar reported in the *New York Times Book Review,* Philips's "name is a guarantee of smooth writing, an ingenious storyline, and convincing characterization." Seargeant Cuff added in *Saturday Review* that the author's work is marked by "complications of the sort only a top pro could handle with clarity and at a brisk pace." "He is never at a loss for a new twist of plot or character," noted a writer for *West Coast Review of Books.* "One can depend on all of his novels to have the power to hold the attention of the reader to the very last page of the book." While, occasionally, reviewers fault the author for producing too many mysteries with too much in common, most appreciate what a *Los Angeles Times Book Review* critic called "vintage Pentecost—tough, taut, immaculately plotted." Concluded Cuff: "Judson Philips . . . is as pro as they come."

BIOGRAPHICAL/CRITICAL SOURCES:

BOOKS

Authors in the News, Volume 1, Gale (Detroit, MI), 1976.

St. James Guide to Crime and Mystery Writers, 4th edition, St. James Press (Detroit, MI), 1996.

PERIODICALS

Books and Bookmen, February, 1968; September, 1973.

Book World, December 17, 1972; June 17, 1973.

Chicago Tribune Book World, March 28, 1982; August 15, 1982; December 19, 1982; May 22, 1983; January 29, 1984.

Hartford Courant, June 30, 1974.

New Yorker, January 8, 1972; September 20, 1976.

New York Times, May 4, 1978.

New York Times Book Review, August 6, 1967; February 23, 1969; March 30, 1969; June 8, 1969; September 21, 1969; April 5, 1970; January 24, 1971; June 20, 1971; October 3, 1971; January 16, 1972; May 28, 1972; August 20, 1972; November 5, 1972; June 10, 1973; June 17, 1973; November 18, 1973; December 9, 1973; March 10, 1974; June 16, 1974; October 20, 1974; January 19, 1975; August 3, 1975; June 12, 1977; January 22, 1978; July 2, 1978.

Observer, August 24, 1969; October 18, 1970; January 24, 1971; May 14, 1972; July 1, 1973; July 14, 1974; April 11, 1976; March 18, 1979.

Punch, March 5, 1969; September 3, 1979.

Saturday Review, March 28, 1970; August 1, 1970; December 26, 1970; September 25, 1971; December 25, 1971; September 9, 1972; November 25, 1972.

Times Literary Supplement, December 2, 1965; February 23, 1967; January 25, 1968; April 24, 1969; June 11, 1970; November 6, 1970; February 26, 1971; May 26, 1972; August 17, 1973; September 6, 1974; July 9, 1976.

OBITUARIES:

PERIODICALS

Chicago Tribune, March 10, 1989.

New York Times, March 9, 1989.*

* * *

PIPHER, Mary (Bray) 1947-

PERSONAL: Born October 21, 1947, in Springfield, MO; daughter of Frank Houston and Avis Ester (Page) Bray; married Jim Pipher (a psychologist), October 18, 1974; children: Zeke, Sara. *Education:* Received Ph.D. from University of Nebraska—Lincoln. *Religion:* Unitarian-Universalist.

ADDRESSES: *Office*—3201 South 33rd, Suite B, Lincoln, NE 68506. *Agent*—Susan Lee Cohen, 2840 Broadway, No. 210, New York, NY 10025.

CAREER: Private practice of psychology in Lincoln, NE, 1979—. Faculty member, University of Nebraska—Lincoln and Nebraska Wesleyan University.

WRITINGS:

Hunger Pains, privately printed, 1987, reprinted as *Hunger Pains: The Modern Woman's Tragic Quest for Thinness,* Ballantine (New York City), 1997.

Reviving Ophelia: Saving the Selves of Adolescent Girls, Putnam (New York City), 1994.

Diets to Eating Disorders, What Every Woman Needs to Know about Food, Dieting, and Self-Concept, Adams Pub. (Holbrook, MA), 1995.

The Shelter of Each Other: Rebuilding Our Families, Putnam, 1996.

WORK IN PROGRESS: Another Country: The Emotional Terrain of the Elderly, publication by Putnam expected in 1999.

SIDELIGHTS: Mary Pipher is a clinical psychologist whose patients include increasing numbers of adolescent girls. She believes, according to *Time* reviewer Elizabeth Gleick, that "adolescence is an especially precarious time for girls." In her book, *Reviving Ophelia: Saving the Selves of Adolescent Girls,* reported *Publishers Weekly,* Pipher "suggests that, despite the advances of feminism, young women continue to be victims of abuse," including self-abuse typified by eating disorders and self-mutilation. The author places the blame on modern culture, with its slick advertising, images of sex and violence in the media, availability of alcohol and drugs, fragmented families, and a population under stress. In *Reviving Ophelia,* wrote Marge Scherer in *Educational Leadership,* "she describes how to rescue young women drowning in a culture that isolates and degrades them."

The book is packed with case studies. "Dozens of troubled teenage girls troop across its pages," commented Gleick, suggesting "[t]here's a girl here for everyone." Gleick attributed the popularity of *Reviving Ophelia* to several factors: many readers can identify with at least one of the wide-ranging case studies, including parents; "for the most part, the culture, not the parents, are to blame"; and "Pipher does offer commonsensical, unthreatening solutions." Pipher describes the varieties of therapy that she offers her own patients and lists suggestions that girls can implement, on their own, to strengthen their self-images. She offers to teachers and parents tips that, according to Scherer, "are sane and simple and within our reach."

Pipher's next book addresses the families to which her patients belong. In *The Shelter of Each Other: Rebuilding Our Families,* according to Scherer, "she examines how to remedy the lack of community that is disorienting families." As she did in *Reviving Ophelia,* the author places the blame on modern society, citing family troubles that have been, as Rose Reissman summarized in *Educational Leadership,* "aggravated by the media . . . corporate values . . . technology, and the isolation wrought by demographic changes." Pipher expressed similar concerns to Scherer: "The media portray families in unrealistic ways—either they are picture perfect or they're grossly dysfunctional."

Pipher also expands on a theme that she introduced in *Reviving Ophelia:* the dynamic of the typical family has changed dramatically since her own Nebraska childhood during the 1950s. In her interview with Scherer, the author said, "There's been a total upending of what was considered a virtuous child." Today's society focuses on independence, rather than traditional obedience, for example, and one result is that parents, teachers (and ultimately children) are uncertain about the proper relationship between responsibility and accountability. Pipher supplies a detailed comparison of an old-fashioned rural family of the past (her grandparents') and today's troubled family, which she describes, according to *Booklist* reviewer Ray Olson, as "multiply stressed by job demands, money worries, conflicting individual schedules, and electronic information overload." Pipher told Scherer, "We also have a culture of narcissism. . . . And there's been a real loss of community between families and schools . . . And there's less communal space for children." She also commented on the increasing demographic mobility that separates today's children from grandparents and other extended family members, replacing them with nameless strangers who cannot provide the nurturing relationships that individuals and families need.

In *The Shelter of Each Other,* Pipher demonstrates that, as Scherer declared, "It is possible to revive our sense of community." She provides examples of families that have succeeded in rebuilding connections and offering mutual support to one another as they grow closer. Theresa Richeson of the *National Catholic Reporter* recommended the book for its "wisdom, common sense, empathy and reality." A *Publishers Weekly* reviewer wrote of Pipher: "She offers plain and practical talk" for parents struggling to take care of their families.

BIOGRAPHICAL/CRITICAL SOURCES:

PERIODICALS

Booklist, February 1, 1996, p. 898.
Educational Leadership, December, 1996, pp. 85-87; May, 1998, pp. 6-12.
National Catholic Reporter, November 21, 1997, p. 14.
Publishers Weekly, February 28, 1994, p. 66; January 29, 1996, pp. 90-92; February 5, 1996, p. 37.
Time, February 19, 1996, p. 73.

* * *

QUILL, Barnaby
See BRANDNER, Gary

* * *

RADZINSKY, Edvard (Stanislavovich) 1936-

PERSONAL: Born September 23, 1936, in Moscow, U.S.S.R. (now Russia); son of Stanislav Adlfovich (a playwright) and Sofia (Kazakova) Radzinsky. *Education:* Attended Institute of History and Archival Science (Moscow).

ADDRESSES: Home—Usievicha Street 8, Flat 96, 125319 Moscow, Russia. *Office*—c/o Union of Writers, 52 Vorovskogo, Moscow, Russia. *Agent*—Lynn C. Franklin Associates, 386 Park Ave. S., Suite 1102, New York, NY 10016.

CAREER: Playwright, biographer, and novelist.

WRITINGS:

The Last Tsar: The Life and Death of Nicholas II (biography), translated from the Russian by Marian Schwartz, Doubleday (New York City), 1992.

Stalin: The First In-Depth Biography Based on Explosive New Documents from Russia's Secret Archives, translated from the Russian by H. T. Willetts, Doubleday, 1996.

The Last Tsar has been published in more than fifteen countries.

PLAYS

Mechta moya . . . Indiya (two-act), produced in Moscow at Youth Theater, 1960.

104 stranitsy pro lyubov (published in *Teatr,* 1964), produced as *Yeshcho raz pro lyubov,* in Leningrad, 1964.

Monolog o brake, produced in Leningrad, 1973.

Besedy s Sokratom (produced in Moscow, 1975), translation by Alma H. Law produced in New York by Jean Cocteau Repertory, 1987.

Lunin, ili smert Zhaka, zapisannaya v prisutstvii Khozyaina (produced in Moscow, 1979; published in *Teatr,* 1979), translation by Alma H. Law, titled *I, Mikhail Sergeevich Lunin,* produced in New York by Jean Cocteau Repertory, 1986.

Teatr vremeen Nerona i Seneki (produced in Moscow, 1987; published in *Sovremennaja dramaturgija,* 1982), translation by Alma H. Law produced in New York by Jean Cocteau Repertory at Bouwerie Lane Theater, 1985.

Staraja aktrisa na rol zeny Dostoevskogo (produced in Moscow at Moscow Arts Theater, 1989; published in *Sovremennaja dramaturgija,* 1984), translation by Alma H. Law, titled *An Old Actress in the Role of Dostoyevsky's Wife,* produced in New York by Jean Cocteau Repertory at Bouwerie Lane Theater, 1992.

Also author of *Vam 22, stariki* (two-act), produced in 1962; *Snimayetsya kino,* published in *Teatr,* 1966; *Obolstitel Kolobashkin* (produced in 1967), published in *Teatr,* 1968; *P'esy,* produced in 1974; *Prijatnaja zenscina s cvetkom i oknami no sever,* published in *Teatr,* 1983; *Ona v otsutstvii ljubvi i smerti,* published in *Besedy s Skratom;* and *Prodolzenie Don Zuana,* published in *Besedy s Skratom.* Also author of an additional untranslated work, produced in Moscow, 1987.

OTHER

Also author of screenplays.

WORK IN PROGRESS: A biography of Rasputin.

SIDELIGHTS: Edvard Radzinsky is a prominent Russian playwright who has gained additional fame as a biographer of two of his country's most significant historical figures: Tsar Nicholas II and Soviet dictator Josef Stalin. Radzinsky has been quoted as saying he was obsessed with these two subjects; indeed, he put his playwrighting career on hold for part of the time he was working on the biography of Nicholas II, the last ruler of imperial Russia. And after the breakup of the Soviet Union in 1991 led to the release of documents on Stalin, Radzinsky immersed himself in research, fearing the new Russian government might reclassify the papers at any time.

Concerning his motivation for writing *The Last Tsar: The Life and Death of Nicholas II,* Radzinsky told Kim Hubbard of *People* magazine: "I decided I had to find the real man and uncover the mystery of his death." Nicholas II was killed in 1918, presumably along with the remainder of his family, the Romanovs, after being held captive by revolutionary forces since the previous year. The Soviet Union's official story had long been that the imperial family was murdered by a group of provincial rebels acting on their own; Radzinsky, however, believes Bolshevik leader V. I. Lenin ordered the killings. Radzinsky was inspired to write his account during the 1970s, while a student at Moscow's Institute of History and Archival Science. His subsequent research spanned the next few decades and was aided in part by *glasnost,* the general loosening of government control in the last years of the Soviet Union. Because of *glasnost,* Radzinsky was able to access many historical records previously concealed from the public, and found not only documents written by Romanov family members, but also a diary—most of it previously unpublished—penned in the Tsar's own hand. "When I found his diaries in the archives—those fantastic diaries that he began when he was 14 and ended three days before his death—I could feel his hands reaching me across a century," the biographer revealed to Sarah Ferrell in the *New York Times Book Review.* Another significant discovery was a firsthand account of the family's killings, written by Yakov Yurovsky, who commanded the executioners. Radzinsky also secured interviews with various individuals associated with the Romanovs and their tragedy, including former servants, acquaintances who lived near the family during its exile, and even descendants of the revolutionaries who slew the family.

The Last Tsar presents a portrait of a ruler unable to handle the complex task of governing Russia in the early twentieth century. By most accounts a kind man, Nicholas was an ineffectual leader. As a commentator for the *Economist* stated, "Nicholas had no grasp of the changes sweeping his own country"; these changes included industrialization and the rise of the middle class. The volatile situation in Russia culminated in revolution, and Tsar Nicholas, Tsarina Alexandra, their five children, and four family servants were captured by the insurgents and moved from town to town in the Ural region. Eventually, they were shot and bayoneted to death in the basement of a house in July of 1918. Radzinsky's account leaves open the possibility that two of the Romanov children, Alexei and Anastasia, may have survived the slaughter. His book also intermingles the story of his investigation with the story of the Romanovs.

Upon its publication in the United States in 1992, *The Last Tsar* became a best-seller and received acclaim from many critics. In a *New York Times Book Review* appraisal, S. Frederick Starr deemed the work "an absorbing tale, the ultimate in last-days-of-the-Romanovs books, and a kind of oncologic report on the disease of history in the last days of the Soviet Union." The biography also garnered praise from Jay Parini, who wrote in the *Los Angeles Times Book Review* that "*The Last Tsar* is an irresistibly readable book. Edvard Radzinsky has done a remarkable job of historical reconstruction, and he has shaped a complex narrative which, in its sweep and particularity, recalls many of the great Russian novels of the 19th Century." *Time* reviewer Brigid O'Hara-Forster lauded *The Last Tsar* as "an unforgettable book in which the evocative power of the dramatist is enriched by scholarship." The account of the killings, she noted, is "a chapter of surpassing sadness and chilling detail."

Other commentators offered more qualified praise. In the *National Review,* David Pryce-Jones remarked that "[t]he entire course of events has been carefully and convincingly reconstructed" and said the book is "a vibrant real-life thriller, though as so often with the genre it is sometimes difficult to follow." *People* contributor Ben Harte asserted that "[c]ompared with Robert Massie's graceful and seamless *Nicholas and Alexandra* of 1967, Radzinsky's rambling narrative sometimes seems cobbled together. But he triumphs in allowing us to hear the voices of protagonists and bit players in diaries (including Nicholas's and Alexandra's), memoirs, letters and oral reminiscences, all of which vividly evoke the imperial twilight and the red dawn."

Stalin: The First In-Depth Biography Based on Explosive New Documents from Russia's Secret Archives is a portrait of the man who ruled the Soviet Union for the 1920s to the 1950s. It traces Stalin's evolution from seminarian to revolutionary to powerful "Boss" of the Soviet regime. It details his role in the revolution, his purges of his enemies within the Communist Party and the military in the 1930s, his leadership of the Soviet Union in World War II, and his postwar campaign against Soviet Jews. It provides new information about his role in the revolution and the events that preceded and followed the 1918 coup; for instance, Radzinsky offers evidence that Stalin may have been a double agent, working both for the Bolsheviks and the Tsarist police. The biography also contends that Stalin was a key aide to Lenin and played a much larger part in the immediate post-revolution era than historians previously believed. Another of Radzinsky's claims is that Stalin tried to provoke another global war in the 1950s. As Paul Richardson stated in *Russian Life,* "Radzinsky asserts that Stalin's 1953 anti-Semitic campaign—the infamous Doctors' Plot—whose immediate goal was mass deportation of Jews to internal exile, was a prelude to his plan to launch a third world war. The Plot would point to foreign imperialists. . . . And the Boss' status as living God would warrant preemptive military attacks." According to Radzinsky, only Stalin's death in 1953 stopped these events from happening; and his death, the biographer speculates, was hastened when Stalin's aides withheld medical treatment after he suffered a stroke.

Richardson found the book valuable but occasionally irritating. "Historians may bridle at Radzinsky's unacademic style of writing," he commented. "And he is good at pulling together compelling, yet circumstantial evidence, then posing intriguing theories that can never be proven or disproven. And he does often confuse the reader by slipping in and out of chronological order to prove a point." *New York Times Book Review* critic Christopher Lehmann-Haupt saw a lack of convincing evidence for many of Radzinsky's claims, including the idea that the anti-Semitic campaign was an effort to start a world war: "[A]s so often happens in this overwrought account, the details make the reader wonder if there may be less here than meets the eye." Also, Lehmann-Haupt complained, Radzinsky raises questions about a plethora of other subjects—Stalin's alteration of his birth date, the circumstances surrounding his wife's and Lenin's deaths—only to reach "anticlimactic conclusions." On the positive side, Lehmann-Haupt observed, Radzinsky uses his experience as a playwright to invest the biography with drama. "Driven by anger . . . and peppered with pungent anecdotes, it sweeps the reader along with its force," the reviewer remarked. Richardson, while voicing some reservations, concluded that "Radzinsky has uncovered many important, new facts and unraveled many mysteries. And he has added some of the clearest evidence yet of Stalin's personal direction of the terror that gripped the USSR for a quarter century."

While Radzinsky's biographical works brought him a new level of prominence in the 1990s, he had long enjoyed considerable popularity as a playwright. As Starr pointed out in the *New York Times Book Review,* Radzinsky is considered "the second most popular playwright in Russia, after [Anton] Chekhov." Radzinsky is known for writing entertaining plays that examine human relationships. Among these works are *Snimayetsya kino,* an exploration of the artist's often antagonistic role in society; *Obolstitel Kolobashkin,* a relatively fantastical play; and "Sporting Scenes of 1981," a well-received drama that revolves around a pair of materialistic married couples.

Among his stage works produced in English translation is 1992's *An Old Actress in the Role of Dostoyevsky's Wife,* about a deranged woman who might possibly be an actress who has played famed writer Fyodor Dostoyevsky's wife. She also recalls other roles from her allegedly illustrious stage career. In turn, she encounters Fedya, an avid gambler who could possibly be Dostoyevsky himself and who wants her to perform a role in one of his plays. "What follows," explained Wilborn Hampton in the *New York Times,* "is not so much a search for what is real in our lives as a metaphysical discourse on the nature of reality itself and whether it even exists apart from one's memories and dreams." Hampton added that the work is "engaging" and contains "flashes of humor and some piercing observations."

BIOGRAPHICAL/CRITICAL SOURCES:

PERIODICALS

Economist, August 29, 1992, p. 79.
Library Journal, July, 1992; April 1, 1996.
Los Angeles Times Book Review, July 26, 1992, pp. 2, 9.
National Review, November 2, 1992, p. 58; July 15, 1996, p. 54.
New York Times, September 19, 1992.
New York Times Book Review, July 19, 1992, pp. 1, 26-27; March 11, 1996.
People, April 6, 1987, p. 20; August 10, 1992, p. 30; October 5, 1992, p. 139.
Publishers Weekly, May 18, 1992, p. 50; November 4, 1996, p. 23.
Russian Life, May, 1996, p. 20.
Time, August 3, 1992, p. 72.
Times (London), July 16, 1992.
Washington Post Book World, August 2, 1992, p. 2.*

* * *

RAPHAEL, Lev 1954-

PERSONAL: Born May 19, 1954, in New York, NY; son of Alex (a limousine driver) and Helen (Klaczko) Steinberg. *Education:* Fordham University at Lincoln Center, B.A., 1975; University of Massachusetts at Amherst, M.F.A., 1978; Michigan State University, Ph.D., 1986. *Politics:* Democrat. *Religion:* Jewish.

ADDRESSES: *Home*—4695 Chippewa Dr., Okemos, MI 48864.

CAREER: Michigan State University, East Lansing, instructor in education, 1983-85, assistant professor of American thought and language, 1985-88; scholar and writer, 1988—. Adjunct instructor, Fordham University at Lincoln Center, 1976-80, and John Jay College of Criminal Justice of the City University of New York, 1979. Intern with Teacher Development and Organizational Change Project, Institute for Research on Teaching, 1984-86; associate editor in College of Education, 1985-86; educational consultant to numerous municipal and state offices in Michigan. Chair of conference on Edith Wharton at Michigan State University, 1990.

AWARDS, HONORS: Harvey Swados Fiction Prize, University of Massachusetts at Amherst, 1977; Reed Smith Prize, *Amelia,* 1988, for "The Life You Have;" Lambda Literary Award, 1990, for *Dancing on Tisha B'av.*

WRITINGS:

(With Gershen Kaufman) *Dynamics of Power: Building a Competent Self,* Schenkman (Cambridge, MA), 1983, revised edition published as *Dynamics of Power: Fighting Shame and Building Self-Esteem,* 1991.

Dancing on Tisha B'Av (short stories), St. Martin's (New York City), 1990.

(With Kaufman) *Stick Up for Yourself: Every Kid's Guide to Personal Power and Positive Self-Esteem,* Free Spirit Press (Minneapolis, MN), 1990, teacher's guide (with Gerry Johnson and Kaufman), 1991.

The Last Novels of Isaac Mayer Wise, University of Alabama Press, 1991.

Edith Wharton's Prisoners of Shame: A New Perspective on Her Neglected Fiction, St. Martin's, 1991.

Winter Eyes: A Novel about Secrets, St. Martin's, 1992.

(With Kaufman) *Coming Out of Shame: Transforming Gay and Lesbian Lives,* Doubleday (New York City), 1996.

Journeys and Arrivals: On Being Gay and Jewish, Faber (Boston), 1996.

Let's Get Criminal: An Academic Mystery, St. Martin's, 1996.

The Edith Wharton Murders, St. Martin's, 1997.

Work represented in anthologies, including *Men on Men 2,* edited by George Stambolian, New American Library, 1988; *Certain Voices,* edited by Darryl Pilcher, Alyson, 1991; and *The Faber Anthology of Short Gay Fiction,* Faber, 1991. Contributor of short stories and articles to scholarly journals, popular magazines, and newspapers, including *Reconstructionist, Christopher Street, Evergreen Chronicles, Commentary, American Imago,* and *Journal of Popular Literature.*

SIDELIGHTS: "The dual identity of being gay and Jewish is [Lev] Raphael's grand theme," according to Ray Olson in *Booklist.* Raphael has written of this theme in such nonfiction titles as *Coming Out of Shame: Transforming Gay and Lesbian Lives* and *Journeys and Arrivals: On Being Gay and Jewish.* In his mystery novels featuring Nick Hoffman, a gay academic, Raphael pokes fun at the pretensions of university life.

In *Coming Out of Shame,* Raphael and co-author Gershen Kaufman "explain how one emotion—shame—affects, overwhelmingly negatively, the lives of homosexuals," as Olson notes in *Booklist.* According to Marny Hall in the *Lambda Book Report,* the authors find the remedy for shame to be "a healthy dose of self-awareness." Olson concludes that *Coming Out of Shame* is "a singularly intelligent example of the psychological self-help game."

Journeys and Arrivals gathers together a number of Raphael's writings, including autobiographical essays first published in magazines. Olson believes that "any of these essays may well become a future anthology piece, for each is that perspicacious and artful, whatever the particular subject." Eric A. Gordon in the *Lambda Book Report* calls the collection "a knowing and loving, if fractionary, autobiography," especially praising Raphael's "poetically sketched portraits of his emotionally deficient father and (later) clinically withdrawn mother."

In his mystery novels, Raphael writes of the fictional State University of Michigan, where Nick Hoffman teaches English. Based in part on Raphael's own experiences teaching at Michigan State University, the Hoffman mysteries revolve around academic rivalries. *Let's Get Criminal* finds Hoffman investigating the murder of a fellow teacher known for his shady past and unscrupulous methods. The critic for *Publishers Weekly* finds that Raphael "delivers literate, witty, mildly suspenseful goods." In *The Edith Wharton Murders,* Hoffman is drawn in when the rivalry between factions in the Wharton academic camp leads to murder. Whitney Scott in *Booklist* calls the novel "a witty, fast-paced gay mystery that is also a hilarious send-up of academia at its quietly snarling worst."

Raphael once told *CA:* "I was born and raised in New York City, the son of Holocaust survivors. Of the thirty short stories I have published, most have appeared in a wide range of Jewish publications. My Jewish and gay stories focus on coming out and finding a lover, coping with the impact of the Holocaust, how gay and straight Jews feel about traditional Judaism, and the place of gay Jews in the Jewish community."

BIOGRAPHICAL/CRITICAL SOURCES:

PERIODICALS

Booklist, January 1, 1996, p. 759; February 1, 1996, p. 902; April 1, 1996, p. 1347; September 1, 1997, p. 66.

Lambda Book Report, July, 1996, p. 13; September-October, 1996, p. 31; February, 1997, p. 33; March, 1998, p. 30.

Los Angeles Times Book Review, November 11, 1990.

Publishers Weekly, February 26, 1996, p. 88.

* * *

RELIS, Harry
See ENDORE, (Samuel) Guy

* * *

RITCHIE-CALDER, Peter Ritchie 1906-1982 (Ritchie Calder)

PERSONAL: Born Peter Ritchie Calder; known after 1966 as Lord Ritchie-Calder, Baron of Balmashannar; born July 1, 1906, in Forfar, Scotland; died January 31, 1982; son of David Lindsay and Georgina (Ritchie) Calder; married Mabel Jane Forbes McKail, 1927; children: Fiona Rudd, Nigel, Angus, Allan, Isla Evans. *Education:* Attended Forfar Academy.

CAREER: Dundee Courier, Dundee, Scotland, police court reporter, 1922-24; *Sunday Post,* Glasgow, Scotland, crime reporter, 1924-26; reporter in London, England for *London Daily News,* 1926-30, *London Daily Chronicle,* 1930, and *London Daily Herald,* 1930-41; science editor, *News Chronicle,* 1945-56; University of Edinburgh, Edinburgh, Scotland, Montague Burton Professor of International Relations, 1961-67; writer and radio and television broadcaster. Charles Beard Lecturer, Ruskin College, Oxford, 1957; Danforth Foundation Lecturer in United States, 1965; Bentwich Lecturer, Hebrew University, 1973; Brodetsky Lecturer, University of Leeds, 1973; visiting professor, Heriot-Watt University, 1973-75. Member of various United Nations delegations and missions, including British delegation to UNESCO, Paris, 1946, and Mexico City, 1947, 1966, and 1968, desert survey mission, 1950, mission to Southeast Asia, 1951 and 1962, the Arctic, 1955, and the Congo, 1960; member of secretariat, Peaceful Uses of Atomic Energy Conference, 1955 and 1958; member, WHO group on mental aspects of atomic energy, 1957. Member of House of Lords Select Committee on Science and Technology, 1980-82. Chair, University of Chicago study group on radiation in the environment, 1960, and United Kingdom Advisory Committee on Oil Pollution of the Sea, 1977-82. Open University, member of planning committee, 1967, member of council, 1969-82; senior fellow, Center for the Study of Democratic Institutions, 1972-75. Special advisor, FAO Famine Conference, 1946; consultant, United Nations Science and Technology Conference, 1963, OXFAM, and U.S. Library of Congress, 1976. President, Mental Health Film Council and National Peace Council. *Military service:* British Foreign Office, director of plans for political warfare, 1941-45, special advisor at supreme headquarters, 1945.

MEMBER: World Academy of Arts and Sciences (fellow), Workers Educational Association (vice-president, 1958-68), Executive United Nations Association, Association of British Science Writers (founder; chair, 1949-55), Royal Society of Arts (fellow), British Sub-Aqua Club (president), Scotland-U.S.S.R. Society (president), American Association for the Advancement of Science (fellow); Society of Visiting Scientists, English Speaking Union, and Savile Club (all London); Scottish Arts Club, University Club (Edinburgh), Edinburgh Press Club, Century Club (New York).

AWARDS, HONORS: Commander of the Order of the British Empire, 1945; Kalinga International Award, 1960, for science writing; New York Public Library Jubilee Medal, 1961; created a life peer (Lord Ritchie-Calder, Baron of Balmashannar) by the Queen of England, 1966, for his professional achievements; Victor Gollancz Award, 1969, for service to humanity; WHO Medical Society Medal, 1974; honorary doctorate, Open University; D.Sc., York University.

WRITINGS:

UNDER NAME RITCHIE CALDER

Birth of the Future, Arthur Barker, 1934.

The Conquest of Suffering, Methuen (London), 1934.

Roving Commission, Methuen, 1935.

Carry On, London, English Universities Press (London), 1941.

The Lesson of London, Secker & Warburg (London), 1941.

Start Planning Britain Now: A Policy for Reconstruction, K. Paul, Trench, Trubner, 1941.

Men against the Desert, Allen & Unwin (London), 1951, 3rd edition, Verry, 1964.

Profile of Science, Allen & Unwin, 1951, Macmillan (New York City), 1952.

Men against Ignorance, UNESCO (New York City), 1953.

Men against the Jungle, Macmillan, 1954.

Born of the Wilderness, News Chronicle (London), 1954.

Science in Our Lives, Michigan State College Press (Lansing, MI), 1954, revised edition, New American Library (New York City), 1962.

Science Makes Sense, Allen & Unwin, 1955.

Men against the Frozen North, Macmillan, 1957.

Medicine and Man: The Story of the Art and Science of Healing, New American Library, 1958.

The Wonderful World of Medicine, Garden City Books (Garden City, NY), 1958, reprinted, Doubleday (Garden City, NY), 1969.

The Hand of Life: The Story of the Weizmann Institute, Weidenfeld & Nicolson (London), 1959.

Agony of the Congo, Gollancz (London), 1961.

After the Seventh Day, Simon & Schuster (New York City), 1961 (published in England as *The Inheritors: The Story of Man and the World He Made,* Heinemann [London], 1961).

The Life Savers, Pan Books (New York City), 1961.

Common Sense about a Starving World, Macmillan, 1962.

Living with the Atom, University of Chicago Press (Chicago, IL), 1962.

Two-Way Passage: A Study of the Give and Take of International Aid, Heinemann, 1964.

Man and the Cosmos: The Nature of Science Today, Praeger (New York City), 1968.

The Evolution of the Machine, American Heritage Publishing (New York City), 1968.

Leonardo and the Age of the Eye, Simon & Schuster, 1970.

The Pollution of the Mediterranean Sea, Herbert Lang, 1972.

How Long Have We Got?, McGill-Queen's University Press (Buffalo, NY), 1972.

The Internationalist in the World of Nationalism, Leeds University Press (Leeds, England), 1973.

Energy: The Fuel of Life, Bantam (New York City), 1979.

(Editor) *The Future of a Troubled World,* Heinemann, 1983.

Also author of booklets for the United Nations and other organizations, including *The Lamp Is Lit,* 1951, and *Ten Steps Forward,* 1958. Member of editorial board, *New Statesman,* 1945-57.

SIDELIGHTS: The late Lord Peter Ritchie-Calder was considered to be a pioneer in the field of "scientific journalism"—that is, the popularization of complex scientific information. His interest in this particular subject began during his early career as a newspaper reporter, when it became evident to him that a huge gap existed between the world of the scientist and that of the layperson. According to E. S. Morison in the *New York Times Book Review,* Calder became "deft in reducing scientific concepts to intelligible simplicity without distorting the essential content." A *Nation* reviewer referred to his work as "the best kind of popularization, inviting, clear, it relies on a mosaic of reference from the whole history of science and plastic art without being patronizing or simplistic."

As a consultant to several specialized United Nations agencies—and as an interested investigator—Calder traveled to nearly all parts of the world. His works range widely over every terrain from the frozen Arctic to the equatorial jungles of South Asia, and his science books treat upon subjects as varied as medicine, chemistry, physics, and mechanics. "Mr. Calder is a superb writer of travelogues, with an eye for significant detail in exotic settings, and a special gift for vivid characterization in a few words," noted Robert Trumbull in the *New York Times.* Likewise, a London *Times* correspondent found Calder's work "not a textbook by an expert but a lively account by a journalist. That is its value."

Calder's reports from far locales include *Men against the Jungle* and *Men against the Frozen North,* both of which describe scientific and medical experiments in challenging environments. In *New Statesman and Nation,* Dorothy Woodman suggested that *Men against the Jungle* "brings to life [the] struggle of men and women in all the countries which lie between the tropical jungles of British Borneo and the remote mountain valleys of Afghanistan." A *Kirkus* reviewer deemed *Men against the Frozen North* "another contribution to Canada's future [which] abounds in good stories of remote regions which are told in personal as well as national terms, and which give a vivid picture of the traditional north in transition."

Calder is perhaps better known for his science books, among them *The Evolution of the Machine, Man and the Cosmos: The Nature of Science Today,* and *Leonardo and the Age of the Eye.* Once again the books range widely, treating such disparate topics as ancient spear design, scientific advances in the Renaissance, and quantum physics. In a review of *Man and the Cosmos, New York Times Book Review* correspondent E. S. Morison wrote: "Probably the most important thing about a book of this sort is that it be both clear and responsible in the report of its information. . . . Calder has furnished accurate accounts of the things he deals with. He has brought off what he sets out to do." In a different *New York Times Book Review* piece, Morison declared *The Evolution of the Machine* "a handsome volume . . . clear and engaging." *Library Journal* contributor Lynda McConnell described the same book as "a distinct success [and a] . . . superior survey history."

His efforts to explain science to popular readers earned Calder a lifetime peerage as Baron of Balmashannar, and he served for many years in England's House of Lords. Following his long career as a journalist, he served as a professor of international relations at Edinburgh University. His later works, one of which was published posthumously, reveal his anxiety over the future of the globe in the face of rampant pollution. His books have been translated into nineteen languages.

BIOGRAPHICAL/CRITICAL SOURCES:

PERIODICALS

Best Sellers, November 1, 1970, p. 302.
Book World, November 29, 1970, p. 5.
Choice, December, 1968, p. 1324; January, 1971, p. 1500.
Christian Science Monitor, June 28, 1954, p. 7.
Kirkus Reviews, October 1, 1957, p. 763.
Library Journal, April 15, 1968, p. 1642; February 15, 1969, p. 882; February 15, 1971, p. 623.
Nation, May 1, 1954, p. 387; December 21, 1970.
Natural History, August, 1968, p. 75.
New Statesman, November 2, 1957, p. 579; December 20, 1968, p. 877.
New Statesman and Nation, March 27, 1954, p. 414.
New York Times, April 25, 1954, p. 18.
New York Times Book Review, June 23, 1968, p. 3.
Observer (London), September 1, 1968.
Pacific Affairs, September, 1954, p. 271.
Spectator, February 21, 1958, p. 239.
Times Literary Supplement, March 12, 1954, p. 173; November 15, 1957, p. 692; October 31, 1968, p. 1228; June 26, 1969; May 14, 1971, p. 552.

OBITUARIES:

Chicago Tribune, February 2, 1982.
New York Times, February 3, 1982.
Times (London), February 2, 1982.*

S

SCHULMAN, Sarah 1958-

PERSONAL: Born July 28, 1958, in New York, NY. *Religion:* Jewish.

ADDRESSES: *Home*—406 East 9th St, New York, NY 10009.

CAREER: Waitress, stagehand, secretary, messenger, and writer. Active in movements for social change, including the peace movement, the reproductive rights movement, the gay liberation movement, and the movement for tenants' rights.

MEMBER: Lesbian Avengers (co-founder).

AWARDS, HONORS: Video grant from Kitchen Media Bureau, 1982; Fulbright fellow, 1984.

WRITINGS:

NOVELS

The Sophie Horowitz Story, Naiad Press (Tallahassee, FL), 1984.
Girls, Visions, and Everything, Seal Press (Seattle, WA), 1986.
After Delores, Dutton (New York City), 1988.
People in Trouble, Dutton, 1990.
Empathy, Dutton, 1992.
Rat Bohemia, Dutton, 1995.

PLAYS

(With Robin Epstein) *Art Failures,* produced in New York City, 1983.
(With Epstein) *Whining and Dining,* produced in New York City, 1984.
(And co-producer) *When We Were Very Young: Radical Jewish Women on the Lower East Side,* produced in New York City, 1984.
(And co-producer) *The Swashbuckler* (based on the story by Lee Lynch), produced in New York City, 1985.
(With Epstein) *Epstein on the Beach* (three-act), produced in New York City, 1985.
Hootenanny Night, produced in New York City, 1986.

OTHER

(Contributor) Melanie Kaye Kantrowitz and Irena Klepfisz, editors, *The Tribe of Dinah: Writings by Jewish Women,* Sinister Wisdom Press, 1985.
(Contributor) Faith Conlon, Rachel Da Silva, and Barbara Wilson, editors, *Things That Divide Us,* Seal Press, 1985.
My American History: Lesbian and Gay Life during the Reagan/Bush Years, Routledge (New York City), 1994.

SIDELIGHTS: Sarah Schulman's work, which includes novels, plays, and a collection of nonfiction articles, is perhaps most notable for the manner in which she gives her readers perspective into the everyday lives of gay and lesbian individuals. Holly Metz gives an introduction to Schulman's style in her article for *Progressive:* "When I called to arrange an interview, Schulman suggested we meet in a cafe in her neighborhood. . . . [that] had been established by waitresses who'd defected from the area's omnipresent Polish/Ukrainian coffee shops and then banded together to start a place of their own. It was the kind of intriguing, class-conscious, real-life detail one finds in a Sarah Schulman novel." Schulman's typical fictional protagonists are "out" lesbians, but, "unlike some gay characters crafted by straight authors or by self-policing gay writers, Schulman's protagonist expresses the full range of human emotion, including rage and jealousy," Metz adds. Kinky Friedman comments in the *New York Times Book Review* that Schulman's 1988 novel *After Delores* "is as raw as fresh-shucked oysters and redolent with ragged charm. The plight of the protagonist is poignantly set out. . . . Ms. Schulman writes with a stumbling grace, and she looks at the world from a fragile, refreshingly jaded angle. It is surprising how long the characters . . . stay with you after you put down the book."

In the *New York Times Book Review,* Edmund White describes Schulman's *Rat Bohemia,* a novel "about a lesbian who is chronicling a community plagued by AIDS," as containing "gimlet-eyed accuracy," "zero-degree honesty," and "charnelhouse humor. AIDS burnout has at last found its bard in Sarah Schulman," White summarizes, adding that "There are few other works of fiction that I could compare with *Rat Bohemia*.. . . Even her own earlier books, like *People in Trouble* and *Empathy,* despite the fact that they, too take place in the East Village and deal with AIDS, carry none of the emotional punch of *Rat Bohemia.* The force of her indignation is savage and has blown the traditional novel off its hinges. If she were contributing to the quilt project, her quilt would be on fire."

Rat Bohemia is a novel that, unusually, is written in four distinct sections. A *Publishers Weekly* critic found the construction disconcerting, remarking that, "other than the presence of the principal characters and a theme of resentment of parents," the story is "a meandering tale of a city so befouled that it leaves the reader wishing for a bath." Vivian Gornick of the *Women's Review of Books* criticizes the novel for unsuccessfully employing the technique of repetition; she writes: "The whole book is a street-smart lament—for these characters the missing parents are an endless devastation—and its problem is the universal problem of the literature of lament. A sense of loss is announced repeatedly, without change and without development." However, Gornick also finds *Rat Bohemia* "oddly moving: It has the power to haunt long after the last page is turned. One feels the melancholy and the grit behind the collective speaking voice."

In an review of Schulman's *My American History: Lesbian and Gay Life during the Reagan/Bush Years* for *Nation,* Jan Clausen notes: "The direct, assertive style and the provocative conclusion . . . are classic Schulman, risking distortion in order to make a valuable point." Another reflection of Schulman's risk-taking as a way to enact change could be seen in 1992, when she and her "major mentor" Maxine Wolfe founded the Lesbian Avenger, a political-action group whose "actions are distinguished by their boldness," according to Metz. Using her book tours to distribute Lesbian Avenger materials, Schulman's organization has spread to several chapters. As Schulman told Metz, "the major goal of the Lesbian Avengers is to transform the lives of the Lesbian Avengers. It's not a vanguardist organization, it's a mass organization . . . the people who are in it are the people who do not have rights, who are trying to win rights for themselves. For them to build community, to learn political skills, to participate in political rebellion, to be a part of a national network, is transforming their own quality of life."

"My goal is to write books with an assumption of lesbianism," Schulman once told *CA,* "so that women who work all week in boring jobs where they have to be in the closet can come home, kick off their shoes, and have something to read that speaks to them. I also see myself in the tradition of populist writing, because my characters are the people who inhabit the urban scenery of New York City but who are rarely recorded in fiction or theater. My audience is composed of the same kind of people who are my characters, and that makes for a very exciting dynamic. My writing has to be emotionally authentic."

BIOGRAPHICAL/CRITICAL SOURCES:

PERIODICALS

Advocate, December 1, 1992, p. 113.
Entertainment Weekly, January 29, 1993, p. 53.
Lambda Book Report, July/August, 1994, p. 16.
Library Journal, January, 1985, p. 89; August, 1995, p. 120.
Los Angeles Times Book Review, January 21, 1990, p. 9; March 7, 1993, p. 11.
Nation, November 14, 1994, p. 583.
New York Times Book Review, May 15, 1988, p. 14; July 8, 1990, pp. 16-17; January 28, 1996, p. 31.
Progressive, October, 1994, p. 37.
Publishers Weekly, October 12, 1984, p. 47; September 19, 1986, p. 139; October 5, 1992, p. 52; September, 25, 1995, p. 44.

San Francisco Review of Books, winter, 1992, p. 28.
Times Literary Supplement, May 3, 1990, p. 456; March 8, 1991, p. 18; December 20, 1991, p. 25; May 14, 1993, p. 24.
Village Voice, August 30, 1988, p. 51; April 17, 1990, p. 79.
Women's Review of Books, March, 1985, pp. 14-15; November, 1994, p. 5: February, 1996, p. 9.*

* * *

SHRIVER, Lionel 1957-

PERSONAL: Born May 18, 1957, in Gastonia, NC; daughter of Donald W. (an ethicist) and Peggy (an administrator for the National Council of Churches; maiden name, Len) Shriver. *Education:* Columbia University, B.A., 1978, M.F.A., 1982.

ADDRESSES: Home—19 Notting Hill, Belfast BT9 5NS, Northern Ireland. *Agent*—Erica Spellman, William Morris Agency, 1350 Avenue of the Americas, New York, NY 10019.

CAREER: Writer. English instructor at various colleges.

MEMBER: PEN, Authors Guild.

WRITINGS:

NOVELS

The Female of the Species, Farrar, Straus (New York City), 1987.
Checker and the Derailleurs, self-illustrated, Farrar, Straus, 1988.
The Bleeding Heart, Farrar, Straus, 1990, published in Britain as *Ordinary Decent Criminals,* HarperCollins (London), 1992.
Game Control, Faber (London), 1994.
A Perfectly Good Family, Faber, 1996.
Double Fault, Doubleday (New York City), 1997.

SIDELIGHTS: Lionel Shriver's first three novels, *The Female of the Species, Checker and the Derailleurs,* and *The Bleeding Heart,* have generated high praise for their energy, imagination, wit, and originality, but are particularly noted for their uncompromisingly lucid, if not at times cynical, perception of human interaction. With a singular emphasis on the charismatic personality, Shriver, who once studied under the renowned anthropologist Margaret Mead at Columbia University, shows a "keen eye for the archetypal characters common to human tribes everywhere," according to *People Weekly* contributor Kim Hubbard. Through her focus on charisma and its accompanying power structures, Shriver exposes what she sees as some of the primitive social dynamics—domination and subordination in academic hierarchy, the "groupie" syndrome in modern music, and thrill-seeking masochism in political activism—that comprise modern civilization. Indeed, Shriver applies her unflinching perspective to her own craft in which, she says, persuasiveness is often taken for truth. "Fiction writers are fakers—it's a trade secret," Shriver said in *Interview* magazine. "The whole idea of novels, in fact, is a conceit, however seductive—as if anyone knows what it's like to be other people. And one of the dangers of all text is that 'truth,' awkwardly put, can seem like a lie, but the dubious assertion will carry because it sounds right." Each of her novels investigates a world in which the powerful but often irrational forces of persuasion rule.

The Female of the Species is the story of highly regarded fifty-nine-year-old anthropologist Gray Kaiser, who is, in her own words, "very tall, and very strong and very brilliant," as quoted from the novel in Ralph Novak's *People* review. Kaiser rose to fame in the 1940s, when she studied a long-lost tribe in Kenya which was under the influence of American pilot Charles Corgie. Corgie, having convinced the tribe that he was a god, briefly shared his power with Kaiser. After a fiasco leading to Corgie's death, however, Kaiser fled back to a more comfortably deified position in the academic world. She returns to Kenya many years later with her longtime platonic living partner and devotee, Errol McEchern, and a young graduate student, Raphael, who is, coincidentally, identical to Corgie in looks and character. In the romantic triangle that arises, the formerly predominant Kaiser subjugates herself to the twenty-five-year-old Raphael, revealing some tortured aspects of human relations.

Critical reaction to *The Female of the Species* was mixed. *Chicago Tribune Books* contributor Celia Hilliard found the novel "convincing, both as a power struggle and a love triangle," but contended that Shriver is "heavy-handed." "Every encounter these characters share is in some way brutal, confused, and painful," she complained. Paul Kincaid, in his *Times Literary Supplement* review, suggested that although the novel "sparkles with ideas,"

Shriver's literary inexperience deters her from answering the provoking questions her work raises. But many critics praised *The Female of the Species* for its accurate, if bleak, representation of life. Novak, calling the work a "terrific first novel," remarked that though disturbing, "it all too often seems all too true."

The world of rock music and a more upbeat protagonist lighten the tone of Shriver's second novel, *Checker and the Derailleurs.* Checker Secretti is a nineteen-year-old drummer in a New York bar band, possessed of such a strong natural charm that people follow him simply to share his joy in life. Checker's magnetism, free of the need and manipulation connected with charisma in *The Female of the Species,* is nevertheless a significant social force that almost magically organizes his followers into harmonious roles around him. In fact, some critics suggested that Checker's appeal beguiles not only the other characters but readers as well. The mysteries that surround Checker's romance with Syria Pyramus, his periodic disappearances, and, most importantly, his unflagging cheerfulness, "keep readers guessing to the end," according to Hubbard. The novel has "adolescent energy and raw appeal," *New York Times Book Review* contributor Margot Mifflin raved. The critic added that "with psychological depth and wry humor" Shriver succeeded in "pulling off a novel that not only works, but rocks."

Shriver's third novel, *The Bleeding Heart,* set in 1988 Northern Ireland, explores the social dynamics of a country perennially at war. The main character, Estrin Lancaster, is a thirty-two-year-old American woman who has spent the last ten years moving from one politically distressed area to another. Living in a bombed-out house on the border between warring Catholic and Protestant neighborhoods in Belfast, she becomes romantically involved with Farrell O'Phelan, a political activist, bomb disposer, and, in the words of Michael Upchurch in his *Washington Post* review, "the most troubled, charismatic character in the place." Even in the danger and self-sacrifice of political rebellion Shriver portrays power as a function of "dubious assertion" rather than heroism. Although Farrell is working tirelessly to unify Catholics and Protestants, he is manipulative, cynical, and masochistic. Like Estrin, he is unwilling or unable to make a commitment and is addicted to the social violence that is a part of everyday existence in Belfast—an atmosphere depicted by Shriver, according to Upchurch, as "partylike." Through the turbulent love affair between Estrin and Farrell in this violent background, the novel explores some frightening manifestations of life in a state of constant crisis.

Shriver's cynicism and an unexpected twist in plot at the end of *The Bleeding Heart* both unnerved and impressed critics. Upchurch observed that "the bracing, acid wit and rich hyperbole are constant and a little terrifying. Who can be this cynical about horrors?" The critic consequently answered: "Shriver can—and for a purpose." Reviewers agreed that Shriver's relentlessly penetrating outlook is gripping and effective in *The Bleeding Heart,* whether or not the reader is comfortable with the picture it paints of human nature. Upchurch hailed this "shrewdly caustic and unexpectedly moving novel" as "challenging, disturbing fiction," which "quivers with enticing energy, seduces you with its nervy amoral appeal."

Game Control, Shriver' fourth novel, is "a sardonic, sexy, salutary novel about, of all things, population control," according to Jonathan Stevenson in *New Scientist.* The book "mixes dark comedy, intellectual sparring, doomsday thrills and psychological scrutiny in a bold and bracing cocktail," remarked *New Statesman and Society* critic Boyd Tonkin. Even though set in Africa, Giles Foden rewarded *Game Control* in *Times Literary Supplement* for "neither trad[ing] on the continent as 'exotica' nor piously making literary capital out of human misery." Stevenson commented that the book "indulges neither the props of the techno-thriller nor the emotional exploitation of the genre suspense yarn," arguing that "Shriver's characters and their aura of feigned sacrifice while living in the Third World simply strike too true a chord." Faulting the novel's characters, *Guardian* contributor Sylvia Brownrigg criticized: "The three [main characters] are not so much people as opportunities for argument. . . . A novel needs an emotional centre, however, not just a line of argument. . . . Shriver . . . is capable of enlivening her stories with slices of vivid prose or surprising description. Ultimately, though, the main characters remain bloodless." Some critics, including Brownrigg, Tonkin, and Stevenson, positively remarked on the appearance of Shriver's intelligence and the true-to-life aspects woven into her story. Foden recognized: "Playing with genres, Shriver encourages the reader to consider serious matters, without serving up tedious ethical fiction, making us aware of shifting issues by shifting our perspective on the action itself."

Shriver's fifth and sixth novels, *A Perfectly Good Family* and *Double Fault,* received mixed reviews from critics. *A Perfectly Good Family* explores the reactions and feelings of three adults with negative memories of their childhood after their mother's death. "The plot moves between detached scenes, and sometimes feels slow," stated Sarah Rigby in *Times Literary Supplement,* continuing: "the characters are believable, but they conform to extreme models." Rigby noted that even though the novel is "inconsistent, Lionel Shriver is clearly a competent writer, and one of her most unambiguous successes is her portrayal of feeling—of the odd, inconstant emotions and the sense of distorted guilt that accompany bereavement." *Double Fault,* called an "earnest narrative" and a "didactic novel" in *Publishers Weekly,* is centered on two professional tennis players; their marriage, and the negative affect of ambitions, competition, and work within the same occupation. "An interesting idea," wrote Jonathan Yardley in *The Washington Post,* but "undone by an artless novel." Yardley specified: "[Shriver] writes well, but she is insufficiently confident of her characters, her plot and her storytelling powers. Her narrative is littered with gratuitous analysis that merely serves to get in the story's way, and toward the end she reaches the novelist's avenue of last resort: She brings a psychologist onto the scene." In contrast, the *Publishers Weekly* critic believes that Shriver is successful with *Double Fault*'s theme, and "all too well" presents "a cautionary tale about the fatal mix of love and ambition." *Library Journal*'s Nancy Pearl commented: "Shriver is a talented enough writer to win over some readers, but many will lose patience with Willy [the story's main female character]."

BIOGRAPHICAL/CRITICAL SOURCES:

PERIODICALS

Guardian, May 3, 1994, section 2, p. 13.
Interview, July, 1987.
Library Journal, July, 1997, p. 128.
New Scientist, April 30, 1994, p. 43.
New Statesman and Society, April 29, 1994.
New York Times Book Review, July 19, 1987; July 24, 1988.
People Weekly, April 27, 1987; July 4, 1988.
Publishers Weekly, June 30, 1997, p. 65.
Times Literary Supplement, March 18, 1988; April 15, 1994, p. 23; April 19, 1996, p. 24.
Tribune Books (Chicago), April 19, 1987.
Washington Post, August 6, 1997, p. C4.
Washington Post Book World, November 20, 1990.*

SMITH, Lillian (Eugenia) 1897-1966

PERSONAL: Born December 12, 1897, in Jasper, FL; died of cancer, September 28, 1966, in Atlanta, GA; daughter of Calvin Warren (in business) and Anne (Simpson) Smith. *Education:* Attended Piedmont College, 1915-16, Peabody Conservatory, 1917-22, and Columbia University, 1927-28. *Politics:* Liberal Democrat.

CAREER: Virginia School, Huchow, Chekiang, China, music teacher, 1922-25; Laurel Falls Camp for Girls, Clayton, GA, director, 1925-48; founder, editor, and publisher of magazine titled successively, *Pseudopodia, North Georgia Review,* and *South Today,* 1936-46; *Chicago Defender,* Chicago, IL, columnist, 1948-49; representative in India of United States State Department, 1954-55; *Chicago Tribune,* Chicago, book reviewer, 1964-66. Taught creative writing at University of Indiana and University of Colorado; lectured at Vassar College, 1955. Rabun County (GA) Hospital, board member, founder of hospital auxiliary. Member, American Famine Commission, 1946.

MEMBER: American Civil Liberties Union (former vice-president; member of the national board), Congress of Racial Equality (member of advisory board; resigned, 1966), Author's Guild, PEN.

AWARDS, HONORS: Julius Rosenwald Foundation fellowship, 1939, 1940; Page One Award, 1944, and Constance Skinner Lindsay Award for "best book by a woman," 1945, both for *Strange Fruit;* Southern Award, 1949, for *Killers of the Dream;* L.H.D., Howard University, 1950; L.H.D., Oberlin College, 1950; L.H.D., Atlanta University, 1957; Sidney Hillman Award for magazine writing, 1962; citation from National Book Award Committee for "distinguished contribution to American letters."

WRITINGS:

Strange Fruit (novel), Reynal (New York City), 1944.
(With Esther Smith) *Strange Fruit* (play; adapted from the novel of same title), produced in New York City, 1945.
Killers of the Dream, Norton (New York City), 1949, revised edition, Doubleday (New York City), 1963.
The Journey, World Publishing (Cleveland), 1954.
Now Is the Time, Viking (New York City), 1955.

One Hour (novel), Harcourt (New York City), 1959, with an introduction by Margaret Rose Gladney, University of North Carolina Press (Chapel Hill), 1994.
Memory of a Large Christmas (autobiography), Norton, 1962.
Our Faces, Our Words, Norton, 1964.
The Journey, Norton, 1965.
From the Mountain: An Anthology of the Magazine Successively Titled Pseudopodia, the North Georgia Review, and South Today, Memphis State University Press, 1972.
The Winner Names the Age: A Collection of Writings, edited by Michelle Cliff, Norton, 1978.
How Am I to be Heard?: Letters of Lillian Smith, edited by Margaret Rose Gladney, University of North Carolina Press, 1993.

Contributor to *Saturday Review, Redbook, Life, New Republic, Nation,* and *New York Times.* Collections of Smith's manuscripts are housed at the University of Florida Libraries, Gainesville, the University of Georgia Libraries, Athens, and the Robert W. Woodruff Library, Emory University, Atlanta, GA.

SIDELIGHTS: Lillian Smith, according to Gary Richards in *Gay and Lesbian Literature,* "was unique among writers of the mid-twentieth century American South for any number of reasons, perhaps the most significant of which was her political activism to combat racism before and during the Civil Rights Movement. . . . Smith stridently condemned the forced separation of races and demanded its immediate end, often much to the irritation of fellow white southerners." Smith's novel *Strange Fruit,* the story of a love affair between a white man and a black woman, brought her notoriety for its frank language and explosive theme.

Strange Fruit, published in 1944, was a book destined for the best-seller lists because of attempts to suppress it. It was "unofficially" banned in Boston and Detroit; used as a test-case by Bernard De Voto in Cambridge, Massachusetts; banned from the mails by an ambitious U.S. postal clerk; and caused a fellow townsman of Smith's to remark: "I'll give you the real facts. Miss Lil is a deeply religious woman. She would never have written that vulgar sexy stuff. Her publishers wrote it. They stuck it in to make the books sell."

The novel told of the love of an educated black girl, Nonnie Anderson, for a white man, Tracy Dean, with murder and lynching a result of that love. Smith presented the couple's sexual relations in graphic scenes which shocked many reviewers. The loud protestations in the North centered around Smith's use of a four-letter word that was regarded as unprintable in 1944. Said Joseph McSorley in the *Catholic World:* "Presumably for the purpose of appealing to a vulgar multitude, she sins against good taste so grossly as to make her story quite unfit for general circulation. It seems curious enough that 'the daughter of one of the South's oldest families' should . . . employ phrases which decent people regard as unprintable." Edward Weeks differed strongly: "I find nothing in the novel that is pornographic. . . . Without the shock, I doubt if the moral would have gone home. At the speed things are moving today, I suspect we shall be needing a new *Uncle Tom's Cabin* for each decade. This one comes from the South, and this time New England seems afraid of it."

Richards pointed out that "miscegenation was and is not, however, the only representation of sexuality to disturb readers. The subplot of *Strange Fruit* features Tracy's sister, Laura, and her homoerotically-charged relationship with Jane Hardy, an older woman who functions as a surrogate mother to Laura since her own mother is cold, calculating, and incessantly preoccupied with social propriety. Smith encodes the eroticism of Jane and Laura's relationship in a clay figurine of a naked woman that Laura sculpts with Jane as her model. Thus, when Alma Deen, Laura's mother, destroys the sculpture, Smith symbolically represents the forces of homophobia and compulsory heterosexuality."

Protest against the novel in the South was not concerned so much with the novel's sexual undercurrent as with its story of racial confrontation. Smith noted that "the lunatic fringe of the fascist groups and the White supremacy crowd . . . were writing editorials and reviews that *Strange Fruit* advocates the mongrelizing of the white race. . . . The *Southern Watchman* screamed in headlines that Alabama must not vote for Roosevelt because the author of *Strange Fruit* once wrote a piece in praise of our President. . . . I thought of my book as a fable about a son in search of a mother, about a race in search of surcease from pain and guilt—both finding what they sought in death and destruction. So when people ask 'Is *Strange Fruit* a race book; is it about the Negro problem?' I say, 'I don't think so.' For it seems to me a book about human beings journeying also back to childhood, always back to the room where they were born, seeking to find, wherever they travel, that which they left there, so long ago."

Smith's novel *One Hour* also includes portraits of gay sexuality. Ostensibly concerned with a girl who accuses a scientist of sexual assault, the novel also tells of the scientist's wife and her hidden relationship with a lesbian lover. Richards explained: "Mark's wife, Grace, confesses to the novel's narrator of a youthful affair with an unnamed camp counselor, designated only as the Woman. It is with horror that Grace eventually realizes that the Woman who taught her 'about tenderness and passion' at the camp, 'who had seemed to her to have come out of a myth, who did not quite belong in the ordinary world, was nothing but a homosexual.' After much struggle with her own sexuality, Grace assumes a heterosexual identity and seemingly exorcises the memory of the Woman. When news of the Woman's suicide reaches Grace, however, she breaks down, forced to admit how much the relationship has meant to her."

Smith once told *CA:* "My deep concern in writing is not simply race relations but the curious and dramatic and subtle ways men have of dehumanizing themselves and others. This is my real theme; and I am fascinated by the deep meanings attached to the word, *segregation.* My writings tend toward depth analysis, the philosophic and ethical implications of segregation, the curious ideas about the body image, etc. I am not a 'reformer' and hate organizations and groups, although sometimes my conscience makes me do chores for them."

This same conscience could also cause her to break relations with an organization. She had worked with the Congress on Racial Equality (CORE) for twenty years but resigned in 1966 when she could no longer sanction its militancy. In a letter to Floyd B. McKissick, CORE's national director, she wrote: "I strongly protest the dangerous and unwise position CORE has taken on the use of violence in effecting racial change. . . . CORE has been infiltrated by adventurers and by nihilists, black nationalists and plain old-fashioned haters, who have finally taken over." She described the new leaders of CORE as "new killers of the dream. . . . We are working for something bigger than civil rights. We are working for better human beings, we are working for excellence in our cultural life."

Smith's personal life evolved around operations, cobalt treatments, and hormone treatments. "I have been struggling with cancer since 1953," she wrote *CA* in 1963, "but during this time have written four books, partially written several others, lectured a number of times, been on television and radio, made tapes, and even went to India for five months. I still have cancer but find it rather a friendly enemy to live with. I have often said more people die of fear of cancer than of the cancer itself; I cannot 'prove' that, but I believe it." She had weaker moments in her prolonged fight as is evidenced in a letter to a friend: "One wants to yowl, sometimes, at this never-ending struggle. It has to be; God, I wish I were as courageous as my friends think I am. But when I can work I am happy and content."

Smith was also "happy and content" with her surroundings. "My home is on a lovely old mountain in north Georgia, where, in spite of my 'controversial' books, the people are friendly and also take me seriously enough to read me. Large quantities of my books are sold in my home town. I love the quietness of the mountain. It affords me a needed seclusion for writing, thinking, studying, painting, listening to music; but I get out into the world often, get into all sorts of activities, know people from the top crust to the bottom ooze; it is my job to, as a writer; but it is also my pleasure to find ways of relating myself to all kinds of people, mean, nasty, bigoted, brave, warm, human, ignorant, brilliant, 'normal' and 'abnormal'—two words I do not believe in."

While discussing her stature as a person and a writer, Smith wrote: "I am small, in height and weight; am called 'vivid, warm, unpretentious.' And this is true, I think; but I have a devil of a temper if people really get too mean; I hate the idea of being a martyr myself and do not like to stress my 'difficult times.' After all, who doesn't have them? After *Strange Fruit,* tons of stuff was written about me. Some fantastic things have been written, too. I have in recent years been 'smothered' somewhat; the critics don't know how to categorize me—and in this age not to be able to file somebody away in a category or pinch them into a stereotype is the signal to bury them! I feel I have been influenced greatly by Dostoevsky, Kafka, and to a certain extent by Freud, Jung, Fromn, Erik Erikson, Maritain, and Charles Williams. Camus I admire; I have not been influenced by him. Faulkner I do not admire; too superficial and anti-woman."

BIOGRAPHICAL/CRITICAL SOURCES:

BOOKS

Blackwell, Louise, and Frances Clay, *Lillian Smith,* Twayne Publishers (New York City), 1971.

Daniel, Bradford, editor, *Black, White and Gray,* Sheed & Ward, 1964.
Downs, Robert B., editor, *The First Freedom,* American Library Association, 1966.
Gay and Lesbian Literature, Volume 2, St. James Press (Detroit), 1998.
Loveland, Anne C., *Lillian Smith, A Southerner Confronting the South: A Biography,* Louisiana State University Press (Baton Rouge), 1986.
Smith, Lillian, *How Am I To Be Heard?: Letters of Lillian Smith,* University of North Carolina Press, 1993.
Sosna, Morton, *In Search of the Silent South: Southern Liberals and the Race Issue,* Columbia University Press (New York City), 1977.
Sullivan, Margaret, *A Bibliography of Lillian Smith and Paula Snelling,* Memphis State University, 1971.

PERIODICALS

Atlantic Monthly, May, 1944.
Catholic World, May, 1944.
Christian Century, October 2, 1957.
Collier's, January 28, 1950.
Life, December 15, 1961.
Newsweek, May 29, 1944.
New York Times, July 6, 1966.
New York Herald Tribune Book Review, October 30, 1949.
Publishers Weekly, March 25, 1944; May 27, 1944; December 2, 1944.
Saturday Review, February 17, 1945; October 22, 1966.
Time, March 20, 1944.*

* * *

STAMBOLIAN, George 1938-1991

PERSONAL: Born April 10, 1938, in Bridgeport, CT; died of complications resulting from AIDS, December 22, 1991, in New York, NY; son of John George (a tailor) and Rose (Alboyagian) Stambolian. *Education:* Dartmouth College, B.A., 1960; University of Wisconsin, M.A., 1961, Ph.D., 1969; also studied at Sorbonne, University of Paris, 1962-63. *Avocational interests:* Archaeology, diplomatic and military history, modern art.

CAREER: Wellesley College, Wellesley, MA, 1965-91, began as assistant professor, became professor of French and comparative literature, chair of department of French, 1975-78.

MEMBER: Modern Language Association of America, American Association of University Professors, Societe des Amis de Marcel Proust, Proust Research Association, Beckett Society, Northeast Theatre Conference, Phi Beta Kappa.

WRITINGS:

Marcel Proust and the Creative Encounter, University of Chicago Press (Chicago), 1972.
(Editor) *Twentieth Century Fiction: Essays for Germaine Bree,* Rutgers University Press (New Brunswick, NJ), 1975.
(Editor with Elaine Marks) *Homosexualities and French Literature: Cultural Contexts, Critical Texts,* Cornell University Press (Ithaca, NY), 1979.
Male Fantasies/Gay Realities: Interviews with Ten Men, SeaHorse Press (New York City), 1984.

EDITOR

Men on Men: Best New Gay Fiction, New American Library (New York City), 1986.
Men on Men 2: Best New Gay Fiction, New American Library, 1988.
Men on Men 3: Best New Gay Fiction, Dutton (New York City), 1990.
Men on Men 4: Best New Gay Fiction, Dutton, 1992.

OTHER

Contributor to *Journal of Popular Culture* and *Christopher Street.*

SIDELIGHTS: George Stambolian, although he taught French literature and contemporary drama at Wellesley College for over twenty-five years, was better known for his championing of gay literature and art. He edited the first volume of *Men on Men,* a series of anthologies of gay male fiction that spotlighted the works of leading gay writers like Edmund White, Ethan Mordden and Felice Picano. Writing in the *New York Times,* Esther B. Fein called Stambolian "an acclaimed editor of gay literature."

Writing in *Gay and Lesbian Literature,* Michael A. Lutes described Stambolian as "an advocate and leader for the recognition of the field of gay literature." Stambolian, Lutes explained, "believed he could reinvigorate the field of American literature by contesting its underlying social and literary assumptions. He provided the initial link between two unrelated spheres: academia and the gay community. He acted as a catalyst for the development of the field of gay literature, and its exponential growth. Because of Stambolian's work gay studies is now taught in schools, giving access to an ever widening audience, who previously lacked the availability to such materials. Gay fiction opened doors to a diverse community whose identity could no longer be ignored."

BIOGRAPHICAL/CRITICAL SOURCES:

BOOKS

Gay and Lesbian Literature, Volume 2, St. James Press (Detroit), 1998.

PERIODICALS

Christopher Street, March, 1980.
New York Times, April 22, 1992.

OBITUARIES:

PERIODICALS

Boston Globe, December 24, 1991.
Christopher Street, Volume 14, number 17, 1992.
Lambda Book Report, March/April, 1992.
New York Times, December 26, 1991, p. D14.*

* * *

STARR, John
See COUNSELMAN, Mary Elizabeth

* * *

STARR, Kevin 1940-

PERSONAL: Born September 3, 1940, in San Francisco, CA; raised in an orphanage, Mendocino County; son of Owen Lee (a production machinist) and Marian Elizabeth (a bank employee; maiden name, Collins) Starr; married Sheila Gordon, June 10, 1963; children: Marian, Jessica. *Education:* Attended a Roman Catholic seminary; University of San Francisco, B.A., 1962; Harvard University, M.A., 1965, Ph.D., 1969; University of California, Berkeley, M.L.S., 1974.

ADDRESSES: Home—445 Chestnut St., San Francisco, CA 94133.

CAREER: Harvard University, Cambridge, MA, assistant professor, 1969-73, associate professor of American literature, 1973-74; San Francisco city librarian, 1973-76; Hearst Newspapers, New York City, daily columnist for San Francisco *Examiner,* 1976-83, correspondent covering Rome and the Vatican, 1978; University of San Francisco, San Francisco, CA, professor of communication arts, 1982—, director of Davies Forum, 1983—; Kevin Starr Associates (communications and development consulting firm), proprietor and principal, 1983-85; State Librarian of California, 1994—; University of Southern California, professor of urban and regional planning in School of Planning and Development, from at least 1994.

University of California, Berkeley, visiting associate professor of English, 1974; San Francisco State University, adjunct professor of humanities, 1975-76; University of California, Berkeley, visiting lecturer in political science, 1976; University of California, Riverside, regents' lecturer in political science, 1977; University of Santa Clara, adjunct professor of English, 1977; University of California, Davis, visiting professor of history, 1985-86.

Executive aide to mayor of San Francisco, worked as a speech writer, 1973; consultant in communications, marketing, and public relations with Beyl & Boyd, 1979-83, Hill & Knowlton USA, 1983-84, Continental Development Corp., 1983—, and Montgomery Gallery, 1985—; San Francisco Taxicab Association, executive director, 1983—; trustee of American Issues Forum, 1975-76, San Francisco Art Institute, 1976, Cathedral School for Boys, 1980-81, and Graduate Theological Union, 1985—; Junior League of San Francisco, adviser, 1982-84; San Francisco/Sydney Sister City Committee, cochair, 1982—; California Library Services Boards, chief executive officer; California Gold Discovery to Statehood Sesquicentennial Commission, chair. Campaigned for the San Francisco Board of Supervisors. *Military service:* U.S. Army, Armor, 1962-64; served in tank battalion in Germany; became lieutenant.

MEMBER: American Studies Association, California Historical Society, California Council of the Humanities, Catholic Commission on Intellectual and Cultural Affairs (member of executive committee, 1985—), Thomas More-Jacques Maritain Institute, Friends of the Bancroft Library, Gleeson Library Associates, Harvard Clubs of New York City and San Francisco, Harvard Graduate Society, Chit Chat Club of San Francisco, Bohemian Club of San Francisco, Olympic Club of San Francisco.

AWARDS, HONORS: Danforth fellowship, 1964-69; *Americans and the California Dream, 1850-1915* was selected by *Time* magazine as one of the best books of 1973, and it won the 1974 gold medal for nonfiction from the Commonwealth Club of California; bicentennial fellowship from the government of Australia, 1976; Guggenheim fellowship, 1976-77; Huntington Library fellow, 1977; D.Litt. from Golden Gate University, 1982; faculty research award from the University of San Francisco, 1985; honorary doctorate from St. Mary's College of California, 1986.

WRITINGS:

"AMERICANS AND THE CALIFORNIA DREAM" SERIES

Americans and the California Dream, 1850-1915, Oxford University Press, 1973.

Inventing the Dream: California Through the Progressive Era, Oxford University Press, 1985.

Material Dreams: Southern California through the 1920's, Oxford University Press, 1990.

Endangered Dreams: The Great Depression in California, Oxford University Press, 1996.

The Dream Endures: California Enters the 1940s, Oxford University Press, 1997.

CONTRIBUTOR

James P. Walsh, editor, *The San Francisco Irish, 1850-1976,* Irish Literary and Historical Society of San Francisco, 1978.

William Bentinck-Smith, editor, *The Harvard Book: Selections From Three Centuries,* Harvard University Press (Cambridge, MA), 1982.

San Francisco: Photographs by Morton Beebe, Abrams (New York City), 1985.

Claudia K. Jurmain and James J. Rawls, editors, *California: A Place, a People, a Dream,* Chronicle Books (San Francisco), 1986.

AUTHOR OF FOREWORD

Lawrence Clark Powell, *An Orange Grove Boyhood: Growing Up in Southern California, 1910-1928,* Capra (Santa Barbara, CA), 1988.

Stephen Vincent, editor (with art selection by Paul Mills), *O California!: Nineteenth and Early Twentieth Century California Landscapes and Observations,* Bedford Arts (San Francisco), 1990.

Santi Visalli, photographer, *San Francisco,* Rizzoli (New York City), 1990.

Bill Pickelhaupt (edited by Judith Robinson), *Shanghaied in San Francisco,* Flyblister Press (San Francisco), 1996.

OTHER

Land's End (novel), McGraw (New York City), 1979.

California!, Peregrine Smith (Layton, UT), 1980.

The Literature of California, Boyd & Fraser (San Francisco), 1986.

The Dream Endures: Value and Expression in California During the Great Depression, Oxford University Press, 1987.

The Rise of Los Angeles as an American Bibliographical Center, California State Library Foundation (Sacramento), 1989.

Over California (photography by Reg Morrison), Collins (San Francisco), 1990.

(With Mark Renneker and Geoff Booth) *Sick Surfers Ask the Surf Docs & Dr. Geoff,* Bull (Palo Alto, CA), 1993.

Senior editor of *New West,* 1976-77; contributing editor to *Los Angeles Times;* contributor of articles to newspapers and magazines.

SIDELIGHTS: A central theme in Kevin Starr's multi-volume history of California, published by Oxford University Press, is how myth and reality combined to shape the development of the Golden State. In *Americans and the California Dream* the author focuses on the northern part of the state and particularly San Francisco, the first center of Anglo-California culture. Starr interprets the history and lore of the region through the writings of such early Californians as novelists Jack London and Mary Austin and philosopher Josiah Royce. He shows how from its earliest days as a state California was seen as a land of promise and opportunity, the bountiful and exotic last western frontier, and how many of the state's leading intellectuals and opinion makers cultivated this image.

Among the various elements that combined to form the California dream, Starr notes, were the lure of gold; the tremendous potential for ranching, agriculture, and lumber; and a Mediterranean climate matched with a landscape of extraordinary beauty, which attracted tourists and others seeking good health and spiritual inspiration. Though reality shattered many individual dreams, he explains, the myth of California endured, beckoning to many thousands of migrants during the state's first fifty years. *Americans and the California Dream* concludes with a description of the San Francisco Exposition of 1915, a celebration of the city's growth and prosperity.

Time selected *Americans and the California Dream* as one of the best books of 1973, while *Nation* critic John Caughey called the book "informative and provocative on a vast number of points." Caughey further remarked that it is "written with verve [and] it offers dozens of gemlike essays within its chapters."

Starr's second book for Oxford, *Inventing the Dream: California Through the Progressive Era,* covers the southern part of the state, including Los Angeles, during roughly the same historical period as the first volume. Unlike the north, Starr points out, southern California had a strong cultural legacy from its long period of settlement by Spaniards and Mexicans, as well as from its Native American inhabitants. He observes that the pattern of land holdings during the period of early statehood reflected this heritage, as the vast Mexican cattle ranches were taken over largely intact by Anglo business interests. As a result, the author notes, small holdings never predominated in southern California, even though the promise of land was one of the early myths that drew migrants to the state.

Starr also examines how cultural and political influences shaped the region. Novelist Helen Hunt Jackson and journalist Charles Fletcher Lummis, for example, romanticized the state's Spanish past, which helped inspire the "mission revival" style of architecture and give California an exotic allure. The Progressive political movement that sprang up in California in the early twentieth century to fight the power of the railroad oligarches, meanwhile, brought about the enactment of a wide range of political reforms and created an image of innovation for the state. Finally, the extraordinarily rapid rise of Hollywood from a middle-class suburb to the world capital of the film industry completed the transformation of southern California into a fantasy land.

Los Angeles Times Book Review critic John Patrick Diggins called *Inventing the Dream* "romance scrupulously documented" and added, "It is vividly written, thoroughly researched, rich in details and alive with interesting, and sometimes, incredible, people." In the *New York Times Book Review,* Wallace Stegner wrote: "The grasp is sure, the learning awesome. The prose . . . has a drive that carries cities and industries and people and decades headlong toward their manifest destiny." The critic concluded, "Posterity is not going to forget this book. For better or for worse, California is not through imagining itself; and definitely for better, Kevin Starr is not through analyzing and reporting the process." In his third book in this series *Material Dreams: Southern California through the 1920s* Starr examines the way in which California social planners' dreams came to fruition. He describes how Los Angeles was transformed into the nation's fifth largest city, tripling its population through the 1920s, and how the groundwork was laid for even greater postwar development. Focusing on water engineering, architecture, culture, land development, and the creation of public agencies, he explores the conflicts between public and private interests and contrasts the development of Santa Barbara with that of Los Angeles. In *The Atlantic* James Fallow says that "Starr retells the water saga in a gripping, vivid way, clearly showing the different moral visions that lay behind different irrigation schemes." He criticizes Starr for using scholarly jargon but concludes that "[m]ost of the time, however, Starr tells his story in strong, clear prose." In *Christian Science Monitor* Merle Rubin concurs stating that "Starr demonstrates a firm grasp on each of the many diverse, often conflicting, tendencies at work in shaping the complex, contradictory world of southern California."

The fourth volume in Starr's "Americans and the California Dream" series, *Endangered Dreams: The Great Depression in California,* "depicts in colorful prose and vivid detail the political conflicts and physical transformations that engulfed California during the Great Depression," stated noted historian William H. Chafe in the *New York Times Book Review.* The book focuses on the struggle between the right and the left, with Starr positing that California was a magnified example of the larger American experience. Chafe notes that Starr's propensity to see the California experience as a metaphor for the nation allows for a "tendency to oversimplify." While Chafe praised Starr's "powerful personal portraits," he conceded that the author sometimes slips into caricature and blanket summarizations. Writing in the *Los Angeles Times Book Review* T. H. Watkins argued that this book is the best in the series and praised Starr's extensive list of sources, his mastery of the narrative tradition, and his coverage of the communist orchestrated agricultural strikes. While he noted that Starr does not always get his details correct, Watkins praised "the triumph of narration and understanding that Starr has given us in the crowded, surprisingly lively pages of Endangered Dreams."

In *The Dream Endures: California Enters the 1940s,* Starr concentrates on the brighter side of California around the time of the Great Depression. The author argues in this fifth volume that in the 1930s Californians were setting the lifestyle and the pursuit of leisure which would be embraced nationwide in the postwar era. In the *New Republic,* Richard White stated that "it is still startling to discover that the California of the Depression years that matters most to Starr is the California of Palm Springs, Carmel, San Diego and Pasadena." However, noted historian and *New York Times Book Review* contributor James T. Patterson commended Starr's focus on the happier side of the Depression in noted contrast to other historians' accounts of misery and blight.

Patterson argued, however, that while Starr describes the activities of elite Californians, he does not provide evidence that this influenced the rest of the nation. Patterson added that Starr "chooses to lavish his attention on well-known individuals who have captured his interest. The activities of more ordinary members of the middle classes tend to slip from view." Patterson concluded that historians must provide more than anecdotal stories and "undisciplined" arguments. In the *Los Angeles Times Book Review,* Herbert Gold presented a favorable review of *The Dream Endures,* stating that Starr "is writing more than a history, but also a philosophical study of the meaning of California." A reviewer for *Kirkus Reviews* pronounced it "[a] penetrating addition to an altogether splendid series, which (thanks to the broad appeal of its subject matter and period) could prove a breakout book."

Throughout the course of his "Americans and the California Dream" series, Gold wrote, "Starr has developed his ability to dramatize the story." Gold concluded that "in his various roles as a professor, lecturer, library official and occasional political aspirant, Kevin Starr is known for his passionate discourses on everything to do with California, from its history to its ecology, its turbulence, its continual promise and the dream of California as a far reach of American dreaming. Fluency of discourse causes impatience in some, but Starr's great ease is matched by a rarer gift: He makes sense."

Starr once told *CA:* "After a decade in the worlds of business and journalism, I am refocusing my energies more exclusively upon historical writing and research. I am never so happy as when I am researching and writing the American past."

BIOGRAPHICAL/CRITICAL SOURCES:

PERIODICALS

American Libraries, November, 1973.
Atlantic, March 1990, pp. 108-11.
Christian Science Monitor, June 12, 1990, p. 12.
Kirkus Reviews, February 1, 1997, p. 209.
Los Angeles Times Book Review, March 24, 1985; January 21, 1996, pp. 1, 10; June 15, 1997, p. 6; November 19, 1994, p. A1.
Nation, October 1, 1973.
New Republic, December 1, 1997, pp. 38-48.
Newsweek, May 27, 1985.
New Yorker, August 12, 1985.
New York Times, February 13, 1985.
New York Times Book Review, August 5, 1973; December 2, 1973; February 24, 1985; February 18, 1996, p. 19; April 20, 1997, p. 26.
San Diego Daily, November 1, 1997.
San Francisco Chronicle, August 31, 1994.

* * *

STERLING, Anthony
See CAESAR, (Eu)Gene (Lee)

* * *

STRAUS, Dorothea 1916-

PERSONAL: Born November 25, 1916, in New York, NY; daughter of Alfred (a brewer and engineer) and Alma (Wallach) Liebmann; married Roger W. Straus, Jr. (a publisher), June 27, 1938; children: Roger W. III. *Education:* Sarah Lawrence College, B.A., 1938. *Politics:* Democrat.

ADDRESSES: *Home*—160 East 65th St., New York, NY 10021. *Agent*—Robert Lescher, 155 East 71st St., New York, NY 10021.

WRITINGS:

Thresholds: Memories of Growing Up, Houghton (Boston), 1971.
Showcases (memoirs), Bodley Head (London), 1975, *Palaces and Prisons* (memoirs), Houghton, 1976.
Under the Canopy (memoirs), G. Braziller (New York City), 1982.

The Birthmark: A Novel (novel), G. Braziller, 1987.

Virgins and Other Endangered Species: A Memoir (memoirs), Moyer Bell, (Wakefield, RI), 1993.

The Paper Trail: A Recollection of Writers (memoirs), Moyer Bell, 1997.

Contributor to national periodicals, including *Harper's* and *Cosmopolitan.*

SIDELIGHTS: Although Dorothea Straus has written a novel, *The Birthmark,* her career as a writer rests on her published memoirs. In her many volumes of memoirs, she presents and explores her German-Jewish ancestry and the people and places associated with her affluent New York childhood. *Thresholds: Memories of Growing Up* is a book of reminiscences "interesting" for "attempting through them to work out for herself the relationship between past and present. . . . [where] remembered past and the imagined, second hand past have equal status," wrote a critic for the *Times Literary Supplement.* A reviewer for *Vogue* writes: "*Thresholds* . . . is nostalgic, but its fragrances are fresh. [Dorothea Straus] does not condemn the present time nor does she in any belligerent way campaign for the restitution of time past. . . . She pauses on the thresholds of many rooms, regarding the appointments and the occupants from angles of refraction that differ with her age and with her recollected mood and with judgments emended by hindsight. Some of the interiors do not exist for her in fact, but have come into the possession of her memory through family stories handed down, diminished and bedimmed by time, or enlarged and illuminated by romantic yearning. . . . Mrs. Straus likens herself to an archeologist in reconstructing the scenes of her forbears' enterprise and tribulations, the forests of much ramified trees that intertwined." Reviewers noted that despite some overstated descriptions, as well as some unclear descriptions, readers are drawn into the book.

"It is her faculty for enthusiasm for a new person of a new cause which gives her writing its very individual intensity," remarked Victoria Glendinning in a *Times Literary Supplement* review of *Showcase,* the sequel to Straus's first memoir. Helen Bevington, writing in the *New York Times Book Review,* described Straus's method in *Thresholds:* "as anecdotal, entertaining, above all searching. Mrs. Straus examines and interprets people to discover what they have meant to her." Not all reviewers, however, have reacted favorably to Straus's writing. "*Showcases,*" argued Glendinning, "could fairly be criticized as being appallingly overwritten. She has the ingenuousness which is both a strength and a weakness."

Continuing her first two memoirs, *Palaces and Prisons* contains "nimbly evocative fragments of a richly interesting life" which, according to Pearl K. Bell in the *New York Times Book Review,* "are as skillful as anything in Mrs. Straus's earlier books, but she also attempted, mistakenly, to make the present volume a different and more ambitious work." Bell specified: "Instead of allowing her versions of the recaptured past to stand on their own, she has interleaved the blocks of actuality with quasi-surrealist episodes of an imaginary cruise." This voyage, argued Bell "seems a pointless distraction from the landscape of the past which Dorothea Straus has explored with intelligence and power." In a *New York Times* review of *Palaces and Prisons,* Christopher Lehmann-Haupt wrote: "There is more to this memoir of places and people than coincidental pleasure or pain. The book has something to do with success or failure at putting down roots in America, something to do with the very idea of rootedness in place."

Straus has published several memoirs which are separate from her original trilogy. *Under the Canopy* is a memoir of Straus's 20 year friendship with the Nobel Prize-winning writer Isaac Bashevis Singer and her struggle with the "Jewish pursuit of 'melting pot' assimilation," noted a commentator for *Kirkus Reviews.* Reviewers warned that the book is thin and contains only a few bits of new information on Singer, and in the words of Frances Taliaferro of the *New York Times Book Review,* "will have the most meaning for those readers who are already partial to Mrs. Straus or Mr. Singer or for those who are rediscovering their own Jewishness." *Virgins and Other Endangered Species: A Memoir,* received mixed critical reviews and is, as her first set of memoirs, a recollection of her privileged New York past and her relationships with prominent individuals. Sections about Straus' literary acquaintances, in this and previous memoirs, were republished, providing the bulk of information in *The Paper Trail: A Recollection of Writers.* Mary Cantwell, a *New York Times Book Review* critic, praised *The Paper Trail* for the "snapshots" Straus provide and declared the book pleasurable. Although, Cantwell, giving similar criticisms as reviewers for Straus's past memoirs, faulted Straus for making some unclear and out-of-context presentations, overstating some descriptions, and at times "overlay[ing] her perceptions with profundity." A commentator for *Publishers Weekly* called Straus "a master impressionist, a quick sketch artist who catches her subjects . . . at moments when they reveal more of themselves than they realize."

BIOGRAPHICAL/CRITICAL SOURCES:

PERIODICALS

Booklist, December 15, 1976.

Kirkus Reviews, July 15, 1974; September 1, 1976; December 15, 1981; February 15, 1987; June 1, 1993; January 15, 1997.

Modern Fiction Studies, summer, 1983.

New York Times, November 19, 1976.

New York Times Book Review, September 12, 1971; October 13, 1974; February 20, 1977; August 29, 1982; April 12, 1987; September 5, 1993; May 11, 1997.

Publishers Weekly, July 12, 1993; January 27, 1997.

Times Literary Supplement, March 10, 1972; May 9, 1975.

Vogue, September 1, 1971.

Washington Post Book World, July 25, 1993.

T-U

TALBOT, Lawrence
See BRYANT, Edward (Winslow, Jr.)

* * *

TALLENT, Elizabeth (Ann) 1954-

PERSONAL: Born August 8, 1954, in Washington, DC; daughter of William Hugh (a research chemist) and Joy (a speech therapist; maiden name, Redfield) Tallent; married Barry Smoots, 1975. *Education:* Illinois State University at Normal, B.A., 1975.

ADDRESSES: *Home*—Espanola, NM. *Agent*—Andrew Wylie, Andrew Wylie Agency, 250 West 57th St., Suite 2331, New York, NY 10019.

CAREER: Writer. Writer-in-residence at the University of Southern Mississippi's Writer's Center, 1983; visiting writer at the University of California at Irvine, spring, 1986. Participates in writers' conferences.

MEMBER: PEN, Poets and Writers.

AWARDS, HONORS: National Endowment for the Arts fiction fellowship, 1983; O. Henry Award, 1984; "No One's a Mystery," a short story, was published in newspapers as a PEN Syndicated Fiction Project selection, 1985; Pushcart Prize from Pushcart Press.

WRITINGS:

Married Men and Magic Tricks: John Updike's Erotic Heroes, (essays), Creative Arts Book Co. (Berkeley, CA), 1982.
Museum Pieces (novel), Knopf (New York), 1985.

SHORT STORIES

In Constant Flight, Knopf, 1983.
Time with Children, Knopf, 1987.
Honey, Knopf, 1993.

OTHER

Work represented in anthologies, including *The Best American Short Stories of 1981; Prize Stories 1984: The O. Henry Awards,* edited by William Abrahams, Doubleday, 1984; *The Pushcart Prize: Best of the Small Presses;* and *Graywolf Annual.* Contributor of short stories to magazines and newspapers, including *Esquire, Harper's, Newsday, New Yorker,* and the *Cincinnati Enquirer.*

SIDELIGHTS: A contributor of short fiction to major periodicals, Elizabeth Tallent wrote and assembled a 1982 collection of essays titled *Married Men and Magic Tricks: John Updike's Erotic Heroes.* In this collection she studies sexuality, particularly male sexuality, as manifested in John Updike's novels. She examines it in light of her thesis that Updike's male characters vacillate between their conflicting desires for Edenic domesticity and marriage on the one hand and worldly experience and adulterous freedom on the other, usually remaining in a state of irresponsibility that Tallent likens to the "realm of childhood." According to Elizabeth Prioleau, in her

American Literature critique of *Married Men and Magic Tricks,* "Intriguing as the central thesis [of Tallent's essays] is, it fails, ultimately, to embrace or explain the complexity of Updike's sexual theme." But Tallent acknowledges in the preface to her book that it "cannot claim to be either methodical or comprehensive." And, Prioleau concluded, "As Updike himself says, you 'should not blame [the author] for not achieving what he [or she] did not attempt,' and *Married Men and Magic Tricks* will surely prove suggestive and lively reading for students of Updike's sexual thought and the general public alike."

Tallent's next book, *In Constant Flight,* is a collection of eleven short stories, a number of which were previously published in the *New Yorker.* Barbara Koenig Quart, reviewing *In Constant Flight* in *Nation,* noted that Tallent's stories, "set in Colorado, but really set nowhere special, . . . are full of exotic and precious characters." Among these characters are a professional ice skater whose skating routine and developing technique parallel her life patterns, an adolescent who refuses to remove a mask during the week that her divorced father leaves her with his lover, an academic couple whose relationship disintegrates in its pettiness when jolted by the perspective of a visiting African scholar, and a woman who has left her husband and joined a lover only to wage a drawn-out battle with her husband for the custody of his Dalmatian, Keats.

Edith Milton, critiquing *In Constant Flight* in the *New York Times Book Review,* observed: "Most of these stories are written in the first person in the voice of a young woman who is always somehow the same young woman. . . . And the men who reject her or whom she rejects . . . are also oddly the same." Perhaps one reason for this similarity is that, according to Milton, the "stories of 'In Constant Flight' are all to one degree or another studies in modern alienation. . . . Though the theme of 'In Constant Flight' is sexual love and each story centers upon a failed romantic relationship . . . , the inability of people to reach one another and speak with warmth and meaning is always projected against a larger and more consuming void." Elaine Kendall, deeming the stories "supremely contemporary tales, so relevant and immediate that it's hard to imagine them being written even 10 years ago," also perceived Tallent's characters as living in a void, and concluded in the *Los Angeles Times:* "The short story seems the perfect medium for these excursions into modern sensibility. . . . Only the short story lends itself to the depiction of characters detached from their pasts, uncommitted to their futures, contextless and placid."

Critics praised Tallent for her sense of detail in writing the stories of *In Constant Flight* and noted her use of meticulous description as opposed to explanatory or metaphorical narration. Clare Sumnor, for instance, observed in the *Times Literary Supplement* that "Tallent has a striking descriptive gift. Each narrative moves through a sequence of images, a technique that places these stories on the borders of poetry, where the eloquence of the image-as-story has gradually acquired dominance." Andrea Barnet remarked in *Saturday Review:* "Elizabeth Tallent is an elegant miniaturist. Her quiet, elegiac stories are shaped less by plot than by immaculately precise imagery." Moreover, concluded Barnet, "what makes these eleven short stories unusual is Tallent's keen and original eye for detail; her characters' obsessions read as though grounded firmly in fact." London *Times* critic Andrew Sinclair noted of Tallent's writing: "Metaphors and explanations are rare in her stories of relationships *In Constant Flight.*" Rather, Sinclair remarked, Tallent "accumulates details and counter-poises conversations" in order to portray her characters' circumstances and attitudes. *New York Times* critic Anatole Broyard, acknowledging that Tallent "can make you think with some of her effects," also observed Tallent's use of counterpoint or juxtaposition of her characters' conversation and action: "Her couples, for example," Broyard explained, "get along in what I can only call a contrapuntal way, and after [reading the stories for] a while I began to feel that this is perhaps how we are meant to be together—at cross purposes, instead of chiming," with "someone always doing something interesting in relation to what one is doing, but not necessarily in response to it."

According to some reviewers, Tallent's descriptive narratives in *In Constant Flight* culminate in what Quart called "moments of poignance," which "are conveyed indirectly, through displaced images, often drawn from the esoterica of natural history." Explained Kendall: "Tallent specializes in capturing the moment when matters could have gone one way or another, but inexplicably stall. She writes of turning points passed by, choices postponed, signals crossed, connections missed, moments of decision when nothing is decided." And Barnet concluded, "Even in the fragile moments when words fail her characters—the moments around which all of these stories pivot—

[Tallent's] meanings surface with the liquid ease of daydreams."

Tallent made her debut as a novelist with the publication of *Museum Pieces* in 1985. That year she was described in *Esquire* magazine as a prominent young writer "whose realistic fiction illuminates the vital trends in modern life and literature" and who draws a connection between the aspiration of her college years—to be an archeologist—and her literary endeavors. She remarked in the *New York Times Book Review:* "Archeologists look at physical evidence of a life that has permanence, a context, intricacy. That's what I'd like in my writing." Moreover, the southwestern settings depicted meticulously in both Tallent's short stories and her novel reflect her affinity for the clarity and spaciousness of the landscape of her home state, New Mexico. Explained Tallent of the American Southwest: "Things aren't crowded together here. I find that visually and morally attractive." So much so, Tallent told *Esquire,* that she began working on *Museum Pieces,* away from New Mexico at the time, in order to recreate its atmosphere: "I *was* homesick," Tallent affirmed. "I think *Museum Pieces* . . . was in part a sort of habitat I constructed for myself, because it is set in Santa Fe, the place I was missing. I wanted its verisimilitude to be a roof over my head." What resulted, according to Tallent, were "characters who, as if in reflection of such an imperfect motive for writing a novel, kept taking refuge—not in each other, but in things they had more or less made up. Yet by the end of the book they did not seem to me to be doing so very badly; if they saw each other only in fragments, at least they sometimes held on to a fragment and burnished it between thumb and forefinger and tried to understand it."

Museum Pieces centers on the separation of Peter and Clarissa Wu-Barnes, their attempts to shape new lives for themselves, and the reaction of their thirteen-year-old daughter, Tara, to the emotional upheaval and changes in her lifestyle brought about by the disintegration of her parents' marriage. Peter, initially unable to establish a new order in life, camps out on an old mattress in the basement of the museum where he works, imagines the house he dreams of building for himself and his daughter, and tries to sort out the present by studying the past. Clarissa, an artist, fills her life by maintaining an orderly household, talking her problems over with a therapist, taking lovers, and fostering a sense of control over her environment by painting still lifes. According to poet and fiction writer Louise Erdrich, who commented in her critique of *Museum Pieces* for the *New York Times Book Review* that there "may be no one who writes as gracefully about debris as Elizabeth Tallent," Peter's work as an archeologist "serves as a metaphor for the book. 'Museum Pieces' is the re-examination of the debris of a marriage, an attempt to describe a once-whole vessel by showing us the fragments. . . . Throughout 'Museum Pieces' the writer . . . has offered the reader fragments of people to be made whole. Through her loving attention they do become whole, understandable, human."

Among the people who "become whole" under Tallent's pen are the adolescent Tara and her friend Natalie, whose gossipy, jargon-filled yet serious conversations reveal, according to Michiko Kakutani's *New York Times* review of *Museum Pieces,* that the "sense of drift and impermanence that haunts the grownups in this book is also handed down to their children." The teenagers' discussions also prompted Erdrich to comment that "Tallent apparently knows a great deal about young girls and their friendships with one another." Moreover, Kakutani continued, Tallent possesses a "finely tuned ear," which "is keyed not only to the nuances of adolescent speech, but also to their elders' elliptical use of language, the circumlocutions, elisions and stammering invocation of psychobabble they employ to cover over their feelings of love and fear and hurt."

With regard to the style employed by Tallent in writing *Museum Pieces,* many critics noted the same sort of accumulation of detailed description as that manifested in Tallent's short stories. Frank Gannon of *Saturday Review* observed that Tallent "builds her superb and moving first novel in a pointilist way using microcosmic sense impressions." Erdrich similarly noted that *Museum Pieces* is an "engrossing and beautifully expressed" story that "grows by the accretion of small discoveries toward a conclusion rather than a climax." And Kakutani concluded: "Writing with a keen, quicksilver appreciation of her characters' inner lives and with a poet's eye for the luminous, skewed details of daily life, . . . Tallent has created a lyrical, resonant novel, a novel about the complicated geometry of emotions between men and women, parents and their children."

Several reviewers noted that *Museum Pieces* resembles, even surpasses, Tallent's short stories in other ways. Elizabeth Kastor, for instance, remarked in her *Washington Post Book World* review of the book: "This is Tallent's first novel. She has been until now a short-story writer, and 'Museum Pieces' is reminiscent of the stories in her 1983 collection, 'In Constant Flight.' The novel shares a certain stillness with the stories, an underlying unease that reveals itself through narrow fissures in the polished surface." In the same vein, Erdrich noted of *Museum Pieces:* "As a novel, it is a sure-handed extension of Elizabeth Tallent's short stories. She has kept the humor and immediacy, the telling quirks, the odd and inventive bits of circumstances, while at the same time rendering her characters in deeper tones." And Gannon concluded: "*Museum Pieces* . . . bears out every bit of promise in her collection of stories, *In Constant Flight*. . . . She gets everything right: the people, the places, and, not least impressively, the children."

Tallent again proved her skill with the short story form with her 1993 collection, entitled *Honey*. Many of the nine stories in the book deal with marriage, or the relationships between parents and children. A *Publishers Weekly* reviewer noted that the author has "a razor-sharp eye" for relating domestic relationships and expresses "an uncanny sense of the minutes shifts of emotion" that can result in the success or failure of a marriage or an affair. Commenting on the story "James Was Here," in which a man calls on two women from his past, *Publishers Weekly* called the ending "mesmerically right and satisfying." In "The Minute I Saw You," which tells of a teenager visiting California, *Publishers Weekly* commented that Tallent's gift for suggesting a sense of place is "extraordinary." Dan Shapiro also praised *Honey* in his *People* review, calling it "a fine new collection . . . [with] brave and unflinching tales of modern marriage." Stepchildren, ex-wives and husbands, half-brothers and sisters, all dance around each other, wounded and determined not to repeat anyone's mistakes. "With actual disintegrations behind them and the threat of disintegration always around them, Tallent's families must make do with habit and the occasional flash of understanding," mused Patricia Moran in *Dictionary of Literary Biography*. "The nature of a family, Tallent seems to say, does not involve absolute certainty."

BIOGRAPHICAL/CRITICAL SOURCES:

BOOKS

Contemporary Literary Criticism, Volume 45, Gale (Detroit), 1987.

Dictionary of Literary Biography, Volume 130: *American Short-Story Writers since World War II,* Gale, 1993.

PERIODICALS

American Literature, March, 1983.
Chicago Tribune, April 28, 1985.
Esquire, August, 1984; April, 1985.
Hudson Review, autumn, 1985, pp. 463-72.
Los Angeles Times, June 9, 1983.
Ms., July, 1983.
Nation, June 11, 1983, pp. 738-41.
New Directions for Women, May-June, 1985, p. 16.
New York Times, April 29, 1983, p. C29; March 30, 1985, p. 13.
New York Times Book Review, August 14, 1983, pp. 12, 26; April 7, 1985, p. 10.
Observer, August 14, 1983.
People, January 17, 1994, p. 31.
Publishers Weekly, September 6, 1993, p. 81.
Saturday Review, June, 1983, pp. 56, 58; March/April, 1985; May/June, 1985.
Times (London), August 11, 1983.
Times Literary Supplement, September 16, 1983, p. 1002.
Washington Post Book World, April 19, 1985.
Western American Literature, August, 1986, pp. 163-64.

* * *

TAPAHONSO, Luci 1953-

PERSONAL: Surname is pronounced "Top-pahonso"; born in 1953, in Shiprock, NM; daughter of Eugene and Lucille (Descheene) Tapahonso; married Earl Ortiz (an artist; divorced, 1987); married Bob G. Martin, 1989; children: (first marriage) Lori Tazbah, Misty Dawn, (stepchildren) Robert Derek, Jonathan Allan, Amber Kristine. *Education:* Participated in a training program for investigative journalism at the National Indian Youth Council; University of New Mexico, B.A., 1980, M.A., 1983.

ADDRESSES: *Home*—Lawrence, KS. *Office*—Department of English, University of Kansas, 3116 Wescoe Hall, Lawrence, KS 66045-2115.

CAREER: Writer and poet. University of New Mexico, Albuquerque, assistant professor of English, 1987-89; University of Kansas, Lawrence, assistant professor, 1990-94, associate professor of English, 1994—. Served on the board of directors of the Phoenix Indian Center, 1974; member of New Mexico Arts Commission Literature Panel, 1984-86, steering committee of *Returning the Gift Writers Festival,* 1989-92, Kansas Arts Commission Literature Panel, 1990, Phoenix Arts Commission, 1990-92, Telluride Institute Writers Forum Advisory Board, 1992—, and commissioner of Kansas Arts Commission, 1992-96.

MEMBER: Modern Language Association, Poets and Writers, Inc., Association of American Indian and Alaska Native Professors, Habitat for Humanity (served on board of directors, 1990-94), New Mexico Endowment for the Humanities, Spooner Museum of Anthropology (member of advisory board, 1990-92); American Indian Law Resource Center (served on board of directors, 1993—).

AWARDS, HONORS: Southwestern Association Indian Affairs Literature fellowship, 1981; honorable mention, American Book Awards, 1983, for *Seasonal Woman;* excellent instructor award, University of New Mexico, 1985; named one of the Top Women of the Navajo Nation, *Maazo* magazine, 1986; New Mexico Eminent Scholar award, New Mexico Commission of Higher Education, 1989; Hall Creative Work fellowship, University of Kansas, 1992; Community Enhancement and Cultural Exchange award, Lawrence Arts Commission, 1993; Outstanding Native American Award, City of Sacramento, 1993; Southwest Book Award, Border Library Association, 1994, for *Saanii Dahataal;* named an Influential Professor, Lady Jayhawks Faculty Recognition, University of Kansas, 1994.

WRITINGS:

One More Shiprock Night: Poems, illustrated by husband, Earl P. Ortiz, Tejas Art Press (San Antonio), 1981.

Seasonal Woman (poems), drawings by R. C. Gorman, Tooth of Time Books (Santa Fe), 1982.

A Breeze Swept Through (poems), West End Press (Los Angeles), 1987.

Saanii Dahataal: The Women Are Singing (poems and stories), University of Arizona Press (Tucson), 1993.

A Song for the Direction of North, Helicon Nine (Kansas City), 1994.

Bah and Her Baby Brother, illustrated by Sam English, Jr., National Organization for Fetal Alcohol Syndrome (Washington, DC), 1994.

(Editor) *Hayoolkaal: Dawn—An Anthology of Navajo Writers,* University of Arizona Press, 1995.

Navajo ABC: A Dine Alphabet Book, illustrated by Eleanor Schick, Macmillan (New York City), 1995.

Blue Horses Rush In: Poems and Stories, University of Arizona Press, 1997.

Also contributor to *Sign Language: Contemporary Southwest Native America,* Aperture (New York City), 1989; *A Circle of Nations: Voices and Visions of American Indians,* Beyond Words (Hillsboro, NM), 1993; and *Open Places, City Spaces: Contemporary Writers on the Changing Southwest,* University of Arizona Press, 1994. Contributor of poems, stories and essays to numerous publications. Contributor to videotape, *The Desert Is No Lady: Women Make Movies,* 1996. Member of editorial board, *Blue Mesa Review,* 1988-92, and *Frontiers,* 1991—.

SIDELIGHTS: Writer Luci Tapahonso grew up on a New Mexico farm in a family of Navajo ancestry, and her body of work often evokes the imagery of this part of the country. While a college student she became acquainted with the acclaimed Native American author Leslie Marmon Silko, who encouraged Tapahonso's efforts at creative writing, and her first book of poems was published in 1981. Entitled *One More Shiprock Night,* the work draws upon her early childhood and Navajo roots in rural New Mexico. Many of the selections reflect the important role of music in the cultural traditions of the area. Although most of her works use everyday language and speech patterns, Tapahonso sometimes writes poems first in Navajo and then translates them into English. "Hills Brothers Coffee" is one such work, a memory of the iconography of her youth and of a beloved uncle.

Tapahonso's second volume of poetry appeared in 1982 under the title *Seasonal Woman.* It contains such pieces as "Listen," in which a woman is warned about marrying a man who can't sing, for lacking this ability is a metaphor for a lack of interest in the Navajo traditions. A character named Leona Grey shows up in many of the selections, a woman who Tapahonso described in an interview with *MELUS* writer Joseph Bruchac III as a composite character. Other poems address issues of violence and racism in the American Southwest.

Having children of her own has also had an impact on Tapahonso's work, and in the interview she questioned the dissonant nature of her children's lives as Navajos in contemporary America. Yet she also reflected that she felt comfortable with this new hybrid culture experienced by her children, one that is distinctly different from her own upbringing, noting that when she was in school there were few contemporary Native American writers to study.

In her third collection, 1987's *A Breeze Swept Through,* Tapahonso returns to these themes of her background and contemporary New Mexico. She further explores her interest in the rhythms of common speech in 1993's *Saanii Dahataal: The Women Are Sining.* The volume incorporates the poet's growing interest in the Navajo tongue, with selections in both this language and English. Many of them center around Tapahonso's New Mexican roots, and the pull she still feels toward it as an adult living several hundred miles away in Kansas.

Saanii Dahataal: The Women Are Singing put Tapahonso among "such writers as Joy Harjo, Louise Erdrich, and Leslie Marmon Silko as an important female voice in the American Indian literary landscape," according to Gretchen M. Bataille in *Dictionary of Literary Biography.* "The book demonstrates her versatility and maturity as a writer and brings together the elements of landscape, tradition, and humor that were evident in earlier works." The book contains both poetry and prose selections, and deals with topics including her childhood, relatives, memories, and pets. "This is a loving collection of voices from the hand of one woman," stated Yolanda Montijo in *Whole Earth Review.*

In one poem, "Navajo Long Walk," Tapahonso recalls Kit Carson's scorched-earth campaign against the Navajo nation. His offensive included slaughtering the Navajo's livestock, destroying their crops and fruit trees, and forcing them to march three hundred miles to a reservation for four years of inadequate food, rampant disease, and death. They were then allowed to return to their homeland. "The poem dwells simultaneously in past and present, jumping time, speaking grief," advised Linda Hogan in *Parabola.* "It reveals a depth of emotion, exquisitely and simply. Although these tales are "simple on the surface," remarked Hogan, they "are enormous and resonant."

Blue Horses Rush In, Tapahonso's next book, commemorates the pleasures and sadness of ordinary life in poems and stories. Debbie Bogenschutz in *Library Journal* called the work "poignant." Although the book draws extensively from Tapahonso's Navaho ancestry, "these stories and poems speak to women of all cultures."

BIOGRAPHICAL/CRITICAL SOURCES:

BOOKS

Bruchac, Joseph, *Survival This Way,* Arizona University Press (Tucson), 1987.

Crawford, John F. and Annie O. Eysturoy, editors, *This Is About Vision: Interviews with Southwestern Writers,* New Mexico Press (Albuquerque), 1990.

Dictionary of Literary Biography, Volume 175: *Native American Writers of the United States,* Gale (Detroit), 1997.

Farah, Cynthia, editor, *Literature and Landscape: Writers in the Southwest,* Texas Western Press (El Paso), 1988.

PERIODICALS

Booklist, March 1, 1993; December 15, 1995, p. 706; July, 1996, p. 1833.

Chicago Tribune, September 5, 1993, sec. 6, p. 2.

Choice, June, 1986, p. 1508; April, 1988, p. 1254.

Library Journal, March 15, 1993, p. 81; August, 1997, p. 88.

MELUS, winter, 1984, pp. 85-91.

New York Times Book Review, October 31, 1993, p. 40.

Parabola, winter, 1993, pp. 96-97.

Publishers Weekly, January 6, 1989, p. 82; July 28, 1997, p. 55.

Whole Earth Review, winter, 1995, p. 22.

* * *

TAPPLY, William G(eorge) 1940-

PERSONAL: Born July 16, 1940, in Waltham, MA; son of H. G. (an outdoor writer) and Muriel (a registered nurse; maiden name, Morgridge) Tapply; married Alice Sandra Knight, 1962 (divorced, 1966); Cynthia Ehrgott (a secretary), March 7, 1970 (divorced, 1995); children: Michael, Melissa, Sarah. *Education:* Amherst College, B.A., 1962; Harvard University, M.A.T., 1963; attended Tufts University, 1966-68.

ADDRESSES: Home and office—47 Ann Lee Rd., Harvard, MA 01451. *Agent*—Jed Mattes, 175 West 73rd St., New York, NY 10023.

CAREER: High school history teacher, Lexington, MA, 1963-66; Tufts University, Medford, MA, director of economic studies, 1968-69; Lexington High School, housemaster and teacher, 1972-90. Writer's Digest School, editorial associate, 1992—. Clark University, writing instructor, 1995—. Contributing editor, *Field and Stream.*

MEMBER: Mystery Writers of America, Authors Guild, Private Eye Writers of America.

AWARDS, HONORS: Scribner Crime Novel award, 1984, for *Death at Charity's Point.*

WRITINGS:

MYSTERY NOVELS

Death at Charity's Point, Scribner (New York City), 1984.
The Dutch Blue Error, Scribner, 1985.
Follow the Sharks, Scribner, 1985.
The Marine Corpse, Scribner, 1986.
Dead Meat, Scribner, 1987.
The Vulgar Boatman, Scribner, 1987.
A Void in Hearts, Scribner, 1988.
Dead Winter, Delacorte (New York City), 1989.
Client Privilege, Delacorte, 1989.
The Spotted Cats, Delacorte, 1991.
Tight Lines, Delacorte, 1992.
The Snake Eater, Otto Penzler (New York City), 1993.
The Seventh Enemy, Otto Penzler, 1995.
(With Linda Barlow) *Thicker than Water,* Signet (New York City), 1995.
Close to the Bone, St. Martin's Press (New York City), 1996.

NONFICTION

Those Hours Spent Outdoors, Scribner, 1988.
Opening Day and Other Neuroses, Lyons & Burford (New York City), 1990.
Home Water Near and Far, Lyons & Burford, 1992.
Sportsman's Legacy, Lyons & Burford, 1993.
The Elements of Mystery Fiction, Writer, Inc. (Boston), 1995.
A Fly-Fishing Life, Lyons & Burford, 1997.

Contributor of numerous articles and stories to magazines, including *Sports Illustrated, Better Homes and Gardens, Organic Gardening, Scholastic Coach, Drummer, Writer, Fins and Feathers, Worcester,* and *Outdoor Life.*

SIDELIGHTS: William G. Tapply is the author of a number of mystery novels featuring Brady Coyne, a Boston attorney serving a wealthy clientele. In an essay for the *St. James Guide to Crime & Mystery Writers,* Jim Huang calls Coyne "a skillful blend of amateur versus professional, serious versus frivolous, and intellectual versus physical." Coyne selects interesting clients to make his otherwise boring legal practice bearable. He also sees his career as a means to finance his avocation, fishing, which is Tapply's great love and the subject of several of the author's nonfiction works.

Over the course of the series, Coyne has dealt with a variety of cases. A murder takes place on what is believed to be sacred Indian land in *Dead Meat,* an author dies under mysterious circumstances in *The Marine Corpse.* and a Vietnam veteran's memoirs cause trouble for many people in *The Snake Eater.* The controversy over gun control is a key plot element in *The Seventh Enemy.* The Brady Coyne series has won Tapply plaudits for his narrative skills. Lauding Tapply for writing "quietly and perceptively" in *Death at Charity's Point,* the story of Coyne's investigation of an apparent suicide, London *Times* contributor Marcel Berlins assessed the book as a "superior" thriller. Marilyn Stasio, critiquing *The Seventh Enemy* for the *New York Times Book Review,* called Tapply "a smooth stylist"; in a piece on *The Snake Eater* for the same publication, she noted, "there's never a break in that practiced, flowing style he has mastered over a dozen books." Huang asserted that "Tapply is among the smoothest storytellers around—his books glide along quickly and effortlessly—but the plots tend towards the straightforward and they're not necessarily fair. He will introduce new elements in the closing chapters in order to facilitate a resolution. . . . But only rarely do Tapply's stories really disappoint."

While lauding the author's portrayal of Coyne's eccentric clients, Huang complained, "If Tapply has a significant flaw, it's in Brady Coyne's peculiar reticence about his own life and feelings. . . . The adventures leave no mark on Coyne." For instance, Huang observed, Coyne remains unperturbed after being nearly blown to bits in *Dead Meat,* and he is largely unaffected by pleas to help the homeless in *The Marine Corpse.* Stasio found *The Snake Eater* an exception to Coyne's usual stoicism. "Tapply wrings some rare passion from Brady Coyne," she remarked, adding "this time his theme of friendship has jagged edges of anger and pain that cut through Coyne's reserve and draw blood." Huang granted that the character's customary restraint has its uses in the series: "Brady Coyne's wry, good-humored narration reminds us not to take it all too seriously."

Tapply once told *CA* that he is reluctant to call his books mystery novels. "I write novels that, like most worthwhile novels, contain mysteries," he said. "I try to avoid formulas, although I suppose with a series character like my attorney Brady Coyne I have conceded that much. I place great emphasis in my writing on characterization, motivation, suspense, and humor—all of which seem to me important in all fiction. I try to tell stories rather than truths, but I think my stories convey some small truths now and then. I have been asked on occasion when I intend to write a 'real novel.' I reply, of course, that I already have."

BIOGRAPHICAL/CRITICAL SOURCES:

BOOKS

St. James Guide to Crime & Mystery Writers, 4th edition, St. James Press (Detroit), 1996.

PERIODICALS

Chicago Tribune, September 25, 1988.
New York Times Book Review, April 18, 1984; December 8, 1985; December 26, 1993; January 22, 1995.
Publishers Weekly, October 4, 1993, p. 66; August 19, 1996, p. 55; July 7, 1997, p. 58.
Times (London), January 31, 1985.*

* * *

THON, Melanie Rae 1957-

PERSONAL: Born August 23, 1957, in Kalispell, MT; daughter of Raymond Albert (an architect) and Lois Ann (a homemaker; maiden name, Lockwood) Thon. *Education:* University of Michigan, B.A., 1980; Boston University, M.A., 1982.

ADDRESSES: *Home*—Cambridge, MA. *Agent*—Irene Skolnick, 121 West 27th St., Ste. 601, New York, NY 10001.

CAREER: Wheelock College, Boston, MA, instructor in writing, 1986-87; Emerson College, instructor in literature, 1986-1992; University of Massachusetts at Boston, instructor in history, 1987-89; Harvard University, Cambridge, MA, instructor in writing, 1989-1992; Syracuse University, professor of writing and literature, 1993—.

AWARDS, HONORS: Hopwood Award, University of Michigan, 1980; A. B. Guthrie, Jr. Award, 1987, for *Cutbank.*

WRITINGS:

Meteors in August (novel), Random House, 1990.
Girls in the Grass (stories), Random House, 1991.
Iona Moon (novel), Poseidon Press, 1993.
First, Body (stories), Houghton Mifflin, 1996.

Contributor of stories to magazines, including *Antaeus, Ontario Review, Ploughshares, Great River Review, Southern Review, Threepenny Review,* and *Hudson Review.*

SIDELIGHTS: Melanie Rae Thon once told *CA* that she writes about "people and situations that trouble me." Nowhere is that theme more apparent than in her 1993 novel *Iona Moon.* The title character, a teenage girl in the mid-1960s, comes of age in hardscrabble rural Idaho. She doesn't stay there for long, though.

"Here in White Falls everyone was one of your own: your neighbor, your cousin, a bad girl you know in high school, your best friend—everything happened to you," narrates Iona. The underprivileged girl finds some happiness when she becomes involved with Jay, the star diver on the high school team. The two find romance in the back seat of a car belonging to Jay's friend Willy; in exchange for borrowing Willy's car, Jay allows Willy to finish first in the swim meet by failing to perform an important dive.

But misfortune comes crashing down on Iona. She drops out of school to care for her mother, who soon dies of cancer. Then, after narrowly escaping abuse by her three roughneck brothers, she hitchhikes away from home. Waiting tables at an all-night truckstop, Iona meets Eddie Birdheart, a one-legged married man; their affair causes Iona to stop eating. Cared for by Eddie's mother, Iona regains her health. In the meantime, back in White Falls, Willy becomes involved with Jay's inebriated mother, and Jay, whose legs were seriously injured in a car crash, leaves school, and is unwilling to learn to walk again. Despite its portrayal of continual misery, *Iona Moon,* said reviewer T. M. McNally of *Washington*

Post Book World, "is . . . not about hardship and grief, but about our interconnected need, and ability, to survive what life brings us."

While general critical reaction to the novel included praise for Thon's passionate style, especially her "luminous, stately prose," as Shelby Hearon noted in a *Chicago Tribune* review, some reviewers questioned the originality of elements in Iona Moon. While praising Thon's "lyrical and lucid" prose, Claire Messud of the *Times Literary Supplement,* faulted her overuse of familiar themes and characters. Messud suggested the need for "a five-year moratorium . . . on tough, sexy girls with hearts of gold from the wrong side of the tracks; on soothsaying women and limbless or mutilated men of all ages and ethnic origins; on incest and child sexual abuse; on alcoholic and/or tranquilized housewives . . . , on high school heroes who don't make good; . . . and, above all, on small towns like White Falls, Idaho." Similarly, *Los Angeles Times* writer Julia Cameron found that *Iona Moon* "resists reading like an overcrowded room resists entry." Citing just too many unhappy events in the story, she declared Thon "a gifted, determined writer," but dismissed the book as "a litany of miseries, lovingly and microscopically detailed, told with claustrophobic intensity."

McNally, however, called the author's efforts "a brave and honest victory." *Iona Moon* is "a dangerous and intricately drawn novel—rich and aching with desire, concluded McNally, with writing that "is wonderfully layered and precise." "Reading *Iona Moon,*" said *Belle Lettres* writer Gale Harris, "is like taking a walk down a dark street where dim lights offer fleeting glimpses of vulnerable young women and men who are overlooked and left unprotected by their families. . . . We return to our own lives with an appreciation of every nuance of affection that we find there."

BIOGRAPHICAL/CRITICAL SOURCES:

BOOKS

Thon, Melanie Rae, *Iona Moon,* Poseidon Press, 1993.

PERIODICALS

Belles Lettres, spring 1994, pp. 40-41.
Booklist, December 1, 1996, p. 642.
Chicago Tribune Book World, June 6, 1993, p. 3.
Los Angeles Times, July 25, 1993, p. 9.
Publishers Weekly, November 4, 1996, p. 62.
Times Literary Supplement, July 23, 1993, p. 19.
Washington Post Book World, July 25 1993, pp. 3, 14.

* * *

TROCCHI, Alexander 1925-1984
(Carmencita de las Lunas, Frances Lengel)

PERSONAL: Surname rhymes with "rocky"; born July 30, 1925, in Glasgow, Scotland; died April 15, 1984; son of Alfredo Luigi (a musician) and Annie Jack (Robertson) Trocchi; married Lyn Hicks, August 13, 1956; children: Mark Alexander. *Education:* University of Glasgow, M.A. (philosophy, with honors), 1950.

CAREER: Painter, sculptor, and writer. *Merlin* (magazine), co-founder and editor-in-chief, 1952-55; *Paris Quarterly,* Paris, editor, 1952-55; *Moving Times,* London, editor. Founding participant and director, Project Sigma (a.k.a. "The Invisible Insurrection"; international cultural engineering project), London; St. Martin's School of Art, London, visiting lecturer in sculpture. Worked as a scow captain on the Hudson River, 1956-59. *Military service:* Royal Navy, 1943-46.

WRITINGS:

(Contributor) *New World Writing,* [New York], 1953.

Sappho of Lesbos, Olympia (Paris), 1955, Castle (New York City), 1960.

What Frank Harris Did Not Say: Being the Tumultuous, Apocryphal Fifth Volume of "My Life and Loves," as Embellished by Alexander Trocchi, with an Apologetic Preface by Maurice Girodias (originally published as spurious fifth volume of Frank Harris's *My Life and Loves,* Olympia, 1958, New English Library (London), 1966), Travellers Companion, 1968.

Cain's Book, Grove (New York City), 1960, with foreword by Griel Marcus and introduction by Richard Seaver, 1992.

The Outsiders (contains *Young Adam* and short stories; also see below), New American Library (New York City), 1961.

(Editor with Terry Southern and Richard Seaver) *Writers in Revolt,* Fell (New York City), 1963.

(Contributor) *New Writers, No. 3,* J. Calder (London), 1965, Transatlantic (Albuquerque, NM), 1967.

(As Carmencita de las Lunas) *Thongs,* Olympia, 1956, with an introduction by Robert Creeley, Brandon House (North Hollywood, CA), 1967. *Drugs of the Mind,* Aldus (London), 1970. *Man at Leisure* (verse), Calder & Boyars (London), 1972.

ORIGINALLY AS FRANCES LENGEL; REVISED EDITIONS AS ALEXANDER TROCCHI

Young Adam, Olympia (Paris), 1954, revised edition, Heinemann (London), 1961, Greenleaf (San Diego), 1966.

Helen and Desire, Olympia, 1954, revised edition, Brandon House, 1967.

The Carnal Days of Helen Seferis, Olympia, 1954, revised edition, Brandon House, 1967.

School for Sin, Olympia, 1955, revised edition as *School for Wives,* Brandon House, 1967.

White Thighs, Olympia, 1955, revised edition, Brandon House, 1967.

TRANSLATOR

(With R. E. Wyngaard) Jan Cremer, *I, Jan Cremer,* Shorewood (New York City), 1965.

Andre Pieyre de Mandiargues, *The Girl on the Motorcycle,* Calder & Boyars, 1966.

Rene de Obaldia, *The Centenarian,* Calder & Boyars, 1970.

Jean Douassot, *La Gana,* Calder & Boyars, 1974.

Contributor to *Botteghe Oscure, Points, Paris Review, Evergreen Review, City Lights Journal,* and other periodicals.

SIDELIGHTS: Alexander Trocchi was an painter, sculptor, editor, translator, novelist, poet, and author of short stories. Joseph Campbell described Trocchi in the *Dictionary of Literary Biography:* "His use of drugs, his readiness to write the then instantly banned pornography, and his preference for experimental and avant-garde art forms are all manifestations of an enduring refusal to accept society's idea of what he, or any man, ought finally to be." Samuel Beckett called Trocchi's work "visual writing" that projects the transcendent element in experience by focusing on that which is immediate. Trocchi is perhaps best remembered for his presence and interactions within the literary and artistic scene, specifically the counter-culture movement, during the 1950s and 1960s. A critic once noted that Trocchi's double misfortune was to be the world's second most famous junkie, author William Burroughs being the first.

Trocchi's first "serious" novel, *Young Adam,* was published in 1954. According to Campbell, it "is a flawed and badly constructed" work of fiction. The book's protagonist, Joe Taylor, a barge worker with an "outsider" stance, is found responsible for a young woman's death. "Descriptions of . . . Joe's experience at large are rendered in an arid, joyless tone," in Campbell's opinion, and "The novel ends weakly with the imposition of a plea for the abolition of capital punishment." While the critic admitted "some passages of vivid writing," he found Trocchi's social protestations at odds with his protagonists' "outsider" persona. "Moreover," Campbell continued, "the frequent intrusion of the author's voice over that of the narrator suggests an authorial presence not sufficiently convinced of its fictional authority." In his 1960 work *Cain's Book,* Trocchi would gain control of his strong narrative, creating a voice distinct from such contemporaries as the Beat writers and Great Britain's "Angry Young Men."

Cain's Book, which explores the life of an author addicted to heroin, gained its author literary notoriety. According to Campbell, most readers ignored the novel's disclaimer as a mere work of fiction; they viewed *Cain's Book* as autobiography. "This assumption is incorrect," maintained Campbell, "since although the narrator, Joe Necchi, is undoubtedly the author himself, other important characters [are fictionalized]. . . experience of actual people." *Cain's Book* is more than a novel concerned with drug addiction. *Village Voice* contributor Mel R. Sabre notes that, in a larger sense, the book "concerns the disciplines of a uniquely perceptive mind driving toward absolute awareness. . . . What has proved so startling to other writers is not Trocchi's attitude to junk, but rather his intensely poetic effort ('poetic' not in the sense of euphony, but in the more profound, traditional sense) to penetrate those areas of experience generally considered inaccessible to language." Sabre adds: "There is much to be said about [*Cain's Book*] and not all commendatory. But the book will be read, now and in the future, because it says so much and says it well." Some critics objected to the novelist's strong language and to his apparent condonation of drug use. The novel was banned in some areas of Great Britain and in France, where Trocchi spent the early 1950s editing the avant-garde reviews *Merlin* and *Paris Quarterly. Merlin* published works by such authors as Eugene Ionesco, Jean Genet, Samuel Beckett, Robert Creeley, Henry Miller, and Jean-Paul Sartre. To help finance the magazine Trocchi wrote pornographic novels under the pseudonym Frances Lengel. These books, including *Helen and Desire, White Thighs,* and *School for Sin,* were also banned in France, England, and the United States.

Trocchi's pornographic books were written to order, their plots designed to fit with titles supplied by Maurice Girodias, owner of Olympia Press. As Campbell quoted Trocchi, "although primarily undertaken to keep the *Merlin* group together . . . the obscene books were serious enough within their own limits. Also we felt it was a very good thing to knock at the bow-leggeds of Grundy [persons of parochial mentality], to bang at doors."

In a review of Trocchi's 1961 short story collection *The Outsiders,* Robert Sage sees Trocchi's characters thus: "Not quite existentialists, not quite beatniks, they are, however, shabby individuals who live without plans or ideals, and who prowl around on the fringes of society." In contrast to other authors using similar characters, Trocchi, according to Sage, "not only has remarkable (albeit rather unsavory) stories to tell, but his manner of telling them is the original and studied one of a man who takes pride in writing well."

BIOGRAPHICAL/CRITICAL SOURCES:

BOOKS

Campbell, Allan, and Tim Niel, *A Life in Pieces: Reflections on Alexander Trocchi,* Rebel (Edinburgh), 1991.

Dictionary of Literary Biography, Volume 15: *British Novelists, 1930-1959,* Gale (Detroit), 1983.

Contemporary Novelists, third edition, St. Martin's Press (New York City), 1982.

PERIODICALS

Gambit (University of Edinburgh), 1962.

Kulchur, autumn, 1962.

Life, February 17, 1967.

New York Herald Tribune (Paris edition), March 11-12, 1961.

New York Times Book Review, March 12, 1961.

Village Voice, September 1, 1960.

Washington Post Book World, December 17, 1967.

OBITUARIES:

PERIODICALS

Times (London), April 21, 1984.*

* * *

UNNERSTAD, Edith (Totterman) 1900-

PERSONAL: Born July 28, 1900, in Helsinki, Finland; daughter of Axel A. and Ingeborg (Boman) Totterman; married Arvid B. Unnerstad (a civil engineer and managing director), January 8, 1924; children: Madeleine. *Education:* Studied at Detthow College, and at art school in Stockholm, Sweden.

ADDRESSES: *Home*—Burevagen 12, Djursholm, Sweden.

CAREER: Writer of children's books, 1932—, novels, 1933—.

MEMBER: Swedish Authors Association, Swedish Childrens Authors Association, Authors Guild (United States).

AWARDS, HONORS: Childrens Book Prize, 1949; Swedish Library Association, Nils Holgersson Plaque for best Swedish children's book, 1957, for *The Spettecake Holiday;* Swedish Government fellowships, 1956, 1959, 1966.

WRITINGS:

FOR CHILDREN

Uffe reser jorden runt, Natur och Kultur, 1932.

Hoppentott i Vanliga skogen, Natur och Kultur, 1938.

Muck, Natur och Kultur, 1939.

Tummelunsarna i Vanliga skogen, Natur och Kultur, 1939.

Pikku-Lotta, Fahlcrantz & Gumaelius, 1941.

Kastrullresan, Raben & Sjogren, 1949, reprinted 1964, translation by James Harker published as *The Saucepan Journey,* illustrated by Louis Slobodkin, Macmillan (New York City), 1951.

Nu seglar Pip-Larssons, Raben & Sjogren, 1950, reprinted, 1971, translation by Lilian Seaton published as *The Pip-Larssons Go Sailing,* M. Joseph (London), 1963, and as *The Peep-Larssons Go Sailing,* illustrated by Ilon Wikland, Macmillan, 1966.

Ankhasten, Raben & Sjogren, 1950.

Pysen, Raben & Sjogren, 1952, translation published as *Pysen,* Macmillan, 1955, translation by Seaton published as *The Urchin,* M. Joseph, 1964, Penguin (New York City), 1967.

Pip-Larssons Lilla O, Raben & Sjogren, 1955, translation published as *Little O,* Macmillan, 1957.

Farmorsresan, Raben & Sjogren, 1956, translation by Inger Boye published as *The Spettecake Holiday,* illustrated by Iben Clante, Macmillan, 1958.

Kattorna fran Sommaron, Raben & Sjogren, 1957, translation by Holger Lundbergh published as *The Cats from Summer Island,* Macmillan, 1963.

Lasseman spelar, Raben & Sjogren, 1958, translation by Gunvor Edwards published as *Larry Makes Music,* illustrated by Ylva Kallstrom, Norton (New York City), 1967.

Bollarulla, Raben & Sjogren, 1958, published as *Bollarulla: sju sagor fran Soederasen,* Raben & Sjogren, 1968.

Mormorsresan, Raben & Sjogren, 1959, translation published as *The Journey with Grandmother,* Macmillan, 1960, published as *Grandmother's Journey,* M. Joseph, 1960.

Englandsresan, Raben & Sjogren, 1960, translation published as *Journey to England,* Macmillan, 1961.

Toppen och jag pa torpet, Raben & Sjogren, 1962, translation by Seaton published as *Toppen and I at the Croft,* M. Joseph, 1966.

Boken om Pip-Larssons, Raben & Sjogren, 1962.

Vi tankte ga till skogen, Raben & Sjogren, 1964, translation published as *The Ditch Picnic,* Norton, 1964 (published in England as *The Picnic,* Oliver, 1964).

Little O's Naughty Day, translation from original Swedish manuscript by M. Turner, Burke Publishing, 1965.

Sagor vid dammen, Raben & Sjogren, 1965.

Tva sma fnissor, Raben & Sjogren, 1966, translation published as *Two Little Gigglers,* pictures by Ylva Kallstrom, Norton, 1967.

Twilight Tales, translation from original Swedish manuscript by Seaton, M. Joseph, 1967.

Kasperssons far till landet, Raben & Sjogren, 1969.

Trollen i Tassuvaara, Ahlen & Akerlund, 1969, translation by Seaton published as *A House for Spinner's Grandmother,* M. Joseph, 1970.

Mickie, illustrated by Ib Ohlsson, Four Winds Press (New York City), 1971.

Cherry Tree Party, translation from original Swedish manuscript by P. Crampton, Dent (London), 1978.

NOVELS, EXCEPT AS INDICATED

Garden vid Rodbergsgatan, Wahlstrom & Widstrand, 1935.

Boken om Alarik Barck, Bonniers, 1936.

Susann, Natur och Kultur, 1943.

Bricken, Natur och Kultur, 1945.

Sara och Lejonkringla, Natur och Kultur, 1946.

Snackhuset, Norstedt & Soner, 1949.

Ensam hemma med Johnny, Norstedt & Soner, 1951.

Leksaksekon (poetry), Norstedt & Soner, 1952.

Bockhornsgrand, Norstedt & Soner, 1954.

Jag alskade Clarinda, Norstedt & Soner, 1957.

Also author of scripts for radio, television, and motion pictures.

SIDELIGHTS: Swedish writer Edith Unnerstad is known for her warm, kindhearted portrayals of life in her native country. Writing mostly in Swedish, the author has produced books for adults, but the main body of her work consists of dozens of novels for children. In translation, several of these, including *The Saucepan Journey, The Spettecake Holiday,* and *The Journey with Grandmother,* have emerged as classics of children's literature.

Writing about her early interest in writing, Unnerstad in a February, 1963, *Horn Book* article cited an observation by A. A. Milne that children's writers are formed early: "Perhaps Mr. Milne was right. Very likely the pattern for my future profession was already minutely drawn when I was seven or eight. For when, many years later, I began to write in real earnest, my first book was a children's book." She went on to say that "Writing for children makes me happy. . . . It is like escaping to a region where the air is fresher and the sky clearer than in the real world. I think maybe this writing is an attempt to revive a little glimpse of the harmony I once possessed but lost together with my childhood."

Several of Unnerstad's novels, beginning with *The Saucepan Journey,* chronicle the adventures of the Larsson family, which consists of two bohemian parents and seven rambunctious children. Later volumes such as *Pysen,* about five-year-old Patrick, and *Little O,* a tale of the youngest child, focus on specific members of the family. Ellen Lewis Buell in the *New York Times Book Review* called the Larsson family "a lively, unpredictable crew," and a critic in the *Junior Bookshelf* wrote that "The story sparkles joyfully from one hugely improbable episode to the next." *The Saucepan Journey* is, in the words of Margery Fisher in *Growing Point,* "[A] frolic. . . . A hilarious story, full of good sense."

Of *Pysen,* a reviewer in *Junior Bookshelf* noted that the author "evokes the unconventional and friendly atmosphere of the home in an excellent manner." The book, wrote Ruth Gagliardo in the *Saturday Review,* "is full of rare, good fun and satisfying adventure." As for *Little O,* a critic in the *Bulletin of the Children's Book Center* called it "an exceptionally fine [story] for reading aloud in family groups."

In *The Spettecake Holiday,* six-year-old Pelle-Goran goes to stay with his grandmother while his mother enters the hospital for treatment of a severe illness. A commentator in *Virginia Kirkus' Service* called the story "A fresh and vigorous portrait of Swedish country life, full of good smells and sounds, and washed through with bright understanding." Noted Frances Lander Spain in the *Saturday Review,* "The humor that characterizes Mrs. Unnerstad's writing pervades this well-told story of real children and their elders."

Translations of *The Journey with Grandmother* and *Journey to England* gave children outside Sweden an exposure to a phenomenon virtually unknown beyond that country's borders, and little remembered even among the Swedish of a younger generation. At one time, the Dalecarlia region of west-central Sweden spawned a group of female artisans whose handiwork lay in their intricate weaving of hair as an accessory. Unnerstad herself explained in *Horn Book* in December, 1963, "Though the use of false hair is an ancient custom, trinkets and ornaments made of hair came into fashion and spread over Europe during the nineteenth century. The production in Dalecarlia began about 1830 or 1840, reached its height in the sixties, seventies, and eighties, when as many as three hundred Vamhus [parish] women every year set out on their travels—and then World War I put an end to all traveling."

Unnerstad, who had known hair-weavers in her youth, conducted extensive research before writing the books, the first of which portrayed a trip into Czarist Russia to sell the grandmother's hair-weavings. To research that journey, Unnerstad herself went to present-day Russia, then just recovering from Stalin's reign, where a state tour guide reluctantly allowed her to visit relevant spots in Leningrad. "Dotted with incidental adventure," wrote a commentator in *Virginia Kirkus' Service,* "[*The Journey with My Grandmother*] is a warm and vivid picture of life in Northern Europe before the advent of Communism." Janet Hitchman in the *New Statesman* asserted that the book "deserves to become a children's classic," and a critic in *Junior Bookshelf* commented that "The grandmother is a wonderful character, and manages to keep everyone happy even when the market for haircraft articles is low."

A Journey to England chronicles a second adventure of the hair-weavers, when the mother of two children disappears during a sales trip to Britain. The children, Margita and Brosus, travel to England to find her, which they do with the help of real-life Swedish opera singer Jenny Lind. "Of all the quests in storybooks," wrote Ruth Hill Viguers in *Horn Book,* "there are probably few more poignant than this of Margita and Brosus." Alice Low in the *New York Times Book Review* wrote that "Although Brosus and Margita may wonder whether their search will end happily, the reader is never in doubt."

BIOGRAPHICAL/CRITICAL SOURCES:

BOOKS

Children's Literature Review, Volume 36, Gale (Detroit, MI), 1995.

PERIODICALS

Bulletin of the Children's Book Center, July-August, 1957, p. 138.
Growing Point, March, 1963, p. 115.
Horn Book, December, 1961, p. 554; February, 1963, p. 110; December, 1963, pp. 580-87.
Junior Bookshelf, October, 1953, p. 163; November, 1960, pp. 310-11; November, 1962, p. 271.
New Statesman, November 19, 1960, p. 794.
New York Times Book Review, May 27, 1951, p. 22; February 28, 1962, p. 38.
Saturday Review, November 1, 1958, p. 46.
Virginia Kirkus' Service, February 1, 1957, p. 67; August 1, 1958, p. 546; August 1, 1960, p. 620.

URQUHART, Fred(erick Burrows) 1912-1995

PERSONAL: Born July 12, 1912, in Edinburgh, Scotland; died December 2, 1995, in Edinburgh, Scotland; son of Frederick Burrows and Agnes (Harrower) Urquhart. *Education:* Attended village and secondary schools in Scotland.

CAREER: Left school at age fifteen and worked in a bookshop, Edinburgh, Scotland, 1927-34; freelance writer; reader for literary agency in London, England, 1947-51, and for Metro-Goldwyn-Mayer, 1951-54; Cassell & Co. Ltd., London, reader, 1951-74. London scout for Walt Disney Productions, 1959-60; reader for J. M. Dent & Sons Ltd., 1967-71.

AWARDS, HONORS: Tom Gallon Award, Society of Authors, 1951-52, for story, "The Ploughing Match"; Arts Council of Great Britain grants, 1966, 1978, and 1985; Scottish Arts Council grant, 1975.

WRITINGS:

Time Will Knit (novel), Duckworth (London), 1938, Penguin (New York City), 1943.
I Fell for a Sailor, and Other Stories, Duckworth, 1940.
The Clouds Are Big with Mercy: Short Stories, William Maclellan, 1946.
Selected Stories, Maurice Fridberg, 1946.
The Last G.I. Bride Wore Tartan: A Novella and Some Short Stories, Serif Books (Edinburgh, Scotland), 1947.
The Ferret Was Abraham's Daughter: A Novel, Methuen (London), 1949.
The Year of the Short Corn, and Other Stories, Methuen, 1949.
The Last Sister, and Other Stories, Methuen, 1950.
Jezebel's Dust, Methuen, 1951.
The Laundry Girl and the Pole: Selected Stories, Arco Publishers (London), 1955.
(Author of text) Kenneth Scowen, *Scotland in Color,* Viking (New York City), 1961.
The Collected Stories of Fred Urquhart, Volume I: *The Dying Stallion,* 1967, Volume II: *The Ploughing Match,* Hart-Davis (London), 1968.
(With William Freeman) *Everyman's Dictionary of Fictional Characters,* 3rd edition (Urquhart was not associated with previous editions), Dent (London), 1973, published as *Dictionary of Fictional Characters,* with indexes of authors and titles by E. N. Pennell, The Writer (Boston), 1974.
Palace of Green Days (novel), Quartet Books (New York City), 1979.
Proud Lady in a Cage, and Other Stories, Paul Harris, 1980.
A Diver in China Seas, and Other Stories, Quartet Books, 1980.
Seven Ghosts in Search, Kimber, 1983.
Full Score: Short Stories, Aberdeen University Press (Aberdeen, Scotland), 1989.

EDITOR

(With Maurice Lindsay) *No Scottish Twilight: New Scottish Short Stories,* William Maclellan, 1947.
W.S.C.: A Cartoon Biography (of Winston Churchill), Cassell (London), 1955.
Scottish Short Stories, 3rd revised edition, Faber (London), 1957.
Great True War Adventures, Arco, 1957.
Men at War: The Best War Stories of All Time, Arco, 1957.
The Cassell Miscellany (1848-1958), Cassell, 1958.
Great True Escape Stories, Arco, 1958.
The Monarch Butterfly, illustrated by the author, University of Toronto Press, 1960.
(With Giles Gordon) *Modern Scottish Short Stories,* Hamish Hamilton (London), 1978.
The Book of Horses, Morrow (London), 1981.

CONTRIBUTOR

Edward J. H. O'Brien, editor, *Best Stories of 1938,* Houghton, 1938.
Cyril Connolly, editor, *Horizon Stories,* Faber, 1945.
Whit Burnett and Hallie Burnett, editors, *Story: The Fiction of the Forties,* Dutton (New York City), 1950.
Derek Hudson, editor, *Modern English Short Stories,* Oxford University Press (New York City), 1956.
John Pudney, editor, *Pick of Today's Short Stories,* Volume 11, Putnam (New York City), 1960.
J. M. Reid, editor, *Scottish Short Stories,* Oxford University Press, 1963.
Michael Rheta Martin, editor, *The Language of Love,* Bantam (New York City), 1964.
James Turner, editor, *Thy Neighbor's Wife,* Cassell, 1964.
Turner, editor, *The Fourth Ghost Book,* Barrie & Rockliff, 1965.
Turner, editor, *Unlikely Ghosts,* Taplinger, 1969.
J. F. Hendry, editor, *Penguin Book of Scottish Short Stories,* Penguin, 1970.

Denys Val Baker, editor, *Stories of Country Life,* Kimber, 1975.

Gordon, editor, *Prevailing Spirits,* Hamish Hamilton, 1976.

Baker, editor, *Stories of the Night,* Kimber, 1976.

Baker, editor, *My Favourite Story,* Kimber, 1977.

Baker, editor, *Stories of Horror and Suspense,* Kimber, 1978.

Baker, editor, *Stories of the Occult,* Kimber, 1978.

James Hale, editor, *The Midnight Ghost Book,* Barrie & Jenkins, 1978.

John Laurie, editor, *My Favourite Stories of Scotland,* Lutterworth, 1978.

Ronald Blythe, editor, *My Favourite Village Stories,* Lutterworth, 1979.

Baker, editor, *Stories of the Supernatural,* Kimber, 1979.

Baker, editor, *Stories of Fear,* Kimber, 1980.

Dedwydd Jones, editor, *2 Plus 2,* Switzerland, 1984-85.

Francis King, editor, *Twenty Stories,* Secker & Warburg (London), 1985.

Amy Myers, editor, *After Midnight Stories,* Kimber, 1985.

Gordon Jarvie, editor, *The Wild Ride,* Viking Kestrel, 1986.

Contributor of over 100 short stories to periodicals, including *London Magazine, London Mercury, Adelphi, Horizon, Life and Letters, Spectator, New Statesman, Story,* and *Harper's*. Book reviewer for periodicals and newspapers, including *Time and Tide, Books of the Month, Sunday Telegraph,* and *Oxford Mail.*

Urquhart's short stories have been read on radio, and have been translated into several European languages.

SIDELIGHTS: Frank Rudman in the *Spectator* called Fred Urquhart "one of our most distinguished writers of the short story. . . . He writes fine Scots dialect as well as supple English, and knows Scottish history down to its minutest detail." Francis King, in the same publication, observed that Urquhart "writes so simply and so effortlessly that it is easy to underrate him." Comparing Urquhart's *Palace of Green Days* to his first novel, *Time Will Knit,* King noted "the same benign enjoyment of human nature in all its inequalities and oddnesses." Urquhart was, in the words of Alexander Reid, "Scotland's leading short story writer of the century."

Working as a clerk in an Edinburgh bookstore during the 1920s, Urquhart first began writing short stories. Several of these were later published in journals, and some were turned into radio-plays. He held positions as a literary reader for agencies in London, as well as for Metro-Goldwyn-Mayer film studios, and also worked as a London scout for Walt Disney Productions. Among his notable works are *The Last G.I. Bride Wore Tartan: A Novella and Some Short Stories, Jezebel's Dust, The Laundry Girl and the Pole: Selected Stories,* and *Full Score: Short Stories.* In addition to his fiction, Urquhart edited many literary anthologies, including *Men at War: The Best War Stories of All Time; Modern Scottish Short Stories,* a collaborative effort with Giles Gordon; and *The Book of Horses.*

Graeme Roberts in the *Reference Guide to Short Fiction* noted that "It was Urquhart's portrayal of female characters that caught the attention of early admirers, such as Compton Mackenzie, who praised his 'remarkable talent for depicting women young and old.'" Most of these women are from the lower echelons of the working class, and the smallest possession, such as the one named in the title of "The Bike," represents a huge investment. Hence when the protagonist of that story sees her drunken boyfriend destroy the bicycle by accident, Urquhart writes, "She knew that something more than her bike had been broken. Nothing would ever be the same again."

Roberts noted the quality of "[s]ympathetic insight" in Urquhart's writing, a quality which he found nowhere more evident than in the award-winning "The Ploughing Match." For fifty years, Annie Dey had envisioned a ploughing match on her family farm, with her as grande dame and hostess. But now that the match finally has come, the weapons of competition are not the handheld ploughs she had known as a girl, but tractors. Worse, Annie is laid up with a stroke, partially paralyzed and unable to speak. She is utterly dependent on others: "The old woman sucked in her lower lip, clamping down her hard gum on it. She looked at her set of false teeth in the tumbler beside the bed, and she closed her eyes in pain. To be beholden to other folk to get them put into her mouth." To top it off, no one attending the match even comes to see her. A lesser writer, Roberts suggested, would have allowed the situation to become "drowned in a welter of pathos"; but "Urquhart's unsentimental conception of Annie's character," as well as "his control of language and tone," makes the story both sharp and sympathetic.

Naomi Mitchison in *Contemporary Novelists* also noted that "Urquhart is best with his women characters, his schoolmistresses and farmers' wives or daughters; his Glasgow lassies on the make or his dirty old wifies." It was ironic, Mitchison suggested, that a man from a country famous for the tough masculinity of its males should write such sensitive portrayals. Ironic, too, was Mitchison's conclusion, written just before Urquhart passed away: "It is hard luck to have to wait till you are dead before you are appreciated. One hopes this won't happen to Fred Urquhart."

Urquhart was, as Mitchison noted, "not a quick writer," though he proved to be prolific in his long career. He was also not inclined to talk about works in progress, even with friends. "I never talk to people about my work," he once said. "When I'm writing a story or novel, I don't want anybody to see it or know anything about it until it is completely finished and it satisfies me. I can't understand the habit of some authors of reading their work aloud to their friends as their work progresses. It is only after I've written a story that I show it to friends, inviting criticism."

BIOGRAPHICAL/CRITICAL SOURCES:

BOOKS

Bold, Alan, *Modern Scottish Literature,* Longman (London), 1983.

Contemporary Novelists, sixth edition, St. James Press, 1996.

Lindsay, Maurice, *History of Scottish Literature,* R. Hale (London), 1977.

Reference Guide to Short Fiction, St. James Press, 1994.

PERIODICALS

Blackwood's Magazine, February, 1968; March, 1980.

Financial Times, August 23, 1980.

Guardian, July 24, 1980; August 21, 1980.

Listener, December 14, 1967.

Observer, July 29, 1979.

Punch, June 5, 1968.

Spectator, December 15, 1967; May 24, 1968; August 18, 1979; September 13, 1980.

Times Literary Supplement, September 19, 1980; December 30, 1983.

OBITUARIES:

PERIODICALS

Times (London), December 18, 1995, p. 19.*

V

VACULIK, Ludvik 1926-

PERSONAL: Surname is pronounced Vaht-*Soo*-leek; born July 23, 1926, in Brumov, Czechoslovakia; son of Martin (a carpenter) and Anna (Lysackova) Vaculik; married Marie Komarkova (a clerk), June 4, 1949; children: Martin, Ondrej, Jan. *Education:* High School for Social and Political Sciences, Prague, B.Soc. and Pol. Sci., 1951.

ADDRESSES: *Office*—c/o Mlada fronta, Panska 8, 11222 Prague 1, Czech Republic.

CAREER: Ceskoslovenska Kolben-Danek (machine works), Prague, Czechoslovakia, educator, 1950-51; Rude pravo (publishing house), Prague, Czechoslovakia, editor, 1953-57; *Beseda venkovske rodiny* (illustrated weekly), Prague, Czechoslovakia, editor, 1957-59; Czechoslovak Radio, Prague, Czechoslovakia, editor, 1959-66; *Literarni noviny* (weekly publication of Writers Union), Prague, Czechoslovakia, editor, 1966-69; writer, 1969—; main organizer, Edice Petlice (Padlock Editions) samizdat series, 1970s; arrested for television interview given to the BBC, 1973, passport revoked. *Military service:* Czechoslovakian Armed Forces, 1951-53.

AWARDS, HONORS: State award for work in the radio youth program, 1964; prize from Ceskoslovensky Spisovatel, 1967, for *Sekyra;* George Orwell Prize, 1976.

WRITINGS:

FICTION

Rusny dum (translated as "The Busy House") Ceskoslovensky Spisovatel (Prague), 1963.

Sekyra, Ceskoslovensky Spisovatel, 1966, translation by Marian Sling published as *The Axe,* Harper (New York City), 1973.

Die Meerschweinchen, Blucher (Lucerne, Switzerland), 1971, published in Czech as *Morcata,* Edice Petlice (samizdat, Prague), 1973, translation by Kaca Polackova published as *The Guinea Pigs,* Third Press (New York City), 1973.

Cesky snar (translated as "A Czech Dreambook"), samizdat (Prague), 1980, Sixty-Eight Publishers (Toronto), 1983, translation published as *Czech Book of Dreams,* Atlantis (Prague), 1990.

NONFICTION

Na farme mladeze (translated as "The Youth Farm"), Statni Nakladatelstvi Politicke Literatury (Prague), 1958.

The Relations Between Citizen and Power: Contribution at the Czechoslovak Writers' Conference 1967, Liberal International/British Group (London), 1968.

(Editor, with Jiri Grusa and Milan Uhde), *Hodina nadeje: almanach ceske literatury 1968-1978* (translated as "Hour of Hope: Anthology of Czech Literature"), Reich (Lucerne), 1978, Sixty-Eight Publishers, 1980.

Mili spouluzaci! Vybor pisemnych praci 1939-1979 (translated as "Dear School-Fellows! A Choice of Written Work, 1939-1979"), Volume 1: *Kniha indiansak* (translated as "Indian Book"), Volume 2: *Kniha delnicka* (translated as "A Worker's Book"), Index (Cologne), 1986.

A Cup of Coffee with My Interrogator: The Prague Chronicles of Ludvik Vaculik, introduction by Vaclav Havel, Readers International (London), 1987.

Jajo je tady: fejetony z let 1981-1987 (translated as "Spring Is Here: Columns from 1981 to 1987"), Index, 1988.

Srpnovy rok: fejetony z roku 1988 (translated as "August Year: Columns from 1988"), Prazska imaginace (Prague), 1989.

Stara dama se bavi (translated as "The Old Lady Is Enjoying Herself"), Lidove noviny (Prague), 1990.

(Editor), *Hlasy nad rukopisem Vaculikova Ceskeho snare* (translated as "Views on the Manuscript of Vaculik's *Cesky snar*"), Torst (Prague), 1991.

Nad jezeem skarede hrat: vyber z publicistiky 1990-1995, Ivo Zelezny (Prague), 1996.

Vaculik's books have been published in German, French, Norwegian, and Serbo-Croat (Yugoslavian) editions.

SIDELIGHTS: Ludvik Vaculik once told *CA,* "I find writing harder than digging in the garden." He also noted that since 1969 he had been a "private writer, without employment." In fact he had been under extensive censure and scrutiny by his nation's government following an abortive attempt by Czech intellectuals and others to overthrown the Communist regime in 1968. The latter event, called "Prague Spring" because it represented a brief thaw in the long winter of totalitarianism, lingered in the memory of Czech writers such as Vaclav Havel, Milan Kundera, and Vaculik as a haunting symbol of unrealized possibilities, of freedom delayed—until the final overthrown of Communism throughout Eastern Europe that began in 1989.

Robert B. Pynsent in *Contemporary World Writers* noted that Vaculik was part of a trend toward "confessional literature" among Czech writers of the 1970s that included Havel, Kundera, and others—"but Vaculik's [books] have been confessional since his debut novel *Rusny dum* ('The Busy House') in 1963." Through this and three subsequent novels, Pynsent wrote, Vaculik "follow(s) the development of an intelligent, streetwise countryman from Communist enthusiasm in *Rusny dum,* to wry quizzicality about the deformation and degradation engendered by the Communist Party in *Sekyra* (*The Axe* [1966]), to a parodic analysis of the rule of fear and inaccessibility of knowledge under Communism in *Morcata* (*The Guinea Pigs* [1971]), and finally, in *Cesky snar* ("A Czech Dreambook" [1980]), to the recognition of freedom as lying in love and responsibility, and being indifferent to the regime. One might say, then, that together the novels depict the formation of a self."

The self developed through Vaculik's work is his own, and the journey from faith to disillusionment to understanding is a journey he took himself. *Rusny dum* is, in Pynsent's words, "essentially a Communist idyll." Its setting is the years from 1951 to 1953, long before Prague Spring, and though the book pokes fun at the system, the perspective is that of an adherent to the faith. *The Axe* is a diffuse tale, a mixture of anecdotes that Pynsent calls "a novel about memory"—and, as Kundera has often pointed out, even the act of remembering, when committed under the shadow of a repressive system, is inherently subversive. "Perhaps it is a measure of the totalitarian pressures on the novelist," wrote Clive Jordan in *Encounter,* "that the present-day activities of his journalist hero are only obliquely suggested, while the picture of childhood stands out in pleasing clarity."

The protagonist of *The Guinea Pigs* is a bank clerk—a bureaucrat who represents millions of other cogs in the state machinery. As the title suggests, the state regards him as little more than a creature for experimentation, a being without choices: hence Vaculik writes, "Most difficult of all, boys and girls, is to change your life of your own free will. Even when you have the most wonderful feeling that you're the driver of your locomotive, someone else always comes along and changes the points." A *Times Literary Supplement* reviewer noted, by reference to Czechoslovakia's most famous writer, the dark tradition to which *The Guinea Pigs* belonged: "What starts out as a cheerful story, ends in the darkest, almost metaphysical horror; there is no faith left, no hope—in anything. Kafka, too, lived in Prague."

Cesky snar almost qualifies as a nonfiction novel rather than a novel per se, since it is the diary of thirteen months (from January of 1979 to February of 1980) that Vaculik spent under police observation. The book had to be published initially in samizdat format—that is, in an underground publication; later, after he had circulated the book among friends and others (including his secret police "minder," Major Fiser), Vaculik published a companion volume whose title translates as "Views on the Manuscript of Vaculik's *Cesky snar.*" In it, he recorded the reactions of Fiser and others to the book.

In the essays collected as *A Cup of Coffee with My Interrogator: The Prague Chronicles of Ludvik*

Vaculik (1987), Vaculik presented a more straightforwardly nonfiction portrayal of his experiences. Presented as a journal, Vaculik writes of his past experiences with Czechoslovakian authorities including his reflections on topics such as coffeehouses, lazy waiters, the bombing of Libya by the United States, and glasnost." Walter Goodman averred in the *New York Times Book Review* that "This is no 'Darkness at Noon' or 'Nineteen Eighty-Four,'" meaning that the world depicted in *A Cup of Coffee* is not as harsh and pitiless as the totalitarian systems depicted by Arthur Koestler and George Orwell respectively in their famous novels. Not only are the examiners "unfailingly polite," but Vaculik manages well by himself. "When, in the title piece, a Lieutenant Colonel Noga asks for his opinion of the way the Western press uses the Prague government's treatment of writers 'for its slanderous campaign against Czechoslovakia,'" Vaculik replies that he will formulate a response once he has reviewed the opinions expressed in the Western press. The anthology, wrote Jeri Laber in the *New York Times Book Review,* "inspires hope, as well as admiration for the strength and dignity that have enabled Czechoslovak intellectuals to survive the long Prague winter."

BIOGRAPHICAL/CRITICAL SOURCES:

BOOKS

Contemporary Literary Criticism, Volume 7, Gale (Detroit, MI), 1977.

Contemporary World Writers, second edition, St. James Press, 1993.

PERIODICALS

Encounter, February, 1974.

New York Times Book Review, August 23, 1987, p. 17; August 27, 1987, section C, p. 25.

Times Literary Supplement, October 12, 1973.

* * *

VANDERHAEGHE, Guy 1951-

PERSONAL: Born April 5, 1951, in Esterhazy, Saskatchewan, Canada; son of Clarence Earl and Alma Beth (Allen) Vanderhaeghe; married Margaret Elizabeth Nagel (a painter), September 2, 1972. *Education:* University of Saskatchewan, B.A. (with honors), 1972, M.A., 1975; University of Regina, B.Ed., 1978.

ADDRESSES: *Home*—Saskatoon, Saskatchewan, Canada. *Office*—c/o Writers Union of Canada, 24 Ryerson Ave., Toronto, Ontario, Canada M5T 2P3.

CAREER: University of Saskatchewan, Saskatoon, archivist, 1973-75; *Journal of Orthomolecular Medicine,* Regina, Saskatchewan, editor, 1976-78; high school English and history teacher in Herbert, Saskatchewan, 1978-79; Access Consulting (health care consultants), Saskatoon, researcher, 1979-81; writer, 1981—. Writer-in-residence at Saskatoon Public Library, 1983-84. Member of Saskatchewan Arts Board, 1983—.

MEMBER: Writers Union of Canada, Saskatchewan Writers Guild.

AWARDS, HONORS: Governor General's Award for English fiction, 1982, for *Man Descending;* Governor General's Award, 1996, for *The Englishman's Boy.*

WRITINGS:

Man Descending (short stories), Macmillan of Canada (Toronto), 1982, Ticknor & Fields (New York City), 1985.

The Trouble With Heroes (short stories), Borealis Press (Ottawa, Canada), 1983.

My Present Age (novel), Macmillan of Canada, 1984, Ticknor & Fields, 1985.

Homesick, McClelland & Stewart (Toronto), 1989, Ticknor & Fields, 1990.

I Had a Job I Liked, Once: A Play, Fifth House (Saskatoon, Canada), 1992.

Things As They Are?: Short Stories, McClelland & Stewart, 1992.

Dancock's Dance, Blizzard Publishers (Winnipeg, Canada), 1996.

The Englishman's Boy, Picador USA (New York City), 1997.

Work represented in anthologies, including *Aurora: New Canadian Writing,* Doubleday, 1978, 1979, 1980; *Best Canadian Short Stories,* Oberon Press, 1980; *Best American Short Stories,* 1982. Contributor to magazines, including *Saturday Night, Wascana Review, Prism International, Journal of Canadian Fiction, Malahat Review,* and *Quarry.*

ADAPTATIONS: *Cages,* a film version of Vanderhaeghe's short story by the same name, was released by Beacon Films (Norwood, MA), 1996.

SIDELIGHTS: Guy Vanderhaeghe once told *CA:* "I have been described as a writer with a singularly bleak outlook. I reject that description. I regard myself as a writer who celebrates endurance—particularly the endurance of the ordinary person whose life is a series of small victories fashioned from small resources and whose hard-won realism is the result of life lived without the buffers that privilege brings."

In a lengthy review of Vanderhaeghe's most noteworthy work to date, *The Englishman's Boy,* John Bemrose of *Maclean's* chronicled the author's career up to that point. His first book, the short collection *Man Descending,* had earned him a Governor General's Award, along with "praise from Canada's master of the genre, Alice Munro, who called the book 'wonderful.'" But though Vanderhaeghe had received great praise for works such as *My Present Age* and *Homesick,* "critical respectability has not translated into financial success. To help support himself and his painter wife, Margaret, Vanderhaeghe teaches creative writing at a Saskatoon night school, and, as he drolly puts it, begs for grants. Yet the begging may end with *The Englishman's Boy.*"

The theme of the latter book—that the myth of heroism does not always survive close scrutiny of heroes—is not an altogether unfamiliar one in Vanderhaeghe's work, which has often found him depicting less than heroic figures. *Man Descending* was characterized thus in *Contemporary Literary Criticism:* "Most of the twelve stories in this collection revolve around characters who are despondent, aimless, and unsuccessful." As for *The Trouble with Heroes and Other Stories,* his second collection, it "likewise depicts unheroic men and their uneventful lives," but juxtaposes these with heroic settings by using backdrops such as stories from the Old Testament.

One of the anti-heroes from *Man Descending,* Ed of the story "Sam, Soren, and Ed," became the protagonist of *My Present Age.* Alberto Manguel wrote, in a review for *Books in Canada,* that "[Vanderhaeghe] has built his novel around (and in the style of) Ed's paranoia: *My Present Age* is the portrait of one man seen by himself in the distorted mirror of his own mind. Too witty for his contemporaries ('Any idea what genius is? The infinite capacity for taking pains?'), too ill-suited for an acceptable place in this world ('I found myself in the unfamiliar position of having no one to disappoint'), Ed is a hero who is also the village idiot." Douglas Barbour in *Canadian Literature* observed that "Vanderhaeghe masterfully shows everything from [Ed's] point of view yet also reveals his failings as an observer. Nevertheless, for all his faults, Ed has an unerring eye and ear for phoniness, and Vanderhaeghe allows that to emerge again and again."

Vera Miller in *Homesick* is a long-suffering anti-heroine, who tells the story of leaving Toronto with her twelve-year-old son Daniel in 1959 to return to her family in a remote Saskatchewan town. She has been estranged from them for seventeen years, and according to Douglas Bauer in the *New York Times Book Review,* has struggled to rear her son "sustained by grit and considerable self-denial." In a drawn-out monologue, Vera voices her grievances "in the guise of selfless strength." Bauer noted that *Homesick* does not compare to Vanderhaeghe's *Man Descending,* and concluded that reading *Homesick* "is like being trapped on a long bus trip next to someone who fills your ear with complaint and self-congratulation."

But with *The Englishman's Boy,* Vanderhaeghe seemed to have hit his stride in the view of numerous critics. "The book is so different from Vanderhaeghe's earlier fiction," Bemrose observed in *Maclean's,* "that it almost seems written by someone else. Vanderhaeghe's past work favored "a dark, almost claustrophobic focus on the conflicts" of relationships. *The Englishman's Boy,* however, "has a clean, exhilarating expansiveness" wrote Bemrose. According to Bemrose, Vanderhaeghe himself says the book developed quickly. " 'Normally I write very slowly,' he says. But after he had spent several years finding his way into *The Englishman's Boy,* it began to draw him rapidly forward."

The Englishman's Boy is really two stories, one set in Montana and Canada during the 1870s, the other in Hollywood in the 1920s. The earlier tale, based on a real event, chronicles the massacre of a group of Native Americans by American and Canadian trappers. A former valet, part Indian, serves as their guide; half a century later, he reappears in Hollywood as an aging cowboy, Shorty McAdoo, whose life is about to become the subject of a blockbuster motion picture intended to rival D. W. Griffith's

1915 epic *Birth of a Nation.* The movie, wrote John Motyka in the *New York Times,* is intended to "[embody] the rather hazy concept of a mythic American identity," and *The Englishman's Boy,* which Motyka called a "fine new novel" exposes the reality behind this myth. With the unfolding of McAdoo's story "into the stuff of patriotic, big-screen legend," noted Megan Harlan in *Entertainment Weekly,* "irony [is set] against idealism" to portray both the American West and Hollywood. Barbara Love in *Library Journal* suggested that it was refreshing to have a gritty adventure tale which doubled as a literary triumph.

The Englishman's Boy won the 1996 Governor General's Award, and was nominated for the 1998 International IMPAC Dublin Literary Award, at $192,000 the world's largest book prize. Though it did not win, the nomination suggested more honors to come.

BIOGRAPHICAL/CRITICAL SOURCES:

BOOKS

Contemporary Literary Criticism, Volume 41, Gale (Detroit, MI), 1987.

PERIODICALS

Books in Canada, October, 1984, p. 31.
Canadian Literature, summer, 1985, pp. 151-52.
Entertainment Weekly, October 31, 1997, p. 100.
Library Journal, September 1, 1997, p. 221.
Maclean's, September 23, 1996, pp. 46-47; March 23, 1998, p. 15.
New York Times, October 5, 1997.
New York Times Book Review, June 17, 1990, section 7, p. 15.
Publishers Weekly, June 16, 197, p. 43.

* * *

VENDLER, Helen (Hennessy) 1933-

PERSONAL: Born April 30, 1933, in Boston, MA; daughter of George (a teacher) and Helen (a teacher; maiden name, Conway) Hennessy; divorced; children: David. *Education:* Emmanuel College, A.B. (summa cum laude), 1954; attended University of Louvain as a Fulbright Fellow,, 1954-55, and Boston University as a special student, 1955-56; Harvard University, Ph.D., 1960.

ADDRESSES: Home—54 Trowbridge St. #2, Cambridge, MA 02138-4113. *Office*—Department of English, Barker Center, 12 Quincy Street, Harvard University, Cambridge, MA 02138-3929.

CAREER: Cornell University, Ithaca, NY, instructor in English, 1960-63; Haverford College, Haverford, PA, lecturer in English, and Swarthmore College, Swarthmore, PA, lecturer in English, both 1963-64; Smith College, Northampton, MA, assistant professor of English, 1964-66; Boston University, Boston, MA, associate professor, 1966-68, professor of English, 1968-85, director of graduate studies, department of English, 1970-75 and 1978-79; Harvard University, Cambridge, MA, visiting professor, 1981-85, professor of English, 1985—, William R. Kenan Professor of English and American Literature and Language, 1986—, associate dean of arts and sciences, 1987-92; Porter University, professor, 1990—; Fulbright lecturer in American literature, University of Bordeaux, 1968-69; Fanny Hurst Visiting Professor, Washington University, St. Louis, fall, 1975. Judge for National Book Award in poetry, 1972, and Pulitzer Prize in poetry, 1974, 1976, 1978, and 1986. Member of subcommittee on literary criticism awards, Guggenheim Foundation, 1974, 1976, 1977, and 1978; jury member for Mellon fellowships and Rockefeller fellowships, both 1979. Member, Rockefeller Commission on the Humanities, 1978-79, and Board of Educational Consultants, National Endowment for the Humanities; Pulitzer Prize Board, 1991-2000; senior fellow Harvard Society Fellows, 1981-93; member of the educational advisory board, Guggenheim Foundation, 1991—.

MEMBER: Modern Language Association of America (member of executive council, 1971-75; second vice-president, 1978; first vice-president, 1979; president, 1980), American Academy of Arts and Sciences (councillor, 1976-80), English Institute (member of supervisory board, 1970-73; trustee, 1977- 86), American Philosophical Society, Norwegian Academy of Letters and Sciences, PEN, Society of Fellows, Harvard University, Phi Beta Kappa.

AWARDS, HONORS: Fulbright fellowship, 1954-55; American Association of University Women fellowship, 1959-60; American Council of Learned Societies, grant-in-aid, 1963, fellowship, 1971; James Russell Lowell Prize, Modern Language Association, and *Explicator* Literary Foundation Award, 1969, both for *On Extended Wings: Wallace Stevens' Longer Poems;* Guggenheim fellowship, 1971; National Institute of Arts and Letters Award, 1975;

Metcalf Teaching Award, Boston University, 1975; National Endowment for the Humanities fellowship, 1977-78, 1986-87 and 1994-95; Graduate Society Medal, Radcliffe College, 1978; National Book Critics Circle Award in criticism, and "Notable Book" citation from American Library Association, 1980, both for *Part of Nature, Part of Us: Modern American Poets;* National Book Critics Circle Award in criticism nomination, 1983, for *The Odes of John Keats,* finalist, 1997, for *The Art of Shakespeare's Sonnets;* Keats-Shelley Association Award, 1994; Charles Stewart Parnell fellow, Magdalene College, Cambridge, 1995; Newton Arvin Prize for Literary Criticism, 1995; recipient of numerous honorary degrees, including those from Smith College, University of Oslo, Kenyon College, University of Hartford, Union College, Columbia University, and Cambridge University.

WRITINGS:

NONFICTION; LITERARY CRITICISM

Yeats's Vision and the Later Plays, Harvard University Press (Cambridge, MA), 1963.

On Extended Wings: Wallace Stevens' Longer Poems, Harvard University Press (Cambridge), 1969.

(Editor with Reuben Brower and John Hollander, and contributor) *I. A. Richards: Essays in His Honor,* Oxford University Press (New York City), 1973.

The Poetry of George Herbert, Harvard University Press, 1975.

Part of Nature, Part of Us: Modern American Poets, Harvard University Press, 1980.

The Odes of John Keats, Harvard University Press, 1983.

Wallace Stevens: Words Chosen Out of Desire, University of Tennessee Press (Knoxville), 1984, Harvard University Press, 1986.

(Editor and author of introduction) *The Harvard Book of Contemporary American Poetry,* Harvard University Press, 1985 (published in England as *The Faber Book of Contemporary American Poetry,* Faber, 1987).

(Contributing editor and author of introduction to contemporary poetry section) Donald McQuade, general editor, *The Harper American Literature,* two volumes, Harper (New York City), 1987.

(Editor, author of introduction, and contributor) *Voices and Visions: The Poet in America* (companion to "Voices and Visions," broadcast on PBS-TV, January 26-April 19, 1988), Random House (New York City), 1987.

The Music of What Happens: Poems, Poets, Critics, Harvard University Press, 1988.

The Given and the Made: Strategies of Poetic Redefinition, Harvard University Press, 1995.

Soul Says: On Recent Poetry, Belknap Press (Cambridge), 1995.

The Breaking of Style: Hopkins, Heaney, Graham, Harvard University Press, 1995.

The Art of Shakespeare's Sonnets, Harvard/Belknap (Cambridge, MA), 1997.

(Editor) *Poems, Poets, Poetry: An Introduction and Anthology,* Bedford Books of St. Martin's Press (Boston), 1997.

Seamus Heaney, Harvard University Press, 1998.

CONTRIBUTOR

Roy Harvey Pearce and Hillis Miller, editors, *The Act of the Mind,* Johns Hopkins University Press (Baltimore, MD), 1964.

Reuben Brower, editor, *Forms of Lyric,* Columbia University Press (New York City), 1970.

Irvin Ehrenpreis, editor, *Wallace Stevens,* Penguin (New York City), 1972.

William H. Pritchard, editor, *William Butler Yeats,* Penguin (New York City), 1972.

W. K. Wimsatt, editor, *Literary Criticism: Idea and Act,* University of California Press (Berkeley), 1974.

Frank Doggett and Robert Buttel, editors, *Wallace Stevens: A Celebration,* Princeton University Press (Princeton, NJ), 1980.

Lloyd Schwartz and Sybil P. Estess, editors, *Elizabeth Bishop and Her Art,* University of Michigan Press (Ann Arbor), 1983.

(Selector and author of introduction) Stevens, Wallace, *Poems,* Arion Press (San Francisco), 1985, Knopf (New York City), 1993.

(Author of introduction) Milosz, Czeslaw, *Swiat = The World* (poetry), Arion Press, 1989.

Keats, John, *Poetry Manuscripts at Harvard,* edited by Jack Stillinger, Belknap Press (Cambridge), 1990.

(Author of foreword) *Polish Poetry of the Last Two Decades of Communist Rule: Spoiling Cannibals' Fun,* edited and translated by Stanislaw Baranczak and Clare Cavanagh, Northwestern University Press (Evanston), 1991.

(Author of introduction) Shakespeare, William, *The Sonnets and Narrative Poems,* edited by William Burto, Knopf, 1992.

OTHER

Also contributor to "Modern Critical Views" series, edited by Harold Bloom, Chelsea House. Contributor of numerous articles to periodicals, including *Atlantic, Mademoiselle, Massachusetts Review, New Republic, New Yorker, New York Times Book Review, Parnassus: Poetry in Review, Salmagundi, New York Review of Books, London Review of Books,* and *Southern Review;* contributor of numerous reviews to periodicals, including *American Scholar, Nation,* and *Yale Review.* Member of advisory board, *Studies in Romanticism;* consulting poetry editor, *New York Times Book Review,* 1971-74; member of editorial board, *American Scholar,* 1978-81; poetry critic, *New Yorker,* 1978—.

SIDELIGHTS: Helen Vendler is regarded by many as one of America's foremost critics of poetry. Since the mid-1960s she has contributed numerous reviews and articles on poetry to prominent literary publications, in particular the *New York Times Book Review,* and since 1978 has served as poetry critic for the *New Yorker.* In addition to her reviews and articles, Vendler is the author of acclaimed book-length studies of poets W. B. Yeats, George Herbert, Wallace Stevens, John Keats, William Shakespeare, and Seamus Heaney. Her most noted work, the award-winning collection of criticism *Part of Nature, Part of Us: Modern American Poets,* is recognized as an extensive and informed view of contemporary American poetry. A second collection, *The Music of What Happens: Poems, Poets, Critics,* further explores the issues that surround contemporary British and American poetry. Regarding Vendler's accomplishments, William H. Pritchard once remarked in the *New Republic:* "To begin with a judgment widely shared, if not a truth universally acknowledged: Helen Vendler is the best poetry reviewer in America."

Vendler is often cited as one of poetry's best "close readers," her criticism frequently praised for its insightful explication of individual poems and its comprehension of individual aesthetic principles. Poetry is the literary art which, she states in the foreword to *Part of Nature, Part of Us,* is "the one form of writing that is to me the most immediate, natural, and accessible." "Poetry, clearly, is Vendler's passion," writes Phoebe Pettingell in the *New Leader.* "She directs her observations straight at the heart of the matter, so that her readers may recognize at once what she finds so marvelous in a poem." Vendler's critical writings have been recognized as assured and illuminating discussions of poetry. Pritchard cites "the pressure of an appetite" and an "unreticent forcefulness" at work in Vendler's poetry criticism, adding that "her virtues are a rigorous attending to verbal structure and texture; the ability to quote appositely and economically; a sure though not a too-exclusive taste; above all, the ability to do the poem one better by putting into words the relevant responses we might have had if we'd been smarter and more feeling." In a review of *Part of Nature, Part of Us* in the *New York Times,* Anatole Broyard describes a respect for poetry that becomes apparent in Vendler's criticism: "Unlike some critics, Helen Vendler puts herself entirely at the service of the poets she is talking about. Although she writes too well to be invisible, she does not compete or pontificate either. . . . What she does is to offer the poetry to you and somehow push and pull you into shape until you can accept it."

Part of Nature, Part of Us was a resounding accomplishment for Vendler, a collection of her reviews and essays published between 1966 and 1979 which "provides a sweeping overview of contemporary American poetry," writes John C. Hawley in *America.* During the time span that these reviews and essays appeared, Vendler's reputation as a formidable literary critic was also bolstered by her extended studies of Stevens and Herbert. *On Extended Wings: Wallace Stevens' Longer Poems* "ought to be read, with care and gratitude, by every reader of Stevens, for no critic before her has understood so well his major poems," says Harold Bloom in the *New York Times Book Review,* adding: "Helen Vendler . . . has written a superb and badly needed book, giving us readings unlikely to be surpassed of Stevens's longer poems, which tend to be his best." Likewise, Vendler's *The Poetry of George Herbert* was praised as an in-depth study of the early seventeenth-century English metaphysical poet. "Vendler is undoubtedly a finely trained and extraordinarily resourceful reader, and I cannot imagine that anybody who cares for Herbert, or more generally for poetry, will fail to learn something from this book," comments Frank Kermode in the *New York Times Book Review.* Kermode adds that although Vendler displays a "willfulness" by examining those of Herbert's poems which most closely "fit her model," she lays the foundations of her study in the works themselves: "Her meditations are nearly always faithful to their texts—she very rarely succumbs to the vice of the 'close reader,' which is to speak more wonders than the poem is considering; and she has brought off a quite notable feat of construction in making a collection of disparate commentaries stand up as a book."

Vendler achieves a similar effect in *Part of Nature, Part of Us* where, instead of extensively treating various aspects of a single poet, she examines diversity among a number of contemporary American poets—in the process giving testament to an entire artistic movement. "The effect of the book is to give a comprehensive and highly authoritative picture of the American poetry scene today," writes John Bayley in the *Times Literary Supplement.* "There is nothing bitty about the technique: the whole sweep of her survey is sure and purposive, and coming to the end of the book one feels that a number of really significant generalizations have been made about the nature of the American poetic phenomenon, and the way it relates to the American consciousness." Forty-five different poets are discussed in Vendler's survey, including Wallace Stevens, Robert Lowell, Elizabeth Bishop, James Merrill, and Adrienne Rich. Vendler's remarks in the foreword to the collection both describe her approach and offer insight into its objectives: "My own preference is to focus on poets one by one, to find in each the idiosyncratic voice wonderfully different from any other. . . . All the poets of the century become part of a common music, but the voices of genius live vividly in their oddness and their intensity. Still, if they had nothing in common with us—if they were not, as Stevens says, part of nature and part of us, their rarities would not be ours, and we could not hear them speak. To write about them is to try to explain, first to oneself and then to others, what common note they strike and how they make it new." Monroe K. Spears in the *Washington Post Book World* comments that "in a time when much criticism seems increasingly academic and autotelic, self-generating and self-absorbed and perhaps self-destructive, it is a relief to find a critic who conceives of her work as having a definite and humane purpose." *Part of Nature, Part of Us* was the unanimous choice of the National Book Critics Circle for its 1980 award in criticism.

Vendler's critical perspective and writing style are central to the impact of *Part of Nature, Part of Us* and emerge as overall strengths of her literary criticism. Irvin Ehrenpreis writes in the *New York Review of Books* that Vendler's critical stance is distinguished in that it does not start with the "poem as a completed object"; rather, "Vendler starts with the act of creation. She stands beside the poet and watches him compose. Reading her essays, one acquires a sense of works of art not laid out in an operating theater but just coming into being." Similarly, Harold Beaver notes in *Parnassus: Poetry in Review* that Vendler's "strategy is not so much to center on the poem, or on the poet, but on the problem of writing such and such a poem." Thus, he explains, "the act of writing is itself treated as a critical act: the critic's role is to ponder and assess that act." Bayley contends that Vendler "is certainly the most thoughtful and humane, as she is the least system-bound, critic of poetry now writing. . . . Her examination of a poet is always as absolutely business-like and thorough as it is sympathetic, like that of a really good doctor."

Vendler's writing style in *Part of Nature, Part of Us* earned particular praise from a number of reviewers. Denis Donoghue writes in the *New York Times Book Review* that "when she likes a poem and sways to its music, she pays it the tribute of paraphrase in terms that are often just as memorable as the poem itself." Ehrenpreis elaborates: "Vendler sparkles with brisk metaphors, colloquial rhythms, newborn phrases, [and] a syntax that evokes a mind endlessly responsive to the article before it. . . . The impression one gets of a wonderfully adaptable sensibility moving in company with the poet's genius is due not only to the wisdom and penetration of her judgement but to the unforeseeable, satisfying notions of her language and phrasing." Beaver describes Vendler's technique as "less a method than an endlessly alert, protracted hesitancy, a hummingbird-like hovering and darting from possibility to possibility."

Vendler attracted much attention with her next book of criticism, *The Odes of John Keats,* a groundbreaking—in some circles, controversial—study of the nineteenth-century English Romantic poet. In the book, Vendler examines several of Keats's most famous odes, not only in regard to their often praised rich language, but, as Ehrenpreis notes, "find[ing] . . . a special relation, dealing progressively with a common theme, the creative imagination." Pettingell explains that "Vendler presents the sequential progression of the odes as a series of tentative solutions, proposed, rejected, then used as building blocks toward the next." A number of reviewers, although impressed with Vendler's reading of the individual odes, point out problems in organizing them as a progressive larger structure. Ehrenpreis writes that "Vendler takes for granted both an order and a progression, with each principle supporting the other. To some readers, therefore, her demonstrations will appear circular." *New Republic* contributor David Bromwich claims that by examining the odes as a progressive development, Vendler "is obliged to discover a fair amount of shortcomings in the earlier odes which readers not attuned to her story have either passed over or refused to consider as faults." And, Frank Kermode comments in the *New York Times Book Review* that Vendler's "overriding need to show development from ode to ode imposes some constraints, perhaps exquisite, on the expositor. It imposes orders, and these orders replace what might be rewarding in a different way, an acceptance of fortuity." Vendler's approach, however, also bears witness to a respect for the strength of Keats's writing, contends Maureen Corrigan in the *Voice Literary Supplement:* "By adopting close reading as her critical technique, she pays Keats the highest compliment of viewing his work as a crystallization of language and culture that anticipates, within its own structures, all the myriad 'outside' frameworks that could be imposed upon it."

While some reviewers take issue with Vendler's thesis in *The Odes of John Keats,* many are quick to point out typical strengths of her literary criticism. "She is a materialist—and in a noble sense of the word," writes Nicholas Bromell in the *Boston Review.* "Vendler roots her discussion of the odes in her deeply felt response to Keats's language. Her ability to *present* what Keats is doing and to describe the effects, registered in our minds, of Keats's verbal facility, is breathtaking." Ehrenpreis concurs, commenting that although "reading the odes as a group is less likely to be successful than individual readings[,] . . . the most appealing feature of Vendler's work remains; and that is her desire to follow the poet in his labor of creation." Ehrenpreis explains that "Vendler's fundamental method is to enter intuitively into the decisions and changes of mind which lie behind the finished work, so that she gives us a dramatic sense of how the poem reached the state in which we know it." Kermode calls Vendler a "virtuoso," adding that "readers should not expect that the task of feeling along her line will be less than arduous for them. Their reward is a renewed sense of what it might be to perform, or even write, these great poems." Similarly, R. Baird Schuman in *English Journal* praises *The Odes of John Keats* as a skillful illumination of the magnitude of Keats's poetic achievement: "To read this book or any major portion of it is to show readers ways of controlling complex detail, of infusing it with sensitivity and imagination, and of bringing forth epiphanies so profound and encompassing as to make one feel a pride in literary accomplishment greater than any that readers have felt before."

In *The Music of What Happens: Poems, Poets, Critics,* Vendler returns to her study of contemporary poetry and, in addition to presenting new studies of poets such as Seamus Heaney, John Ashbery, and A. R. Ammons, offers further insight into the foundations of her critical work. Aligning her methods with what she terms "aesthetic criticism," Vendler is first concerned with approaching a particular poem as a distinct artistic expression, understandable within its own context. She writes in the book's introduction that her aim "is to describe the art work in such a way that it cannot be confused with any other art work (not an easy task), and to infer from its elements the aesthetic that might generate this unique configuration." Vendler distinguishes her approach from "both ideological and hermeneutic (or interpretation-centered) critics [who] want to place the literary work principally within the sphere of history and philosophy." An "aesthetic critic," she explains, "would rather place it in the mimetic, expressive, and constructivist sphere of the fine arts—theater, painting, music, sculpture, dance—where it may more properly belong." Outside of such theoretical bearings, however, *The Music of What Happens* is primarily devoted to offering new insights into a range of contemporary poetry. "These essays confirm Vendler's authority as a subtle, shrewd and demanding critic of recent American poetry," writes James E. B. Breslin in the *Los Angeles Times Book Review,* while Anthony Thwaite comments in the *Washington Post Book World* that "some of Vendler's most incisive, balanced, and sometimes astringent pieces are on poets who are not Americans: Ted Hughes, Stephen Spender, [Donald] Davie." The essays in *The Music of What Happens,* according to Breslin, "aim not to display the cleverness of the critic but to make poetry a habitable place."

In 1995, Helen Vendler did what William T. Hamilton in the *Bloomsbury Review* called "nearly unprecedented: three books of poetry criticism by the same author, published in the same year, by the same press," though he suggests that may not be such an unusual occurrence if that writer is "probably the most influential critic of poetry at work in this country today." These three books—*Soul Says, The Breaking of Style,* and *The Given and the Made*—offer, according to James Wood in the *London Review of Books,* "many examples of the critic as rhapsodic explicator, and the critic in formidable command of an artistic language of metaphor."

Soul Says: On Recent Poetry offers a collection of twenty-one essays published between 1987-1995, generally to mark the appearance of each author's newest work. Here, Vendler's focus is on lyric poetry, where poets truly reflect the mind at work, for, as Robert Beum notes in *Sewanee Review,* Vendler believes that "the normal home for the 'soul' is the lyric, where the human being becomes a set of warring passions independent of time and space." Though neither hermetically canonical nor forcibly inclusive, the only flaw may be in its geographical restriction, for, as Hamilton points out, "The American West . . . is hardly represented except for a fine essay on Gary Snyder."

The Given and the Made: Strategies of Poetic Redefinition, the 1993 T. S. Eliot Memorial Lectures at the University of Kent, explores how each poet's work is shaped by a particular 'given,' in his or her life. Of the four poets treated, Robert Lowell, given his family, was shaped by history; John Berryman, given what James Morris in *Wilson Quarterly* calls "his alcoholic manic-depression" was shaped by "the Freudian concept of the id"; Rita Dove was shaped by the blackness given her at birth; and Jorie Graham, according to Morris, "given her trilingual upbringing" was shaped by "the arbitrary attachment of word to thing." Still, as Hamilton points out, "these 'givens' are only the starting place," for it is what these poets make of their particular backgrounds "that makes their verse as vital as it is."

The Breaking of Style: Hopkins, Heaney, Graham, the 1994 Richard Ellmann Lectures in Modern Literature at Emory University, traces changes in style of three poets—one English, one Irish, one American—which also reflect a change in each poet's worldview. For Gerard Manley Hopkins, it was the development of "sprung rhythm" which, as Hamilton notes, "matched his radical new approach to the world of his senses when he resumed his poetic career after seven years of silence as a newly ordained Jesuit priest." For Seamus Heaney, it is the turning of a poem upon a grammatical moment, which Vendler suggests marks the shift from public to private, thought to action, violence to art. For Jorie Graham, it is the shift from short lines to longer lines, allowing for the inclusion of dichotomies and irreconcilables, for a shift from "deliberation" to "desire." In each case, the poet is casting off an old body for a new one, so that both poet and poetic style shed the chrysalis and emerge in a new shape.

The Art of Shakespeare's Sonnets goes to the heart of perhaps the most famous and intriguing sequence of lyric poems, and in doing so, Vendler has generated what may become the new standard text for the study of Shakespeare's famous sonnets by including close readings of all 154 sonnets, offering both the 1609 facsimile and modernized versions, accompanied by a CD of Vendler reading sixty-five of the sonnets. Disregarding the stock considerations of possible homoeroticism or the identity of the mysterious dark lady, Vendler, according to Frank Kermode in *New Republic,* makes it her "main tasks" just "to deal with the sonnets as poems, in themselves," arguing for a close reading of the text and utilizing a formalist approach, and though, as Kermode points out, this makes Vendler's commentary "addressed primarily to the scholar and serious student," Vendler's book is, nonetheless, "a great achievement, the work of an author with an almost devout passion for good poems." Still, this book, like all of Vendler's books, will be a success with readers with a passion for good poems, for, as A. O. Scott has stated in the *Nation,* "Vendler holds to the old-fashioned, fundamentally democratic belief that the job of a critic is to help readers understand and better appreciate poems."

BIOGRAPHICAL/CRITICAL SOURCES:

BOOKS

Vendler, Helen, *Part of Nature, Part of Us: Modern American Poets,* Harvard University Press, 1980.

Vendler, *The Music of What Happens: Poems, Poets, Critics,* Harvard University Press, 1988.

PERIODICALS

America, July 25, 1981.

American Poetry Review, May/June, 1996, pp. 37-45.

Bloomsbury Review, March/April, 1996, p. 26.

Book World, February 25, 1996, p. 4.

Boston Review, April, 1984.

Chicago Tribune, May 18, 1988.

English Journal, October, 1984.

Globe and Mail (Toronto), December 14, 1985.

Hudson Review, winter, 1980.

Library Journal, April 15, 1995, p. 78; November 15, 1997, p. 59.

London Review of Books, June 21-July 4, 1984; March 21, 1996, p. 22.

Los Angeles Times Book Review, December 22, 1985; February 7, 1988; February 21, 1988; September 17, 1995, p. 2.

Nation, March 9, 1970; December 25, 1995, p. 841.

New Leader, June 2, 1980; January 9, 1984; December 18, 1995, p. 22.

New Republic, March 29, 1980; December 5, 1983; November 17, 1997, p. 27.
New York Review of Books, May 29, 1980; April 12, 1984.
New York Times, March 29, 1980.
New York Times Book Review, October 5, 1969; July 6, 1975; March 23, 1980; November 27, 1983.
Parnassus: Poetry in Review, Volume 8, number 2, 1980.
Publishers Weekly, October 13, 1997, p. 65.
Sewanee Review, winter, 1996, p. iii.
South Atlantic Quarterly, summer, 1976.
Times (London), January 29, 1987.
Times Literary Supplement, August 22, 1980; March 2, 1984; May 24, 1985; May 1, 1987; May 22, 1987; October 20, 1995, p. 9.
Virginia Quarterly Review, summer, 1976; autumn, 1980; spring, 1985.
Voice Literary Supplement, December, 1983.
Washington Post Book World, April 6, 1980; January 31, 1988.
Wilson Quarterly, spring, 1996, p. 84.
World Literature Today, spring, 1981.
Yale Review, summer, 1984.

—Sketch by Robert Miltner

* * *

VINGE, Joan (Carol) D(ennison) 1948-

PERSONAL: Surname is pronounced *Vin-jee;* born April 2, 1948, in Baltimore, MD; daughter of Seymour W. (an engineer) and Carol (an executive secretary; maiden name, Erwin) Dennison; married Vernor S. Vinge (a science-fiction writer), January 17, 1972 (divorced December, 1979), James R. Frenkel (a publisher), 1980; children. *Education:* San Diego State University, B.A. (with highest honors), 1971. *Avocational interests:* Horseback riding, needlework, aerobic dance.

ADDRESSES: *Home*—26 Douglas Rd., Chappaqua, NY 10514. *Agent*—Merrilee Heifetz, Writers House Inc., 21 West 26th Street, New York, NY 10010.

CAREER: San Diego County, San Diego, CA, salvage archaeologist, 1971; writer, 1974—.

MEMBER: Science Fiction Writers of America, Phi Kappa Phi, Alpha Mu Gamma.

AWARDS, HONORS: Hugo Award for best novelette from 36th World Science Fiction Convention, 1977, for "Eyes of Amber," 1980, for *The Snow Queen; Locus* award, 1981.

WRITINGS:

SNOW QUEEN SERIES

The Snow Queen (novel), Dial (New York City), 1980.
World's End, Bluejay Books (New York City), 1984.
The Summer Queen, Warner Books, 1991.

CAT SERIES (FOR YOUNG READERS)

Psion, Delacorte Press (New York City), 1982.
Catspaw, Warner Books, 1988, published as *Cats Paw,* Gollancz (London), 1989.
Alien Blood: Psion, Catspaw (collection), Doubleday (New York City), 1988.
Dreamfall, Warner Books, 1996.

ADAPTATIONS

Tarzan, King of the Apes (for children; adapted from *Tarzan of the Apes* by Edgar Rice Burroughs), Random House (New York City), 1983.
Return of the Jedi: The Storybook Based on the Movie, Random House, 1983.
The Dune Storybook, Putnam (New York City), 1984.
Santa Claus, the Movie Storybook (for children), Grosset and Dunlap (New York City), 1985.
Santa Claus: The Movie: A Novel, Berkley (New York City), 1985.
Ladyhawke, Signet (New York City), 1985.
Mad Max Beyond Thunderdome: A Novelization, Warner Books, 1985.
Return to Oz: A Novel, Ballantine (New York City), 1985.
Star Wars—The First Ten Years—Storybook Trilogy: The Storybook Based on the Movies,, Random House, 1987.
Willow: Based on the Motion Picture,, Random House, 1988.
Lost in Space (audiocassette), HarperAudio (New York City), 1998.

OTHER

(With Vonda N. McIntyre and Marta Randall) *The Crystal Ship: Three Original Novellas of Science Fiction,* edited and with an introduction by Robert Silverberg, T. Nelson (Nashville, TN), 1976.

Fireship (story collection), Signet, 1978 (see also below), published as *Fireship, and Mother and Child: Science Fiction,* Sidgwick & Jackson (London), 1980.

The Outcasts of Heaven Belt (novel), Signet, 1978 (see also below).

Eyes of Amber and Other Stories, Signet, 1979.

Joan D. Vinge Omnibus (collection; includes *Fireship* and *The Outcasts of Heaven Belt*), Sidgwick & Jackson, 1983.

(With others) *Suzy McKee Charnas,* Borgo Press (San Bernardino, CA), 1986.

(Contributor) *Women of Vision,* edited by Denise Dupont, St. Martin's (New York City), 1988.

(Author of *Tin Soldier;* with Norman Spinrad, author of *Riding the Torch*) *Tin Soldier/Riding the Torch,* Tor (New York City), 1990.

Heaven Chronicles (includes "Legacy" and *The Outcasts of Heaven Belt*), Warner Books (New York City), 1991.

Work represented in anthologies, including *Orbit 14,* 1974, and *Millennial Women.* Contributor to science fiction magazines, including *Analog, Galileo,* and *Isaac Asimov's Science Fiction Magazine.*

Vinge has adapted numerous screenplays and stories for books such as *Tarzan, King of the Apes* (1983), *Return of the Jedi: The Storybook Based on the Movie* (1983), *Mad Max Beyond Thunderdome: A Novelization* (1985), and *Willow: Based on the Motion Picture* (1988).

SIDELIGHTS: Joan Vinge once told *CA:* "I've been a science fiction reader since junior high school, although I've only been writing it for a few years. I write full time, but do most of my best writing after midnight, when there are no interruptions. I have written some poetry, although now I concentrate on prose.

"Originally I had planned to be an artist, but I wound up getting a degree in anthropology, and have worked as a salvage archaeologist. Anthropology is very similar to science fiction: they both give you fresh viewpoints for looking at 'human' behavior. Archaeology is the anthropology of the past, and science fiction is the anthropology of the future. I am very interested in mythology and mythological archetypes. *The Snow Queen* contains many elements inspired by Robert Graves's *The White Goddess.*"

Carl Yoke, in *The Feminine Eye: Science Fiction and the Women Who Write It,* elaborated on the latter theme: "While it occurs in a number of variations, the death and revival of vegetation story occurs in many of the world's mythologies. It is a personification of the fate of most vegetation during the changing seasons." Though it appears in much of Vinge's fiction, "it is most obvious in *The Snow Queen.*" Graves identified the idea in *The White Goddess,* Yoke wrote: "She is a goddess of the moon. . . . As such, she goes thorough a cyclical process each month that results in renewal."

Vinge herself discussed many of the motivations behind her work in an essay for *Women of Vision:* "There used to be an ad for the Famous Writers School that ran on matchbook covers. It read, *Do You Have the Restless Urge to Write?* Whenever I think about my career as a writer, it always comes back into my mind, because it seems to sum up creativity better than anything I've ever seen. I never expected to become a science-fiction writer; probably no one was more surprised than I was. And yet I've had a restless urge to create *something*—not always in the form of writing—and share it, ever since childhood." She and her best friend, she said, "were always reading the sort of books that listed 'other books boys will enjoy' on the back flap. We each had a male alter/ego 'secret identity' we used when playing pretend." Another pivotal influence came when her father bought a telescope: "on summer evenings we used to go out and look at the moon and planets through it. That was probably the beginning of my fascination with space, and eventually with science fiction."

Later, Andre Norton's *The Time Traders* had an impact on Vinge, sparking an interest in a type of science fiction with an overlay of anthropology. The fact that Norton was a woman helped her to overcome the stereotype that women didn't write science fiction: "I was in college in the late Sixties, a time that seemed very much in sync with the world view I'd started to form from reading science fiction, especially Andre Norton's work. My support of the peace, ecology, and equal-rights movements grew naturally out of the values I'd found in her books, and the kind of person that reading them had made me want to become. These values also inspired my support of one more thing—the women's movement." Her first husband, Vernor Vinge, was a science-fiction writer, and "He gave me the encouragement I needed to work seriously on a story and send it out. I actually sold the story ('Tin Soldier'), and after that there was no turning back."

Vinge's first novel was *The Outcasts of Heaven Belt.* The Heaven Belt is a ring of planets and asteroids, inhabited by descendants of earthlings, which has been devastated by a long civil war. It is in part an interplanetary love story between Betha Torgussen, captain of a spaceship called the *Ranger,* and a government negotiator, Wadie Abdhiamal. She followed this with *The Snow Queen,* the first in a series.

The protagonist of *The Snow Queen* is Moon Dawntreader, whose fate it is to become queen of the planet Tiamat. She finds herself opposed by the reigning queen, Arienrhod, of whom Moon—without knowing it—is a clone. Moon, as Yoke noted in the *St. James Guide to Science Fiction Writers,* "is opposite to Arienrhod in both values and philosophies. Moon represents good. Arienrhod's story is one of Machiavellian manipulation." *World's End* focuses on the character of BZ Gundhalinu from *The Snow Queen.* Driven by guilt, he travels into "both the physical wasteland of *World's End* and his own psychological wasteland," Yoke wrote, in a search "for his sanity and [to save] his soul." *The Summer Queen* returns to the saga of Moon in a story that Yoke called "monumental. It bucks and weaves, twists and turns, as it neatly knots up loose ends."

With *Psion,* Vinge began a series of books built around a half-breed with strange powers—a psion—named Cat. The latter, wrote Yoke, "resembles many of her characters: disenfranchised, isolated, scorned, and both physically and mentally different from those around him." He finds and then loses a love, undergoes "mind-rape," and after taking his revenge on the rapist, loses his powers. "Despite these setbacks, however," wrote Yoke, "Cat has undergone an initiation into manhood that has taught him how to survive and permitted him to mature."

Catspaw, which Yoke called "a 'palace-intrigue,'" takes up the story of Cat a few years later in his life. In a lengthy study of the novel published in *Extrapolation,* Joe Sanders observed that "Once again, Vinge gives readers what they expect in genre fiction, but once again she subverts comfortable expectations to communicate a personal moral vision." In Sanders's view, Cat is like the archetypal antihero of detective fiction, a loner outside society who must enter the world of others in order to work out their problems for them. Vinge "understands how attractive the elements of detective fiction are to readers who feel almost overwhelmed by the corruption and deceit around them. *Catspaw* uses the same elements in the same pattern. But not quite." For instance, "Rather than operating from a hard-boiled detective's established position, Cat begins with maximum insecurity. . . . Part of the pleasure of detective fiction is watching the detective make stuck-up people squirm; in *Catspaw* readers watch as Cat squirms through one blunder after another."

Cat's adventures continue in *Dreamfall,* in which he travels to the planet Refuge and finds a remnant of Hydrans, or psions, still managing to survive. His aim is to discover his own origins, but as in *Catspaw,* he finds himself drawn into other people's conflicts. "Vinge deftly twists together multilayered plot strands," wrote a reviewer in *Publishers Weekly,* while unwise allegiances set destructive events in motion.

BIOGRAPHICAL/CRITICAL SOURCES:

BOOKS

Contemporary Literary Criticism, Volume 30, Gale (Detroit, MI), 1984.

Barr, Marleen S., *Suzy Charnas, Joan Vinge, and Octavia Butler, [and others]* Borgo Press, 1986.

Dupont, Denise, editor, *Women of Vision,* St. Martin's, 1988.

Short Story Criticism, Volume 24, Gale, 1997.

St. James Guide to Science Fiction Writers, fourth edition, St. James Press, 1996.

Staicar, Tom, editor, *The Feminine Eye: Science Fiction and the Women Who Write It,* Frederick Ungar, 1982.

PERIODICALS

Extrapolation, summer, 1996, pp. 120-25.

Library Journal, May 15, 1998, p. 133.

New York Times Book Review, May 2, 1982, section 7, p. 11.

Publishers Weekly, May 13, 1996, p. 60.

* * *

VISSER, Margaret 1940-

PERSONAL: Surname is pronounced "*Fiss*-ser"; born May 11, 1940, in Germiston, South Africa; naturalized Canadian citizen; daughter of John H. (an engineer) and Margaret (a teacher; maiden name, O'Connell) Barclay-Lloyd; married Colin Visser (a professor), June 9, 1962; children: Emily,

Alexander. *Education:* University of Toronto, B.A. (classics, with honors), 1970, M.A. (Greek), 1973, Ph.D. (classics), 1980. *Religion:* Roman Catholic.

ADDRESSES: Home—Toronto, Ontario, Canada. *Office*—Department of Classics, York University, Toronto, Ontario, Canada. *Agent*—Colbert Agency, 303 Davenport, Toronto, Ontario, Canada.

CAREER: Mansfield Chronicle-Advertiser, Mansfield, England, reporter, 1958-60; British Council, London, schoolteacher in Baghdad, Iraq, 1962-64; University of Rochester, Rochester, NY, secretary, 1964-66; York University, Toronto, Ontario, lecturer in classics, 1974-79; CBC-Radio, Toronto, broadcaster, 1980—. York University, Toronto, course director and lecturer in classics, 1982—. Regular appearances on CBC-Radio's *Morningside.*

AWARDS, HONORS: Glenfiddich Award, Foodbook of the Year, 1990; International Association of Culinary Professionals' Literary Food Writing Award, 1991; Jane Grigson Prize, 1991.

WRITINGS:

Much Depends on Dinner: The Extraordinary History and Mythology, Allure and Obsessions, Perils and Taboos of an Ordinary Meal, McClelland & Stewart (Toronto), 1986, Collier (New York City), 1988.

(Contributor) Martin Cropp, Elaine Fantham, and S. E. Scully, editors, *Greek Tragedy and Its Legacy,* University of Calgary Press, 1986.

The Rituals of Dinner: The Origins, Evolution, Eccentricities, and Meaning of Table Manners, Grove Weidenfeld (New York City), 1991.

The Way We Are, HarperCollins (Toronto), 1994, Faber (Boston), 1996.

Writer for "Siblings," a feature on CBC-Radio program *Ideas,* 1983. Contributor to journals, including *Journal of the History of Ideas* and *Harvard Theological Review.* Author of monthly column, "The Way We Are," in *Saturday Night* magazine, 1988—.

SIDELIGHTS: Margaret Visser is a university professor of classics, a columnist, the author of several well-received books, and has worked in radio and television. Toronto's *Globe and Mail* critic Bart Kreps described Visser's work as "endlessly entertaining. . . . She is consistently illuminating in describing the mix of luck, ingenuity and centuries of hard work it took us to develop our staple foods." "Visser's forte is to take the ordinary and turn it into the extraordinary by providing a cultural history of its evolution," according to a *Publishers Weekly* review of *The Way We Are.* Accepting a last minute invitation to speak on the CBC-Radio program *Morningside,* "Visser, seldom at a loss for something to say, came right over and delivered an authoritative and captivating recitation on just why it is that North Americans don't eat insects," reported *Los Angeles Times* contributor Mary Williams Walsh. According to Walsh, the audience loved Visser, who later became a regular on the well-known radio show, and "the essay on insect-eating was the prototype for what would ultimately become Visser's stock-in-trade: Learned but accessible explanations of commonplace items and practices that most North Americans take for granted."

Encouraged by the requests of radio listeners, Visser wrote a book. "She settled on food, she say, because 'everybody's interested in food,'" according to Walsh. Her first book, *Much Depends on Dinner: The Extraordinary History and Mythology, Allure and Obsessions, Perils and Taboos of an Ordinary Meal,* begins with a simple, generic dinner menu: corn with salt and butter, chicken with rice, lettuce with olive oil and lemon juice, and ice cream. The rest of the work is devoted to a history of the food items contained in such a meal. "In a discursive way, she examines the historical, mythological, religious, medicinal, agricultural, and social aspects of each [food item]," notes Janet Fetherling in *Quill & Quire.* Novelist Robertson Davies commented on the book's jacket that *Much Depends on Dinner* is "a wonderfully learned, intelligent book about food; in every few lines one learns something one did not know before, about something important, conveyed with the easy command of a truly learned writer." Fetherling similarly remarked that the book "offers fascinating trivia, yet it is also a serious project, leavened with [an appealing] voice." *New York Times Book Review* contributor Laura Shapiro called the book "a lively and perceptive guide" and commented: "Despite a fascinating subject and Mrs. Visser's graceful writing style, *Much Depends on Dinner,* never quite comes to life, a problem that may be called the no-primary-sources syndrome. . . . [she] has relied almost entirely on secondary source, ignoring those unmediated voices from the past that give focus, immediacy and a human dimension to scholarship. . . . Still [her unconvincing] assertions inspire the sorts of arguments for which one should thank Mrs. Visser, not bury her." Keith Jeffery, in *Times Literary Supplement,* also recommended the book and remarked that it has "no detailed source references," but specified: "The approach, however, is so infectious, and the writing generally so engaging and stimulating that passing references prompt one to further speculation."

Visser's second book, *The Rituals of Dinner: The Origins, Evolution, Eccentricities, and Meaning of Table Manners,* "is, for all its good-naturedness, a scary work, devoted as it is to the mystery and menace of entertaining, the politics that underlie each decision confronting a host, the risks borne in each seemingly innocent gesture of hospitality," described Walsh. Called a "fascinating work" by P. N. Furbank in *London Review of Books,* it "is crammed to overflowing with things that one would want to know. . . . ranged as widely as possible, both in space and time, and [Visser] explores her theme in a logical progression." Hilary Mantel was not alone when she clearly noted in a *Spectator* review that, unlike many books involving etiquette, the book is "descriptive not prescriptive." Mantel praised: "Visser's style seems heavy, for a page or so; then you notice the subterranean drollness seeping through. Her book is a learned, fascinating and wide-ranging survey of eating customs from prehistoric times to the present day; it is one of those rare books that, because it touches on the essence of everyday experience, transforms your world while you are reading it. . . . There is something quotable, interesting or alarming on every page of this book." In *New York Times Book Review,* Molly O'Neil commented that Visser's "dense learned patter could ground a frivolous cocktail hour, but it might become a little pedantic over the course of a long meal. Read [*The Rituals of Dinner*] in small doses. But read it, because you'll never look at a table knife the same way again."

A critic for *Kirkus Reviews* similarly warned that *The Way We Are* should be read "at random and in short bursts" so that "Visser's warmth and humor" can overcome "a tendency to the pedantic, which . . . in larger swallows becomes almost overwhelming." Comments on food are part, but not all, of what comprise *The Way We Are.* This, Visser's third publication, is a compilation of about fifty short essays previously published in the popular Canadian magazine, *Saturday Night.* The book's topics vary widely and, according to Thomas Blaikie in *Spectator,* "There will be readers who will protest that too much of the material is incidental, that the open-minded, suggestive approach leads nowhere. . . . [but] it can be said unequivocally that in Margaret Visser's hands to read a history of knitting or of Christmas Pudding is pure pleasure." Positively highlighting the book, Sandra Martin called the book "witty, erudite, and succinct" and stated in *Quill & Quire:* "If I have one complaint . . . it is that Visser does tend to circle the same ground . . . more than once, but can a columnist ignore Christmas or spring just because she covered it last year?"

A Canadian citizen, Visser was raised in what is now Zambia, and lived in Iraq, France, England, and the United States, as well as Canada. She once told *CA:* "My intention, in my radio and television work as well as in my books, is to celebrate the 'ordinary' in such a way that people who listen, watch, or read it will never feel quite the same about everyday things again. After all, the word 'ordinary' derives from 'order'; the more you take a thing or a custom for granted, the more it organizes you and directs your actions. Nothing 'ordinary' can be unimportant.

"My academic training is in ancient Greek and Latin, with a specialty in Greek drama, mythology, and religion. The ideas and methods I learned from this scholarly pursuit have formed the basis of my work outside the university." Visser's scholarly research is conducted in French, German, and Italian, as well as in the classical languages.

BIOGRAPHICAL/CRITICAL SOURCES:

PERIODICALS

Booklist, March 15, 1996, p. 1227.
Chicago Tribune, November 12, 1995.
Denver Post, March 31, 1996.
Globe and Mail (Toronto), October 25, 1986; January 3, 1987.
Kirkus Reviews, January 1, 1996, p. 58.
Library Journal, January, 1988, p. 133; August, 1991, p. 108.
London Review of Books, December 3, 1992, p. 27.
Los Angeles Times, August 6, 1992.
New York, July 22, 1991, p. 50.
New York Times Book Review, February 21, 1988, p. 18; July 28, 1991, p. 7.
Psychology Today, November, 1988, p. 70.
Publishers Weekly, May 17, 1991, p. 49; January 8, 1996, p. 52.
Quill & Quire, October, 1986, p. 46; July, 1994.
Spectator, September 9, 1992; January 6, 1996, pp. 30-31.

Times Literary Supplement, July 27, 1990, p. 809.
Washington Post, April 2, 1996.
Wilson Library Bulletin, June, 1988.*

* * *

VIVANTE, Arturo 1923-

PERSONAL: Born October 17, 1923, in Rome, Italy; son of Leone (a philosopher) and Elena (a painter; maiden name, De Bosis) Vivante; married Nancy Bradish, April 19, 1958; children: Lucy, Lydia, Benjamin. *Education:* McGill University, B.A., 1945; University of Rome, M.D., 1949. *Politics:* Liberal.

ADDRESSES: Home—Wellfleet, MA. *Agent*—Curtis Brown, 575 Madison Ave., New York, NY 10022.

CAREER: Short story writer, novelist, poet. Physician in practice of general medicine, Rome, Italy, 1950-58. Writer-in-residence, University of North Carolina, 1968, Boston University, 1970, Purdue University, 1972-74, Brandeis University, 1976, University of Michigan, 1977, University of Iowa, 1977, University of Texas, 1978, College of the Holy Cross, 1979, University of Idaho, 1980, and Bennington College, 1980-89; Massachusetts Institute of Technology, part-time teacher in writing program, 1990—.

MEMBER: PEN American Center.

AWARDS, HONORS: Fulbright travel grant, 1952; Italian Communication Media Award, 1976; National Endowment for the Arts grant, 1979; Guggenheim fellowship, 1985; award in literature, American Academy of Arts and Letters, 1989.

WRITINGS:

Poesie, Ferrari (Venice), 1951.
A Goodly Babe (novel), Little, Brown (Boston), 1966.
The French Girls of Killini (short stories), Little, Brown, 1967.
Doctor Giovanni (novel), Little, Brown, 1969.
English Stories, illustrated by Ann Mikolowski, Street Fiction (Ann Arbor, MI), 1975.
Run to the Waterfall (short stories), Scribner (New York), 1979.
Writing Fiction, Writer, Inc. (Boston), 1980.
(Translator) Leone Vivante, *Essays on Art and Ontology,* Utah University Press, 1980.
The Tales of Arturo Vivante, selected and with an introduction by Mary Kinzie, Sheep Meadow Press (Riverdale-on-Hudson, NY), 1990.
(Translator) Giacomo Leopardi, *Poems: Giacomo Leopardi,* Delphinium Press (Wellfleet, MA), 1988.
(Selector and translator) *Italian Poetry: An Anthology: From the Beginnings to the Present* (bilingual edition), Delphinium Press, 1996.

Contributor of short stories and travel essays to periodicals, including *New Yorker, Guardian, Botteghe Oscure, Vogue, Southern Review, Cornhill, London Magazine, New York Times, Bennington Review,* and *Canto.*

Author of plays, including *Evening Light, The Moon Doesn't Care, Live Well,* and *Curtain Flutter,* all performed in Provincetown, MA, and Bennington, VT.

WORK IN PROGRESS: Short stories; a play; a novel.

SIDELIGHTS: Arturo Vivante's short story collection *Run to the Waterfall* is an autobiographical account of a half-Jewish family in Siena, Italy, before and after World War II. Like Vivante's own family, the family in the stories includes a father who is a philosopher, a mother who is a painter, and a doctor who abandons his practice to become an artist. Discussing the autobiographical nature of his work, Vivante once told *CA:* "My writing is mainly a study of life as I've known it. I write to know the mystery that even a small matter holds. Through my writing I have come on some of the calmest, clearest and brightest moments of my life."

Because the stories in *Run to the Waterfall* are based on real people in real situations, it is hard for some reviewers to see them as stories. "Most of them lack the shape, the tension, the nerve, of fiction," Jonathan Penner writes in the *Washington Post Book World.* "Their principal method is not scenic but synoptic: there is a quality of summary, of looking back from a safe distance, many years later. Often they are less like fiction than reminiscence, less like stories than anecdotes. Or like a series of meditations, whose subjects (or occasions) are stated, like headings, in their titles: 'The Orchard,' 'The Chest,' 'The Room,' 'The Bell' and so on."

But A. G. Mojtabai interprets the collection differently. "In this book," he writes in the *New York Times Book Review,* "a vanished world is evoked fragment by fragment, rather than delivered full-blown to a single steady gaze. The cumulative effect is as complex as many a novel and, with its sudden stops and starts, its restless hoverings, hesitations and searchings, is truer to our sense of man as a temporal being, haunted by past and future, with an eye that is ever adrift between the two horizons." Or, in the words of *New Republic*'s Marc Granetz: "There is no manufactured drama, no exaggeration, no attempt at psychological analysis. The past can only be put into a larger perspective, and accepted. Again and again in that acceptance Vivante convincingly affirms life . . . and that alone is reason enough to read this book."

Similarly, *The Tales of Arturo Vivante,* a selection of the author's short stories spanning three decades, was warmly received for its nostalgic portrayal of Vivante's family memories. These simple, autobiographical stories are "aptly presented as tales, experiences told, with the double force of memory and invention," writes Beverly Fields in the *New York Times.* Those set in Italy, depicting the give-and-take in the relationship between a philosopher-father and his son, are favored by Fields. "The wrench of these father-son encounters is not the only tender spot in the collection," observes the reviewer, who notes the sympathetic portrayal of the author's artist-mother and sister in several pieces, and several homages to the author's favorite writers.

Vivante's childhood in rural Siena, Italy, was overshadowed by the worldwide economic depression of the 1930s and the rise of fascism. Being part Jewish, the family decided to take refuge in England when restrictions against Jews were put into place, but when England joined the war and Vivante attained the age of sixteen, he was taken into custody as an "enemy alien" and eventually sent to an internment camp in Canada. He was there a year before he was released, but spent the remaining war years in Canada, attending school. He was reunited with his family in England in 1945. "Of my early influences what can I say?" Vivante wrote in an essay for *Contemporary Authors Autobiography Series.* "My father's appreciation and my mother's help were probably the most important. As a painter she looked more at what she was painting than at the canvas. I tried to do the same while writing. Even before that I remember her bedtime stories, how they held me, especially those that she said were 'from the truth.' Later she would sometimes help me with an essay. Through her I learned how one detail, accurately drawn, or one right word, can bring life to a picture."

BIOGRAPHICAL/CRITICAL SOURCES:

BOOKS

Contemporary Authors Autobiography Series, Volume 12, Gale, 1990.

PERIODICALS

Hudson Review, August, 1980.
New Republic, September 15, 1979.
New York Times, December 23, 1990.
New York Times Book Review, November 11, 1979.
Washington Post Book World, December 23, 1979.

WARD, Jonas
See ARD, William (Thomas)

* * *

WHEATLEY, Dennis (Yeats) 1897-1977

PERSONAL: Born January 8, 1897, in London, England; died November 11, 1977, in London, England; son of Albert David and Florence Baker (Lady Newton) Wheatley; married Nancy Madelaine Leslie Robinson, 1923 (divorced, 1931); married Joan Gwendoline Johnstone, August 8, 1931; children: (first marriage) Anthony Marius. *Education:* Educated at Dulwich College, 1908, aboard H.M.S. *Worcester,* 1909-13, and privately in Germany, 1913. *Politics:* Conservative. *Avocational interests:* Travel; books; building (Wheatley once estimated he had laid more than sixty thousand bricks in his garden); collecting Georgian furniture, Persian rugs, stamps, and fine wines.

CAREER: Wheatley & Son (wine merchants), London, England, 1919-31, became sole owner upon father's death in 1926; free-lance writer, 1932-77. *Wartime service:* British Army, 1914-19; became lieutenant. Member of National Service Recruiting Panel, 1940-41; member of Joint Planning Staff of War Cabinet, 1941-44; wing commander on Sir Winston Churchill's staff, 1945; decorated, awarded U.S. Bronze Star.

MEMBER: Royal Society of Literature (fellow), Royal Society of Arts (fellow), Old Comrades Association (president, 1960), St. James' Club, Paternoster Club.

WRITINGS:

CRIME NOVELS

Such Power Is Dangerous, Hutchinson (London), 1933.
The Fabulous Valley, Hutchinson, 1934.
The Eunuch of Stamboul, Little, Brown (Boston, MA), 1935.
They Found Atlantis (also see below), Hutchinson, 1936.
(With J. G. Links) *Crimefile Number One: File on Bolitho Blane,* Morrow (New York City), 1936, published in England as *Murder off Miami,* Hutchinson, 1936.
The Secret War, Hutchinson, 1937.
(With Links) *File on Robert Prentice,* Greenberg (New York City), 1937, published in England as *Who Killed Robert Prentice?,* Hutchinson, 1937.
Uncharted Seas (also see below), Hutchinson, 1938.
(With Links) *The Malinsay Massacre,* Hutchinson, 1938.
(With Links) *Herewith the Clues,* Hutchinson, 1939.
Sixty Days to Live, Hutchinson, 1939.
The Man Who Missed the War (also see below), Hutchinson, 1946.
The Haunting of Toby Jugg, Hutchinson, 1948.
The Star of Ill-Omen, Hutchinson, 1952.
Worlds Far from Here (contains *Uncharted Seas, The Man Who Missed the War,* and *They Found Atlantis*), Hutchinson, 1952.
Curtain of Fear, Hutchinson, 1953.

Black Magic Omnibus (contains *The Devil Rides Out, Strange Conflict,* and *To the Devil—a Daughter*), Hutchinson, 1956.
The Ka of Gifford Hillary, Hutchinson, 1956.
Death in the Sunshine, Hutchinson, 1958.
Mayhem in Greece, Hutchinson, 1962.
Unholy Crusade, Hutchinson, 1967.
The Strange Story of Linda Lee, Hutchinson, 1972.
The Devil Rides Out, Gateway to Hell, Chancellor Press (London), 1992.

"ROGER BROOK" SERIES; CRIME NOVELS

The Launching of Roger Brook (also see below), Hutchinson, 1947.
The Shadow of Tyburn Tree (also see below), Hutchinson, 1948.
The Rising Storm (also see below), Hutchinson, 1949.
Early Adventures of Roger Brook (contains *The Launching of Roger Brook* and *The Shadow of Tyburn Tree*), Hutchinson, 1951.
The Man Who Killed the King (also see below), Hutchinson, 1951, Putnam, 1965.
The Dark Secret of Josephine, Hutchinson, 1955.
Roger Brook in the French Revolution (contains *The Rising Storm* and *The Man Who Killed the King?*), Hutchinson, 1957.
The Rape of Venice, Hutchinson, 1959.
The Sultan's Daughter, Hutchinson, 1963.
The Wanton Princess, Hutchinson, 1966, published as *The Wanton Princess: A Roger Brook Story,* Hutchinson, 1971.
Evil in a Mask, Hutchinson, 1969.
The Ravishing of Lady Mary Ware, Hutchinson, 1971.
The Irish Witch, Hutchinson, 1973.
Desperate Measures, Hutchinson, 1974.

"JULIAN DAY" SERIES; CRIME NOVELS

The Quest of Julian Day, Hutchinson, 1939.
The Sword of Fate, Hutchinson, 1941.
Bill for the Use of a Body, Hutchinson, 1964, new edition, Arrow Books, 1972.

"MOLLY FOUNTAIN" SERIES; CRIME NOVELS

To the Devil—a Daughter (also see below), Hutchinson, 1953.
The Satanist, Hutchinson, 1960.

"DUKE DE RICHLEAU" SERIES; CRIME NOVELS

The Forbidden Territory (also see below), Hutchinson, 1933.
The Devil Rides Out (also see below), Hutchinson, 1935.
The Golden Spaniard (also see below), Hutchinson, 1938.
Those Modern Musketeers (contains *Three Inquisitive People, The Forbidden Territory,* and *The Golden Spaniard*), Hutchinson, 1939.
Three Inquisitive People (previously published in *Those Modern Musketeers*), Hutchinson, 1940.
Strange Conflict (also see below), Hutchinson, 1941.
Codeword: Golden Fleece, Hutchinson, 1946.
The Second Seal, Hutchinson, 1950.
The Prisoner in the Mask, Hutchinson, 1957.
Vendetta in Spain, Hutchinson, 1961.
Dangerous Inheritance, Hutchinson, 1965, published as *Dangerous Inheritance: A Duke de Richleau Story,* Hutchinson, 1971.
Gateway to Hell, Hutchinson, 1970.

"GREGORY SALLUST" SERIES; CRIME NOVELS

Black August (also see below), Hutchinson, 1934.
Contraband (also see below), Hutchinson, 1936.
The Scarlet Impostor, Hutchinson, 1940.
Faked Passports, Hutchinson, 1940, Macmillan (New York City), 1943.
The Black Baroness, Hutchinson, 1940, Ryerson Press (New York City), 1941.
"V" for Vengeance, Hutchinson, 1942.
Come into My Parlor, Hutchinson, 1946.
The Island Where Time Stands Still (also see below), Hutchinson, 1954.
Secret Missions of Gregory Sallust, Hutchinson, 1955.
Traitor's Gate, Hutchinson, 1958.
Plot and Counterplot: Three Adventures of Gregory Sallust (contains *Black August, Contraband,* and *The Island Where Time Stands Still*), Hutchinson, 1959.
They Used Dark Forces, Hutchinson, 1964.
The White Witch of the South Seas, Hutchinson, 1968.

OTHER

"Old Rowley": A Private Life of Charles II, Hutchinson, 1933, Dutton (New York City), 1934, published as *A Private Life of Charles II,* Hutchinson, 1938, published as *"Old Rowley": A Very Private Life of Charles II,* Arrow Books, 1977.

(Editor) *A Century of Horror Stories,* Hutchinson, 1935, selections published as *Shafts of Fear,* Arrow Books, 1965 (published as *Dennis Wheatley's First Book of Horror Stories: Tales of Strange Doings,* Hutchinson, 1968), further selections published as *Quiver of Horror,* Arrow Books, 1965 (published as *Dennis Wheatley's Second Book of Horror Stories: Tales of Strange Happenings,* Hutchinson, 1968).

Red Eagle: The Story of the Russian Revolution and of Klementy Efremovitch Voroshilov, Marshal and Commissar for Defence of the Union of Socialist Soviet Republics, Hutchinson, 1938, published as *Red Eagle: A Story of the Russian Revolution and of Klementy Efremovitch Voroschilov,* Arrow Books, 1964, Hutchinson, 1967.

(Editor) *A Century of Spy Stories,* Hutchinson, 1938.

Invasion (war game), Hutchinson, 1938.

Blockade (war game), Hutchinson, 1939.

Total War: A Paper, Hutchinson, 1941.

Mediterranean Nights (short stories), Hutchinson, 1942, revised edition, 1965.

Gunmen, Gallants, and Ghosts (short stories), Hutchinson, 1943, revised edition, Arrow Books, 1968.

The Seven Ages of Justerini's: 1749-1949, Riddle Books, 1949, revised edition published as *1749-1965, The Eight Ages of Justerini's,* Dolphin Publishing, 1965.

Alibi (war game), Geographia (London), 1951.

Stranger than Fiction, Hutchinson, 1959.

Into the Unknown, Hutchinson, 1960.

Selected Works, Hutchinson, 1961.

Saturdays with Bricks, and Other Days under Shell-Fire, Hutchinson, 1961.

The Devil and All His Works, American Heritage Press (New York City), 1971.

Uncanny Tales, Sphere Books, Volumes I-II, 1974, Volume III, 1977.

Satanism and Witches: Essays and Stories, Sphere Books, 1975.

The Time Has Come: The Memoirs of Dennis Wheatley, Hutchinson, Volume I: *The Young Man Said, 1897-1914,* 1977, Volume II: *Officer and Temporary Gentleman, 1914-1919,* 1978, Volume III: *Drink and Ink, 1919-1977,* 1979.

The Deception Planners: My Secret War, edited by Anthony Lejeune, Hutchinson, 1980.

Also author, with others, of screenplay *An Englishman's Home (Madmen of Europe),* 1939. Editor of "Dennis Wheatley's Library of the Occult" series, Sphere Books, 1974-77. Author of personalities page column, *Sunday Graphic,* 1939. Contributor to periodicals, including London *Times, Daily Mail, Daily Express,* and *Cosmopolitan.*

ADAPTATIONS: J. H. Hoffberg filmed *Forbidden Territory* in 1938 and *The Eunuch of Stamboul*—released as *The Secret of Stamboul*—in 1941. In 1968 Warner Bros. produced *The Lost Continent,* a filmed version of *Uncharted Seas,* and Twentieth Century-Fox produced *The Devil's Bride,* a filmed version of *The Devil Rides Out. To the Devil—A Daughter,* taken from the novel of the same title, was filmed in 1975.

SIDELIGHTS: Best-selling author Dennis Wheatley was "one of the twentieth century's most prolific and best-selling authors," according to a writer in the *Washington Post.* He "was called 'Prince of Thriller Writers' by a critic in the *Times Literary Supplement,"* explained *Dictionary of Literary Biography* contributor J. Randolph Cox, "and this motto was emblazoned on the spines of the collected edition of his works." His more than sixty books have sold over 45 million copies and have been translated into twenty-nine languages.

Wheatley began his career as a writer after having lost his successful family business during the Great Depression. He had enlisted in the Royal Field Artillery at the beginning of World War I and had served with the City of London Brigade until 1917. He later transferred to the Thirty-sixth Ulster Division but was invalided out of the service when he was gassed. "His father and grandfather before him had been vintners," wrote Cox in the *Dictionary of Literary Biography,* "so it was natural for him to join the family wine firm, Wheatley and Son, in 1919 after his military service." Wheatley led the firm as sole owner following his father's death in 1927.

However, Cox revealed in his *Dictionary of Literary Biography* entry, "the firm of Dennis Wheatley, Ltd., was affected by the Great Depression in the early-1930s, and the company went into liquidation with Wheatley himself sustaining a loss of several hundred thousand pounds." He turned to writing as a way of supporting himself and his family. Wheatley once stated in the *Writer:* "Numerous distinguished critics said of my first novel, *The Forbidden Territory,* and of its successors, that I had broken every rule in the game, that my punctuation was lamentable and my English appalling—but they praised the story. It was reprinted seven times in seven weeks and within a year translated into a dozen foreign languages."

Thriller stories made Wheatley's reputation and proved to be his most successful books. *The Forbidden Territory* was the first volume in one of many continuing series featuring "the Duke de Richleau, Gregory Sallust, Roger Brook, and Julian Day," wrote Cox in the *St. James Guide to Crime and Mystery Writers.* "Some of these," the critic explained, "were influenced by one of his own favorite writers, Alexandre Dumas." For instance, "the characters in *The Forbidden Territory* have direct counterparts in Dumas," Cox wrote in the *Dictionary of Literary Biography.* "The Duke de Richleau himself is Athos, the conservative Richard Eaton is d'Artagnan, Simon Aron (the liberal Jew) is Aramis, and the democratic American, Rex van Ryn, is Porthos. Wheatley readily acknowledged that *The Golden Spaniard* (1938) was his version of Dumas's *Twenty Years After* (1845), while *The Prisoner in the Mask* (1957) was inspired by the Man in the Iron Mask section of Dumas's *The Vicomte de Bragelonne* (1848-1850)."

Another series hero, Gregory Sallust, took his inspiration less from prototypes established by Dumas and more on the experiences of Wheatley himself and his friends and acquaintances. Sallust, said Cox in the *Dictionary of Literary Biography,* "was based in part (his appearance and personality) on a friend of Wheatley's from World War I, Gordon Eric Gordon-Tombe." Although Sallust's first adventures were set in Britain in an indeterminate future, Wheatley soon "conceived the idea of using him in a series set during the early years of World War II," Cox continued. The stories, which began to see print during the late 1930s, were often published only shortly after the events that provided their setting. The series ran to another ten volumes, making it one of Wheatley's most popular extended works. Wheatley also launched a historical melodramatic series featuring master spy Roger Brook, who worked for the British government during the years of the French Revolution and the Napoleonic Wars. "The series has received much praise," Cox concluded, "for the skillful way in which Wheatley combined his melodramatic plots with accurate historical detail."

Yet, despite his reputation as a writer of exciting adventure stories, Wheatley also wrote extensively on many other subjects. "Dennis Wheatley was the master of the macabre to some, the creator (with Joe Links) of a series of detective games, the 'Crime Dossiers,' to others," stated Cox in the *St. James Guide to Crime and Mystery Writers.* His *The Devil and All His Works,* a comprehensive survey of the black arts, "is considered a modern textbook on satanism," according to a *New York Times* writer. He also wrote works on political analysis, historical biography, and personal history. "Though Wheatley became known for his stories of black magic (and followers of this subgenre sought out his books) fewer than a dozen of the novels deal with that theme," Cox concluded in the *St. James Guide to Crime and Mystery Writers.* "His supernatural manifestations are often described in too much detail for them to be truly frightening; they could just as well have been replaced by gunmen or exotic villains."

Urging novice authors to be conscientious and persistent, Wheatley wrote that anyone "who is prepared to face hard, hard work can achieve—and maintain—success. In my case it has meant writing two books for each one published: a factual, accurate account of a war or period of history or travel, which will interest the better-educated reader, and a thriller with plenty of throat-cutting and boy jumping into bed with girl, then dovetailing the two. But don't let any pedantic idiot tell you that because, like myself, you haven't the faintest idea what the word 'syntax' means, you can't write a best seller."

BIOGRAPHICAL/CRITICAL SOURCES:

BOOKS

Dictionary of Literary Biography, Volume 77: *British Mystery Writers, 1920-1939,* Gale (Detroit, MI), 1989.

Hedman, Iwan and Jan Alexandersson, *Fyra Decennier med Dennis Wheatley: En Biografi & Bibliografi,* privately printed, 1963, revised edition, Straegnaes (Sweden), DAST, 1973.

St. James Guide to Crime and Mystery Writers, 4th edition, St. James Press (Detroit, MI), 1996.

PERIODICALS

Booklist, December 15, 1992, p. 757.
Books and Bookmen, September, 1965.
Library Journal, October 15, 1992, p. 118.
Los Angeles Times, November 13, 1980.
Times Literary Supplement, June 8, 1940.
Writer, October, 1969.

OBITUARIES:

PERIODICALS

AB Bookman's Weekly, February 6, 1978.
New York Times, November 12, 1977.
Washington Post, November 12, 1977.*

* * *

WILCOX, James (P.) 1949-

PERSONAL: Born April 4, 1949, in Hammond, LA; son of James Henry (a music professor) and Marie (a homemaker and oboist; maiden name, Wiza) Wilcox. *Education:* Yale University, B.A. (magna cum laude), 1971. *Avocational interests:* "Though I have not kept up with playing the cello, I do practice piano dutifully and with great enjoyment. My current repertoire includes etudes and ballades by Frederic Chopin, an Aleksandr Scriabin etude, Maurice Ravel's 'Gaspard de la Nuit,' and Sergey Prokofiev's Seventh Sonata."

ADDRESSES: Home—239 East 24th St., No. 9, New York, NY 10010. *Agent*—Amanda Urban, International Creative Management, 40 West 57th St., New York, NY 10019.

CAREER: Random House, New York City, editorial assistant, 1971-72, assistant editor, 1973-76, associate editor, 1976-77; Doubleday, New York City, associate editor, 1977-78; full-time writer, 1978—.

MEMBER: PEN, Authors Guild, Authors League of America.

AWARDS, HONORS: Guggenheim fellowship.

WRITINGS:

NOVELS

Modern Baptists, Dial (New York City), 1983.
North Gladiola, Harper (New York City), 1985.
Miss Undine's Living Room, Harper, 1987.
Sort of Rich, Harper, 1989.
Polite Sex, Harper, 1991.
Guest of a Sinner, Harper, 1993.
Plain and Normal, 1998.

OTHER

Author of short stories "Mr. Ray," "Camping Out," and "The Ivy in the Chimney." Contributor of short stories to periodicals, including *New Yorker, Avenue,* and *Louisiana Literature,* and of reviews to *New York Times Book Review.*

SIDELIGHTS: An acclaimed Southern novelist and short story writer, James Wilcox has written comedies that take place in the fictional town of Tula Springs, Louisiana, a present-day community somewhere to the north of New Orleans. Based largely on Wilcox's impressions growing up in the South, the world presented by his 1983 novel *Modern Baptists* and enlarged in *North Gladiola, Miss Undine's Living Room,* and *Sort of Rich* has regularly drawn comparisons to such composite regional portraits as William Faulkner's Yoknapatawpha County. Noting the author's eye for comic incongruity and humorous detail, critics have admired Wilcox's elaborate plots as well as his caricatures of the eccentric, often unsophisticated people who populate his writing.

Wilcox first introduced Tula Springs in short stories published in such periodicals as the *New Yorker;* he established his reputation as a novelist with *Modern Baptists,* which also takes place there. Located near a creosote plant and soon to accommodate a toxic waste disposal site, Tula Springs is home to a variety of characters ranging from movie theater ushers to cellists, social activists to hot-tub saleswomen. "It's the sort of town," noted *New York Times* reviewer Michiko Kakutani, "where the Old Jefferson Davis Highway and Azalea Manor co-exist on the map with the Tiger Unisex Hair Styling Salon and Dick's China Nights restaurant." The critic went on to state that unlike many other Southern writers who explore themes of alienation characteristic of much contemporary fiction, Wilcox is concerned with "examining the comic possibilities afforded . . . by the clash of cultures and the acceleration of change."

Modern Baptists is the story of Bobby Pickens, the middle-aged assistant manager of Tula Springs's Sonny Boy Bargain Store. Believing that he is terminally ill, Pickens has invited his recently paroled half-brother F. X. to live with him, a decision that helps put into motion a complex plot involving mistaken identities and misinterpreted events. Pickens' life is further complicated by a chain of romantic entanglements: the already engaged Burma LaSteele loves him, while Toinette Quaid, the woman Pickens loves, is interested in F. X.

Critics found much to praise in *Modern Baptists.* Jim Crace, for example, appreciated the novel's authentic humor, noting in the *Times Literary Supplement* that Wilcox displays "a sophisticated control of comic pace, his humour [has] the chill of home truth, and his squibs at the expense of small-town America are rarely off-target." *New York Times Book Review* contributor Anne Tyler admired Wilcox's "sense of particularity—a granting of a full measure of individualism to the most incidental character, place or fact—that makes 'Modern Baptists' seem startlingly alive, exuberantly overcrowded." And Art Seidenbaum, writing for the *Los Angeles Times,* commented that *Modern Baptists* places the reader "in a community of lost industry and losing residents, in the company of absurd characters whose meager reaches exceed their minimal grasps." "We come to like them," the critic asserted, "because dimness is made lovable by down homeness."

Wilcox followed *Modern Baptists* with *North Gladiola,* a comedy that focuses on Ethyl Mae Coco, a forty-year resident of Tula Springs and the mother of six rather eccentric grown children. Bored with her marriage, disapproving of her children's occupations and spouses, and trying to believe in the Catholicism that she uses mainly to judge others, Mrs. Coco perseveres in her attempts to bring some culture to Tula Springs. She leads the Pro Arts Quartet, an ensemble that plays—for lack of better engagements—at such events as hamburger stand openings. She finds herself the object of the affections of violinist Duk-Soo Yoon, a middle-aged graduate student and tourism major at the nearby St. Jude State College, and faces personal crisis when the rumor mill links her to, among other scandals, the death of the local beauty school's pet Chihuahua. During the course of the novel, in which Pickens and several other characters from *Modern Baptists* also make appearances, Mrs. Coco reconciles her beliefs with her seemingly spiritually barren surroundings.

North Gladiola also won favor with reviewers, who considered the work subtler and less animated than *Modern Baptists.* Critics admired, for instance, Wilcox's sharp but compassionate presentation of the Tula Springs inhabitants. *New York Times Book Review* contributor Lisa Zeidner, in particular, praised the author's talent for creating "just the right combination of affection for and detachment from his characters." James Idema, writing in Chicago's *Tribune Books,* applauded a scene in which Mrs. Coco expresses her doubts about religion to a Tula Springs priest, who finds her confessions of uncertainty and questioning to be routine, inconsequential, and ultimately unresolvable. Describing the conversation as "a splendid set piece, a gentle fusion of humor and despair," Idema deemed *North Gladiola* "wise as well as witty." Zeidner noted as well Mrs. Coco's and Duk-Soo's contrasting outlooks, commenting that "the clash of [their] beliefs makes for fine intellectual slapstick, especially played out against the distinctly unintellectual backdrop of beauty pageants, diners, rodeos and Daughters of the American Revolution luncheons."

Wilcox's third novel, *Miss Undine's Living Room,* concerns, among several others, Olive Mackie, a fired city hall secretary who embarks on a political campaign for the Tula Springs office of Superintendent of Streets, Parks, and Garbage. Olive's political aspirations are endangered by the town's suspicion that her elderly step-great-uncle L. D. Loraine has murdered his home attendant, Mr. Versey, by pushing him out of the second floor window above the Sonny Boy Bargain Shop. Olive's personal life is disrupted, too, as she must contend with her crush on dental student Martin Bates, her unemployed and unfaithful husband, and her self-righteous son Felix, who lectures her about her behavior. The climax of the novel occurs in the parlor of Bates' landlady and ex-mother-in-law, Mrs. Undine, where Olive unravels the mystery of Mr. Versey's death.

Like *Modern Baptists* and *North Gladiola, Miss Undine's Living Room* was critically well received. "The novel is by turns hilarious, silly, tacky, tender, maddeningly digressive, and as brimming with off-the-wall canniness as any modern comedy of manners I know," declared Marianne Gingher in the *Washington Post Book World.* She added that "*Miss Undine's Living Room* feels as if it were peopled by a cast of thousands—mostly twangy loudmouths, all holding forth on assorted dissatisfactions and dilemmas." *Village Voice* contributor Walter Kendrick was similarly impressed with Wilcox's third book, noting that "each time out, Wilcox gets better—subtler, more complex, closer to the fusion of pathos and joy that makes for the highest comedy." And although *New York Times* contributor Kakutani criticized the novel's ending as too "contrived," Wilcox was judged as having "lost neither his gift for slapstick nor his instinct for finding and describing the incongruities of modern life."

Wilcox's fourth novel, *Sort of Rich,* also takes place in Tula Springs, but it centers on an outsider—a middle-aged native New Yorker who has recently married the successful entrepreneur and widower Frank Dambar. Moving to Tula Springs with her husband, Gretchen hopes to trade her Manhattan distractions for life in a quieter town, where she plans to finish a book about her experience as a Peace Corps volunteer in the Philippines. Her expectations for serenity are crushed, however, as she finds herself at odds with the strange members of Dambar's household, including Frank's niece, a bullying German housekeeper, and Leo, the enigmatic handyman. *Sort of Rich*'s complex plot unfolds with Dambar's sudden death, a visit from Gretchen's New York cousin Henry, and her associations with a private detective and a new therapist, who has a previous connection to Leo.

Reviews of *Sort of Rich* were mixed. Some critics, such as *Tribune Books* contributor L. J. Davis, saw the novel's characters as too superficial to be engaging, calling Gretchen "a crashing bore" and Dambar "living proof that an unexamined life is not worth living." Other critics, however, were more enthusiastic; while finding less outright comedy in the themes of self-delusion and dashed expectations than in Wilcox's previous novels, reviewers nevertheless noted the humor contributing to the characterizations and plot. "Mr. Wilcox employs the zany eye for comic detail that has become a trademark of his fiction and makes his characters wholly original," remarked Jill McCorkle, for instance, in her *New York Times Book Review* critique. Similarly, a *Publishers Weekly* reviewer noted that while the author's "antic humor is less evident" in *Sort of Rich,* it provides "an undercurrent to the pathos he evokes" in the novel. McCorkle also admired *Sort of Rich*'s intricate narrative and commented that Wilcox "surrounds the facts of his plot with . . . amusing exchanges and outlandish speculation," adding that the author "gives us just enough slack in the story line to keep us off balance . . . ; then with a sharp sobering twist in events he pulls it tightly together."

A number of critics have seemed to agree with Peter Heinegg's *Los Angeles Times Book Review* assessment that Wilcox "create[s] a thoroughly convincing and fully realized micro-universe in Tula Springs." And Rosemary Daniell, another *New York Times Book Review* writer, remarked that "life in Tula Springs is like that in a terrarium: looking from the outside in, we see everything; and the microcosm of small lives, small problems, makes amusing, even soothing, reading. . . . Wilcox has created a delicious little world." Concluded Zeidner, "Ten novels and a decade from now, we may know Mr. Wilcox's testy, endearing townsfolk as well as they know each other."

In a *New Yorker* profile of Wilcox by James B. Stewart, titled "*Moby Dick* in Manhattan," Stewart described the trajectory of Wilcox's career, from his childhood in Hammond, Louisiana, where his father taught him classical piano, to studies at Yale under such luminaries as Robert Penn Warren and Harold Bloom, to his job working with editor Albert Erskine at Random House in the early 1970s. James Michener, Stewart reported, had been so happy with Wilcox's comments on the manuscript of his novel *Centennial* that he invited the young editor to travel anywhere in Europe at his expense; thus Wilcox got to spend ten days in Paris in 1974, courtesy of the famous author. But he was restless to become a famous author himself, especially because his coworker Toni Morrison had already published two books, so eventually he went out on his own.

By the early 1990s Wilcox had published two more novels, each of which takes place far from the setting of the previous four. Both are set in New York, although 1991's *Polite Sex* involves characters from Tula Springs. In this work, Emily Brix arrives in the big city hoping for a career as a serious actress, but instead she lands a job reading scripts at a shabby production company, and winds up dating an unromantic seminary student. Hugh Vanderbilt asks Emily to marry him because she "did not exhaust him with her wiles, her need for attention. Neither was he distracted by passion or lust." Emily accepts his proposal, and the results—which the reader witnesses in another part of the book, set twenty years later—are predictably dreary. Meanwhile, things go quite differently for Clara Edward Tilman, who came to New York to get away from her boyfriend, F. X. from *Modern Baptists.* Clara gets an acting job, albeit in a soap opera, and takes as a lover a man who had once been a friend of Emily's. Naturally Emily is jealous of all this, especially in light of the fact that Clara is her little sister's best friend, a mere upstart.

A number of reviewers noted that the humor was more muted in *Polite Sex* than in its four predecessors. Elinor Lipman of the *New York Times Book Review* assumed that this was intentional: "Mr. Wilcox doesn't draw as much on his comedic talents throughout 'Polite Sex' as readers of his four earlier novels . . . might expect. But we trust that this is deliberate, that he cares too much about these characters to make us laugh at them out loud." A critic in *Kirkus Reviews* concluded that the book had "little humor to steer it straight," and a *Publishers Weekly* contributor observed that "A jolting last-minute revelation comes too late [to give] this tale the poignancy and credibility it never quite achieves." But a *Booklist* commentator held that "Wilcox writes with empathy, depicting the light and restless sleep of those with shattered dreams."

Wilcox was on firmer ground with *Guest of a Sinner,* another story set in New York, but without any characters from Tula Springs. The plot is a comedy of errors centering around the gorgeous but aloof Eric Thorsen, a fortyish pianist; Wanda Skopinski, a secretary with a crush on him; and Una Merton, an eighty-three-year-old woman with twenty-two cats. The plot revolves in part around a struggle to acquire a rent-controlled apartment, but there are numerous subplots and quirky peripheral characters. "What a nest of ninnies!" Eric Kraft wrote in a delighted tone for the *New York Times Book Review.* He concluded by listing the characters' many foibles and absurdities, and ended with the pronouncement: "In short, they would be exactly like everyone else if James Wilcox hadn't made them much funnier." Cheryl Mercer in Chicago's *Tribune Books* noted that "The author is sympathetic and affectionate toward this motley group, and adept at enticing the reader to be patient with them, too." A reviewer in *Publishers Weekly* observed that Wilcox had "recover[ed] his characteristic wit," and *Time* magazine began a short blurb with the announcement, "Come along, fiction lovers, James Wilcox writes your kind of book." Eloise Kinney of *Booklist* called it "A fine, funny read," and Carolyn See wrote in the *Los Angeles Times* that *Guest of a Sinner* would "help to explain to Los Angeles-lovers why New Yorkers are so homesick." Speaking as a New Yorker, and very much caught up in the spirit of the book, See concluded with the words, "Everyone here ends up very happily, and the best part of all, when absolutely everything is said and done, there seems at the end to be one or two or even three relatively new, absolutely usable, attractive apartments in the extended family, and they're all rent-controlled."

BIOGRAPHICAL/CRITICAL SOURCES:

PERIODICALS

Booklist, May 1, 1991, p. 1695; March 15, 1993, p. 1300.

Detroit News, July 17, 1983.

Globe and Mail (Toronto), September 8, 1984.

Kirkus Reviews, March 15, 1991, pp. 359-60.

Los Angeles Times, August 17, 1983; June 5, 1989; May 17, 1993, p. E6.

Los Angeles Times Book Review, October 4, 1987; September 1, 1991, p. 6.

National Review, August 23, 1985.

Newsweek, June 10, 1985.

New Yorker, July 18, 1983; June 27, 1994, pp. 46-60.

New York Times, August 12, 1987.

New York Times Book Review, July 31, 1983; June 30, 1985; October 18, 1987; May 28, 1989; July 7, 1991, p. 10; May 16, 1993, p. 18.

Publishers Weekly, March 17, 1989; April 26, 1991, p. 47; February 22, 1993, p. 83; July 6, 1998, p. 48.

Time, April 26, 1993, p. 71.

Times (London), January 12, 1984.

Times Literary Supplement, January 20, 1984.

Times-Picayune (New Orleans), May 23, 1993, p. E10.

Tribune Books (Chicago) July 7, 1985; April 25, 1993, pp. 14-18.

Village Voice, August 25, 1987.

Voice Literary Supplement, June, 1985.

Washington Post, May 5, 1985.

Washington Post Book World, August 16, 1987; June 16, 1991, p. 12.

* * *

WILLOUGHBY, Lee Davis
See BRANDNER, Gary

* * *

WILLS, Thomas
See ARD, William (Thomas)

* * *

WOMACK, Steven (James) 1952-

PERSONAL: Born July 31, 1952, in Nashville, TN; son of Harry Womack (a printing salesperson) and Katherine Raines (a homemaker; maiden name, Fudge); married Cathryn Yarbrough (a psychologist), May 5, 1990. *Education:* Tulane University, B.A. (with honors), 1974; attended Tennessee State University, Northwestern University, and PTC, Inc. (property tax school). *Politics:* Libertarian. *Religion:* Episcopalian.

ADDRESSES: Home and office—Nashville, TN. *Agent*—Carole Abel, 160 West 87th St., New York, NY 10024.

CAREER: Daily Record, New Orleans, LA, city editor, reporter, and photographer, 1975-77; Vanderbilt University, Nashville, TN, development researcher, 1977-78; United Press International (UPI), Nashville, reporter, 1978; freelance writer and photographer in Nashville, 1978; American Bible Society, New York City, writer and photographer for news bureau, 1979-80, typographer, graphic artist, and photographer, 1980-82; Thomas Nelson Publishers, Nashville, operations manager of typesetting department, 1983-86; Tennessee State University, Nashville, instructor in screenwriting, 1988—; Equitax of Tennessee (property tax management firm), senior partner, 1990—; writer.

MEMBER: Mensa.

AWARDS, HONORS: Top five finish, Houston International Film Festival, 1987, for screenplay *Murder at Vanderbilt,* 1988, for script *The Days and Nights of Molly Dodd;* honorable mention, Wisconsin Screenwriter's Forum, 1988; Edgar Award, 1993, for *Dead Folk's Blues.*

WRITINGS:

"JACK LYNCH" MYSTERY SERIES

Murphy's Fault, St. Martin's (New York City), 1990.
Smash Cut, St. Martin's, 1991.
The Software Bomb, St. Martin's, 1993.

"HARRY JAMES DENTON" MYSTERY SERIES

Dead Folk's Blues, Ballantine (New York City), 1993.
Torch Town Boogie, Ballantine, 1993.
Way Past Dead, Ballantine, 1995.
Chain of Fools, Ballantine, 1996.
Murder Manual, Ballantine, 1998.

OTHER

Author of script for ABC television movie *Fire on the Mountain* and of script for series *The Days and Nights of Molly Dodd.* Also author of unpublished screenplays. Contributor of articles, photographs, and reviews to periodicals.

ADAPTATIONS: The "Harry James Denton" books have been optioned for film and television adaptations.

SIDELIGHTS: Steven Womack is the author of two detective series, both set in the American South. The Jack Lynch books feature a public relations man who doubles as a crime solver in New Orleans. In Womack's more recent series, a newspaper reporter named Harry James Denton becomes a private eye in Nashville.

Marilyn Stasio favorably reviews *Murphy's Fault,* the first book in the Lynch series. It is a twisted tale of corruption and shady land deals. Stasio was impressed with Womack's sense of place, writing in the *New York Times Book Review:* "New Orleans, so often called the city that care forgot, is not a pretty place in this pained novel. The streets stink and so do the people who play politics in the gutter, during this hot summer in the city that care finally caught up with. Maybe this side of town doesn't have 'the aura of memory and myth' that lures strangers to the old quarters, but there's a powerful throbbing in 'the mean reality of a living, breathing place full of people' so vividly evoked."

In the next entry in the series, *Smash Cut,* Womack again summoned up memorably corrupt characters, "reveling in their blatant political cynicism and the glee they take in their own deviltry," noted Stasio in another *New York Times Book Review* evaluation. Lynch's third appearance, in *The Software Bomb,* is praised as "an effective work" by a *Publishers Weekly* reviewer who also notes: "There's no shortage of New Orleans atmosphere here; the author is especially unforgiving toward gullible tourists and inefficient restaurants with inflated reputations."

Womack used the country musical capital of Nashville, Tennessee, as the backdrop for his second series. Harry James Denton, the central character, "bears the markings of his breed," notes Stasio. "He talks too much, he jokes too hard, and, broke all the time, he has to scrounge for work from repo outfits and cheapo insurance companies." Wes Lukowsky, reviewing *Way Past Dead* in *Booklist,* calls the book "a little jewel" and comments: "Denton is a Rockford-like private eye who'd like to avoid danger but has just enough integrity to follow his cases through to the end. Toss him into the colorful Nashville musical milieu, and you get a mystery in which the mournful wail of a pedal steel guitar represents death as well as heartbreak."

Womack once told *CA:* "I began writing novels at the age of eighteen. By the time I was thirty-eight, I had six of them. There were also four screenplays, all unsold, and probably two hundred articles, essays, and reviews. The struggle for book publication was long and painful. I can only hope it winds up being worth it."

BIOGRAPHICAL/CRITICAL SOURCES:

PERIODICALS

Booklist, March 1, 1995, p. 1182.
New York Times Book Review, March 4, 1990, section 7, p. 35; November 24, 1991; April 16, 1995.
Publishers Weekly, May 17, 1993, p. 69; April 1, 1996, p. 70.

* * *

WOODS, Stuart 1938-

PERSONAL: Original surname Lee, legally changed to stepfather's surname in 1955; born January 9, 1938, in Manchester, GA; son of Stuart Franklin (in business) and Dorothy (in business; maiden name, Callaway) Lee. *Education:* University of Georgia, B.A., 1959. *Politics:* Democrat.

ADDRESSES: Home—Santa Fe, NM. *Agent*—Peter Shepherd, Harold Ober Associates, Inc., 40 East 49th St., New York, NY 10017.

CAREER: Advertising writer and creative director with firms in New York City, 1960-69, including Batten, Barton, Durstine & Osborne, Paper, Koenig & Lois, Young & Rubicam, and J. Walter Thompson; creative director and consultant with firms in London, England, 1970-73, including Grey Advertising and Dorland; consultant to Irish International Advertising and Hunter Advertising, both in Dublin, both 1973-74; freelance writer, 1973—. Past member of board of directors of Denham's, Inc. *Military service:* Air National Guard, 1960-68, active duty, 1961; served in Germany.

MEMBER: Authors Guild, Georgia Conservancy, New York Yacht Club, Royal Oak Yacht Club, Royal Ocean Racing Club, Galway Bay Sailing Club (honorary member).

AWARDS, HONORS: Advertising awards from numerous organizations in New York, including Clio award for television writing and Gold Key award for print writing; Edgar Award, Mystery Writers of America, 1980, for *Chiefs.*

WRITINGS:

NONFICTION

Blue Water, Green Skipper (Dolphin Book Club selection), Norton (New York City), 1977.
A Romantic's Guide to the Country Inns of Britain and Ireland, Norton, 1979.
A Romantic's Guide to London, Norton, 1980.
A Romantic's Guide to Paris, Norton, 1981.
A Romantic's Guide to the Country Inns of France, Norton, 1981.

NOVELS

Chiefs, Norton, 1980.
Run Before the Wind, Norton, 1983.
Deep Lie, Norton, 1986.
Under the Lake, Simon & Schuster (New York City), 1987.
White Cargo, Simon & Schuster, 1988.
Grass Roots, Simon & Schuster, 1989.
Palindrome, HarperCollins (New York City), 1991.
New York Dead, HarperCollins, 1991.
Santa Fe Rules, HarperCollins, 1992.
L.A. Times, HarperCollins, 1993.
Dead Eyes, HarperCollins, 1994.
Heat, HarperCollins, 1994.
Imperfect Strangers, HarperCollins, 1995.
Choke, HarperCollins, 1995.
Dirt, HarperCollins, 1996.
Dead in the Water, HarperCollins, 1997.
Swimming to Catalina, HarperCollins, 1998.
Orchid Beach, HarperCollins, 1998.

OTHER

Contributor to magazines, including *Yachting.* Contributing editor and restaurant critic for *Atlanta.*

SIDELIGHTS: Stuart Woods is best known as a writer of suspenseful thrillers, but he has also authored several nonfiction books. His first publication, *Blue Water, Green Skipper,* was the story of his own sailing experiences. He explained to *CA:* "*Blue Water, Green Skipper* is a memoir deriving from my decision to sail in the 1976 *Observer* Single-Handed Transatlantic Race (OSTAR), though I had only eighteen months to build a boat and learn to sail it. I also sailed in the 1979 Fastnet race, in which many lives were lost." He added: "I expect to continue ocean racing and cruising, including a transatlantic crossing from England to Antigua."

In reviewing *Blue Water, Green Skipper,* Holger Lundbergh of *Yachting* declares, "The step-by-step account of how this green skipper in a remarkably short time became a seasoned blue-water sailor is beautifully told by a young American from Georgia, a brilliant stylist, a man of humor, courage, and patience," adding that the book is "dramatic and inspiring reading of rare quality."

Woods's novels are fast-paced adventures that are frequently set in high society or the entertainment world. Among his most popular works are those featuring the character of Stone Barrington, an ex-cop turned New York City lawyer and detective. In *Dirt,* Barrington is hired by a sexually voracious gossip columnist to find out who is faxing damaging information about her to influential people around the city. June Vigor, a reviewer for *Booklist,* finds *Dirt* to have "the jaded, waspish tone of a society gossip column, which necessarily keeps [Woods's] characters at a certain remove but makes for an amusingly catty novel. Fans of glitzy pop fiction will find brisk sex, designer name-dropping, and the voyeuristic tingle of dishing dirt on the rich and famous." A *Publishers Weekly* also praises *Dirt,* noting: "This slickly entertaining suspenser displays Woods at the top of his game with no signs of flagging. . . . [This] superbly paced tale [is] subtly reminiscent of the waggish P. G. Wodehouse, [and] Woods delivers a marvelously sophisticated, thoroughly modern old-fashioned read." Emily Melton approves of *Swimming to Catalina,* another Barrington adventure, stating in *Booklist:* "Despite the fact that his book is definitely politically incorrect and Barrington had apparently never heard of safe sex, it's a highly entertaining read that's chock-full of slam-bang action, fast cars, beautiful women, fine wine, and tart, tongue-in-cheek humor. Another outstanding effort."

Woods once told *CA:* "Writing fiction is terribly hard work, and I intend to alleviate this oppression by continuing to write about yachting, travel, food and wine, and whatever else takes my fancy. I have found the secret to happiness: finding a way to make a living doing all the things you like best, or, to put it another way, finding a way to make all the things you like to do best tax-deductible."

BIOGRAPHICAL/CRITICAL SOURCES:

PERIODICALS

Atlanta Journal/Constitution Magazine, February 8, 1977.

Booklist, December 1, 1994, p. 635; August, 1996, p. 1857; July, 1997, p. 1777; March 15, 1998, p. 1180.

Cosmopolitan, January, 1994, p. 18.

Entertainment Weekly, May 7, 1993, p. 53; January 20, 1995, p. 47.

Library Journal, March 1, 1997, p. 141; August, 1997, p. 136; September 15, 1997, p. 118.

New York Times, November 24, 1991; October 8, 1995.

People, September 16, 1996, p. 48; May 11, 1998, p. 48.

Publishers Weekly, April 12, 1993, p. 48; June 7, 1993, p. 26; November 1, 1993, p. 65; May 30, 1994, p. 36; December 5, 1994, p. 66; August 12, 1996, p. 65; July 14, 1997, p. 63; September 1, 1997, p. 40; April 6, 1998, p. 58.

Yachting, September, 1977; September, 1978.